Tolle

Capital Ga

2006–07

by
Kevin Walton BA (Hons)
Andrew Flint MA CTA

LexisNexis®
Tolley

Members of the LexisNexis Group worldwide

United Kingdom	LexisNexis Butterworths, a Division of Reed Elsevier (UK) Ltd, Halsbury House, 35 Chancery Lane, LONDON, WC2A 1EL, and RSH, 1–3 Baxter's Place, Leith Walk, EDINBURGH EH1 3AF
Argentina	LexisNexis Argentina, BUENOS AIRES
Australia	LexisNexis Butterworths, CHATSWOOD, New South Wales
Austria	LexisNexis Verlag ARD Orac GmbH & Co KG, VIENNA
Benelux	LexisNexis Benelux, AMSTERDAM
Canada	LexisNexis Canada, MARKHAM, Ontario
Chile	LexisNexis Chile Ltda, SANTIAGO
China	LexisNexis China, Beijing and Shanghai
France	LexisNexis SA, Paris
Germany	LexisNexis Deutschland, Gmbh, MUNSTER
Hong Kong	LexisNexis Hong Kong, HONG KONG
India	LexisNexis, NEW DELHI
Italy	Giuffrè Editore, MILAN
Japan	LexisNexis Japan, TOKYO
Malaysia	Malayan Law Journal Sdn Bhd, KUALA LUMPUR
Mexico	LexisNexis Mexico, Mexico
New Zealand	LexisNexis NZ Ltd, WELLINGTON
Poland	Wydawnictwo Prawnicze LexisNexis Sp, WARSAW
Singapore	LexisNexis Singapore, SINGAPORE
South Africa	LexisNexis Butterworths, DURBAN
USA	LexisNexis, DAYTON, Ohio

Published by LexisNexis Butterworths

A CIP Catalogue record for this book is available from the British Library.
ISBN 10: 0 7545 2975 4
ISBN 13: 9 780754 529750

Typeset by Kerrypress Ltd, Luton, Bedfordshire

Printed and bound in Great Britain by CPI Bath Press, Bath

Visit LexisNexis Butterworths at www.lexisnexis.co.uk

About This Book

This is the 29th annual edition of Tolley's Capital Gains Tax, one of Tolley's principal Tax Reference Annuals. It includes the provisions of Finance Act 2006 as far as they concern capital gains tax and corporation tax on chargeable gains. It also includes all relevant case law, HMRC pronouncements and other information up to 1 July 2006. A summary of the relevant contents of *FA 2006* is included in Chapter 68.

The book includes the law and practice relating to capital gains tax and corporation tax on chargeable gains for at least six years (i.e. for 2000/01 onwards, and sometimes earlier) as well as the current year, and so provides comprehensive information for claims, late assessments etc. An index and tables of cases and statutes provide quick reference to the subject and legislation, and, in addition, the text is arranged into chapters alphabetically for ease of reference. Worked examples are included. Chapter 69 comprises a digest of relevant cases.

Comments and suggestions for improvement are always welcome.

Consolidation of Tax Enactments

With effect generally for 1992/93 and subsequent years of assessment (and for companies' accounting periods beginning after 5 April 1992) the *Taxes Acts* provisions relating to the taxation of chargeable gains are consolidated in the *Taxation of Chargeable Gains Act 1992 (TCGA 1992)*. The consolidation does not affect the application of the provisions concerned, but references to provisions which ceased to have effect before 6 April 1992 are omitted, as is the commencement date of the consolidated provisions (unless still relevant to the application of the current provisions).

Tolley's Capital Gains Tax 2006/07 continues, as in previous years, to set out the position for the six years prior to 2006/07, i.e. for 2000/01 to 2005/06, but occasional references are still required to earlier years. In strictness, the legislation applicable to the years before 1992/93 etc. is that in force prior to the consolidation referred to above, and the Revenue (while acknowledging that 'on previous consolidation, inspectors, Commissioners and taxpayers alike got used to the new references in dealing with previous periods') indicated that claims etc. for those years should refer to the statute then applicable.

Accordingly, the approach which has been adopted to statutory references in this work is as follows.

(i) References to current legislation invariably quote the *TCGA 1992* reference in the familiar form, i.e. '*TCGA 1992, s XXX*' to identify a section thereof and '*TCGA 1992, Sch XX*' to identify a Schedule thereto. Remaining references to pre-consolidation legislation are in the same form. Where there has been no change in the legislation in the last six years, no statutory reference other than the current legislation is quoted.

(ii) Where the legislation has changed during the last six years, the earlier provisions continue to be described in the text, and the appropriate earlier statutory reference is quoted. Legislation current during those six years but now repealed is similarly dealt with. Where any part of the current legislation was introduced during those six years, the commencement date is quoted.

(iii) Where a full pre-consolidation statutory reference is required, this may be obtained from Tolley's Capital Gains Tax 1991/92 or an earlier edition.

Following the re-enactment of the capital allowances legislation in the *Capital Allowances Act 2001* as part of the 'simplification' programme, both the old and the new references are quoted in the text, as the revised wording and layout of the legislation may be relevant, particularly in cases where minor changes have been incorporated. A similar approach has been adopted in relation to the *Income Tax (Employment and Pensions) Act 2003* and the *Income Tax (Trading and Other Income) Act 2005*.

Contents

Notes

Simon's Direct Tax Service. Numerous references are made in the text to this comprehensive work published by LexisNexis Butterworths (enquiries 020–8662 2000, fax 020–8662 2012).

Years of Assessment (or tax years) run from 6 April. Thus '2006/07' or 'the year 2006/07' means the year from 6 April 2006 to 5 April 2007.

HMRC explanatory publications may be obtained from local tax offices (except where otherwise stated, see list in Chapter 30) and are mostly free. Most are also on the internet.

Tolley's Income Tax 2006/07 is a comprehensive detailed guide to income tax and includes the provisions of the Finance Acts 2006.

Tolley's Corporation Tax 2006/07 is the companion publication to Tolley's Income Tax and is a comprehensive detailed guide to corporation tax and includes the provisions of the Finance Acts 2006.

Tolley's Capital Gains Tax 2006/07 is a comprehensive detailed guide to capital gains tax and corporation tax on chargeable gains and includes the provisions of the Finance Acts 2006.

Tolley's Inheritance Tax 2006/07 is a comprehensive detailed guide to inheritance tax and includes the provisions of the Finance Acts 2006.

Tolley's Tax Cases 2006 contains over 2,500 summaries of cases up to 1 January 2006 relevant to current legislation.

Tolley's Tax Computations 2006/07 contains copious worked examples covering income tax, corporation tax, capital gains tax, inheritance tax and value added tax.

Tolley's Income Tax, Corporation Tax and **Capital Gains Tax Workbooks 2006/07** contain comprehensive, clearly presented and up-to-date examples covering income tax, corporation tax and capital gains tax respectively.

Tolley's Yellow Tax Handbook 2006/07 contains the text of the current legislation relating to income tax, corporation tax, capital gains tax and inheritance tax, plus non-statutory material, and includes the Finance Acts 2006.

Abbreviations and References

ABBREVIATIONS

A-G	Attorney-General.
Art	Article.
BES	Business Expansion Scheme.
CA	Court of Appeal.
CAA	Capital Allowances Act.
CCA	Court of Criminal Appeal.
CCAB	Consultative Committee of Accountancy Bodies.
CES	Court of Exchequer (Scotland).
Cf.	compare.
CGT	Capital Gains Tax.
CGTA	Capital Gains Tax Act.
CJEC	Court of Justice of the European Communities.
Ch D	Chancery Division.
CIR	Commissioners of Inland Revenue ('the Board' or 'the Revenue').
CRCA	Commissioners for Revenue and Customs Act.
DC	Divisional Court.
EC	European Community.
ECHR	European Court of Human Rights.
EIS	Enterprise Investment Scheme.
ESC	Inland Revenue Extra-Statutory Concession.
EU	European Union.
Ex D	Exchequer Division (now part of Chancery Division).
FA	Finance Act.
Fam D	Family Division.
HC	House of Commons.
HL	House of Lords.
HMRC	Her Majesty's Revenue and Customs.
I	Ireland.
ICAEW	Institute of Chartered Accountants in England and Wales.
ICTA	Income and Corporation Taxes Act.
IHT	Inheritance Tax.
IHTA	Inheritance Tax Act.
ISA	Individual Savings Account.
ITEPA	Income Tax (Earnings and Pensions) Act.
ITTOIA	Income Tax (Trading and Other Income) Act.
KB	King's Bench Division.
LLP	Limited Liability Partnership.
LLPA	Limited Liability Partnership Act.
NI	Northern Ireland.
OEIC	Open-ended Investment Company
PC	Privy Council.
PDA	Probate, Divorce and Admiralty Division (now Family Division).
PEP	Personal Equity Plan.
QB	Queen's Bench Division.
QIS	Qualified Investor Scheme
R	Regina or Rex (i.e. The Crown).
Reg	Regulation.
RPI	Retail Prices Index.
s	Section.
SC(I)	Supreme Court (Ireland).

SCS	Scottish Court of Session.
Sch	Schedule.
SE	*Societas Europaea* (European Company)
SI	Statutory Instrument.
SP	Inland Revenue Statement of Practice.
Sp C	Special Commissioners.
TCGA	Taxation of Chargeable Gains Act.
TMA	Taxes Management Act.

REFERENCES
(*denotes a series accredited for citation in court).

All E R	*All England Law Reports (Butterworths, Halsbury House, 35 Chancery Lane, London WC2A 1EL).
All ER(D)	All England Reporter Direct (Butterworths).
AC	*Law Reports, Appeal Cases (Incorporated Council of Law, Reporting for England and Wales, 3 Stone Buildings, Lincoln's Inn, London, WC2A 3XN).
ATC	*Annotated Tax Cases (publication discontinued).
Ch	*Law Reports, Chancery Division.
CMLR	Common Market Law Reports.
Ex D	*Law Reports, Exchequer Division (1875–1880; see also below).
Fam D	*Law Reports, Family Division.
KB	*Law Reports, King's Bench Division (1900–1952).
IR	*Irish Reports (Law Reporting Council, Law Library, Four Courts, Dublin).
ITC	*Irish Tax Cases (Government Publications, 1 and 3 G.P.O. Arcade, Dublin 1).
LR Ex	*Law Reports, Exchequer Division (1865–1875; see also above).
NILR	Northern Ireland Law Reports.
QB	*Law Reports, Queen's Bench Division (1891–1901 and 1952 onwards).
QBD	Law Reports, Queen's Bench Division (1875–1890).
SLT	Scots Law Times.
Sp C	Special Commissioner's Decisions (Tax Tribunals, 15–19 Bedford Avenue, London, WC1B 3AS).
SSCD	Simon's Tax Cases—Special Commissioners' Decisions (Butterworths).
STC	Simon's Tax Cases (Butterworths).
STI	Simon's Tax Intelligence (Butterworths).
TC	*Official Reports of Tax Cases (The Stationery Office, P.O. Box 276, London, SW8 5DT).
TR	Taxation Reports (publication discontinued).
WLR	*Weekly Law Reports (Incorporated Council of Law Reporting above).

The first number in the citation refers to the volume, and the second to the page, so that *[1978] 2 WLR 10* means that the report is to be found on page ten of the second volume of the Weekly Law Reports for 1978. Where no volume number is given, only one volume was produced in that year. Some series have continuous volume numbers.

Where legal decisions are very recent and in the lower courts, it must be remembered that they may be reversed on appeal. However, references to the official Tax Cases ('*TC*'), and to the Appeal Cases ('*AC*') may be taken as final.
In English cases, Scottish and Northern Irish decisions (unless there is a difference of law between the countries) are generally followed but are not binding, and Republic of Ireland decisions are considered (and vice versa).

Acts of Parliament, Command Papers, 'Hansard' Parliamentary Reports and Statutory Instruments (SI) are obtainable from The Stationery Office, (bookshops at 123 Kingsway,

London, WC2B 6PQ and elsewhere). Publications can be purchased using their online bookshop (at www.tso.co.uk). Fax orders should be made to 0870 600 5533. General enquiries and telephone orders should be made to 0870 600 5522. **Hansard** (referred to as HC Official Report or H L Official Report) references are to daily issues and do not always correspond to the columns in the bound editions. **N.B.** Statements in the House, while useful as indicating the intention of enactments, have no legal authority except in the limited circumstances mentioned in 4.24 appeals.

1 Introduction

1.1 BASIC PRINCIPLES OF CAPITAL GAINS TAX

Capital gains tax is charged in respect of chargeable gains accruing to individuals, personal representatives and trustees on the disposal of ASSETS (6.1). The tax is chargeable on the total gains on disposals in a 'year of assessment', after deductions, including LOSSES (40), TAPER RELIEF (61) and the annual exemption (see 2 ANNUAL RATES AND EXEMPTIONS). Every gain is a chargeable gain unless expressly excluded (see 22 EXEMPTIONS AND RELIEFS). For this purpose, a '*year of assessment*', otherwise known as a '*tax year*', is a year ending on 5 April. Thus '2006/07' indicates the year of assessment ending on 5 April 2007 (and so on). [*TCGA 1992, s 288*(*1*)].

Companies and other corporate bodies within the scope of corporation tax do not pay capital gains tax as such but instead are chargeable to corporation tax on their chargeable gains. The computation of their gains is broadly in accordance with the general principles applying for capital gains tax, but in recent years there has been considerable divergence between the capital gains tax and the corporation tax provisions (see 13.1 COMPANIES). Companies pay corporation tax by reference to accounting periods rather than years of assessment.

A gain is computed by reference to the excess of the disposal consideration over the acquisition consideration, received and given, for an asset. In certain circumstances the legislation deems a disposal or acquisition to take place where there is no actual disposal or acquisition. Certain types of expenditure are deductible in computing the gain. See 15 COMPUTATION OF GAINS AND LOSSES. An allowance, known as the indexation allowance (see 34 INDEXATION), was introduced by *FA 1982* with the intention of adjusting for the effects of inflation. For CGT purposes, indexation allowance was frozen at its April 1998 level. Assets acquired after 31 March 1998 do not attract indexation allowance at all. For disposals after 5 April 1998, the allowance is replaced by a taper relief whereby a chargeable gain is progressively reduced according to the length of time the asset has been held, with more generous reductions for business assets (as defined) than for other assets (see 61 TAPER RELIEF). These changes do *not* apply for the purposes of corporation tax on chargeable gains.

Capital gains tax (CGT) was introduced by *FA 1965* and commenced on 6 April 1965. The legislation was consolidated by *CGTA 1979* and subsequently by *TCGA 1992*. Assets acquired before 7 April 1965 are within the charge if they are disposed of on or after that date, but there are special provisions dealing with the computation of gains on the disposal of such assets (see 7 ASSETS HELD ON 6 APRIL 1965). *FA 1988* replaced the 1965 base date with 31 March 1982, subject to the detailed provisions of 8 ASSETS HELD ON 31 MARCH 1982. Both CGT and corporation tax are administered and paid under SELF-ASSESSMENT (56). For individuals, the amount chargeable to CGT for a year of assessment is treated as if it were the top slice of the taxpayer's income. To the extent that the gains fall within the starting rate band, they are taxable at a rate equivalent to the income tax starting rate (currently 10%). To the extent that they fall within the basic rate band they are taxable at the lower rate of income tax (currently 20%) and, where they exceed the basic rate limit, at the higher rate of income tax (currently 40%). Trustees of settlements and personal representatives are normally chargeable to CGT at 40%. See 2 ANNUAL RATES AND EXEMPTIONS. For companies, chargeable gains form part of the profits chargeable to corporation tax and are accordingly taxable at the appropriate corporation tax rate. See 13 COMPANIES.

1.2 THE CHARGE TO TAX

Subject to exceptions and special provisions, a person is chargeable to capital gains tax in respect of chargeable gains accruing to him in a year of assessment during any part of which he is resident in the UK, or during which he is ordinarily resident in the UK. [*TCGA 1992, s 1(1), s 2(1)*]. Companies are chargeable to corporation tax in respect of their chargeable gains. [*TCGA 1992, s 1(2)*]. Although *TCGA 1992, s 2(1)* refers to a 'person' (i.e. including a company) and ordinary residence, the key factor in charging companies is residence in the UK. See 13 COMPANIES, 45.7 OVERSEAS MATTERS, and 52.6 RESIDENCE AND DOMICILE.

Special rules apply to persons not resident or individuals not domiciled in the UK, to temporary visitors to the UK and to persons becoming temporarily non-UK resident. See 44 OFFSHORE SETTLEMENTS, 45 OVERSEAS MATTERS, 51 REMITTANCE BASIS and 52 RESIDENCE AND DOMICILE.

Married persons and civil partners are taxed independently. Transfers between spouses or civil partners living together are made on a 'no gain, no loss' basis. See 42 MARRIED PERSONS AND CIVIL PARTNERS.

Persons may be assessed in a representative capacity. See 5 ASSESSMENTS, 11 CHILDREN, 18 DEATH, 56 SELF-ASSESSMENT and 57 SETTLEMENTS.

There are special rules for UK resident or ordinarily resident shareholders of certain overseas resident companies. See 45.6 OVERSEAS MATTERS. See 44 OFFSHORE SETTLEMENTS for the provisions applying to trustees, settlors and beneficiaries of settlements which are or become overseas resident.

For unit and investment trusts, real estate investment trusts, open-ended investment companies and qualifying investor schemes, see 65 UNIT TRUSTS ETC. For venture capital trusts, see 66.10 VENTURE CAPITAL TRUSTS.

See Tolley's Corporation Tax under Friendly Societies and Life Insurance Companies for provisions of *TCGA 1992* (and related provisions) which are integral with the corporation tax regime applicable to life assurance business carried on by such entities.

TCGA 1992, ss 194–198, which deal with matters relating to oil exploration taxed under the *Oil Taxation Act 1975* and in practice apply mainly to companies, are not dealt with in this book.

2 Annual Rates and Exemptions

Cross-reference. See 13.3 COMPANIES as regards the rate of corporation tax on chargeable gains.

2.1 RATES OF TAX — INDIVIDUALS

Subject to the provisions below, the rate of capital gains tax applicable to an individual for 1999/2000 and subsequent years of assessment is equivalent to the lower rate of income tax for the year. [*TCGA 1992, s 4(1); FA 1999, s 26(2)(6)*]. For 1999/2000 to 2006/07 inclusive, this rate is **20%**. [*ICTA 1988, s 1A(1B); FA 1999, s 22(7)(a)*].

For 1999/2000 only, the starting rate for income tax does not apply for capital gains tax purposes. For 2000/01 and subsequent years, the starting rate does so apply to the extent that taxable gains, if treated as though they were the top slice of taxable income, fall within the starting rate band. [*TCGA 1992, s 4(1AB)(1AC); FA 2000, s 37*]. For 2000/01 to 2006/07 inclusive, the starting rate is **10%**. For 2006/07 the starting rate band applies to the first **£2,150** of taxable income and gains; for 2005/06 it applies to the first £2,090; for 2004/05 it applies to the first £2,020; for 2003/04 it applies to the first £1,960; for 2002/03, it applies to the first £1,920; for 2001/02, it applies to the first £1,880; for 2000/01, it applies to the first £1,520. [*ICTA 1988, s 1; FA 2000, s 31; FA 2001, ss 50, 51; FA 2002, s 26; FA 2003, s 131; FA 2004, s 23; FA 2005, s 8; FA 2006, s 23; SI 2000 No 806; SI 2002 No 707; SI 2003 No 840; SI 2004 No 772; SI 2005 No 716; SI 2006 No 872*].

If income tax is chargeable at the higher rate (or dividend upper rate) in respect of any part of an individual's income for a year of assessment, the rate of capital gains tax is equivalent to the higher rate. If no income tax is chargeable at the higher rate (or dividend upper rate) in respect of his income, but the amount on which he is chargeable to capital gains tax exceeds the unused part of his basic rate band, the rate of capital gains tax on the excess is equivalent to the higher rate of income tax for the year. The unused part of an individual's basic rate band is the amount by which the basic rate limit exceeds his total income (as reduced by any statutory deductions, e.g. the personal allowance). [*TCGA 1992, s 4(2)(3)(4); F(No 2)A 1997, Sch 4 para 24(2)(3)(6); FA 1999, s 26(5)(6); ITTOIA 2005, Sch 1 para 427*]. For 1999/2000 to 2006/07 inclusive, the higher rate of income tax is **40%**. [*FA 1999, s 23; FA 2000, s 31; FA 2001, s 50; FA 2002, s 26; FA 2003, s 131; FA 2004, s 23; FA 2005, s 8; FA 2006, s 23*]. For 2006/07 the basic rate limit is **£33,300**; for 2005/06 it is £32,400; for 2004/05 it is £31,400; for 2003/04 it is £30,500; for 2002/03 it is £29,900; for 2001/02 it is £29,400; for 2000/01 it is £28,400; for 1999/2000 it is £28,000. [*ICTA 1988, s 1; SI 1999 No 597; SI 2000 No 806; SI 2001 No 638; SI 2002 No 707; SI 2003 No 840; SI 2004 no 772; SI 2005 No 716; SI 2006 No 872*]. (The dividend upper rate is the special higher rate applicable to dividend income in excess of the basic rate limit — see Tolley's Income Tax.)

Although income tax rates are used in determining the charge to capital gains tax, it remains an entirely separate tax. Unused personal allowances and other income tax reliefs *cannot* be set against gains (though see 10.7 CHARITIES, 40.7 LOSSES for exceptions).

Example

Emile, a single man under 65, owns an established business and has taxable profits of £26,940 for his accounting year ended 31 March 2007. In 2006/07, he receives building society interest of £3,200 (net of tax) and dividends of £5,400. He also has chargeable gains of £12,200 (after losses and taper relief but before deducting the annual exemption). His income tax and capital gains tax liabilities for 2006/07 are computed as follows.

		£	£
Income tax payable:			
Trade profits			26,940.00
Building society interest		3,200.00	
Tax deducted £3,200 × 20/80		800.00	4,000.00
Dividends		5,400.00	
Tax credit 1/9		600.00	6,000.00
Total income			36,940.00
Deduct Personal allowance			5,035.00
Taxable income			£31,905.00
£		£	£
2,150.00	@ 10% (starting rate)		215.00
19,755.00	@ 22% (basic rate)		4,346.10
4,000.00	@ 20% (savings rate)		800.00
6,000.00	@ 10% (dividend rate)		600.00
31,905.00			5,961.10
Deduct	Tax on savings income (20%)	800.00	
	Tax credit on dividend income (10%)	600.00	1,400.00
Net income tax liability			£4,561.10

Unused basic rate band = £1,395 (£33,300 – £31,905)

		£
Capital gains tax payable:		
Chargeable gains		12,200.00
Deduct Annual exemption (see 2.3 below)		8,800.00
Taxable gains		£3,400.00
£		
1,395.00	@ 20% (lower rate)	279.00
2,005.00	@ 40% (higher rate)	802.00
3,400.00		£1,081.00

Note that the basic rate limit may in some cases be extended by tax deductible payments made — see, for example, 10.7 CHARITIES as regards Gift Aid payments and *ICTA 1988, s 639(5A)* (as extended by ESC A101) as regards personal/stakeholder pension contributions for 2001/02 onwards.

Where for any year of assessment

(*a*) under *ITTOIA 2005, s 539* (gains from contracts for life insurance etc.), a deduction of an amount is made from a person's total income for the purposes of extra liability, or

(*b*) under *ITTOIA 2005, s 669(1)(2)* (reduction in residuary income: inheritance tax on accrued income) the residuary income of an estate is treated as reduced so as to reduce a person's income by any amount for those purposes, the ascertainment of the unused part of the basic rate band referred to above has effect as if his income for the year were reduced by that amount. [*TCGA 1992, s 6*(*2*); *FA 1995, Sch 29 Pt VIII*(*8*); *ITTOIA 2005, Sch 1 para 428*(*2*)].

Where under *ITTOIA 2005, s 465* (gains from contracts for life insurance etc.) a person's total income for a year of assessment is deemed to include any amount(s),

(i) the ascertainment of the unused part of the basic rate band referred to above has effect as if his total income included not the whole of the amount(s) concerned but only the annual equivalent within the meaning of *ITTOIA 2005, s 536*(*1*) or (as the case may be) the total annual equivalent within the meaning of *ITTOIA 2005, s 537*, and

(ii) if relief is given under *ITTOIA 2005, s 535* and the calculation under *section 536*(*1*) or *section 537* does not involve the higher rate of tax, the ascertainment of the rate of tax applicable under *TCGA 1992, s 4* above is to have effect as if no income tax were chargeable at the higher rate (or the dividend upper rate) in respect of his income.

[*TCGA 1992, s 6*(*3*); *F*(*No 2*)*A 1997, Sch 4 para 25; ITTOIA 2005, Sch 1 para 428*(*3*)].

Nothing in *TCGA 1992, s 6*(*2*)(*3*) above is to be taken to increase the amount of a deduction which a person is entitled to make from his total income under any provision of *ICTA 1988, Pt VII Ch I* (personal reliefs) which limits any allowance by reference to the level of total income. [*TCGA 1992, s 6*(*4*)].

See Tolley's Income Tax for the income tax provisions mentioned above.

2.2 RATES OF TAX — PERSONAL REPRESENTATIVES ETC.

Personal representatives. For 1998/99 and subsequent years, the rate of capital gains tax in respect of gains accruing to the personal representatives of a deceased person is equivalent to the 'rate applicable to trusts' in *ICTA 1988, s 686*. [*TCGA 1992, s 4*(*1AA*); *FA 1998, s 120; FA 1999, s 26*(*3*)]. For 2004/05 to 2006/07 inclusive, this is **40%**. For 1998/99 to 2003/04 inclusive, it is 34%.

Settlements. Special provisions apply as regards the rate of tax for SETTLEMENTS (57.1).

2.3 ANNUAL EXEMPTION

For 2006/07 an individual is exempt from capital gains tax on the first **£8,800** of his 'taxable amount' (see below for the figures for earlier years). For 1998/99 onwards, the '*taxable amount*' is the amount of chargeable gains for the year after deducting current year and brought-forward allowable losses and applying TAPER RELIEF (61). It also includes any of the following gains that might be attributed to the individual (after deducting losses and applying taper relief where appropriate — see 40.1 LOSSES):

(*a*) gains treated under *TCGA 1992, s 77* as accruing to him as settlor from a UK resident settlement in which he has an interest (see 57.5 SETTLEMENTS);

(*b*) gains treated under *TCGA 1992, s 86* as accruing to him as settlor from a non-UK resident settlement in which he has an interest (see 44.5 OFFSHORE SETTLEMENTS);

(*c*) gains treated under *TCGA 1992, s 87* or *s 89*(*2*) as accruing to him as a beneficiary of a non-UK resident settlement (an offshore trust) (see 44.14 OFFSHORE SETTLEMENTS).

Where an individual's 'adjusted net gains' are equal to or less than the annual exempt amount, any allowable losses brought forward from a previous year or carried back from the year of death (see 18.5 DEATH) need not be deducted and are thus preserved for further carry-forward (or, if possible, carry-back). Where the 'adjusted net gains' exceed the annual exempt amount, such losses are deducted only to the extent necessary to wipe out the excess. The '*adjusted net gains*' are the chargeable gains for the year *before* TAPER RELIEF (61) *less* any current year allowable losses. They also include gains attributed under (*a*), (*b*) and (*c*) above to the following extent.

- For 2003/04 onwards and for any of the years 2000/01, 2001/02 or 2002/03 for which an election is made under *FA 2002, Sch 11 para 8* (see 40.1 LOSSES), attributed gains under (*a*) and (*b*) above are included net of any remaining current year allowable losses.
- Wherever the law prohibits the set-off of personal losses against attributed gains (see 40.1 LOSSES), any such gains are included in adjusted net gains only to the extent that they do not exceed the annual exempt amount and will thus be covered by that amount. See the examples below.

These provisions also apply to personal representatives for the year of death and the following two years (see 18.7 DEATH).

The annual exempt amounts for earlier years were as follows:

2005/06	£8,500
2004/05	£8,200
2003/04	£7,900
2002/03	£7,700
2001/02	£7,500
2000/01	£7,200
1999/2000	£7,100

[*TCGA 1992, s 2(2), s 3(1)(2)(5)–(5C)(7); FA 1998, s 121(3)(4), Sch 21 para 3; SI 1999 No 591; SI 2000 No 808; SI 2001 No 636; SI 2002 No 702; SI 2003 No 842; SI 2004 No 774; SI 2005 No 721; SI 2006 No 871*].

The exempt amount for the year (see above), unless Parliament determines otherwise, is the previous year's exempt amount as increased by a percentage which is the same as the percentage increase in the retail prices index for the September preceding the year of assessment over the index for the previous September. The resulting figure is rounded up to the nearest £100 and is announced before the relevant year of assessment in a Treasury statutory instrument (see list of references above). [*ICTA 1988, s 833(2); TCGA 1992, s 3(3)(4), s 288(2); FA 1993, s 83*].

See 57.10 and 57.11 SETTLEMENTS for further applications of the above rules.

The annual exemption is available regardless of the residence, ordinary residence or domicile status of the individual and is available separately to husband and wife.

Examples

For 2006/07, Paul has chargeable gains (after indexation but before taper relief) of £12,000 and allowable losses of £1,200. He also has allowable losses of £12,000 brought forward.

	£
Adjusted net gains (£12,000 – £1,200)	10,800
Losses brought forward (part)	2,000
	8,800
Annual exempt amount	8,800
Taxable gains	Nil

Losses brought forward	12,000
Less utilised in 2006/07	2,000
Losses carried forward	£10,000

Taper relief, if otherwise available, is effectively lost as the taxable gains are reduced to nil in any case.

For 2006/07, Mary has the same gains and losses (including brought-forward losses) as Paul above, but is also a beneficiary of an offshore trust. Trust gains of £9,000 are attributed to her for 2006/07 under *TCGA 1992, s 87*.

	£
Adjusted net gains (£12,000 – £1,200 + £8,800*)	19,600
Losses brought forward (part)	10,800
	8,800
Annual exempt amount	8,800
	Nil
Add: TCGA 1992, s 87 gains not brought in above	200
Taxable gains	£200
Losses brought forward	12,000
Less utilised in 2006/07	10,800
Losses carried forward	£1,200

* Gains attributed under *TCGA 1992, s 87* are included in adjusted net gains only to the extent that they do not exceed the annual exempt amount. Such gains cannot be covered by personal losses and will already have been reduced by any taper relief available to the trustees.

For 2006/07, Peter is in the same position as Mary except that his attributed gains are only £6,100.

	£
Adjusted net gains (£12,000 – £1,200 + £6,100)	16,900
Losses brought forward (part)	8,100
	8,800
Annual exempt amount	8,800
Taxable gains	Nil
Losses brought forward	12,000
Less utilised in 2006/07	8,100
Losses carried forward	£3,900

In Peter's case, £6,100 of the annual exempt amount is set against the attributed gains. Losses brought forward are used only to the extent necessary to reduce the personal gains to the balance of the annual exempt amount (£2,700).

3 Anti-Avoidance

Cross-references. See 13.4 COMPANIES for provisions relating to corporate losses; 16 CONNECTED PERSONS; 19.8 DOUBLE TAX RELIEF for schemes and arrangements designed to increase such relief; 44 OFFSHORE SETTLEMENTS for provisions relating to overseas resident settlements; 45.7, 45.8 OVERSEAS MATTERS for interests in controlled foreign companies and in offshore funds respectively; 46.18 PARTNERSHIPS; 57.5 SETTLEMENTS for charge on settlors with interests in settlements; 57.15 SETTLEMENTS for restrictions on transfer of settlement losses to beneficiary becoming absolutely entitled to settled property; 57.18–57.21 SETTLEMENTS for further anti-avoidance provisions.

The headings in this chapter are as follows.

3.1 APPROACH OF THE COURTS

For the general approach of the Courts to transactions entered into solely to avoid or reduce tax liability, leading cases are *Duke of Westminster v CIR HL 1935, 19 TC 490*; *W T Ramsay Ltd v CIR; Eilbeck v Rawling HL 1981, 54 TC 101*; *CIR v Burmah Oil Co Ltd HL 1981, 54 TC 200*; *Furniss v Dawson (and related appeals) HL 1984, 55 TC 324*. See also *Coates v Arndale Properties Ltd HL 1984, 59 TC 516*; *Reed v Nova Securities Ltd HL 1985, 59 TC 516*; *Magnavox Electronics Co Ltd (in liquidation) v Hall CA 1986, 59 TC 610*; *Commissioner of Inland Revenue v Challenge Corporation Ltd PC, [1986] STC 548*; *Craven v White; CIR v Bowater Property Developments Ltd*; *Baylis v Gregory HL 1988, 62 TC 1*; *Dunstan v Young Austen Young Ltd CA 1988, 61 TC 448*; *Shepherd v Lyntress Ltd*; *News International plc v Shepherd Ch D 1989, 62 TC 495*; *Ensign Tankers (Leasing) Ltd v Stokes HL 1992, 64 TC 617*; *Moodie v CIR and another (and related appeals) HL 1993, 65 TC 610*; *Countess Fitzwilliam and others v CIR (and related appeals) HL 1993, 67 TC 614*; *Pigott v Staines Investments Co Ltd Ch D 1995, 68 TC 342*; *CIR v McGuckian HL 1997, 69 TC 1*; *MacNiven v Westmoreland Investments Ltd HL 2001, 73 TC 1*; *CIR v Scottish Provident Institution HL 2004, [2005] STC 15* and *Mawson v Barclays Mercantile Business Finance Ltd HL 2004, [2005] STC 1*.

The classical interpretation of the constraints upon the Courts in deciding cases involving tax avoidance schemes is summed up in Lord Tomlin's statement in the *Duke of Westminster* case that 'every man is entitled if he can to order his affairs so that the tax attaching ...

is less than it otherwise would be'. The judgment was concerned with the tax consequences of a single transaction, but in *Ramsay*, and subsequently in *Furniss v Dawson*, the House of Lords has set bounds on the ambit within which this principle can be applied in relation to modern sophisticated and increasingly artificial arrangements to avoid tax. In *CIR v McGuckian*, it was observed that while Lord Tomlin's words in the *Duke of Westminster* case 'still point to a material consideration, namely the general liberty of the citizen to arrange his financial affairs as he thinks fit, they have ceased to be canonical as to the tax consequences of a tax avoidance scheme'. It was further observed that the *Ramsay* principle was 'more natural and less extreme' than the majority decision in *Duke of Westminster*.

Ramsay concerned a complex 'circular' avoidance scheme at the end of which the financial position of the parties was little changed but it was claimed that a large capital gains tax loss had been created. It was held that where a preconceived series of transactions is entered into to avoid tax and with the clear intention to proceed through all stages to completion, once set in motion, the Duke of Westminster principle does not compel a consideration of the individual transactions and of the fiscal consequences of such transactions in isolation. The opinions of the House of Lords in *Furniss v Dawson* are of outstanding importance, and establish, *inter alia*, that the *Ramsay* principle is not confined to 'circular' devices, and that if a series of transactions is 'preordained', a particular transaction within the series, accepted as genuine, may nevertheless be ignored if it was entered into solely for fiscal reasons and without any commercial purpose other than tax avoidance, even if the series of transactions as a whole has a legitimate commercial purpose.

However, in *Craven v White* the House of Lords indicated that for the *Ramsay* principle to apply all the transactions in a series have to be preordained with such a degree of certainty that, at the time of the earlier transactions, there is no practical likelihood that the transactions would not take place. It is not sufficient that the ultimate transaction is simply of a kind that was envisaged at the time of the earlier transactions. See, however, *CIR v Scottish Provident Institution* below. In the unanimous decision of the House of Lords in *Ensign Tankers (Leasing) Ltd v Stokes*, the lead judgment drew a clear distinction between 'tax avoidance' and 'tax mitigation', it being said that the *Duke of Westminster* principle is accurate as far as the latter is concerned but does not apply to the former.

Fitzwilliam involved five transactions entered into over a short period of time to avoid capital transfer tax on appointments from a will trust, the last four transactions being determined by the Revenue to form a preordained series of transactions subject to the *Ramsay* principle but which the taxpayers claimed should be viewed separately with the result that by reason of a number of available reliefs no liability to capital transfer tax arose. The House of Lords stated that the correct approach to a consideration of steps 2 to 5 was to ask whether realistically they constituted a single and indivisible whole in which one or more of the steps was simply an element without independent effect and whether it was intellectually possible so to treat them. It was held that both questions should be answered in the negative. The case put by the Revenue did not depend on disregarding for fiscal purposes any one or more of steps 2 to 5 as having been introduced for fiscal purposes only and as having no independent effect, nor on treating the whole of steps 2 to 5 as having no such effect. Each of the four steps had a fiscal effect of giving rise to an income tax charge on two of the taxpayers for a period of time, and there was a potential capital transfer tax charge should either have died whilst in enjoyment of the income associated with the transactions. Although steps 2 to 5 were 'preordained', in the sense that they formed part of a pre-planned tax avoidance scheme and that there was no reasonable possibility that they would not all be carried out, the fact of preordainment in that sense was not sufficient in itself to negative the application of an exemption from liability to tax which the series of transactions was intended to create, unless the series was capable of being construed in a manner inconsistent with the application of the exemption. In the particular circumstances of the case, the series of transactions could not be so construed. Two or more transactions in the series could not be run together, as in *Furniss v Dawson*, nor could any one or more of them be disregarded. There was no rational basis on which the four separate steps could be treated as effective for the purposes of one provision which created a charge to tax on a termination of an interest in possession but ineffective for the purposes of two other provisions which gave exemptions from that charge where the interest was disposed of for a consideration and where the interest reverted to the settlor. Accordingly, the case was one to which the *Ramsay* principle, as extended by *Furniss v Dawson*, did not apply.

In *MacNiven v Westmoreland Investments Ltd*, where the HL held that the *Ramsay* principle did not apply to a payment of interest, Lord Nicholls held that 'the very phrase "the *Ramsay* principle" is potentially misleading. In *Ramsay* the House did not enunciate any new legal principle. What the House did was to highlight that, confronted with new and sophisticated tax avoidance devices, the courts' duty is to determine the legal nature of the transactions in question and then relate them to the fiscal legislation'. Lord Hoffmann held that 'what Lord Wilberforce was doing in the *Ramsay* case was no more ... than to treat the statutory words "loss" and "disposal" as referring to commercial concepts to which a juristic analysis of the transaction, treating each step as autonomous and independent, might not be determinative'. Lord Hutton held that 'an essential element of a transaction to which the *Ramsay* principle is applicable is that it should be artificial'.

In *Mawson v Barclays Mercantile Business Finance Ltd* the HL held that Lord Hoffman's distinction in *Westmoreland* between 'legal' and 'commercial' concepts was not 'intended to provide a substitute for a close analysis of what the statute means'. It 'does not justify the assumption that an answer can be obtained by classifying all concepts a priori as either "commercial" or "legal" '. Instead, in applying any statutory provision, it is necessary 'first, to decide, on a purposive construction, exactly what transaction will answer to the statutory description and secondly, whether the transaction in question does so'.

In *CIR v Scottish Provident Institution* the issue was whether the decision in *Craven v White* meant that a series of transactions could not be treated as a composite transaction under the *Ramsay* principle because there was a real commercial risk that the transactions would not take place. The HL held that 'it would destroy the value of the *Ramsay* principle ... as referring to the effect of composite transactions if their composite effect had to be disregarded simply because the parties had deliberately included a commercially irrelevant contingency, creating an acceptable risk that the scheme might not work as planned'.

In *Hitch and Others v Stone CA, [2001] STC 214*, the Revenue mounted a successful challenge to a complex and artificial tax avoidance scheme on the grounds that agreements on which it was based were shams. It was noted that 'sham' meant acts done or documents executed by the parties thereto which were intended by them to give to third parties or to the court the appearance of creating between the parties legal rights and obligations different from the actual legal rights and obligations (if any) which the parties intended to create. The law did not require that in every situation every party to the act or document should be a party to the sham, although a case where a document was properly held to be only in part a sham would be the exception rather than the rule and would occur only where the document reflected a transaction divisible into several parts.

Simon's Direct Tax Service. See A1.315, A1.316.

3.2 DISCLOSURE OF TAX AVOIDANCE SCHEMES

With effect on and after 1 August 2004, there are provisions requiring 'promoters' of, and, in some cases, taxpayers making use of, tax avoidance schemes to disclose details to HMRC. [*FA 2004, s 319(2)*]. The detailed provisions are mostly contained in regulations. Originally, the provisions required disclosure only of schemes connected with employment or involving financial products, but with effect, broadly, from 1 August 2006, the provisions are extended to cover the whole of income tax, capital gains tax and corporation tax. From that date, the disclosure requirements are triggered where arrangements feature one of seven hallmarks.

Disclosure can be made online via HMRC's Anti-Avoidance Group website (www.hmrc.gov.uk), or alternatively, forms for making disclosures can be downloaded from the same location.

Legal professional privilege. The provisions do not require the disclosure of any information with respect to which a claim to legal professional privilege (or, in Scotland, to confidentiality of communications) could be maintained in legal proceedings. [*FA 2004, s 314*]. Note, however, that where a person who would otherwise be a promoter is not required to make a disclosure as a result of this provision, he is treated as not being a promoter, and the obligation to disclose the arrangements will (if there is no other person who is a promoter) fall on the taxpayer making use of the scheme (as the scheme will be one with no promoter). See further below.

Arrangements requiring disclosure. '*Notifiable arrangements*' requiring disclosure under the provisions are 'arrangements' which

- fall within any description prescribed by Treasury regulations (see below),
- enable, or might be expected to enable, any person to obtain an 'advantage' in relation to any tax (which may include capital gains tax and corporation tax) that is so prescribed in relation to arrangements of that description, and
- are such that the main benefit, or one of the main benefits, that might be expected to arise from the arrangements is the obtaining of that advantage.

The provisions also require disclosure of '*notifiable proposals*', i.e. proposals for arrangements which would be notifiable arrangements if entered into, whether the proposal relates to a particular person or to any person who may seek to take advantage of it.

For these purposes, '*arrangements*' include any scheme, transaction or series of transactions. An '*advantage*', in relation to any tax, means

- relief or increased relief from, or repayment or increased repayment of, that tax,
- the avoidance or reduction of a charge or assessment to that tax,
- the avoidance of a possible assessment to that tax,
- the deferral of any payment of tax,
- the advancement of any repayment of tax, or
- the avoidance of any obligation to deduct or account for any tax.

[*FA 2004, ss 306, 318(1)*].

Prescribed arrangements — August 2006 onwards. With effect as indicated below, any arrangements which fall within any of the descriptions (or '*hallmarks*') listed below are prescribed by the Treasury for the purposes of these provisions. The taxes covered are income tax, capital gains tax and corporation tax. The hallmarks are as follows.

(1) *Confidentiality in cases involving a promoter.* Arrangements fall within this hallmark if it might be reasonably expected that a promoter would wish the way in which the arrangements secure a tax advantage to be kept confidential from any other promoter at any time in the period beginning with the date of the first transaction forming part of the arrangements and ending with the date by which the user of the arrangements must notify HMRC of the reference number (see below). Arrangements also fall within this hallmark if either

- the promoter would, but for these provisions, wish to keep the way in which the arrangements secure a tax advantage confidential from HMRC for some or all of that period, and a reason for doing so is to facilitate repeated or continued use of the element of the arrangements which secure the advantage or of substantially the same element; or

- where there is no promoter by virtue only of the provision relating to legal professional privilege in (C) below, or the promoter is not UK resident, the user of the arrangements wishes to keep confidential from HMRC the way that the arrangements secure a tax advantage for some or all of that period.

(2) *Confidentiality in cases not involving a promoter.* Arrangements fall within this hallmark if there is no promoter and

- the intended user of the arrangements is a business (as defined) which is not a '*small or medium-sized enterprise*' (broadly, a micro, small or medium-sized enterprise as defined in the Commission Recommendation of 6 May 2003);
- the user wishes the way in which the arrangements secure a tax advantage to be kept confidential from HMRC for some or all of the period beginning with the date on which he enters into the first transaction forming part of the arrangements and ending with the latest date by which he must notify HMRC of the reference number; and
- a reason for doing so is to facilitate repeated or continued use of the element of the arrangements which secure the advantage or of substantially the same element.

(3) *Premium fee.* Arrangements fall within this hallmark if they are such that it might reasonably be expected that a promoter or a person connected with a promoter of arrangements that are the same as, or substantially similar to, the arrangements in question, would, but for these provisions, be able to obtain a 'premium fee' from a person experienced in receiving services of the type being provided. Arrangements where there is no promoter or where the tax advantage is intended to be obtained by an individual, or business that is a small or medium-sized enterprise, are excluded. A '*premium fee*' for this purpose is one chargeable by virtue of any element of the arrangements from which the tax advantage is expected to arise and which is to a significant extent attributable to, or to any extent contingent on the obtaining of, that advantage.

(4) *Off market terms.* Arrangements fall within this hallmark if

- the tax advantage expected from the arrangements arises, to more than an incidental degree, from the inclusion of one or more 'financial products';
- a promoter or person connected with the promoter becomes party to one or more of those products; and
- the price of the product or products differs significantly from that which might reasonably be expected to apply in the open market.

For this purpose, the following are '*financial products*':

(*a*) loans (excluding finance leases);

(*b*) derivative contracts under *FA 2002, Sch 26*, including contracts otherwise excluded by virtue of their underlying subject matter (see 14.7 COMPANIES—CORPORATE FINANCE AND INTANGIBLES);

(c) contracts which would be within (*b*) above if they were contracts of a company;

(*d*) agreements for the sale and repurchase of securities as described in *ICTA 1988, s 730A*(*1*);

(*e*) stock lending arrangements within *TCGA 1992, s 263B*(*1*) (see 58.21 SHARES AND SECURITIES);

(*f*) shares; and

(*g*) any contract (other than the above) whether on its own or in combination with other contracts (including any of the above) which in accordance with UK generally accepted accounting practice is in substance and so treated as a loan, or the advancing or depositing of money in whatever form (excluding finance leases).

Financial products held within an ISA (see 22.29 EXEMPTIONS AND RELIEFS) are excluded.

(5) *Standardised tax products.* Arrangements fall within this hallmark if they are 'tax products' which are made available by a promoter for implementation by more than one person. A 'product' is a '*tax product*' for this purpose if it would be reasonable for an informed observer who had studied the arrangements to conclude that their main purpose was to enable a client to obtain a tax advantage. Arrangements are a '*product*' if:

- they have substantially standardised documentation to enable implementation of the arrangements by the client and the form of that documentation is determined by the promoter and not tailored to any material extent to the client;
- the client must enter into a specific transaction or series of transactions; and
- the transaction or series of transactions are substantially standardised in form.

Arrangements which are the same, or substantially the same, as arrangements first made available for implementation before 1 August 2006 are excluded, as are arrangements consisting solely of one or more plant or machinery leases (see (7) below), an ENTERPRISE INVESTMENT SCHEME (21) or ISA, arrangements using the CORPORATE VENTURING SCHEME (17) or VENTURE CAPITAL TRUSTS (66), arrangements qualifying for community investment tax relief, specified approved EMPLOYEE SHARE SCHEMES (20), certain pension schemes and schemes to which *ITTOIA 2005, s 731* (periodical payments of personal injury damages) applies.

(6) *Loss schemes.* Arrangements are within this hallmark if the promoter expects more than one individual to implement them or to implement arrangements which are substantially the same and an informed observer, having studied them, could reasonably conclude that the main benefit of the arrangements for some or all of the participants would be the provision of losses which they would be expected to use to reduce their liability to income tax or capital gains tax.

(7) *Leasing arrangements.* This hallmark covers certain arrangements which include high-value plant or machinery leases. See Tolley's Corporation Tax for further details.

For the purpose only of determining whether arrangements are prescribed by (1)–(3) or (7) above, (C) below is disregarded.

The above provisions apply with effect from 1 August 2006 but do not apply to:

- notifiable proposals where the relevant date (see below) is before that date;
- notifiable arrangements, in relation to which the disclosure requirement falls on a promoter, where the promoter first becomes aware of any transaction forming part of the arrangements before that date; and
- notifiable arrangements, in relation to which the disclosure requirement falls on a person other than a promoter, where any transaction forming part of the arrangements is entered into before that date.

[*SI 2006 No 1543*].

See also HMRC's guidance published on their website on 16 June 2006.

Prescribed arrangements — pre-August 2006. Prior to the introduction of the hallmark system above, there were two types of arrangements prescribed by the Treasury. They were arrangements connected with employment (for details of which see Tolley's Income Tax), and arrangements in relation to financial products. The taxes covered were income tax, capital gains tax and corporation tax.

The arrangements in relation to financial products which had to be disclosed were those where the tax advantage was expected to be gained, to a significant degree, from the inclusion of any financial products (defined as above).

Disclosure of arrangements relating to financial products was not required where:

- the only financial products involved in the arrangements were assets held within an ISA or a PEP (see 58.18 SHARES AND SECURITIES); or
- the promoter (or person connected with the promoter) became a party to the financial product which did not differ significantly from that which might reasonably be expected to be offered in the open market.

Disclosure was also not required where

- the arrangements were such that no promoter (or person connected with a promoter) of arrangements that were substantially similar to the arrangements in question would reasonably have been expected to generate a premium fee (as above) from a person experienced in receiving services of the type provided; and
- the tax advantage expected to be obtained did not arise from any element of the arrangements which the promoter might reasonably have expected to be kept confidential from other promoters.

[*SI 2004 No 1863, Sch paras 6–8; SI 2006 No 1543, Reg 18*].

For examples of transactions which would and would not fall within these provisions, see HMRC's guidance material published on their website (www.hmrc.gov.uk) on 29 July 2004.

Disclosure by promoter. Subject to the transitional rules below, a 'promoter' must provide HMRC with specified information on any notifiable proposal within five business days of the '*relevant date*' (i.e. the date on which he makes the proposal available for implementation by any person or, if earlier, the date he first becomes aware of any transaction forming part of arrangements implementing the proposal) or by 30 September 2004 if later. The time limit for disclosure is extended where the promoter reasonably expects to make a clearance application to HMRC under certain specified provisions (see *SI 2004 No 1864, Reg 5*).

There is a separate requirement for a promoter to provide HMRC with specified information relating to notifiable arrangements and to do so within five business days of the date on which he first becomes aware of any transaction forming part of those arrangements, or by 30 September 2004 if later; but this does not apply if the arrangements implement a proposal which has been notified as above.

The disclosure under these provisions must provide sufficient information as might be reasonably expected to enable a Revenue officer to comprehend the manner in which the proposal or arrangements are intended to operate, including the details specified in *SI 2004 No 1864, Reg 3*.

Where two or more persons are promoters in relation to the same proposal or arrangements, notification by one promoter discharges the obligations of the others. If a promoter has discharged his obligations in relation to a proposal or arrangements, he is not required to notify proposals or arrangements which are substantially the same as those already notified (whether or not they relate to the same parties).

Transitional provisions. The above requirements do not apply in the case of any notifiable proposal for which the relevant date fell before 18 March 2004, any notifiable arrangements which implement such a proposal or any notifiable arrangements which include a transaction entered into before that date. In the case of notifiable proposals or arrangements relating to financial products, the requirements do not apply if the relevant date or, as appropriate, the date on which the promoter first becomes aware of any transaction forming part of the arrangements, falls before 22 June 2004. The time limit for disclosure of all notifiable proposals or arrangements is extended to 31 October 2004 where the relevant date or, as appropriate, the date on which the promoter first becomes aware of any transaction forming part of the arrangements, falls before 1 August 2004.

Meaning of promoter. A '*promoter*' is a person who conducts a 'relevant business' and who in the course of that business

(*a*) in relation to a notifiable proposal

- (i) is to any extent responsible for the design of the proposed arrangements, or
- (ii) makes a notifiable proposal available for implementation by another person, or

(*b*) in relation to notifiable arrangements

- (i) is a promoter by virtue of (*a*)(ii) above in relation to a notifiable proposal which is implemented by the arrangements,
- (ii) is to any extent responsible for the design of the arrangements, or
- (iii) is to any extent responsible for the organisation or management of the arrangements.

A person is not, however, a promoter by reason of anything done in circumstances prescribed in regulations.

A '*relevant business*' for this purpose is a trade, profession or business which involves the provision to other persons of services relating to taxation or which is carried on by a bank (within *ICTA 1988, s 840A*) or securities house (within *ICTA 1988, s 209A*(*4*)). Anything done by a company which is a member of the same 51% group (as defined) as a bank or securities house is taken to be done in the course of a relevant business if it is done for the purposes of the trade etc. of the bank or securities house.

The following exclusions apply.

(A) A company providing services within (*a*) or (*b*) above to a company which is a member of the same group (as defined) is not a promoter.

(B) Neither is an employee of (or of a person connected (within *ICTA 1988, s 839*) with) either a promoter or a person entering into any transaction forming part of the proposed arrangements.

(C) A person is not treated as a promoter where his involvement in the proposal or arrangements is such that he is not required to provide all of the required information because of the legal professional privilege rules above.

(D) A person is not treated as a promoter by virtue of (*a*)(i) or (*b*)(ii) above where

- in the course of providing tax advice, he is not responsible for the design of any element of the proposed arrangements or arrangements from which the tax advantage expected to be obtained arises;

- his relevant business is the provision of tax services but he does not provide tax advice in the course of carrying out his responsibilities in relation to the proposed arrangements or arrangements; or
- he is not responsible for the design of all the elements of the proposed arrangements or arrangements from which the tax advantage is expected to be obtained arises and could not reasonably be expected to have sufficient information to comply with the disclosure requirements or to know whether a disclosure is required.

(E) A person is not treated as a promoter by virtue of (*b*)(iii) above if he is not connected (within *ICTA 1988, s 839*) with another person who is a promoter by virtue of (*a*)(i) or (*b*)(ii) above in relation to the arrangements or substantially similar arrangements.

[*FA 2004, ss 307, 308, 319(3); SI 2004 No 1864, Regs 1, 3(1)(2), 4(1)–(3), 5, 6; SI 2004 No 1865; SI 2004 No 2613*].

Disclosure by person dealing with non-UK promoter. A person who enters into any transaction forming part of notifiable arrangements in relation to which there is a non-UK resident promoter (and no UK resident promoter) must himself provide HMRC with specified information relating to those arrangements. He must do so within five business days after entering into the first such transaction or by 30 September 2004 if later. The information to be supplied to HMRC is similar to that which promoters must provide (see above). This obligation is discharged if a promoter makes disclosure of the notifiable arrangements in question.

This provision does not apply in relation to any notifiable arrangements which include a transaction entered into before 23 April 2004. In the case of notifiable arrangements relating to financial products, the provision does not apply if the date on which any transaction forming part of the arrangements is entered into falls before 22 June 2004. The time limit for disclosure of all notifiable arrangements is extended to 31 October 2004 where the date on which any transaction forming part of the arrangements is entered into falls before 1 August 2004.

[*FA 2004, ss 309, 319(4); SI 2004 No 1864, Regs 1, 3(3), 4(4)(7), 6*].

Disclosure by parties to arrangements not involving a promoter. A person who enters into any transaction forming part of notifiable arrangements in respect of which neither he nor any other person in the UK has a disclosure obligation under the above provisions must himself provide HMRC with specified information relating to those arrangements. Such disclosure must normally be made within 30 days beginning with the day after the day in which he enters into the first transaction forming part of the arrangements. Where, however, there is no promoter only because the person who would otherwise be the promoter is not required to make a disclosure because of the legal professional privilege rules above, the disclosure by the client must be made within five days after the day on which he enters into the first transaction. Before 1 August 2006, a disclosure under these provisions could, unless the five-day time limit applied, be made at any time after the date of the first transaction and before the person was first required to notify HMRC of the reference number for the arrangements (see below). The information to be supplied to HMRC is similar to that which promoters must provide (see above).

This provision does not apply in relation to any notifiable arrangements which include a transaction entered into before 23 April 2004. In the case of notifiable arrangements relating to financial products, the provision does not apply if the date on which any transaction forming part of the arrangements is entered into falls before 22 June 2004. The time limit for disclosure of all notifiable arrangements is extended to 31 October 2004 where the date on which any transaction forming part of the arrangements is entered into falls before 1 August 2004.

[*FA 2004, ss 310, 319(4); SI 2004 No 1864, Regs 1, 3(4), 4(5)(5A), 6; SI 2004 No 2613, Reg 2; SI 2006 No 1544, Reg 4*].

Reference numbers allocated to arrangements. Where a person has made a disclosure as above, HMRC may allocate a reference number to the arrangements in question and notify the number to that person within 30 days after the disclosure. (The allocation of a reference number does not in itself indicate that HMRC accept that the arrangements could as a matter of law result in the obtaining by any person of a tax advantage.) A promoter who is providing services to a client in connection with notifiable arrangements must pass on to the client the reference number for those arrangements or the number for arrangements which are substantially the same as those arrangements. He must do so within 30 days after the date he first becomes aware of any transaction forming part of the arrangements or, if later, the date on which the reference number is notified to him by HMRC.

Any person who is a party to any notifiable arrangements must quote the allocated reference number in his tax return for the tax year or accounting period in which he is notified of the number (or, if earlier, the year or period in which the tax advantage is expected to arise) and in all subsequent returns until the advantage ceases to apply. The person must also state the tax year or accounting period in which, or the date on which, the advantage is expected to arise. In the case of arrangements relating to a partnership, the reference number must be quoted in the partnership returns. For arrangements under which a tax advantage is expected to arise by reason of a person's employment, the obligation falls on the employer to quote the reference number etc. on a return in such form as HMRC may specify. Where the arrangements are connected with employment under the pre-August 2006 regulations (see above), the employer must quote the reference number etc. in the annual return on form P35 for the appropriate tax year. Persons not required to file a tax return or, as the case may be, a P35 return must instead provide HMRC with specified information, including the reference number, no later than what would have been the filing date for such a return.

[*FA 2004, ss 311–313; SI 2004 No 1864, Reg 8; SI 2006 No 1544, Reg 6*].

Penalties. See 48.16 PENALTIES for the penalties applicable for failure to fulfil the above requirements.

3.3 LEGISLATION

Anti-avoidance legislation is intended to counteract transactions designed to avoid taxation but bona fide transactions may sometimes be caught also. The provisions relating to capital gains tax and corporation tax on chargeable gains and dealt with in this chapter are as listed below, and see also the cross-references given at the beginning of the chapter.

3.4	UK domiciled and UK resident or ordinarily resident participator in overseas resident company. [*TCGA 1992, s 13*]. See 45.6 OVERSEAS MATTERS for full coverage.
3.5	Value shifting. [*TCGA 1992, s 29*].
3.7–3.14	Value shifting to give tax-free benefit. [*TCGA 1992, ss 30–34*].
3.15	Connected persons. [*TCGA 1992, s 18*].
3.16	Assets disposed of in a series of transactions. [*TCGA 1992, ss 19, 20*].
3.17	Close company transferring asset at undervalue. [*TCGA 1992, s 125*].
3.18–3.19	Restrictions on company reconstructions. [*TCGA 1992, ss 137, 138*]. For schemes involving the transfer of a business owned by a company under *TCGA 1992, s 139*, see 13.10 COMPANIES for full coverage.
3.20	Groups of companies. See 3.7–3.14, 3.21 and 3.22 below and 27 GROUPS OF COMPANIES for full coverage.
3.21	Depreciatory transactions within groups of companies. [*TCGA 1992, s 176*].
3.22	Dividend stripping. [*TCGA 1992, s 177*].
3.23	Transactions in land. [*ICTA 1988, ss 776–778*]. See 38.4 LAND for full coverage.

3.24 Land sold and leased back. [*ICTA 1988, s 780*]. See 38.21 LAND for full coverage.
3.25 Provisions to deter abuse of concessions involving deferral of gains. [*TCGA 1992, ss 284A, 284B*].
3.26 Tax arbitrage. [*F(No 2)A 2005, ss 24–31, Sch 3*].

3.4 **UK PARTICIPATOR IN OVERSEAS RESIDENT COMPANY** [*TCGA 1992, s 13*]

Subject to *de minimis* limits, a participator in an overseas resident company which would be a close company if it were resident in the UK is assessable on a part of any chargeable gain made by the company provided that at the time the gain accrues the person is resident or ordinarily resident in the UK and, if an individual, is domiciled in the UK. See 45.6 OVERSEAS MATTERS.

3.5 **VALUE SHIFTING** [*TCGA 1992, s 29*]

Without prejudice to the generality of *TCGA 1992*, any of the following transactions are to be treated as giving rise to a disposal of an asset for capital gains tax purposes and, if made gratuitously or at an undervalue, the consideration (or additional consideration) for the disposal which could have been obtained in an arm's length transaction is treated as having been actually received. The same disposal value is treated as the cost of acquisition to the person or persons acquiring value as a result of the transaction. [*TCGA 1992, s 29(1)*].

(*a*) If a person having control of a company exercises his control so that value passes out of shares in the company owned by him (or by CONNECTED PERSONS (16)) or out of rights over the company exercisable by him (or by connected persons) and passes into other shares in or rights over the company, a disposal is deemed to have been made out of those shares or rights. Losses arising from such a deemed disposal are not allowable. [*TCGA 1992, s 29(2)(3)*]. An omission to act may be treated as an exercise of control and 'person' includes the plural i.e. the provisions apply where two or more persons have control (*Floor v Davis HL 1979, 52 TC 609*).

(*b*) Where an owner of property enters into a transaction whereby he becomes the lessee of that property (e.g. a sale and lease-back) and there is a subsequent adjustment of the rights and liabilities under the lease (whether or not including the grant of a new lease) which is as a whole favourable to the lessor, such an adjustment is a disposal by the lessee of an interest in the property. [*TCGA 1992, s 29(4)*].

(*c*) If an asset is subject to any right or restriction, the extinction or abrogation, in whole or part, of that right etc. by the person entitled to enforce it is treated as a disposal thereof. [*TCGA 1992, s 29(5)*].

The aim of the legislation is to tax the amount of value passing *into* the transferee holdings, not (if different) the amount passing from the transferor. The disposal value is thus the value received by the transferee(s). (HMRC Capital Gains Manual CG 58855). This will be of relevance where value passes from a majority shareholding into one or more minority holdings — see the *Example* at 3.6 below.

3.6 *Example*

Jak owns all the 1,000 £1 ordinary shares of K Ltd. The shares were acquired on subscription in 1978 for £1,000 and had a value of £65,250 on 31 March 1982. In December 2006, the trustees of Jak's family settlement subscribed at par for 250 £1 ordinary shares in K Ltd, thereby acquiring 20% of the voting power in the company. It is agreed that the value per share of Jak's holding immediately before the December 2006 share issue was £175 and immediately afterwards was £150. The value per share of the trust's holding, on issue, was £97 per share.

The proceeds of the deemed disposal are computed as follows

Value passing out of Jak's 1,000 shares is £25,000 (1,000 × £25 per share (£175 – £150)).

Value passing into the trust's 250 shares is £24,250 (250 × £97 per share) *less* the subscription price paid of £250 (250 × £1 per share) = £24,000.

The proceeds of the deemed disposal are equal to the value passing into the new shares, i.e. £24,000. (The trust's acquisition cost is £24,250, i.e. actual plus deemed consideration given).

The disposal is a part disposal (see 15.7 COMPUTATION OF GAINS AND LOSSES), the value of the part retained being £150,000 (1,000 × £150 per share).

Jak will have a capital gain for 2006/07 as follows (subject to indexation allowance to April 1998 and TAPER RELIEF (61))

	£
Proceeds of deemed disposal	24,000
Allowable cost $\dfrac{24{,}000}{24{,}000 + 150{,}000} \times £65{,}250$	9,000
Unindexed gain	£15,000

Simon's Direct Tax Service. See C2.115, C1.335.

3.7 VALUE SHIFTING TO GIVE TAX-FREE BENEFIT [*TCGA 1992, ss 30–34*]

These provisions apply to the disposal of an asset (the *section 30* disposal) if a scheme has been effected or arrangements have been made (whether before or after the disposal) whereby the value of the asset or a 'relevant asset' has been materially reduced and a 'tax-free benefit' is conferred at any time on

(*a*) the person making the disposal or a person connected with him (see 16 CONNECTED PERSONS), or

(*b*) any other person, except in a case where tax avoidance was not a main purpose of the scheme or arrangements.

Where the disposal of an asset precedes its acquisition, references to a reduction include references to an increase.

Any allowable loss or chargeable gain accruing on the *section 30* disposal is to be calculated as if the consideration were increased by such amount as is 'just and reasonable' having regard to the scheme or arrangements and the tax-free benefit. Where such an increase of consideration has been made for one asset and the tax-free benefit was an increase in value of another asset, the consideration for the first subsequent disposal of that other asset is to be reduced by such amount as is 'just and reasonable' in the circumstances. (There is no provision for the acquirer's cost of the asset to be correspondingly increased or reduced.)

These provisions do not apply to disposals by personal representatives to legatees (see 18.9 DEATH), or between spouses living together (see 42.4 MARRIED PERSONS AND CIVIL PARTNERS) or between companies in a group (see 27.2 GROUPS OF COMPANIES).

[*TCGA 1992, s 30(1)(4)–(7)(9); FA 1996, Sch 20 paras 46, 47(a)*].

An asset ('the second asset') is a '*relevant asset*' if

(1) the disposal of an asset (here called 'the first asset') is made by a company ('the disposing company'),

(2) the first asset comprises shares in, or securities (within *TCGA 1992, s 132* as in 22.5 EXEMPTIONS AND RELIEFS) of, a company, and

(3) the second asset is owned at the time of disposal of the first asset by a company 'associated' (see 3.12 below) with the disposing company.

A reduction in value of a relevant asset is not taken into account except in a case where

(A) during the period from the reduction in value to the time immediately before the disposal of the first asset there is no disposal of it other than one within *TCGA 1992, s 171* (intra-group transfers at no gain/no loss price as in 27.2 GROUPS OF COMPANIES),

(B) no disposal of that asset is treated as occurring during that period under *TCGA 1992, s 179* (company ceasing to be member of group as in 27.9 GROUPS OF COMPANIES), and

(C) if the reduction had not occurred, but any consideration given for the relevant asset and any other material circumstances (including any consideration given before the disposal for the first asset disposed of) were unchanged, the value of the first asset would have been materially greater at the time of its disposal.

Where the disposal of an asset precedes its acquisition, references to a reduction include references to an increase.

[*TCGA 1992, s 30(2)(9); FA 2000, Sch 40 Pt II(12)*].

A '*tax-free benefit*' arises to a person if he becomes entitled to money or money's worth or his interest in the value of any asset is increased or he is wholly or partly relieved from any liability to which he is subject *and* none of the foregoing benefits when conferred is otherwise liable to income tax, capital gains tax or corporation tax. [*TCGA 1992, s 30(3)*].

HMRC do not regard ordinary commercial group relief transactions (e.g. the purchase of group relief) as falling within *TCGA 1992, s 30.*

A lease of a farm at a rack-rent by a retiring farmer to his son, followed by a sale of the reversion at market value to an outside investor, would likewise be outside it (HMRC Statement of Practice D18).

Where a disposal within *TCGA 1992, s 30* would otherwise form the basis for a claim for loss relief against income under *ICTA 1988, s 573* or *s 574* these provisions apply if *any* benefit is conferred, whether tax-free or not. [*ICTA 1988, s 576(2)*]. See also 40.13 and 40.15 LOSSES.

The Revenue confirmed that where a person was caught by the value shifting provisions before 14 March 1989, the deemed gain could be held over under the then applicable provisions of *FA 1980, s 79* (provided that the other conditions were satisfied). This may also apply to the other reliefs mentioned in 33 HOLD-OVER RELIEFS which are still current.

See 3.13 below for modification of these provisions in relation to chargeable intangible assets.

Simon's Direct Tax Service. See C2.116

3.8 **Certain disposals of shares by companies.** The provisions at 3.9–3.11 below apply where a disposal within 3.7 above ('the *section 30* disposal') occurs and is of shares ('the principal asset') which are owned by a company ('the first company') in another company ('the second company'). [*TCGA 1992, s 30(8)*].

See 3.13 below for modification of these provisions in relation to chargeable intangible assets.

3.9 **Distributions within a group followed by a disposal of shares.** If a reduction in the value of an asset is attributable to the payment of a dividend by the second company while the two companies are 'associated' (see 3.12 below), it is not treated as a reduction for the purposes of 3.7 above except to the extent (if any) that the dividend is attributable (see below) to 'chargeable profits' of the second company; and, in such a case, the tax-free benefit is ascertained without regard to any part of the dividend that is not attributable to such profits.

'*Chargeable profits*' are

(*a*) the 'distributable profits' of a company, to the extent that they arise from a 'transaction caught by this *section*', and

(*b*) the distributable profits of a company, to the extent that they represent so much of a distribution received from another company as was attributable to chargeable profits of that company (including ones similarly representing a distribution).

'*Distributable profits*' are such profits computed on a commercial basis as, after allowance for any provision properly made for tax, the company is empowered, assuming sufficient funds, to distribute to persons entitled to participate in its profits. So far as possible in ascertaining distributable profits, losses and other amounts to be set against profits must be set against profits other than ones which could be chargeable profits.

Profits arising on a '*transaction caught by this section*' are profits of a company (here called 'company X') where the three conditions in (1)–(3) below are met but the three exceptions to them (see (A)–(C) below) do not apply.

(1) The transaction is

(i) a no gain/no loss disposal by company X to another group company within *TCGA 1992, s 171(1)* (see 27.2 GROUPS OF COMPANIES), or

(ii) an exchange, or deemed exchange, of shares in or debentures of a company held by company X for shares in or debentures of another company which, immediately after the transaction, is associated with company X, being a transaction treated by virtue of *TCGA 1992, s 135* (see 58.4 SHARES AND SECURITIES) or *s 136* (see 58.6 SHARES AND SECURITIES) as a reorganisation of share capital, or

(iii) a revaluation of an asset in the accounting records of company X.

(2) No disposal of the 'asset with enhanced value'

(i) occurs, other than one within *TCGA 1992, s 171(1)*, during the period beginning with the transaction within (1) above and ending immediately before the *section 30* disposal, or

(ii) is treated as having occurred during that period by virtue of *TCGA 1992, s 179* (company ceasing to be member of group as in 27.9 GROUPS OF COMPANIES).

(3) Immediately after the *section 30* disposal the asset with enhanced value is owned by a person other than the disposing company or a company associated with it (see 3.12 below).

'*Asset with enhanced value*' is defined as follows, according to which transaction within (1)(i), (1)(ii) or (1)(iii) above occurs respectively: the asset acquired from company X; the shares or debentures acquired by company X as a result of the exchange; and the revalued asset.

The three exceptions to the foregoing three conditions are as follows.

(A) At the time of the transaction within (1) above, company X carries on a trade, and a profit on a disposal of the asset with enhanced value would form part of the trading profits.

(B) By reason of the nature of the asset with enhanced value, there could be no chargeable gain or allowable loss on its disposal.

(C) Immediately before the *section 30* disposal, the company owning the asset with enhanced value carries on a trade, and a profit on disposal would form part of the trading profits.

Attribution of profits to a distribution is made by determining the total distributable profits and chargeable profits which remain at the time of distribution, after allowing for all earlier distributions and distributions to be made then or subsequently in respect of other classes of shares etc. and so far as possible by attributing distributable profits other than chargeable profits.

Chargeable profits are treated as arising to shareholders etc. proportionately to their holdings of shares, etc.

[*TCGA 1992, s 31; FA 2000, Sch 40 Pt II(12); FA 2002, Sch 9 paras 5(2), 7*].

3.10 **Asset-holding company leaving the group.** Where the *section 30* disposal (see 3.7 above) occurred before 9 March 1999, the provisions at 3.9 above were not triggered if that disposal was to a non-UK resident subsidiary such that the asset with enhanced value (see 3.9 above) continues to be owned within the capital gains group of which the company making the disposal is a member. This is because the condition at 3.9(3) above is not then satisfied. That asset could subsequently be sold by the non-resident subsidiary to a third party with impunity from the value shifting provisions. The provisions described below were introduced to counteract this avoidance device as regards any disposal of an asset on or after 9 March 1999. They apply wherever profits of a company would be profits on a transaction caught by *TCGA 1992, s 31* (see 3.9 above) but for the fact that condition 3.9(3) above is not satisfied.

Where the above-mentioned provisions apply, the said profits are treated as profits arising on a transaction caught by *section 31* (with the result that *TCGA 1992, s 30* at 3.7 above has effect with the consequences described below) if either:

(*a*) at any time during the period of six years beginning with the date of the *section 30* disposal, an event occurs which consists of the 'asset-holding company' ceasing to be a member of the 'disposal group' (otherwise than by virtue of the principal company of the group becoming a member of another group, i.e. the group being taken over); or

(*b*) at any time during the said six-year period, the asset-holding company ceases to be a member of the disposal group by virtue only of the principal company of the group becoming a member of another group *and* at any time in that period an event occurs as a result of which

- there is no member of the disposal group of which the asset-holding company is a 75% subsidiary, or
- there is no member of the disposal group of which the asset-holding company is an effective 51% subsidiary (see 27.1 GROUPS OF COMPANIES).

However, these provisions do not apply (and there is thus no double charge) if, during the said six-year period but prior to the occurrence of an event within (*a*) or (*b*) above, a disposal of the asset with enhanced value has been treated as having occurred by virtue of *TCGA 1992, s 179* (company leaving a group after acquiring an asset intra-group — see 27.9 GROUPS OF COMPANIES).

In relation to any particular time, the '*asset-holding company*' is the company holding the asset with enhanced value at that time. The '*disposal group*' is the group of which the company which made the *section 30* disposal was a member at the time of that disposal (or a group regarded as being the same as that group under *TCGA 1992, s 170(10)* — see 27.1 GROUPS OF COMPANIES).

Where *section 30* has effect by virtue of the above, the consideration for the *section 30* disposal is not adjusted but a chargeable gain is treated as accruing to the 'chargeable company' immediately before the event within (*a*) or (*b*) above. The '*chargeable company*' is normally the company which made the disposal but if that company is at that time no longer a member of the disposal group, the chargeable company is (for disposals on or after 1 April 2000) any other company which is at that time a member of that group and which is designated as the chargeable company by HMRC notice.

The amount of the gain is the shortfall between the allowable loss or chargeable gain which accrued on the *section 30* disposal and the allowable loss or chargeable gain which would have accrued on that disposal if the consideration had been notionally increased as in 3.7 above.

If an allowable loss arose on the *section 30* disposal and has not been otherwise utilised, it may be set against the notional gain arising above, notwithstanding the connected persons rule in *TCGA 1992, s 18*(*3*) (see 40.5 LOSSES).

[*TCGA 1992, s 31A; FA 1999, s 74, Sch 9 paras 2, 5; FA 2000, Sch 29 para 17*].

3.11 **Disposals within a group followed by a disposal of shares.** A reduction in the value of an asset is not treated as a reduction for the purposes of 3.7 above if it is attributable to the disposal of any asset ('the underlying asset') by the second company while the two companies are 'associated' (see 3.12 below) and the disposal is within *TCGA 1992, s 171*(*1*) (no gain/no loss disposals in a group as in 27.2 GROUPS OF COMPANIES), unless

(*a*) the actual consideration for the disposal of the underlying asset is less than both its market value and its 'cost',

(*b*) the disposal is not effected for bona fide commercial reasons and forms part of a scheme or arrangements of which the main purpose, or one of the main purposes, is the avoidance of a corporation tax liability, and

(*c*) the first company is not treated as disposing of an interest in the principal asset by virtue of a distribution in a dissolution or winding up of the second company.

For the purpose of (*a*) above, the '*cost*' of an asset is the aggregate of any capital expenditure incurred by the company in acquiring or providing it, or in respect of it while owned after its acquisition.

In the case of a part disposal of an underlying asset,

(A) the market value in (*a*) above is the market value of the asset acquired by the transferee, and

(B) the amounts attributed to the cost of the underlying asset are reduced to the '*appropriate proportion*' thereof; i.e.,

(i) the proportion of capital expenditure properly attributed in the company's accounting records to the asset acquired by the transferee; or

(ii) if (i) does not apply, such proportion as is 'just and reasonable'.

[*TCGA 1992, s 32; FA 1996, Sch 20 para 47*(*b*)].

3.12 **Interpretation of the value shifting provisions.** The following interpretational provisions apply to the value shifting provisions described at 3.7–3.11 above.

As regards any asset ('the original asset'), the provisions in (1)–(5) below apply in relation to the enactments mentioned in (*a*) and (*b*) below.

(*a*) The enactments concerning relevant assets in *TCGA 1992, s 30*(*2*): namely, in 3.7 above, (1)–(3) and (A)–(C).

(*b*) The enactments concerning distributions within a group followed by a disposal of shares in *TCGA 1992, s 31(7)–(9)*: namely, in 3.9 above, the second and third conditions ((2) and (3)) and the three exceptions ((A)–(C)) to the three conditions.

The provisions in (1)–(5) below also apply in connection with *TCGA 1992, s 31A* (see 3.10 above) for the purposes of determining any question in relation to the asset with enhanced value.

(1) In (A) and (B) in 3.7 above and in condition (2) in 3.9 above, references to the disposal of an asset do not include a part disposal. The same applies as regards the reference in 3.10 above to a disposal occurring by virtue of *TCGA 1992, s 179*.

(2) For the purposes of the enactments mentioned in (*a*) and (*b*) above, references to an asset are to the original asset; except that if subsequently one or more assets are treated under (4) or (5) below as the same as the original asset,

(i) if there has been no disposal falling within (A) or (B) in 3.7 above or (2) in 3.9 above, the references are to the asset(s) so treated; and

(ii) in any other case, the references are to the asset(s) representing that part of the value of the original asset remaining after allowing for earlier disposals within the relevant provision.

For the above purposes a disposal includes a part disposal which would have been within (A) or (B) in 3.7 above or (2) in 3.9 above if it had not been excluded by (1) above.

For the purposes of *TCGA 1992, s 31A* at 3.10 above, the following apply where one or more assets are treated under (4) or (5) below as the same as the asset with enhanced value.

(I) If in the period beginning with the transaction in 3.9(1) and ending with the event in 3.10(*a*) or (*b*),

- there is no disposal of the asset with enhanced value to any person other than a no gain/no loss intra-group disposal within *TCGA 1992, s 171(1)* (see 27.2 GROUPS OF COMPANIES), and
- no disposal of that asset is treated as having occurred by virtue of *TCGA 1992, s 179* (company leaving a group after acquiring an asset intra-group — see 27.9 GROUPS OF COMPANIES),

references to the asset with enhanced value are to the asset(s) treated under (4) or (5) below as the same as that asset.

(II) In any other case, references to the asset with enhanced value are to the asset(s) representing that part of the value of the asset with enhanced value remaining after allowing for disposals of either kind mentioned in (I) above.

(3) If, by virtue of (2) above, a reference to an asset is treated as a reference to two or more assets,

(i) the assets are treated as a single asset,

(ii) a disposal of any of them is a part disposal, and

(iii) the reference to the second asset in (3) in 3.7 above, to the asset in condition (3) in 3.9 above and to the asset in the definition of 'asset-holding company' in 3.10 above is in each case a reference to all or any of those two or more assets.

(4) If there is a part disposal of an asset, that asset and the asset acquired by the transferee are treated as the same.

(5) Where

(i) the value of an asset is derived from another asset owned by the same or an 'associated company' (see below), and

(ii) assets have been merged or divided or have changed their nature, or rights or interests in or over assets have been created or extinguished,

the two assets are treated as the same.

Where a reduction in the value of a relevant asset is to be taken into account under *TCGA 1992, s 30(2)* (see (1)–(3) and (A)–(C) in 3.7 above) and at the time of the disposal of the first asset in 3.7(1) by the disposing company

(A) references to the relevant asset are treated under (1)–(5) above as references to two or more assets treated as a single asset, and

(B) one or more, but not all, of those assets is owned by a company 'associated' (see below) with the disposing company,

the amount of the reduction in the value of the relevant asset to be taken into account is reduced to such amount as is 'just and reasonable'.

For the purposes of the provisions in TCGA 1992, s 31 concerning distributions within a group followed by a disposal of shares (see 3.9 above), the reduction in value of the principal asset (see 3.8 above) is to be reduced to such amount as is 'just and reasonable' if

(*aa*) a dividend paid by the second company is attributable to that company's chargeable profits, and

(*bb*) the criterion in (2), (3) or (C) in 3.9 above is satisfied by reference to an asset, or assets treated as a single asset, treated under (2)(ii) above as the same as the asset with enhanced value.

Where *TCGA 1992, s 31A* (see 3.10 above) treats profits as arising on a transaction caught by *section 31* (see 3.9 above) and either condition (2) in 3.9 above or a condition in 3.10 above is satisfied by reference to an asset (or assets treated as a single asset) treated by virtue of (2)(II) above as the same as the asset with enhanced value, the reduction in value of the principal asset (see 3.8 above) is to be reduced to such amount as is 'just and reasonable'.

The definitions relating to groups of companies in *TCGA 1992, s 170(2)–(11)* apply as in 27.1 GROUPS OF COMPANIES; and companies are '*associated*' if they are members of the same group. The change in the residence requirement as regards groups of companies (see 27.1 GROUPS OF COMPANIES) has effect for the purposes of the value shifting provisions, including those at 3.14 below, in relation to disposals on or after 1 April 2000.

[*TCGA 1992, s 33; FA 1996, Sch 20 para 47(c); FA 1999, s 74, Sch 9 paras 3, 5; FA 2000, Sch 29 para 17(4)*].

The provisions of *TCGA 1992, ss 30–33* are considered by HMRC at HMRC Capital Gains Manual CG 46800–46922.

3.13 **Modification of value shifting provisions in relation to chargeable intangible assets.** The provisions at 3.7 to 3.12 above have effect in relation to an asset which is a 'chargeable intangible asset' for the purposes of the corporation tax intangible asset regime of *FA 2002, Sch 29* (see 14.13 COMPANIES—CORPORATE FINANCE AND INTANGIBLES and Tolley's Corporation Tax under Intangible Assets) with the following modifications.

(1) References in 3.7 to 3.12 above to a disposal or part disposal of an asset are to be read as references to its 'realisation' or 'part realisation', as defined in *FA 2002, Sch 29 para 19*.

(2) References to a disposal of an asset under *TCGA 1992, s 171(1)* (intra-group transfers — see 27.2 GROUPS OF COMPANIES) are to be read as references to its transfer under the analogous provisions of *FA 2002, Sch 29 para 55*.

(3) References to a sale of an asset under *TCGA 1992, s 179* (degrouping charge — see 27.9 GROUPS OF COMPANIES) are to be read as references to its realisation under the analogous provisions of *FA 2002, Sch 29 para 58* or *60*.

(4) Sub-paragraph 3.9(1)(iii) above does not apply to a revaluation of an asset the profit on which is wholly taken into account as a credit under the intangible assets regime.

(5) None of the exceptions at 3.9(A)–(C) above can be treated as satisfied if the asset with enhanced value is a chargeable intangible asset.

(6) The reference in 3.11(*a*) above to the cost of the underlying asset is to be read, in the case of a chargeable intangible asset, as a reference to the capitalised value of the asset recognised for accounting purposes.

[*TCGA 1992, s 33A; FA 2002, s 84(2), Sch 30 para 6*].

An asset is a '*chargeable intangible asset*' if a gain on its realisation would give rise to a credit falling to be brought into account under the intangible assets regime. [*FA 2002, Sch 29 para 137(1)*].

3.14 **Transactions treated as a reorganisation of share capital.** If the following conditions apply, a 'disposing company' is treated as receiving the amount specified in (*b*) below on a part disposal within *TCGA 1992, s 128(3)* (see 58.1 SHARES AND SECURITIES) of the 'original holding'.

(*a*) But for the rules whereby shares etc. held after a reorganisation, reconstruction etc. are treated as the same as those held beforehand (see 58.1, 58.4, 58.6 SHARES AND SECURITIES), *TCGA 1992, s 30* in 3.7 above would apply on an exchange by a company (the 'disposing company') of shares, etc. in another company (the 'original holding') for shares etc. in a further company which immediately afterwards is not in the same 'group' (see the note on definitions in 3.12 above) as the disposing company.

(*b*) If *section 30* had applied, and the reduction in value causing them to apply had occurred after 13 March 1989, any allowable loss or chargeable gain on the disposal would have been calculated as if the consideration had been increased by an amount.

Similarly, if, but for the rules mentioned in (*a*) above, *section 30* would have applied by virtue of *TCGA 1992, s 31A* (asset-holding company leaving the group — see 3.10 above) on an exchange of the kind mentioned in (*a*) above, *section 31A* is applied (with appropriate modification) as if the said rules did not apply. In the computation of the shortfall mentioned in 3.10 above, an allowable loss is in this case regarded as a chargeable gain of nil.

[*TCGA 1992, s 34; FA 1999, s 74, Sch 9 paras 4, 5; FA 2002, Sch 9 paras 5(3), 7*].

3.15 **CONNECTED PERSONS** [*TCGA 1992, s 18*]

Simon's Direct Tax Service. See C2.110.

A transaction between CONNECTED PERSONS (16) is treated as having been made by way of a non-arm's length bargain so that acquisition and disposal are treated as being made at market value in most cases (see 41.1 MARKET VALUE). [*TCGA 1992, s 18(1)(2)*]. There are restrictions on losses in such circumstances. See 40.5 LOSSES.

Where the asset disposed of is subject to a right or restriction enforceable by the person making the disposal or a person connected with him, then if the acquisition consideration is treated as being the market value of the asset, that value is ascertained by deducting from the market value of the unencumbered asset either the market value of the right or restriction or, if less, the amount by which its extinction would enhance the value of the asset to its owner. Rights or restrictions the enforcement of which might effectively destroy or substantially impair the value of the asset without bringing any countervailing advantage either to the person making the disposal or to a person connected with him are disregarded, e.g. rights to extinguish incorporeal assets by way of forfeiture or merger (but see below). Options and other rights to acquire assets are also disregarded.

The valuation provisions outlined above do not apply to rights of forfeiture etc. exercisable on the breach of a covenant in a lease, nor to any right or restriction under a mortgage or other charge. [*TCGA 1992, s 18(6)–(8)*].

3.16 ASSETS DISPOSED OF IN A SERIES OF TRANSACTIONS [*TCGA 1992, ss 19, 20*]

Simon's Direct Tax Service. See C2.114.

Where by way of two or more 'material transactions' which are 'linked' (a '*series of linked transactions*')

(*a*) a person disposes of assets to another person with whom he is connected (or to two or more other persons with each of whom he is connected) (see 16 CONNECTED PERSONS); and

(*b*) the 'original market value' of the assets disposed of by any of the transactions in the series is less than the appropriate portion of the 'aggregate market value' of the assets disposed of by all the transactions in the series,

the disposal effected by the linked transaction in (*b*) is deemed to be for a consideration equal to the appropriate portion referred to in that paragraph. The above is not, however, to affect the consideration for any disposals between married persons (see 42 MARRIED PERSONS AND CIVIL PARTNERS) living together.

A '*material transaction*' is any transaction, whether by gift or otherwise (subject to the exception below as regards intra-group transfers). Two or more such transactions are '*linked*' if they occur within the period of **six years** ending on the date of the last of them.

The provisions apply *both* when a second material transaction causes a series of linked transactions to come into being *and* when an existing series is extended by a further material transaction (whether or not an earlier transaction ceases to form part of the series). Assessments and adjustments are made accordingly.

'*Original market value*'. If a transaction is the most recent in the series, the original market value of the assets disposed of by it is the market value which would otherwise be deemed to be the consideration for it under the general capital gains tax rules (e.g. 41 MARKET VALUE). In the case of any other transaction in the series, the original market value of the assets disposed of by it is the value which, prior to the occurrence of the most recent transaction in the series, was or would have been deemed to be the consideration, whether under the general capital gains tax rules or by the previous operation of these provisions.

'*Aggregate market value*'. Subject to further provisions below, aggregate market value is the amount which would have been the market value of all the transactions in the series under the general capital gains tax rules if, 'considering all the assets together', they had been disposed of by one disposal occurring at the time of the transaction concerned. The appropriate portion of the aggregate market value is that portion which it is reasonable to apportion to those of the assets which were actually disposed of by the transaction concerned.

'*Considering all the assets together*' refers not only to considering them as a group or holding or collection of assets retaining their separate identities but also (if it gives a higher market value) to considering them as brought together, physically or in law, so as to constitute either a single asset or a number of assets which are distinct from those which were comprised in each of the transactions concerned.

Groups of companies. Intra-group transfers of assets which are treated as taking place on a no gain/no loss basis (see 27.2 GROUPS OF COMPANIES) are not material transactions. In a case where

(*a*) a company ('company A') disposes of an asset by way of a material transaction; and

(*b*) company A acquired the asset (after 19 March 1985) by way of an intra-group transfer as above; and

(*c*) the disposal by company A is to a person who is connected with another company ('company B') which at some time (after 19 March 1985) disposed of the asset by way of an intra-group transfer as above; and

(*d*) either the disposal by way of intra-group transfer which is referred to in (*c*) above was the occasion of the acquisition in (*b*) above or, between that disposal and acquisition, there has been no disposal of the asset which was not an intra-group transfer as above,

then, in determining whether the above provisions apply in relation to a series of linked transactions, the disposal by company A is treated as having been made by company B; but any increase in the consideration for that disposal resulting from the application of the new provisions has effect with respect to company A.

Disposal preceding acquisition. If any of the assets disposed of by all the transactions in a series of linked transactions were acquired after the time of the first of those transactions, then, in considering aggregate market value in relation to each of the transactions in the series, no account is taken of any assets which were acquired after the time of that transaction (unless they were acquired by way of an intra-group transfer). Further, the number of assets taken into account is limited to the maximum number held at any time in the period beginning immediately before the first transaction and ending immediately before the last; and in arriving at this figure any intra-group transfers prior to the first transaction are treated as taking place after that transaction. For identification purposes, fungible assets are treated as disposed of on a 'first in/first out' basis.

For further commentary and examples, see HMRC Capital Gains Manual CG 14650–14742.

Example

L purchased a set of 6 antique chairs in June 1991 at a cost of £12,000. He gave 2 chairs to his daughter in February 2001, another pair to his son in November 2003, and sold the final pair to his brother for their market value in August 2006.

The market value of the chairs at the relevant dates were

	2 chairs	4 chairs	6 chairs
	£	£	£
February 2001	6,000	14,000	26,000
November 2003	7,800	18,000	34,200
August 2006	10,400	24,000	46,200

The indexation factor for the period June 1991 to April 1998 is 0.213.

The capital gains tax computations are as follows

February 2001

Disposal to daughter

Deemed consideration	£6,000

As the consideration does not exceed £6,000, the disposal is covered by the chattel exemption (see note (*a*)).

November 2003

(i) *2000/01 disposal to daughter recomputed*

Original market value (deemed disposal consideration at February 2001)	£6,000
Reasonable proportion of aggregate market value as at February 2001 of all assets disposed of to date:	
£14,000 × 2/4	£7,000
	£
Deemed consideration (greater of £6,000 and £7,000)	7,000
Cost $\frac{7,000}{7,000+14,000} \times £12,000$	4,000
Unindexed gain	3,000
Indexation allowance £4,000 × 0.213	852
Chargeable gain 2000/01	£2,148

(ii) *2003/04 disposal to son*

Original market value (deemed disposal consideration)	£7,800
Reasonable proportion of aggregate market value as at November 2003 of all assets disposed of to date:	
£18,000 × 2/4	£9,000
	£
Deemed consideration (greater of £7,800 and £9,000)	9,000
Cost $\frac{9,000}{9,000+7,800} \times (£12,000 - £4,000)$	4,286
Unindexed gain	4,714
Indexation allowance £4,286 × 0.213	913
Chargeable gain 2003/04 (subject to TAPER RELIEF (61))	£3,801

August 2006

(i) *Gain on 2000/01 disposal to daughter recomputed*

Original market value (deemed consideration in recomputation at November 2003)	£7,000
Reasonable proportion of aggregate market value as at February 2001 of all assets disposed of to date:	
£26,000 × 2/6	£8,667

	£
Deemed consideration (greater of £7,000 and £8,667)	8,667
Cost $\frac{8,667}{8,667+14,000} \times £12,000$	4,588
Unindexed gain	4,079
Indexation allowance £4,588 × 0.213	977
Revised chargeable gain 2000/01	£3,102

(ii) *Gain on 2003/04 disposal to son recomputed*

Original market value (deemed consideration in computation at November 2003)	£9,000
Reasonable proportion of aggregate market value as at November 2003 of all assets disposed of to date: £34,200 × 2/6	£11,400

	£
Deemed consideration (greater of £9,000 and £11,400)	11,400
Cost $\frac{11,400}{11,400+7,800} \times (12,000-4,588)$	4,401
Unindexed gain	6,999
Indexation allowance £4,401 × 0.213	938
Revised chargeable gain 2003/04 (subject to TAPER RELIEF (61))	£6,061

(iii) *Gain on 2006/07 disposal to brother*

	£
Original market value (actual consideration)	£10,400
Reasonable proportion of aggregate market value as at August 2006 of all assets disposed of to date: £46,200 × 2/6	£15,400

	£
Deemed consideration (greater of £10,400 and £15,400)	15,400
Cost (£12,000 – £4,588 – £4,401)	3,011
Unindexed gain	12,389
Indexation allowance £3,011 × 0.213	641
Chargeable gain 2006/07 (subject to TAPER RELIEF (61))	£11,748

Notes to the example

(*a*) The disposal in February 2001 is at first covered by the chattel exemption (£6,000). As the second disposal in November 2003 is to a person connected with the recipient of the first disposal, the two must then be looked at together for the purposes of the chattel exemption, and, as the combined proceeds exceed the chattel exemption limit, the exemption is not available. [*TCGA 1992, s 262*].

(*b*) The three disposals are linked transactions within *TCGA 1992, s 19* as they are made by the same transferor to persons with whom he is connected, and take place within a six-year period.

(*c*) It is assumed in the above example that it is 'reasonable' to apportion the aggregate market value in proportion to the number of items. In other instances a different basis may be needed to give the 'reasonable' apportionment required by *TCGA 1992, s 20(4)*.

3.17 CLOSE COMPANY TRANSFERRING ASSET AT UNDERVALUE [*TCGA 1992, s 125*]

Where, on or after 31 March 1982, a close company (as defined by *ICTA 1988, ss 414, 415*) transfers (other than within a group of companies under *TCGA 1992, s 171(1)*, see 27.2 GROUPS OF COMPANIES) an asset to any person otherwise than at arm's length and for a consideration of an amount or value less than the market value of the asset, an amount equal to the difference is apportioned among the issued shares of the company. On a disposal of the shares by the person who owned them at the date of transfer, an amount equal to the amount so apportioned is not treated as allowable expenditure. Where the owner of such shares is itself a close company, an amount equal to the amount apportioned to those shares is apportioned among the issued shares of that close company, the owners thereof being treated as above, and so on through any number of close companies.

Where the gain or loss on disposal of shares held at 31 March 1982 falls to be computed *other than* by reference to their value at that date (see 8.2 ASSETS HELD ON 31 MARCH 1982), any transfers of assets as above which were made before that date (but not before 6 April 1965) are also taken into account.

Where the asset is transferred to a settlement for the benefit of employees, etc. (see 22.85 EXEMPTIONS AND RELIEFS), the amount apportioned is the difference between the market value of the asset or the amount of the allowable expenditure attributable to the asset, whichever is the less, and the consideration. [*TCGA 1992, s 239(3)*].

By concession, *TCGA 1992, s 125* is not applied in two sets of circumstances. The first is where the transferee is a participator or an associate of a participator in the company and the transfer is treated as an income distribution within *ICTA 1988, s 209(2)(b)* or (*4*) or the transfer is treated as a capital distribution within *TCGA 1992, s 122* (see 58.10 SHARES AND SECURITIES). The second is where the transferee is an employee of the company and the excess of the market value of the asset over the price paid for it is charged to income tax as employment income (HMRC Extra-Statutory Concession D51).

3.18 RESTRICTIONS ON COMPANY RECONSTRUCTIONS [*TCGA 1992, ss 137, 138; FA 2002, Sch 9 paras 5(5)(6), 7; CRCA 2005, s 5*]

TCGA 1992, s 135 applies to the takeover of one company by another wholly or partly for shares or debentures and provides that the original holding and the new holding are to be treated as the same asset. See 58.4 SHARES AND SECURITIES. *TCGA 1992, s 136* deals with company reconstructions where a company issues shares or debentures to another company's shareholders whose original holdings are either retained or cancelled. The original and new holdings are likewise treated as the same asset. See 58.6 SHARES AND SECURITIES. Neither of these provisions applies, however, unless the exchange of securities or scheme of reconstruction is for 'bona fide commercial reasons', and not part of a scheme or arrangement for the main or only purpose of avoiding capital gains tax or corporation tax. This restriction does not apply where a recipient of the shares, etc. holds 5% or less of, or of any class of, the relevant shares, etc. (including holdings by connected persons) in the company being acquired etc., or where the Commissioners for HMRC (or, before 18 April 2005, the Board of Inland Revenue), on written application by either company, have given clearance before the issue is made. In determining whether a recipient holds 5% or less of the shares concerned for this purpose, any of its own shares that the company holds as treasury shares (see 58.14 SHARES AND SECURITIES) do not count (HMRC Capital Gains Manual CG 52623).

See *Snell v HMRC (Sp C 532), [2006] SSCD 296* in which the above provisions were held to apply where the taxpayer became non-resident after exchanging his shareholding in a company for loan notes and before selling the loan notes.

Application for clearance must contain particulars of operations contemplated and the Commissioners may, within thirty days of receipt, call for further particulars (to be supplied within thirty days, or longer if the Commissioners allow). If the particulars are not supplied, the application lapses. Subject to this, the Commissioners must indicate their decision within a further thirty days. If not so notified, or if dissatisfied with the decision, the applicants may within a further thirty days require the Commissioners to refer the particulars to the Special Commissioners for their decision. All material facts and considerations must be disclosed, otherwise any decision is void.

Applications for clearance should be directed to the Clearance and Counteraction Team, Anti-Avoidance Group Intelligence, First Floor, 22 Kingsway, London, WC2B 6NR for the attention of Mohini Sawhney (or, if market-sensitive information is included, Eric Gardner). Applications may be faxed to 020–7438 4409 or emailed to reconstructions@gtnet.gov.uk (in both cases after telephoning Eric Gardner (on 020–7438 6585) if market-sensitive information is included). A hard copy need not then be sent. From 1 November 2002, only a single application need be made as above for clearances under any one or more of: *ICTA 1988, s 215* (demergers), *ICTA 1988, s 225* (purchase of own shares), *ICTA 1988, s 707* (transactions in securities), *TCGA 1992, s 138(1)* (as above), *TCGA 1992, s 139(5)* (reconstructions involving the transfer of a business — see 13.10 COMPANIES), *TCGA 1992, s 140B* (transfer of a UK trade between EU member states — 45.10 OVERSEAS MATTERS), *TCGA 1992, s 140D* (transfer of a non-UK trade between EU member states — 45.11 OVERSEAS MATTERS) and *FA 2002, Sch 29 para 88* (various clearances under the corporation tax intangible assets regime). (Before 1 November 2002, applications under *section 138(1)* were sent to Capital and Savings division at Solihull.) (Revenue Internet Statement 23 October 2002).

The above provisions also apply to interests in a company without share capital (where relevant — see 58.4, 58.6 SHARES AND SECURITIES) and certain quoted options.

Tax assessed on a person (the '*chargeable person*') by virtue of the above provisions and not paid within six months of the date when it is payable may be recovered, in whole or in part, from certain third parties, in the name of the chargeable person, within two years of that date. There is a right of recourse to the chargeable person for the tax so paid together with, in the case of corporation tax, interest paid in respect of that tax. The third parties are restricted to persons holding the shares, etc. issued to the chargeable person who acquired them as a result of one or more disposals within *TCGA 1992, s 58(1)* (spouses or civil partners living together) or *s 171(1)* (companies within same group) without any intervening disposals not within those provisions.

Seeking to retain family control of a company may be a 'bona fide commercial reason', see *CIR v Brebner HL 1967, 43 TC 705*; *Clark v CIR Ch D 1978, 52 TC 482* and *CIR v Goodwin HL 1976, 50 TC 583*, which deal with the similar phrase in *ICTA 1988, s 703(1)*.

Under the law as it stood for shares or debentures issued on or before 16 April 2002, the reconstructed company or amalgamated companies should, strictly speaking, carry on substantially the same business and have substantially the same members as the original company or companies, but in practice the latter requirement may be waived if the scheme was carried out for bona fide commercial reasons. Where new companies are formed to take over separate parts of the original company's business, this provision may be applied even if the new companies have no common shareholder, provided that there is an actual segregation of trades or businesses which can be carried on in their own right, and not merely a segregation of assets. (HMRC Statement of Practice 5/85). For shares or debentures issued after 16 April 2002, a revised statutory definition of 'scheme of reconstruction' was introduced (for which, see 58.6 SHARES AND SECURITIES), partly to incorporate the aforementioned practice, which consequently no longer applies.

For the Revenue's response to a number of concerns regarding aspects of clearances under *TCGA 1992, s 138*, see ICAEW Guidance Note TR 657, 10 April 1987.

3.19 **Schemes involving the transfer of a business owned by companies.** [*TCGA 1992, s 139*]. See 13.10 COMPANIES where a scheme of reconstruction involves the transfer of a UK resident company's business to another UK resident company for no consideration other than the assumption of liabilities of the business.

3.20 GROUPS OF COMPANIES

There are a number of anti-avoidance provisions relating to groups of companies generally. See 27 GROUPS OF COMPANIES and in particular 27.9 for a company ceasing to be a member of a group. In addition, see 3.7–3.14 above for value shifting to give a tax-free benefit which may involve groups, 3.21 below for depreciatory transactions within groups of companies and 3.22 for dividend stripping treated as a depreciatory transaction.

3.21 DEPRECIATORY TRANSACTIONS WITHIN GROUPS OF COMPANIES

[*TCGA 1992, s 176; FA 1996, Sch 20 para 57; FA 2000, Sch 29 para 24*]

Simon's Direct Tax Service. See D2.665.

Where, on or after 31 March 1982, two or more members of a group of companies are parties to a 'disposal of assets' at other than market value which has the effect of materially reducing the value of the shares or 'securities' of one of those companies ('a depreciatory transaction'), any loss arising on the ultimate disposal of those shares or securities by a member or a former member of the group (having been a member when the transaction took place) is to be allowable only so far as is 'just and reasonable'. Account may be taken of any other post-30 March 1982 transaction which has

(i) enhanced the value of the assets of the company the shares in which are being disposed of, and

(ii) depreciated the assets of any other group member.

Where the loss on the ultimate disposal of an asset held at 31 March 1982 falls to be computed *other than* by reference to its value at that date (see 8.2 ASSETS HELD ON 31 MARCH 1982), depreciatory (and other) transactions before that date (but not before 6 April 1965) are also taken into account.

Where a loss has been wholly or partly disallowed as above, any chargeable gain accruing within six years of the depreciatory transaction on the disposal of shares or securities of another company which was a party to it is reduced as is just and reasonable (but not so as to exceed the reduction in the allowable loss). Regard is to be had to the effect of the depreciatory transaction on the value of the shares at the date of disposal. All adjustments, by discharge or repayment of tax, or otherwise, as are required to give effect to these provisions may be made at any time.

A '*depreciatory transaction*' also includes any other transaction where

(*a*) the company, the shares or securities in which are the subject of the ultimate disposal, or any 75% subsidiary of that company, was party to that transaction; and

(*b*) the parties to the transaction were, or included, two or more companies which, when the transaction occurred, were in the same group.

A transaction is not depreciatory to the extent that it is a payment which is required to be, or has been, brought into account in computing a chargeable gain or allowable loss of the company making the ultimate disposal. Cancellation within *Companies Act 1985, s 135* of shares or securities of one member of a group which are owned by another is deemed to be a depreciatory transaction unless it falls within this exemption. The deemed disposal arising under a claim that shares or securities have become of negligible value under *TCGA 1992, s 24(2)* (see 40.9 LOSSES) may constitute a depreciatory transaction.

References to '*disposal of assets*' include appropriation by one member of a group of the goodwill of another member.

'*Securities*' includes loan stock or similar securities whether secured or unsecured.

A group of companies, and related expressions, are construed for these purposes in accordance with 27.1 GROUPS OF COMPANIES, except that a group could include non-UK resident companies even before the change in the residence requirement there mentioned.

Where a subsidiary company pays dividends to its parent out of post-acquisition profits, HMRC do not regard the payment as being a depreciatory transaction (HMRC Capital Gains Manual CG 46580).

For consideration of these provisions, see HMRC Capital Gains Manual CG 46500–46683.

3.22 **DIVIDEND STRIPPING** [*TCGA 1992, s 177; F(No 2)A 1992, s 46(1)(6); FA 2000, Sch 29 para 25*]

Simon's Direct Tax Service. See D2.667.

Where a company (the 'first company') holds 10% or more of a class of shares in another company (the 'second company') otherwise than as a dealing company, and a distribution is or has been made to the first company which materially reduces or has reduced the value of the holding, the distribution is to be treated as a depreciatory transaction under *TCGA 1992, s 176* (see 3.21 above) in relation to any disposal of the shares. This applies whether the disposal is by the first company or any other company to which the holding has been transferred under the provisions of *TCGA 1992, s 140A* (transfer of UK trade between companies in different EC member states, see 45.10 OVERSEAS MATTERS), *s 171* (transfers within a group, see 27.2 GROUPS OF COMPANIES) or *s 172* (now repealed — see 45.3 OVERSEAS MATTERS). If the first and second companies are not members of the same group, they are deemed to be so.

For these purposes, a company's holding of different classes in another company are treated as separate holdings and holdings of the same class which differ in the entitlements or obligations they confer are treated as holdings of different classes. Subject to this, all of a company's holdings of the same class in another company must be treated as a single holding and other holdings of the same class held by connected persons are aggregated in determining whether the 10% test is satisfied. For the meaning of connected persons, see 16 CONNECTED PERSONS. For the above provisions only, the persons mentioned in 16.6 specifically include persons acting together to secure or acquire a holding in a company (and not just control).

A distribution need not be treated as a depreciatory transaction under these provisions to the extent that it consists of a payment which is required to be, or has been, brought into account in calculating a chargeable gain or allowable loss by the person making the ultimate disposal.

3.23 **TRANSACTIONS IN LAND** [*ICTA 1988, ss 776–778; ITTOIA 2005, Sch 1 paras 312, 313*]

Where land in the UK is acquired or developed with the sole or main object of realising a gain from disposing of it or is held as trading stock, any capital gain from 'disposal' of the land is, subject to certain exemptions, treated as *income* of the person realising the gain (or the person who transmitted to him the opportunity of making that gain). See 38.4 LAND.

3.24 LAND SOLD AND LEASED BACK [*ICTA 1988, s 780; ITTOIA 2005, Sch 1 para 315*]

As regards certain arrangements within *ICTA 1988, s 779,* part of the consideration received by the lessee for giving up the original lease (or undertaking to pay an increased rent) is treated as an income receipt and not a capital one. See 38.21 LAND.

3.25 ABUSE OF CONCESSIONS

Prior to 9 March 1999, there was no statutory authority for a charge to tax arising by virtue of a concession under the terms of which a gain was initially deferred with the intention that it be brought back into charge (whether directly or indirectly) on the occasion of a subsequent event in a later chargeable period. As a result it was difficult for the Revenue to enforce payment of the tax. A statutory charge was therefore introduced by *Finance Act 1999* to have effect where the deferred gain is to be brought back into charge under the terms of the concession and that gain is not returned (i.e. included in a tax return).

The statutory charge applies where a person (the '*original taxpayer*') has at any time obtained the benefit of a capital gains relief in reliance on a 'concession' and circumstances arise in a subsequent chargeable period and on or after 9 March 1999, which, if that benefit had been obtained under a statutory relief, would have resulted in the whole (or part) of the benefit falling to be recouped from any person (whether or not the original taxpayer). A chargeable gain equal to the full amount of that benefit is deemed to accrue to the latter person for the chargeable period in which the circumstances arise. The chargeable gain is not eligible for TAPER RELIEF (61) (or ROLLOVER RELIEF (55) — see HMRC Capital Gains Manual CG 13659). The total recouped under these provisions cannot exceed the original benefit (which might otherwise have been the case where there are part disposals, such that the said circumstances arise in more than one chargeable period — see HMRC Capital Gains Manual CG 13655).

The above provision does not, however, apply where the person to whom the deemed chargeable gain would otherwise accrue indicates in writing to HMRC that he accepts that the benefit obtained by the original taxpayer may be recouped from him. Such acceptance may be indicated simply by the making or amending of a self-assessment to include the deferred gain. Where, *following* an assessment under this provision,

- such indication of acceptance is given on or before the latest of the deadlines listed below, or
- it transpires that the original taxpayer did not, or was not entitled to, rely on the concession and *his* tax position for the earlier period is finally determined on that basis,

such adjustments are to be made to ensure that the chargeable person's liability is no greater than would have been the case had such an event occurred earlier such that no assessment would have been necessary. The above-mentioned deadlines are:

- twelve months after an assessment is made under the above provision;
- the latest date for amending the self-assessment tax return or company tax return for the period in which the gain accrues (see 54.6, 54.18 RETURNS); and,
- where a claim for further relief (for example, rollover relief) is possible against the gain and is made, the latest possible date for making that claim.

For the purpose of the above provision, '*concession*' means any concession which

- was first published by the Revenue before 9 March 1999 or replaces a concession so published and having similar effect;

- was available generally to any person falling within its terms at the time it was relied upon by the original taxpayer;

and which has the effect of

- applying (with or without modifications) the provisions of any enactment to a case to which they would not otherwise have applied; or
- treating, without applying a specific enactment,
  - (i) any asset as the same as any other asset and acquired as the other asset was acquired;
  - (ii) any two or more assets as a single asset; or
  - (iii) any disposal as having been a disposal on which neither a gain nor a loss accrued.

For these purposes, the term 'concession' is not restricted to those listed as EXTRA-STATUTORY CONCESSIONS (33) but includes any practice, interpretation or other statement in the nature of a concession and within the above definition.

[*TCGA 1992, ss 284A, 284B; FA 1999, s 76*].

The following extra-statutory concessions are *examples* of concessions at which the above provisions are aimed.

- D15 (which extends rollover relief on business assets to cover gains on assets of a company which is 90% owned by an unincorporated association — see 55.5 ROL-LOVER RELIEF).
- D16 (which extends rollover relief on business assets where the proceeds from the disposal of an asset are reinvested in the repurchase of the same asset — see 55.3 ROLLOVER RELIEF).
- D22 (which extends rollover relief on business assets where the proceeds from the disposal of an asset are used to enhance the value of another asset — see 55.3 ROLLOVER RELIEF).
- D39 (which treats a lease of property which is surrendered before its expiry date as the same asset as a new lease to replace it — see 38.14 LAND).

(Treasury Explanatory Notes to the Finance Bill 1999). For further commentary and examples, see HMRC Capital Gains Manual CG 13650–13659. For the Revenue's practice where the said circumstances arose *before* 9 March 1999 and the taxpayer attempts to repudiate the previous concessionary relief, maybe retrospectively by means of error or mistake relief claim (see 12.7 CLAIMS), see HMRC Capital Gains Manual CG 13662.

3.26 TAX ARBITRAGE

F(No 2)A 2005 introduced anti-avoidance provisions to prevent the exploitation by companies of differences between or within national tax codes using hybrid entities or instruments (known as tax arbitrage). The provisions operate by reducing or disallowing deductions or by bringing receipts into charge, but apply only where HMRC issue a notice to the company. Separate provisions apply in relation to deductions cases and receipts cases. See below for the commencement rules. HMRC published guidance to the provisions on their website (www.hmrc.gov.uk) on 2 August 2005.

The following apply for the purposes of the provisions. A '*scheme*' is any scheme, arrangements or understanding of any kind, whether or not legally enforceable, involving a single transaction or two or more transactions. The circumstances in which any two or more transactions are to be taken as forming part of a series of transactions or a scheme include any case in which it would be reasonable to assume that one or more of them would not have been entered into independently of the others or if entered into independently would not have taken the same form or been on the same terms. It is immaterial in determining whether any transactions form part of a series of transactions that the parties to any of the transactions are different from the parties to another of the transactions. A scheme achieves a '*UK tax advantage*' for a person if in consequence of the scheme that person is in a position to obtain, or has obtained,

- a relief (including a tax credit) or increased relief from,
- a repayment or increased repayment of, or
- the avoidance or reduction of a charge to

income tax or corporation tax. In particular, avoidance or reduction of a charge to tax may be effected by receipts accruing in such a way that the recipient does not pay or bear tax on them or by a deduction in computing profits or gains. [*F(No 2)A 2005, s 30*].

Deductions cases. Subject to the commencement rules below, the following provisions apply to a company which is resident in the UK, or a non-resident company which is within the charge to corporation tax, if the following conditions are satisfied in relation to a transaction to which the company is a party.

(*a*) The transaction forms part of a scheme which is a 'qualifying scheme' (see below).

(*b*) The scheme is such that for corporation tax purposes the company is in a position to claim, or has claimed, an amount by way of deduction in respect of the transaction or is in a position to set off, or has set off, against profits in an accounting period an amount relating to the transaction.

(*c*) The main purpose, or one of the main purposes, of the scheme is to achieve a UK tax advantage for the company.

(*d*) The amount of the UK tax advantage is more than a minimal amount.

If the Commissioners for HMRC consider, on reasonable grounds, that the above conditions are or may be satisfied they may give the company a notice specifying the transaction involved, the accounting period in respect of which condition (*b*) above is or may be satisfied and informing the company that as a consequence the provisions apply. The Commissioners may issue such a notice to a company in respect of two or more transactions.

If a company receives a notice and conditions (*a*)–(*d*) above are in fact satisfied at the time it is given, the company must compute (or recompute) its income or chargeable gains for corporation tax purposes or its liability to corporation tax for the specified accounting period and any subsequent accounting period in accordance with the following two rules.

The first rule is that no deduction is allowable in respect of the transaction specified in the notice to the extent that an amount in relation to the expense in question may be otherwise deducted or allowed in computing the income, profits or losses of any person for the purposes of any tax (including foreign tax (within the meaning of *ICTA 1988, s 403D*) but excluding petroleum revenue tax and tax chargeable under *ICTA 1988, s 501A(1)* in respect of ring fence trades), or would be so deductible or allowable but for a rule (whether a UK or non-UK tax provision) that has the same effect as this provision.

The second rule applies where a transaction or series of transactions forming part of the scheme involves a payment which creates a deduction or allowance for tax purposes (including foreign tax purposes) for the payer or another party to the scheme but the payee is not liable to tax on the receipt or has his tax liability reduced as a result of the scheme. For this purpose, the circumstances in which a payee is treated as having his liability to tax reduced as a result of the scheme include where he can set off against his income an expense or relief arising out of the scheme. A payee is not treated as not liable to tax on the receipt if he is not liable to tax on any income or gains under the tax law of any territory or if he is not liable to tax on the receipt because of a statutory exemption which exempts him from tax in respect of income or gains without providing that those income or gains are to be treated as those of another person. Where the rule applies, the aggregate of the amounts allowable as a deduction in computing profits for corporation tax purposes arising from the transaction specified in the notice and any other transactions forming part of the scheme and to which the company is party must be reduced. If the payee is not liable to tax on the receipt (as above), the aggregate is reduced to nil. If the payee is liable to tax on part of the receipt or his liability to tax is reduced as above, the aggregate is reduced proportionately to correspond to the payee's liability (treating the amount by which the payee's liability is reduced as an amount on which the payee is not liable to tax).

Instead of applying the above two rules, the company may choose to incorporate in its tax return for the specified accounting period any adjustments that are necessary to counteract the effects of the scheme that are referable to the purpose mentioned in (*c*) above. The adjustments to be made are to treat all or part of a deduction as not being allowable, or all or part of an amount which may be set off against profits as not falling to be set off. If the adjustments fully counteract the effects of the scheme the company is treated as having complied with the provisions.

See below for further provisions governing the effects of a notice under the above provisions.

The above provisions apply for accounting periods of a company beginning on or after 16 March 2005. Accounting periods straddling that date are treated for this purpose as consisting of two accounting periods, the first ending on 15 March 2005, and the second beginning on 16 March 2005. The provisions do not, however, apply in the case of a transaction to which a company is party on 16 March 2005 if the company is not on that date connected (within *ICTA 1988, s 839*) with any other person who is on that date a party to, or concerned in, the scheme, and the scheme ceases to exist before 31 August 2005.

[*F(No 2)A 2005, ss 24, 25, 31(1)–(3)(5)*].

Qualifying scheme. A scheme is a '*qualifying scheme*' for the purposes of the above provisions if it is one of the following types.

(1) A scheme in which a party to a transaction forming part of it is a 'hybrid entity'. For this purpose, an entity is a '*hybrid entity*' if under the tax law of any territory it is regarded as a person but its profits or gains are, for the purposes of a '*relevant tax*' (i.e. income tax, corporation tax or similar non-UK tax) under the law of any territory, treated as the profits or gains of a different person or persons. An entity is not so treated by reason only of its profits or gains being subject to a non-UK tax rule similar to that in *ICTA 1988, s 747(3)* (imputation of profits of controlled foreign company — see 45.7 OVERSEAS MATTERS).

(2) A scheme one of the parties to which is party to an instrument of which, under the law of a particular territory, a 'relevant characteristic' may be altered on the election of any party to it. A characteristic of an instrument is a '*relevant characteristic*' if, under the law of a particular territory, altering it has the effect of determining whether or not, for that territory's tax purposes, the instrument is taken into account as giving rise to income or capital. For this purpose, an instrument is taken into account as giving rise to capital if a gain on disposal would be a chargeable gain, or would be if the person making the disposal were UK-resident.

(3) A scheme which includes the issuing by a company of shares subject to conversion or the amendment of rights attaching to shares issued by a company such that the shares become shares subject to conversion. Shares of a company are subject to conversion for this purpose if the rights attaching to them include provision by virtue of which a holder is entitled, on the occurrence of an event, to acquire securities (within the meaning of *ICTA 1988, s 254(1)*) in that or another company by conversion or

exchange and the occurrence of that event is within the reasonable expectation of the company either at the time when the shares are issued or at the time the rights attaching to the shares are amended.

(4) A scheme which includes the issuing by a company of securities (within the meaning of *ICTA 1988, s 254(1)*) subject to conversion or the amendment of rights attaching to securities issued by a company such that the securities become securities subject to conversion. Securities of a company are subject to conversion for this purpose if the rights attaching to them include provision by virtue of which a holder is entitled, on the occurrence of an event, to acquire shares in that or another company by conversion or exchange and the occurrence of that event is within the reasonable expectation of the company either at the time when the securities are issued or at the time the rights attaching to the securities are amended.

(5) A scheme which includes a 'debt instrument' issued by a company that is treated as equity in the company under generally accepted accounting practice (within *FA 2004, s 50*). A '*debt instrument*' for this purpose is an instrument issued by a company that represents a loan relationship (see 14.5 COMPANIES—CORPORATE FINANCE AND INTANGIBLES), or would do if the company were UK-resident.

(6) A scheme which includes the issue by a company to a connected person (within *ICTA 1988, s 839*) of shares other than shares which, on their issue, are ordinary shares that are fully paid-up, which confer a 'qualifying beneficial entitlement' at all times in the accounting period in which they are issued and in respect of which there is no arrangement or understanding at the time of issue under which the rights attaching to the shares may be amended. A share in a company confers a '*qualifying beneficial entitlement*' if it confers a beneficial entitlement to the same proportion of any profits available for distribution to equity holders of the company and of any assets available for distribution to equity holders on a winding-up as the proportion of the issued share capital represented by that share. *ICTA 1988, Sch 18* (equity holders and profits or assets available for distribution) applies for this purpose as it applies for the purposes of group relief.

(7) A scheme which includes a transaction or series of transactions under which a person transfers rights to receive a payment under a 'relevant security' to one or more other persons or otherwise secures that one or more other persons are similarly benefited (i.e. that they receive a payment which would, but for the transaction or series of transactions, have arisen to the transferor) and

- the transferor and at least one of the persons to whom a transfer of rights is made or similar benefit is secured are connected (within *ICTA 1988, s 839*), and
- following the transfer of rights or securing of the similar benefit, two or more persons either hold rights to receive a payment under the security or enjoy a similar benefit and the rights held and benefits enjoyed by such of those persons as are connected have, taken together, a market value equal to or greater than the market value of any other such rights and benefits, taken together.

For this purpose, a '*relevant security*' is a security within the meaning of *ICTA 1988, s 254(1)* or any agreement under which a person receives an annuity or other annual payment (whether payable annually or at shorter or longer intervals) for a term which is not contingent on the duration of a human life or lives.

[*F(No 2)A 2005, Sch 3*].

Receipts cases. The following provisions apply to a company resident in the UK if the following conditions are satisfied.

(i) A scheme makes or imposes provision (the '*actual provision*') as between the company and another person (the '*paying party*') by means of a transaction or series of transactions.

(ii) The actual provision includes the making by the paying party, by means of a transaction or series of transactions, of a 'qualifying payment'. For this purpose, a '*qualifying payment*' is a contribution to the capital of the company made on or after 16 March 2005.

(iii) As regards the qualifying payment there is an amount that is available for deduction for UK tax purposes or that may be deducted or otherwise allowable under the tax law of a territory outside the UK. (Such an amount is, however, disregarded for this purpose if or to the extent that it is set for tax purposes against any income arising to the paying party from the transaction or transactions forming part of the scheme.) This condition is not treated as satisfied if the paying party is a dealer (as defined) who incurs losses in the ordinary course of his business in respect of the transaction or transactions and the amount by reference to which this condition would otherwise be satisfied is an amount in respect of those losses.

(iv) At least part of the qualifying payment is not

(A) income or gains arising to the company in the accounting period in which the qualifying payment was made;

(B) income arising to any other company resident in the UK in a 'corresponding' accounting period (i.e. an accounting period with at least one day in common with the accounting period in (A) above); or

(C) taken into account in determining the loan relationship credits or debits to be brought into account by a company as respects a share in another company under *FA 1996, ss 91A, 91B* (shares treated as loan relationships — see 14.5 COMPANIES—CORPORATE FINANCE AND INTANGIBLES).

(v) The company and the paying party expected on entering into the scheme that a benefit would arise as a result of (iv) above being satisfied (whether by reference to all or part of the qualifying payment).

If the Commissioners for HMRC consider, on reasonable grounds, that the above conditions are or may be satisfied they may give the company a notice specifying the qualifying payment involved, the accounting period in which the payment is made and informing the company that as a consequence the following provisions apply.

If a company receives a notice and conditions (i)–(v) above are in fact satisfied at the time it is given, the company must compute (or recompute) its income or chargeable gains for corporation tax purposes or its liability to corporation tax for the specified accounting period as if the part of the qualifying payment by reference to which (iii) and (iv) above are satisfied were an amount of income arising to the company in that period and chargeable under Schedule D, Case VI. If (iii) and (iv) above are satisfied in relation to the whole of the qualifying payment, the whole of the payment is so chargeable.

See below for further provisions governing the effects of a notice under the above provisions.

[*F(No 2)A 2005, ss 26, 27, 31(4)(5)*].

Effects of a notice. If a notice under either of the above provisions is given before the company has made its return for the specified accounting period then, if the return is made in the period of 90 days beginning with the day on which the notice is given, it may disregard the notice, and at any time before the end of the 90 days the company may amend the return in order to comply with the notice.

If no notice has been given before the company's return has been made, a notice may only be given if the company has been given a notice of enquiry (see 54.18 RETURNS) in respect of the return. After an enquiry has been completed, a notice may only be given if

- at the time the enquiry was completed the Commissioners for HMRC could not have reasonably been expected, on the basis of the information made available (within *FA 1998, Sch 18 para 44(2)(3)*— see 5.2 ASSESSMENTS) to them or an officer of Revenue and Customs before that time, to have been aware that the circumstances were such that a notice could have been given; and
- the company was requested to provide information during the enquiry and, if it had been so provided, the Commissioners could reasonably have been expected to give the company a notice.

If the notice is given after the company has made its return, it may amend the return to comply with the notice within 90 days beginning with the day on which the notice is given. If the notice is given after an enquiry into the return has started, a closure notice (see 54.11 RETURNS) may not be issued until the end of the period of 90 days beginning with the issue of the notice or, if earlier, an amendment is made to the return complying with the notice. If the notice is given after the completion of an enquiry, a discovery assessment (see 5.2 ASSESSMENTS) in relation to the income or chargeable gain to which it relates may not be made until the end of the period of 90 days beginning with the issue of the notice or, if earlier, an amendment is made to the return complying with the notice.

Where a notice is issued and no amendment is made to the return for the purpose of complying with it, the above provisions do not prevent a return becoming incorrect if such an amendment should have been made.

[*F(No 2)A 2005, s 28*].

Clearance. HMRC operate an advance clearance scheme for the above provisions and will give a decision wherever possible as to whether a notice will be issued in respect of proposed transactions. Sufficient information must be provided to enable HMRC to reach a view as to whether the provisions apply and procedures for clearance applications are set out in Annex C to the HMRC guidance to the provisions published on their website on 2 August 2005. HMRC will consider themselves bound by any clearance given in accordance with those procedures. Clearance applications and any queries about the procedures should be sent to Andrew Hoar, HMRC (International CT), 100 Parliament Street, London SW1A 2BQ.

3.27 FACTORING OF INCOME RECEIPTS

FA 2006 introduced anti-avoidance provisions to counter schemes (referred to in the legislation as 'structured finance arrangements') involving the factoring of income receipts. The schemes involve the transfer of an asset on which there is a predictable income stream or a transfer of the right to such an income stream, in return for a lump sum. The income stream acquired by the transferee is then sufficient to repay both the lump sum and interest. The transferor then claims that the income or receipts arising during the period of the arrangement are not taxable on him and that the lump sum is either a capital receipt giving rise to a chargeable gain only or is not taxable at all. Broadly, the provisions operate by deeming the intended effects of the arrangements not to have effect for tax purposes. See *ICTA 1988, ss 774A–774G* (inserted by *FA 2006, Sch 6 para 3B*) and Tolley's Income Tax for full details.

For capital gains purposes, where:

(*a*) *ICTA 1988, s 774B* applies to a structured finance arrangement;

(*b*) the 'borrower' or a person connected with him (other than the 'lender') makes a disposal at any time of any 'security' under the arrangement to or for the benefit of the lender or a person connected with him (other than the borrower); and (*c*) either

- the person making the disposal subsequently reacquires under the arrangement the asset disposed of; or
- that asset subsequently ceases to exist, having been held continuously by the lender (or connected person) from the time of the disposal,

then the disposal of the security in (*b*) above and any subsequent reacquisition of the asset are disregarded.

An 'arrangement' is a '*structured finance arrangement*' in relation to a person (the '*borrower*') for these purposes if:

(i) under the arrangement the borrower receives from another person (the '*lender*') any money or other asset (the '*advance*') in any period;

(ii) the accounts of the borrower for that period record a financial liability in respect of the advance in accordance with generally accepted accounting practice (or would so record a financial liability if accounts were drawn up in accordance with generally accepted accounting practice);

(iii) the borrower or a person connected with him (other than the lender) makes a disposal (including anything which would constitute a disposal for capital gains purposes) under the arrangement of an asset (the '*security*') to or for the benefit of the lender or a person connected with him (other than the borrower);

(iv) the lender or a person connected with him (other than the borrower) is entitled to 'payments' in respect of the security under the arrangements; and

(v) those payments reduce the amount of the financial liability in respect of the advance recorded in the accounts of the borrower in accordance with generally accepted accounting practice (or would so reduce the amount if accounts were drawn up in accordance with generally accepted accounting practice).

The circumstances in which the borrower is treated for the purposes of (i) above as receiving an asset include the borrower's obtaining directly or indirectly the value of the asset or otherwise deriving directly or indirectly any benefit from it. Similarly, the circumstances in which the lender or other person is treated as entitled to payments in respect of the security for the purposes of (iv) above include the person's obtaining directly or indirectly the value of the security or otherwise deriving directly or indirectly any benefit from it. Where the borrower is a partnership, references above to the accounts of the borrower include the accounts of any member of the partnership. Where the borrower is a company, references to the accounts of the borrower include the consolidated group accounts of any group of companies of which it is a member. An '*arrangement*' includes any agreement or understanding, whether or not legally enforceable.

These provisions apply to disposals on or after 6 June 2006 and to disposals before that date where the person making the disposal makes a claim to that effect.

[*ICTA 1988, ss 774A, 774G; TCGA 1992, s 263E; FA 2006, Sch 6 paras 6, 9*].

4 Appeals

Cross-references. See 5 ASSESSMENTS; 12.3 CLAIMS for appeals in connection with claims and elections made outside the annual tax return; 23.8 FRAUDULENT OR NEGLIGENT CONDUCT for investigatory powers of HMRC; 28.2 HMRC: ADMINISTRATION as regards the Appeal Commissioners; 37.2, 37.3 INTEREST AND SURCHARGES ON UNPAID TAX as regards assessments raised before 6 April 1998 for 1995/96 and earlier years; 47.3, 47.4 PAYMENT OF TAX for postponement provisions; 48.18, 48.20 PENALTIES; 52.8 RESIDENCE AND DOMICILE.

Simon's Direct Tax Service. See A3.5, A3.7.

The headings in this chapter are as follows.

4.1 CAPITAL GAINS TAX (AND INCOME TAX) APPEALS

An appeal may be made against

(*a*) any assessment other than a self-assessment;

(*b*) any conclusion stated, or amendment made, by a closure notice on completion of an enquiry into a personal, trustees' or partnership tax return (see 54.11 RETURNS);

(*c*) any HMRC amendment (of a self-assessment) made, during an enquiry, to prevent potential loss of tax to the Crown (see 54.12 RETURNS);

(*d*) any amendment of a partnership return where loss of tax is 'discovered' (see 5.3 ASSESSMENTS).

Notice of appeal must be given, in writing to the officer of Revenue and Customs concerned and specifying grounds of appeal, within 30 days after the date of issue of the assessment in (*a*) above, the closure notice in (*b*) above or the notice of amendment in (*c*) or (*d*) above. An appeal within (*c*) above cannot be heard and determined until the enquiry has been completed. The Appeal Commissioners may allow the appellant to put forward grounds omitted from the notice of appeal, if satisfied that the omission was not wilful or unreasonable. [*TMA 1970, ss 31*(*1*)(*2*)(*4*), *31A; FA 2001, s 88, Sch 29 para 11*(*1*); *CRCA 2005, s 7*].

The above provisions apply as from, broadly, 11 May 2001, though comparable provisions applied previously (i.e. under self-assessment for 1996/97 onwards), the changes being in consequence of the revised procedure at 54.11 RETURNS for completion of an enquiry. [*FA*

2001, Sch 29 para 11(*2*)]. An appeal may be made in similar fashion against HMRC amendments made under the rules in 54.12 RETURNS to a self-assessment (or partnership statement) following completion of an enquiry before 11 May 2001, or against a disallowance (or partial disallowance) of a claim or election included in a return (now covered by (*b*) above and no longer a separate matter). [*TMA 1970, s 31*(*1*)(*1AA*)(*1A*)(*2*)(*5*)(*6*) *as previously enacted; FA 1994, ss 196, 199*(*2*)*, Sch 19 para 7; FA 1996, Sch 19 para 6*].

An appeal within (*a*) above is to the Special Commissioners if the assessment was made by the Commissioners for HMRC or the Board of Inland Revenue or under *ICTA 1988, s 350* (see Tolley's Income Tax under Deduction of tax at source). Otherwise, appeals are normally to the General Commissioners, subject to specific statutory exceptions and subject also to the appellant's right of election to bring an appeal before the Special Commissioners (see 4.5, 4.6 below). However, where a question has been referred to the Special Commissioners (see 54.13 RETURNS) during an enquiry into a return, an appeal within (*b*), (*c*) or (*d*) above relating to that return must also be to the Special Commissioners (unless they otherwise direct), and this applies even if notice of referral was given but subsequently withdrawn. [*TMA 1970, s 31*(*3*)(*6*) *as previously enacted, ss 31B, 31C; FA 1996, Sch 22 para 4; FA 2001, s 88, Sch 29 para 11; CRCA 2005, s 7*].

A number of enactments give right of appeal against a decision of HMRC in specified circumstances or an HMRC notice or determination. Where relevant, such right of appeal is referred to at the appropriate place in this book. There is no right of appeal against a determination of liability made by HMRC in the event of non-submission of a self-assessment tax return (see 54.14 RETURNS). Appeals in connection with claims and elections, where made outside the tax return, are dealt with at 12.3 CLAIMS. Unless otherwise stated or required by context, the remainder of this chapter applies to all appeals and all matters treated as appeals, and not only to appeals within (*a*)–(*d*) above or 4.2 below.

An appeal once made cannot be withdrawn unilaterally (see *R v Special Commissioners (ex p. Elmhirst) CA 1935, 20 TC 381* and *Beach v Willesden General Commissioners Ch D 1981, 55 TC 663*) but see 4.7 below for the withdrawal of appeals by agreement and 4.24 below as regards appeals to the High Court.

For postponement of tax pending appeal and for payment of tax on determination of the appeal, see respectively 47.3, 47.4 PAYMENT OF TAX.

4.2 CORPORATION TAX APPEALS

Provisions broadly similar to those in 4.1 above apply to corporation tax appeals and are found in *FA 1998, Sch 18 paras 30*(*3*)–(*5*)*, 34*(*3*)–(*5*)*, 48, 49, 92, 93*. See Tolley's Corporation Tax for detailed coverage. An appeal against an assessment to corporation tax is an appeal against the total amount of profits charged to tax in the assessment (*Owton Fens Properties Ltd v Redden Ch D 1984, 58 TC 218*).

See 13.18 COMPANIES regarding the application of these provisions where a company ceases to be UK-resident in the course of the formation of an SE and where an SE becomes non-UK resident.

Unless otherwise stated or required by context, the remainder of this chapter applies to corporation tax appeals as it does to CGT (and income tax) appeals.

4.3 SPECIAL REGULATIONS FOR CAPITAL GAINS TAX APPEALS

The Capital Gains Tax Regulations 1967 (*SI 1967 No 149*) make special provisions in relation to CGT appeals and are summarised below. In particular, they lay down procedures under which a question of market value or apportionment which affects the liability of two or more persons (e.g. a donor and donee, or a vendor and purchaser in a transaction not at arm's length) can be settled.

Joinder of third parties in appeals. Where the market value of an asset on a particular date or the apportionment of any amount or value is a material question in an appeal, any person whose liability to CGT for any period may be affected by that market value may apply to be joined in the appeal. Application is in writing to the inspector and should state, *inter alia*, how the applicant's liability may be affected and his contention in relation to the matters under appeal. A copy of the application is sent by the inspector to the appellant and any other party to the appeal. If the application is received more than thirty days before the date of the appeal hearing, or before that date is set, then if the inspector is satisfied with the propriety of the applicant's case, the applicant will be joined as a third party and appropriate notice given to the other parties. Otherwise, the inspector will refer the application to the Commissioners who may allow or refuse the application at their discretion. Insofar as his interest is being considered, the third party has the same rights as the appellant. [*SI 1967 No 149, Reg 8*].

Applications for determination of market value. Where the market value of an asset or the apportionment of any amount or value may affect the liability to CGT of two or more persons, either or any of them may apply to the Commissioners (General or Special) for a ruling if the point is not, nor has been, a material question in an appeal brought by any of them. The inspector is a party to such proceedings. [*SI 1967 No 149, Reg 9*].

Conclusive effect of determination on appeal. The values as determined are conclusive between HMRC, the parties to the appeal and any third party who was given notice of the appeal in reasonable time unless that person's application (made without undue delay) to be joined as a party to the appeal was refused. [*SI 1967 No 149, Reg 11*].

Agreements in writing. There can be no binding agreement on the value of an asset between HMRC and the taxpayer unless the agreement is joined by any proper third party to the appeal. A written agreement will be effective against the taxpayer's personal representatives, trustee in bankruptcy etc. An agreement conclusive against trustees of a settlement will be effective against any person becoming absolutely entitled to the settled property. [*SI 1967 No 149, Regs 12, 13*].

4.4 LATE APPEALS

The normal time limit for giving notice of appeal is as stated in 4.1 above. A late appeal may be accepted by HMRC if satisfied that there was a reasonable excuse for the delay. If not accepted, HMRC must refer the application to the Commissioners (normally the General Commissioners) for their decision. [*TMA 1970, s 49*]. In the event of refusal to accept a late appeal, the decision is not subject to appeal by way of stated case (*R v Special Commrs (ex p. Magill) QB (NI) 1979, 53 TC 135*, but is subject to judicial review (see *R v Hastings and Bexhill General Commrs and CIR (ex p. Goodacre) QB 1994, 67 TC 126*, in which a refusal was quashed and the matter remitted to a different body of Commissioners). In *R (oao Browallia Cal Ltd) v General Commissioners of Income Tax QB 2003, [2004] STC 296*, it was held that the Appeal Commissioners have a wider discretion than HMRC in considering a late appeal. The court held that the Commissioners in that case had misunderstood their powers and that the lack of any reasonable excuse was 'potentially relevant' but was 'not conclusive'.

4.5 ELECTION TO BRING APPEAL BEFORE SPECIAL COMMISSIONERS

As stated at 4.1 above (with the exceptions there stated), and subject to 4.6 below, an appeal is normally brought to the General Commissioners. However, an appellant may elect to bring an appeal within 4.1(*a*)–(*d*) above before the Special Commissioners instead. The election must be made either with the notice of appeal or by separate notice given within the time limit for giving the notice of appeal.

The election is, however, disregarded if the appellant and HMRC so agree in writing before the appeal is determined. Alternatively, HMRC may refer the election to the General Commissioners (after notifying the appellant). The General Commissioners must then direct that the election be disregarded unless satisfied that the appellant has arguments to present or evidence to adduce on the merits of the appeal. Such a direction may be revoked at any time before determination of the appeal if that condition is subsequently satisfied. The decision to give or revoke a direction is final.

[*TMA 1970, s 31(5A)–(5E) as previously enacted, ss 31D, 46(1); FA 1984, Sch 22 para 3; FA 2001, s 88, Sch 29 para 11*].

Similar provision applies in the case of corporation tax appeals; these are in part to be found in *FA 1998, Sch 18 para 94*.

Appeals to the General Commissioners may, if the parties so apply and the Commissioners consent, be transferred to the Special Commissioners (and vice versa) despite the expiry of the time limit for election above or the making of such an election. [*TMA 1970, s 44(3)*].

4.6 JURISDICTION OF APPEAL COMMISSIONERS

Certain specified questions in dispute on an appeal must be determined by the Special Commissioners. These include any question as to the value of unquoted shares or securities of a UK-resident company which arises in relation to the taxation of chargeable gains. [*TMA 1970, s 46B; FA 1996, Sch 22 para 7; FA 1998, Sch 19 para 24; FA 2001, s 88, Sch 29 para 27; ITEPA 2003, Sch 6 para 129; ITTOIA 2005, Sch 1 para 373*].

Where, on an appeal, the question in dispute concerns a claim made (in a return) to the Commissioners for HMRC (or, before 18 April 2005, to the Board of Inland Revenue) or made under any one or more specified provisions, the question must be determined by the Special Commissioners. The specified provisions cover double taxation relief, (before *ITTOIA 2005* came into effect) management expenses of the owner of mineral rights, exemptions for certain friendly societies, trade unions and employers' associations, and reliefs in respect of royalties, copyright payments etc. This applies in relation to appeals against conclusions and amendments following an enquiry into a return and appeals against certain HMRC amendments to returns and self-assessments to prevent loss of tax. [*TMA 1970, s 46C; FA 1996, Sch 22 para 7; FA 2001, s 88, Sch 29 para 28; ITTOIA 2005, Sch 1 para 374; CRCA 2005, s 5*]. Comparable provisions apply under *TMA 1970, Sch 1A* (see 12.3 CLAIMS) as regards claims not included in returns.

Insofar as an appeal involves the question of the value of any land, or of a lease of land, and it arises in relation to the taxation of chargeable gains, that question is to be determined by the Lands Tribunal (in England and Wales, Scotland or Northern Ireland depending on where the land is situate). [*TMA 1970, s 46D; FA 1996, Sch 22 para 7; FA 1998, Sch 19 para 26; FA 2001, s 88, Sch 29 para 29*].

Appeals to the General Commissioners may, if the parties so apply and the Commissioners consent, be transferred to the Special Commissioners (and vice versa) despite the expiry of the time limit for election in 4.5 above or the making of such an election. [*TMA 1970, s 44(3)*].

The General Commissioners may arrange that an appeal brought before them be transferred to the Special Commissioners, with the Special Commissioners' consent, if, after considering any representations made to them by the parties to the appeal, the General Commissioners consider that, because of the complexity of, or likely time required to hear, the appeal, it should be so transferred. [*TMA 1970, s 44(3A); FA 1984, Sch 22 para 5; SI 1984 No 1836*].

The Special Commissioners go on circuit to the chief provincial towns, but appeals to them may generally by arrangement be heard in London, which is usually more convenient if it is intended to engage counsel.

Rules for assigning procedures to General Commissioners. For proceedings relating to CGT or income tax for 1996/97 and subsequent years (except those concerning PAYE or partnerships or where a direction is made, see below), either the taxpayer or

HMRC (whichever commences the proceedings) may elect by notice to the other in writing for the proceedings to be heard in the division situated in either the taxpayer's place of residence, his place of business (as defined) or his place of employment (as defined and regardless of whether the proceedings are in connection with the employment). An officer may make the election if the taxpayer fails to exercise his right to do so when giving notice of appeal (or otherwise commencing proceedings) or by such later time as the Commissioners for HMRC (or, before 18 April 2005, the Board of Inland Revenue) allow. (In practice, HMRC will admit a late election by the taxpayer up to the point where the case is set down for hearing — Revenue Tax Bulletin May 1993 p 70 (comments made there about Schedule E appeals are believed to apply equally to CGT appeals).) The taxpayer's election is irrevocable. Proceedings relating to a partnership to which a partner is a party are brought before the division in the place where the partnership business is, or is mainly, carried on. For proceedings relating to corporation tax (or income tax where a UK resident company is a party) under the self-assessment regime, there are rules similar, but suitably modified, to those above for CGT and income tax.

Notwithstanding the above, the Commissioners for HMRC (or, before 18 April 2005, the Board of Inland Revenue) may direct that specified proceedings be brought before the General Commissioners for a specified division. An HMRC officer must serve on the taxpayer written notice stating the effect of the direction, and the taxpayer may object in writing within 30 days of the notice being served, in which case the direction has no effect. The Commissioners (or Board) may also give directions for determining the appropriate division, other than in PAYE appeals, where there is no place of residence, business or employment (or corporation tax equivalents) in the UK; procedure is as above except that the taxpayer has no right of objection.

The parties to proceedings may supersede the above rules by coming to an agreement that the proceedings be brought before the General Commissioners for a division specified therein. In general, HMRC will agree to transfer jurisdiction for an appeal to be heard in a division more convenient for the taxpayer (Revenue Tax Bulletin May 1993 p 70 — comments made there about Schedule E appeals are believed to apply equally to CGT appeals.) The rules are also subject to specified provisions for questions involving two or more parties (other than HMRC), which have their own rules.

[*TMA 1970, s 44(1)(2), Sch 3; FA 1988, s 133(2); FA 1996, Sch 22 para 10; ITEPA 2003, Sch 6 para 142; ITTOIA 2005, Sch 1 para 383; CRCA 2005, s 5*].

The power to make a direction as above is used broadly where HMRC have no expectation that the taxpayer will attend the hearing, but HMRC will withdraw it if the taxpayer objects because of an inconvenient journey (Revenue Tax Bulletin May 1993 p 70 — comments made there about Schedule E appeals are believed to apply equally to CGT appeals.)

Comparable rules under earlier legislation were held to be directory and not mandatory (*CIR v Adams CA 1971, 48 TC 67*; *Murphy v Elders Ch D 1973, 49 TC 135*). A determination of the General Commissioners cannot be invalidated for want of jurisdiction if there was no objection to jurisdiction before the determination. [*TMA 1970, s 44(4)*]. See also *R v Kingston & Elmbridge Commrs (ex p. Adams) QB 1972, 48 TC 75*; *R v St Pancras Commrs (ex p. Church of Scientology of California) QB 1973, 50 TC 365*; *Parikh v Birmingham North Commrs CA, [1976] STC 365*.

4.7 SETTLEMENT OF APPEALS BY AGREEMENT

Where agreement, written or otherwise, has been reached at any time between HMRC and the appellant or his agent on any appeal to the Commissioners against any assessment or decision, the assessment or decision as upheld, varied, discharged, or cancelled by that agreement, is treated as if it had been determined on appeal, provided that

- the taxpayer may withdraw from the agreement by giving written notice within 30 days of making it, and

- oral agreements are ineffective unless confirmed in writing by either side (the date of such confirmation then being the effective date of agreement).

[*TMA 1970, s 54*].

The agreement must specify the figure for assessment or a precise formula for ascertaining it (*Delbourgo v Field CA 1978, 52 TC 225*). The inspector has no power unilaterally to withdraw ('vacate') an assessment (*Baylis v Gregory HL 1988, 62 TC 1*). See *Gibson v General Commissioners for Stroud Ch D 1989, 61 TC 645* for a case where there was held not to have been a determination and *R v Inspector of Taxes, ex p. Bass Holdings Ltd*; *Richart v Bass Holdings Ltd QB 1992, 65 TC 495* for one where rectification of an agreement was ordered where a relief had been deducted twice contrary to the intention of Revenue and taxpayer. An agreement based on a mutual mistake of fact was thereby vitiated, so that the taxpayer could proceed with his appeal (*Fox v Rothwell (Sp C 50), [1995] SSCD 336*). The agreement only covers the assessments which are the subject of the appeal, and does not bind HMRC for subsequent years, for example where relievable amounts are purported to be carried forward from the year in question (*MacNiven v Westmoreland Investments Ltd HL 2001, 73 TC 1*). See *CIR v West CA 1991, 64 TC 196* for a case where the taxpayer was unsuccessful in seeking leave to defend a Crown action for payment of tax on the ground that the accountant who had entered into an agreement had no authority to do so given him by the taxpayer.

The issue of an amended notice of assessment cannot in itself constitute an offer for the purposes of a *section 54* agreement; nor can a lack of response by the taxpayer constitute acceptance of an offer (*Schuldenfrei v Hilton CA 1999, 72 TC 167*).

A taxpayer cannot withdraw an appeal made to the Commissioners (see 4.1 above), but if, having appealed, he or his agent gives the inspector oral or written notice of his desire not to proceed, then unless the inspector gives written notice of objection within 30 days thereof, the appeal is treated as if settled by agreement, as above. Agreement is effective from the date of the taxpayer's notification that the assessment etc. be upheld without variation. [*TMA 1970, s 54(4)*].

In *Tod v South Essex Motors (Basildon) Ltd Ch D 1987, 60 TC 598*, the taxpayer company's agent and the inspector agreed in 1974 that a disposal by the company in 1968 (details of which had been fully disclosed) had resulted in an allowable loss available for carry forward. However, neither party had appreciated that a correct application of the law would have resulted in the disposal being treated as giving rise to neither a gain nor a loss. In 1977 a new inspector and new agent agreed that part of the previously agreed loss should be allowed against gains arising in 1975. In 1981 the company made a substantial gain against which it claimed to set the balance of the loss but the then inspector's refusal to allow the claim was upheld. The binding effect of an agreement under *TMA 1970, s 54(1)* could be no wider than the binding effect of a determination by Commissioners or by a court on appeal. There was nothing to prevent the parties agreeing under *TMA 1970, s 54* to correct a previous agreement (as was done here); the corrected agreement became operative both for the ordinary law of contract as well as this taxing statute. Provided that full disclosure had been made, the fact that the correction proceeded upon an erroneous view of fact or law made no difference. See also HMRC Capital Gains Manual CG 40234. (For 1996/97 onwards, capital losses are subject to a formal notification procedure — see 40.3 LOSSES).

4.8 NOTIFICATION OF HEARING

Appeal meetings must be notified to the appellant and the inspector (or other HMRC party). In practice the inspector normally gives details of appeals ready for hearing to the Clerk to the Commissioners, who, after consulting the inspector and, in important appeals, the taxpayer or his agent as appropriate, makes the necessary arrangements, notifies the inspector and issues notices of the hearing to the appellant. In some Divisions he may, by arrangement, also notify the appellant's agent. See also 4.11, 4.18 below.

4.9 **APPEAL COMMISSIONERS — INTRODUCTION**

The Lord Chancellor has wide regulatory powers in relation to the practice and procedure to be followed in connection with appeals, including the power to make different provision for different cases and different circumstances. Regulations may also provide for the transfer of appeals between the General and Special Commissioners or between General Commissioners for different divisions, and for varying the number of General or Special Commissioners required or permitted to hear appeals. [*TMA 1970, ss 46A, 56B–56D; F(No 2)A 1992, Sch 16 paras 3, 4; FA 1994, s 254*]. With effect from 1 September 1994, regulations [*SI 1994 No 1812*] were introduced governing the jurisdiction of the General Commissioners and the procedure for proceedings before them (see 4.10–4.15 below). At the same time, similar regulations [*SI 1994 No 1811*] were introduced in relation to the Special Commissioners (see 4.16–4.19 below).

The Department for Constitutional Affairs publishes a leaflet containing guidance on taking appeals to the Commissioners. The leaflet, 'Tax Appeals: A guide to appealing against decisions of the Revenue on tax and other matters', can be obtained from HMRC.

4.10 **GENERAL COMMISSIONERS**

Constitution of tribunal. Two or more, but not more than five, General Commissioners for a division may hear any proceedings. [*SI 1994 No 1812, Reg 2*]. They will themselves decide which one of them will preside at the hearing. Where possible at least three will sit, and, with the consent of all the parties, proceedings may be continued by any one or more of them. [*SI 1994 No 1812, Reg 11*]. For the effect of personal business connection between a Commissioner and a party to proceedings, see *R v Holyhead Commrs (ex p. Roberts) QB 1982, 56 TC 127*.

The Clerk to the Commissioners, who is frequently a local solicitor, normally attends the meeting to take minutes and to advise them as required, but a meeting without the Clerk would not be invalid (*Venn v Franks CA 1958, 38 TC 175*).

4.11 **Preparation for hearing.** *Listing and notice of hearing*. Except in relation to proceedings under *TMA 1970, s 100C* (see 48.21 PENALTIES), any party to the proceedings may serve notice on the Clerk to the Commissioners that he wishes a date for the hearing to be fixed, on receipt of which the Clerk must send notice to each party of the place, date and time of the hearing. Unless the parties otherwise agree, or the Commissioners otherwise direct, the date must not be earlier than 28 days after the date of the Clerk's notice. [*SI 1994 No 1812, Reg 3*].

Witnesses. A General Commissioner, on the application of any party to the proceedings, may issue a witness summons (in Scotland, a witness citation) requiring any person in the UK either to attend the hearing of those proceedings to give evidence or to produce any relevant document in his possession, custody or power. The party applying for issue of the summons is responsible for its service (for which see *Reg 4(3)*), and attendance may not be required within seven days of service unless the witness informs the Clerk that he accepts shorter notice. That party must also agree to meet the witness's reasonable travelling expenses. The witness may apply, by notice served on the Clerk, for the Commissioner to set aside the summons (in whole or part), on which application the party on whose application the summons was issued is entitled to be heard.

Except in Scotland, a witness so summoned to give evidence may only be cross-examined by the party on whose application the summons was issued if the Commissioners decide that the witness is a hostile witness and give leave.

A witness cannot be compelled to give evidence or produce documents which he could not be compelled to give or produce in an action in a court of law. An auditor or tax adviser (within *TMA 1970, s 20B(10)*) cannot be compelled to produce any document which he would not be obliged to deliver or make available by notice under *TMA 1970, s 20(3)* or

(*8A*) (having regard to *TMA 1970, s 20B*(*9*)–(*13*)), and copies of, or of parts of, documents may similarly be produced in certain cases (see 23.8 FRAUDULENT OR NEGLIGENT CONDUCT).

In the event of failure by a witness to attend in obedience to the summons, or refusal to be sworn or to affirm, or refusal to answer any lawful question or to produce a document he is required to produce by the summons, the Commissioners may summarily determine a penalty not exceeding £1,000, to be treated as tax charged by an assessment and due and payable.

[*SI 1994 No 1812, Reg 4*].

Joint hearings. The Commissioners have powers to direct that two or more proceedings, in one or more divisions, with common issues be heard at the same time or consecutively within one division, either of their own motion or on an application by any of the parties to any of those proceedings. All the parties must be notified, and are entitled to be heard before such a direction is given. On the giving of a direction, the Clerk must send notice of its date and terms to all parties. [*SI 1994 No 1812, Reg 6*]. The Commissioners have an inherent power to deal with two or more appeals simultaneously where the appellants' affairs are so intermingled as to be incapable of separation, and where they are satisfied that it would result in no injustice to either party (*Johnson v Walden; King v Walden CA 1995, 68 TC 387*).

Postponements and adjournments. The Commissioners may postpone or adjourn the hearing of any proceedings, the Clerk being responsible for notifying all parties of the place, date and time of the postponed or adjourned hearing (unless announced before an adjournment in the presence of all parties). Where a hearing is adjourned for the obtaining of further information or evidence, the Commissioners may direct the parties regarding the disclosure of such information or evidence prior to resumption. [*SI 1994 No 1812, Reg 8*]. In *Packe v Johnson Ch D 1991, 63 TC 507*, a determination was quashed because of the Commissioners' refusal to consider all relevant information in deciding to refuse an adjournment at a second hearing.

Other matters in preparation for hearing. There are also regulations dealing with the agreement of documents [*Reg 5*], the joinder of additional parties to the proceedings [*Reg 7*] and the admission of expert evidence [*Reg 9*].

4.12 **Hearing and determination of proceedings.** Where proceedings are commenced after 30 December 2002, the hearing is in public. The Commissioners may, however, direct (dependent on certain criteria, e.g. national security, interests of justice, protection of private life etc., and subject to all parties having opportunity to make representations) that all or part of a hearing be in private, such direction to be made of their own volition or on the application (by written notice to the Clerk) of any or all of the parties. In such circumstances, they may also direct that *information* about the proceedings should not be made public. Certain persons with official responsibilities may be present at *any* hearing, and may remain present during, but not take part in, the Commissioners' deliberations. With the consent of the parties, the Commissioners may permit any other person to attend an otherwise private hearing. They may exclude a person from all or part of any hearing on grounds of disruptive or potentially disruptive conduct. Before 31 December 2002, hearings were in private, though with similar provision as above as to the presence of others. [*SI 1994 No 1812, Reg 13; SI 2002 No 2976, Regs 1, 10*].

Preliminary points will be considered prior to the hearing of the substantive appeal only in cases where the facts are complicated and the legal issue is short and easily decided (*Investment Trust v CIR (Sp C 173), [1998] SSCD 287*).

Power to obtain information. The Commissioners may, at any time before final determination of the proceedings, serve on any party to the proceedings (other than HMRC) notice (a 'precept') requiring that party, within a specified time, (*a*) to deliver such particulars as may be required to determine any issue of the proceedings, and

(*b*) to make available for inspection by the Commissioners or by an HMRC officer such specified or described books, accounts etc. in his possession or power as may, in their opinion, contain information relevant to the proceedings.

The Commissioners may summarily determine a penalty (to be treated as tax charged in an assessment and due and payable) of up to £300 for failure to comply with such a notice, plus up to £60 per day for continuing failure after such a penalty is determined. Any HMRC officer (and the Commissioners in the case of (*b*)) may, at all reasonable times, take copies of, or extracts from, any such particulars, books etc. [*SI 1994 No 1812, Reg 10*].

Representation at hearing. A party to the proceedings may be represented by any person, except that the Commissioners may, if satisfied that there are good and sufficient reasons for doing so, refuse to permit a party to be represented by a particular person, not being a legally qualified person or a person who is currently (see *Cassell v Crutchfield (No 1) Ch D 1995, 69 TC 253*) a member of an incorporated society of accountants. In practice, most bodies of Commissioners permit the taxpayer to be represented by any person who they are satisfied is competent to present the appellant's case. HMRC may be represented by a barrister, advocate, solicitor or any HMRC officer. [*SI 1994 No 1812, Reg 12*]. The HMRC representative is normally an inspector. The secretary or 'other proper officer' represents a company (the liquidator if in liquidation or (where the company enters administration on or after 15 September 2003) the administrator if in administration). [*TMA 1970, s 108; FA 2003, s 196, Sch 41 para 2; SI 2003 No 2093*].

Failure to attend hearing. Where a party fails to attend or be represented at a hearing of which he has been duly notified, the Commissioners may postpone or adjourn a hearing or (unless satisfied that there is good and sufficient reason for such failure, and after considering any written or other representations) hear and determine the proceedings. [*SI 1994 No 1812, Reg 14*]. Determinations in the absence of the taxpayer or his agent have been upheld where notice of the meeting was received by the appellant (*R v Tavistock Commrs (ex p. Adams) (No 1) QB 1969, 46 TC 154*; *R v Special Commr (ex p. Moschi) CA, [1981] STC 465* and see *Fletcher & Fletcher v Harvey CA 1990, 63 TC 539*), but Commissioners were held to have acted unreasonably in refusing to re-open proceedings when the taxpayer's agent was temporarily absent when the appeal was called (*R & D McKerron Ltd v CIR CS 1979, 52 TC 28*). Where the taxpayer was absent through illness, a determination was quashed because the Commissioners, in refusing an adjournment, had failed to consider whether injustice would thereby arise to the taxpayer (*R v Sevenoaks Commrs (ex p. Thorne) QB 1989, 62 TC 341* and see *Rose v Humbles CA 1971, 48 TC 103*). See also *R v O'Brien (ex p. Lissner) QB, [1984] STI 710* where the determination was quashed when the appellant had been informed by the inspector that the hearing was to be adjourned.

Procedure and evidence at hearing. The Commissioners have wide discretion as to the manner in which the proceedings are conducted, and should seek to avoid inappropriate formality. They may require any witness to give evidence on oath or affirmation, and may admit evidence which would be inadmissible in a court of law. Evidence may be given orally or, if they so direct, by affidavit or statement recorded in a document (and they may, on their own motion or on the application of any party, at any stage require the personal attendance as a witness of the maker of such a statement or affidavit or the person who recorded the statement). They may take account of the nature and source of any evidence, and the manner in which it is given, in assessing its truth and weight. The parties may be heard in any order, but are entitled to give evidence, to call witnesses, to question witnesses (including other parties who give evidence), and to address the Commissioners both on the evidence and on the subject matter of the proceedings. [*SI 1994 No 1812, Reg 15*]. A party to the proceedings cannot insist on being examined on oath (*R v Special Commrs (in re Fletcher) CA 1894, 3 TC 289*). False evidence under oath would be perjury under criminal law (*R v Hood Barrs CA, [1943] 1 All ER 665*). A taxpayer was held to be bound by an affidavit he had made in other proceedings (*Wicker v Fraser Ch D 1982, 55 TC 641*). A remission to Commissioners to hear evidence directed at the credit of a witness was refused in *Potts v CIR Ch D 1982, 56 TC 25*. Rules of the Supreme Court under which evidence can be obtained from a witness abroad cannot be used in proceedings before the Commissioners (*Leiserach v CIR CA 1963, 42 TC 1*). As to hearsay evidence under *Civil Evidence Act 1968*, see *Forth Investments Ltd v CIR Ch D 1976, 50 TC 617* and *Khan v Edwards Ch D 1977, 53 TC 597*.

The Commissioners are under no obligation to adjourn an appeal for the production of further evidence (*Hamilton v CIR CS 1930, 16 TC 28; Noble v Wilkinson Ch D 1958, 38 TC 135*), and were held not to have erred in law in determining assessments in the absence abroad of the taxpayer (*Hawkins v Fuller Ch D 1982, 56 TC 49*).

The taxpayer has no general right to conduct his appeal in writing without attending the hearing (*Banin v Mackinlay CA 1984, 58 TC 398*), although written pleadings may, at the Commissioners' discretion, be taken into account (*Caldicott v Varty Ch D 1976, 51 TC 403*).

In reaching their decision, the Commissioners may not take into account matters appropriate for application for judicial review (*Aspin v Estill CA 1987, 60 TC 549*). They do not generally have the power to review on appeal the exercise of a discretion conferred on HMRC by statute (see *Slater v Richardson & Bottoms Ltd Ch D 1979, 53 TC 155*; *Kelsall v Investment Chartwork Ltd Ch D 1993, 65 TC 750*).

For the extent to which Commissioners may use their local knowledge, see *Forest Side Properties (Chingford) Ltd v Pearce CA 1961, 39 TC 665*.

Onus of proof. The onus is on the appellant to displace an assessment (but see 23.2 FRAUDULENT OR NEGLIGENT CONDUCT for onus on Crown to prove fraud or wilful default to support extended time limit assessments). See *Brady v Group Lotus Car Companies plc CA 1987, 60 TC 359* where the onus of proof remained with the taxpayer where the amount of normal time limit assessment indicated contention of fraud. The general principle emerges in appeals against estimated assessments in 'delay cases', which, before self-assessment, made up the bulk of appeals heard by the General Commissioners. For examples of cases in which the Commissioners have confirmed estimated assessments in the absence of evidence that they were excessive, see *T Haythornthwaite & Sons Ltd v Kelly CA 1927, 11 TC 657*; *Stoneleigh Products Ltd v Dodd CA 1948, 30 TC 1*; *Rosette Franks (King St) Ltd v Dick Ch D 1955, 36 TC 100*; *Pierson v Belcher Ch D 1959, 38 TC 387*. In a number of cases, the courts have supported the Commissioners' action in rejecting unsatisfactory accounts (e.g. *Cain v Schofield Ch D 1953, 34 TC 362*; *Moll v CIR CS 1955, 36 TC 384*; *Cutmore v Leach Ch D 1981, 55 TC 602*; *Coy v Kime Ch D 1986, 59 TC 447*) or calling for certified accounts (e.g. *Stephenson v Waller KB 1927, 13 TC 318*; *Hunt & Co v Joly KB 1928, 14 TC 165*; *Wall v Cooper CA 1929, 14 TC 552*). In *Anderson v CIR CS 1933, 18 TC 320*, the case was remitted where there was no evidence to support the figure arrived at by the Commissioners (which was between the accounts figure and the estimated figure assessed), but contrast *Bookey v Edwards Ch D 1981, 55 TC 486*. The Commissioners are entitled to look at each year separately, accepting the appellant's figures for some years but not all (*Donnelly v Platten CA(NI) 1980, [1981] STC 504*). Similarly, the onus is on the taxpayer to substantiate his claims to relief (see *Eke v Knight CA 1977, 51 TC 121*; *Talib v Waterson Ch D, [1980] STC 563*).

For the standard of proof required in evidence, see *Les Croupiers Casino Club v Pattinson CA 1987, 60 TC 196*.

4.13 **The Commissioners' decision.** The HMRC representative must not be present while the Commissioners are deliberating their decision unless the other party or parties (or their representative(s)) are also present (*R v Brixton Commrs KB 1912, 6 TC 195*). The Commissioners' determination was quashed where the Clerk had discussed the case with

Revenue representatives between hearing and announcement of determination (*R v Wokingham Commrs (ex p. Heron) QB 1984, [1984] STI 710*).

If, on an appeal, it appears to the Commissioners

(*a*) that the appellant is overcharged or undercharged by a self-assessment;

(*b*) that any amounts in a partnership statement (see 54.16 RETURNS) are excessive or insufficient; or

(*c*) that the appellant is overcharged or undercharged by an assessment other than a self-assessment,

they must reduce or increase the assessment or amounts accordingly, but otherwise the assessment or statement stands good. The Commissioners are given the power to vary the extent to which a claim or election included in a tax return is disallowed following an enquiry. (Separate rules apply to claims and elections made outside returns, for which see 12.3 CLAIMS.) In a case within (*c*) above, the Commissioners can normally only reduce or increase the amount assessed, and this determines the appeal; they are not obliged to determine the revised tax payable. In a case within (*b*) above, HMRC must amend the partners' own tax returns to give effect to the reductions or increases made. These provisions apply as from, broadly, 11 May 2001, though comparable provisions applied previously (i.e. under self-assessment for 1996/97 onwards and for company accounting periods ending on or after 1 July 1999), the changes being in consequence of the revised procedures for completion of an enquiry (see 54.11 RETURNS). [*TMA 1970, s 50(6)–(9); F(No 2)A 1975, s 67(2); FA 1994, ss 196, 199(2)(3), Sch 19 para 17; FA 1996, Sch 19 para 7; FA 2001, s 88, Sch 29 para 30; SI 1994 No 1813*].

See 37.4 INTEREST AND SURCHARGES and 48.2 PENALTIES for Commissioners' options in an appeal against a surcharge or a late filing penalty, which turns on the question of whether the appellant had a 'reasonable excuse' for his non-compliance.

Any decision is by a majority of the Commissioners hearing the proceedings, with the presiding Commissioner having a casting vote where necessary. The final determination may be announced orally at the end of the hearing or may be reserved. In either case, the Clerk to the Commissioners must send to each party a notice (including details of the procedure for appeals from the General Commissioners) setting out the determination, and unless the determination was given at the hearing, the date of such notice is the date of the determination. [*SI 1994 No 1812, Reg 16; SI 1999 No 3293, Reg 3*]. Where the Clerk announced the decision wrongly, it was held that the correct decision stood good (*R v Morleston & Litchurch Commrs KB 1951, 32 TC 335*) (and see 4.15 below under Irregularities).

Where Commissioners determined appeals in principle and held a further hearing to adjust assessments, their action in refusing to admit further evidence for the taxpayer at the later hearing was upheld (*R v St Marylebone Commrs (ex p. Hay) CA 1983, 57 TC 59*). They are entitled, however, to alter their decision in principle at a later hearing (*Larner v Warrington Ch D 1985, 58 TC 557*). See also *Gibson v Stroud Commrs Ch D 1989, 61 TC 645*.

A decision of the Commissioners is not legally binding on them or any other Commissioners in any other proceedings, even on appeal by the same taxpayer against a similar assessment for another year (*CIR v Sneath CA 1932, 17 TC 149* and cf. *Edwards v 'Old Bushmills' Distillery HL 1926, 10 TC 285*; *Abdul Caffoor Trustees PC 1961, 40 ATC 93*).

The Commissioners may dismiss an appeal where there is no appealable matter, as in *Merani (Personal Representative of Merani deceased) v CIR (Sp C 285), [2001] SSCD 178*, an inheritance tax case where the amount of tax was not in dispute and the taxpayer merely wanted to negotiate new instalment terms.

Review of the Commissioners' final determination. A decision of the Commissioners is generally final and conclusive [*TMA 1970, s 46(2)*], but the Commissioners may review and set aside or vary their final determination on the application of any party or of their own motion where they are satisfied that either

- it was wrongly made as a result of administrative error, or
- a party entitled to be heard failed to appear or be represented for good and sufficient reason, or
- relevant information had been supplied to the Clerk or to the appropriate inspector or other HMRC officer prior to the hearing but was not received by the Commissioners until after the hearing.

A written application for such a review must be made to the Commissioners not later than 14 days after the date of the notice of the determination (or by such later time as the Commissioners may allow), stating the grounds in full. Where the Commissioners propose of their own motion to review a determination, they must serve notice on the parties not later than 14 days after the date of the notice of the determination.

The parties are entitled to be heard on any such review or proposed review. If practicable, the review is to be determined by the Commissioners who decided the case, and if they set aside the determination, they may substitute a different determination or order a rehearing before the same or different Commissioners. A decision to vary or substitute a final determination is to be notified in the same way as the original determination (see above).

[*SI 1994 No 1812, Reg 17*].

See 4.26 below as regards application for judicial review where the Commissioners have acted unfairly or improperly.

4.14 **Special procedures.** *Proceedings relating to tax on chargeable gains.* Where material, the market value of an asset or the apportionment of an amount or value is, if so required by any party, to be recorded in the final determination. They may be proved in any proceedings relating to tax on chargeable gains by a certificate signed by the Clerk to the Commissioners (in certain cases the clerk or registrar of another tribunal), or by the inspector where the appeal was settled by agreement, stating the material particulars. [*SI 1994 No 1812, Reg 18; SI 1999 No 3293, Reg 4*].

Reference to other tribunals. Certain questions relating to the value of land or of a lease of land must be referred to the appropriate Lands Tribunal, and questions in relation to unquoted shares and to certain specified claims must be referred to the Special Commissioners (see *TMA 1970, ss 46B, 46C, 46D* at 4.6 above). The instant proceedings are to be determined without awaiting the outcome of such referral. [*SI 1994 No 1812, Reg 19; SI 1999 No 3293, Reg 5*].

4.15 **Miscellaneous.** *Irregularities.* Any irregularity resulting from failure to comply with regulations or with any Commissioners' direction given before a final determination is reached, shall not, of itself, render the proceedings void, and before reaching that determination the Commissioners may, and if they consider that any person has been prejudiced by the irregularity must, give such direction as they think just to cure or waive any irregularity which comes to their attention. Clerical errors in any document recording a direction or decision of the Commissioners may be corrected by any of the Commissioners concerned (or by the Clerk if all the Commissioners have died or ceased to be Commissioners) by certificate under his hand. [*SI 1994 No 1812, Reg 24*].

Notices must be in writing unless the Commissioners authorise them to be given orally. [*SI 1994 No 1812, Reg 25*].

Service of any notice or document (other than a witness summons, see 4.11 above) may be by post, by (legible) facsimile transmission etc. or by delivery at the proper address.

[*SI 1994 No 1812, Reg 26(1)*]. The persons and addresses to whom and which a document may be sent or delivered are set out in *Reg 26(2)(3)*, and the provisions for substituted or waived service in certain cases in *Reg 27*.

Penalties. Any appeal against summary penalties determined pursuant to regulations under 4.9 above lies to the High Court (in Scotland, the Court of Session). [*TMA 1970, s 53(1); SI 1994 No 1813*].

Guidance notes on Appeals to the General Commissioners (TAXGUIDE 4/00) were published in June 2000 by the Tax Faculty of the ICAEW.

Protection of General Commissioners. From 1 April 2001 (except in Scotland), the following apply. There is no right of action against a General Commissioner in respect of any act or omission of his in the execution of his duty, except with respect to matters outside his jurisdiction and then only if it is proved that he acted in bad faith. [*TMA 1970, s 2(9)(10); Access to Justice Act 1999, s 101; SI 2001 No 916*]. With limited exceptions, such as if his having acted in bad faith is proved, a General Commissioner cannot be ordered by a court to pay *costs* in respect of any act or omission of his in the execution of his duty. The court may, however, order the Lord Chancellor to make such payment instead, subject to such exceptions and procedures (for determining costs) as are provided for by regulations. [*TMA 1970, s 2A; Access to Justice Act 1999, s 102; SI 2001 Nos 916, 1304*]. There are provisions for the Lord Chancellor to indemnify a General Commissioner or his clerk from certain sums incurred, i.e. costs, damages etc., in connection with proceedings in respect of any act or omission of his in the execution of his duty, again unless it is proved that he acted in bad faith. [*TMA 1970, s 3A; Access to Justice Act 1999, s 103; SI 2001 No 916*].

4.16 SPECIAL COMMISSIONERS

Except where otherwise stated or required by context, the provisions applicable to the General Commissioners in 4.10–4.15 above) apply equally to the Special Commissioners, with the variations and additions in 4.17–4.19 below.

4.17 **Constitution of tribunal.** Any one, two or three of the Special Commissioners may hear any proceedings. If two or three Commissioners are sitting, the Presiding Special Commissioner, or, if he is not sitting, the Commissioner nominated by him, shall preside at the hearing. With the consent of all parties, proceedings may be continued by any one or two of the Commissioners unless the Presiding Special Commissioner otherwise directs. [*SI 1994 No 1811, Regs 2, 13*].

4.18 **Preparation for hearing.** *Listing and notice of hearing.* Before notifying the parties of the place, date and time of a hearing, the Clerk to the Commissioners must satisfy himself that the Special Commissioners have jurisdiction over the proceedings and that he has sufficient particulars for determination. The Presiding Special Commissioner may direct that such notifications are not to be sent. [*SI 1994 No 1811, Reg 3*].

General power to give directions. The Commissioner(s) have wide direction-giving powers, on the application of any of the parties to proceedings or of their own motion. Applications by the parties (otherwise than during the hearing) must be in writing to the Clerk, and if not made with the consent of all the parties, must be served by the Clerk on any affected party, who may object. [*SI 1994 No 1811, Reg 4*].

Witnesses. The maximum penalty which the Commissioner(s) may summarily determine for failure to attend or refusal to be sworn or affirm, to answer any lawful question or to produce documents as required is £10,000. [*SI 1994 No 1811, Regs 5, 24(2)*].

Preliminary hearing. Where it appears to a Special Commissioner that any proceedings would be facilitated by holding a preliminary hearing, he may, on the application of a party or of his own motion, give directions for such a hearing to be held. The Clerk to the Special Commissioners must give to all the parties 14 days' notice (or such shorter time as the parties agree or the Commissioner sees fit to impose) of the time and place of the hearing.

On a preliminary hearing, the Commissioner has wide direction-giving powers, and may, if the parties so agree, determine the proceedings without any further hearing. [*SI 1994 No 1811, Reg 9*]. See 4.19 below as regards powers of Commissioner to obtain information on preliminary hearing of any proceedings.

4.19 **Hearing and determination of proceedings.** Hearings before the Special Commissioner(s) are normally in public. Where proceedings are commenced after 30 December 2002, rules equivalent to those for the General Commissioners in 4.12 above apply as regards private hearings in certain cases and the right to attend. Broadly similar rules applied before 31 December 2002, although an explicit direction for a hearing to be in private was required only where the application was made by the Revenue. [*SI 1994 No 1811, Reg 15; SI 2002 No 2976, Regs 1, 6*].

Power to obtain information. The powers of General Commissioners to obtain information apply to both a preliminary hearing before a Special Commissioner and to the hearing of the proceedings, except that the specific penalty provisions for failure to comply with a notice do not apply (although the general penalty for failure to comply with Commissioner's direction, see below, *does* apply). [*SI 1994 No 1811, Regs 10, 24(1)*].

The Commissioners' decision. The recording of the Commissioner(s)' decision must contain a statement of the facts found and the reasons for the determination. After reserving the final determination, the Commissioner(s) may give a written decision in principle on one or more of the issues arising, and adjourn the making of the final determination until after that decision has been issued and any further questions arising from it have been agreed by the parties or decided by the Commissioner(s) after hearing the parties. A decision in principle must contain a statement of the facts and the reasons for the decision, and these need not be repeated in the document recording the final determination. [*SI 1994 No 1811, Reg 18; SI 1999 No 3292, Reg 4*].

Review of the Commissioners' decision in principle may proceed in the same way as a review of a final determination. [*SI 1994 No 1811, Reg 19*].

Publication of decisions in principle or final determinations. The Presiding Special Commissioner may arrange for the publication of such reports of decisions in principle and final determinations as he considers appropriate. If the proceedings (or any part) were held in private, he must ensure that the report is in a form which, so far as possible, prevents the identification of any person whose affairs are dealt with. [*SI 1994 No 1811, Reg 20*]. A substantial number of cases is now reported, and these are referred to in the text of this publication where relevant. The Special Commissioners expect to have their attention drawn in appropriate cases to any of their previous published decisions which is relevant, unless superseded by a higher court decision. HMRC considers that, whilst not creating any binding legal precedent, these decisions may be relevant in other cases, particularly if not appealed against, but that it would be inappropriate to enter into any discussion of a case which is, or may be, the subject of appeal to the High Court etc. (Revenue Tax Bulletin October 1995 pp 258, 259).

Orders for costs. The Commissioner(s) may make an order awarding costs (in Scotland expenses) of, or incidental to, the hearing of any proceedings against any party who has, in their opinion, acted wholly unreasonably in connection with the hearing, but not without giving that party the opportunity of making representations against the award. The award may be of all or part of the costs of the other party or parties, such costs to be taxed in the county court (in Scotland the sheriff court) if not agreed. In Northern Ireland, the Commissioners may determine the costs. [*SI 1994 No 1811, Reg 21*]. For this purpose an act 'in connection with the hearing' includes any action taken once the appeal has been consigned by one or both parties to the Special Commissioners (*Carter v Hunt 1999 (Sp C 220), [2000] SSCD 17*). Failure by the taxpayer to attend or be represented at the hearing without giving prior notification may be a contributory factor in an award of costs, as may a failure to comply with a Commissioners' direction (*Phillips v Burrows 1998 (Sp C 229, 229A), [2000] SSCD 107, 112*).

For cases in which costs/expenses were awarded against HMRC, see *Scott and another (trading as Farthings Steak House) v McDonald (Sp C 91), [1996] SSCD 381*, *Robertson v CIR (No 2) (Sp C 313), [2002] SSCD 242* and *Carvill v Frost (Sp C 447), [2005] SSCD 208.*

In *McEwan v O'Donoghue (No 2) (Sp C 488), [2005] SSCD 681* the appellant was denied costs even though it was held that the Revenue had behaved wholly unreasonably, because the result of the appeal was that each party succeeded in roughly equal amounts. In *Salt v Young (Sp C 205), [1999] SSCD 249*, the Revenue were refused costs on the grounds that although the taxpayer had, on an objective test, behaved unreasonably, he had not been *wholly* unreasonable, and his unreasonableness was connected with the hearing only to a very minor extent. Only in 'a very rare case' would the Court interfere with the Commissioners' decision as regards costs (see *Gamble v Rowe Ch D 1998, 71 TC 190* in which a refusal of costs was upheld). For the basis for assessment of costs see *Carvill v Frost (No 2) (Sp C 468), [2005] SSCD 422.*

Dismissal of appeal without full hearing. An appeal may be dismissed without a full hearing if there is no longer any live issue between the parties and it would not be in the public interest to proceed (*Self-assessed v Inspector of Taxes (No 2) 1999 (Sp C 224), [2000] SSCD 47*).

Penalty for failure to comply with Commissioner(s)' direction. The Commissioner(s) may summarily determine a penalty of up to £10,000 for any such failure, to be treated as if it were tax charged in an assessment and due and payable. [*SI 1994 No 1811, Reg 24(1)(3)*].

4.20 APPEALS TO THE HIGH COURT — INTRODUCTION

Prior to the determination of an appeal by the Commissioners, the court may be prepared to consider an application seeking a determination as to whether HMRC may make use of certain 'tax-altering' provisions in relation to the assessments under appeal (*Balen v CIR Ch D 1976, 52 TC 406; Beecham Group plc v CIR Ch D 1992, 65 TC 219*).

4.21 APPEAL FROM THE GENERAL COMMISSIONERS

Case stated procedure. Within 30 days of the date of final determination of an appeal (or of the variation or substitution of such a determination, see 4.13 above) any party dissatisfied with the determination as being erroneous in point of law (for which see e.g. *Billows v Robinson CA 1991, 64 TC 17*) may serve notice on the Clerk requiring the Commissioners to state and sign a case for the opinion of the High Court (in Scotland the Court of Session, in Northern Ireland the Court of Appeal (NI)), setting forth the facts and final determination of the Commissioners. See *Grainger v Singer KB 1927, 11 TC 704* as regards receipt of the case. The 30-day time limit for requesting a case does not apply to the payment of the fee (*Anson v Hill CA 1968, 47 ATC 143*). The Commissioners may serve notice on the person who required the stated case requiring him, within a specified period of not less than 28 days, to identify the question of law on which he requires the case to be stated. They may refuse to state a case until such notice is complied with, or if they are not satisfied that a question of law is involved, or if the requisite fee (see below) has not been paid. A requirement for a case to be stated becomes invalid if the determination to which it relates is set aside or varied. After 31 December 1999, the case stated procedure does not apply to a final determination by the General Commissioners of an appeal in which a question has been referred to another tribunal (the Lands Tribunal or the Special Commissioners — see *TMA 1970, ss 46B, 46C, 46D* at 4.6 above) and all appeal rights have been exhausted. [*SI 1994 No 1812, Regs 20, 23; SI 1999 No 3293, Reg 6*].

A fee of £25 is payable to the Clerk by the person requiring the case before he is entitled to have it stated. [*TMA 1970, s 56(3); FA 1984, Sch 22 para 6; SI 1994 No 1813*]. A single case may have effect as regards each of a number of appeals heard together (*Getty Oil Co v Steele and related appeals Ch D 1990, 63 TC 376*).

If the taxpayer dies, his personal representatives stand in his shoes (*Smith v Williams KB 1921, 8 TC 321*).

Although the case stated procedure envisages the determination of the proceedings before the Commissioners, where an appeal has been decided in principle but there may be considerable delay in reaching figures for the formal determination, the Court will accept a case stated in principle (see e.g. *Rank Xerox Ltd v Lane HL 1979, 53 TC 185*).

The case stated procedure is not open to a successful party to an appeal (*Sharpey-Schafer v Venn Ch D 1955, 34 ATC 141*), but where another party requires a case, the successful party may invite the Commissioners to include in the case an additional question relating to another ground on which the Commissioners had found against it (*Gordon v CIR CS 1991, 64 TC 173*). In the case of a partnership, the procedure is available to any one of the partners, with or without the consent of the others (*Sutherland & Partners v Barnes and Another CA 1994, 66 TC 663*).

4.22 **Consideration of draft case.** Within 56 days of receipt of a notice requiring a stated case (or of the Commissioners being satisfied as to the question of law involved), the Clerk must send a draft of the case to all the parties. Written representations thereon may be made to the Clerk by any party within 56 days after the draft case is sent out, with copies to all the other parties, and within a further 28 days further representations may similarly be made in response. Any party to whom copies of representations are not sent may apply to the Clerk for a copy. The validity of a case after it has been stated and signed (see 4.23 below), and of any subsequent proceedings, is not affected by a failure to meet these time limits or by a failure to send copies of representations to all parties. [*SI 1994 No 1812, Reg 21*].

An application for the taxpayer's name to be withheld was refused (In re *H Ch D 1964, 42 TC 14*) as was an application for the deletion of a passage possibly damaging the taxpayer (*Treharne v Guinness Exports Ltd Ch D 1967, 44 TC 161*). An application for judicial review on the ground that the case did not cover all matters in dispute was refused in *R v Special Commrs (ex p. Napier) CA 1988, 61 TC 206*. In *Danquah v CIR Ch D 1990, 63 TC 526*, an application for the statement of a further case was refused where the case did not set out all the questions raised by the taxpayer in the originating motion by which he had sought an order directing the Commissioners to state a case. The proper course was for the taxpayer to apply for remission of the case for amendment under *TMA 1970, s 56(7)*. See also *Consolidated Goldfields plc v CIR Ch D 1990, 63 TC 333* (dealt with further at 4.24 below) in which a request to remit a case to the Commissioners for further findings of fact was refused.

4.23 **Preparation and submission of final case.** As soon as may be after the final date for representations (see 4.22 above), the Commissioners, after taking into account any representations, must state and sign the case. In the event of the death of a Commissioner, or of his ceasing to be a Commissioner, the case is to be signed by the remaining Commissioner(s) or, if there are none, by the Clerk. The case is then sent by the Clerk to the person who required it to be stated, and the other parties notified accordingly.

In England, Wales and Scotland, the party requiring the case must transmit it to the High Court (in Scotland, the Court of Session) within 30 days of receiving it, and at or before the time he does so must notify each of the other parties that the case has been stated on his application and send them a copy of the case. The 30 day time limit (under the similar earlier provisions of *TMA 1970, s 56(4)*) is mandatory (*Valleybright Ltd (in liquidation) v Richardson Ch D 1984, 58 TC 290*; *Petch v Gurney CA 1994, 66 TC 473*), may run from the date the case is received by the taxpayer's authorised agent (*Brassington v Guthrie Ch D 1991, 64 TC 435*), and requires the case to be *received* by the High Court within the 30 days (*New World Medical Ltd v Cormack Ch D, [2002] STC 1245*). The notification (and copy) to the other parties is required only to give 'adequate notice' of the appeal and not to be 'too long delayed' (*Hughes v Viner Ch D 1985, 58 TC 437*). In Northern Ireland, slightly different rules apply (and see *CIR v McGuckian CA(NI) 1994, 69 TC 1*).

[*SI 1994 No 1812, Regs 22, 23*].

4.24 **The Hearing.** The High Court (or Court of Session or Court of Appeal (NI)) hears and determines any question(s) of law arising on the case, and may reverse, affirm or amend the determination of the Commissioners, or may remit the matter to the Commissioners with the opinion of the Court thereon, or may make such other order as to the Court seems fit. It may also cause the case to be sent back for amendment. An appeal from the decision of the High Court lies (in England and Wales) to the Court of Appeal and thence (with leave) to the House of Lords. In certain cases, 'leap-frog' appeals direct from the High Court to the House of Lords may be permitted under *Administration of Justice Act 1969, s 12* (see e.g. *Fitzleet Estates Ltd v Cherry HL 1977, 51 TC 708*). In the case of an appeal against a decision on an appeal against an assessment, tax must be paid in accordance with the Commissioners' decision. Following the decision on appeal, any tax overpaid is refunded with such interest as the Court may allow, and any amount undercharged is due and payable 30 days after the inspector issues a notice of the amount due. [*TMA 1970, s 56(6)–(9); SI 1994 No 1813*].

Once set down for hearing, a case cannot be declared a nullity (*Way v Underdown CA 1974, 49 TC 215*) or struck out under *Order 18, Rule 19 of the Rules of the Supreme Court* (*Petch v Gurney CA 1994, 66 TC 473*), but the appellant may withdraw (*Hood Barrs v CIR (No 3) CA 1960, 39 TC 209*, but see *Bradshaw v Blunden (No 2) Ch D 1960, 39 TC 73*). Where the appellant was the inspector and the taxpayer did not wish to proceed, the Court refused to make an order on terms agreed between the parties (*Slaney v Kean Ch D 1969, 45 TC 415*).

The Court may, however, return a case for amendment. [*TMA 1970, s 56(7)*]. In *Consolidated Goldfields plc v CIR Ch D 1990, 63 TC 333*, the taxpayer company's request that the High Court remit a case to the Commissioners for further findings of fact was refused. Although the remedy was properly sought, it would only be granted if it could be shown that the desired findings were (*a*) material to some tenable argument, (*b*) reasonably open on the evidence adduced, and (*c*) not inconsistent with the findings already made. However, in *Fitzpatrick v CIR CS 1990, [1991] STC 34*, a case was remitted where the facts found proved or admitted, and the contentions of the parties, were not clearly set out, despite the taxpayer's request for various amendments and insertions to the case, and in *Whittles v Uniholdings Ltd (No 1) Ch D, [1993] STC 671*, remission was appropriate in view of the widely differing interpretations which the parties sought to place on the Commissioners' decision (and the case was remitted a second time (see *[1993] STC 767*) to resolve misunderstandings as to the nature of a concession made by the Crown at the original hearing and apparent inconsistencies in the Commissioners' findings of fact). If a case is remitted, the taxpayer has the right to attend any further hearing by the Commissioners (*Lack v Doggett CA 1970, 46 TC 497*) but the Commissioners may not, in the absence of special circumstances, admit further evidence (*Archer-Shee v Baker CA 1928, 15 TC 1*; *Watson v Samson Bros Ch D 1959, 38 TC 346*; *Bradshaw v Blunden (No 2) Ch D 1960, 39 TC 73*), but see *Brady v Group Lotus Car Companies plc CA 1987, 60 TC 359* where the Court directed the Commissioners to admit further evidence where new facts had come to light suggesting the taxpayers had deliberately misled the Commissioners. Errors of fact in the case may be amended by agreement of the parties prior to hearing of the case (*Moore v Austin Ch D 1985, 59 TC 110*). See *Jeffries v Stevens Ch D 1982, 56 TC 134* as regards delay between statement of case and motion for remission.

A new question of law may be raised in the courts on giving due notice to the other parties (*Muir v CIR CA 1966, 43 TC 367*) but the courts will neither admit evidence not in the stated case (*Watson v Samson Bros Ch D 1959, 38 TC 346*; *Cannon Industries Ltd v Edwards Ch D 1965, 42 TC 625*; *Frowd v Whalley Ch D 1965, 42 TC 599*, and see *R v Great Yarmouth Commrs (ex p. Amis) QB 1960, 39 TC 143*) nor consider contentions of which evidence in support was not produced before the Commissioners (*Denekamp v Pearce Ch D 1998, 71 TC 213*).

Following the decision in *Pepper v Hart HL 1992, 65 TC 421*, the courts are prepared to consider the parliamentary history of legislation, or the official reports of debates in Hansard, where all of the following conditions are met.

- Legislation is ambiguous or obscure, or leads to an absurdity.
- The material relied upon consists of one or more statements by a Minister or other promoter of the Bill together if necessary with such other parliamentary material as is necessary to understand such statements and their effect.
- The statements relied upon are clear.

Any party intending to refer to an extract from Hansard in support of any argument must, unless otherwise directed, serve copies of the extract and a brief summary of the argument intended to be based upon the extract upon all parties and the court not less than five clear working days before the first day of the hearing (Supreme Court Practice Note, 20 December 1994) (1995 STI 98).

Many court decisions turn on whether the Commissioners' decision was one of fact supported by the evidence, and hence final. The courts will not disturb a finding of fact if there was reasonable evidence for it, notwithstanding that the evidence might support a different conclusion of fact. The leading case is *Edwards v Bairstow & Harrison HL 1955, 36 TC 207*, in which the issue was whether there had been an adventure in the nature of trade. The Commissioners' decision was reversed on the ground that the *only* reasonable conclusion from the evidence was that there had been such an adventure. For a recent discussion of the application of this principle, see *Milnes v J Beam Group Ltd Ch D 1975, 50 TC 675.*

A court decision is a binding precedent for itself or an inferior court except that the House of Lords, while treating its former decisions as normally binding, may depart from a previous decision should it appear right to do so. For this see *Fitzleet Estates Ltd v Cherry HL 1977, 51 TC 708*. Scottish decisions are not binding on the High Court but are normally followed. Decisions of the Privy Council and of the Irish Courts turning on comparable legislation are treated with respect. A court decision does not affect other assessments already final and conclusive (see 5.6 ASSESSMENTS) but may be followed, if relevant, in the determination of any open appeals against assessments and in assessments made subsequently irrespective of the years of assessment or taxpayers concerned (*Re Waring decd Ch D, [1948] 1 All ER 257*; *Gwyther v Boslymon Quarries Ltd KB 1950, 29 ATC 1*; *Bolands Ltd v CIR SC(I) 1925, 4 ATC 526*). Further, a court decision does not estop the Crown from proceeding on a different basis for other years (*Hood Barrs v CIR (No 3) CA 1960, 39 TC 209*). A general change of practice consequent on a court decision may affect error or mistake relief (see 12.7 CLAIMS).

For joinder of CIR in non-tax disputes, see In *re Vandervell's Trusts HL 1970, 46 TC 341.*

4.25 APPEAL FROM THE SPECIAL COMMISSIONERS

In the case of an appeal to the Special Commissioners, if the appellant or HMRC is dissatisfied in point of law with a decision (whether in principle or on final determination) or with a decision varying or substituting such a decision, appeal may be made to the High Court. (This does not apply after 31 December 1999 in the case of a final determination by the Special Commissioners of an appeal in which a question has been referred to the Lands Tribunal and all appeal rights have been exhausted.) Further appeal may be made to the Court of Appeal and thence (with leave) to the House of Lords. A 'leap-frog' appeal to the Court of Appeal may be made if all the parties agree, the Commissioners certify that a point of law is involved relating wholly or mainly to the construction of an enactment which was fully argued and considered before them, and the leave of the Court of Appeal has been obtained. In Scotland appeals are to the Court of Session, in Northern Ireland to the Court of Appeal (NI), and thence in either case to the House of Lords. When a decision against which an appeal has been made is set aside or varied under *SI 1994 No 1811, Reg 19* (see 4.19 above), the appeal is treated as withdrawn.

In the case of an appeal against a decision on an appeal against an assessment, tax must be paid in accordance with the Commissioners' decision. Following the decision on appeal, any tax overpaid is refunded with such interest as the Court may allow, and any amount undercharged is due and payable 30 days after the inspector issues a notice of the amount due.

[*TMA 1970, ss 56A, 58; ITTOIA 2005, Sch 1 para 375; SI 1994 No 1813; SI 1999 No 3294*].

For case law applicable equally to appeals from the Special Commissioners, see 4.24 above in relation to appeals from the General Commissioners.

4.26 JUDICIAL REVIEW

A taxpayer who is dissatisfied with the exercise of administrative powers may in certain circumstances (e.g. where HMRC has exceeded or abused its powers or acted contrary to the rules of natural justice, or where the Appeal Commissioners have acted unfairly or improperly) seek a remedy in one of the prerogative orders of mandamus, prohibition and certiorari. This is now done by way of application for judicial review under *Supreme Court Act 1981, s 31* and *Order 53* of the *Rules of the Supreme Court.*

The issue on an application for leave to apply for judicial review is whether there is an arguable case (*R v CIR (ex p. Howmet Corporation and another) QB, [1994] STC 413*). The procedure is generally used where no other, adequate, remedy, such as a right of appeal, is available. See *R v Special Commr (ex p. Stipplechoice Ltd) (No 1) CA, [1985] STC 248* and *(No 3) QB 1988, 61 TC 391*, *R v HMIT (ex p. Kissane and Another) QB, [1986] STC 152*, *R v CIR (ex p. Goldberg) QB 1988, 61 TC 403* and *R v Dickinson (ex p. McGuckian) CA(NI) 1999, 72 TC 343.*

There is a very long line of cases in which the courts have consistently refused applications where a matter should have been pursued through the ordinary channels as described earlier in this chapter. See, for example, *R v Special Commrs (ex p. Morey) CA 1972, 49 TC 71*; *R v Special Commrs (ex p. Emery) QB 1980, 53 TC 555*; *R v Walton General Commrs (ex p. Wilson) CA, [1983] STC 464*; *R v Special Commrs (ex p. Esslemont) CA, 1984 STI 312*; *R v Brentford General Commrs (ex p. Chan and Others) QB 1985, 57 TC 651*; *R v Special Commr (ex p. Napier) CA 1988, 61 TC 206*; *R v North London General Commrs (ex p. Nii-Amaa) QB 1999, 72 TC 634.* See, however, *R v HMIT and Others (ex p. Lansing Bagnall Ltd) CA 1986, 61 TC 112* for a successful application where the inspector issued a notice under a discretionary power on the footing that there was an obligation to do so, and *R v CIR (ex p. J Rothschild Holdings plc) CA 1987, 61 TC 178* where the Revenue were required to produce internal documents of a general character relating to their practice in applying a statutory provision. See also *R v CIR (ex p. Taylor) (No 1) CA 1988, 62 TC 562* where an application for discovery of a document was held to be premature, and *R v Inspector of Taxes, Hull, ex p. Brumfield and others QB 1988, 61 TC 589*, where the court was held to have jurisdiction to entertain an application for judicial review of a failure by the Revenue to apply an established practice not embodied in an extra-statutory concession (cf. *R v CIR (ex p. Fulford-Dobson) QB 1987, 60 TC 168* at 28.3 HMRC: ADMINISTRATION, which see for 'care and management' powers of the Revenue). It was held that there had been no unfairness by the Revenue when it refused to assess on the basis of transactions that would have been entered into by the applicants had a Revenue Statement of Practice been published earlier (*R v CIR, ex p. Kaye QB 1992, 65 TC 82*). A similar view was taken in *R v CIR (ex p. S G Warburg & Co Ltd) QB 1994, 68 TC 300* where the Revenue declined to apply a previously published practice because not only was it not clear that the taxpayer's circumstances fell within its terms but also the normal appeal procedures were available. The underlying facts in *Carvill v CIR (No 2); R (oao Carvill) v CIR Ch D, [2002] STC 1167* were that in two separate appeals relating to different tax years, income from an identical source had been held liable to tax for some years (the earlier years) but not others; an application for judicial review of the Revenue's refusal to refund tax, and interest on tax, paid for the earlier years was rejected; the assessments for those years were valid assessments which the Sp C in question had had jurisdiction to determine, and the taxpayer the right to challenge, and those assessments had not been set aside.

The first step is to obtain leave to apply for judicial review from the High Court. Application for leave is made ex parte to a single judge who will usually determine the application without a hearing. The Court will not grant leave unless the applicant has a sufficient interest in the matter to which the application relates. See *CIR v National Federation of Self-Employed and Small Businesses Ltd HL 1981, 55 TC 133* for what is meant by 'sufficient interest' and for discussion of availability of judicial review generally.

Time limit. Applications must be made **within three months** of the date when the grounds for application arose. The Court has discretion to extend this time limit where there is good reason, subject to conditions, but is generally very reluctant to do so. Grant of leave for review does not amount to a ruling that application is made in good time (*R v Tavistock Commrs (ex p. Worth) QB 1985, 59 TC 116*).

4.27 **COSTS**

Costs may be awarded by the courts in the usual way. In suitable cases, e.g. 'test cases', HMRC may undertake to pay the taxpayer's costs. There is no provision for the award of costs of appearing before the General Commissioners. See 4.19 above as regards costs awarded by the Special Commissioners. Costs awarded by the courts may include expenses connected with the drafting of the case stated (*Manchester Corporation v Sugden CA 1903, 4 TC 595*). Costs of a discontinued application for judicial review were refused where the Revenue were not informed of the application (*R v CIR (ex p. Opman International UK) QB 1985, 59 TC 352*). Law costs of appeals are not allowable for tax purposes generally (*Allen v Farquharson KB 1932, 17 TC 59; Smith's Potato Estates Ltd v Bolland HL 1948, 30 TC 267; Rushden Heel Co v Keene HL 1948, 30 TC 298; Spofforth & Prince v Golder KB 1945, 26 TC 310*); and see 15.4 COMPUTATION OF GAINS AND LOSSES.

5 Assessments

Cross-references. See 4 APPEALS; 11.3 CHILDREN as regards assessments on trustees, guardians etc. where tax due from a child or other 'incapacitated person'; 12.5 CLAIMS; 23 FRAUDULENT OR NEGLIGENT CONDUCT; 45.3 OVERSEAS MATTERS as regards UK representatives of non-residents; 46.4 PARTNERSHIPS; 54.14 RETURNS for HMRC determinations of tax liability in the event of the non-filing of a self-assessment tax return; 56 SELF-ASSESSMENT.

5.1 ASSESSMENTS

Notwithstanding the introduction of SELF-ASSESSMENT (56) for 1996/97 and subsequent years and corporation tax self-assessment for accounting periods ending on or after 1 July 1999, HMRC retain the power to make assessments where necessary, most notably 'discovery' assessments (see 5.2–5.4 below). Income tax assessments and CGT assessments on individuals (including individual members of partnerships), trustees and personal representatives are made for years of assessment (tax years). Corporation tax assessments on companies are made for accounting periods.

An assessment is made by an officer of Revenue and Customs (or, before 18 April 2005, by an officer of the Board) by the giving of a notice of assessment. The notice must be served on the person assessed (normally by post) and must state its date of issue and the time limit for giving notice of appeal (4.1 APPEALS). All income tax falling to be charged by such an assessment, even if chargeable under more than one Schedule or more than one Part or Chapter of *ITTOIA 2005*, may be included in one assessment, but there is no provision for income tax and CGT to be charged in the same assessment. Where any statutory provision gives the Commissioners for HMRC (or, before 18 April 2005, the Board of Inland Revenue) the power to make an assessment, the assessment is nevertheless to be made by an officer in like manner as aforesaid. [*TMA 1970, s 30A(1)–(3)(5); FA 1994, ss 196, 199, Sch 19 para 5; FA 1998, Sch 18 para 47(1); ITTOIA 2005, Sch 1 para 370; CRCA 2005, ss 5, 7, Sch 4 para 68*].

An assessment must include a statement of the tax actually payable (*Hallamshire Industrial Finance Trust Ltd v CIR Ch D 1978, 53 TC 631*). An assessment defective in form or containing errors may be validated by *TMA 1970, s 114(1)*, or in some cases the court may choose to use its powers under *TMA 1970, s 56(6)* (see 4.24 APPEALS) to alter an assessment on appeal (*Pickles v Foulsham HL 1925, 9 TC 261*; *Bath & West Counties Property Trust Ltd v Thomas Ch D 1977, 52 TC 20*). However, *section 114(1)* does *not* extend to integral fundamental parts of the assessment such as an error in the year of assessment for which it is made (*Baylis v Gregory HL 1988, 62 TC 1*).

A taxpayer may authorise HMRC (on form 64–8) to automatically provide his agent with a copy of any assessment made on him. If an assessment is not dealt with promptly, interest (or additional interest) may arise on unpaid tax, and any appeal may be out of time.

An officer's power of assessment is not limited to persons (or sources of income) within the area of his tax office (*R v Tavistock Commrs (ex p. Adams) (No 2) CA 1971, 48 TC 56*).

See 5.7 below for the normal time limits within which an assessment may be made. For extended time limits in cases of fraudulent or negligent conduct, see 23.4 FRAUDULENT OR NEGLIGENT CONDUCT.

See 54.14 RETURNS for HMRC's power to make a determination of the tax liability in a case where an annual self-assessment tax return has been issued but not filed. Tax is payable as if the determination were a self-assessment, with no right of appeal, and the determination can only be displaced by the filing of a return and the making of a self-assessment based thereon.

See 13.18 COMPANIES regarding the application of the corporation tax provisions where a company ceases to be UK-resident in the course of the formation of an SE or where an SE becomes non-UK resident.

Prior to self-assessment, it was specifically provided that in the absence of a satisfactory return the inspector of taxes could make an assessment 'to the best of his judgment'. [*TMA 1970, s 29(1)(b) as previously enacted*]. As to this, see *Blackpool Marton Rotary Club v Martin CA 1989, 62 TC 686, Phillimore v Heaton Ch D 1989, 61 TC 584* and *Van Boeckel v Customs & Excise Commissioners QB 1980, [1981] STC 290* (which related to the comparable value added tax provision of what is now *VATA 1994, s 73(1)*).

5.2 **DISCOVERY**

If, as regards 1996/97 and subsequent years of assessment or company accounting periods ending on or after 1 July 1999, HMRC 'discover', as regards any person (the taxpayer) and a chargeable period (i.e. for income tax and CGT purposes, a year of assessment or for corporation tax, an accounting period), that

(*a*) any profits (i.e. income or chargeable gains) which ought to have been assessed to tax have not been assessed, or

(*b*) an assessment is or has become insufficient, or

(*c*) any relief given is or has become excessive,

then with the exceptions below, an assessment (a discovery assessment) may be made to make good to the Crown the apparent loss of tax.
In a case where a return under *TMA 1970, s 8* or *s 8A* (see 54.2 RETURNS), or a company tax return (see 54.18 RETURNS), has been filed in respect in respect of a chargeable period,

(1) no discovery assessment may be made in respect of that chargeable period if it would be attributable to an error or mistake in the return as to the basis on which the liability ought to have been computed and the return was, in fact, made on the basis, or in accordance with the practice, generally prevailing at the time when it was made;

(2) no discovery assessment may be made in respect of that chargeable period unless either

  (i) the loss of tax is attributable to fraudulent or negligent conduct by the taxpayer or a person acting on his behalf, or

  (ii) at the time when HMRC either ceased to be entitled to enquire (see 54.8 RETURNS) into the return or completed their enquiries, they could not have been reasonably expected, on the basis of the information so far made available to them, to be aware of the loss of tax.

For the purposes of (2)(ii) above, information is regarded as having been made available to HMRC if it has been included in

(A) the return (or accompanying accounts, statements or documents) for the chargeable period concerned or for either of the two immediately preceding it, or

(B) a partnership return (see 54.15 RETURNS), where applicable, in respect of the chargeable period concerned or either of the two immediately preceding it, or

(C) any claim for the chargeable period concerned, or

(D) documents, etc. produced for the purposes of any enquiries into such a return or claim,

or is information the existence and relevance of which could reasonably be expected to be inferred from the above-mentioned information or are notified in writing to HMRC. See also below.

The requirement for either of the conditions in (i) or (ii) in (2) above to be met does not apply in respect of chargeable gains (and income) in relation to which the taxpayer has been given, after the completion of an enquiry, a notice under *ICTA 1988, s 804ZA* (schemes and arrangements designed to increase DOUBLE TAX RELIEF (19.8)), *TCGA 1992, s 184G* or *s 184H* (avoidance utilising losses — see 13.5 COMPANIES) or *F(No 2)A 2005, s 24* or *s 26* (tax arbitrage — see 3.26 ANTI-AVOIDANCE).

An objection to a discovery assessment on the grounds that neither (i) nor (ii) in (2) above applies can be made only on an appeal against the assessment. (See 4.1 APPEALS for right of appeal.)

[*TMA 1970, s 29; FA 1994, s 191(1), s 199(2)(3); FA 1998, s 117, Sch 18 paras 41–45, Sch 19 para 12; FA 2001, s 88, Sch 29 para 22; FA 2005, s 88(2)(4); CRCA 2005, s 5, Sch 4 para 68; F(No 2)A 2005, s 29(2); FA 2006, s 71(3)*].

See 47.1 PAYMENT OF TAX as regards due date of payment of income tax and CGT under these provisions. For time limits for making assessments, see 5.7 below and, in cases of fraudulent or negligent conduct, 23.4 FRAUDULENT OR NEGLIGENT CONDUCT.

A change of HMRC opinion on information previously made available to them is not grounds for a discovery assessment. See 54.3 RETURNS for the use of discovery assessments in amending provisional figures in a self-assessment.

Particularly in large or complex cases, the standard accounts information details and other information included in the personal tax return may not provide a means of disclosure adequate to avoid falling within (2)(ii) above. The submission of further information, including perhaps accounts, may be considered appropriate but will not necessarily provide protection against a discovery assessment beyond that arising from submission of the return alone. The reasonable expectation test (see (2)(ii) above) must be satisfied. Where voluminous information beyond the accounts and computations is sent with the return, HMRC do not accept that the test is satisfied if the information is so extensive that an officer could not reasonably be expected to be aware of the significance of particular information and the officer's attention has not been drawn to it by the taxpayer. HMRC will accept that for *TMA 1970, s 29* purposes documents submitted within a month of the return 'accompany' it (see (A) above) provided the return indicates that such documents have been or will be submitted. They will consider sympathetically a request that this condition be treated as satisfied where the time lag is longer than a month. (Revenue Tax Bulletin June 1996 pp 313–315; HMRC Statement of Practice 1/06).

In *Veltema v Langham CA, [2004] STC 544* a company director (V) was liable to income tax on the value of a house, and in his tax return he submitted a valuation of £100,000. After the deadline for making an enquiry into the return (see 54.8 RETURNS) had passed, the Revenue formed the opinion that the value of the house had been more than £100,000, and they subsequently issued a further assessment on the basis that the true value had been £145,000. V appealed, contending that the issue of a further assessment was not authorised by *TMA 1970, s 29*.The CA rejected this contention and upheld the assessment, holding that the assessment was not prohibited by *TMA 1970, s 29(5)* (i.e. (2)(ii) above). Prior to the enquiry deadline, the Revenue 'could not have been reasonably expected' to be aware that the valuation was inadequate. The CA observed that 'it would frustrate the aims of the self-assessment scheme, namely simplicity and early finality of assessment to tax, to interpret *s 29(5)* so as to introduce an obligation on tax inspectors to conduct an immediate and possibly time consuming scrutiny of self-assessment returns ... when they do not disclose insufficiency, but only circumstances further investigation of which might or might not show it'. Furthermore, the definition of 'information made available' to the Revenue given above was exhaustive for the purpose of (2)(ii) above. The key to the scheme was that the inspector was precluded from making a discovery assessment under *section 29* only when the taxpayer or his representatives, in making an honest and accurate return, had clearly alerted him to the insufficiency of the assessment. He was not precluded from making an assessment where he might be able to obtain some other information, not normally part of his checks, that might put the sufficiency of the assessment in question.

Following the decision in this case the Revenue issued guidance on the amount of information which taxpayers need to provide to reduce or remove the risk of a discovery assessment in certain circumstances. That guidance has subsequently been formalised as HMRC Statement of Practice 1/06.

Where an entry in a return depends on the valuation of an asset, HMRC consider that most taxpayers who state in the additional information space at the end of the return that a valuation has been used, by whom it has been carried out, and that it was carried out by a named independent and suitably qualified valuer if that was the case, on the appropriate basis, will be able to rely on protection from a later discovery assessment after the enquiry period, provided those statements are true. Alternatively, in capital gains cases, completion of the entry in the capital gains pages indicating that a valuation has been made and inclusion of a copy of the valuation with the return will be sufficient to provide protection if the copy of the valuation includes all the information mentioned above. In some circumstances provision of the above information will not protect against a discovery assessment, particularly where other parties to the same transaction subsequently include a (different) valuation of the asset in their return.

Where a properly advised taxpayer adopts a different view of the law from that published as HMRC's view, to protect against a discovery assessment after the enquiry period HMRC consider that the return would have to indicate that a different view had been adopted. This might be done by an entry in the additional information space to the effect that HMRC guidance has not been followed on the issue or that no adjustment has been made to take account of it. In HMRC's view it is not necessary for the taxpayer to provide with the return enough information for the HMRC officer to be able to quantify any resulting under assessment of tax.

(Revenue Internet Statement 23 December 2004; HMRC Statement of Practice 1/06).

In *Hancock v CIR (Sp C 213), [1999] SSCD 287*, it was held that a taxpayer who had made errors in his tax return had exhibited standards of competence beneath those to be reasonably expected, that his conduct thus amounted to negligence (see (2)(i) above), and that the Revenue did therefore have the power to make a discovery assessment.

In *McEwan v Martin Ch D, [2005] STC 993*, a capital gains tax computation prepared by a professional adviser was held to constitute negligent conduct on the taxpayer's behalf, so that a discovery assessment could be made. The Revenue were entitled to assume that a professionally prepared tax computation was prepared properly, and the fact that they accepted a negligent computation at face value did not mean that it somehow ceased to be prepared negligently.

There is nothing to stop HMRC raising a discovery assessment (or recognising the potential for doing so in setting the amount of a contract settlement — see 23.9 FRAUDULENT OR NEGLIGENT CONDUCT) where an enquiry window is still open (see 54.8 RETURNS). See Revenue Tax Bulletin August 2001 pp 875, 876 for a note of the circumstances in which they would do so.

See 12.5 CLAIMS for extended time limits for claims where a discovery assessment is made in a case where no fraudulent or negligent conduct is involved.

5.3 **Amendment of partnership return on discovery.** Provisions broadly similar to those in 5.2 above apply as regards an understatement of profits or excessive claim for relief or allowances in a partnership statement (see 54.16 RETURNS), although HMRC's remedy in this case is to amend the partnership return, with consequent amendment of partners' own returns. [*TMA 1970, s 30B; FA 1994, s 196, s 199(2)(3), Sch 19 para 6; FA 1995, s 103(7), s 115(5); FA 2001, s 88, Sch 29 para 24*].

5.4 **Discovery before introduction of self-assessment regime.** See the 2005/06 and earlier editions for the provisions which applied in respect of years of assessment before 1996/97 (1997/98 as regards partnership businesses commenced (or deemed to commence) before 6 April 1994) and company accounting periods ended before 1 July 1999.

5.5 DOUBLE ASSESSMENT

Where there has been 'double assessment' for the same cause and for the same chargeable period, a claim may be made to the Commissioners for HMRC (or, before 18 April 2005, the Board of Inland Revenue) for the assessment reflecting the overcharge to be vacated. An appeal on a claim may be made to the Commissioners having jurisdiction to hear an appeal against the assessment, or the later of the assessments, to which the claim relates. [*TMA 1970, s 32; CRCA 2005, s 5*]. See 12.7 CLAIMS for error or mistake relief and 35.1 INTERACTION WITH OTHER TAXES as regards alternative income tax and CGT assessments.

5.6 FINALITY OF ASSESSMENTS

An assessment cannot be altered after the notice has been served except in accordance with the express provisions of the *Taxes Acts* (for example where the taxpayer appeals — see 4 APPEALS). [*TMA 1970, s 29(6) as previously enacted, s 30A(4); FA 1994, ss 196, 199, Sch 19 para 5; FA 1998, Sch 18 para 47(2)*]. Where over-assessment results from an *error or mistake* in a return, see 12.7 CLAIMS. An assessment as determined on appeal, or not appealed against, is final and conclusive (but see 47.15 PAYMENT OF TAX for HMRC 'equitable liability' treatment).

5.7 TIME LIMITS

The normal time limit for the making of an assessment to income tax and capital gains tax for 1996/97 onwards, i.e. under the self-assessment regime, is five years after 31 January following the year of assessment in question. For companies, the equivalent time limit, both under the corporation tax self-assessment regime and previously, is six years after the end of the corporation tax accounting period. [*TMA 1970, s 34(1); FA 1994, ss 196, 199, Sch 19 para 10; FA 1998, s 117, Sch 18 para 46(1), Sch 19 para 17*].

For 1996/97 onwards, the latest time for assessing the personal representatives of a deceased person in respect of gains accruing before his death is the third anniversary of 31 January following the tax year in which he died. [*TMA 1970, s 40(1)(3); FA 1994, ss 196, 199, Sch 19 para 12*].

In certain cases, specific provisions extend the normal time limits (see, for example, 12.5 CLAIMS, 47.12, 47.14 PAYMENT OF TAX; 64.1 UNDERWRITERS AT LLOYD'S). For extended time limits in cases of FRAUDULENT OR NEGLIGENT CONDUCT, see 23.3–23.5.

An objection to the making of any assessment on the grounds that it is out of time can only be made on an appeal against the assessment. [*TMA 1970, s 34(2); FA 1998, s 117, Sch 18 para 46(3)*].

An assessment is made on the date on which the officer authorised to make it signs a certificate in the appropriate assessments volume that he made certain assessments including the assessment in question (*Honig v Sarsfield CA 1986, 59 TC 337*).

5.8 TRUSTEES AND PERSONAL REPRESENTATIVES

For 1996/97 and subsequent years, CGT due from trustees or personal representatives may be assessed and charged on and in the name of any one or more of the 'relevant trustees' or, as the case may be, 'relevant personal representatives'. In relation to chargeable gains, the '*relevant trustees*' means the trustees in the tax year in which the gains accrue and any subsequent trustees of the settlement, and '*relevant personal representatives*' has a corresponding meaning. See 44.2 OFFSHORE SETTLEMENTS for the modification of this rule in relation to the 'exit charge' under *TCGA 1992, s 80* on trustees ceasing to be resident in the UK.

Unless the assets are held by the trustees or personal representatives as nominees or bare trustees for another person absolutely (see 57.2 SETTLEMENTS), chargeable gains accruing to, and CGT chargeable on, the trustees or personal representatives are not to be regarded as accruing to, or chargeable on, any other person. No trustee or personal representative is to be regarded as an individual for the purposes of *TCGA 1992*.

[*TCGA 1992, s 65(1)(2)(4); FA 1995, s 103(7), s 114*].

See also 57.4, 57.7 SETTLEMENTS.

5.9 NON-CORPORATE BODIES, PERSONAL REPRESENTATIVES AND RECEIVERS

Assessments may be made on the treasurer etc. of bodies which are not corporations; on personal representatives in respect of disposals made *by the deceased person*; and receivers appointed by a court. [*TMA 1970, ss 71, 74, 75, 77*]. As regards receivers, however, see *CIR v Piacentini and others QB 2003, 75 TC 288*.

Simon's Direct Tax Service. See C1.102.

6 Assets

Cross-references. See 7 ASSETS HELD ON 6 APRIL 1965; 8 ASSETS HELD ON 31 MARCH 1982; 22 EXEMPTIONS AND RELIEFS for assets exempt from capital gains tax; 24 FURNISHED HOLIDAY ACCOMMODATION; 26 GOVERNMENT SECURITIES; 38 LAND; 40.9 LOSSES for assets of negligible value; 43 MINERAL ROYALTIES; 49 PRIVATE RESIDENCES; 50 QUALIFYING CORPORATE BONDS; 58 SHARES AND SECURITIES; 65 UNIT TRUSTS ETC.; 67 WASTING ASSETS.

The headings in this chapter are as follows.

6.1 GENERAL

Capital gains tax is charged in respect of chargeable gains accruing to a person on the disposal of 'assets'. [*TCGA 1992, s 1*(*1*)].

'*Assets*' comprise all forms of property, wherever situated, including incorporeal property (goodwill, options, debts, etc.), currency other than sterling, and any form of property created by the disposer, or otherwise coming to be owned without being acquired. [*TCGA 1992, s 21*(*1*); *FA 2006, Sch 12 para 9*]. Sovereigns minted after 1837 are still sterling currency and as such are not within this definition.

The restating in euros of a holding of a participating EU currency on or after 1 January 1999 is not treated as involving the disposal of the original currency or the acquisition of a new holding of euros. The original currency and the new holding are treated as the same asset, acquired as the original currency was acquired. [*SI 1998 No 3177, Reg 36*].

For the treatment of currency other than sterling when disposed of by a 'qualifying company' in certain circumstances, see 22.5 and 22.8 EXEMPTIONS AND RELIEFS.

There is no general principle that assets must have a market value or that they must be transferable or assignable (*O'Brien v Benson's Hosiery (Holdings) Ltd HL 1979, 53 TC 241*). A right to share in a statutory fund for compensation to owners of expropriated foreign property is a form of property and therefore an asset (*Davenport v Chilver Ch D 1983, 57 TC 661*). (To a great extent this decision was superseded by ESC D50 announced in Revenue Press Release 19 December 1994 (see 9.1 CAPITAL SUMS DERIVED FROM ASSETS)). Tax is only chargeable in relation to an asset which existed at the time of disposal and not to an asset coming into existence only on a disposal which created it. 'Property' has the meaning of that which is capable of being owned in a normal legal sense and thus does not extend to include the right of freedom to trade and compete in the market place, but such a right must be distinguished from the goodwill in respect of the trade in question and which is an asset for capital gains tax purposes (*Kirby v Thorn EMI plc CA 1987, 60 TC 519*). The right to unquantified and contingent future consideration on the disposal of an asset is itself an asset (*Marren v Ingles HL 1980, 54 TC 76*).

The right to bring an action to enforce a bona fide claim, and which can be turned to account by negotiating a compromise yielding a capital sum, constitutes an asset. Such a right is acquired otherwise than by way of a bargain made at arm's length and at the time when the cause of action arises. Any capital sum received derives only from the right and not from other assets which may have been associated with the existence of the right (*Zim Properties Ltd v Proctor Ch D 1984, 58 TC 371*). However, in similar cases not involving contractual or statutory rights of action (see HMRC Capital Gains Manual CG 13010) by concession HMRC now treat damages and compensation payments as derived from any underlying asset (and therefore exempt or taxable like that asset), and as exempt if there is no underlying asset. Entitlement to other reliefs is also determined on this basis, and HMRC are prepared to consider extending time limits for claims where there has been a delay in obtaining compensation (HMRC Extra-Statutory Concession D33). For notes and examples on the effect of ESC D33 on computations of TAPER RELIEF (61), ROLLOVER RELIEF (55) and PRIVATE RESIDENCES relief (49), see Revenue Tax Bulletin October 2002 pp 967–970.

See also 9.1 CAPITAL SUMS DERIVED FROM ASSETS.

Corporation tax: intellectual property, goodwill and other intangible fixed assets. *FA 2002, Sch 29* introduced a new corporation tax regime for the treatment of expenditure and receipts in respect of 'intangible fixed assets' created after 31 March 2002 or acquired after that date from an unrelated party or from a related party in whose hands the asset was within the regime. Such assets are therefore removed from the charge to corporation tax on chargeable gains, subject to transitional provisions. The regime applies only *for corporation tax purposes* and the treatment of such assets for individuals etc. for capital gains tax purposes is unaffected. See 14.13 COMPANIES—CORPORATE FINANCE AND INTANGIBLES for further details. See also 55.1, 55.3 ROLLOVER RELIEF and 64.5 UNDERWRITERS AT LLOYD'S.

6.2 LOCATION OF ASSETS ('SITUS')

Where liability depends on where the assets are actually situated (e.g. a non-resident trading in the UK or individuals not domiciled here, see 45 OVERSEAS MATTERS) the following provisions apply to determine the location of assets.

(*a*) The situation of rights or interests (otherwise than by way of security) in or over *immovable property* is that of the immovable property.

(*b*) Subject to the following provisions, the situation of rights or interests (otherwise than by way of security) in or over *tangible movable property* is that of the tangible movable property.

(*c*) Subject to the following provisions, *a debt*, secured or unsecured, is situated in the UK if, and only if, the creditor is resident in the UK.

(*d*) *Shares or debentures* (*before 16 March 2005, shares or securities*) *issued by any municipal or governmental authority*, or by any body created by such an authority, are situated in the country of that authority.

(*e*) With effect on or after 16 March 2005 and subject to paragraph (*d*) above, *shares in or debentures of a company incorporated in the UK* are situated in the UK.

(*f*) Subject to paragraphs (*d*) and (*e*) above, *registered shares or debentures* (before 16 March 2005, registered shares or securities) are situated where they are registered and, if registered in more than one register, where the principal register is situated. A depositary receipt (see 58.17 SHARES AND SECURITIES) issued outside the UK for shares registered in the UK does not alter the location of the underlying shares, to which any consideration on disposal of the receipt will be largely, if not totally, attributable (HMRC Capital Gains Manual CG 50243).

(*g*) A *ship or aircraft* is situated in the UK if, and only if, the owner is then resident in the UK, and an interest or right in or over a ship or aircraft is situated in the UK if, and only if, the person entitled to the interest or right is resident in the UK.

(*h*) The situation of *goodwill* as a trade, business or professional asset is at the place where the trade, business or profession is carried on.

(*j*) *Patents, trade-marks and registered designs* are situated where they are registered, and if registered in more than one register, where each register is situated, and rights and licences in respect of a patent, trade-mark or registered design are situated in the UK if they, or any rights derived from them, are exercisable in the UK. With effect from 16 March 2005 this provision applies equally to rights under the law of a country or territory outside the UK which correspond or are similar to rights under patents, trade-marks or registered designs.

(*k*) *Copyright, design right and franchises*, and rights or licences in respect of any copyright work or design in which design right subsists, are situated in the UK if they or any right derived from them are exercisable in the UK. With effect from 16 March 2005 this provision applies equally to rights under the law of a country or territory outside the UK which correspond or are similar to copyright, design right or franchises.

(*l*) A *judgment debt* is situated where the judgment is recorded.

(*m*) A *non-sterling debt owed by a bank* and represented by a sum standing to the credit of an individual not domiciled in the UK is situated in the UK if, and only if, that individual is resident in the UK and the branch or other place of business of the bank where the account is maintained is itself situated in the UK.

Note that the amendments made to the above provisions with effect from 16 March 2005 apply in determining the situation of an asset at all times on or after that date irrespective of when the asset was acquired. In relation to a company that has no share capital, references in paragraphs (*d*), (*e*) and (*f*) above to shares or debentures include any interests in the company possessed by members of the company. References to 'debentures' in (*d*) and (*f*) above include, in relation to a person other than a company, securities.

[*TCGA 1992, s 275; Trade Marks Act 1994, Sch 5; F(No 2)A 2005, Sch 4 paras 4, 10(1)*].

With effect from 16 March 2005 (as above), where the situation of an 'intangible asset' is not '*otherwise determined*' (under the above provisions or any other provision of *TCGA 1992*), the asset is taken at all times to be situated in the UK if it is 'subject to UK law' at the time it is created. For this purpose, an '*intangible asset*' is intangible or incorporeal property including a thing in action or anything which corresponds to or is similar to intangible or incorporeal property or a thing in action under the law of a country or territory outside the UK. An asset is '*subject to UK law*' at a particular time if any right or interest which comprises or forms part of it is at that time governed by or otherwise subject to, or enforceable under, the law of any part of the UK.

Special rules apply in the case of an intangible asset ('*asset A*') which is a 'future' or 'option' which is not subject to UK law at the time it is created. Broadly, whether asset A is treated as situated in the UK will depend on its 'underlying subject matter' (as defined). If the underlying subject matter consists of or includes a future or option, asset A is treated as situated in the UK at all times if that future or option is subject to UK law at the time it is created and, on the assumption that there were no rights in or over that contract, its situation would not be otherwise determined. Where there is a nested sequence of futures or options, in which the underlying subject matter of each contract in the sequence consists of or includes the next contract in the sequence, asset A is taken to be situated in the UK at all times if any contract in the sequence meets those conditions. Asset A is also treated as situated in the UK at any time at which its underlying subject matter either consists of or includes shares or debentures of a company incorporated in the UK which had not been issued at the time the contract was created or is otherwise treated for capital gains purposes as being situated in the UK. Again, where there is a nested sequence of futures or options, asset A is taken to be situated in the UK if any contract in the sequence meets those conditions. For these purposes, '*future*' and '*option*' have the same meaning as for the derivative contract provisions (see 14.8 COMPANIES—CORPORATE FINANCE AND INTANGIBLES).

[*TCGA 1992, ss 275A, 275B; F(No 2)A 2005, Sch 4 paras 5, 10(1)*].

Under the general law, *bearer shares and securities* transferable by delivery are situated where the certificate, etc. is kept (*Winans v A-G (No 2) HL, [1910] AC 27*).

See also *Standard Chartered Bank Ltd v CIR Ch D, [1978] STC 272* where share certificates lodged in the UK by a person who was resident and domiciled abroad were held to be situated abroad, being registered in South Africa and effectively transferable only in that country. Renounceable letters of allotment of registered shares in a company are documents evidencing rights against the company and are only enforceable (and thus situated) where the register is kept (*Young and Another v Phillips Ch D 1984, 58 TC 232*).

Securities issued by designated European Communities or international organisations (e.g. The Asian Development Bank, The African Development Bank and The European and International Banks for Reconstruction and Development) or the European Investment Bank are taken for capital gains purposes to be situated outside the UK. Organisations are designated by Treasury order. [*TCGA 1992, s 265; F(No 2)A 2005, Sch 4 para 3*]. A similar treatment applies to securities issued by the Inter-American Development Bank [*TCGA 1992, s 266*] and by the OECD Support Fund [*OECD Support Fund Act 1975, s 4*].

Interests of co-owners. In determining the situation of any asset at any time on or after 16 March 2005, the situation of an 'interest' in an asset is taken to be the same as the situation of the asset, determined on the assumption that the asset is wholly-owned by the person holding the interest in it. An '*interest*' in an asset for this purpose means an interest as a co-owner of the asset, whether the asset is owned jointly or in common, and whether or not the interests of the co-owners are equal. [*TCGA 1992, s 275C; F(No 2)A 2005, Sch 4 paras 5, 10(1)*].

Simon's Direct Tax Service. See C1.604.

6.3 APPROPRIATIONS TO AND FROM TRADING STOCK

Where an asset acquired by a person otherwise than as trading stock is appropriated by him for the purposes of his trade as trading stock (whether on the commencement of the trade or otherwise) and a chargeable gain or allowable loss would have accrued to him if he had then sold the asset for its market value, he is treated as having then disposed of the asset at its then market value. Where the asset is appropriated for the purposes of a trade carried on wholly or partly in the UK and chargeable to income tax or corporation tax under Schedule D, Case I or under *ITTOIA 2005, Pt 2 Ch 2* (income tax charge on trading income for 2005/06 onwards), the person may alternatively elect (under *TCGA 1992, s 161(3)*) that, in computing the assessable profits of the trade, the market value of the asset is reduced by the amount of the chargeable gain or increased by the allowable loss that would otherwise arise (i.e. he may treat the gain or loss as subject to income tax rather than capital gains tax). A partner must have the agreement of all his co-partners to make the election effective.

For 1996/97 onwards for CGT purposes, the election must be made on or before the first anniversary of 31 January following the tax year in which ends the period of account in which the asset is appropriated. For corporation tax purposes for accounting periods ending on or after 1 July 1999, it must be made within two years after the end of the accounting period in which the asset is appropriated.

[*TCGA 1992, s 161(1)(3)(3A)(4), s 288(1); FA 1996, Sch 21 para 36; FA 2002, s 103(3), Sch 40 Pt 3(16); SI 2006 No 959, Art 3(3)*].

The above provisions apply equally if any gain (or loss) on a sale of the asset would have been exempt (or non-allowable) under the provisions of *TCGA 1992, Sch 7AC* (see 60 SUBSTANTIAL SHAREHOLDINGS OF COMPANIES). [*TCGA 1992, Sch 7AC para 36*].

Where an asset forming part of a person's trading stock is

(*a*) appropriated by him for any other purpose, or

(*b*) retained by him on his ceasing to carry on the trade,

he is treated as having acquired it at the time for a consideration equal to the amount brought into the accounts of the trade for tax purposes. [*TCGA 1992, s 161*(*2*)]. For the valuation of trading stock in such circumstances, see Tolley's Income Tax under Schedule D, Cases I and II.

See 13.13 COMPANIES for appropriations of gilt-edged securities and qualifying corporate bonds and see also 27.4 GROUPS OF COMPANIES for intra-group transfers of assets which are trading stock of one of the companies but not of the other and for acquisition 'as trading stock' generally.

See 38.4 LAND for deemed appropriation as trading stock where transactions in land are within *ICTA 1988, s 776*(*2*)(*c*).

6.4 KNOW-HOW

For corporation tax purposes, 'know-how' is generally within the definition of an intangible fixed asset for the purposes of the intangible assets regime (see 14.13 COMPANIES—CORPORATE FINANCE AND INTANGIBLES). Broadly, know-how created after 31 March 2002 or acquired by a company from an unrelated party after that date falls within that regime (and see 14.13 COMPANIES—CORPORATE FINANCE AND INTANGIBLES for the detailed transitional provisions).

The following provisions apply where know-how does not fall within that regime.

Consideration for a disposal of know-how used in a trade which continues to be carried on by the disposer after the disposal is treated, for all purposes, as a trading receipt unless

(i) the consideration is brought into account as a disposal value for the purposes of *CAA 2001, s 462* or is otherwise chargeable as a revenue or income receipt; or

(ii) the buyer is a body of persons (this term, here and in (iii) and (iv) below, includes a partnership), exercising control over the seller; or

(iii) the seller is a body of persons exercising control over the buyer; or

(iv) the buyer and seller are bodies of persons together controlled by a third person.

Where a person disposes of know-how in connection with the disposal of part or the whole of the trade in which it was used, any consideration for the know-how is treated as a capital payment for goodwill. This provision does not apply to

(*a*) both parties where a written joint election is made within two years of the disposal; or

(*b*) the acquirer only where the trade concerned was, before the acquisition, carried on wholly outside the UK.

If the consideration is, under (*a*) or (*b*), not regarded as a payment for goodwill, the acquirer is treated, for the purpose of claiming writing-down allowances, as if he had acquired the know-how for use in a trade previously carried on by him. However, the exclusion at (*a*) or (*b*) does not apply where any of (ii)–(iv) above applies.

Where consideration for the disposal of know-how is not taxed as a deemed trading receipt, or otherwise as an income or revenue receipt, or as a payment for goodwill, it is charged to income tax under *ITTOIA 2005, s 583* (or, for 2004/05 and earlier years, under Schedule D, Case VI) or to corporation tax under Schedule D, Case VI unless any one of (ii)–(iv) above applies. The consideration received is subject to the deduction of expenditure wholly and exclusively incurred in the acquisition or disposal of the know-how concerned.

For the above purposes, '*know-how*' is defined as any industrial information and techniques likely to assist in the manufacture or processing of goods or materials, in the working of a mine, oil-well or other source of mineral deposits (including the searching for, discovery or testing of deposits or the winning of access thereto), or in the carrying out of any agricultural, forestry or fishing operations.

[*TCGA 1992, s 261A; ICTA 1988, ss 530, 531, 533(7); CAA 2001, Sch 2 para 47; ITTOIA 2005, ss 192–195, 583–586, Sch 1 paras 207, 444*].

6.5 PATENTS

Except where the corporation tax intangible assets regime applies (see 14.13 COMPANIES—CORPORATE FINANCE AND INTANGIBLES and Tolley's Corporation Tax under Intangible Assets), capital sums received from the sale of patent rights are specifically taxable as income (see Tolley's Income Tax under Intellectual Property). In either case, the consideration for the sale is not therefore taxable as a chargeable gain.

6.6 PLANT OR MACHINERY USED FOR LONG FUNDING LEASE

Where plant or machinery is used for the purpose of leasing under a 'long funding lease', the 'lessor' is treated for chargeable gains purposes as disposing of and immediately reacquiring the plant or machinery at the 'commencement' of the 'term' of the lease for an amount equal to:

- where the lease is a 'long funding finance lease', the amount that would fall to be recognised as the lessor's investment in the lease if accounts were prepared in accordance with generally accepted accounting practice on the date on which the lessor's net investment in the lease is first recognised in the books or other financial records of the lessor; or
- where the lease is a 'long funding operating lease', the market value (determined on the assumption of a disposal by an absolute owner free from all leases and other encumbrances) of the plant or machinery at the commencement of the term of the lease.

On 'termination' of the lease, the lessor is treated as having disposed of and immediately reacquired the asset for a consideration equal to the 'termination amount'.

For the purposes of these provisions, a '*long funding lease*' is, broadly (and subject to further exclusions), a lease of plant or machinery with a term of more than five years (seven years in certain cases) which at its inception meets one or more of the following tests:

- the lease would fall, under generally accepted accounting practice, to be treated as a finance lease or a loan;
- the present value of the minimum lease payments equals 80% or more of the fair value of the leased plant or machinery; or
- the term of the lease is more than 65% of the remaining useful economic life of the leased plant or machinery.

The expressions '*lessor*', '*commencement*', '*term*', '*long funding finance lease*', '*long funding operating lease*', '*termination*' and '*termination amount*' are defined as in *CAA 2001, Pt 2 Ch 6A*. See Tolley's Income Tax or Tolley's Corporation Tax.

These provisions apply where the commencement of the term of the lease is on of after 1 April 2006.

[*TCGA 1992, s 25A; CAA 2001, ss 70G–70U, 70YI(2); FA 2006, Sch 8 para 7, Sch 9 para 4*].

For the restriction of a loss arising on the disposal of an asset which includes plant or machinery which is a fixture and which has been used for leasing under a long funding lease, see 15.6 COMPUTATION OF GAINS AND LOSSES.

6.7 OPTIONS

As regards **companies**, see 14.7–14.12 COMPANIES—CORPORATE FINANCE AND INTANGIBLES for a summary of the special rules on **derivative contracts** introduced by *FA 2002, Sch 26* for accounting periods beginning on or after 1 October 2002. An option is a derivative contract for those purposes unless falling within one of the exclusions. See 14.16 COMPANIES—CORPORATE FINANCE AND INTANGIBLES for the financial instruments rules that preceded the derivative contracts rules. Both subjects are covered in detail in Tolley's Corporation Tax under Financial Instruments and Derivative Contracts.

For **employee share options**, see 20 EMPLOYEE SHARE SCHEMES.

The grant of an option is the disposal of an asset (i.e. the option). This applies in particular to the grant of an option under which the grantor binds himself to sell what he does not own, and because the option is abandoned, never has occasion to own, and the grant of an option under which the grantor binds himself to buy that which he does not acquire because the option is abandoned. This treatment is without prejudice to *TCGA 1992, s 21* (see 6.1 ASSETS and 15.7 COMPUTATION OF GAINS AND LOSSES) and is subject to the provisions below as to treating the grant of an option as part of a larger transaction. [*TCGA 1992, s 144*(*1*)]. A grant of an option is not a part disposal of an asset that was the subject of the option even though the grantor possessed that asset at the time of the grant (*Strange v Openshaw Ch D 1983, 57 TC 544*).

Subject to the treatment of cash-settled options below, if an option is exercised, the grant of the option and the transaction entered into by the grantor in fulfilment of his obligations under the option are treated as a single transaction, so if a sale by the grantor can be called for under the option, the option consideration is part of the consideration for the sale, and if the grantor can be called on to buy, the option consideration is deducted from the acquisition cost incurred by him in buying in accordance with his option obligations. The exercise of an option by the grantee is not a disposal, but on that event the acquisition of the option (whether directly from the grantor or not) and the transaction entered into by the grantee (or his assignee etc.) on the exercise are treated as a single transaction. Therefore if a sale by the grantor can be called for under the option, the option cost is part of the cost of acquiring what is sold, and if the grantor can be called on to buy, the option cost is treated as an incidental cost of disposal of what is bought by the grantor. [*TCGA 1992, s 144*(*2*)(*3*)]. The time of the 'single transaction' is taken to be the time the option is exercised (and see below re taper relief). [*TCGA 1992, s 28*(*2*)].

As a consequence of the option being exercised, any tax paid on the gain arising on the grant of the option should be set off or repaid (and, for years before self-assessment, any assessment should be discharged) (HMRC Capital Gains Manual CG 12317).

If an option binds the grantor both to sell and to buy, it is treated for this purpose (and for the purposes of *TCGA 1992, ss 144ZA–144ZD* below) as two separate options with half the consideration attributable to each. [*TCGA 1992, s 144*(*5*)]. Any reference to an 'option' includes a reference to an option binding the grantor to grant a lease for a premium, or enter into any other transaction that is not a sale, so that references to 'buying' and 'selling' under an option are construed accordingly. [*TCGA 1992, s 144*(*6*)].

Application of market value rule. Subject to the exclusion below, the following provisions apply to options exercised after 9 April 2003 to which the above 'single transaction' treatment applies where the market value rule in *TCGA 1992, s 17*(*1*) (see 41.1 MARKET VALUE) applies (or would apply but for these provisions) in relation to the grant of the option, the acquisition of the option by the person exercising it (whether or not the acquisition was directly from the grantor) or the transaction resulting from its exercise.

Where the option binds the grantor to sell, the market value rule does not apply for determining the consideration for the sale, except to the extent (if any) that it applies for determining the option consideration (which forms part of the sale consideration as indicated above). Likewise, the rule does not apply for determining the acquisition cost of the person exercising the option, except to the extent (if any) that it applies for determining the cost of acquiring the option.

Where the option binds the grantor to buy, the market value rule does not apply for determining the acquisition cost of the grantor, except to the extent (if any) that it applies for determining the option consideration. Likewise, it does not apply for determining the disposal consideration, but without prejudice to its application for determining the cost of the option.

To the extent that the market value rule is disapplied in determining an amount or value by the above provisions, the amount or value to be taken into account is:

- where the option is exercised on or after 2 December 2004, the 'exercise price' (subject to the inclusion of any amount by virtue of *TCGA 1992, s 119A*—see 20.6, 20.8, 20.14, 20.16 and 20.24 EMPLOYEE SHARE SCHEMES); or
- where the option is exercised before that date, the *actual* amount or value (subject to the inclusion of any amount by virtue of *TCGA 1992, s 120*—see 20.6, 20.8, 20.13, 20.15 and 20.17 EMPLOYEE SHARE SCHEMES).

The '*exercise price*' for this purpose is the amount of value of the consideration which, under the terms of the option, is receivable (where the option binds the grantor to buy) or payable (if it binds the grantor to sell) as a result of the exercise of the option, but does not include the amount or value of any consideration for the acquisition of the option.

[*TCGA 1992, s 144ZA; FA 2003, s 158; F(No 2)A 2005, Sch 5 paras 1, 6(1)*].

Exclusion. For options to which the above provision would otherwise apply which are exercised 'non-commercially' on or after 2 December 2004, the provision does not apply, and *TCGA 1992, s 144(2)(3)* above applies in modified form. The 'single transaction' rule continues to apply, but, if the option binds the grantor to buy, his cost of acquisition in buying in pursuance of his obligations, and the disposal consideration for what he buys are deemed for chargeable gains purposes to be the market value of what is bought at the time of exercise. If the option binds the grantor to sell, the consideration for the sale and the cost to the person exercising the option are deemed to be the market value of what is sold at the time of exercise. If the whole or any part of the 'underlying subject matter' of the option is subject to any right or restriction which is enforceable by the person disposing of it or a connected person, the market value of the underlying subject matter is determined for the purposes of these provisions as if the right or restriction did not exist and *TCGA 1992, s 18(6)(7)* (disposal to connected person of asset subject to right or restriction — see 3.15 ANTI-AVOIDANCE) is disapplied.

For this purpose, the '*underlying subject matter*' of an option is, if the option binds the grantor to sell, what falls to be sold on exercise, and, if the option binds the grantor to buy, what falls to be bought on exercise.

This provision does not apply if the option is a 'share option' to which the income tax provisions at 20.6 EMPLOYEE SHARE SCHEMES apply, or would apply but for *ITEPA 2003, s 474*. It also does not apply if:

- at the time the option is exercised the 'open market price' of the underlying subject matter differs from its open market price at the time the option was granted;
- some or all of that change in open market value results, directly or indirectly, from 'relevant arrangements';
- the exercise of the option would not be non-commercial if there were to be disregarded so much of that change in open market value as results to any extent, directly or indirectly, from the relevant arrangements; and

- the grantor and the person exercising the option would otherwise obtain, or might be expected to obtain, a tax advantage (as defined) directly or indirectly in consequence of, or otherwise in connection with, the exercise of the option.

For these purposes, the '*open market price*' of the underlying subject matter of an option is the price which that subject matter might reasonably be expected to fetch on a sale in the open market at the time of exercise, with no allowance made for any reduction arising out of the whole of the assets being placed on the market at one and the same time. Where the underlying subject matter includes unquoted shares or securities, the open market price is determined on the assumption that all information is available which a prudent prospective purchaser might reasonably require before purchase by private treaty at arm's length from a willing vendor. If any part of the underlying subject matter is subject to a right or restriction enforceable by the person disposing of it or a connected person, the open market price is determined as if the right or restriction did not exist.

'*Relevant arrangements*' are arrangements (including any agreement, understanding, scheme, transaction or series of transactions, whether or not legally enforceable) to which, or which include one or more transactions to which, a '*relevant person*' (i.e. the grantor, any person holding the option at any time, or any person connected with either of them) is or has been a party.

An option is exercised '*non-commercially*' if, in the case of an option which binds the grantor to buy, the exercise price (as above) is less than the open market price of what is bought. In the case of an option binding the grantor to sell, the option is exercised non-commercially if the exercise price is greater than the open market price of what is sold.

[*TCGA 1992, ss 144ZB–144ZD; F(No 2)A 2005, Sch 5 paras 2, 6(1)*].

TCGA 1992, s 144ZA above was introduced to reverse the effect of the decision in *Mansworth v Jelley CA 2002, 75 TC 1*. In that case, an employee (J) was granted options to acquire shares in his employer's parent company. He was not resident in the UK at the time he was granted these options, but subsequently became UK-resident, exercised the options, and then sold the shares. The Revenue issued CGT assessments on the basis that the acquisition cost of the shares was the sum of the price paid for the shares on the exercise of the options and the market value of the options when they were originally granted (which was treated as nil). However, in the CA, Chadwick LJ held that the acquisition of the shares was clearly 'an incident of the taxpayer's employment', and was therefore within *TCGA 1992, s 17(1)(b)* (see 41.1 MARKET VALUE). In the CGT computation, the cost of acquisition of the shares was 'the market value of the underlying asset' at the time when the options were exercised.

Following this case, HMRC accept that where an asset is acquired via an option exercised before 10 April 2003 and granted otherwise than by way of a bargain at arm's length or by reason of employment (so that the market value rule applies in respect of the grant (or would apply but for *TCGA 1992, s 149A* — see 20.3 EMPLOYEE SHARE SCHEMES)), the acquisition cost of the asset is equal to the market value of the asset at the time the option is exercised (plus any amount charged to income tax on the exercise — see 20.6 and 20.24 EMPLOYEE SHARE SCHEMES). Any corresponding disposal proceeds are also equal to the market value at that time, but HMRC have indicated that they will implement this only in the case of returns made on or after 12 December 2002 (Revenue Internet Statement, 8 January 2003). For examples of how HMRC seek to implement this approach in different circumstances see Revenue Internet Statements, 17 March 2003 and 8 August 2003.

Taper relief. For the purposes of TAPER RELIEF (61), the time of disposal of any asset disposed of in pursuance of the 'single transaction' referred to above, is as follows:

- where the option binds the grantor to sell, the time of the disposal made in fulfilment of the grantor's obligations under the option; and
- where the option binds the grantor to buy, the time of the disposal made to the grantor in consequence of the exercise of the option.

Any question as to whether the asset disposed of or acquired was a business asset (see 61.4 TAPER RELIEF) at any time is determined by reference to the asset to which the option related and not the option. The time of acquisition for taper relief purposes of any asset acquired in pursuance of an option, or in consequence of its exercise, is the time of the exercise of the option.

[*TCGA 1992, Sch A1 para 13; FA 1998, s 121(2)(4), Sch 20*].

Cash-settled options. In relation to an option granted after 29 November 1993, alternative provisions to those in *TCGA 1992, s 144(2)(3)* above apply to a 'cash-settled' option, i.e. an option which is exercised where the nature of the option (or its exercise) is such that the grantor is liable to make, and the grantee is entitled to receive, a payment in full settlement (for partial settlement, see below) of all obligations under the option. [*TCGA 1992, s 144A(1); FA 1994, s 96*].

Under the alternative provisions, the grantor of a cash-settled option is treated as having disposed of an asset consisting of the liability to make the payment and the payment is treated as an incidental cost of making the disposal. Here, the grant of the option and the disposal are treated as a single transaction and the consideration for the option is treated as the consideration for the disposal. Whereas, the grantee of the cash-settled option is treated as having disposed of an asset consisting of the entitlement to receive the payment and the payment received is treated as the consideration for the disposal. In this case the acquisition of the option and the disposal are treated as a single transaction and the cost of acquiring the option and related expenses is treated as allowable expenditure deductible under *TCGA 1992, s 38(1)(a)* (acquisition and incidental costs; see 15.4 COMPUTATION OF GAINS AND LOSSES). [*TCGA 1992, s 144A(2)(3)(a)(b); FA 1994, s 96*].

Where a payment is only in partial settlement of all obligations under a cash-settled option, *TCGA 1992, s 144(2)(3)* and *s 144A(2)(3)* above both apply subject to the modification that, in those provisions, any reference to the grant or acquisition of an option is replaced by a reference to the grant or acquisition of so much of the option as relates to the making and receipt of the payment or, as the case may be, the sale or purchase by the grantor, and any reference to the consideration for, or the cost of or of acquiring, the option is replaced by a reference to a just and reasonable proportion of that consideration or cost. [*TCGA 1992, s 144A(4)(5); FA 1994, s 96*].

Other matters. The above applies generally but the further treatment of options depends on the circumstances as under.

(*a*) **Options to acquire assets for trading use.** An option to acquire an asset exercisable by a person intending to use it, if acquired, for the purpose of a trade carried on by him, is not a wasting asset, and abandonment of such an option constitutes a disposal of it (such that an allowable loss may accrue). [*TCGA 1992, s 144(4)(c), s 146(1)(c)*].

(*b*) **Traded options.** A 'traded option', i.e. an option listed on a 'recognised stock exchange', or on a 'recognised futures exchange', is not a wasting asset, and an abandonment of such an option constitutes a disposal of it (such that an allowable loss may accrue). [*TCGA 1992, s 144(4)(b), (8)(b), s 146(1)(b), (4)(a); FA 1996, Sch 38 para 10(1)–(3)*].

'*Recognised stock exchange*' means the London Stock Exchange and any overseas stock exchange designated as such by Order. [*ICTA 1988, s 841; TCGA 1992, s 288(1)*]. See also 58.23 SHARES AND SECURITIES.

'*Recognised futures exchange*' means the London International Financial Futures and Options Exchange and any other UK or non-UK futures exchange designated by order. [*TCGA 1992, s 288(6)(7)*]. A list of recognised futures exchanges appears in Simon's Direct Tax Service, Binder 1, p 7521 *et seq.*

Gains arising in the course of dealing in traded options, which, but for the exemption in *ICTA 1988, s 128* or *ITTOIA 2005, s 779*, would have been chargeable to tax under Schedule D otherwise than as profits of a trade or under *ITTOIA 2005, Pt 5 Ch 8* are instead within the scope of capital gains tax. Losses are treated similarly. [*TCGA 1992, s 143(1)(2)(b); SI 2006 No 959, Art 3(2)*]. See also 6.8 below.

Where a person ('the grantor') who has granted a traded option ('the original option') closes it out by acquiring a traded option of the same description ('the second option'), any disposal by the grantor involved in closing out the original option is disregarded for the purposes of capital gains tax. The allowable expenditure attributable to the incidental costs to the grantor of making the disposal constituted by the original option is treated as increased by the aggregate of the amount or value of the consideration, in money or money's worth, given by him or on his behalf wholly and exclusively for the acquisition of the second option and the incidental costs of that acquisition. [*TCGA 1992, s 148*].

(*c*) **Quoted options to subscribe for shares.** An option to *subscribe* for shares in a company, which option is itself quoted on a recognised stock exchange (see (*b*) above), is not a wasting asset and an abandonment of such an option constitutes a disposal of it (such that an allowable loss may accrue). [*TCGA 1992, s 144(4)(a), (8)(a), s 146(1)(a), (4)(a)*]. (The term 'quoted option' is understood to have become virtually otiose following the introduction of the term 'traded option'; the technical differences between the definitions, which have changed from time to time, are believed to have few, if any, practical consequences.)

(*d*) **Financial options.** 'Financial options' are treated in the same way as traded options in (*b*) above, except that *TCGA 1992, s 148* does not apply to financial options. A '*financial option*' is an option, other than a traded option, which:

(i) relates to currency, shares, securities or an interest rate and is granted (otherwise than as agent) by a member of a recognised stock exchange, an 'authorised person' (defined by reference to *Financial Services and Markets Act 2000, s 31* and *SI 2001 No 544*); or

(ii) relates to shares or securities which are quoted on a recognised stock exchange (see (*b*) above) and is granted by a member of such an exchange, acting as agent; or

(iii) relates to currency, shares, securities or an interest rate and is granted to an authorised person and concurrently and in association with an option falling within (i) above which is granted by the authorised person concerned to the grantor of the first-mentioned option; or

(iv) relates to shares or securities which are quoted on a recognised stock exchange and is granted to a member of such an exchange, including such a member acting as agent; or

(v) is of a description specified in a Treasury order.

[*TCGA 1992, s 144(4)(b), (8)(c), (9), s 146(1)(b), (4)(a); SI 2001 No 3629, Art 65*].

Two options, purchased by the taxpayer company from the same fellow group company, intended to have effect together, and undoubtedly financial options within (i) above when considered separately, could not be re-characterised as a loan (*Griffin v Citibank Investments Ltd Ch D 2000, 73 TC 352*).

(*e*) **Options to acquire or dispose of gilt-edged securities and qualifying corporate bonds.** Disposals of any such options are exempt. [*TCGA 1992, s 115(1)(b)*].

(*f*) **Options not within (a)–(e) above.** Such options are WASTING ASSETS (67) and the abandonment of such an option is not a disposal. Options (other than those in (*b*), (*c*) or (*d*) above) to buy or sell quoted shares and securities (being shares or securities which are listed on a recognised stock exchange in the UK or elsewhere — see 58.23 SHARES AND SECURITIES) are regarded as wasting assets, the life of which end when the right to exercise the option ends, or when the option becomes valueless, whichever is the earlier. [*TCGA 1992, s 144(4), s 146(2)(3)(4)(b); FA 1996, Sch 38 para 11*].

Example

On 1 February 2002 F granted an option to G for £10,000 to acquire freehold land bought by F for £50,000 in September 1995. The option is for a period of five years, and the option price is £100,000 plus 1% thereof for each month since the option was granted. On 1 February 2004, G sold the option to H for £20,000. On 30 June 2006, H exercises the option and pays F £141,000 for the land. Neither G nor H intended to use the land for the purposes of a trade.

Indexation factor	September 1995 to April 1998	0.080

2002 Grant of option by F

	£
Disposal proceeds	10,000
Allowable cost	—
Chargeable gain	£10,000

2004 Disposal of option by G

	£	£
Disposal proceeds		20,000
Allowable cost	10,000	
Less: Wasted — ⅖ × £10,000	4,000	
		6,000
Chargeable gain		£14,000

2006 Exercise of option

	£
(i) Earlier assessment on F vacated	
(ii) Aggregate disposal proceeds	
(£10,000 + £141,000)	151,000
Allowable cost of land	50,000
Unindexed gain	101,000
Indexation allowance £50,000 × 0.080	4,000
Chargeable gain (on F) (subject to TAPER RELIEF (61))	£97,000

H's allowable expenditure is

	£
Cost of option (month of acquisition February 2004, so no indexation due)	20,000
Cost of land (month of acquisition June 2006, so no indexation due)	141,000
	£161,000

A sum paid to a person to relinquish his rights to call on another person to buy property from him (a put option) is a capital sum derived from an asset (the option) and can bring about a chargeable event as regards gains although such a transaction is not able to give rise to an allowable loss. Properly construed, the provision above that an abandonment of an option is not to be treated as a disposal is a specific exception to the general rule that the extinction of an asset constitutes a disposal of it (see 9.1 CAPITAL SUMS DERIVED FROM ASSETS) for the purpose of allowable losses. However, the provision does not exempt a gain made from such a transaction (*Golding v Kaufman Ch D 1984, 58 TC 296*; *Powlson v Welbeck Securities Ltd CA, 1987, 60 TC 269*). The consideration to be taken into account in respect of the receipt of a contingently repayable sum in return for the grant of an option to purchase land is valued subject to the contingency, provided the contingency is not within 15.6(*f*) and (*g*) COMPUTATION OF GAINS AND LOSSES (*Randall v Plumb Ch D 1974, 50 TC 392*). If, however, a contingency is related to matters which do not directly bear upon the value of the consideration, it does not necessarily have to be taken into account (*Garner v Pounds Shipowners & Shipbreakers Ltd (and related appeal) HL 2000, 72 TC 561*).

If, under *Building Societies Act 1986*, the whole of a building society's business is transferred to a successor company, and in connection therewith rights are conferred on members to acquire shares in priority to other persons, at a discount or for no payment, the rights are treated as options within *TCGA 1992, s 144* having no value and granted for no consideration. [*TCGA 1992, s 216(1), s 217(1)(6)*]. See also 58.22 SHARES AND SECURITIES. Similar provisions apply where a building society confers on its members or former members (or any class of them) similar acquisition rights after 24 July 1991 over 'qualifying shares' in the society (meaning, generally, permanent interest bearing shares (PIBS) — see 50.2 QUALIFYING CORPORATE BONDS for full definition). [*TCGA 1992, s 149*].

HMRC have set out in a Statement of Practice their views, with examples, on the tax treatment of transactions in financial futures and options otherwise within *TCGA 1992, s 143* (see (*b*) and (*d*) above and 6.8 below) and relating to shares, securities, foreign currency or other financial instruments, with particular reference to whether or not such transactions are to be regarded as profits or losses of a trade (in which case *section 143* is of no application) or taxed under the chargeable gains rules. The principles they set out are of relevance to

- UK residents such as unauthorised unit trusts, charities and others (including companies but not approved pension schemes), and
- non-UK resident collective investment vehicles, pension funds and others (including companies),

which either do not trade or whose principal trade is outside the financial area. As regards companies, principles do not apply to derivative contracts within 14.7–14.12 COMPANIES—CORPORATE FINANCE AND INTANGIBLES or to contracts within the predecessor financial instruments legislation at 14.16 COMPANIES—CORPORATE FINANCE AND INTANGIBLES. Whilst each case must be judged on its merits, HMRC consider that an *individual* is unlikely to be regarded as trading as a result of purely speculative transactions in financial futures or options, whereas transactions in financial futures or options by a company may be either trading or capital in nature. In *all* cases where the transaction is clearly ancillary to another transaction, the question of whether it is trading or capital will depend on the nature of the other transaction. The Statement lists factors to be considered in determining whether an ancillary relationship exists between the financial futures or options transaction and another transaction. In particular, such a relationship exists if the intention is to eliminate or reduce risk, or to reduce transaction costs, in respect of the other transaction, and the financial futures or options transaction is 'economically appropriate' (as defined) to such elimination or reduction. Even if the other transaction is abandoned, these principles will normally be applied, although it is politic to close out the financial futures or options transaction as soon thereafter as is practicable.

(HMRC Statement of Practice 3/02, replacing SP 14/91).

See 22.56 EXEMPTIONS AND RELIEFS for options contracts entered into by pension schemes.

See 58.8 SHARES AND SECURITIES and 20 EMPLOYEE SHARE SCHEMES for quoted options granted following a reorganisation and options granted to employees respectively.

See 55.3 ROLLOVER RELIEF for options over land as regards that relief.

See 34.7 INDEXATION for indexation allowance provisions relating to options generally.

Transactions with guaranteed returns. For chargeable periods ending after 4 March 1997 in relation to profits realised, and losses sustained, after that date, special provisions apply to a disposal of futures or options if it is one of two or more related transactions and it is reasonable to assume that a main purpose of the transactions, taken together, is or was to produce a guaranteed return, either from the disposal itself or together with another such disposal or disposals. Broadly, any profits arising are treated as income rather than, where such would otherwise be the case, as capital gains (and any losses are treated accordingly). For these purposes, the existence or timing of a disposal is determined in accordance with *TCGA 1992, s 143(5)(6)* (see 6.8 below) and *ss 144, 144A* (see above), modified as necessary. [*ITTOIA 2005, ss 551–569, Sch 1 paras 109, 344, 435, Sch 2 paras 91–95; TCGA 1992, ss 148A–148C; ICTA 1988, s 127A, Sch 5AA; FA 1997, s 80, Sch 11; FA 2002, ss 78, 83, Sch 27 paras 14, 25*]. With effect from 6 February 1998, these provisions are extended to cover the exercise, as well as the disposal, of an option. [*ITTOIA 2005, s 564, FA 1998, s 99; FA 2002, Sch 40 Pt 3(13)*]. See Tolley's Income Tax under Anti-Avoidance for detailed coverage. These provisions **cease to apply for the purposes of corporation tax for accounting periods beginning on or after 1 October 2002**, being replaced by specific corporation tax provisions (to similar effect) in *FA 2002, Sch 26 para 6* (see 14.8 COMPANIES—CORPORATE FINANCE AND INTANGIBLES and Tolley's Corporation Tax under Financial Instruments and Derivative Contracts); see also the transitional provision at *FA 2002, Sch 28 para 6*.

Derivatives over assets which are the subject of euroconversion. The following applies where: (A) a 'derivative' represents rights or obligations in respect of an asset, liability or other amount; (B) there is a 'euroconversion' of the underlying asset; (C) a transaction is entered into that would otherwise result in a disposal of the original derivative and the acquisition of a new derivative; (D) the terms of the new derivative differ from those of the original only to the extent necessary to reflect the euroconversion; *and* (E) no party to the transaction receives any consideration other than the new derivative. The transaction is not treated as involving a disposal or acquisition for CGT purposes. Instead, the original derivative and the new derivative are treated as the same asset, acquired as the original derivative was acquired. '*Derivative*' means any commodity or financial futures or an option. A '*euroconversion*', in relation to an asset, liability, contract or instrument, is the redenomination into euros of that asset etc. where it was previously expressed in the currency of an EU member state participating in the European single currency. [*SI 1998 No 3177, Regs 2, 3, 38*].

6.8 FUTURES CONTRACTS

As regards **companies,** see 14.7–14.12 COMPANIES—CORPORATE FINANCE AND INTANGIBLES for a summary of the special rules on **derivative contracts** introduced by

FA 2002, Sch 26 for accounting periods beginning on or after 1 October 2002. A future (as there defined) is a derivative contract for those purposes unless falling within one of the exclusions. See 14.16 COMPANIES—CORPORATE FINANCE AND INTANGIBLES for the financial instruments rules that preceded the derivative contracts rules. Both subjects are covered in detail in Tolley's Corporation Tax under Financial Instruments and Derivative Contracts.

Commodity and financial futures. Gains arising in the course of dealing in '*commodity or financial futures*' (which here means commodity futures or financial futures which are for the time being dealt in on a 'recognised futures exchange' (as in 6.7(*b*) above)) which would otherwise (apart from *ICTA 1988, s 128* (corresponding treatment for Schedule D) or *ITTOIA 2005, s 779* (corresponding treatment for income tax for 2005/06 onwards) have been chargeable to tax under Schedule D otherwise than as profits of a trade or under *ITTOIA 2005, Pt 5 Ch 8*, are instead brought within the scope of tax on chargeable gains. Losses are treated similarly. In addition, the following transactions, not being entered into in the course of dealing on a recognised futures exchange and except in so far as any gain or loss arising to any person from any such transaction arises in the course of a trade, are regarded as being so dealt in.

(*a*) A transaction under which an 'authorised person' (defined by reference to *Financial Services and Markets Act 2000, s 31* and *SI 2001 No 544*) enters into a commodity or financial futures contract with another person.

(*b*) A transaction under which the outstanding obligations under a commodity or financial futures contract to which an authorised person is a party are brought to an end by a further contract between the parties to the futures contract.

[*TCGA 1992, s 143(1)(2)(a), (3)(4)(8); FA 1994, s 95, Sch 26 Pt V; SI 2001 No 3629, Art 64; SI 2006 No 959, Art 3(2)*].

For the purposes of *TCGA 1992*, where, in the course of dealing in commodity or financial futures (whether or not, it seems, ones dealt in on a recognised futures exchange) a person who has entered into a futures contract closes out that contract by entering into another futures contract with reciprocal obligations to those of the first contract, the transaction is regarded as the disposal of an asset consisting of the outstanding obligations under the first contract. Any money received or paid on the transaction is treated, respectively, as consideration for the disposal or as incidental costs of the disposal. [*TCGA 1992, s 143(5)*].

In any case where, in the course of dealing in commodity or financial futures (whether or not, it seems, ones dealt in on a recognised futures exchange) a person has entered into a futures contract and has not closed out that contract as above, and he becomes entitled to receive, or liable to make, a payment, whether under the contract or otherwise, in full or partial settlement of any obligations under the contract, he is treated for the purposes of *TCGA 1992* as having disposed of an asset consisting of that entitlement or liability. The payment received or made is treated, respectively, as consideration for, or as incidental costs of, the disposal. [*TCGA 1992, s 143(6); FA 1994, s 95*].

TCGA 1992, s 46 (WASTING ASSETS (67)) does not apply to obligations under a commodity or financial futures contract which is entered into by a person in the course of dealing in such futures on a recognised futures exchange, or a commodity or financial futures contract to which an authorised person is a party. [*TCGA 1992, s 143(7)(8); FA 1994, s 95; SI 2001 No 3629, Art 64*].

See 6.7 above as regards SP 3/02 setting out HMRC's views on whether isolated transactions in financial futures are to be regarded as trading or taxed under the chargeable gains rules.

See 22.56 EXEMPTIONS AND RELIEFS for futures contracts entered into by pension schemes.

Gilt-edged securities and qualifying corporate bonds. The disposal of the outstanding obligation under any contract to acquire or dispose of such securities and bonds is exempt. Without prejudice to the provisions within *TCGA 1992, s 143(5)* above regarding the closing out of futures contracts generally, where a person closes out a contract for gilts or bonds as above by entering into another, reciprocal, contract, that transaction is treated as a disposal of the outstanding obligation under the first-mentioned contract. [*TCGA 1992, s 115(1)(b), (2)(3)*].

Transactions with guaranteed returns. For chargeable periods ending after 4 March 1997 in relation to profits realised, and losses sustained, after that date, special provisions apply to a disposal of futures or options if it is one of two or more related transactions and it is reasonable to assume that a main purpose of the transactions, taken together, is or was to produce a guaranteed return, either from the disposal itself or together with another such disposal or disposals. Broadly, any profits arising are treated as income rather than, where such would otherwise be the case, as capital gains (and any losses are treated accordingly). For these purposes, the existence or timing of a disposal is determined in accordance with *TCGA 1992, s 143(5)(6)* (see above) and *ss 144, 144A* (see 6.7 above), modified as necessary. [*ITTOIA 2005, ss 551–569, Sch 1 paras 109, 344, 435, Sch 2 paras 91–95; TCGA 1992, ss 148A–148C; ICTA 1988, s 127A, Sch 5AA; FA 1997, s 80, Sch 11; FA 2002, ss 78, 83, Sch 27 paras 14, 25*]. With effect from 6 February 1998, these provisions are extended so as to apply in the case of the exercise of an option or the running to delivery of a futures contract. [*ITTOIA 2005, s 564; FA 1998, s 99; FA 2002, Sch 40 Pt 3(13)*]. See Tolley's Income Tax under Anti-Avoidance for detailed coverage. These provisions **cease to apply for the purposes of corporation tax for accounting periods beginning on or after 1 October 2002**, being replaced by specific corporation tax provisions (to similar effect) in *FA 2002, Sch 26 para 6* (see 14.8 COMPANIES—CORPORATE FINANCE AND INTANGIBLES and Tolley's Corporation Tax under Financial Instruments and Derivative Contracts); see also the transitional provision at *FA 2002, Sch 28 para 6*.

Derivatives over assets which are the subject of euroconversion; see 6.7 above.

6.9 MILK QUOTA

The milk quota system was introduced by the European Community in 1984 in order to regulate overall milk production (EC Council Regulation 856/84). Under the scheme, each member state was allocated a production quota. The national quota was then divided between all of the country's milk producers. If total UK production for any year exceeds the national quota then a levy is payable to the European Union by the Intervention Board (previously the Milk Marketing Board). This levy is then charged on to individual producers who have exceeded their own quota.

Quota was originally allocated to milk producers in the UK by reference to levels of production for 1983 and was attached both to the producer and to the producer's land in use for milk production at 1 April 1984 (his 'holding'). Originally it was only possible to transfer milk quota permanently to another producer as part of a disposal of all or part of the holding to which it was attached (*SI 1984 No 1047*). This could be by outright sale of the land or by use of a scheme by which a permanent transfer of the quota is achieved by granting a short lease of the land. From 1 April 1994, it is possible in limited circumstances to sell milk quota without selling the land (*SI 1994 No 160*).

HMRC consider that milk quota is an asset separate from the land to which it is attached, and does not constitute an interest in or right over land. The decision in *Cottle v Coldicott (Sp C 40), [1995] SSCD 239* supports this view. The taxpayer sold part of his quota using the scheme involving a short lease of land referred to above. The Special Commissioners held that the sale of milk quota amounted to the disposal of a separate asset. It was not a part disposal of the taxpayer's land, as he had contended, and neither were the proceeds a capital sum derived from the land within *TCGA 1992, s 22(1)* (see 9.1 CAPITAL SUMS DERIVED FROM ASSETS). Since the quota was a separate asset which had been allocated without cost in 1984, it followed that the allowable cost of acquisition was nil. The decision was followed in *Foxton v HMRC (Sp C 485), [2005] SSCD 661*.

For HMRC's view of the treatment of milk quota as a separate asset, see HMRC Capital Gains Manual CG 77820–77860. See also Revenue Tax Bulletin February 1993 pp 49–51 and December 1995 p 265. Where land and milk quota are acquired in a single transaction and the consideration is not allocated separately to each, an apportionment is required on a just and reasonable basis under *TCGA 1992, s 52(4)*.

For corporation tax purposes, milk quota is generally within the definition of an intangible fixed asset for the purposes of the intangible assets regime (see 14.13 COMPANIES—CORPORATE FINANCE AND INTANGIBLES). Broadly, milk quota acquired by a company from an unrelated party after 31 March 2002 is therefore outside the scope of corporation tax on chargeable gains (but see 14.13 COMPANIES—CORPORATE FINANCE AND INTANGIBLES for the detailed transitional provisions). A gain on disposal of milk quota not falling within that regime remains within the charge to corporation tax on chargeable gains (but see below as regards rollover relief).

Milk quota is a *fungible* asset, i.e. one which grows or diminishes as parts are acquired or disposed of but the individual parts of which cannot be separately identified. Acquisitions and disposals of quota are expressed in terms of a specific number of litres. Quota acquired in stages before 6 April 1998 form a single asset for the purposes of both capital gains tax and corporation tax on chargeable gains. For the latter purposes, this treatment continues on and after that date (for acquisitions not falling within the corporation tax intangible assets regime — see above). Any quota allocated without cost on 1 April 1984 forms part of that asset but without contributing to its overall acquisition cost. Expenditure is allocated to a part disposal of the single asset in accordance with the formula in *TCGA 1992, s 42* (see 15.7 COMPUTATION OF GAINS AND LOSSES). For capital gains tax purposes only (i.e. not for corporate producers), each acquisition of quota after 5 April 1998 forms a separate asset, and disposals are matched with acquisitions in accordance with the rules summarised at 59.1 SHARES AND SECURITIES — IDENTIFICATION RULES (generally last in/first out, the pre—6 April 1998 single asset being equivalent to the 'section 104 holding' of shares). (HMRC Capital Gains Manual CG 77900–77911).

For taper relief purposes (not applicable to corporate producers), the qualifying holding period (see 61.2 TAPER RELIEF) begins on 6 April 1998 as regards the pre-6 April 1998 single asset and on the actual date of acquisition as regards each post-5 April 1998 acquisition of milk quota. Quota will normally be a business asset for taper relief purposes, unless, for example, milk production has ceased and all the quota is being leased out. (HMRC Capital Gains Manual CG 77916–77919).

Tenant farmers. On the termination of a tenancy, the milk quota reverts to the landlord. The tenant and the landlord may agree compensation for the tenant's loss of milk quota. If not, the tenant is entitled to statutory compensation under *Agriculture Act 1986, s 13*. Where the compensation is paid under a contract, the time of the disposal is the time the contract is made. If the contract is conditional, it is the time the condition is satisfied. Where the compensation is statutory or is paid under a contractual agreement which does not provide for the reversion of the quota, the date of the disposal is the date of receipt of the compensation.

Tenant farmers require the consent of the landlord before selling milk quota. If the tenant makes a payment to the landlord in consideration of such consent the expenditure qualifies as a deduction in computing the chargeable gain on disposal of the milk quota. The landlord will have received a capital sum derived from an asset, taxable under *TCGA 1992, s 22(1)* (see 9.1 CAPITAL SUMS DERIVED FROM ASSETS).
(HMRC Capital Gains Manual CG 77885, 77942–77946).

Compensation payments.

(1) '*Outgoers Schemes*'. On the introduction of the scheme, existing milk producers not wishing to receive quota and preferring to cease production were paid compensation under

the Milk Supplementary Levy (Outgoers) Scheme 1984. Any farmer claiming payment under that scheme had the option to apply either for compensation for loss of profits in the five years immediately after ceasing to produce milk, or for compensation for the surrender of his milk quota. Payments in respect of loss of profits were treated as receipts of the farming business and therefore liable to tax as income. Payments in respect of surrender of quota were treated as capital and liable to capital gains tax (Hansard 18 July 1984, col 218 and 15 April 1985, col 27). Similar comments apply to the Milk (Community Outgoers) and Milk (Partial Cessation of Production) Schemes (Hansard 13 February 1987, col 384). Where compensation is so chargeable to CGT, it is chargeable for the year in which the producer was accepted into the scheme, although deferral of tax may be due under *TCGA 1992, s 280* (consideration receivable in instalments — see 47.6 PAYMENT OF TAX) (HMRC Capital Gains Manual CG 77867).

(2) Compensation was paid to certain producers, (known as 'SLOM' producers), who were initially not allocated quota because of their participation in another scheme for temporary non-production of milk at the time the milk quota scheme was introduced. These producers were later allocated quota and were able to claim compensation for the loss of income arising from their temporary exclusion from the scheme. Claims had to be made by 30 September 1993. The compensation is for loss of profits and is treated as a receipt of the farming business, liable to tax as income. See Revenue Tax Bulletin May 1994 pp 127, 128.

(3) Compensation in respect of the temporary suspension of a proportion of quota is treated as a receipt of the farming trade, taxable as income. Such compensation was paid for 1987/88 and 1988/89. (HMRC Capital Gains Manual CG 77921).

(4) Compensation paid for a permanent reduction in milk quota is a capital sum derived from an asset, chargeable to capital gains tax under *TCGA 1992, s 22(1)* (see 9.1 CAPITAL SUMS DERIVED FROM ASSETS). Compensation for cuts announced between 1987 and 1990 was chargeable in the year in which the first instalment was received, but with deferral due under *TCGA 1992, s 280* as in (1) above. A further cut was announced in 1991 and the compensation was paid in five annual instalments starting in June 1992. A further instalment for UK producers, arising as a result of changes in rules which affected the conversion of the compensation into sterling, was announced in January 1997 and paid in 1996/97 or, in a few cases, 1997/98. Each of these instalments is chargeable in the year of receipt. The last-mentioned instalment included an element described as 'compensation in lieu of interest'; this is not chargeable to CGT but is instead taxable as income under Schedule D, Case III. (HMRC Capital Gains Manual CG 77922–77924 and Revenue Tax Bulletins May 1994 p 128, October 1997 p 474).

Rollover relief etc. For capital gains tax purposes, and for corporation tax purposes in relation to acquisitions of 'new assets' before 1 April 2002, milk quota is a qualifying asset for rollover relief purposes (see 55.3 ROLLOVER RELIEF).

For corporation tax purposes, where milk quota would be the new asset for rollover relief purposes, it is not a qualifying asset where it is acquired on or after 1 April 2002 and falls within the intangible assets regime (see 14.13 COMPANIES—CORPORATE FINANCE AND INTANGIBLES). Disposals of milk quota (whether or not within the regime) on or after 1 April 2002 qualify for chargeable gains rollover relief only where the acquisition of the new asset takes place before that date. See 55.1 ROLLOVER RELIEF.

Milk quota is not regarded as a WASTING ASSET (67) (HMRC Capital Gains Manual CG 77940). The concessionary rollover relief available for the exchange of joint interests in land also includes the parallel exchange of joint interests in milk quota (see 38.12 LAND).

6.10 **Bonus issue of Milk Marque shares to dairy farmers.** In October 1998, milk producers who supplied Milk Marque Ltd in the year to 31 March 1998 were awarded a bonus consisting of preference shares (or in some cases loan stock) in the company. HMRC consider that the cost of acquisition of the shares or loan stock for capital gains tax purposes is equal to their nominal value. Such value should also be included in the producer's accounts as a trading receipt. (Revenue Tax Bulletin August 1999 p 685).

6.11 **BOOKMAKERS' PITCHES**

A bookmaker's pitch is a specified position at a racecourse on which the bookmaker may erect a stand and take bets. HMRC take the view that the right to occupy a particular pitch at a particular racecourse is an asset for capital gains tax purposes. A disposal of such a right by way of auction, which is permitted with effect from 8 October 1998, is therefore a disposal of a chargeable asset. The date of disposal is the date on which the purchaser's bid is accepted. Where a pitch has not previously changed hands by way of auction, it will normally have no acquisition cost and no 31 March 1982 value. The exception is where the pitch was acquired by inheritance on or after 8 October 1998, in which case its acquisition cost to the legatee will be its market value at date of death, under the general rule at 18.1 DEATH.

A pitch qualifies as a business asset for the purposes of TAPER RELIEF (61). It does not fall within any of the classes of asset qualifying for ROLLOVER RELIEF (55.3).

(Revenue Tax Bulletin October 1999 pp 699, 700).

6.12 **DOMAIN NAMES**

The sale of an internet domain name is a disposal of an asset for the purposes of capital gains tax and corporation tax on chargeable gains. The exception is where a business deals in domain names as, or as part of, its trade, in which case such sales contribute to its trading profits for income tax or corporation tax purposes. (Revenue Technical Note: Guide to the Tax Consequences of Trading over the Internet, November 2000).

7 Assets held on 6 April 1965

Cross-reference. See 8 ASSETS HELD ON 31 MARCH 1982 for the restricted circumstances in which disposals after 5 April 1988 of such assets will be assessed by reference to the provisions of this chapter.

Simon's Direct Tax Service. See C2.610–C2.614.

7.1 Assets held on 6 April 1965 (the original base date for the purposes of capital gains tax) are still subject to special provisions contained in *TCGA 1992, s 35(9), Sch 2* and for this purpose may be divided into three categories.

(i) Quoted securities (see 7.2–7.5 below).

(ii) Land subsequently disposed of at a price including development value (see 7.6 below).

(iii) Other assets and miscellaneous aspects (see 7.7–7.12 below).

Married persons and civil partners. The provisions relating to assets held on 6 April 1965 apply in relation to the disposal of an asset by one spouse or civil partner, and who acquired it from the other spouse or civil partner in a year of assessment when they were living together, as if the other's acquisition or provision of the asset had been the acquisition etc. of the asset by the spouse or partner making the disposal. [*TCGA 1992, Sch 2 para 22; SI 2005 No 3229, Reg 124(b)*].

Groups of companies. The provisions relating to assets held on 6 April 1965 apply in relation to the disposal of an asset by a company which is or has been a member of a group of companies (within 27.1 GROUPS OF COMPANIES), and which acquired the asset from another member of the group at the time when both were members of the group, as if all members of the group for the time being were the same person, and as if the acquisition or provision of the asset by the group, taken as a single person, had been the acquisition or provision of it by the member disposing of it. *After 31 March 1980*, this does not apply where the disposing company is an investment trust or acquired the asset after that date from an investment trust. [*TCGA 1992, s 174(4)(5)*].

7.2 QUOTED SECURITIES: GENERAL RULES

The provisions apply to 'quoted securities', namely

(i) Shares and securities which on 6 April 1965, or at any time within six years prior to that date, had quoted market values on a 'recognised stock exchange' in the UK or elsewhere.

(ii) Interests in unit trusts (see 65 UNIT TRUSTS ETC.), the prices of which are published regularly by the scheme's managers.

Shares or securities issued to an employee on terms restricting his right to dispose of them are excluded. [*TCGA 1992, Sch 2 para 1*].

'*Recognised stock exchange*' has its natural meaning. So far as the UK is concerned, it is understood that HMRC accept that all the stock exchanges in the UK during the six years ended on 6 April 1965 were within this meaning but that the Provincial Brokers Exchange was outside it.

Subject to the election in 7.3 below, on a disposal of such assets after 5 April 1965, computation of the gain or loss accruing is made

(*a*) by reference to allowable expenditure computed according to the normal rules (i.e. cost/value at the *actual* date of acquisition and other allowable expenditure) (see 15.4 COMPUTATION OF GAINS AND LOSSES), *and* (*b*) by reference to allowable expenditure, etc. calculated according to identical rules, except that market value at 6 April 1965 is treated as the acquisition cost. Market value at 6 April 1965 (except where special circumstances may affect the value, see *Hinchcliffe v Crabtree HL 1971, 47 TC 419*) is the greater of

(i) a price half-way between the prices quoted in The Stock Exchange Daily Official List (or, for unit trusts, those published by the managers) and

(ii) for shares and securities, the average of the highest and lowest prices for normal bargains, if any, on that day.

Of the computations under (*a*) and (*b*), the one which prevails is that which produces (after, if available, any indexation allowance) the smaller gain or the smaller loss. But if one computation produces a gain and the other a loss, the disposal is treated as giving rise to neither a chargeable gain nor an allowable loss. [*TCGA 1992, Sch 2 para 2*(*1*), *Sch 11 para 6*].

Where the original cost of the shares is not known and no election (see 7.3 below) has been made, it is HMRC's practice to compute gains by reference to the value of the shares at 6 April 1965 and to disallow losses (computed on the same basis) altogether.

7.3 **Elections.** The taxpayer (or his personal representatives) may, however, elect (under *TCGA 1992, Sch 2 para 4*) that in respect of *all* disposals after 19 March 1968 (including those made before the election) of

(*a*) fixed interest securities and preference shares, or

(*b*) other quoted securities etc., or

(*c*) both kinds of securities etc. under (*a*) and (*b*),

their actual cost be ignored and computations made by reference to their market value at 6 April 1965 only. The election, which is irrevocable, must be made, by notice in writing to HMRC. An election for pooling may be made for the purposes of capital gains tax on or before the first anniversary of the 31st January next following the year of assessment in which the first relevant disposal is made. In the case of an election for the purposes of corporation tax not later than two years after the end of the accounting period in which the first relevant disposal is made. In either case, HMRC may allow an extension. [*TCGA 1992, Sch 2 para 11; FA 1996, Sch 21 para 42*(*2*)].

After 5 April 1985 (31 March 1985 for companies), another opportunity is available for an election to be made where the time limit given above has expired by reference to the first relevant disposal after 19 March 1968. The time limit is extended so as to apply by reference to the first relevant disposal after 5 April 1985 (31 March 1985 for companies).

'Fixed interest security' is as defined in 58.7 SHARES AND SECURITIES.

'Preference share' means any share the holder of which has a right to a dividend at a fixed rate but no other right to share in the profits of the company. Fixed rate dividends include those payable before 6 April 1973 and which varied at a rate fluctuating in accordance with the standard rate of income tax.

Married persons and civil partners. An election does not cover quoted securities which the holder acquired from his spouse or civil partner on a disposal after 19 March 1968 (or, again, after 31 March 1985) but such securities continue to be covered by an election which the transferor may have made. Where it is necessary to identify securities disposed of, earliest acquisitions are deemed to be disposed of first.

Example

H acquired 3,000 U plc ordinary shares in 1962 for £15,000. Their market value was £10 per share on 6 April 1965 and £12 per share on 31 March 1982. In September 2006, H sells 2,000 of the shares for £30 per share. The indexation factor for March 1982 to April 1998 is 1.047.

	£	£	£
Sale proceeds	60,000	60,000	60,000
Cost	10,000		
6 April 1965 value		20,000	
31 March 1982 value			24,000
Unindexed gain	50,000	40,000	36,000
Indexation allowance			
£24,000 × 1.047	25,128	25,128	25,128
Indexed gain	£24,872	£14,872	£10,872
Chargeable gain (subject to TAPER RELIEF (61))			£10,872

Notes to the example

(1) The comparison is firstly between the gain arrived at by deducting cost and that arrived at by deducting 6 April 1965 value. The smaller of the two gains is taken. If, however, an election had been made under either *TCGA 1992, Sch 2 para 4* or *TCGA 1992, s 109(4)* for 6 April 1965 value to be used in computing all gains and losses on quoted shares held at that date, this comparison need not be made and the taxable gain, subject to (2) below, would be £14,872.

(2) The second comparison is between the figure arrived at in (1) above and the gain using 31 March 1982 value. As the latter is smaller, it is substituted for the figure in (1) above by virtue of *TCGA 1992, s 35(2)*. If, however, an election had been made under *TCGA 1992, s 35(5)* for 31 March 1982 value to be used in computing all gains and losses on assets held at that date, neither this comparison nor that in (1) above need be made and the taxable gain would still be £10,872.

(3) Indexation is based on 31 March 1982 value in all three calculations as this gives the greater allowance.

(4) All comparisons are between gains *after* indexation and *before* taper relief.

Groups of companies. An election does not cover quoted securities which a company acquired from another group company (see 27.1 GROUPS OF COMPANIES and note that the change in the residence requirement therein mentioned has effect for this purpose after 31 March 2000) on a disposal after 19 March 1968 (or, again, after 31 March 1985) but such securities continue to be covered by an election which the transferor company may have made. Where it is necessary to identify securities disposed of, earliest acquisitions are deemed to be disposed of first. An election by a company which is at the 'relevant time' the principal company of the group has effect as an election by any other company which at that time is a member of the group. No election may be made by any other company which is a member of the group at that time. The '*relevant time*' is the first occasion after 19 March 1968 (or, again, after 31 March 1985) when any company which is then a member of the group disposes of quoted securities of a kind covered by the election. These provisions apply notwithstanding that a company ceases to be a member of the group at any time after the relevant time. They do not apply to securities owned by a company which, after 19 March 1968 (or, again, after 31 March 1985) and before the relevant time, was not a member of the group and in relation to which either an election was made or no election was made within the time limit following a disposal.

[*TCGA 1992, s 109(4)(5), Sch 2 para 3, para 4(1)(2)(8)–(13), paras 5, 8; FA 2000, Sch 29 para 37; SI 2005 No 3229, Reg 124(a)*].

For the position as regards *partnerships*, see 46.17 PARTNERSHIPS.

7.4 **QUOTED SECURITIES: IDENTIFICATION RULES**

Where quoted securities of the same class are held on 6 April 1965, the identification rules for matching acquisitions with disposals depend on whether an election for 6 April 1965 market values under 7.3 above has been made or not. In addition, the rules are further governed by the general identification rules for securities etc. at 59 SHARES AND SECURITIES—IDENTIFICATION RULES. Consequently this paragraph (dealing with the situation on or after the '1985 date') should be read with those general rules. For the position where there has been a reorganisation or exchange etc. of quoted securities following an election under 7.3(*a*) or (*b*) but not both, see 7.5 below. Where it is necessary to re-establish which shares remain following a disposal before the '1985 date' (see below), see the 2005/06 and earlier editions for the identification rules for disposals in the period before that date but on or after the '1982 date' (i.e. 6 April 1982 (1 April 1982 for companies)) and for the period before the '1982 date'.

After the '1985 date', the identification rules given in (*a*) or (*b*) below apply to quoted securities held on 6 April 1965 excluding any 'relevant securities' so held. Note that for disposals after 5 April 1998, 'relevant securities' are no longer excluded from the general identification rules for capital gains tax purposes as opposed to those of corporation tax on chargeable gains. The full definition of 'relevant securities' is given at 59.6 SHARES AND SECURITIES—IDENTIFICATION RULES as are the identification rules. So far as concerns quoted securities held on 6 April 1965, this definition is only relevant to securities within the accrued income provisions (bondwashing) of *ICTA 1988, ss 710–728* (broadly any government, public authority, or company loan stock). Government securities retain their own identification rules for disposals before 2 July 1986, being exempt from capital gains tax for disposals on or after that date.

(*a*) Where *no* election has been made, pre-7 April 1965 acquisitions are treated as disposed of on a 'last-in, first-out' basis and only identified with disposals after all post-6 April 1965 acquisitions have been identified under the general identification rules. See 59.2–59.5 SHARES AND SECURITIES—IDENTIFICATION RULES.

(*b*) Where an election *is* made, pre-7 April 1965 acquisitions (at 6 April 1965 market values) form part, or the whole, of the '1982 holding' which is treated as a single asset (but one which cannot grow by further acquisitions). See 59.5 SHARES AND SECURITIES—IDENTIFICATION RULES. Disposals are only identified with the '1982 holding' after any subsequent acquisitions have been identified.

The '*1985 date*' is 6 April 1985 (1 April 1985 for companies).

[*TCGA 1992, s 104*(*3*), *ss 105, 106A, 107, 108, Sch 2 para 2*(*2*), *para 3, para 4*(*3*)–(*7*); *FA 1998, s 123*(*3*), *s 124; FA 2006, s 72*(*2*)].

7.5 **Reorganisation, exchange etc. following partial election.** Where an election has been made under 7.3(*a*) *or* under 7.3(*b*) above *but not both* and there is a disposal out of a 'new holding' (see definition below) following a reorganisation or exchange etc. of quoted securities held on 6 April 1965, the election applies according to the nature of the securities in the new holding, notwithstanding that it is to be treated as one with the 'original holding' and that the election would have applied differently to the original holding.

Where the election does cover the disposal out of the new holding, but does not cover quoted securities of the kind comprised in the original holding, the question of how much of the new holding derives from securities held on 6 April 1965, and how much derives from other quoted securities is decided on the assumption that an election does not apply.

Where the election does not cover a disposal out of the new holding, but does cover quoted securities of the kind comprised in the original holding, then, in computing the gain accruing on the disposal out of the new holding, the question of what remained undisposed of on any disposal out of the original holding is calculated on the footing that an election did not apply to that earlier disposal.

[*TCGA 1992, Sch 2 para 6*].

'*Original holding*' means securities held before and concerned in the reorganisation etc. and '*new holding*' means, in relation to any original holding, the shares in and debentures of the company which, following the reorganisation etc., represent the original holding, together with any remaining original holding. [*TCGA 1992, ss 126, 127*]. See 58.1 SHARES AND SECURITIES for full coverage of reorganisations etc. generally.

Note. Where (i) disposals are made on or after the '1982 date' (see 7.4 above) out of the new holding and (ii) there were disposals out of the original holding before the '1982 date', the legislation does not make clear whether the 'last-in, first-out' basis applying on or after the '1982 date' in respect of original shares held on 6 April 1965 (as under 7.4(*a*) above) is the appropriate identification procedure for disposals in (ii) or if it is the 'first-in/first-out' basis applying before the 1982 date. In addition it should be noted that there is no provision to adjust the original *computation* of any gain arising on a disposal out of the original shares.

7.6 LAND REFLECTING DEVELOPMENT VALUE

If land in the UK held on 6 April 1965 is disposed of after 17 December 1973 either

(i) at a price exceeding 'current use value' (as defined and see *Morgan v Gibson Ch D 1989, 61 TC 654*) at the time of the disposal, or

(ii) if any 'material development' (as defined) has been carried out after 17 December 1973 by the disposer,

on the disposal, computations of the gain or loss accruing are made

(*a*) by reference to the original cost, or market value when acquired if appropriate—see 41 MARKET VALUE, and

(*b*) by reference to market value on 6 April 1965.

Of these two computations, the one which produces the smaller gain or the smaller loss prevails, but if one computation produces a gain and the other a loss, the result is treated as giving rise to neither gain nor loss. The provisions apply only if before 6 April 1965, expenditure was *incurred* which would otherwise have been deductible in computing the gain on the disposal. A deemed acquisition cost by virtue of *TCGA 1992, s 17* (or similar previous legislation) is 'expenditure incurred' for this purpose. See *Mashiter v Pearmain CA 1984, 58 TC 334*. [*TCGA 1992, Sch 2 paras 9–15*].

Example

K sells a building plot, on which planning permission has just been obtained, in November 2006 for £200,000. He acquired the plot by gift from his father in 1958 when its value was £2,000. The market value was £5,000 at 6 April 1965 and £10,000 at 31 March 1982, and the current use value in November 2006 is £15,000. The indexation factor for March 1982 to April 1998 is 1.047.

	£	£	£
Sale proceeds	200,000	200,000	200,000
Cost	2,000		
Market value 6.4.65		5,000	
Market value 31.3.82			10,000
Unindexed gain	198,000	195,000	190,000
Indexation allowance			
£10,000 × 1.047	10,470	10,470	10,470
Gain after indexation	£187,530	£184,530	£179,530
Chargeable gain (subject to TAPER RELIEF (61))			£179,530

Notes to the example

(1) Time apportionment would have substantially reduced the gain of £187,530, using cost, such that re-basing to 31 March 1982 would have given a greater gain than that based on cost and would not therefore have applied. However, as the plot has been sold for a price in excess of its current use value, no time apportionment can be claimed.

(2) Gains are compared after applying the indexation allowance, which is based on 31 March 1982 value, this being greater than either cost or 6 April 1965 value. The comparison is made before applying taper relief.

(3) In this case, the gain is computed in accordance with the rules in 8 ASSETS HELD ON 31 MARCH 1982 as the gain by reference to 31 March 1982 value is lower than the lowest of the alternatives at (*a*) and (*b*) above.

See 38.7 LAND for part disposals with development value of an estate of land acquired before 6 April 1965.

7.7 OTHER ASSETS AND MISCELLANEOUS ASPECTS

Special provisions apply to other assets not falling within 7.2–7.6 above (including unquoted shares and land not covered by 7.6 above) held on 6 April 1965.

Subject to 7.8 below, gains on disposals of such assets which are held on 6 April 1965 are apportioned (on the basis of relative costs) between the original asset and any additions to it, and are deemed to have arisen evenly over the period from acquisition (or addition), or from 6 April 1945 if later, to the date of disposal. Only the part of the gain or loss attributable, on this basis, to the period from 6 April 1965 to disposal is taxable or allowable. [*TCGA 1992, Sch 2 para 16*]. This basis is known as **time apportionment**. According to HMRC Statement of Practice 3/82, indexation allowance, where available, is calculated and deducted before applying such apportionment, and the case of *Smith v Schofield HL 1993, 65 TC 669* subsequently confirmed this practice.

Example

On 6 April 1953, A acquired 5,000 shares in C Ltd, an unquoted company, for £15,201. He sells these shares (his entire holding in the company) on 6 April 2006 for £75,000. The retail prices index for March 1982 is 79.44 and for April 1998 it is 162.6. No election for universal 31 March 1982 re-basing is made but the market value of the holding on that date is agreed at £17,000.

The chargeable gain is computed thus

7.7 Assets held on 6 April 1965

Total period of ownership	53 years
Period after 6 April 1965	41 years
Unindexed gain	
£(75,000 – 15,201)	£59,799
Indexation allowance	
$\dfrac{162.6 - 79.44}{79.44} \times £17{,}000$	£17,799 (indexation factor 1.047)
Overall gain £(59,799 – 17,799)	£42,000
Chargeable gain (subject to TAPER RELIEF (61))	£42,000 × 41/53 = £32,490
The gain by reference to 31 March 1982 value is	
£(75,000 – 17,000 – 17,799)	£40,201

31 March 1982 re-basing does not apply as a higher gain would thereby result. See also 7.8 below re election for 6 April 1965 value (not illustrated above).

Assume, however, that in April 1960, A, having discovered a defect in his title to the shares, incurred legal costs of £1,500 in order to correct it.

The gain would then be computed as follows

Overall gain (as revised)

£75,000 – £(15,201 + 1,500 + 17,799) £40,500

Proportion of gain attributable to original expenditure (E(0)) $\dfrac{£15{,}201}{£16{,}701} \times £40{,}500 = £36{,}862$

Proportion of gain attributable to enhancement expenditure (E(1)) $\dfrac{£1{,}500}{£16{,}701} \times £40{,}500 = £3{,}638$

$$\frac{\text{Period of ownership since 6 April 1965}}{\text{Total period of ownership}} \times E(0)$$

= 41/53 × £36,862 = £28,516

$$\frac{\text{Period of ownership since 6 April 1965}}{\text{Total period of ownership since enhancement}} \times E(1)$$

= 41/46 × £3,638 =£3,242

Total chargeable gain £28,516 + £3,242 = £31,758

The gain by reference to 31 March 1982 value is again £40,201 so re-basing at that date does not apply.

The formulae for apportionment of gains are contained in *TCGA 1992, Sch 2 para 16* (whence the designations 'E(0)' and 'E(1)' are taken).

Where the original expenditure (compared with the enhancement expenditure) is disproportionately small having regard to the value of the asset immediately before the enhancement expenditure was incurred (or where there is no original expenditure) the *actual gain* attributable to the enhancement expenditure is substituted for the figure arrived at under the formula, and the balance is treated as attributable to original expenditure. This is done in practice by establishing as a fact what the proceeds for the asset would have been without any of the enhancement expenditure in question.

HMRC are prepared to accept a period of tenancy prior to a period of ownership as part of the time apportionment denominator e.g. where farm land was gifted by a father to his son in 1956 and subsequently sold by the son in 1980, if the son had been a tenant since 1945 a time apportionment factor of 15/(20+15) would apply rather than 15/(15+9). The existence of an ordinary tenancy is sufficient to allow the extended time apportionment formulae to apply even though no formal lease or tenancy agreement was in existence, provided sufficient rent was paid. Any sale of land, including buildings, follows the same pattern but any 'wasted cost' of a lease has to be added to the cost of the 'freehold reversion'. (CCAB Statement TR 500, 10 March 1983).

For the circumstances in which HMRC will require a valuation of the asset transferred where a claim for hold-over relief is made, see 33.1 HOLD-OVER RELIEFS.

7.8 **Election.** Alternatively (except in the case of an asset which has been the subject of a previous part disposal after 5 April 1965; see 15.7 COMPUTATION OF GAINS AND LOSSES) the taxpayer may elect, by notice in writing that the gain should be computed by reference to the market value at 6 April 1965 of the asset disposed of. An election for the purposes of capital gains tax must be made on or before the first anniversary of 31st January following the year of assessment in which the disposal is made. In the case of corporation tax, it must be made within two years after the end of the accounting period in which the disposal is made.

HMRC have discretion to extend the time limit for instances of which see *Whitaker v Cameron Ch D 1982, 56 TC 97*, 3.16 ANTI-AVOIDANCE and 27.9 GROUPS OF COMPANIES. The election is irrevocable, and HMRC will not normally discuss a valuation before an election is made. On a part disposal, an election will affect all later such disposals, or the ultimate disposal, made by the same person. [*TCGA 1992, Sch 2 para 17(1)(3)–(5); FA 1996, Sch 21 para 42(3)*].

If the election to use 6 April 1965 value results in a gain, it is valid irrespective of all other figures (and the election will thus be to the detriment of the taxpayer if the time apportionment basis would have produced a smaller gain or a loss). If the election results in a loss, that loss is allowable, unless

(i) there is a smaller loss by reference to cost in which case that smaller loss is taken (and this means that the full loss by reference to cost is taken instead of the time apportionment loss, so that the election has been beneficial to the taxpayer), or

(ii) there is a gain by reference to cost, in which case the disposal will be treated as producing neither a gain nor a loss.

[*TCGA 1992, Sch 2 para 17(2)*].

Part disposals out of an estate of land may be able to be treated as disposals of separate assets and thus allow 6 April 1965 value to be used in relation only to parts. See 38.7 LAND.

7.9 **Identification rules for unquoted securities, commodities etc. where no election under 7.8 above.** *After 5 April 1982* (*31 March 1982 for companies*) on the realisation of part of an unquoted shareholding or other fungible assets, any shares held on 6 April 1965 are not pooled but are identified with shares disposed of on a last-in, first-out basis. *Before 6 April 1982* (*1 April 1982 for companies*) the part sold was identified on a first-in, first-out basis with shares held on 6 April 1965 which again were not pooled. [*TCGA 1992, Sch 2 para 18; CGTA 1979, Sch 5 para 13*].

Post-6 April 1965 acquisitions are treated as in 59 SHARES AND SECURITIES—IDENTIFICATION RULES.

7.10 **Time apportionment restrictions.** Where, after the date of acquisition and before 6 April 1965,

(*a*) there was a *reorganisation* of a company's share capital (see 58.1 SHARES AND SECURITIES), time apportionment is not available. In such a case, 6 April 1965 value must be used. [*TCGA 1992, Sch 2 para 19*(*1*)], or

(*b*) a *part disposal* was made, time apportionment is calculated from the date of that part disposal by reference to market value at that time. [*TCGA 1992, Sch 2 para 16*(*7*)].

Where, after 5 April 1965,

(i) there is a *reorganisation* of a company's share capital, the new holding is treated as having been sold and immediately re-acquired at that time by the owner at the then market value. The amount of any gain on the disposal of the new holding, or part thereof, is computed by time apportioning any gain or loss over the period ending at that time and bringing into account the full gain or loss from that time to the date of disposal, computed by reference to the ultimate disposal value and the aforesaid market value. [*TCGA 1992, Sch 2 para 19*(*2*)], or

(ii) there is a *part disposal*, the asset is treated as having been sold and immediately re-acquired at that time by the owner at the then market value. The amount of any gain on the disposal is calculated as under (i) above. [*TCGA 1992, Sch 2 para 16*(*8*)].

The provisions under (*a*) and (i) above do not apply (i.e. normal time apportionment applies) in relation to a reorganisation of a company's share capital if the new holding differs only from the original shares in being a different number of shares of the same class as the original shares. [*TCGA 1992, Sch 2 para 19*(*3*)]. Following the decision in *CIR v Beveridge CS 1979, 53 TC 178*, in all cases where liability is finalised after 19 July 1979, HMRC do not consider this provision to apply where the shares comprised in the new holding are in a different company from the old shares. Previously, the practice of the Revenue had been to apply the wording to such a reorganisation (HMRC Statement of Practice 14/79). In *Unilever (UK) Holdings Ltd v Smith CA, 2002 STI 1806*, in which a scheme of arrangement involved the cancellation of preference shares without altering the rights attaching to the ordinary shares, it was held that there had been no 'reorganisation' and that, consequently, (i) above could not apply.

Where (*a*) or (i) above has applied, gains chargeable on the disposal of the entire new holding are limited to the actual gains realised. Separate transactions in the year or accounting period are treated as a single disposal provided the entire holding is so disposed of. (HMRC Extra-Statutory Concession D10).

Where the provisions in (ii) above would normally apply to unquoted shares in a winding-up, the time apportionment fraction determined at the date of the first distribution may be able to be used to calculate the gain on each additional distribution without further adjustment (HMRC Statement of Practice D3). See also 58.11 SHARES AND SECURITIES.

Part disposals out of an estate of land may be able to be treated as disposals of separate assets and so prevent the operation of (*b*) and (ii) above. See 38.7 LAND.

7.11 **Capital allowances.** Where the gain on the disposal of an asset is calculated by reference to its value on 6 April 1965, the restriction of relief given for losses accruing on assets which have qualified for capital allowances (*TCGA 1992, s 41*, see 15.6(*j*) COMPUTATION OF GAINS AND LOSSES) and the provisions relating to wasting assets qualifying for capital allowances (*TCGA 1992, s 47*, see 67.1 WASTING ASSETS) apply as if the capital allowances for 1965/66 and subsequent years were allowances in respect of expenditure incurred on the asset on 6 April 1965. [*TCGA 1992, Sch 2 para 20*].

7.12 **Assets transferred to close companies.** Where, at any time, a person who has 'control' of a 'close company', or a person 'connected' with him, transfers an asset to the company, and subsequently the first person (or any person with a 'substantial holding' of shares in the company) disposes of shares in circumstances such that the chargeable gain is to be determined by time apportionment, to the extent that the gain accruing on the disposal is attributable to a profit on the asset transferred, the shares are deemed to have been acquired at the date when the asset was transferred. The provisions do not apply where a loss accrues on the disposal. [*TCGA 1992, Sch 2 para 21*].

'*Control*' is as given by *ICTA 1988, s 416*. '*Close company*' has the meaning given by *ICTA 1988, ss 414, 415*. '*Connected*' is as given at CONNECTED PERSONS (16). '*Substantial holding*' is not defined.

8 Assets held on 31 March 1982

Cross-references. See 59.5 SHARES AND SECURITIES—IDENTIFICATION RULES for identification of certain share pools held by companies at 31 March 1982 and by others at 5 April 1982; 46.7, 46.17 PARTNERSHIPS for partnership transactions involving assets held on 31 March 1982.

Simon's Direct Tax Service. See Division C2.6.

8.1 RE-BASING TO 31 MARCH 1982

Subject to certain exceptions, disposals after 5 April 1988 of assets which were held on 31 March 1982 by the person making the disposal are re-based by reference to the market value of the assets on the last-mentioned date; see 8.2 below. However, the taxpayer may irrevocably (with one exception mentioned in 8.3 below), subject to the modification in 8.2 below concerning certain disposals of 'oil industry assets', elect for such re-basing to apply to all assets held on 31 March 1982 regardless of the exceptions; see 8.3 below. Subject to certain exceptions and such election, re-basing applies to both the unindexed gain and the indexation allowance.

A 50% reduction is made in taxing certain deferred gains (except, in certain cases, where the deferred gain is never deemed to accrue at all) which arise after 5 April 1988 where such gains are wholly or partly attributable to an increase in value of an asset before 31 March 1982; see 8.12 below.

In addition, disposals after 5 April 1985 (31 March 1985 for companies) and before 6 April 1988 of assets held on 31 March 1982 could, on a claim, be the subject of a similar re-basing treatment as regards indexation allowance only; see 8.13 below.

8.2 GENERAL RE-BASING RULE

The general re-basing rule is that on a disposal after 5 April 1988 of an asset held on 31 March 1982 it is to be assumed that the asset was sold on the last-mentioned date by the person making the disposal and immediately reacquired by him at its market value on that date. [*TCGA 1992, s 35*(*1*)(*2*)].

Subject to the irrevocable election in 8.3 below and subject to the modification below concerning certain disposals of 'oil industry assets', the general re-basing rule is not applied to a disposal where

(*a*) a gain would accrue on the disposal if the general rule applied, and either a smaller gain or a loss would accrue if it did not, or

(*b*) a loss would accrue if the general rule applied, and either a smaller loss or a gain would accrue if it did not, or

(*c*) either on the facts of the case or by virtue of the provisions for ASSETS HELD ON 6 APRIL 1965 (7) in *TCGA 1992, Sch 2*, neither a gain nor a loss would accrue if the general rule did not apply, or

(*d*) the disposal is a 'no gain/no loss disposal' as in 8.7 below.

[*TCGA 1992, s 35*(*3*)].

Where the effect of the general re-basing rule would be to substitute a loss for a gain or a gain for a loss, but under (*a*)–(*d*) the application of that rule is excluded, it is to be assumed in relation to the disposal that the asset was acquired for a consideration such that, on the disposal, neither a gain nor a loss accrues. [*TCGA 1992, s 35*(*4*)].

Indexation allowance on the disposal after 5 April 1988 of an asset held on 31 March 1982 is calculated, without need for a claim, on the assumption that the asset was sold on the last-mentioned date by the person making the disposal and immediately reacquired by him at its market value on that date. [*TCGA 1992, s 55(1)*]. Except where an irrevocable election as in 8.3 below has effect and subject to the modification below concerning certain disposals of 'oil industry assets', neither this provision nor the general re-basing rule of *TCGA 1992, s 35(1)(2)* above is to apply for the purposes of calculating indexation allowance in a case where that allowance would be greater if they did not apply. [*TCGA 1992, s 55(2)*].

Valuations. Where, for the purposes of the re-basing provisions in *TCGA 1992, s 35* and the indexation provisions in *TCGA 1992, s 55*, it is necessary to determine the market value of shares or securities of the same class in any company on 31 March 1982, all the shares or securities held at that date will be valued as a single holding whether they were acquired on or before 6 April 1965 or after that date. If the shares or securities in the relevant disposal represent some but not all of those valued at 31 March 1982 then the allowable cost or indexation allowance as appropriate will be based on the proportion that the shares or securities disposed of bears to the total holding at 31 March 1982 (HMRC Extra-Statutory Concession D34). See also 8.7 below for HMRC's practice as to the valuation of shares deemed held on 31 March 1982 by reason of 'no gain/no loss disposals' since that date.

Where a valuation at 31 March 1982 of unquoted shares is required for a number of shareholders, all of whom agree to be bound by the valuation, HMRC's Shares Valuation Division may initiate valuation procedures before receiving a formal request to do so from the inspector, provided that a full list of the company's shareholders and the size of their holdings, both at 31 March 1982 and at the date of disposal, is supplied, together with details of the tax offices involved, if available. It should be noted that entering into negotiations with Shares Valuation Division does not constitute a return for taxation purposes (Revenue Press Release 18 November 1991).

After 20 March 2000, companies and groups of companies may ask HMRC to agree the value of land and buildings held by them at 31 March 1982 in advance of a statutory need for such valuations (the 'Pre-disposal Portfolio Valuation Scheme'). The application should extend to the entire property portfolio of the company or group (but see below as regards part portfolios). The service is available only if the company or group have at least 30 properties held since 31 March 1982 or fewer such properties but with an aggregate current value greater than £20 million (£30 million for applications made before 17 October 2003). Companies must provide values for checking, prepared by qualified valuers (whether independent or in-house). Companies may obtain further information on this service from HMRC, Capital Taxes Technical Group, Room 133, Sapphire House, 550 Streetsbrook Road, Solihull, West Midlands, B91 1QU. (Revenue News Release BN2G, 21 March 2000). Further details are given in Revenue Tax Bulletin October 2003 pp 1064, 1065; part portfolios are admissible if they are clearly distinguishable from other property held and they meet the minimum size requirement; a portfolio which includes overseas as well as UK properties is admissible but only the values of the UK properties can be agreed. The information required on initial application is summarised in Revenue Tax Bulletin October 2003 pp 1064, 1065. Using the service does not prevent a company from agreeing individual valuations, either under normal procedures or using the pre-return valuation service (see 54.18 RETURNS), if it sells a property before the portfolio valuations have been agreed (Revenue Tax Bulletin February 2002 p 918).

A pre-existing scheme (the 'Multiple Land Valuation Scheme') is available to persons (including companies) who dispose of 30 or more interests in land in a single year of assessment or company accounting period. (A group of companies is considered together to determine if the threshold has been reached.) The scheme involves a sampling process carried out by the Land Portfolio Valuation Unit of the HMRC Valuation Office Agency and designed to avoid, if possible, the need to agree individual valuations for all properties disposed of. Further information is available at Revenue Tax Bulletin February 2002 pp 917, 918 and by contacting Land Portfolio Valuation Unit, District Valuer Services, 5th Floor, Sherbourne House, 1 Manor House Drive, Coventry, CV1 2TG (Tel. 0121–633 1271).

8.2 Assets held on 31 March 1982

Example 1

An asset (which is neither tangible movable property nor otherwise exempt) was acquired for £900 in 1980 and, after having been held continuously by the same owner, is disposed of in 2006/07. For *illustration purposes*, the indexation factor is taken to be 80%. The disposal proceeds are £1,900. The capital gains tax consequences, for differing 31 March 1982 values, are as follows. 'N/A' means that indexation allowance is not applicable and 'NGNL' means that the disposal is treated as giving rise to neither a gain nor a loss. Amounts shown as chargeable gains are subject to TAPER RELIEF (61) (assuming the owner not to be a company).

Example 1A

	(1)	(2)
	£	£
Sale proceeds	1,900	1,900
(1) Cost; (2) 31.3.1982 value	900	1,000
Unindexed gain	1,000	900
Indexation allowance		
at 80% of higher of (1) and (2)	800	800
Gain arising	£200	£100
Chargeable gain		£100

Example 1B

	(1)	(2)
	£	£
Sale proceeds	1,900	1,900
(1) Cost; (2) 31.3.1982 value	900	1,200
Unindexed gain	1,000	700
Indexation allowance		
at 80% of higher of (1) and (2)	960	N/A
Gain/NGNL arising	£40	£NGNL

The disposal is treated as giving rise to neither a gain nor a loss. The corresponding acquisition is unaffected by this treatment.

Example 1C

	(1)	(2)
	£	£
Sale proceeds	1,900	1,900
(1) Cost; (2) 31.3.1982 value	900	800
Unindexed gain	1,000	1,100
Indexation allowance		
at 80% of higher of (1) and (2)	720	720
Gain arising	£280	£380
Chargeable gain	£280	

Example 1D

	(1)	(2)
	£	£
Sale proceeds	1,900	1,900
(1) Cost; (2) 31.3.1982 value	900	3,000
Unindexed gain/(Loss)	1,000	(1,100)
Indexation allowance		
at 80% of higher of (1) and (2)	N/A	N/A
NGNL/(Loss) arising	NGNL	£(1,100)

The disposal is treated as giving rise to neither a gain nor a loss. The corresponding acquisition is unaffected by this treatment.

Example 2

An asset (which is neither tangible movable property, land with development value, quoted securities nor otherwise exempt) was acquired in 1960 for £500. After having been held continuously by the same owner, the asset is completely destroyed in 2006/07. For *illustration purposes*, the indexation factor is taken to be 80%. The asset was under-insured and, later in the month of disposal, £1,900 only was recovered from the insurers. The owner elects for valuation at 6 April 1965, which value is later agreed with HMRC to be £2,000. The value at 31 March 1982 was similarly agreed at £1,700.

	(1)	(2)
	£	£
Insurance proceeds	1,900	1,900
(1) Cost; (2) 6.4.1965 value	500	2,000
	1,400	(100)
Indexation allowance		
at 80% of 31.3.1982 value (£1,700) for (1) only	1,360	N/A
Gain/(Loss) arising	£40	£(100)

Re-basing at 31 March 1982 does not apply since, under *TCGA 1992, Sch 2 para 17(2)* (see 7.8 ASSETS HELD ON 6 APRIL 1965), the disposal is deemed to have given rise to neither a gain nor a loss. The corresponding acquisition is unaffected by this treatment.

8.3 ELECTION FOR UNIVERSAL RE-BASING AT 31 MARCH 1982

If a person so elects (under *TCGA 1992, s 35(5)*), disposals made by him (including any made by him before the election) after 5 April 1988 of assets which he held on 31 March 1982 will all have the general re-basing rule of *TCGA 1992, s 35(1)(2)* in 8.2 above applied to them regardless of the exclusion of that rule that might otherwise apply under *TCGA 1992, s 35(3)*. Similarly in such a case, indexation allowance will always be calculated under the equivalent provision of *TCGA 1992, s 55(1)* as in 8.2 above regardless of the exclusion of that provision that might otherwise apply under *TCGA 1992, s 55(2)*. [*TCGA 1992, s 35(5), s 55(2)*].

An election is irrevocable and must be made by notice in writing to HMRC at any time before 6 April 1990 or at any time during the period beginning with the time of the first disposal after 5 April 1988 of an asset held on 31 March 1982 or treated (see 8.7 below) as so held ('*the first relevant disposal*') and ending in the case of an election for capital gains tax by the first anniversary of 31 January next following the year of assessment in which the disposal is made, and in the case of an election for corporation tax within two years after the end of the accounting period in which the disposal is made and in either case such later period as HMRC may allow. An election made by a person in one capacity does not cover disposals made by him in another capacity. Adjustments as required may be made, whether by way of discharge or repayment of tax, the making of assessments or otherwise, to give effect to an election. [*TCGA 1992, s 35(6)–(8); FA 1996, Sch 21 para 35*].

HMRC will always exercise their discretion to extend the time limit for an election to at least the date on which the statutory time limit would expire if certain disposals did not count as a first relevant disposal. There are three such kinds of disposal, as follows.

(1) Disposals on which the gain would not be chargeable by virtue of a particular statutory provision. The main examples of these provisions are as follows.

- (*a*) Private cars (see 22.11 EXEMPTIONS AND RELIEFS).
- (*b*) Chattels, except commodity futures and foreign currency, worth less than the chattel exemption (see 22.4 EXEMPTIONS AND RELIEFS).
- (*c*) Chattels which are wasting assets, except plant and machinery used in business and commodity futures (see 22.4 EXEMPTIONS AND RELIEFS).
- (*d*) Non-marketable government securities (see 22.14 EXEMPTIONS AND RELIEFS).
- (*e*) Gilt-edged securities and qualifying corporate bonds, except ones received in exchange for shares or other securities (see 26 GOVERNMENT SECURITIES and 50 QUALIFYING CORPORATE BONDS).
- (*f*) Life assurance policies and deferred annuity contracts, unless purchased from a third party (see 39.1 LIFE ASSURANCE POLICIES AND DEFERRED ANNUITIES).
- (*g*) Foreign currency acquired for personal or family expenditure abroad (see 22.8 EXEMPTIONS AND RELIEFS).
- (*h*) Rights of compensation for a wrong or injury suffered by an individual in his person, profession or vocation (see 22.23 EXEMPTIONS AND RELIEFS).
- (*j*) Debts, not on a security, held by the original creditor, his personal representative or his legatee (see 22.5 EXEMPTIONS AND RELIEFS).

(*k*) Business expansion scheme shares issued after 18 March 1986 for which relief has been given and not withdrawn (see 22.20 EXEMPTIONS AND RELIEFS).

(*l*) Personal equity plan shareholdings (see 58.18 SHARES AND SECURITIES).

(*m*) Gifts of eligible property, including works of art, for the benefit of the public (see 22.28, 22.37 EXEMPTIONS AND RELIEFS).

(*n*) Decorations for valour or gallantry (see 22.6 EXEMPTIONS AND RELIEFS).

(*o*) Betting winnings (see 22.19 EXEMPTIONS AND RELIEFS).

(*p*) A right to or to any part of an allowance, annuity or capital sum from a superannuation fund or any other annuity (but not under a deferred annuity policy) or annual payments received under a covenant which is not secured on property (see 22.3 EXEMPTIONS AND RELIEFS).

(2) Disposals which, in practice, do not give rise to a chargeable gain or allowable loss. The main examples of these disposals are as follows.

(*a*) Withdrawals from building society accounts.

(*b*) The disposal of an individual's private residence where the whole of the gain is exempt under *TCGA 1992, s 223*(*1*) (see 49.1 PRIVATE RESIDENCES).

(*c*) Disposals which give rise to neither a chargeable gain nor an allowable loss by virtue of the statutory 'no gain/no loss' provisions listed at *TCGA 1992, s 35*(*3*)(*d*) (see 8.7 below).

(3) Excluded disposals (see 8.4 below).

As sterling is not an asset for capital gains tax purposes (see 6.1 ASSETS), a disposal of it cannot be a first relevant disposal.

Where a person holds assets in more than one capacity (for example, as an individual, trustee, partner or member of a European Economic Interest Grouping), there will be a first relevant disposal and a separate time limit for each group of assets which the person holds in a different capacity. An individual who holds assets in different capacities should indicate at the time an election under *TCGA 1992, s 35*(*5*) is made in what capacity it should be regarded as applying. See also 46.17 PARTNERSHIPS.

Where a person who is non-UK resident on 6 April 1988 makes a disposal which would otherwise count as a first relevant disposal between that date and the date on which they first become UK resident, HMRC will give sympathetic consideration to extending the time limit to the end of the second year of assessment (for companies, the second accounting period) after the year in which the first disposal is made *after becoming UK resident*. In other words, the disposal made while non-resident may be disregarded at the discretion of HMRC. The extension will not be available where the assets are within *TCGA 1992, s 10* (non-resident with UK branch or agency — see 45.3 OVERSEAS MATTERS).

Where, after 5 April 1988, an individual who is resident but not domiciled in the UK disposes of an asset situated outside the UK, the date of the first relevant disposal will be the date on which the proceeds of an overseas gain are remitted to the UK or the date of the first disposal of a UK asset, whichever is earlier.

Where an individual who was resident in the UK on 6 April 1988 has a period of non-residence before resuming UK residence, the first relevant disposal will be the first disposal made after 5 April 1988 on which the individual is chargeable to UK capital gains tax.

There are a variety of other circumstances where, having regard to the facts of each case, HMRC will or may exercise their discretion to extend the statutory time limit.

(HMRC Statement of Practice 4/92).

In circumstances other than those covered by SP 4/92, a late election may be accepted if the delay in making it is less than twelve months from the statutory time limit and resulted from events outside the taxpayer's control or any other reasonable cause (HMRC Capital Gains Manual CG 16821 and 46374). The mere fact that a gain is covered by the annual exemption does *not* prevent a disposal from being a first relevant disposal (*Liddell v CIR SCS 1997, 72 TC 62*).

HMRC point out that in special cases elections need to be made by a person other than the person assessed. In the case of an assessment under *TCGA 1992, s 13* (charge on UK resident shareholder of an overseas resident company — see 45.6 OVERSEAS MATTERS), the election needs to be made by the company concerned. Similarly, the trustees concerned should make an election where the gains of a settlement are assessed under *TCGA 1992, s 77* (charge on settlor of UK resident — see 57.5 SETTLEMENTS), *s 86* (charge on UK resident settlor of overseas resident settlement — see 44.5 OFFSHORE SETTLEMENTS) or *s 87* (charge on UK resident beneficiary of overseas resident settlement — see 44.14 OFFSHORE SETTLEMENTS) (HMRC Capital Gains Manual CG 16762–16764).

8.4 **Excluded disposals.** An election does not cover a disposal of (or of an interest in): plant or machinery; an asset which the person making the disposal held at any time for the purposes of or in connection with a trade or part of a trade involving the working of a 'source of mineral deposits' (within *CAA 2001, s 394*, formerly *CAA 1990, s 121*); a licence under *Petroleum Act 1998, Pt I* (or earlier corresponding legislation) or *Petroleum* (*Production*) *Act* (*Northern Ireland*) *1964*; or, for disposals after 21 January 1990, 'shares' which, on 31 March 1982, were 'unquoted' and derived their value, or the greater part thereof, directly or indirectly from 'oil exploration or exploitation assets' situated in the UK or a 'designated area' or from such assets and 'oil exploration or exploitation rights' taken together (the quoted terms having the meanings given by the legislation). However, disposals within the first two of these four categories are not excluded unless a capital allowance in respect of any expenditure attributable to the asset has been made to the person making the disposal or would have been made to him had he made a claim. Where that person acquired the asset on a 'no gain/no loss disposal' (see 8.7 below), references in the foregoing to the person making the disposal are references to that person, the person who last acquired the asset other than on a no gain/no loss disposal or any person who subsequently acquired the asset on such a disposal. [*TCGA 1992, Sch 3 para 7; Petroleum Act 1998, Sch 4 para 32; CAA 2001, Sch 2 para 81*].

8.5 **Married persons.** Where a spouse disposes of an asset acquired by him from the other spouse after 5 April 1988 and the no gain/no loss basis of *TCGA 1992, s 58* applied to the acquisition (see 42.4 MARRIED PERSONS AND CIVIL PARTNERS and 8.7 below), an election made by the transferee spouse does not apply to the disposal, and, whether or not an election is made by that spouse, the making of such an election by the transferor spouse applies to the ultimate disposal made by the transferee spouse. Where the transferor spouse also acquired the asset after 5 April 1988 and *TCGA 1992, s 58* applied to that acquisition, an election made by him does not have effect on the ultimate disposal, but an election made by the last person by whom the asset was acquired after 5 April 1988 otherwise than on an acquisition to which *TCGA 1992, s 58* applied or, if there is no such person, the person who held the asset on 5 April 1988, does have effect on the ultimate disposal. [*TCGA 1992, Sch 3 para 2*].

8.6 **Groups of companies.** Where a member of a group of companies disposes of an asset acquired by it from another group member after 5 April 1988 and the no gain/no loss basis of *TCGA 1992, s 171* applied to the acquisition (see 27.2 GROUPS OF COMPANIES and 8.7 below), an election made by the transferee company does not apply to the disposal, and, whether or not an election is made by that company, the making of such an election by the transferor company applies to the ultimate disposal made by the transferee company. Where the transferor company also acquired the asset after 5 April 1988 and *TCGA 1992, s 171* applied to that acquisition, an election made by it does not have effect on the ultimate disposal, but an election made by the last company by which the asset was acquired after 5 April 1988 otherwise than on an acquisition to which *TCGA 1992, s 171* applied or, if there is no such company, the company which held the asset on 5 April 1988, does have effect on the ultimate disposal. [*TCGA 1992, Sch 3 para 2*].

Election by principal company. Only a company which is the 'principal company' of a 'group' (for both of which see 27.1 GROUPS OF COMPANIES and note that the change in the residence requirement therein mentioned has effect for this purpose after 31 March 2000) may make an election unless the company did not become a group member until after the 'relevant time'. For this purpose the time limit for the making of an election (see 8.3 above) applies with the modification that a reference to 'the first relevant disposal' is a reference to the first disposal after 5 April 1988 of an asset held on 31 March 1982 by a company which is *either* a group member but not an 'outgoing company' in relation to the group *or* an 'incoming company' in relation to the group. An election made by the principal company also has effect as one made by any other company which is a group member at the relevant time; but this treatment does not extend to a company which, in some period after 5 April 1988 and before the relevant time, is not a member of the group if during that period the company makes a disposal of an asset which it held on 31 March 1982 and the time limit for the making of an election expires without an election having been made. However, the effect of an election continues to extend to a company notwithstanding that it ceases to be a group member after the relevant time except where it is an outgoing company in relation to the group and the election relating to the group is made after it ceases to be a group member. [*TCGA 1992, Sch 3 para 8, para 9(3); FA 2000, Sch 29 para 38*].

'*The relevant time*', in relation to a group, is the earliest of: the first time when any company which is then a group member, and is not an outgoing member in relation to the group, makes a disposal after 5 April 1988 of an asset which it held on 31 March 1982; the time immediately following the first occasion when a company which is an incoming company in relation to the group becomes a group member; and the time when an election is made by the principal company. [*TCGA 1992, Sch 3 para 9(1)*].

'*Incoming company*', in relation to a group, means a company which makes its first disposal after 5 April 1988 of an asset which it held on 31 March 1982 at a time when it is not a group member, and which becomes a group member before the expiry of the time limit for the making of an election which would apply to it and at a time when no such election has been made.

'*Outgoing company*', in relation to a group, means a company which ceases to be a group member before the expiry of the time limit for the making of an election which would apply to it and at a time when no such election has been made. [*TCGA 1992, Sch 3 para 9(2)*].

See HMRC Capital Gains Manual CG 46330–46395 for consideration of the above provisions (including extension of time limits in certain cases).

8.7 SUPPLEMENTARY PROVISIONS FOR RE-BASING AT 31 MARCH 1982

Previous no gain/no loss disposals. Where

(*a*) a person makes a disposal, other than a 'no gain/no loss disposal', after 5 April 1988 of an asset which he acquired after 31 March 1982, and

(*b*) the disposal by which he acquired the asset and any previous disposal of the asset after 31 March 1982 was a no gain/no loss disposal,

he is treated for the purposes of the re-basing provisions of *TCGA 1992, s 35* and the equivalent provisions for indexation allowance of *TCGA 1992, s 55(1)* in 8.2 and 8.3 above as having held the asset on 31 March 1982. HMRC have confirmed that where a person is treated as having held an asset on 31 March 1982 under these provisions, enhancement expenditure on the asset incurred after 31 March 1982 by a previous owner may be taken into account for indexation and re-basing purposes on a disposal by the current owner (Revenue Tax Bulletin, August 1992, p.32).

A '*no gain/no loss disposal*' is one under the following enactments (being enactments by virtue of which neither a gain nor a loss accrues).

(i) *TCGA 1992, s 58* (transfers between spouses living together, see 42.4 MARRIED PERSONS AND CIVIL PARTNERS), *s 73* (reversion of settled property to settlor on death of person entitled to life interest, see 57.17 SETTLEMENTS), *s 139* (company reconstructions, see 13.10 COMPANIES), *s 140A* (transfer of UK trade between companies in different EC member states, see 45.10 OVERSEAS MATTERS), *s 140E* (formation of SE by merger: assets left within UK tax charge, see 13.18 COMPANIES), *s 171* (intra-group disposals of assets, see 27.2 GROUPS OF COMPANIES), *s 172* (transfer of UK branch or agency before 1 April 2000, see 45.3 OVERSEAS MATTERS), *s 215* (amalgamation of building societies, see 13.10 COMPANIES), *s 216* (transfer of building society's business to company, see 13.10 COMPANIES), *s 217A* (transfer of assets on incorporation of registered friendly society, see 22.47 EXEMPTIONS AND RELIEFS), *ss 218–220* (housing associations, see 22.49 EXEMPTIONS AND RELIEFS), *s 221* (harbour authorities, see 22.73 EXEMPTIONS AND RELIEFS), *s 257(2)* (gifts to charities etc., see 10.5 CHARITIES), *s 257(3)* (gifts to charities etc. out of settlements, see 10.6 CHARITIES), *s 258(4)* (gifts of national heritage property, see 22.80 EXEMPTIONS AND RELIEFS), *s 259(2)* (gifts to housing associations, see 22.49 EXEMPTIONS AND RELIEFS), *s 264* (transfers between constituency associations, see 22.67 EXEMPTIONS AND RELIEFS) and *s 267(2)* (sharing of transmission facilities, see 13.10 COMPANIES);

(ii) *CGTA 1979, s 148* (assets transferred to maintenance funds for historic buildings, see 22.78 EXEMPTIONS AND RELIEFS);

(iii) *FA 1982, s 148* (transfers by Hops Marketing Board, see 22.75 EXEMPTIONS AND RELIEFS);

(iv) *Trustee Savings Banks Act 1985, Sch 2 para 2* (see 13.10 COMPANIES);

(v) *Transport Act 1985, s 130(3)* (see 13.10 COMPANIES);

(vi) *ICTA 1988, s 486(8)* (amalgamation of industrial and provident societies, see 13.10 COMPANIES);

(vii) *FA 1990, Sch 12 para 2(1)* (broadcasting undertakings, see 13.10 COMPANIES);

(viii) *F(No 2)A 1992, Sch 17 para 5(3)* (privatisation of Northern Ireland Electricity, see 13.10 COMPANIES);

(ix) *FA 1994, Sch 24 para 2(1), para 7(2), para 11(3)(4), para 25(2)* (provisions relating to *Railways Act 1993*, see 13.10 COMPANIES);

(x) *FA 1994, Sch 25 para 4(2)* (Northern Ireland Airports Ltd, see 13.10 COMPANIES);

(xi) *Coal Industry Act 1994, Sch 4 para 2(1)*;

(xii) *Broadcasting Act 1996, Sch 7 para 2(1)*;

(xiii) *Transport Act 2000, Sch 7 para 2(1)*; and

(xiv) *Transport Act 2000, Sch 26 paras 3, 9*.

[*TCGA 1992, s 35(3)(d)(10), s 55(5)(6)(a), Sch 3 para 1; F(No 2)A 1992, s 46(1)(2), ss 56, 77, Sch 9 para 21(1)(2), Sch 17 para 5(9); FA 1994, ss 252, 253, Sch 24 para 2(2), Sch 25 para 4(3); Coal Industry Act 1994, s 21, Sch 4 para 2(3); Broadcasting Act 1996, Sch 7 para 3; FA 2000, Sch 40 Pt II(12); Transport Act 2000, ss 64, 250, Sch 7 para 2, Sch 26 para 37; F(No 2)A 2005, s 59(2)*].

(*Note.* Neither *TCGA 1992, s 257(2)* nor *s 259(2)* is in strictness included as no gain/no loss provisions for the purposes of re-basing under *TCGA 1992, s 35* although they are for the equivalent provisions for indexation allowance under *TCGA 1992, s 55(1)*. However, both provisions deem (for the purposes of *TCGA 1992*) the original acquisition by the transferor making the disposal to which the provision concerned applies to be the acquisition of the transferee on the occasion of the transferee making a subsequent disposal. Consequently it seems that in practice both provisions are no gain/no loss provisions for the purposes of re-basing under *TCGA 1992, s 35*. It appears that the reason that both provisions have to be specifically included as no gain/no loss provisions for the purposes of *TCGA 1992, s 55(1)* is because of the effect of *TCGA 1992, s 56(2)* (see further below).)

Certain disposals of a share in partnership assets may be treated as if they were no gain/no loss disposals. See 46.7 PARTNERSHIPS.

Where (*a*) and (*b*) above apply on the disposal of an asset so that, as stated above, the person making the disposal is treated for the purposes of computing the indexation allowance on the disposal as having held the asset on 31 March 1982 [*TCGA 1992, s 55(6)(a)*], then for the purpose of determining any gain or loss on the disposal, the consideration which otherwise that person would be treated as having given for the asset is reduced by the amount of indexation allowance brought into account under *TCGA 1992, s 56(2)* (consideration on disposal treated as giving rise to neither a gain nor a loss to be computed on assumption that on the disposal an unindexed gain accrues equal to the indexation allowance on the disposal; see 34.3 INDEXATION) on any disposal falling within (*b*) above. [*TCGA 1992, s 55(6)(b)*].

Further rules as below apply (after the application of the computation of any indexation allowance under *TCGA 1992, s 53* (see 34.1 INDEXATION) but before the application of the provisions of *TCGA 1992, s 35(3)* or *(4)* (which disapply or amend the general re-basing rule of *TCGA 1992, s 35(1)(2)* in certain cases; see 8.2 above) in relation to disposals on or after 30 November 1993. The rules apply where (*a*) and (*b*) above apply to the disposal ('*the disposal in question*') of an asset by any person ('*the transferor*') and, but for *TCGA 1992, s 55(6)(b)* above, the consideration the transferor would be treated as having given for the asset would include an amount or amounts of indexation allowance brought into account under *TCGA 1992, s 56(2)* on any disposal made before 30 November 1993. [*TCGA 1992, s 55(7); FA 1994, s 93(4)(11)*]. The rules are that

(A) where otherwise there would be a loss, an amount equal to the 'rolled-up indexation' is added to it so as to increase it,

(B) where otherwise the unindexed gain or loss would be nil, a loss is deemed to accrue equal to the rolled-up indexation, and

(C) where otherwise there would be an unindexed gain and the gain or loss would be nil but the amount of the indexation allowance used to extinguish the gain would be less than the rolled-up indexation, the difference is deemed to constitute a loss.

[*TCGA 1992, s 55(8); FA 1994, s 93(4)(11)*].

For the purposes of the above, the '*rolled-up indexation*' means, subject to *TCGA 1992, s 55(10)* and *(11)* below (which provisions, as well as applying on the disposal in question, are also treated as having applied on any previous part disposal by the transferor), the amount or, as the case may be, the aggregate of the amounts of indexation allowance which, but for *TCGA 1992, s 55(6)(b)* above, would be brought into account under *TCGA 1992, s 56(2)* on any disposal made before 30 November 1993. [*TCGA 1992, s 55(9); FA 1994, s 93(4)(11)*].

Where, for the purposes of any disposal of the asset made by the transferor on or after 30 November 1993, any amount, amounts or combination of amounts within *TCGA 1992, s 38(1)(a)–(c)* (acquisition consideration etc., enhancement expenditure etc. and incidental disposal costs respectively; see 15.4 COMPUTATION OF GAINS AND LOSSES) is required to be excluded, reduced or written down, the amount or amounts constituting the rolled-up indexation (or so much of it as remains after the application of this provision and *TCGA 1992, s 55(11)* below on a previous part disposal) are reduced in proportion to any reduction made in the amount falling within one or any combination of *TCGA 1992, s 38(1)(a)–(c)*. [*TCGA 1992, s 55(10); FA 1994, s 93(4)(11)*].

Where the transferor makes a part disposal of the asset at any time on or after 30 November 1993, then, for the purposes of that and any subsequent part disposal, the amount or amounts constituting the rolled-up indexation (or so much of it as remains after the application of this provision and *TCGA 1992, s 55(10)* above on a previous part disposal by him or after the application of *TCGA 1992, s 55(10)* on the part disposal) is apportioned between the property disposed of and the property which remains in the same proportions as the amounts within *TCGA 1992, s 38(1)(a)* and *(b)*. [*TCGA 1992, s 55(11); FA 1994, s 93(4)(11)*].

Example

X Ltd, Y Ltd and Z Ltd are all members of the same group within *TCGA 1992, s 170* (see 27.1 GROUPS OF COMPANIES), all three companies having joined the group before 1 April 1987 (see 27.20 GROUPS OF COMPANIES) and making up annual accounts for calendar years. No election under *TCGA 1992, s 35(5)* (universal re-basing — see 8.3 and 8.6 above) is in force. An asset was acquired by X Ltd from outside the group for £90,000 in 1980 and at 31 March 1982 the value of the asset is £100,000. The asset was transferred to Y Ltd in October 1985 such that the no gain/no loss basis of *TCGA 1992, s 171* (see 27.2 GROUPS OF COMPANIES) applied. X Ltd made the appropriate election under *FA 1985, s 68(4)(5)* (indexation allowance to be calculated by reference to value at 31 March 1982 rather than original cost — see 8.13, 8.14 below). In January 1995 Y Ltd transferred the asset to Z Ltd such that *TCGA 1992, s 171* again applied. Z Ltd sells the asset outside the group in March 2007 for £80,000. The relevant retail prices indices are

March 1982	79.44	January 1995	146.00
October 1985	95.59		

	£
Original cost of asset to X Ltd in 1980	90,000
Indexation allowance: March 1982–October 1985	
on 31 March 1982 value under *FA 1985, s 68(4)(5)*	
$\frac{95.59 - 79.44}{79.44} \times$ £100,000 (indexation factor 0.203)	20,300
Deemed consideration under *TCGA 1992, s 56(2)*	£110,300

	£
Deemed cost of asset to Y Ltd in October 1985	110,300
Indexation allowance: October 1985–January 1995	
$\frac{146.0-95.59}{95.59}$ × £110,300 (indexation factor 0.527)	58,128
Deemed consideration under *TCGA 1992, s 56(2)*	£168,428

Under *TCGA 1992, s 35(10), s 55(6)(a), Sch 3 para 1*, Z Ltd is treated as having held the asset on 31 March 1982 for the purposes of re-basing under *TCGA 1992, s 35* and calculating indexation allowance.

	Cost	Re-base
	£	£
Proceeds received by Z Ltd	80,000	80,000
Deemed consideration under *TCGA 1992, s 55(6)(b)* (£168,428 – £58,128 – £20,300)	90,000	
Market value at 31 March 1982		100,000
Loss before *TCGA 1992, s 55(8)* adjustment	10,000	20,000
Rolled-up indexation under *TCGA 1992, s 55(9)*	20,300	20,300
Loss after *TCGA 1992, s 55(8)* adjustment	£30,300	£40,300

TCGA 1992, s 35(3) applies, so the allowable loss arising is £30,300.

Note to the example

(1) It should be noted that the effect of the legislation in force for disposals before 30 November 1993 meant that Z Ltd would not have been prejudiced on the ultimate disposal outside the group if X Ltd had not made a valid claim under *FA 1985, s 68(4)(5)* within the time limit in respect of the transfer of the asset to Y Ltd in October 1985. However, the legislation in force for disposals on or after 30 November 1993 means that, in the absence of such an election in respect of that disposal, the rolled-up indexation in the above example would have to be computed by reference to the original cost to X Ltd (i.e. 0.203 × £90,000 = £18,270). The allowable loss would then be £28,270 (i.e. £18,270 + £10,000). It is not known whether the Revenue would use the discretion it had in similarly affected cases to extend the time limit of two years after the end of the year of assessment or accounting period in which the disposal fell.

Shares or securities of the same class in any company which are *treated* as above as held on 31 March 1982 by a person will be treated as a single holding with any shares or securities of the same class in the same company *actually* held by that person in determining the market value for re-basing purposes of the shares or securities. If the shares or securities in the relevant disposal represent some but not all of those valued at 31 March 1982 then the allowable cost or indexation allowance as appropriate will be based on the proportion that the shares or securities disposed of bears to the total holding (HMRC Statement of Practice 5/89). See also 8.2 above regarding the concessional valuation of a holding of shares or securities at 31 March 1982 where part of the holding was held on 6 April 1965.

Where SP 5/89 above applies, HMRC will also apply the following concessional valuation treatment where shares or securities of the same class are acquired by way of no gain/no loss transfer under *TCGA 1992, s 58* (spouses living together) or *s 171* (intra-group disposals). The concessional treatment applies to disposals within the scope of SP 5/89 made before 16 March 1993 in relation to which a claim is made before liabilities are finally determined, and all such disposals made after 15 March 1993 provided that a claim is made within two years (or such further time as HMRC may allow) of the end of the year of assessment or accounting period in which the disposal is made. Under the concessional valuation treatment the value of a single holding may be regarded as the appropriate proportion of the value of any larger holding of shares or securities of the same class which were held by a spouse or another company at 31 March 1982 and from which part or all of the single holding was derived by one or more transfers within *TCGA 1992, s 58* or *s 171* respectively (HMRC Extra-Statutory Concession D44).

8.8 **Capital allowances.** If, under either the re-basing provisions of *TCGA 1992, s 35* or the equivalent provisions for indexation allowance of *TCGA 1992, s 55(1)* (see 8.2 and 8.3 above), it is to be assumed that any asset was on 31 March 1982 sold by the person making the disposal and immediately reacquired by him, *TCGA 1992, s 41* (restriction of losses by reference to capital allowances, see 15.6(*j*) COMPUTATION OF GAINS AND LOSSES) and *s 47* (wasting assets qualifying for capital allowances, see 67.1 WASTING ASSETS) apply with suitable modifications on the assumed reacquisition at 31 March 1982. [*TCGA 1992, s 55(3), Sch 3 para 3*].

8.9 **Part disposals etc.** Where, on a disposal to which the general re-basing rule of *TCGA 1992, s 35(1)(2)* in 8.2 above applies, *TCGA 1992, s 42* (allowable expenditure on a part disposal, see 15.7 COMPUTATION OF GAINS AND LOSSES) has effect by reason of an earlier disposal made after 31 March 1982 and before 6 April 1988, the sums to be apportioned under that provision on the later disposal are to take the general re-basing rule into account. [*TCGA 1992, Sch 3 para 4(1)*].

If in relation to disposals after 5 April 1989 the general re-basing rule of *TCGA 1992, s 35(1)(2)* applies, and if that rule did not apply expenditure would under specified enactments not be allowable in computing a gain arising on the disposal, and the disallowance would be attributable to the reduction of the amount of the consideration for a disposal made after 31 March 1982 but before 6 April 1988, the amount otherwise allowable as a deduction on the disposal is reduced by the amount of the disallowance that would have been made if the general re-basing rule had not applied. The enactments specified are

(i) *TCGA 1992, s 23(2)* (disallowance of allowable expenditure where allowance already given against receipts of compensation or insurance money, see 9.2 CAPITAL SUMS DERIVED FROM ASSETS);

(ii) *TCGA 1992, s 122(4)* (disallowance where allowance already given against capital distribution, see 58.10 SHARES AND SECURITIES);

(iii) *TCGA 1992, s 133(4)* (disallowance where allowance already given against premium on conversion of securities, see 58.7 SHARES AND SECURITIES); and

(iv) *TCGA 1992, s 244* (disallowance where allowance already given against gain from small part disposal of land, see 38.8 and 38.10 LAND).

[*TCGA 1992, Sch 3 para 4(2)*].

8.10 **Assets derived from other assets.** The re-basing provisions of *TCGA 1992, s 35* in 8.2 and 8.3 above apply with the necessary modifications in relation to a disposal of an asset which was not held on 31 March 1982, if its value is derived from another asset which is taken into account under *TCGA 1992, s 43* (assets derived from other assets, see 15.7 COMPUTATION OF GAINS AND LOSSES). [*TCGA 1992, Sch 3 para 5*]. For indexation allowance purposes, where, after 31 March 1982, an asset which was held on that date has been merged or divided or has changed its nature or rights in or over the asset have been created, then *TCGA 1992, s 55(1)(2)* (re-basing for indexation allowance purposes) in 8.2

above has effect to determine for the purposes of *TCGA 1992, s 43* the amount of the consideration for the acquisition of the asset which was so held. [*TCGA 1992, s 55(4)*].

8.11 **Time apportionment of pre-6 April 1965 gains and losses.** If *TCGA 1992, Sch 2 para 16* (time apportionment of gains and losses accruing on ASSETS HELD ON 6 APRIL 1965; see 7.7) applies so that only part of a gain or loss is a chargeable gain or an allowable loss, the exclusion of the general re-basing rule of *TCGA 1992, s 35(1)(2)* under 8.2(*a*) and (*b*) above has effect as if the amount of the gain or loss that would accrue if the general re-basing rule did not apply were equal to that part. [*TCGA 1992, Sch 3 para 6*].

8.12 DEFERRED CHARGES ON GAINS BEFORE 31 MARCH 1982

Where, before 6 April 1988, a gain was deferred in respect of one or more disposals which related in whole or in part to an asset acquired before 31 March 1982, and the deferred gain is brought into charge on a disposal or other occasion after 5 April 1988, the deferred gain will, subject to conditions and on a claim, be halved (except, in certain cases, where the deferred gain is never deemed to accrue at all) when the charge to tax is computed in respect of it.

The provisions under which a gain can be deferred effectively fall into two groups for this purpose. In the first group (*TCGA 1992, Sch 4 para 2*), which includes the hold-over provisions for gifts made before 14 March 1989 and rollover relief on the replacement of business assets, the deferred gain is deducted from the expenditure allowable in computing the gain on a later disposal. In the second group (*TCGA 1992, Sch 4 paras 3, 4*), the deferred gain is brought into charge on the occurrence of a subsequent event. For both groups, the deferred gain will be half of what it would otherwise be. [*TCGA 1992, s 36, Sch 4 para 1*].

As regards the first group of provisions, both of the following circumstances must be fulfilled in order to bring about the halving of the deferred gain.

(*a*) There is a disposal, other than a 'no gain/no loss disposal' (see 8.7 above), after 5 April 1988 of an asset acquired after 31 March 1982 by the person making the disposal.

(*b*) A deduction from allowable expenditure falls to be made under any of the first group of provisions in computing the gain on that disposal and is attributable directly or indirectly, in whole or in part, to a chargeable gain accruing on the disposal before 6 April 1988 of an asset acquired before 31 March 1982 by the person making that disposal.

No relief is given under *TCGA 1992, Sch 4* where, by reason of the previous operation of it, the amount of the deduction in (*b*) is less than it otherwise would be. Where the disposal takes place after 18 March 1991, no relief under *TCGA 1992, Sch 4* is available if the amount of the deduction would have been less had relief by virtue of a previous application of it been duly claimed. (In effect, for disposals after 18 March 1991, the relief for the first group of provisions (*TCGA 1992, Sch 4 para 2*) cannot be claimed twice for the same gain and must be claimed in respect of the earliest possible occasion. For disposals after 5 April 1988 and before 19 March 1991, it was possible to claim other than on the earliest possible occasion. See below as regards time limits for claims affected by this change.) [*TCGA 1992, Sch 4 para 2(1)–(3)*].

Where the asset was acquired after 18 March 1991, the deduction is partly attributable to a claim under *TCGA 1992, s 154(4)* (rollover into non-depreciating asset instead of into depreciating asset, see 55.7 ROLLOVER RELIEF), and the claim applies to the asset, no relief under *TCGA 1992, Sch 4* is available by virtue of its application in respect of the first group of provisions below (*TCGA 1992, Sch 4 para 2*) (but see below as regards the relief available in respect of the second group of provisions). [*TCGA 1992, Sch 4 para 2(4)*].

In the case of rollover relief on the replacement of business assets and subject to the usual time limits, the disposal of the old asset may be before 31 March 1982, and the replacement asset may be acquired afterwards (Revenue Press Release 8 July 1988).

For the circumstances in which HMRC will require a valuation of the asset transferred where a hold-over relief claim is made, see 33.1 HOLD-OVER RELIEFS.

The first group of provisions mentioned above is as follows.

(i) *TCGA 1992, s 23(4)(5)* (rollover where replacement asset acquired after receipt of compensation or insurance money, see 9.3 CAPITAL SUMS DERIVED FROM ASSETS);

(ii) *TCGA 1992, s 152* (rollover where replacement asset acquired on disposal of business asset, see 55 ROLLOVER RELIEF);

(iii) *TCGA 1992, s 162* (hold-over where shares acquired on disposal of business to company, see 33.10 HOLD-OVER RELIEFS);

(iv) *TCGA 1992, s 165* (hold-over where business asset acquired by gift, see 33.1–33.6 HOLD-OVER RELIEFS);

(v) *TCGA 1992, s 247* (rollover where replacement land acquired on compulsory acquisition of other land, see 38.11 LAND);

(vi) *FA 1980, s 79* (hold-over where asset acquired by gift after 5 April 1980 and before 14 March 1989, see 33.9 HOLD-OVER RELIEFS).

[*TCGA 1992, Sch 4 para 2(5)*].

As regards the second group of provisions and subject to the exception below, both of the following circumstances must be fulfilled in order to bring about the halving of the deferred gain.

(A) Under any of the second group of provisions a gain is treated as accruing in consequence of an event occurring after 5 April 1988.

(B) The gain is attributable directly or indirectly, in whole or in part, to the disposal before 6 April 1988 of an asset acquired before 31 March 1982 by the person making that disposal.

[*TCGA 1992, Sch 4 para 4(1)*].

Where a gain is treated as accruing in consequence of an event after 18 March 1991, relief under *TCGA 1992, Sch 4* does not apply if the gain is attributable directly or indirectly, in whole or in part, to the disposal of an asset after 5 April 1988, or the amount of the gain would have been less had relief by virtue of a previous application of *TCGA 1992, Sch 4* been duly claimed. [*TCGA 1992, Sch 4 para 4(4)*]. (In effect, for events after 18 March 1991, the relief for the second group of provisions (*TCGA 1992, Sch 4 paras 3, 4*, and see below as regards *TCGA 1992, Sch 4 para 3*) cannot be claimed twice for the same gain and must be claimed in respect of the earliest possible occasion. For events after 5 April 1988 and before 19 March 1991, it was possible to claim other than on the earliest possible occasion and more than once. See below as regards time limits for claims affected by this change.)

The second group of provisions mentioned above is as follows (and see also below).

(I) *TCGA 1992, s 116(10)(11)* (postponement of charge on reorganisation etc. involving acquisition of qualifying corporate bonds, see 50.3 QUALIFYING CORPORATE BONDS).

(II) *TCGA 1992, s 134* (postponement of charge where gilts acquired on compulsory acquisition of shares, see 58.7 SHARES AND SECURITIES);

(III) *TCGA 1992, s 140* (postponement of charge where securities acquired in exchange for business acquired by overseas resident company until transferor company disposes of securities as mentioned in *s 140(4)* or transferee company within six years of exchange disposes of assets acquired on exchange as mentioned in *s 140(5)*, see 45.9 OVERSEAS MATTERS);

(IV) *TCGA 1992, s 154(2)* (postponement of charge where depreciating asset acquired as replacement for business asset, see 55.7 ROLLOVER RELIEF) (and see below as regards *TCGA 1992, Sch 4 para 3*);

(V) *TCGA 1992, s 168* (as modified by *TCGA 1992, s 67(6)*) (activation of charge held over under *FA 1980, s 79* on emigration of donee in relation to a gift after 5 April 1981 and before 14 March 1989, see 33.9 HOLD-OVER RELIEFS);

(VI) *TCGA 1992, s 179(3)* (or earlier equivalent) (charge on company leaving group of companies in respect of asset acquired from another member of same group within previous six years, see 27.9 GROUPS OF COMPANIES, but only if the asset was acquired by the chargeable company before 6 April 1988, so no longer relevant);

(VII) *TCGA 1992, s 248(3)* (postponement of charge where depreciating asset acquired on compulsory acquisition of land, see 38.11 LAND);

[*TCGA 1992, Sch 4 para 4(2)(3); FA 2000, Sch 40 Pt II(12)*].

Where relief under *TCGA 1992, Sch 4* would have applied on a disposal but for the effect of *TCGA 1992, Sch 4 para 2(4)* (exclusion of relief under *TCGA 1992, Sch 4 para 2* where deduction partly attributable to claim under *TCGA 1992, s 154(4)*) above, then such relief (on the same lines as for the second group of provisions above) is available (under *TCGA 1992, Sch 4 para 3*) if the relief for the second group of provisions (*TCGA 1992, Sch 4 para 4*) would have applied had *TCGA 1992, s 154(2)* (see (IV) above) continued to apply to the gain carried forward as a result of the claim under *TCGA 1992, s 154(4)*, and the time of disposal been the time when that gain was treated as accruing by virtue of *TCGA 1992, s 154(2)*. [*TCGA 1992, Sch 4 para 3*].

There is an exception to the bringing about of the halving of the deferred gain in respect of certain provisions contained in the second group. Neither *TCGA 1992, s 134, s 140(4), s 154(2)* nor *s 248(3)* (see (II)–(IV) and (VII) above) is to apply in consequence of an event occurring after 5 April 1988 if its application would be *directly* attributable to the disposal of an asset before 1 April 1982. [*TCGA 1992, Sch 4 para 4(5)*]. In effect the deferred gain is in such circumstances never deemed to accrue. See also below regarding views expressed by HMRC.

Relief is available as regards both groups of provisions where a person makes a disposal of an asset which he acquired after 30 March 1982 where the disposal by which he acquired it and any previous disposal of it after that date was a 'no gain/no loss disposal' (see 8.7 above). In such a case, the person is treated for the purposes of (*b*) and (B) above as having acquired the asset before 31 March 1982. [*TCGA 1992, Sch 4 paras 5, 7*].

Where deferral has been claimed under one of the first group of provisions and there is a subsequent no gain/no loss disposal (or continuous series of such disposals) as in 8.7 above, relief is available (subject to the conditions in (*a*) and (*b*) above) in computing the gain on the first later disposal which is not a no gain/no loss disposal. [*TCGA 1992, Sch 4 paras 6, 7*].

Relief is available as regards both groups of provisions for an asset which was not acquired before 31 March 1982 if its value was derived from another asset which was so acquired and which is taken into account under *TCGA 1992, s 43* (see 15.7 COMPUTATION OF GAINS AND LOSSES). [*TCGA 1992, Sch 4 para 8*].

No relief is available under *TCGA 1992, Sch 4* unless a claim is made

(*a*) in respect of gains accruing to a person chargeable to corporation tax within two years of the end of the accounting period, and (*b*) in respect of gains accruing to a person chargeable to capital gains tax, on or before the first anniversary of the 31st January next following the year of assessment in which the disposal is made or the gain in question is treated as accruing,

(*c*) on or before such later date as HMRC may allow,

in which, for the first group of provisions, the disposal to which the claim relates is made, or for the second group of provisions, the deferred gain is treated as accruing (except where (VI) above applied where the claim had to be made within two years of the end of the accounting period in which the chargeable company ceased to be a member of the group). A claim must be supported by any particulars the inspector may require for establishing the validity and quantum of any relief. [*TCGA 1992, Sch 4 para 9; FA 1996, Sch 21 para 43; FA 2000, Sch 40 Pt II(12)*]. A late claim may be accepted if the delay in making it is less than twelve months and resulted from events outside the taxpayer's control or any other reasonable cause (HMRC Capital Gains Manual CG 16821, 17012).

It is understood that HMRC accept that the crystallisation under *TCGA 1992, s 67(4)(5)* of a gain deferred by *FA 1980, s 79* (as extended by *FA 1981, s 78* and *FA 1982, s 82*) (clawback of deferred gain on death of life tenant, see 33.5 and 33.9 HOLD-OVER RELIEFS) can by concession be treated as if it were amongst the second group of provisions in (I)–(VII) above. In addition, a gain deferred on a transfer into settlement occurring before 1 April 1982 and which would otherwise crystallise on the death after 5 April 1988 of a life tenant will by concession be deemed never to accrue (and so treated in the same way as for the exception given by *TCGA 1992, Sch 4 para 4(5)* above).

Example

1980 A acquires an asset for £10,000

1983 The asset is gifted to B with a hold-over election under *FA 1980, s 79* when worth £12,000. Indexation allowance is taken to be £500 (for illustration purposes only).

Gain held over £12,000 – £10,000 – £500 = £1,500

B's cost of the asset £12,000 – £1,500 = £10,500

1985 B sells the asset for £15,000 and replaces it by one costing £17,000 at the same time. Indexation allowance is taken to be £750 by reference to the reduced base cost of £10,500. Full rollover under *TCGA 1992, s 152* (formerly *CGTA 1979, s 115*) is available and claimed.

Gain rolled over £15,000 – £10,500 – £750 = £3,750

Base cost of second asset £17,000 – £3,750 = £13,250

1987 B sells the replacement asset for £20,000 replacing it by one costing £22,000 at the same time. Indexation allowance is taken to be £1,250 by reference to the reduced base cost of £13,250. Full rollover as in 1985 is claimed.

Gain rolled over £20,000 – £13,250 – £1,250 = £5,500

Base cost of third asset £22,000 – £5,500 = £16,500 (but see below)

2006 B sells the third asset for £35,000 and does not replace it. The increase in the retail prices index between the month of acquisition in 1987 and April 1998 is taken to be 60%.

On a claim the deduction (£5,500) otherwise taken into account in arriving at the base cost of the third asset is reduced by half because it is partly attributable to the gain arising in 1983 in respect of the asset acquired in 1980.

Revised base cost of third asset £22,000 – £2,750 = £19,250

Chargeable gain (subject to TAPER RELIEF (61))
£35,000 – £19,250 – (60% × £19,250) = £4,200

8.13 **INDEXATION ALLOWANCE: CLAIM BEFORE 6 APRIL 1988 FOR RE-BASING AT 31 MARCH 1982**

For disposals on or after the '1985 date' (1 April 1985 for companies and 6 April 1985 for others) and before 6 April 1988, a claim could be made for the indexation allowance (but not the unindexed gain or loss) arising on a disposal of an asset held on 31 March 1982 by the person making the disposal to be calculated on the assumption that on that date the asset was sold by the person concerned and immediately reacquired by him at its market value on that date. Such a claim had to be made within two years of the end of the year of assessment or accounting period in which the disposal occurred or within such longer period as the Revenue by notice in writing allowed. [*FA 1985, s 68(4)(5)* (*as originally enacted*)].

Although allowable expenditure relating to an asset held on 31 March 1982 may have been reduced (e.g. by rollover relief), there was no corresponding restriction applied to the market value on that date for the purposes of any deemed reacquisition on that date.

The Revenue in practice allowed a claim to be withdrawn within the time limit for making the claim provided the relevant assessment had not become final and conclusive (Tolley's Practical Tax 1986 pp 33, 88).

8.14 **Previous no gain/no loss disposals.** Where

(*a*) a person made a disposal, other than a 'no gain/no loss disposal', of an asset which he acquired after 31 March 1982, and

(*b*) the disposal by which he acquired the asset and any previous disposal of the asset after 31 March 1982 was a no gain/no loss disposal,

he was treated for the purposes of the re-basing provisions of *FA 1985, s 68(4)(5)* in 8.13 above as having held the asset on 31 March 1982.

A '*no gain/no loss disposal*' was one under the following enactments (being enactments by virtue of which neither a gain nor a loss accrues): *TCGA 1992, ss 58, 139, 171* and *264*; and *FA 1982, s 148*. See 8.7 above for details of these enactments and note the wider definition given there to a no gain/no loss disposal.

In computing the gain or loss on a person's disposal (not being a no gain/no loss disposal) of an asset which he was treated as having held on 31 March 1982, the no gain/no loss acquisition value which otherwise would have been deductible as allowable expenditure (see 34.3 INDEXATION) was reduced by any indexation allowance given on the disposal to him or any previous no gain/no loss disposal. [*FA 1985, s 68(7)(8)* (*as originally enacted*)].

8.15 **Assets derived from other assets.** For indexation allowance purposes, where, after 31 March 1982, an asset which was held on that date was merged or divided or changed its nature or rights in or over the asset were created, then the re-basing provisions of *FA 1985, s 68(4)(5)* in 8.13 above had effect to determine for the purposes of *TCGA 1992, s 43* (assets derived from other assets, see 15.7 COMPUTATION OF GAINS AND LOSSES) the amount of the consideration for the acquisition of the asset which was so held. [*FA 1985, s 68(6)*].

9 Capital Sums Derived from Assets

Cross-references. See 6 ASSETS; 35.1 INTERACTION WITH OTHER TAXES; 38.8 and 38.10 LAND for small part disposals of land.

Simon's Direct Tax Service. See C1.319.

9.1 Subject to 9.2 and 9.3 below, there is a disposal of assets by their owner where any 'capital sum' is *derived from* them, 'notwithstanding that no asset is acquired by the person paying the capital sum' (which means 'whether or not an asset is acquired', see *Marren v Ingles HL 1980, 54 TC 76*, and thus not following *CIR v Montgomery Ch D 1974, 49 TC 679*). See also *Zim Properties Ltd v Proctor Ch D 1984, 58 TC 371* (which has been superseded by extra-statutory concession; see 6.1 ASSETS) and *Kirby v Thorn EMI plc CA 1987, 60 TC 519.*

For general consideration of what constitutes an 'asset' for tax purposes, see 6.1 ASSETS.

'*Capital sum*' means any money or money's worth which is not otherwise excluded from the computation of chargeable gains.

The provisions apply in particular to capital sums received as follows (other than those brought into charge to income tax — see Revenue Tax Bulletin December 1997 pp 490, 491 for the treatment of compensation received by a business).

(*a*) By way of compensation for any kind of damage or injury to assets or for the loss, destruction or dissipation of assets or for any depreciation or risk of depreciation of an asset.

Following *Stoke-on-Trent City Council v Wood Mitchell & Co Ltd CA 1978, [1979] STC 197*, any element of compensation paid for the acquisition of business property by an authority possessing powers of compulsory acquisition which relates to temporary loss of profits is treated as a trading receipt. Compensation for losses on trading stock and to reimburse revenue expenditure, such as removal expenses and interest, are similarly treated. (HMRC Statement of Practice 8/79). See also *Lang v Rice CA (NI) 1983, 57 TC 80* and 35.1 INTERACTION WITH OTHER TAXES.

In *Pennine Raceway Ltd v Kirklees Metropolitan Borough Council CA, 1988, [1989] STC 122*, to which the Revenue was not a party, the company held a licence to conduct motor racing in accordance with existing planning permission. Compensation under *Town and Country Planning Act 1971* paid by the local authority for revoking the planning permission was held to be derived from the licence, the value of which had been depreciated.

See 6.9 ASSETS re compensation receivable in respect of milk quota.

(*b*) Under a policy of insurance of the risk of any kind of damage or injury to, or the loss or depreciation of, assets.

(*c*) In return for the forfeiture or surrender of rights or for refraining from exercising rights.

Statutory compensation payable to agricultural tenants under *Agricultural Holdings Act 1986, ss 60, 64* or under *Agricultural Tenancies Act 1995, s 16* and to business tenants under *Landlord and Tenant Act 1954, s 37* is not chargeable to capital gains tax. This follows the decision in (*Davis v Powell Ch D 1976, 51 TC 492*) where a tenant quit the holding in consequence of a notice to quit.

Following the decisions in *Davis v Henderson (Sp C 46), [1995] SSCD 308* and *Pritchard v Purves (Sp C 47), [1995] SSCD 316*, where a tenant is issued with a notice to quit and quits before the expiry of the notice period in return for payments made by his landlord under a surrender agreement, HMRC does not consider that the part of the landlord's payment that represents statutory compensation is chargeable to capital gains tax. (Revenue Tax Bulletin April 1996 pp 303, 304). (Grants for giving up agricultural land may be specifically exempt. See 22.18 EXEMPTIONS AND RELIEFS.) Compensation under *Landlord and Tenant Act 1954, Pt II* to a tenant giving up possession is similarly excluded (*Drummond v Austin Brown CA 1984, 58 TC 67*).

(*d*) As consideration for use or exploitation of assets.

Time of disposal under (*a*) to (*d*) above is when the capital sum is received (see Revenue Tax Bulletin October 2002 pp 967–970 for the effect on the computation of taper relief; both the qualifying holding period and the relevant period of ownership, see respectively 61.2, 61.11 TAPER RELIEF, run to the date of receipt of the capital sum).

[*TCGA 1992, s 22*].

See *British Telecommunictions plc v HMRC (Sp C 535), [2006] SSCD 347* where a payment received (in unusual circumstances) on the termination of a merger agreement was held not to constitute a capital sum derived from an asset.

A right to unquantified and contingent future consideration on the disposal of an asset is itself an asset and the future consideration, if received, is a capital sum derived from that asset (*Marren v Ingles* above and *Marson v Marriage Ch D 1979, 54 TC 59*), but see 58.5 SHARES AND SECURITIES for mitigation of this principle in the case of 'earn-outs'.

A grant received under *Farm Amalgamations Scheme 1973* is regarded as a capital sum derived from an asset (an interest in land) within *TCGA 1992, s 22* (HMRC Capital Gains Manual CG 15290).

In HMRC's view, the receipt for a grant of indefeasible rights to use a telecommunications cable system, where falling to be treated as a capital (rather than a trading) receipt, falls within (*d*) above; the only allowable costs will be incidental costs such as those of drawing up the relevant contracts (Revenue Tax Bulletin December 2000 p 816).

Where under *Matrimonial Causes Act 1973, s 31* the court effectively replaces in whole or in part an order for periodic payments by an order for a lump sum payment, it is HMRC's view that the lump sum is not a capital sum derived from an asset and that the recipient is not liable to capital gains tax (Revenue Tax Bulletin April 2001 p 840).

The *entire* loss, destruction, dissipation or extinction of an asset (whether or not any capital sum is received as above) constitutes a disposal of that asset (with certain exceptions for options as in 6.7 ASSETS). (The fact that the asset may be a capital asset employed in a business makes no difference to this tax treatment — see Revenue Tax Bulletin December 1997 pp 490, 491.) For this purpose, land and buildings may be regarded as separate assets so that where there is a deemed disposal of a building, the land comprising the site of the building (including any land occupied for purposes ancillary to the use of that building) is treated as if it were sold and immediately reacquired at its then market value. [*TCGA 1992, s 24(1)(3)*]. See also the treatment under *TCGA 1992, s 23(4)(5)* in 9.2 below. For relief where the value of an asset becomes *negligible*, see 40.9 LOSSES.

By concession, and subject to the conditions below, a capital sum is not treated as giving rise to a chargeable gain on the person entitled to receive it, where it is received as compensation for the loss or deprivation of property then situated outside the UK, and the payment of such compensation is

(i) by virtue of a statutory order under *Foreign Compensation Act 1950* or under directly analogous arrangements set up by foreign governments, or

(ii) in consequence of a recommendation of the Spoliation Advisory Panel (set up by the Government to consider claims for the return of cultural items looted during the Nazi era (1933–1945)) or of any non-UK equivalent body, or

(iii) in settlement of legal claims to the effect that the original confiscation of the property was wrong and should be declared illegal.

Loss or deprivation of property includes its sale under duress for less than market value. The concession applies only where no form of legal redress was available to the owner at the time the property was confiscated, expropriated or destroyed. It applies only if the person entitled to the compensation

- was the owner of the property at the time of confiscation etc., or
- acquired his title (directly or indirectly) from the owner of the property at that time.

If an allowable capital loss has been established in consequence of the loss or deprivation, the concession does not apply to so much of the gain as is equal to the allowable loss claimed. In deciding whether the concession applies to any person, any no gain/no loss transfers between spouses or group companies are ignored. The concession does not in any case apply where the right to compensation has itself been acquired for consideration in money or money's worth.

The concession applies in the above form to compensation received on or after 20 December 2000 or in respect of which the liability was not finally determined before that date. In its original form, it applied only to compensation within (i) above where received on or after 19 December 1994 or in respect of which the liability was not finally determined before that date. (HMRC Extra-Statutory Concession D50). For a list of countries covered by (i) above, see HMRC Capital Gains Manual CG 78706.

HMRC consider that *TCGA 1992, s 22* does not change the normal meaning of the word 'owner' so all that the provision needs for it to apply is that the person receiving the capital sum has, or had, beneficial ownership of the asset, and the receipt of a capital sum derived from that ownership. They cite the case of an asset being damaged prior to its sale where a claim for compensation results in compensation being received after the time of sale. Unless the owner has assigned his rights to compensation, the receipt of compensation will be chargeable within the provision. In certain cases, the sale itself will require to be treated as a part disposal depending on the 'hope value' of the compensation. (HMRC Capital Gains Manual CG 12975, 12976).

9.2 CAPITAL SUMS APPLIED IN RESTORING ASSETS AND SMALL CAPITAL SUMS

Where a capital sum within 9.1(*a*)–(*d*) above is derived from an asset which is not lost or destroyed, the recipient may claim under *TCGA 1992, s 23(1)* that the asset is not treated as disposed of, provided the capital sum is:

(*a*) wholly applied in restoring the asset (not being a wasting asset in relation to a capital sum received before 6 April 1996); or

(*b*) (subject to the following) applied in restoring the asset (not being a wasting asset) except for a part which is not reasonably required for the purpose and which is 'small' compared with the whole capital sum; or

(*c*) (subject to the following) 'small' as compared with the value of the asset (not being a wasting asset).

'*Small*' for the purposes of (*b*) and (*c*) above has normally been taken by HMRC to mean not exceeding 5%. With effect from **24 February 1997**, HMRC also regard any amount of £3,000 or less as being 'small', whether or not it would pass the 5% test (Revenue Tax Bulletin February 1997 p 397). Additionally, for small part disposals of land, see 38.8 and 38.10 LAND.

If the receipt is not treated as a disposal, the capital sum is deducted from the allowable expenditure on a subsequent disposal. [*TCGA 1992, s 23(1)(6)(8)(a); FA 1996, Sch 39 para 3*].

Where the allowable expenditure relating to the asset (not being a wasting asset) immediately prior to the receipt of the capital sum (including the cost of any restoration work before receipt) is less than the capital sum (or is nil), (*b*) and (*c*) above do not apply, but the recipient may elect under *TCGA 1992, s 23*(*2*) to reduce the capital sum by the amount of any allowable expenditure. The balance of the capital sum is treated as a part disposal. The capital sum so utilised cannot be deducted again either on the part disposal or any subsequent disposal of the asset by the recipient. [*TCGA 1992, s 23*(*2*)(*6*)(*8*)(*a*); *FA 1996, Sch 39 para 3*]. Where the capital sum received is subsequently wholly applied in restoring the asset, the recipient may alternatively make a claim as under (*a*) above for the asset not to be disposed of.

If part only of the capital sum within 9.1(*a*) or (*b*) derived from an asset (not being a wasting asset in relation to capital sums received before 6 April 1996) is applied in restoring the asset (but not sufficient so as to fall within (*b*) above) the recipient may claim under *TCGA 1992, s 23*(*3*) to have the part so applied deducted from any allowable expenditure on a subsequent disposal. The balance of the capital sum is treated as a part disposal of the asset. [*TCGA 1992, s 23*(*3*)(*6*)(*8*); *FA 1996, Sch 39 para 3*]. In the part disposal computation, HMRC take the market value after any restoration work.

Where *TCGA 1992, s 23*(*1*) or (*3*) above applies in the case of a wasting asset in relation to capital sums received after 5 April 1996, the amount of the allowable expenditure from which the appropriate deduction is made is the amount that would have been allowable if the asset had been disposed of immediately after the application of the capital sum. [*TCGA 1992, s 23*(*8*)(*b*); *FA 1996, Sch 39 para 3*].

The above provisions supersede ESC D1 (see 38.22 LAND) in respect of capital sums received after 5 April 1996.

Examples

An Old Master painting belonging to X and worth £100,000 (in its undamaged state) is damaged in June 2006. Subsequently, X successfully claims £20,000 from his insurance company. The picture cost X £40,000 in 1995 and in its damaged state in 2006 is valued at £60,000. The following possibilities arise, the capital gains tax calculations being as shown.

(i) X retains the insurance moneys and does nothing to restore the picture. He is treated as having made a part disposal, and the unindexed gain is computed according to the formula for part-disposals (see 15.7 COMPUTATION OF GAINS AND LOSSES). The allowable expenditure apportioned to the disposal is thus £10,000.

(ii) X subsequently expends the whole of the sum on restoration of the picture, but *does not* make a claim under (*a*) above. He will be treated as having made a part disposal as in (i) above, and his allowable expenditure on a future disposal is computed as follows.

	£
Original allowable expenditure	40,000
Deduct: apportioned allowable expenditure	10,000
	30,000
Add: Expenditure on restoration	20,000
Revised allowable expenditure	£50,000

(iii) X expends the whole of the sum on restoration of the asset *and* makes a claim under (*a*) above. The position is as follows

	£
Original allowable expenditure	40,000
Deduct: compensation moneys received	20,000
	20,000
Add: Expenditure incurred on the asset after compensation received	20,000
Revised allowable expenditure	£40,000

(iv) X expends £19,000 on restoration of the asset and makes a claim under (*b*) above. The shortfall of £1,000 is small in relation to the compensation moneys received, and will effectively be treated as a deferred capital gain.

	£
Original allowable expenditure	40,000
Deduct: compensation	20,000
	20,000
Add: Expenditure out of compensation	19,000
Revised allowable expenditure	£39,000

(v) X manages to have the asset restored for £15,000. The shortfall is not small in relation to the compensation moneys received. X makes a claim under *TCGA 1992, s 23*(*3*). The market value of the restored asset is £95,000.

	£
Consideration deemed to have been received for the part disposal (£20,000 – £15,000)	5,000
Deduct: Allowable expenditure on that disposal $\frac{5,000}{(5,000+95,000)} \times £(40,000+15,000)$	2,750
Unindexed gain	£2,250

The allowable expenditure on a future disposal is as follows

	£
Allowable expenditure after part disposal £(40,000 + 15,000 – 2,750)	52,250
Deduct: Compensation expended on asset	15,000
Revised allowable expenditure	£37,250

Indexation allowance will be computed at (i), (ii) and (v) above in respect of the expenditure attributable to the part disposed of as in 34.2 INDEXATION, but not beyond April 1998. All gains are subject to TAPER RELIEF (61).

9.3 **ASSETS LOST AND REPLACED OUT OF COMPENSATION**

Where an asset (other than a wasting asset in relation to capital sums received before 6 April 1996) is lost or destroyed and a capital sum is received in compensation, there is a disposal of the asset under *TCGA 1992, s 22(1)* as in 9.1 above. Where, however, within one year of receipt (or such longer period as the inspector allows; inspectors are instructed to allow two years from receipt where the delay can reasonably be regarded as unavoidable (HMRC Capital Gains Manual CG 15744)) the whole capital sum is applied in acquiring a replacement asset (other than a wasting asset in relation to capital sums received before 6 April 1996), the owner may claim under *TCGA 1992, s 23(4)* to have the disposal of the old asset (if otherwise greater) treated as made at a consideration giving rise to neither a gain nor a loss. The consideration for the acquisition of the new asset is then reduced by the amount of the excess of the capital sum received plus any residual or scrap value of the old asset over the amount of the deemed consideration. [*TCGA 1992, s 23(4)(6)(8); FA 1996, Sch 39 para 3*].

Where all of the gain on the disposal of the old asset is not chargeable as it was acquired before 6 April 1965, the amount of the reduction in the acquisition cost of the new asset is the amount of the chargeable gain and not the whole amount of the gain. [*TCGA 1992, Sch 2 para 23*].

If part only of the capital sum received in respect of the old asset (other than a wasting asset in relation to capital sums received before 6 April 1996) is applied in acquiring the new asset (other than a wasting asset in relation to capital sums received before 6 April 1996), the relief above cannot be claimed. However, provided that the amount not applied is less than the gain (whether chargeable or not) accruing on the disposal of the old asset, the owner can claim under *TCGA 1992, s 23(5)* to reduce the gain arising to the amount not applied (and if not all chargeable, with a proportionate reduction in the amount of the chargeable gain). The amount of the consideration for the acquisition of the new asset is reduced by the same amount as the original gain. [*TCGA 1992, s 23(5)(6)(8); FA 1996, Sch 39 para 3*].

Where all of the gain on the disposal of the old asset is not chargeable as it was acquired before 6 April 1965, the amount of the reduction in acquisition cost is the amount by which the chargeable gain is reduced and not the amount by which the original gain is reduced. [*TCGA 1992, Sch 2 para 23*].

If a building (including a structure in the nature of a building) is destroyed or irreparably damaged, and all or part of any capital sum received after 5 April 1996 is applied by the recipient in constructing or otherwise acquiring a replacement building (but excluding the land on which the building stands) situated elsewhere, then for the purposes of a claim under *TCGA 1992, s 23(4)* or *(5)* above each of the old building and the new building are regarded as an asset separate from the land on which it was or is situated and the old building treated as lost or destroyed. Just and reasonable apportionments of expenditure, compensation or consideration are made for this purpose. [*TCGA 1992, s 23(6)(7); FA 1996, Sch 39 para 3*]. Cf. the treatment under *TCGA 1992, s 24(1)(3)* in 15.8 COMPUTATION OF GAINS AND LOSSES.

In respect of capital sums received after 5 April 1996 the provisions of *TCGA 1992, s 23(6)(7)* replace ESC D19 which was similar in its effect but did not apply where the interest in the land on which the old building stood was a wasting asset.

Examples

(*a*) A bought an asset for £50,000 in February 1992. It is subsequently destroyed by fire in October 2006 and A receives £90,000 compensation later in that month. A buys a new asset six months later for £100,000 and makes a claim under *TCGA 1992, s 23(4)*. The indexation factor for the period February 1992 to April 1998 is 0.193.

	£
Cost of destroyed asset	50,000
Indexation allowance £50,000 × 0.193	9,650
Deemed consideration	£59,650
Compensation received	90,000
Deemed consideration	59,650
Excess (i.e. the gain otherwise accruing)	£30,350

Consideration for acquisition of new asset	100,000
Excess as above	30,350
Reduced allowable expenditure on new asset	£69,650

(*b*) Facts as in *Example* (*a*) above except that A buys another asset to replace the old at a cost of £80,000 and makes a claim under *TCGA 1992, s 23(5)*.

	£	
Gain on disposal (see above)		£30,350
Compensation moneys received	90,000	
Compensation moneys expended	80,000	
Excess (being less than the gain of £30,350)	£10,000	

The chargeable gain is treated as reduced to the balance arrived at as above and, subject to TAPER RELIEF (61), is	£10,000
Amount by which the gain otherwise chargeable is reduced (£30,350 – £10,000)	£20,350

The allowable expenditure on the new asset is reduced as follows

	£
Actual expenditure	80,000
Amount by which chargeable gain is reduced	20,350
Total allowable expenditure	£59,650

10 Charities

Simon's Direct Tax Service. See C1.415, C4.524; Division C4.5.

10.1 DEFINITIONS AND GENERAL PRINCIPLES

For certain income tax purposes, '*charity*' means any body of persons or trust established for charitable purposes only. [*ICTA 1988, s 506*(*1*)]. The meaning of charity is also governed by general law. These meanings apply for capital gains tax for all practical purposes.

Under *Recreational Charities Act 1958, s 1,* the provision, in the interests of social welfare, of facilities for recreation or other leisure occupation is deemed to be charitable (subject to the principle that, unless the trust is for the relief of poverty (*Dingle v Turner HL, [1972] 1 All E R 878*) a trust or institution to be charitable must be for the public benefit). See in this connection *Guild v CIR HL, [1992] STC 162.*

Charities are regulated under the *Charities Acts 1992* and *1993* in England and Wales by the Charity Commissioners. In Scotland, charities recognised as such by HMRC are regulated by the Scottish Charities Office, on behalf of the Lord Advocate, under the *Law Reform* (*Miscellaneous Provisions*) (*Scotland*) *Act 1990.* Registers of charities are kept by the Charity Commissioners and the Financial Intermediaries and Claims Office (Scotland), Trinity Park House, South Trinity Road, Edinburgh EH5 3SD (Tel. 031 551 8127), as appropriate. A leaflet CB(1), available from the address quoted, provides further information on how to apply for recognition in Scotland and the tax reliefs available. Under *Charities Act 1993, s 10* and *Law Reform* (*Miscellaneous Provisions* (*Scotland*) *Act 1990, s 1,* HMRC may disclose information regarding charities to the Charity Commissioners and the Lord Advocate, as appropriate.

Subject to the above, what is a charity rests largely on judicial interpretation. A leading case is *Special Commrs v Pemsel HL 1891, 3 TC 53* in which Lord Macnaghten laid down that 'charity' should be given its technical meaning under English law and comprises 'four principal divisions; trusts for the relief of poverty, trusts for the advancement of education, trusts for the advancement of religion and trusts beneficial to the community and not falling under any of the preceding heads. The trusts last referred to are not the less charitable ... because incidentally they affect the rich as well as the poor'. In the same case it was held that, in relation to tax, the English definition should be applied to Scottish cases (and cf. *Jackson's Trustees v Lord Advocate CS 1926, 10 TC 460* and *CIR v Glasgow (City) Police Athletic Assn HL 1953, 34 TC 76*). A trust established to pay income to 'any one or more religious, charitable or educational institutions operating for the public good' was held not to be exclusively charitable; Lord Browne-Wilkinson observed that 'general words are not to be impliedly limited to charitable purposes only' (*Attorney-General of the Cayman Islands v Wahr-Hansen PC, [2000] 3 WLR 869*). The concept of 'charity' may change with changes in social values (cf. *CIR v Trustees of Football Association Youth Trust HL 1980, 54 TC 413*).

The charity reliefs are not available to charities established overseas (*CIR v Gull KB 1937, 21 TC 374*; *Dreyfus Foundation Inc v CIR HL 1955, 36 TC 126*). The *Charitable Trusts* (*Validation*) *Act 1954* provides for validating as charitable a pre-1953 trust if its property was in fact applied for charitable purposes only, notwithstanding that the trust also authorised its application for non-charitable purposes (cf. *Vernon & Sons Ltd Employees Fund v CIR Ch D 1956, 36 TC 484*; *Buxton v Public Trustees Ch D 1962, 41 TC 235*).

The Revenue published Guidelines on the Tax Treatment of Appeal Funds (May 2001) to assist people organising appeals to raise money in the wake of an accident, disaster or other misfortune. These are available on the internet (at www.hmrc.gov.uk).

10.2 **CHARITY, CHARITABLE PURPOSES — EXAMPLES**

Relevant cases are summarised below under appropriate headings.

(*a*) **Almshouse.** Inmates need not be destitute (*Mary Clark Home Trustees v Anderson KB 1904, 5 TC 48*).

(*b*) **Arts.** A musical festival association and the Royal Choral Society have been held to be charitable (*Glasgow Musical Festival Assn CS 1926, 11 TC 154*; *Royal Choral Society v CIR CA 1943, 25 TC 263*) but not companies formed to produce plays in association with the Arts Council (*Tennent Plays Ltd v CIR CA 1948, 30 TC 107*) or with the aim of furthering the theatre and dramatic taste (*Associated Artists Ltd v CIR Ch D 1956, 36 TC 499*).

(*c*) **Benevolent funds, etc.** for the relief of widows and orphans of members were held charitable (*Society for the Relief of Widows and Orphans of Medical Men KB 1926, 11 TC 1*; *Baptist Union, etc. Ltd v CIR KB (NI) 1945, 26 TC 335*) but not a death benefit fund (*Royal Naval etc. Officers' Assn Ch D 1955, 36 TC 187*) nor a fund set up to promote the formation of mutual provident associations (*Nuffield Foundation v CIR*; *Nuffield Provident Guarantee Fund v CIR KB 1946, 28 TC 479*).

(*d*) **Education.** A trust for the advancement of education does not require an element of poverty to be charitable (*R v Special Commrs (ex p. University College of N. Wales) CA 1909, 5 TC 408*). The technical college of a trade association was held to be charitable (*Scottish Woollen Technical College v CIR CS 1926, 11 TC 139*) as was the Students' Union of a medical college (*London Hospital Medical College Ch D 1976, 51 TC 365*) and a trust to promote sports in schools, etc. (*CIR v Trustees of Football Association Youth Trust HL 1980, 54 TC 413*). See also *Educational Grants Assn Ltd CA 1967, 44 TC 93*; *Abdul Caffoor Trustees v Ceylon Income Tax Commr PC 1961, 40 ATC 93*. For 'public school' see (*h*) below.

(*e*) **Hospital.** A friendly society's convalescent home was exempted (*Royal Antediluvian Order of Buffaloes v Owens KB 1927, 13 TC 176*).

(*f*) **Political and similar objects** (including the reform of the law) are not charitable purposes. Objects held not to be charitable include the reform of the law on vivisection (*National Anti-Vivisection Society HL 1947, 28 TC 311*) and temperance (*Temperance Council etc. of England KB 1926, 10 TC 748*), the securing of worldwide observance of the Universal Declaration of Human Rights (*McGovern and Others v Attorney-General & CIR Ch D 1981, [1982] 2 WLR 222*), the education of the public in militarism and disarmament (*Southwood & Another v Attorney-General CA, [2000] All ER(D) 886*), simplified spelling (*Hunter 'C' Trustees v CIR KB 1929, 14 TC 427*), fostering Anglo-Swedish relations (*Anglo-Swedish Society v CIR KB 1931, 16 TC 34*), Jewish resettlement (*Keren Kayemeth Le Jisroel Ltd v CIR HL 1932, 17 TC 27*) and a memorial fund for Bonar Law (*Bonar Law Memorial Trust v CIR KB 1933, 17 TC 508*).

(*g*) **Professional associations etc.** Professional associations are generally not admitted to be established for charitable purposes; they benefit their members, any wider public advantage being incidental (*R v Special Commrs (ex p. Headmasters' Conference) KB 1925, 10 TC 73*; *General Medical Council v CIR CA 1928, 13 TC 819*; *Geologists' Assn v CIR CA 1928, 14 TC 271*; *Midland Counties Institution of Engineers v CIR KB 1928, 14 TC 285*; *General Nursing Council for Scotland v CIR CS 1929, 14 TC 645*; *Master Mariners (Honourable Company of) v CIR KB 1932, 17 TC 298*). But contrast *Institution of Civil Engineers v CIR CA 1931, 16 TC 158*, where the Institution was held to be charitable, any benefit to members being incidental. Members' clubs and social clubs are not charitable (*Scottish Flying Club v CIR CS 1935, 20 TC 1*; *Sir H J Williams's Trustees v CIR HL 1947, 27 TC 409*). An agricultural society for the general promotion of agriculture was held charitable (*CIR v Yorkshire Agricultural Society CA 1927, 13 TC 58*) but not a statutory pig marketing board (*Pig Marketing Board (Northern Ireland) v CIR KB (NI) 1945, 26 TC 319*) nor a society to promote foxhound breeding (*Peterborough Royal Foxhound Show Society v CIR KB 1936, 20 TC 249*) (but it was given relief under *ICTA 1988, s 510* on its annual show).

(*h*) **Public school.** A school may be for the public benefit and qualify for the relief notwithstanding that it derives substantial receipts from fees (*Blake v Mayor etc. of London CA 1887, 2 TC 209*; *Ereaut v Girls' Public Day School Trust Ltd HL 1930, 15 TC 529*, and contrast *Birkenhead School Ltd v Dring KB 1926, 11 TC 273*). A Quaker school exclusively for children of members of the Society of Friends was refused relief (*Ackworth School v Betts KB 1915, 6 TC 642*) but a Roman Catholic school which admitted non-Catholic pupils qualified for relief (*Cardinal Vaughan Memorial School Trustees v Ryall KB 1920, 7 TC 611*).

(*i*) **Religion.** Charitable relief was refused for trusts to advance the 'religious, moral, social and recreative life' of Presbyterians in Londonderry (*Londonderry Presbyterian Church House Trustees v CIR CA (NI) 1946, 27 TC 431*), for the promotion and aiding of 'Roman Catholicism' in a particular district (*Ellis v CIR CA 1949, 31 TC 178*) and for the 'religious, educational and other parochial requirements' of the Roman Catholic inhabitants of a parish (*Cookstown Roman Catholic Church Trustees v CIR QB (NI) 1953, 34 TC 350*). In each case, the objects included non-charitable elements which prevented the whole being charitable. Relief was also refused to the Oxford Group (*Oxford Group v CIR CA 1949, 31 TC 221*).

(*j*) **Miscellaneous.** A nursing home (*Peebleshire Nursing Assn CS 1926, 11 TC 335*) and a holiday home (*Roberts Marine Mansions Trustees CA 1927, 11 TC 425*) providing services for members etc. at reduced fees were held to be charitable, as was a non-profit making company for publishing law reports (*Incorporated Council of Law Reporting v A-G CA 1971, 47 TC 321*). Relief was refused to a trust to maintain an historic building because it also had a non-charitable object (*Trades House of Glasgow v CIR CS 1969, 46 TC 178*) and to a Society established mainly with philanthropic objects which, in the event, were not achieved (*Hugh's Settlement Ltd v CIR KB 1938, 22 TC 281*). A training and enterprise council was denied charitable status, despite having *some* charitable objects, on the grounds that one of its main objects enabled it to 'promote the interests of individuals engaged in trade, commerce or enterprise and provide benefits and services to them' (*CIR v Oldham Training and Enterprise Council Ch D 1996, 69 TC 231*).

10.3 EXEMPTION AVAILABLE

Subject to the restriction in 10.4 below, a gain accruing to a charity is not a chargeable gain provided it is 'applicable and applied for charitable purposes only'. [*TCGA 1992, s 256(1)*; *FA 2006, s 55(4)*]. For the scope of 'applicable and applied for charitable purposes only', see *Lawrence v CIR KB 1940, 23 TC 333*, *Slater (Helen) Charitable Trust Ltd CA 1981, 55 TC 230* and *Guild and others v CIR CS 1993, 66 TC 1*.

Where a UK charity is a beneficiary of an offshore trust and receives a capital payment, such that a gain would otherwise be treated as accruing to the charity under *TCGA 1992, s 87* (see 44.14 OFFSHORE SETTLEMENTS), the above exemption is available to the extent that the capital payment is applicable and applied for charitable purposes. This represents a change of practice by the Revenue following legal advice and applies to capital payments made on or after 10 August 1998 and also to any earlier payments where the tax liability remained open at that date. The Revenue had previously taken the view that the exemption was unavailable in such circumstances. (Revenue Tax Bulletin August 1998 pp 573, 574).

Where property held on charitable trusts ceases to be subject to those trusts, the trustees are deemed to have disposed of, and immediately reacquired, the property at its market value at that time. Any gain arising is not treated as accruing to a charity. Furthermore, insofar as the property represents, directly or indirectly, the consideration for the disposal of assets by the trustees, any gain accruing on that earlier disposal (and previously exempt) is treated as not having accrued to a charity and capital gains tax is chargeable as if the exemption had never applied. A cumulative liability may therefore arise and an assessment may be made within three years of the end of the year of assessment in which the property ceases to be subject to charitable trusts. [*TCGA 1992, s 256(2)*]. Such an assessment seems to be able to be made even where the gain arising on an earlier disposal is outside the normal time limit for assessment.

By concession, where land given for educational and certain other charitable purposes ceases after 16 August 1987 to be used for such purposes and, under *Reverter of Sites Act 1987*, is held by the trustees on a trust for sale for the benefit of the revertee, then unless the revertee is known to be a charity, there is a deemed disposal and reacquisition for capital gains purposes under *TCGA 1992, s 256(2)* above, which may give rise to a chargeable gain. Any income arising from the property will be liable to income tax, and a chargeable gain may also arise on a subsequent sale of the land. By concession, where the revertee is subsequently identified as a charity or disclaims all entitlement to the property (or where certain orders are made by the Charity Commissioners or the Secretary of State), provided that charitable status is re-established within six years of the date on which the land ceased to be held on the original charitable trust, any capital gains tax paid as above in the interim period will be discharged or repaid (with repayment supplement where appropriate) as will any income tax (provided that the income charged was used for charitable purposes). Partial relief will be given where the above conditions are only satisfied in respect of part of the property concerned. A request by the trustees for postponement of the tax payable will be accepted by HMRC where the revertee has not been identified and this concession may apply (HMRC Extra-Statutory Concession D47).

10.4 **Restriction of exemption—Chargeable periods beginning on or after 22 March 2006.** If, in any 'chargeable period' (i.e. tax year or accounting period), a charity incurs (or is treated as incurring) 'non-charitable expenditure', the amount of relief given under the following exemptions is reduced by an amount equal to that expenditure. The exemptions are those under:

- *TCGA 1992, s 256* (see 10.3 above);
- *ICTA 1988, s 505(1)* (general exemption for income of charities);
- *ICTA 1988, s 56(3)(c)* (exemption for certain income from certificates of deposit);
- *ICTA 1988, s 761(6)* (exemption for offshore income gains); and
- *FA 2000, s 46* (exemption for profits of small trades).

The charity may by notice in writing to HMRC specify against which items of income or gains the reduction is to be treated as made. If, within 30 days of a request to do so, the charity does not give such notice, HMRC determine the attribution.

If the charity's non-charitable expenditure for a chargeable period exceeds the aggregate for the period of:

- income and gains which, but for the application of these provisions, would qualify for any of the above exemptions;
- other income and gains chargeable to tax; and
- donations, legacies and other similar receipts that are not chargeable to tax,

the excess is treated as non-charitable expenditure of previous chargeable periods ending not more than six years before the end of the chargeable period in which the expenditure was actually incurred. Attributions are made to later periods in priority to earlier periods. Adjustments by way of assessment or otherwise are made in consequence of an attribution to a previous period. Where an amount is so attributed to a chargeable period beginning before 22 March 2006, the amount of relief to be disallowed is limited to the amount which would have been disallowed under the provisions applying for such periods (see below).

For the purposes of these provisions, expenditure incurred in a particular period may be treated as incurred in another period if it is properly chargeable against income of that other period and is referable to commitments (contractual or otherwise) entered into before or during that other period.

'*Non-charitable expenditure*' is expenditure which is not 'charitable expenditure'. Subject to the following, '*charitable expenditure*' is expenditure which is exclusively for charitable purposes. A payment made (or to be made) to a body situated outside the UK is not charitable expenditure unless the charity concerned has taken such steps as may be reasonable in the circumstances to ensure that the payment will be applied for charitable purposes.

If the charity invests any funds in an investment which is not a 'qualifying investment' or makes a loan (not as an investment) which is not a 'qualifying loan', the amount invested or lent is treated as non-charitable expenditure. Where the investment or loan is realised or repaid in whole or in part in the period in which it was made, any further investment or lending of the sum realised or repaid in that period is, to the extent that it does not exceed the sum originally invested or lent, ignored in arriving at non-charitable expenditure of the period.

The following are '*qualifying investments*'.

(A) Investments within *Trustee Investments Act 1961, Sch 1 Pts I, II* (*para 13* excepted; mortgages etc.) and *III*.

(B) Investments in a common investment fund established under *Charities Act 1993, s 24* (or NI equivalent), a common deposit fund established under *Charities Act 1960, s 25* or similar funds under other enactments.

(C) Any interest in land other than a mortgage, etc.

(D) Shares or securities of a company listed on a recognised stock exchange (within *ICTA 1988, s 841* — see 58.23 SHARES AND SECURITIES) or dealt in on the Unlisted Securities Market (now closed).

(E) Units in unit trusts and shares in an open-ended investment company (as statutorily defined).

(F) Deposits with a recognised bank or licensed institution in respect of which interest is payable at a commercial rate but excluding a deposit made as part of an arrangement whereby the bank, etc. makes a loan to a third party.

(G) Uncertificated eligible debt securities within *ITTOIA 2005, s 552(2)*.

(H) Certificates of deposit within *ICTA 1988, s 56(5)* or *ITTOIA 2005, s 552(2)*.

(J) Loans or other investments as to which HMRC are satisfied, on a claim, that the loans or other investments are made for the benefit of the charity and not for tax avoidance purposes (whether by the charity or by a third party). Loans secured by mortgage etc., over land are eligible.

A loan which is not made by way of investment is a '*qualifying loan*' if it is one of the following.

(1) A loan made to another charity for charitable purposes only.

(2) A loan to a beneficiary of the charity which is made in the course of carrying out the purposes of the charity.

(3) Money placed on a current account with a recognised bank or licensed institution otherwise than under arrangements as in (F) above.

(4) A loan, not within (1)–(3) above, as to which HMRC are satisfied, on a claim, that the loan is made for the benefit of the charity and not for tax avoidance purposes (whether by the charity or by a third party).

[*ICTA 1988, s 505(3)–(7), s 506, Sch 20; FA 2006, s 55, Sch 26 Pt 3(5); SI 1997 No 1154, Reg 16; SI 2006 No 964, Reg 94(7)*].

Payments to substantial donors. Anti-avoidance provisions apply to restrict the transactions that can take place between a 'substantial donor' and a charity without loss of the tax exemptions listed above. The provisions operate by treating certain payments and deemed payments to be non-charitable expenditure for the purposes of *ICTA 1988, s 505*. The provisions apply to transactions occurring on or after 22 March 2006. Transactions entered into in pursuance of a contract made before 22 March 2006, otherwise than in pursuance of a variation on or after that date, are excluded.

The following are treated as non-charitable expenditure under the provisions:

(I) a payment made by a charity to a substantial donor in the course of, or for the purposes of, one of the transactions listed below;

(II) where the terms of such a transaction are less beneficial to the charity than terms which might be expected at arm's length, the amount that the Commissioners for HMRC determine as the cost to the charity of the difference in terms (the deemed expenditure being treated as incurred at such time or times as the Commissioners determine); and

(III) a payment by a charity of remuneration to a substantial donor other than remuneration for services as a trustee which is approved by the Charity Commission or other body with responsibility for regulating charities by virtue of legislation having effect in respect of any part of the UK, or a court. Where the remuneration is not paid in money, the cash equivalent under the employment benefits rules of *ITEPA 2003, Pt 3* is used to determine the amount of the non-charitable expenditure.

Payments and benefits arising to a donor are disregarded for these purposes to the extent that they relate to a donation by the donor and do not exceed the limits on donor benefits for the purposes of the gift aid provisions (see 10.7 below for donations by individuals and *ICTA 1988, s 339* for donations by companies).

Non-charitable expenditure may be deemed to be incurred in respect of a single transaction under both (I) and (II) above, but any amount treated as incurred under (I) above is deducted from any amount which the charity would otherwise be treated as incurring under (II) above. A transaction entered into in a chargeable period falls within the provisions even if it occurs before the donor first satisfied the definition of substantial donor in respect of that period.

Two or more charities which are connected in a matter relating to the structure, administration or control of a charity are treated as a single charity for the purposes of the provisions.

Subject to the exclusions below, (I) and (II) above apply to the following transactions:

- the sale or letting of property by a charity to a substantial donor or by a substantial donor to a charity;
- the provision of services by a charity to a substantial donor or by a substantial donor to a charity;
- an exchange of property between a charity and a substantial donor;
- the provision of financial assistance (including, in particular, the provision of a loan, guarantee or indemnity or entering into alternative financial arrangements within *FA 2005, s 46* (see 15.9 COMPUTATION OF GAINS AND LOSSES)) by a charity to a substantial donor or by a substantial donor to a charity; and

- investment by a charity in the business of a substantial donor other than by purchase of shares or securities listed on a recognised stock exchange (see 58.23 SHARES AND SECURITIES).

The sale or letting of property, or the provision of services, to a charity by a substantial donor is excluded if the Commissioners for HMRC determine that the transaction occurs in the course of the donor's business on terms which are no less beneficial to the charity than those to be expected at arm's length and that the transaction is not part of an arrangement for the avoidance of tax. The provision of services to a substantial donor is excluded if the Commissioners determine that the services are provided in the course of carrying out a primary purpose of the charity on terms which are no more beneficial to the donor than those on which services are provide to others. The provision of financial assistance to a charity by a substantial donor is excluded if the Commissioners determine that the assistance is on terms which are no less beneficial to the charity than those which might be expected at arm's length and is not part of an arrangement for the avoidance of tax.

A disposal at an undervalue to which *ICTA 1988, s 587B* or *TCGA 1992, s 257(2)* (gifts of assets to charities — see 10.5 below) apply is not itself a transaction to which the above provisions apply, but it may be taken into account in determining whether a person is a substantial donor to the charity.

A person is a '*substantial donor*' to a charity for a chargeable period if the charity receives 'tax relievable' gifts (including non-monetary gifts) from him to a value of at least:

- £25,000 in a period of twelve months in which the chargeable period wholly or partly falls; or
- £100,000 in a period of six years in which the chargeable period wholly or partly falls.

Where a person qualifies as a substantial donor for a chargeable period in this way, he continues to be treated as a substantial donor for the following five chargeable periods. The Treasury may by regulations vary these amounts or periods of time. A company that is wholly owned by a charity (within *ICTA 1988, s 339(7AB)*) is not treated as a substantial donor to that charity. A registered social landlord or housing association (as defined) is not treated as a substantial donor to a charity with which it is connected (i.e. where one owns or controls the other or both are under common ownership or control). Note that a person may be a substantial donor by reference to gifts made at any time, including those made before 22 March 2006.

References above to a substantial donor are to be taken to include any person connected (within *ICTA 1988, s 839* — see 16 CONNECTED PERSONS) with him.

Gifts are '*tax relievable*' if they qualify for relief under any of the following provisions:

- *ICTA 1988, s 83A* (gifts of trading stock by companies);
- *ICTA 1988, s 339* (gift aid for donations by companies);
- *ICTA 1988, ss 587B, 587C* (gifts of assets);
- *FA 1990, s 25* (gift aid for donations by individuals, see 10.7 below);
- *TCGA 1992, s 257* (gifts of chargeable assets, see 10.5, 10.6 below);
- *CAA 2001, s 63* (gifts of plant and machinery);
- *ITEPA 2003, ss 713–715* (payroll giving);
- *ITTOIA 2005, s 108* (gifts of trading stock by individuals); or
- *ITTOIA 2005, ss 628, 630* (gifts from settlor-interested trusts).

Appeals against decisions of the Commissioners for HMRC under the above provisions are to the Special Commissioners.

[*ICTA 1988, ss 506A–506C; FA 2006, s 54*].

Restriction of exemption — chargeable periods beginning before 22 March 2006. If, in any chargeable period beginning before 22 March 2006, a charity:

(*a*) has 'relevant income and gains' of £10,000 or more (but see below); and

(*b*) has relevant income and gains exceeding the amount of its 'qualifying expenditure'; and

(*c*) incurs, or is treated as incurring 'non-qualifying expenditure',

exemption under *TCGA 1992, s 256* (and *ICTA 1988, s 505(1)* for income tax) is not available for so much of the excess at (*b*) as does not exceed the non-qualifying expenditure incurred in that period. Where the exemption is not so available, the charity may, by notice in writing, specify which items of its relevant income and gains are wholly or partly to be attributed to the amount concerned. Covenanted payments to the charity (within *ICTA 1988, s 347A(7)*) are treated as a single item. If, within thirty days of a request to do so, the charity does not give notice, the Commissioners for HMRC (or, before 18 April 2005, the Board of Inland Revenue) determine the attribution.

The £10,000 limit in (*a*) above is proportionately reduced where a chargeable period is less than twelve months, and does not apply where two or more charities acting in concert are engaged in transactions aimed at tax avoidance and where the Commissioners (or Board), by notice in writing, so direct. An appeal, as against a decision on a claim, may be made against such a notice.

'*Relevant income and gains*'. This means the aggregate of

(i) income which, apart from *ICTA 1988, s 505(1)*, would not be exempt from tax, together with any income which is taxable notwithstanding *ICTA 1988, s 505(1)*; and

(ii) gains which, apart from *TCGA 1992, s 256*, would be chargeable gains, together with any gains which are chargeable gains notwithstanding *TCGA 1992, s 256*.

'*Non-qualifying expenditure*'. This is expenditure other than 'qualifying expenditure'. If the charity invests any funds in an investment which is not a 'qualifying investment' or makes a loan (not as an investment) which is not a 'qualifying loan', the amount invested or lent is treated as non-qualifying expenditure. Where the investment or loan is realised or repaid in whole or in part in the period in which it was made, any further investment or lending of the sum realised or repaid in that period is, to the extent that it does not exceed the sum originally invested or lent, ignored in arriving at non-qualifying expenditure of the period.

Where the aggregate of the qualifying and non-qualifying expenditure incurred in a chargeable period (the '*primary period*') exceeds the relevant income and gains of that period, so much of the excess as does not exceed the non-qualifying expenditure constitutes '*unapplied non-qualifying expenditure*'. Except to the extent (if any) that it represents the expenditure of 'non-taxable sums' received in the primary period, the unapplied non-qualifying expenditure may be treated as non-qualifying expenditure of an '*earlier period*' (a chargeable period ending not more than six years before the end of the primary period). '*Non-taxable sums*' are donations, legacies and other sums of a similar nature which, apart from *ICTA 1988, s 505(1)* and *TCGA 1992, s 256*, are not within the charge to tax.

Where an amount of unapplied non-qualifying expenditure (the '*excess expenditure*') falls to be treated as non-qualifying expenditure of earlier periods, it is attributed only to those periods in which, apart from the attribution in question but taking account of any previous attribution, the relevant income and gains exceed the aggregate of the qualifying and non-qualifying expenditure in that period; and such attribution is not to be greater than the excess. Attributions are made to later periods in priority to earlier periods. Any excess expenditure which cannot be attributed to an earlier period is ignored for attribution purposes altogether. Adjustments by way of further assessment etc. are made in consequence of an attribution to an earlier period.

'*Qualifying expenditure*'. This is expenditure incurred for charitable purposes only. A payment made (or to be made) to a body situated outside the UK is not qualifying expenditure unless the charity concerned has taken such steps as may be reasonable in the circumstances to ensure that the payment will be applied for charitable purposes.

Expenditure incurred in a particular period may be treated as incurred in another period if it is properly chargeable against income of that other period and is referable to commitments (contractual or otherwise) entered into before or during that other period.

'*Qualifying investments*' are defined as above except that uncertificated eligible debt securities within *ITTOIA 2005, s 552(2)* (see (G) above) are qualifying investments only after 23 June 2003. '*Qualifying loans*' are as defined above.

[*ICTA 1988, s 505, s 506, Sch 20; Charities Act 1993, Sch 6 para 25; FA 1995, Sch 17 para 7; FA 1996, s 146, s 198, Sch 37 para 2(3)(4), para 5, para 10, Sch 38 para 6(1)(2)(l)(11); FA 2002, s 84(2), Sch 30 para 3; ITTOIA 2005, Sch 1 paras 198, 347; CRCA 2005, s 5; SI 2001 No 3629, Art 50*].

10.5 GIFTS OF ASSETS TO CHARITIES

Where a disposal of an asset is made otherwise than under a bargain at arm's length to a charity, the normal MARKET VALUE (41) provisions (which deem the acquisition and disposal as being made at market value) do not apply.

If the disposal is by way of gift (including a gift into settlement) or for a consideration not exceeding the allowable expenditure which would be available on a disposal of the asset (see 15.4 COMPUTATION OF GAINS AND LOSSES) the transaction is treated as made for a consideration producing neither a gain nor a loss. Where the asset is subsequently disposed of by the charity, its acquisition by the person making the original disposal is treated as the acquisition of the asset by the charity. See 8.7 ASSETS HELD ON 31 MARCH 1982 and 34.3 INDEXATION for consequential re-basing and indexation provisions. Where the asset is a qualifying investment for the purposes of *ICTA 1988, s 587B* (gifts of shares, securities and real property to charities) and the disposal qualifies for income tax or corporation tax relief under that *section* (see Tolley's Income Tax under Charities), the amount treated as the charity's acquisition cost is reduced by the amount on which income tax or corporation tax relief is given or, if this would otherwise produce a negative figure, is reduced to nil.

If the disposal to the charity is for a consideration exceeding the allowable expenditure, the market value is not substituted for the actual consideration.

For gifts made to a registered community amateur sports club (see 10.8 below) after 5 April 2002, these provisions have effect as if the club were a charity.

See 50.3 QUALIFYING CORPORATE BONDS as regards making a gift of such a bond received on a reorganisation of share capital.

These provisions do not apply to disposals in relation to which venture capital trust relief is available (see 66 VENTURE CAPITAL TRUSTS).

The above provisions do apply to disposals made otherwise than under a bargain at arm's length to any of the bodies mentioned in *IHTA 1984, Sch 3.*

[*TCGA 1992, s 257(1)(2)(4); ICTA 1988, s 587B; FA 1995, s 72(5)(8); FA 2000, s 43; FA 2002, s 58(1)(4), s 97, Sch 18 para 9; FA 2004, s 139, Sch 26 para 10; ITTOIA 2005, Sch 1 para 249*].

The bodies listed in *IHTA 1984, Sch 3* (as amended) comprise

The National Gallery.

The British Museum.

The National Museum of Scotland.

The National Museum of Wales.

The Ulster Museum.

Any other similar national institution which exists wholly or mainly for the purpose of preserving for the public benefit a collection of scientific, historic or artistic interest and which is approved for this purpose by the Treasury (see list at HMRC Capital Gains Manual Appendix 4).

Any museum or art gallery in the UK which exists wholly or mainly for that purpose and is maintained by a local authority or university in the UK.

Any library the main function of which is to serve the needs of teaching and research at a university in the UK.

The Historic Buildings and Monuments Commission for England.

The National Trust for Places of Historic Interest or Natural Beauty.

The National Trust for Scotland for Places of Historic Interest or Natural Beauty.

The National Art Collections Fund.

The Trustees of the National Heritage Memorial Fund.

The National Endowment for Science, Technology and the Arts.

The Friends of the National Libraries.

The Historic Churches Preservation Trust.

Nature Conservancy Council for England.

Scottish National Heritage.

Countryside Council for Wales.

Any local authority.

Any Government department (including the National Debt Commissioners).

Any university or university college in the UK.

A health service body within *ICTA 1988, s 519A*.

10.6 **Gifts of assets out of settlements.** Where, subject to below, a charity becomes absolutely entitled to any assets (or part thereof) which were previously settled property and those assets are deemed to be disposed of and reacquired by the trustees on that occasion (under *TCGA 1992, s 71* — see 57.15 SETTLEMENTS) then, if no consideration is received by any person for or in connection with the transaction, the disposal is deemed to take place on a no gain, no loss basis. This does *not* apply where the charity becomes absolutely entitled to the assets on the termination of a life interest (within the meaning of *TCGA 1992, s 72*, see 57.13 SETTLEMENTS) by the death of the person entitled to it. These provisions also apply to a gift to any of the bodies mentioned in *IHTA 1984, Sch 3* (gifts for national purposes). See 10.5 above. [*TCGA 1992, s 257*(*3*)].

For gifts made to a registered community amateur sports club (see 10.8 below) after 5 April 2002, the above provisions have effect as if the club were a charity. [*FA 2002, s 58*(*1*)(*4*), *Sch 18 para 9*].

In *Prest v Bettinson Ch D 1980, 53 TC 437*, the residue of an estate was held on trust for five institutions, four of which were charities, subject to the payment of annuities to six individuals. No specific fund was set aside, but distributions of capital and income were made annually to the five institutions, the income of the residuary fund being more than sufficient to pay the annuities. The trustee failed in his claim that four-fifths of any capital gain arising was exempt as accruing for charitable purposes. Since no fund had been set aside to pay the annuities, the trustee retained full control of the trust property until the distribution of the proceeds of sale, and any gain from a disposal thereof had accrued to him as trustee and not to the charities.

10.7 GIFT AID DONATIONS BY INDIVIDUALS

Gifts of money made by individuals to charities which are 'qualifying donations' attract relief under the Gift Aid provisions described below. Significant modifications were made to the rules with effect from 6 April 2000. The Gift Aid provisions applying before 6 April 2000 had no direct significance for CGT purposes and are not covered here. See Tolley's Income Tax under Charities for those provisions. For the Gift Aid provisions applicable to companies, see the corresponding chapter of Tolley's Corporation Tax.

The provisions described below apply to gifts made on or after 6 April 2000 which are not covenanted payments, and to covenanted payments due on or after that date. For the purposes of these provisions, '*charity*' has the same meaning as in 10.1 above and also includes the bodies listed in *ICTA 1988, s 507*. [*FA 1990, s 25(12)(a); FA 2000, s 39(10)*].

For gifts made after 5 April 2002, these provisions have effect as if a registered community amateur sports club (see 10.8 below) were a charity, but club membership fees are not gifts for the purposes of these provisions. [*FA 2002, s 58(1)(4), Sch 18 para 9*].

The donor. Where a qualifying donation is made by an individual ('*the donor*') in a tax year, then, for that year,

(*a*) he is treated for the purposes of income tax and CGT as if:

- the gift had been made after deduction of income tax at the basic rate; and
- the basic rate limit were increased by an amount equal to the 'grossed up amount of the gift' (i.e. the amount which, after deducting income tax at the basic rate for the tax year in which the gift is made, leaves the amount of the gift);

(*b*) references in specified income tax provisions to income tax which an individual is entitled to charge against any person are taken in his case to include a reference to the tax treated as deducted from the gift; and

(*c*) to the extent, if any, necessary to ensure that he is charged to an amount of income tax and CGT equal to the tax treated as deducted from the gift, he is not entitled to income tax personal reliefs.

As the basic rate limit is used in determining the CGT liability of a higher rate taxpayer (see 2.1 ANNUAL RATES AND EXEMPTIONS), the increase mentioned in (*a*) above gives potential CGT relief in a case where *income* is insufficient to fully obtain higher rate relief on the amount of the gift. For this purpose, higher rate relief means relief for the excess of tax at the higher rate over tax at the basic rate for which relief is effectively given at source. The increase in the basic rate limit does not apply for the purposes of computing top-slicing relief on life assurance policy gains chargeable to income tax.

Where the tax treated as deducted from a gift by virtue of (*a*) above exceeds the amount of income tax and CGT with which the donor is charged for the tax year, the donor is liable to income tax at the basic rate on so much of the gift as is necessary to recover an amount of tax equal to the excess. In determining for this purpose the total amount of income tax and CGT with which the donor is charged for the year, the following are disregarded:

- any tax charged at the basic rate by virtue of *ICTA 1988, s 348* or *s 349* (annual payments — see Tolley's Income Tax under Deduction of tax at source);

- for 2006/07 and subsequent years, any tax paid to meet the lifetime allowance charge or the annual allowance charge under *FA 2004, Pt 4* (registered pension schemes);
- any notional tax treated as having been paid under *ITTOIA 2005, ss 399(2)* or *400(2)* (taxation of certain recipients of distributions), *ITTOIA 2005, s 414(1)* (stock dividends treated as income), *ITTOIA 2005, s 421(1)* (release of loan to participator in close company), *ITTOIA 2005, s 530(1)* (method of charging life policy gain to tax) or *ITTOIA 2005, s 685A(2)* (payments from settlor-interested settlements);
- any personal reliefs, or any relief for maintenance payments, falling to be given by way of an income tax reduction;
- any double tax relief (whether given under a double tax agreement or unilaterally);
- any set-off of tax deducted, or treated as deducted, from income *other than* tax treated as deducted from estate income under *ITTOIA 2005, s 656(3)* or *s 657(4)* so far as that income is treated under *ITTOIA 2005, s 679* as paid from sums within *ITTOIA 2005, s 680(3)(b)(4)* (see Tolley's Income Tax); and
- any set-off of tax credits on dividends.

For the purposes of age-related income tax allowances, which are dependent on the level of total income, the donor's total income is treated as reduced by the aggregate grossed up amount of his qualifying donations for the year.

[*FA 1990, s 25(1)(6)–(9A)(12)(d); FA 2000, s 39(1)(6); FA 2002, s 57, Sch 17 para 4; FA 2004, s 284, Sch 35 para 37; ITTOIA 2005, Sch 1 para 415; FA 2006, Sch 13 para 30; SI 2005 No 3229, Reg 104*].

A person making a qualifying donation after 5 April 2003 can elect for it to be treated, for the purposes of the above provisions, as if it were a qualifying donation made in the previous tax year. An election cannot be made unless the grossed up amount of the gift would, if made in the previous tax year, be payable out of profits or gains brought into charge to income tax or capital gains tax. The election must be made by notice in writing to an officer of HMRC on or before the date on which the donor delivers his tax return for the previous tax year, and not later than 31 January in the tax year in which the gift is actually made. [*FA 2002, s 98(1)–(4)(6)*].

An individual making a tax return for 2003/04 or a subsequent year which results in a tax repayment becoming payable in respect of one or more tax years may make a direction in the return for the repayment to be paid on his behalf to a single specified charity. The direction may also require that the gift be treated as a qualifying donation (provided that it meets the necessary conditions noted below). The gift is then treated as a qualifying donation made by the individual at the time it is received by the charity, and it is not possible to elect for the gift to be treated as made in the previous tax year as above. The charity to which the gift is made must be one which is included in a list published by HMRC for the purposes of this provision. The tax repayments in respect of which a direction can be made are repayments of income tax, payments on account of income tax and CGT, plus repayment supplement (see 36.1 INTEREST ON OVERPAID TAX). [*FA 2004, s 83(1)–(3)(5)–(7)*].

The charity. The receipt by a charity of a qualifying donation is treated as the receipt, under deduction of income tax at the basic rate for the tax year in which the gift is made, of an annual payment of an amount equal to the 'grossed up amount of the gift' (see (*a*) above). [*FA 1990, s 25(10)*]. An election by the donor to treat a qualifying donation as being made in the previous tax year does not affect the position of the charity; the donation is grossed up by reference to the basic rate for the tax year in which payment is *actually* made. [*FA 2002, s 98(5)*]. Charities wishing to receive gifts of tax repayments under *FA 2004, s 83* must request inclusion in HMRC's list of eligible charities. [*FA 2004, s 83(5)*].

Qualifying donations. A '*qualifying donation*' is a gift to a charity by the donor which meets the following conditions:

(i) it takes the form of a payment of a sum of money;

(ii) it is not subject to a condition as to repayment;

(iii) it is not deductible under the payroll deduction scheme — see Tolley's Income Tax under Charities);

(iv) neither the donor nor any person connected with him (within *ICTA 1988, s 839*) receives any benefit in consequence of making it which exceeds specified limits (see below);

(v) it is not conditional on or associated with, or part of an arrangement involving, the acquisition of property by the charity, otherwise than by way of gift, from the donor or a person connected with him;

(vi) either

- at the time it is made the donor is UK-resident or is in Crown employment as defined in *ITEPA 2003, s 28(2)* (previously *ICTA 1988, s 132(4)(a)*), or
- the grossed up amount of the gift (see (*a*) above) would, if in fact made, be payable out of profits or gains brought into charge to income tax or CGT; and

(vii) the donor gives the charity an 'appropriate declaration' in relation to it.

An '*appropriate declaration*' for the purposes of (vii) above is a declaration which is given in the form and manner prescribed by regulations. The regulations include provision for declarations to be made orally (by telephone, for example), in writing or via the internet.

[*FA 1990, s 25(1)–(3A)(11); FA 2000, s 39(1)–(4); ITEPA 2003, Sch 6 para 166; FA 2004, s 92, Sch 17 para 5; SI 2000 No 2074; SI 2005 No 2790*].

Limits on donor benefits. Where the donor or a person connected with him receives a benefit or benefits in consequence of making the gift, the gift will not be a qualifying donation if either:

(1) the aggregate value of the benefits received exceeds

- where the gift is £100 or less, 25% of the amount of the gift;
- where the gift is greater than £100 but not more than £1,000, £25;
- where the gift is greater than £1,000, 2.5% of the amount of the gift; or

(2) the aggregate of the value of the benefits received in relation to the gift and the value of any benefits received in relation to any qualifying donations previously made to the charity by the donor in the same tax year exceeds £250.

Where a benefit:

- consists of the right to receive benefits at intervals over a period of less than twelve months;
- relates to a period of less than twelve months; or
- is one of a series of benefits received at intervals in consequence of making a series of gifts at intervals of less than twelve months,

the value of the benefit and the amount of the gift are 'annualised' for the purposes of (1) above. Where a one-off benefit is received in consequence of making a gift which is one of a series of gifts made at intervals of less than twelve months, the amount of the gift (but not the value of the benefit) is likewise annualised. For these purposes a gift or benefit is '*annualised*' by multiplying the amount or value by 365 and dividing the result by the number of days in the period of less than twelve months or the average number of days in the intervals of less than twelve months as appropriate.

For gifts made after 5 April 2006, in applying the above limits, the benefit of a 'right of admission' is disregarded provided that

- the opportunity to make a gift and to receive the right of admission in consequence is available to the public;
- the right of admission is a right granted by the charity for the purpose of viewing property preserved, maintained, kept or created by a charity in pursuance of its charitable purposes, including buildings, grounds or other land, plants, animals, works of art (but not performances), artefacts and property of a scientific nature; and
- either
  - a member of the public could purchase the same right of admission (i.e. a right relating to the same property, classes of person and period of time) and the amount of the gift is at least 10% greater than the amount payable for that right, or
  - the right of admission applies, for a period of at least one year, at all times at which the public can obtain admission other than certain days specified by the charity on which an event is to take place on the premises to which the right relates. Where the right is for a period of one year, there must be no more than five specified days in the period. Where the right is for a period of more than one year, there must be no more than five specified days in each calendar year during all or part of which the right applies.

For this purpose, a '*right of admission*' is a right of free or reduced-price admission for the person making the gift (or for that person and one or more family members, whether or not the right must be exercised by all those persons at the same time) to premises or property to which the public are admitted on payment of an admission fee.

For gifts made before 6 April 2006, the rules relating to admission benefits are more restrictive. For such gifts, the benefit of a right of free or reduced-price admission for the donor or a member of his family

- to view property, the preservation of which for the public benefit is the sole or main purpose of the charity; or
- to observe wildlife, the conservation of which for the public benefit is the sole or main purpose of the charity;

is disregarded provided that the opportunity to make gifts which attract such a right is available to members of the public.

[*FA 1990, s 25(2)(e), (4)–(5J)(11); FA 2000, s 39(1)(3)(5); F(No 2)A 2005, s 11*].

HMRC have published guidance on the right of free admission to charity property. See HMRC Guidance Note 22 September 2005 on HMRC's website.

10.8 **COMMUNITY AMATEUR SPORTS CLUBS**

An exemption for certain gains accruing in accounting periods ending after 31 March 2002 can be claimed by sports clubs which are registered with HMRC as community amateur sports clubs ('*registered clubs*').

For a club to be eligible to register, it must, and its constitution must require it to,

- be 'open to the whole community';
- be 'organised on an amateur basis'; and
- have as its main purpose the provision of facilities for, and promotion of participation in, one or more 'eligible sports'.

For the above purposes, a club is '*open to the whole community*' if membership is open to all, and the club facilities are available to members, without discrimination (leaving aside necessary differentiation on grounds of age, gender or disability relative to a particular sport). Additionally, fees must be set at a level which does not pose a significant obstacle to membership or use of the facilities.

A club is '*organised on an amateur basis*' if it meets the following three conditions.

(*a*) The club must be non-profit making, i.e. its constitution must require surplus income or gains to be reinvested in the club and must not permit the distribution of club assets (whether in cash or in kind) to members or third parties. However, donations by a club to charities or other registered clubs are allowed.

(*b*) It must provide only the following benefits for members and their guests:

- provision of sporting facilities and suitably qualified coaches;
- reasonable provision and maintenance of club-owned sports equipment;
- provision of, or reimbursement of the costs of, coaching courses;
- provision of insurance cover and medical equipment;
- reimbursement of reasonable travel expenses incurred by players and officials travelling to away matches;
- reasonable provision of post-match refreshments for players and match officials; and
- sale or supply of food or drink as a social adjunct to the sporting purposes of the club.

Payments to members as employees of the club or for goods or services supplied to the club are permitted subject to conditions.

(*c*) The club's constitution must provide for any net assets on the dissolution of the club to be applied for the purposes of

- a charity,
- another registered club, or
- the governing body of an eligible sport for the purposes of which the club existed, for use in related community sport,

as approved by the members of the club in general meeting or by its governing body.

An '*eligible sport*' is one designated as such by Treasury order for the purposes of these provisions. See now *SI 2002 No 1966* which designates for these purposes sports appearing on the National Sports Councils list of activities recognised by them. The full list as at July 2002 is reproduced in a Treasury Press Release of 25 July 2002.

[*FA 2002, s 58(1)–(3), Sch 18 paras 1–3, 14*].

HMRC have published guidance on their website (www.hmrc.gov.uk) making it easier for multi-sports clubs to qualify and clarifying the position regarding prize-giving (see Revenue Internet Statement 19 November 2004).

Registration. Applications for registration are made to HMRC. The applicant club must provide the such information as HMRC may reasonably require, and, if required to do so, produce for inspection any relevant books, documents or other records in the club's possession or under its control. Registration may be backdated (possibly to before the date of the application, but not before 1 April 2002).

HMRC may terminate a club's registration (possibly with retrospective effect) if it appears to them that the club is not, or is no longer, entitled to be registered.

HMRC must notify a club of a decision to register it, to refuse its application or to terminate its registration. The club may appeal to the General Commissioners against any such decision by notice in writing to HMRC within 30 days of the date of the notification. The notice of appeal must specify the grounds of appeal. The provisions of *TMA 1970* relating to APPEALS (4) apply to such an appeal. On the hearing of an appeal, the Commissioners may allow the club to put forward grounds not specified in the appeal notice if they are satisfied that the omission was not wilful or unreasonable. If they do not dismiss the appeal, the Commissioners may either remit the matter to HMRC for reconsideration, or, as applicable, direct that the club be registered from a particular date, rescind a termination of registration, or direct that a termination take effect on a particular date.

HMRC publishes the names and addresses of registered clubs. This enables potential donors to confirm that they are donating to a registered club (and, therefore, that the donation may qualify for gift aid relief — see below). A list of the names of registered clubs is available electronically (HMRC Internet Statement 5 June 2006).

[*FA 2002, s 58(1)(2), Sch 18 paras 11–13, 15*].

Tax exemptions. Subject to the restriction noted below, a gain accruing to a registered club in an accounting period ending after 31 March 2002 is not a chargeable gain if it is wholly applied for 'qualifying purposes' and the club makes a claim to that effect. '*Qualifying purposes*' means purposes of providing facilities for, and promoting participation in, one or more eligible sports (and in the following paragraphs, '*non-qualifying purposes*' are to be construed accordingly). [*FA 2002, s 58(1)(3), Sch 18 paras 7, 16(b)*].

In addition to the exemption for gains, registered clubs also enjoy tax exemptions relating to trading income, interest and gift aid income and property income. For full details, see Tolley's Corporation Tax under Clubs and Societies.

Restriction of exemption. The above exemptions are restricted where a registered club incurs any expenditure for non-qualifying purposes in an accounting period and any of the club's income or gains for that period are exempted from tax (or would be but for the restriction).

The restriction operates by comparing the amount of the expenditure incurred in the accounting period for non-qualifying purposes ('*the non-qualifying expenditure*') with the aggregate of the club's income (whether or not taxable, and before deducting expenses) and gains (whether chargeable gains or gains exempted as above) for the accounting period ('*the total income and gains*'), as follows.

(1) Where the non-qualifying expenditure is less than the total income and gains, the amount of exempt income and gains is restricted in the proportion that the non-qualifying expenditure bears to the total income and gains.

(2) Where the non-qualifying expenditure equals the total income and gains, the amount of exempt income and gains is reduced to nil.

(3) Where the non-qualifying expenditure exceeds the total income and gains, the amount of exempt income and gains is reduced to nil, and the 'surplus amount' is carried back to previous accounting periods (latest first) ending not more than six years before the end of the current period, and deducted from income and gains exempted for those periods. To the extent that the amount exempted for an accounting period has already been reduced under this provision or (1) or (2) above, it cannot be reduced again by reference to expenditure of a later accounting period. The '*surplus amount*' is the excess of (i) an amount equal to the proportion of the originally exempt income and gains that the non-qualifying expenditure bears to the total income and gains, over (ii) the amount of the originally exempt income and gains.

Where, as a consequence of this restriction, a registered club has an amount of income and gains for which exemption is not available, the club may, by notice to HMRC, specify which items of income and gains are, in whole or part, to be attributed to that amount. If no such notice is given by the club within 30 days of being required to do so by HMRC, it falls to HMRC to make the attribution.

[*FA 2002, Sch 18 para 8*].

Property ceasing to be held for qualifying purposes. Where, in an accounting period ending after 31 March 2002, a club holds property and, without disposing of it, ceases at any time to be a registered club or to hold the property for 'qualifying purposes' (see under 'Tax Exemptions' above), it is treated for the purposes of *TCGA 1992* as having disposed of, and immediately reacquired, the property at that time at its then market value. Any gain resulting from the deemed disposal is treated as accruing otherwise than to a registered club, with the result that it cannot attract the above exemption. Additionally, to the extent that any of the property represents, directly or indirectly, the consideration for the disposal of assets by the club, any gain that accrued on that disposal is also treated as having accrued otherwise than to a registered club. Assessments in respect of resulting chargeable gains can be made at any time not later than three years after the end of the accounting period in which falls the event giving rise to this treatment. [*FA 2002, s 58(1)(3), Sch 18 para 10*].

Reliefs for donations. For gifts to registered clubs made after 5 April 2002, the following provisions relevant for capital gains purposes have effect as if a registered club were a charity:

- *FA 1990, s 25* (gift aid donations by individuals — see 10.7 above), and
- *TCGA 1992, s 257* (gifts of assets to charities — see 10.5, 10.6 above).

Club membership fees are not gifts for gift aid purposes.
[*FA 2002, s 58(1)(4), Sch 18 para 9*].

11 Children

Cross-reference. See 22.22 EXEMPTIONS AND RELIEFS for Child Trust Funds; 52.7 RESIDENCE AND DOMICILE for domicile of children.

11.1 GENERAL

There is no general bar to the chargeable gains made by an infant (i.e. an individual under 18 years of age) being assessed and charged on him personally (see *R v Newmarket Commissioners (ex p. Huxley) CA 1916, 7 TC 49*). HMRC can, therefore, resort directly to the infant, whether or not there is a guardian etc. to charge. Whether or not, in practice, they will do so will depend on particular circumstances.

A child is entitled to the same capital gains tax reliefs and exemptions as an adult (subject to specific exclusions).

11.2 NOMINEES AND BARE TRUSTEES

Where property is held by a person as nominee, or as trustee for any person who would be absolutely entitled against him but for being an infant, the provisions of *TCGA 1992* apply as if the acts of the nominee or trustee are the acts of the infant. Acquisitions from or to the trustee or nominee to or from the infant are accordingly disregarded. References in *TCGA 1992* to a person being absolutely entitled against the trustee mean that the person has the exclusive right (subject only to satisfying any outstanding charge, lien or other right of the trustee to resort to the relevant property for payment of duty, taxes, costs or other outgoings) to direct how the property shall be dealt with. (Note that before 6 April 2006, the legislation referred to 'assets' rather than 'property'.) [*TCGA 1992, s 60; FA 2006, Sch 12 para 10*]. For the wider implications of nominees and bare trustees generally, see 57.2 SETTLEMENTS.

11.3 ASSESSMENT OF GUARDIANS ETC.

In practice, HMRC often makes use of the machinery of *TMA 1970*, which enables it to charge and assess the tax due from an 'incapacitated person' (this term includes an 'infant': see *TMA 1970, s 118*), on the trustee, guardian, tutor, curator or committee, having the direction, control or management of that person's property. Such machinery applies whether or not the incapacitated person resides in the UK. The person chargeable in this way is answerable for all matters required to be done under the capital gains tax provisions, for the purpose of assessment of that tax, but is given a right of retention and indemnity in respect of tax charges or payments made on the incapacitated person's behalf. [*TMA 1970, ss 72, 77*].

11.4 DEFAULT OF INFANT

Where the person chargeable to tax is an infant, then his parent, guardian, or tutor is liable for the tax in the event of the infant's default. On neglect or refusal of payment, the parent etc. may be proceeded against for sums due to HMRC. [*TMA 1970, ss 73, 77*].

12 Claims

Cross-reference. See 40.3 LOSSES for requirement to notify capital losses.

12.1 For details of the formal procedures applying for 1996/97 and subsequent years of assessment under self-assessment, see 12.2 below.

Claims are personal matters and (except in the case of trustees for persons under disability etc.) can be made only by the person entitled to the relief (cf. *Fulford v Hyslop Ch D 1929, 8 ATC 588*). See 54.3 RETURNS for the signing of claims by an attorney.

From 1998 onwards, HMRC accept certain income tax claims by telephone (see Tolley's Income Tax). At present, this facility does not extend to capital gains tax claims.

For corporation tax claims see 12.4 below.

12.2 CLAIMS AND ELECTIONS UNDER SELF-ASSESSMENT

A formal procedure applies for 1996/97 and subsequent years of assessment as regards the making of claims, elections and notices. A claim for a relief, allowance or tax repayment (other than one to be given effect by a PAYE coding adjustment) must be for an amount quantified at the time of the claim. Where notice has been given by HMRC requiring the delivery of a return (see 54.2, 54.15 RETURNS), a claim etc. (other than one to be given effect by a PAYE coding adjustment) can only be made at any time by inclusion in such a return (or by virtue of an amendment to a return) *unless it could not be so included* either at that time or subsequently (but see below re claims involving two or more years).

In the case of a partnership business, a claim under any of numerous provisions specified in *TMA 1970, s 42(7)* must be made by a partner nominated by the partnership if it cannot be included in a partnership return (or amendment thereto). See 12.3 below for provisions applying where a claim etc. is made otherwise than by inclusion in a return.

Where a claimant discovers that an error or mistake has been made in a claim (whether or not made in a return), he may make a supplementary claim within the time allowed for making the original claim.

[*TMA 1970, s 42; FA 1994, s 196, s 199(2)(3), Sch 19 para 13; FA 1995, s 103(7), s 107; FA 1996, s 128(1), s 130(1)–(4)(7)–(9); FA 2001, s 88, Sch 29 para 26; ITEPA 2003, Sch 6 para 128; ITTOIA 2005, Sch 1 para 372*].

Claims for relief involving two or more years. A claim for a loss incurred or payment made in one year of assessment to be carried back to an earlier year or years need not be made in a return, is treated as a claim for the year of loss or payment (the later year), must be for an amount equal to what would otherwise have been the tax saving for the earlier year, and is given effect *in relation to the later year* by repayment, set-off etc. or by treating the said amount as a tax payment made on account under SELF-ASSESSMENT (56.4). The tax position for the earlier year is not adjusted. [*TMA 1970, Sch 1B para 2; FA 1996, s 128(2)(11), Sch 17*]. See Tolley's Income Tax for more details. The non-reopening of the earlier year's self-assessment does not prevent the making or revising of other claims for that earlier year that are consequential to the carry-back (Revenue Tax Bulletin August 2000 pp 774, 775). In relation to the carry-back claim, repayment supplement may be due as in 36.1 INTEREST ON OVERPAID TAX, though only from 31 January following the *later year* (as above). This applies by law to income tax repayments made on or after 11 May 2001 [*ICTA 1988, s 824; FA 2001, s 90*] but was also applied in practice by the Revenue in relation to earlier repayments and will presumably continue to be so applied in relation to capital gains tax repayments. An example of a capital gains provision affected by these rules is the potential three-year carry-back of capital losses incurred by an individual in the tax year in which he dies — see 18.5 DEATH.

12.3 **Claims etc. not included in returns.** Subject to any specific provision requiring a claim, etc. to be made to the Commissioners for HMRC (or the Board of Inland Revenue), an income tax or capital gains tax claim or election made otherwise than in a return (see 12.2 above) must be made to an officer of Revenue and Customs (or, before 18 April 2005, to an officer of the Board). The claim, etc. must include a declaration by the claimant that all particulars are correctly stated to the best of his information or belief. No claim requiring a tax repayment can be made unless the claimant has documentary proof that the tax has been paid or deducted. The claim must be made in a form determined by HMRC and may require, inter alia, a statement of the amount of tax to be discharged or repaid and supporting information and documentation. In the case of a claim by or on behalf of a person who is not resident (or who claims to be not resident or not ordinarily resident or not domiciled) in the UK, HMRC may require a statement or declaration in support of the claim to be made by affidavit.

A person who may wish to make a claim must keep all such records as may be requisite for the purpose and must preserve them until such time as HMRC may no longer enquire into the claim (see below) or any such enquiry is completed. There is a maximum penalty of £3,000 for non-compliance in relation to any claim actually made. Similar provisions and exceptions apply as in 54.7 RETURNS as to the preservation of copies of documents instead of originals.

Provisions similar to those in 54.6 RETURNS above (amendments of self-assessments) apply to enable a claimant (within twelve months of the claim) or HMRC officer (within nine months of the claim) to amend a claim etc. HMRC has power of enquiry into a claim, etc. (or amendment thereof) similar to that in 54.8 RETURNS (enquiries into returns). Notice of intention to enquire must be given by the first anniversary of 31 January following the year of assessment (or where the claim relates to a period other than a year of assessment, the first anniversary of the end of that period) or, if later, the quarter day (meaning 31 January, 30 April, etc.) next following the first anniversary of the date of claim, etc. In the event of such an enquiry, HMRC has power to call for documents similar to that in 54.10 RETURNS. Where an enquiry is in progress, an HMRC officer may give provisional effect to the claim, etc. (or amendment thereof) to such extent as he thinks fit. Provisions similar to those in 54.11, 54.12 RETURNS apply as regards completion of enquiries and amendments of claims upon completion. HMRC must give effect (by assessment, discharge or repayment) to an amendment arising out of an enquiry within 30 days after the date of issue of the closure notice (for enquiries completed before 11 May 2001 within 30 days after the amendment is made). An appeal may be made against any conclusion stated, or amendment made, by a closure notice by giving written notice to the relevant officer within 30 days after the date of issue of the closure notice (for enquiries completed before 11 May 2001 within 30 days after the amendment is made), extended to three months where certain specified issues concerning residence are involved. If an amendment is varied on appeal, HMRC must give effect to the variation within 30 days.

Where a claim etc. does not give rise to a discharge or repayment of tax, there are provisions for disallowance of the claim on completion of enquiry, with appeal procedures similar to those above.

Appeals as above are normally made to the General Commissioners. Where the claim was made to the Commissioners for HMRC (or the Board of Inland Revenue) or under certain specified provisions, appeal is to the Special Commissioners, and in other cases, there are rules, similar to those in 4.5 APPEALS, enabling the taxpayer to elect to bring the appeal before the Special Commissioners. If the taxpayer also has an appeal pending concerning an assessment and the appeals relate to the same income, both appeals must be to the same body of Commissioners.

[*TMA 1970, s 42(11), Sch 1A; FA 1994, s 196, s 199(2)(3), Sch 19 paras 13, 35; FA 1995, s 103(7), s 107(10)(11), Sch 20; FA 1996, s 124(4), s 130(5), Sch 19 paras 8–10, Sch 22 para 9; FA 1998, s 117, Sch 19 paras 20, 42; FA 2001, s 88, Sch 29 paras 10, 12, 34; ITEPA 2003, Sch 6 para 141; ITTOIA 2005, Sch 1 para 381; CRCA 2005, ss 5, 7*].

12.4 CORPORATION TAX CLAIMS

Under corporation tax self-assessment (for accounting periods ending on or after 1 July 1999 — see 13.2 COMPANIES), provisions having broadly similar effect as those in 12.2 above (other than those of *TMA 1970, Sch 1B*) apply to companies. Subject to any express provision to the contrary, claims and elections made after notice has been given requiring the delivery of a company tax return must be made in the return, or by amendment of the return, if they can be so made (see 54.18 RETURNS) and must be quantified. A claim etc. made by a company which could have been made by amending the return is treated for this purpose as an amendment of the return. Otherwise, *TMA 1970, Sch 1A* (see 12.3 above) provides the procedure for claims etc. A supplementary claim (where there was an error or mistake in the original claim) may be made within the time limit for the original claim. A group relief or capital allowances claim *must* be made in a return or by amendment of a return. [*FA 1998, Sch 18 paras 9, 10, 54, 56-60*].

12.5 TIME LIMITS FOR CLAIMS

See 62 TIME LIMITS—FIXED DATES and 63 TIME LIMITS—MISCELLANEOUS for check-lists of claims and elections.

The following general time limits apply where no specific time limit is prescribed. A claim **for 1996/97 or a subsequent year** must be made within **five years after 31 January** following the year of assessment to which it relates. For corporation tax purposes, the general time limit is **six years** after the end of the accounting period to which the claim relates. [*TMA 1970, s 43(1); FA 1998, s 117, Sch 18 para 55, Sch 19 para 21*].

By concession, where an overpayment of tax arises because of an error by HMRC or another Government department and where there is no dispute as to the facts, claims to repayment of the tax overpaid made outside of the statutory period will be allowed (HMRC Extra-Statutory Concession B41).

A claim (including a supplementary claim) which could not have been allowed but for the making of an assessment to capital gains tax after the year of assessment to which it relates, may be made at any time before the end of the year of assessment following that in which the assessment was made. [*TMA 1970, s 43(2)*].

If an assessment makes good loss of tax arising from fraudulent or negligent conduct (see 23.3 FRAUDULENT OR NEGLIGENT CONDUCT), the person assessed can require effect to be given to reliefs or allowances to which he would have been entitled had he made the necessary claims within the relevant time limits. [*TMA 1970, s 36(3); FA 1989, s 149; FA 1998, s 117, Sch 18 para 65*].

Where HMRC issue an amendment to a return as part of an enquiry closure notice (see 54.11 RETURNS) after 10 July 2003, the above extended time limits apply in relation to the amendment as they apply in relation to assessments. [*TMA 1970, s 43C(1)–(3); FA 2003, s 207(1)(3)*].

Discovery etc. In the case of a 'discovery' assessment (see 5.2 ASSESSMENTS), which is *not* for making good loss of tax attributable to fraudulent or negligent conduct,

(*a*) any 'relevant' claim, election, application or notice which could have been made or given within the normal time limits of the *Taxes Acts* may be made or given within a year of the end of the chargeable period in which the assessment is made, and

(*b*) any 'relevant' claim, etc. previously made or given, except an irrevocable one, can, with the consent of the person(s) by whom it was made or given (or their personal representatives), be revoked or varied in the manner in which it was made or given.

A claim, etc. is *'relevant'* to an assessment for a chargeable period if

(i) it relates to, or to an event occurring in, the chargeable period, and

(ii) it, or its revocation or variation, reduces, or could reduce,

(A) the increased tax liability resulting from the assessment, or

(B) any other liability of the person for that chargeable period or a later one ending not more than one year after the period in which the assessment is made.

These extended time limits cannot be used for the purpose of making an election for universal re-basing under *TCGA 1992, s 35(5)* (see 8.3 ASSETS HELD ON 31 MARCH 1982) after 10 July 2003.

The normal APPEALS (4) provisions apply, with any necessary modifications.

If the making, etc. of a claim, etc. would alter another person's tax liability, the consent of that person (or his personal representatives) is needed. If such alteration is an increase, the other person cannot make, etc. a claim, etc. under the foregoing provisions.

If the reduction in tax liability resulting from one or more claims etc. would exceed the additional tax assessed, relief is not available for the excess. If the reduction involves more than one period, or more than one person, the inspector will specify by notice in writing how it is to be apportioned; but within 30 days of the notice being given, or the last notice being given if there is more than one person, the person (or persons jointly) can specify the apportionment by notice in writing to the inspector. [*TMA 1970, ss 43A, 43B; FA 1989, s 150; FA 1993, Sch 14 para 2; FA 1998, s 117, Sch 19 para 22; FA 2003, s 207(2)*].

Where HMRC issue an amendment to a return as part of an enquiry closure notice (see 54.11 RETURNS) after 10 July 2003, these provisions apply in relation to the amendment as they apply in relation to assessments. [*TMA 1970, s 43C(2)(3); FA 2003, s 207(1)(3)*].

The provisions broadly apply to companies under corporation tax self-assessment. [*FA 1998, s 117, Sch 18 paras 61–64*].

Extended time limits for assessment. Where it is necessary to make an assessment after 10 July 2003 on any person to give effect to, or as a result of allowing, a claim, supplementary claim, election, application or notice given or made under the extended time limits of *TMA 1970, ss 36(3)*, *43(3)*, *43A* or *43C* above, the assessment is not out of time if made within one year of the final determination of the claim etc. For this purpose a claim etc. is finally determined when it can no longer be varied, on appeal or otherwise. [*TMA 1970, s 43C(4)(5); FA 2003, s 207(1)*].

12.6 APPEALS IN RESPECT OF CLAIMS

As regards 1996/97 and later years of assessment see 12.3 above and 4.1 APPEALS. As regards company accounting periods ending on or after 1 July 1999, see 12.3 above (applied for corporation tax purposes by *FA 1998, Sch 18 paras 57–59*) and 4.2 APPEALS.

12.7 ERROR OR MISTAKE RELIEF

Relief may be claimed in writing against any over-assessment (including a self-assessment) due to an error or mistake (including an omission) in any return. The time limit for claiming error or mistake relief, in the case of an income tax or capital gains tax assessment, is five years after 31 January following the year of assessment to which the return in question relates, and, in the case of an assessment to corporation tax, six years after the end of the accounting period to which the return relates. The relief is given because the return was wrong and hence does not apply where the assessment is not on the basis of the return. No relief is allowed if the return was made on the basis or in accordance with the practice generally prevailing at the time or in respect of an error or mistake in a claim which is included in the return (but see 12.2 above as regards supplementary claims). Otherwise, HMRC will give such relief as is reasonable and just, having regard to all the relevant circumstances.

The relief is determined by the Commissioners for HMRC (or, before 18 April 2005, by the Board of Inland Revenue) with appeal from them to the Special Commissioners and from them, but only on a point of law *arising in connection with the computation of profits*, to the High Court. (See *Rose Smith & Co Ltd v CIR KB 1933, 17 TC 586*; *Carrimore Six Wheelers Ltd v CIR CA 1944, 26 TC 301*; *R v Special Commrs (ex p. Carrimore Six Wheelers Ltd) CA 1947, 28 TC 422*; *Arranmore Investment Co Ltd v CIR CA (NI) 1973, 48 TC 623*; *Eagerpath Ltd v Edwards CA 2000, 73 TC 427*.)

[*TMA 1970, s 33; FA 1994, s 196, s 199(2)(3), Sch 19 para 8, Sch 26 Pt V; FA 1998, s 117, Sch 18 para 51, Sch 19 para 15; CRCA 2005, s 5*].

The fact that a taxpayer has agreed an amendment to his self-assessment following an HMRC enquiry does not preclude his subsequently making a claim for error or mistake relief (*Wall v CIR (Sp C 303), [2002] SSCD 122*). Where, however, the subject matter is covered in an agreement under *TMA 1970, s 54* (see 4.7 APPEALS), an error or mistake relief claim is precluded (*Thompson v CIR (Sp C 458), 2005 STI 222*).

Error or mistake relief cannot be used to rectify a failure to claim a particular tax relief within a stipulated time limit where that claim could have been made outside a return (*Howard v CIR (Sp C 329), [2002] SSCD 408*).

Error or mistake in partnership return. Error or mistake relief is extended to cover an error or mistake in a partnership return (see 54.15 RETURNS) by reason of which the partners allege that their self-assessments were excessive. The claim to relief must be made by one of the partners within five years after the filing date for the return. Where the claim results in an amendment to the partnership return, HMRC will, by notice, make any necessary amendments to the tax returns of all persons who were partners at any time in the period covered by the partnership return. Otherwise, provisions similar to those above apply, with appropriate modifications. [*TMA 1970, s 33A; FA 1994, s 196, s 199(2)(3), Sch 19 para 9; FA 1996, Sch 22 para 5; FA 1998, s 117, Sch 19 para 16; FA 2001, s 88, Sch 29 para 25*].

See 54.3 RETURNS for the use of error or mistake relief claims in amending provisional figures in a self-assessment.

For relief for double assessment, see 5.5 ASSESSMENTS.

12.8 CLAIM FOR RESTITUTION OF PAYMENT MADE UNDER MISTAKE OF LAW

It was confirmed in *R v CIR (ex p. Woolwich Equitable Building Society), HL 1990, 63 TC 589* that a claim can be made through the courts, under common law, for restitution of tax payments made to the Revenue under an unlawful statutory demand and that interest is payable from the dates of the payments. In *Deutsche Morgan Grenfell Group plc v CIR CA, [2005] STC 329* the company sought to obtain this remedy in respect of tax paid under a mistake of law. In making its claim the company contended that under *Limitation Act 1980, s 32(1)(c)* it could make the claim for restitution within six years of the time it discovered the mistake (or could with reasonable diligence have discovered it), rather than within the normal time limit of six years from the time of payment under *Limitation Act 1980, s 5*. It argued that the date of such discovery was 8 March 2001, the date of the decision in *Metalgesellschaft Ltd & Others v CIR CJEC 2001; [2001] STC 452*. The Court of Appeal held that the company was entitled to a 'restitutionary remedy' under the principles laid down in *Woolwich*, but that this was subject to the six-year limitation period of *Limitation Act 1980, s 5*. The extended period of limitation available under *Limitation Act 1980, s 32(1)(c)* was only applicable to 'private law' transactions, and was not applicable to claims for the repayment of tax.

Following the High Court decision in this case (which found in the taxpayer's favour), provisions were included in *FA 2004* to prevent the application of the extended time limit of *Limitation Act 1980, s 32(1)(c)* to taxation matters. Accordingly, *section 32(1)(c)* (and the NI equivalent) does not apply in relation to any action or claim for relief from the consequences of a mistake of law relating to a taxation matter under the care and management of HMRC brought after 7 September 2003, whether the action or claim is expressed to be brought on the grounds of mistake or on some other ground (such as unlawful demand or *ultra vires*). [*FA 2004, s 320(1)(6)*]. The effect of this provision is that court actions for restitution based on mistake of law must generally be brought within six years of the tax having been paid. *FA 2004, s 321* makes a similar change to Scottish law, so that claims for relief for tax paid under an error of law must generally be made within five years of the tax having been paid.

FA 2004, s 320 also includes provisions to prevent a claim to amend an existing action, seeking to introduce claims for a different payment, transaction, period or other matter, from being treated by the courts under *Limitation Act 1980, s 35* as being a separate action commenced on the same date as the original action (and thereby in some cases potentially circumventing the above provisions). This applies to amendment claims made after 19 November 2003, and for this purpose, such a claim is treated as made before 20 November 2003 if the Revenue consented to the making of it in writing before that date or if, immediately before that date, the Revenue's consent had been sought and not refused or an application to the court for permission to make the claim had been made and not refused. [*FA 2004, s 320(2)(5)*].

The above provisions take legal effect only on 22 July 2004 (the date of Royal Assent to *FA 2004*). *FA 2004, s 320(3)* therefore deems an action begun before that date but after 7 September 2003, or a claim to amend an existing action made before 22 July 2004 but after 19 November 2003 to be discontinued on 22 July 2004 and provides for the recovery (with interest) of any amount paid out by the Revenue in relation to such an action or amendment.

13 Companies

Cross-references. See 14 COMPANIES—CORPORATE FINANCE AND INTANGIBLES; 27 GROUPS OF COMPANIES; 52.6 RESIDENCE AND DOMICILE for company residence; 58 SHARES AND SECURITIES; 59.7 SHARES AND SECURITIES—IDENTIFICATION RULES for parallel pooling provisions before 1 April 1985; 60 SUBSTANTIAL SHAREHOLDINGS OF COMPANIES; 65 UNIT TRUSTS ETC.; 66 VENTURE CAPITAL TRUSTS.

Simon's Direct Tax Service. See Division D2.3.

The headings in this chapter are as follows.

13.1 LIABILITY OF COMPANIES TO CORPORATION TAX ON THEIR CHARGEABLE GAINS

Companies resident in the UK (and non-resident companies in respect of UK permanent establishment (previously branch or agency) assets, see 45.3 OVERSEAS MATTERS) are liable to corporation tax on their chargeable gains. These gains are included in their profits liable to corporation tax as described in 13.3 below. [*ICTA 1988, s 6, s 11(2)(2A); TCGA 1992, ss 10(3), 10B; FA 2003, s 149(1)(4); ITTOIA 2005, Sch 1 para 6*].

Companies accordingly do not pay 'capital gains tax' as such, but their chargeable gains less allowable losses are computed in accordance with provisions relating to capital gains tax, except that

(i) computations are made by reference to accounting periods instead of years of assessment [*TCGA 1992, s 8(3)*],

(ii) provisions in the legislation confined to individuals do not apply to companies [*TCGA 1992, s 8(4)(5)*],

(iii) the indexation allowance and share identification rules apply (subject to transitional provisions) to disposals after 31 March 1982 and again after 31 March 1985 instead of 5 April 1982 and 5 April 1985 respectively,

(iv) an alternative method was available of identifying particular shares and securities which were disposed of after 31 March 1982 and before 1 April 1985 ('parallel pooling'; see 59.7 SHARES AND SECURITIES—IDENTIFICATION RULES),

(v) for disposals by companies after 14 March 1988 and before 30 November 1993, indexation allowance was restricted or excluded in certain cases involving a debt on a security owed by, or shares in, a 'linked company' (see Tolley's Corporation Tax under Capital Gains),

(vi) special provisions apply to tax as income gains and losses in respect of loan relationships, derivative contracts, financial instruments and foreign exchange (see 14 COMPANIES—CORPORATE FINANCE AND INTANGIBLES),

(vii) TAPER RELIEF (61) applies to disposals after 5 April 1998 by individuals, trustees etc., but not by companies; but indexation allowance is not frozen at its April 1998 level for companies as it is for individuals etc. (see 34.1 INDEXATION),

(viii) as regards acquisitions after 5 April 1998, the rules for matching shares and securities sold with those acquired are not the same for corporation tax as for capital gains tax (see 59.1 SHARES AND SECURITIES—IDENTIFICATION RULES),

(ix) gains and losses on intangible fixed assets created or acquired by a company after 31 March 2002 are taxed as income within the intangible fixed assets regime (see 14.13 COMPANIES—CORPORATE FINANCE AND INTANGIBLES) and are outside the scope of corporation tax on chargeable gains, and

(x) certain provisions, as contained in this chapter, apply only to companies.

See Tolley's Corporation Tax under Friendly Societies and Life Insurance Companies for provisions of *TCGA 1992* (and related provisions) which are integral with the corporation tax regime applicable to life assurance business carried on by such entities.

See also 5 ASSESSMENTS; 36 INTEREST ON OVERPAID TAX; 37 INTEREST AND SURCHARGES ON UNPAID TAX; 47 PAYMENT OF TAX; 48 PENALTIES; and 54 RETURNS for matters applicable to companies generally.

The definition of 'company' includes any body corporate or unincorporated association but does not include a partnership. [*TCGA 1992, s 288(1)*]. References to 'persons' in the capital gains tax legislation generally include unincorporated associations (*CIR v Worthing Rugby Football Club Trustees CA 1987, 60 TC 482*).

Regulations (*SI 1998 No 3177*) have been made to modify the application of the Taxes Acts on the introduction of the European single currency in certain countries other than the UK on 1 January 1999. The regulations are meant to prevent unintended tax consequences arising as a result of the conversion of the currencies of participating EU member states into euros. Broadly, they provide for continuity of treatment for assets, contracts, financial instruments etc. redenominated in euros, and grant tax relief, by means of a deduction from profits, for the costs of converting a company's shares or other securities into euros. (Revenue Press Release 17 December 1998). See 6.1 ASSETS, 22.5 EXEMPTIONS AND RELIEFS and 58.7 SHARES AND SECURITIES for specific CGT measures included.

13.2 CORPORATION TAX SELF-ASSESSMENT

For company accounting periods ending on or after 1 July 1999, a SELF-ASSESSMENT (56) regime applies for corporation tax purposes. Corporation tax self-assessment is covered in this work where appropriate and in detail in Tolley's Corporation Tax.

13.3 RATE OF CORPORATION TAX IN RESPECT OF CHARGEABLE GAINS

The whole of the chargeable gains (net of allowable losses under 13.4 below) of a company is included in the profits chargeable to corporation tax. The rate of corporation tax applicable will be dependent upon, inter alia, the residence position of the company, its status, the number of associated companies and the level of the chargeable profits and certain franked investment income but the rate so determined applies to both income and chargeable gains included in the chargeable profits. If the company's accounting period straddles different financial years, chargeable profits are apportioned on a time basis between the years. [*ICTA 1988 s 8(3); TCGA 1992, s 8(1)*]. For the level and applicability of the various rates of corporation tax, see Tolley's Corporation Tax.

Alternative rules apply as in 65 UNIT TRUSTS ETC. and 66 VENTURE CAPITAL TRUSTS.

13.4 CAPITAL LOSSES

The amount of chargeable gains to be taken into account for an accounting period is the amount of the chargeable gains accruing to the company in that period less the aggregate amount of the allowable losses in that period and allowable losses brought forward from any previous period. Allowable losses include short-term losses accruing under Schedule D, Case VII for years before 1971/72 which remain unrelieved. [*TCGA 1992, s 8(1), Sch 11 para 12*].

For corporation tax on chargeable gains purposes an allowable loss does not include:

(*a*) any loss which, if it had been a gain, would have been exempt from corporation tax in the hands of the company; or

(*b*) any loss accruing on a disposal on or after 5 December 2005 directly or indirectly in consequence of, or otherwise in connection with, any 'arrangements' the main purpose of which, or one of the main purposes of which, is to secure a 'tax advantage'.

For the purposes of (*b*) above, it does not matter whether the loss accrues at a time when there are no chargeable gains against which it could be set or whether the tax advantage would be secured for the company incurring the loss or another company. '*Arrangements*' include any agreement, understanding, scheme, transaction or series of transactions, whether or not legally enforceable. '*Tax advantage*' means relief or increased relief from, or repayment or increased repayment of, corporation tax or the avoidance or reduction of a charge or assessment to corporation tax or the avoidance of a possible assessment to corporation tax.

[*TCGA 1992, ss 8(2), 184D; FA 2006, ss 69, 70(2)*].

HMRC consider that interdependence of transactions or of the terms on which transactions take place is a strong indicator (although not a necessary condition) of the existence of an arrangement. In their view, if, on the facts, any participant in arrangements is found to have a main purpose of achieving a tax advantage, that is sufficient to demonstrate that one of the main purposes of the arrangements is the securing of a tax advantage. HMRC is likely to examine carefully any relevant case in which a normal commercial objective is lacking, or where commercial objectives are not being sought in a genuine and straightforward manner. Where there is more than one way of achieving a commercial objective and a course of action is chosen on commercial grounds, any incidental tax advantage is not relevant. However, where the tax advantage was material to the choice the anti-avoidance legislation may be in point, but HMRC have indicated that this is unlikely to be the case unless there is evidence of additional, complex or costly steps included solely for tax reasons. (HMRC Guidance 'Avoidance through the creation and use of capital losses by companies', 22 March 2006).

Allowable losses for the purposes of corporation tax on chargeable gains cannot normally be offset against trading profits or other income but see 40.15 LOSSES. Since chargeable gains are included in profits chargeable to corporation tax as in 13.1 above, claims under *ICTA 1988, s 393A* to set trading losses against such profits mean that trading losses can be set against chargeable gains arising in the same accounting period and, to the extent permitted by that *section*, preceding accounting periods. See Tolley's Corporation Tax under Losses for the detailed provisions.

Management expenses of a company with investment business (before 1 April 2004, an investment company) may be offset against chargeable gains within the same or succeeding accounting periods. [*ICTA 1988, s 75(1)(3)(8)(9); FA 2004, ss 38(1), 42(1), 43*].

There are a number of anti-avoidance provisions relating specifically to corporate capital losses. In particular, *FA 2006* introduced three targeted provisions attacking arrangements entered into which have as a main purpose the obtaining of a tax advantage. For details of the provisions, see (*b*) above, 13.5–13.7 below (avoidance utilising losses) and 27.18, 27.19 GROUPS OF COMPANIES (gain buying and loss buying).

See also 27.20 GROUPS OF COMPANIES for the restriction, where the provisions at 27.18, 27.19 GROUPS OF COMPANIES do not apply, on set-off of pre-entry losses where a company joins a group, and see 27.31 GROUPS OF COMPANIES for the restriction (now repealed) on set-off of losses against pre-entry gains where a company joins a group.

13.5 **AVOIDANCE UTILISING LOSSES**

As part of a general initiative countering various avoidance schemes (see 13.4 above) provisions were introduced by *FA 2006* to ensure that capital losses cannot be used against income profits. HMRC have indicated that the provisions are intended to affect only companies that deliberately and knowingly enter into arrangements to avoid tax (HMRC Guidance 'Avoidance through the creation and use of capital losses by companies', 22 March 2006). The provisions apply to disposals on or after 5 December 2005. [*FA 2006, s 71*(*4*)].

Two strategies to utilise capital losses are targeted by the provisions. The first is to turn an income receipt into capital (see 13.6 below). The second is to generate a deduction from income as part of arrangements to crystallise a capital gain (see 13.7 below). The effect is to restrict the use of capital losses. In both cases, the provisions apply only where HMRC issue a notice to the company concerned (see below).

Both sets of provisions require that there be 'arrangements' the main purpose, or one of the main purposes, of which is to secure a 'tax advantage' (although each contains a qualification of the definition of tax advantage given below — see 13.6 and 13.7 below). [*TCGA 1992, s 184G*(*2*)(*5*), *184H*(*2*)(*4*); *FA 2006, s 71*(*1*)].

'*Arrangements*' for this purpose include any agreement, understanding, scheme, transaction or series of transactions, whether or not legally enforceable. A '*tax advantage*' means obtaining or increasing relief from, or repayment of, corporation tax, the avoidance or reduction of a corporation tax charge or assessment or the avoidance of a possible assessment to corporation tax. [*TCGA 1992, s 184D, 184G*(*10*), *184H*(*10*); *FA 2006, ss 70*(*2*), *71*(*1*)].

For HMRC's view on the application of the terms 'arrangements', 'tax advantage' and 'main purpose', see 13.4 above and HMRC Guidance 'Avoidance through the creation and use of capital losses by companies', 22 March 2006, available on their website (www.hmrc.gov.uk).

HMRC notices. As noted above, the application of the provisions is contingent upon the issue of a notice to the company by HMRC. Such a notice may be issued if HMRC have reasonable grounds for considering that the statutory conditions triggering the legislation are present. It must specify the arrangements in question, the accounting period (or periods) involved and the effect of the anti-avoidance provisions.

If the company has not yet made a return for the accounting period it may, if it makes a return within the 90-day period beginning with the day on which the notice is given, make the return disregarding the notice and make any necessary amendment later within the same 90-day period.

If the company has already made a return for the accounting period, HMRC may only issue a notice if a notice of enquiry (see 54.18 RETURNS) has been given in respect of that return. The company may amend its return in light of the notice at any time within the 90-day period beginning with the day on which the notice is given. A closure notice in respect of the enquiry may not be issued before the earlier of the company amending its return or the end of the 90-day period.

If enquiries into the return have been completed the power enjoyed by HMRC to issue a notice is subject to two requirements, both of which must be met. The first is that at the time enquiries were completed HMRC could not, on the basis of information made available to them (within *FA 1998, Sch 18 para 44*(*2*)(*3*) — see 5.2 ASSESSMENTS) before that time, reasonably have been aware of circumstances indicating that a notice could have been issued. The second is that a request for information was made during the enquiry which, if duly complied with, would have resulted in a reasonable expectation that HMRC would issue a notice. If a notice is issued in these circumstances no discovery assessment may be made before the earlier of the company amending its return or the end of the 90-day period beginning with the day on which the notice is given. However, the normal restrictions on making discovery assessments in *FA 1998, Sch 18 paras 43, 44* do not apply (see 5.2 ASSESSMENTS).

On receiving a notice containing HMRC's view of the position, it is up to the company to decide if it needs to amend its self-assessment. If it fails to make an amendment which ought to have been made its return will be incorrect (with all the resulting implications for penalties, etc.).

[*TCGA 1992, ss 184G(6)(8)(9), 184H(6)(8)(9), 184I; FA 2006, s 71(1)*].

Clearances. HMRC operate an informal clearance procedure and will give advice on actual or proposed transactions. Applications for clearance procedure should be sent to HM Revenue & Customs, Clearance & Counteraction Team, Anti Avoidance Group Intelligence, First floor, 22 Kingsway, London WC2B 6NR. HMRC will aim to give a response within 30 days of receipt of a clearance application. A clearance will state the terms on which it has been given and HMRC will regard itself bound by a clearance provided that all relevant facts are accurately given and (where the clearance is sought in advance) the transaction is executed in accordance with the proposals set out in the clearance application. Where a clearance cannot be given HMRC will state the reasons, but taxpayers are not bound by their decision. For details of the information required by HMRC in clearance applications, see HMRC Guidance 'Avoidance through the creation and use of capital losses by companies', 22 March 2006, available on their website (www.hmrc.gov.uk).

13.6 **Schemes converting income into capital.** HMRC may issue a notice (see 13.5 above) invoking anti-avoidance measures where it has reasonable grounds for considering that the following four conditions are, or may be, satisfied:

- any receipt arises to a company (the '*relevant company*') on the disposal of an asset and that receipt arises directly or indirectly in consequence of, or otherwise in connection with, any arrangements (see 13.5 above);
- a chargeable gain (the '*relevant gain*') accrues to the relevant company on the disposal and that company has allowable losses available;
- but for the arrangements an amount would have been taken into account wholly or partly instead of the capital receipt as income of the relevant company (or as the income of a company in the same capital gains tax group (see 27.1 GROUPS OF COMPANIES) at any time in the period beginning with the time at which the arrangements were made and ending when the matters, other than the tax advantage, intended to be secured by the arrangements are secured); and
- the main purpose, or one of the main purposes, of the arrangements was the obtaining of a tax advantage (see 13.5 above) involving the deduction of the capital losses from the relevant gain.

If all these conditions are satisfied when the HMRC notice is given, the relevant company may not deduct any loss from the relevant gain.

[*TCGA 1992, s 184G(1)–(5)(7)(10); FA 2006, s 71(1)*].

13.7 **Schemes securing deductions.** HMRC may issue a notice (see 13.5 above) invoking anti-avoidance measures where it has reasonable grounds for considering that the following four conditions are, or may be, satisfied:

- a chargeable gain (the '*relevant gain*') accrues to a company (the '*relevant company*') directly or indirectly in consequence of, or otherwise in connection with, any arrangements (see 13.5 above) and that company has capital losses available;

- the relevant company, or a company connected with it, incurs expenditure in connection with the arrangements which is deductible in calculating total profits but not in calculating chargeable gains;
- the main purpose, or one of the main purposes, of the arrangements was the obtaining of a tax advantage (see 13.5 above) involving both the deduction of the expenditure in calculating total profits and the deduction of losses from the relevant gain; and
- the arrangements are not 'excluded arrangements' (see below).

It does not matter whether the tax advantage is secured for the relevant company or any other company.

'*Excluded arrangements*' are certain arm's length sale and leaseback transactions involving land where there is no connection between the lessor and the lessee.

If all the above conditions are satisfied when the HMRC notice is given, the relevant company may not deduct any loss from the relevant gain.

[*TCGA 1992, s 184H(1)–(5)(7)(10)(11); FA 2006, s 71(1)*].

13.8 LIQUIDATION

The vesting of a company's assets in a liquidator is disregarded. All the acts of the liquidator in relation to such assets are treated as acts of the company. [*TCGA 1992, s 8(6)*].

All expenses properly incurred in a voluntary winding-up, including the remuneration of the liquidator, are payable out of the company's assets in priority to all other claims. [*Insolvency Act 1986, s 115*]. *Insolvency Rules 1986, Rule 4.218(1)* provides that expenses of a liquidation are to be paid out of the assets in the order of priority therein specified, subject to a discretionary power of the court under *Insolvency Act 1986, s 156* to vary the order where assets are insufficient to satisfy liabilities. [*SI 1986 No 1925, Rule 4.218(1), Rule 4.220*]. Included in the normal order of priority is the amount of any corporation tax on chargeable gains accruing on the realisation of any asset of the company (*Rule 4.218(1)(p)*).

Notwithstanding the specific inclusion of corporation tax on chargeable gains, corporation tax chargeable on a company's post-liquidation profits is to be treated as a 'necessary disbursement' of the liquidator (within *Insolvency Rules 1986, Rule 4.218(1)(m)*), and thus as an expense requiring priority as above (*Re Toshoku Finance UK plc; Kahn and another v CIR HL, [2002] STC 368*).

See also 58.10, 58.11 and 58.12 SHARES AND SECURITIES.

13.9 RECOVERY FROM SHAREHOLDERS

Where a person connected with a UK resident company (see 16 CONNECTED PERSONS) receives, or becomes entitled to receive, in respect of shares in that company, a capital distribution within *TCGA 1992, s 122* (see 58.10 SHARES AND SECURITIES) which is not a reduction of capital but which constitutes, or is derived from, a disposal of assets from which a chargeable gain accrues to the company, and the company does not pay, within six months after the later of the due date and the date the assessment was made, the corporation tax due for the accounting period in which the gain accrued, the recipient of the distribution may be required to pay so much of that corporation tax as relates to chargeable gains but not exceeding the lesser of

(i) part of that tax, at the rate in force when the gain accrued, proportionate to his share of the total distribution made by the company, and

(ii) the value of the distribution he received or became entitled to receive.

The recipient then has a right of recovery against the company, which extends to any interest on unpaid tax which he has paid on the outstanding tax. The assessment on the recipient must be made within two years after the later of the date the tax became due and payable by the company and the date the assessment was made on the company. These provisions do not affect any liability of the recipient in respect of any chargeable gain accruing to him as a result of the capital distribution. [*TCGA 1992, s 189*].

For coverage of *ICTA 1988, ss 767A–767C*, which broadly allow HMRC to recover any corporation tax unpaid by a company from persons controlling the company in certain circumstances where there has been a change of ownership of the company, see Tolley's Corporation Tax under Payment of Tax.

13.10 RECONSTRUCTIONS INVOLVING TRANSFER OF BUSINESS

See also 58.4 and 58.6 SHARES AND SECURITIES and 13.16 below.

Subject to the following, where a 'scheme of reconstruction' involves the transfer of a company's business to another company for no consideration (other than the assumption of liabilities of the business), capital assets (not used as trading stock by either company) are regarded as being transferred at a 'no gain/no loss' disposal value and the acquiring company takes over the disposing company's acquisition date for the purposes of ASSETS HELD ON 6 APRIL 1965 (7). In relation to shares or debentures issued after 16 April 2002, '*scheme of reconstruction*' is as defined by *TCGA 1992, s 136, Sch 5AA* (see 58.6 SHARES AND SECURITIES). For practical illustrations of schemes of reconstruction, see HMRC Capital Gains Manual CG 52720–52729. In relation to shares or debentures issued on or before that date, the legislation referred instead to a '*scheme of reconstruction or amalgamation*', which was defined as 'a scheme for the reconstruction of any company or companies or the amalgamation of any two or more companies'. For further detail, see HMRC Capital Gains Manual CG 52730–52733.

For disposals before 1 April 2000, the above is conditional on both companies being UK-resident at the time of transfer. For disposals on or after that date, the conditions are:

- that *either* the transferee company is UK-resident at time of acquisition *or* the assets are 'chargeable assets' in relation to that company immediately after that time; *and*
- that *either* the transferor company is UK-resident at that time *or* the assets are 'chargeable assets' in relation to that company immediately before that time.

For these purposes, an asset is a '*chargeable asset*' in relation to a company at a particular time if, on a disposal by that company at that time, any gain would be a chargeable gain and would be within the charge to corporation tax by virtue of *TCGA 1992, s 10* or *s 10B* (non-UK resident company trading in the UK through a permanent establishment (previously a branch or agency) — see 45.3 OVERSEAS MATTERS).

[*TCGA 1992, s 139(1)(1A)(2)(9); FA 2000, Sch 29 para 5; FA 2002, Sch 9 paras 5(7), 7, Sch 40 Pt 3(2); FA 2003, Sch 27 para 2*].

Under the law as it stood for shares or debentures issued on or before 16 April 2002, the second company should, strictly speaking, carry on substantially the same business and have substantially the same members as the first, but in practice the identity of shareholdings is not insisted upon where the scheme is for bona fide commercial reasons or where there is segregation of trades or businesses into identifiable parts which are capable of being carried on in their own right. (HMRC Statement of Practice 5/85). For shares or debentures issued after 16 April 2002, a revised statutory definition of 'scheme of reconstruction' (referred to above and covered at 58.6 SHARES AND SECURITIES) was introduced, partly to incorporate the aforementioned practice, which consequently no longer applies. Under the old definition, *TCGA 1992, s 139* could be used on its own to transfer a business (see the example at HMRC Capital Gains Manual CG 52833). This is no longer possible under the revised definition; there must be a scheme of reconstruction that meets the conditions of *TCGA 1992, Sch 5AA* and includes an issue of shares under *TCGA 1992, s 136*.

Anti-avoidance, disapplication of relief and advance clearance. *TCGA 1992, s 139* will not apply to any transfer unless the scheme is for bona fide commercial reasons and not to avoid corporation tax, capital gains tax or income tax, or HMRC, on written application by the acquiring company, has notified its satisfaction with the scheme before the transfer is made. HMRC may, within 30 days of receipt, call for further particulars to be supplied within 30 days, or longer if HMRC allows; if the information is not supplied, the application lapses. Subject to this, HMRC must notify its decision within a further 30 days. If not so notified, or if dissatisfied with the decision, the applicant may within a further 30 days require HMRC to refer the application to the Special Commissioners for their decision. All material facts and considerations must be disclosed, otherwise any decision is void. [*TCGA 1992, s 138(2)–(5), s 139(5); FA 2002, Sch 40 Pt 3(2)*].

Applications for clearance should be directed to the Clearance and Counteraction Team, Anti-Avoidance Group Intelligence, First Floor, 22 Kingsway, London, WC2B 6NR for the attention of Mohini Sawhney (or, if market-sensitive information is included, Eric Gardner). Applications may be faxed to 020–7438 4409 or emailed to reconstructions@gtnet.gov.uk (in both cases after telephoning Eric Gardner (on 020–7438 6585) if market-sensitive information is included). A hard copy need not then be sent. From 1 November 2002, only a single application need be made as above for clearances under any one or more of: *ICTA 1988, s 215* (demergers), *ICTA 1988, s 225* (purchase of own shares), *ICTA 1988, s 707* (transactions in securities), *TCGA 1992, s 138(1)* (share exchanges — see 3.18 ANTI-AVOIDANCE), *TCGA 1992, s 139(5)* (as above), *TCGA 1992, s 140B* (transfer of a UK trade between EU member states — 45.10 OVERSEAS MATTERS), *TCGA 1992, s 140D* (transfer of a non-UK trade between EU member states — 45.11 OVERSEAS MATTERS) and *FA 2002, Sch 29 para 88* (various clearances under the corporation tax intangible assets regime). (Before 1 November 2002, applications under *section 139(5)* were sent to Capital and Savings division at Solihull.) (Revenue Internet Statement 23 October 2002).

Where, if the disposing company had not been wound up, tax could have been assessed on it because of the effect of *TCGA 1992, s 139(5)* above, that tax can be assessed and charged (in the name of the disposing company) on the acquiring company. Subject to this, tax assessed on either company which is unpaid six months after the date when it is payable, may be similarly assessed and charged on certain third parties. The third parties are restricted to any person holding all or any part of the assets in respect of which the tax is charged and who either is the acquiring company or subsequently acquired them as a result of one or more disposals within *TCGA 1992, s 139* or *s 171(1)* (companies within same group) without any intervening disposals not within those provisions. Tax assessed on the third party is restricted to the proportion held of the assets in respect of which the tax was originally charged and may be recovered from the company originally assessed, along with any interest which the third party has paid on the outstanding tax. The assessment on the third party must be made within two years after the later of the date the tax became due and payable by the company and the date the assessment was made on the company. [*TCGA 1992, s 139(6)–(8); SI 1992 No 3066*].

The provisions of *TCGA 1992, s 139* do not apply in the case of a transfer of the whole or part of a company's business to a unit trust scheme (including an umbrella scheme), within *TCGA 1992, s 100(2)* or which is an authorised unit trust, to an investment trust or, for transfers after 16 March 1998, to a venture capital trust (see 65 UNIT TRUSTS ETC. and 66 VENTURE CAPITAL TRUSTS). [*TCGA 1992, ss 99A(3), 139(4); FA 1998, s 134(1)(4); FA 2004, s 118(3)*].

Where *TCGA 1992, s 139* has applied in relation to a transfer to a company which was not then an investment trust but which subsequently becomes one for an accounting period, then any assets transferred and still owned by the company at the beginning of that accounting period are deemed to have been sold and immediately reacquired by the transferee company, immediately after the transfer, at their market value at that time. For accounting periods ending on or after 1 July 1999 (the appointed day for corporation tax self-assessment — see 13.2 above), the resulting chargeable gain or allowable loss arising is deemed to accrue to the transferee company not at the time of the deemed disposal but at the end of the accounting period preceding the accounting period in which the company becomes an investment trust. Notwithstanding normal time limits, a corporation tax assessment in respect of any resulting liability can be made within six years after the end of the last-mentioned accounting period.

Similar provisions apply where, after a transfer to which *TCGA 1992, s 139* applied and after 16 March 1998, the transferee company becomes a venture capital trust (within *ICTA 1988, s 842AA* — see 66 VENTURE CAPITAL TRUSTS). They apply by reference to the time at which HMRC's approval for the purposes of *section 842AA* comes into effect, and the resulting gain or loss is deemed to accrue immediately before that time rather than at the time of the deemed disposal. In a case in which HMRC's approval has effect as from the beginning of an accounting period, any consequential corporation tax assessment can be made, notwithstanding normal time limits, within six years after the end of that accounting period. These provisions do not apply if those above relating to investment trusts have already applied (in relation to the same transfer of assets) and *vice versa*.

[*TCGA 1992, ss 101, 101B; FA 1996, s 140; FA 1998, s 134(2)(3)(5)*].

In respect of disposals after 19 March 1990, the provisions of *TCGA 1992, s 139* did not apply in relation to an asset acquired before 30 November 1993 (the latter date being the date of the coming into force of *FA 1994, s 249*; companies otherwise regarded as UK resident but under double tax relief arrangements already regarded as non-UK resident to be treated as non-UK resident for *Taxes Acts* purposes after 29 November 1993; see 52.6 RESIDENCE AND DOMICILE) if the company which acquired it, though resident in the UK, was regarded as resident elsewhere by virtue of DOUBLE TAX RELIEF (19.2) arrangements such that it would not under those arrangements be taxable in the UK on any gain arising on a disposal of the asset immediately after its acquisition. [*TCGA 1992, s 139(3); FA 1994, s 251(1)(5), Sch 26 Pt VIII*].

FOREX. The following applies where there is a disposal or acquisition of currency; a 'qualifying asset' consisting of the right to settlement under a debt which is not a debt on a security (within *TCGA 1992, s 132*; see 22.5 EXEMPTIONS AND RELIEFS); a 'qualifying asset' consisting of the right to settlement under a debt on a security; or an obligation which by virtue of *TCGA 1992, s 143* (futures contracts; see 6.8 ASSETS) is regarded as an asset to the disposal of which *TCGA 1992* applies and which is a duty under a currency contract. It applies where the disposal or acquisition is by a 'qualifying company' and is made on or after the company's 'commencement day' (the first day of its first accounting period beginning after 22 March 1995, subject to transitional provisions) and in an accounting period beginning before 1 October 2002 (see 14.15 COMPANIES—CORPORATE FINANCE AND INTANGIBLES). Where, immediately before the disposal or after the acquisition, as the case may be, the asset is held wholly for 'qualifying purposes', and *TCGA 1992, s 139* would otherwise apply, that provision does not apply as regards the disposal or acquisition and the corresponding acquisition or disposal. '*Qualifying purposes*' are purposes of long-term or mutual insurance business. [*FA 1993, s 169, Sch 17 para 7; FA 2002, Sch 40 Pt 3(10); SI 2001 No 3629, Art 81*]. See 14.15 COMPANIES—CORPORATE FINANCE AND INTANGIBLES for a note of the terms quoted and not otherwise defined.

Life assurance business. The provisions of *TCGA 1992, s 139* are adapted for certain transfers of an insurance company's long-term business. See Tolley's Corporation Tax under Life Insurance Companies.

Privatisations etc. In connection with privatisations, and reorganisations of public corporations, various specific provisions have been enacted, mainly to cause transfers of assets to be treated on a 'no gain/no loss' basis, and to preclude a liability from arising under *TCGA 1992, s 179* (see 27.9 GROUPS OF COMPANIES) when a company leaves a group. See, for example, *British Telecommunications Act 1981, s 82*; *Telecommunications Act 1984, s 72*; *Trustee Savings Bank Act 1985, Sch 2 paras 2–6*; *Transport Act 1985,* *s 130(3)(4)*; *Airports Act 1986, s 77*; *Gas Act 1986, s 60*; *ICTA 1988, s 513*; *Water Act 1989, s 95*; *Electricity Act 1989, Sch 11*; *FA 1990, Sch 12* (broadcasting undertakings); *TCGA 1992, s 267* (sharing of transmission facilities); *F(No 2)A 1992, Sch 17* (privatisation of Northern Ireland Electricity); *FA 1994, Sch 24* (provisions relating to *Railways Act 1993*); and *FA 1994, Sch 25* (Northern Ireland Airports Ltd).

Building society's business etc. transferred to a company or other building society. Similar provisions apply as for privatisations etc. above where there is a transfer of the whole of a building society's business to a successor company in accordance with the relevant provisions of *Building Societies Act 1986* [*TCGA 1992, s 216*] and where there is a disposal by one society to another as part of an amalgamation etc. of societies. [*TCGA 1992, s 215*].

Industrial and provident societies etc. Similar provisions apply as for privatisations etc. above where there is a union or amalgamation of two or more registered industrial and provident societies or a transfer of engagements from one society to another. This treatment also applies to certain co-operative associations established and resident in the UK, the primary purposes of which are to assist members in carrying on husbandry in the UK or fishery operations. [*ICTA 1988, s 486(8)(9)*].

13.11 OVERSEAS MATTERS

See 45.3 OVERSEAS MATTERS for the transfer before 1 April 2000 of a UK branch or agency owned by a non-UK resident company to a UK resident company.

Various provisions apply where a UK resident company has an interest in a controlled foreign company. See 45.7 OVERSEAS MATTERS.

Where a UK resident company transfers all or part of a trade carried on by it outside the UK to a company not resident in the UK in exchange, wholly or partly, for shares, see 45.9 OVERSEAS MATTERS. Where the transferee company is resident in an EC member state, see 45.11 OVERSEAS MATTERS. Where the UK company's trade is carried on in the UK and is transferred to a company resident in another EC member state, see 45.10 OVERSEAS MATTERS.

There are 'exit charges' and provisions for the recovery of unpaid tax where a company ceases to be UK resident etc., is a dual resident company or is not resident in the UK. See 45.12 and 45.13 OVERSEAS MATTERS.

See also 13.18 below as regards European Companies (SEs).

13.12 INTEREST CHARGED TO CAPITAL

For interest paid in accounting periods beginning after 31 March 1981, interest on money borrowed by a company for the construction of any building, structure or works, and referable to a time before disposal of it, may be added to the expenditure allowable as a deduction under *TCGA 1992, s 38* in computing the gain on the disposal of the building etc. by the company, provided the expenditure on the construction was itself so allowable. No such relief is given for interest referable to any accounting period ending after 31 March 1996 (in consequence of the loan relationship provisions at 14.2 COMPANIES—CORPORATE FINANCE AND INTANGIBLES) or for interest treated as a charge on income under *ICTA 1988, s 338*. This restriction also applies to any amount which is allowable as a deduction in computing income, profits, gains or losses for corporation tax purposes (or would be so but for an insufficiency of profits or gains) or which would be allowable if the building etc. was held as a fixed asset of a trade. The practical effect of these restrictions is that a payment of interest is unlikely to qualify as allowable expenditure in computing a chargeable gain.

For interest paid in accounting periods ending before 1 April 1981, the provisions and comment made in the last two sentences above do not apply. Instead, interest had to be charged to capital in order to qualify as allowable expenditure, which treatment prevented it being treated as a charge on income by virtue of *ICTA 1970, s 248(5)(a) as originally enacted.*

[*TCGA 1992, s 40; FA 2002, s 82, Sch 25 para 60*].

13.13 GILTS AND BONDS

See 26 GOVERNMENT SECURITIES, 14.2–14.6 COMPANIES—CORPORATE FINANCE AND INTANGIBLES and 50 QUALIFYING CORPORATE BONDS for the exemption available for gilt-edged securities and qualifying corporate bonds.

For accounting periods ended on or before 31 March 1996, if gilt-edged securities or qualifying corporate bonds are appropriated by a company *from* trading stock in such circumstances that any gain accruing on their disposal would be exempt from corporation tax on chargeable gains, there is a deemed disposal and re-acquisition at market value immediately before the appropriation. Where the securities are appropriated *to* trading stock, any trading loss arising on a subsequent disposal cannot exceed the loss which would have arisen if the securities had been acquired at their market value at the time of the appropriation. As a consequence of the introduction of the loan relationships provisions (see 14.2–14.6 COMPANIES—CORPORATE FINANCE AND INTANGIBLES), this ceases to be of application for accounting periods ended after 31 March 1996, subject to the transitional provisions outlined in that chapter. [*ICTA 1988, s 126A; TCGA 1992, Sch 10 para 14(6); FA 1996, s 105, Sch 41 Pt V(3)*].

See 6.3 ASSETS for appropriations to and from trading stock generally and see also 27.4 GROUPS OF COMPANIES for intra-group transfers of assets which are trading stock of one of the companies but not of the other.

13.14 SHARES—ACQUISITIONS AND DISPOSALS WITHIN SHORT PERIOD

The ordinary rules for matching disposals with 'acquisitions' are modified for disposals before 5 December 2005 by a company of shares (including securities, as defined in 58.7 SHARES AND SECURITIES) if

(*a*) the company acquired shares of the same class within one month before or after the disposal where the disposal was through a stock exchange, or otherwise within six months before or after the disposal, and

(*b*) the number of that class of shares held by the company during the said prescribed period before the disposal was not less than 2% of the number issued.

Shares acquired within (*a*) above are called '*available shares*'.

Where the company making the disposal (Company X) is a member of a group and the prescribed period as above begins on or after 1 April 2000, the following apply.

(A) Where shares of the same class are held by another group member and at any time in the prescribed period before the disposal

- (i) the other group member is UK-resident, or
- (ii) the shares are 'chargeable shares' in relation to that other group member,

those shares are treated for the purposes of (*b*) above as held by Company X.

(B) Where shares of the same class are acquired by another group member, and either (A)(i) or (A)(ii) applies at the time of acquisition, those shares are treated for the purposes of (*a*) above as acquired by Company X.

(C) Where shares of the same class are acquired by Company X from a company which was a member of the group throughout the prescribed period before and after the disposal, and either (A)(i) or (A)(ii) applies throughout that part of the said period during which the other group member held the shares, those shares are disregarded for the purposes of (*a*) above.

Shares are '*chargeable shares*' in relation to a company at a particular time if, on a disposal by that company at that time, any gain would be a chargeable gain and would be within the charge to corporation tax by virtue of *TCGA 1992, s 10* or *s 10B* (non-UK resident company trading in the UK through a permanent establishment (previously a branch or agency) — see 45.3 OVERSEAS MATTERS). The question whether a company is a member of a group is determined as in 27.1 GROUPS OF COMPANIES, taking into account the change in the residence requirement.

Where the company making the disposal is a member of a group and the prescribed period as above begins before 1 April 2000, similar provisions apply but taking into account the fact that under 27.1 GROUPS OF COMPANIES, as it applies before the change in the residence requirement, a group is restricted to UK-resident companies.

Disposals are matched with available shares before other shares and with available shares acquired by the disposing company before those acquired by a fellow group member, and then with acquisitions before the disposal (latest ones first) rather than after (when earlier ones are taken first). Where disposals are identified with acquisitions of another group member, the cost to that member will be allowed to the disposing company plus the usual incidental costs of disposal. Shares identified with one disposal are precluded from further identification with a later disposal.

'*Acquisitions*' do not include shares acquired as trading stock or acquired from another group member.

For disposals after 31 March 1985, the above identification rules have priority over those in 59 SHARES AND SECURITIES—IDENTIFICATION RULES generally, but not where shares acquired and disposed of on the same day are matched under *TCGA 1992, s 105*(*1*) (see 59.3 SHARES AND SECURITIES—IDENTIFICATION RULES). For disposals after 31 March 1982 and before 1 April 1985 the above rules had priority over the then identification rules pertaining to the indexation provisions. For disposals before 1 April 1982 the above rules were subject to *TCGA 1992, s 105*(*1*) solely.

[*TCGA 1992, s 106; FA 2000, Sch 29 para 18; FA 2003, Sch 27 para 2; FA 2006, s 72*(*1*)(*3*), *Sch 26 Pt 3*(*10*)].

These provisions are repealed with effect for disposals on or after 5 December 2005. They are considered to be unnecessary following the introduction of the provision at 13.4(*b*) above which denies relief for losses arising from arrangements intended to secure a tax advantage and therefore provides an alternative mechanism to prevent loss creation using bed and breakfasting of shares. (Treasury Explanatory Notes to the Finance (No 2) Bill 2006.)

13.15 CLOSE COMPANY TRANSFERRING ASSET AT UNDERVALUE

See 3.17 ANTI-AVOIDANCE where a close company transfers an asset otherwise than at arm's length for a consideration less than market value.

13.16 DEMERGERS

The provisions of *ICTA 1988, ss 213–218* have effect for facilitating certain transactions whereby trading activities carried on by a single company or 'group' are divided so as to be carried on by two or more companies not belonging to the same group or by two or more independent groups. '*Group*' means a company and all of its 75 per cent subsidiaries (with the effect of direct and indirect ownership of shares held as trading stock being ignored in deciding whether one company is a 75 per cent subsidiary of another).

An exempt distribution (as in *ICTA 1988, s 213(2)*) within *ICTA 1988, s 213(3)(a)* (transfer by company of shares in one or more 75 per cent subsidiaries) is not a capital distribution within *TCGA 1992, s 122* (see 58.10 SHARES AND SECURITIES). *TCGA 1992, ss 126–130* (see generally 58.1 SHARES AND SECURITIES) are applied as if that company and the subsidiary whose shares are transferred were the same company and the distribution were a reorganisation of share capital.

A charge under *TCGA 1992, s 179* (see 27.9 GROUPS OF COMPANIES) on a company ceasing to be a member of a group does not apply where the cessation is by reason only of an exempt distribution. However, this exemption does not apply if there is a chargeable payment (within *ICTA 1988, s 214(2)*: payment not made for *bona fide* reasons or made for tax avoidance purposes) within five years of the exempt distribution, and will result in the *TCGA 1992, s 179* charge being able to be the subject of an assessment made within three years of the chargeable payment.

[*TCGA 1992, s 192; FA 2000, Sch 29 para 29, Sch 40 Pt II(12)*].

For full details of the provisions see Tolley's Corporation Tax under Groups of Companies. For the treatment of distributions arising from demergers in the hands of trustees, see HMRC Capital Gains Manual CG 33900–33936.

13.17 USE OF NON-STERLING CURRENCIES

There are provisions (see now *FA 1993, ss 92–92E* as substituted by *FA 2004, Sch 10 para 77*) under which a currency other than sterling is used to determine profits and losses of a company that fall to be computed in accordance with generally accepted accounting practice for corporation tax purposes. For full details see Tolley's Corporation Tax.

Chargeable gains and allowable capital losses do not fall to be computed in accordance with generally accepted accounting practice and are therefore effectively excluded from the provisions. Such gains and losses are translated into sterling using the rules at 15.4(*a*) COMPUTATION OF GAINS AND LOSSES, subject to the exception there noted. Prior to the substitution of the provisions by *FA 2004*, chargeable gains and allowable losses were subject to a specific exclusion from the provisions then applicable. [*FA 1993, ss 93(7), 93A(9); FA 2000, s 105; FA 2002, s 80, Sch 24 para 4; FA 2004, Sch 10 para 77*].

13.18 EUROPEAN COMPANY (SOCIETAS EUROPAEA)

Council Regulation (EC) No 2157/2001 provided for the creation of a new type of company, the European Company or *Societas Europaea* ('SE'). The *Regulation* came into effect on 8 October 2004. It permits the formation of new SEs and also allows for the 'transformation' of existing companies into SEs and for the merger between two (or more) companies in different member states into an SE. For most tax purposes, an SE based in the UK is treated like a UK-resident plc, but special provisions are required to deal with, among other matters, the formation of SEs by cross-border merger. The provisions, described below, are intended to be broadly tax-neutral. (Revenue Technical Note, 'Implementation of the European Company Statute', January 2005).

Formation of SE by merger. The following provisions apply where an SE is formed on or after 1 April 2005 by the merger of two or more companies in accordance with *Council Regulation (EC) No 2157/2001, Arts 2(1), 17(2)* and each merging company is resident in a member state but not all of them are resident in the same member state.

A company is resident in a member state for this purpose if is within a charge to tax under the law of the State as being resident for that purpose and it is not regarded, for the purposes of any DOUBLE TAX RELIEF (19) arrangements to which the state is a party, as resident in a territory not within a member state.

Treatment of securities issued on merger. If it does not constitute or form part of a scheme of reconstruction within the meaning of *TCGA 1992, s 136* (see 58.6 SHARES AND SECURI-

TIES), the merger is nevertheless treated as if it were a scheme of reconstruction for the purposes of that section, but the anti-avoidance provision at *section 136(6)* does not apply (and neither does *section 137* (restrictions on company reconstructions — see 3.18 ANTI-AVOIDANCE)). See, however, the anti-avoidance provision below.

Assets left within UK tax charge. If *TCGA 1992, s 139* (reconstruction involving transfer of business — see 13.10 above) does not apply to the merger, any 'qualifying transferred assets' are treated for chargeable gains purposes as acquired by the SE for a consideration resulting in neither gain nor loss for the transferor.

For this purpose, an asset transferred to the SE as part of the merger process is a '*qualifying transferred asset*' if

- either the transferor was resident in the UK at the time of the transfer or any gain accruing on disposal of the asset immediately before that time would have been a chargeable gain forming part of the transferor's chargeable profits by virtue of *TCGA 1992, s 10B* (trade carried on via UK permanent establishment — see 45.3 OVERSEAS MATTERS); and
- either the SE is resident in the UK on formation or any gain accruing to it on disposal of the asset immediately after the transfer would have been a chargeable gain forming part of its chargeable profits by virtue of *TCGA 1992, s 10B*.

Assets not left within UK tax charge. If

- in the course of the merger a company resident in the UK (company A) transfers to a company resident in another member state all the assets and liabilities relating to a business carried on by company A in a member state other than the UK through a permanent establishment, and
- the aggregate chargeable gains accruing to company A on the transfer exceed the aggregate allowable losses,

the allowable losses are treated as set off against the chargeable gains and the transfer is treated as giving rise to a single chargeable gain equal to the excess. See 45.11 OVERSEAS MATTERS for special double tax relief provisions applying where this provision applies.

Anti-avoidance. The above provisions do not apply if the formation of the SE is not effected for *bona fide* commercial reasons or if it forms part of a scheme or arrangements of which the main purpose, or one of the main purposes, is avoiding liability to UK tax. The advance clearance provisions of *TCGA 1992, s 138* (see 3.18 ANTI-AVOIDANCE) apply, with any necessary modifications, for this purpose as they apply for the purposes of *TCGA 1992, s 137*.

[*TCGA 1992, ss 140E–140G; F(No 2)A 2005, s 51*].

Held-over gains. For the effect of the formation of an SE by merger on various hold-over reliefs, see 13.12 above, 45.9 OVERSEAS MATTERS, 50.3 QUALIFYING CORPORATE BONDS and 55.7 ROLLOVER RELIEF.

Residence. For the residence for tax purposes of an SE transferring its registered office to the UK, see 52.6 RESIDENCE AND DOMICILE.

Continuity on ceasing to be UK resident. If at any time a company ceases to be resident in the UK in the course of the formation of an SE by merger (whether or not the company continues to exist following the merger), *FA 1998, Sch 18* (company RETURNS (54.18), ASSESSMENTS (5), APPEALS (4), etc.) applies after that time in relation to liabilities accruing and other matters arising before that time as if the company were still UK-resident and, if the company has ceased to exist, as if the SE were the company.

Where an SE transfers its registered office outside the UK and ceases to be UK-resident, *FA 1998, Sch 18* applies after that time in relation to liabilities accruing and other matters arising before that time as if the SE were still UK-resident.

[*F(No 2)A 2005, s 61*].

Groups of companies. See 27.1 GROUPS OF COMPANIES.

14 Companies—Corporate Finance and Intangibles

14.1 **INTRODUCTION**

There are a number of sets of special corporation tax rules which seek to apply accepted accounting principles to particular types of profits and gains. Broadly (and with certain exceptions), under each of the regimes all profits are treated for corporation tax purposes as income and all losses as income losses, including those which would ordinarily be capital. Currently, the regimes concerned are those which cover:

- loan relationships (see 14.2–14.6 below);
- derivative contracts (see 14.7–14.12 below); and
- intangible fixed assets (see 14.13, 14.14 below).

The derivative contracts rules replaced, with effect for accounting periods beginning on or after 1 October 2002, a similar but narrower regime dealing with financial instruments, for which see 14.16 below. A further set of rules dealing with foreign exchange gains and losses ('FOREX') applied for accounting periods beginning before 1 October 2002: see 14.15 below. For later accounting periods, such gains and losses are brought within the loan relationships and derivative contracts provisions.

This chapter describes these regimes in detail only insofar as they interact with chargeable gains provisions. For full coverage see Tolley's Corporation Tax.

14.2 **LOAN RELATIONSHIPS**

Subject to transitional provisions, the loan relationships rules of *FA 1996, ss 80–110, Schs 8–15* apply for company accounting periods ending after 31 March 1996. [*FA 1996, s 105*]. For accounting periods beginning on or after 1 October 2002 (subject to anti-avoidance provisions to prevent forestalling), following the abolition of the FOREX provisions introduced by *FA 1993* (see 14.15 below), foreign exchange gains and losses arising to a company from its loan relationships are brought within the loan relationships rules.

As noted at 14.1 above, the intention of the provisions is for the corporate taxation of income and expenditure from corporate and government debt to equate with its accepted accounting treatment. This is brought about by first establishing the existence of a 'loan relationship' and secondly, by treating all company profits and losses from such relationships as income and not capital, regardless of whether the company is borrower or lender.

See also 26 GOVERNMENT SECURITIES, 50 QUALIFYING CORPORATE BONDS and HMRC Corporate Finance Manual CFM 3000 onwards.

14.3 **Summary of provisions.** As the underlying criteria is for the tax treatment of each loan relationship to follow generally accepted accounting practice, the terms *debit* and *credit* are used to describe the method of accounting for individual items of income and expenditure. The debits and credits will include all profits, gains and losses, including those of a capital nature, interest payments, charges and expenses appertaining to the company's loan relationship or its attributed rights and liabilities. [*FA 1996, s 84*(*1*); *FA 2004, Sch 10 para 1*(*2*)]. Charges and expenses appertaining to loan relationships include only those incurred directly

(i) in bringing any of the loan relationships into existence,

(ii) in entering into or giving effect to any of the related transactions,

(iii) in making payments under any of the relationships or in pursuance of any of the related transactions, or

(iv) in taking steps for ensuring the receipt of payments under any of the relationships or in pursuance of any of the related transactions.

[*FA 1996, s 84(3)*].

Interest on money debts which are not themselves loan relationships is also brought into account as debits and credits under the provisions. Profits from disposals of interest and from discounts are also brought into account, generally with effect from 16 March 2005. [*FA 1996, s 100; FA 2002, Sch 2 paras 1, 6; F(No 2)A 2005, Sch 7 para 12; FA 2006, Sch 6 para 17*].

For the calculation of credits and debits, see *FA 1996, ss 84–90A*.

Debits and credits arising from loan relationships to which a company is party are brought into account according to the purposes for which the company is party to it. Where the loan relationship is one to which the company is party for trading purposes, debits and credits are treated as receipts and expenses to be brought into account in computing the profits of the trade under Schedule D, Case I. Credits and debits in respect of non-trading loan relationships are aggregated and, where the aggregate credits exceed the aggregate debits, that excess is taxable under Schedule D, Case III. Relief is available for deficits. If only part of a loan relates to trading purposes the debits and credits should be apportioned accordingly. [*FA 1996, s 82(1)–(3)*].

Foreign exchange gains and losses. For accounting periods beginning on or after 1 October 2002 (subject to anti-avoidance provisions to prevent forestalling — see 14.15 below), with specified exceptions, the reference above to profits, gains and losses to be included in debits and credits includes foreign exchange gains and losses arising to a company in relation to any asset or liability representing a loan relationship of the company. [*FA 1996, ss 84A, 103(1A)(1AA)(1B); FA 2002, s 79, Sch 23 paras 3, 7; FA 2004, Sch 10 para 2; FA 2005, Sch 4 para 29; F(No 2)A 2005, Sch 6 para 10, Sch 11 Pt 2(6); SI 2004 No 3256, Regs 3, 5; SI 2005 No 2012, Regs 4, 6; SI 2005 No 3374, Regs 3, 4, 6; SI 2005 No 3422*].

F(No 2)A 2005, Sch 6 paras 9, 10 give the Treasury powers to repeal *FA 1996, s 84A* and replace it with new provisions by statutory instrument.

Matching of exchange differences on chargeable assets generally with those on borrowings, available by election under the superseded 'FOREX' rules (see 14.15(*f*) below) continues for accounting periods beginning on or after 1 October 2002 under a non-elective regime which seeks to follow generally accepted accounting practice. Matched differences are normally brought into account, as chargeable gains or allowable capital losses as appropriate, when the matched asset is disposed of (see *SI 2002 No 1970* as amended by *SI 2004 No 3259; SI 2005 No 2013*).

14.4 **Loan relationships with embedded derivatives.** Special provisions apply, for periods for which companies draw up accounts beginning on or after 1 January 2005, to loan relationships with 'embedded derivatives'. This is where a company in accordance with generally accepted accounting practice splits the rights and liabilities under the loan relationship into those under the loan relationship (the '*host contract*') and '*embedded derivatives*', which are those under one or more derivative financial instruments or equity instruments (as defined). In this case, the host contract will fall, for corporation tax purposes, within the loan relationship rules and the embedded derivative within the derivative contracts rules (see 14.7 below) which provide, in certain cases, for the embedded derivative to be taxed on a chargeable gains basis. The embedded derivative is treated as having the character (be it an option, a future or a contract for differences) which the rights and liabilities would have if contained in a separate contract. [*FA 1996, s 94A; FA 2004, s 52, Sch 10 para 13*].

Election for embedded derivatives provision to apply. A company which, for a period of account beginning on or after 1 January 2005, is subject to '*old UK GAAP*' (i.e. UK generally accepted accounting practice as it applied for periods of account beginning before that date) and holds assets ('*relevant assets*') which it is not permitted under old UK GAAP to split as above (so that the above provision does not apply), may make an election for the loan relationship and derivative contract rules to have effect as if the above provision did apply. The election can only be made if the company would have been permitted so to split the assets had it been subject to international accounting standards or '*new UK GAAP*' (i.e. UK generally accepted accounting practice as it applies for periods of account beginning on or after 1 January 2005).

An election has effect in relation to all relevant assets held by the company, including any acquired later. It must be made in writing to an officer of Revenue and Customs, generally on or before 31 December 2005. The deadline is extended if the company does not hold any relevant assets at the beginning of its first period of account beginning on or after 1 January 2005 but subsequently acquires one or more; in such a case the deadline is 90 days after the acquisition of the first relevant asset. The deadline is also extended if the company does not have a period of account beginning in 2005 and holds a relevant asset at the beginning of its first period of account beginning after the end of that year, in which case the election must be made no later than 90 days after the beginning of that period.

The election takes effect from the beginning of the company's first period of account beginning on or after 1 January 2005, unless it is made after 31 December 2005 as a result of the company acquiring its first relevant asset, in which case it takes effect from the beginning of the period of account in which that asset is acquired.

Where an election is made, the provisions of *FA 1996, Sch 9 para 19A* and *FA 2002, Sch 26 para 50A* (adjustments on change of accounting policy) apply as if there were a change of accounting policy consisting in the company splitting its relevant assets as above as from the date the election takes effect.

These provisions replace a similar election available under *FA 2005, Sch 4 para 28* (repealed by *F(No 2)A 2005, Sch 11 Pt 2(6)*). A valid election under the *FA 2005* provisions is treated as an election under the above provisions.

[*F(No 2)A 2005, Sch 6 para 7*].

Simon's Direct Tax Service. See D2.1819D.

14.5 **Definition of 'loan relationship'**. A '*loan relationship*' exists whenever a company is in the position of debtor or creditor to a 'money debt' which arises from the lending of money. [*FA 1996, s 81(1)*].

A '*money debt*' is defined as a debt which is, or at any time has been, one that falls (or that may at the option of the debtor or of the creditor fall) to be settled

(*a*) by the payment of money;

(*b*) by the transfer of a right to settlement under a debt which is itself a money debt; or

(*c*) for relationships to which a company is a party on or after 22 March 2006, by the issue or transfer of shares in any company;

disregarding any other option exercisable by either party. For accounting periods beginning before 1 October 2002, a '*money debt*' was defined more simply as a debt which fell to be settled as in (*a*) or (*b*) above.

[*FA 1996, s 81(2); FA 2002, s 82, Sch 25 para 2; FA 2006, s 76, Sch 6 para 10(2)(3)*].

Transitional provisions apply where a creditor relationship (see below) to which a company is party becomes a loan relationship on 22 March 2006 as a result of the application of (*c*) above and immediately before that date the asset representing the relationship was an asset in respect of which any gain on disposal would be a chargeable gain. The company is treated as if it had disposed of that asset immediately before 22 March 2006 at its 'fair value' (see below). Any resulting chargeable gain or loss is deferred until the company ceases to be a party to the relationship. [*FA 2006, Sch 6 para 10(4)–(7)*].

The legislation does not define a *debtor* or *creditor* and therefore the accepted meaning is understood to apply. The meaning of 'money debt' and 'the lending of money' were considered in *HSBC Life (UK) Ltd v Stubbs (and related appeals) (Sp C 295), [2002] SSCD 9* (although these appeals pre-dated the tightening of the statutory definition of 'money debt' for accounting periods beginning on or after 1 October 2002).

Examples of loan relationships are: bank overdrafts, bank borrowings and third party borrowings plus corporate bonds and gilt-edged securities (subject to special rules for 3½% Funding Stock 1999–2004 and 5½% Treasury Stock 2008–2012 held by non-financial traders).

However, normal debtor/creditor relationships are not included as these do not arise from the lending of money and a debt arising from shareholders' rights is specifically excluded. Thus, ordinary shares and preference shares are not loan relationships. The same applied for accounting periods beginning before 1 October 2002 as regards permanent interest bearing shares (PIBS) issued by building societies, although only in respect of gains (and losses), which were, therefore, brought within the charge to corporation tax on chargeable gains. Interest on PIBS was within the loan relationship rules by virtue of *ICTA 1988, s 477A(3)*. (See HMRC Company Taxation Manual CTM 51190 and Life Assurance Manual para 3B.44.) For accounting periods beginning on or after 1 October 2002, all building society shares, including PIBS, are brought *fully* within the loan relationships rules and thus outside the scope of corporation tax on chargeable gains.

The legislation does not provide a definition of *money* but it is not restricted to sterling. [*FA 1996, s 81(5)(6), s 103(1); FA 2002, s 82, Sch 25 para 14*].

Alternative finance arrangements within *FA 2005, ss 47, 47A, 49* or *49A* are also loan relationships. [*FA 2005, s 50; FA 2006, ss 95(4), 96(4)*].

A '*creditor relationship*', in relation to a company, is a loan relationship of that company in the case of which it stands in the position of a creditor as respects the debt in question. A '*debtor relationship*' has a corresponding meaning. The '*fair value*' of a loan relationship is the amount which, at the time at which the value falls to be determined, the company would obtain from, or would have to pay to, an independent person for the transfer of all its rights and liabilities under the relationship. Before 22 March 2006 (subject to transitional rules) only amounts which at the relevant time were not yet due and payable were taken into account in arriving at the fair value. [*FA 1996, s 103(1); FA 2004, s 52, Sch 10 para 17; FA 2006, Sch 6 para 18*].

Shares treated as creditor relationships. For accounting periods ending on or after 22 March 2006, a share in one company (the '*issuing company*') held by another company (the '*investing company*') is treated in the hands of the investing company as if it were rights under a creditor relationship of that company during any period in which it is 'subject to outstanding third party obligations' and an 'interest-like investment'. Previously, for such shares held on or after 16 March 2005, the shares were treated as creditor relationships throughout an accounting period of the investing company if at any time in that period they were subject to outstanding third party obligations and an interest-like investment.

For this purpose, a share is '*subject to outstanding third party obligations*' if it is subject to, or will or might, under any 'relevant arrangements', be subject to, undischarged obligations ('*third party obligations*') to meet unpaid calls on it or to make a contribution to the capital of the issuing company that could affect the share's value. The obligations must be either obligations of a person other than the investing company or obligations of the investing company which, under any relevant arrangements, will or might be discharged directly or indirectly by any other person. '*Relevant arrangements*' are arrangements (including any agreement or understanding, whether or not legally enforceable) entered into at any time on or before the share was issued.

At any time before 22 March 2006, a share is treated as subject to outstanding third party obligations only in more restricted circumstances. The share must be subject to undischarged obligations to meet unpaid calls on it or to make a contribution to the capital of the issuing company that could affect the share's value where those obligations are obligations of a person other than the investing company.

A share is an '*interest-like investment*' if its nature is such that its fair value (see above) is likely to increase at a rate which represents a return on an investment of money at a commercial rate of interest (as defined) and is unlikely (ignoring fluctuations resulting from exchange rate changes) to deviate to a substantial extent from that rate of increase. It is assumed for this purpose that any third party obligations will be met in the amounts and at the time at which they are due and that no transaction (or series of transactions) intended to cause the share not to be an interest-like investment will be entered into.

A share is treated as continuing to be held by a company notwithstanding that it has been transferred to another person under a repo or stock lending arrangement or under a transaction treated as not involving a disposal by *TCGA 1992, s 26* (transfer of asset by way of security — see 15.2 COMPUTATION OF GAINS AND LOSSES).

[*FA 1996, s 91A; F(No 2)A 2005, Sch 7 paras 10(2)(7), 13; FA 2006, Sch 6 para 13*].

A share held on or after 16 March 2005 is also treated as rights under a creditor relationship of an investing company during any period in which the above provisions do not apply and the share is a 'non-qualifying share' and not in any event treated as such rights under *FA 1996, Sch 10 para 4* (holdings in unit trusts and offshore funds). For accounting periods ending before 22 March 2006, this provision applied for the whole of any accounting period if at any time in that period the share met the conditions. For accounting periods beginning before that date and ending on or after that date, amounts are to be brought into account as a result of the above amended provision only if they relate to any time on or after that date.

A share is a 'non-qualifying share' if *ICTA 1988, s 95* (taxation of dealers in respect of distributions) does not apply to distributions in respect of it and if one or more of the conditions listed below is satisfied. Broadly, and subject to further conditions and exclusions, those conditions are as follows.

1. The assets of the issuing company are of such a nature that the fair value of the share is likely to increase at a rate which represents a return on an investment of money at a commercial rate of interest and is unlikely (ignoring fluctuations resulting from exchange rate changes) to deviate to a substantial extent from that rate of increase. This condition is not satisfied if the whole or substantially the whole by fair value of the assets of the issuing company are 'income producing' (as defined).
2. The share is 'redeemable' (as defined), is designed to produce a return which equates, in substance, to the return on an investment of money at a commercial rate of interest and is not an 'excepted share' (as defined).
3. There is a scheme or arrangement under which the share and one or more 'associated transactions' (as defined) are together designed to produce a return which equates, in substance, to the return on an investment of money at a commercial rate of interest. This condition is not satisfied if the share by itself is within either of the above conditions, or would be but for falling within the income producing assets or excepted share exemptions from those conditions.

The Treasury has the power to add, vary or remove conditions by regulations.

[*FA 1996, ss 91B–91F; F(No 2)A 2005, Sch 7 paras 10(3)–(5)(7), 13; FA 2006, Sch 6 paras 13–15*].

Where, at any time after 15 March 2005, either *FA 1996, s 91A* or *s 91B* above begins to apply in the case of any shares, the investing company is deemed for chargeable gains purposes to have disposed of the share immediately before that time, and to have immediately reacquired it, at its fair value. This does not apply in the case of a share held by a company at the end of 15 March 2005 and at the beginning of 16 March 2005 if either of the provisions applies at the beginning of 16 March 2005. In the latter case, *TCGA 1992, s 116* (reorganisations involving QUALIFYING CORPORATE BONDS (50.3)) applies on the assumption that the share became an asset representing a creditor relationship of the company, and therefore a qualifying corporate bond, as a result of a 'relevant transaction' on 16 March 2005 in relation to which the share immediately before 16 March 2005 was the 'old asset' and the asset representing the creditor relationship immediately after the beginning of that day was the 'new asset'. (See 50.3 QUALIFYING CORPORATE BONDS for the meaning of these expressions.)

Where at any time, either *FA 1996, s 91A* or *s 91B* above cease to apply to a share, the investing company is deemed for chargeable gains purposes to have disposed of the share immediately before that time, and to have immediately reacquired it, at its fair value. If the deemed disposal occurs before 1 January 2006 in respect of a share to which *TCGA 1992, s 116* applied in the circumstances indicated above, the disposal is not regarded as a disposal for the purposes of *TCGA 1992, s 116(10)(b)(c)* (see 50.3(*b*) QUALIFYING CORPORATE BONDS) and the share continues to be treated as the new asset for the purposes of that section.

[*FA 1996, ss 91G, 103(1); F(No 2)A 2005, Sch 7 para 10(6)*].

Simon's Direct Tax Service. See D2.1803.

14.6 **Chargeable gains.** The **general rule** is that no chargeable gain will arise on the disposal of any loan relationship because every asset representing a loan relationship of a company is a QUALIFYING CORPORATE BOND (see 50.2). [*TCGA 1992, s 117(A1); FA 1996, Sch 14 para 61, Sch 15 para 7(c); FA 2002, Sch 40 Pt 3(10)*].

Exceptions to the general rule are described below.

(i) **Convertible securities etc.** *Creditor relationships.* The following provisions are repealed for periods for which a company draws up accounts beginning on or after 1 January 2005. See below for the transitional rules applying to the repeal of the provisions.

Subject to the above, the provisions apply to an asset if:

(*a*) it represents a creditor relationship of a company (see 14.5 above);

(*b*) the rights attached to it include provision by virtue of which the company is, or may become, entitled to acquire any shares in a company (subject to (*c*) below);

(*c*) for accounting periods ending on or after 26 July 2001, the only shares which may be acquired under (*b*) above are 'qualifying ordinary shares' or 'mandatorily convertible preference shares';

(*d*) the extent to which shares may be acquired under (*b*) is not determined using a cash value specified in the provision or ascertainable by reference to its terms;

(*e*) it is neither a 'deeply discounted security' (see 58.16 SHARES AND SECURITIES) nor, for accounting periods ending on or after 26 July 2001, an 'excluded indexed security' (within *ITTOIA 2005, s 433*);

(*f*) for accounting periods ending on or after 26 July 2001, the company holding the asset does not have the right to require any person other than the issuing company to acquire it for an amount involving a 'deep gain' on redemption (see 58.16 SHARES AND SECURITIES);

(*g*) when it came into existence, there was more than a negligible likelihood that the rights to acquire shares (as in (*b*) above) would in due course be exercised to a significant extent;

(*h*) for accounting periods ending on or after 26 July 2001, the rights to acquire shares (as in (*b*) above), when fully exercised, would result in the replacement of the entire asset by shares (plus any cash in respect of a fractional share entitlement, which must not exceed 5% of the value of the shares), and the ending of the creditor relationship; and

(*j*) its disposal by the company would not be treated as in the course of activities forming an integral part of a trade carried on by the company.

In those circumstances, the amounts falling to be brought into account under the loan relationship rules in respect of the creditor relationship are confined to those relating to interest and, for accounting periods beginning on or after 1 October 2002, foreign exchange gains and losses. The normal chargeable gains provisions apply to the asset as if it did not represent a loan relationship, with the appropriate adjustment to exclude interest accrued but not received.

For accounting periods beginning on or after 1 October 2002, an adjustment is also to be made for exchange gains and losses in an accounting period where this provision applies, or for a just and reasonable fraction of the exchange gains or losses where an asset does not fall within this provision for the whole of the accounting period. The consideration for disposal of the asset is to be increased to include any net exchange losses and decreased to exclude any net exchange gains brought into account as loan relationship debits or credits. Where the exclusion of net exchange gains would reduce the consideration to below nil, the excess gain is to be treated as part of the incidental costs incurred on disposal of the asset (under *TCGA 1992, s 38(1)(c)* — see 15.4(*d*) COMPUTATION OF GAINS AND LOSSES).

As regards (*c*) above, '*mandatorily convertible preference shares*' are shares (other than 'qualifying ordinary shares') which must, within 24 hours of acquisition, be converted into or exchanged for 'qualifying ordinary shares'. '*Qualifying ordinary shares*' are shares which are either listed on a recognised stock exchange or shares in a 'holding company' or 'trading company' (both defined as in 61.5 TAPER RELIEF), and which are not shares carrying no right to payment of a dividend or other profit share in the company or a right only to a dividend at a fixed rate. In either case these conditions must have been met when the asset in question came into existence and at all times since.

If an asset continuing to represent a creditor relationship ceases after 14 February 1999 to be a convertible security within these provisions (which would be the case if it becomes a relevant discounted security), there is deemed to be a disposal and reacquisition by the company at current value (adjusted for accrued interest and any exchange gains and losses as above) under the loan relationships provisions, with the resulting gain or loss deferred under the provisions concerning share reorganisations etc. involving the issue of a qualifying corporate bond (see 50.3 QUALIFYING CORPORATE BONDS). For disposals after 1 April 2002, the gain held over may be exempt under *TCGA 1992, Sch 7AC* (see 60 SUBSTANTIAL SHAREHOLDINGS OF COMPANIES).

Those of the above provisions which apply to accounting periods ending on or after 26 July 2001 do not apply to determine, in relation to any part of an accounting period falling before that date, whether or not an asset falls within *FA 1996, s 92*. Nor do they apply, for accounting periods straddling that date, to any assets representing a loan relationship to which the company ceased to be a party before that date. An asset held on 26 July 2001 to which *section 92* ceases to apply by virtue only of the changes applicable from that date will be treated for capital gains purposes as disposed of and reacquired immediately before that date.

Issuing company not to be connected company. The above provisions do not apply for accounting periods ending *on or after 19 December 2001* to assets held on or after that date where there is a 'connection' between the issuer and the holder. They cease to apply where such a connection arises after the issue of the security, in which case a deemed disposal will arise for chargeable gains purposes (as above). However, they continue to apply where either:

- the parties were not so connected in an accounting period ending before 19 December 2001 when the creditor company held the asset; or
- immediately before 19 December 2001, one of the companies was not a '100% subsidiary' of the other company and they were not both 100% subsidiaries of a third company.

'*Connection*' for these purposes is as defined by *FA 1996, s 87(3)* (see Tolley's Corporation Tax under Loan Relationships).

'*Subsidiary*' is as defined by *ICTA 1988, s 838* (substituting 100% for 75% in the definition of '75% subsidiary').

This provision does not apply to determine, in relation to any part of an accounting period falling before 19 December 2001, whether or not an asset falls within *FA 1996 s 92*. Nor does it apply to any assets representing the loan relationship which the company ceased to hold before that date even though held in that accounting period. An asset held on 19 December 2001, to which *section 92* ceases to apply by virtue only of the changes applicable from that date, will be treated for capital gains purposes as disposed of and reacquired immediately before that date.

Repeal of provisions. These provisions are repealed by *FA 2004* with effect as indicated above. An asset within the provisions immediately before the repeal takes effect is treated as ceasing to fall within the provisions at that time, without ceasing to be a creditor relationship of the company. The rules described above as to deemed disposal and reacquisition for such assets are then applied to the asset at that time. See also 14.4 above for the election to treat assets within these provisions immediately before their repeal as loan relationships with embedded derivatives.

[*FA 1996, s 92; FA 1999, s 65(7)(9); FA 2002, ss 72, 73, Sch 23 para 5; FA 2004, s 52, Sch 10 para 9; ITTOIA 2005, Sch 1 para 486; FA 2005, Sch 4 para 50*].

Debtor relationships. The following provision is repealed for periods for which a company draws up accounts beginning on or after 1 January 2005. Subject to this, the provision applies to amounts falling to be paid on or after 26 July 2001, and to related expenses accruing on or after that date, with respect to a liability if:

- the liability represents a debtor relationship of a company (see 14.5 above); and
- the rights attached to the asset representing the corresponding creditor relationship include provision by virtue of which a company is or may become entitled to acquire (by conversion, exchange or otherwise) any shares in the debtor or another company.

In these circumstances, amounts are *not* to be treated as loan relationship debits of the debtor company where they are:

- amounts payable in connection with rights to acquire any shares in another company except where the debtor has entered into the loan relationship in the ordinary course of a banking or securities dealing business (securities being defined as under *ICTA 1988, s 473*); or
- charges or expenses (within 14.3(ii)–(iv) above) incurred by the debtor company in connection with the acquisition of shares by another person in the debtor or other company as under (B) above.

[*FA 1996, s 92A; FA 2002, s 74; FA 2004, s 52, Sch 10 para 10; FA 2005, Sch 4 para 50*].

(ii) Asset-linked loan relationships. The following provisions are repealed for periods for which a company draws up accounts beginning on or after 1 January 2005. See below for the transitional rules applying to the repeal of the provisions.

Subject to the above, where a loan relationship is 'linked' to the value of chargeable assets, the amounts falling to be brought into account in respect of the relationship are confined to those relating to interest, and must be ascertained using an authorised accruals basis of accounting. The normal chargeable gains provisions apply to the asset representing the relationship as if it did not represent a loan relationship, with the appropriate adjustment for interest accrued but not received.

This provision does not, however, apply to a loan relationship the disposal of which would fall to be treated as in the course of activities forming an integral part of a trade carried on by the company. For accounting periods ending on or after 26 July 2001, this exclusion is extended to refer to assets the disposal of which would fall to be treated as in the course of activities forming an integral part of such a trade, to liabilities entered into in the course of such activities, and to loan relationships within *FA 1996, s 93A* (guaranteed return — see below).

A loan relationship is '*linked*' to the value of chargeable assets if, in pursuance of any provision having effect for the purposes of the relationship, the discharge payment is determined by applying to the amount of the original loan a percentage change over the 'relevant period' in the value of chargeable assets of any particular description (or, for accounting periods ending before 26 July 2001, in an index of the value of such assets — neither the retail prices index nor any similar foreign general prices index is such an index). If, however, there is such a provision which is made subject to any other provision applying to the determination of the amount of the discharge payment, whose only effect is to place a lower limit on the discharge payment of a specified percentage (which must not be more than 10%) of the original loan, then that other provision is disregarded for this purpose.

An asset is for these purposes a chargeable asset if, for accounting periods ending before 26 July 2001, any gain on disposal would be a chargeable gain (assuming the asset to belong to the company and not to be one the disposal of which would fall to be treated as in the course of activities forming an integral part of a trade carried on by the company, and disregarding any postponed gains that might accrue under *TCGA 1992, s 116(10)* — see 50.3 QUALIFYING CORPORATE BONDS). For accounting periods ending on or after 26 July 2001, an asset is only a chargeable asset for these purposes where the loan relationship is linked to an estate or interest in land or 'qualifying ordinary shares' listed on a recognised stock exchange. '*Qualifying ordinary shares*' are shares other than shares carrying no right to payment of a dividend or other profit share in the company or carrying a right only to a dividend at a fixed rate.

The new provisions for accounting periods ending on or after 26 July 2001 do not apply where the company ceased to be a party to the loan relationship concerned before that date, even though it may have been a party to the loan relationship in the accounting period. They also do not apply to determine, in relation to a part of an accounting period falling before that date, whether a loan relationship is within *FA 1996, s 93*.

The '*relevant period*' is the period between the time of the original loan and the discharge of the debt, or any other period in which almost all of that period is comprised and which differs from it exclusively for valuation purposes.

[*FA 1996, s 93; FA 2002, s 75; FA 2004, s 52, Sch 10 para 11(1); FA 2005, Sch 4 para 50*].

Asset-linked loan relationships involving guaranteed returns. As noted above, with effect for accounting periods ending *on or after 26 July 2001* (and where the company had not ceased to be a party to the loan relationship in question before that date), *FA 1996, s 93* (which provides for chargeable gains treatment for asset-linked loan relationships) does not apply to loan relationships within *FA 1996, s 93A*. This applies to any creditor loan relationship where that loan relationship and one or more other transactions (consisting of the disposal of futures or options) are 'associated transactions' designed to produce a guaranteed return comprising the repayment of the loan relationship and the disposal of the futures or options.

The loan relationship and other transactions are for this purpose designed to produce a guaranteed return where it is reasonable to assume when considering the likely effect of the transactions, and/or the circumstances in which they are entered into, that such result was the main purpose (or one of the main purposes) of the transactions. A 'guaranteed return' is produced when the risks from fluctuations in the underlying subject matter are reduced or eliminated so as to produce a return which in substance equates to a return of interest on an investment. This includes cases where the main reason for the choice of the underlying subject matter is that there is little or no risk of fluctuation (e.g. shares in a company the assets of which comprise debt instruments with a fixed or predictable return). References to the underlying subject matter are, in the case of loan relationships, references to the value of chargeable assets to which the loan relationship is linked. In the case of a disposal of futures or options, such references are to, or to the value of, the commodities, shares, stocks or securities, interest rates, indices or other matters to which, or to the value of which, the futures or options are referable.

For these purposes, for accounting periods beginning before 1 October 2002, references to returns from or disposals of futures or options and to 'associated transactions' are to be construed in accordance with *ICTA 1988, Sch 5AA paras 4–6* (as amended by *FA 2002, s 78*) (guaranteed returns on transactions in futures and options — see 6.7, 6.8 ASSETS, and see Tolley's Income Tax under Anti-Avoidance for detailed coverage). Where profits and losses arising from such futures or options fall within *ICTA 1988, Sch 5AA* (now *ITTOIA 2005, ss 555–569*), the return is to be treated as income in accordance with that *Schedule*. *Schedule 5AA* no longer applies for corporation tax purposes with effect for accounting periods beginning on or after 1 October 2002, after which time *FA 1996, s 93A* has effect for loan relationships and *FA 2002, Sch 26 para 6* has effect in relation to derivative contracts (14.8 below and Tolley's Corporation Tax under Financial Instruments and Derivative Contracts). For such accounting periods, references above to disposals of futures or options and to their underlying subject matter are references to derivative contracts and to their underlying subject matter.

[*FA 1996, s 93A; FA 2002, ss 76, 78, Sch 27 paras 18, 25; FA 2004, s 52, Sch 10 para 11*(*1*)].

Loan relationships ceasing to be asset-linked. With effect for accounting periods ending *on or after 26 July 2001* (and provided that the company had not ceased to be a party to the loan relationship in question before that date), where, after 25 July 2001, a loan relationship ceases to be linked to the value of assets (within *FA 1996, s 93*, as detailed above) but the company continues to be a party to that loan relationship, there is a deemed disposal and reacquisition by the company for chargeable gains purposes of the asset representing the loan relationship immediately before it ceased to be within *section 93*. The amount to be used for the deemed disposal and reacquisition of the asset is the current value (adjusted for any accrued interest) under the loan relationships provisions, with the resulting gain or loss deferred under the provisions concerning share reorganisations etc. involving the issue of a qualifying corporate bond (see 50.3 QUALIFYING CORPORATE BONDS). [*FA 1996, s 93B; FA 2002, s 77; FA 2004, s 52, Sch 10 para 11*(*1*)].

Repeal of provisions. FA 1996, ss 93, 93A and *93B* are repealed by *FA 2004* with effect as indicated above. An asset to which *FA 1996, s 93* applies immediately before the repeal takes effect is treated as ceasing to fall within the provisions at that time, without ceasing to be a creditor relationship of the company. The provisions of *FA 1996, s 93B* described above as to deemed disposal and reacquisition for such assets are then applied to the asset at that time. [*FA 2004, s 52, Sch 10 para 11*(*2*)(*3*)]. See also 14.4 above for the election to treat assets within *FA 1996, s 93* immediately before its repeal as loan relationships with embedded derivatives.

Simon's Direct Tax Service. See D2.1805.

14.7 DERIVATIVE CONTRACTS

The regime for the taxation of 'derivative contracts' (see 14.8 below) of companies replaced the more limited regime for the taxation of financial instruments (see 14.16 below) for accounting periods beginning on or after 1 October 2002. [*FA 2002, s 83,*

Sch 26]. This is subject to an anti-avoidance rule to prevent a company delaying the coming into effect of the regime to its advantage by shortening an accounting period beginning on or after 1 October 2001 so that it ends before 30 September 2002. [*FA 2002, s 83, Sch 28 para 1*]. See 14.12 below for transitional provisions. Subject to the special rules below for certain contracts which are taxed on a chargeable gains basis, under the regime, all profits/(losses) arising to a company from its derivative contracts are taxed as/(relieved against) income, using credits and debits under rules analogous to those for taxing loan relationships (see 14.3 above). Non-trading credits and debits are, in fact, taken into account under the loan relationships rules themselves. Such profits/(losses) are thus outside the charge to corporation tax on chargeable gains. [*FA 2002, s 83, Sch 26 paras 14, 15, 17–21; FA 2004, Sch 10 paras 47, 50, 51; SI 2005 No 2082, Art 9*]. The same treatment is applied to certain foreign exchange gains and losses arising to a company from its derivative contracts, and there are non-elective 'matching' rules similar to those referred to at 14.3 above (see *Sch 26 para 16*). Note that *F(No 2)A 2005, Sch 6 paras 9, 11* gives the Treasury powers to repeal *Sch 26 para 16* and replace it with new provisions by statutory instrument. There are special rules for bad debts (see *Sch 26 para 22*), anti-avoidance and other special computational provisions (see *Sch 26 paras 23–31A*), and special rules for collective investment schemes such as unit trusts (see *Sch 26 paras 32–40*) and for insurance and mutual trading companies (see *Sch 26 paras 41–43*).

For '*periods of account*' (i.e. periods for which companies draw up accounts) beginning on or after 1 January 2005, the derivative contracts regime is modified by *SI 2004 No 2201* and *SI 2004 No 3270*. The changes provide for comprehensive provisions to deal with certain derivatives previously excluded from the regime including contracts whose value derives essentially from land and certain 'embedded derivatives'. Non-trading profits, gains and losses on such derivative contracts are treated as capital gains and allowable losses (see 14.9 below). [*SI 2004 No 2201, Art 1*]. Further changes were made by statutory instrument in 2005.

See Tolley's Corporation Tax under Financial Instruments and Derivative Contracts for detailed coverage.

14.8 **Definition of 'derivative contract'.** For the purposes of 14.7 above, a company's '*derivative contracts*' are 'relevant contracts' entered into or acquired by it which are not excluded under the accounting tests etc. referred to below or by virtue of their underlying subject matter (see below). A '*relevant contract*' is any of the following:

- an option (including a warrant (as defined)); or
- a future, i.e. a contract for the sale of property under which delivery is to be made at a date and price agreed (as defined) when the contract is made; or
- a contract for differences, i.e. a contract the purpose or pretended purpose of which is to make a profit or avoid a loss by reference to fluctuations in the value or price of property described in the contract or fluctuations in an index or other factor designated in the contract. None of the following is a contract for differences: an option, a future, a contract of insurance, a capital redemption policy (as defined), a contract of indemnity, a guarantee, a warranty or a loan relationship.

A contract which can only be cash settled, and which does not provide for the delivery of any property, is excluded from being an option or a future but not from being a contract for differences. This does not apply if the underlying subject matter (see below) of the contract is currency.

For periods of account beginning on or after 1 January 2005, where a company, in accordance with generally accepted accounting practice, treats rights and liabilities under a contract to which it is party and which is not a loan relationship, as divided between rights and liabilities under one or more derivative financial instruments ('embedded derivatives') and the remaining rights and liabilities (the 'host contract'), the company is treated for the purposes of these provisions as party to a relevant contract (or contracts) whose rights and liabilities consist only of those of the embedded derivative (or derivatives). The embedded derivative is treated as having the character (be it an option, a future or a contract for differences) which the rights and liabilities would have if contained in a separate contract. (See *FA 2002, Sch 26 para 45L* for the tax treatment of such derivatives.)

[*FA 2002, Sch 26 paras 2, 12, 53(1)(2); SI 2004 No 2201, Arts 3, 13; SI 2004 No 3270, Art 3; SI 2005 No 3440, Arts 4, 6*].

Accounting tests etc. A relevant contract is *not* a derivative contract for the purposes of these provisions for an accounting period unless

- it is treated for accounting purposes as a derivative financial instrument in accordance with the relevant accounting standard (as defined) used by the company (or would be so treated if the company applied a relevant accounting standard to the relevant contract); or
- for periods of account beginning on or after 1 January 2005 and ending on or after 16 March 2005, it is not so treated solely because it does not meet the requirement in paragraph 9(d) of FRS 26 issued in December 2004 but is treated for accounting purposes as, or as forming part of, a financial asset or liability in accordance with the relevant accounting standard used by the company (or would be so treated if the company applied a relevant accounting standard to the relevant contract); or
- for periods of account beginning on or after 1 January 2005 and ending before 16 March 2005, it is a contract falling within *Sch 26 para 6* (contracts producing a guaranteed return — see (ii) below), *para 7* (contracts with a guaranteed amount payable on maturity — see (iii) below) or *para 8* (contracts held by company to provide insurance benefits — see (iv) below); or
- for periods of account beginning before 1 January 2005, it is a contract falling within *Sch 26 para 6* or *para 7* and it is treated for accounting purposes as a financial asset in accordance with the relevant accounting standard (as defined) (or would be so treated if the company applied that standard to the relevant contract); or
- its 'underlying subject matter' (see below) is commodities; or
- it is a contract for differences (see above) and its underlying subject matter is
  - for contracts entered into on or after 1 August 2004 in an accounting period ending after 16 September 2004, land (wherever situated);
  - for contracts entered into on or after 1 August 2004 in an accounting period ending after 16 September 2004, tangible movable property other than commodities which are tangible assets;
  - intangible fixed assets (see 14.13 below);
  - weather conditions; or
  - creditworthiness.

[*FA 2002, Sch 26 paras 3, 12(11); SI 2004 No 2201, Arts 1, 4, 13(3); SI 2005 Nos 646, Art 3, 2082, Art 4*].

Contracts excluded by virtue of their underlying subject matter. Subject to the qualifications below, a relevant contract is *not* a derivative contract for the purposes of these provisions if its underlying subject matter consists wholly of one or more types of 'excluded property'.

For periods of account beginning on or after 1 January 2005 and ending on or after 16 March 2005, the following are '*excluded property*':

(A) intangible fixed assets (see 14.13 below) (but these are not excluded if the relevant contract is a contract for differences);

(B) shares in a company (as defined);

(C) rights of a unit holder under a unit trust scheme.

Exclusions (B) and (C) above apply only where, broadly, the contract is entered into for non-trading purposes or by a life assurance company or mutual trading company or where the contract is part of a hedging relationship.

Previously, the following were '*excluded property*':

(*a*) for contracts entered into before 1 August 2004 and for contracts entered into on or after that date in accounting periods ending before 17 September 2004, land (whether in the UK or elsewhere);

(*b*) for contracts entered into before 1 August 2004 and for contracts entered into on or after that date in accounting periods ending before 17 September 2004, tangible movable property, other than commodities which are tangible assets;

(*c*) intangible fixed assets (but not if the relevant contract is a contract for differences);

(*d*) shares in a company;

(*e*) rights of a unit holder under a unit trust scheme;

(*f*) for periods of account beginning before 1 January 2005, assets representing loan relationships which are within *FA 1996, s 92* or *s 93* (convertible or asset-linked securities — see 14.6 above).

The underlying subject matter of a relevant contract is *treated* as consisting wholly of one or more of the above in certain circumstances if it consists partly of such property and partly of other property, where the latter is subordinate to the former or of small value compared with the whole. See also 14.11 below for the splitting of a contract into two notional contracts (applicable only to futures and options).

The '*underlying subject matter*' of a relevant contract is

- (in the case of an option) the property which would fall to be delivered if the option were exercised; or, where such property is itself a derivative contract, the underlying subject matter of that contract;
- (in the case of a future) the property which, if the future were to run to delivery, would fall to be delivered at the date and price agreed when the contract is made; or, where such property is itself a derivative contract, the underlying subject matter of that contract;
- (in the case of a contract for differences), where the contract relates to fluctuations in the value or price of property described in the contract, the property so described; or, where the contract designates an index or factor, the matter by reference to which the index or factor is determined (and in particular, underlying subject matter may include interest rates, weather conditions or creditworthiness, but the use of interest rates to establish the amount of a payment whose due date may vary does not make those rates the underlying subject matter of the contract).

For contracts entered into on or after 1 August 2004 in an accounting period ending on or after 17 September 2004, where the underlying subject matter of a relevant contract consists of or includes income from shares in a company or rights of a unit trust holder or unit trust scheme (or, for periods of account beginning before 1 January 2005 and ending before 16 March 2005, land), the underlying subject matter is not to be treated, by reason only of that income, as being such shares or rights (or land).

[*FA 2002, Sch 26 paras 4, 9, 11, 12; SI 2004 No 2201, Arts 5, 11, 12; SI 2005 No 646, Arts 1, 4; SI 2005 No 2082, Arts 5, 8; SI 2005 No 2440, Arts 5, 6*].

Exclusions (*d*)–(*f*) above do not apply where:

(i) the relevant contract is entered into or acquired by the company for the purposes of a trade carried on by it;

(ii) the relevant contract is designed, either by itself or together with certain 'associated transactions' (as defined), to produce a 'guaranteed return' (as defined); or

(iii) the relevant contract is designed, either by itself or together with certain 'associated transactions' (as defined), to secure that the amount payable on maturity does not fall below a guaranteed amount (defined as, broadly, 80% of the consideration payable for entering into, or acquiring, the contract or associated transactions); or

(iv) the company is carrying on long-term insurance business and the relevant contract is designed to provide certain benefits under life insurance or capital redemption policies.

For periods of account beginning on or after 1 January 2005 and ending before 16 March 2005, exclusion (*d*) above does not apply where the contract of a company is a deemed relevant contract to which the company is treated as party under the above embedded derivatives rules or under the embedded derivatives rules of *FA 1996, s 94A*(*2*) (see 14.4 above).

[*FA 2002, Sch 26 paras 5–8, 10; SI 2004 No 2201, Arts 6–10; SI 2004 No 3270, Art 4; SI 2005 No 646, Arts 1, 6, 8*].

For periods of account beginning before 1 January 2005 and ending before 16 March 2005, a company may elect to treat a contract within (iii) above as divided on a just and reasonable basis into two separate contracts, one a creditor loan relationship (see 14.5 above) which is a 'relevant zero coupon bond' (as defined), and the other an option to which (ii)–(iv) above do not apply and which may therefore be excluded property. [*FA 2002, Sch 26 para 48; FA 2004, Sch 10 para 64; SI 2005 No 646, Arts 1, 20*].

Transitional provisions for contracts becoming derivative contracts. The following provisions apply where a company is a party to a relevant contract immediately before and immediately after 3 p.m. on 16 March 2005, and the contract becomes a derivative contract immediately after that time having previously been a 'chargeable asset' (i.e. an asset in respect of which a gain on disposal would be a chargeable gain). When the company ceases to be a party to the contract it has to bring into account, for the accounting period in which it so ceases, the amount of any chargeable gain or allowable loss that would have accrued to the company on a disposal of the asset immediately before 3 p.m. on 16 March 2005 for a consideration equal to the value given to the contract in the company accounts at the end of the accounting period immediately before its first new period. [*FA 2002, Sch 26 para 4A; SI 2005 No 646, Art 5*].

Further transitional provisions apply where a company is party to a relevant contract both immediately before and on 28 July 2005 and the contract was a chargeable asset and not a derivative contract immediately before that date but would have been a derivative contract on that date had an accounting period of the company begun on that date. The contract is treated as a derivative contract entered into by the company on 28 July 2005 for a consideration equal to the fair value (within *FA 2002, Sch 26 para 54*(*1*)) of the contract on that date. When the company ceases to be a party to the contract it has to bring into account, for the accounting period in which it so ceases, the amount of any chargeable gain or allowable loss that would have accrued to the company on a disposal, at fair value, of the contract immediately before 28 July 2005.

A relevant contract to which a company becomes a party on or after 28 July 2005 is treated in the hands of the company as a derivative contract if, on the date on which the company so becomes a party to it, it is a chargeable asset but would be a derivative contract if an accounting period began on that date.

[*FA 2002, Sch 26 paras 4B, 4C; SI 2005 No 2082, Art 6*].

Treasury power to vary definition of derivative contract. Any of *FA 2002, Sch 26 paras 2–12* may be amended by Treasury order so as to vary the above definition of a 'derivative contract'. This is so that account can be taken of developments in markets, the creation of new types of derivatives, and changes to applicable accounting standards (in which case the amendment may have effect for accounting periods current at the time the order comes into force). Following *FA 2004*, the Treasury may also amend *FA 2002, Sch 26 Pt 9* (including *para 48* above) by order (see 14.9 and 14.11 below). [*FA 2002, Sch 26 para 13; FA 2004, s 49, Sch 9 para 2*].

14.9 **Derivative contracts taxed on a chargeable gains basis.** Non-trading debits and credits in respect of certain types of derivative contract are not brought into account under the loan relationship rules as outlined at 14.7 above. Instead, where such credits of a company for an accounting period exceed the debits for that period, a chargeable gain is deemed to accrue to the company in that period. Where the debits exceed the credits an allowable loss arises. See below for the carry back of allowable losses arising under these provisions.

This treatment applies to the following types of contract where the contract is not one to which the company is party at any time in the accounting period concerned for the purposes of a trade carried on by it (other than life assurance business or mutual trading):

(*a*) contracts entered into on or after 1 August 2004 in an accounting period ending on or after 17 September 2004 where the underlying subject matter relates to land (wherever situated) or tangible movable property other than commodities which are tangible assets;

(*b*) for periods of account beginning on or after 1 January 2005, certain 'embedded derivatives' which are options or exactly tracking contracts for differences (see further below); and

(*c*) contracts entered into on or after 1 August 2004 in an accounting period ending on or after 17 September 2004 which are 'property-based total return swaps'.

As regards (*a*) and (*c*) above, chargeable gains treatment does not apply where the company is an authorised unit trust, an investment trust, an open-ended investment company or a venture capital trust. Nor, as regards (*a*) above, does it apply in the case of an embedded derivative which is an exactly tracking contract for differences whose underlying subject matter is land within (*b*) above or (for periods of account beginning on or after 1 January 2005 and ending on or after 16 March 2005) where *FA 2002, Sch 26 para 45K* (issuers of securities with embedded derivatives — deemed contracts for differences; see 14.10 below) applies to the contract. Where the underlying subject matter includes income, this is ignored in determining the underlying subject matter of the contract, where it is subordinate to the land or property in question, or small in value in comparison with the underlying subject matter of the contract as a whole.

[*FA 2002, Sch 26 paras 45A, 45C, 45D((2)(a)(3), 45F(2)(a)(3), 45G(1A)(1B); SI 2004 No 2201, Arts 1, 15; SI 2004 No 3270, Art 8; SI 2005 No 2082, Art 12; SI 2005 No 3440, Art 8*].

Where the loan relationship in which a derivative is embedded is one to which *FA 1996, s 87* (accounting method where parties have a connection) applies, no loss arising from the derivative gives rise to a debit under the derivative contracts provisions (including the above provisions). [*FA 2002, Sch 26 para 48A; SI 2004 No 3270, Art 11*].

Embedded derivatives. Chargeable gains treatment as above applies to two types of embedded derivative where the loan relationship in which the derivative is embedded is a creditor relationship of the company. Subject to further conditions and exclusions, these are:

(i) options whose underlying subject matter is 'qualifying ordinary shares' or 'mandatorily convertible preference shares' (both as defined); and

(ii) contracts for differences whose subject matter is land or qualifying ordinary shares and which are 'exactly tracking contracts' (as defined).

For the meaning of '*embedded derivative*' for this purpose see 14.4 above.

Chargeable gains treatment does not apply in the case of (i) above where the substantial shareholdings exemptions under *TCGA 1992, Sch 7AC para 2* (see 60.5 SUBSTANTIAL SHAREHOLDINGS OF COMPANIES) would apply to a gain arising on the disposal at the end of the accounting period in question of the option if it were contained in a separate contract.

Where chargeable gains treatment applies to embedded derivatives within (i) or (ii) above, the loan relationship in which they are embedded are not QUALIFYING CORPORATE BONDS (50).

[*FA 2002, Sch 26 paras 45A, 45D–45F; SI 2004 No 2201, Arts 1, 15; SI 2004 No 3270, Arts 6, 7, 9; SI 2005 No 646, Art 15; SI 2005 No 2082, Arts 13–15*].

For periods of account beginning on or after 1 January 2005 and ending on or after 16 March 2005, see *FA 2002, Sch 26 para 45M* for the tax treatment of host contracts and embedded derivatives whose underlying subject matter is shares or rights of a unit trust holder in a unit trust scheme.

Property-based total return swaps. A '*property-based total return swap*' is a contract for differences in which one or more indices is designated where at least one of the indices is an index of changes in the value of land (wherever situated) and the underlying subject matter of the contract also includes interest rates. Special rules apply to determine the debits and credits to be taken into account in computing the chargeable gains and allowable losses under the above provisions. [*FA 2002, Sch 26 para 45G; SI 2002 No 2201, Art 15*].

Carry back of losses. Where there is a 'net loss' under the above provisions in an accounting period and, in a previous accounting period falling wholly or partly within 24 months immediately preceding the start of the loss period, there is a 'net gain' under the above provisions, a claim can be made for the loss to be wholly or partly carried back and set against part or all of the gain (but not so as to reduce either the loss or the gain below nil). The claim must be made within two years of the end of the period in which the net loss arose. Losses must be set against gains of a later period before those of an earlier period. Where a gain period falls partly before the 24-month period mentioned above, the loss can be only offset against the proportion of the gain falling within the 24-month period (time-apportioned based on the number of days).

A '*net loss*' in this case is the sum of any allowable losses arising under the above provisions ('*paragraph 45A losses*') in a period less the sum of any chargeable gains arising under the above provisions ('*paragraph 45A gains*') in the same period, in both cases in respect of the company's derivative contracts. A '*net gain*' is the excess of paragraph 45A gains over paragraph 45A losses, further reduced by any 'non-paragraph 45A allowable losses' (i.e. allowable losses arising other than under the above provisions). Any non-paragraph 45A allowable losses must be set against any non-paragraph 45A gains before the remainder is deducted from paragraph 45A gains.

[*FA 2002, Sch 26 para 45B; SI 2004 No 2201, Art 15*].

Terminal exercise of options. For periods of account beginning on or after 1 January 2005 and ending on or after 1 August 2005 there are provisions dealing with the chargeable gains consequences of the exercise or, for accounting periods ending on or after 31 December 2005, disposal of rights to acquire shares comprised in a derivative contract which is, or is treated as, an option.

Where the contract is an embedded derivative within (i) above, the following applies.

(A) In computing any chargeable gain accruing on a disposal of the asset representing the creditor relationship associated with the embedded derivative, the acquisition cost is increased by the amount by which G (see below) exceeds L or, where L exceeds G, is reduced by the excess.

(B) In computing any chargeable gain accruing on a disposal of all the shares acquired in exercising the rights where, for accounting periods ending on or after 31 December 2005, the acquisition was in circumstances such that no disposal was deemed to arise by virtue of *TCGA 1992, s 127* (reorganisation of share capital — see 58.1 SHARES AND SECURITIES), the acquisition cost is increased by the amount by which G (see below) exceeds L or, where L exceeds G, is reduced by the excess. In the case of a part disposal of the shares, the part disposal apportionment rule at 15.7 COMPUTATION OF GAINS AND LOSSES applies accordingly.

In either case, where L exceeds G and the excess is greater than the acquisition cost, any remaining amount is added to the disposal consideration.

For these purposes, G is the sum of the 'initial carrying value' of the contract and any chargeable gains accruing under *FA 2002, Sch 26 para 45A* above in respect of the contract for the accounting period in which the disposal is made and any previous accounting periods so far as they are referable, on a just and reasonable apportionment, to the shares. L is the sum of any allowable losses accruing for those accounting periods so far as they are so referable. The '*initial carrying value*' of a contract is the amount treated in accordance with *FA 1996, s 94A(2)* as the carrying value of the contract at the time the company became party to the loan relationship.

Where the contract is not an embedded derivative, in computing any chargeable gain accruing on a disposal of all the shares acquired in exercising the rights, the acquisition cost is increased by the amount by which X (see below) exceeds Y or, where Y exceeds X, is reduced by the excess and, in the case of a part disposal of the shares, the part disposal apportionment rule at 15.7 COMPUTATION OF GAINS AND LOSSES applies accordingly. Where Y exceeds X and the excess is greater than the acquisition cost, any remaining amount is added to the disposal consideration.

For this purpose, X is the sum of any credits brought into account as trading receipts in respect of the derivative contract for the accounting period in which the disposal is made and any previous accounting periods so far as they are referable, on a just and reasonable apportionment, to the shares. Y is the sum of any debits so brought into account for those accounting periods so far as they are so referable.

[*FA 2002, Sch 26 paras 45H, 45HA; SI 2005 No 2082, Arts 1, 17; SI 2005 No 3440, Arts 9, 10*].

14.10 *Issuers of securities with embedded derivatives — deemed options.* There are also provisions dealing with certain embedded derivatives on a chargeable gains basis where the loan relationship in which the derivative is embedded is a *debtor* relationship of the company. Subject to further conditions, the following provisions apply for periods of account beginning on or after 1 January 2005 to embedded derivatives which are deemed to be options and whose underlying subject matter is shares.

Where the provisions apply, non-trading and, for periods of account ending on or after 17 August 2005, trading debits and credits are not brought into account under the loan relationship rules as outlined at 14.7 above. Instead, the following applies.

(*a*) Where the option is exercised and shares are issued or transferred in fulfilment of the obligations under the option (the '*relevant disposal*'), *TCGA 1992, s 144(2)* (see 6.7 ASSETS) applies to the relevant disposal as if the 'initial carrying value' was the consideration for the grant of the option. For periods of account ending on or after 17 August 2005, the market value rule at *TCGA 1992, s 17(1)* (see 41.1 MARKET VALUE) is disapplied.

(*b*) Where the option is exercised, there is no relevant disposal and an amount is paid in fulfilment of the obligations under the option, a chargeable gain is treated as accruing to the company equal to the excess of the initial carrying value over the amount paid by the debtor in fulfilment of the obligation or, if a single amount is paid in fulfilment of the obligations under the debtor relationship, the part of the amount falling for accounting purposes to be treated as the amount relating to the option. For periods of account ending before 17 August 2005, the gain is the excess of the initial carrying value over the amount paid in fulfilment of the obligation, reduced by the aggregate of the initial carrying value and the carrying amount of the host contract at the time the company became party to the loan relationship. In either case, an allowable loss will accrue if the initial carrying value is less than the latter amount.

(*c*) Where the debtor relationship comes to an end without the option having been exercised, the company is treated for the purposes of corporation tax on chargeable gains as having disposed of the option for an amount equal to the initial carrying value. For periods of account ending on or after 17 August 2005, the acquisition cost of the option is deemed to be so much of the amount paid by the company in consideration for it ceasing to be a party to the debtor relationship as falls to be treated for accounting purposes as the amount relating to the option.

If the company was a party to the debtor relationship immediately before its first accounting period beginning on or after 1 January 2005, (*a*) and (*c*) above do not apply and for the purposes of (*b*) above, the initial carrying value is taken to be nil.

For these purposes, the '*initial carrying value*' means the amount treated in accordance with *FA 1996, s 94A(2)* as the carrying value of the option at the time the company became party to the loan relationship.

[*FA 2002, Sch 26 para 45J; SI 2004 No 3270, Art 10; SI 2005 No 646, Art 16; SI 2005 No 2082, Arts 1, 18; SI 2005 No 3440, Art 11*].

Issuers of securities with embedded derivatives — equity instruments. Subject to further conditions, the following applies for periods of account beginning on or after 1 January 2005 and ending on or after 16 March 2005 where a debtor relationship is divided under the embedded derivatives provisions between the loan relationship and an equity instrument, such that the equity instrument is a relevant contract treated as an option but is not a derivative contract. Where the company pays an amount to the person who is party to the loan relationship as creditor in discharge of any obligations under the relationship, an allowable loss is treated as accruing to the extent that RA exceeds E. For this purpose, RA is the amount so paid less so much of that amount as is treated for accounting purposes as paid in discharge of the liabilities under the loan relationship element, and E is the amount treated in accordance with *FA 1996, s 94A(2)* as the carrying value of the relevant contract at the time the company became party to the loan relationship. These provisions do not apply where the liability representing the debtor relationship was owed by the company immediately before its first accounting period beginning on or after 1 January 2005. [*FA 2002, Sch 26 para 45JA; SI 2005 No 2082, Arts 1, 19*].

Issuers of securities with embedded derivatives — deemed contracts for difference. Subject to further conditions, the following applies for periods of account beginning on or after 1 January 2005 where a debtor relationship is divided under the embedded derivatives provisions such that the relevant contract to which the company is treated as being party is a derivative contract whose underlying subject matter is land or shares and which is a contract for differences (other than one falling within *FA 2002, Sch 26 para 45J* above). The contract must be an exactly tracking contract (as defined) or, for periods of account ending on or after 17 August 2005, must be excluded from being such a contract only by a specific condition (see *FA 2002, Sch 26 para 45K(1)(d)*).

Non-trading and, for periods of account ending on or after 17 August 2005, trading debits and credits are not brought into account under the loan relationship rules as outlined at 14.7 above. For periods of account ending on or after 17 August 2005, where the debtor relationship comes to an end and an amount is paid to discharge all of the company's obligations (the '*discharge amount*'), a chargeable gain or allowable loss is treated as accruing, calculated on the assumption that the derivative contract is an asset of the company, that there is a disposal of that asset at the time the relationship comes to an end, that the consideration for the disposal is equal to the amount of the proceeds of issue of the security representing the relationship, and that the cost of the asset is the discharge amount.

For periods of account ending on or after 17 August 2005, these provisions do not apply where the liability representing the debtor relationship was owed by the company immediately before its first accounting period beginning on or after 1 January 2005.

[*FA 2002, Sch 26 para 45K; SI 2005 No 2082, Arts 1, 20*].

14.11 **Miscellaneous rules with potential chargeable gains consequences.** *Transfers between trade and non-trade use.* Where a relevant contract is a derivative contract by virtue of 14.8(i) above but ceases to be held for the purposes of the trade without the company's ceasing to be a party to it, the company is deemed to have disposed of and immediately reacquired the relevant contract for an amount equal to its fair value (within *FA 2002, Sch 26 para 54*(*1*)). [*FA 2002, Sch 26 para 44*]. Where it thereby ceases to be a derivative contract and comes instead within the scope of corporation tax on chargeable gains, *TCGA 1992, s 161*(*2*) (see 6.3 ASSETS) will apply so as to treat it for chargeable gains purposes as acquired at that fair value.

The following consequence ensues where a relevant contract whose underlying subject matter is within 14.8(B) or (C) above (or, for periods of account beginning before 1 January 2005 and ending before 16 March 2005, within 14.8(*d*)–(*f*) above), is a chargeable asset rather than a derivative contract, i.e. it is within the scope of corporation tax on chargeable gains, and it is appropriated by the company for the purposes of a trade carried on by it (such that it becomes a derivative contract). *TCGA 1992, s 161*(*1*) (see 6.3 ASSETS) applies to the appropriation, so that the contract is deemed to have been disposed of for chargeable gains purposes at its market value. However, the election under *TCGA 1992, s 161*(*3*) (see 6.3 ASSETS) is *not* available in these circumstances. [*FA 2002, Sch 26 para 45; SI 2005 No 646, Arts, 1, 14*].

Contracts treated as two separate contracts. Where a relevant contract is an option or a future and its underlying subject matter consists partly of excluded property (as in 14.8 above) and partly of non-excluded property, it is treated, for all corporation tax purposes (including those of corporation tax on chargeable gains), as split (on a just and reasonable basis) into two separate notional contracts. This treatment does not apply if the contract is excluded under the accounting tests etc. referred to above or if the non-excluded property meets the 'subordinate' or 'small value' tests referred to immediately following 14.8(*f*) above (in which case it is merely disregarded rather than dealt with separately). [*FA 2002, Sch 26 para 46; SI 2004 No 2201, Art 16; SI 2005 No 646, Arts 1, 19*].

For contracts entered into before 1 August 2004 and for contracts entered into on or after that date in accounting periods ending before 17 September 2004, similar treatment applies (with similar exceptions) where a relevant contract is an option or a future and its underlying subject matter consists partly of excluded property within 14.8(*a*)–(*c*) above and partly of excluded property within 14.8(*d*)–(*f*) above (exclusions subject to qualifications). [*FA 2002, Sch 26 para 47; SI 2004 No 2201, Arts 1, 17*].

Treasury power to amend provisions. Following *FA 2004*, the Treasury may amend *FA 2002, Sch 26 Pt 9* (including *paras 44–47* above and the provisions at 14.8–14.10 above) by order. [*FA 2002, Sch 26 para 13; FA 2004, s 49, Sch 9 para 2*]. A number of such orders have been made, and these are covered above and at 14.8–14.10.

14.12 **Transitional provisions with potential chargeable gains consequences.** The following applies where:

- a company is party to a contract immediately before and on its commencement day, i.e. the first day of its first accounting period beginning on or after 1 October 2002;

- the contract was outside the financial instruments regime at 14.16 above but is a derivative contract within the *FA 2002, Sch 26* regime; and
- the contract was, immediately before the company's commencement day, a chargeable asset, i.e. it was within the scope of corporation tax on chargeable gains.

When the company ceases to be a party to the contract, it is deemed to have made a chargeable gain or allowable loss equal to that which it would have made had it disposed of the asset immediately before its commencement day at the accounting value (if any) given to the contract at the end of the accounting period immediately preceding its first accounting period beginning on or after 1 October 2002. The gain or loss is to be brought into account in the accounting period in which the company ceases to be a party to the contract. In the case of an allowable loss, the company may elect, within two years after the end of that accounting period, that it be treated instead as a non-trading debit under the loan relationships rules.

Where the above conditions are satisfied and the contract is a derivative contract within *FA 2002, Sch 26 para 7* (contracts with a guaranteed amount payable on maturity — see 14.8(iii) above), the company may irrevocably elect to treat the contract for all corporation tax purposes as divided into two separate contracts in similar manner as under *FA 2002, Sch 26 para 48* (see 14.8 above). The election must be made within two years after the end of the company's first accounting period beginning on or after 1 October 2002 and has effect for that and all subsequent accounting periods. Where this election is made, the same consequences ensue as above (with the same election entitlement in the case of an allowable loss).

[*FA 2002, Sch 28 paras 4, 5, 7*].

14.13 INTANGIBLE FIXED ASSETS

FA 2002, Sch 29 introduced a new corporation tax regime for the treatment of expenditure and receipts in respect of 'intangible fixed assets' (see 14.14 below). Such assets are therefore removed from the charge to corporation tax on chargeable gains, subject to the commencement provisions described below. [*FA 2002, Sch 29 para 1(1)(3)*]. For full details of the regime, see Tolley's Corporation Tax under Intangible Assets.

In summary, the regime encompasses expenditure on the creation, acquisition and enhancement of intangibles (including abortive expenditure) as well as on their preservation and maintenance, and also applies to payments for the use of such assets, e.g. royalties. Profits on disposal of such assets are taxed as income. Losses on disposal and payments are relievable against income. The tax treatment of amortisation normally follows the accounts treatment, but for assets with an indefinite or longer life, a company can elect for a fixed allowance of 4% per annum. The rules extend to agricultural and fishing quotas, payment entitlements under the single payment scheme and Lloyd's syndicate capacity. A form of rollover relief (similar to, but not to be confused with, capital gains tax rollover relief) is available where realisation proceeds of intangibles are reinvested in new intangibles. The relief is available even on the disposal (after 31 March 2002) of an intangible asset excluded from the regime by the commencement provisions, and in such a case may reduce or eliminate a chargeable gain (and reduce the tax-recognised cost of the new intangible asset for the purposes of the regime). See also 55.1, 55.3 ROLLOVER RELIEF and 64.5 UNDERWRITERS AT LLOYD'S.

Commencement. The regime applies only to intangible fixed assets of a company that are:

(*a*) created by the company after 31 March 2002; or

(*b*) acquired by the company after 31 March 2002 from a person who is not a 'related party' (as defined at 41.2 MARKET VALUE); or (*c*) acquired by the company after 31 March 2002 from a related party in the following cases:

(i) where the asset is acquired from a company in whose hands the asset fell within the intangible assets regime;

(ii) where the asset is acquired from an intermediary who acquired the asset after 31 March 2002 from a third party which was not a related party of the intermediary (at the time of the intermediary's acquisition of the asset) or of the company (at the time of the company's acquisition); or

(iii) where the asset was created by any person after 31 March 2002.

It should be noted, therefore, that an asset cannot be brought within the regime simply by means of a transfer between related parties, for example from a sole trader to a company in which he has a major interest. Anti-avoidance provisions apply, broadly, to treat an asset created after commencement and acquired by a company from a related party as excluded from the regime by the above provisions where either the asset is derived from assets themselves so excluded, or the acquisition is directly or indirectly in consequence of, or in connection with, the disposal of an excluded asset. The provisions apply in relation to the debits and credits to be brought into account for accounting periods ending on or after 5 December 2005 (treating, for this purpose only, accounting periods straddling that date as two separate periods, the first ending on 4 December 2005 and the second beginning on 5 December 2005).

For the above purposes and subject to the exceptions below, an asset is treated as acquired or created after 31 March 2002 to the extent that expenditure on its acquisition or creation is incurred after that date. Where only part of such expenditure was incurred after that date, the asset is treated as two separate assets, one falling within the regime and one not; expenditure on the asset is apportioned between the two notional assets on a just and reasonable basis. In general, expenditure is regarded as incurred for this purpose when it is recognised for 'accounting purposes' (see 14.14 below). In certain cases, however, either the capital gains rule (see 15.3 COMPUTATION OF GAINS AND LOSSES), or the capital allowances rule governing the date expenditure is treated as incurred is applied.

Internally-generated goodwill is treated as created before 1 April 2002 if the business in question was carried on at any time before that date by the company concerned or a 'related party' (as defined at 41.2 MARKET VALUE). There is therefore no division of such goodwill into two notional assets, and on disposal it will remain within the charge to corporation tax on chargeable gains. A similar rule applies in the case of an internally-generated asset, other than goodwill, which represents expenditure which would not be qualifying expenditure for capital allowances purposes under the law applicable prior to the introduction of the intangible assets regime. Such an asset is treated as created before 1 April 2002 if it was held at any time before that date by the company concerned or a related party. Where part of the expenditure on such an asset would have qualified for capital allowances, the asset is treated as two separate assets, one qualifying for capital allowances and one not. The notional asset which would have qualified for capital allowances is then treated as created or acquired at the time given by the general provisions above (but using the capital allowances rule to determine the date the expenditure is deemed to have been incurred). Necessary apportionments are made for this purpose on a just and reasonable basis.

Assets acquired by means of certain no gain/no loss transfers made after 27 June 2002 are excluded from the intangible assets regime in the hands of the transferee company if they fell outside the regime in the hands of the transferor company. The transfers in question are those within *TCGA 1992, s 139* (company reconstructions involving transfer of business — see 13.10 COMPANIES), *TCGA 1992, s 140A* (transfer of UK trade between companies resident in different EC member states — see 45.10 OVERSEAS MATTERS) or *TCGA 1992, s 140E* (formation of SE by merger: assets left within UK tax charge — see 13.18 COMPANIES).

Special commencement provisions apply in the case of assets consisting of licences or other rights within *FA 2000, Sch 23* (certain telecommunications rights) and Lloyd's syndicate capacity (see 64.5 UNDERWRITERS AT LLOYD'S). The intangible assets regime applies to such assets in respect of any amounts to be brought into account for tax purposes in accounting periods ending after 31 March 2002.

Special commencement provisions also apply in the case of fungible assets, such as milk quota (see 6.9 ASSETS). For the purpose of the intangible assets regime, fungible assets of the same kind held by the same person in the same capacity are generally pooled and treated as indistinguishable parts of a single asset. Where, however, only part of the single asset would fall within the intangible assets regime under the above commencement provisions, the single asset is divided into two assets, one falling within the regime (the '*new regime pool*') and the other not so falling (the '*existing asset pool*'). Realisations of assets are treated as diminishing the existing asset pool in priority to the new regime pool. Assets acquired are allocated to the existing asset pool (and therefore do not fall within the intangible assets regime) to the extent that they can be identified with assets realised by the company from the existing asset pool in accordance with the following rules. The rules are that acquisitions are to be identified with assets realised from the existing asset pool within the period beginning 30 days before and ending 30 days after the acquisition; assets realised earlier fall to be identified before those realised later, and acquisitions are considered in the date order in which they take place.

Royalties from intangible fixed assets which are recognised for accounting purposes after 31 March 2002 fall within the intangible assets regime regardless of whether or not the asset in respect of which they are payable does so. Transitional provisions apply to prevent royalties being taken into account for tax purposes more than once.

[*FA 2002, s 84(1), Sch 29 paras 107, 117–129; F(No 2)A 2005, s 59(6); FA 2006, s 77(6)–(8)(10)(11)*].

14.14 **Definition of 'intangible fixed asset'.** The term '*intangible asset*' has the same meaning for the purposes of the intangible assets regime as it has for '*accounting purposes*' (as defined in *ICTA 1988, ss 832(1), 836A; FA 2004, s 50* i.e. for the purposes of accounts drawn up in accordance with generally accepted accounting practice). The definition includes also any '*intellectual property*', being:

- any patent, trade mark, registered design, copyright or design right, plant breeders' rights or rights under *Plant Varieties Act 1997, s 7*; or
- any corresponding non-UK right; or
- any information or technique not protected by any of the rights above but having industrial, commercial or other economic value; or
- any licence or other right in respect of any of the above rights, information or techniques.

An '*intangible fixed asset*' is an intangible asset acquired or created by a company for use on a continuing basis in the course of the company's activities, and includes options or other rights to acquire or dispose of an intangible fixed asset. An intangible asset is an intangible fixed asset if it falls within this definition, whether or not it is capitalised in the company's accounts.

'Goodwill' (defined as for accounting purposes — see above) is specifically included within the intangible assets regime.

[*ICTA 1988, ss 832(1), 836A; FA 2002, ss 84(1), 103(1)(2)(6), Sch 29 paras 2–4; FA 2004, s 50; FA 2005, Sch 4 paras 25, 49*].

In effect, these provisions apply the intangible assets regime to assets within the scope of Financial Reporting Standard (FRS) 10, *Goodwill and Intangible Assets*. Broadly, FRS 10 defines intangible assets as non-financial fixed assets which do not have physical substance but are identifiable and which are controlled through custody or legal rights. 'Purchased' goodwill is defined as the difference between the cost of an acquired entity and the aggregate of the fair values of its identifiable assets and liabilities.

Assets excluded. The following types of intangible fixed asset (and options or other rights to acquire or dispose of such assets) are excluded from the intangible assets regime:

(*a*) assets representing rights enjoyed by virtue of an estate, interest or right in or over land;

(*b*) assets representing rights in relation to tangible movable property (see 22.4 EXEMPTIONS AND RELIEFS);

(*c*) an oil licence (as defined) or an interest in an oil licence;

(*d*) financial assets (as defined for accounting purposes (see above) and including loan relationships (see 14.2 above), derivative contracts (see 14.7 above) (or, for accounting periods beginning before 1 October 2002, qualifying contracts within the financial instruments regime — see 14.16 below)), contracts or policies of insurance or capital redemption policies, and rights under a collective investment scheme within the meaning of *Financial Services and Markets Act 2000*);

(*e*) an asset representing shares or other rights in relation to the profits, governance or winding up of a company;

(*f*) an asset representing rights under a trust (other than rights that for accounting purposes fall to be treated as representing an interest in trust property that is an intangible fixed asset within the regime);

(*g*) an asset representing the interest of a partner in a partnership (other than an interest that for accounting purposes falls to be treated as representing an interest in partnership property that is an intangible fixed asset within the regime);

(*h*) assets held for a purpose that is not a business or commercial purpose;

(*j*) assets held for the purpose of activities of a company in respect of which the company is outside the charge to corporation tax;

(*k*) an asset held by a film production company to the extent that it represents production expenditure on a film to which *FA 2006, Sch 4* (taxation of activities of film production company in relation to films that commence principal photography on or after 1 April 2006) applies;

(*l*) (except in relation to royalties) an asset (other than computer software) held for the purposes of a life assurance business;

(*m*) (except in relation to royalties) an asset held for the purposes of a mutual trade or business (other than life assurance business);

(*n*) (except in relation to royalties) an asset representing expenditure on the production of, or on the acquisition before 1 October 2007 of, the original master version (as defined) of a film that commenced principal photography before 1 April 2006;

(*p*) (except in relation to royalties) an asset representing expenditure on the production or acquisition of the master version of a sound recording;

(*q*) (except in relation to royalties) an asset which represents expenditure on computer software that is to be treated for accounting purposes as part of the cost of the related hardware; and

(*r*) (in relation to periods for which a company draws up accounts beginning on or after 1 January 2005) assets previously treated as tangible assets in accounts of the company concerned and in respect of which capital allowances have been made to the company under *CAA 2001, Pt 2* (plant and machinery).

Category (*r*) above is intended specifically to exclude certain expenditure on websites treated as a tangible asset under UK generally accepted accounting practice, but treated as an intangible asset under international accounting standards (Treasury Explanatory Notes to the Finance Bill 2004). The dates in (*k*) and (*n*) above are subject to alteration by Treasury order.

Where an asset does not wholly fall within one of the above categories, it is treated as if it were two separate assets, one falling within the intangible assets regime and one not so falling; any necessary apportionment is to be made on a just and reasonable basis. Assets representing expenditure on research and development or (by election) computer software are excluded from the regime to a limited extent, but proceeds from a disposal of such an asset do fall within the regime to the extent that they are not brought into account for capital allowances purposes.

[*FA 2002, Sch 23 para 24, Sch 27 para 26, Sch 29 paras 72–83; FA 2004, s 52, Sch 10 para 71; FA 2005, Sch 4 para 50; FA 2006, ss 51, 53, 77(4)(5)*].

After 14 August 2002, but subject to the commencement rules above (as modified for this purpose), the intangible assets regime is applied (with exceptions and modifications), in relation to corporate finance lessors, to any intangible asset that is the subject of a finance lease (notwithstanding that the asset may be accounted for by the finance lessor as a financial asset — see exclusions above). [*SI 2002 No 1967*].

Assets excluded from the intangible assets regime are not excluded from the charge to corporation tax on chargeable gains as a result of the introduction of the regime (although assets within a number of the above categories are not within the charge in any event).

14.15 FOREIGN EXCHANGE GAINS AND LOSSES (FOREX)

The so-called FOREX legislation was introduced in 1993, its main effect being to tax exchange gains and losses on monetary assets and liabilities of companies as income. For accounting periods beginning on or after 1 October 2002, the original legislation, as briefly summarised below, is repealed (by *FA 2002, s 79, Sch 23, Sch 40 Pt 3(10)*), and foreign exchange gains and losses of companies are instead taxed under the loan relationships rules, which are amended accordingly. There are rules (at *FA 2002, Sch 23 para 25*) to prevent a company forestalling by bringing to a premature end an accounting period beginning on or after 1 October 2001 (i.e. by changing its accounting date) to delay the coming into effect of the *FA 2002* provisions.

The main elements of the now repealed provisions in *FA 1993, ss 60, 125–170, Schs 15–18* (as amended), which are described in detail in Tolley's Corporation Tax under Exchange Gains and Losses (wherein the terms referred to in the following are defined), are as below.

(*a*) The provisions apply, subject to transitional rules, to 'qualifying companies' (broadly all companies excepting authorised unit trusts, investment trusts and open-ended investment companies) becoming entitled to 'qualifying assets', subject to 'qualifying liabilities', or entitled or subject to 'currency contracts', for accounting periods beginning after 22 March 1995.

(*b*) Exchange gains and losses in respect of qualifying assets and liabilities and currency contracts are recognised as they accrue between set 'translation times'.

(*c*) Trading exchange gains and losses are treated as trading items within Schedule D, Case I, net non-trading exchange gains are assessed under Schedule D, Case VI, and there are special provisions for the relief of net non-trading exchange losses.

(*d*) Certain unrealised exchange gains on long-term capital items may be deferred.

(*e*) Exchange differences are generally calculated in sterling, subject to 13.17 COMPANIES.

(*f*) A company can elect for 'matching' of exchange differences on borrowings with exchange differences on certain non-qualifying assets (see *SI 1994 No 3227* as amended, and as modified by *SI 2000 No 3315*). Matched exchange differences are left out of account until the matched asset is disposed of (other than by way of no gain/no loss disposal) and are then treated as chargeable gains or allowable capital losses. See Tolley's Corporation Tax for details.

(*g*) The charge to corporation tax in respect of chargeable gains does not apply to qualifying assets (subject to transitional provisions).

(*h*) Anti-avoidance rules operate to prevent abuse of the provisions.

There are a number of exclusions from the operation of the provisions, and special rules in relation to insurance companies and cases where assets or contracts are held, or liabilities owed, in '*exempt circumstances*' (broadly, for the purposes of long-term insurance business; for the purposes of mutual insurance business; for the purposes of the occupation for profit of commercial woodlands in the UK; by an approved housing association; or by an approved self-build society).

As regards (*d*) above, the deferral facility is not continued under the loan relationships regime for accounting periods beginning on or after 1 October 2002. Transitional rules (at *FA 2002, Sch 23 para 26*) ensure that previously deferred amounts are brought in as credits under the loan relationship rules in the first accounting period beginning on or after 1 October 2002, but companies may elect to spread such amounts equally over its first six accounting periods so beginning.

As regards (*f*) above, 'matching' continues for accounting periods beginning on or after 1 October 2002, with similar consequences where the matched asset is disposed of, under a non-elective regime which seeks to follow UK generally accepted accounting practice (see *SI 2002 No 1970*).

The principal provisions consequential to (*g*) above are mentioned at 13.10 COMPANIES; 22.5 and 22.8 EXEMPTIONS AND RELIEFS; 27.2 GROUPS OF COMPANIES; 45.3 OVERSEAS MATTERS and 50.2 QUALIFYING CORPORATE BONDS.

14.16 FINANCIAL INSTRUMENTS INVOLVING INTEREST RATE AND CURRENCY CONTRACTS

The corporation tax provisions in *FA 1994, Pt IV Ch II* (i.e. *ss 147–177, Sch 18* (as amended)) relating to the treatment of financial instruments to manage interest rate and currency risk are given in Tolley's Corporation Tax under Financial Instruments and Derivative Contracts (wherein the following quoted terms are defined). For the purposes of those provisions, an 'interest rate contract' or 'interest rate option', or a 'currency contract' or 'currency option', is a 'qualifying contract' as regards a 'qualifying company' if the company becomes entitled to rights or subject to duties under the contract or option on or after its 'commencement day', i.e. the first day of its first accounting period beginning after 22 March 1995 (subject to transitional provisions). The *FA 1994* provisions, as summarised below, **are repealed** for accounting periods beginning on or after 1 October 2002 (see further below).

Under the *FA 1994* rules, any amount which under or by virtue of the above provisions is chargeable to corporation tax as profits of a qualifying company, or which falls to be taken into account as a receipt in computing for the purposes of those provisions (which are deemed to include certain provisions in 14.15 above dealing with non-trading exchange gains), the profits or losses of such a company, is excluded for the purposes of *TCGA 1992* from the consideration for a disposal of assets taken into account in the computation of the gain. Similarly, any amount (irrespective of whether effect is or would be given to the deduction of it in computing the amount of tax chargeable or by discharge or repayment of tax or in any other way), which is allowable as a deduction in computing for the above purposes (as similarly extended) the profits or losses of a qualifying company, or which under or by virtue of the above provisions is allowable as a deduction in computing any other income or profits or gains or losses of such a company for the purposes of the *Tax Acts*, or which, although not so allowable as a deduction in computing any losses, would be so allowable as a deduction but for an insufficiency of income or profits or gains, is excluded from the sums allowable under *TCGA 1992, s 38* (allowable expenditure on disposal) as a deduction in the computation of the gain. [*FA 1994, s 173*].

Finance Act 1996 extended the *Finance Act 1994* rules, with effect for accounting periods ending after 31 March 1996 but subject to transitional provisions, to debt contracts or options.

A debt contract is a contract which may or may not be subject to conditions whereby a qualifying company has an entitlement or requirement to become a party to a loan relationship, details of which will be contained in the contract.

Payments allowed under the contract apart from those under the loan relationship are:

(*a*) a payment of an amount representing the price for becoming a party to the relationship;

(*b*) a payment of an amount determined by reference to the value at any time of the money debt by which the relationship subsists;

(*c*) a settlement payment of an amount determined by reference at specified times to the difference between —

(i) the price for becoming a party to the relationship, and

(ii) the value of the money debt by reference to which the relationship subsists or (if the relationship were in existence) would subsist.

[*FA 1994, s 150A(1)–(6); FA 1996, Sch 12*].

In addition payments under *FA 1994, s 151* are also allowed. These will include payments for entering into a contract or option, arrangement fees, variation or termination fees and compensation fees on non-compliance.

If the contract is a hybrid of debt contract and non-debt contract provisions, the clauses relating to the debt contract shall be treated as a separate contract.

[*FA 1994, s 150A(7)(8); FA 1996, Sch 12*].

A debt contract is not a loan relationship if it is convertible or its value is linked to the value of chargeable assets.

[*FA 1994, s 150A(10); FA 1996, Sch 12*].

For accounting periods beginning on or after 1 October 2002, the above rules are replaced by the derivative contracts regime (see 14.7–14.12 above), which widens the scope of the financial instruments regime to cover new types of instrument that have become available since the *FA 1994* rules were enacted, and remodels the core provisions along the lines of the loan relationships rules.

15 Computation of Gains and Losses

Cross-references. See 2.3 ANNUAL RATES AND EXEMPTIONS; 6.7 ASSETS for options; 7 ASSETS HELD ON 6 APRIL 1965; 8 ASSETS HELD ON 31 MARCH 1982; 9 CAPITAL SUMS DERIVED FROM ASSETS; 34 INDEXATION; 35 INTERACTION WITH OTHER TAXES; 38 LAND for disposals of land and leases; 40 LOSSES; 41 MARKET VALUE; 59 SHARES AND SECURITIES—IDENTIFICATION RULES; 67 WASTING ASSETS.

Simon's Direct Tax Service. See C1.105.

The headings in this chapter are as follows.

15.1 BASIC PRINCIPLES

Gains and losses accruing on disposals of assets are computed by deducting allowable expenditure (see 15.4–15.6 below) from the amount realised or deemed to be realised on the disposal (i.e. the actual or deemed consideration). [*TCGA 1992, ss 15, 38*]. In certain circumstances a disposal (and/or acquisition) may be deemed by the legislation to be made at MARKET VALUE (see 41.1) or on a no gain/no loss basis (see, in particular, 27.2 GROUPS OF COMPANIES and 42.4 MARRIED PERSONS AND CIVIL PARTNERS). See also 15.9 below for alternative finance arrangements, and 35.1 INTERACTION WITH OTHER TAXES for the exclusion of amounts charged to income tax from disposal consideration.

There are special computational provisions in respect of certain types of assets. See 38.14 LAND for leases, 59 SHARES AND SECURITIES—identification rules, and 67 WASTING ASSETS.

Where a bundle of assets is sold together, it is necessary to consider each disposal separately, in the light of the rules which apply to that asset (*Aberdeen Construction Group Ltd v CIR HL 1978, 52 TC 281*). See also *Fullarton and others v CIR Sp C, [2004] SSCD 207*. The consideration for the sale of an asset is the agreed purchase price regardless of how it is to be applied (*Spectros International plc v Madden Ch D 1996, 70 TC 349*). No deduction is allowable more than once from any sum or from more than one sum. [*TCGA 1992, s 52(1)*].

See 15.3 below for date of disposal. See 15.7 below for part disposals.

Indexation. The gain (if any) arrived at as above is termed the '*unindexed gain*'. Any indexation allowance due is deducted from the unindexed gain to give the gain for the purposes of *TCGA 1992* unless otherwise provided. If the allowance equals or exceeds the unindexed gain, no gain or loss arises. If a loss arises as above, no indexation allowance is available. For disposals after 5 April 1998 for capital gains tax purposes (although not those of corporation tax on chargeable gains), indexation allowance is frozen at its April 1998 level and is not available at all in respect of expenditure incurred after 31 March 1998. See 34.1 INDEXATION.

Losses. See 40 LOSSES for the deduction of allowable losses from chargeable gains.

Taper relief. For disposals after 5 April 1998, a taper relief applies to gains realised by individuals, trustees and personal representatives, whereby the otherwise chargeable gain (after deducting any indexation allowance and allowable losses (but see 61.3 TAPER RELIEF)) is reduced according to the length of time the asset has been held after 5 April 1998 and whether it is a business or non-business asset. See 61 TAPER RELIEF.

Annual exemption. Individuals are exempt from capital gains tax in respect of so much of their taxable gains for a tax year as do not exceed the annual exempt amount. Where the gains exceed that amount, only the excess is taxable. Personal representatives (for a limited period) and trustees of settlements are also entitled to an annual exempt amount, but companies are not. See 2.3 ANNUAL RATES AND EXEMPTIONS.

Assets held on 6 April 1965. There are special computational provisions for assets held on 6 April 1965, the broad purpose of which is to exclude from tax that part of the eventual gain on disposal which accrued before that date. See 7 ASSETS HELD ON 6 APRIL 1965. For most disposals after 5 April 1988, the provisions are displaced by the rebasing provisions for assets held on 31 March 1982 (see below), but they still apply in certain cases.

Assets held on 31 March 1982. Special provisions also apply to the disposal after 5 April 1988 of assets held on 31 March 1982. Broadly, on the disposal of such an asset, the acquisition cost for tax purposes is rebased to its market value on 31 March 1982 where this results in a smaller gain or loss than would be the case using the actual acquisition cost (or applying the rules for assets held on 6 April 1965) in the computation. Taxpayers are able to make a universal rebasing election for such rebasing to apply to all of their assets held on 31 March 1982 and so avoid the need for comparative computations on each disposal. See 8 ASSETS HELD ON 31 MARCH 1982.

15.2 DISPOSAL

Simon's Direct Tax Service. See C1.104.

'*Disposal*' is not defined in the legislation. The term includes a part disposal (see 15.7 below) and there are numerous circumstances in which the legislation deems there to be a disposal for tax purposes even though there has been no actual disposal. See in particular 9 CAPITAL SUMS DERIVED FROM ASSETS, 15.3 below for assets lost or destroyed and 40.9 LOSSES for assets becoming of negligible value.

A conveyance or transfer of an asset or of a right therein *by way of security* (e.g. a mortgage) is not a disposal, but if the creditor or any person appointed as receiver, manager, etc. deals with the asset in order to enforce the security, his activities are imputed to the giver of the security. The existence of a security is ignored for both acquisition and disposal of an asset save that the amount of liability assumed forms part of the acquisition and disposal consideration in addition to any other consideration. [*TCGA 1992, s 26*]. Relief is available if there has been a sale of an asset at arm's length in circumstances such that the vendor granted the purchaser a mortgage (in full or in part) in order for the purchaser to buy and where there has later been a default on the mortgage loan. If, as a result, the vendor regains beneficial ownership of the asset he has contracted to sell he may elect that the gain realised by him on that sale be taken as limited to the net proceeds (after incidental costs of disposal) retained by him and for the loan to be treated as never coming into existence (although interest on the loan would be subject to income tax in the usual way). On any subsequent disposal of the asset concerned, the computation will be by reference to the original date and costs of acquisition etc. (HMRC Extra-Statutory Concession D18).

A taxpayer who, in consideration of a loan, promised his parents 60% of the net proceeds of any sale of his shares in his personal company, whilst retaining beneficial ownership of the shares in the meantime, was held liable to capital gains tax in respect of the total proceeds of the eventual sale (*Burca v Parkinson Ch D 2001, 74 TC 125*).

15.3 DATE OF DISPOSAL

Simon's Direct Tax Service. See C1.322.

Contracts. Where an asset is disposed of and acquired under a contract, the disposal and acquisition are made at the time the contract is made (and not, if different, the time at which the asset is conveyed or transferred, e.g. on a contract for the sale of land). This rule applies even if the contract is unenforceable, provided that the disposal is actually completed (*Thompson v Salah Ch D 1971, 47 TC 559*). (However, HMRC points out that the authority of this case is no longer valid where the general law provides that contracts entered into in respect of land must be made in writing (as is required under *Law of Property* (*Miscellaneous Provisions*) *Act 1989* and which applies in England and Wales although a similar requirement applies in Scotland (HMRC Capital Gains Manual CG 18162, 25860 and 70280)). If the contract is conditional (and, in particular, if it is conditional on the exercise of an option), the disposal and acquisition are made at the time the condition is satisfied. [*TCGA 1992, s 28*].

See *Eastham v Leigh London & Provincial Properties Ltd CA 1971, 46 TC 687*; *Johnson v Edwards Ch D 1981, 54 TC 488*. In *Jerome v Kelly HL, [2004] STC 887; [2004] All ER(D) 168(May)*, in which there was an intermediate disposal of part of the asset to a Bermudan trust between contract and completion, the taxpayer was held not to be liable to CGT on the original disposal of the part of the asset covered by the intermediate disposal. Lord Hoffmann observed that the draftsman responsible for what is now *TCGA 1992, s 28*(*1*) 'did not think about what should happen in the situation which has arisen in this case'. He held that it would be wrong 'to attribute to Parliament an intention to impose a liability to tax upon a person who would not be treated as having made a disposal under the carefully constructed scheme for taxing the disposals of assets held on trust'. *TCGA 1992, s 28*(*1*) should be treated as 'concerned solely with fixing the time of disposal by a person whose identity is to be ascertained by other means'.

See also under hire purchase below.

Gifts. A gift is treated as having been made when the donor has done everything within his power to transfer the property to the donee (*Re Rose, Rose and Others v CIR CA, [1952] 1 All ER 1217*).

Hire purchase. A transaction under which the assets may pass to the hirer at the end of the hire is treated as a disposal of the whole asset at the beginning of that period, with subsequent adjustments if the agreement terminates without the hirer acquiring the asset. [*TCGA 1992, s 27*]. For consideration of hire-purchase and conditional contracts (see above), see *Lyon v Pettigrew Ch D 1985, 58 TC 452*.

Capital sums. Deemed disposals covered by 9 CAPITAL SUMS DERIVED FROM ASSETS take place on the receipt of the capital sum. [*TCGA 1992, s 22*(*2*)]. See *Chaloner v Pellipar Investments Ltd Ch D 1996, 68 TC 238* in which it was held, by reference to the particular facts of the case, that a capital sum received by the taxpayer in 'money's worth' fell outside *section 22* and that the date of disposal had thus to be determined by reference to the contract date as above.

Options. See 6.7 ASSETS.

Assets lost or destroyed are deemed to be disposed of at the time of loss etc. [*TCGA 1992, s 24*(*1*)]. It seems that this provision does not override *TCGA 1992, s 22*(*2*) above where an actual capital sum is received subsequent to the loss etc. (see comments by Hoffman J in the Ch D in *Powlson v Welbeck Securities Ltd CA 1987, 60 TC 269*).

Assets becoming of negligible value. See 40.9 LOSSES.

Land compulsorily acquired. See 38.9 LAND for acquisition of land by an authority possessing any power of compulsory purchase.

Rollover relief. See 55.1 ROLLOVER RELIEF.

15.4 ALLOWABLE EXPENDITURE—GENERAL PROVISIONS

Simon's Direct Tax Service. See Division C2.2.

Except as otherwise expressly provided, the sums allowable as a deduction from the consideration in the computation of any gain accruing to a person on the disposal of an asset are restricted to the following.

(*a*) **The amount or value of the consideration, in money or money's worth, given wholly and exclusively for the acquisition of the asset** (plus 'incidental costs') or expenditure incurred wholly and exclusively in providing the asset [*TCGA 1992, s 38*(*1*)(*a*)]. See *Cleveleys Investment Trust Co v CIR (No 2) CS 1975, 51 TC 26*; *Allison v Murray Ch D 1975, 51 TC 57*; *Garner v Pounds Shipowners & Shipbreakers Ltd (and related appeal) HL 2000, 72 TC 561*.

'*Incidental costs*' of acquisition are (strictly) limited to expenditure wholly and exclusively incurred for the purposes of the acquisition, being

(i) fees, commission or remuneration for the professional services of a surveyor, valuer, auctioneer, accountant, agent or legal adviser;

(ii) transfer/conveyancing charges (including stamp duty); and

(iii) advertising to find a seller.

[*TCGA 1992, s 38*(*2*)].

Where the purchaser is a company, and the purchase price is satisfied by the issue of fully paid-up shares in the company, the consideration is the shares and their value is normally that placed on them by the parties, i.e. the purchase price satisfied by the issue. 'Value' in *TCGA 1992, s 38*(*1*)(*a*) (see above) does not mean 'market value' (*Stanton v Drayton Commercial Investment Co Ltd HL 1982, 55 TC 286*). Disposals which are deemed to take place at market value will, generally speaking, give rise to an equivalent base cost in the acquirer's hands (but see 41.1 MARKET VALUE). No allowance is given for notional costs of disposal or reacquisition, where there is a deemed disposal and reacquisition. [*TCGA 1992, s 17, s 38*(*4*)].

See (*b*) below for capital contributions by shareholders.

A company with an annual turnover of not less than £5 million may round incidental costs of acquisition to the nearest £1,000 subject to certain conditions and exceptions (HMRC Statement of Practice 15/93).

Foreign currency. Where the cost (or deemed cost) of an asset is in foreign currency, it is converted into sterling at the exchange rate ruling at the time of acquisition. Similarly, consideration is converted at the date of disposal. (*Bentley v Pike Ch D 1981, 53 TC 590*; *Capcount Trading v Evans CA 1992, 65 TC 545*). Where a company borrowed foreign currency and entered into a forward contract to purchase sufficient foreign currency to repay the loan some ten months later, which in effect commercially was a single composite transaction, these were treated as separate transactions for chargeable gains purposes. As a result, the forward currency contract produced a chargeable gain and the repayment of the currency loan produced a loss on exchange that was not an allowable loss for capital gains tax. (*Whittles v Uniholdings Ltd (No 3) CA, [1996] STC 914*).

A 'qualifying company' was excepted from the above, as regards a 'qualifying asset', by the introduction of the 'FOREX' regime for foreign exchange gains and losses introduced by *FA 1993*, which is summarised at 14.15 COMPANIES—CORPORATE FINANCE AND INTANGIBLES and covered in detail in Tolley's Corporation Tax under Exchange Gains and Losses. For accounting periods beginning on or after 1 October 2002 (subject to forestalling rules), this regime no longer applies; instead, foreign exchange gains and losses arising to a company in relation to any asset or liability representing a loan relationship of the company are dealt with under the rules at 14.2–14.6 COMPANIES—CORPORATE FINANCE AND INTANGIBLES (again covered in detail in Tolley's Corporation Tax). Matching of exchange differences on chargeable assets generally with those on borrowings was available by election under the superseded 'FOREX' rules (see 14.15(*f*) COMPANIES—CORPORATE FINANCE AND INTANGIBLES). Matching continues for accounting periods beginning on or after 1 October 2002 under a non-elective regime — see 14.3 COMPANIES—CORPORATE FINANCE AND INTANGIBLES.

(*b*) **Expenditure wholly and exclusively incurred for the purpose of enhancing the value of the asset being expenditure reflected in the state or nature of the asset at the time of disposal.** [*TCGA 1992, s 38*(*1*)(*b*)]. Expenditure on initial repairs (including decoration) to a property, undertaken to put it into a fit state for letting, and not allowable in computing taxable property business profits, is regarded as allowable expenditure under this heading (HMRC Statement of Practice D24). HMRC consider that capital contributions made to a company by shareholders are not allowable expenditure under this heading, but that if made at the time of issue of the shares they might be treated as in the nature of a share premium (ICAEW Guidance Note TR 713, 23 August 1988 and HMRC Capital Gains Manual CG 43500). See also 15.6(*a*) below.

'*Expenditure*' does not include the value of personal labour and skill (*Oram v Johnson Ch D 1980, 53 TC 319*). However, it may be in the form of providing money's worth and may be first reflected in the state or nature of the asset before completion even if this is after the time of disposal (*Chaney v Watkis Ch D 1985, 58 TC 707*).

(*c*) **Expenditure wholly and exclusively incurred in establishing, preserving or defending title to, or to a right over, the asset.** [*TCGA 1992, s 38*(*1*)(*b*)]. This includes resealing Scottish confirmation and other probate etc. expenses incurred to establish the title of the personal representatives (*Richards' Executors HL 1971, 46 TC 626* and see 18.8 DEATH) and see 57.15 SETTLEMENTS.

In *Lee v Jewitt (Sp C 257), [2000] SSCD 517*, legal costs incurred by a partner in defending an action by fellow partners resulting in dissolution of the partnership were held to have been incurred under this heading.

(*d*) **Incidental costs of disposal.** [*TCGA 1992, s 38*(*1*)(*c*)]. Strictly, such costs are limited to expenditure wholly and exclusively incurred for the purposes of the disposal, being

(i) fees, commission or remuneration for the professional services of a surveyor, valuer, auctioneer, accountant, agent or legal adviser;

(ii) transfer/conveyancing charges (including stamp duty);

(iii) advertising to find a buyer; and

(iv) any other costs reasonably incurred in making any valuation or apportionment for capital gains tax purposes, including, in particular, expenses reasonably incurred in ascertaining market value where this is required under *TCGA 1992*.

[*TCGA 1992, s 38*(*2*)].

Stamp duty and other expenses of terminating a settlement incurred to bring about a chargeable occasion within *TCGA 1992, s 71* are allowable (*Chubb's Trustee CS 1971, 47 TC 353*).

Costs within (iv) above extend only to costs reasonably incurred in making the valuation or apportionment, and not to any subsequent costs incurred in negotiating a value with the Revenue or in litigation with it concerning the value (Revenue Tax Bulletin February 1994 p 116) and see *Caton's Administrators v Couch CA 1997, 70 TC 10*. The same principle applies where the costs are incurred in relation to a post-transaction valuation check (see 54.4 RETURNS) (HMRC Capital Gains Manual CG 15261, 16615).

A company with an annual turnover of not less than £5 million may round incidental costs of disposal to the nearest £1,000 subject to certain conditions and exceptions (HMRC Statement of Practice 15/93).

15.5 ALLOWABLE EXPENDITURE—SPECIAL CASES

In addition to the general provisions relating to allowable expenditure in 15.4 above, specific items of expenditure are allowed as follows.

(*a*) **Interest in certain (now very rare) circumstances** on money borrowed by a *company* for financing allowable expenditure on the construction of a building, structure, or work. There is no such provision for individuals, trustees, etc. See 13.12 COMPANIES.

(*b*) **Income tax paid by a close company participator** on income which has been apportioned to him (broadly in relation only to accounting periods ending before 1 April 1989) but which remains undistributed is an allowable deduction. [*TCGA 1992, s 124*]. Alternatively, the Revenue will restrict a participator's 'excess liability' on an apportionment for a period after commencement of winding-up to the excess, if any, over capital gains tax paid on distributions made in respect of the participator's share by the liquidator during that period. Where post liquidation income is apportioned to trust beneficiaries or residuary legatees, account will be taken of any relevant capital gains tax paid by the trustees or personal representatives (see HMRC Extra-Statutory Concession A36). Where tax on the apportioned income is borne by a beneficiary under a trust or by a residuary legatee, the relief is extended to a disposal of the relevant shares by the trustees or by the personal representatives (see HMRC Extra-Statutory Concession D12). The reliefs in ESCs A36 and D12 are in the alternative. See also 3.17 ANTI-AVOIDANCE regarding *TCGA 1992, s 125* (close company transferring assets at undervalue).

(*c*) **Foreign tax** borne by the disposer on the disposal is deductible. See 19.5 DOUBLE TAX RELIEF.

(*d*) **Inheritance tax** is a deduction in some circumstances. See 35.2 INTERACTION WITH OTHER TAXES.

(*e*) **Acquisitions from persons neither resident nor ordinarily resident in the UK.** Where, *after 9 March 1981 and before 6 April 1983*,

(i) a person acquired an asset for no valuable consideration, or for a consideration lower than the asset's market value, and no other amount or value was imputed to the consideration by operation of *CGTA 1979* (e.g. under the MARKET VALUE (41) rules), and

(ii) there was a corresponding disposal of the asset by a person neither resident nor ordinarily resident in the UK, and

(iii) a charge to income tax, corporation tax or capital gains tax arose in respect of the acquisition in (i) above,

a deduction is given on the subsequent disposal of the asset by the acquirer, equal to the amount in respect of which the charge in (iii) above arises. The condition in (iii) above was taken to be satisfied where, under *FA 1981, s 80(3)* (now *TCGA 1992, s 87(4)*; see 44.14 OFFSHORE SETTLEMENTS), in any year of assessment, gains were attributed to a beneficiary of a non-resident settlement, by reason of that beneficiary's acquisition of an asset in that or an earlier fiscal year. In such circumstances, the deduction is the amount of the gains attributed to the beneficiary because of the acquisition of the said asset.

After 5 April 1983, the market value rules were amended so that, subject to the election below, an acquisition under the circumstances in (i) to (iii) is treated as being made at market value and the above provisions do not apply. Where, however, the corresponding disposal under (ii) is made *after 5 April 1983 and before 6 April 1985* the persons acquiring and disposing of the asset may jointly elect that both the acquisition and disposal are excepted from the amended market value rules in which case the above provisions still apply. [*CGTA 1979, s 32(5)(6); FA 1981, s 90(2); FA 1984, s 66(3)*]. See 41.1 MARKET VALUE for further details.

(*f*) **Stock dividends.** The 'appropriate amount in cash' relating to a stock dividend is deductible. See 58.9 SHARES AND SECURITIES.

(*g*) **Offshore funds.** Certain sums charged to income tax on the disposal of interests in offshore funds. See 45.8 OVERSEAS MATTERS.

(*h*) **Shares acquired by employees.** See 20 EMPLOYEE SHARE SCHEMES.

(*j*) **Legatees and beneficiaries.** Where a person disposes of an asset held by a personal representative or trustee to which he became absolutely entitled as legatee or as against the trustee, any incidental expenditure incurred by that person, the personal representative or the trustee in relation to the transfer of the asset to him, is allowable. [*TCGA 1992, s 64(1); FA 2006, Sch 12 para 12*]. See 18.9 DEATH and 57.15 SETTLEMENTS.

(*k*) **Devaluation of sterling in November 1967.** In computing gains on the disposal of foreign securities purchased out of foreign currency borrowed before 19 November 1967 for that purpose (by permission given, subject to specified conditions, under *Exchange Control Act 1947*) the deduction under 15.4(*a*) above is increased by one-sixth. A similar increase applies to disposals after 18 November 1967 of foreign securities which at that date formed part of a trust fund established abroad by a Lloyd's underwriter, etc., or a company engaged in marine protection or indemnity assurance on a mutual basis, which consists of premiums received and used mainly for meeting business liabilities arising in the country in which the fund is set up. [*TCGA 1992, Sch 11 paras 13, 14*].

15.6 NON-ALLOWABLE EXPENDITURE

In no case is allowance given for the following.

(*a*) Expenditure which is deductible in computing profits or losses for income tax purposes [*TCGA 1992, s 39(1)*] or would be so deductible if the asset were held as a fixed asset of a trade [*TCGA 1992, s 39(2)*]. See *Emmerson v Computer Time International Ltd CA 1977, 50 TC 628.*

(*b*) Premiums paid to cover the risk of damage to, or loss or depreciation of, the asset. [*TCGA 1992, s 205*].

(*c*) Any expenditure recoverable from any government or public or local authority in the UK or elsewhere. Where such a grant is subsequently repaid, the consideration on disposal of the asset may be treated, by concession, as reduced by the amount repaid. (HMRC Extra-Statutory Concession D53). [*TCGA 1992, s 50*]. (See Revenue Tax Bulletin April 1999 pp 642–645 (in particular, Example 2) re the application of this provision to land introduced by a public sector body into a Private Finance Initiative contract as a contribution to the private sector operator's construction costs.) This provision has no effect on the quantum of rollover relief available under *TCGA 1992, s 152* (see 55.1 ROLLOVER RELIEF) where the asset attracting the grant is the new asset for the purposes of that relief (*Wardhaugh v Penrith Rugby Union Football Club Ch D 2002, 74 TC 499*).

(*d*) Interest, except as under 15.5(*a*) above. [*TCGA 1992, s 38(3)*].

(*e*) Income tax chargeable on shares acquired under certain employee schemes. See 20 EMPLOYEE SHARE SCHEMES.

(*f*) Liabilities remaining with, or assumed by, the disposer contingent upon the default of the assignee of a lease, or upon the breach of covenants in a conveyance or lease of land, or of warranties, or representations made on the sale or lease of other property. If the contingent liability subsequently becomes enforceable and is enforced, relief is given by way of discharge or repayment. [*TCGA 1992, s 49; FA 1996, Sch 20 para 49*]. An amount received under a warranty or indemnity is normally deductible from the purchaser's acquisition cost (HMRC Extra-Statutory Concession D33 and HMRC Capital Gains Manual CG 13043, 13044). See further 38.24 LAND.

(*g*) Any discount for postponement of receipt of the consideration and, in the first instance, for any risk of non-recovery, or for any contingency in the right to receive any part of the consideration. If, however, any part of the consideration subsequently proves to be irrecoverable, on a claim to that effect the tax liability will be adjusted accordingly which may result in a discharge or repayment of tax. On or after 20 July 2005 this provision does not apply to so much of any consideration as consists of rights under a creditor relationship (see 14.5 COMPANIES—CORPORATE FINANCE AND INTANGIBLES) to which a company becomes a party as a result of the disposal. Instead, the amount to be brought into account in respect of that consideration is the 'fair value' (within *FA 1996, s 103(1)*) of the creditor relationship. [*TCGA 1992, s 48; FA 1996, Sch 20 para 48; F(No 2)A 2005, Sch 7 para 7*]. (See *Marson v Marriage Ch D 1979, 54 TC 59.*) See also 9.1 CAPITAL SUMS DERIVED FROM ASSETS and 47.6 PAYMENT OF TAX for the possibility of payment by instalments.

Where consideration for a disposal is fixed in a foreign currency, any subsequent loss on exchange is not irrecoverable consideration for the purposes of a claim under *TCGA 1992, s 48*. See *Goodbrand v Loffland Bros North Sea Inc CA 1998, 71 TC 57.*

A subsequent payment, by the vendor of an option to a third party, to release restrictive covenants did not alter the consideration received for the option and was not allowable expenditure in computing the gain (*Garner v Pounds Shipowners & Shipbreakers Ltd (and related appeal) HL 2000, 72 TC 561*).

(*h*) Notional expenses on deemed disposals and acquisitions. [*TCGA 1992, s 38(4)*].

(*j*) Where a 'loss' would otherwise be shown, expenditure otherwise allowable as a deduction is reduced to the extent that capital allowances have been made in respect of it. The capital allowances taken into account are those granted (less any balancing charge) to the disposer. Where the asset was treated for capital allowance purposes as acquired at written-down value, allowances granted to any former owner which were not taken into account in restricting his loss are also deducted from allowable expenditure.

'*Loss*' seemed to refer to the unindexed loss for disposals before 30 November 1993 and after 5 April 1985 (after 31 March 1985 for companies), when the restriction of allowable expenditure above also applied in the calculation of the indexation allowance so that, broadly, the allowable loss was the indexation allowance arising. HMRC maintain that '*loss*' is the indexed loss, i.e. the loss after indexation (HMRC Capital Gains Manual CG 17450), though this is arguable.

Where the loss-making disposal is of plant or machinery in relation to expenditure on which allowances or charges have been made for capital allowance purposes and which has been used solely for trade purposes and has not attracted partial depreciation subsidies which would deny capital allowances, the capital allowances (if any) are deemed to be the difference between the qualifying expenditure incurred (or treated as incurred) by the disposer, and the disposal value. [*TCGA 1992, s 41(1)–(7), s 53(3); CAA 2001, Sch 2 para 78; ITTOIA 2005, Sch 1 para 430*]. See also 7.11 ASSETS HELD ON 6 APRIL 1965, 8.8 ASSETS HELD ON 31 MARCH 1982 and 27.6 GROUPS OF COMPANIES for further applications of these rules.

In *Smallwood v HMRC Sp C 2005 (Sp C 509), [2006] SSCD 12*, *TCGA 1992, s 41* was held not to restrict a loss on units in an enterprise zone unit trust where the trustees of the unit trust had used the funds subscribed for the units to acquire land and buildings, in respect of which the taxpayer had been credited with capital allowances. The Special Commissioner held that capital allowances had not been made in respect of the taxpayer's expenditure in subscribing for the units. It was the trustees' expenditure that had resulted in capital allowances for the taxpayer.

(*k*) Where a loss would otherwise be shown on the disposal on or after 1 April 2006 of an asset which includes plant or machinery which is a fixture for the purposes of *CAA 2001, Pt 2 Ch 6A* (long-funding leases: interpretation) and which has been used by the person making the disposal for the purpose of leasing under one or more 'long funding leases', expenditure otherwise allowable as a deduction is reduced by an amount equal to the fall in value of the plant or machinery during the period of that lease (or, where there was more than one such lease, the periods of those leases). For this purpose, the fall in value of plant or machinery during the period of a lease is equal to the excess of the 'market value' of the plant or machinery at the 'commencement' of the 'term' of the lease over its market value at the 'termination' of the lease.

For the meaning of '*long funding lease*' see 6.6 ASSETS. '*Market value*' is determined on the assumption of a disposal by an absolute owner free from all leases and other encumbrances. The expressions '*commencement*', '*term*', and '*termination*' are defined as in *CAA 2001, Pt 2 Ch 6A*. See Tolley's Income Tax or Tolley's Corporation Tax.

[*TCGA 1992, s 41A, FA 2006, Sch 9 para 5*].

15.7 PART DISPOSALS

Simon's Direct Tax Service. See Division C2.4.

References to a disposal for the purposes of the capital gains tax legislation include, unless otherwise required, references to a part disposal. There is a part disposal of an asset where an interest or right in or over the asset is created by the disposal, as well as where it subsists before the disposal, and generally, there is a part disposal of an asset where, on a person making a disposal, any description of property derived from the asset remains undisposed of. [*TCGA 1992, s 21*(2)].

Where a disposal is partial, those deductions which are not wholly attributable either to the part retained or to the part disposed of are apportioned over the total value of the asset, including the part retained, and only the portion relative to the part disposed of is deductible from the consideration received for it. This apportionment also applies for indexation allowance purposes. The apportioned allowable expenditure is calculated by reference to the formula

$$\frac{A}{A+B}$$

where

A is the consideration received or deemed to have been received; and

B is the market value of the part retained.

Any such apportionment is to be made before applying the following provisions.

(*a*) *TCGA 1992, s 41* (restriction of losses by reference to capital allowances, see 15.6(*j*) above). (If after the part disposal there is a subsequent disposal of the asset, the capital allowances to be taken into account on that subsequent disposal are those referable to the expenditure incurred under 15.4(*a*)–(*c*) above whether before or after the part disposal, but those allowances are reduced by the amount, if any, by which the loss on the earlier disposal was restricted under *TCGA 1992, s 41*.)

(*b*) *TCGA 1992, s 58(1)* (transfers between spouses or civil partners, see 42.4 MARRIED PERSONS AND CIVIL PARTNERS).

(*c*) *TCGA 1992, ss 152–158* (replacement of business assets, see 55 ROLLOVER RELIEF).

(*d*) *TCGA 1992, s 171(1)* (transfers within GROUPS OF COMPANIES (27.2)).

(*e*) Any other provision making an adjustment to secure that neither a gain nor a loss occurs on disposal.

(*f*) The computation of any indexation allowance. [*TCGA 1992, s 56(1); FA 1994, Sch 26 Pt V*].

[*TCGA 1992, s 42*].

Similar apportionments of allowable deductions are made where assets have been merged or divided, have changed their nature, or have had interests created out of them, etc. [*TCGA 1992, s 43*].

See 8 ASSETS HELD ON 31 MARCH 1982 for further applications of *TCGA 1992, s 42* and *s 43*.

Any other necessary apportionment is to be made as may be 'just and reasonable'. [*TCGA 1992, s 52(4), Sch 11 para 11; FA 1996, Sch 20 para 50*]. HMRC cites the case of *EV Booth (Holdings) Ltd v Buckwell Ch D 1980, 53 TC 425* as authority for its view that if the inspector is satisfied with the allocation contained in a contract made between parties bargaining at arm's length, it is not open to either the vendor or the purchaser to seek to alter that apportionment for capital gains tax purposes. In contrast, where the terms of the contract are artificial it takes the view that *TCGA 1992, s 52(4)* may be applied irrespective of the way in which the vendor and purchaser have agreed to allocate the overall price (HMRC Capital Gains Manual CG 14772).

Example

X buys a piece of land in 1989 for £182,000. He subsequently sells half of it to Y in May 2005 for £150,000. The remainder of the land, because of its better position, is estimated to be then worth £200,000.

X's unindexed gain is computed as follows

A = £150,000

B = £200,000

Allowable expenditure attributable to the part disposed of

$$\frac{150{,}000}{(150{,}000+200{,}000)} \times £182{,}000 = £78{,}000$$

Unindexed gain (subject to indexation to April 1998 and TAPER RELIEF (61)): £150,000 – £78,000 = £72,000

The allowable expenditure on a disposal of the remaining land will be £104,000, i.e. £182,000 less £78,000.

In *Anders Utkilens Rederi A/S v O/Y Lovisa Stevedoring Co A/B and Another Ch D 1984, [1985] STC 301*, a plaintiff had initially obtained judgment for a liquidated sum against a defendant, but the action was then compromised by an agreement for the defendant's property to be sold and the proceeds divided between the parties. It was held that there had been a part disposal of an interest in the property by the defendant to the plaintiff followed by a disposal by each party of his interest then held to the final purchaser.

A 1995 assignment, for a capital sum, of the right to receive rental income for a fixed period (a 'rent factoring' transaction) was held to be a *part* disposal of the property in question (*CIR v John Lewis Properties plc CA 2002, [2003] STC 117*), but note that, under subsequent legislation, rent factoring receipts are now chargeable as income (see Tolley's Corporation Tax under Property Income).

See 38.7 LAND for relief for certain part disposals of land and 38.16 where part of the premium received for a lease is liable to income tax.

Simon's Direct Tax Service. See C2.4.

15.8 FORFEITED DEPOSIT OF PURCHASE MONEY

A forfeited deposit of purchase money or other consideration money for a prospective purchase or other transaction which is abandoned is treated in the same way as consideration given for an option to purchase which is not exercised. [*TCGA 1992, s 144(7)*]. There is no disposal for capital gains tax purposes by the person who abandons his deposit and no loss relief is available (except in the case of a forfeited deposit on an asset intended to be used, if acquired, for the purposes of a trade carried on by the forfeiter (see 6.7(*a*) ASSETS)). There is, however, a disposal of an asset to which no allowable expenditure attaches by the person receiving the forfeited deposit the amount of which is treated as the consideration received. See 6.7 ASSETS.

15.9 ALTERNATIVE FINANCE ARRANGEMENTS

Where, under certain 'alternative finance arrangements', an asset is sold by one party to the arrangements to the other party, the 'effective return' is excluded in determining for capital gains purposes the consideration for the sale and purchase of the asset. This does not affect the operation of any provision providing for the consideration to be treated as an amount other than the actual consideration.

This provision applies to two types of '*alternative financial arrangements*': those within *FA 2005, s 47* and those within *FA 2005, s 47A*.

For this purpose, alternative finance arrangements within *FA 2005, s 47* are, broadly, arrangements entered into after 5 April 2005 between two persons (A and B), at least one of whom is a 'financial institution' (as defined), under which:

(*a*) A purchases an asset and sells it to B;

(*b*) the amount payable by B in respect of the sale (the '*sale price*') is greater than the amount paid by A in respect of the purchase (the 'purchase price');

(*c*) all or part of the sale price does not have to be paid until a time after the sale; and

(*d*) the difference between the sale price and the purchase price equates, in substance, to the return on an investment of money at interest.

The sale of the asset in (*a*) above must take place immediately after the purchase unless A is a financial institution and the asset was purchased by A for the purpose of entering into the arrangements. The '*effective return*' is so much of the sale price as exceeds the purchase price.

Alternative finance arrangements within *FA 2005, s 47A* are, broadly, arrangements entered into after 5 April 2006 (31 March 2006 for corporation tax purposes) under which a financial institution acquires a beneficial interest in an asset and another person (the '*eventual owner*'):

(i) also acquires a beneficial interest in the asset;

(ii) is to make payments to the financial institution amounting in aggregate to the consideration paid for the acquisition of its beneficial interest;

(iii) is to acquire (whether or not in stages) the financial institution's beneficial interest as a result of those payments;

(iv) is to make other payments to the financial institution (whether under a lease forming part of the arrangements or otherwise);

(v) has the exclusive right to occupy or otherwise use the asset; and

(vi) is exclusively entitled to any income, profit or gain attributable to the asset (including any increase in its value).

The '*effective return*' is equal to the payments made by the eventual owner under the arrangements other than payments within (ii) above and payments in respect of any arrangement fee or legal or other costs or expenses which the eventual owner is required to pay under the arrangements.

[*FA 2005, ss 46, 47(1)–(4), ss 47A, 53, 56(1); FA 2006, s 96(1)(3)(6)(8)*].

The Treasury has the power to amend the above provisions by statutory instrument to make provision for other types of arrangements which equate in substance to a loan, deposit, or other transaction of a kind which generally involves the payment of interest but which achieve a similar effect without providing for the payment of interest. [*FA 2006, s 98*].

See Tolley's Income Tax and Tolley's Corporation Tax for the detailed provisions governing alternative finance arrangements.

16 Connected Persons

[*ICTA 1988, s 839; TCGA 1992, s 286; FA 1995, Sch 17 paras 20, 31; ITTOIA 2005, Sch 1 paras 341, 446; FA 2006, Sch 12 paras 25, 43, Sch 13 para 25; SI 2005 No 3229, Regs 100, 121*]

Cross-references. See 3.15, 3.16 ANTI-AVOIDANCE for certain disposals between connected persons; 40.5 LOSSES for losses on disposals to connected persons; 46.14 PARTNERSHIPS for transactions between partners; and 57.12 SETTLEMENTS for settlors and trustees being connected persons.

16.1 An **individual** is connected with his spouse or civil partner, any 'relative' (see 16.7 below) of himself or of his spouse or civil partner, and with the spouse or civil partner of any such relative. It appears that a widow or widower is no longer a spouse (*Vestey's Exors and Vestey v CIR HL 1949, 31 TC 1*). Spouses divorced by decree nisi remain connected persons until the divorce is made absolute (*Aspden v Hildesley Ch D 1981, 55 TC 609*).

16.2 A **'trustee' of a 'settlement'**, in his capacity as such, is connected with

(*a*) the 'settlor' (if an individual) (see 16.7 below),

(*b*) any person connected with the settlor,

(*c*) a 'body corporate connected with the settlement' (see 16.7 below),

(*d*) if the settlement is the principal settlement in relation to one or more sub-fund settlements (see 57.8 SETTLEMENTS), the trustees of those settlements, and

(*e*) if the settlement is a sub-fund settlement, the trustees of any other sub-fund settlements of its principal settlement.

HMRC has confirmed (*a*) above applies as regards the time when a settlement is created and property first transferred to it. On the death of the settlor, neither (*a*) nor (*b*) apply (Revenue Tax Bulletin February 1993 p 56).

16.3 **Partners** are connected with each other and with each other's spouses (see 16.1 above), civil partners and relatives (see 16.7 below), except in connection with acquisitions and disposals of partnership assets made pursuant to *bona fide* commercial arrangements. See also 16.5 below.

16.4 **A company is connected with another company** if

(*a*) the same person 'controls' both (see 16.7 below), or

(*b*) one is controlled by a person who has control of the other in conjunction with persons connected with him, or

(*c*) a person controls one company and persons connected with him control the other, or

(*d*) the same group of persons controls both, or

(*e*) the companies are controlled by separate groups which can be regarded as the same by interchanging connected persons.

16.5 A **company is connected with another person who** (either alone or with persons connected with him) **has control of it**. It is understood that HMRC will accept that a partnership and a company under common control are connected for some purposes (see Tolley's Practical Tax 1981 p 142).

16.6 **Persons acting together to secure or exercise control of a company** are treated in relation to that company as connected with each other and with any other person acting on the direction of any of them to secure or exercise such control (see *Steele v EVC*

International NV CA 1996, 69 TC 88). Control may be 'exercised' passively. See *Floor v Davis HL 1979, 52 TC 609*. See 3.22 ANTI-AVOIDANCE for an extension of this provision in connection with dividend stripping.

16.7 '*Company*' includes any body corporate, unincorporated association or unit trust scheme but does not include a partnership.

'*Control*' is as defined in *ICTA 1988, s 416*. [*TCGA 1992, s 288(1)*]. See Tolley's Corporation Tax under Close Companies.

'*Relative*' means brother, sister, ancestor or lineal descendant. [*TCGA 1992, s 286(8)*].

'*Settlement*' includes any disposition, trust, covenant, agreement, arrangement or transfer of assets. [*ITTOIA 2005, s 620(1); ICTA 1988, s 660G(1); FA 1995, Sch 17 para 1*]. It must contain an element of bounty. It does not include a transfer of assets for full consideration (*CIR v Plummer HL 1979, 54 TC 1*). After 5 April 2006, '*trustee*' specifically includes, where otherwise a settlement would have no trustees, any person in whom the settled property or its management is vested. [*TCGA 1992, s 286(3ZA); FA 2006, Sch 12 para 25(2)(3)*].

'*A body corporate connected with the settlement*' is a close company (or one which would be so if resident in the UK) the participators in which include the trustees of the settlement, or a company controlled by such a close company. Control for these purposes is as under *ICTA 1988, s 840*: namely, the power of a person by shareholding or voting power (whether directly or through another company), or under Articles of Association, to secure that the company's affairs are conducted according to his wishes. Prior to 27 July 1981 it was defined as a close company (or one which would be so if resident in the UK), the participators in which include the trustees of, or a beneficiary under, the settlement. [*ICTA 1988, s 682A; FA 1995, Sch 17 para 11*].

After 5 April 2006 (in relation to all settlements, whenever created), '*settlor*' is as at 57.3 SETTLEMENTS. Previously, a '*settlor*' was any person by whom the settlement was made or who has directly or indirectly (or by a reciprocal arrangement) provided, or undertaken to provide, funds for the purpose of the settlement. [*ITTOIA 2005, s 620(2)(3); ICTA 1988, s 660G(1)(2); FA 1995, Sch 17 para 1*]. See *Countess Fitzwilliam and others v CIR (and related appeals) HL 1993, 67 TC 614*.

17 Corporate Venturing Scheme

17.1 **INTRODUCTION**

For shares issued on or after 1 April 2000 but before 1 April 2010, a scheme is introduced whereby most trading companies are able to obtain corporation tax relief at 20% ('*investment relief*') on corporate venturing investments, i.e. acquisitions (by cash subscription) of minority shareholdings in 'small higher risk' trading companies. In addition, investing companies are able to postpone chargeable gains ('*deferral relief*') on disposals of corporate venturing investments where they reinvest in other shares attracting investment relief. Also, an allowable capital loss on the disposal of a corporate venturing investment, computed net of investment relief, can be relieved against *income* of the accounting period in which the loss arises and accounting periods ending in the previous 12 months (but may alternatively be relieved against chargeable gains in the normal way). [*FA 2000, s 63*(*1*)(*4*), *Sch 15 para 1*].

Investee companies are limited to those with gross assets not exceeding £15 million immediately before the investment and £16 million immediately afterwards. Such companies must exist for the purpose of carrying on trading activities other than the kind of 'lower risk' activity excluded under the ENTERPRISE INVESTMENT SCHEME (21) or the provisions for VENTURE CAPITAL TRUSTS (66). Potential investee companies may request advance clearance from HMRC. The maximum investment qualifying for relief is 30% of the issued ordinary share capital of the investee company, and no minimum investment is stipulated. It is a further condition that at least 20% of the ordinary share capital of the investee company be held by individuals (other than directors and employees of the investing company). To qualify for the relief, the investing company must retain the shares acquired for at least three years. Investing companies carrying on financial trades (e.g. banking, share dealing etc.) are not eligible.

See generally HMRC Venture Capital Schemes Manual VCM 10000–17320, 50000 *et seq.* See also **Simon's Direct Tax Service**, Division D2.13.

The remainder of this chapter is set out under the following headings.

17.2 **INVESTMENT RELIEF**

Eligibility. An investing company is eligible for investment relief (see 17.3 below) in respect of an amount subscribed by it for shares in an investee company (the '*issuing company*') if

(*a*) the shares (the '*relevant shares*') are issued to the investing company;

(*b*) the investing company is a 'qualifying investing company' (see 17.5 below);

(*c*) the issuing company is a 'qualifying issuing company' (see 17.6 below) in relation to the relevant shares; and

(*d*) the general requirements at 17.8 below are met.

For advance clearance as regards (*c*) and (*d*) above, see 17.9 below.

Qualification period. In these provisions, the '*qualification period*' is normally the three-year period beginning with the date of issue of the relevant shares. If, however, the money raised by the issue is employed wholly or mainly for the purposes of a qualifying trade (or trades) (see 17.7 below) which, on the date of issue, was not being carried on by the issuing company or a qualifying 90% subsidiary (or, for shares issued before 17 March 2004, a qualifying subsidiary (see 17.6 below)), the qualification period begins on the date of issue and ends immediately before the third anniversary of the date of commencement of the trade (or the latest such date where there is more than one such trade). In relation to shares issued after 16 March 2004, any carrying on of a trade by a subsidiary before it became a qualifying 90% subsidiary is disregarded in determining when the trade commences for this purpose.

[*FA 2000, Sch 15 paras 2, 3, 102(8); FA 2004, s 95, Sch 20 paras 2, 13, 15*].

17.3 **Form of relief.** Where an investing company is eligible for investment relief (see 17.2 above) in respect of amounts subscribed by it for shares, its corporation tax liability for the accounting period in which the shares are issued is reduced, on a claim (see 17.4 below), by the lesser of

- 20% of the amount (or aggregate amount) subscribed, and
- the amount which reduces the liability to nil.

[*FA 2000, Sch 15 para 39*].

The reduction in corporation tax liability is made in priority to any reduction in respect of community investment tax relief (see Tolley's Income Tax) but before any DOUBLE TAX RELIEF (19). [*FA 1998, Sch 18 para 8(1); FA 2002, s 57, Sch 16 para 20, Sch 17 para 5*].

Investment relief is said to be 'attributable to shares' if relief as above has been obtained in respect of those shares and has not been withdrawn (as opposed to reduced) — see 17.10 below. Where for any one accounting period relief has been obtained by reason of more than one issue of shares, the relief is attributed to those issues in proportion to the amounts subscribed. Relief attributable to any one issue of shares is attributed *pro rata* to each share in that issue, and any reduction of relief (see 17.10 below) is similarly apportioned between the shares in question. For these purposes, any bonus shares, issued in respect of the original shares and being shares in the same company, of the same class and carrying the same rights, are treated as if comprised in the original issue, and relief is apportioned to them accordingly. This applies only if the original shares have been held continuously since issue (as in 17.20(*a*) below), and, where it does apply, the bonus shares are themselves treated as having been held continuously since the time of the original issue. [*FA 2000, Sch 15 para 45*].

17.4 **Claims for relief.** No deadline is specified for making a claim, so the general six-year time limit applies as in 12.5 CLAIMS. A claim for relief cannot be made in respect of any investment until

- in respect of shares issued after 16 March 2004, the 'funded trade' has been carried on by no person other than the issuing company or a qualifying 90% subsidiary (see 17.6 below) of that company for at least four months disregarding
  - time spent *preparing* to carry on the trade), and
  - where the funded trade is carried on by a partnership or joint venture, the other partners or parties to the joint venture; and
- the investing company has received from the issuing company a 'compliance certificate' (see below).

In respect of shares issued before 17 March 2004, the first requirement above is simply that the funded trade must have been carried on by the issuing company or a subsidiary for at least four months (disregarding time spent preparing to carry on the trade).

No postponement of tax pending appeal (see 47.3 PAYMENT OF TAX) can be made on the grounds of eligibility for investment relief until a claim for that relief can be and has been made. The '*funded trade*' is the trade or trades by reference to which the requirement at 17.8 below as to 'use of money raised' is met (or, where applicable, the notional trade of research and development therein mentioned). A claim *can* be made if the funded trade is carried on as above for less than four months by reason of the winding-up or dissolution of any company (or, for shares issued before 17 March 2004, the issuing company or subsidiary) or its going into administration or receivership (both as defined), provided that this is for commercial reasons and not part of tax avoidance arrangements.

A '*compliance certificate*' is a certificate issued, with the authority of HMRC and in such form as they may direct, by the issuing company in respect of the relevant shares and confirming that, from the issuing company's point of view, the requirements for investment relief are for the time being met in relation to the shares. To obtain authority for the issue of a certificate, the issuing company must provide HMRC with a 'compliance statement' in respect of the issue of shares which includes the relevant shares. Where notice of an event giving rise to withdrawal etc. is given to HMRC by or in relation to the issuing company (see 17.10 below), any authority already given is invalid unless renewed.

A '*compliance statement*' is a statement, in respect of an issue of shares, to the effect that, from the issuing company's point of view, the requirements for investment relief are for the time being met in relation to the shares and have been met at all times since the shares were issued. The statement must be in required form and must contain any additional information as HMRC reasonably require, a declaration that it is correct to the best of the company's knowledge and belief, and such other declarations as HMRC reasonably require. A compliance statement cannot be made until such time as the funded trade has been carried on for at least four months (or such shorter time as is specified above). It *must* be made within two years after the end of the accounting period in which the shares were issued or, if later, two years after the minimum period of trading condition is satisfied.

The issuing company may give notice of appeal, within 30 days, against an HMRC refusal to authorise a compliance certificate (as if that refusal were the disallowance of a claim other than for discharge or repayment of tax — see 12.3 CLAIMS).

The issuing company is liable to a penalty of up to £3,000 for issuing a compliance certificate which is made fraudulently or negligently or without HMRC authority, or for making a compliance statement fraudulently or negligently.

[*FA 2000, Sch 15 paras 40–44, 102(4); FA 2004, Sch 20 paras 12, 15*].

17.5 QUALIFYING INVESTING COMPANY

The investing company is a '*qualifying investing company*' (see 17.2(*b*) above) in relation to the relevant shares if it meets all the requirements below as to absence of material interest, reciprocal arrangements, control and tax avoidance, the nature of its activities, and the relevant shares being a chargeable asset. [*FA 2000, Sch 15 para 4*].

'No material interest' requirement. At no time in the qualification period (see 17.2 above) must the investing company have a material interest in the issuing company. For this purpose, a person has a material interest in a company if he (alone or together with any person connected with him — within *ICTA 1988, s 839* — see 16 CONNECTED PERSONS) directly or indirectly possesses, or is entitled (or will in future be entitled) to acquire (at present or at a future date), more than **30%** of

- the 'ordinary share capital' of, or
- the voting power in,

the company or any 51% subsidiary. In applying the test, there must be attributed to a person any rights or powers of any associate of his (as defined by *FA 2000, Sch 15 para 99*). For these purposes, a company's '*ordinary share capital*' comprises (*a*) all of its issued share capital other than 'relevant preference shares', and

(*b*) all of its loan capital (as widely defined but excluding a bank overdraft or an ordinary business debt) that carries a right to convert into, or to acquire, shares which would fall within (*a*) above.

'*Relevant preference shares*' are, broadly, non-voting, non-convertible shares issued for new consideration and carrying no right to dividends other than dividends which

- are of a fixed amount or at a rate which is fixed or which varies according to a standard published interest rate, a tax rate, a retail price index or an official share price index, and
- which are not dependent on the company's business results or asset values and do not represent more than a reasonable commercial return on the investment.

[*FA 2000, Sch 15 paras 5, 7, 9, 102(3)*].

'No reciprocal arrangements' requirement. The investing company's subscription for the relevant shares must not be part of any arrangements which provide for any other person to subscribe for shares in a 'related company'. A '*related company*' is a company in which the investing company, or any other person who is party to the arrangements, has a material interest (as defined immediately above). Arrangements are disregarded to the extent that they provide for the issuing company to subscribe for shares in any qualifying subsidiary (see 17.6 below). [*FA 2000, Sch 15 para 6*].

'No control' requirement. At no time in the qualification period must the investing company 'control' the issuing company. '*Control*' is determined in accordance with *ICTA 1988, s 416(2)–(6)* as modified for this purpose. [*FA 2000, Sch 15 para 8; SI 2005 No 3229, Reg 132*].

'No tax avoidance' requirement. The relevant shares must be subscribed for by the investing company for commercial reasons and not as part of a tax avoidance scheme or arrangement. [*FA 2000, Sch 15 para 14*].

Non-financial activities requirement. Throughout the qualification period, the investing company,

- if a single company (i.e. a company which is not a parent company or a 51% subsidiary), must exist wholly for the purpose of carrying on one or more 'non-financial trades'; and,
- if a group company, must be part of a 'non-financial trading group' and must either exist wholly for the purpose of carrying on one or more 'non-financial trades' or businesses other than trades or be the parent company of the group.

In determining the purpose for which a company exists, purposes having no significant effect (other than in relation to incidental matters) on the extent of the company's activities are disregarded. Purposes for which a company exists are also disregarded to the extent that they consist of

- (as regards a single company) the holding and managing of property used by the company for one or more 'non-financial trades' carried on by it;
- (as regards a group company) any activities within (*a*) or (*b*) below; or
- (as regards any company) holding shares to which investment relief is attributable (see 17.3 above) unless the holding of such shares is a substantial part of the company's business.

A trade is a '*non-financial trade*' if

- it is conducted on a commercial basis and with a view to profit, and

- it does not consist, wholly or as to a substantial part, in the carrying on of 'financial activities'.

'*Financial activities*' include for this purpose

- banking, or money-lending, carried on by a bank, building society or other person;
- debt factoring, finance-leasing or hire-purchase financing;
- insurance;
- dealing in shares, securities, currency, debts or other assets of a financial nature; and
- dealing in commodity or financial futures or options.

A group is a '*non-financial trading group*' unless the business of the group (treating the activities of the group companies, taken together, as a single business) consists, wholly or as to a substantial part, in the carrying on of trades other than non-financial trades (as above) and/or businesses other than trades. Activities of a group company are disregarded to the extent that they consist of

(*a*) holding shares in or securities of, or making loans to, another group company;

(*b*) holding and managing property used by a group company for the purposes of one or more non-financial trades carried on by a group company; or

(*c*) holding shares to which investment relief is attributable (see 17.3 above), unless the holding of such shares is a substantial part of the company's business.

Amendments to the non-financial activities requirement may be made in the future by Treasury Order.

[*FA 2000, Sch 15 paras 10–12, 101, 102*(*1*)].

Requirement as to shares being a chargeable asset. The relevant shares must be a chargeable asset of the investing company immediately after they are issued to it. For this purpose, an asset is a chargeable asset at a particular time if, on a disposal at that time, a gain would be a chargeable gain. [*FA 2000, Sch 15 para 13*].

17.6 QUALIFYING ISSUING COMPANY

The issuing company is a '*qualifying issuing company*' (see 17.2(*c*) above) in relation to the relevant shares if it meets all the requirements below as to unquoted status, independence, individual-owners, partnerships and joint ventures, qualifying subsidiaries, property managing subsidiaries, gross assets, and trading activities. [*FA 2000, Sch 15 para 15; FA 2004, Sch 20 para 3*].

Unquoted status requirement. At the time of issue of the relevant shares, none of the issuing company's shares, debentures or other securities must be listed on a recognised stock exchange (see 58.23 SHARES AND SECURITIES) or a 'designated' exchange outside the UK or be dealt in outside the UK by 'designated' means, and there must be no arrangements in existence for such a listing or such dealing. This applies whether or not the company is UK-resident. '*Designated*' means designated by order for the purposes of *ICTA 1988, s 312*(*1B*) (enterprise investment scheme). The company does not fail to meet the requirement simply because a designation order is made, or a stock exchange obtains recognition, after the time of issue of the shares.

If, at the time of issue of the relevant shares, arrangements are in existence for the issuing company to become a wholly-owned subsidiary of a new holding company by means of a share exchange within 17.24 below, there must be no arrangements made for any of the new company's shares, debentures or other securities to be listed or dealt in as above.

[*FA 2000, Sch 15 para 16*].

Independence requirement. At no time in the qualification period (see 17.2 above) must the issuing company be a 51% subsidiary of another company or otherwise under the control (within *ICTA 1988, s 840*) of another company or of another company and persons connected with it (within *ICTA 1988, s 839* — see 16 CONNECTED PERSONS). No arrangements must exist at any time during that period whereby the company could become such a subsidiary or fall under such control (whether during that period or otherwise). Arrangements with a view to a company reconstruction within 17.24 below are disregarded for this purpose. [*FA 2000, Sch 15 paras 17, 102(3)*].

Individual-owners requirement. Throughout the qualification period, at least **20%** of the issued ordinary share capital of the issuing company must be beneficially owned by one or more 'independent individuals'. An '*independent individual*' is one who is not, at any time during the qualification period when he holds ordinary shares in the issuing company, a director or employee of the investing company or of any company connected with it (within *ICTA 1988, s 839* — see 16 CONNECTED PERSONS), or a relative (i.e. husband, wife, civil partner, forebear or issue) of such a director or employee. Where an independent individual owned shares immediately prior to his death, they are treated for these purposes as continuing to be owned by an independent individual until they cease to form part of the deceased's estate. [*FA 2000, Sch 15 paras 18, 102(3); SI 2005 No 3229, Reg 132*].

Partnerships and joint ventures requirement. At no time in the qualification period must the issuing company or any qualifying subsidiary (see below) be a member of a partnership or a party to a joint venture where

- a trade by reference to which the trading activities requirement (see below) is met by the issuing company is being carried on, or is to be carried on, by the partners in partnership or, as the case may be, by the company or a qualifying subsidiary (see below) as a party to the joint venture;
- the other partners or parties to the joint venture include at least one other company; and
- the same person(s) is/are the beneficial owner(s) of more than 75% of the issued share capital or the ordinary share capital of both the issuing company and at least one of the other partners/parties.

For these purposes, there must be attributed to any person any share capital held by an associate of his (within *FA 2000, Sch 15 para 99*).

[*FA 2000, Sch 15 para 19*].

Qualifying subsidiaries requirement. At no time in the qualification period must the issuing company have a 'subsidiary' other than a 'qualifying subsidiary'. For this purpose, a '*subsidiary*' of a company is any company which it controls (within *ICTA 1988, s 416(2)–(6)*), with or without the aid of CONNECTED PERSONS (16). In relation to shares issued after 16 March 2004, a subsidiary is a '*qualifying subsidiary*' of another company (the '*relevant company*') if the following conditions are met.

(*a*) The subsidiary is a 51% subsidiary (within *ICTA 1988, s 838*) of the relevant company;

(*b*) No other person has control (within *ICTA 1988, s 840*) of the subsidiary; and

(*c*) No arrangements exist whereby (*a*) or (*b*) could cease to be satisfied (though see also below).

In relation to shares issued on or before that date, a subsidiary is a qualifying subsidiary of a company if the following conditions are met.

(i) The relevant company, or another of its subsidiaries, possesses at least 75% of the issued share capital of, and the voting power in, the subsidiary, and is beneficially entitled to at least 75% of the assets available for distribution to shareholders on a winding-up etc. and of the profits available for distribution to shareholders;

(ii) No other person has control (within *ICTA 1988, s 840*) of the subsidiary; and

(iii) No arrangements exist whereby (i) or (ii) could cease to be satisfied (though see also below).

The fact that a subsidiary or another company is wound up or otherwise dissolved or goes into administration or receivership (both as defined) does not mean the subsidiary ceases to be a qualifying subsidiary, provided that the winding-up etc., and anything done as a consequence of administration or receivership, is for genuine commercial reasons and not part of a tax avoidance scheme or arrangements. Similarly, the fact that arrangements may exist to dispose of the entire interest held in the subsidiary does not prevent the subsidiary from being a qualifying subsidiary of the relevant company if the disposal is to be for commercial reasons and is not to be part of a tax avoidance scheme or arrangements.

[*FA 2000, Sch 15 paras 20, 21, 102(3)(4); FA 2004, s 95, Sch 20 paras 4, 5, 15, Sch 42 Pt 2(12)*].

Property managing subsidiaries requirement. In relation to shares issued after 16 March 2004, the issuing company must not have, at any time in the qualification period, a 'property managing subsidiary' other than one which is its 'qualifying 90% subsidiary'. For this purpose, a '*property managing subsidiary*' is a qualifying subsidiary (see above) whose business consists wholly or mainly in the holding or managing of land or any property deriving its value from land (and the terms 'land' and 'property deriving its value from land' have the same meaning as in 38.4 LAND).

A subsidiary is a '*qualifying 90% subsidiary*' of the issuing company if the following conditions are met.

(1) The issuing company possesses at least 90% of the issued share capital of, and the voting power in, the subsidiary, and is beneficially entitled to at least 90% of the assets available for distribution to shareholders on a winding-up etc. and of the profits available for distribution to shareholders;

(2) No other person has control (within *ICTA 1988, s 840*) of the subsidiary; and

(3) No arrangements exist whereby (1) or (2) could cease to be satisfied (though see also below).

The fact that a subsidiary or another company is wound up or otherwise dissolved or goes into administration or receivership (both as defined) does not mean the subsidiary ceases to be a qualifying 90% subsidiary of the issuing company, provided that the winding-up etc., and anything done as a consequence of administration or receivership, is for genuine commercial reasons and not part of a tax avoidance scheme or arrangements. Similarly, the fact that arrangements may exist to dispose of the entire interest held in the subsidiary does not prevent the subsidiary from being a qualifying 90% subsidiary of the issuing company if the disposal is to be for commercial reasons and is not to be part of a tax avoidance scheme or arrangements.

[*FA 2000, Sch 15 paras 21A, 23(1)(11); FA 2004, Sch 20 paras 6, 7(d), 15*].

Gross assets requirement. The value of the company's gross assets must not exceed £7 million immediately before the issue of the relevant shares or £8 million immediately afterwards. For shares issued before 6 April 2006 or subscribed for before 22 March 2006 the limits were £15 million immediately before the issue and £16 million immediately afterwards. If the company is the parent company of a group, those limits apply by reference to the aggregate value of the gross assets of the group (disregarding certain assets held by any member of the group which correspond to liabilities of another member). The limits may be amended in the future by Treasury Order. [*FA 2000, Sch 15 paras 22, 101; FA 2006, Sch 14 para 3*].

HMRC's approach to the gross assets requirement is the same as for the similar requirement under the EIS (for which see 21.5 ENTERPRISE INVESTMENT SCHEME) (HMRC Statement of Practice 2/00).

Trading activities requirement. Throughout the qualification period, the issuing company must meet the trading activities requirement, which is as follows. If the company is a single company (i.e. neither the parent company of a group nor a subsidiary), it must exist wholly for the purpose of carrying on one or more qualifying trades (see 17.7 below) and must actually be carrying on such a trade or preparing to do so. Purposes having no significant effect (other than in relation to incidental matters) on the extent of the company's activities are disregarded.

If the company is a parent company, the business of the group (treating the activities of the group companies, taken together, as a single business) must not consist wholly or as to a substantial part in any 'non-qualifying activities', and at least one company in the group (which, in relation to shares issued after 16 March 2004, must be either the issuing company or a qualifying 90% subsidiary (see above) of the issuing company) must satisfy the above trading activity requirement for a single company. '*Non-qualifying activities*' means 'excluded activities' (as in 17.7 below, and with similar exceptions in relation to the letting of ships and the receiving of royalties or licence fees) and non-trading activities.

Where the trading activities requirement would otherwise be met by reason of a company *preparing* to carry on a qualifying trade, the requirement is treated as not having been met at any time if that trade does not commence within two years after the issue of the relevant shares. In relation to shares issued after 16 March 2004, any carrying on of a trade by a subsidiary before it became a qualifying 90% subsidiary is disregarded in determining when the trade commences for this purpose.

Purposes for which a company exists are disregarded to the extent that they consist of

- (as regards a single company) the holding and managing of property used by the company for one or more qualifying trades carried on by it;
- (as regards a group company) any activities within (*a*), (*b*) or (*d*) below; or
- (as regards any company) holding shares to which investment relief is attributable (see 17.3 above), unless the holding of such shares is a substantial part of the company's business.

For the purposes of determining the business of a group, activities of a group company are disregarded to the extent that they consist of

(*a*) holding shares in or securities of, or making loans to, another group company;

(*b*) holding and managing property used by a group company for the purposes of one or more qualifying trades carried on by a group company;

(*c*) holding shares to which investment relief is attributable (see 17.3 above), unless the holding of such shares is a substantial part of the company's business; or

(*d*) incidental activities of a company which meets the above trading activities requirement for a single company.

A company does not cease to meet the trading activities requirement purely by reason of it or a qualifying subsidiary (see above) being wound up or otherwise dissolved, provided that the winding-up or dissolution is for commercial reasons and not part of a tax avoidance scheme or arrangements. A similar let-out applies in relation to a company or its qualifying subsidiary going into administration or receivership (both as defined) and to anything done as a consequence thereof.

Amendments to the trading activities requirement (including the provisions at 17.7 below) may be made in the future by Treasury Order.

[*FA 2000, Sch 15 paras 23, 24, 101, 102(1)(4)(8); FA 2004, Sch 20 paras 7, 8, 13, 15, Sch 27 para 6(2), Sch 42 Pt 2(12)*].

17.7 **Qualifying trades.** A trade is a qualifying trade (see the trading activities requirement at 17.6 above) if

(i) it is carried on wholly or mainly in the UK;

(ii) it is conducted on a commercial basis and with a view to profit; and

(iii) it does not consist wholly or as to a 'substantial' part in the carrying on of any 'excluded activities' (see below).

In considering the requirement at (i) above, HMRC will take into account the totality of the activities of the trade; a company can satisfy the requirement if the major part of the trade, i.e. over half of the trading activity, taken as a whole, is carried on within the UK. See HMRC Statement of Practice 3/00. '*Substantial*' in (iii) above is not defined, but where, judged by any measure which is reasonable in the circumstances (normally turnover or capital employed), excluded activities account for less than 20% of the activities of the trade as a whole, HMRC do not regard them as amounting to a substantial part of the trade (HMRC Venture Capital Schemes Manual VCM 17040).

Activities of research and development (within *ICTA 1988, s 837A*) from which it is intended that a 'connected qualifying trade' will be derived or will benefit are treated as a notional qualifying trade, but preparing to carry on such activities is not treated as preparing to carry on a qualifying trade. A '*connected qualifying trade*' is a qualifying trade carried on either by the company carrying out the research and development or, where applicable, by another member of the group (which, in relation to shares issued after 16 March 2004, must be either the issuing company or a qualifying 90% subsidiary (see 17.6 above) of the issuing company).

'*Excluded activities*' are as follows:

(*a*) dealing in land, commodities or futures, or in shares, securities or other financial instruments;

(*b*) dealing in goods otherwise than in an ordinary trade of wholesale or retail distribution (for more detail, see the similar exclusion at 66.5 VENTURE CAPITAL TRUSTS);

(*c*) banking, insurance, money-lending, debt-factoring, hire purchase financing or other financial activities;

(*d*) leasing or receiving royalties or licence fees (see further below);

(*e*) providing legal or accountancy services;

(*f*) property development (see further below);

(*g*) farming or market gardening;

(*h*) holding, managing or occupying woodlands, any other forestry activities or timber production;

(*j*) operating or managing hotels or comparable establishments (including guest houses, hostels and other establishments whose main purpose is to offer overnight accommodation with or without catering) or property used as such (see further below);

(*k*) operating or managing nursing homes or residential care homes (both as defined) or property used as such (see further below);

(*l*) providing services or facilities for any business consisting to a substantial extent of activities within (*a*)–(*k*) above and carried on by another person, where a person has a controlling interest (see below) in both that business and the business of the provider company.

The term 'leasing' in (*d*) above includes the letting of ships on charter or other assets on hire. A trade will be not be excluded by reason only of its consisting of letting ships, other than pleasure craft (as defined) or, for shares issued on or after 6 April 2004, offshore installations (within *ICTA 1988, s 837C*) or, for shares issued before that date, oil rigs (as defined), on charter, provided certain conditions are satisfied.

As regards the receiving of royalties or licence fees (see (*d*) above), a trade is not excluded from being a qualifying trade solely because at some time in the qualification period (see 17.2 above) it consists to a substantial extent in the receiving of royalties or licence fees substantially attributable (in terms of value) to the exploitation of intangible assets, such as intellectual property, which have been created by the company carrying on the trade or by a fellow group company — for more details, see the similar let-out at 66.5 VENTURE CAPITAL TRUSTS.

As regards (*f*) above, see the comments at 66.5 VENTURE CAPITAL TRUSTS, which apply equally here. The exclusions at (*j*) and (*k*) above apply only if the person carrying on the activity has an estate or interest (e.g. a lease) in the property concerned or occupies that property.

As regards (*l*) above, see the comparable exclusion at 66.5 VENTURE CAPITAL TRUSTS as regards the meaning of 'controlling interest', which applies similarly here, though without the modifications there mentioned to *ICTA 1988, s 416*.

[*FA 2000, Sch 15 paras 25–33, 102(1); FA 2004, Sch 20 paras 9, 15, Sch 27 para 6(3)–(6)*].

As regards (*e*) above, the provision of accounting staff by a company to a firm of accountants was held in an EIS case to be synonymous with the provision of accountancy services, with the result that the company's trade was not a qualifying trade (*Castleton Management Service Ltd v Kirkwood (Sp C 276), [2001] SSCD 95*).

17.8 GENERAL REQUIREMENTS

For investment relief to be available in respect of the relevant shares (see 17.2 above), the following requirements (see 17.2(*d*) above) must be met as to the shares, the use of money raised by the issue, the absence of pre-arranged exits and the absence of a tax avoidance motive. [*FA 2000, Sch 15 para 34*].

The shares. The relevant shares must be ordinary, fully paid up, shares and must be subscribed for wholly in cash. Shares issued after 16 March 2004 are not fully paid up for this purpose if there is any undertaking to pay cash to any person at a future date in respect of the acquisition of the shares. Shares issued on or before that date are not fully paid up for this purpose only if there is an undertaking to pay cash to the issuing company at a future date. At no time in the qualification period (see 17.2 above) must the shares carry any present or future preferential right to dividends or to assets on a winding-up, or any present or future right to be redeemed. [*FA 2000, Sch 15 para 35; FA 2004, Sch 20 paras 10, 15*].

Use of money raised. The money raised by the 'relevant issue of shares' must be employed wholly (disregarding any insignificant amount) for the purposes of a 'relevant trade' within 24 months after the issue, and 80% of that money must be so employed within 12 months after the issue. These 24-month and 12-month periods begin with the date of commencement of the relevant trade where this is later than the date of issue. This applies in relation to shares issued on or after 7 March 2001, and also applies on and after that date in relation to shares issued before then to which investment relief was attributable (see 17.3 above) immediately before that date. Previously, *all* the money had to be so employed within the said 12-month period. In relation to shares issued after 16 March 2004, any carrying on of the relevant trade by a subsidiary before it became a qualifying 90% subsidiary (see 17.6 above) is disregarded in determining the date of commencement of the relevant trade for this purpose.

For these purposes, employing money for the purposes of *preparing* to carry on a trade (other than a notional trade of research and development — see 17.7 above) is equivalent to employing it for the purposes of a trade.

The '*relevant issue of shares*' means the issue of shares which includes the relevant shares. A '*relevant trade*' is a trade by reference to which the issuing company meets the trading activities requirement in 17.6 above. Where the trade by reference to which the trading activities requirement is met is a notional trade of research and development (see 17.7 above), the term 'relevant trade' also refers to any qualifying trade which is derived or benefits from that notional trade and is carried on by the issuing company or a qualifying 90% subsidiary (or, in relation to shares issued before 17 March 2004, a qualifying subsidiary; see 17.6 above); in this case, all the money raised by the issue must be employed for the purposes of that trade before the third anniversary of the date of issue of the shares (notwithstanding that a later date may be given by the rules above), and the 80% requirement does not apply.

[*FA 2000, Sch 15 paras 36, 102(8); FA 2001, Sch 16 para 5; FA 2004, Sch 20 paras 11, 13, 15*].

No pre-arranged exits. The arrangements (as very broadly defined) under which the relevant shares are issued to the investing company (including arrangements preceding the issue but relating to it and, in certain cases, arrangements made on or after the issue and within the qualification period) must not

(*a*) provide for the eventual disposal by the investing company of the relevant shares or other shares or securities of the issuing company;

(*b*) provide for the eventual cessation of a trade of the issuing company or a person connected with it;

(*c*) provide for the eventual disposal of all, or a substantial part of, the assets of the issuing company or of a person connected with it; or

(*d*) provide (by means of any insurance, indemnity, guarantee or otherwise) partial or complete protection for investors against the normal risks attaching to the investment (but excluding commercial arrangements which merely protect the issuing company and/or its subsidiaries against normal business risks).

Arrangements with a view to a company reconstruction within 17.24 below are excluded from (*a*) above. Arrangements applicable only on an unanticipated winding-up of the issuing company for commercial reasons are excluded from (*b*) and (*c*) above.

[*FA 2000, Sch 15 paras 37, 102(1)*].

No tax avoidance motive. The relevant shares must be issued for commercial reasons and not as part of a tax avoidance scheme or arrangement. [*FA 2000, Sch 15 para 38*].

17.9 ADVANCE CLEARANCE

A *potential* qualifying issuing company (see 17.6 above) may apply to HMRC for an advance clearance notice in respect of an issue of shares. An application must contain particulars, declarations and undertakings as required and must disclose all material facts and circumstances. An advance clearance notice states that, on the basis of the particulars etc. provided by the applicant, HMRC are satisfied that, at the time the shares are issued, the requirements of 17.6–17.8 above will be met (or, in the case of a requirement that can only be met in the future, will for the time being be met).

Within 30 days after receiving an application (or within 30 days after an 'information notice' is complied with), HMRC must either issue an information notice (or further information notice), issue an advance clearance notice, or refuse the application. An '*information notice*' is a notice requiring further particulars to be provided within such time, not being less than 30 days, as is stated therein. If the applicant fails to comply timeously with an information notice, HMRC need not proceed further with the application. If the shares in question are issued before the advance clearance notice is given or the application refused, then again HMRC need not proceed further.

Within 30 days after a refusal of an application, or a failure to give a decision, the applicant can require HMRC to transmit the application, together with any information notices given and further particulars provided, to the Special Commissioners, whose approval, if given, has effect as if it were an advance clearance notice given by HMRC.

An advance clearance notice is rendered void if it transpires that any particulars provided did not fully and accurately disclose all facts and circumstances material for the decision, or if the applicant or any subsidiary (including any new subsidiary) fails to act in accordance with any declaration or undertaking given as part of the application.

[*FA 2000, Sch 15 paras 89–92*].

HMRC have published guidance for companies wishing to obtain advance clearance. These include an outline of the information, documents and undertakings HMRC will require. Any clearance given applies only to the single issue of shares in respect of which it was sought. Applications for clearance should be sent to HMRC, Small Company Enterprise Centre, Ty Glas, Llanishen, Cardiff, CF14 5ZG. See HMRC Statement of Practice 1/00.

17.10 WITHDRAWAL OR REDUCTION OF INVESTMENT RELIEF

Investment relief falls to be withdrawn or reduced on a disposal of the relevant shares (see 17.11 below), if value is received in respect of the shares (see 17.12–17.15 below), or on the grant of certain options relating to the shares (see 17.16 below).

Where investment relief given falls to be withdrawn or reduced, and also where it is found not to have been due, the withdrawal etc. is achieved by means of an assessment under Schedule D, Case VI for the accounting period of the investing company *in which the relief was given*. For relief to be withdrawn on the grounds that the issuing company is not a qualifying issuing company (see 17.6 above), or that the general requirements at 17.8 above are not met, or by virtue of value received by the investing company (see 17.12 below) or other persons (see 17.15 below), certain statutory notice procedures must be followed. The investing company may give notice of appeal, within 30 days, against an HMRC notice pending withdrawal of relief on such grounds (as if the giving of that notice were the disallowance of a claim other than for discharge or repayment of tax — see 12.3 CLAIMS).

HMRC cannot make an assessment to withdraw (or reduce) investment relief, or give statutory notice pending withdrawal of relief on the above-mentioned grounds, more than six years after the end of whichever is the later of the following accounting periods:

- the accounting period in which falls the deadline for employing money raised by the issue of the shares (see 17.8 above);
- the accounting period in which occurs the event giving rise to withdrawal (or reduction) of relief.

The above is subject to the extended time limit for assessments in cases of fraud or negligence (see 23.4 FRAUDULENT OR NEGLIGENT CONDUCT).

In most cases, interest on overdue tax runs from the date of the event giving rise to withdrawal (or reduction) of relief, if this is later than the normal due date, or the latest such date, for payment of corporation tax for the accounting period for which the assessment is made (see 47.2 PAYMENT OF TAX).

[*FA 2000, Sch 15 paras 60–63*].

Information. Certain events giving rise to withdrawal or reduction of investment relief must be notified to HMRC, generally within 60 days, by the investing company or the issuing company (or any person connected with the issuing company and having knowledge of the matter), as the case may be. HMRC have power to require information from such persons where they have reason to believe that such notice should have been given or from a person whom they believe to have given or received value which would have triggered a requirement to give such notice but for the amount of value being insignificant (see 17.12 below). The penalty provisions of *TMA 1970, s 98* apply in the event of non-compliance with these information provisions. [*FA 2000, Sch 15 paras 64–66, Sch 16 para 1*].

17.11 **Disposal.** Where, during the qualification period (see 17.2 above), the investing company disposes of any shares to which relief is attributable (see 17.3 above) and which it has held continuously since their issue (see 17.20(*a*) below), relief is withdrawn or reduced as set out below. See 17.10 above re consequences of withdrawal etc.

If the disposal is either

- by way of bargain at arm's length for full consideration; or
- by way of a distribution on a dissolution or winding-up of the issuing company; or
- a disposal within *TCGA 1992, s 24(1)* (entire loss, destruction etc. of asset — see 9.1 CAPITAL SUMS DERIVED FROM ASSETS); or
- a deemed disposal under *TCGA 1992, s 24(2)* (assets of negligible value — see 40.9 LOSSES),

the relief attributable to the shares disposed of is withdrawn, or is reduced by 20% of the disposal consideration (if such reduction would not amount to full withdrawal). If the relief initially obtained was less than 20% of the amount subscribed for those shares (i.e. because the company's corporation tax liability was insufficient to fully absorb the available relief), the reduction is correspondingly restricted.

In the case of any other disposal, for example a transaction not at arm's length, the relief attributable to the shares disposed of is withdrawn.

[*FA 2000, Sch 15 para 46*].

For the above purposes, shares are regarded as being disposed of if they are so regarded for the purposes of corporation tax on chargeable gains, and see also 17.23 below (certain company reconstructions treated as disposals). [*FA 2000, Sch 15 para 96; FA 2002, Sch 9 paras 6(5), 8(1)*]. In the case of a part disposal, see 17.17 below for the rules for identifying shares disposed of.

17.12 **Value received by investing company.** Subject to 17.14 below (replacement value), where during the 'period of restriction' the investing company 'receives value' (see 17.13 below), other than an 'amount of insignificant value', from the issuing company, investment relief attributable to the relevant shares is withdrawn, or is reduced by 20% of the amount of value received (if such reduction would not amount to full withdrawal). If the relief initially obtained was less than 20% of the amount subscribed for those shares (i.e. because the company's corporation tax liability was insufficient to fully absorb the available relief), the reduction is correspondingly restricted. These provisions apply equally to receipts of value by and from persons connected (within *ICTA 1988, s 839* — see 16 CONNECTED PERSONS), at any time in the period of restriction, with the investing company or, as the case may be, the issuing company. See 17.13 below for the meaning of 'value received' and the determination of the amount of value received. See 17.10 above for consequences of withdrawal etc.

The '*period of restriction*' in relation to the relevant shares is the period beginning one year before their issue and ending at the end of the qualification period in 17.2 above.

Where two or more issues of shares have been made by the same issuing company to the same investing company, in relation to each of which investment relief is claimed, and value is received during a period of restriction relating to more than one such issue, the value received is apportioned between them by reference to the amounts subscribed for each of those issues.

An '*amount of insignificant value*' is an amount of value which

- does not exceed £1,000, or
- in any other case is insignificant in relation to the amount subscribed by the investing company for the relevant shares.

If at any time in the period beginning one year before the date of issue of the relevant shares and ending with the date of issue, there are in existence arrangements (as very broadly defined) providing for the investing company to receive, or become entitled to receive, any value from the issuing company at any time in the period of restriction (see above), no amount of value received by the investing company is treated as an amount of insignificant value.

There are provisions to aggregate a receipt of value, whether insignificant or not, with amounts of insignificant value received previously, and treating that aggregate, if it is not itself an amount of insignificant value, as an amount of value received at the time of the latest actual receipt.

Where relief is withdrawn or reduced by reason of a disposal (see 17.11 above), the investing company is not treated as receiving value from the issuing company in respect of the disposal.

[*FA 2000, Sch 15 paras 47, 48, 51–53, 102(1)*].

17.13 Meaning *of, and amount of, value received.* The investing company '*receives value*' from the issuing company if the latter (and see 17.12 above re connected persons)

(*a*) repays, redeems or repurchases any part of the investing company's holding of the issuing company's share capital or securities, or makes any payment to the investing company in respect of the cancellation of any of the issuing company's share capital or any security;

(*b*) repays, in pursuance of any arrangements for or in connection with the acquisition of the relevant shares, any debt owed to the investing company other than one incurred by the issuing company on or after the date of issue of the shares and otherwise than in consideration of the extinguishment of a debt incurred before that date;

(*c*) makes any payment to the investing company in respect of the cancellation of any debt owed to it;

(*d*) releases or waives any liability of the investing company to the issuing company (which it is deemed to have done if discharge of the liability is twelve months or more overdue) or discharges, or undertakes to discharge, any liability of the investing company to a third person;

(*e*) makes a loan or advance to the investing company which has not been repaid in full before the issue of the relevant shares; for this purpose a loan includes any debt incurred, other than an ordinary trade debt (as defined), and any debt due to a third person which is assigned to the issuing company;

(*f*) provides a benefit or facility for the directors or employees of the investing company or any of their associates (as defined), except in circumstances such that, if a *payment* had been made of equal value, it would have been a 'qualifying payment';

(*g*) disposes of an asset to the investing company for no consideration or for consideration less than market value (as defined), or acquires an asset from the investing company for consideration exceeding market value; or

(*h*) makes a payment to the investing company other than a 'qualifying payment'.

References above to a debt or liability do not include one which would be discharged by making a 'qualifying payment'. References to a payment or disposal include one made indirectly to, or to the order of, or for the benefit of, the person in question.

Each of the following is a '*qualifying payment*':

(i) a reasonable (in relation to their market value) payment for any goods, services or facilities provided by the investing company in the course of trade or otherwise;

(ii) the payment of interest at no more than a reasonable commercial rate on money lent;

(iii) the payment of a dividend or other distribution which represents no more than a normal return on investment;

(iv) a payment to acquire an asset at no more than its market value;

(v) a payment not exceeding a reasonable and commercial rent for property occupied;

(vi) a payment discharging an ordinary trade debt.

The *amount of value received* is

- in a case within (*a*), (*b*) or (*c*) above, the amount received or, if greater, the market value of the shares, securities or debt in question;
- in a case within (*d*) above, the amount of the liability;
- in a case within (*e*) above, the amount of the loan etc. less any amount repaid before the issue of the relevant shares;
- in a case within (*f*) above, the cost (net of any consideration given for it by the recipient or his associate) of providing the benefit etc.;
- in a case within (*g*) above, the difference between market value and the consideration received (if any); and
- in a case within (*h*) above, the amount of the payment.

[*FA 2000, Sch 15 paras 49, 50, 99, 102(5); ITTOIA 2005, Sch 1 para 521*].

17.14 *Replacement value.* The provisions at 17.12 above are disapplied if the person from whom the value was received (the '*original supplier*') receives, by way of a 'qualifying receipt' and whether before or after the original receipt of value, at least equivalent replacement value from the original recipient. A receipt is a '*qualifying receipt*' if it arises by reason of

(*a*) any one, or any combination, of the following:

  (i) a payment by the original recipient to the original supplier other than an 'excepted payment';

  (ii) the acquisition of an asset by the original recipient from the original supplier for consideration exceeding market value (as defined);

  (iii) the disposal of an asset by the original recipient to the original supplier for no consideration or for consideration less than market value; or

(*b*) (where the original receipt of value falls within 17.13(*d*) above) an event having the effect of reversing the original event.

The amount of replacement value is

- in a case within (*a*) above, the amount of any such payment plus the difference between the market value of any such asset and the consideration received; and
- in a case within (*b*) above, the same as the amount of the original value.

The receipt of replacement value is disregarded if

- it occurs before the start of the period of restriction (see 17.12 above);
- there was an unreasonable delay in its occurrence; or
- it occurs more than 60 days after the relief falling to be withdrawn (or reduced) has been determined on appeal.

Each of the following is an '*excepted payment*' for the purposes of (*a*)(i) above:

(1) a reasonable (in relation to their market value) payment for any goods, services or facilities provided (in the course of trade or otherwise) by the original supplier;

(2) a payment of interest at no more than a reasonable commercial rate on money lent to the original recipient;

(3) a payment not exceeding a reasonable and commercial rent for property occupied by the original recipient;

(4) a payment within 17.13(iii)(iv) or (vi) above;

(5) a payment for any shares or securities in any company in circumstances not within (*a*)(ii) above.

Each reference in (1)–(3) above to the original supplier or recipient includes a reference to any person who at *any* time in the period of restriction is an associate (as defined) of his or connected with him (within *ICTA 1988, s 839* — see 16 CONNECTED PERSONS).

The above provisions apply in relation to shares issued after 6 March 2001 and, for shares issued previously, in relation to value received after that date. Under earlier provisions, (*a*)(ii) and (iii) above applied only where the original receipt of value fell within 17.13(*g*) above, and an '*excepted payment*' meant a payment within 17.13(i)–(vi) above or within (5) above.

Where

- the receipt of replacement value is a qualifying receipt (as above), and
- the event giving rise to the receipt is (or includes) a subscription for shares by the investing company or a person connected (as above) with it at any time in the period of restriction,

the subscriber is not eligible for investment relief, EIS income tax relief or EIS capital gains deferral relief in relation to those shares or any other shares in the same issue.

In relation to shares issued after 6 March 2001 and, for shares issued previously, in relation to value received after that date, any apportionment made as in 17.12 above (where there are two or more share issues) is taken not to reduce the original value for the above purposes.

[*FA 2000, Sch 15 paras 54, 55, 99, 102(3)(5); FA 2001, Sch 16 paras 6, 7; ITTOIA 2005, Sch 1 para 521*].

17.15 **Value received by other persons.** Investment relief is withdrawn (or reduced) in certain cases of value received by persons other than the investing company (see 17.10 above re consequences of withdrawal etc.). This applies where, during the period of restriction (as in 17.12 above), the issuing company or a 'subsidiary'

(*a*) repays, redeems or repurchases any part of its share capital belonging to a member (other than the investing company) who does not thereby suffer a withdrawal or reduction of any investment relief, EIS income tax relief or EIS capital gains deferral relief attributable to his shares; or

(*b*) makes any payment to any such member in respect of the cancellation of any of the share capital of the issuing company or subsidiary.

In relation to shares issued after 6 March 2001 and, for shares issued previously, in relation to repayments etc. made after that date, the fact that no withdrawal or reduction of the kind referred to in (*a*) above falls to be made is disregarded if this is due only to the insignificance of the value received (see, for example, 17.12 above).

The investment relief attributable to the relevant shares held by the investing company is withdrawn, or is reduced by 20% of the amount received by the member (if such reduction would not amount to full withdrawal). If the relief initially obtained was less than 20% of the amount subscribed for those shares (i.e. because the company's corporation tax liability was insufficient to fully absorb the available relief), the reduction is correspondingly restricted. The amount received is also apportioned between investing companies (by reference to amounts subscribed) where the receipt of value causes a withdrawal or reduction of more than one such company's investment relief. Where the receipt of value falls into overlapping periods of restriction in relation to more than one issue of shares which includes shares to which investment relief is attributable, the value received is similarly apportioned between issues.

If the amount received by the member in question is insignificant in relation to the remaining issued share capital of the issuing company or, as the case may be, subsidiary, it is disregarded. In applying this test, the market value, immediately before the event concerned, of the shares to which the event relates is substituted for the amount received if this would give a greater amount. The assumption is made that the shares in question are cancelled at the time of the event. This let-out does not apply if at any time in the period beginning one year before the date of issue of the relevant shares and ending with the date of issue, there are in existence arrangements (as very broadly defined) providing for a payment within these provisions to be made, or entitlement to such a payment to come into being, at any time in the period of restriction. In relation to shares issued before 7 March 2001, in relation to repayments etc. made before that date, this disregard applied if the amount received was insignificant in relation to remaining share capital, issued or otherwise.

For the above purposes, a '*subsidiary*' is a company which is a 51% subsidiary of the issuing company at any time in the period of restriction, whether or not at the time of receipt of value.

The above provisions do not apply to the redemption, within twelve months of issue, of any share capital of nominal value equal to the authorised minimum issued to comply with *Companies Act 1985, s 117* (or NI equivalent).

[*FA 2000, Sch 15 paras 56–58, 102(1); FA 2001, Sch 16 paras 8, 9*].

17.16 **Put options and call options.** Where there is granted during the qualification period (see 17.2 above)

- an option, the exercise of which would bind the grantor to purchase any of the relevant shares from the investing company, or
- an option, the exercise of which would bind the grantor, in this case the investing company, to sell any of the relevant shares,

investment relief attributable (see 17.3 above) to those of the relevant shares which would (on given assumptions) be treated as disposed of on exercise of the option is withdrawn. See 17.10 above re consequences of withdrawal.

[*FA 2000, Sch 15 para 59*].

17.17 IDENTIFICATION RULES

The rules below apply, for the purpose of identifying shares disposed of, where a company makes a part disposal of a holding of shares of the same class in the same company, and the holding includes shares to which investment relief is attributable (see 17.3 above) and which have been held continuously (see 17.19(*a*) below) since the time of issue. The rules apply for the purposes of the corporate venturing scheme and for the purposes of corporation tax on chargeable gains generally. As regards the latter, the normal rules at 59.3 SHARES AND SECURITIES — IDENTIFICATION RULES are disapplied.

Where shares comprised in the holding have been acquired on different days, a disposal is identified with acquisitions on a first in/first out basis. In matching the shares disposed of with shares acquired on a particular day, shares to which investment relief is attributable and which have been held continuously since issue are treated as being disposed of *after* any other shares acquired on that day.

If, on a reorganisation of share capital (e.g. a scrip issue), a new holding falls, by virtue of *TCGA 1992, s 127* (or any other chargeable gains enactment which applies that *section* — see, for example, 58.1, 58.4, 58.6, 58.7 SHARES AND SECURITIES, and see also 17.22 below), to be equated with the original shares, shares comprised in the new holding are deemed for the above purposes to have been acquired when the original shares were acquired.

[*FA 2000, Sch 15 para 93; FA 2002, Sch 9 paras 6(4), 8(1); FA 2006, s 72(2)(e)*].

17.18 **CHARGEABLE GAINS AND ALLOWABLE LOSSES**

A gain on the disposal at any time by the investing company of shares to which investment relief is attributable (see 17.3 above) is a chargeable gain, though see 17.21 below as regards possibility of deferral relief. A loss on such a disposal is an allowable loss — see 17.19 below as to the computation of the loss and 17.20 below as regards possibility of setting the loss against income rather than gains. For the rules for identifying disposals with acquisitions, see 17.17 above.

17.19 **Computation of allowable loss.** If a loss would otherwise accrue on a disposal by the investing company of shares to which investment relief is attributable, and the investment relief does not fall to be withdrawn (as opposed to reduced) as a result of the disposal (see 17.10 above), the company's acquisition cost for the purposes of corporation tax on chargeable gains is reduced by the amount of investment relief attributable to the shares immediately after the disposal, but not so as to convert the loss into a chargeable gain. This applies only if the condition at 17.20(*a*) below (shares held continuously) is met from issue to disposal. [*FA 2000, Sch 15 para 94*].

17.20 **Set-off of allowable loss against income.** Subject to all the conditions at (*a*)–(*c*) below being satisfied and a claim being made, an allowable loss, on a disposal by the investing company of shares to which investment relief is attributable (see 17.3 above), may be set against *income* (as an alternative to setting it against chargeable gains in the normal way — see 13.4 COMPANIES). The loss is as computed after applying the reduction at 17.19 above. The conditions are as follows.

(*a*) The shares must have been held continuously by the company from time of issue to time of disposal. If, during any period,

- the company was deemed under any provision of *TCGA 1992* to have disposed of and immediately reacquired the shares; or,
- following a scheme of reconstruction within *TCGA 1992, s 136* — see 58.6 SHARES AND SECURITIES (or which would have been within that *section* but for the provisions at 3.18 ANTI-AVOIDANCE), the company was deemed by virtue of 17.23 below to have made a disposal of shares which it retained under the scheme;

it is not treated for the purposes of the corporate venturing scheme provisions as having held the shares continuously throughout that period.

(*b*) The investment relief must not fall to be withdrawn (as opposed to reduced) as a result of the disposal.

(*c*) The disposal must be either

- by way of bargain at arm's length for full consideration; or
- by way of a distribution on a dissolution or winding-up of the issuing company; or
- a disposal within *TCGA 1992, s 24*(*1*) (entire loss, destruction etc. of asset — see 9.1 CAPITAL SUMS DERIVED FROM ASSETS); or
- a deemed disposal under *TCGA 1992, s 24*(*2*) (assets of negligible value — see 40.9 LOSSES).

The set-off is against income of the accounting period in which the loss is incurred. As regards any unrelieved balance, the claim may be extended to income of accounting periods ending within the 12 months immediately preceding the accounting period in which the loss is incurred. Income of an accounting period beginning before, and ending within, that 12 months is apportioned on a time basis so as to exclude income thereby deemed to have accrued prior to that 12-month period. The income of each accounting period included in the claim is treated as reduced by the loss, or by so much of it as cannot be relieved in a later accounting period. Where claims are made to relieve two or more losses, they are relieved in the order in which they were incurred. Relief is given before any relief claimed under *ICTA 1988, s 573* (loss incurred by investment company on disposal of unlisted shares — see 40.15 LOSSES) and before any deduction for charges on income or other deductible amounts. Once relief has been obtained under these provisions for an amount of loss, that amount cannot be relieved under *section 573* or against chargeable gains.

Claims must be made within two years after the end of the accounting period in which the loss is incurred.

Where a claim is made under these provisions, *TCGA 1992, s 30* (value shifting to give tax-free benefit) has effect in relation to the disposal if *any* benefit is conferred, whether tax-free or not. No loss relief against income is available if the disposal is the result of a company reconstruction effected for tax avoidance rather than commercial reasons, such that it falls within the ambit of 3.18 ANTI-AVOIDANCE.

[*FA 2000, Sch 15 paras 67–72, 97; FA 2002, Sch 9 paras 6*(*2*), *8*(*1*)].

17.21 **Deferral relief.** Deferral relief is available where a chargeable gain would otherwise accrue to the investing company

- on a disposal of shares to which investment relief was attributable (see 17.3 above) immediately before the disposal and which satisfy the condition at 17.20(*a*) above (shares held continuously) from issue to disposal; or
- on the occurrence of a chargeable event under these provisions,

and the company makes a 'qualifying investment'. A '*qualifying investment*' is a subscription for shares ('*qualifying shares*') on which investment relief is obtained under the corporate venturing scheme, other than shares issued by a 'prohibited company'. The qualifying shares must be issued to the investing company within the one year immediately preceding or the three years immediately following the time the chargeable gain in question accrues. If the qualifying shares are issued *before* the gain accrues, they must have been held continuously (see 17.20(*a*) above) by the investing company from issue until the time the gain accrues, and investment relief must still be attributable to them. A '*prohibited company*' means either

(*a*) the company whose shares are disposed of or, or as the case may be, in relation to whose shares the chargeable event occurred; or (*b*) a company which, when the gain accrues or when the qualifying shares are issued, is a member of the same group as the company in (*a*) above.

Deferral relief is said to be 'attributable to shares' if expenditure on those shares has been used to defer the whole or part of a chargeable gain and no chargeable event has occurred resulting in the deferred gain being brought back into charge.

The following themselves become qualifying shares:

- any bonus shares, issued in respect of the qualifying shares and being shares in the same company, of the same class and carrying the same rights;
- any shares issued on a company reconstruction within 17.24 below in exchange for qualifying shares.

Postponement of the original gain. On a claim by the investing company, the whole or part of the chargeable gain can be deferred. The amount to be deferred is the lower of

- the amount of the gain (or the amount remaining in charge after any previous deferral relief claim);
- the amount subscribed for the qualifying shares (to the extent that it has not been used in previous deferral relief claims); and
- the amount specified by the company in the claim.

No time limit is specified for making a claim, so the general six-year time limit applies as in 12.5 CLAIMS.

Deferred gain becoming chargeable. The deferred gain will become chargeable on the occurrence of, *and at the time of*, one of the following chargeable events:

(i) a disposal of qualifying shares by the investing company; or

(ii) any other event giving rise to a withdrawal of, or reduction in, the investment relief attributable to qualifying shares (see 17.10 above).

If the qualifying investment is made before the gain accrues, there is disregarded for the purposes of (ii) above any reduction made by reason of an event occurring before the gain accrues.

The chargeable gain accruing to the investing company at the time of the chargeable event is equal to so much of the deferred gain as is attributable to the shares in relation to which the chargeable event occurs. For these purposes, a proportionate part of the net deferred gain (i.e. the deferred gain less any amount brought into charge on an earlier chargeable event, e.g. a part disposal) is attributed to each of the qualifying shares held immediately before the chargeable event. Thus, a part disposal of qualifying shares brings into charge a proportionate part of the deferred gain.

Provision is made to ensure that a previously deferred gain accruing as above is brought into charge under *TCGA 1992, s 10B* (previously *TCGA 1992, s 10*) (see 45.3 OVERSEAS MATTERS) in the case of a non-UK resident company carrying on a trade or vocation through a UK permanent establishment (previously a branch or agency).

[*FA 2000, Sch 15 paras 73–79; FA 2003, Sch 27 para 9*].

17.22 COMPANY RESTRUCTURING

Reorganisations of share capital. The following applies where a company holds shares in another company, being shares of the same class, held in the same capacity and forming part of the ordinary share capital of that other company, and there is a reorganisation within the meaning of *TCGA 1992, s 126* (see 58.1 SHARES AND SECURITIES). If the shares fall within two or more of the categories below, *TCGA 1992, s 127* (see 58.1 SHARES AND SECURITIES), or, where appropriate, *TCGA 1992, s 116* (reorganisations involving QUALI-

FYING CORPORATE BONDS (50.3)), applies separately to each category. (This is subject to the disapplication of those provisions in the circumstances set out below.) The categories are:

- shares to which deferral relief is attributable (see 15.21 above);
- shares to which investment relief, but not deferral relief, is attributable (see 15.3 above) and which have been held continuously (see 17.20(*a*) above) by the company since they were issued; and
- shares in neither of the categories above.

[*FA 2000, Sch 15 para 80*].

Rights issues etc. Where

- a reorganisation (within *TCGA 1992, s 126* — see 58.1 SHARES AND SECURITIES) involves an allotment of shares or debentures in respect of and in proportion to an existing holding,
- investment relief is attributable (see 17.3 above) to the shares in the existing holding or to the allotted shares, and,
- if investment relief is attributable to the shares in the existing holding, those shares have been held continuously (see 17.20(*a*) above) by the company since they were issued,

the share reorganisation rules of *TCGA 1992, ss 127–130* (see 58.1 SHARES AND SECURITIES) are disapplied. The effect is that the allotted shares are treated as a separate holding acquired at the time of the reorganisation. This does not apply in the case of bonus shares where these are issued in respect of shares comprised in the existing holding and are of the same class and carry the same rights as those shares.

If, in a case otherwise within 50.3 QUALIFYING CORPORATE BONDS,

- the old asset consists of shares to which investment relief is attributable and which have been held continuously (see 17.20(*a*) above) by the company since they were issued, and
- the new asset consists of a qualifying corporate bond,

the usual treatment is disapplied. The effect is that the investing company is deemed to have disposed of the shares at the time of the relevant transaction, and the resulting chargeable gain or allowable loss crystallises *at that time*.

[*FA 2000, Sch 15 para 81*].

17.23 **Company reconstructions.** Subject to 17.24 below, *TCGA 1992, s 135* (exchange of securities for those in another company — see 58.4 SHARES AND SECURITIES) and *s 136* (schemes of reconstruction involving issue of securities — see 58.6 SHARES AND SECURITIES), which equate the new holding with the original shares, are disapplied in the following circumstances:

- a company holds shares in another company (Company A),
- investment relief is attributable (see 17.3 above) to those shares,
- those shares have been held continuously (see 17.20(*a*) above) by the investing company since they were issued, and
- there is a reconstruction whereby a third company issues shares or debentures in exchange for, or in respect of, Company A shares or debentures.

The result is that the transaction is treated, both for the purposes of the corporate venturing scheme provisions and for the purposes of corporation tax on chargeable gains generally, as a disposal of the original shares (and an acquisition of a new holding).

[*FA 2000, Sch 15 paras 82, 96; FA 2002, Sch 9 para 6(3)(5), para 7, para 8(1)*].

17.24 **Issuing company becoming wholly-owned subsidiary of new holding company.** Notwithstanding 17.23 above, *TCGA 1992, s 135* is not disapplied (and there is thus no disposal and acquisition) where, by means entirely of an exchange of shares, all the shares in one company (the '*old shares*') are acquired by another company, and the conditions below are satisfied. Following such a share exchange, the shares thereby issued by the acquiring company (the '*new shares*') stand in place of the old shares, so that

- any investment relief or deferral relief attributable to the old shares (see, respectively, 15.3, 15.21 above) is attributed to the new shares for which they were exchanged;
- the new shares are treated as having been issued at the time the old shares were issued and as having been held continuously (see 17.20(*a*) above) by the investing company since that time (provided the old shares had been so held);
- generally speaking, anything done, or required to be done, by or in relation to the acquired company is treated as having been done etc. by or in relation to the acquiring company; and
- certain of the requirements of 17.5, 17.6 above which were met to any extent in relation to the old shares are deemed to be met to the same extent in relation to the new shares.

The conditions to be satisfied are as follows.

(*a*) The consideration for the old shares consists entirely of the issue of the new shares.

(*b*) New shares are issued only at a time when the issued shares in the acquiring company consist entirely of subscriber shares (and any new shares already issued in consideration of old shares).

(*c*) The consideration for new shares of each description consists entirely of old shares of the 'corresponding description'.

(*d*) New shares of each description are issued to holders of old shares of the 'corresponding description' in respect of, and in proportion to, their holdings.

(*e*) Before any exchange of shares takes place, HMRC have given an 'approval notification'.

For the purposes of (*c*) and (*d*) above, old and new shares are of a '*corresponding description*' if, assuming they were shares in the same company, they would be of the same class and carry the same rights. All references above to 'shares' (other than to 'subscriber shares') include references to 'securities'. An '*approval notification*' (see (*e*) above) is given by HMRC, on an application by either company involved, if they are satisfied that the share exchange will be effected for commercial reasons and does not form part of a scheme or arrangements to avoid liability to corporation tax or capital gains tax.

The provisions of *FA 2000, Sch 15 para 80* (see 17.23 above) are applied to a reconstruction within the above provisions where a company's holding of 'old shares' falls within more than one of the categories there mentioned.

For interaction between these provisions and the exemptions relating to SUBSTANTIAL SHAREHOLDINGS OF COMPANIES, see 60.14.

[*FA 2000, Sch 15 paras 83–87; FA 2002, s 44, Sch 8 para 5*].

18 Death

Cross-references. See 35.2 INTERACTION WITH OTHER TAXES for inheritance tax (or capital transfer tax); 37.7 INTEREST AND SURCHARGES ON UNPAID TAX for relief given if probate is delayed; 41 MARKET VALUE; 54.2 RETURNS for simplified procedures for small deceased estates; 57.2 SETTLEMENTS for death of a bankrupt etc. and 57.15–57.17 for termination of a life interest by the death of the person entitled thereto; 58.15 SHARES AND SECURITIES.

Simon's Direct Tax Service. See Divisions C1.2 and C4.1.

18.1 GENERAL PROVISIONS

All 'assets of which a deceased person was competent to dispose' are deemed to have been acquired on his death by his personal representatives (or other person on whom they devolve) for a consideration equal to their market value at the date of death. However, they are not deemed to be disposed of by the deceased on his death (whether or not they were the subject of a testamentary disposition), i.e. no chargeable gain or allowable loss arises on death and any gain or loss arising on the disposal of the asset by the personal representatives, etc. after the death is calculated by reference to the market value of the asset at the date of death (subject to the further provisions in this chapter).

'*Assets of which the deceased was competent to dispose*' are those assets which (otherwise than in right of a power of appointment or of the testamentary power conferred by statute to dispose of entailed interests) he could, if of full age and capacity, have disposed of by his will, assuming that all the assets were situated in England and, if he was not domiciled in the United Kingdom, that he was domiciled in England, and include references to his severable share in any assets to which, immediately before his death, he was beneficially entitled as joint tenant. [*TCGA 1992, s 62*(*1*)(*10*)].

18.2 **Scotland.** So far as the provisions in *TCGA 1992* relate to the consequences of the death of

(*a*) for deaths before 6 April 2006, an heir of entail in possession of any property in Scotland subject to an entail (whether *sui juris* or not), or

(*b*) a proper liferenter of any property,

then, on the death of any such heir or liferenter, the heir next entitled or, as the case may be, the person (if any) who, on the death of the liferenter, becomes entitled to possession of the property as heir, is deemed to have acquired all the assets forming part of the property at the date of the deceased's death for a consideration equal to their market value at that date. [*TCGA 1992, s 63; FA 2006, Sch 12 para 11*(*1*)(*3*)].

Northern Ireland. For deaths after 5 April 2006, so far as the provisions in *TCGA 1992* relate to the consequences of the death of a person to whom property in Northern Ireland stands limited for life, a person who acquires property in fee simple absolute or fee tail in possession as a consequence of the deceased's death, is deemed to have acquired all the assets forming part of the property at the date of death for a consideration equal to their market value at that date. [*TCGA 1992, s 63; FA 2006, Sch 12 para 11*(*2*)(*3*)].

18.3 **Valuation.** Where on the death of any person, inheritance tax is chargeable on the value of his estate immediately before his death and the value of an asset forming part of his estate has been ascertained for those purposes, that value is taken to be the market value at the date of death for capital gains tax purposes. [*TCGA 1992, s 274*]. See also Revenue Tax Bulletin April 1995 p 209. In practice (see HMRC Pamphlet IHT 15 page 15), unless there are special circumstances, quoted shares and securities are valued in the same way as for capital gains tax (see 41.3 MARKET VALUE). In the case of land and quoted shares and securities, proceeds of certain post-death sales within a specified period may be substituted for values at date of death for inheritance tax purposes. The value of related property (as defined for inheritance tax purposes) may also be revised in the event of a post-death sale. If such substitutions/revisions are made for inheritance tax purposes, they must be made for CGT purposes also (but see *Stonor and Another (Executors of Dickinson deceased) v CIR (Sp C 288), [2001] SSCD 199* in which the executors failed in an attempt to use this rule to upgrade values of freehold properties for CGT purposes where there was no inheritance tax liability). See Tolley's Inheritance Tax for details and also HMRC Capital Gains Manual CG 32290–32310.

Where, in consequence of a death before 31 March 1971 (when death *was* an occasion of charge for CGT), capital gains tax was chargeable or an allowable loss accrued, then if the market value of any property on the date of death which was subject to charge has been depreciated *by reason of the death*, then any later estimate of the market value is to take that depreciation into account. [*TCGA 1992, Sch 11 para 8*]. This provision may still, therefore, be relevant in computing allowable expenditure on a first disposal subsequent to the date of death. The legislation now refers to deaths before 31 March 1973 but the reasoning for this is not clear; see *FA 1965, s 44(2) proviso* as repealed by *FA 1971, Sch 14 Pt V* for deaths occurring after 30 March 1971 and cf. *CGTA 1979, Sch 6 para 2(2)*).

Following the decision in *Gray v CIR CA, [1994] STC 360*, HMRC's view is that two or more different assets comprised in an estate can be treated as a single unit of property if disposal as one unit was the course that a prudent hypothetical vendor would have adopted in order to obtain the most favourable price without undue expenditure of time and effort.

This principle will apply for capital gains tax purposes in the following cases:

(*a*) An acquisition by personal representatives or legatees under *TCGA 1992, s 62* of assets which a deceased person was competent to dispose.

(*b*) An acquisition of settled property under *TCGA 1992, s 71(1)* on the occasion of a person becoming absolutely entitled to that settled property.

There are certain situations when a single valuation will still apply, such as:

(i) the disposal of an asset for consideration deemed to be equal to its market value under *TCGA 1992, s 17*;

(ii) when a valuation of an asset is required for the purpose of re-basing to 31 March 1992 under *TCGA 1992, s 35*.

The single asset valuation for *TCGA 1992, s 17* is modified by *TCGA 1992, s 19* where there is a series of linked transactions between connected persons. Each disposal in the series may be treated as being made for consideration equal to a proportion of the aggregate value of all the assets in the series.

18.4 **Donatio mortis causa.** No chargeable gain arises on the making of a disposal by way of '*donatio mortis causa*' i.e. a gift of personal property made in 'contemplation of the conceived approach of death' (see *Duffield v Elwes Ch D 1827, 1 Bligh's Reports (New Series) 497*), and the recipient is treated as a legatee acquiring it at the date of death. [*TCGA 1992, s 62(5), s 64(2)*].

18.5 CARRY-BACK OF LOSSES

Allowable losses in excess of chargeable gains incurred by the deceased in the tax year in which death occurs can be carried back and set off against chargeable gains in the three preceding tax years. See 2.3 ANNUAL RATES AND EXEMPTIONS for the interaction between losses carried back and the annual exempt amount. Subject to this, chargeable gains accruing in a later year must be relieved before those of an earlier year. Losses carried back to 1998/99 or a subsequent year cannot be set against any of the following that might be attributed to the individual (*except* to the extent noted at 40.1 LOSSES as regards gains for 2003/04 onwards or, by election, for any of the years 2000/01 to 2002/03):

- gains treated under *TCGA 1992, s 77* as accruing to him as settlor from a UK resident settlement in which he has an interest (see 57.5 SETTLEMENTS);
- gains treated under *TCGA 1992, s 86* as accruing to him as settlor from a non-UK resident settlement in which he has an interest (see 44.5 OFFSHORE SETTLEMENTS);
- gains treated under *TCGA 1992, s 87* or *s 89(2)* as accruing to him as a beneficiary of a non-UK resident settlement (an offshore trust) (see 44.14 OFFSHORE SETTLEMENTS).

Losses carried back are treated in the same way as current year and brought-forward losses for the purposes of the application of TAPER RELIEF (61) and are thus set against chargeable gains *before* applying that relief (see 61.2).

[*TCGA 1992, s 62(2)–(2B); FA 1998, s 121(3)(4), Sch 21 para 5*].

Any remaining unused losses *cannot* be carried forward and set off against gains made by the personal representatives or legatees.

Where the year of death is **1996/97 or a later year** (i.e. where self-assessment applies), a carry-back of a loss under *TCGA 1992, s 62(2)* is brought within the scope of *TMA 1970, Sch 1B* (claims for relief involving two or more years). This provision is fully covered in Tolley's Income Tax (and see also 12.2 CLAIMS) and its effect is that whilst the resulting tax saving/repayment is computed by reference to the facts for the tax year(s) to which the loss is carried back (the earlier year), it is then treated as a reduction or repayment of tax for the tax year in which the loss is incurred (the later year). The tax position for the earlier year is not adjusted. The general requirement that claims be made in a self-assessment tax return (see 12.2 CLAIMS) does not apply to a carry-back under *section 62(2)*. [*TMA 1970, Sch 1B para 2; FA 1996, s 128(2)(11), Sch 17*]. Repayment supplement may be due as in 36.1 INTEREST ON OVERPAID TAX, though only from 31 January following the *later year* (as above). This applies by law to income tax repayments made on or after 11 May 2001 (see 12.2 CLAIMS) but was also applied in practice by the Revenue in relation to earlier repayments and will presumably continue to be so applied by HMRC in relation to capital gains tax repayments.

18.6 DEEDS OF FAMILY ARRANGEMENT ETC.

Variations or disclaimers of the dispositions (whether effected by will, under the intestacy rules or otherwise) of the 'property of which the deceased was competent to dispose' (see 18.1 above) which are made by deed of family arrangement (or similar instrument in writing) within two years of death do not constitute disposals but are related back to the date of death. Such treatment does not apply in respect of variations or disclaimers made for any consideration in money or money's worth other than consideration consisting of the making of a variation or disclaimer in respect of another of the dispositions.

In the case of a variation (as opposed to a disclaimer), the above treatment applies only if the instrument contains a statement by the persons making the instrument to the effect that they intend the treatment to apply. This has effect in relation to instruments made after 31 July 2002. For instruments of variation made on or before that date, no such statement was required but it was necessary for an election to be made (under *TCGA 1992, s 62(7)*) for the above treatment to apply. The election had to be made to the Revenue in writing by the parties to the instrument within six months after the date of the instrument or such longer time as the Revenue would allow. Under the post-31 July 2002 procedure, it is necessary to send HMRC a copy of the instrument only if it has immediate tax consequences or if it is requested as part of an enquiry (see Revenue Tax Bulletin August 2002 pp 957–959).

The above provisions apply whether or not the administration of the estate is complete or the property has been distributed in accordance with the original dispositions.

[*TCGA 1992, s 62(6)–(9); FA 2002, s 52*].

In HMRC's view, the above provisions apply to a variation of the deceased's interest in jointly held assets, which pass on death to the surviving joint owner(s) (Revenue Tax Bulletin October 1995 p 254).

In a case based upon the original *FA 1965* legislation, it was held that the equivalent provisions to *TCGA 1992, s 62(6)* above and *s 62(4)* (see 18.9 below), although deeming provisions, were to be given their normal and natural meaning. But, where such construction would lead to an injustice or absurdity, the application of the statutory fiction should be limited to the extent needed to avoid such injustice or absurdity. Thus, nothing in *TCGA 1992, s 62(6)* requires one to assume something which is inconsistent with the legatee under an original will, who then varies dispositions under *TCGA 1992, s 62(6)* to a third party, as having been the actual settlor of the arrangement. The deeming provisions apply only to assets of which the testator was competent to dispose at his death. However, the property settled by the legatee comprised, not the assets in the deceased's estate which eventually came to be vested in the third party, but a separate chose in action, i.e. the right to due administration of the estate, and this could only have been settled by the legatee and not by the deceased. (*Marshall v Kerr HL 1994, 67 TC 56*). Where, in the rare event, the administration of an estate has been completed before a deed of variation is made, a different analysis may follow.

For HMRC's comments on the provisions affecting the variation of the devolution of a deceased estate, see HMRC Capital Gains Manual CG 31400–32100. For cases bearing on the effectiveness of similar deeds used for inheritance tax purposes, see Tolley's Inheritance Tax under Deeds Varying Dispositions on Death.

18.7 PERSONAL REPRESENTATIVES

Personal representatives are treated as a single and continuing body (distinct from persons who may from time to time be the personal representatives) which has the deceased's residence, ordinary residence and domicile at the date of death. [*TCGA 1992, s 62(3)*].

They are liable to capital gains tax on disposals of assets made by them by reference to the disposal proceeds and the market value at the date of death (but see 18.8 below). They may be assessed in respect of disposals made by the deceased prior to death as well as in respect of their own disposals. See 5.7, 5.8 ASSESSMENTS.

For the year of assessment in which death occurs and the following two years of assessment, the personal representatives are entitled to the same annual exempt amount as individuals, with the same general provisions applying. [*TCGA 1992, s 3(7)(7A); FA 2003, s 159, Sch 28 para 3(3)(4)*]. See 2.3 ANNUAL RATES AND EXEMPTIONS.

See 2.2 ANNUAL RATES AND EXEMPTIONS for the rate of capital gains tax applicable to personal representatives.

Losses made by personal representatives during the administration period cannot be passed on to the legatees. The position should be compared with that for losses made by trustees as in 57.15 SETTLEMENTS.

For 1996/97 and subsequent years, CGT due from personal representatives may be assessed and charged on and in the name of any one or more of the 'relevant personal representatives'. In relation to chargeable gains, the '*relevant personal representatives*' means the personal representatives in the tax year in which the gains accrue and any subsequent personal representatives of the deceased. Previously, CGT could be assessed on any personal representative, except that where an assessment was raised otherwise than on all the personal representatives the persons assessed could not include a person who was not resident or ordinarily resident in the UK. [*TCGA 1992, s 65(1)((4); FA 1995, s 103(7), s 114*].

18.8 **Allowable expenditure.** The decision in *Richards' Executors HL 1971, 46 TC 626* enables personal representatives, in computing chargeable gains on the disposal of assets, to add to the cost of acquiring the assets from the testator (i.e. the market value at the date of death) those legal and accountancy costs that are involved in preparing the inheritance tax or capital transfer tax account and obtaining the grant of probate etc. See also 15.4 COMPUTATION OF GAINS AND LOSSES.

Because of the practical difficulty of identifying the costs applicable to individual assets comprised in the estate, HMRC have agreed expenditure based on the following scales (HMRC Statements of Practice 8/94 and 2/04).

Personal representatives

Deaths after 5 April 2004

	Gross value of estate	*Allowable expenditure*
A	Up to £50,000	1.8% of the probate value of the assets sold by the personal representatives.
B	Between £50,001 and £90,000	A fixed amount of £900, to be divided between all the assets in the estate in proportion to the probate values, and allowed in those proportions on assets sold by the personal representatives.
C	Between £90,001 and £400,000	1% of the probate value of the assets sold.
D	Between £400,001 and £500,000	A fixed amount of £4,000, to be divided as at B above.
E	Between £500,001 and £1,000,000	0.8% of the probate value of the assets sold.
F	Between £1,000,001 and £5,000,000	A fixed amount of £8,000, to be divided as at B above
G	Over £5,000,000	0.16% of the probate value of the assets sold, subject to a maximum of £10,000

Deaths before 6 April 2004

	Gross value of estate	*Allowable expenditure*
A	Up to £40,000	1.75% of the probate value of the assets sold by the personal representatives.
B	Between £40,001 and £70,000	A fixed amount of £700, to be divided between all the assets in the estate in proportion to the probate values, and allowed in those proportions on assets sold by the personal representatives.
C	Between £70,001 and £300,000	1% of the probate value of the assets sold.
D	Between £300,001 and £400,000	A fixed amount of £3,000, to be divided as at B above.
E	Between £400,001 and £750,000	0.75% of the probate value of the assets sold.

The scale does not extend to gross estates that exceed £750,000 for deaths before 6 April 2004. In those cases, the allowable expenditure has to be determined according to the facts of the particular case.

In practice, HMRC will accept computations based either on these scales or on the actual expenditure incurred.

Corporate trustees

HMRC have also agreed the following scales of allowable expenditure for expenses incurred by corporate trustees in the administration of estates and trusts. They will accept computations based either on these scales or on the actual allowable expenditure incurred.

Acquisitions and disposals, or deemed disposals, after 5 April 2004

(*a*) *Transfers of assets to beneficiaries etc.*

(1)	Publicly marketed shares and securities	
	(A) One beneficiary	£25 per holding transferred.
	(B) More than one beneficiary between whom a holding must be divided	As (A), to be divided in equal shares between the beneficiaries.
(2)	Other shares and securities	As (1) above, with the addition of any exceptional expenditure.
(3)	Other assets	As (1) above, with the addition of any exceptional expenditure.

Shares and securities are regarded as marketed to the general public for this purpose if buying and selling prices are regularly published in the financial pages of a national or regional newspaper, magazine or journal.

(*b*) *Actual disposals and acquisitions*

(1)	Publicly marketed shares and securities	The investment fee as charged by the trustees.
(2)	Other shares and securities	As (1) above, plus actual valuation costs.
(3)	Other assets	The investment fee as charged by the trustees, subject to a maximum of £75, plus actual valuation costs.

Where a comprehensive annual management fee is charged, covering both the cost of administering the trust and the expenses of actual disposals and acquisitions, the investment fee for (1)–(3) above will be taken to be £0.25 per £100 on the sale or purchase moneys.

(*c*) *Deemed disposals by trustees*

(1)	Publicly marketed shares and securities	£8 per holding disposed of.
(2)	Other shares and securities	Actual valuation costs.
(3)	Other assets	Actual valuation costs.

Acquisitions and disposals, or deemed disposals, before 6 April 2004

(*a*) *Transfers of assets to beneficiaries etc.*

(1)	Quoted stocks and shares	
	(A) One beneficiary	£20 per holding.
	(B) More than one beneficiary between whom a holding must be divided	As (A), to be divided in equal shares between the beneficiaries.
(2)	Unquoted shares	As (1) above, with the addition of any exceptional expenditure.
(3)	Other assets	As (1) above, with the addition of any exceptional expenditure.

(*b*) *Actual disposals and acquisitions*

(1)	Quoted stocks and shares	The investment fee as charged by the trustee.
(2)	Unquoted shares	As (1) above, plus actual valuation costs.
(3)	Other assets	The investment fee as charged by the trustee, subject to a maximum of £60, plus actual valuation costs.

Where a comprehensive annual management fee is charged, covering both the cost of administering the trust and the expenses of actual disposals and acquisitions, the investment fee for (1)–(3) above will be taken to be £0.25 per £100 on the sale or purchase moneys.

(*c*)	*Deemed disposals by trustees*	
(1)	Quoted stocks and shares	£6 per holding.
(2)	Unquoted shares	Actual valuation costs.
(3)	Other assets	Actual valuation costs.

18.9 LEGATEES

A '*legatee*' includes any person taking under a testamentary disposition or an intestacy or partial intestacy, whether he takes beneficially or as trustee. [*TCGA 1992, s 64*(*2*)].

On a 'person acquiring any asset as legatee', no chargeable gain accrues to the personal representatives, and the legatee is treated as if the personal representatives' acquisition of the asset had been his acquisition of it. [*TCGA 1992, s 62*(*4*)]. The consequences of this are that the asset is taken as acquired at either the market value at the date of death or, if the asset was acquired subsequent to death, the allowable expenditure incurred by the personal representatives in providing etc. the asset. See also 18.6 above.

For the purposes of '*legatee*' and '*person acquiring an asset as legatee*', property taken under a testamentary disposition or on an intestacy or partial intestacy includes any asset appropriated by the personal representative in or towards satisfaction of a pecuniary legacy or any other interest or share in the property devolving. [*TCGA 1992, s 64*(*3*)].

Where a person disposes of an asset held by a personal representative to which he became absolutely entitled as legatee, any incidental expenditure incurred by that person or the personal representative in relation to the transfer of the asset to him is allowable as a deduction in the computation of the gain arising on the disposal. [*TCGA 1992, s 64*(*1*); *FA 2006, Sch 12 para 12*]. The expenditure incurred by the person concerned, but not that incurred by the personal representative, may qualify for indexation allowance (HMRC Capital Gains Manual CG 31192).

19 Double Tax Relief

(See also HMRC Pamphlet IR 20 and Capital Gains Manual CG 14380–14427.)

Cross-references. See 20.40 EMPLOYEE SHARE SCHEMES; 44 OFFSHORE SETTLEMENTS; 45 OVERSEAS MATTERS; 46.4 PARTNERSHIPS; 51 REMITTANCE BASIS; and 52 RESIDENCE AND DOMICILE.

Simon's Direct Tax Service. See C1.615–618.

19.1 Where the same gains are liable to be taxed in both the UK and another country, relief may be available as follows.

(*a*) Under the specific terms of a double tax agreement between the UK and that other country — see 19.2 below.

(*b*) Under special arrangements with Ireland — see 19.3 below.

(*c*) Under the unilateral double tax relief provisions contained in UK tax legislation — see 19.4 below.

(*d*) By deduction — see 19.5 below.

See 19.9 below for provisions dealing with special withholding tax.

19.2 **DOUBLE TAX AGREEMENTS** [*TCGA 1992, s 277; ICTA 1988, ss 788, 789, 791–816, 828 as amended; FA 2002, s 88*]

A list is given below of the bilateral agreements made by the UK which are currently operative. Under these agreements, exemption from taxes in the country where they arise may be granted for gains realised by UK residents, whether individuals or companies. Reciprocal relief is given to overseas residents from UK capital gains tax and corporation tax. See 19.6(*b*) below as regards claims.

The specific provisions of the particular agreement concerned must be examined carefully. For relevant court decisions, see Tolley's Tax Cases. Where tax on overseas gains is not relieved, or is only partly relieved, under an agreement, unilateral relief (see 19.4 below) will normally apply.

Where double tax relief by agreement applies, no deduction for foreign tax is allowed in computing the foreign gains (see 19.6(*a*)(ii) below). If a taxpayer chooses not to take relief by way of credit, any foreign tax paid is treated as allowable expenditure for the purposes of the UK assessment. See 19.5 below.

Reciprocal agreements with the following countries supersede the provisions of *ICTA 1988, s 790* (unilateral relief) to the extent, and as from the operative dates, specified therein (SI numbers in round brackets).

Antigua and Barbuda (1947/2865; 1968/1096), **Argentina** (1997/1777), **Australia** (1968/305; 1980/707; 2003/3199), **Austria** (1970/1947; 1979/117; 1994/768), **Azerbaijan** (1995/762),

Bangladesh (1980/708), **Barbados** (1970/952; 1973/2096), **Belarus** (1995/2706 — see notes below), **Belgium** (1987/2053), **Belize** (1947/2866; 1968/573; 1973/2097), **Bolivia** (1995/2707), **Bosnia-Herzegovina** (see note below), **Botswana** (1978/183), **Brunei** (1950/1977; 1968/306; 1973/2098), **Bulgaria** (1987/2054), **Burma** (see Myanmar below),

Canada (1980/709; 1980/1528; 1985/1996; 2003/2619 — protocol applies in UK from 1 April 2005 for corporation tax and from 6 April 2005 for capital gains tax (1980/780, 1987/2071, 1996/1782 all revoked from 1 April 2001 — see SI 2000/3330)), **Chile** (2003/3200 — applies in UK from 1 April 2005 for corporation tax and from 6 April 2005 for capital gains tax), **China** (1984/1826; 1996/3164), **Croatia** (see note below), **Cyprus** (1975/425; 1980/1529), **Czech Republic** (see note below),

Denmark (1980/1960; 1991/2877; 1996/3165),

Egypt (1980/1091), **Estonia** (1994/3207),

Falkland Islands (1997/2985), **Faroe Islands** (1961/579; 1971/717; 1975/2190 until 6 April 1997), **Fiji** (1976/1342), **Finland** (1970/153; 1980/710; 1985/1997; 1991/2878; 1996/3166), **France** (1968/1869; 1973/1328; 1987/466; 1987/2055),

Gambia (1980/1963), **Georgia** (2004/3325 — applies in UK from 1 April 2006 for corporation tax and from 6 April 2006 for capital gains tax), **Germany** (1967/25; 1971/874), **Ghana** (1993/1800), **Greece** (1954/142), **Grenada** (1949/361; 1968/1867), **Guernsey** (1952/1215; 1994/3209), **Guyana** (1992/3207),

Hungary (1978/1056),

Iceland (1991/2879), **India** (1981/1120; 1993/1801), **Indonesia** (1994/769), **Ireland** (see 19.3 below), **Isle of Man** (1955/1205; 1991/2880; 1994/3208), **Israel** (1963/616; 1971/391), **Italy** (1990/2590), **Ivory Coast** (1987/169),

Jamaica (1973/1329), **Japan** (1970/1948; 1980/1530), **Jersey** (1952/1216; 1994/3210), **Jordan** (2001/3924),

Kazakhstan (1994/3211; 1998/2567), **Kenya** (1977/1299), **Kiribati** (as per Tuvalu), **Korea, Republic of (South)** (1996/3168), **Kuwait** (1999/2036),

Latvia (1996/3167), **Lesotho** (1997/2986), **Lithuania** (2001/3925; 2002/2847), **Luxembourg** (1968/1100; 1980/567; 1984/364),

Macedonia (see note below), **Malawi** (1956/619; 1964/1401; 1968/1101; 1979/302), **Malaysia** (1997/2987), **Malta** (1995/763), **Mauritius** (1981/1121; 1987/467; 2003/2620), **Mexico** (1994/3212), **Mongolia** (1996/2598), **Montserrat** (1947/2869; 1968/576), **Morocco** (1991/2881), **Myanmar** (1952/751),

Namibia (1962/2352; 1962/2788; 1967/1490), **Netherlands** (1967/1063 revoked by SI 2000/3330 from 1 April 2001; 1980/1961; 1983/1902; 1990/2152), **New Zealand** (1984/365; 2004/1274), **Nigeria** (1987/2057), **Norway** (1985/1998; 2000/3247),

Oman (1998/2568),

Pakistan (1987/2058), **Papua New Guinea** (1991/2882), **Philippines** (1978/184), **Poland** (1978/282), **Portugal** (1969/599),

Romania (1977/57), **Russia** (1994/3213),

St. Christopher (St. Kitts) and Nevis (1947/2872), **Serbia and Montenegro** (see note below), **Sierra Leone** (1947/2873; 1968/1104), **Singapore** (1997/2988), **Slovak Republic (Slovakia)** (see note below), **Slovenia** (see note below), **Solomon Islands** (1950/748; 1968/574; 1974/1270), **South Africa** (1969/864; 2002/3138), **Spain** (1976/1919; 1995/765), **Sri Lanka** (1980/713), **Sudan** (1977/1719), **Swaziland** (1969/380), **Sweden** (1961/619 revoked by SI 2000/3330 from 1 April 2001; 1984/366), **Switzerland** (1978/1408; 1982/714; 1994/3215),

Taiwan (2002/3137), **Thailand** (1981/1546), **Trinidad and Tobago** (1983/1903), **Tunisia** (1984/133), **Turkey** (1988/932), **Tuvalu** (1950/750; 1968/309; 1974/1271),

Uganda (1952/1213; 1993/1802), **Ukraine** (1993/1803), **U.S.A.** (1980/568; 2002/2848 — see notes below (1946/1331, 1955/499, 1961/985, 1980/779, 1994/418, 1996/1781 all revoked from 1 January 2001 — see SI 2000/3330)), **USSR** (see note below), **Uzbekistan** (1994/770),

Venezuela (1996/2599), **Vietnam** (1994/3216),

Yugoslavia (1981/1815 and see note below),

Zambia (1972/1721; 1981/1816), **Zimbabwe** (1982/1842).

Shipping & Air Transport only—Algeria (Air Transport only) (1984/362), Brazil (1968/572), Cameroon (Air Transport only) (1982/1841), Ethiopia (Air Transport only) (1977/1297), Hong Kong (Air Transport) (1998/2566), Hong Kong (Shipping Transport) (2000/3248), Iran (Air Transport only) (1960/2419), Jordan (1979/300), Lebanon (1964/278), Saudi Arabia (Air Transport only) (1994/767), Zaire (1977/1298).

Notes.

Agreements not yet in force. The above-mentioned Agreement with Belarus had not yet entered into force at 1 April 2002. (Revenue Tax Bulletin June 2002 p 940). A new agreement was signed with France on 28 January 2004. A new agreement was signed with Botswana on 9 September 2005. A new agreement was signed with Japan on 2 February 2006.

China. The Agreement published as *SI 1984 No 1826* does not apply to the Hong Kong Special Administrative Region which came into existence on 1 July 1997. (Revenue Tax Bulletin October 1996 p 357).

Czechoslovakia. The Agreement published as *SI 1991 No 2876* between the UK and Czechoslovakia is treated as remaining in force between the UK and, respectively, the Czech Republic and the Slovak Republic. (HMRC Statement of Practice 5/93).

USA. Applies in UK from 1 April 2003 for corporation tax and from 6 April 2003 for capital gains tax. For HMRC's understanding of how certain provisions of the Agreement published as *SI 2002 No 2848* are interpreted and applied, see Revenue Tax Bulletin Special Edition 6, April 2003.

USSR. The Agreement published as *SI 1986 No 224* (which also continued in force the Air Transport agreement published as *SI 1974 No 1269*) between the UK and the former Soviet Union was to be applied by the UK as if it were still in force between the UK and the former Soviet Republics until such time as new agreements took effect with particular countries. It later came to light that Armenia, Georgia, Kyrgyzstan, Lithuania and Moldova did not consider themselves bound by the UK/USSR convention and were not operating it in relation to UK residents. Accordingly, the UK ceased to apply it to residents of those countries from 1 April 2002 for corporation tax and from 6 April 2002 for income tax and capital gains tax. (The Agreement published as *SI 2001 No 3925* between the UK and Lithuania has effect from those dates.) The position for other former Republics (Belarus, Tajikistan and Turkmenistan) with which new conventions are not yet in force remains as before. (HMRC Statement of Practice 4/01 (replacing SP 3/92) and Revenue Tax Bulletin June 2001 p 864).

Yugoslavia. The Agreement published as *SI 1981 No 1815* between the UK and Yugoslavia is regarded as remaining in force between the UK and, respectively, Bosnia-Herzegovina, Croatia, Slovenia, Macedonia and Serbia and Montenegro. (HMRC Statement of Practice 3/04).

Copies of double tax agreements and other statutory instruments published from 1987 onwards are available on the Stationery Office website at www.hmso.gov.uk/stat.htm

Representations about new double tax treaties, or suggestions about desirable changes to existing ones, should be made to HMRC Policy International, HMRC, Victory House, 30–34 Kingsway, London, WC2B 6ES. Questions about a particular double tax treaty and its effects on an individual's own tax affairs should be addressed to his local tax office.

Representations for new or revised double tax treaties in connection with estates, inheritances and gifts should be made to HMRC Policy Capital and Savings, HMRC, Room 121, 3rd Floor, New Wing, Somerset House, Strand, London WC2R 1LB.

19.3 **IRELAND** [*TCGA 1992, s 277; ICTA 1988, ss 788, 789, 791–816, 828 as amended; SI 1976 Nos 2151, 2152; SI 1995 No 764; SI 1998 No 3151*]

Broadly, capital gains on immovable property (and on business assets of a permanent establishment) are taxed in the country where it is situate. The same applies to gains on certain assets deriving their value from immovable property. Gains on other property are normally taxed in the taxpayer's country of residence. See also 52.10 RESIDENCE AND DOMICILE.

19.4 **UNILATERAL RELIEF BY UK** [*TCGA 1992, s 277; ICTA 1988, ss 790, 794 as amended; FA 2002, s 88; FA 2003, s 153(2)(a)(4)*]

Tax on chargeable gains, *other than that for which credit is available under the bilateral double tax agreements in* 19.2 *above,* payable under the law of any territory outside the UK (and see 19.3 above for Ireland) and computed by reference to gains *arising in that territory* is allowed (to the extent defined below) as a credit against UK tax paid on those gains by *UK residents.* The machinery and limits (with modifications as below) are substantially the same as those under which the bilateral agreements operate and the credit given is, basically, such as would be allowable were a double taxation agreement in force with the territory concerned.

The modifications are as follows.

(*a*) The foreign taxes must be charged on gains and correspond to capital gains tax in the UK but may include similar taxes payable under the law of a province, state or part of a country, or a municipality or other local body. See *Yates v GCA International Ltd (and cross-appeal) Ch D 1991, 64 TC 37.* Following that decision, the Revenue amended its practice from 13 February 1991. For claims made on or after that date, and earlier claims unsettled at that date, foreign taxes will be examined to determine whether, in their own legislative context, they serve the same function as UK taxes, and are thus eligible for unilateral relief. (HMRC Statement of Practice SP 7/91). The overseas taxes which the HMRC consider admissible or inadmissible for relief are listed country by country in the HMRC Double Taxation relief Manual at D2100 *et seq.* See also HMRC Inspector's Manual IM 1121 and Revenue Tax Bulletins August 1995 p 244 and October 1996 p 358 as regards recent reclassification of certain South African, Algerian, Argentine, Brazilian and Peruvian taxes.

(*b*) The restriction to tax on '*income arising in the territory*' does not apply in the case of the Channel Islands or the Isle of Man, and credit is given for CI or IOM tax if the claimant is resident for the particular year of assessment or accounting period *either in the UK or the Channel Islands or IOM*, as the case may be.

For accounting periods ending after 20 March 2000, unilateral relief is extended to foreign tax paid in respect of the chargeable gains of a UK branch or agency of a non-UK resident person or (for accounting periods beginning after 31 December 2002) a UK permanent establishment of a non-UK resident company. The relief does not extend to taxes of the non-resident's home state, and it is limited to that which would have been available if the branch or agency had been a UK-resident person to whom such gains had accrued.

In relation to double tax agreements made after 20 March 2000, unilateral relief will not be given in particular circumstances if the agreement expressly precludes relief by credit under the agreement in those circumstances. As regards claims made after 20 March 2000, it is made expressly clear that where relief or credit for foreign tax is available under a double tax agreement, unilateral relief cannot be claimed. [*ICTA 1988, s 793A; FA 2000, Sch 30 para 5; FA 2002, s 88(2)(3)*].

19.5 **RELIEF BY DEDUCTION**

Subject to 19.2–19.4 above and 19.6 and 19.9 below, foreign tax on the disposal of an asset which is borne by the disposer is an *allowable deduction* in computing UK chargeable gains.

This is on the assumption that no relief is claimed by way of credit. See HMRC Capital Gains Manual CG 14410, 14425–14427. Where the amount of any deduction allowed is rendered excessive or insufficient by reason of any adjustment made after 20 March 2000 of any tax payable either in the UK or under the law of any other territory, the time limit for revising the UK liability accordingly is extended to six years after the time when all material assessments etc. have been made to give effect to the adjustment. In a case where a deduction is rendered excessive by reason of adjustment after 20 March 2000 of a foreign tax charge, the taxpayer must give HMRC written notification of the adjustment within one year of its being made. The maximum penalty for non-compliance is equal to the additional tax payable for the tax year or company accounting period in question. [*TCGA 1992, s 278; FA 2000, Sch 30 para 30; FA 2002, s 88(2)(3); FA 2004, s 115(3)*].

19.6 SPECIFIC MATTERS

(*a*)

(i) **Amounts assessable in UK on the remittance basis.** Where double tax credit for foreign tax is allowable in respect of it, any gain which is assessable on the basis of remittance is treated, for UK assessment purposes, as increased by the foreign tax on that gain. An increase may also be required in respect of special withholding tax, calculated as indicated at 19.9 below. [*ICTA 1988, s 795(1)(3)(5); TCGA 1992, s 277(1)–(1C); FA 2004, s 112(2)(5)(6)*].

(ii) **Amounts assessable in UK on the arising basis.** Where gains are assessable to capital gains tax on the basis of the full amount arising (not on remittances as in (i) above) and double tax credit is allowable in respect of foreign tax suffered on a gain, no deduction may be made in the computation of the gain for foreign tax, or special withholding tax in respect of which a claim under 19.9 below has been made, on that, or any other gain. [*ICTA 1988, s 795(2)(5); TCGA 1992, s 277(1); FA 2004, s 112(3)(4)*].

(*b*) **Claims** for credit under double tax arrangements must normally be made on or before the fifth anniversary of 31 January following the year of assessment for which the gain is chargeable to CGT; or within six years after the end of the company accounting period for which the gain is chargeable to corporation tax. In relation to claims made after 20 March 2000, the deadline is extended to 31 January following the year of assessment in which the foreign tax is paid or one year after the end of the company accounting period in which the foreign tax is paid, where this is later than the deadline given above. [*ICTA 1988, s 806(1); TCGA 1992, s 277; FA 1996, Sch 21 para 23; FA 2000, Sch 30 para 20; FA 2002, s 88(2)(3)*]. Claims for credit are made to the officer of Revenue and Customs (or, before 18 April 2005, the inspector) responsible for the relevant assessment but other claims for relief are to the Commissioners for HMRC (or, before 18 April 2005, the Board of Inland Revenue). [*ICTA 1988, s 788(6); CRCA 2005, ss 5, 7*]. Pending final agreement, a provisional allowance can usually be obtained on application to the inspector.

Written notice must be given to HMRC where any credit allowed for foreign tax has become excessive by reason of an adjustment of the amount of any foreign tax payable (except in the case of UNDERWRITERS AT LLOYD'S (64) where the consequences of such an adjustment are dealt with under regulations). This applies to adjustments made on or after 17 March 1998, and the notice must be given within one year after the making of the adjustment. The maximum penalty for failure to comply is the amount by which the credit was rendered excessive by the adjustment. [*ICTA 1988, s 806(3)–(6); FA 1998, s 107*]. For what constitutes an adjustment and when an adjustment should be considered to have been made for these purposes, see Revenue Tax Bulletin June 1999 p 673.

(*c*) **Limit of relief.** Where gains are chargeable to UK capital gains tax, credit for foreign tax suffered on a gain is set against the capital gains tax chargeable in respect of the double-taxed gain. [*ICTA 1988, s 790(4), s 793*]. See *George Wimpey International Ltd v Rolfe Ch D 1989, 62 TC 597* and *Yates v GCA International Ltd (and cross-appeal) Ch D 1991, 64 TC 37*. But the relief is limited to the difference between the capital gains tax (before double tax relief) which would be payable by the claimant

(i) if he were charged on his total capital gains (as computed under (*a*) above), and

(ii) if he were charged on those gains excluding the gains in respect of which the credit is to be allowed.

Where double tax relief is due from more than one source, the above limitation is applied successively to each source, but so that on each successive application, (i) above applies to the total capital gains exclusive of the capital gains to which the limitation has already been applied. [*ICTA 1988, s 796(1)(2)*].

In no case may total double tax credits exceed the total capital gains tax payable by the claimant for the year of assessment. [*ICTA 1988, s 796(3)*].

HMRC take the view that if the UK chargeable gain (before deducting any losses and taper relief) is less than the sterling equivalent of the gain chargeable in the overseas territory, the foreign tax eligible for relief must be proportionately restricted. They are also of the view that where the gain chargeable abroad has accrued over a longer period than the UK chargeable gain, the foreign tax must again be proportionately restricted. See, in both cases, HMRC Helpsheet IR 261 (as in 30.3 HMRC EXPLANATORY PUBLICATIONS). Neither of these views appears to have any basis in either statute or case law, and they are thus open to challenge.

(*d*) **Minimisation of foreign tax.** In relation to claims made after 20 March 2000, relief by credit under double tax arrangements is restricted to the foreign tax that would have been payable had all reasonable steps been taken, under the law of the territory concerned and under the agreement itself, and on the assumption that no double tax relief were available, to minimise the liability. Such steps include the claiming of available reliefs and allowances and the making of available elections. [*ICTA 1988, s 795A; FA 2000, Sch 30 para 6; FA 2002, s 88(2)(3)*].

19.7 **HMRC practice.** The standard credit article in double tax agreements provides for overseas tax to be allowed as a credit against UK tax on the gain in respect of which the overseas tax was computed. Unilateral relief operates similarly. There is no requirement for the two liabilities to arise at the same time or on the same persons; and therefore HMRC consider that relief is available in the following situations.

(*a*) A capital gain is taxed overseas as income.

(*b*) Tax is charged overseas on a no gain/no loss transfer within a group of companies, and a UK liability arises on a subsequent disposal (see 27.2, 27.9 GROUPS OF COMPANIES).

(*c*) An overseas trade carried on through a branch or agency is transferred to a local subsidiary, with an immediate overseas tax charge; and a UK tax charge arises on a subsequent disposal of the securities or on a disposal of the assets by the subsidiary within six years (see 45.9 OVERSEAS MATTERS).

(*d*) UK liability arises on a disposal of assets after overseas tax has become payable by reference to an increase in value without a disposal.

This relief is not available where a gain is rolled over in the UK (see 55 ROLLOVER RELIEF); but the overseas tax can be deducted from the gain (see 19.5 above) (HMRC Statement of Practice 6/88).

19.8 SCHEMES AND ARRANGEMENTS DESIGNED TO INCREASE RELIEF

FA 2005 introduced anti-avoidance provisions intended to defeat schemes designed to increase credit relief for foreign tax. The provisions apply to a credit for foreign tax which relates to a payment of foreign tax made on or after 16 March 2005 (or to income received on or after that date in respect of which foreign tax has been deducted at source). Where the scheme involved is within (4) below, the provisions apply to foreign tax paid (or income received) on or after 10 February 2005.

The provisions apply where the following conditions are satisfied.

(*a*) In relation to any chargeable gains (or income) taken or to be taken into account for the purposes of determining a person's liability to tax in a chargeable period there is an amount of foreign tax for which, under any double tax arrangements, credit is allowable against UK tax for that period.

(*b*) There is a scheme or arrangement the main purpose, or one of the main purposes, of which is to cause an amount of foreign tax to be taken into account in the case of that person for that chargeable period.

(*c*) The scheme or arrangement is a 'prescribed scheme or arrangement'.

(*d*) The aggregate of the amount of the claims for credit made by the person for that chargeable period and the amount of claims for credit made by all the persons connected to that person for a corresponding chargeable period is more than a minimal amount. For this purpose, a chargeable period of one person corresponds with a chargeable period of another if they have at least one day in common.

If HMRC consider, on reasonable grounds, that the above conditions are or may be satisfied in relation to any person they may give that person a notice informing him of their view and that as a consequence he will be required, in his tax return for the period concerned, to make such adjustments as are necessary to counteract the effects of the scheme or arrangement that are referable to the purpose in (*b*) above. The notice may (but is not required to) specify the adjustments required.

Where a person receives such a notice and the conditions at (*a*)–(*d*) above are in fact satisfied, that person must, in his tax return for the period concerned, make such adjustments as are necessary to counteract the effects of the scheme or arrangement that are referable to the purpose in (*b*) above.

If the notice is given before the person has made his return for the chargeable period concerned then, if the return is made in the period of 90 days beginning with the day on which the notice is given, it may disregard the notice, and at any time before the end of the 90 days the person may amend the return in order to comply with the notice.

If no notice has been given before the person's return has been made, a notice may only be given if the person has been given a notice of enquiry (see 54.8 RETURNS) in respect of the return. After an enquiry has been completed, a notice may only be given if

- at the time the enquiry was completed HMRC could not have reasonably been expected, on the basis of the information made available (within *TMA 1970, s 29(6)(7)*— see 5.2 ASSESSMENTS) to them before that time, to have been aware that the circumstances were such that a notice could have been given; and
- the person was requested to provide information during the enquiry and, if it had been so provided, HMRC could reasonably have been expected to give the person a notice.

If the notice is given after the person has made his return, he may amend the return to comply with the notice within 90 days beginning with the day on which the notice is given. If the notice is given after an enquiry into the return has started, a closure notice (see 54.11 RETURNS) may not be issued until the end of the period of 90 days beginning with the issue of the notice or, if earlier, an amendment is made to the return complying with the notice. If the notice is given after the completion of an enquiry, a discovery assessment (see 5.2 ASSESSMENTS) in relation to the gains (or income) to which it relates may not be made until the end of the period of 90 days beginning with the issue of the notice or, if earlier, an amendment is made to the return complying with the notice.

Where a notice is issued and no amendment is made to the return for the purpose of complying with it, the above provisions do not prevent a return becoming incorrect if such an amendment should have been made.

[*ICTA 1988, ss 804ZA–804ZC; FA 2005, s 87*].

Prescribed scheme or arrangement. A '*prescribed scheme or arrangement*' is one which falls within one or more of the following types.

(1) A scheme or arrangement which enables a person who is party to it or concerned in it to pay, in respect of a chargeable gain (or source of income), an amount of foreign tax all or part of which is properly attributable to one or more other gains (or sources of income).

(2) A scheme or arrangement under which an amount of foreign tax is paid by a person (the '*claimant*') who has claimed, or is in a position to claim, for a chargeable period, an allowance under any double tax arrangements by way of credit for foreign tax where, at the time the claimant entered into the scheme or arrangement, it could reasonably be assumed that the effect of the payment of that amount of foreign tax on the 'foreign tax total' would be to increase it by less than the amount allowable as a credit in respect of that payment. For this purpose, the '*foreign tax total*' is the amount found by aggregating the amounts paid or payable in respect of the transactions forming part of the scheme or arrangement by persons party to it or concerned in it and taking into account any reliefs, deductions, reductions or allowances against or in respect of any tax that arise to those persons (including any such reliefs etc. arising as a consequence of the payment by the claimant of the amount of foreign tax).

(3) A scheme or arrangement under which a step is taken by a person who is party to it or concerned in it or a step that could have been taken by such a person is not taken where that action or omission has the effect of increasing a claim made by such a person for an allowance by way of credit or of giving rise to such a claim. The steps concerned are those that may be made under the law of any territory or under double tax arrangements made in relation to any territory and include claiming or otherwise securing the benefit of reliefs, deductions, reductions or allowances, and making elections for tax purposes.

(4) A scheme or arrangement under which 'amount A' is less than 'amount B' in relation to a person who has claimed, or is in a position to claim, for a chargeable period an allowance by way of credit for foreign tax under any double tax arrangements. For this purpose, '*amount A*' is the amount of UK tax payable in respect of income and chargeable gains arising in the chargeable period and '*amount B*' is the amount of UK tax that would be payable in respect of income and chargeable gains for the period if, in determining that amount, the transactions forming part of the scheme or arrangement were disregarded.

(5) A scheme or arrangement which includes the making by a person (A) of a 'relevant payment' or payments and the giving, for that payment or payments, of consideration, all or part of which consists of a payment or payments made to A, or a person connected (within *ICTA 1988, s 839*) with A, which is chargeable to tax under the law of a territory outside the UK. For this purpose, a '*relevant payment*' is a payment by A all or part of which may be brought into account in computing A's income for UK tax purposes. A '*payment*' includes the transfer of money's worth.

[*ICTA 1988, Sch 28AB; FA 2005, s 87(2), Sch 5*].

HMRC published draft guidance on the above provisions on their website (www.hmrc.gov.uk) on 6 May 2005.

19.9 SPECIAL WITHHOLDING TAX

The following provisions apply to give relief by way of set-off against UK income tax or capital gains tax liabilities for 'special withholding tax' levied on foreign 'savings income'. To the extent that the tax cannot be so set off, relief is given by repayment.

'*Special withholding tax*' is withholding tax (however described) levied under the law of a territory outside the UK which implements either Article 11 of the EU Savings Directive (Council Directive 2003/48/EC) or, in the case of a territory which is not a member state, any corresponding provisions of 'international arrangements'. The Directive came into effect on 1 July 2005 (HMRC Internet Statement, 1 July 2005). '*International arrangements*' in relation to a particular territory are arrangements made to ensure the effective taxation of savings income under the law of the UK or under that law and the law of that territory. '*Savings income*' has the same meaning as the expression 'interest payment' has for the purposes of the Directive or, in relation to territories which are not member states, the same meaning as the corresponding expression has for the purposes of the international arrangements concerned.

[*FA 2004, s 107*].

Under the terms of the Directive, three EU member states, Austria, Belgium and Luxembourg, will impose special withholding tax for a transitional period. The other member states will instead adopt the system of automatic exchange of information on cross-border payments for which the Directive provides. Certain non-EU states are also expected to apply special withholding tax during the transitional period, and agreements to this effect have been made between the UK and the British Virgin Islands (*SI 2005 No 1457*), Jersey (*SI 2005 No 1261*), Guernsey (*SI 2005 No 1262*), the Isle of Man (*SI 2005 No 1263*), the Netherlands Antilles (*SI 2005 No 1460*) and Gibraltar (*SI 2006 No 1453*) (HMRC Internet Statements, 2 February 2005, 17 May 2005, 21 December 2005). The rate of special withholding tax is expected to be 15% for the first three years, 20% for the next three years and 35% thereafter.

Income tax credit. Where a person is chargeable to income tax for a tax year in respect of a payment of savings income which has suffered special withholding tax (or would be so chargeable but for an exemption or relief), income tax of an amount equal to the special withholding tax is deemed for tax purposes to have been paid by or on behalf of that person and to have been deducted at source from the income. For this treatment to apply, the person concerned must be UK resident for the tax year in question and must make a claim. If the deemed tax exceeds the person's income tax liability for the year, the excess is first set against any capital gains tax liability for the year, with any remaining balance relieved by way of a repayment of income tax. [*FA 2004, s 108*].

Capital gains tax credit. Where

- a person disposes of assets in a tax year so that any chargeable gain accruing on the disposal would accrue to him and he would be chargeable to capital gains tax on it (if the annual exempt amount, any allowable losses and *TCGA 1992, s 77(1)* (charge on settlor with interest in settlement — see 57.5 SETTLEMENTS) were disregarded), and
- the consideration for the disposal consists of or includes savings income which has suffered special withholding tax

capital gains tax of an amount equal to the special withholding tax is deemed for tax purposes to have been paid by or on behalf of that person for that year and to have been deducted at source. For the purposes of INTEREST ON OVERPAID TAX (36), the deemed tax is, however, treated as paid on 31 January following that year. If the deemed tax exceeds the person's capital gains tax liability for the year, the excess is first set against any income tax liability for the year, with any remaining balance relieved by way of a repayment of income tax. For this treatment to apply, the person concerned must be UK resident for the tax year in question and must make a claim. This treatment only applies to the extent that income tax credit relief as above is not available in respect of the special withholding tax concerned.

[*FA 2004, s 109*].

Interaction with other double tax relief provisions. A person cannot obtain relief under the above provisions if double tax relief has been obtained in respect of the special withholding tax under the law of a territory outside the UK and the person was resident in that territory (or treated as so resident under any double tax arrangements) in the tax year in question. Similarly, a person cannot obtain double tax relief under the normal income tax double tax relief provisions for special withholding tax.

Credit for foreign tax due by agreement (see 19.2 above) or unilaterally (see 19.4 above) is given in priority to relief for special withholding tax. This enables overall relief to be maximised, as excess foreign tax other than special withholding tax is not repayable.

[*FA 2004, ss 107(5), 108(5), 109(6), 110*].

Computation of chargeable gains subject to special withholding tax. Where a chargeable gain accrues to a person on a disposal of assets in circumstances where the consideration consists of or includes an amount of savings income which has suffered special withholding tax in respect of which a claim has been made under the above provisions, and the REMITTANCE BASIS (51) does not apply, no deduction may be made in the computation of the gain for any special withholding tax in respect of that or any other gain.

Where the remittance basis applies, the amount of the gain received in the UK is treated as increased by the proportion of the special withholding tax suffered that the chargeable gain received in the UK bears to the total gain less the special withholding tax.

[*ICTA 1988, s 795; TCGA 1992, s 277(1)–(1C); FA 2004, ss 111, 112*].

Certificates to avoid levy of special withholding tax. On receipt of a valid application, HMRC will issue a certificate (valid for up to three years) which can be forwarded to a person's paying agent so that he will not levy special withholding tax on payments of savings income. An application for such a certificate must be in writing and must include certain required information listed in *FA 2004, s 113(3)*. There is a right of appeal to the Special Commissioners against an HMRC decision not to issue such a certificate. The appeal must be in writing and must be given to HMRC within 30 days of the date of HMRC's notice refusing a certificate. [*FA 2004, ss 113, 114*].

20 Employee Share Schemes

Cross-reference. See also 22.84 EXEMPTIONS AND RELIEFS re employee trusts.

20.1 INTRODUCTION

Income tax and capital gains tax (CGT) legislation applies where there are arrangements to allow employees (which term includes for these purposes directors) to acquire shares in their employing companies. Tax reliefs and exemptions apply where such arrangements take the form of one or more of the various statutory schemes and have been granted HMRC approval. This chapter is concerned with the CGT consequences of both approved schemes and unapproved schemes (and for these purposes the term 'scheme' encompasses any such arrangements as mentioned above). The expression 'shares' is used in its broadest sense. For the application of the chapter to stocks and securities, as well as shares, see 20.2 below. For context, the coverage includes in most cases a brief note of the income tax position, but for the full provisions (and, as regards approved schemes, the conditions for approval) see Tolley's Income Tax under Share Related Employment Income and Exemptions. For the general income tax liability in respect of shares given to employees as part of their earnings see Tolley's Income Tax under Employment Income. See HMRC Capital Gains Manual CG 56300–56554 for HMRC's own notes on the CGT provisions, and see generally Simon's Direct Tax Service at E4.5.

The remainder of this chapter is set out under the following headings.

20.40 Double tax relief

See 59.2, 59.4 SHARES AND SECURITIES—IDENTIFICATION RULES for special rule where shares are acquired as an employee and are subject to restricted disposal rights.

See also 6.7 ASSETS and 67 WASTING ASSETS for CGT treatment of options generally.

20.2 EXTENDED MEANING OF 'SHARES'

For the purposes of 20.13 and 20.15 below, and also of 20.6, 20.8 and 20.9 below as they had effect before the *FA 2003* changes detailed therein, 'shares' includes stocks and also includes most securities issued by companies (though with little clarification as to exactly which types of security are and are not included).

For the purposes of 20.10, 20.11, 20.12, 20.14, and 20.16 below, and also of 20.6, 20.8 and 20.9 below as they have effect after the *FA 2003* changes detailed therein, the meaning of 'shares' is extended to embrace a broader range of financial products, including, for example, government and local authority stocks. All of the following are now 'shares' for these purposes:

- shares (including stock) in any body corporate, wherever incorporated, or in any unincorporated body constituted under the law of a foreign country;
- rights under 'contracts of insurance' other than 'excluded contracts' (but see further below);
- debentures, debenture stock, loan stock, bonds, certificates of deposit and other instruments creating or acknowledging indebtedness (other than contracts of insurance);
- warrants and other instruments entitling the holders to subscribe for securities;
- certificates and other instruments conferring rights in respect of securities held by persons other than the persons on whom the rights are conferred and which may be transferred without the consent of those persons;
- units in a collective investment scheme (as defined by *ITEPA 2003, s 420*(*2*));
- futures (as defined by *ITEPA 2003, s 420*(*3*)) and options (other than 'share options' — see below) acquired on or after 2 December 2004;
- rights under contracts for differences (or under similar contracts — as defined by *ITEPA 2003, s 420*(*4*)), other than contracts of insurance.

However, none of the following are 'shares' for these purposes:

- cheques, bills of exchange, bankers' drafts and letters of credit (other than bills of exchange accepted by a banker);
- money and statements showing balances on a current, deposit or savings account;
- leases and other dispositions of property and heritable securities;
- options acquired before 2 December 2004; and
- share options (within the meaning given at 20.6 below) acquired on or after 2 December 2004.

The above lists can be amended by Treasury order.

Note that contracts of insurance are brought within the definition of shares on and after 2 December 2004. This applies to rights under contracts acquired before that date as well as those acquired on or after that date. Previously such contracts were not shares. A contract is an '*excluded contract*' if it is:

- a contract for an annuity which is, or will be, pension income within *ITEPA 2003, Pt 9*;
- a 'contract of long-term insurance', other than an annuity contract, which does not have, and cannot acquire (whether on conversion or otherwise), a surrender value; or
- a 'contract of general insurance' other than one falling in accordance with generally accepted accounting practice (as defined in *FA 2004, s 50*) to be accounted for as a financial asset or liability.

For the above purposes, 'contract of insurance', 'contract of long-term insurance' and 'contract of general insurance' all have the same meaning as in *Financial Services and Markets Act 2000 (Regulated Activities) Order 2001 SI 2001 No 544*.

It is important to note that the above extended meaning of 'shares' does *not* apply for the purposes of the HMRC-approved schemes at 20.19 *et seq.* below. For the purposes of 20.24 and 20.29 below, 'shares' includes stock but not securities, and there are specific rules restricting the types of shares eligible under the other schemes. For details see Tolley's Income Tax under Share-Related Employment Income and Exemptions.

An '*interest in shares*', for the purposes of 20.10, 20.11, 20.12, 20.14, and 20.16 below, and also of 20.6, 20.8 and 20.9 below as they have effect after the *FA 2003* changes detailed therein, means an interest which is less than full beneficial ownership. It includes an interest in their sale proceeds but not a right to acquire them.

[*ITEPA 2003, s 420, ss 434(1), 470(1), 487(1) as originally enacted, ss 516(4), 521(4), 548(1), Sch 5 para 58; ICTA 1988, s 136(5), s 139(11), s 140A(9), s 140H(8), s 187(2); FA 1988, s 87(1); TCGA 1992, ss 119A(7), 120(1)(7)(8); FA 2000, Sch 14 para 71(1); FA 2003, s 140, Sch 22 paras 1, 2, 50, 51; F(No 2)A 2005, Sch 2 para 2; FA 2006, s 92(2)(3)(5)*].

For the purposes of this chapter, '*employment-related shares*' are shares or an interest in shares (as above) acquired by a person by virtue of a right or opportunity made available by reason of the employment (past, present or prospective) of that or any other person. For this purpose, shares are deemed to be acquired when the beneficial entitlement to them is acquired and not, if different, at the time of conveyance or transfer. Any right or opportunity made available by a person's employer, or by a person connected (within *ICTA 1988, s 839*) with a person's employer, is treated as made available by reason of the employment of that person, other than in the case of an individual conferring a right or opportunity in the normal course of his domestic, family or personal relationships. There are rules dealing with company reorganisations (such as conversions, scrip issues and rights issues); these treat replacement shares or additional shares acquired on such a reorganisation as acquired by virtue of the same right or opportunity as the original interest and treat any consequent reduction in the market value of the original shares as consideration given for the replacement shares or additional shares. [*ITEPA 2003, ss 421B, 421D; FA 2003, Sch 22 para 2; FA 2005, s 20(3)*].

20.3 CONSIDERATION FOR GRANT OF SHARE OPTION

Where an option is granted after 27 November 1995 and

- for options granted on or after 2 December 2004, the option is a 'share option' to which the income tax provisions at 20.6 below apply, or would apply but for *ITEPA 2003, s 474*; or
- for options granted before 2 December 2004, the option is to acquire shares in a company and is obtained by an individual by reason of his office or employment as a director or other employee of that or any other company,

then *TCGA 1992, s 17(1)* (see 41.1 MARKET VALUE) is disapplied (where it would otherwise apply), so that, for CGT purposes, the amount or value of the consideration for the grant, as regards both the company and employee, is the actual value or consideration passing (if any). However, in computing actual value for this purpose, any value put on the employee's services, past or present, is ignored. [*TCGA 1992, s 149A; FA 1993, s 104; FA 1996, s 111; F(No 2)A 2005, Sch 5 paras 4, 6(2)*]. Before 28 November 1995, the above applied only to options granted under approved schemes (see 20.25 below) and then only as regards the company and not the employee.

20.4 **RELEASE AND REPLACEMENT OF OPTIONS**

The following applies where an option to acquire shares in a company (*'the old option'*) which was obtained by an individual by reason of his office or employment as director or other employee of that or any other company is released after 27 November 1995 in whole or in part for a consideration which consists of or includes the grant to him of another option (*'the new option'*) to acquire shares in that or any other company. The new option is not regarded for CGT purposes as consideration received by him for the release of the old option. Any consideration given by him for the old option is taken to be the consideration given for the new option and any additional expenditure paid by him for the acquisition of the new option is treated as allowable expenditure. The release of the old option is disregarded in determining the consideration received for the new option by the grantor company. [*TCGA 1992, s 237A; FA 1996, s 112*].

20.5 **UNAPPROVED EMPLOYEE SHARE SCHEMES**

Where an employee (including a director) receives shares by reason of his employment and otherwise than under an approved scheme (see 20.19–20.30 below), he is generally treated by virtue of *TCGA 1992, s 17* (see 41.1 MARKET VALUE) as acquiring them at their market value at the time of acquisition. Likewise, any disposal by the employer is treated as made at market value (but see Revenue Tax Bulletin December 1994 p 181 for concessional treatment applied in certain cases to pre-6 April 1995 transactions). As regards certain shares subject to risk of forfeiture, *section 17* is disapplied as regards the employee only (see 20.15 below).

See also, at 41.1 MARKET VALUE, the **exception to the market value rule** where an asset is acquired for nil consideration or at less than its market value *and* there is no corresponding disposal. This would apply, for example, where *new* shares are *issued* by a company to an employee (as opposed to existing shares being transferred), as an issue of shares is not a disposal by a company for the purposes of corporation tax on chargeable gains; in such a case, the employee's CGT acquisition cost of the shares is restricted to the actual consideration given (if any). (This exception to the rule did not apply to pre-10 March 1981 transactions.)

A transfer of shares to a director or other employee for nil consideration or at less than market value normally gives rise to a charge to income tax if regarded as part of his general earnings. The amount so charged does not form part of the acquisition cost of the shares for CGT purposes (cf. 20.6 below re shares acquired on the exercise of an option).

See 20.39 below for disapplication of market value rules where employees receive priority allocations in public share offers.

Before 28 November 1995, the market value rule of *TCGA 1992, s 17* could also be applied in determining the cost of acquisition of an *option* to acquire shares, but see now 20.3 above.

See 20.6 below where shares are acquired as a result of the *exercise* of an option.

20.6 **Exercise of unapproved employee share option.** An income tax charge may arise on the exercise of an unapproved share option. The provisions apply to a 'share option' (an '*employment-related share option*') acquired by a person where the right or opportunity to acquire it is available by reason of the employment (past, present or prospective) of that person or any other person.

A '*share option*' is a right to acquire 'shares'. For options acquired on or after 2 December 2004, a right to acquire shares which is acquired pursuant to a right or opportunity made available under arrangements the main purpose, or one of the main purposes, of which is the avoidance of tax or national insurance contributions is not a share option. This applies also to any option acquired before that date where something is done on or after that date as part of the arrangements under which it was made available. Before 1 September 2003, '*shares*', for the purposes of these provisions, includes stock and also includes securities as defined in *ICTA 1988, s 254(1)*. This definition was amended by *FA 2003* so that, on and after that date, '*shares*' is given the extended meaning in 20.2 above. This extended meaning applies from the earlier date of 16 April 2003 in relation to options to acquire securities that would not have fallen within the original definition of 'shares'.

Subject to exclusions, the acquisition of shares on the exercise of the option by an employee results in the chargeable amount being taxed as employment income of the employee for the tax year in which the exercise occurs under *ITEPA 2003, s 476* (or, for 2002/03 and earlier years, under *ICTA 1988, s 135*). The chargeable amount is the difference between the open market value of the acquired shares at the time of exercise and the aggregate of the consideration given for the shares and any given for the option. Certain other amounts may be deducted in arriving at the chargeable amount, including any amount charged on *grant* of the option. Relief is given by deduction from the chargeable amount in respect of any liability to secondary Class 1 national insurance contributions (i.e. employer contributions) in respect of the exercise of the option borne by the employee under a voluntary agreement or a joint election under *Social Security Contributions and Benefits Act 1992, Sch 1 para 3A* or *para 3B* (or NI equivalent). Consideration given for an option does not include any value placed on the performance of duties in connection with the employment. (In specified circumstances, a person is likewise chargeable even though the gain in question is realised by another person.)

[*ITEPA 2003, ss 419, 420(8), 421–421B, 421D, 471–484, ss 485, 487 as originally enacted, ss 718, 721(1), Sch 7 paras 62–67; ICTA 1988, ss 135, 136, 140, 187A; FA 1998, s 49; FA 2000, s 56(1)(3)(4); FA 2002, Sch 6 para 1; FA 2003, Sch 22 paras 2, 10, 46(20)–(26); FA 2004, s 90, Sch 16 paras 3, 7; ITTOIA 2005, Sch 1 paras 598, 599; FA 2006, s 92(4)(5); SI 2003 No 1997*].

For shares in research institution spin-out companies, see 20.18 below.

Capital gains tax. From the dates indicated above for the commencement of the *FA 2003* changes, all employment-related share options to which the above provisions apply (or would apply but for the exclusions in *ITEPA 2003, s 474*) are treated as options for capital gains tax purposes, whether or not they would ordinarily be regarded as such. The acquisition of shares pursuant to such an option is accordingly treated as the exercise of an option. [*TCGA 1992, s 288(1A); FA 2003, Sch 22 para 54; F(No 2)A 2005, Sch 5 para 5*].

The acquisition of an option and the transaction entered into by the grantee on the exercise of the option, being in this case an acquisition of shares, are treated for CGT purposes as a single transaction taking place at the time the option is exercised (see also 6.7 ASSETS).

Any sum charged to income tax as employment income under the above provisions forms part of the cost of acquisition of the shares for CGT purposes (within *TCGA 1992, s 38(1)(a)* — see 15.4(*a*) COMPUTATION OF GAINS AND LOSSES). For this purpose only, however, any deduction made in arriving at the amount chargeable to income tax in respect of any tax charged on *grant* of the option (see above) is added back and no account is taken of any relief given for national insurance contributions met by the employee. Where the shares would otherwise have ceased to be 'employment-related shares' (see 20.2 above) by virtue of *ITEPA 2003, s 421B(6)* (death of employee) or *s 421B(7)* (shares ceasing to be employment-related shares seven years after employee leaves the employer, the company which issued the shares or connected person), they are treated as continuing to be employment-related shares until they are next disposed of (so that on that disposal, any amounts counting as employment income under the above provisions can be added to the acquisition cost).

[*TCGA 1992, ss 119A, 120(2)(4)(9), s 144(3); ITEPA 2003, Sch 6 para 210(4); FA 2003, Sch 22 paras 50, 51; FA 2004, Sch 16 para 6*].

In respect of options exercised after 9 April 2003, where *TCGA 1992, s 144ZA* (see 6.7 ASSETS) applies, the cost of acquisition will therefore consist of the aggregate of

- the amount counting as employment income (with the adjustments indicated above),
- the consideration given for the shares acquired on the exercise of the option, and
- any consideration given for the option (for options granted before 28 November 1995, the market value of the option at the time it was granted — see 20.3 above).

This is the same aggregate that the Revenue took to make up the acquisition cost prior to the decision in *Mansworth v Jelley CA 2002, 75 TC 1*. Following that decision, the Revenue accepted that the market value rule at 20.5 above applies to shares acquired as a result of the exercise of an option. Accordingly, in respect of options exercised before 10 April 2003 (i.e. where *TCGA 1992, s 144ZA*, which is intended to reverse the effect of the decision (see 6.7 ASSETS), does not apply), the cost of acquisition will consist of the aggregate of

- the amount counting as employment income (with adjustments), and
- the market value of the shares at the time the option is exercised

(Revenue Internet Statement 8 January 2003).

For further details of how HMRC implement the *Mansworth v Jelley* decision in different circumstances see Revenue Internet Statements 8 January 2003, 17 March 2003 and 8 August 2003.

Where the cost of acquisition of shares acquired on the exercise of an option includes the market value of the shares at the time of exercise, the proceeds of any corresponding disposal are likewise treated as the market value at that time (see 41.1 MARKET VALUE). However, the Revenue implemented this provision only in the case of returns made on or after 12 December 2002, the date of the judgment in *Mansworth v Jelley* (Revenue Internet Statement 8 January 2003).

See 20.40 below for relief from double taxation where a tax charge also arises in a country other than the UK.

20.7 **Other charges in respect of unapproved share options.** A charge to income tax under *ITEPA 2003, s 476* (previously *ICTA 1988, s 135*) also arises on the happening of certain other events in relation to unapproved share options. The events are the assignment, release (including the cancellation or surrender) or abandonment of the option or, following the *FA 2003* changes (see 20.6 above for the commencement provisions), the receipt of a benefit in connection with the option.

The assignment or release of an option is a CGT disposal, and the amount charged to income tax is excluded by *TCGA 1992, s 37* (see 35.1 INTERACTION WITH OTHER TAXES) from the proceeds to be taken into account for CGT purposes (HMRC Capital Gains Manual CG 56387). See 20.4 above re the release of an option in return for a replacement option. By virtue of *TCGA 1992, s 144(4)* (see 6.7(*f*) ASSETS), the abandonment (i.e. the lapse) of an employee share option is not a disposal for CGT purposes, so no capital loss may be claimed in respect of any consideration given for the option. Any amount charged to income tax in respect of a benefit in connection with an option is *not* added to the acquisition cost of the option or shares for CGT purposes.

20.8 SHARES ACQUIRED FOR LESS THAN MARKET VALUE

A charge to income tax may apply where an employee obtains shares for less than their market value. The provisions operate by creating the fiction of a notional interest-free loan on the amount of the under-value. In relation to shares acquired on or after 16 April 2003 the provisions apply to all employees acquiring 'employment-related shares' (see 20.2

above) or an interest in such shares. In relation to shares acquired before that date but after 6 April 1976, the provisions apply only where the shares (or interest in shares) are acquired by the employee, or by a person connected with him, by reason of the employee's employment, and do not apply to those in 'lower-paid employment' (i.e. those earning less than £8,500 per year). See 20.2 above for the meaning of 'shares' for the purposes of these provisions.

Subject to the anti-avoidance provisions of *ITEPA 2003, s 446UA*, the provisions apply where, at the time of acquisition of the shares, either no payment is (or has been) made for them or a payment below market value is (or has been) made for them. The employee is regarded as having the benefit of an interest-free loan, which attracts a charge under the employment income benefits code. The amount of the notional loan is the market value less any payment made for the shares and any amounts treated as earnings or counting as employment income under other provisions (see in particular 20.5, 20.6 above). The notional loan terminates on the happening of specified chargeable events, viz. (i) the making good of the loan by payments or further payments for the shares, (ii) any obligation to make further payment ceasing to bind the employee (or connected person), (iii) the disposal of the shares, (iv) the doing of something on or after 2 December 2004 which affects the shares as part of a scheme or arrangement the main purpose, or one of the main purposes, of which is the avoidance of tax or National Insurance contributions, or (v) the death of the employee. Where the notional loan terminates as a result of any of (ii), (iii) or (iv), then the amount of the loan thus deemed to be written off is treated as employment income.

[*ITEPA 2003, ss 192–197, 419, 421, 421B–421D, 421E(2)–(5), 421F–421H, 446Q–446W, Sch 7 paras 28, 29; ICTA 1988, s 162(1)–(5)(9)–(11); FA 2003, Sch 22 paras 2, 7, 22; FA 2004, ss 86, 88(2), 89, 90(2); F(No 2)A 2005, Sch 2 paras 12–15*].

These provisions are most likely to be applied where shares are issued partly-paid, where payment is due in instalments or on the exercise of an option where the employment is outside the scope of *ITEPA 2003, s 476* in 20.6 above. See Tolley's Income Tax under Employment Income for further detail.

For shares in research institution spin-out companies, see 20.18 below.

Capital gains tax. Where a chargeable event is also a disposal of the shares for CGT purposes, and in any other case on the first disposal after a chargeable event, the aggregate of any amount counting as employment income in respect of that chargeable event and any other chargeable events occurring after the last disposal to which this provision applied, is added to the cost of acquisition (within *TCGA 1992, s 38(1)(a)* — see 15.4(*a*) COMPUTATION OF GAINS AND LOSSES) of the person making the disposal. Where shares acquired after 15 April 2003 would otherwise cease to be employment-related shares by virtue of *ITEPA 2003, s 421B(6)* (death of employee) or *s 421B(7)* (shares ceasing to be employment-related shares seven years after employee leaves the employer, the company which issued the shares or connected person), they are treated as continuing to be employment-related shares until they are next disposed of (so that on that disposal, any amounts counting as employment income in respect of chargeable events can be added to the acquisition cost). [*TCGA 1992, ss 119A, 120(2)(3); ITEPA 2003, Sch 6 para 210(3); FA 2003, Sch 22 paras 50, 51*].

20.9 SHARES DISPOSED OF FOR MORE THAN MARKET VALUE

A charge to income tax may apply where shares are disposed of for more than their market value. In relation to shares disposed of on or after 16 April 2003 the provisions apply to all employees where 'employment-related shares' (see 20.2 above) or an interest in such shares are acquired by an 'associated person' (as defined). In relation to shares disposed of before that date but acquired after 6 April 1976, the provisions apply only where the shares (or interest in shares) are acquired by the employee, or by a person connected with him, by reason of the employee's employment, and do not apply to those in 'lower-paid employment' (i.e. those earning less than £8,500 per year). See 20.2 above for the meaning of 'shares' for the purposes of these provisions.

Where shares within these provisions are disposed of (such that no associated person (or, in relation to disposals before 16 April 2003, neither the employee nor any person connected with him (within *ICTA 1988, s 839*)) any longer has a beneficial interest) at more than their market value at the time of disposal, the excess over market value is chargeable to income tax as employment income. For disposals on or after 16 April 2003, any expenses incurred in connection with the disposal are also deductible in arriving at the chargeable amount.

[*ITEPA 2003, ss 198–200, 419, 421, 421, 421A–421D, 421E(2)–(5), 421F–421H, 446X–446Z, Sch 7 paras 30, 31, 61A; ICTA 1988, s 162(6); FA 2003, Sch 22 paras 2, 8, 46(2)(19)(26); FA 2004, ss 88(2), 89, 90(2)*].

The amount charged to income tax is excluded by *TCGA 1992, s 37* (see 35.1 INTERACTION WITH OTHER TAXES) from the proceeds to be taken into account for CGT purposes.

20.10 ANTI-AVOIDANCE — SHARES WITH ARTIFICIALLY DEPRESSED MARKET VALUE

FA 2003 introduced provisions 'designed to ensure that if the value of employment-related securities is depressed by means of non-commercial transaction(s), then that reduction in value is taxed on the employee.' (Treasury Explanatory Notes to Finance Bill 2003). Broadly, the provisions apply on and after 16 April 2003 irrespective of the date the shares in question were acquired. Subject to exclusions, they apply in certain cases where the market value of 'employment-related shares' (see 20.2 above) (or, where relevant, other shares or interests in shares) is reduced by things done otherwise than for genuine commercial purposes; this specifically includes anything done as part of a scheme or arrangement a main purpose of which is to avoid tax *or national insurance contributions* and any transaction (other than a payment for corporation tax group relief) between members of a 51% group of companies otherwise than on arm's length terms. See 20.2 above for the extended meaning of 'shares', in relation to these provisions.

If anything done otherwise than for genuine commercial purposes within the seven years ending with the acquisition reduces the market value of employment-related shares at acquisition by at least 10%, there is a charge to income tax on the employee for the tax year in which the acquisition occurs; the amount chargeable counts as employment income for tax purposes. The provisions may also modify the operation of those at 20.9 above and 20.12, 20.14, 20.15, and 20.16 below, broadly with the effect of replacing, in computing various amounts, the artificially reduced market value with what would have been the market value if it were not for the reduction.

[*ITEPA 2003, ss 419, 421, 421A–421D, 421E(2)–(5), 421F–421I, 446A–446J; FA 2003, Sch 22 paras 2, 5; FA 2004, s 86(6)(8), ss 87, 88(2), 89, 90(2)*].

See Tolley's Income Tax under Share-Related Employment Income and Exemptions for the detailed provisions.

Amounts charged to income tax under these provisions on the acquisition of shares are *not* added to the acquisition cost of the shares for CGT purposes.

20.11 ANTI-AVOIDANCE — SHARES WITH ARTIFICIALLY ENHANCED MARKET VALUE

FA 2003 introduced provisions 'designed to ensure that if the value of employment-related securities is enhanced by means of non-commercial transaction(s) during any tax year, then that appreciation in value is taxed on the employee at the earlier of the disposal of the employment-related securities or 5 April.' (Treasury Explanatory Notes to Finance Bill 2003). The provisions apply, broadly, on and after 16 April 2003 irrespective of the date the shares in question were acquired. Subject to exclusions, they apply in certain cases where the market value of 'employment-related shares' (see 20.2 above) is increased by things done otherwise than for genuine commercial purposes (a '*non-commercial increase*'); this specifically includes anything done as part of a scheme or arrangement a main purpose of which is to avoid tax *or national insurance contributions* and any transaction (other than a payment for corporation tax group relief) between members of a 51% group of companies otherwise than on arm's length terms. See 20.2 above for the extended meaning of 'shares', in relation to these provisions.

Where, on the 'valuation date' for a 'relevant period', the market value of employment-related shares is at least 10% greater than it would be if any 'non-commercial increases' (see above) during the relevant period were disregarded, the whole of the excess is taxed as employment income of the employee for tax purposes for the tax year in which the valuation date falls. For these purposes,

- the '*valuation date*' is the last day of the 'relevant period'; and
- the '*relevant period*' means any tax year, except that the first such period runs from date of acquisition (or from 16 April 2003 if later) to the following 5 April and the last runs from 6 April to the date in the tax year on which the provisions cease to apply. If the provisions cease to apply to an interest in the shares, the relevant period ends at that time in relation to that interest, but these provisions apply separately to that interest and to what remains.

[*ITEPA 2003, ss 419, 421, 421B–421D, 421E(2)–(5), 421F–421H, 446K–446P; FA 2003, Sch 22 paras 2,; FA 2004, ss 86(7)(8), 88(2), 89, 90(2)*].

See Tolley's Income Tax under Share-Related Employment Income and Exemptions for the detailed provisions.

Amounts charged to income tax under these provisions are *not* added to the acquisition cost of the shares for CGT purposes.

For shares in research institution spin-out companies, see 20.18 below.

20.12 POST-ACQUISITION BENEFITS AFTER FA 2003

The following provisions supersede those at 20.13 below and generally have effect on and after 16 April 2003 irrespective of when the shares were acquired. See, however, Tolley's Income Tax under Share-Related Employment Income and Exemptions for the detailed transitional provisions. Subject to exclusions, the provisions apply if an 'associated person' (as defined) receives a benefit in connection with 'employment-related shares' (see 20.2 above) (before 2 December 2004, by virtue of the ownership of employment-related shares, whether by him or another associated person). The amount or market value (determined as for capital gains tax purposes) of the benefit is taxed as employment income of the employee for the tax year in which the benefit is received. [*ITEPA 2003, ss 421, 421B–421D, 421E(1)(3)–(5), 421F–421H, 447–450, Sch 7 para 54; FA 2003, Sch 22 paras 2, 9, 46(13)(26); FA 2004, ss 86, 88(2), 89, 90(2); F(No 2)A 2005, Sch 2 paras 17–19*].

For shares in research institution spin-out companies, see 20.18 below.

Capital gains tax. On a disposal of employment-related shares after 5 April 2005, where that disposal is the first following the receipt of a benefit within the above provisions which is an increase in the market value of the shares, the aggregate of any amount counting as employment income in respect of that benefit and any other such benefits occurring after the last disposal to which this provision applied, is added to the cost of acquisition of the person making the disposal. Where shares would otherwise cease to be employment-related shares by virtue of *ITEPA 2003, s 421B(6)* (death of employee) or *s 421B(7)* (shares ceasing to be employment-related shares seven years after employee leaves the employer, the company which issued the shares or connected person), they are treated as continuing to be employment-related shares until they are next disposed of (so that on that disposal, any amounts counting as employment income in respect of chargeable events can be added to the acquisition cost). [*TCGA 1992, s 119A; FA 2005, s 22(2)(b)(4)*].

Where the above does not apply, amounts charged to income tax under these provisions are *not* added to the acquisition costs of the shares for CGT purposes.

20.13 POST-ACQUISITION BENEFITS BEFORE FA 2003

The following provisions are superseded by those at 20.12 above generally with effect on and after 16 April 2003 irrespective of when the shares were acquired. See, however, Tolley's Income Tax under Share-Related Employment Income and Exemptions for the detailed transitional provisions.

As regards shares (or an interest in shares) in a company acquired (other than in pursuance of a public offer) by a person after 25 October 1987 (and subject to *ITEPA 2003, s 427* (or, for 2002/03 and earlier years, *ICTA 1988, s 140A*) in 20.15 below for interests acquired after 16 March 1998) by reason of his being a director or other employee, past, present or future, within *ITEPA 2003, ss 15* or *21* (previously Schedule E, Case I), of that or any other company, a subsequent income tax charge may arise in either of the following circumstances (in addition to any charge arising on acquisition).

- The imposition, removal or variation of a restriction, or the creation, removal or variation of a right, relating to the acquired shares or to other shares in the company, such that the acquired shares increase in value (or would do so but for another event). [*ITEPA 2003, ss 449–452; FA 1988, s 78*].
- The receipt by the employee of a 'chargeable benefit' by virtue of his ownership of the shares. [*ITEPA 2003, ss 457–460; FA 1988, s 80; F(No 2)A 1992, s 37*].

In addition, where the company concerned is a 'dependent subsidiary' (as defined by *ITEPA 2003, s 467*), an income tax charge arises on any increase in value of the acquired shares from time of acquisition to the earlier of

- the employee's ceasing to have a beneficial interest in the shares (such an interest normally being treated as retained for this purpose where a disposal is made to a connected person and/or other than at arm's length — see *ITEPA 2003, s 463* (previously *FA 1988, s 83(2)(3)*)), and
- seven years after acquisition.

Slightly different rules apply where the company becomes a dependent subsidiary after the acquisition in question. [*ITEPA 2003, ss 453–456, Sch 7 para 59; FA 1988, s 79; FA 1998, s 50(3), s 51(2)*].

Where a person acquires shares (or an interest in shares) by reason of his being connected (within *ICTA 1988, s 839*) with a director or employee, the shares are deemed for the purposes of these provisions to have been acquired by the director or employee. [*ITEPA 2003, s 447(5); FA 1988, s 83(1)*].

Where an amount is chargeable as employment income under these provisions on a person who acquires (or is treated as acquiring) shares (or an interest in shares), then on the first disposal of the shares following that acquisition (whether that disposal is made by that or any other person, for example a connected person), the amount of the employment income forms part of the CGT acquisition cost of the shares to the person making the disposal. [*TCGA 1992, s 120(1)–(1B)(9); ITEPA 2003, Sch 6 para 210(2); FA 2003, Sch 22 para 51*].

The above provisions replaced the broadly comparable provisions of *ICTA 1988, s 138*, which continue to apply, subject to transitional provisions in *ITEPA 2003, Sch 7 paras 55–57* (previously *FA 1988, s 88*), in respect of shares acquired before 26 October 1987. The earlier provisions and the transition continue to be covered in Tolley's Income Tax under Share Related Employment Income and Exemptions. Where an amount is chargeable under *section 138* on a person who acquired shares (or an interest in shares), then on the first disposal of the shares following that acquisition (whether that disposal is made by that or any other person), the amount so chargeable forms part of the CGT acquisition cost of the shares to the person making the disposal. [*TCGA 1992, s 120(2)(5)*].

20.14 RESTRICTED SHARES

The following provisions have effect in relation to shares (or interests in shares) acquired after 15 April 2003 but only from 1 September 2003. See 20.15 below as regards shares etc. acquired on or before that day and for the position before these provisions take effect in relation to shares etc. acquired subsequently. The provisions apply, subject to exclusions, to 'employment-related shares' (see 20.2 above) if, at the time of acquisition, they are 'restricted shares' (or a 'restricted interest in shares'). For the extended meaning of 'shares', in relation to these provisions, see 20.2 above. Employment-related shares are '*restricted shares*' (or a '*restricted interest in shares*') if there is a contract, agreement, arrangement or condition that imposes any of three types of restriction *and* the market value of the shares or interest (determined as for capital gains purposes) is less than it otherwise would have been. The types of restriction covered are any provision for the transfer, reversion or forfeiture of the shares, any restriction on the freedom of the holder to dispose of the shares (or to retain the proceeds if they are sold) or on his right to retain the shares or proceeds or on any right conferred by the shares themselves, and any provision whereby the disposal or retention of the shares, or the exercise of a right conferred by them, may result in a disadvantage to the holder or (if different) the employee or a connected person.

No liability to income tax under the general provisions at 20.5 above arises on the acquisition of employment-related shares if the shares are subject to transfer, reversion or forfeiture and will cease to be so within five years after the acquisition. If a 'chargeable event' occurs in relation to restricted shares, there is a charge to tax on the employee for the tax year in which it occurs, the amount chargeable (which is calculated by applying a complex formula) counting as employment income for tax purposes. From 1 September 2004, relief is given by deduction from the chargeable amount in respect of any liability to secondary Class 1 national insurance contributions (i.e. employer contributions) in respect of that amount which is borne by the employee under a voluntary agreement or a joint election under *Social Security Contributions and Benefits Act 1992, Sch 1 para 3A* or *para 3B* (or NI equivalent).

Broadly, a chargeable event occurs when the shares cease to be restricted shares or a restriction is varied or removed, or the shares are disposed of for consideration by an 'associated person' (as defined) at a time when they are still restricted shares. Various elections can be made jointly by the employer and employee to disapply or moderate these provisions.

[*ITEPA 2003, ss 419, 421, 421A–421D, 421E(1)(3)–(5), 421F–421I, 422–432, 721(1); FA 2003, Sch 22 paras 2, 3; FA 2004, ss 85, 86, 88, 89, 90(2), Sch 16 paras 1, 7; F(No 2)A 2005, Sch 2 paras 3–7; SI 2003 No 1997; SI 2004 No 1945*].

See Tolley's Income Tax under Share-Related Employment Income and Exemptions for full details of the provisions.

For shares in research institution spin-out companies, see 20.18 below.

Capital gains tax. Where an individual acquires, on or after 1 September 2003, employment-related shares which are restricted shares (or a restricted interest in shares), the consideration for the acquisition of the shares is taken as the aggregate of

- the actual amount or value given for the restricted shares (or restricted interest in shares), and
- any amount charged to income tax as earnings in relation to the acquisition.

This does not affect the calculation of the consideration received by the person from whom the acquisition is made.

On a disposal of employment-related shares after 15 April 2003, where that disposal constitutes a chargeable event under the restricted share provisions or is the first disposal of the shares following a chargeable event not involving disposal, the aggregate of any amount counting as employment income in respect of that chargeable event and any other chargeable events occurring after the last disposal to which this provision applied, is added to the cost of acquisition of the person making the disposal. In determining amounts counting as employment income for this purpose, no account is taken of any relief given for national insurance contributions borne by the employee (see above). Where shares would otherwise cease to be employment-related shares by virtue of *ITEPA 2003, s 421B(6)* (death of employee) or *s 421B(7)* (shares ceasing to be employment-related shares seven years after employee leaves the employer, the company which issued the shares or connected person), they are treated as continuing to be employment-related shares until they are next disposed of (so that on that disposal, any amounts counting as employment income in respect of chargeable events can be added to the acquisition cost).

[*TCGA 1992, ss 119A, 149AA; FA 2003, Sch 22 paras 50, 52; FA 2004, Sch 16 para 6*].

20.15 CONDITIONAL INTERESTS IN SHARES

The following provisions are replaced by those at 20.14 above but still have effect in relation to shares (or interests in shares) acquired before 16 April 2003. In relation to shares etc. acquired subsequently, these provisions continue to have effect prior to 1 September 2003.

The provisions apply where, after 16 March 1998, a beneficial interest in shares in or securities of a company is acquired by an employee or director (of that or another company) on terms such that, subject to certain exclusions, his interest is only conditional, i.e. subject to the risk of forfeiture. Employment income chargeable to income tax may arise on the interest ceasing to be conditional or on an earlier disposal. As regards shares acquired after 16 March 1998 and before 27 July 1999, employment income could also arise under the provisions on the employee's acquisition of the shares if the terms were such that his interest might have remained conditional for more than five years. For shares acquired on or after 27 July 1999 on such terms, no charge arises under the provisions, but a charge may still arise under the general employment earnings provisions referred to at 20.5 above. There is no charge on acquisition, whether before, on or after 27 July 1999, if the terms are such that the interest will cease to be conditional within five years or less, except for any charge that may arise under *ITEPA 2003, s 476* (previously *ICTA 1988, s 135*) (see 20.6 above) or *ss 192–197* (previously *ICTA 1988, s 162*) (see 20.8 above). [*ITEPA 2003, ss 422–434 as originally enacted, Sch 6 para 18, Sch 7 paras 44–48; ICTA 1988, ss 140A, 140C; FA 1998, s 50; FA 1999, ss 42, 43; FA 2003, Sch 22 para 46(6)–(9); SI 2003 No 1997*]. For CGT purposes, the consideration given for the interest (see below) is increased by any amount counting as employment income under the above provisions. [*TCGA 1992, s 120(2)(5A)(8); FA 1998, s 54(2)(4)(6); ITEPA 2003, Sch 6 para 210(5)(10)*].

TCGA 1992, s 17 (see 41.1 MARKET VALUE) is disapplied (where it would otherwise apply) so that, instead of his being deemed to have acquired the interest at market value, the consideration given by the individual for the interest is the actual amount or value of the consideration given as computed under *ITEPA 2003, s 429 as originally enacted* (previously *ICTA 1988, s 140B*) (which does not include the value of duties performed in the office or employment concerned). However, this does not apply in calculating the consideration received for the interest by the person from whom the individual acquired it. [*TCGA 1992, s 149B; FA 1998, s 54(5)(6); ITEPA 2003, Sch 6 para 211; FA 2003, Sch 22 para 53*].

As regards shares acquired before 17 March 1998 and subject to risk of forfeiture, it was originally the Revenue's view that an income tax charge arose when that risk was lifted and by reference to the value of the shares at that time. Following legal advice received on

26 May 1995, they now take the view that a charge arises at the time of acquisition and by reference to the then value of the shares taking into account the risk of forfeiture, with no charge arising on the risk being lifted. The CGT acquisition cost of the shares is whatever value has been taken into account for income tax purposes. See Revenue Tax Bulletin June 1998 pp 545–548.

The employee's acquisition date for CGT purposes of employee shares held in trust and subject to risk of forfeiture or other restrictions is the date the employee becomes absolutely entitled as against the trustees, normally the date the risk of forfeiture or other restrictions are removed. This applies regardless of when or whether an income tax charge arises as above. Where the employee makes a payment for the shares, the terms of the employee's agreement with the trustees establish when 'absolute entitlement' occurs. Separate rules apply as regards share incentive plans (see 20.19 below) and approved profit sharing schemes (see 20.30 below). (Revenue Tax Bulletin February 2001 pp 828, 829).

20.16 CONVERTIBLE SHARES AFTER FA 2003

The following provisions replace those at 20.17 below and have effect on and after 1 September 2003 irrespective of when the shares were acquired, except that the tax relief on acquisition (see below) applies only to acquisitions on and after that date. The provisions apply, subject to exclusions, to 'employment-related shares' (see 20.2 above) if, at the time of acquisition, they are 'convertible shares' (or an interest in 'convertible shares'). For the extended meaning of 'shares', in relation to these provisions, see 20.2 above. Employment-related shares are '*convertible shares*' if they confer on the holder any entitlement (for shares acquired before 2 December 2004, an immediate or conditional entitlement) to convert them into shares of a different description, or a contract, agreement, arrangement or condition authorises or requires the grant of such an entitlement to the holder if certain circumstances arise, or do not arise, or makes provision for the conversion of the shares (otherwise than by the holder) into shares of a different description.

In relation to acquisitions on and after 1 September 2003, for the purposes of any liability to income tax in respect of the acquisition of shares (under the general charging rules at 20.5 above, under 20.6 above (unapproved share options) or under 20.8 above (acquisition for less than market value)), the market value of the employment-related shares is to be determined as if they were not convertible shares or an interest in convertible shares. For acquisitions on or after 2 December 2004, this does not apply if the shares are acquired as part of an arrangement to avoid tax or NICs. Instead, in such cases the market value is computed as if there were an immediate and unfettered right to convert (if this is greater than the value without the right to convert).

If a chargeable event occurs in relation to convertible shares, there is a charge to tax on the employee for the tax year in which it occurs, the amount chargeable counting as employment income for tax purposes. Broadly, the conversion of the employment-related shares (or the shares in which they are an interest) into shares of a different description, the disposal for consideration of the shares (or any interest in them), the release, for consideration, of the conversion right and the receipt by an 'associated person' (as defined) of a benefit in money or money's worth in connection with the conversion right are chargeable events. The chargeable amount is found by computing the gain (if any) realised on the occurrence of the chargeable event and deducting from it any consideration given for the conversion right and any expenses incurred by the shareholder in connection with the conversion, disposal, release or receipt (whichever is applicable). An adjustment is made where the market value on acquisition was computed under the alternative rules for avoidance cases above. From 1 September 2004, relief is given by deduction from the chargeable amount in respect of any liability to secondary Class 1 national insurance contributions (i.e. employer contributions) in respect of that amount which is borne by the employee under a voluntary agreement or a joint election under *Social Security Contributions and Benefits Act 1992, Sch 1 para 3A* or *para 3B* (or NI equivalent).

[*ITEPA 2003, ss 419, 421, 421A–421D, 421E(1)(3)–(5), 421F–421I, 435–444, 721(1); FA 2003, Sch 22 paras 2, 4; FA 2004, ss 85, 86, 88(2), 89, 90(2), Sch 16 paras 2, 7; F(No 2)A 2005, Sch 2 paras 8–11; SI 2003 No 1997; SI 2004 No 1945*].

See Tolley's Income Tax under Share-Related Employment Income and Exemptions for full details of the provisions.

For shares in research institution spin-out companies, see 20.18 below.

Capital gains tax. Where an individual acquires, on or after 1 September 2003, employment-related shares which are convertible shares (or an interest in convertible shares), the consideration for the acquisition of the shares is taken as the aggregate of

- the actual amount or value given for the convertible shares (or interest in convertible shares), and
- any amount charged to income tax as earnings in relation to the acquisition.

This does not affect the calculation of the consideration received by the person from whom the acquisition is made.

On a disposal of employment-related shares after 15 April 2003, where that disposal constitutes a chargeable event under the convertible share provisions or is the first disposal of the shares following a chargeable event not involving disposal, the aggregate of any amount counting as employment income in respect of that chargeable event and any other chargeable events occurring after the last disposal to which this provision applied, is added to the cost of acquisition of the person making the disposal. In determining amounts counting as employment income for this purpose, no account is taken of any relief given for national insurance contributions borne by the employee (see above). Where shares would otherwise cease to be employment-related shares by virtue of *ITEPA 2003, s 421B(6)* (death of employee) or *s 421B(7)* (shares ceasing to be employment-related shares seven years after employee leaves the employer, the company which issued the shares or connected person), they are treated as continuing to be employment-related shares until they are next disposed of (so that on that disposal, any amounts counting as employment income in respect of chargeable events can be added to the acquisition cost).

[*TCGA 1992, ss 119A, 149AA; FA 2003, Sch 22 paras 50, 52; FA 2004, Sch 16 para 6; SI 2003 No 1997*].

20.17 CONVERTIBLE SHARES BEFORE FA 2003

The following provisions have effect before 1 September 2003.

Where convertible shares in a company are acquired after 16 March 1998 by a director or employee of that or another company, employment income chargeable to income tax arises on the conversion of the shares to shares of a different class whilst the employee etc. still has a beneficial interest. [*ITEPA 2003, ss 435–446 as originally enacted, Sch 6 para 18, Sch 7 paras 49–53; ICTA 1988, s 140D; FA 1998, s 51; FA 2003, Sch 22 para 46(10)–(12)(26); SI 2003 No 1997*]. For CGT purposes, the cost of acquiring the shares is increased by the amount so counting as employment income. [*TCGA 1992, s 120(2)(5B)(9); FA 1998, s 54(2)(6); ITEPA 2003, Sch 6 para 210(6); FA 2003, Sch 22 para 51*].

20.18 RESEARCH INSTITUTION SPIN-OUT COMPANIES

FA 2005 introduced provisions to ensure, broadly, that no income tax charge arises on an increase in the value of academics' shares in 'spin-out companies' due to the transfer of intellectual property from a research institution or a company controlled by it. Subject to the commencement provisions below, the provisions apply where

- an agreement is made for one or more transfers of intellectual property from one or more research institutions to a company (a '*spin-out company*');

- a person acquires shares in the spin-out company either before the making of the agreement or within 183 days beginning with the date of the agreement;
- the right or opportunity to acquire the shares was available by reason of employment by any of the research institutions or the company; and
- the person is involved in research in relation to any of the intellectual property which is the subject of the agreement.

The provisions do not apply if the avoidance of tax or national insurance is one of the main purposes of the arrangements under which the shares are acquired.

Where the provisions apply, the following income tax consequences follow.

(*a*) On acquisition, the market value of the shares is calculated disregarding the effect of both the transfer agreement and the transfer itself.

(*b*) If the shares are acquired before the agreement is made or before any transfer, the taxable amount under the provisions at 20.12 above in respect of any benefit received by the employee deriving from the agreement or transfer in connection with the shares is treated as nil.

(*c*) If the shares are restricted shares, the employer and employee are (subject to a right to make an irrevocable agreement to the contrary) deemed to make an election disapplying the provisions at 20.14 above.

(*d*) For the purposes of 20.11 above, neither the transfer agreement nor any transfer pursuant to it are treated as things done otherwise than for genuine commercial purposes.

For the purposes of these provisions, the extended meaning of shares at 20.2 above does not apply, but '*shares*' includes stock and an interest in shares.

The above provisions apply where either the shares are acquired or the transfer agreement is made on or after 2 December 2004. More limited relief, enabling the deferment of the tax charge, is available where both the shares are acquired and the transfer agreement is made before that date if the employer and employee make an irrevocable election to that effect before 16 October 2005. Where an election is made, a chargeable event giving rise to a tax liability will occur either when the shares are disposed of for consideration by an 'associated person' (as defined) or on the date specified in an irrevocable election by the employee, the amount chargeable counting as employment income. The relief is broadly equivalent to that available for structures covered by the memorandum of understanding between the Inland Revenue and the University Companies Association (see Revenue Internet Statement, 23 April 2004 and 2004 STI 1070).

[*ITEPA 2003, ss 451–460; FA 2005, ss 20, 21*].

Capital gains tax. Where an individual acquires shares (or an interest in shares) in circumstances such that (*a*) above applies (including where it applies by virtue of the election for pre-2 December 2004 cases referred to above), the consideration for the acquisition is taken as the aggregate of

- the actual amount or value given for the shares or interest, and
- any amount charged to income tax as earnings in relation to the acquisition.

This does not affect the calculation of the consideration received by the person from whom the acquisition is made.

On a disposal of employment-related shares which is the first disposal of the shares following a chargeable event fixed by an employee election under the provisions above for pre-2 December 2004 cases, the amount counting as employment income in respect of that chargeable event is added to the cost of acquisition of the person making the disposal. Where shares would otherwise cease to be employment-related shares by virtue of *ITEPA*

2003, s 421B(6) (death of employee) or *s 421B(7)* (shares ceasing to be employment-related shares seven years after employee leaves the employer, the company which issued the shares or connected person), they are treated as continuing to be employment-related shares until they are next disposed of (so that on that disposal, any amounts counting as employment income in respect of chargeable events can be added to the acquisition cost). [*TCGA 1992, ss 119A, 149AB; FA 2005, s 22*].

HMRC have issued guidance on the operation of the above provisions (HMRC Internet Statement 28 April, 2005).

20.19 SHARE INCENTIVE PLANS

Subject to HMRC approval **on or after 28 July 2000**, a company may set up a Share Incentive Plan (SIP) (originally known as an All-Employee Share Ownership Plan), which is a tax-advantaged all-employee share plan of which the main features are as follows.

- A plan is operated by trustees, who buy or subscribe for shares with funds provided by the company (or, in the case of partnership shares, the employees) and appropriate them to the participating employees.
- With limited exceptions, the plan must be open to all employees (other than those with a material interest where the company is a close company), but may incorporate performance-related awards within certain parameters.
- An employer can appropriate to an employee free shares in the company valued at up to £3,000 per tax year without any charge to income tax at that time ('*free share plans*').
- An employee can buy shares in the company out of amounts deducted from his salary up to a limit of £1,500 in any tax year or, if less, 10% of salary (or such lower limits as the employer's particular plan may specify), these being allowable deductions for income tax ('*partnership share plans*'). For 2002/03 and earlier years, these limits were expressed in terms of months, so that the amount deducted from salary could not exceed £125 in any month (or 10% of salary if less).
- In respect of each partnership share an employee buys, the employer may appropriate to him up to two free '*matching shares*', again without any charge to income tax at that time.
- Free and matching shares must normally be kept in the plan for a specified period which must be not less than three years nor more than five (the '*holding period*') — no such restriction applies to partnership shares. The employer's plan may provide that free and/or matching shares be forfeited in certain circumstances (see further below under Capital gains tax).
- An employee who keeps shares in the plan for at least five years after they are awarded to him receives them free of income tax. With some exceptions (e.g. on death, disability, normal retirement or redundancy), an employee who withdraws shares from the plan within three to five years pays income tax on the lower of their value at the time of award (or, for partnership shares, their cost) and their value at withdrawal. With similar exceptions, an employee who withdraws shares from the plan within three years of appropriation pays income tax on their value at withdrawal.
- An employer's plan may provide for reinvestment of up to £1,500 worth of dividends on plan shares per tax year, in which case such dividends are tax-free. Shares acquired by such reinvestment are known as '*dividend shares*'.
- The employer's costs of setting up and running the scheme are tax deductible as is the market value at acquisition of free and matching shares awarded to employees under the plan.

[*ICTA 1988, ss 68A–68C, 85B, 251A–251D, Sch 4AA; FA 2000, s 47, Sch 8; ITEPA 2003, ss 488–515, Sch 2, Sch 6 paras 10,109, Sch 7 paras 68–70; FA 2003, Sch 21 paras 1–8, Sch 22 paras 26–28, 43*); *FA 2004, s 88(4)(5); ITTOIA 2005, ss 392–396, 405–408, 770, Sch 1 paras 41, 122, 599–604, 617*].

For detailed coverage of the above, see Tolley's Income Tax under Share Related Employment Income and Exemptions.

Capital gains tax. Notwithstanding anything in the plan or the trust instrument, an employee (a '*participant*') is treated for CGT purposes as absolutely entitled as against the plan trustees to any shares awarded to him under an approved SIP. [*TCGA 1992, s 238A, Sch 7D para 3; FA 2000, Sch 8 para 99; ITEPA 2003, Sch 6 paras 216, 221*]. Shares are awarded to a participant when free or matching shares are appropriated to him or when partnership shares are acquired on his behalf. [*ITEPA 2003, Sch 2 para 5(1); FA 2000, Sch 8 para 3(1)*]. For the purpose of applying 59.2 SHARES AND SECURITIES — IDENTIFICATION RULES, plan shares (including free, matching, partnership and dividend shares) are treated as of a different class from any shares (otherwise of the same class) held by the participant outside the plan. [*TCGA 1992, Sch 7D para 4(1); FA 2000, Sch 8 para 100(1); ITEPA 2003, Sch 6 para 221*]. A company reconstruction is not normally treated as a disposal of plan shares (see Tolley's Income Tax for details and for a note on rights issues).

Shares cease to be subject to a plan when either the shares are withdrawn from the plan, or the participant ceases to be in relevant employment, or in certain circumstances the trustees dispose of shares in order to meet PAYE obligations. See Tolley's Income Tax for full details. Shares are withdrawn from the plan when on the direction of the participant (or, after his death, of his personal representatives) the plan trustees either transfer them (whether to the participant etc. or to another person) or dispose of them and similarly account for the proceeds, or when the participant etc. assigns, charges or otherwise disposes of his beneficial interest in them. [*ITEPA 2003, Sch 2 para 96; FA 2000, Sch 8 para 122*]. Shares which cease to be subject to a plan at any time are deemed to have been disposed of and immediately reacquired by the participant at their then market value, but no chargeable gain (or allowable loss) arises on the deemed disposal. [*TCGA 1992, Sch 7D para 5; FA 2000, Sch 8 para 101; ITEPA 2003, Sch 6 para 221*]. It follows that on a subsequent disposal the period of ownership for TAPER RELIEF (61) purposes begins on the date of the deemed disposal and reacquisition.

Shares (but not securities or other rights) which have ceased to be subject to the plan but remain in the participant's beneficial ownership may be transferred without CGT consequences to an Individual Savings Account (see 22.29 EXEMPTIONS AND RELIEFS), subject to the annual subscription limits for such an Account (applied by reference to market value transferred) and provided the transfer is made within 90 days after the shares ceased to be subject to the plan.

Plan trustees. A gain (or loss) accruing in respect of shares to the trustees of an approved SIP is not a chargeable gain (or an allowable loss) if the shares

- satisfy the requirements of *ITEPA 2003, Sch 2 Pt 4* (previously *FA 2000, Sch 8 paras 59–67*) as to the type of share that may be used in a plan (see Tolley's Income Tax); and
- are awarded to employees (see above), or acquired on their behalf as dividend shares, in accordance with the plan within the 'relevant period'; for these purposes, shares of a particular class acquired by the trustees are deemed to be awarded on a first in/first out basis (subject to special rules for shares acquired by qualifying transfer from an employee share ownership trust).

The '*relevant period*' depends on whether or not any of the shares in the company are 'readily convertible assets' within *ITEPA 2003, ss 701, 702* (previously *ICTA 1988, s 203F*) — broadly, whether or not they are capable of being readily converted into cash (see Tolley's Income Tax under Pay As You Earn). In determining whether shares are readily convertible assets, one may disregard any market for the shares which is created by virtue of the trustees acquiring shares for the plan and exists solely for the purposes of the plan. If any of the shares in the company are readily convertible assets at the time of acquisition by the trustees, the relevant period is the two years beginning with that time. If none of them are, the relevant period is extended to five years, but if within that period any of the shares in the company become readily convertible assets the relevant period ends no later than two years beginning with the date on which they did so. For shares acquired before 11 May 2001, these provisions operated by reference to the shares acquired by the trustees as opposed to shares in the company generally.

A payment made after 5 April 2003 by the employer company to the trustees sufficient to enable them to acquire a significant block of shares (at least 10% of the company's ordinary share capital) attracts an 'up-front' corporation tax deduction under *ICTA 1988, Sch 4AA para 9* (i.e. the deduction will not, as normal, be deferred until the shares are awarded to employees). The deduction will, however, be clawed back unless at least 30% of those shares are awarded within five years of acquisition by the trustees and all of the shares are awarded within ten years. As a consequence, the 'relevant period' above is extended to ten years in relation to shares acquired by virtue of such a payment.

[*TCGA 1992, Sch 7D para 2; FA 2000, Sch 8 paras 98, 128; FA 2001, Sch 13 para 8; ITEPA 2003, Sch 6 para 221*].

If the plan trustees acquire shares from the trustees of an approved profit sharing scheme (see 20.29 below), the disposal by the scheme trustees and acquisition by the plan trustees are deemed to be made for such consideration as to secure that neither a gain nor a loss accrues on the disposal. For the purpose *only* of determining the relevant period as above (and *not* for taper relief purposes), the shares are deemed to have been acquired by the plan trustees at the time they were acquired by the trustees of the profit sharing scheme. [*ITEPA 2003, Sch 7 para 86; FA 2000, Sch 8 para 103*].

An approved SIP *may* provide for free or matching shares to be forfeited in certain circumstances, i.e. if, other than for a permitted reason, the participant leaves the relevant employment within a specified forfeiture period of up to three years or withdraws the shares, or any related partnership shares, from the plan within that period. [*ITEPA 2003, Sch 2 para 32; FA 2000, Sch 8 para 65*]. Forfeited shares are deemed to have been disposed of by the participant and acquired by the plan trustees at their market value at the date of forfeiture, but no chargeable gain (or allowable loss) arises on the deemed disposal. [*TCGA 1992, Sch 7D para 7; FA 2000, Sch 8 para 102; ITEPA 2003, Sch 6 para 221*].

Subject to their duty to act in accordance with the participant's directions, the plan trustees may dispose of some of the rights under a rights issue in respect of a participant's plan shares in order to raise funds to take up other rights under the issue. [*ITEPA 2003, Sch 2 para 77; FA 2000, Sch 8 para 72*]. Provided similar rights are conferred in respect of all ordinary shares in the company, the gain (or loss) arising on such a disposal is not a chargeable gain (or an allowable loss). [*TCGA 1992, Sch 7D para 8; FA 2000, Sch 8 para 104; ITEPA 2003, Sch 6 para 221*].

For the purpose of applying 59.2 SHARES AND SECURITIES — IDENTIFICATION RULES,

- any shares transferred to the plan trustees by way of qualifying transfer from an employee share ownership trust (see Tolley's Income Tax) are treated as of a different class from any other shares (otherwise of the same class) held by the trustees; and
- any shares acquired by the trustees by virtue of a payment by the employer made after 5 April 2003 and attracting an up-front corporation tax deduction under *ICTA 1988, Sch 4AA para 9* are treated as of a different class from any other shares (otherwise of the same class) held by the trustees.

[*TCGA 1992, Sch 7D para 4(2)–(6); FA 2000, Sch 8 para 100(2)(3); ITEPA 2003, Sch 6 para 221*].

20.20 **Rollover relief on disposals of shares to a SIP.** A form of capital gains rollover relief is available, as described below, on a disposal after 27 July 2000 of shares, or an interest in shares, to the trustees of an approved share incentive plan and the reinvestment of the proceeds into a chargeable asset. The relief is not available where the person making the disposal is a company. [*TCGA 1992, s 236A, Sch 7C; FA 2000, s 48, Sch 9; ITEPA 2003, Sch 6 paras 214, 220*].

Requirements for relief. The relief (see 20.21 below) applies only where all the following requirements are met.

(*a*) The person making the disposal (the claimant) obtains consideration for the disposal and, at any time in the '*acquisition period*' (the period of 6 months beginning with the date of disposal or, if later, the date on which the requirement at (*d*) below is first met) or under an unconditional contract made within that period, he either

(i) applies the whole of the consideration in acquiring 'replacement assets', or

(ii) applies part of the consideration as in (i) above, and the part *not* so applied is less than the gain on the disposal (whether all chargeable gain or not).

A '*replacement asset*' is one which, immediately after the acquisition, is a 'chargeable asset' in relation to the claimant. The term includes an interest in an asset but does not include shares in, or debentures of, the company whose shares are the subject of the disposal or a company which, at the time of the acquisition, is in the same CGT group (see 27.1 GROUPS OF COMPANIES, as amended by *FA 2000*) as that company. A '*chargeable asset*' is broadly an asset the immediate disposal of which would give rise to a chargeable gain which would not be outside the charge to CGT as a result of the claimant's residence status or the terms of a double tax agreement.

(*b*) The share incentive plan is HMRC-approved at the time of the disposal (though the relief is not withdrawn if the plan subsequently loses approval — HMRC Capital Gains Manual CG 61970).

(*c*) The shares disposed of

- are not of a class listed on a recognised stock exchange (within *ICTA 1988, s 841* — see 58.23 SHARES AND SECURITIES),
- are not shares in a company which is under the control (within *ICTA 1988, s 840*) of a company (other than a close company or non-resident equivalent) whose shares are so listed,

but otherwise meet the requirements of *ITEPA 2003, Sch 2 paras 25–33* (see Tolley's Income Tax) as to the types of share that may be awarded under an approved plan. (This appears to be what the draftsman intended, and is confirmed by HMRC Capital Gains Manual CG 61973, though the wording of the legislation is ambiguous.)

(*d*) At some time in the '*entitlement period*' (the period of 12 months beginning with the date of disposal), the plan trustees hold (for the beneficiaries) shares in the company concerned that constitute at least 10% of ordinary share capital and carry rights to at least 10% of distributable profits and of distributable assets on a winding-up. Shares appropriated under the plan, or acquired on a beneficiary's behalf, but still subject to the plan count towards this requirement.

(*e*) At no time in the '*proscribed period*' (the period beginning with the date of disposal and ending with the date of acquisition of the replacement asset or, if later, the date on which the requirement at (*d*) above is first met) are there any unauthorised arrangements under which the claimant (or a person connected with him — see 16 CONNECTED PERSONS) may be entitled to acquire (directly or indirectly) from the plan trustees any shares (or an interest in or right deriving from any shares). For this purpose, all arrangements are unauthorised unless they only allow shares to be appropriated to or acquired on behalf of an individual under the plan.

[*TCGA 1992, Sch 7C paras 1–4, 8; FA 2000, Sch 29 para 40; ITEPA 2003, Sch 6 para 220*].

20.21 *Form of relief.* Where the requirements at 20.20 are met, the person making the disposal may make a claim for rollover relief under these provisions, such claim to be made within the two years beginning with the acquisition.

Where the whole of the consideration was reinvested (as in 20.20(*a*)(i) above), the effect of the claim is that for CGT purposes the disposal is deemed to have been made for such consideration (if it would otherwise be greater) as would result in no gain and no loss. The acquisition cost of the replacement asset is reduced by the excess of the actual consideration over the deemed consideration.

Where part only of the consideration was reinvested (as in 20.20(*a*)(ii) above), the effect of the claim is that for CGT purposes the gain on the disposal is reduced to the amount of consideration not reinvested. The acquisition cost of the replacement asset is reduced by the amount by which the gain is reduced.

The other parties to the disposal and acquisition are not affected by a claim for relief. Any provision of *TCGA 1992* fixing deemed consideration for a disposal or acquisition is applied before the above adjustments are made.

[*TCGA 1992, Sch 7C para 5*].

Where a claim relates to more than one replacement asset, the relief is to be allocated between them on a just and reasonable basis (HMRC Capital Gains Manual CG 61979).

20.22 *Special rules where replacement asset is a dwelling-house.* Special rules may apply where

- a rollover relief claim is made under 20.21 above,
- any replacement asset (as in 20.20(*a*) above) is a dwelling-house, part of a dwelling-house or land, and,
- as is required, that asset was a chargeable asset in relation to the claimant immediately after the acquisition.

The said rules apply where the property later comes within the private residence exemption (see 49 PRIVATE RESIDENCES) (or would do if it were disposed of) by reference to the claimant or the claimant's spouse or civil partner (whether as an individual taxpayer or as a person entitled to occupy the property under the terms of a settlement).

If there is a time after the acquisition and *before* the making of the rollover relief claim when the dwelling-house etc. would fall within the private residence exemption, it is treated as if it had not been a chargeable asset in relation to the claimant immediately after the acquisition, with the result that the rollover relief claim fails. If, instead, there is a time *after* the making of the rollover relief claim when the dwelling-house etc. would fall within the private residence exemption, it is similarly treated, but in this case the gain rolled over is treated as not having accrued until that time (or until the earliest of such times if there is more than one).

Similar rules apply where the replacement asset is an option to acquire (or to acquire an interest in) a dwelling-house etc., and the option is exercised.

[*TCGA 1992, Sch 7C para 6; SI 2005 No 3229, Reg 129*].

20.23 *Special rules where replacement asset is EIS shares.* Special rules apply where

- a rollover relief claim is made under 20.21 above,
- any replacement asset (as in 20.20(*a*) above) is shares,

- that asset was a chargeable asset in relation to the claimant immediately after the acquisition, and
- the claimant makes a claim for Enterprise Investment Scheme (EIS) income tax relief in respect of the shares (see 21.2 ENTERPRISE INVESTMENT SCHEME).

Regardless of whether the EIS relief claim is made before or after the rollover relief claim, the shares are treated if they had not been a chargeable asset in relation to the claimant immediately after the acquisition, with the result that the rollover relief claim fails (and any relief already given is treated as if never due).

[*TCGA 1992, Sch 7C para 7*].

20.24 ENTERPRISE MANAGEMENT INCENTIVES

With effect **on and after 28 July 2000**, 'small higher risk' trading companies are able to grant options over shares worth up to £100,000 (at time of grant) to eligible employees without income tax consequences (except to the extent that the option is to acquire shares at less than their market value at time of grant). In relation to options granted on or after 11 May 2001, the total value of shares in respect of which unexercised options exist must not exceed £3 million. This replaced a rule limiting the number of employees who could hold options at any one time to 15. The company may be quoted or unquoted but must be an independent company trading or preparing to trade wholly or mainly in the UK and whose gross assets do not exceed £30 million (£15 million in relation to options granted before 1 January 2002). A company carrying on certain specified activities deemed to be lower risk activities does not qualify, such exclusions being similar to those at 66.5 VENTURE CAPITAL TRUSTS. Broadly, an employee is eligible if he is employed by the company for at least 25 hours per week or, if less, at least 75% of his total working time, and he controls no more than 30% of the company's ordinary share capital. Companies are not required to obtain HMRC approval to schemes but must give notification to HMRC within 92 days after an option is granted (30 days for options granted before 11 May 2001). [*ITEPA 2003, ss 527–541, Sch 5, Sch 7 paras 77–83; FA 2000, s 62, Sch 14; FA 2001, Sch 14; SI 2001 No 3799; FA 2003, Sch 22 paras 36–41, 45; FA 2004, s 96, Sch 27 para 17; ITTOIA 2005, Sch 1 para 620; FA 2005, Sch 4 para 48*]. For full details, see Tolley's Income Tax under Share-Related Employment Income and Exemptions.

Capital gains tax. On a disposal of shares acquired under an option satisfying the requirements of the enterprise management incentives (EMI) scheme (hereafter referred to as a '*qualifying option*'), where the option was exercised after 9 April 2003 so that *TCGA 1992, s 144ZA* (see 6.7 ASSETS) applies, the cost of acquisition of the shares for CGT purposes (within *TCGA 1992, s 38(1)(a)* — see 15.4(*a*) COMPUTATION OF GAINS AND LOSSES) consists of the aggregate of

- (by virtue of *TCGA 1992, ss 119A, 120(2)(4)* — see 20.6 above) any amount counting as employment income under *ITEPA 2003, s 476* (or, for 2002/03 and earlier years, *ICTA 1988, s 135*) after the deductions mentioned at 20.6 above, which might be the case if the option was to acquire shares at less than their market value at the time of grant or if a disqualifying event (see below) occurred while the option remained unexercised,
- the consideration given for the shares acquired on the exercise of the option, and
- any consideration given for the option.

This is the same aggregate that the Revenue took to make up the acquisition cost prior to the decision in *Mansworth v Jelley CA 2002, 75 TC 1*. Following that decision, the Revenue accepted that the market value rule at 20.5 above applies to shares acquired as a result of the exercise of an option. Accordingly, in respect of options exercised before 10 April 2003 (i.e. where *TCGA 1992, s 144ZA*, which is intended to reverse the effect of the decision (see 6.7 ASSETS), does not apply), the cost of acquisition will consist of the aggregate of

- any amount counting as employment income, and
- the market value of the shares at the time the option is exercised

(Revenue Internet Statement 8 January 2003).

For further details of how HMRC implement the *Mansworth v Jelley* decision in different circumstances see Revenue Internet Statements 8 January 2003, 17 March 2003 and 8 August 2003.

The provisions at 20.7 above (as regards release of options) and 20.9–20.17 above apply to options under an EMI scheme and to shares acquired under such options. Those at 20.8 above are disapplied (see Tolley's Income Tax).

Modification of taper relief provisions. On a disposal of 'qualifying shares', the shares are treated for the purposes of taper relief as if they had been acquired when the option was granted. Thus, the qualifying holding period (see 61.2 TAPER RELIEF) begins with the date of grant and not with the date of exercise (which is contrary to the normal rule in 6.7 ASSETS).

'*Qualifying shares*' are shares acquired by the exercise of a qualifying option, but also include 'replacement shares'. '*Replacement shares*' are shares treated under *TCGA 1992, s 127* (reorganisation of share capital — see 58.1 SHARES AND SECURITIES) as the same asset as shares acquired under a qualifying option and which meet the statutory requirements as to the type of share that may be acquired under such an option (broadly, fully paid up, non-redeemable ordinary shares). A 'disqualifying event' occurs in relation to a qualifying option if any of a number of specified conditions ceases to be satisfied whilst the option remains unexercised (for details, see Tolley's Income Tax under Share-Related Employment Income and Exemptions). Where such an event occurs (whether in relation to the original option or a replacement option — see below), shares acquired by the exercise of the option are qualifying shares, and thus attract the advantageous taper relief treatment, *only* if the option is exercised within 40 days after that event.

Where a qualifying option is exchanged on one or more occasions for a 'replacement option', the above modification to the taper relief rules applies by reference to the time the original option was granted. A '*replacement option*' is an option issued by a company which in specified circumstances takes over the company that granted the original qualifying option and which is issued, on equivalent terms, in place of the original option (see Tolley's Income Tax for details).

Rights issues. If there is a rights issue affecting qualifying shares, the share reorganisation rules of *TCGA 1992, ss 127–130* (see 58.1 SHARES AND SECURITIES) are disapplied, with the result that the rights shares are treated as a separate acquisition and are not qualifying shares.

[*TCGA 1992, Sch 7D paras 14–16; FA 2000, Sch 14 paras 56–58; ITEPA 2003, Sch 6 para 221*].

Identification rules. For an election to modify the normal rules in a case where EMI scheme shares are acquired on the same day as other shares in the same company and after 5 April 2002, see 59.2 SHARES AND SECURITIES — IDENTIFICATION RULES.

20.25 OTHER APPROVED SHARE OPTION SCHEMES

Assignment, release or abandonment of approved employee share option. The same comments apply as for unapproved options at 20.7 above.

Identification rules. For an election to modify the normal rules in a case where approved share option scheme shares are acquired on the same day as other shares in the same company and after 5 April 2002, see 59.2 SHARES AND SECURITIES — IDENTIFICATION RULES.

Earlier CGT provisions applicable to approved schemes generally. The following applied as regards all Revenue-approved share option schemes.

Consideration for grant of share option. Where an option to acquire shares in a company was granted after 15 March 1993 and before 28 November 1995 under an approved share option scheme, the grantor company was treated for CGT purposes as if *TCGA 1992, s 17(1)* (see 41.1 MARKET VALUE) did not apply so that the company was treated as if the amount or value of the consideration for the grant was the actual value or consideration passing (if any). In computing actual value for this purpose, any value put on the employee's services, past or present, was ignored. These provisions did not affect the CGT position of the person to whom the option was granted. [*TCGA 1992, s 149A; FA 1993, s 104*]. This treatment applies to *all* employee share options granted after 27 November 1995 and does so with regard to both grantor and grantee (see 20.3 above).

Release and replacement of options. Where approved share option schemes are permitted to make provision for the release of options over one company's shares in consideration of the grant of options over another company's shares (for example on a company takeover), any such transaction before 28 November 1995 was not treated as a disposal or acquisition, the new options and old options being treated as the same asset. [*TCGA 1992, s 238(4); FA 1996, s 112(2)(3)*]. For transactions after 27 November 1995, the position as regards *all* employee share options is governed by *TCGA 1992, s 237A* — see 20.4 above.

20.26 **Save as you earn (SAYE) share option schemes.** Under a SAYE share option scheme approved by HMRC, a company grants to an employee of itself or its group an option to acquire ordinary shares in the company at a specified price (the option price) at a specified future date. No income tax charge arises on either the grant of the option or, on exercise of the option, on any excess of the then value of the shares over the option price. The option price must not be less than 80% of the market value of shares of the same class at the time the option is granted. The scheme is linked to an approved certified contractual savings (CCS) scheme with a bank, building society or other authorised provider, to which the employee makes regular contributions by deduction from salary and to which a tax-free bonus is added at maturity (the bonus date), the funds then being used to purchase the agreed number of shares at the option price (though the funds may alternatively be repaid to the employee if he so chooses, the option being allowed to lapse). Savings contracts of between three years and five years are available (the former from April 1996), and five-year contracts may offer the choice of an extension to seven years. Aggregate monthly contributions to all such schemes to which an employee contributes at any one time cannot exceed £250, and the minimum monthly contribution set for any scheme must not exceed £10 (although monthly contributions as low as £5 are permitted).

Other than in specified circumstances, the option cannot be exercised before the bonus date, nor can it be exercised, except in the case of death (for which special rules apply), more than six months after that date. The circumstances under which early exercise may be permitted include *inter alia* (i) the takeover of the company whose shares are scheme shares, (ii) where the eligible employment is in a subsidiary company, the company which established the scheme ceasing to have control of that subsidiary, and (iii) the transfer (to a person other than a subsidiary or associated company) of the business (or part thereof) to which the employment relates. In each case, the option can be exercised within six months of the change but if, in any of these three instances, the option is thus exercised within three years of its being granted, the income tax exemption on exercise is lost and a charge may arise under *ITEPA 2003, s 476* (previously *ICTA 1988, s 135*) (see 20.6 above); the income tax exemption on the *grant* of the option does, however, continue to apply.

The scheme *must* be available on similar terms (subject to any variations by reference to salary level, period of service etc.) to all employees and full-time directors within *ITEPA 2003, ss 15* or *21* (previously Schedule E, Case I) and with a stipulated minimum period of service, which cannot be more than five years. It *may* be made available to other employees and directors. Where the company is a close company, those with material interests are excluded.

[*ITEPA 2003, ss 516–520, Sch 3, Sch 7 paras 71, 72; ICTA 1988, s 185(1)–(4)(10), s 187, Sch 9; FA 2003, Sch 21 paras 9–12, Sch 22 paras 29–31, 44; FA 2004, s 88(6); ITTOIA 2005, Sch 1 paras 605, 618*].

See Tolley's Income Tax for the full provisions and conditions for approval.

Capital gains tax. Other than where early exercise of the option results in the loss of the income tax exemption as mentioned above (in which case see 20.6 above), the provisions of *TCGA 1992, s 17* (see 41.1 MARKET VALUE) are specifically disapplied both in calculating the CGT acquisition cost of the shares to the employee and for the purposes of any corresponding disposal to him. Those provisions are likewise disapplied where an option is exercised following the death of the employee in accordance with a rule included in the scheme by virtue of *ITEPA 2003, Sch 3 para 32*. [*TCGA 1992, Sch 7D para 10; ICTA 1988, s 185(3)(b), (4); FA 1991, s 39(2)(4)(8); ITEPA 2003, Sch 6 para 221*]. On a disposal of the shares by the employee, his allowable expenditure consists of the actual consideration given on the exercise of the option, i.e. the amount saved plus the tax-free bonus (plus, if applicable, any consideration given for the option itself, or, for options granted before 28 November 1995, the market value, if any, of the option at the time it was granted — see 20.3 above). The date of acquisition of the shares for CGT purposes is the date the option is exercised.

Shares acquired through an approved SAYE share option scheme may be transferred without CGT consequences to an Individual Savings Account (see 22.29 EXEMPTIONS AND RELIEFS), or, before 6 April 1999, to a single company PEP (see 58.18 SHARES AND SECURITIES), subject to the annual subscription limits for those investment vehicles (applied by reference to market value transferred) and provided the transfer is made within 90 days after the option is exercised.

20.27 **Company share option plan (CSOP) schemes.** CSOP schemes were introduced by *FA 1996* to replace executive share option schemes (see 20.28 below). Unlike SAYE share option schemes and profit sharing schemes, company share option plans and their predecessors are not required to be open to all employees, and are more likely to be used to reward directors and key employees. CSOP schemes are more restrictive than their predecessors in that they place a lower ceiling on the value of options an individual may hold at any one time and do not permit the option price to be discounted by reference to the current share price. New CSOP schemes could be established from 29 April 1996, but under transitional provisions the new rules also apply to pre-existing approved executive schemes with effect for options granted on or after 17 July 1995 (other than within 30 days of a written offer or invitation to apply for them made before that date). An executive share option scheme had until 1 January 1997 to opt out of the new rules if it wished and thus cease to be an approved scheme.

Under a CSOP scheme approved by HMRC, a company grants to an employee of itself or its group an option to acquire ordinary shares in the company at a specified price (the option price) at a specified future date. The option price should not be less than the market value of the shares at the time of the grant. Normally, no income tax charge arises on either the grant of the option or, on exercise of the option, on any excess of the then value of the shares over the option price. In the exceptional case where the aggregate of the option price and any amount paid for the option itself is less than the market value of the shares at the time of the grant, the amount of the difference counts as employment income for the tax year in which the option is granted. The normal tax exemption on *exercise* of the option does not apply if the scheme is no longer approved at the time of exercise or if the option is exercised less than three years or more than ten years after it was granted. There is an exception for options exercised within three years of grant but no later than six months after the individual ceases to be a qualifying employee of the scheme organiser (or of a constituent company in a group scheme) because of injury, disability, redundancy or retirement. For options exercised before 9 April 2003, this exception did not apply, and the income tax exemption further depended on the condition that the individual concerned had not within the last three years (other than earlier that same day) exercised an option under the scheme or under another approved CSOP scheme and obtained the tax exemption. Special rules apply in cases of death.

Only full-time directors (generally taken to mean those working at least 25 hours per week) are eligible. For schemes approved after 30 April 1995, or altered accordingly after that date, part-time employees (other than directors) may be included. Where the company is a close company, employees and directors with material interests are excluded.

It is a condition of approval that the aggregate market value (at the time of grant) of shares over which an individual may hold unexercised rights under the scheme (and any other approved CSOP scheme established by the company or an associated company) must at no time exceed £30,000.

[*ITEPA 2003, ss 521–526, Sch 4, Sch 7 paras 73–76; ICTA 1988, ss 185, 187, Sch 9; FA 1996, s 114, Sch 16; FA 2003, Sch 21 paras 13–18, Sch 22 paras 32–35*); *FA 2004, s 88(7)*; *ITTOIA 2005, Sch 1 para 619*].

See Tolley's Income Tax for the full provisions and conditions for approval.

Capital gains tax. Where the income tax exemption on exercise of the option applies (see above), the provisions of *TCGA 1992, s 17* (see 41.1 MARKET VALUE) are specifically disapplied both in calculating the CGT acquisition cost of the shares to the employee and for the purposes of any corresponding disposal to him. Those provisions are likewise disapplied where an option is exercised following the death of the employee in accordance with a rule included in the scheme by virtue of *ITEPA 2003, Sch 4 para 25*. [*TCGA 1992, Sch 7D para 13; ICTA 1988, s 185(3)(b); ITEPA 2003, Sch 6 para 221*]. Where, exceptionally, an income tax liability arises on the grant of the option (due to the option price being discounted — see above), the amount counted as employment income is included in the cost of acquisition of the shares for CGT purposes. This applies whether or not the exercise is in accordance with the provisions of the scheme and whether or not the scheme is still approved at the time of the exercise. [*TCGA 1992, s 120(2)(6)(c), Sch 7D para 12; ICTA 1988, s 185(7); FA 1996, s 114(7)(8); ITEPA 2003, Sch 6 paras 210(7), 221*]. Thus, on a disposal of the shares by the employee, his allowable expenditure within *TCGA 1992, s 38(1)(a)* (see 15.4(*a*) COMPUTATION OF GAINS AND LOSSES) consists of

- the actual consideration given on the exercise of the option,
- any consideration given for the option itself (or, for options granted before 28 November 1995, the market value, if any, of the option at the time it was granted — see 20.3 above), and
- the amount, if any, counting as employment income.

The date of acquisition of the shares for CGT purposes is the date the option is exercised. Any deemed expenditure corresponding to an amount chargeable to income tax is also deemed to have been incurred on that date.

20.28 **Executive share option schemes** were superseded by CSOP schemes in relation to (broadly) options granted on or after 17 July 1995. See 20.27 above for the new plans and for transitional provisions.

The executive share option scheme rules differed from the current rules for CSOP schemes in the following respects.

(*a*) The aggregate market value (at the time of grant) of shares over which an individual could hold unexercised rights under the scheme (and any other approved share option scheme, other than a SAYE scheme, established by the company or an associated company) could at no time exceed the greater of £100,000 and four times his emoluments (as defined).

(*b*) Subject to certain conditions being fulfilled, and with effect after 31 December 1991, the scheme could contain provision for the option price (i.e. the price at which shares may be acquired) to be set at 85% (at least) of the market value of the shares at the time of grant.

Where the conditions referred to in (*b*) above were fulfilled and the scheme contained the appropriate provision, an income tax charge on grant of the option arose only if the aggregate of the option price and any consideration for the option itself was less than 85% of the then market value of the shares.

[*ICTA 1988, ss 185, 187, Sch 9; FA 1991, s 39*].

Capital gains tax. The same comments apply as for CSOP schemes in 20.27 above. [*TCGA 1992, s 120(2)(6)(a)(b); ICTA 1988, s 185(7); FA 1991, s 39*].

20.29 APPROVED PROFIT SHARING SCHEMES

Approved profit sharing schemes are being **phased out** following the introduction of share incentive plans (see 20.19 above). Applications for approval of new schemes, accompanied by necessary particulars, had to be received by the Revenue before 6 April 2001, and no appropriations of shares to employees under approved schemes may be made after 31 December 2002. [*ICTA 1988, s 186(1); FA 2000, s 49*]. Approval is withdrawn if shares are appropriated to a participant who has already had *free shares* appropriated to him in the same tax year under an approved share incentive plan established by the same company (or by a 'connected company', as defined) (or to a participant who would have had such shares appropriated to him but for his failure to meet set performance targets). [*ICTA 1988, Sch 9 para 3(2)(4)–(6); FA 2000, s 51*].

Otherwise, under a profit sharing scheme approved by the Revenue, a company provides funds to trustees who use them to acquire ordinary shares in the company for appropriation free-of-charge to employees of the company or group. The scheme *must* be available on similar terms (subject to any variations by reference to salary level, period of service etc.) to all employees and full-time directors within Schedule E, Case I (i.e. within what is now *ITEPA 2003, ss 15* or *21*) and with a stipulated minimum period of service, which cannot be more than five years. It *may* be made available to other employees and directors with at least 18 months' service. Where the company is a close company, those with material interests are excluded. The limit on the market value of shares which may be appropriated to any one individual in any tax year is the greater of £3,000 and 10% of salary (excluding benefits and net of pension contributions) for that year or, if greater, the preceding year, subject to a ceiling of £8,000.

There is no income tax charge on the appropriation of shares to an eligible employee (the participant) nor on the transfer of shares to him after three years. On a disposal before the third anniversary of the date of appropriation (the release date), the 'locked-in value' counts as employment income of the participant, chargeable to income tax for the tax year of disposal. The '*locked-in value*' is normally the market value of the shares at date of appropriation (less any capital receipts previously giving rise to an income tax charge — see below) or, if less, the disposal proceeds. The charge is reduced to 50% of the locked-in value if the disposal follows the cessation of employment due to injury, disability, redundancy or on reaching a specified retirement age of between 60 and 75. Before 29 April 1996, the release date was the fifth anniversary of the date of appropriation but the normal charge was reduced to 75% of the locked-in value if the disposal occurred between the fourth and fifth anniversaries. Where an appropriation of shares is made to a non-eligible employee or in excess of the permitted limit (see above), an income tax charge arises at the earlier of the date of disposal, the release date or the employee's death and is on the market value at that time.

[*ICTA 1988, ss 186, 187, Schs 9, 10*].

There is also an income tax charge on any capital receipts (e.g. proceeds of a sale of rights) between date of appropriation and release date. The charge varies according to the length of time that has elapsed since appropriation. [*ICTA 1988, s 186(3)(12), Sch 10 para 4; FA 1996, s 118*].

See Tolley's Income Tax for the full provisions and conditions for approval.

20.30 **Capital gains tax.** Notwithstanding any period of retention or other restriction imposed by an approved profit sharing scheme, the participant who has shares appropriated to him in pursuance of such a scheme is treated as absolutely entitled as against the trustees for CGT purposes. [*TCGA 1992, s 238(1)(3)*]. The date of the participant's acquisition of the shares for CGT purposes is the date of appropriation. By virtue of *TCGA 1992, s 17* (see 41.1 MARKET VALUE), the participant's acquisition cost is the market value of the shares at the date of appropriation (HMRC Capital Gains Manual CG 56478). On a disposal of the shares, neither this acquisition cost nor the proceeds are adjusted to take account of any amount chargeable to income tax as in 20.29 above in relation to the shares at that or any earlier time. [*TCGA 1992, s 238(2)(a); ITEPA 2003, Sch 6 para 215*].

The fact that a capital receipt may have been charged to income tax under the provisions in 20.29 above does not prevent its being a capital distribution within *TCGA 1992, s 122* (see 58.10 SHARES AND SECURITIES). [*TCGA 1992, s 238(2)(b)*].

Part disposals of scheme shares acquired at different times are subject to the normal IDENTIFICATION RULES (59) notwithstanding anything to the contrary in the income tax provisions. [*TCGA 1992, s 238(2)(c)*]. For as long as the shares remain subject to restrictions on their disposal, i.e. until the release date (see 20.29 above), they are regarded as a separate holding as compared to other shares of the same class in the same company held by the participant. [*TCGA 1992, s 104(4); FA 1998, s 123(4)*]. Thus, scheme shares cannot be pooled with non-scheme shares before 6 April 1998 and disposals of scheme shares cannot be identified with acquisitions of non-scheme shares (and *vice versa*) on or after that date. See 59.2, 59.4 SHARES AND SECURITIES — IDENTIFICATION RULES. See also HMRC Capital Gains Manual CG 56480.

Shares acquired through an approved profit sharing scheme may be transferred without CGT consequences to an Individual Savings Account (see 22.29 EXEMPTIONS AND RELIEFS), or, before 6 April 1999, to a single company PEP (see 58.18 SHARES AND SECURITIES), subject to the annual subscription limits for those investment vehicles (applied by reference to market value transferred) and provided the transfer is made within 90 days after the shares leave the scheme.

Trustees. The appropriation of shares to participants is a disposal by the trustees. However, no chargeable gain (or allowable loss) arises to the extent that shares are appropriated within a period of 18 months beginning with the date of their acquisition by the trustees. For the purpose of deciding whether or not this condition has been met, shares are deemed to be appropriated on a first in/first out basis. [*TCGA 1992, s 238(2)(d); ICTA 1988, s 186(11)*]. Following appropriation, the trustees act as bare trustees (see 57.2 SETTLEMENTS) for the participant, so the eventual transfer of the shares to the participant does not constitute a disposal (HMRC Capital Gains Manual CG 56482).

20.31 EMPLOYEE SHARE OWNERSHIP TRUSTS

Under provisions contained in *FA 1989, ss 67–74, Sch 5*, payments made by a UK resident company in an accounting period beginning before 1 January 2003 to a 'qualifying employee share ownership trust' (broadly, a trust set up to acquire shares in a company and distribute them to employees of that company) are, subject to conditions, deductible for corporation tax purposes. On the happening of a 'chargeable event', any tax relief given to the company is clawed back by means of an income tax charge on the trustees of the trust, and if they fail to pay the tax it can be recovered from the company. The relief is abolished for payments in accounting periods beginning on or after 1 January 2003 by *FA 2003, s 142*, in consequence of the introduction of the general corporation tax relief for employee share acquisition in *FA 2003, s 141, Sch 23* (see Tolley's Corporation Tax). An employee share ownership trust and its beneficiaries do not qualify for any special income tax or CGT reliefs, but may be used in conjunction with an approved SAYE share option scheme (see 20.26 above) or an approved profit sharing scheme (see 20.29 above). See Tolley's Income Tax under Share-Related Employment Income and Exemptions for the detailed provisions.

20.32 **Rollover relief on disposals of shares to a trust.** On a disposal of shares, or an interest in shares, **before 6 April 2001** to a qualifying employee share ownership trust, a relief in the form of a rollover of a chargeable gain applies subject to the detailed conditions below. The relief is abolished for disposals on or after that date by *FA 2000, s 54*.

The relief given under *TCGA 1992, s 229(1)* below is available where the following conditions are met.

(*a*) The claimant makes a disposal of, or of his interest in, shares to the trustees of a trust which is a 'qualifying employee share ownership trust' at the time of the disposal and which was established by a company (the 'founding company') which, immediately after the disposal, was a 'trading company' or the 'holding company' of a 'trading group'.

(*b*) The shares are fully paid up, not redeemable, form part of the 'ordinary share capital' of the founding company, and are not subject to any restrictions other than those which attach to all shares of the same class or are authorised by *FA 1989, Sch 5 para 7(2)*.

(*c*) At any time in the 'entitlement period', the trustees are beneficially entitled to at least 10% of the 'ordinary share capital' of the founding company and of any 'profits available for distribution to equity holders' therein, and would be beneficially entitled to at least 10% of any of the founding company's 'assets available for distribution to equity holders' on a winding-up.

(*d*) The claimant obtains consideration for the disposal and, at any time in the 'acquisition period', applies all (but see below under *TCGA 1992, s 229(2)(3)*) the consideration in acquiring assets ('replacement assets') (or an interest therein) which are, immediately thereafter, 'chargeable assets' in relation to the claimant and which are not shares in, or debentures issued by, the founding company or a company which, at the time of the acquisition, is in the same 'group' as the founding company. The requirement that the consideration be applied in the 'acquisition period' is satisfied if the acquisition is made pursuant to an unconditional contract entered into in that period.

(*e*) At all times in the 'proscribed period', there are no 'unauthorised arrangements' under which the claimant or a person connected with him may be entitled to acquire any of the shares, or an interest in or right deriving from any of the shares, which are the subject of the disposal by the claimant.

(*f*) No 'chargeable event' occurs in relation to the trustees in the chargeable period(s) in which the claimant makes the disposal and acquisition or in any other chargeable period between those of the disposal and the acquisition, 'chargeable period' meaning year of assessment or (if the claimant is a company) claimant company accounting period.

[*TCGA 1992, s 227*].

Where relief is available as above, the claimant may, within two years of the acquisition, claim that, for the purposes of *TCGA 1992*, the disposal be treated as made at a no gain/no loss consideration (if it otherwise would be greater), the consideration for the acquisition being treated as reduced by the excess of the actual consideration for the disposal over that no gain/no loss consideration. [*TCGA 1992, s 229(1)*].

Partial relief is available on a claim made within the same time limit where part only of the consideration for the disposal is applied as under (*d*) above and the amount of the consideration not so applied is less than the gain (whether all chargeable gain or not) accruing on the disposal. In such a case, the amount of the gain on the disposal is treated as reduced to the amount of the consideration not so applied, and the consideration for the acquisition is treated as reduced by the reduction so made to the amount of the gain. [*TCGA 1992, s 229*(*2*)(*3*)].

The other parties to the disposal and acquisition are not affected by such claims for relief. Any provision of *TCGA 1992* fixing deemed consideration for a disposal or acquisition is applied before the above adjustments are made. [*TCGA 1992, s 229*(*4*)(*5*)].

For the purposes of *TCGA 1992, s 227* above, the following applies.

(A) The '*entitlement period*' is the period beginning with the disposal and ending twelve months after the date of the disposal.

(B) The '*acquisition period*' is the period beginning with the disposal and ending six months after the date of the disposal or, if later, the date on which the condition at (*c*) above first becomes fulfilled.

(C) The '*proscribed period*' is the period beginning with the disposal and ending on the date of the acquisition or, if later, the date on which the condition at (*c*) above first becomes fulfilled.

(D) Arrangements are '*unauthorised arrangements*' unless either they arise wholly from a restriction authorised by *FA 1989, Sch 5 para 7*(*2*), or they only allow, as regards shares, interests or rights, acquisition by a beneficiary under the trust and/or appropriation under an approved profit sharing scheme (within *ICTA 1988, Sch 9*).

(E) An asset is a '*chargeable asset*' at a particular time in relation to the claimant if

(i) he is at that time resident or ordinarily resident in the UK and, were the asset to be disposed of at that time, a gain accruing to him would be a chargeable gain; or

(ii) were it to be disposed of at that time, any gain accruing to him would be a chargeable gain under *TCGA 1992, s 10*(*1*) or form part of his corporation tax profits under *TCGA 1992, s 10*(*3*) or *s 10B* (see 45.3 OVERSEAS MATTERS),

but not if, were he to dispose of it at that time, double tax relief arrangements under *ICTA 1988, s 788* (as extended to CGT by *TCGA 1992, s 277*) would render him not liable to UK tax on any gain accruing to him on the disposal.

(F) '*Qualifying employee share ownership trust*' has the same meaning as under *FA 1989, Sch 5*, and '*chargeable event*' in relation to the trustees has the same meaning as under *FA 1989, s 69*.

(G) '*Holding company*', '*trading company*' and '*trading group*' have the same meanings as under *TCGA 1992, Sch 6 para 1* (see 53.3 RETIREMENT RELIEF); and '*group*' (except in the expression 'trading group') is construed in accordance with 27.1 GROUPS OF COMPANIES, with the change in the residence requirement there mentioned having effect in relation to disposals on or after 1 April 2000.

(H) '*Ordinary share capital*' means all issued share capital other than that carrying a right to a dividend at a fixed rate but with no other right to share in profits.

(J) As regards the condition at (*c*) above, the provisions of *ICTA 1988, Sch 18* (suitably adapted) apply as appropriate.

[*TCGA 1992, s 228, s 288*(*1*); *FA 2000, Sch 29 para 33, Sch 40 Pt II*(*11*); *FA 2003, s 155, Sch 27 para 2*(*3*)].

20.33 *Chargeable event when replacement assets owned.* Where

(*a*) relief under *TCGA 1992, s 229*(*1*) or (*3*) is given as in 20.32 above,

(*b*) a 'chargeable event' in relation to the trustees (within *FA 1989, s 69* as amended) occurs on or after the date on which the disposal is made,

(*c*) the claimant was neither an individual who died before the occurrence of the chargeable event nor trustees of a settlement which ceased to exist before that occurrence, and

(*d*) at the time of the occurrence of the chargeable event, the claimant or a person connected with him (within *TCGA 1992, s 286*) is beneficially entitled to all the replacement assets acquired as under 20.32(*d*) above,

the claimant or the connected person (as the case may be) is deemed, immediately before the occurrence of the chargeable event, to have disposed of, and immediately reacquired, all the replacement assets at the 'relevant value'.

The '*relevant value*' is such value as secures on the deemed disposal a chargeable gain equal to the amount of the gain carried forward by virtue of *TCGA 1992, s 229*(*1*) or (*3*), i.e. the amount by which the consideration for the acquisition was treated as reduced as a result of a claim for that relief to apply.

Where only a part of the replacement assets falls within 20.32(*d*) above, there is a deemed disposal and reacquisition of that part, the relevant value being reduced as is just and reasonable.

An adjustment may be made where there is a deemed disposal and reacquisition under these provisions, and before the occurrence of the chargeable event it can be said that, because of something which has happened as regards any of the replacement assets, a charge has accrued in respect of any gain carried forward as a result of relief having been given under *TCGA 1992, s 229*(*1*) or (*3*). In these circumstances, the deemed disposal and reacquisition rules apply, if it is just and reasonable, as if the relevant value either were such value as secures that the deemed disposal produces neither gain nor loss (if that is just and reasonable), or, unless it produces a lower value, were reduced to whatever value is just and reasonable.

[*TCGA 1992, s 232*].

Where a charge can be said, on a just and reasonable basis, to accrue by virtue of a deemed disposal as above in respect of any of the gain carried forward by virtue of *TCGA 1992, s 229*(*1*) or (*3*), so much of the gain charged is not to be capable of being carried forward for the purposes of ROLLOVER RELIEF (55) under *TCGA 1992, ss 152–158*. For the purposes of ROLLOVER RELIEF (55.5) under *TCGA 1992, s 154* (new assets which are depreciating assets), a charge will arise under that provision by reference to the earlier of the disposal of the replacement asset, the deemed disposal of it under the above and the expiration of ten years beginning with the acquisition of the replacement asset. [*TCGA 1992, s 154*(*3*), *s 236*(*1*)(*2*)].

20.34 *Chargeable event when replacement property owned.* Where

(*a*) the conditions described in 20.33(*a*)–(*c*) above are fulfilled,

(*b*) before the time when the chargeable event occurs all the gain carried forward by virtue of *TCGA 1992, s 229*(*1*) or (*3*) (see 20.32 above) was in turn carried forward from all the replacement assets to other property by virtue of a claim for ROLLOVER RELIEF (55) to apply under *TCGA 1992, ss 152–158*, and

(*c*) at the time of the occurrence of the chargeable event, the claimant or a person then connected with him (as above) is beneficially entitled to all the property, the claimant or the connected person (as the case may be) is deemed, immediately before the occurrence of the chargeable event, to have disposed of, and immediately reacquired, all the property at the 'relevant value'.

The '*relevant value*' is as defined for *TCGA 1992, s 232* in 20.33 above.

Where the conditions at (*b*) and (*c*) above were satisfied as regards only part of the gain carried forward, the replacement assets from which it was in turn carried forward or the beneficial entitlement to the property into which it was further carried forward, there is a deemed disposal and reacquisition of the property concerned, the relevant value being reduced as is just and reasonable.

An adjustment may be made where there is a deemed disposal and reacquisition under these provisions, and before the occurrence of the chargeable event it can be said that, because of something which has happened as regards any of the replacement assets or any other property, a charge has accrued in respect of any gain carried forward by virtue of *TCGA 1992, s 229*(*1*) or (*3*). In these circumstances, the deemed disposal and reacquisition rules apply, if it is just and reasonable, as if the relevant value either were such value as secures that the deemed disposal produces neither gain nor loss (if that is just and reasonable), or, unless it produces a lower value, were reduced to whatever value is just and reasonable.

[*TCGA 1992, s 233*].

Where a charge can be said to accrue, on a just and reasonable basis, by virtue of a deemed disposal as above in respect of any of the gain carried forward by virtue of *TCGA 1992, s 229*(*1*) or (*3*), so much of the gain charged is not to be capable of being carried forward for the purposes of ROLLOVER RELIEF (55) under *TCGA 1992, ss 152–158*. [*TCGA 1992, s 236*(*1*)(*2*)].

20.35 ***Chargeable event when qualifying corporate bonds owned.*** Where

(*a*) the conditions described in 20.33(*a*)–(*c*) above are fulfilled,

(*b*) all the replacement assets were shares in a company or companies (referred to below as 'new shares'),

(*c*) there has been a transaction within *TCGA 1992, s 116*(*10*) (see 50.3 QUALIFYING CORPORATE BONDS) as regards which all the new shares constitute the 'old asset' and qualifying corporate bonds constitute the 'new asset', and

(*d*) at the time of the occurrence of the chargeable event, the claimant or a person then connected with him (as above) is beneficially entitled to all the bonds,

a chargeable gain of the 'relevant amount' is deemed to have accrued to the claimant or the connected person (as the case may be) immediately before the time when the chargeable event occurs.

The '*relevant amount*' is the lesser of the 'first amount' and the 'second amount'.

The '*first amount*' is the amount of the chargeable gain that would be deemed to accrue under *TCGA 1992, s 116*(*10*)(*b*) if there were a disposal of all the bonds at the time the chargeable event occurs (or nil if an allowable loss would arise). The '*second amount*' is the relevant value as for *TCGA 1992, s 232* in 20.33 above.

Where the conditions at (*b*), (*c*) and (*d*) above were satisfied as regards only part of the replacement assets, the new shares constituting the old asset or the bonds to which there is beneficial entitlement, a chargeable gain is nevertheless deemed to arise as above, but the first amount is determined only by reference to the bonds concerned, the second amount is reduced as is just and reasonable, and the relevant amount is reduced accordingly.

An adjustment may be made where a chargeable gain arises as above, and before the occurrence of the chargeable event it can be said that, because of something which has happened as regards any of the new shares or any of the bonds, a charge has accrued in respect of any gain carried forward by virtue of *TCGA 1992, s 229(1)* or (*3*) (see 20.32 above). In these circumstances, the chargeable gain is, if it is just and reasonable, calculated as if the second amount were reduced as is just and reasonable (but not so as to reduce it below nil) and the relevant amount reduced (if appropriate) accordingly.

[*TCGA 1992, s 234*].

Where a charge arises as above in the case of qualifying corporate bonds and subsequently a chargeable gain accrues under *TCGA 1992, s 116(10)(b)* on a disposal of them (see above), the chargeable gain is reduced by the relevant amount or (if the amount exceeds the gain) reduced to nil. The relevant amount is apportioned for this purpose where the subsequent disposal is of only some of the bonds. [*TCGA 1992, s 236(3)(4)*].

20.36 *Dwelling-houses: special provisions.* As regards 20.32(*d*) above, a replacement asset which is a dwelling-house (or part thereof) or land is not treated (where it would otherwise be so treated) as being a chargeable asset in relation to the claimant immediately after the asset's acquisition if on a disposal of it (or an interest in it) at some time in the period from its acquisition to the time a claim is made under *TCGA 1992, s 229(1)* or (*3*) (see 20.32 above), the PRIVATE RESIDENCES (49.1) exemption of *TCGA 1992, s 222(1)* would apply to the asset (or interest in it) and the 'individual' (which includes references to a person entitled to occupy the dwelling-house etc. under the terms of a settlement; see 49.5 PRIVATE RESIDENCES) mentioned in *TCGA 1992, s 222(1)* would be the claimant or his spouse or civil partner.

A similar treatment applies retrospectively where the replacement asset is a dwelling-house etc. which would otherwise be a chargeable asset in relation to the claimant immediately after its acquisition and which becomes eligible for the private residences exemption at some time after a claim under *TCGA 1992, s 229(1)* or (*3*) is made. In such a case, any gain thereby treated as having accrued is deemed not to have accrued until the time (or the earliest time) on which a disposal of the dwelling-house would be within the private residences exemption.

Similar provisions apply in relation to a replacement asset which is an option to acquire (or to acquire an interest in) a dwelling-house and the application of the private residences exemption in the period from the exercise of the option and the time of claim, and subsequent to the time of claim, respectively.

[*TCGA 1992, s 230; SI 2005 No 3229, Reg 119*].

20.37 *Shares qualifying for EIS relief: special provisions.* As regards 20.32(*d*) above, a replacement asset which consists of shares is not treated (where it would otherwise be so treated) as being a chargeable asset in relation to the claimant immediately after the asset's acquisition if at some time in the period from its acquisition to the time a claim is made under *TCGA 1992, s 229(1)* or (*3*) (see 20.32 above) Enterprise Investment Scheme (EIS) income tax relief (see 21.2 ENTERPRISE INVESTMENT SCHEME) is claimed in respect of it.

A similar treatment applies retrospectively where the replacement asset consists of shares which would otherwise be a chargeable asset in relation to the claimant immediately after their acquisition and EIS relief is claimed at some time after a claim under *TCGA 1992, s 229(1)* or (*3*) is made.

Similar provisions applied as regards relief under the Business Expansion Scheme for shares issued before 1 January 1994 (see 22.20 EXEMPTIONS AND RELIEFS).

[*TCGA 1992, s 231; FA 1994, s 137, Sch 15 para 34*].

20.38 *Information powers.* The Inspector may, by notice in writing, require a return containing specified information by the trustees of an employee share ownership trust (within *FA 1989, Sch 5*) where a disposal of shares (or an interest therein) has been made to them and a claim is made under *TCGA 1992, s 229(1)* or (*3*) (see 20.32 above). The information specified must be needed for the purposes of *TCGA 1992, ss 232–234* (see 20.33–20.35 above), and may include information about: expenditure incurred by the trustees (including the purpose of the expenditure and the recipients); assets acquired by them (including the persons from whom the assets were acquired and the consideration); and transfers of assets made by them (including the persons to whom they were transferred and the consideration). Penalties under *TMA 1970, s 98* apply for failure to comply with a notice. Where relief has been given by virtue of *TCGA 1992, s 229(1)* or *(3)*, the Inspector must send to the trustees a certificate that it has been given, stating the effect on the consideration for the disposal or on the gain accruing on the disposal. [*TCGA 1992, s 235*].

20.39 PRIORITY ALLOCATIONS IN PUBLIC SHARE OFFERS

If a benefit derived by an employee from a priority allocation of shares in a public offer is exempted from income tax by *ITEPA 2003, ss 542* or *544* (previously *FA 1988, s 68*) (see Tolley's Income Tax under Employment Income), the usual MARKET VALUE (41) rules do not apply and the allowable expenditure for CGT on a disposal of the shares is the consideration given. [*TCGA 1992, s 149C; FA 1988, s 68(4); ITEPA 2003, Sch 6 para 212*].

20.40 DOUBLE TAX RELIEF

Where an employee is internationally mobile, a tax charge may arise both in the UK and in another country when a share option is exercised, assigned or released. An article in the Revenue Tax Bulletin October 2001 pp 883–887 sets out the HMRC practice for dealing with possible double taxation in the most common scenarios. The article is concerned with options granted under unapproved schemes and those granted under one of the approved schemes where the circumstances are such that a UK income tax charge nevertheless arises.

The article is concerned primarily with the income tax aspects, but does consider the position of an employee who is not resident and not ordinarily resident in the UK when an option is granted, moves to the UK and exercises the option whilst performing the duties of the employment there, and then disposes of the shares. There would normally be no UK income tax charge in such a case but there may well be a CGT charge on the disposal, i.e. under general principles. Strictly, the exercise of the option and the disposal of the shares are distinct events and the UK is not obliged to grant relief against UK CGT for any foreign tax paid on the grant or exercise of, or otherwise in connection with, the option. However, where such foreign tax is that of a country with which the UK has a double tax agreement (see 19.2 DOUBLE TAX RELIEF), HMRC will by concession allow a proportion of the foreign tax as a credit against the UK CGT liability on all or part of the gain depending on the circumstances — see p 886 of the Tax Bulletin for more details.

21 Enterprise Investment Scheme

Cross-references. See 20.23, 20.37 EMPLOYEE SHARE SCHEMES for restriction on rollover relief arising from disposal of shares to, respectively, an approved share incentive plan and, before 6 April 2001, an employee share ownership trust, where replacement asset is shares and a claim for EIS income tax relief is made; 58 SHARES AND SECURITIES; 66 VENTURE CAPITAL TRUSTS.

Simon's Direct Tax Service. See Division C3.10.

The headings in this chapter are as follows.

21.1 INTRODUCTION

The Enterprise Investment Scheme (EIS) offers income tax relief to a qualifying individual to whom eligible shares (see 21.4 below) in a qualifying company (see 21.5 below) have been issued after 31 December 1993 by subscription. The company concerned must use the money raised within the specified time limit for a qualifying business activity (see 21.6 below). See 21.2(*a*) below.

For more detailed coverage of the income tax provisions, see Tolley's Income Tax under Enterprise Investment Scheme. As regards both income tax and CGT, see also HMRC Venture Capital Schemes Manual VCM 10000 *et seq.*

See 21.9 below re capital gains deferral relief.

From 25 September 2000, a new centralised service became operational for companies newly raising money under the EIS. All enquiries about whether a company meets the requirements should be made to Small Company Enterprise Centre, Ty Glas, Llanishen, Cardiff, CF14 5ZG (Tel. 029 2032 7400; fax 029 2032 7398; e-mail: enterprise.centre@ir.gsi.gov.uk). This initial point of contact is supported by specialist HMRC units that also deal with the corporation tax affairs, and the monitoring, of such companies as well as companies raising money under other types of venture capital scheme or granting options under enterprise management incentives. (Revenue Press Release 25 September 2000).

21.2 INCOME TAX RELIEF

Conditions for relief. A qualifying individual (see 21.3 below) is eligible for income tax relief under the Enterprise Investment Scheme (EIS) if

(*a*) eligible shares (see 21.4 below) in a qualifying company (see 21.5 below) for which he has subscribed are issued to him

(*b*) he subscribes for the shares (other than, for shares issued after 16 March 2004, any of them which are 'bonus shares') wholly in cash (and see below),

(*c*) for shares issued after 5 April 1998, the shares are fully paid up (see below) at the time of issue (other than, for shares issued after 16 March 2004, any of them which are bonus shares), (*d*) those shares (other than, for shares issued after 16 March 2004, any of them which are bonus shares) are issued to raise money for the purpose of a qualifying business activity (see 21.6 below),

(*e*) the money raised by the issue of the shares and all other eligible shares in the company of the same class issued on the same day (or, for shares issued after 5 April 1998 and before 17 March 2004, the money raised by the issue of the shares and all other shares comprised in the same issue) is employed wholly (disregarding insignificant amounts) for that purpose by the end of the 24 months following the issue or, if the only qualifying business activity falls within 21.6(*a*) below, and if later, by the end of the 24 months starting when the company (or subsidiary) began to carry on the qualifying trade (see 21.6 below), and 80% of that money is so employed within 12 months after the issue/commencement of trade. This applies after 6 March 2001; previously, *all* the money had to be so employed within 12 months after the issue/ commencement of trade, and

(*f*) the condition as to the person carrying on the required activity is met (see below).

'*Bonus shares*' are shares issued otherwise than for payment, whether in cash or otherwise.

The requirement in (*b*) above that the shares are subscribed for wholly in cash is explicit in the legislation only for shares issued after 5 April 1998. However, HMRC would consider it implicit in the legislation that shares issued before 6 April 1998 also had to be issued for a money consideration and not for money's worth, and that view was supported by the Court in the BES case of *Thompson v Hart Ch D 2000, 72 TC 543*.

Shares issued after 16 March 2004 are not fully paid up for the purposes of (*c*) above if there is any undertaking to pay cash to any person in respect of the acquisition of the shares at a future date. In determining whether shares issued before 17 March 2004 are fully paid up, any undertaking to pay cash to the company at a future date is disregarded.

In relation to shares issued after 5 April 1998 and before 17 March 2004, the requirement in (*d*) above is that the shares in question, *and all other shares comprised in the same issue*, are issued to raise money for the purpose of a qualifying business activity.

In relation to shares issued after 16 March 2004, in determining for the purposes of (*e*) above when a qualifying trade is begun to be carried on by a subsidiary, any carrying on of the trade by it before it became a qualifying 90% subsidiary (see below) is disregarded.

The application of (*d*) and (*e*) above was considered in *4Cast Ltd v Mitchell (Sp C 455), [2005] SSCD 287.*

[*ICTA 1988, s 289(1)(3)(3A)(8A), s 312(1); FA 1994, Sch 15 para 2; FA 1998, Sch 13 para 1(1); FA 2001, Sch 15 paras 6, 40; FA 2004, s 93, Sch 18 paras 1(2)(5)–(7), 11(2), 21*].

Person carrying on required activity. In relation to shares issued after 16 March 2004, the required qualifying trade or preparations for the trade (see 21.6(*a*) below) or any 'relevant research and development' must not be carried on at any time in the relevant period (as defined in 21.6 below) by any person other than the qualifying company or a 'qualifying 90% subsidiary' of that company. This requirement is not, however, treated as not met

(i) by reason only of the carrying on of the qualifying trade by a person other than the qualifying company or a qualifying 90% subsidiary at a time when such a company has not yet carried on the trade but is preparing to do so; or

(ii) if, by reason only of anything done as a consequence of any company being in administration or receivership (both as defined by *ICTA 1988, s 312(2A)*) or of any company being wound up or dissolved without winding-up, the qualifying trade ceases to be carried on in the relevant period (as in 21.6 below) by the qualifying company or any of its qualifying 90% subsidiaries and is subsequently carried on within that period by any person who is not connected (within *ICTA 1988, s 839*) with the qualifying company at any time in the 'period of restriction' (defined as in 21.12

below). The winding-up etc. or the entry into, and everything done as a consequence of being in, administration or receivership must be for genuine commercial reasons and not part of a tax avoidance scheme or arrangement.

For this purpose, '*relevant research and development*' means research and development within 21.6(*b*) below which is the subject of the qualifying business activity in (*d*) above and any other preparations for the carrying on of the qualifying trade which is the subject of that activity. A subsidiary is a '*qualifying 90% subsidiary*' of another company if

(*aa*) that company possesses at least 90% of both the issued share capital of, and the voting power in, the subsidiary, and is beneficially entitled to at least 90% of the assets available for distribution to equity holders on a winding-up etc. (see *ICTA 1988, Sch 18 paras 1, 3*) and of the profits available for distribution to equity holders,

(*bb*) no other person has control (within *ICTA 1988, s 840*) of the subsidiary, and

(*cc*) no arrangements exist whereby (*aa*) or (*bb*) could cease to be satisfied.

The provisions of *ICTA 1988, s 308(3)(3A)(4)* described at 21.5 below which deal with the winding-up, administration and disposal of qualifying subsidiaries apply to qualifying 90% subsidiaries as they apply to qualifying subsidiaries.

In relation to shares issued before 17 March 2004, the 'active company' must, throughout the relevant period (as defined in 21.6 below), either:

(I) exist wholly for the purpose of carrying on one or more 'qualifying trades' (see 21.6 below) (disregarding purposes incapable of having any significant effect on the company's activities); or

(II) fall within (I) above if the company's purposes were disregarded to the extent that they consist

- in holding shares in or securities of, or making loans to, any of the company's subsidiaries, or
- in holding and managing property used by the company or any of its subsidiaries either for research and development (as defined) from which a qualifying trade (see 21.6 below) to be carried on by any of them is intended to be derived, or for the purposes of a 'qualifying trade' or trades carried on by any of them, or
- in making loans to the parent company; or

(III) be a '90% subsidiary' of the qualifying company which either

- apart from purposes capable of having no significant effect (other than on incidental matters) on the extent of its activities, exists wholly for the purpose of carrying on activities consisting in holding and managing property used by the company or any of its subsidiaries either for research and development (as defined) from which a qualifying trade to be carried on by any of them is intended to be derived, or for the purposes of a qualifying trade or trades carried on by any of them, or
- has no corporation tax profits and no part of its business consists in the making of investments.

Although a winding-up or dissolution in the 'relevant period' (as in 21.6 below) generally prevents a company meeting these requirements, they are deemed met if the winding-up or dissolution is for *bona fide* commercial reasons and not part of a scheme a main purpose of which is tax avoidance, with the additional proviso before 21 March 2000 that any net assets are distributed to members (or dealt with as *bona vacantia*) before the end of the relevant period or (if later) the end of three years from the commencement of winding-up. After 20 March 2000 (both in relation to shares issued after that date and to pre-existing shares to which EIS income tax relief or capital gains tax deferral relief remains attributable), a company does not cease to meet the above conditions by reason of anything done as a consequence of its being in administration or receivership (both as defined by *ICTA 1988, s 312(2A)*), provided everything so done and the making of the relevant order are for *bona fide* commercial (and not tax avoidance) reasons.

The '*active company*' is the qualifying company unless the qualifying business activity consists in a subsidiary of the qualifying company carrying on or preparing to carry on a qualifying trade, research and development or, before 7 March 2001, oil exploration, in which case it is that subsidiary. Due to a defect in *Finance Act 1998*, it was sufficient as regards shares issued after 5 April 1998 and before 6 April 1999 for the active subsidiary to be a 75% subsidiary of the qualifying company (except for the purpose of satisfying condition (III) above). As regards shares issued after 5 April 1999, reverting to the rules for those issued before 6 April 1998, it must be a '90% subsidiary'. A '*90% subsidiary*' is a subsidiary that would satisfy the conditions for a qualifying subsidiary given at 21.5 below, as they apply for shares issued before 17 March 2004, if references to 90% were substituted for references to 75% and the let-out for *bona fide* commercial disposals of interests in the subsidiary were disregarded.

[*ICTA 1988, s 289(1A)–(1E)(9)–(13), s 312(1)(2)(2A); FA 1997, Sch 8 paras 1, 2; FA 1998, s 74, Sch 13 para 1(2)(5); FA 1999, s 71; FA 2000, Sch 17 para 9(2)(4), paras 12, 15; FA 2001, Sch 15 paras 2(a), 40; FA 2004, Sch 18 paras 1(3)(8), 21*].

Method of relief. On the making of a claim (see 21.7 below), EIS income tax relief is given in the year of assessment in which the subscription is made. The relief is given as a reduction from the individual's income tax liability, the reduction being equal to the smaller of tax at the lower rate (currently 20%) of the amount subscribed for the shares (subject to (*c*) below) and the amount which reduces the tax liability to nil. For the purposes of calculating an individual's total tax liability, EIS income tax relief is given before any other reliefs or allowances granted in terms of tax except for top-slicing relief on chargeable event gains and Venture Capital Trust relief (see HMRC Venture Capital Schemes Manual VCM 25400). [*ICTA 1988, s 289A(1)(2)(5); FA 1994, s 137(1)(2), Sch 15 para 2; FA 2002, s 57, Sch 17 para 2*].

Income tax relief is said to be attributable to EIS shares if a reduction has been made in the individual's income tax liability in respect of them, and that relief has not been fully withdrawn. [*ICTA 1988, s 289B(1); FA 1994, s 137(1)(2), Sch 15 para 2*].

Example

W is a married man who on 2 January 2007 subscribes £20,000 for 20,000 EIS shares in E Co Ltd. His pension income for the year ended 5 April 2007 amounts to £60,000. PAYE deducted amounts to £15,499.00. He has no other sources of income. W and his wife were born on 27 April 1943 and 25 September 1934 respectively.

W's 2006/07 income tax liability is calculated as follows:

	£
Pension Income	60,000
Less Personal Allowance	5,035
Taxable Income	£54,965

Tax Liability			£
	£2,150	@ 10%	215.00
	£31,150	@ 22%	6,853.00
	£21,665	@ 40%	8,666.00
	£54,965		15,734.00
Less EIS relief £20,000 @ 20%			4,000.00
			11,734.00
Less Married Couple's Allowance (minimum) £2,350 @ 10%			235.00
Income tax liability			11,499.00
Less PAYE deducted			15,499.00
Income tax repayment due			£4,000.00

Maximum and minimum amounts. The respective total maximum and minimum amounts per tax year on which income tax relief is granted to an individual are £400,000 (£200,000 before 2006/07, £150,000 as regards shares issued before 6 April 2004 and £100,000 as regards shares issued before 6 April 1998) and £500 respectively. The relief is granted for the tax year in which the shares were issued. [*ICTA 1988, s 290(1)(2); FA 1994, Sch 15 paras 1, 3; FA 1998, s 74, Sch 13 para 4; FA 2004, Sch 18 para 4; FA 2006, Sch 14 para 6, Sch 26 Pt 3(17)*]. The individual will obtain Form EIS 3 from the EIS company for the purposes of making the claim. Where the shares in the company are issued between 6 April and 5 October inclusive in any year the investor can request that up to one half of those shares be treated as being issued in the previous tax year, subject to an overall limit of £50,000 (£25,000 as regards shares issued before 6 April 2006 and £15,000 as regards shares issued before 6 April 1998) on the amount of subscriptions which may be so treated. [*ICTA 1988, s 289A(3)(4); FA 1994, s 137(1)(2), Sch 15 paras 1, 2; FA 1998, s 74, Sch 13 para 2; FA 2006, Sch 14 para 5, Sch 26 Pt 3(16)*].

Approved investment funds. Income tax relief for investments made through approved investment funds is due in the year of assessment in which the fund closes and should be claimed on Form EIS 5 obtainable from the fund manager. For any fund closing before 6 October the investor may treat part of the investment as relating to the previous year as described in (*c*) above. [*ICTA 1988, s 311(2B); FA 1994, s 137(1)(2), Sch 15 para 26*].

Issue of shares. Shares or debentures shall be treated as issued if they are included in a letter of allotment or similar instrument except in circumstances where the allotment is dependent upon acceptance and such acceptance is not obtained. [*TCGA 1992, s 288(5)*].

Withdrawal of relief on disposal. Where the investor disposes of EIS shares before the end of the 'relevant period' (as in 21.3 below), EIS income tax relief given falls to be withdrawn. This does not apply on a transfer to the investor's spouse or civil partner made at a time they are living together; the transferee stands in the shoes of the transferor as regards any subsequent disposal. If a disposal is not made by way of bargain at arm's length, the relief is fully withdrawn in all cases. Otherwise, the relief given is fully withdrawn unless it is greater than tax at the lower rate (for the tax year for which the relief was given) on the amount or value of the consideration received on disposal, in which case only the lower amount is withdrawn. [*ICTA 1988, s 299(1)–(3), s 304; FA 1994, Sch 15 paras 12, 18; FA 1998, s 74, Sch 13 para 12(1)(2)(8), para 16; SI 2005 No 3229, Reg 65*]. Withdrawal is given effect by income tax assessment for the tax year for which the relief was given (under Schedule D, Case VI for 2004/05 and earlier years). [*ICTA 1988, s 307(1); ITTOIA 2005, Sch 1 para 127*]. Disposals are identified with acquisitions on a first in/first out (FIFO) basis, and for disposals after 5 April 1998 further rules apply as to the order in which shares acquired on the same day are deemed to be disposed of where only some of those shares have attracted income tax relief and/or CGT deferral relief (see 21.9 below). These rules are the same as those described at 21.8 below (under 'Identification rules') for CGT purposes. [*ICTA 1988, s 299(6)–(6D); FA 1998, Sch 13 para 12(5)(6)(8); FA 2002, Sch 9 paras 4(2), 8(1)*]. A share exchange is treated as a disposal for these purposes (HMRC Venture Capital Schemes Manual VCM 26030), unless it occurs after 5 April 1998 and is within *ICTA 1988, s 304A* — see 21.5 below. For further details and for other circumstances in which EIS income tax relief falls to be withdrawn, see Tolley's Income Tax.

Loan-linked investments. An individual is not eligible for income tax relief in respect of EIS shares if there is a loan made by any person at any time in the 'relevant period' (as in 21.3 below) to that individual or to an associate of his, and the loan would not have been made (or would not have been made on the same terms) if the individual had not subscribed for the shares or had not been proposing to do so. The giving of credit, and the assignment of a debt due from the individual or an associate, are also caught by these provisions. [*ICTA 1988, s 299A; FA 1993, s 111(1)(4); FA 1994, Sch 15 para 13*]. For HMRC's views on loan-linked investments, see HMRC Statement of Practice 6/98.

Pre-arranged exits. In relation to shares issued after 1 July 1997, an individual is not eligible for income tax relief in respect of EIS shares if arrangements (as very broadly defined) under which the shares are issued to him (or arrangements preceding the issue but relating to it)

- provide for the eventual disposal by the investor of the shares in question or other shares or securities of the company; or
- provide for the eventual cessation of a trade of the company or of a person connected with it; or
- provide for the eventual disposal of all, or a substantial part of, the assets of the company or of a person connected with it; or
- provide (by means of any insurance, indemnity, guarantee or otherwise) complete or partial protection for investors against the normal risks attaching to EIS investment (but excluding arrangements which merely protect the company and/or its subsidiaries against normal trading risks).

Certain types of arrangements, i.e. those applicable only on an unanticipated winding-up of the company for commercial reasons and those for certain share exchanges not counted as a disposal by the investor, are excluded from the above.

[*ICTA 1988, ss 299B, 312(1); FA 1998, s 71(1)(5); FA 2000, Sch 17 para 14, Sch 40 Pt II(5)*].

21.3 QUALIFYING INDIVIDUAL

Unconnected with the company. The individual must be unconnected with the company throughout the designated period (as regards shares issued before 6 April 1998 at any time in the 'relevant period') and must subscribe for the shares on his own behalf. Relief is not available to individuals acting in the capacity of trustees.

The designated period for these purposes is

- (for shares issued after 5 April 2000) the period beginning two years before the issue of the shares and ending immediately before the third anniversary of the issue date or, if later and where relevant, the third anniversary of the date of commencement of the intended trade referred to in 21.6(*a*) below; or
- (for shares issued before 6 April 2000) the seven-year period beginning two years before the issue of the shares.

The '*relevant period*' for the purposes of this and certain other specified EIS provisions is the period beginning with the incorporation of the company or, if later, two years before the date of issue of the shares and ending

- (for shares issued after 5 April 2000, where relevant) immediately before the third anniversary of the issue date or, if later and where relevant, the third anniversary of the date of commencement of the intended trade referred to in 21.6(*a*) below; or
- (for shares issued before 6 April 2000) five years after the issue date.

[*ICTA 1988, s 291(1)(5)(6), s 312(1)(1A)(a); FA 1994, s 137(1)(2), Sch 15 paras 1, 5; FA 1998, s 74, Sch 13 para 6(1)(4); FA 2000, Sch 17 paras 2, 6(2)–(4), para 8; FA 2001, Sch 15 paras 10, 40, Sch 33 Pt II(3)*].

Residence. There is no requirement for the individual to be UK resident and ordinarily resident at the time the shares are issued but EIS relief is only available against income chargeable to UK income tax.

Circumstances in which an individual/director may be connected with the company. An individual is connected with the issuing company if he or an 'associate' of his is

- employed by the company (or a subsidiary) or by a partner of the company (or of a subsidiary);
- a partner of the company (or a subsidiary); or
- (subject to what is said below) a director of the company (or a subsidiary) or of a company which is a partner of the company (or of a subsidiary);

and see also the provisions of *ICTA 1988, s 291B* outlined below.

References above to a subsidiary are to any company which is a 51% subsidiary of the issuing company at any time in the 'relevant period' (see (*a*) above) regardless of whether or not the individual etc. was an employee etc. at that particular time.

[*ICTA 1988, s 291(2)–(5), s 312(1)(1A)(a); FA 1994, s 137(1)(2), Sch 15 paras 1, 5; FA 1998, s 74, Sch 13 para 6(2)(3), Sch 27 Pt III(14); FA 2000, Sch 17 para 6(3)(4), para 8*].

If the individual or his associate is a director he will *not* be regarded as connected with the company unless the company or a related person (as defined) makes or accrues a payment to him (or to his associate or his or his associate's partnership) during the designated period — see (*a*) above (as regards shares issued before 6 April 1998, the 'relevant period' — see (*a*) above). The following normal business expenditure is disregarded for this purpose:

- reimbursement of travelling or other expenses wholly, exclusively and necessarily incurred by the individual or his associate in the performance of the individual's duties as a director;
- interest at a commercial rate for money lent to the company;
- distributions at a reasonable return for the investment;
- payment for use of goods at a commercial rate;
- rent for any property occupied by the issuing company and related person that does not exceed a reasonable and commercial rent;
- remuneration at a reasonable rate for services supplied by the director in the course of a trade or profession carried on wholly or partly in the UK, excluding secretarial or managerial services, which is taken into account in computing for tax purposes the profits of that trade or profession.

A director who receives reasonable remuneration *can* receive EIS relief if, when the shares are issued,

- he has never been connected with the issuing company, and
- he has never been involved (as sole trader, employee, partner or director) in carrying on its (or its subsidiary's) trade (or any part thereof) (in relation to shares issued before 6 April 1998, he has never been an employee of a person who had previously carried on the issuing company's trade).

If additional EIS shares are issued within three years (five years for shares issued before 6 April 2000) after the previous EIS issue these new shares will also qualify for relief. Where relevant, and in relation only to shares issued after 5 April 2000, the said three-year period is replaced by a longer period beginning with the date of the last such issue and ending with the third anniversary of the date of commencement of the intended trade referred to in 21.6(*a*) below.

[*ICTA 1988, ss 291A, 312(1)(1A)(a); FA 1994, s 137(1)(2), Sch 15 paras 1, 5; FA 1998, s 74, Sch 13 para 7, Sch 27 Pt III(14); FA 2000, Sch 17 paras 3, 6(2)–(4), para 8; FA 2001, Sch 15 paras 11, 40; ITTOIA 2005, Sch 1 para 126*].

Individuals who own or are entitled to acquire more than 30% of the issued ordinary share capital, loan capital, voting power or the assets available to equity holders on a winding-up are deemed to be connected with the company. [*ICTA 1988, s 291B(1)–(3); FA 1994, s 137(1)(2), Sch 15 paras 1, 5*]. For this purpose, the interests of an individual and his associates fall to be aggregated (*Cook v Billings & Others CA 2000, [2001] STC 16*, a BES case which is nevertheless considered relevant to the EIS as the wording of the disputed provisions is identical). An individual is also connected if he controls the voting power by holding a majority of shares or has the power granted to him in the Articles of Association or other document [*ICTA 1988, s 291B(4); FA 1994, s 137(1)(2), Sch 15 paras 1, 5*]. Bank overdrafts arising in the normal course of banking business are not treated as loan capital for this purpose. [*ICTA 1988, s 291B(9)*]. An individual is not connected with the company by virtue only of the fact that he or an associate is a shareholder if at that time the company has issued no shares other than subscriber shares and has neither commenced business nor made preparations for doing so. [*ICTA 1988, s 291B(5A); FA 1998, s 74, Sch 13 para 8*]. This applies by statute in relation to shares issued after 5 April 1998, but a similar exclusion previously applied by concession (ESC A76 now withdrawn).

'*Associate*' for the above purposes has the same meaning as *ICTA 1988, s 417(3)(4)* except that a 'relative' does not include a brother or sister. [*ICTA 1988, s 312(1)*]. See Tolley's Corporation Tax under Close Companies.

21.4 ELIGIBLE SHARES

Types of share. The shares must be new ordinary shares issued for *bona fide* commercial purposes and not as part of a scheme or arrangement the main purpose of which is the avoidance of tax. Throughout the three years beginning with the date of issue (five years for shares issued before 6 April 2000) the shares must carry no present or future preferential right to dividends or to a company's assets on its winding up and no present or future right (for shares issued before 6 April 1998, present or future preferential right) to redemption. If, for shares issued after 5 April 2000, the company satisfied the qualifying business activity requirement by virtue of 21.6(*a*) below and the trade had not yet commenced on the issue date, this condition must be satisfied throughout the period from date of issue to immediately before the third anniversary of commencement. [*ICTA 1988, s 289(6)(7), s 312(1); FA 1994, s 137(1)(2), Sch 15 paras 1, 2; FA 1998, s 74, Sch 13 para 1(3)(4), Sch 27 Pt III(14); FA 2000, Sch 17 paras 1, 6(3), para 8*]. Shares are not issued until the company's register of members has been completed. (*National Westminster Bank plc v CIR; Barclays Bank plc v CIR HL 1994, 67 TC 1* and see Revenue Tax Bulletin June 1995 p 217).

Permitted maximum. As regards shares issued before 6 April 1998, there was a restriction on the total amount of eligible shares which could be issued by a company within a specified period (see below) and attract relief. Where the money raised in such a period exceeded £1m (£5m in the case of certain shipping concerns) the excess did not qualify for relief. The period specified was the longer of

(*a*) six months ending with the date of issue of the shares, and

(*b*) the period from the preceding 6 April to the date of issue.

Amounts raised which did not attract relief because the subscriber was not a qualifying individual (see 21.3 above), or had exceeded his personal limit or invested under the permitted minimum (see 21.2(*c*) above), or because of an earlier application of these provisions, were not taken into account for the purposes of this restriction.

There were provisions which reduced the limit where the issuing company or a subsidiary carried on a trade in partnership, or as a joint venture, with other companies.

Where the application of the permitted maximum restricted the amount of relief available to two or more individuals, the total relief available was apportioned amongst them according to the respective amounts subscribed for shares giving rise to the restriction and which would otherwise be eligible for the relief.

The permitted maximum is abolished as regards shares issued after 5 April 1998.

[*ICTA 1988, s 290A; FA 1988, s 51(1); FA 1994, Sch 15 para 4; FA 1997, Sch 8 paras 1, 3; FA 1998, s 74, Sch 13 para 5, Sch 27 Pt III(14)*].

21.5 QUALIFYING COMPANY

A '*qualifying company*' may be resident in the UK or elsewhere. It must, throughout the 'relevant period' (defined as in 21.6 below), either

(*a*) exist wholly for the purpose of carrying on one or more 'qualifying trades' (see 21.6 below) (disregarding purposes incapable of having any significant effect on the company's activities), or

(*b*) be 'the parent company of a trading group'.

The above conditions are not considered to be breached by reason only of the winding-up or dissolution of the company (or, in relation to shares issued after 16 March 2004, any of its subsidiaries), or anything done after 20 March 2000 as a consequence of it (or, in relation to shares issued after 16 March 2004, any of its subsidiaries) being in administration or receivership, provided certain conditions are met.

Before 7 March 2001, it was also a condition that the company be 'unquoted' throughout the 'relevant period' (as in 21.6 below). This is replaced by a condition that it be 'unquoted' at the beginning of the said period (i.e. when the shares are issued) and that no arrangements then exist for it to cease to be unquoted. If, at the time of issue, arrangements exist for the company to become a wholly-owned subsidiary of a new holding company by means of a share exchange within *ICTA 1988, s 304A* (see below), no arrangements must exist for the new company to cease to be unquoted. A company is '*unquoted*' if none of its shares etc. are listed on a recognised stock exchange (see 58.23 SHARES AND SECURITIES) or designated foreign exchange, or dealt in outside the UK by such means as may be designated. Securities on the Alternative Investment Market ('AIM') are treated as unquoted for these purposes. (Revenue Press Release 20 February 1995). If the company is unquoted at the time of the share issue, it does not cease to be unquoted in relation to those shares solely because they are listed on an exchange which becomes a recognised stock exchange or is designated by an order made after the date of issue.

The '*parent company of a trading group*' is a company all of whose subsidiaries are 'qualifying subsidiaries' provided that, in relation to the business consisting of the activities, taken together, of the company and its subsidiaries, neither the business nor a 'substantial part' of it consists in either or both of

(I) excluded activities within 21.6(A)–(M) below, and

(II) non-trading activities (not including, as regards shares issued after 5 April 1998, research and development (as defined) and, before 7 March 2001, oil exploration).

Activities are for this purpose disregarded to the extent that they consist (*a*) in holding shares in or securities of, or making loans to, any of the company's subsidiaries, or (*b*) in holding and managing property used by the company or any of its subsidiaries either for research and development (as defined) from which a 'qualifying trade' (see 21.6 below) to be carried on by any of them is intended to be derived, or for the purposes of a 'qualifying trade' or trades carried on by any of them. They are similarly disregarded to the extent that they consist in making loans to the company or, in the case of a 'mainly trading subsidiary' (as defined), in activities not in pursuance of its main purpose.

During the debates on the 1997 Finance Bill, the Government stated that a '*substantial part*' means 80% of the business activity (HC Official Report, Standing Committee B (Twelfth sitting), cols 418, 419).

The company must not at any time in the 'relevant period' (defined as in 21.6 below) either

(i) (in relation to shares issued before 6 April 1998) have share capital which includes any issued shares not fully paid up (or which would not be fully paid up if any undertaking to pay cash to the company at a future date were disregarded), or

(ii) control another company other than a 'qualifying subsidiary' (see below), 'control' being construed in accordance with *ICTA 1988, s 416(2)–(6)* and being considered with or without connected persons within *ICTA 1988, s 839*, or

(iii) be a 51% subsidiary of another company or otherwise under the control of another company, 'control' being construed in accordance with *ICTA 1988, s 840* (after 20 March 2000, previously in accordance with *ICTA 1988, s 416(2)–(6)*) and again being considered with or without connected persons, or

(iv) be capable of falling within (ii) or (iii) by virtue of any arrangements (as very broadly defined).

The above is subject to provisions in *ICTA 1988, s 304A* (inserted by *FA 1998, Sch 13 para 17*) which enable an EIS company to become, after 5 April 1998, a wholly-owned subsidiary of a new holding company in certain circumstances. The investors receive shares in the new company in exchange for their original shares, and the new shares then stand in the shoes of the old for the purposes of EIS income tax relief. See Tolley's Income Tax for details.

Gross assets test. This test applies in relation to shares issued after 5 April 1998. The value of the company's gross assets must not exceed £7 million immediately before the issue of EIS shares and must not exceed £8 million immediately afterwards. For shares issued before 6 April 2006 or subscribed for before 22 March 2006 the limits were £15 million immediately before the issue and £16 million immediately afterwards. The latter limits continue to apply in relation to shares issued on or after 6 April 2006 to the managers of an approved investment fund (see 21.2 above) as nominee for an individual investor provided that the fund was approved before 22 March 2006 and investments in the fund have been accepted before 6 April 2006.

If the company has 'qualifying subsidiaries', the test applies by reference to the aggregate gross assets of the company and all such subsidiaries (disregarding certain assets held by any such company which correspond to liabilities of another).

HMRC's approach is that the value of a company's gross assets at any time is the aggregate of the values of its assets (without any deduction for liabilities) as would be shown in a balance sheet drawn up as at that time. Any advance payment received for the share issue itself is ignored immediately before the issue but the right to the unpaid portion of shares issued partly paid is taken as included in gross assets immediately after the issue. See HMRC Statement of Practice 2/00.

As regards shares issued after 16 March 1998, any of the above provisions may be amended by Treasury Order.

[*ICTA 1988, s 293, s 298(4), s 312(1)–(1E); FA 1994, Sch 15 para 7; FA 1997, Sch 8 paras 1, 4; FA 1998, s 70(2)(4), s 74, Sch 13 paras 9, 23, Sch 27 Pt III(14); FA 2000, Sch 17 para 9(1)(4), paras 10–12, 14, 15; FA 2001, Sch 15 paras 4, 12–14, 40; FA 2004, Sch 18 paras 5(1)–(5), Sch 27 para 4(2); FA 2006, Sch 14 para 1*].

Land and buildings. Subject to an exemption for small issues, there was an additional exclusion if at any time during the relevant period (defined as in 21.6 below) and before 29 November 1994, the value of the company's 'interests in land' exceeded half the value of all its assets. See Tolley's Income Tax for full details.

Advance assurance. A company may submit its proposals for using the EIS to the inspector who normally deals with its tax affairs. If satisfied as to the purposes for which the money raised will be used, the company's status as a qualifying company and the eligibility of the shares to be issued under the proposals, the inspector may grant advance assurance, of which investors may be informed, although in the end the question of whether the company qualifies for the scheme is one of fact which cannot be determined in advance. Any assurance supplied to a company can only be given on the basis of the information provided and the inspector is under no obligation to check the accuracy of that information. No assurance as to the availability of relief to a particular subscriber can be given either to the company or to the subscriber in question. (HMRC Venture Capital Schemes Manual VCM 21010–21040). From 25 September 2000, requests for informal advance assurance are dealt with by the Small Company Enterprise Centre (see 21.1 above).

Subsidiaries. The existence of certain subsidiaries in the 'relevant period' (defined as in 21.6 below) does not prevent the parent being a qualifying company. The conditions imposed on any such subsidiary (a '*qualifying subsidiary*') are that:

(i) in relation to shares issued after 16 March 2004, the subsidiary is a 51% subsidiary (within *ICTA 1988, s 838*) of the qualifying company,

(ii) in relation to shares issued before 17 March 2004, the qualifying company, or another of its subsidiaries, must possess at least 75% (90% in relation to EIS shares issued before 6 April 1998) of both the issued share capital and the voting power, and be beneficially entitled to at least 75% (90% in relation to EIS shares issued before 6 April 1998) of the assets available for distribution to equity holders on a winding-up etc. (see *ICTA 1988, Sch 18 paras 1, 3*) and of the profits available for distribution to equity holders,

(iii) no other person may have control (within *ICTA 1988, s 840*) of the subsidiary, and

(iv) no arrangements (as very broadly defined) may exist whereby (i), (ii) or (iii) would cease to be satisfied.

The conditions must continue to be satisfied until the end of the relevant period, except that the winding-up or dissolution, during that period, of the subsidiary, the qualifying company or, in relation to shares issued after 16 March 2004, any other company does not prevent those conditions being satisfied, provided that the winding-up meets certain conditions. Likewise, in relation to shares issued after 16 March 2004, the fact that a subsidiary or any other company goes into administration or receivership (both as defined) does not mean that the subsidiary ceases to be a qualifying subsidiary provided that the entry into, and everything done as a consequence of being in, administration or receivership is for genuine commercial reasons and is not part of a tax avoidance scheme or arrangements. The above conditions are also not regarded as ceasing to be satisfied by reason only of the disposal of the interest in the subsidiary within the relevant period if it is to be for *bona fide* commercial reasons and is not to be part of a tax-avoidance scheme.

In relation to shares issued after 16 March 2004, the parent company must not have a 'property managing subsidiary' other than one which is its qualifying 90% subsidiary (see 21.2 above). For this purpose, a '*property managing subsidiary*' is a subsidiary whose business consists wholly or mainly in the holding or managing of land or any property deriving its value from land (and the terms 'land' and 'property deriving its value from land' have the same meaning as in 38.4 LAND).

[*ICTA 1988, s 293(3)(6ZA)–(6ZC), ss 308, 312(1); FA 1994, Sch 15 paras 23, 24; FA 1997, Sch 8 paras 1, 6; FA 1998, s 74, Sch 13 para 21; FA 2000, Sch 17 paras 14, 15; FA 2004, Sch 18 paras 5(6), 9, 21*].

21.6 QUALIFYING BUSINESS ACTIVITY

Any of the following is a '*qualifying business activity*' (see 21.1 above) in relation to the issuing company, provided that, at any time in the 'relevant period' (see below) when it is carried on, it is carried on wholly or mainly in the UK.

(*a*)

(i) In relation to shares issued after 16 March 2004, the issuing company or any 'qualifying 90% subsidiary' (see 21.2 above) of that company

- carrying on a 'qualifying trade' (see below) which the company or any such subsidiary is carrying on on the date of issue of the shares, or
- preparing to carry on or carrying on such a trade which, on the date of issue of the shares, is intended to be carried on wholly or mainly in the UK by the company or any such subsidiary and which is begun to be carried on by the company or any such subsidiary within two years after that date. For this purpose, any carrying on of a trade by a subsidiary before it became a qualifying 90% subsidiary is disregarded in determining when the trade commences.

(ii) In relation to shares issued before 17 March 2004, the issuing company or any 'qualifying subsidiary' (see 21.5 above) carrying on a 'qualifying trade' (see below) which it is carrying on on the date of issue of the shares, or preparing to carry on such a trade which, on the date of issue of the shares, it intends to carry on wholly or mainly in the UK and which it begins to carry on within two years after that date.

(*b*)

(i) In relation to shares issued after 16 March 2004, the issuing company or any qualifying 90% subsidiary carrying on research and development which the company or any qualifying 90% subsidiary is carrying on on the date of issue of the shares or begins to carry on immediately afterwards, and from which it is intended will be derived a 'qualifying trade' which the company or any such subsidiary will carry on wholly or mainly in the UK. For this purpose, any carrying on of research and development by a subsidiary before it became a qualifying 90% subsidiary is disregarded in determining when the research and development commences.

(ii) In relation to shares issued before 17 March 2004, the issuing company or any subsidiary carrying on either research and development (as defined) or, before 7 March 2001, oil exploration, which it is carrying on on the date of issue of the shares, or which it begins to carry on immediately afterwards, and from which it is intended will be derived a 'qualifying trade' which the company or a subsidiary will carry on wholly or mainly in the UK.

Note that, for shares issued after 16 March 2004, it is possible for the identity of the company carrying on the qualifying business activity to change during the relevant period. Under the previous rules, the same company had to be carrying on the activity throughout.

As regards (*a*) above, 'preparing' to carrying on a trade covers both the setting up of a new trade and the acquisition of an existing trade from its present owner. It does not cover preliminary activities such as market research aimed at discovering whether a trade would be likely to succeed or raising capital or research and development. (HMRC Venture Capital Schemes Manual VCM 20030). As regards (*b*) above, in relation to oil exploration, there were further conditions relating to exploration and appraisal or development licences.

In considering whether a trade is carried on '*wholly or mainly in the UK*', HMRC will take into account the totality of the activities of the trade; a company can satisfy the requirement if the major part of the trade, i.e. over half of the trading activity, taken as a whole, is carried on within the UK. See HMRC Statement of Practice 3/00. As to how the scheme operates where a company raises money by a single share issue for more than one qualifying business activity, see Revenue Tax Bulletin April 1996 pp 305, 306.

Relevant period. The '*relevant period*' for these purposes is the period beginning with the date of issue of the shares and ending three years after that date or, where (*a*) above applies and the company (or subsidiary) was not carrying on the 'qualifying trade' on that date, three years after the date on which it begins to carry on the trade.

[*ICTA 1988, s 289(2)(3A)(4)(5)(8), s 312(1)(1A)(b); FA 1994, Sch 15 para 2; FA 2000, Sch 17 para 6(4), paras 8, 15; FA 2001, Sch 15 paras 2(b)(c), 40; FA 2004, Sch 18 paras 1(4)(6), 21*].

Qualifying trades. To be a '*qualifying trade*' a trade may *not*, at any time in the relevant period (as defined above) consist to a substantial extent of, or of a combination of:

(A) dealing in land, commodities or futures, or in shares, securities or other financial instruments; or

(B) dealing in goods otherwise than in an ordinary trade of wholesale or retail distribution (see the similar exclusion at 66.3(*b*) VENTURE CAPITAL TRUSTS for further details); or

(C) banking, insurance or any other financial activities; or

(D) (before 7 March 2001) oil extraction activities (but without prejudice to relief in respect of oil exploration (see (*b*) above) for which the activities would otherwise qualify), or

(E) leasing or letting or receiving royalties or licence fees (see below re letting of ships, and see the similar exclusion at 66.3(*b*) VENTURE CAPITAL TRUSTS for further details as regards these items generally); or

(F) providing legal or accountancy services;

(G) 'property development' (see below);

(H) farming or market gardening;

(J) holding, managing or occupying woodlands, any other forestry activities or timber production;

(K) operating or managing hotels or comparable establishments (including guest houses, hostels and other establishments whose main purpose is to offer overnight accommodation with or without catering) or property used as such;

(L) operating or managing nursing homes or residential care homes (both as defined in *ICTA 1988, s 298(5)*) or property used as such;

(M) providing services or facilities for any trade, profession or vocation consisting to a substantial extent of activities within (A)–(L) above and carried on by another person (other than a parent company), where one person has a controlling interest (as defined) in both trades.

Exclusions (G)–(L) (and the reference to those in exclusion (M)) apply in relation to shares issued **after 16 March 1998**. Exclusions (K) and (L) apply only if the person carrying on the activity in question has an estate or interest (e.g. a lease) in the property concerned or occupies that property.

Adventures and concerns in the nature of trade, and trades not carried on commercially and with a view to the realisation of profits, are also generally excluded.

HMRC regard as 'substantial' for the above purposes a part of a trade which consists of 20% or more of total activities, judged by any reasonable measure (normally turnover or capital employed). (HMRC Venture Capital Schemes Manual VCM 17040).

'*Property development*' in (G) above means the development of land by a company, which has (or has had at any time) an 'interest in the land' (as defined by *ICTA 1988, s 298(5B)(5C)*), with the sole or main object of realising a gain from the disposal of an interest in the developed land.

As regards (E) above, a trade will not be excluded by reason only of its consisting of letting ships, other than pleasure craft (as defined) or, for shares issued on or after 6 April 2004, offshore installations (within *ICTA 1988, s 837C*) or, for shares issued before that date, oil rigs (as defined), on charter, provided certain conditions are satisfied.

[*ICTA 1988, ss 297, 298; FA 1994, Sch 15 paras 10, 11; FA 1997, Sch 8 para 5; FA 1998, s 70(1), Sch 12 paras 1, 2, 5(1); FA 2000, Sch 17 para 13; FA 2001, Sch 15 paras 5, 40; FA 2004, Sch 27 para 4(3)–(6)*].

As regards (F) above, the provision of accounting staff by a company to a firm of accountants was held to be synonymous with the provision of accountancy services, with the result that the company's trade was not a qualifying trade (*Castleton Management Service Ltd v Kirkwood (Sp C 276), [2001] SSCD 95*).

21.7 CLAIMS FOR RELIEF

A claim by the individual for EIS income tax relief cannot be made until the trade or other qualifying business activity has been carried on for at least four months. It cannot be made later than the fifth anniversary of 31 January following the tax year in which the shares were issued (or treated as issued, in a case where relief is carried back one year as in 21.2(*c*) above). A claim cannot be made until, with the authority of HMRC, the company has furnished the individual with a certificate (on form EIS 3) to the effect that, from its point of view, the conditions for the relief are satisfied. [*ICTA 1988, s 289A(6)–(8A), s 306; FA 1994, Sch 15 para 21; FA 1996, Sch 20 para 22, Sch 21 para 7; FA 1998, s 74, Sch 13 para 19, Sch 27 Pt III(14); FA 2000, Sch 17 para 9(3), para 12; FA 2001, Sch 15 paras 3, 22, 40; FA 2004, Sch 18 para 2*]. For more details, see Tolley's Income Tax.

21.8 CAPITAL GAINS TAX

See also 21.9 below re EIS deferral relief.

Gains arising on the disposal by the investor, after the end of the 'relevant period' (see below), of shares on which EIS income tax relief has been given are not chargeable gains. (There is no such exemption for shares disposed of before the end of the relevant period, and any EIS income tax relief given will be withdrawn — see 21.2 above.) Where EIS income tax relief was not given on the full amount subscribed for the shares (other than by reason of the income tax liability being insufficient to support the relief), the capital gains tax exemption is restricted to a proportion of the gain. Where this arises, it will usually be because the investor's EIS subscriptions exceeded the annual maximum on which relief is available (see 21.2 above). The exempt gain is the proportion of the gain (after any indexation allowance available) found by applying the multiple A/B where

A = the actual income tax relief given (expressed in terms of the reduction in the tax liability); and

B = tax at the lower rate (for the tax year for which EIS relief was given) on the amount subscribed for the issue.

The '*relevant period*' for these purposes is the period beginning with the incorporation of the company or, if later, two years before the date of issue of the shares and ending

- (for shares issued after 5 April 2000) immediately before the third anniversary of the issue date or, if later and where relevant, the third anniversary of the date of commencement of the intended trade referred to in 21.6(*a*) above; or

- (for shares issued before 6 April 2000) five years after the issue date.

[*TCGA 1992, s 150A(2)(3); ICTA 1988, s 312(1A)(a); FA 1994, Sch 15 paras 28–30; FA 1995, Sch 13 para 2(3); FA 1998, Sch 13 para 24(1)(8); FA 2000, Sch 17 paras 6(4), 8; SI 2005 No 3229, Reg 110*].

See *Example 1* below. See also 21.13 below for special taper relief rules where a gain on EIS shares is chargeable but is deferred by reinvestment in further EIS shares.

Losses. If a disposal of shares on which EIS income tax relief has been given results in a capital loss, the loss is allowable *regardless* of whether the disposal occurs within or without the 'relevant period' (see above). However, in calculating the loss, or in ascertaining whether a loss has indeed arisen, the cost of the shares for CGT purposes is reduced by the amount of EIS income tax relief attributable to the shares disposed of (expressed in terms of the reduction in the tax liability) to the extent that this has not been, or does not fall to be, withdrawn. See *Examples 2 & 3* below. The loss qualifies for relief against income, if claimed, under the provisions of *ICTA 1988, ss 574–576* (losses on shares in unlisted trading companies), which are specifically applied for these purposes — see 40.13 LOSSES.

[*TCGA 1992, s 150A(1)(2A); ICTA 1988, s 305A; FA 1994, Sch 15 paras 20, 28–30; FA 1995, Sch 13 para 2(2); FA 1998, Sch 13 paras 18, 24(1)(8)*].

Example 1

On 8 November 2006 P subscribes £675,000 for 450,000 shares in the EIS company, S Ltd, and obtains the maximum EIS income tax relief of £80,000 (£400,000 × 20%) for 2006/07. On 3 April 2011 he sells the entire holding for £1,395,000.

The chargeable gain arising is calculated as follows:

	£
Disposal proceeds	1,395,000
Cost	675,000
Gain	720,000
Less TCGA 1992, s 150A(3) exemption	
£720,000 x (£80,000(A)/£135,000(B))	426,667
Chargeable gain (subject to TAPER RELIEF (61))	£293,333

Note:

A = relief given (£400,000 × 20%)	£80,000
B = £675,000 × 20%	£135,000

Example 2

Assuming the facts are as in *Example 1* above except that the shares are sold for £450,000 on 3 April 2011.

The allowable loss arising is calculated as follows:

	£	£
Disposal proceeds		450,000
Less Cost	675,000	
Less income tax relief given (and not withdrawn)	80,000	595,000
Allowable loss		£145,000

Example 3

Assuming the facts are as in *Example 1* above except that the shares are sold on 3 April 2008 for £450,000. Income tax relief of £450,000 × 20% × 80,000/135,000 = £53,333 is withdrawn (see below). The balance of £26,667 is not withdrawn and is attributable to the shares sold.

	£	£
Disposal proceeds		450,000
Less Cost	675,000	
Less income tax relief given (and not withdrawn)	26,667	648,333
Allowable loss		£198,333

In calculating the EIS withdrawal, as not all the subscriber shares qualified for EIS income tax relief, the consideration must be reduced by applying the formula A/B, to the amount of the consideration received. [*ICTA 1988, s 299(4); FA 1994, Sch 15 para 12; FA 1998, s 74, Sch 13 para 12(3)(8)*]. For this purpose, A is the actual income tax reduction and B is the tax at the lower rate for that year on the amount subscribed for the issue, i.e. £450,000 × 80,000/135,000 = £266,667. The EIS relief withdrawn is then calculated on this result, i.e. £266,667 × 20% = £53,333.

See HMRC Venture Capital Schemes Manual VCM 31300 for an example involving a part disposal.

Identification rules. The normal pooling arrangements for shares acquired before 6 April 1998 (see 59.3, 59.4 SHARES AND SECURITIES—IDENTIFICATION RULES) and the normal identification rules for disposals on or after that date (see 59.2 SHARES AND SECURITIES—IDENTIFICATION RULES) are each disapplied as regards EIS shares. Instead, the rules described below apply to match disposals with acquisitions of shares of the same class in the same company, and they apply where at least some of those shares have attracted EIS income tax relief. Shares are not treated as being of the same class unless they would be so treated if dealt with on the Stock Exchange.

Disposals **after 5 April 1998** are identified with acquisitions on different days on a first in/first out (FIFO) basis. Shares transferred between spouses living together are treated as if they were acquired by the transferee spouse on the day they were issued. Shares comprised in a 'new holding' following a reorganisation to which *TCGA 1992, s 127* applies (including a case where it applies by virtue of any other chargeable gains enactment — see, for example, 58.1, 58.4, 58.6, 58.7 SHARES AND SECURITIES) are treated as having been acquired when the original shares were acquired. Where shares within two or more of the categories listed below were acquired on the same day, any of those shares disposed of (applying the FIFO basis) are treated as disposed of in the order in which they are listed, as follows:

- shares to which neither EIS income tax relief nor EIS deferral relief (see 21.9 below) is attributable;
- shares to which EIS deferral relief, but not EIS income tax relief, is attributable;
- shares to which EIS income tax relief, but not EIS deferral relief, is attributable;
- shares to which both of those reliefs are attributable.

Any shares within either of the last two categories which are treated as issued on an earlier day by virtue of the carry-back provisions at 21.2 above (under 'Maximum and minimum amounts') are to be treated as disposed of before any other shares within the same category.

Disposals before 6 April 1998 are identified with acquisitions on a FIFO basis.

[*TCGA 1992, s 150A(4)(5); ICTA 1988, s 299(6)–(6D)(8)(a), s 312(4B); FA 1994, Sch 15 paras 12, 28, 30; FA 1998, Sch 13 para 12(5)(7)(8), para 23(5), para 24(2)(3)(8), Sch 27 Pt III(14); FA 2002, Sch 9 para 4(2), 8(1)*].

The above rules are appropriately modified where an individual makes the election described at 59.2 SHARES AND SECURITIES — IDENTIFICATION RULES for alternative treatment of same-day acquisitions after 5 April 2002 and the shares covered by the election include EIS shares. [*TCGA 1992, s 105A(4)(7)(8); FA 2002, s 50*].

Reorganisations of share capital. Where EIS income tax relief has been given on some shares in a particular company but not others and there is a reorganisation (including a bonus issue) within the meaning of *TCGA 1992, s 126*, then *TCGA 1992, s 127* (see 58.1 SHARES AND SECURITIES) applies separately as regards the shares attracting and not attracting relief so that, in each case, the new shares will stand in the place of the old shares. For reorganisations taking effect after 5 April 1998, a distinction is also made, as regards shares attracting income tax relief, between those (if any) to which EIS deferral relief (see 21.9 below) is attributable and those to which it is not, and the separate treatment described above also applies to each of those two categories.

Rights issues. If, immediately following a rights issue, EIS relief is attributable either to the original holding or the rights shares, the share reorganisation rules of *TCGA 1992, ss 127–130* (see 58.1 SHARES AND SECURITIES) are disapplied, with the result that the rights shares are treated as a separate acquisition.

[*TCGA 1992, s 150A(6)(6A)(7); FA 1994, Sch 15 paras 28, 30; FA 1998, Sch 13 para 24(4)(8)*].

Special rules applied to reduce the EIS relief given where a rights issue occurred before 29 November 1994 and the market value of the shares immediately afterwards was less than both the market value immediately before the rights issue and the amount subscribed for the shares. The rules applied *mutatis mutandis* where the individual sold his rights instead of taking up his allotment. [*ICTA 1988, s 305; FA 1995, s 66(4)*]. In any case where these rules have applied, an amount equal to the reduction made is added to the cost for CGT purposes of the allotted shares and deducted from the cost for CGT purposes of the original shares, in each case being apportioned between shares in a just and reasonable manner. [*TCGA 1992, s 150A(9); FA 1994, Sch 15 paras 28, 30; FA 1996, Sch 20 para 54*].

Company reconstructions. If as part of a reconstruction, shares or debentures in another company are issued to an EIS shareholder in exchange for EIS shares to which income tax relief remains attributable, then the shares in the new company are not generally deemed to stand in the place of shares in the old company under *TCGA 1992, s 135* or *s 136* (see 58.4, 58.6 SHARES AND SECURITIES) and there is thus a disposal of the shares in the old company. However, *section 135* or *136* does apply in the normal way if

- the new holding consists of new ordinary shares issued after 28 November 1994 and after the end of the 'relevant period' (as defined above under Gains and applied by reference to the original shares and the company which issued them) and carrying no present or future preferential rights to dividends or assets or right to redemption (no preferential right to redemption where the new shares were issued before 6 April 1998); and

- the company issuing the new shares has previously issued shares under the EIS and has issued the appropriate certificate (see 21.7 above) enabling investors to obtain relief on that earlier issue.

In addition, *TCGA 1992, s 135* is not disapplied in a case to which *ICTA 1988, s 304A* (inserted by *FA 1998, Sch 13 para 17*) applies. That provision enables an EIS company to become, after 5 April 1998, a wholly-owned subsidiary of a new holding company in certain circumstances. The investors receive shares in the new company in exchange for their original shares, and the new shares then stand in the shoes of the old for the purposes of EIS income tax relief. This treatment is generally applied for CGT purposes also. See Tolley's Income Tax for details.

[*TCGA 1992, s 150A(8)(8A)–(8D); FA 1994, Sch 15 paras 28, 30; FA 1995, Sch 13 para 2(4); FA 1998, Sch 13 para 24(5)(6)(8), Sch 27 Pt III(14)*].

Reduction of relief where value received etc. Where a gain on disposal of EIS shares would otherwise be exempt due to their having been held until after the end of the 'relevant period' (see above), a special rule applies if EIS income tax relief has been, or falls to be, reduced (though not fully withdrawn) as a result of either or both of the following events occurring before the disposal and after 28 November 1994:

- the investor receives value from the company within the meaning of *ICTA 1988, s 300* (see Tolley's Income Tax);

- there is a repayment, redemption, repurchase or payment in circumstances within *ICTA 1988, s 303* (see Tolley's Income Tax).

The CGT exemption applies only to so much of the gain as remains after deducting so much of it as is represented by the fraction X/Y where

X = the reduction(s) made, as mentioned above, to the income tax relief given, and

Y = the income tax relief given before applying such reductions.

Where the CGT exemption has already been restricted because EIS income tax relief was not given on the full amount subscribed for the shares (see above), the fraction is applied to the part of the gain otherwise exempt and the deduction made from that part.

[*TCGA 1992, s 150B; FA 1995, Sch 13 para 3; FA 1998, Sch 13 para 25, Sch 27 Pt III(14)*].

Example 4

On 9 November 2006, Q subscribed for 20,000 EIS £1 shares at par in H Ltd. The EIS relief given was £4,000. On 2 January 2008 he received £2,000 from the company, as a result of which EIS relief of £2,000 @ 20% = £400 is withdrawn under *ICTA 1988, s 300(1B)*. In June 2011, the shares were sold for £60,000.

The CGT computation is as follows:

	£
Disposal consideration	60,000
Less Cost	20,000
Gain	£40,000
Chargeable gain (subject to TAPER RELIEF (61))	
$£40,000 \times \frac{400}{4,000}$ (TCGA 1992, s 150B)	£4,000
Exempt gain (balance)	£36,000

If only £3,000 EIS relief were given (say because the investor was also given £77,000 EIS relief on another investment in 2006/07, the maximum relief for that year being £80,000) the relief withdrawn would be 3,000/4,000 × £2,000 × 20% = £300 (see *ICTA 1988, s 300(1B)* applying *ICTA 1988, s 299(4)*).

The chargeable gain restriction would be calculated in two stages:

Gain as above	£40,000
Stage 1 (*TCGA 1992, s 150A(3)* restriction)	
Gain exempt:	
$£40,000 \times \frac{3,000}{4,000}$	£30,000
Gain chargeable (balance)	£10,000

Stage 2 (*TCGA 1992, s 150B* restriction)

	Exempt £	Chargeable £
Gain chargeable as above		10,000
Gain otherwise exempt	30,000	
Reduced by value received		
$£30,000 \times \frac{300}{3,000}$	(3,000)	3,000
Total chargeable gain (subject to TAPER RELIEF (61))		£13,000
Exempt gain	£27,000	

21.9 EIS: CAPITAL GAINS DEFERRAL RELIEF

Introduction. General reinvestment relief was available for reinvestment into qualifying shares acquired before 6 April 1998 (see 22.81 EXEMPTIONS AND RELIEFS) but relief under those rules for reinvestment into shares on which EIS income tax relief is claimed was prohibited by *TCGA 1992, s 164MA*. However, a specific relief was introduced by *FA 1995, s 67, Sch 13 para 4*(*3*) whereby any chargeable gain accruing after 28 November 1994 could be deferred to the extent that it could be matched with an investment in EIS shares to which income tax relief (see 21.2 above) was attributable.

In relation to EIS shares issued after 5 April 1998, significant changes were made to the deferral relief provisions. In particular, it is no longer a requirement that the shares qualify for income tax relief nor that the individual be unconnected with the company. The provisions are also extended to trustees. These changes are intended to compensate for the abolition of general reinvestment relief. There is no limit on the amount of the gain that can be deferred under the new provisions (previously the income tax relief annual maximum at 21.2 above would have applied), but the gross assets test at 21.5 above does limit the amount that may be invested in any one EIS company (or group).

The main provisions of the revamped EIS deferral relief are described at 21.10 below, with further provisions at 21.12 below. Their application to trustees is covered at 21.11 below. Special rules on the application of taper relief in certain cases are dealt with at 21.13 below. The provisions as they related to shares issued before 6 April 1998 are described at 21.14 below.

Deferral relief is attributable to any EIS shares if expenditure on them has been used to defer the whole or part of any gain and there has been no chargeable event (see 21.10 and 21.14 below) in relation to those shares resulting in the deferred gain being brought back into charge. [*TCGA 1992, Sch 5B para 19*(*2*)].

21.10 **Reinvestment into EIS shares issued after 5 April 1998.** Deferral relief applies where

- a chargeable gain would otherwise accrue to an individual
  - on the disposal by him of any asset; or
  - on the occurrence of a chargeable event under these provisions or the provisions governing reinvestment into VCT shares (see 66.12 VENTURE CAPITAL TRUSTS); or
  - to give effect to a withdrawal under *TCGA 1992, s 164F* or *s 164FA* of general reinvestment relief (see 22.81 EXEMPTIONS AND RELIEFS);
- the individual makes a 'qualifying investment'; and
- the individual is UK resident or ordinarily resident both when the chargeable gain accrues to him and when he makes the qualifying investment, and is not, at the time he makes the investment, regarded as resident outside the UK for the purposes of any double taxation arrangements the effect of which would be that he would not be liable to tax on a gain arising on a disposal, immediately after their acquisition, of the shares comprising the qualifying investment, disregarding any exemption available under *TCGA 1992, s 150A* (see 21.8 above).

See 21.11 below re the application of these provisions to trustees.

Subject to the further conditions below, a '*qualifying investment*' is a subscription for eligible shares (broadly, *new* ordinary, non-preferential, shares — see 21.4 above) in a company which are issued within the one year immediately preceding or the three years immediately following the time the chargeable gain in question accrues. These time limits may be extended by HMRC in individual cases. If the shares are issued *before* the gain accrues, they must still be held at the time it accrues. For these purposes, shares are not treated as issued merely by being comprised in a letter of allotment or similar instrument. The further conditions are as follows:

(*a*) the shares (other than, for shares issued after 16 March 2004, any of them which are 'bonus shares') must be subscribed for wholly in cash;

(*b*) the company must be a qualifying company (within 21.5 above) in relation to the shares;

(*c*) the shares must be fully paid up (see below) at time of issue (other than, for shares issued after 16 March 2004, any of them which are bonus shares);

(*d*) the shares must be subscribed for and issued for *bona fide* commercial purposes and not as part of tax avoidance arrangements;

(*e*) the requirements of *ICTA 1988, s 289(1A)–(1E)* (see 21.2 above under 'Person carrying on required activity') must be satisfied in relation to the company; in practice, this condition need be considered only if the company is part of a group (HMRC Venture Capital Schemes Manual VCM 38020);

(*f*) the shares (other than, for shares issued after 16 March 2004, any of them which are bonus shares) must be issued to raise money for the purpose of a qualifying business activity (see 21.6 above); and

(*g*) the money raised by the issue of the shares and all other eligible shares in the company of the same class issued on the same day (or, for shares issued before 17 March 2004, the money raised by the issue of the shares and all other shares comprised in the same issue) must be employed wholly (disregarding insignificant amounts) for that purpose by the end of the 24 months following the issue or, if the only qualifying business activity falls within 21.6(*a*) above, and if later, by the end of the 24 months starting when the company (or subsidiary) began to carry on the qualifying trade (see 21.6 above), and 80% of that money must be so employed within 12 months after the issue/commencement of trade. This applies after 6 March 2001; previously, *all* the money had to be so employed within 12 months after the issue/commencement of trade.

These conditions draw on those applicable to income tax relief (see 21.2 above). However, there is no requirement that any income tax relief be attributable to the shares, and, in contrast to the position for income tax relief, the individual does not have to be unconnected with the company. '*Bonus shares*' are shares issued otherwise than for payment, whether in cash or otherwise.

Shares issued after 16 March 2004 are not fully paid up for the purposes of (*c*) above if there is any undertaking to pay cash to any person in respect of the acquisition of the shares at a future date. In determining whether shares issued before 17 March 2004 are fully paid up, any undertaking to pay cash to the company at a future date is disregarded.

In relation to shares issued before 17 March 2004, the requirement in (*f*) above is that the shares in question, *and all other shares comprised in the same issue*, are issued to raise money for the purpose of a qualifying business activity.

In relation to shares issued after 16 March 2004, in determining for the purposes of (*g*) above when a qualifying trade is begun to be carried on by a subsidiary, any carrying on of the trade by it before it became a qualifying 90% subsidiary (see 21.2 above) is disregarded.

In *R (oao Devine) v CIR QB 2003, TL 3713*, the taxpayer unsuccessfully applied for judicial review of the Revenue's decision not to extend the reinvestment time limits noted above.

Postponement of the original gain. Where a chargeable gain would otherwise accrue to an individual ('the investor'), and he acquires a qualifying investment, a claim can be made by him to defer the whole or part of that gain against his investment up to an amount specified in the claim (limited to the amount of the gain or, where applicable, the amount of the gain not already relieved under either these provisions or those at 66.12 VENTURE CAPITAL TRUSTS). The amount of investment available to be matched with gains in this way is limited to the amount of the qualifying investment (to the extent that it has not already been so matched). The gain eligible for deferral is the gain after all available reliefs (including indexation allowance and (before 2003/04) retirement relief where available) other than taper relief (see *Example* below and also 21.13 below) (HMRC Venture Capital Schemes Manual VCM 38010).

Claims. Subject to what is said at 12.2 CLAIMS re claims being included in a self-assessment tax return if possible, there is no statutory form in which a claim *must* be made (though the claim form attached to form EIS 3 — see below — *may* be used, with or without a tax return). The provisions for income tax relief claims (see 21.7 above) are applied, with modifications, to deferral relief claims. Thus, a deferral relief claim cannot be made until the company has carried on the trade or other qualifying business activity for at least four months and cannot be made later than the fifth anniversary of 31 January following the tax year in which the shares were issued. A claim cannot be made until, with the authority of HMRC, the company has furnished the individual with a certificate (on form EIS 3) to the effect that, from its point of view, the conditions for deferral relief are satisfied. For more details relating to the issue of the certificate, see Tolley's Income Tax.

Deferred gain becoming chargeable. The deferred gain will become chargeable upon the occurrence of, *and at the time of*, any of the chargeable events listed below. The amount of the gain accruing at the time of the chargeable event is equal to so much of the deferred gain as is attributable to the EIS shares in relation to which the chargeable event occurs. For these purposes, a proportionate part of the net deferred gain (i.e. the deferred gain less any amount brought into charge on an earlier part disposal) is attributed to each of the 'relevant shares' held, immediately before the chargeable event, by the investor or by a person who acquired them from the investor on a transfer between spouses or civil partners within *TCGA 1992, s 58*. The '*relevant shares*' are the shares acquired in making the qualifying investment and, in a case where the original gain accrued at a later time than the making of the qualifying investment, still held at that time. They also include any bonus shares issued in respect of the relevant shares and of the same class and carrying the same rights. These rules were modified by *FA 1999, Sch 8* and are described here in their modified form. The modifications affect part disposals (see the *Example* below) and give statutory effect in relation to shares issued after 5 April 1999 to the Revenue's interpretation of the previous rules (Treasury Explanatory Notes to Finance Bill 1999). The said chargeable events are as follows.

(i) The investor disposes of the EIS shares otherwise than by way of a transfer between spouses or civil partners to which *TCGA 1992, s 58* applies.

(ii) Subsequent to a transfer within *TCGA 1992, s 58*, the shares are disposed of by the investor's spouse or civil partner (otherwise than by way of transfer back to the investor).

(iii) Within the designated period (see below), the investor becomes neither resident nor ordinarily resident in the UK.

(iv) Within the designated period (see below), the investor's spouse or civil partner, having acquired the shares by way of transfer within *TCGA 1992, s 58*, becomes neither resident nor ordinarily resident in the UK.

(v) The shares cease to be eligible shares or are treated as so ceasing (see below).

For these purposes, the designated period is

- (for shares issued after 5 April 2000) the period ending immediately before the third anniversary of the date of issue of the shares or, if later and where relevant, the third anniversary of the date of commencement of the intended trade referred to in 21.6(*a*) above; or
- (for shares issued before 6 April 2000) the five years beginning with the issue of the shares.

In the case of (iii) or (iv) above (non-residence), the deferred gain does not become chargeable where the investor (or, where applicable, spouse or civil partner) becomes neither resident nor ordinarily resident through temporary working outside the UK and again becomes resident or ordinarily resident within three years of that event, without having disposed of any of the relevant shares in the meantime in circumstances such that a chargeable event would have occurred had he been UK resident. No assessment is to be made until it is clear that the person concerned will not regain UK resident status within the three-year period.

EIS shares are *treated* as ceasing to be eligible shares (in which case a chargeable event occurs under (v) above) in any of the following circumstances (and see also the further provisions in 21.12 below).

(1) The condition at (*b*) above (qualifying company) ceases to be satisfied in consequence of an event occurring after the issue of the shares: the shares cease to be eligible shares at the time of that event. HMRC have confirmed that the company is required to retain its qualifying status only for the duration of the 'relevant period' (as defined in 21.6 above), so no chargeable event can occur under this heading by reason of anything happening beyond the end of that period (*Taxation 18 February 1999 p 486*).

(2) The condition at (*e*) above (compliance with *ICTA 1988, s 289(1A)*) ceases to be satisfied in consequence of an event occurring after the issue of the shares: the shares cease to be eligible shares at the time of that event.

(3) The condition at (*g*) above (money raised to be used for purpose of qualifying business activity within a specified time period) is not satisfied and the deferral claim was made before the end of the time period of 12 or 24 months (whichever is relevant): the shares cease to be eligible shares at the end of that time period. (If the deferral claim has not been made by then, or if the condition at (*f*) above is not satisfied at all, the shares are treated as never having been eligible shares.)

Death. The deferred gain does not become chargeable on the death of the investor (or, where applicable, spouse or civil partner) or on the occurrence after death of any event which would otherwise have been a chargeable event.

Identification rules. In determining whether any shares disposed of after 5 April 1998 are shares to which deferral relief is attributable (see 21.9 above), the normal identification rules (see 59.2 SHARES AND SECURITIES—IDENTIFICATION RULES) are disapplied and, instead, the same rules as in 21.8 above apply (broadly, first in/first out but with special rules where shares acquired on the same day fall into different specified categories — see examples at HMRC Venture Capital Schemes Manual VCM 38290).

Where at the time of the chargeable event, any of the relevant shares are regarded under capital gains tax legislation as represented by assets which consist of or include assets other than such shares, the deferred gain attributable to those shares is to be apportioned between those assets on a just and reasonable basis. As between different assets regarded as representing the same shares, the identification of those assets follows the same identification rules as for shares.

Persons chargeable. The chargeable gain is treated as accruing, depending on which type of chargeable event occurs, to

- the individual who makes the disposal;
- the individual who becomes non-resident;
- the individual who holds the shares in question when they cease (or are treated as ceasing) to be eligible shares.

Where the last category applies and some of the shares are held by the investor and some by a person who acquired them from the investor by way of transfer between spouses or civil partners within *TCGA 1992, s 58*, the gain is computed separately as regards each individual without reference to the shares held by the other.

[TCGA 1992, s 105A(4)(7)(8), s 150C, Sch 5B paras 1–6, 19; FA 1995, s 67, Sch 13 para 4(3)(4); FA 1998, s 74, Sch 13 paras 26–33, 36, Sch 27 Pt III(14); FA 1999, s 73, Sch 8; FA 2000, Sch 17 para 7(2)(3), para 8; FA 2001, Sch 15 paras 26–29, 37, 40, Sch 33 Pt II(3); FA 2002, s 50; FA 2004, s 93, Sch 18 paras 13, 14, 20(1)(b), 21, Sch 19 para 6, Sch 42 Pt 2(12); SI 2005 No 3229, Reg 127].

See the further provisions at 21.12 below.

Example

Frank realises a gain of £270,000 (before taper relief) in May 2006 on the disposal of a business asset he had acquired in August 2004. He makes no other disposals in 2006/07. On 1 March 2008, he subscribes £234,000 for 60% of the issued ordinary share capital in a new company, ABC Ltd. The investment is a qualifying investment for the purposes of EIS deferral relief, and the shares represent a business asset for the purposes of taper relief. Frank makes a claim to defer the maximum £234,000 of the May 2006 gain against the qualifying investment.

The CGT position for 2006/07 is as follows.

	£
Gain	270,000
Less deferred under EIS provisions	234,000
	36,000
Less taper relief £36,000 @ 50%	18,000
	18,000
Less annual exemption	8,800
Taxable gain 2006/07	£9,200

On 1 August 2012, he sells 40% of his holding of ABC Ltd shares for £213,600. He makes no other disposals in 2012/13. His CGT position for that year is as follows.

Gain on ABC Ltd shares	£
Disposal proceeds	213,600
Less cost (£234,000 × 40%)	93,600
	120,000
Less taper relief £120,000 @ 75%	90,000
Gain	£30,000
Deferred gain brought into charge	
Total gain deferred	£234,000
	£
Clawback restricted to expenditure to which disposal relates	93,600
Less taper relief £93,600 @ 50%	46,800
Gain	£46,800
Taxable gains 2012/13 (subject to annual exemption) (£30,000 + £46,800)	£76,800

Gain remaining deferred until any future chargeable event (£234,000 – £93,600) £140,400

Notes to the example

(*a*) Frank's subscription for ABC Ltd shares cannot qualify for EIS income tax relief. He is connected with the company by virtue of his shareholding being greater than 30%. (In practice, the holdings of his associates, e.g. wife and children, need to be taken into account as well.) See 21.3 above.

(*b*) As the ABC Ltd shares do not qualify for income tax relief, there is no exemption as in 21.8 above for the gain arising on part disposal, despite the shares having been held for over three years.

(*c*) Taper relief on the deferred gain becoming chargeable is given by reference to the time and circumstances of the original disposal, not the disposal of the EIS shares which gives rise to the chargeable event (see 61.15 TAPER RELIEF), but see 21.13 below re cases of serial reinvestment. See 61.2 for the calculation of taper relief and 61.4 for the definition of a business asset.

21.11 **Reinvestment into EIS shares issued after 5 April 1998 — application to trustees.** The deferral provisions for individuals at 21.10 above (and the further provisions at 21.12 below) also apply to trustees of a settlement where, in a case where the gain to be deferred accrues to them on the disposal of an asset, that asset (the '*trust asset*') is comprised in settled property of the kind mentioned in either (*a*) or (*b*) below.

(*a*) Settled property on discretionary trusts (i.e. settlements where the beneficiaries' interests are not interests in possession, an interest in possession for this purpose excluding an interest for a fixed term; and see generally 57.13 SETTLEMENTS) where all of the beneficiaries are either individuals or charities.

(*b*) Settled property on non-discretionary trusts (i.e. settlements where the beneficiaries' interests are interests in possession as in (*a*) above) where any of the beneficiaries is an individual or a charity.

Where there is at least one beneficiary holding a non-discretionary interest and at least one beneficiary holding a discretionary interest (i.e. a mixed settlement), all of the discretionary interests are treated for these purposes as if they were a single interest in possession, and as if that interest were held, where all the discretionary beneficiaries are individuals or charities, by an individual or charity, and, in any other case, by a person who is not an individual or charity.

If, at the time of the disposal of the trust asset, the settled property comprising that asset is within (*b*) above but not all of the beneficiaries are individuals or charities, then only the 'relevant proportion' of the gain on the disposal is taken into account for the purposes of deferral relief. The '*relevant proportion*' at any time is the proportion which the aggregate amount of the income of the settled property interests in which are held by individuals or charities bears to the total amount of all of the income of the settled property.

If the settled property qualifies under (*a*) above at the time of the disposal of the trust asset, deferral relief is available only if, immediately after the acquisition of the EIS shares, the settled property comprising the EIS shares also qualifies under (*a*) above. This also applies *mutatis mutandis* to settled property qualifying under (*b*) above but, if not all the beneficiaries are individuals or charities, with the additional condition that the relevant proportion immediately after the acquisition of the EIS shares must be not less than the relevant proportion at the time of the disposal of the trust asset.

[*TCGA 1992, Sch 5B para 17; FA 1998, s 74, Sch 13 para 36*].

Note that neither EIS income tax relief nor the CGT disposal relief at 21.8 above applies to trustees.

21.12 Reinvestment into EIS shares issued after 5 April 1998 — further provisions

(1) *Reorganisations.* Provisions identical to those of *TCGA 1992, s 150A(6)(6A)(7)* (see 21.8 above under 'Reorganisations of share capital'), as they apply for reorganisations taking effect after 5 April 1998, apply in relation to shares to which deferral relief is attributable (see 21.9 above).

Acquisition of share capital by new company. Provisions similar to those of *ICTA 1988, s 304A* (which enables an EIS company to become a wholly-owned subsidiary of a new holding company in certain circumstances — see 21.8 above under 'Company reconstructions' and also Tolley's Income Tax) apply for the purposes of deferral relief. Provided all the conditions are satisfied, deferral relief attributable to shares in the original EIS company is regarded as being attributable to the shares in the new company for which the original shares are exchanged.

Other reconstructions. Provisions similar to those of *TCGA 1992, s 150A(8)(8A)–(8D)* (see 21.8 above under 'Company reconstructions') apply in relation to shares to which deferral relief is attributable. These provisions treat an exchange of shares as a disposal, except in specified circumstances.

[*TCGA 1992, Sch 5B paras 7–9, 19; FA 1998, s 74, Sch 13 paras 34, 36; FA 1999, Sch 8 para 3; SI 2005 No 3229, Reg 127*].

(2) *Anti-avoidance provisions.*

Reinvestment in same company etc. If an individual realises a gain on disposal of shares in or securities of a company (Company A), he cannot defer that gain by virtue of a subscription for shares in an EIS company which is either Company A itself or is, either at the time of the disposal or the time of the issue of the EIS shares, a member of the same 'group' as Company A. For disposals of shares or securities after 16 March 2004, a '*group*' is defined for this purpose as consisting of a company which has one or more 51% subsidiaries (within *ICTA 1988, s 838*) and those subsidiaries. Previously, no definition of the term was given.

Further provisions apply where an individual defers a gain by subscribing for EIS shares, disposes of any of those shares and makes a further subscription for shares in the same company (or member of the same group); no deferral relief is allowed in respect of the second subscription. This also applies where there has been no disposal of the original EIS shares but the further subscription is for shares in a company a disposal of shares in which resulted in the initial deferral (or a member of the same group as that company). The definition of a group given above applies for these purposes in relation to further subscriptions for shares after 16 March 2004.

Investment-linked loans. Provisions analogous to those at 21.2 above apply where an investment-linked loan etc. is made to the investor or his associate in the 'relevant period' (as in 21.3 above). For deferral relief purposes, the EIS shares are treated as never having been eligible shares (with the result that no such relief is available) if the loan is made on or before the date of their issue and as otherwise ceasing to be eligible shares (with the result that a chargeable event occurs in respect of deferral relief claimed — see 21.10(v) above) on the date the loan is made.

Where the shares are subscribed for by trustees, and relief claimed by virtue of 21.11 above, the above applies to loans made not only to the trustees but to any individual (or associate) or charity (or connected person) by virtue of whose interest (at the time the shares are issued and/or at the time the loan is made) deferral relief is available in respect of the settled property.

Pre-arranged exits. Provisions identical to those at 21.2 above apply to prevent EIS shares from being eligible shares for deferral relief purposes where certain exit arrangements are made in relation to their issue.

Put and call options. The granting of a put option or call option prevents the EIS shares to which it relates from being eligible shares for deferral relief purposes if the option is granted on or before the date of issue of the shares, or otherwise causes them to be treated as ceasing to be eligible shares (with the result that a chargeable event occurs in respect of deferral relief claimed — see 21.10(v) above) at the time the option is granted. The provisions apply where an individual subscribes for EIS shares (or acquires them on a no gain/no loss transfer from a subscriber spouse or civil partner) and, during the 'relevant period' (defined as in 21.3 above), either

- an option for the grantor to purchase such shares (a '*put option*') is granted to the individual, or
- an option for the individual to sell such shares (a '*call option*') is granted by the individual.

Comparable provisions apply for the purposes of EIS income tax relief.

Value received by the investor from the EIS company. Where the EIS investor (or his associate — within 21.3 above) receives any value from the company during the 'period of restriction' (see below), the shares are treated as never having been eligible shares for deferral relief purposes if the value is received on or before the date of the share issue or as otherwise ceasing to be eligible shares (with the result that a chargeable event occurs in respect of deferral relief claimed — see 21.10(v) above) at the time value is received. Note that the full amount of the deferred gain falls to be clawed back even if the investor receives back only a proportion of the value of his investment. The provisions of *TCGA 1992, Sch 5B para 13* which determine whether value is received from a company are based on the EIS income tax relief withdrawal provisions of *ICTA 1988, ss 300–301A*. They are fairly widely drawn but *not* so as to catch, for example, reasonable remuneration (or reimbursement of expenses) to the individual as an officer or employee of the company, interest at a commercial rate on a loan made to the company or dividends which represent no more than a normal return on investment in that company. The provisions *do* include, for example, any repayment, redemption or repurchase by the company of any of its share capital or securities which belong to the individual, any loan or advance by the company to the individual which is not repaid before the EIS shares are issued, and the provision of a benefit or facility for the individual. Value received from a connected person of the company (within *TCGA 1992, s 286* — see 16 CONNECTED PERSONS) falls within the provisions if it would have done so had it been received from the EIS company itself.

In relation to shares issued after 6 March 2001 and, for shares issued previously, in relation to value received after that date, value received is disregarded if its amount is *insignificant*, i.e. if it does not exceed £1,000 or, in any other case, if it is insignificant in relation to that part of the amount expended on subscribing for the shares that has been used as in 21.10 above to defer chargeable gains. In applying this let-out, multiple receipts of value must be aggregated (see examples at HMRC Venture Capital Schemes Manual VCM 40350), and the let-out is disapplied in certain cases where value received is pre-arranged. Value received is also disregarded if the person from whom the value was obtained receives at least equivalent *replacement value* from the original recipient, though certain types of payment are treated as not giving rise to a receipt of replacement value.

Where the shares are subscribed for by trustees, and relief claimed by virtue of 21.11 above, the above provisions apply to value received not only by the trustees but by any individual (or associate) or charity (or connected person) by virtue of whose interest (at the time the shares are issued and/or at the time the value is received) deferral relief is available in respect of the settled property.

For these purposes, the '*period of restriction*' is

(*a*) (for shares issued after 6 March 2001 and also as regards value received after that date in respect of shares issued on or before that date) the period beginning one year before the issue of the shares and ending immediately before the third anniversary of the issue date or, if later and where relevant, the third anniversary of the date of commencement of the intended trade referred to in 21.6(*a*) above; or

(*b*) (as regards value received before 7 March 2001 in respect of shares issued after 5 April 2000 and before 7 March 2001) the period beginning two years before the issue of the shares and ending immediately before the third anniversary of the issue date or, if later and where relevant, the third anniversary of the date of commencement of the intended trade referred to in 21.6(*a*) above; or

(*c*) (as regards value received before 7 March 2001 in respect of shares issued before 6 April 2000) the seven-year period beginning two years before, and ending five years after, the issue of the shares.

In relation to shares issued after 16 March 2004, where the trade is begun to be carried on by a subsidiary after the date of issue of the shares, in determining for the purposes of (*a*) above when the trade commenced, any carrying on of the trade by the subsidiary before it became a 'qualifying 90% subsidiary' (see 21.2 above) is disregarded.

See the corresponding chapter of Tolley's Income Tax for detailed coverage of the broadly equivalent income tax provisions.

Value received by other persons from the EIS company. Provisions based on the EIS income tax relief withdrawal provisions of *ICTA 1988, ss 303–303A* apply where, at any time in the period of restriction (as defined immediately above), the EIS company (or one which is a 51% subsidiary at some time in the 'relevant period' — defined as in 21.3(*a*) above) repays, redeems or repurchases any of its share capital from a member (other than the EIS investor in question) who does not thereby lose EIS income tax relief or deferral relief or CORPORATE VENTURING SCHEME (17) investment relief. They apply equally where the company or such subsidiary makes any payment to any such member for the giving up of rights to share capital on its cancellation or extinguishment. The shares are treated as never having been eligible shares for deferral relief purposes if such an event occurs on or before the date of the share issue or as otherwise ceasing to be eligible shares (with the result that a chargeable event occurs in respect of deferral relief claimed — see 21.10(v) above) at the time such event occurs.

In relation to shares issued after 6 March 2001 and, for shares issued earlier, in relation to repayments etc. made after that date, the absence of any loss of EIS income tax relief etc., as referred to above, is disregarded if it is due only to the amount received being of insignificant value. A repayment etc. is itself disregarded if the amount received by the member in question is insignificant in relation to the market value immediately after the event of the remaining issued share capital of the company or, as the case may be, 51% subsidiary. The assumption is made that the shares in question are cancelled at the time of the event. In applying the test, the market value, immediately before the event, of the shares to which the event relates is substituted for the amount received if this would give a greater amount. This let-out is disapplied in certain cases where a repayment etc. is pre-arranged. 'Insignificant' is taken by HMRC to mean 'trifling or completely unimportant' (HMRC Venture Capital Schemes Manual VCM 40300).

[*TCGA 1992, Sch 5B paras 10–15, 18, 19; FA 1998, s 74, Sch 13 para 35*); *FA 2000, Sch 16 para 4, Sch 17 para 7(4), para 8; FA 2001, Sch 15 paras 30–34, 36, 37, 40; FA 2004, Sch 18 paras 15–18, 20; ITTOIA 2005, Sch 1 para 450; SI 2005 No 3229, Reg 127*].

(3) *Information.* Certain chargeable events and failures of conditions must be notified to the inspector, generally within 60 days, by either the investor, the EIS company or any person connected with the EIS company having knowledge of the matter. The inspector may require such notice where he has reason to believe it should have been made, and is given broad powers to require information generally.

[*TCGA 1992, Sch 5B para 16; FA 1998, s 74, Sch 13 para 36; FA 1999, Sch 8 para 4(i); FA 2000, Sch 17 para 7(3), para 8; FA 2001, Sch 15 paras 28, 35, 40; FA 2004, Sch 18 para 19; SI 2005 No 3229, Reg 127*].

21.13 **Taper relief.** Except where the special rule below has effect, taper relief is applied to a gain deferred under 21.10 above at the time it becomes chargeable but by reference to the period for which the original asset was held — see 61.15 TAPER RELIEF.

A special rule applies in consequence of the disposal after 5 April 1999 of a holding of EIS shares (the initial investment) which were issued after 5 April 1998 and to which either (or both) CGT deferral relief or income tax relief is attributable (see, respectively, 21.9 above and 21.2 above under 'Method of relief'). The rule has effect only where the whole or part of the gain otherwise accruing is deferred under 21.10 (or 21.11) above by reinvestment in further EIS shares (the second investment). Upon a disposal of the second investment (the '*relevant disposal*'), with the result that all or part of the deferred gain on the initial investment is revived (i.e. becomes chargeable), taper relief is calculated in respect of the revived gain as if the qualifying holding period (see 61.2 TAPER RELIEF) for the initial investment began with the date of acquisition of that investment and ended with the date of the relevant disposal. In other words, the holding periods of the two investments are combined. Where all or part of the revived gain is itself deferred by means of a third EIS investment, such that taper relief does not fall to be calculated until the third investment is disposed of, the holding periods of all three investments are combined to form the qualifying holding period, and so on as regards fourth and subsequent investments.

The above applies only to the revived gain and not to any other gain accruing on the relevant disposal or to any part of the original gain which was not deferred. The extension of the qualifying holding period as above is subject to the anti-avoidance provisions at 61.19–61.22 TAPER RELIEF, which provide *inter alia* for certain periods to be left out of account for taper relief purposes. In addition, any gap in time between disposal of the initial investment and acquisition of the second investment (or between disposal and acquisition of subsequent investments in the chain) does not count towards the qualifying holding period or the relevant period of ownership (see 61.11 TAPER RELIEF).

In determining the extent (if any) to which the revived gain is a gain on a business asset and thus the rate of taper relief to be applied (see 61.2, 61.4 TAPER RELIEF), the combined period of ownership is calculated as above. The initial investment and each subsequent investment in the chain is treated as having been held for the actual time it was held and its character (as a business or non-business asset) resolved accordingly. For the duration of any overlap period during which more than one such investment was held, it is assumed for these purposes that only the first-acquired of those investments was held. If these rules result in the revived gain being of mixed character, the rules at 61.12 TAPER RELIEF apply to determine the relief available.

[*TCGA 1992, s 150D, Sch 5BA; FA 1999, s 72, Sch 7*].

Example

Annabelle realises a gain of £270,000 (before taper relief) on 1 May 2006 on the disposal of a complete holding of shares in ABC Ltd (an EIS company) for which she had subscribed on 1 May 2005 and in respect of which she had deferred a gain of £50,000 which would otherwise have accrued in 2003/04 on a disposal of a non-business asset acquired in 2001. The ABC Ltd shares were a business asset throughout for taper relief purposes. She makes no other disposals in 2006/07. On 1 November 2007, she subscribes £210,000 for new ordinary shares in a new company, EIS Ltd. The investment is a qualifying investment for the purposes of EIS deferral relief (but not income tax relief) and a business asset for the purposes of taper relief. Annabelle makes a claim to defer the maximum £210,000 of the May 2006 gain against her investment in EIS Ltd.

The CGT position for 2006/07 is as follows.

	£
Gain on ABC Ltd shares	270,000
Less deferred under EIS provisions	210,000
	60,000
Less taper relief £60,000 @ 50% (Qualifying holding period 1.5.05–1.5.06 = 1 year)	30,000
	30,000
Previously deferred gain now chargeable*	50,000
	80,000
Less annual exemption	8,800
Taxable gain 2005/06	£71,200

* The taper relief period for the first asset (a non-EIS investment) ends on the date of disposal of that asset (see 61.15 TAPER RELIEF) and does not fall to be extended under these provisions. No taper relief is due in this case as the asset is a non-business asset held for less than three years.

On 1 May 2011, Annabelle sells her holding of EIS Ltd shares for £500,000. She makes no other disposals in 2011/12. Her CGT position for that year is as follows.

Gain on EIS Ltd shares	£
Disposal proceeds	500,000
Less cost	210,000
	290,000
Less taper relief £290,000 @ 75% (Qualifying holding period 1.11.07–1.5.11 = 3 years)	217,500
Gain	£72,500

Deferred gain brought into charge	£
Gain deferred	210,000
Less taper relief £210,000 @ 75%*	157,500
Gain	£52,500

* Qualifying holding period:
1.5.05–1.5.06 — 1 year
1.11.07–1.5.11 — 3.5 years
Total — 4.5 years
Number of whole years in qualifying holding period = 4

Taxable gains 2011/12 (subject to annual exemption) (£72,500 + £52,500)	£125,000

21.14 **Reinvestment into EIS shares issued before 6 April 1998.** The deferral rules described below apply where the EIS shares are issued before 6 April 1998 (see 21.10 above re later issues and 21.9 above generally).

The relief applies where

(*a*) a chargeable gain would otherwise accrue to an individual after 28 November 1994 on the disposal by him of any asset (or on the occurrence of a chargeable event either under these provisions or the similar provisions governing reinvestment into VCT shares (see 66.12 VENTURE CAPITAL TRUSTS));

(*b*) the individual makes a 'qualifying investment'; and

(*c*) the individual is UK resident or ordinarily resident both when the chargeable gain accrues to him and when he makes the 'qualifying investment', and is not, at the time he makes the investment, regarded as resident outside the UK for the purposes of any double taxation arrangements the effect of which would be that he would not be liable to tax on a gain arising on a disposal, immediately after their acquisition, of the shares comprising the 'qualifying investment', disregarding the exemption under *TCGA 1992, s 150A* (see 21.8 above).

A '*qualifying investment*' is a subscription for shares to which any income tax relief given under the EIS to the individual is attributable and which are issued within the one year immediately preceding or the three years immediately following the time the chargeable gain in question accrues. These time limits may be extended by HMRC in individual cases. If the shares are issued *before* the gain accrues, they must still be held at the latter time. For these purposes, shares are not treated as issued merely by being comprised in a letter of allotment or similar instrument.

Postponement of the original gain. Where a chargeable gain would otherwise accrue to an individual ('the investor'), and he acquires a qualifying investment, a claim can be made by him to defer the whole or part of that gain against his investment up to an amount specified in the claim (limited to the amount of the gain or, where applicable, the amount of the gain not already relieved under either these provisions or those at 66.12 VENTURE CAPITAL TRUSTS). The amount of investment available to be matched with gains in this way is limited to the amount in respect of which income tax relief is given under the EIS and which has not already been so matched.

Subject to what is said at 12.2 CLAIMS re claims being included in a self-assessment tax return if possible, there is no statutory form in which a claim must be made. The deferral claim must be made by the fifth anniversary of 31 January following the 'relevant tax year'. The '*relevant tax year*' is the tax year in which the *later* of the following events occurred:

- the gain to be deferred arose;
- the EIS shares were issued.

(HMRC Venture Capital Schemes Manual VCM 36360).

Deferred gain becoming chargeable. The deferred gain will become chargeable upon the occurrence of, *and at the time of*, any of the chargeable events listed below. The amount of the gain accruing at the time of the chargeable event is equal to so much of the original gain as was matched under these provisions with expenditure on the EIS shares in question.

(i) The investor disposes of the EIS shares otherwise than by way of a transfer to which *TCGA 1992, s 58* (see 42.4 MARRIED PERSONS AND CIVIL PARTNERS) applies. As regards part disposals, HMRC interpret the law as requiring a proportionate part of the deferred gain to be brought into account.

(ii) Subsequent to a transfer within *TCGA 1992, s 58*, the shares are disposed of by the investor's spouse (otherwise than by way of transfer back to the investor).

(iii) Within five years after the issue of the shares, the investor becomes neither resident nor ordinarily resident in the UK.

(iv) Within five years after the issue of the shares, the investor's spouse, having acquired the shares by way of inter-spouse transfer within *TCGA 1992, s 58*, becomes neither resident nor ordinarily resident in the UK.

(v) The company which issued the shares ceases to be a qualifying company under the EIS (see 21.5 above) within the 'relevant period' (defined as in 21.6 above).

(vi) The EIS income tax relief is withdrawn or reduced (see Tolley's Income Tax) in circumstances not falling within (i)–(v) above.

In the case of (iii) or (iv) above (non-residence), the deferred gain does not become chargeable where the investor (or, where applicable, spouse) becomes neither resident nor ordinarily resident through temporary working outside the UK and again becomes resident or ordinarily resident within three years of that event, without having disposed of any of the relevant EIS shares in the meantime in circumstances such that a chargeable event would have occurred had he been UK resident. No assessment is to be made until it is clear that the person concerned will not regain UK resident status within the three-year period.

Death. The deferred gain does not become chargeable on the death of the investor (or, where applicable, spouse) or on the occurrence after death of any event which would otherwise have been a chargeable event.

Identification rules. In determining whether any EIS shares to which a chargeable event relates are shares the expenditure on which has been matched with any gain, disposals of shares are first identified with those acquired earlier rather than later (i.e. first in, first out). On a part disposal of shares in a company acquired by the same person on the same day, shares the expenditure on which has been matched under these provisions are regarded as disposed of subsequent to any others (see Venture Capital Schemes Manual VCM 35400–35500).

Where at the time of the chargeable event, the relevant EIS shares are regarded under capital gains tax legislation as represented by assets which consist of or include assets other than such shares, the expenditure on those shares is to be apportioned between those assets on a just and reasonable basis. As between different assets regarded as representing the same shares, the identification of those assets follows the share identification rules above.

Persons chargeable. The chargeable gain is treated as accruing, depending on which type of chargeable event occurs, to

(A) the individual who makes the disposal;

(B) the individual who becomes non-resident;

(C) the individual who holds the shares in question at the time that the company ceases to be a qualifying company; or

(D) the individual who holds the shares in question at the time that the EIS income tax relief is withdrawn or reduced.

Where (C) or (D) apply and some of the shares are held by the investor and some by a person who acquired them from the investor by way of inter-spouse transfer within *TCGA 1992, s 58*, the gain is computed separately as regards each individual without reference to the shares held by the other.

[*TCGA 1992, s 150C, Sch 5B; FA 1995, s 67, Sch 13 para 4(3)(4)*].

22 Exemptions and Reliefs

Cross-references. See 7 ASSETS HELD ON 6 APRIL 1965; 8 ASSETS HELD ON 31 MARCH 1982; 10 CHARITIES; 17 CORPORATE VENTURING SCHEME; 18 DEATH; 19 DOUBLE TAX RELIEF; 21 ENTERPRISE INVESTMENT SCHEME; 26 GOVERNMENT SECURITIES; 33 HOLD-OVER RELIEFS; 34 INDEXATION; 40 LOSSES; 45 OVERSEAS MATTERS; 49 PRIVATE RESIDENCES; 50 QUALIFYING CORPORATE BONDS; 52 RESIDENCE AND DOMICILE; 53 RETIREMENT RELIEF; 55 ROLLOVER RELIEF; 58 SHARES AND SECURITIES; 60 SUBSTANTIAL SHAREHOLDINGS OF COMPANIES; 65 UNIT TRUSTS ETC.; 66 VENTURE CAPITAL TRUSTS.

22.1 INTRODUCTION

A person is chargeable to capital gains tax on chargeable gains accruing to him on the disposal of assets in any year of assessment during any part of which he is resident in the UK, or during which he is ordinarily resident in the UK. [*TCGA 1992, s 1*(*1*), *s 2*(*1*)]. All forms of property except sterling are regarded as assets for these purposes [*TCGA 1992, s 21*(*1*)] and every gain, except as otherwise expressly provided, is a chargeable gain. [*TCGA 1992, s 28*(*2*)]. There are, however, a number of exemptions and reliefs. These may broadly be classified as follows.

(*a*) Exempt assets (see 22.2–22.16 below).

(*b*) Exempt gains and transactions (see 22.17–22.37 below).

(*c*) Exempt organisations and individuals (see 22.38–22.62 below).

In addition, a number of reliefs are available to reduce or defer the amount of capital gains tax payable. See 22.63–22.88 and certain provisions in 22.49 and 22.58 below.

22.2 EXEMPT ASSETS

Gains accruing on the disposal of certain assets are exempt from capital gains tax. The exemption (total or partial) of the various types of asset is examined in 22.3–22.16 below. Losses arising from such disposals are similarly not allowable unless expressly provided otherwise. [*TCGA 1992, s 16*(*2*)].

22.3 **Annuities and annual payments.** A gain accruing on the disposal of a right to or to any part of an allowance, annuity, or capital sum from a *superannuation fund* or annual payments receivable under a 'covenant' not secured on property, is exempt. [*TCGA 1992, s 237*(*a*)(*c*)]. '*Covenant*' means a gratuitous promise enforceable solely due to the form in which it is evidenced (i.e., in England, in a document under seal). It does not include contracts enforceable as such (*Rank Xerox Ltd v Lane HL 1979, 53 TC 185*).

A gain accruing on the disposal of, or of an 'interest' in, rights under a contract for a 'non-deferred annuity' or an annuity granted (or deemed to be granted) under *Government Annuities Act 1929* is also exempt. For this purpose, a '*non-deferred annuity*' is an annuity (including an annuity which includes instalments of capital) which is not granted under a contract for a deferred annuity and which is granted in the ordinary course of a business granting annuities on the life of any person. For disposals before 5 December 2005, only annuities granted by a company were included. An '*interest*' in rights means an interest as co-owner of the rights, and it is immaterial whether the rights are owned jointly or in common or whether or not the interests of the co-owners are equal. [*TCGA 1992, s 204*(*5*)(*7*)–(*9*), *s 237*(*b*); *FA 2006, s 73*].

22.4 **Chattels.** A tangible movable asset (other than a commodity disposed of by or through a dealer on a terminal market) is entirely exempt, provided that the asset is not 'currency of any description' and that the disposal is for a consideration of £6,000 or less. If the consideration exceeds £6,000, the chargeable gain is limited to five-thirds of the excess.

[*TCGA 1992, s 262(1)(2)(6)*]. Sovereigns minted before 1837 are not legal tender and are thus within the exemption (HMRC Capital Gains Manual CG 78309).

Examples

(i) A chattel which cost £5,000 in May 1998 is disposed of in May 2006 for £8,000. Assume expenses of disposal of £300. The chargeable gain is ascertained as follows.

Excess of consideration over £6,000	£2,000
£2,000 × 5/3	£3,333
Actual gain is £2,700 which is less than £3,333	
Chargeable gain (subject to TAPER RELIEF (61))	£2,700

(ii) A chattel which cost £2,000 in May 1998 is disposed of in May 2006 for £8,000. Assume expenses of disposal of £280.

Excess of consideration over £6,000	£2,000
£2,000 × 5/3	£3,333
Actual gain is £5,720 which is more than £3,333	
Chargeable gain (subject to TAPER RELIEF (61))	£3,333

Part disposal. Where the disposal is of a right or interest in or over a tangible movable asset, and the sum of the consideration received plus the value of what remains exceeds £6,000, a similar limitation of the chargeable gain applies but the excess for this purpose is computed as follows.

$$(\text{consideration received} + \text{value of remainder} - £6{,}000) \times \frac{\text{consideration received}}{\text{total value}}$$

[*TCGA 1992, s 262(5)*].

Losses. For the purposes of loss relief, a disposal of a tangible movable asset for a consideration of less than £6,000 is deemed to be made for a consideration of £6,000. In the case of a partial disposal of an asset the total value of which is less than £6,000, the deemed consideration for loss relief purposes is computed as follows.

$$(£6{,}000 - \text{total value}) \times \left(\frac{\text{consideration received}}{\text{total value}}\right) + \text{consideration received}$$

Simplified, this becomes (£6,000 × consideration/total value).

[*TCGA 1992, s 262(3)*].

Assets forming a set. Where these are owned by the same disposer they are to be treated as a single asset where they are disposed of, whether on the same or on different occasions, to the same person or to persons acting in concert, or to CONNECTED PERSONS (16). [*TCGA 1992, s 262(4)*]. For HMRC's views on the circumstances in which a number of bottles of wine may constitute a set, see Revenue Tax Bulletin August 1999 p 686. For an article on pairs of shotguns, see Revenue Tax Bulletin February 2000 pp 726, 727.

Wasting assets. Tangible movable assets which are WASTING ASSETS (67) are exempt whatever the consideration received, but this exemption is restricted or eliminated to the extent that the asset, by reason of its having been used in trade or otherwise, has been or could have been the subject of a capital allowance. This exemption is not applicable to a disposal of commodities on a terminal market. [*TCGA 1992, s 45*]. Where capital allowances were initially granted in respect of qualifying expenditure on movable machinery but were later withdrawn because the machinery was sold without it having been brought into use by the taxpayer, it was held that the taxpayer should be treated as if the allowance had never been made, with the result that the disposal on sale was exempt (*Burman v Westminster Press Ltd Ch D 1987, 60 TC 418*). If a restriction by reference to capital allowances would otherwise arise, relief as under *TCGA 1992, s 262* above may be available.

HMRC accept that any of the following is machinery and is thus a tangible movable wasting asset (see 67.1 WASTING ASSETS) which will be exempt where owned privately and not used in a business: antique clocks and watches; motor vehicles which are not normal private passenger vehicles and are thus outside the exemption at 22.11 below, e.g. taxi cabs, vans, motor cycles etc.; trawlers, fishing vessels, tankers and other vessels propelled by engines (and see below re boats generally). (Revenue Tax Bulletin October 1994 pp 166, 167). They 'generally accept' that all types of gun are within the general description of machinery (Revenue Tax Bulletin February 2000 p 727).

Boats 'will generally be tangible movable wasting assets' and thus exempt (except where qualifying for capital allowances). (HMRC Capital Gains Manual CG 64328 and see also above). This will not always apply to yachts, barges or boats used as a residence, as these may have a longer useful life. A houseboat which is permanently located on a site and connected to all mains services may in some circumstances be regarded as a dwelling house. (HMRC Capital Gains Manual CG 64329, 64330).

For HMRC's views on the circumstances in which *bottled wine* may qualify as a wasting asset and thus an exempt chattel, see Revenue Tax Bulletin August 1999 p 686.

22.5 **Debts.** A debt, other than a 'debt on a security' (see below), disposed of by the original creditor or his personal representative or legatee is exempt. Where the trustees of a settlement are the original creditor (or, for debts created before 6 April 2006, where the original creditor is a trustee and the debt, when created, is settled property), a person becoming absolutely entitled to the debt is treated as a personal representative or legatee as is his own personal representative or legatee. [*TCGA 1992, s 251(1)(5); FA 2006, Sch 12 para 23*].

The foregoing does not apply to the disposal of a bank balance in foreign currency, except to the extent that it represents currency acquired by an individual for purposes similar to those in *TCGA 1992, s 269* or, in the case of a company, the disposal is exempted under (the now repealed) *FA 1993, Sch 17 paras 1–3* (see, in both cases, 22.8 below). [*TCGA 1992, s 252*]. A taxpayer may treat all bank accounts in his name containing a particular foreign currency as one account and so disregard direct transfers among such accounts which would otherwise constitute disposals (withdrawals) and acquisitions (deposits) under *section 252*. The practice, once adopted, must be applied to all future direct transfers among bank accounts in the taxpayer's name designated in that currency until such time as all debt represented in the accounts has been repaid to the taxpayer. Accounts held as in 6.2(*l*) ASSETS (non-domiciled individuals) do not qualify for this treatment. (HMRC Statement of Practice 10/84). (See 3.25 ANTI-AVOIDANCE for the charge arising where concessions involving deferral of gains are abused.)

By concession, as long as the practice is followed consistently and produces a reasonable overall result, a net figure for deposits into and withdrawals from a foreign currency bank account may be computed for each calendar month or part month within a tax year or company accounting period to ease the task of computing gains and losses on numerous withdrawals. The net deposit or withdrawal thus computed is then converted to sterling at the average exchange rate for the month. (HMRC Capital Gains Manual CG 78333).

The redenomination into euros of a debt, other than a debt on a security, from the currency of a State participating in the European single currency on or after 1 January 1999 is not treated as involving the disposal of that debt or the acquisition of a new debt. The original debt and the new debt are treated as the same asset, acquired as the original debt was acquired. [*SI 1998 No 3177, Reg 37*]. Accordingly the disposal of the new debt by the original creditor retains its exemption.

Loss relief is available to the maker of a 'qualifying loan' or a guarantor of a qualifying loan. See 40.10 LOSSES. See 40.11 LOSSES for a corresponding relief where the borrower's debt is a debt on a security which is a qualifying corporate bond.

A right possibly to receive an unidentifiable sum at an unascertainable date is not a 'debt' (*Marren v Ingles HL 1980, 54 TC 76*; *Marson v Marriage Ch D 1979, 54 TC 59*).

Subject to the foregoing, the satisfaction of a debt (including a debt on a security) or part of it is treated as a disposal of the debt by the creditor made at the time when the debt is satisfied. Where a debt on a security is involved this rule is subject to the provisions in *TCGA 1992, ss 132, 135, 136* covering reorganisations of share capital (see 58.4, 58.6 and 58.7 SHARES AND SECURITIES). [*TCGA 1992, s 251(2)*; *FA 2002, Sch 9 paras 5(12), 7*].

Where property is acquired by a creditor in satisfaction of a debt then, subject to any reorganisation of share capital as above, the property is not treated as disposed of by the debtor or acquired by the creditor for a consideration greater than its market value at the time of the creditor's acquisition of it. But if no chargeable gain accrues as regards the debt either because the creditor is the original creditor or under the share capital reorganisation rules *and* a chargeable gain accrues to the creditor on a disposal by him of the property, then any resulting chargeable gain is reduced so as not to exceed the chargeable gain that would have accrued if he had acquired the property for a consideration equal to the amount of the debt. [*TCGA 1992, s 251(3)*; *FA 2002, Sch 9 paras 5(12), 7*].

Where the original creditor and a subsequent creditor are CONNECTED PERSONS (16), a loss incurred by the subsequent creditor on the disposal of a debt is not an allowable loss. See 40.5 LOSSES.

A '*debt on a security*' is defined by reference to *TCGA 1992, s 132(3)(b)*, '*security*' thereby including any loan stock or similar security of any government or public or local authority in the UK or elsewhere, or of any company, and whether secured or unsecured. The existence of a document may be indicative of a 'debt on a security', but it cannot be concluded from the absence of a document that the debt is not 'on a security' (*Aberdeen Construction Group Ltd v CIR HL 1978, 52 TC 281*; *W T Ramsay Ltd v CIR HL 1981, 54 TC 101*; *Cleveleys Investment Trust Co v CIR (No 1) CS 1971, 47 TC 300*). An intra-group loan secured on a promissory note was held not to be a marketable security in any realistic sense and was not a 'debt on a security' (*Taylor Clark International Ltd v Lewis CA 1998, 71 TC 226*). For further discussion of the meaning of 'security' see the income tax case of *Williams v Singer and Others HL 1920, 7 TC 387*, and for 'debt on security' see *Tarmac Roadstone Holdings Ltd v Williams (Sp C 95), [1996] SSCD 409.*

HMRC's view, based principally on the HL judgments of Lords Wilberforce and Fraser in *Ramsay*, is set out in HMRC Capital Gains Manual CG 53420–53436. This guidance states that for a debt to be a debt on a security it should be capable of being *both*

- held as an investment, and
- realised at a profit.

The position is to be judged by reference to circumstances prevailing at the time the debt is created, though these may include *anticipated* changes in market interest rates. For a debt to be capable of being held as an investment it should carry a commercial rate of interest, or offer an equivalent return by virtue of its being repayable at a premium or issued at a discount. It should also be marketable. Whether it can be realised at a profit depends not only on the rate of interest, premium etc. but also on whether the debt will last long enough to cover the costs of acquisition and obtain a worthwhile return. HMRC will accept that any loan which cannot be terminated by the borrower within a year of commencement will be outstanding long enough to have the required 'structure of permanence'. But a debt will not have a structure of permanence merely because the borrower is not in a position to repay it in the foreseeable future. A debt can, however, be capable of being realised at a profit if the terms require the lender to be adequately compensated in the event of early repayment. Standard clauses requiring early repayment on the happening of events considered improbable, such as the default or liquidation of the borrower, should not be seen as displacing any stated terms for repayment. The existence of a formal document constituting or evidencing the debt is not an *essential* feature of a debt on a security. Neither realised, nor potential, foreign exchange gains or losses should be taken into account in deciding whether a debt is a debt on a security.

In relation to any chargeable period ending after 15 March 1993, a debenture issued by any company after 15 March 1993 is deemed to be a security within *TCGA 1992, s 132(3)(b)* above if

(1) it is issued on a reorganisation or reduction of a company's share capital or in pursuance of its allotment on any such reorganisation or reduction;

(2) it is issued in exchange for shares in or debentures of another company and in a case to which *TCGA 1992, s 135* (see 58.4 SHARES AND SECURITIES) applies and which is unaffected by *TCGA 1992, s 137(1)* (restriction on application of share reorganisation rules in *TCGA 1992, ss 135, 136* — see 3.18 ANTI-AVOIDANCE);

(3) it is issued under any such arrangements as are mentioned in *TCGA 1992, s 136(1)(a)* (arrangement between company and share or debenture holders in connection with a scheme of reconstruction) and in a case unaffected by *TCGA 1992, s 137* where *s 136* requires shares or debentures in another company to be treated as exchanged for, or for anything that includes, that debenture; or

(4) it is issued in pursuance of rights attached to any debenture issued after 15 March 1993 and falling within (1), (2) or (3) above.

In relation to any disposal after 25 November 1996, any debenture resulting from a conversion of securities (within *TCGA 1992, s 132* — see 58.7 SHARES AND SECURITIES — and whether occurring before or after that date), or which is issued in pursuance of rights attaching to such a debenture, is similarly deemed to be a security.

[*TCGA 1992, s 251(6); FA 1993, s 84(2)(3); FA 1997, s 88(5)(6); FA 2002, Sch 9 paras 5(12), 7*].

For the purposes of *section 251*, the following instruments are deemed to be 'securities' where this would not otherwise be the case, but this fiction does not apply for the purposes of determining what is or is not an allowable loss in any case.

(i) Any instrument falling to be treated as an asset representing a company loan relationship if it were not for the exclusions at 14.6 COMPANIES—CORPORATE FINANCE AND INTANGIBLES.

(ii) Any instrument which, even apart from the exclusions mentioned in (i) above, is not a loan relationship of a company but which would be a deeply discounted security if it were not an 'excluded indexed security' (see 58.16 SHARES AND SECURITIES).

[*TCGA 1992, s 251(7)(8); FA 1996, s 104, s 105(1), Sch 14 para 64; ITTOIA 2005, Sch 1 para 442*].

See also 50.2 QUALIFYING CORPORATE BONDS for a provision corresponding to *TCGA 1992, s 251(6)* and regarding the definition of 'corporate bond', so that combined the two provisions prevent, in the circumstances stated, the issue of a debenture which neither represents a debt on a security nor is a qualifying corporate bond.

22.6 **Decorations.** A decoration for valour or gallantry (unless acquired by the vendor for money or money's worth) is exempt. [*TCGA 1992, s 268*].

22.7 **Dwelling-houses.** A gain accruing to an individual on the disposal of (or of an interest in) a dwelling-house which has been his only or main residence during his period of ownership is exempt (or partly exempt). See 49 PRIVATE RESIDENCES for this exemption which is also extended, in certain circumstances, to trustees and personal representatives.

22.8 **Foreign currency.** Foreign currency acquired for an individual's (or his dependant's) personal expenditure outside the UK (including the provision or maintenance of his residence outside the UK) is exempt. [*TCGA 1992, s 269*].

No chargeable gain or allowable loss accrues on the disposal by a 'qualifying company' (see 14.15 COMPANIES—CORPORATE FINANCE AND INTANGIBLES), on or after its 'commencement day' (the first day of its first accounting period beginning after 22 March 1995) and in an accounting period beginning before 1 October 2002 (see 14.15 COMPANIES—CORPORATE FINANCE AND INTANGIBLES), of currency other than sterling, provided that immediately before the disposal the company did not hold the currency in 'exempt circumstances'. '*Exempt circumstances*' are when the currency is held

(*a*) for the purposes of long-term insurance business;

(*b*) for the purposes of mutual insurance business;

(*c*) for the purposes of the occupation for profit of commercial woodlands in the UK;

(*d*) by an approved housing association; or

(*e*) by an approved self-build society.

[*FA 1993, s 169, Sch 17 paras 1–3; FA 2002, Sch 40 Pt 3(10); SI 2001 No 3629, Art 81*].

See also 22.5 above. (For accounting periods beginning on or after 1 October 2002, the rules for taxing exchange gains and losses of companies (FOREX) are assimilated into the loan relationships regime — see 14.15 COMPANIES—CORPORATE FINANCE AND INTANGIBLES.)

22.9 **Government securities.** Disposals of specified government and public corporation securities are exempt from capital gains tax whatever the period of ownership. This also applies to options or contracts to acquire or dispose of such securities. See 26 GOVERNMENT SECURITIES, 14.2–14.6 COMPANIES—CORPORATE FINANCE AND INTANGIBLES, and also 6.7, 6.8 ASSETS as regards options and contracts.

22.10 **Insurance policies.** A gain on the disposal of, or of an 'interest' in, the rights conferred by a 'non-life insurance policy' is exempt, but where the policy is for damage to, or loss or depreciation of, assets, the exemption applies only so far as the rights do not relate to assets which on disposal could give rise to a chargeable gain. (This does not prevent sums received under such policies for loss, damage, etc. to assets from being chargeable; see 9 CAPITAL SUMS DERIVED FROM ASSETS.)

For this purpose, a '*non-life insurance policy*' is a contract made in the course of a capital redemption business within *ICTA 1988, s 458(3)* (i.e. a capital redemption policy) or any other policy of insurance which is not a policy of insurance on the life of any person. An '*interest*' in rights means an interest as co-owner of the rights, and it is immaterial whether the rights are owned jointly or in common or whether or not the interests of the co-owners are equal.

For disposals before 5 December 2005, these provisions did not refer to interests in rights and the definition of 'non-life insurance policy' did not explicitly include capital redemption policies. HMRC's view, however, is that the exemption has always applied to capital redemption policies and that the addition of such policies to the definition for disposals on or after 5 December 2005 is simply a clarification (Treasury Explanatory Notes to the Finance Bill 2006).

[*TCGA 1992, s 204(1)–(4)(7)(8)(10); FA 2006, s 73(2)(4)*].

See also 39 LIFE INSURANCE POLICIES AND DEFERRED ANNUITIES.

22.11 **Motor cars etc.** A mechanically propelled road vehicle constructed or adapted for the carriage of passengers, except for a vehicle of a type not commonly used as a private vehicle and unsuitable to be so used, is not a chargeable asset, and thus no chargeable gain or allowable loss accrues on its disposal. [*TCGA 1992, s 263*]. This exemption applies regardless of whether or not the vehicle was eligible for capital allowances (cf. 22.4 above). For the interpretation of 'commonly used as a private vehicle' in relation to capital allowances, see cases mentioned in Tolley's Capital Allowances. Vehicles outside this exemption include taxi cabs, racing cars, single seat sports cars, vans, lorries, other commercial vehicles, motor cycles, scooters and motor cycle/sidecar combinations (HMRC Capital Gains Manual CG 76907).

Motor vehicles which are outside the above exemption, and which are privately owned and not used in a business, are exempt as tangible movable wasting assets (see 22.4 above and Revenue Tax Bulletin October 1994 p 166).

Personalised car number plates are not covered by either exemption. The value of the number plate itself is usually negligible, and the plate is regarded as part of the car when sold attached thereto. However, the disposal of the inherent intangible right to use a specific combination of letters or numbers when registering a vehicle is neither a disposal of a motor car as above nor of a chattel as in 22.4 above, and any gain arising will be a chargeable gain. (HMRC Capital Gains Manual CG 76920–76928).

22.12 **Qualifying corporate bonds.** Qualifying corporate bonds are exempt whatever the period of ownership. This also applies to options or contracts to acquire or dispose of such bonds. See 50 QUALIFYING CORPORATE BONDS, and see 6.7 and 6.8 ASSETS as regards options and contracts. For loans to traders evidenced by qualifying corporate bonds, see 40.11 LOSSES.

22.13 **Right to receive interest on deposit of victim of National-Socialist persecution.** A gain accruing on the disposal of a right, or an 'interest' in a right, to receive the whole or any part of a payment of interest eligible for income tax exemption under *ITTOIA 2005, s 756A* is not a chargeable gain. That section provides, broadly, for income tax exemption for interest paid under certain compensation schemes for deposits made on or before 5 June 1945 by, or on behalf of, victims of National-Socialist persecution. See Tolley's Income Tax for further details.

An '*interest*' in a right is for this purpose an interest as a co-owner of the right and it is immaterial whether the right is owned jointly or in common, or whether or not the interests of the co-owners are equal.

This exemption was introduced in *FA 2006* and applies with retrospective effect to disposals on or after 6 April 1996. No loss accruing on a disposal before 6 April 2006 is, however, to cease to be an allowable loss as a consequence. All necessary adjustments, whether by assessment, discharge or repayment of tax or otherwise, can be made for 2005/06 or any earlier year to give effect to the exemption for those years, provided that the person entitled to it makes a claim on or before 31 January 2012.

[*TCGA 1992, s 268A; FA 2006, s 64(4)(8)(10)–(12)*].

See also 22.25 below for compensation from foreign governments for assets confiscated, destroyed etc.

22.14 **Savings certificates, savings schemes and savings accounts etc.** Savings certificates, and non-marketable securities issued under the *National Loans Acts 1939* and *1968* and corresponding NI enactments are not 'chargeable assets' and accordingly no chargeable gain accrues on their disposal. Interest resulting from certified SAYE savings arrangements and tax-exempt special savings accounts are ignored for capital gains tax purposes. [*TCGA 1992, s 121, s 271(4); ITTOIA 2005, Sch 1 para 445(3)*]. No provision of *TCGA 1992* defines 'chargeable asset' but the subsequent words of the provision seem to put the position beyond doubt.

22.15 **Settlements.** With certain exceptions, no chargeable gain accrues on the disposal of an interest created by or arising under a settlement by the original beneficiary or any other person (other than one who acquired, or derives his title from one who acquired, his interest for money or money's worth). See 57.14 SETTLEMENTS.

22.16 **Ships and other assets within the tonnage tax regime.** Under this ring-fenced regime introduced for accounting periods beginning on or after 1 January 2000, a shipping company or group may elect to have its taxable profits computed by reference to the net tonnage of each of the qualifying ships it operates. The initial period for making an election was the 12 months beginning with 28 July 2000 (the date of Royal Assent to *FA 2000*), but a further period, 1 July 2005 to 31 December 2006 has been added. An election is normally expected to remain in force for at least 10 years, although *FA 2005* provided a limited opportunity to withdraw from an election in 2005 (and further such opportunities may be provided for by Treasury order). Qualifying ships must be seagoing, of at least 100 tons gross tonnage and be engaged in qualifying activities, e.g. the transportation of goods or passengers by sea. Certain vessels are excluded, e.g. fishing and factory support vessels, harbour and river ferries, oil rigs, pleasure craft, floating restaurants etc. The strategic and commercial management of ships within the regime must be undertaken from the UK. *FA 2005* also introduced a requirement for new ships entering tonnage tax to be registered in the EU (but this rule is disapplied for the financial year 2006). *Capital gains* accruing during the currency of the election are not chargeable gains (and losses are not allowable losses) to the extent that the assets disposed of were used exclusively for the qualifying shipping activity. In the event of a company leaving the regime for certain specified reasons, anti-avoidance provisions apply to bring into charge a previously exempt gain arising in the last six years. [*FA 2000, s 82, Sch 22; FA 2005, s 93, Sch 7; SI 2005 No 1449; SI 2006 No 333*]. HMRC have published guidance on the practical operation of the regime (see HMRC Statement of Practice 4/00 — in particular, para 131 on exemptions from exit charges).

22.17 EXEMPT GAINS AND TRANSACTIONS

The gains or transactions detailed in 22.18–22.37 below do not give rise to a liability to capital gains tax.

22.18 **Agricultural grants.** Grants made to an individual under *Agriculture Act 1967, s 27* (grants for relinquishing occupation of uncommercial agricultural units) are not treated as part of the consideration obtained, or otherwise accruing, on the disposal of any asset. [*TCGA 1992, s 249*]. See also 9.1(*c*) CAPITAL SUMS DERIVED FROM ASSETS.

22.19 **Betting, lottery etc.** Winnings from betting, including pool betting, or lotteries or games with prizes are not chargeable gains, and no chargeable gain or allowable loss accrues on the disposal of rights to such winnings obtained by participating. [*TCGA 1992, s 51*(*1*)]. Included is the betting on future price movements of precious and base metals, soft commodities and currencies etc. (see Tolley's Practical Tax 1982 p 59).

Where prize winnings take the form of an asset, the recipient is regarded as having acquired the asset at its market value at the time of acquisition (HMRC Capital Gains Manual CG 12604).

22.20 **Business expansion scheme (BES).** Any gain accruing to an individual, to whom BES income tax relief has been given, on the disposal of eligible shares **issued after 18 March 1986** and before 1 January 1994 (when the scheme was abolished) is exempt from CGT provided the income tax relief has not been withdrawn. Similarly, any loss is not allowable. [*TCGA 1992, s 150*(*2*)]. If the BES shares have been disposed of to a spouse and the inter-spouse exemption applies under *TCGA 1992, s 58*, the BES exemption for capital gains will still apply to disposals by the recipient spouse to third parties (see 42.4 MARRIED PERSONS AND CIVIL PARTNERS).

Only a complete withdrawal of relief, and not a partial one, will affect the CGT position, i.e. exemption for a gain, no allowance for a loss (Tolley's Practical Tax 1987, p 115). If relief is withdrawn completely, any allowable loss which results on a disposal of the shares may be eligible for relief under *ICTA 1988, s 574* — CGT loss accruing to individual in respect of unquoted shares in a trading company converted to an income tax loss — see 40.13 LOSSES.

Further rules dealing with identification and other matters apply as follows.

(*a*) The normal share identification rules (and, for shares acquired before 6 April 1998, share pooling arrangements) (see 59 SHARES AND SECURITIES—IDENTIFICATION RULES) do not apply to BES shares. Each acquisition is treated as a separate acquisition and shares are matched on a first in/first out (FIFO) basis. Where a disposal after 5 April 1998 is so matched with shares acquired on the same day as one another, only some of which still have BES income tax relief attributable to them, it is first matched with shares in respect of which no such relief is still attributable. For these purposes and that in (*d*) below shares are only treated as being of the same class if they would be so treated if dealt with on the Stock Exchange and the grant after 18 March 1986 of an option the exercise of which would bind the grantor to sell shares is treated as a disposal of those shares.

(*b*) If there is a reorganisation within the meaning of *TCGA 1992, s 126* then the new ordinary shares will stand in the place of the old ordinary shares and each is treated as a new holding.

(*c*) If, as part of a reconstruction, shares or debentures in another company are issued to a BES shareholder in exchange for the BES shares, then, unless the income tax relief is withdrawn, the shares in the new company are not generally deemed to stand in the place of shares in the old company under *TCGA 1992, s 135* or *s 136* (see 58.4, 58.6 SHARES AND SECURITIES) and there is thus a disposal of the shares in the old company. However, *section 135* or *136* does apply in the normal way if

- the new holding consists of new ordinary shares issued after 28 November 1994 and more than five years after the issue of the original shares and carrying no present or future preferential rights to dividends or assets or right to redemption (no preferential right to redemption where the new shares were issued before 6 April 1998); and

- the company issuing the new shares has previously issued shares under the BES and has issued the appropriate certificate enabling investors to obtain relief on that earlier issue.

In addition, *TCGA 1992, s 135* is not disapplied in a case to which *ICTA 1988, s 304A* (inserted by *FA 1998, Sch 13 para 41*) applies. That provision enables a BES company to become, after 5 April 1998, a wholly-owned subsidiary of a new holding company in certain circumstances. The investors receive shares in the new company in exchange for their original shares, and the new shares then stand in the shoes of the old for the purposes of BES income tax relief. This treatment is generally applied for CGT purposes also.

(*d*) Where an original holding has been subject to the relief, a disposal of the whole or part of a new holding, allotted other than for payment as a result of a reorganisation within *TCGA 1992, s 126(2)(a)* after 18 March 1986 (allotments in respect of, and in proportion to, existing holdings or of any class of shares, e.g. a bonus issue within 58.1 SHARES AND SECURITIES above), will be treated, for the purposes of deciding whether relief given is to be withdrawn, as a disposal of the whole or a corresponding part of the original holding with which, by reason of *TCGA 1992, s 127*, the new holding is identified. Any reallocated shares under *section 127* will be deemed to stand in the place of the original shares.

(*e*) The general share reorganisation provisions of *TCGA 1992, ss 127–130* (see 58.1–58.3 SHARES AND SECURITIES above) do not apply after 18 March 1986 to ordinary shares in respect of which relief has been given if

(i) there is, by virtue of an allotment for payment within *TCGA 1992, s 126(2)(a)* (see also (*d*) above), a reorganisation affecting those shares; and

(ii) immediately following the reorganisation, the relief has not been withdrawn in respect of those shares or relief has been given in respect of the allotted shares and not withdrawn.

On such reorganisations occurring before 29 November 1994 where immediately before it the relief has not been withdrawn, and where both the amount of relief (or the amount remaining where it has been reduced) and the market value of the shares immediately before the reorganisation exceed their market value immediately after the reorganisation, the relief is reduced by an amount equal to whichever is the smaller of those excesses. This reduction also applies *mutatis mutandis* where the individual sells his rights instead of taking up his allotment. Where the relief is so reduced an amount equal to the reduction is treated as additional expenditure for CGT purposes on a disposal of the allotted shares or debentures and such expenditure is apportioned between the allotted shares etc. in a just and reasonable manner. Where a disposal of the original holding of ordinary shares is not ultimately exempt (e.g. because all relief has been withdrawn), the allowable expenditure relating to such shares is reduced by an amount equal to the above reduction and is again apportioned in a just and reasonable manner.

In computing gains or losses arising on an individual's disposal of shares **issued before 19 March 1986** in respect of which BES relief has been given and not withdrawn, that relief is disregarded *except* to the extent that an unindexed loss would otherwise accrue, in which case the deductible expenditure is reduced by the smaller of the BES relief given (and not withdrawn) and the amount of the loss. [*TCGA 1992, s 150(3)*]. It was held in *Quinn v Cooper Ch D 1998, 71 TC 44* that indexation allowance should be based on the reduced cost. *Section 150(3)* does not apply to disposals within *TCGA 1992, s 58(1)* (see 42.4 MARRIED PERSONS AND CIVIL PARTNERS) but will apply on a subsequent disposal to a third party by the transferee. In determining whether any sums are excluded under *TCGA 1992, s 39(1)(2)* (exclusion of expenditure allowable against income — see 15.6 COMPUTATION OF GAINS AND LOSSES), the existence of any relief given and not withdrawn is ignored.

The provisions in (*a*) (except in relation to a grant of an option etc.) and (*b*) above also apply to shares issued before 19 March 1986 as do those in (*d*) in respect of reorganisations before that date. The provisions in (*c*) do not apply to shares issued before 19 March 1986 and those in (*e*) do not apply to reorganisations before that date. (*Note.* A Revenue Press Release of 19 December 1989 announced that an unintended change in the law had been made by *ICTA 1988* so as to apply the provisions in (*c*) above to shares issued before 19 March 1986 where a reconstruction involving an exchange or cancellation of shares occurs after 5 April 1988 with the result that the exchange or cancellation would give rise to a disposal. *FA 1990, Sch 14 paras 17, 19* restored the position for exchanges etc. occurring after 5 April 1988 save that in respect of an exchange before 1 January 1990 the shareholder could irrevocably elect to have the exchange treated as a disposal by giving written notice at any time before 6 April 1991.)

Where an allowable loss still arose after the above reduction in consideration, the loss may have been eligible for relief under *ICTA 1988, s 574* (CGT loss accruing to individual in respect of unquoted shares in a trading company converted to an income tax loss — see 40.13 LOSSES).

General. Where relief has been granted or withdrawn, consequential adjustments may be made to the individual's CGT position.

[*TCGA 1992, s 39(3), s 150; FA 1985, Sch 19 para 16(3); ICTA 1988, ss 289, 299, 305; FA 1991, s 99(2)(4); F(No 2)A 1992, s 38; FA 1994, s 137, Sch 15 para 29; FA 1995, ss 68, 69; FA 1998, s 74, Sch 13 paras 37, 39, 42; FA 2002, Sch 9 paras 4(2), 8(1); SI 2005 No 3229, Reg 109*].

It should be noted that 'relief' refers to the deduction falling to be made from a person's income and not to any amount of income tax which is not chargeable due to such a deduction.

For consideration of the determination of the time shares are issued under the scheme, see *National Westminster Bank plc v CIR; Barclays Bank plc v CIR HL 1994, 67 TC 1.*

22.21 **Cashbacks.** A cashback is a lump sum received by a customer as an inducement for entering into a transaction for the purchase of goods, investments or services and received as a direct consequence of having entered into that transaction. An example of such a transaction is the taking out of a mortgage. The payer may be either the provider of the goods etc. or an interested third party. The term 'cashback' does not include a cash payment by a building society to its members on a takeover or conversion (for which see 58.22 SHARES AND SECURITIES), or by other mutual organisations such as insurance companies or friendly societies to their policy holders on demutualisation.

A cashback does not derive from a chargeable asset for CGT purposes. No chargeable gain therefore arises on its receipt. (An ordinary retail customer purchasing goods etc. at arm's length will not be liable to income tax on a cashback either.)

(HMRC Statement of Practice 4/97).

22.22 **Child Trust Funds.** The Child Trust Fund scheme commences on 6 April 2005 for any child born after 31 August 2002 where, broadly, there is an entitlement to child benefit (an '*eligible child*'). The scheme provides for HMRC to make an initial contribution in the form of a voucher (initially worth £250, or £500 for children in lower income families), which is then used to open an account. Anyone, including the child, may then pay money into the account up to a yearly limit of £1,200. HMRC will make a further contribution when the child reaches the age of seven. The account provider, acting on the instructions of a nominated responsible person (the '*registered contact*'), or the child if over 16, may invests the funds in a limited range of qualifying investments. Normally no withdrawals are permitted before the fund matures when the child reaches 18. For further details see Tolley's Income Tax.

Tax treatment. No tax is chargeable in respect of interest, dividends, distributions, gains or (from 27 December 2005) alternative financial arrangement return on account investments. Capital losses on account investments are disregarded. Any income from account investments is not to be regarded as income for any income tax purposes. For capital gains tax purposes, any assets held as account investments are regarded as held by the child concerned in a separate capacity from that in which he holds any other assets of the same description. The child is treated as having sold all the account investments, and as having reacquired them in his personal capacity, for their market value immediately before attaining the age of 18.

It is up to the account provider to make tax claims, conduct appeals, and agree liabilities and reliefs on behalf of the child or registered contact. It is unlikely therefore that the child or registered contact will have to deal with any tax matters arising from the account. However, there is power for HMRC to make an assessment as an alternative to the account provider in order to withdraw relief or recover tax.

[*Child Trust Funds Act 2004, s 13; SI 2004 No 1450, Regs 24–38; SI 2005 No 3349*].

22.23 **Damages and compensation.** Sums received by way of compensation or damages for any wrong or injury suffered by an individual 'in his person' or in his profession or vocation are not chargeable gains. [*TCGA 1992, s 51(2)*]. The words 'in his person' are distinct from 'in his finances', but are construed widely (see HMRC Capital Gains Manual

CG 13032). The exemption given in relation to vocation is extended by concession to an individual's trade or employment. See HMRC Extra-Statutory Concession D33 (referred to at 6.1 ASSETS). If the compensation relates to an asset (e.g. insurance recoveries), payment does constitute a disposal; see 9 CAPITAL SUMS DERIVED FROM ASSETS.

22.24 **Enterprise investment scheme (EIS).** In respect of shares issued after 31 December 1993, any gain arising on a disposal more than, broadly, three years after the issue of them (five years for shares issued before 6 April 2000), where an amount of EIS income tax relief is attributable to them, is wholly or partly exempt. If a loss would otherwise arise on a disposal of shares where an amount of such relief is attributable to them, a reduction is made in the amount of allowable expenditure equal to the amount of relief. See 21 ENTERPRISE INVESTMENT SCHEME).

Venture capital trusts. In respect of shares issued after 5 April 1995, any gain arising on a disposal of them where an amount of such relief is attributable to them is wholly or partly exempt. A loss arising on a disposal of shares is not an allowable loss, except to the extent that a gain on the disposal would have been a chargeable gain. See 66.11 VENTURE CAPITAL TRUSTS.

22.25 **Compensation from foreign governments.** Gains on sums received by individuals from foreign governments by way of compensation for assets confiscated, destroyed or expropriated are exempt provided certain conditions are met. See 9.1 CAPITAL SUMS DERIVED FROM ASSETS.

22.26 **Exempt amount for the year.** A specified amount of the taxable amount of gains for a year of assessment is exempt. See 2.3 ANNUAL RATES AND EXEMPTIONS.

22.27 **Gains arising partly before 6.4.1965 or 31.3.1982.** Assets held on, and gains arising partly before, these dates are subject to special provisions. See 7 ASSETS HELD ON 6 APRIL 1965 and 8 ASSETS HELD ON 31 MARCH 1982.

22.28 **Gifts for public benefit.** Gifts **before 17 March 1998** of 'eligible property' to bodies not established or conducted for profit will, if the Revenue so direct (whether before or after the transfer), be exempt from capital gains tax.

'*Eligible property*' is

(*a*) land which in the opinion of the Revenue is of outstanding scenic, historic or scientific interest;

(*b*) a building for the preservation of which special steps should in the opinion of the Revenue be taken by reason of its outstanding historic, architectural or aesthetic interest and the cost of preserving it;

(*c*) land used as the grounds of a building within (*b*) above;

(*d*) an object which at the time of the transfer is ordinarily kept in, and is given with, a building within (*b*) above;

(*e*) property given as a source of income for the upkeep of property within these sub-paragraphs;

(*f*) a picture, print, book, manuscript, work of art or scientific collection which in the opinion of the Revenue is of national, scientific, historic or artistic interest. ('*National interest*' includes interest within any part of the UK.)

The Revenue must not give a direction (i) unless in their opinion, the body who receives the property is an appropriate one to be responsible for its preservation; or (ii) in relation to property within (*e*) above, if or to the extent that the property will, in their opinion, produce more income than is needed (with a reasonable margin) for the upkeep of the other property in question.

Before giving a direction, the Revenue may require undertakings (which may be varied by agreement) concerning the use, disposal, and preservation of the property and reasonable access to it for the public.

The above exemption is abolished for disposals after 16 March 1998.

[*TCGA 1992, s 258(1); IHTA 1984, s 26; FA 1998, s 143(1), Sch 27 Pt IV*].

See also 33.7 HOLD-OVER RELIEFS for relief for gifts for public benefit.

22.29 **Individual Savings Accounts (ISAs).** ISAs are available **after 5 April 1999** to individuals over 18 (though see below) who are both resident and ordinarily resident in the UK and will continue to be available for a minimum of ten years. The accounts can be made up of cash, stocks and shares and, before 6 April 2005, life insurance (see below). They were introduced as a replacement for PEPs and TESSAs, although see 22.31 below as regards PEPs already in existence at the end of 1998/99 and note that neither the value of PEP holdings nor any capital transferred to an ISA from a TESSA (tax-exempt special savings account) will affect the amount which can be subscribed to an ISA. Investors can subscribe up to £7,000 to an ISA in each tax year up to and including 2009/10, of which a maximum of £3,000 can go into cash and, for 2004/05 and earlier years, £1,000 into life insurance. See further details below. After 5 April 2001, the availability of cash ISAs is extended to 16 and 17-year olds. There is no statutory lock-in, minimum subscription, minimum holding period or lifetime subscription limit. Withdrawals may be made at any time without loss of tax relief but not so as to allow further subscriptions in breach of the annual maximum.

Interest and dividends are free of income tax (and a 10% tax credit is payable on dividends received from UK equities before 6 April 2004). Gains arising from assets held within an ISA are not chargeable gains for CGT purposes (and losses are not allowable).

[*TCGA 1992, s 151; ICTA 1988, ss 333, 333A; FA 1998, ss 75, 76, Sch 27 Pt III(15); ITTOIA 2005, ss 694–701, Sch 1 paras 141, 436, 503*].

The Individual Savings Account Regulations 1998 (*SI 1998 No 1870* as amended) provide for the setting up by HMRC-approved accounts managers of plans in the form of an account (an ISA) under which individuals may make certain investments, for the conditions under which they may invest and under which the accounts are to operate, for relief from tax in respect of account investments, and for general administration. The regulations generally took effect on 6 April 1999 and are summarised below.

General. An application to subscribe to an ISA may be made by an individual who is 18 or over (though see below as regards children under 18) and who is resident and ordinarily resident in the UK (or who is a non-UK resident Crown employee performing duties treated under *ICTA 1988, s 132(4)(a)* (see Tolley's Income Tax) as performed in the UK or, after 5 April 2001, who is married to, or a civil partner of, such an employee). Joint accounts are not permitted. An investor who subsequently fails to meet the residence requirement may retain the account and the right to tax exemptions thereunder but can make no further subscriptions to the account until he again comes to meet that requirement. After 7 January 2003, an application made on behalf of an individual suffering from mental disorder, by a parent, guardian, spouse, civil partner, son or daughter of his, is treated as if made by that individual. This replaced a rule specific to Scotland whereby a *curator bonis* appointed in respect of a qualifying individual incapable of managing his affairs could subscribe to an ISA in his capacity as such without affecting his right to subscribe in any other capacity.

An ISA is made up of *one or more* of the following: a stocks and shares component, a cash component and, for 2004/05 and earlier years, an insurance component. For details of investments qualifying for inclusion in each component, see Tolley's Income Tax. It must be designated from the outset as a maxi-account, mini-account or TESSA only account, such designation continuing to have effect for any year in which the investor makes a subscription to the account. The insurance component is abolished after 5 April 2005.

After that date, life insurance products instead go into the stocks and shares component, except that certain low-risk products providing a 'cash-like' return go into the cash component. As regards insurance components in existence immediately before 6 April 2005, these are merged into either the stocks and shares component or the cash component, as appropriate. Where the insurance component was part of a maxi-account it is treated as merging on that date into the stocks and shares, or, as appropriate, cash component of that account. If the insurance component constituted a mini-account, it is treated as becoming on that date the stocks and shares, or, as appropriate, cash component of the same account.

A *maxi-account* must comprise a stocks and shares component (*with or without* other components). The maximum subscription per tax year (up to and including 2009/10) is £7,000 of which a maximum of £3,000 may be allocated to a cash component and, for 2004/05 and earlier years, £1,000 to an insurance component. In any tax year in which an investor subscribes to a maxi-account he cannot subscribe to any other ISA apart from a TESSA only account.

A *mini-account* must consist of a single specified component. The maximum subscription (per tax year) is £4,000 (£3,000 for 2004/05 and earlier years) if that component is stocks and shares, £3,000 if it is cash and, for 2004/05 and earlier years, £1,000 if it is insurance. In any tax year in which an investor subscribes to a mini-account, he cannot subscribe to another mini-account consisting of the same component or to a maxi-account.

A *TESSA only account* is an account consisting of a cash component only and limited to capital (*not* accumulated interest) transferred from a TESSA (see Tolley's Income Tax) within six months following its maturity after 5 April 1999 (or after 5 January 1999 where no follow-up TESSA is opened). Such transfers are not subject to any annual subscription limit, and may also be made to a maxi-account or to a cash component mini-account without counting towards the annual subscription limits for such accounts. Continuing subscriptions after 5 April 1999 to a TESSA or follow-up TESSA do not affect an individual's ISA annual subscription limits.

Subscriptions to an ISA must be made in cash (and must be allocated irrevocably to the agreed component or single component) except that

- shares acquired by the investor under a savings-related (SAYE) share option scheme (see 20.26 EMPLOYEE SHARE SCHEMES); or
- shares appropriated to him under an approved profit sharing scheme (see 20.29 EMPLOYEE SHARE SCHEMES); or
- plan shares (but not securities or other rights) of an approved share incentive plan (see 20.19 EMPLOYEE SHARE SCHEMES) which have ceased to be subject to the plan but remain in his beneficial ownership

may be transferred to a stocks and shares component. Such transfers count towards the annual subscription limits, by reference to the market value of the shares at the date of transfer. No chargeable gain or allowable loss arises on the transfer. A transfer of SAYE scheme shares must be made within 90 days after the exercise of the option. A transfer of shares appropriated under a profit sharing scheme must be made within 90 days after the earlier of the release date and the date on which the investor instructed the scheme trustees to transfer ownership of the shares to him. A transfer of share incentive plan shares must be made within 90 days after the shares ceased to be subject to the plan. In all cases, after 12 December 2000, 'shares' includes a reference to shares held in the form of depositary interests (see (*j*) below).

ISA investments cannot be purchased otherwise than out of cash held by the account manager and allocated to the particular component concerned, and cannot be purchased from the investor or his spouse or civil partner.

The title to ISA investments (other than cash deposits, national savings products and certain insurance policies) is vested in the account manager (or his nominee) either alone or jointly with the investor, though all ISA investments are in the beneficial ownership of the investor. The investor may elect to receive annual reports and accounts etc. in respect of ISA investments and/or to attend and vote at shareholders' etc. meetings.

The statements and declarations to be made when applying to subscribe to an ISA are specified. The maximum penalty for an incorrect statement or declaration is the amount (if any) of income tax and/or capital gains tax underpaid as a result. Assessments to withdraw tax relief or otherwise recover tax underpaid may be made on the account manager or investor. HMRC have power to require information from, and to inspect records of, account managers and investors.

From 1 October 2002 (and with reference to pre-existing ISAs as well as new ones), the terms and conditions of an ISA cannot prevent the investor from withdrawing funds or from transferring his account (or a part of it) to another HMRC-approved account manager (subject to the conditions governing such transfers). The account manager is allowed a reasonable business period (not exceeding 30 days) to comply with the investor's instructions in this regard. By concession, an ISA opened before 24 August 2002 offering a fixed or guaranteed return under terms requiring the funds to be locked in for a period of up to five years may, if the manager wishes and with HMRC agreement, continue to maturity under its original terms, though no further subscriptions can be made after 5 April 2003 (Revenue Press Release 26 July 2002).

Children under 18. For 2001/02 onwards, 16 and 17-year olds who otherwise satisfy the general conditions above may subscribe to a cash mini-account or to a cash component of a maxi-account. The maximum subscription for a tax year at the end of which the individual is under 18 is £3,000. The maximum ISA subscriptions for the tax year in which the individual reaches 18 are the same as for any other 18-year old, but no more than £3,000 can be subscribed before the individual's 18th birthday. See also under Tax Exemptions below.

Tax exemptions. Except as stated below, no income tax or capital gains tax is chargeable on the account manager or the investor in respect of interest, dividends, distributions, gains or (from 27 December 2005) alternative financial arrangement return on ISA investments. Capital losses are not allowable. As stated in the introduction above, tax credits on UK dividends paid before 6 April 2004 are repayable (via the account manager). An investor who ceases to be UK-resident is treated as continuing to be so resident as regards his entitlement to repayment of tax credits.

Interest on a cash deposit held within a stocks and shares component or insurance component is, however, taxable at the lower rate of income tax, such tax to be accounted for by the account manager (by set-off against tax repayments or otherwise). There is no further liability; the interest does not form part of the investor's total income and the tax paid cannot be repaid to the investor.

As regards children under 18 (see above), the exemption for interest on a cash mini-account or cash component of a maxi-account does not prevent the application of the settlements legislation of *ITTOIA 2005, s 629* (see Tolley's Income Tax under Settlements) whereby (subject to a *de minimis* limit) the income of an unmarried minor on capital provided by a parent is taxable as if it were the parent's income. Such income arising in an ISA is therefore taxable.

Life assurance gains on policies held within an insurance component are not subject to income tax (and a deficiency on termination is not deductible from the investor's total income). If it comes to the account manager's notice that such a policy is invalid, i.e. its terms and conditions do not provide (or no longer provide) that it be held only as a qualifying insurance component investment, a chargeable event then occurs, with any gain taxable as income. If the policy has already terminated, the chargeable event is deemed to have occurred at the end of the final policy year (see Tolley's Income Tax). Any previous chargeable event which actually occurred in relation to the policy is similarly taxed, by reference to the time it occurred. Lower rate income tax (for 2004/05 and earlier years, basic rate income tax) is payable by the account manager (with HMRC also having power to assess the investor). Any higher rate tax due is payable by the investor by assessment within five years after 31 January following the year of assessment in which the chargeable event occurred or was deemed to occur. Top-slicing relief (see Tolley's Income Tax) is available in the same way as for non-ISA-related chargeable events.

Exempt income and gains do not have to be reported in the investor's personal tax return.

Further capital gains matters. A transfer of ISA investments by an account manager to an investor is deemed to be made at market value, with no capital gain or allowable loss arising. An investor is treated as holding shares or securities in an ISA in a capacity other than that in which he holds any other shares etc. of the same class in the same company, so that share identification rules (see 59.1 SHARES AND SECURITIES—IDENTIFICATION RULES) are applied separately to ISA investments (and separately as between different ISAs held by the same investor). The normal share reorganisation rules are disapplied in respect of ISA investments in the event of a reorganisation of share capital involving an allotment for payment, e.g. a rights issue. Shares transferred to an ISA in the limited circumstances described above are deemed for these purposes to have been ISA investments from,

- in the case of SAYE option scheme shares, their acquisition by the investor; or
- in the case of profit sharing scheme shares, the earlier of the release date and the date on which the investor instructed the scheme trustees to transfer ownership of the shares to him; or
- in the case of share incentive plan shares, the date when they ceased to be subject to the plan.

Where the investor held shares eligible for transfer to an ISA and other shares of the same class but not so eligible, disposals are generally identified primarily with the latter, thus preserving to the greatest possible extent the eligibility of the remaining shares.

Repairing of invalid accounts. Where, within a single tax year, an investor opens a valid ISA, closes it and opens a new ISA of the same designation and component, the new ISA used to be technically invalid (because transfers between ISAs can only be carried out by account managers). For 2003/04 onwards, where the account is a mini-account or TESSA only account, the new ISA (i.e. the first such ISA to be opened after the said closure and in the same tax year) is treated as valid (and thus qualifying for tax relief) from the date it is opened.

Where the above circumstances occurred in 2001/02 or 2002/03 and HMRC give notice after 7 January 2003 that the new account is invalid, the account becomes 'eligible for repair', i.e. it qualifies for tax relief *but only from the date of the notice*. Similar consequences ensue for 2001/02 and all subsequent years (where the resulting HMRC notice is given after 7 January 2003) where an investor subscribes to an incompatible combination of maxi-accounts and mini-accounts in a single tax year. Accounts thus eligible for repair are the earliest invalid account opened in the year and any account to which the capital proceeds of a matured TESSA are transferred. Repairing of accounts is subject to normal subscription limits, and where necessary HMRC will apportion (i.e. between valid accounts and any one or more accounts eligible for repair) the total amount subscribed in the tax year.

Account managers. The regulations cover qualification as an account manager, HMRC approval and withdrawal thereof, appointment of UK tax representatives of non-UK account managers, account managers ceasing to act or to qualify, claims for tax relief and agreement of liabilities, annual returns of income and of information, annual and interim tax repayment claims, record-keeping, and information to be provided to investors.

[*SI 1998 Nos 1870, 3174; SI 2000 Nos 809, 2079, 3112; SI 2001 No 908; SI 2001 No 3629, Arts 168–178; SI 2001 No 3778; SI 2002 Nos 453, 1974, 3158; SI 2003 No 2747; SI 2004 Nos 1677, 2996; SI 2005 Nos 609, 2561, 3230, 3350*].

Separate regulations modify existing tax legislation so far as it concerns individual savings account business of insurance companies. [*SI 1998 No 1871 as amended*].

Closure and death. Subject to the ISA terms and conditions, an investor may close an ISA at any time without affecting tax exemptions up to the date of closure. Where an investor dies, income and gains in respect of ISA investments which arise after the date of death but before the date of closure are not exempt.

See generally HMRC Pamphlet IR 2008.

22.30 **Legatees.** No chargeable gain accrues to the personal representatives where a person acquires an asset from them as legatee, and the legatee is treated as if the personal representatives' acquisition of the asset had been his acquisition of it. See 18.9 DEATH.

22.31 **Personal Equity Plans (PEPs). Before 6 April 1999,** an individual could make, subject to conditions, investments under a plan and obtain exemption from capital gains tax (as well as income tax) in respect of transactions covered by the plan. No further subscriptions to PEPs can be made after 5 April 1999, but existing PEPs may continue, and independently of individual savings accounts (see 22.29 above). See 58.18 SHARES AND SECURITIES.

22.32 **Recovery of assets under Proceeds of Crime Act 2002, Pt 5.** *Proceeds of Crime Act 2002, Pt 5 Ch 2* provides for the recovery, in civil proceedings before the High Court (or, in Scotland, the Court of Session), of property which is, or represents, property obtained through 'unlawful conduct' (as defined in the *Act*). If the Court is satisfied that any property is recoverable under the provisions, it will make a '*recovery order*', vesting the property in an appointed trustee for civil recovery. Alternatively, the Court may make an order under *section 276* of the *Act* staying (or, in Scotland, sisting) proceedings on terms agreed by the parties. [*Proceeds of Crime Act 2002, ss 240(1), 266(1)(2), 276, 316(1)*].

A gain which is attributable to the vesting of property in a trustee for civil recovery or any other person either under a recovery order or in pursuance of an order under *section 276* (a '*Pt 5 transfer*'), and which accrues to the person who held the property immediately before the transfer (the '*transferor*'), is not a chargeable gain, unless a 'compensating payment' is made to the transferor. In the latter event, the amount of the compensating payment is treated as the consideration for the transfer of the property. Where property belonged, immediately before the *Pt 5* transfer, to joint tenants, and a compensating payment is made to one or more (but not all) of them, these provisions apply separately to each joint tenant.

A '*compensating payment*' for these purposes is any amount paid in respect of a *Pt 5* transfer by the trustee for civil recovery or another to a person who held the property in question immediately before the transfer. If a recovery order, or the terms on which an order under *section 276* is made, provides for the creation of any interest in favour of such a person, that person is treated as receiving (in addition to any actual compensating payment) a compensating payment equal to the value of the interest.

[*Proceeds of Crime Act 2002, s 448, Sch 10 paras 2(1)(3)–(5), 3(1)(2)*].

Proceeds of Crime Act 2002, s 298 provides for the forfeiture of 'cash' (which term includes coins and notes in any currency, postal orders, cheques of any kind (including travellers' cheques), bankers' drafts, bearer bonds and bearer shares) in summary proceedings before a magistrates' court (or, in Scotland, the sheriff). A gain attributable to such a forfeiture is not a chargeable gain if it accrues to the person who held the property immediately before the forfeiture and is attributable to property consisting of notes or coins in any currency other than sterling, of postal orders, cheques or bankers' drafts if expressed in any currency other than sterling or of bearer bonds or bearer shares. [*Proceeds of Crime Act 2002, s 289(6), Sch 10 para 3(3)*].

22.33 **Settled property.** No charge to capital gains tax arises

(*a*) where a person disposes of an interest in settled property provided the interest either was created for his benefit or was not acquired for money or money's worth (see 57.14 SETTLEMENTS); or (*b*) when a person becomes absolutely entitled to settled property on the termination of a life interest by the death of the person entitled to it (see 57.15 and 57.17 SETTLEMENTS); or

(*c*) on the termination, on the death of the person entitled to it, of a life interest in possession in settled property where the property does not cease at that time to be settled property (see 57.16 SETTLEMENTS).

22.34 **Special reserve funds of individual Lloyd's underwriters.** Disposals of assets held in an individual underwriter's special reserve fund set up in respect of the 1992 or a subsequent underwriting year of account are exempt. See 64.1 UNDERWRITERS AT LLOYD'S.

22.35 **Substantial shareholdings of companies.** A gain on a disposal by a company of shares after 31 March 2002 is exempt (and a loss is not allowable) where, throughout a continuous twelve-month period beginning not more than two years before the disposal, the company held a 'substantial shareholding' (broadly, at least a **10%** interest) in the company whose shares are the subject of the disposal. The exemption extends to assets 'related to shares' (as defined). The investing company must be a trading company or a member of a trading group and the investee company must be a trading company or the holding company of a trading group (or subgroup). See 60 SUBSTANTIAL SHAREHOLDINGS OF COMPANIES.

22.36 **Woodlands.** Where woodlands are managed by the occupier on a commercial basis and with a view to the realisation of profits

(*a*) any consideration for the disposal of trees (whether standing, felled or cut thereon) and saleable underwood; and

(*b*) any capital sum received under an insurance policy in respect of the destruction of, or damage or injury to, trees or saleable underwood by fire or other hazard thereon

is excluded from any capital gains tax computation on the disposal if the person making the disposal is the occupier.

In *any* capital gains tax computation on the sale of woodlands in the UK, there is excluded so much of the cost of the woodlands and/or consideration for the disposal as is attributable to trees, including saleable underwood, growing on the land. [*TCGA 1992, s 250*].

The cultivation of 'short rotation coppice' is regarded as farming for capital gains purposes and not as forestry, and any land on which such activity takes place is regarded as farm land or agricultural land, as the case may be, and not as woodlands. '*Short rotation coppice*' means a perennial crop of tree species at high density, the stems of which are harvested above ground level at intervals of less than ten years. [*FA 1995, s 154; ITTOIA 2005, Sch 1 para 481*].

HMRC regard the initial cultivation of the land including any spraying, ploughing, fencing and planting of the cuttings as capital costs against which any Woodland Grants received should be matched. The stools from planting form part of the land and as such will be allowable for capital gains purposes. The cost of the stools will not be allowable for capital gains if they are grubbed up before the land is sold. Revenue Tax Bulletin October 1995 p 253.

22.37 **Works of art etc.** A gain is not a chargeable gain if it accrues on the disposal of an asset with respect to which an undertaking has been given and where the disposal is

(*a*) by way of sale by private treaty to a body mentioned in *IHTA 1984, Sch 3* (see 10.5 CHARITIES); or

(*b*) to such a body as in (*a*) above otherwise than by sale; or

(*c*) to HMRC in satisfaction of the payment of inheritance tax or capital transfer tax.

[*TCGA 1992, s 258(2)*].

See 22.80(*a*)–(*e*) below for types of national heritage property which may be sold by private treaty within (*a*) above and also the undertakings required generally. See also 33.7 HOLD-OVER RELIEFS for relief for gifts of works of art etc.

The standard of objects which can be accepted under (*c*) above is very much higher. They have to satisfy a test of 'pre-eminence' either in the context of a national, local authority, or university collection, or through association with a particular building.

22.38 EXEMPT ORGANISATIONS AND INDIVIDUALS

The organisations and individuals detailed in 22.39–22.62 below are completely exempt from capital gains tax except where otherwise indicated.

22.39 **Atomic Energy Authority.** For gains accruing before 1 April 2005, the authority is exempt from corporation tax in respect of chargeable gains. In addition, before that date, gains arising from investments or deposits held by a pension scheme provided and maintained by the Authority are exempt. [*TCGA 1992, s 271(7); F(No 2)A 2005, s 46(3)(5)*].

22.40 **Bare trustees and nominees.** Where property is held by bare trustees or nominees for another person, capital gains tax is chargeable as if the property were held by that other person. Consequently, there is no liability where the property is transferred from the bare trustees etc. to that other person. (Note that before 6 April 2006, the legislation referred to 'assets' rather than 'property'.) [*TCGA 1992, s 60; FA 2006, Sch 12 para 10*]. See further 57.2 SETTLEMENTS.

22.41 **British Museum** and the **Natural History Museum** are entitled, on a claim, to exemption from tax on chargeable gains. [*TCGA 1992, s 271(6)(a); Museums and Galleries Act 1992, Sch 8 para 1(8)(9)*].

22.42 **Central banks.** Non-resident central banks as specified by Order in Council and the issue departments of the Reserve Bank of India and the State Bank of Pakistan are exempt from tax on chargeable gains. [*ICTA 1988, s 516(3)–(5); TCGA 1992, s 271(8)*].

22.43 **Charities.** Subject to restrictions after 11 June 1986, a gain is not a chargeable gain if it accrues to a charity and is applicable and applied for charitable purposes. See 10.3 and 10.4 CHARITIES.

22.44 **Community amateur sports clubs.** On a claim, and subject to restrictions, a gain is not a chargeable gain if it accrues to a registered community amateur sports club and is wholly applied for qualifying purposes. See 10.8 CHARITIES.

22.45 **The Crown.** The Crown is not liable to tax unless statute otherwise provides; see *Bank voor Handel v Administrator of Hungarian Property HL 1954, 35 TC 311* and *Boarland v Madras Electric Supply Corporation HL 1955, 35 TC 612*. In addition, gains arising on the disposal of stock belonging to the Crown, or in the name of the Treasury or National Debt Commissioners under statutory schemes under which transfers are made in accounts at the Bank of England, are not chargeable gains. [*TCGA 1992, s 271(1)(a)*]. Property held under trusts contained in *Chevening Estate Act 1959* is exempt from capital gains tax. [*TCGA 1992, s 270*].

22.46 **Diplomatic agents.** Diplomatic agents (i.e. heads of mission or members of the diplomatic staff) of foreign states are exempt from capital gains tax except on gains arising from private investments or immovable property in the UK. [*Diplomatic Privileges Act 1964*]. Similar exemption is given to agents-general and to their personal staffs. Consular officers and their personal staffs are exempt from gains arising out of disposals of assets which are situated outside the UK at the time of disposal. [*TCGA 1992, s 11(2)–(4), s 271(1)(f); ICTA 1988, ss 320, 322; ITTOIA 2005, Sch 1 para 445(2)*].

An order made under *Arms Control and Disarmament (Privileges and Immunities) Act 1988, s 1(2)* can extend a similar exemption to the above to persons designated by states other than the UK.

22.47 **Friendly societies.** A friendly society registered under *Friendly Societies Act 1974* (a registered friendly society) is an unincorporated society of individuals. Under *Friendly Societies Act 1992*, societies are able to incorporate, take on new powers and form subsidiary companies. *TCGA 1992, ss 217A–217C* provide continuity of tax treatment between registered societies and incorporated societies and removes adverse tax consequences which would otherwise arise as a result of incorporation.

Friendly societies which are neither registered nor incorporated, the incomes of which do not exceed £160 per annum, are wholly exempt from corporation tax on chargeable gains, but a claim must be made. Exemption for other friendly societies is broadly restricted in respect of life or endowment business to the assurance of gross sums under contracts under which the total premiums payable in any period of twelve months do not exceed £270 or the granting of annuities not exceeding £156. The figure of £270 is reduced to £200 for contracts made after 24 July 1992 and before 1 May 1995, and to £150 for contracts made after 31 August 1990 and before 25 July 1991, previously £100. Where the premium under a contract made after 31 August 1987 and before 1 May 1995 is increased by a variation after 24 July 1991 and before 1 August 1992, or after 1 May 1995 and before 1 April 1996, the contract is treated for these purposes as having been made at the time of the variation. For contracts before 1 September 1987 the restriction was by reference to the assurance of gross sums not exceeding £750 and of annuities not exceeding £156. The limits were £500 for gross sums and £104 for annuities for contracts before 14 March 1984. Exemption also applied before that date provided that the society's rules did not enable it to write business above £2,000 and £416 respectively for years of account ending after 31 May 1980. Some policies made before 20 March 1991 were written on the mistaken assumption that they fell outside the required conditions for the tax-exempt policies above. A society may treat the policies as not being tax-exempt by election made before 1 August 1992, but a member surrendering or allowing a policy to mature will not be affected (see Revenue Press Release 12 June 1991). [*ICTA 1970, ss 331–337; FA 1976, s 48; FA 1980, s 57; FA 1984, s 73; Friendly Societies Act 1984, s 2(4); FA 1985, s 41, Sch 8; FA 1987, s 30; F(No 2)A 1987, Sch 2 para 2; ICTA 1988, ss 459–466; FA 1990, ss 49, 50; FA 1991, s 50, Sch 9; TCGA 1992, ss 217A–217C; F(No 2)A 1992, s 56, Sch 9; SI 1993 No 236; FA 1995, Sch 10 para 1; FA 2000, Sch 29 para 32; FA 2004, Sch 35 paras 21, 22; SI 2005 No 2014*]. See also Tolley's Income Tax and Tolley's Corporation Tax under Friendly Societies.

22.48 **The Historic Buildings and Monuments Commission for England** is exempt from tax in respect of chargeable gains. [*TCGA 1992, s 271(7)*].

22.49 **Housing associations** approved under *ICTA 1988, s 488* (see Tolley's Corporation Tax under Housing Associations Etc.) may make a claim to the inspector (within two years of the end of the relevant accounting period) for exemption from corporation tax on chargeable gains arising from the sale of property which is, or has been, occupied by a tenant of the association. [*ICTA 1988, s 488(5)*].

Relief from corporation tax generally by specific grant made by the Secretary of State for the Environment may also be obtainable under *Housing Act 1988, s 54* for registered non-profit making housing associations which are approved as above. See Tolley's Corporation Tax under Housing Associations Etc.

Disposals of land and other assets by a housing association (as defined) to the Housing Corporation (or the Secretary of State (formerly Housing for Wales) or Scottish Homes) under certain statutory schemes, and subsequent disposals of those assets by the Corporation etc. to a single housing association, are treated as taking place on a no gain/no loss basis. The same applies to

(*a*) transfers of land between the Housing Corporation etc. and registered housing associations (as defined and see 22.58 below regarding self-build societies);

(*b*) transfers of land between such associations; and

(*c*) transfers under a direction from the Corporation etc. of property other than land between such associations.

Similar relief applies to NI housing associations.

[*TCGA 1992, ss 218–220; Government of Wales Act 1998, Sch 16 paras 77–80; Housing* (*Scotland*) *Act 2001, Sch 10 paras 18, 19; SI 1996 No 2325; SI 1998 No 2244*].

The disposal and corresponding acquisition of an estate or interest in land in the UK made after 13 March 1989 otherwise than under a bargain at arm's length to a registered housing association (as defined) is treated as being made for a no gain/no loss consideration (or for the actual consideration if the latter exceeds the disposer's allowable expenditure; see 15.4 COMPUTATION OF GAINS AND LOSSES) if a joint claim for such relief is made. On a subsequent disposal of the land by the association after a no gain/no loss acquisition its acquisition by the original donor is treated as the acquisition of the association. [*TCGA 1992, s 259*]. See 8.7 ASSETS HELD ON 31 MARCH 1982 and 34.3 INDEXATION for the consequential re-basing and indexation provisions which apply.

22.50 **International organisations** (e.g. the United Nations) may be specified by Order in Council as exempt from certain taxes [*International Organisations Act 1968*], as may certain financial bodies under the *Bretton Woods Agreement Act 1945* (e.g. the International Monetary Fund). Also exempt are the International Development Association [*International Development Association Act 1960, s 3* and *SI 1960 No 1383*]; the International Finance Corporation [*International Finance Corporation Act 1955, s 3* and *SI 1955 No 1954*]; and signatories to the Convention on the International Maritime Satellite Organisation in respect of capital gains tax on any payment received by the signatory from the Organisation in accordance with the Convention. [*TCGA 1992, s 271*(*5*)]. Bodies may be specified by Order as exempt under *European Communities Act 1972, s 2*(*2*).

Securities issued by designated international organisations are treated as situated outside the UK. See 6.2 ASSETS.

22.51 **Local authorities, local authority associations and health service bodies** (as defined) are exempt from capital gains tax. [*TCGA 1992, s 271*(*3*)].

22.52 **London Olympic Games.** The London Organising Committee of the Olympic Games Ltd, the company established to organise, manage and promote the London Olympic Games in 2012, is exempt from corporation tax (including tax on chargeable gains). The Treasury has wide powers to restrict or remove the exemption by regulations and to extend it to wholly-owned subsidiaries of the company. [*FA 2006, ss 65, 66*].

The Treasury also has powers to make regulations providing for the International Olympic Committee, and certain persons owned or controlled by it, to be exempt from capital gains tax, and to provide for certain activities undertaken by non-UK resident athletes and others in connection with the London Games to be disregarded for corporation tax and capital gains tax purposes. [*FA 2006, ss 67, 68*].

22.53 **National Debt.** Gains accruing to trustees of a settlement the property of which is for the reduction of the National Debt and which qualifies under statute are not chargeable. [*TCGA 1992, s 271*(*1*)(*e*)].

22.54 **The National Heritage Memorial Fund** is exempt from tax on chargeable gains. [*TCGA 1992, s 271*(*7*)].

22.55 **The National Radiological Protection Board** is exempt from tax on chargeable gains accruing before 2 April 2005. [*TCGA 1992, s 271*(*7*); *F*(*No 2*)*A 2005, s 46*(*3*)(*5*)]. The Board ceased to exist on that date.

22.56 **Pension schemes.** Subject to the following, gains accruing to a person from investments forming part of the funds of certain pension schemes are not chargeable gains. For

2006/07 onwards, the schemes covered by this exemption are registered pension schemes within *FA 2004, s 150(2)*, the House of Commons Members' Fund and certain overseas pension funds. For 2005/06 and earlier years, the pension schemes covered are exempt approved schemes, retirement annuity schemes, approved personal pension schemes, parliamentary pension schemes, National Insurance supplementary benefit schemes and certain overseas pension funds. Also exempt for those years are gains arising from the disposal of units in an authorised unit trust (including an umbrella scheme) which is also an approved personal pension scheme. Futures contracts and options contracts are included as investments (notwithstanding that one party to the contract will not be involved with a transfer of assets other than money) as regards exempt approved schemes and approved personal pension schemes (for 2005/06 and earlier years) and registered pension schemes (for 2006/07 onwards). For HMRC's treatment of options and futures in other cases, see 6.7 ASSETS.

For 2006/07 onwards, the above exemption does not prevent a scheme sanction charge to income tax arising in the case of an investment-regulated pension scheme (as defined) on a gain on the disposal of certain taxable property (broadly, and subject to exceptions, residential and tangible moveable property). See Tolley's Income Tax.

[*TCGA 1992, s 99A(3), s 271(1)(b)(c)(d)(g)(h)(j), (1A)(1B)(10)(11), s 288(1); FA 1996, Sch 20 para 63; ITEPA 2003, Sch 6 para 218; FA 2004, ss 118(3), 187(2)–(4)(6), s 284, Sch 35 para 41, Sch 42 Pt 3; FA 2006, Sch 21 para 1*].

Life assurance companies, registered friendly societies and qualifying incorporated friendly societies are also exempt from tax on chargeable gains arising from their 'pension business' (as defined). [*ICTA 1988, ss 431B, 438(1), s 460(1)(2), s 461(1), s 461B(1), s 463, s 466; FA 2004, Sch 35 paras 20, 22*].

The above chargeable gains exemptions do not apply to gains accruing to a person as a member of a property investment limited liability partnership (see 46.19 PARTNERSHIPS). [*TCGA 1992, s 271(12); ICTA 1988, s 460(2), s 461(3A), s 461B(2A); FA 2001, s 76, Sch 25 paras 4, 8; FA 2004, s 187(7)*].

Pension scheme surpluses. For 2005/06 and earlier years, the exemption provided by *TCGA 1992, s 271(1)(g)* applies only to a prescribed percentage of any gain accruing on a disposal where an exempt approved scheme of a prescribed kind fails to carry out a reduction of its actuarial surplus. [*ICTA 1988, s 603, Sch 22; FA 2004, s 284, Sch 42 Pt 3; ITTOIA 2005, Sch 1 para 348; SI 1987 No 412*]. For 2006/07 onwards, such schemes are registered pension schemes for the purposes of *FA 2004, Pt 4* (unless the administrator opts out under *FA 2004, Sch 36 para 2*). [*FA 2004, s 284, Sch 36 para 1(1)(a)(3)*]. For full coverage, see Tolley's Income Tax under Retirement Schemes for Employees.

Deregistration or withdrawal of approval of pension schemes. Where

(i) in 2005/06 or an earlier year, a retirement benefits scheme ceases to be tax approved, and accordingly there is a charge to income tax under *ICTA 1988, s 591C*;

(ii) in 2005/06 or an earlier year and after 16 March 1998, an approved personal pension scheme has its tax approval withdrawn and accordingly there is a charge to income tax under *ICTA 1988, s 650A*; or

(iii) in 2006/07 or a subsequent year, the registration of a registered pension scheme (within *FA 2004, s 150(2)*) is withdrawn and accordingly there is a charge to income tax under *FA 2004, s 242*,

for capital gains purposes, the assets held for the purposes of the scheme in question are deemed to have been acquired immediately before the date of withdrawal of approval or registration (without any corresponding disposal) by the person who would be chargeable if there had been a disposal at that time giving rise to a gain, and the acquisition cost of the assets is deemed to be equal to the amount on which income tax is charged as above. In all cases, that amount is the market value of the assets in question immediately before the date of withdrawal of approval or registration. Accordingly, only the gain accruing on the assets since approval or registration was withdrawn will be brought into account on a subsequent disposal. [*TCGA 1992, ss 239A, 239B, 288(1); FA 1995, s 61(2)(3); FA 1998, s 95(3)(4); FA 2004, s 284, Sch 35 para 40*].

Mis-sold pensions. Capital sums received by way of compensation for 'bad investment advice' received during the period beginning on 29 April 1988 and ending on 30 June 1994 in connection with a person's membership of certain occupational pension schemes and his entry into a personal pension scheme or retirement annuity contract is not regarded as the disposal of an asset for capital gains tax purposes. [*FA 1996, s 148(2)*]. The same applies, by concession, to capital sums received by way of compensation for mis-sold free standing additional voluntary contribution schemes (FSAVCS), where such compensation is paid as a result of the Financial Services Authority (FSA)/Personal Investment Authority Policy Statement issued on 28 February 2000 and is determined under the related FSA Guidance. The Policy Statement required a review of specified categories of FSAVCS sold during the period 28 April 1988 to 15 August 1999 inclusive. (HMRC Extra-Statutory Concession A99).

Pension Protection Fund. The Treasury may make regulations providing for the application of certain taxes, including capital gains tax and corporation tax, in relation to the Board of the Pension Protection Fund and the funds that it controls. The Regulations provide that any gain accruing to the Board from disposals of investments are not chargeable gains if, or to the extent that, they were held for the purposes of the Pension Protection Fund or Fraud Compensation Fund. Receipt of certain specified fraud compensation payments from the Board is not a disposal of an asset for tax purposes. [*FA 2005, s 102; SI 2005 No 1907; SI 2006 No 575*].

22.57 **Scientific research associations**, provided that in each case

(*a*) its object is scientific research (i.e. research in the fields of natural or applied science) which may lead to an extension of trade and which is approved by the Department of Trade and Industry (DTI), and

(*b*) it is prohibited by its Memorandum or similar instrument from distributing its income or property to its members in any form other than that of reasonable payments for supplies, labour, power, services, interest and rent.

With effect from a date to be fixed by statutory instrument, (*a*) above is to be replaced by a requirement that the association have as its object the undertaking of 'research and development' (within the meaning of *ICTA 1988, s 837A*) which may lead to or facilitate an extension of any class or classes of trade. The Treasury will have power to make regulations prescribing circumstances in which associations are deemed to comply, or not to comply, with the conditions. [*TCGA 1992, s 271(6)(b); ICTA 1988, s 508; F(No 2)A 2005, s 13*]. On 4 September 1998, the DTI issued new guidance on the criteria for approval. By concession, the tax exemption continued for accounting periods beginning before 1 September 1999 as regards scientific research associations established before 4 September 1998 which either were approved or would have obtained approval under DTI practice before 1 January 1997. Capital gains on disposals of assets on or after 4 September 1998 qualify for exemption under this concession provided the proceeds are applied for qualifying scientific research by a body approved by the DTI for accounting periods beginning on or after 1 September 1999. (HMRC Extra-Statutory Concession C31).

22.58 **Self-build society.** An approved self-build society (as defined) may claim relief from corporation tax on chargeable gains arising on the disposal of any land to a member, provided that none of its land is occupied by a non-member. Claims must be made to the inspector within two years of the end of the accounting period. [*ICTA 1988, s 489*]. Disposals of land by unregistered self-build societies (as defined) to the Housing Corporation (or the Secretary of State (formerly Housing for Wales) or Scottish Homes) are treated as made at a no gain/no loss price. [*TCGA 1992, s 219; Government of Wales Act 1998,*

Sch 16 para 79; Housing (Scotland) Act 2001, Sch 10 para 19; SI 1996 No 2325; SI 1998 No 2244]. See Tolley's Corporation Tax under Housing Associations Etc. and 22.49 above.

22.59 **Superannuation funds.** For 2005/06 and earlier years, approved superannuation funds which, immediately before 6 April 1980, enjoyed exemption under *ICTA 1970, s 208* (repealed after 5 April 1980 by *FA 1971, Sch 3 para 1*) may claim exemption for chargeable gains arising from the disposal of investments (for which see 22.56 above) held for the purposes of the fund. The following conditions must be satisfied.

(*a*) The fund has not been approved under *FA 1970, Pt II Ch II* or *ICTA 1988, Pt XIV Ch I*.

(*b*) No contribution has been made to it since 5 April 1980.

(*c*) The terms on which benefits are payable from the fund have remained unaltered since 5 April 1980.

This exemption does not apply to gains accruing to a person as a member of a property investment limited liability partnership (see 46.19 PARTNERSHIPS).

[*TCGA 1992, s 271(2)(10)(11)(12); FA 1980, s 36; FA 1984, s 45; FA 1987, Sch 16 Pt VI; ICTA 1988, s 431(5), s 608, s 659, Sch 29 para 26; FA 1990, s 81(3)(4)(6)(8); FA 1994, s 146, Sch 17 para 4; FA 1996, Sch 20 para 63; FA 2001, s 76, Sch 25 para 4; FA 2004, ss 187(5), 284, Sch 42 Pt 3*].

For 2006/07 onwards, the above funds are registered pension schemes for the purposes of *FA 2004, Pt 4* (unless the administrator opts out under *FA 2004, Sch 36 para 2*) and therefore fall within the exemption at 22.56 above. [*FA 2004, s 284, Sch 36 para 1(1)(b)(3)*].

22.60 **Trade unions.** Registered trade unions, provided that they are precluded from assuring more than £4,000 by way of gross sum or £825 by way of annuity (excluding approved annuities under *ICTA 1988, s 620(9)*) in respect of any one person. The Treasury has power to increase the limits by order. Exemption is granted in respect of chargeable gains which are applicable and are applied to 'provident benefits' i.e. sickness, injury and superannuation payments, payment for loss of tools, etc. [*ICTA 1988, s 467; FA 1991, s 74; FA 2004, Sch 35 para 23; SI 2005 No 3229, Reg 74*]. Provident benefits also include legal expenses incurred in representing members at Industrial Tribunal hearings of cases alleging unfair dismissal, or incurred in connection with a member's claim in respect of accident or injury suffered, and general administrative expenses of providing provident benefits (HMRC Statement of Practice 1/84).

The above exemption also applies to employers' associations registered as trade unions [*ICTA 1988, s 467(4)(b)*], and to the Police Federations for England and Wales, Scotland, and Northern Ireland and other police organisations with similar functions. [*ICTA 1988, s 467(4)(c)*].

22.61 **Unit and investment trusts, open-ended investment companies and venture capital trusts.** Authorised unit trusts, investment trusts, open-ended investment companies and venture capital trusts are exempt from corporation tax on their chargeable gains. See 65 UNIT TRUSTS ETC. and 66.10 VENTURE CAPITAL TRUSTS.

22.62 **Visiting forces etc.** A period during which a member of a visiting force to whom *ITEPA 2003, s 303(1)* (previously *ICTA 1988, s 323(1)*) applies is in the UK solely because of such membership is not treated either as a period of residence here or as creating a change in his residence or domicile. [*TCGA 1992, s 11(1); ICTA 1988, s 323; ITEPA 2003, s 303, Sch 6 paras 45, 209*].

22.63 RELIEFS AND DEFERRALS

In addition to the exemption from capital gains tax detailed in 22.2–22.62 above, a number of reliefs are available to reduce or defer the amount of tax payable. The more common of these are outlined in 22.64–22.88 below as well as in certain provisions in 22.49 and 22.58 above.

22.64 **Capital distributions and sale of rights.** If small as compared with the value of the shares in respect of which it is made, a capital distribution may be treated not as a disposal but the proceeds deducted from the acquisition cost of the shares on a subsequent disposal. See 58.10 SHARES AND SECURITIES. This treatment also applies to any consideration received for the disposal of rights. See 58.3 SHARES AND SECURITIES.

22.65 **Companies.**

(*a*) *Intra-group transfers of capital assets* are treated as if made at a no gain, no loss consideration (with certain exceptions). See 27.2 GROUPS OF COMPANIES.

(*b*) *Transfers of assets to non-UK resident company.* Where a UK resident company carrying on a trade outside the UK through a permanent establishment or, for accounting periods beginning before 1 January 2003, through a branch or agency, transfers that trade and its assets to a non-UK resident company partly or wholly for shares in that company, a proportion of the net chargeable gains relating to those shares may be claimed by the transferor company as being deferred. See 45.9 OVERSEAS MATTERS.

(*c*) *Transfers of UK trades between companies resident in different EC member states* are treated as if made at a no gain, no loss consideration. See 45.10 OVERSEAS MATTERS.

22.66 **Company reconstructions.** These do not normally constitute disposals, the original holding and the new holding being treated as the same asset acquired at the same date as the original shares. See 58.4 and 58.6 SHARES AND SECURITIES and 13.10 COMPANIES.

22.67 **Constituency associations.** Where, as a result of the redistribution of parliamentary constituencies, an existing constituency association in a former parliamentary constituency disposes, after 5 April 1983, of any land

(*a*) to a new association which is its successor, or

(*b*) to a body which is an organ of the political party (within *IHTA 1984, s 24*) and which, as soon as practicable thereafter, disposes of the land to a new association which is a successor to the existing association,

the disposal is treated as being made for such consideration as would secure that neither a gain nor loss accrues on disposal.

If the asset was originally held on 6 April 1965, time apportionment will be available (see 7.7 ASSETS HELD ON 6 APRIL 1965) to the new association as if it had held the land from the original date of acquisition.

Where, as a result of the redistribution of parliamentary constituencies, an existing constituency association in a former parliamentary constituency disposes, after 5 April 1983, of any land used and occupied by it for the purposes of its functions and transfers the whole or part of the proceeds to a new association which is its successor, ROLLOVER RELIEF (55) may be claimed as if the land disposed of had been the property of the new association since its acquisition. Where only part of the proceeds is transferred, rollover relief may be claimed on a corresponding share. [*TCGA 1992, s 264*].

22.68 **Corporate venturing scheme.** Companies may defer all or part of a chargeable gain on a corporate venturing scheme investment against a further subscription for shares (other than those of the same company or a company in its group) on which investment relief is obtained under the corporate venturing scheme. The deferred gain becomes chargeable on a disposal of the shares and in certain other circumstances. See 17.21 CORPORATE VENTURING SCHEME.

22.69 **Disposals: capital sums received as compensation etc.** Where such a sum is received in respect of an asset which is damaged or, alternatively, lost or destroyed, a number of reliefs are available provided the capital sum is expended on restoration of, or a replacement for, the asset. See 9.2 and 9.3 CAPITAL SUMS DERIVED FROM ASSETS.

22.70 **Enterprise investment scheme (EIS).** Individuals and most trustees may defer all or part of a chargeable gain against a subscription for eligible shares under the EIS. The deferred gain becomes chargeable on a disposal of the EIS shares and in certain other circumstances. See 21.9 ENTERPRISE INVESTMENT SCHEME.

22.71 **Gifts of business assets and assets on which inheritance tax is chargeable etc.** A form of holdover relief applies to

(*a*) gifts of business assets before 14 March 1989 (see 33.6 HOLD-OVER RELIEFS);

(*b*) gifts of business assets after 13 March 1989 (see 33.1 HOLD-OVER RELIEFS); and

(*c*) gifts after 13 March 1989 of assets on which inheritance tax is chargeable etc. (see 33.7 HOLD-OVER RELIEFS).

22.72 **Gifts to charities etc.** Disposals (otherwise than under a bargain at arm's length), by way of gift or at a consideration not exceeding the allowable expenditure, to charities or any of the bodies mentioned in *IHTA 1984, Sch 3* are deemed to have been made for a consideration giving neither a gain nor a loss. See 10.5 CHARITIES.

22.73 **Harbour reorganisation schemes.** Where the trade of any body corporate, other than a limited company, is transferred to a harbour authority by or under a certified harbour reorganisation scheme which provides for the dissolution of the transferor, any assets transferred on the transfer of trade are treated as giving rise to neither gain nor loss and, for the purposes of any assets acquired before 6 April 1965, the transferor's acquisition of the asset is treated as the transferee's acquisition of it. The transferee is also entitled to relief for any amount for which the transferor would have been entitled to claim relief in respect of allowable losses if it had continued to trade. [*TCGA 1992, s 221; ICTA 1988, s 518*].

22.74 **Hold-over: general relief for gifts.** After 5 April 1980 and before 14 March 1989, a general relief for gifts applied to the disposal of an asset otherwise than at arm's length. Any gain otherwise chargeable could be deferred by deduction from the transferee's acquisition cost. For full details of the relief and claims required, together with the possible clawback of relief, see 33.9 HOLD-OVER RELIEFS.

22.75 **Hops Marketing Board.** Certain transfers of assets by the Hops Marketing Board were deemed to be for a consideration which gives rise to neither a gain nor a loss and the Board's period of ownership is imputed to the transferee for the purposes of applying (where relevant) the provisions relating to ASSETS HELD ON 6 APRIL 1965 (7). [*FA 1982, s 148; TCGA 1992, Sch 12*].

22.76 **Land — compulsory acquisition.** Where *part* of a holding of land is transferred under a compulsory acquisition order, in certain circumstances the transferor may claim not to treat the transfer as a disposal and the consideration is then deducted from the allowable expenditure on a subsequent disposal. See 38.10 LAND for this and 38.11 for deferral of any gain arising on the compulsory purchase of land by means of a claim for rollover relief where the proceeds are re-invested in new land.

22.77 **Land — part disposals.** Where the value of the consideration for a part disposal of a larger holding of land does not exceed £20,000, in certain circumstances the transferor may claim that the transfer is not treated as a disposal and the consideration is then deducted from the allowable expenditure on a subsequent disposal. See 38.7 LAND.

22.78 **Maintenance funds for historic buildings.** After 5 April 1982 and before 6 April 1984, assets disposed of by a person to trustees for the purposes of maintenance, repair, preservation or reasonable improvement of, or for making provision for public access to, property of historic, scientific, etc. interest (see 22.80 below) where the transfer was exempt from capital transfer tax were deemed to be made for a consideration which gave neither a gain nor a loss for capital gains tax purposes. These provisions also applied in certain other circumstances. [*CGTA 1979, s 148; FA 1980, s 82; FA 1982, s 85; FA 1984,* *s 68*]. Broadly similar capital gains tax provisions existed for disposals after 30 July 1980 and before 6 April 1982, except that there was no provision for *improvement* of the buildings concerned.

In view of the general relief for gifts (see 33.9 HOLD-OVER RELIEFS but note that relief in turn was abolished for gifts after 13 March 1989) the above relief was abolished for disposals after 5 April 1984. For gifts after 13 March 1989, a specific deferral relief is again introduced in the form of the hold-over relief for gifts on which inheritance tax is chargeable etc. See 33.7 HOLD-OVER RELIEFS.

22.79 **Married persons and civil partners.** Transfers between married persons and between civil partners are regarded as made on a no gain, no loss basis where the spouses or partners are living together. See 42.4 MARRIED PERSONS AND CIVIL PARTNERS.

22.80 **National heritage property.** The following types of property are within the term 'national heritage property' provided they are so designated by HMRC.

(*a*) Any picture, print, book, manuscript, work of art or scientific object, any collection or group of such items taken as a whole, and any other item not yielding income, which appears to HMRC to be pre-eminent for its national, scientific, historic or artistic interest (with regard being taken of any significant association of the item, collection or group with a particular place). Slightly less stringent criteria applied before 31 July 1998. '*National interest*' includes interest within any part of the UK;

(*b*) Land which in the opinion of HMRC is of outstanding scenic or historic or scientific interest;

(*c*) A building for the preservation of which special steps should in the opinion of HMRC be taken by reason of its outstanding historic or architectural interest;

(*d*) Any area of land which in the opinion of HMRC is essential for the protection of the character and amenities of such a building as is mentioned in (*c*) above. For events before 19 March 1985 the land had to *adjoin* the building;

(*e*) An object which in the opinion of HMRC is historically associated with such a building as is mentioned in (*c*) above.

[*IHTA 1984, s 31(1)(5); FA 1985, s 94, Sch 26 para 2(1)(2); FA 1998, Sch 25 para 4*].

Where any of the above assets, which have been (or could be) designated by HMRC under *IHTA 1984, s 31*, are disposed of by gift (including a gift into settlement) or deemed to be disposed of by trustees on a person becoming absolutely entitled to settled property (other than on the death of the life tenant), then the person making the disposal and the person acquiring the asset are treated for capital gains tax purposes as making the transaction for a consideration giving neither gain nor loss. [*TCGA 1992, s 258(3)(4)*].

Certain undertakings must be given by such persons as HMRC think appropriate in the circumstances of the case that, until the person beneficially entitled to the property dies or the property is disposed of, certain conditions regarding the property are kept, e.g. reasonable access to the public. [*TCGA 1992, s 258(9); IHTA 1984, s 30(1), s 31(2)(4); FA 1985, s 94, Sch 26 para 2(2)–(4)*]. An undertaking given on or after 31 July 1998 may be varied by agreement between HMRC and the person bound by the undertaking or, in the absence of such agreement, by a Special Commissioner at HMRC's behest. Earlier undertakings, where access to the asset is by public appointment only (disregarding special exhibitions), may be similarly varied so as to include an extended access requirement and/or a requirement that certain information be published. This does not apply to earlier undertakings in relation to which a chargeable event for inheritance tax purposes (see Tolley's Inheritance Tax) occurs before 31 July 1998. [*TCGA 1992, s 258(8A); IHTA 1984, s 35A; FA 1998, Sch 25 para 8(1)(4), para 9, para 10*].

If the asset is sold and inheritance tax is chargeable under *IHTA 1984, s 32* (or would be chargeable if an undertaking under that provision had been given), the person selling the asset is treated as having sold the asset for its market value. Similarly, if HMRC are satisfied that at any time during the period for which any undertaking was given that it has not been observed in a material respect, the owner is treated as having sold and immediately reacquired the asset for its market value. An undertaking for the purposes of these provisions is given for the period until the person beneficially entitled to the asset dies or disposes of the asset (whether by sale, gift or otherwise). [*TCGA 1992, s 258(5)(6)*].

If the asset subject to the undertaking is disposed of otherwise than on sale and without a further undertaking being given, the asset is treated as having been sold to an individual for its market value. [*TCGA 1992, s 258(6)*].

Where a person is treated as having sold for market value any asset within (*c*), (*d*) or (*e*) above, he is also treated as having sold and immediately reacquired at market value any asset 'associated' with it (unless HMRC direct otherwise). '*Associated*' assets are a building within (*c*) above and land or objects which, in relation to that building, fall within (*d*) or (*e*) above. [*TCGA 1992, s 258(7)*].

Where a person is treated as having sold an asset under these provisions and inheritance tax becomes chargeable on the same occasion, any capital gains tax payable is deductible in determining the value of the asset for inheritance tax purposes. [*TCGA 1992, s 258(8)*].

An undertaking to grant access will not be regarded as breached where suspension of access is due to foot and mouth disease restrictions, and nor will missed visiting days have to be made up later in 2001 (Revenue Tax Bulletin, Special Foot and Mouth Disease Edition, May 2001 p 4).

See also 33.7 HOLD-OVER RELIEFS for relief for gifts of works of art etc.

Exceptions. The above provisions do not apply where the disposal is by way of gift or sale by private treaty to a body within *IHTA 1984, Sch 3* or if the disposal is to HMRC in satisfaction of inheritance tax (or capital transfer tax). Such disposals are exempt. See 22.37 above.

22.81 **Reinvestment relief.** Reinvestment relief enabled individuals and trustees to claim to roll-over chargeable gains accruing on any assets if the disposal proceeds were reinvested in a 'qualifying investment' within the 'qualifying period' and **before 6 April 1998**. The relief was given effect by reducing the sale proceeds of the disposed assets and the acquisition cost of the newly acquired investment by the lowest of the following amounts:

- the otherwise chargeable gain (net of any amount deferred by virtue of a previous claim for reinvestment relief);
- the acquisition cost of the new asset;
- if the new asset is not acquired at arm's length, the market value at the time of its acquisition;
- the amount specified by the individual in the claim.

These adjustments only affected the reinvestor claiming the relief and there was no consequential effect for either the complementary purchaser or vendor.

A '*qualifying investment*' was an acquisition of any 'eligible shares' in a 'qualifying company' unless, where the asset disposed of consisted of shares in or securities of any company, the qualifying company is that company or a member of that company's group. Where the eligible shares were acquired by their being issued to the taxpayer, the company was required to have an intention to employ the money raised by the issue wholly for the purposes of a 'qualifying trade' carried on by it

'*Eligible shares*' means any '*ordinary shares*' (i.e. shares forming part of a company's '*ordinary share capital*' (as defined)) in a company which do not carry any present or future preferential rights to dividends or the company's assets on a winding up or right to be redeemed.

Subject to further provisions and exclusions, a company is a '*qualifying company*' if it is an unquoted company which exists wholly for the purpose of carrying on one or more 'qualifying trades' or which is the 'parent company of a trading group'. A company is the '*parent company of a trading group*' for this purpose if it is the principal company of a group of companies (as defined) and, treating all the activities of the company and its qualifying subsidiaries as one business, its business is carried on wholly or mainly in the UK and neither the business nor a substantial part of it consists in specified excluded activities or activities carried on otherwise than in the course of a trade. A company ceases to be a qualifying company if a resolution is passed or an order is made for its winding up, or any other act is done for a like purpose under foreign law or the company is dissolved without winding up. Note that different rules applied before 26 November 1996.

A trade is a '*qualifying trade*' if it complies with the requirements below. For this purpose the carrying on of any activities of research and development (as defined) from which it is intended that a trade meeting those requirements will be derived is treated as the carrying on of a qualifying trade. A trade cannot be a qualifying trade unless it is conducted on a commercial basis and with a view to profit realisation. With effect, broadly, after 26 November 1996, there is the additional requirement that the trade be carried on wholly or mainly in the UK.

Subject to further provisions, a trade is a qualifying trade if neither that trade nor a substantial part of it consists in one or more of the following activities:

- dealing in land, in commodities or futures or in shares, securities or other financial instruments;
- dealing in goods, otherwise than in the course of an ordinary trade of wholesale or retail distribution;
- banking, insurance, money-lending, debt-factoring, hire-purchase financing or other financial activities;
- leasing or receiving royalties or licence fees;
- providing legal or accountancy services;
- providing services or facilities for any trade which consists, to a substantial extent, in activities within any of the above and is carried on by another person (except the principal company of a group of companies) who has a controlling interest in both trades.

The acquisition of a qualifying investment was in the '*qualifying period*' if it took place at any time in the period beginning twelve months before and ending three years after the disposal of the asset disposed of (subject to such extension as the Board allowed). No reinvestment relief is available under these provisions where the reinvestment takes place after 5 April 1998.

[*TCGA 1992, ss 164A, 164B, 164FF, 164G, 164I, s 164J, 164N(1)(2)(5); FA 1993, Sch 7 para 3; FA 1994, Sch 11 paras 2, 3, 7; FA 1995, s 46(1)(4); FA 1997, Sch 17 paras 2, 4–7; FA 1998, s 141(1)(2), Sch 27 Pt III(32)*].

For full coverage of the provisions, see the 2005/06 and earlier editions. For continuing deferral reliefs applying for reinvestment in EIS and VCT shares, see respectively 21.9 ENTERPRISE INVESTMENT SCHEME and 66.12 VENTURE CAPITAL TRUSTS.

Withdrawal of relief. In certain circumstances an effective withdrawal of reinvestment relief applies as follows.

Subject to the following, if at any time in the 'relevant period' (see below),

(*a*) the shares forming the acquired holding cease to be eligible shares, (*b*) the company whose shares form the acquired holding ceases to be a qualifying company,

(*c*) the person who acquired the acquired holding becomes neither resident nor ordinarily resident in the UK, or

(*d*) any of the shares forming the acquired holding are, on a reorganisation, conversion or reconstruction, exchanged for qualifying corporate bonds so that the transaction is within *TCGA 1992, s 116* (gain on original shares not deemed to crystallise until bonds disposed of; see 50.3 QUALIFYING CORPORATE BONDS),

a chargeable gain equal to 'the appropriate proportion' of the held-over gain is treated as accruing to that person immediately before that time or, in a case within (*d*) above, immediately before the disposal that is hypothecated under *TCGA 1992, s 116(10)(a)* immediately before the transaction concerned.

[*TCGA 1992, s 164F(1)(2), s 164N(1); FA 1993, Sch 7 para 3; FA 1994, Sch 11 para 9(1)(a), (2)(a); FA 1997, Sch 17 para 3(1)*].

'*The appropriate proportion*' of the held-over gain is so much, if any, of that gain as has not already been charged on any disposal or under the provisions below. However, where (*d*) above applies, or where (*a*) or (*b*) above applies in accordance with (A)–(D) below, the proportion is a just and reasonable one having regard to the extent to which the acquired holding forms the original shares. [*TCGA 1992, s 164F(3); FA 1993, Sch 7 para 3; FA 1994, Sch 11 para 9(1)(b), (2)(b), (3)*].

The whole or a part of any held-over gain on the acquisition of the acquired holding is treated as below as charged on any disposal in relation to which the whole or any part of the held-over gain falls to be taken into account in determining the chargeable gain or allowable loss on the disposal, and as charged under these provisions so far as it falls to be disregarded under *TCGA 1992, s 164F(11)* below. For a disposal other than a part disposal, the amount of the held-over gain charged on that disposal is the amount taken into account in determining the amount of the chargeable gain etc. as above. In the case of a part disposal, the corresponding amount charged on that disposal is calculated by multiplying so much of the amount of the held-over gain as has not already been charged on a previous disposal (as similarly reduced by any reduction made under *TCGA 1992, s 164D(3)(a)*) by the A/(A + B) fraction of *TCGA 1992, s 42(2)* (see 15.7 COMPUTATION OF GAINS AND LOSSES) used. This is subject to any deductions under the reinvestment relief provisions, in computing the apportioned allowable expenditure on the disposal in question. [*TCGA 1992, s 164F(4)(4A); FA 1993, Sch 7 para 3; FA 1994, Sch 11 para 9(1)(c), (2)(c), (3)*].

Where the acquired holding or any asset treated as comprised in a single asset (e.g. a share pool) with the whole or any part of that holding has been disposed of under *TCGA 1992, s 58* (transfers between spouses at no gain/no loss; see 42.4 MARRIED PERSONS AND CIVIL PARTNERS) by the individual who acquired that holding to another person ('*the spouse*'):

(I) the spouse is not (subject to below) treated for the purposes of these provisions as a person who has acquired eligible shares for a consideration which is treated as reduced by reinvestment relief;

(II) the disposal is not included in the disposals on which the whole or any part of the held-over gain may be treated as charged for the purposes of these provisions;

(III) disposals by the spouse, as well as disposals by that individual, are taken into account under *TCGA 1992, s 164F(4)(4A)* above;

(IV) any charge under (*a*), (*b*) or (*d*) above is apportioned between that individual and the spouse according to the extent to which the appropriate proportion of the held-over gain would be charged on the disposal by each of them of their respective holdings (if any);

(V) (*c*) above has effect as if the reference there to that individual included a reference to the spouse;

(VI) a charge under (*c*) above is imposed only on a person who becomes neither resident nor ordinarily resident in the UK; and

(VII) the amount of the charge imposed on any person under (*c*) above is that part of the charge on the appropriate proportion of the held-over gain which would be apportioned to that person under (IV) above.

[*TCGA 1992, s 164F(5); FA 1993, Sch 7 para 3; FA 1994, Sch 11 para 9(1)(d)*].

Subject to (A)–(D) below, where the qualifying company in which the acquired holding subsists ceases to be an unquoted company these provisions have effect as if the relevant period ended immediately before it so ceased. (For the reason that to be a qualifying company a company has to be unquoted, this provision seems to prevent a charge arising under (*b*) above because the cessation of qualifying status will not arise in the relevant period.) Subject to this, '*the relevant period*' means the period of three years after the acquisition of the acquired holding. [*TCGA 1992, s 164F(6)(12), s 164N(1); FA 1993, Sch 7 para 3*].

Where there is a transaction involving shares in a company which applies *TCGA 1992, s 127* (see 58.1 SHARES AND SECURITIES) so that those shares are regarded as the same asset as the acquired holding or the whole or any part of an asset comprising that holding, no charge arises as a result of the event in (*a*) or (*b*) above except where:

(A) those shares are not, or cease to be, eligible shares in that company;

(B) neither that company nor (if different) the company in which the acquired holding subsisted is or continues to be a qualifying company, or would be or continue to be a qualifying company if it were an unquoted company;

(C) the transaction is one resulting in the shares comprised in the acquired holding ceasing to be eligible shares under *TCGA 1992, s 164L* (see below); or

(D) there is a transaction under which any shares at any time comprised in the acquired holding would have ceased to be eligible shares under *TCGA 1992, s 164L*.

[*TCGA 1992, s 164F(7), s 164N(1); FA 1993, Sch 7 para 3*].

A charge (*a*) or (*b*) above does not apply where the company in which the acquired holding subsists is wound up or dissolved without winding up and:

(*aa*) the winding-up or dissolution is for bona fide commercial reasons and not part of a scheme or arrangement the main purpose of which, or one of the main purposes of which, is the avoidance of tax; and

(*bb*) the company's net assets (if any) are distributed to its members or dealt with as *bona vacantia* before the end of the period of three years from the commencement of the winding up or dissolution.

[*TCGA 1992, s 164F(8); FA 1993, Sch 7 para 3; FA 1996, Sch 20 para 55*].

A charge will not apply under (*c*) above in relation to any person if:

(AA) the reason for his becoming neither resident nor ordinarily resident in the UK is that he works in an employment or office all the duties of which are performed outside the UK; and

(BB) he again becomes resident or ordinarily resident in the UK within the period of three years from the time he ceases to be so, without having meanwhile disposed of any eligible shares in the company in question.

HMRC are precluded from making an assessment under (*c*) above before the end of the three-year period mentioned in (BB) above where the person has satisfied the condition in

(AA) above and may satisfy that in (BB). A person is taken to have disposed of an asset under (BB) if there has been such a disposal as would, if the person making the disposal had been resident in the UK, have been a disposal on which the whole or any part of the held-over gain would have been charged. [*TCGA 1992, s 164F(9)(10), s 164N(1); FA 1993, Sch 7 para 3*].

Where otherwise a chargeable gain would arise under (*a*)–(*d*) above but the person who acquired the acquired holding also acquires, within a specified period, a qualifying investment, he is treated as respects the qualifying investment on making a claim

(1) as if the amount of the gain were reduced by whichever is the smallest of the following amounts:

 (i) the actual amount or value of the consideration for the acquisition of the qualifying investment,

 (ii) in the case of a qualifying investment acquired otherwise than by a transaction at arm's length, the market value of that investment at the time of its acquisition,

 (iii) the amount specified for these purposes in the claim;

 and

(2) as if the amount or value of the consideration for the acquisition of the qualifying investment were reduced by the amount of the reduction made under (1) above (but without affecting the treatment for the purposes of *TCGA 1992* of the other party to the transaction involving the qualifying investment).

FA 1995 introduced measures to prevent excess relief being claimed in respect of shares acquired by way of gift if the qualifying investment was acquired after 19 June 1994, or a claim under the preceding paragraph is made in relation to a gain which would otherwise accrue after that date. Thus, where a claim for the above relief is made after 19 June 1994 and the qualifying investment in respect of which the claim is made was acquired by the reinvestor through an inter-spouse (no gain/no loss) transfer under *TCGA 1992, s 58*, the relief claimed cannot exceed the transferor spouse's allowable base cost of the qualifying investment, after any reduction in that cost due to gains already rolled over into that investment. This is irrespective of the re-basing rules in *TCGA 1992, s 35, Sch 3 para 1* or *TCGA 1992, s 55* in situations where the qualifying investment was held by the transferor spouse since 31 March 1982. Similarly, the re-basing provisions are disapplied where the claimant returns the qualifying investment to his spouse on a no gain/no loss basis.

In addition, rules were introduced with regard to the making of multiple claims for relief against the same qualifying investment to ensure that aggregate gains rolled over do not exceed the cost thereof. These rules have effect where claims under the penultimate paragraph above are made in respect of gains which would otherwise accrue after 19 June 1994. Where multiple reductions are claimed under the above relief in respect of the same qualifying investment, the reductions shall be treated as claimed separately in such order as the claimant elects. On the second and subsequent claims the amount of gain able to be rolled over will be limited to the remaining acquisition cost ((1)(i) above) or market value ((1)(ii) above) of the qualifying investment left after any previous claims have been made. A claim that has become final (i.e. it may not be amended or is finally determined, whichever occurs first) will be treated as made earlier than any claim which is not final.

The specified period mentioned above is the period (not including any period before the acquisition of the acquired holding) beginning twelve months before and ending three years after the time the chargeable gain accrues or would otherwise accrue, together with any such further time after the disposal as the Board may by notice allow. [*TCGA 1992, s 164F(10A)–(10C), s 164FF, s 164FG; FA 1993, Sch 7 para 3; FA 1994, Sch 11 para 9(1)(f); FA 1995, s 47(1)(3)–(8); FA 1996, Sch 20 para 56*].

Gains on disposals made after a chargeable gain has been deemed to accrue under (*a*)–(*d*) above to any person in respect of the acquired holding are computed as if so much of the held-over gain as is equal to the amount of the chargeable gain were to be disregarded. [*TCGA 1992, s 164F(11); FA 1993, Sch 7 para 3*].

Where a withdrawal is of reinvestment relief given to trustees, the resulting chargeable gain is taxable at whichever is the relevant of the rates given at 57.1 SETTLEMENTS. This applies even if the settlor has an interest in the settlement, as the 'charge on settlor' provisions in *TCGA 1992, s 77* (see 57.5 SETTLEMENTS) apply only in the event of a disposal, whilst the withdrawal of relief provisions above treat a gain as accruing without any disposal being deemed to have occurred. (See *Taxation 15 May 1997 p 194*).

A clawback of relief under the above provisions or those below can be sheltered by a qualifying investment in EIS shares issued after 5 April 1998 (see 21.10 ENTERPRISE INVESTMENT SCHEME).

Additional withdrawal provisions. The provisions detailed below apply after 26 November 1996 where a person acquired the shares by their being issued to him. They apply equally to shares acquired on or before 26 November 1996, held until that time and continuing until that time to be eligible shares in a qualifying company; however, in their application to such shares the provisions cannot give rise to a withdrawal of relief at any time within three years after the acquisition of the shares. For reinvestment relief purposes, an allotment of shares before their issue is disregarded in determining whether and when a person acquires shares by their issue to him.

Where a person acquired eligible shares in a qualifying company by their being issued to him and the consideration given has been treated as reduced by a held-over gain under the reinvestment relief provisions, a loss of relief applies in *any* of the following circumstances.

(X) The money raised by the issue was, at the time of acquisition, intended to be employed for the purposes of a qualifying trade then being carried on, but that money has not been wholly employed for 'permissible purposes' (see below) by the end of the 'initial utilisation period' (see below).

(Y) The money raised by the issue was, at the time of acquisition, intended to be employed for the purposes of a qualifying trade *not* then being carried on; the trade begins to be carried on within two years after that time, but that money has not been wholly employed for the purposes of the trade by the end of one year from commencement of trading. (Any part of the money wholly employed for 'permissible purposes' within the 'initial utilisation period' is disregarded for this purpose.)

(Z) The money raised by the issue was, at the time of acquisition, intended to be employed for the purposes of a qualifying trade *not* then being carried on; the trade *does not begin* to be carried on within two years after that time and that money has not been wholly employed for permissible purposes by the end of the initial utilisation period.

'*Permissible purposes*' means the purposes of any qualifying trade carried on by the company concerned or by any of its 'qualifying subsidiaries' (as defined). The '*initial utilisation period*' is the period of one year after the acquisition of the shares in question. Money is treated as employed wholly for particular purposes even if an amount thereof is employed for other purposes, provided such amount is not significant. Money employed for the purpose of preparing to carry on a qualifying trade is taken to be employed for the purposes of that trade.

Where any of the above circumstances applies, the held-over gain (or such part of it as has not been charged on any disposal, or under the above withdrawal provisions or under these provisions) is treated as accruing to the person in question immediately before the end of:

- where (X) above applies, the initial utilisation period;

- where (Y) above applies, the first year of trading; or
- where (Z) above applies, the period of two years therein mentioned.

Where only part of the money raised by the issue of shares has been permissibly employed within the time allowed in (X), (Y) or (Z) above (and the other part is a significant amount), there are provisions whereby a person's shareholding is treated for reinvestment relief purposes as two separate holdings, one from which that part of the money was raised and one from which the remainder was raised, the value of the holding being apportioned accordingly between the two notional holdings.

TCGA 1992, s 164F(4)(4A)(5)(11) (see above) apply for the purposes of these provisions, except that (V)–(VII) do not so apply. *TCGA 1992, s 164F(10A)–(10C)* also apply, so that the gain treated as accruing under these provisions may itself be deferred upon the acquisition of a further qualifying investment.
[*TCGA 1992, s 164FA, s 164N(5); FA 1997, Sch 17 para 3(2), para 6(2), para 7*].

Return of value. If an individual, having acquired eligible shares in a qualifying company, has returned to him afterwards the whole or any part of the value of his investment, the shares are treated as ceasing to be eligible shares under *TCGA 1992, Pt V Ch IA* (reinvestment relief) (for the consequences of which event when it occurs in the relevant period, see above). A return of the whole or part of the value of the investment of an individual who is to acquire or has acquired shares in a company is treated as being made if the company:

- repays, redeems or repurchases any of its shares or other securities belonging to that individual or makes any payment to him for giving up rights on the cancellation or extinguishment of any of the company's shares or securities;
- repays any debt owed to that individual, other than a debt that was incurred by the company on or after the acquisition of the shares and otherwise than in consideration of the extinguishment of a debt incurred before the acquisition;
- makes any payment to that individual for giving up his rights to any debt on its extinguishment;
- releases or waives any liability of that individual to the company (which is deemed to occur if the liability remains undischarged twelve months after the time it should have been discharged) or discharges, or undertakes to discharge, any liability of his to a third party;
- provides a benefit or facility for that individual;
- disposes of an asset to that individual for no or an insufficient consideration;
- acquires an asset from that individual for more than a sufficient consideration; or
- makes any payment to that individual other than a 'qualifying payment'.

Similarly, a whole or partial return of the value of an individual's investment is treated as being made where there is a loan made (including the giving of credit and the assignment of debt) by any person to that individual such that either no loan would have been made or the terms of it would have been different had the individual not have acquired, or been proposing to acquire, the shares. For the Revenue's views on 'loan-linked' investments, see Revenue Statement of Practice 6/98.

Debts and liabilities that could be discharged by the company making a qualifying payment are ignored for the purposes of the above, as are benefits or facilities provided in circumstances such that a payment made to the value of them would be a 'qualifying payment'. A '*qualifying payment*' means:

- reasonable payment by a company of remuneration to an officer or employee;

- reimbursement by a company of an officer's or employee's travel or other expenses incurred wholly, exclusively and necessarily in the performance of his duties;
- interest paid by a company on money lent to it on reasonable commercial terms;
- payment by a company of a dividend etc., not exceeding a normal return on the investment in shares etc. of the company;
- a payment not exceeding market value for the supply of goods;
- a payment by a company, as rent for any property occupied by the company, of an amount not exceeding a reasonable and commercial rent for the property;
- any reasonable and necessary remuneration paid by a company for services rendered to it in the course of a trade assessed under Schedule D, Case I or II;
- a payment in discharge of an '*ordinary trade debt*' (meaning any debt for goods or services supplied in the ordinary course of trade or business where any credit given does not exceed six months and is not longer than that normally given to customers generally).

[*TCGA 1992, s 164L, s 164N(1)(1A)(3); FA 1993, Sch 7 para 3; FA 1994, Sch 11 paras 6, 10, 11*].

22.82 **Reorganisation of share capital.** Reorganisations do not normally constitute disposals, the original holding and the new holding being treated as the same asset acquired at the same date as the original shares. See 58.1 SHARES AND SECURITIES. See also 58.7 for conversion of securities into shares where the same principles apply.

22.83 **Retirement relief.** Subject to certain conditions, where an individual who has attained the age of 50 (or at a lesser age through ill-health) makes, **before 6 April 2003**, a 'material disposal of business assets' at a gain, the gains qualifying for relief are reduced in accordance with the provisions in 53 RETIREMENT RELIEF.

22.84 **Rollover relief: replacement of business assets.** A person disposing of certain qualifying assets used exclusively for the purposes of a trade who used the proceeds to purchase other qualifying assets so used may claim to defer the capital gains tax payable by deducting the otherwise chargeable gain on the old asset from the cost of the newly acquired one. See 55 ROLLOVER RELIEF.

22.85 **Settlements for the benefit of employees.** Where the circumstances surrounding a disposal are as in one of (*a*)–(*c*) below, the MARKET VALUE (41.1) rules do not apply to it; and if made gratuitously or for a consideration of an amount not exceeding the allowable expenditure attributable to the asset, the disposal, and the corresponding acquisition by the trustees, is treated as taking place on a no gain/no loss basis and the transferor's acquisition of the asset is imputed to the trustees.

The circumstances mentioned above are as follows.

(*a*) A close company (as in *ICTA 1988, ss 414, 415* but additionally including a non-UK resident company which would be close as defined by those provisions) disposes of an asset to trustees in circumstances such that the disposition is not a transfer of value for IHT purposes by virtue of *IHTA 1984, s 13* (employee trusts).

(*b*) An individual disposes of an asset to trustees in circumstances such that the disposal is an exempt transfer for IHT purposes by virtue of *IHTA 1984, s 28* (employee trusts).

(*c*) A company other than a close company (as in (*a*) above) disposes of property to trustees otherwise than under a bargain at arm's length in circumstances such that, broadly, had the disposition been made by a close company it would not be a transfer of value by virtue of *IHTA 1984, s 13*.

[*TCGA 1992, s 239(1)(2)(4)–(8)*].

For coverage of *IHTA 1984, s 13* and *s 28* (each of which refers to the provisions of *IHTA 1984, s 86*), see Tolley's Inheritance Tax under Trusts for Employees.

If the trustees of an 'employee trust' transfer an asset to a beneficiary for no payment, no charge under *TCGA 1992, s 71* will, by concession, be levied on the trustees provided there is an income tax charge of the full market value of the asset on the employee. For this purpose, '*employee trust*' means a trust within *IHTA 1984, s 86* but ignoring the restriction in *s 86(3)* (class defined by employment with a particular body to include all or most employees), and the employee must not be a person of the kind described in *IHTA 1984, s 28(4)* (participators, connected persons etc.) and not excluded by *s 28(5)* (participators with 5% or more of a class of shares etc.). The concession does not apply where special statutory rules restrict either the liability to capital gains tax or the income tax liability (HMRC Extra-Statutory Concession D35). For notes on the application of ESC D35 in given situations, see Revenue Tax Bulletin April 2000 p 738.

For the position of the shareholders in a close company transferor which makes a transfer within *(a)*–*(c)* above at less than market value, see 3.17 ANTI-AVOIDANCE.

See also 33 HOLD-OVER RELIEFS and 20.20, 20.32 EMPLOYEE SHARE SCHEMES for alternative reliefs which may be available in respect of transfers to settlements for the benefit of employees.

22.86 **Transfer of a business to a company—incorporation relief.** Where a person transfers a business and its assets to a company in return for shares in that company, any chargeable gain on disposal of the assets is deferred by reducing the amount otherwise chargeable in the proportion of the value of the shares received to the value of the overall consideration received by the transferor in exchange for the business. See 33.10 HOLD-OVER RELIEFS. For transfers after 5 April 2002 an election is available for the relief not to apply. See 33.11 HOLD-OVER RELIEFS.

22.87 **Unremittable overseas gains.** On a claim, such gains may be treated as gains of the year in which conditions preventing remittance cease to apply. See 45.5 OVERSEAS MATTERS. See also 37.6 INTEREST AND SURCHARGES ON UNPAID TAX.

22.88 **Venture capital trusts (VCTs).** For 2003/04 and earlier years, individuals may defer all or part of a chargeable gain against subscriptions of up to £100,000 per tax year for shares in VCT companies by reference to which income tax investment relief is obtained. The deferred gain becomes chargeable on a disposal of the VCT shares and in certain other circumstances. The relief is abolished for VCT shares issued on or after 6 April 2004. See 66.12 VENTURE CAPITAL TRUSTS.

23 Fraudulent or Negligent Conduct

Cross-references. See 5 ASSESSMENTS; 12 CLAIMS; 37 INTEREST AND SURCHARGES ON UNPAID TAX; 47 PAYMENT OF TAX; 48 PENALTIES.

23.1 Where HMRC consider tax to have been lost by a taxpayer's fraudulent or negligent conduct (or by his fraud, wilful default or neglect) they will seek to recover that tax, whether by formal assessment or by way of a contract settlement (see 23.12 below). In such cases, the normal time limits for assessments are extended (see 23.3 below) and INTEREST AND SURCHARGES ON UNPAID TAX (37) and PENALTIES (48) are incurred, which HMRC may mitigate in appropriate circumstances. In cases of serious fraud, HMRC may seek a criminal prosecution. In most cases, the amount of tax lost will be established by use of HMRC's enquiry powers, which are explained at 54.8–54.13 RETURNS, or the investigatory powers explained at 23.8–23.11 below. For cases relating to fraudulent or negligent conduct, see Tolley's Tax Cases.

23.2 CASE LAW ON FRAUDULENT OR NEGLIGENT CONDUCT

The following cases relate to old legislation for 'fraud, wilful default or neglect' assessments which has now been replaced by 'fraudulent or negligent conduct' assessments. The latter expression is not defined, and the cases may be of continued assistance in this respect.

The onus of proving fraud or wilful default is on the Crown but the onus then shifts to the taxpayer to prove the revised assessments incorrect if he wishes to do so (*Johnson v Scott CA 1978, 52 TC 383*; *Jonas v Bamford Ch D 1973, 51 TC 1*; *Hurley v Taylor CA 1998, 71 TC 268*; *Nicholson v Morris CA 1977, 51 TC 95* and cf. *Barney v Pybus Ch D 1957, 37 TC 106*; *R v Special Commrs (ex p. Martin) CA 1971, 48 TC 1* and *Arumugam Pillai v Director General of Inland Revenue PC, [1981] STC 146*). For the standard of proof required, see *Les Croupiers Casino Club v Pattinson CA 1987, 60 TC 196*.

Unexplained capital increases or admitted omissions may be held evidence of fraud or wilful default (*Amis v Colls Ch D 1960, 39 TC 148*; *Woodrow v Whalley Ch D 1964, 42 TC 249*; *Hudson v Humbles Ch D 1965, 42 TC 380*; *Hillenbrand CS 1966, 42 TC 617*; *Young v Duthie Ch D 1969, 45 TC 624*; *James v Pope Ch D 1972, 48 TC 142*; and cf. *Brimelow v Price Ch D 1965, 49 TC 41*). Fraud or wilful default may be by an agent (*Clixby v Pountney Ch D 1967, 44 TC 515*; *Pleasants v Atkinson Ch D 1987, 60 TC 228*).

'*Neglect*' means negligence or a failure to give any notice, make any return, or produce or furnish any document or other information required by or under the *Taxes Acts*. [*TMA 1970, s 118; FA 1989, Sch 17 Pt VIII*]. Neglect may be by an agent (*Mankowitz v Special Commrs Ch D 1971, 46 TC 707*).

23.3 EXTENDED TIME LIMITS

The normal time limits for making assessments are stated at 5.7 ASSESSMENTS. Extended time limits as in 23.4 below apply to assessments made for the purpose of making good to the Crown a loss of tax attributable to fraudulent or negligent conduct. There is an overriding deadline for deceased persons (see 23.5 below). See 5.7 ASSESSMENTS as regards the date on which an assessment is made.

23.4 **Assessments made after 26 July 1989 relating to 1983/84 and subsequent years (or to company accounting periods ending after 31 March 1983).** Where a loss of capital gains tax (or income tax) arises due to the fraudulent or negligent conduct of a person (or of a person acting on his behalf), an assessment may be made at any time not later than 20 years after 31 January following the tax year to which it relates. The equivalent corporation tax time limit is 21 years after the end of the accounting period. If the person assessed so requires, the assessment may give effect to reliefs or allowances to which he would have been entitled had he made the necessary claims within the relevant time limits (with some exceptions for income tax).

For 1995/96 and earlier years and for corporation tax accounting periods ended before 1 July 1999 (i.e. before the introduction of self-assessment), the equivalent time limit for capital gains tax, income tax *and* corporation tax was 20 years after the end of the chargeable period (i.e. the tax year or the corporation tax accounting period).

[*TMA 1970, s 36*(*1*)(*3*)(*3A*); *FA 1989, s 149*; *F*(*No 2*)*A 1992, Sch 5 para 9*(*2*); *FA 1994, ss 196, 199, Sch 19 para 11*; *FA 1998, s 117, Sch 18 paras 46*(*2*), *65, Sch 19 para 18*].

An objection to the making of any assessment on the grounds that it is out of time can only be made on an appeal against the assessment. [*TMA 1970, s 34*(*2*); *FA 1998, s 117, Sch 18 para 46*(*3*)].

23.5 **Deceased persons.** As stated at 5.7 ASSESSMENTS, assessments on a deceased person's chargeable gains accrued before death must be made on the deceased's personal representatives no later than the third anniversary of 31 January following the tax year in which death occurred. Assessments to recoup loss of tax due to the deceased's fraudulent or negligent conduct can be made, *no later* than that third anniversary, for any year of assessment ending *not earlier* than six years before the death. [*TMA 1970, s 40*(*2*)(*3*); *FA 1989, s 149*(*4*), *Sch 17 Pt VIII*; *FA 1994, ss 196, 199, Sch 19 para 12*]. See 5.7 ASSESSMENTS as regards the date on which an assessment is made.

23.6 EVIDENCE

Statements made or documents produced by or on behalf of a taxpayer are admissible as evidence in proceedings against him, notwithstanding that reliance on the Board's practice in cases of full disclosure may have induced him to make or produce them. [*TMA 1970, s 105*; *FA 1989, s 168*(*1*)(*5*)]. See 23.7, 23.12 below and 48.23 PENALTIES.

23.7 CERTIFICATES OF FULL DISCLOSURE

Where it is established that tax has been lost due to fraudulent or negligent conduct, HMRC may request that the taxpayer complete a certificate of full disclosure stating that complete disclosure has been made of, inter alia, all banking, savings and loan accounts, deposit receipts, building society accounts and accounts with other financial institutions; all investments including savings certificates and premium bonds and loans (whether interest-bearing or not); all other assets, including cash and life assurance policies, which the taxpayer now possesses, or has possessed, or in which he has or has had any interest or power to operate or control during the stated period; all gifts in any form, by the taxpayer to his spouse, domestic partner, children or other persons during the stated period; all sources of income and all income derived therefrom; and all facts bearing on liability to income tax, capital gains tax and other duties for the stated period. Great care must be exercised before signing such a certificate, since subsequent discovery of an omission could lead to heavy penalties including, in serious cases, criminal prosecution. See also 48.17 PENALTIES.

23.8 INVESTIGATORY POWERS

The self-assessment enquiry procedures are explained at 54.8–54.11 RETURNS; these operate in tandem with the provisions below and incorporate a separate power to call for documents.

HMRC powers to require documents and other particulars. For the following purposes, '*document*' has the same meaning as in *Civil Evidence Act 1968, Pt I* (or Scottish or Northern Ireland equivalent), but does not include personal records or journalistic material (within *Police and Criminal Evidence Act 1984, ss 12, 13*) (and those exclusions apply also to particulars contained in such records or material). The documents concerned are those in the possession or power of the person receiving the notice. Photographic, etc. facsimiles may be supplied provided the originals are produced if called for, and documents relating to any pending tax appeal need not be delivered. In practice, the latter also applies to documents relating to a pending referral of questions during an enquiry (see 54.13 RETURNS) (Hansard Standing Committee A, 8 May 2001, Cols 172–174). There are special provisions relating to computer records (see *FA 1988, s 127*). Documents in a person's 'possession or power' are those actually in existence at the time the notice is given, and not any which would have to be brought into existence in order to satisfy the notice.

Note that, before 18 April 2005, the functions of the Commissioners for HMRC referred to below were vested in the Board of Inland Revenue. Functions to be carried out by an officer of Revenue and Customs were to be carried out by an inspector (or, in certain cases, an officer of the Board).

(*a*) Where an officer of Revenue and Customs is of the reasonable opinion that documents contain, or may contain, information relevant to the tax liability of a person, he may (with the authority of the Commissioners for HMRC and the consent of a General or Special Commissioner) by notice in writing require that person to deliver such documents to him (but only after that person has been given reasonable opportunity to produce them).

The officer must give a written summary of his reasons for applying for consent to the giving of the notice. He is not required to identify any informant in the summary and no summary need be provided if the Special or General Commissioner giving consent so directs, and the Commissioner concerned must not so direct unless he is satisfied that the officer has reasonable grounds for believing that disclosure of the information in question would prejudice the assessment or collection of tax. The Commissioner concerned must not take part in or be present at any subsequent proceedings concerning an appeal made by the person if the Commissioner concerned has reason to believe that any of the documents which were the subject of the notice is likely to be adduced in evidence in those proceedings.

For an unsuccessful challenge to the validity of a notice, see *Kempton v Special Commrs & CIR Ch D 1992, 66 TC 249*. In *R v CIR (ex p. Banque International à Luxembourg SA) QB 2000, 72 TC 597*, an application for judicial review based *inter alia* on the protections afforded by the European Convention on Human Rights was refused. In *R (oao Morgan Grenfell & Co Ltd) v Special Commr HL, [2002] STC 786*, the HL quashed a notice on the grounds that the Revenue were not entitled to require delivery of documents subject to legal professional privilege, a fundamental human right not expressly overridden by *TMA 1970, s 20(1)*.

(*b*) An officer of Revenue and Customs may similarly by notice in writing require a person to furnish him with such particulars as he may reasonably require as being relevant to any tax liability of that person.

The notice is subject to the same authority and giving of consent requirements as at (*a*) above, and the requirements there relating to the giving of a written summary and the obligation imposed on the Special or General Commissioner giving consent apply similarly in relation to particulars as they do there to documents.

(*c*) An officer of Revenue and Customs may similarly by notice in writing require any other person (including the Director of Savings) to deliver to him (or, if the person so elects, make available for inspection by a named officer of Revenue and Customs) documents relevant to any tax liability of a 'taxpayer'. A copy of the notice must be given to the taxpayer concerned unless, in a case involving suspected fraud, a General or Special Commissioner so directs. Production of documents originating more than six years before the notice cannot be required (unless the Commissioner who gave consent to the notice specifically allows it on being satisfied that there is reasonable ground for believing loss of tax through fraud).

'*Taxpayer*' includes an individual who has died (but any notice must be given no more than six years after the death) and a company which has ceased to exist.

The notice is subject to the same authority and giving of consent requirements as at (*a*) above, and the requirements there relating to the giving of a written summary and the obligation imposed on the Special or General Commissioner giving consent apply similarly, except that the summary must be given to, and the obligation imposed relates to an appeal brought by, the taxpayer rather than the person to whom the notice is given, and no summary need be given if the taxpayer is not, as above, given a copy of the notice.

A notice cannot require the production by a statutory auditor of his audit papers, nor by a tax adviser of communications with a client (or with any other tax adviser of his client) relating to advice about the client's tax affairs. This exemption does not, however, apply to explanatory documents concerning any other documents prepared with the client for, or for delivery to, HMRC, unless HMRC already has access to the information contained therein in some other document. Where the exemption is so disapplied, either the document must be delivered or made available to HMRC or a copy of the relevant parts must be supplied (which parts must be available if required for inspection).

HMRC's application of these provisions relating to papers of a statutory auditor or client communications of a tax adviser is set out in HMRC Statement of Practice 5/90. In particular, it is made clear that accountants' working papers will be called for only where voluntary access has not been obtained and it is considered absolutely necessary in order to determine whether a client's accounts or returns are complete and correct. Requests for access may on occasion extend to the whole or a particular part of the working papers, rather than just to information explaining specific entries, and HMRC will usually be prepared to visit the accountants' or clients' premises to examine the papers and to take copies or extracts.

For guidance on the question of whether documents and records are the property of a statutory auditor or tax adviser, or of the client of such a person, see ICAEW Memorandum TR 781, 23 February 1990.

For an unsuccessful challenge to the validity of a notice, see *R v CIR (ex p. TC Coombs & Co.) HL 1991, 64 TC 124*.

(*d*) An officer of Revenue and Customs may similarly, on an application authorised by the Commissioners for HMRC, give a notice in writing as under (*c*) above without naming the taxpayer concerned. Consent to the application must be obtained from a Special Commissioner, who must be satisfied that: it relates to a taxpayer or class of taxpayers whose identity(ies) is (are) not known; there are reasonable grounds to believe the taxpayer(s) to have failed to comply with the *Taxes Acts*, with the likelihood of serious prejudice to the assessment or collection of tax; and the information is not reasonably available from elsewhere. The recipient can object (with a right of appeal to the Special Commissioners), by notice in writing, within 30 days on the ground that it would be onerous for him to comply.

The requirements at (*a*) above relating to the giving of a written summary and the obligation imposed on the Special or General Commissioner giving consent do not apply. The exemption, and disapplication of the exemption, from the requirements of a notice under (*d*) above relating to the production of the papers of a statutory auditor or client communications of a tax adviser apply similarly, except that the exemption does not apply to any document giving the identity or address of any taxpayer to whom the notice relates or of any person who has acted on behalf of any such person, unless HMRC already has access to the information contained therein in some other document.

The power of the Commissioners for HMRC to authorise an application may be delegated to one of their officers, and the authorisation may be given orally (*R v Special Commr (ex p. CIR); R v CIR (ex p. Ulster Bank Ltd) QB 2000, 73 TC 209*).

(*e*) An officer may similarly (with the authority of the Commissioners for HMRC and the consent of a Circuit judge in England and Wales, a sheriff in Scotland or a county court judge in Northern Ireland) by notice in writing require a '*tax accountant*' (i.e. a person who assists another in the preparation of returns, etc. for tax purposes) who has been convicted by or before any UK court of a tax offence or incurred a penalty under *TMA 1970, s 99* (see 48.13 PENALTIES) to deliver documents in his possession or power relevant to any tax liability of any of his clients. The notice must be issued within twelve months of the final determination of the conviction or penalty award.

Neither the requirements at (*a*) above relating to the giving of a written summary nor the exemption from the requirements of a notice under (*d*) above relating to the production of the papers of a statutory auditor or client communications of a tax adviser apply to the giving of a notice as above.

(*f*) The Commissioners for HMRC may require, by notice in writing, a person to deliver or furnish to a named officer of theirs documents or information as specified in (*a*) and (*b*) above relevant to the tax liability of that person.

The requirements at (*a*) above relating to the giving of consent and a written summary do not apply. However, notices cannot be given on or after 26 July 1990 under this power unless there are reasonable grounds for believing that that person may have failed, or may fail, to comply with any provision of the *Taxes Acts*, and that any such failure is likely to have led, or to lead, to serious prejudice to the proper assessment or collection of tax.

For procedural matters in relation to such a notice, see *R v CIR (ex p. Taylor) (No 1) CA 1988, 62 TC 562; (No 2) CA 1990, 62 TC 578.*

The notice must specify or describe the documents or particulars required, the time limit for production (generally not less than 30 days) and, except as above, the name of the taxpayer or client, as appropriate; and the person to whom they are delivered may take copies.

The penalty for failure to comply with a notice is given by *TMA 1970, s 98* (see 48.15 PENALTIES for this and the penalty for failure to allow access to computers). In addition there are severe penalties (in summary proceedings, a fine of the statutory maximum, and on indictment, imprisonment for two years and/or an unlimited fine) for the falsification, concealment, destruction or disposal of a document which is the subject of a notice, unless strict conditions and time limits are observed.

[*TMA 1970, s 20, s 20A, s 20B(1)(1A)(1B)(2)(4)–(7)(9)–(14), s 20BB, s 20D; FA 1976, Sch 6; FA 1988, s 126(2)(3); FA 1989, ss 142–145, s 148, s 168(1)(2); FA 1990, s 93; FA 1994, s 255; FA 2000, s 149(3)(4); CRCA 2005, ss 5, 7*].

The person to whom notice is to be given is not entitled to attend or be legally represented at the meeting at which HMRC seek the consent of a Commissioner (*Applicant v Inspector of Taxes (Sp C 189), [1999] SSCD 128*).

Notices other than those under (*d*) and (*e*) above may relate to tax liabilities in EU member states other than the UK [*FA 1990, s 125(1)(2)(6)*] or in any other territory with which the UK has entered into a tax enforcement agreement or other arrangements providing for the obtaining of information (see 29.2(*c*) HMRC: CONFIDENTIALITY OF INFORMATION). [*FA 2000, s 146(3)(4); FA 2006, s 174, Sch 26 Pt 8(2)*].

For an article setting out HMRC's view on the question of claims to legal or professional privilege in relation to requests for information under these provisions (other than where tax evasion or tax fraud is suspected), see Revenue Tax Bulletin April 2000 pp 743–746 (updated by Revenue Tax Bulletin December 2002 p 993 following the *Morgan Grenfell* case at (*a*) above) (and see 23.11 below).

23.9 **Order for delivery of documents in serious tax fraud cases.** Under *TMA 1970, s 20BA, Sch 1AA*, introduced by *FA 2000, s 149, Sch 39*, HMRC may apply to the appropriate judicial authority (a Circuit judge in England and Wales, a sheriff in Scotland or a County Court judge in NI) for an order requiring any person who appears to have in his possession or power documents specified or described in the order to deliver them to an HMRC officer within ten working days after the day of service of the notice, or such longer or shorter period as may be specified in the order. The judicial authority must be satisfied, on information on oath given by an authorised HMRC officer, that there is reasonable ground for suspecting that an offence involving serious tax fraud has been or is about to be committed, and that the documents may be required as evidence in proceedings in respect of the offence. In Scotland, a single sheriff may make orders in respect of persons anywhere in Scotland as long as one of the orders relates to a person residing or having a place of business at an address in the sheriff's own sherriffdom. Orders may not be made in relation to items subject to legal privilege (as defined) unless they are held with the intention of furthering a criminal purpose. Failure to comply with an order is treated as contempt of court, and there are severe penalties for falsification of documents.

Schedule 1AA lays down detailed requirements in relation to such applications, and these may be supplemented by regulations (see now *SI 2000 No 2875*). In particular, a person is entitled to at least five days' notice of intention to apply for such an order, and to appear and be heard at the application, unless the judicial authority is satisfied that this would seriously prejudice investigation of the offence. Until the application has been dismissed or abandoned, or an order made or complied with, any person given such notice must not conceal, destroy, alter or dispose of any document to which the order sought relates, or disclose information etc. likely to prejudice the investigation, except with the leave of the judicial authority or the written permission of the Commissioners for HMRC (or, before 18 April 2005, the Board of Inland Revenue). Professional legal advisers may, however, disclose such information etc. in giving legal advice to a client or in connection with legal proceedings, provided that it is not disclosed with a view to furthering a criminal purpose. Failure to comply with these requirements is treated as failure to comply with an order under these provisions. The procedural rules where documents are delivered in accordance with an order are as for Search and seizure (see 23.10 below) under *TMA 1970, s 20CC(3)–(9)*. The regulations include procedural rules for resolving any dispute between HMRC and a person against whom an order is made as to whether a document (or part thereof) is an item subject to legal privilege.

23.10 **Search and seizure.** Where there is a reasonable suspicion of serious tax fraud, and there are reasonable grounds for believing that use of the procedure under *TMA 1970, s 20BA* (see 23.9 above) might seriously prejudice the investigation, HMRC may apply to a Circuit judge (a sheriff in Scotland or a County Court judge in NI) for a warrant to enter premises within 14 days to search and seize any things which may be relevant as evidence. There are detailed procedural rules governing searches and the removal of documents etc. [*TMA 1970, ss 20C, 20CC, 20D; FA 1976, Sch 6; FA 1989, ss 146–148; FA 2000, s 150*].

The taxpayer is not entitled to be told the nature of the offence, the ground of suspicion, or the person suspected (*CIR and Another v Rossminster Ltd and Others HL 1979, 52 TC 160*). For the proper procedure in seeking and obtaining judicial review of a decision to grant a warrant as above, and interim injunctions, see *R v CIR (ex p. Kingston Smith) QB 1996, 70 TC 264*. As regards the validity of warrants, see *R v CIR (ex p. Tamosius & Partners) QB, [1999] STC 1077*. If an HMRC officer executing a warrant has reasonable cause to believe that the data on a computer's hard drive might be required as evidence, he can seize and remove that computer even though it may also contain irrelevant material (*R (oao H) v CIR QB 2002, 75 TC 377*).

23.11 **Barristers, advocates or solicitors.** A notice under 23.8(*a*), (*b*), (*c*) or (*e*) above to a barrister, advocate or solicitor can be issued only by the Commissioners for HMRC (or, before 18 April 2005, the Board of Inland Revenue), although they may nevertheless delegate their powers (see *R v CIR (ex p. Davis Frankel & Mead) QB 2000, 73 TC 185*). The requirements at 23.8(*a*) above relating to the giving of consent and a written summary do not apply. The barrister etc. cannot (without his client's consent) be required to deliver under 23.8(*c*), (*d*) or (*e*) documents protected by professional privilege but, subject to that, the exemption, and disapplication of the exemption, from the requirements of a notice under, as the case may be, 23.8(*c*), (*d*) or (*e*) relating to the production of the papers of a statutory auditor or client communications of a tax adviser apply similarly. [*TMA 1970, s 20B(3)(8)*]. As regards the Search and seizure powers above, there is similarly an exclusion for documents protected by professional privilege or, from 28 July 2000, 'legal privilege' as more widely defined (but excluding items held with the intention of furthering a criminal purpose) [*TMA 1970, s 20C(4)–(4B); FA 1989, s 146(4); FA 2000, s 150(4)*], and see above as regards similar protection in relation to an order under *TMA 1970, s 20BA* in cases involving serious tax fraud.

See *R v CIR (ex p. Goldberg) QB 1988, 61 TC 403* and cf. *Dubai Bank Ltd v Galadari CA, [1989] 3 WLR 1044* (a non-tax case). In relation to search and seizure, it was held in *R v CIR (ex p. Tamosius & Partners) QB, [1999] STC 1077* that the presence of independent counsel to determine the issue of professional privilege was 'to be encouraged', although it would not prevent action by the courts if counsel was wrong. The issue and execution of warrants to search a lawyer's offices was held not to be in breach of *Article 8* of the *European Convention on Human Rights* (*Tamosius v UK ECHR, [2002] STC 1307*). The professional privilege exemption does not extend to the direction of notices against lawyers in their capacity as taxpayers rather than their professional capacity (*R v CIR (ex p. Lorimer) QB 2000, 73 TC 276*).

For an article setting out HMRC's view on the question of claims to legal or professional privilege in relation to requests for information under these provisions (other than where tax evasion or tax fraud is suspected), see Revenue Tax Bulletin April 2000 pp 743–746 (updated by Revenue Tax Bulletin December 2002 p 993 following the *Morgan Grenfell* case at 23.8(*a*) above).

23.12 CONTRACT SETTLEMENTS

In cases of fraudulent or negligent conduct the taxpayer may be invited to offer a sum in settlement of liability of tax, interest and penalties (a 'contract settlement') and such offers are often accepted by HMRC without assessment of all the tax. A binding agreement so made cannot be repudiated afterwards by the taxpayer or his executors. Where the liability is agreed and the tax etc. paid, this cannot afterwards be set aside, notwithstanding any alleged overcharge and no formal assessment (see cases at 48.17 PENALTIES and *CIR v Nuttall CA 1989, 63 TC 148* and *CIR v Woollen CA 1992, 65 TC 229*). See generally HMRC Pamphlet IR 160 regarding negotiation of settlements.

23.13 HMRC PRACTICE IN CASES OF SERIOUS TAX FRAUD

From 18 April 2005, criminal prosecutions for serious tax fraud in England and Wales are conducted by the Revenue and Customs Prosecutions Office, which is independent of HMRC. The Office has its own investigatory powers under *Serious Organised Crime and Police Act 2005, ss 60–62*. Before 18 April 2005, the Inland Revenue was itself a prosecuting authority and conducted its own prosecutions.

For new cases opened from 1 September 2005, the policy of the Commissioners of HMRC in cases of suspected serious tax fraud, as set out in Code of Practice COP 9 (2005), is as follows

1. The Commissioners reserve complete discretion to pursue a criminal investigation with a view to prosecution where they consider it necessary and appropriate.

2. Where a criminal investigation is not considered necessary or appropriate the Commissioners may decide to investigate using the civil investigation of fraud procedure.
3. Where the Commissioners decide to investigate using the civil investigation of fraud procedure they will not seek a prosecution for the tax fraud which is the subject of that investigation. The taxpayer will be given an opportunity to make a full and complete disclosure of all irregularities in their tax affairs.
4. However, where materially false statements are made or materially false documents are provided with intent to deceive, in the course of a civil investigation, the Commissioners may conduct a criminal investigation with a view to a prosecution of that conduct.

If the Commissioners decide to investigate using the civil investigation of fraud procedure the taxpayer will be given a copy of the above statement by an authorised officer.

Previously, the practice of the Board of Inland Revenue (and, after 18 April 2005, of HMRC) in cases of suspected serious tax fraud was set out in the so-called 'Hansard Statement' (last revised on 7 November 2002). This practice continues for investigations commenced before 1 September 2005. The practice was as follows.

(i) The Board reserved complete discretion to pursue prosecutions in the circumstances they considered appropriate.

(ii) Where serious tax fraud has been committed, they might accept a money settlement instead of pursuing a criminal prosecution.

(iii) They would accept a money settlement, and would not pursue a criminal prosecution, if the taxpayer, in response to being given a copy of the Hansard Statement by an authorised officer (meaning a current serving member of Inland Revenue Special Compliance Office), made a full and complete confession of all tax irregularities.

(Revenue Internet Statement 8 November 2002; Revenue Tax Bulletin December 2002 pp 979–981). This replaced the previous Hansard Statement of 18 October 1990, which did not include the undertaking in (iii) above. Instead, the Board retained full discretion as to the course they would pursue. In considering this, it was the Board's practice to be *influenced* by the taxpayer's having made a full confession and given full co-operation during the investigation, but they gave no explicit assurance that they would not prosecute in such cases.

See also HMRC Code of Practice COP 9 (2005) and HMRC Internet Statement 20 December 2005.

A decision by HMRC to enter into a contract settlement (see 23.12 above) and not to prosecute does not preclude the Crown Prosecution Service (CPS) from instituting criminal proceedings (*R v W and another CA, [1998] STC 550*). However, the Revenue in commenting on this case stated that the CPS will ordinarily bring proceedings that encompass tax evasion charges only where that evasion is incidental to allegations of non-fiscal criminal conduct (Revenue Tax Bulletin June 1998 pp 544, 545).

HMRC's policy is to use the civil investigation of fraud procedure wherever possible. Criminal investigation is reserved for cases where HMRC needs to send a strong deterrent message or where the conduct involved is such that only a criminal sanction is appropriate. Circumstances in which HMRC will usually consider commencing a criminal, rather than civil, investigation include:

- cases of organised or systematic fraud including conspiracy;
- where an individual holds a position of trust or responsibility;
- where materially false statements are made or materially false documents are provided in the course of a civil investigation;

- where deliberate concealment, deception, conspiracy or corruption is suspected;
- cases involving the use of false or forged documents;
- cases involving money laundering;
- where the perpetrator has committed previous offences or there is a repeated course of unlawful conduct or previous civil action;
- cases involving theft, or the misuse or unlawful destruction of HMRC documents;
- where there is evidence of assault on, threats to, or the impersonation of HMRC officials; and
- where there is a link to suspected wider criminality, whether domestic or international, involving offences not under the administration of HMRC.

When considering whether a case should be investigated under the civil investigation of fraud procedure or will be the subject of a criminal investigation, one factor considered by HMRC is whether the taxpayer has made a complete and unprompted disclosure of the offences committed.

(HMRC Internet Statement 20 December 2005).

The Board of Inland Revenue sought to prosecute where a taxpayer, having had his attention formally drawn to the Hansard statement, was given an opportunity to disclose irregularities and made false denials of irregularities or incomplete or incorrect disclosures. The Board were also likely to prosecute where there was evidence of tax fraud involving accountants, lawyers and other tax advisers (whether the fraud was on their own account or in connection with a client), persons involved in the administration of taxation or occupying a prominent position in the field of law or government, or personnel in government departments who were administering tax, benefits or law enforcement (including Revenue personnel).

(Revenue Internet Statement 15 July 2004).

See also 28.3 HMRC: ADMINISTRATION.

From 1 January 2001, the fraudulent evasion of *income tax* (not capital gains tax) on behalf of oneself or another person is itself a criminal offence. [*FA 2000, s 144*].

24 Furnished Holiday Accommodation

24.1 DEFINITIONS

Special provisions apply to the treatment for the purposes of tax on chargeable gains of the commercial letting of furnished holiday accommodation in the UK.

'*Commercial letting*' is letting (whether or not under a lease) on a commercial basis and with a view to the realisation of profits (see *Brown v Richardson (Sp C 129), [1997] SSCD 233* and Revenue Tax Bulletin October 1997 p 472), and accommodation is let '*furnished*' if the tenant is entitled to the use of furniture.

'*Holiday accommodation*' is accommodation which

(*a*) must be available for commercial letting to the public generally as holiday accommodation for at least 140 days in a twelve month period (see below), and

(*b*) is so let for at least 70 such days.

It must, however, not normally be in the same occupation for more than 31 consecutive days at any time during a period (although not necessarily a continuous period) of seven months in that twelve month period which includes any months in which it is let as in (*b*) above. In the case of an individual or partnership, these conditions must be satisfied in the tax year in which the profits or gains arise, unless

(i) the accommodation was not let furnished in the preceding tax year but is so let in the following tax year, in which case they must be satisfied in the twelve months from the date such letting commenced in the tax year, or

(ii) the accommodation was let furnished in the preceding tax year but is not so let in the following tax year, in which case they must be satisfied in the twelve months ending with the date such letting ceased in the tax year.

In the case of a company, the conditions must be satisfied in the twelve months ending on the last day of the accounting period in which the profits or gains arise, with similar variations as in (i) and (ii) above where the accommodation was not let furnished in the twelve months preceding or following the period in question.

In satisfying the 70 day test ((*b*) above) averaging may be applied to letting periods of holiday accommodation already treated as such ('*qualifying accommodation*') and letting periods of any or all of other accommodation let by the same person which would be holiday accommodation if it satisfied the 70 day test. Any such other accommodation is then treated as holiday accommodation if the average of the days let in the twelve month period is at least 70. For persons other than companies, a claim for averaging must be made on or before the first anniversary of 31 January following the tax year for which it is to apply. For companies, the time limit is two years after the end of the accounting period for which the averaging claim is to apply. Only one such claim may be made in respect of qualifying accommodation in any tax year or accounting period.

Where there is a letting of accommodation only part of which is holiday accommodation, apportionments are made as are just and reasonable.

[*ICTA 1988, s 504; TCGA 1992, s 241(1)(2)(7); FA 1996, Sch 20 para 62, Sch 21 para 14; ITTOIA 2005, ss 323–326, Sch 1 paras 196, 441(2)*].

Furnished holiday accommodation may include caravans (Revenue Press Release 17 May 1984).

The Revenue operated a concession whereby if a furnished holiday lettings business satisfied the tests as to availability for letting, actual letting, and occupation, in 1999/2000 or 2000/01 but is prevented from doing so, *by foot and mouth disease restrictions*, in 2000/01 or 2001/02, the failure will be disregarded and the furnished holiday lettings rules will be deemed to be satisfied (Revenue Tax Bulletin, Special Foot and Mouth Disease Edition, May 2001 p 4).

See Tolley's Income Tax regarding income tax provisions in respect of furnished holiday accommodation.

24.2 CAPITAL GAINS TAX TREATMENT

For the purposes of the following provisions, any UK property business or Schedule A business which consists of, or so far as it consists of, the commercial letting of furnished holiday accommodation in the UK is treated as a trade, and all such lettings made by a particular person, partnership or body of persons are treated as one trade.

(*a*) (Before 2003/04) RETIREMENT RELIEF (53).

(*b*) ROLLOVER RELIEF (55).

(*c*) Relief for gifts of business assets (see 33.1–33.6 HOLD-OVER RELIEFS).

(*d*) Relief for loans to traders (see 40.10 LOSSES).

(*e*) TAPER RELIEF (61).

(*f*) The exemptions relating to SUBSTANTIAL SHAREHOLDINGS OF COMPANIES (60).

A notable omission from (*a*)–(*f*) above, which may be of advantage to the taxpayer, are the provisions applying in respect of a non-UK resident trading in the UK through a branch or agency or permanent establishment (see 45.3 OVERSEAS MATTERS).

Where, in any chargeable period, a person makes a commercial letting within these provisions, the let property is to be taken for the purposes of (*a*)–(*e*) above as being used throughout that period only for the purposes of the deemed trade of making such lettings except for any period when it is neither commercially let nor available to be so let (unless it is only works of construction or repair that make this the case).

For the purposes of (*b*) above, the replacement asset must be acquired after 5 April 1982. However, where the only or main residence exemption in *TCGA 1992, s 222* (see 49 PRIVATE RESIDENCES) is also available to any extent, the gain to which *TCGA 1992, s 222* applies is reduced by the amount of the rolled-over gain.

[*TCGA 1992, s 241(3)–(6)(8); FA 1995, Sch 6 para 36; FA 1998, s 121(3)(4), Sch 5 para 62, Sch 21 para 8; FA 2002, s 44, Sch 8 para 3; ITTOIA 2005, Sch 1 para 441(3)*].

The Revenue indicated in 1984 that the relief at (*a*) or (*b*) is available if the holiday accommodation is sold within three years of its ceasing to be let so long as the owner does not occupy it or use it for some other non-qualifying purpose (CCAB Statement TR 551, June 1984).

Simon's Direct Tax Service. See C2.1114, C3.319.

25 Gifts

Cross-references. See 35.2 INTERACTION WITH OTHER TAXES for inheritance tax interaction on lifetime gifts; and 47.6 PAYMENT OF TAX for payment by instalments on certain gifts etc.

25.1 GENERAL

The fact that no proceeds are received on a disposal of an asset does not mean that capital gains tax will not apply. With certain exceptions, where a person acquires or disposes of an asset, otherwise than by way of a bargain made at arm's length *and in particular where he acquires or disposes of it by way of gift,* his acquisition or disposal of the asset is deemed to be for a consideration equal to the market value of the asset. [*TCGA 1992, s 17*(*1*)(*a*)]. See 41 MARKET VALUE for the full market value rules and the exceptions where the provisions do not apply.

Thus, the donor of an asset is normally treated as incurring a chargeable gain computed by reference to market value at the date of disposal. For the purposes of gifts, the date of disposal is the time when the donor has done everything within his power to transfer the property to the donee (see *Re Rose, Rose and Others v CIR CA, [1952] 1 All ER 1217*).

25.2 SPECIAL EXEMPTIONS RELATING TO GIFTS

Once the market value of a gift has been established, the ordinary capital gains tax provisions relating to exemptions apply to that gift. See 22 EXEMPTIONS AND RELIEFS. For example, the gift of a chattel with a market value of £6,000 or less is exempt. The following gifts are expressly exempt.

(*a*) Gifts for public benefit (see 22.28 EXEMPTIONS AND RELIEFS).

(*b*) Gifts of property to bodies mentioned in *IHTA 1984, Sch 3* for national purposes (see 22.37 EXEMPTIONS AND RELIEFS).

(*c*) Donatio mortis causa (see 18.3 DEATH).

25.3 SPECIAL RELIEFS RELATING TO GIFTS

Reliefs are available for:

(*a*) gifts after 5 April 1980 and before 14 March 1989 (see 33.9 HOLD-OVER RELIEFS);

(*b*) gifts of business assets before 14 March 1989 (see 33.6 HOLD-OVER RELIEFS);

(*c*) gifts of business assets after 13 March 1989 (see 33.1 HOLD-OVER RELIEFS);

(*d*) gifts to charities (see 10.5 CHARITIES);

(*e*) gifts after 13 March 1989 of assets on which inheritance tax etc. is chargeable (see 33.7 HOLD-OVER RELIEFS);

(*f*) gifts to housing associations after 13 March 1989 (see 22.49 EXEMPTIONS AND RELIEFS);

(*g*) gifts to maintenance trusts for historic buildings before 6 April 1984 (see 22.78 EXEMPTIONS AND RELIEFS);

(*h*) gifts of national heritage property subject to certain undertakings (see 22.80 EXEMPTIONS AND RELIEFS); and

(*i*) gifts to settlements for the benefit of employees (see 22.85 EXEMPTIONS AND RELIEFS).

25.4 RECOVERY OF TAX FROM DONEE

Where capital gains tax arising on a disposal made by way of gift (including any transaction otherwise than at arm's length) is not paid by the donor (or, if he being an individual has died, his personal representatives) within twelve months from the date it became payable, it may be recovered, subject to the coverage below, from the donee within two years after the date on which it became payable. The donee then has a right of recovery from the donor or his personal representatives. The recovery is done by assessment and the donee is assessed and charged (in the name of the donor) to capital gains tax on an amount not exceeding the amount of the chargeable gain arising on the disposal, and not exceeding the grossed-up amount of the capital gains tax unpaid at the time such assessment is made, grossing up at the marginal rate of tax (i.e. by taking capital gains tax on a chargeable gain at the amount which would not have been chargeable but for that chargeable gain).

These provisions apply in relation to a chargeable gain accruing to a transferor under *TCGA 1992, s 169C(7)* (clawback of relief under *TCGA 1992, s 165* or *s 260* if settlement becomes settlor-interested — see 33.5 HOLD-OVER RELIEFS) as they apply in relation to a gain accruing on the disposal of an asset by way of a gift. For this purpose, the transferor is taken to be the donor, and the trustees to whom the relevant disposal in question (see 33.5 HOLD-OVER RELIEFS) was made are taken to be the donee.

[*TCGA 1992, s 282; FA 2004, s 116, Sch 21 para 7*].

26 Government Securities

Cross-reference. See also 14 COMPANIES—CORPORATE FINANCE AND INTANGIBLES.

26.1 EXEMPTION RULES

Gains on disposals of any of the UK government and public corporation stocks ('gilts') specified in 26.2 below are not chargeable gains, and losses are not allowable. [*TCGA 1992, s 115(1)(a)*].

The same applies to disposals of options or contracts to acquire or dispose of such gilts. See 6.7 and 6.8 ASSETS.

Gains and losses on disposals by companies of such assets are within the company loan relationship provisions described in 14.2–14.6 COMPANIES—CORPORATE FINANCE AND INTANGIBLES. They are thus treated for corporation tax purposes as *income* (and not capital) gains and losses, and are chargeable/allowable accordingly.

See 13.13 COMPANIES for appropriations of gilts to and from trading stock by companies.

See 58.7 SHARES AND SECURITIES regarding government stock issued as compensation for shares compulsorily acquired.

26.2 EXEMPT SECURITIES

Government (and certain public corporation securities guaranteed by the Treasury) are specified as exempt, as described in 26.1 above, by the Treasury in the form of a statutory instrument. In practice, all UK government securities charged on the National Loans Fund are so specified.

Any security which is a strip (within *FA 1942, s 47*) of a security which is a gilt specified as exempt is also itself a gilt specified for the purposes of the exemption. The Treasury are given powers to amend the legislation by regulations in connection with the introduction of gilt strips. [*TCGA 1992, s 288(8), Sch 9 Pt I; FA 1996, s 202, Sch 40 para 8*].

Those securities specified as exempt are listed in *TCGA 1992, Sch 9 Pt II* as supplemented by *SI 1993 No 950*, *SI 1994 No 2656*, *SI 1996 No 1031*, *SI 2001 No 1122*, *SI 2002 No 2849*, *SI 2004 No 438*, *SI 2005 No 276* and *SI 2006 No 184*. A list of the exempt securities has been made available on the HMRC website (www.hmrc.gov.uk).

27 Groups of Companies

Cross-references. See 7.1, 7.3 ASSETS HELD ON 6 APRIL 1965 and 8.3, 8.6 ASSETS HELD ON 31 MARCH 1982 for irrevocable election by principal company of a group; 13 COMPANIES.

Simon's Direct Tax Service. See Division D2.6.

The headings in this chapter are as follows.

27.1 DEFINITIONS

For the purposes of this chapter, the following definitions apply.

Company. '*Company*' means a company within the meaning of the *Companies Act 1985* or the corresponding enactment in Northern Ireland or a company (other than a limited liability partnership — see 46.19 PARTNERSHIPS) which is constituted under any other Act, Royal Charter, or letters patent or under the law of a country outside the UK. It also includes a registered industrial and provident society, a trustee savings bank, a building society and, from 17 March 1998, an incorporated friendly society within the meaning of *Friendly Societies Act 1992*.

Residence requirement. Before, broadly, April 2000, and in all cases, except those referred to in 27.13 below, 27.16 below and 45.3, 45.6 OVERSEAS MATTERS, the company had to be resident in the UK. The law is amended by *FA 2000* to remove this condition and thus enable any company, whatever its country of residence, to be a member of a group for the purposes of UK corporation tax on chargeable gains. The change is generally effective on and after 1 April 2000, though consequential changes to pre-existing anti-avoidance legislation took effect on 21 March 2000. The consequences, and effective dates, of the change in the residence requirement are dealt with in this publication wherever appropriate (see, for example, 27.2 below). Transitional measures ensure continuity of treatment as regards a pre-existing group of companies (see also (3) below). For an example of the effect of the change in the residence requirement on a worldwide group, see HMRC Capital Gains Manual CG 45141.

[*TCGA 1992, s 170(2)(a)(9); FA 1998, s 136(1)(4); FA 2000, s 102, Sch 29 paras 1, 46(1)–(3); FA 2001, s 75(4)*].

Group. A '*group*' comprises

(*a*) a company ('*the principal company of the group*') and

(*b*) that company's '75% subsidiaries' (as in *ICTA 1988, s 838* i.e. where not less than 75% of the 'ordinary share capital' (see below under 'General') is beneficially owned directly or indirectly by the principal company), and those subsidiaries' 75% subsidiaries (and so on), except that any 75% subsidiary which is not 'an effective 51% subsidiary' of the principal company is excluded.

This definition is subject to the following rules.

(1) A company ('the subsidiary') which is a 75% subsidiary of another company cannot be a principal company of a group, unless,

- (i) because of the exclusion in (*b*) above, the two companies are not in the same group,
- (ii) the requirements of the definition of a group in (*a*) and (*b*) are otherwise satisfied, and
- (iii) no further company could, under this provision, be the principal company of a group of which the subsidiary would be a member.

(2) If a company would otherwise belong to more than one group (the principal company of each of which is called the 'head of a group' below), it belongs only to the group which can first be determined under the following tests.

- (i) The group to which it would belong if the exclusion of a company which is not an effective 51% subsidiary in (*b*) above were applied without the inclusion of any amount to which the head of a group is entitled of any profits available for distribution to equity holders of a head of another group or would be entitled to any assets of a head of another group available for distribution to its equity holders on a winding up.
- (ii) The group the head of which is entitled to a greater percentage than any other head of a group of its profits available for distribution to equity holders.
- (iii) The group the head of which would be entitled to a greater percentage than any other head of a group of its assets available for distribution to equity holders on a winding-up.
- (iv) The group the head of which owns (as in *ICTA 1988, s 838(1)(a)*) directly or indirectly more of its ordinary share capital than any other head of a group.

(3) *Transitional.* If a group is regarded as reconstituted purely because of the amendment made by *FA 2000* to the residence requirement (see above), such that the principal company of the 'old' group is not the principal company of the 'new' group, a subsidiary which is not 'an effective 51% subsidiary' of the new principal company remains part of the group for as long as it remains 'an effective 51% subsidiary' of the company which was the principal company of the old group. For examples, see HMRC Capital Gains Manual CG 45130, 45162.

A company ('the subsidiary') is '*an effective 51% subsidiary*' of another company ('the parent') at any time if and only if

(A) the parent is entitled to more than 50% of any profits available for distribution to equity holders of the subsidiary, and

(B) the parent would be entitled to more than 50% of any assets available for distribution to the equity holders on a winding up.

ICTA 1988, Sch 18 as amended (group relief: equity holders and profits or assets available for distribution) applies with suitable modifications for the purposes of (2) and (A) and (B) above. One modification for these purposes disapplies the requirement that certain arrangements for changes in profit or asset shares are assumed to take place in applying the 50% tests above.

[*TCGA 1992, s 170(2)(b)(3)–(8); ICTA 1988, s 838; F(No 2)A 1992, s 24, Sch 6 paras 5, 10; FA 2000, Sch 29 para 46(4)–(6), Sch 40 Pt II(11)*].

For consideration of beneficial ownership of a company's shares where they are subject to cross-options by shareholders, see *J Sainsbury plc v O'Connor CA 1991, 64 TC 208.* Although legislation overturning the *Sainsbury* decision in respect of arrangements entered into after 14 November 1991 was introduced by *F(No 2)A 1992* for group relief purposes, it does not apply for the purposes of the taxation of chargeable gains.

A group remains the same group so long as the same company remains the principal company of the group, and if at any time the principal company of a group becomes a member of another group, the first group and the other group are regarded as the same, and the question whether or not a company has ceased to be a member of a group is determined accordingly. [*TCGA 1992, s 170(10)*].

Where the principal company of a group

- becomes an SE (see 13.18 COMPANIES) on or after 1 April 2005 by reason of being the acquiring company in the formation of an SE by merger by acquisition (in accordance with *Council Regulations (EC) No 2157/2001, Arts 2(1), 17(2) and 29(1)*);
- becomes a subsidiary of a holding SE (formed on or after 1 April 2005 in accordance with *Art 2(2)*); or
- is transformed on or after 1 April 2005 into an SE (in accordance with *Art 2(4)*),

the group and any group of which the SE is a member on formation are regarded as the same, and the question whether or not a company has ceased to be a member of a group is determined accordingly. [*TCGA 1992, s 170(10A); F(No 2)A 2005, s 62*].

The passing of a resolution, or the making of an order, or any other act for the winding-up of a member of a group is not treated as an occasion on which any company ceases to be a member of the group. [*TCGA 1992, s 170(11)*].

General. '*Ordinary share capital*' means all issued share capital of a company except that carrying a fixed rate of dividend only. Any share capital of a registered industrial and provident society is treated as ordinary share capital.

'*Group*' and '*subsidiary*' are construed with any necessary modifications where applied to a company incorporated under the law of a country outside the UK.

'*Profits*' means income and gains. '*Trade*' includes a vocation, office or employment (including the occupation of UK woodlands before 6 April 1993).

[*TCGA 1992, s 170(1)(2)(c)(d); ICTA 1988, s 832(1)*].

For HMRC's own notes on the capital gains definition of a group of companies, see HMRC Capital Gains Manual CG 45100–45231.

HMRC have confirmed that it is possible for a Delaware Limited Liability Company that issues shares to be a member of a capital gains group (Revenue Tax Bulletin February 2001 p 827). With effect for disposals on or after 1 April 2006, it is specifically provided that an open-ended investment company (see 65.6 UNIT TRUSTS, ETC.) cannot be the principal company of a group [*TCGA 1992, s 170(4A) treated as inserted by SI 2006 No 964, Reg 107*] or a member of a group (see HMRC Capital Gains Manual, CG 45173).

As regards nationalised industries, etc., see *TCGA 1992, s 170(12)–(14)*.

See also 45.6, 45.9, 45.14 OVERSEAS MATTERS.

27.2 DISPOSALS OF CAPITAL ASSETS BY ONE MEMBER OF A GROUP TO ANOTHER

Disposals of capital assets by one member of a group to another member are treated as if made at a 'no gain/no loss' disposal value except for the following.

(i) Assumed (as opposed to actual) disposals.

(ii) A disposal of a debt due from a group member effected by satisfying it (or part of it).

(iii) A disposal on redemption of redeemable shares.

(iv) A disposal of an interest in shares in consideration of a capital distribution within *TCGA 1992, s 122* whether or not involving a reduction of capital.

(v) The receipt of compensation for destruction etc. of assets (in that the disposal is treated as being to the insurer or other person who ultimately bears the burden of furnishing the compensation).

(vi) A disposal by or to an investment trust within *ICTA 1988, s 842* (and see also 27.14 below).

(via) A disposal by or to a venture capital trust within *ICTA 1988, s 842AA* (and see 27.15 below).

(vib) A disposal by or to a qualifying friendly society, i.e. an incorporated friendly society within *ICTA 1988, s 461A* which is entitled to income tax and corporation tax exemptions on certain profits.

(vii) A disposal to a 'dual resident investing company' within *ICTA 1988, s 404*.

(viia) A disposal by or to a real estate investment trust (see 65.4 UNIT TRUSTS ETC.).

(viii) An exchange of securities which is treated by *TCGA 1992, s 127* as it applies by virtue of *TCGA 1992, s 135* as not involving a disposal by the member of the group first mentioned above (see 58.1 and 58.4 SHARES AND SECURITIES).

The position for exchanges of shares before 14 March 1988 in reorganisations within a group was examined in *Westcott v Woolcombers Ltd CA 1987, 60 TC 575* and *NAP Holdings UK Ltd v Whittles HL 1994, 67 TC 166*. The decision in the former case, which involved consideration of the original *FA 1965* legislation and a reorganisation occurring prior to the introduction by *FA 1968* of certain anti-avoidance provisions was approved in the judgements given in the latter case, which involved a reorganisation which occurred when the provisions of *ICTA 1970* and *CGTA 1979* were extant and subsequent to further anti-avoidance provisions introduced by *FA 1977*.

For HMRC's views on this topic, see HMRC Capital Gains Manual CG 45550–45573.

(ix) A disposal after 15 March 2005 where *FA 1996, s 91A* (certain shares subject to outstanding third party obligations — see 14.5 COMPANIES—CORPORATE FINANCE AND INTANGIBLES) does not apply to the asset in relation to the company making the disposal immediately before the disposal but does apply in relation to the acquiring company immediately after its acquisition, or where that section applies immediately before the disposal but not immediately afterwards.

(x) A disposal after 19 March 1990 and before 30 November 1993 (the latter date being the date of the coming into force of *FA 1994, s 249*; companies otherwise regarded as UK resident but under double tax relief arrangements already regarded as non-UK resident to be treated as non-UK resident for *Taxes Acts* purposes after 29 November 1993; see 52.6 RESIDENCE AND DOMICILE) to a company which, though resident in the UK, was regarded as resident elsewhere by virtue of DOUBLE TAX RELIEF (19.2) arrangements such that it would not under those arrangements be taxable in the UK on any gain arising on a disposal of the asset immediately after its acquisition.

The change in the residence requirement in 27.1 above has effect for these purposes in relation to disposals on or after 1 April 2000. The conditions for intra-group transfers of assets on or after that date to be treated as no gain/no loss disposals are:

- that *either* the transferor company is UK-resident at time of disposal *or* the asset is a 'chargeable asset' in relation to that company immediately before that time; *and*
- that *either* the transferee company is UK-resident at time of disposal *or* the asset is a 'chargeable asset' in relation to that company immediately after that time.

For these purposes, an asset is a '*chargeable asset*' in relation to a company at a particular time if, on a disposal by that company at that time, any gain would be a chargeable gain and would be within the charge to corporation tax by virtue of *TCGA 1992, s 10* or *s 10B* (non-UK resident company trading in the UK through a permanent establishment (previously a branch or agency) — see 45.3 OVERSEAS MATTERS).

For disposals before 1 April 2000, the effect of the residence requirement was that both transferor and transferee had to be UK-resident and members of the same group of UK-resident companies.

[*TCGA 1992, s 171; FA 1994, s 251(1)(7), Sch 26 Pt VIII; FA 1998, s 135(1)(4), s 136(2)(3)(5); FA 2000, Sch 29 para 2; FA 2002, Sch 9 paras 5(10), 7; FA 2003, Sch 27 para 2; F(No 2)A 2005, Sch 7 para 9; FA 2006, s 135*].

HMRC accept that the no gain/no loss rule can apply to the grant or surrender of a lease by one group company to another (HMRC Capital Gains Manual CG 45351).

As regards (iv) above, the assets acquired in the capital distribution are nevertheless transferred at a 'no gain/no loss' price (see *Innocent v Whaddon Estates Ltd Ch D 1981, 55 TC 476*).

For the Revenue's views as to the application of the principles established by *Furniss v Dawson HL 1984, 55 TC 324* with regard to the use of 'capital loss' companies within a group, see ICAEW Guidance Note TR 588, 25 September 1985 (but note the provisions in 27.20 below).

FOREX. The following applies where there is a disposal or acquisition of currency; a 'qualifying asset' consisting of the right to settlement under a debt which is not a debt on a security (within *TCGA 1992, s 132*; see 22.5 EXEMPTIONS AND RELIEFS); a 'qualifying asset' consisting of the right to settlement under a debt on a security; or an obligation which by virtue of *TCGA 1992, s 143* (futures contracts; see 6.8 ASSETS) is regarded as an asset to the disposal of which *TCGA 1992* applies and which is a duty under a currency contract. It applies where the disposal or acquisition is by a 'qualifying company' and is made on or after the company's 'commencement day' (the first day of its first accounting period beginning after 22 March 1995, subject to transitional provisions) and in an accounting period beginning before 1 October 2002 (see 14.15 COMPANIES—CORPORATE FINANCE AND INTANGIBLES). Where, immediately before the disposal or after the acquisition, as the case may be, the asset is held wholly for 'qualifying purposes', and

TCGA 1992, s 171 would otherwise apply, that provision does not apply as regards the disposal or acquisition and the corresponding acquisition or disposal. '*Qualifying purposes*' are purposes of long-term or mutual insurance business. [*FA 1993, s 169, Sch 17 para 7; FA 2002, Sch 40 Pt 3(10); SI 2001 No 3629, Art 81*]. See 14.15 COMPANIES—CORPORATE FINANCE AND INTANGIBLES for a note of the terms quoted and not otherwise defined.

27.3 DISPOSAL OUTSIDE A GROUP TREATED AS HAVING BEEN PRECEDED BY INTRA-GROUP TRANSFER

Where two companies, X and Y, are members of a group, and X disposes of an asset on or after 1 April 2000 to a person outside the group (the actual disposal), X and Y may make a joint election to the effect that for the purposes of corporation tax on chargeable gains:

- the asset (or a specified part of it) be deemed to have been transferred by X to Y immediately before the actual disposal;
- that transfer be deemed to be a no gain/no loss disposal within *TCGA 1992, s 171* (see 27.2 above);
- the actual disposal (or the part of it to which the election relates) be deemed to have been made by Y; and
- any incidental costs incurred by X in making the actual disposal be deemed to have been incurred by Y in making the deemed disposal.

The election must be made in writing to an HMRC officer on or before the second anniversary of the end of the accounting period of X in which the actual disposal was made. It can be made only if an actual transfer of the asset (or part) from X to Y would have been a no gain/no loss disposal within *TCGA 1992, s 171*. This provision is intended to facilitate the bringing together of chargeable gains and allowable losses within one group company. Any payment made by X to Y, or vice versa, in connection with the election is not to be taken into account in computing profits or losses of either company or treated as a distribution or, for payments made before 16 March 2005, a charge on income, *provided* it does not exceed the chargeable gain or allowable loss deemed to accrue to Y on the disposal.

For disposals on or after 16 March 2005, where Y is not resident in the UK but is carrying on a trade in the UK through a permanent establishment there, the asset deemed to be transferred by X to Y is treated for the purposes of these provisions as having been acquired by Y for use by or for the purposes of the permanent establishment (so that, if the asset is situated in the UK, the deemed transfer is a no gain/no loss disposal and the deemed disposal by Y is a deemed disposal of a chargeable asset). This treatment is not taken to affect the question of whether the asset or part is situated in the UK.

[*TCGA 1992, s 171A; FA 2000, s 101; FA 2001, s 77; F(No 2)A 2005, s 36, Sch 11 Pt 2(7)*].

Where the election has been made, Y's chargeable gain may be adjusted under *TCGA 1992, s 49* (see 15.6(*f*) COMPUTATION OF GAINS AND LOSSES) as extended by ESC D33 para 13 to reflect any payments to the purchaser by X under warranties or indemnities (HMRC Capital Gains Manual CG 45359).

27.4 INTRA-GROUP TRANSFERS OF ASSETS WHICH ARE TRADING STOCK OF ONE OF THE COMPANIES BUT NOT OF THE OTHER

Where a company (Company A) acquires an asset as trading stock of a trade from another member of the group (Company B), and the asset did not form part of the trading stock of a trade carried on by Company B, Company A is treated for the purposes of *TCGA 1992, s 161* (see 6.3 ASSETS) as acquiring the asset otherwise than as trading stock and immediately appropriating it to trading stock. The effect is that, subject to an election being made for the alternative treatment in 6.3 ASSETS, a chargeable gain or allowable loss accrues to Company A based on the difference between market value and the no gain/no loss (see 27.2 above) transfer value.

Where a company (Company C) disposes of an asset forming part of the trading stock of a trade to another member of the group (Company D), and the asset is acquired by Company D otherwise than as trading stock of a trade carried on by it, Company C is treated for the purposes of *TCGA 1992, s 161* as appropriating the asset immediately before the disposal for a purpose other than use as trading stock. The effect is that Company C is deemed to have acquired the asset at that time at the amount brought into the accounts of the trade for tax purposes (see 6.3 ASSETS).

In relation to acquisitions and disposals on or after 1 April 2000, the change in the residence requirement in 27.1 above applies in determining whether a company is a member of a group for the above purposes, but references above to a trade do not include a trade carried on by a non-UK resident company other than in the UK through a permanent establishment or, for accounting periods beginning before 1 January 2003, through a branch or agency.

[*TCGA 1992, s 173; FA 2000, Sch 29 para 11; FA 2003, s 153(1)(b)(4)*].

Acquisition 'as trading stock' implies a commercial justification for the acquisition, see *Coates v Arndale Properties Ltd HL 1984, 59 TC 516*, *Reed v Nova Securities Ltd HL 1985, 59 TC 516*, *N Ltd v Inspector of Taxes (Sp C 90), [1996] SSCD 346* and *New Angel Court Ltd v Adam CA, [2004] STC 779; [2004] EWCA Civ 242.*

27.5 INTRA-GROUP TRANSFERS: INDEXATION ALLOWANCES

See 8.7 ASSETS HELD ON 31 MARCH 1982 and 34.3 INDEXATION for re-basing and indexation provisions on 'no gain/no loss' disposals.

27.6 DISPOSAL OR ACQUISITION OUTSIDE A GROUP — MISCELLANEOUS

Where there is a disposal of an asset which was acquired in circumstances in which *TCGA 1992, s 140A* (see 45.10 OVERSEAS MATTERS), *s 171* (see 27.2 above) or (before 1 April 2000) *s 172* (see 45.3 OVERSEAS MATTERS) applied or in which *TCGA 1992, s 171* would have applied but for the exclusions mentioned in 27.2(ii)–(iv)(vi)–(vii)(ix) above, restriction of allowable losses by reference to capital allowances (see 15.6(*j*) COMPUTATION OF GAINS AND LOSSES) applies in relation to capital allowances made to the person from whom it was acquired (so far as not taken into account in relation to a disposal by that person) and so on as respects previous such acquisitions. The above does not affect the 'no gain/no loss' consideration for which the asset is deemed under the above-mentioned provisions to have been acquired. [*TCGA 1992, s 41(8), s 174(1)–(3); F(No 2)A 1992, s 46(1)(5); FA 2000, Sch 29 para 12, Sch 40 Pt II(12)*].

Where a company which is or has been a group member disposes of an asset which it acquired from another group member as a result of a no gain/no loss disposal within 27.2 above, the provisions relating to ASSETS HELD ON 6 APRIL 1965 (7) apply as if all group members were one person. As regards acquisitions before 1 April 2000, this provision was dependent on the asset having been acquired at a time when both parties to the transaction were members of the group, regardless of whether or not the transfer was within 27.2 above, except that it did not apply if the transfer was within 27.2(iv) (transfer by or to an investment trust). The change in the residence requirement in 27.1 above applies in determining whether a company is a member of a group for these purposes at any time on or after 1 April 2000. [*TCGA 1992, s 174(4)(5); FA 2000, Sch 29 para 13*].

27.7 ROLLOVER RELIEF ON THE REPLACEMENT OF BUSINESS ASSETS

See 55.5 ROLLOVER RELIEF for provisions relating to groups of companies.

27.8 COLLECTION OF UNPAID TAX FROM OTHER MEMBERS OF THE GROUP AND CONTROLLING DIRECTORS

Gains accruing after 31 March 2000. Where a chargeable gain accrues to a company (hereafter referred to as the taxpayer company) after 31 March 2000 and either

- that company is UK-resident at the time the gain accrues, or
- the gain is within the charge to corporation tax by virtue of *TCGA 1992, s 10* or *s 10B* (non-UK resident company trading in the UK through a permanent establishment (previously a branch or agency) — see 45.3 OVERSEAS MATTERS),

the following rules apply where all or part of the corporation tax assessed on the company for the relevant accounting period (i.e. the accounting period in which the gain accrues) remains unpaid six months after it became payable.

HMRC may serve on any of the following persons a notice requiring that person to pay, within 30 days, the unpaid tax or, if less, an amount equal to corporation tax on the chargeable gain at the appropriate rate.

(*a*) If the taxpayer company was a member of a 'group' at the time the gain accrued:

- a company which was at that time the 'principal company of the group'; and
- any other company which, in any part of the period of 12 months ending with that time, was a member of the group *and* owned the asset, or any part of the asset, disposed of (or, where that asset is an interest in, or a right over, another asset, owned either asset or any part of either asset).

(*b*) If the gain is within the charge to corporation tax by virtue of *TCGA 1992, s 10* or *s 10B*, any person who is, or has been during the 12 months ending with the time the gain accrued, a controlling director of the taxpayer company or of a company which has, or has had within that 12-month period, control over the taxpayer company.

For the purpose of (*a*) above, '*group*' and '*principal company of the group*' are construed as in 27.1 above but as if references there to 75% subsidiaries were references to 51% subsidiaries. The change in the residence requirement in 27.1 above applies in determining whether a company is a member of a group at any time (including a time before 1 April 2000). For the purposes of (*b*) above and in determining whether a director is a controlling director, 'control' is construed in accordance with *ICTA 1988, s 416*, and 'director' has the wide meaning given by *ITEPA 2003, s 67(1)(2)* (previously *ICTA 1988, s 168(8)(9)*) and *ICTA 1988, s 417(5)(6)*.

The notice must state the amount of tax assessed, the original due date and the amount required from the person on whom it is served. It has effect, for the purposes of collection, interest and appeals, as if it were a notice of assessment on that person. The notice must be served within three years beginning with the date on which the liability of the taxpayer company for the relevant accounting period is finally determined. That date varies according to whether the unpaid tax is charged in a self-assessment (and, if so, whether there is an enquiry into the tax return in question), in a discovery assessment (and, if so, whether there is an appeal) or in consequence of a 'determination' (see Tolley's Corporation Tax under Self-Assessment). In the simplest case of a self-assessment and no enquiry, the liability is determined on the last date on which notice of enquiry could have been given.

A person paying an amount under these provisions may recover it from the taxpayer company, but such an amount is not deductible for any tax purpose.

[*TCGA 1992, s 190; FA 2000, Sch 29 para 9(1)(3)(4); FA 2003, Sch 27 para 2*].

Gains accruing before 1 April 2000 (and see also 45.13 OVERSEAS MATTERS as regards non-resident companies). If corporation tax on a chargeable gain of a group member is not paid within six months of the time when it becomes payable or it is assessed (whichever is the later), then, within two years after that time, the tax may be assessed on (*a*) the principal company of the group when the gain accrued or (*b*) any other company which at any time in the two years preceding the time the gain accrued was a group member and owned the asset disposed of (or the right, interest, etc. therein). The company paying the tax then has a right of recovery from the company to which the gain accrued, or from the principal company of the group when the gain accrued, if that is a different company. In the latter instance, a right is given to that principal company of recovery from the company to which the gain accrued and, insofar as the tax is not so recovered, of a just proportion from any present member of the group which has previously owned, whilst still a group member, the asset disposed of. These provisions extend to interest on overdue tax. [*TCGA 1992, s 190*].

General. For coverage of:

- *ICTA 1988, ss 767A–767C*, which provide for unpaid corporation tax due from a company to be recovered from persons controlling the company, in certain circumstances where there has been a change of ownership; and
- *FA 2000, s 98, Sch 28*, effective for accounting periods ending on or after 1 April 2000, which provide for unpaid corporation tax due from a non-UK resident company to be recovered from other companies within the same group (defined by reference to 51% subsidiaries), from any member of a consortium (defined as for CT group relief purposes) owning the company, or from any member of the same group (defined as for CT group relief purposes) as a member of that consortium,

see Tolley's Corporation Tax under Payment of Tax.

27.9 COMPANY LEAVING GROUP AFTER ACQUIRING ASSET INTRA-GROUP — DEGROUPING CHARGE

Broadly, where a company ceasing to be a member of a group owns a capital asset which has been transferred to it by another group member (such status being determined at the time of transfer) **within the preceding six years**, that company is treated as if, immediately after its acquisition of the asset (subject to 27.12 below), it had sold, and immediately reacquired, the asset at its then market value. There will thus be a gain or loss by reference to the market value of the asset at that time and its 'no gain/no loss' acquisition consideration under 27.2 above. See below as to the time at which the gain or loss is deemed to accrue. For relieving provisions, see 27.10–27.13 below. The time limit for electing for 6 April 1965 value (normally two years from the end of the accounting period in which the disposal took place) is concessionally extended (HMRC Statement of Practice D21).

The provision applies to a company ('*the chargeable company*') leaving a group which acquired an asset as described above where it or an 'associated' company also leaving the group at the same time owns (otherwise as trading stock) the asset at that time, replacement property to which a gain on the disposal of the original asset has been carried forward under ROLLOVER RELIEF (55) or an asset the value of which is wholly or partly derived from the original asset.

Companies are '*associated*' if they would form a group by themselves.

These provisions do not apply if, before the chargeable company leaves the group (or leaves a second group — see below), it has already been deemed to have sold and reacquired the asset in question at the time mentioned above by virtue of its having since become an investment trust or a venture capital trust (see, respectively, 27.14 and 27.15 below).

The companies involved in the asset transfer do not both have to be members of the group at the time of transfer for this degrouping charge to apply. It is sufficient that the transferee company leaves the group of which the transferor company was a member at the time of transfer, though in practice a charge can only arise if the transfer was other than at market value and in particular if it was at no gain/no loss. (HMRC Capital Gains Manual CG 45411).

In relation to assets acquired by intra-group transfer on or after 1 April 2000, the degrouping charge can apply only if the asset is within the charge to UK corporation tax both before and after the transfer, the precise conditions being similar to those for intra-group transfers at 27.2 above. Where the transfer occurred before 1 April 2000 and the degrouping charge would otherwise arise on or after that date, transitional provisions in *FA 2000, Sch 29 para 47* ensure that there can be no such charge where the transferee company leaves the group whilst remaining in a wider world-wide group of which it became a member by virtue of the change in the residence requirement at 27.1 above. The fact that the company may not be an effective 51% subsidiary of the principal company of the world-wide group does not prevent it being a member of that group, *for so long as* it remains an effective 51% subsidiary of the company that, prior to the change in the residence requirement, was the principal company of the narrower group. See HMRC Capital Gains Manual CG 45406 for an example.

The gain or loss on the deemed sale is normally treated as accruing immediately after the beginning of the accounting period in which (or at the end of which, if that be the case) the company ceases to be a member of the group. This will apply in most cases but it is subject to the proviso that the time of accrual cannot be earlier than the time of transfer of the asset (see above). It is possible under these rules for the transferee company not to be a member of the group at the time of accrual.

Where, for group relief purposes, the accounting period of the claimant or surrendering company ends after 1 July 1997 and the overlapping period for the purposes of *ICTA 1988, s 403A* falls at least partly after that date, *ICTA 1988, ss 403A, 403B* (limits on group relief — see Tolley's Corporation Tax) have effect as if the actual circumstances were as they are treated above as having been. For earlier accounting periods, an apportionment under *ICTA 1988, s 409(2)* (profits and losses for group relief etc. when two or more companies join or leave a group) is to take the timing of the gain or loss on the deemed sale into account but not so as to require any reference in that provision to an accounting period to have effect for any of the purposes mentioned in *ICTA 1988, s 409(3)* (surrendering and claimant companies) as a reference to any accounting period other than a true accounting period.

The provision does not apply in relation to transfers of assets between associated companies which cease to be members of the group at the same time.

[*TCGA 1992, s 179(1)(1A)(2)(2C)(2D)(3)(4)(10); FA 1993, s 89; F(No 2)A 1997, Sch 7 para 8; FA 1998, s 133(2)(3), s 135(3)(5); FA 2000, Sch 29 para 4(2)(6), para 47; FA 2001, s 79; FA 2002, s 44(2)(5), Sch 8 para 2; FA 2003, Sch 27 para 2*].

However, where a company in a group transfers an asset intra-group and both transferor and recipient then leave that group to form a second group 'connected' with the first, with the recipient company then departing from the second group after 28 November 1994, the provision will apply (in relation to the departure from the second group) if the intra-group transfer, which is deemed for this purpose to have taken place in the second group, occurred within the preceding six years. The two groups are '*connected*' for this purpose if, broadly, at the time the chargeable company ceases to be a member of the second group, the second group is under the control of the first group or both groups are under the common control of a company which controls or has controlled the first group at any time since the chargeable company left the first group. The general definitions of *ICTA 1988, s 416(2)–(6)* (meaning of 'control') apply for this purpose (except for banking businesses). See Tolley's Corporation Tax under Close Companies. Where the recipient company's departure from the second group takes place after 16 March 1998, the definition of '*connected*' groups is widened so that this provision will apply where common control of the two groups is exercised by any person or persons (which thus includes natural persons as well as companies). [*TCGA 1992, s 179(2A)(2B)(9A); FA 1995, s 49; FA 1998, s 139; FA 2000, Sch 29 para 4(3)(4)(6)*].

'*Ceasing to be a member of a group*' does not apply to cases where a company ceases to be a member of a group in consequence of another member of the group ceasing to exist. For a company ceasing to be a member of a group before 15 November 1991, the phrase did not apply to cases where a company ceased to be a member of a group by being wound up or dissolved or in consequence of another member of the group being wound up or dissolved. [*TCGA 1992, s 179(1); F(No 2)A 1992, s 25*]. For events after 14 November 1991, HMRC takes the view that this 'liquidation let out' only applies to the case of a parent company ceasing to be a member of a group on the occasion of its only subsidiary ceasing to exist on dissolution (or all its subsidiaries ceasing to exist simultaneously on dissolution). (HMRC Capital Gains Manual CG 45441–45445). See also *Burman v Hedges & Butler Ltd Ch D 1978, 52 TC 501*. In relation to events at any time, HMRC has confirmed it does not apply the deemed sale and reacquisition where the company receiving the asset ceases to be a group member as a result of its only subsidiary leaving the group except where the parent company emigrates before 1 April 2000, thereby causing the group to break up (HMRC Capital Gains Manual CG 45450 and see *Dunlop International AG v Pardoe CA 1999, 72 TC 71*).

Where, as part of a process of merger to form an SE in circumstances in which *TCGA 1992, s 140E* applies (formation of SE by merger: assets left within UK tax charge — see 13.18 COMPANIES), a company which is a member of a group ceases to exist and as a consequence assets, or shares in one or more companies which were also members of the group, are transferred to the SE, the company which has ceased to exist and any company whose shares have been transferred to the SE are, for the purposes of these provisions, not treated as having left the group. The SE and the company which ceased to exist are treated as the same entity and, if the SE is itself a member of a group on its formation, any company which was a member of the first group and became a member of the SE's group as a result of the SE's formation is treated as if the two groups were the same. [*TCGA 1992, s 179(1B)(1C); F(No 2)A 2005, s 64(4)*].

If

(*a*) a company ceases to be a member of a group only through the principal company becoming a member of another group (e.g. it is not an 'effective 51% subsidiary' of the principal company of the other group as in 27.1 above), and

(*b*) under the provisions described above, it would be treated as selling an asset at any time,

the following provisions apply.

(1) The company in question is not treated as selling the asset at that time.

(2) If

   (i) within six years of that time the company in question ceases at any time ('*the relevant time*') to satisfy the following conditions: namely that it is a '75% subsidiary' (as defined in 27.1 above) of one or more members of the other group mentioned in (*a*) above and an 'effective 51% subsidiary' (as defined in 27.1 above) of one or more of those members; and

   (ii) at the relevant time the company in question or a company in the same group, owns (otherwise than as trading stock) the asset, or property to which a chargeable gain has been rolled over from the asset, or an asset the value of which is wholly or partly derived from the original asset,

   the company in question is treated as if, immediately after acquiring the asset (subject to 27.12 below), it had sold and reacquired it at its market value at the time of acquisition.

(3) Any gain or loss on the deemed sale is treated as arising at the relevant time.

[*TCGA 1992, s 179(5)–(8)*].

If under any of the foregoing provisions a deemed sale arises at any time, and if on an actual sale at market value at that time any loss or gain would, under the value shifting provisions (see 3.7–3.14 ANTI-AVOIDANCE), have been calculated as if the consideration were increased by an amount, the market value at the time of the deemed sale is treated as having been greater by that amount. [*TCGA 1992, s 179(9)*].

In relation to gains accruing before 1 April 2000, if any corporation tax assessed on a company in consequence of the above is still unpaid six months after the later of the date when the tax becomes due and payable by the company and the date when the assessment was made on the chargeable company, it may instead be assessed and charged (in the name of the chargeable company), within two years from the date determined above, on the principal company of the group on that date or immediately after the time the chargeable company ceased to be a member of the group, or on a company which owned the asset on that date or immediately after that time. A company paying tax and interest under such an assessment is given a right of recovery against the chargeable company. As regards gains accruing on or after 1 April 2000, see the general recovery provisions at 27.8 above. [*TCGA 1992, s 179(11)(12); FA 2000, Sch 29 para 4(5)(7)*].

Any adjustment of tax or recomputation of liability on a disposal may be made by assessment or otherwise as a result of any deemed disposal and reacquisition mentioned above. [*TCGA 1992, s 179(13)*].

Example

C Ltd had the following transactions.

1.3.88	Purchased a freehold property £20,000.
1.12.02	Sold the freehold to D Ltd (a wholly-owned subsidiary) for £40,000 (market value £100,000).
31.7.06	Sold its interest in D Ltd (at which time D Ltd continued to own the freehold property).

Both C Ltd and D Ltd prepare accounts to 30 April.

Relevant values of the RPI are: March 1988 104.1, December 2002 178.5.

(i) C Ltd's disposal of the property to D Ltd is to be treated as one on which, after taking account of the indexation allowance, neither gain nor loss arises (see 27.2 above and 34.3 INDEXATION).

Indexation factor 178.5 – 104.1/104.1 = 0.715

	£
Cost to C Ltd	20,000
Indexation allowance £20,000 × 0.715	14,300
Deemed cost to D Ltd	£34,300

(ii) Following the sale of C Ltd's shares in D Ltd on 31.7.06 (i.e. within six years after the transaction in (i) above), *D Ltd* will have a deemed disposal as follows.

Deemed disposal on 1.12.02

	£
Market value at 1.12.02	100,000
Cost (as above)	34,300
Chargeable gain subject to CT	£65,700
D Ltd's new base cost for future gains	£100,000

Although the deemed disposal occurs on 1 December 2002, i.e. immediately after D Ltd's acquisition, the gain is treated as accruing on 1 May 2006, i.e. the beginning of the accounting period in which D Ltd left the group, being later than the date of the deemed disposal. The gain thus forms part of D Ltd's profits for the year ended 30 April 2007.

27.10 **Transfer of degrouping charge to another company in the group.** Where, after 31 March 2002, a company (Company A) ceases to be a member of a group such that the provisions of *TCGA 1992, s 179* in 27.9 above apply, the company may jointly elect with another company (Company C) for the resultant gain or loss to be treated as accruing to Company C instead of Company A. Where the degrouping charge arises under *TCGA 1992, s 179(5)–(8)*, the election is available only where the 'relevant time' (see 27.9(2)(i) above) falls after 31 March 2002.

Except where the degrouping charge arises under *TCGA 1992, s 179(5)–(8)*, the two parties to the election must be members of the same group at the 'time of accrual'; the '*time of accrual*' is the time at which the gain or loss is treated as accruing and not, if earlier, the time at which the deemed sale and reacquisition in 27.9 above is treated as occurring. Where the charge arises under *TCGA 1992, s 179(5)–(8)*, Company C must be a member of the second group referred to at 27.9(*a*) above at the 'time of accrual'; the '*time of accrual*' is the latest time that Company A satisfies the conditions at 27.9(2)(i) above.

In either case, the following further conditions must all be met at the time of accrual.

- Company C must either be UK-resident or own assets that are chargeable assets in relation to it. For this purpose, an asset is a chargeable asset in relation to a company at a particular time if, on a disposal by that company at that time, any gain would be a chargeable gain and would be within the charge to corporation tax by virtue of *TCGA 1992, s 10B* (non-UK resident company trading in the UK through a permanent establishment — see 45.3 OVERSEAS MATTERS) or, before 16 March 2005, *TCGA 1992, s 10* (company trading in the UK through a branch or agency — see 45.3 OVERSEAS MATTERS).
- Company C cannot be an investment trust (within *ICTA 1988, s 842*), a venture capital trust (within *ICTA 1988, s 842AA*) or a dual resident investing company (within *ICTA 1988, s 404*).
- Neither Company A nor Company C can be a qualifying friendly society (as defined at 27.2(vib) above).

On the making of a joint election by Company A and Company C, the chargeable gain or allowable loss on the deemed sale under *TCGA 1992, s 179*, or such part of that gain or loss as is specified in the election, is treated as accruing not to Company A but to Company C. The election must be made by notice in writing to an HMRC officer within two years after the end of the accounting period of Company A in which the time of accrual fell. More than one election may be made, with more than one other company, within the time limit, each specifying part of the gain or loss (but the sum of the parts cannot exceed the whole).

If Company C is a non-UK resident company, the gain or loss is treated as accruing in respect of a chargeable asset held by it and thus remains within the charge to corporation tax. Any payment made by Company A to Company C, or vice versa, in connection with the election is not to be taken into account in computing profits or losses of either company or treated as a distribution or, for payments made before 16 March 2005, a charge on income, provided it does not exceed the chargeable gain or allowable loss thereby treated as accruing to Company C.

[*TCGA 1992, s 179A; FA 2002, s 42(1)(4); F(No 2)A 2005, Sch 4 paras 8, 10(3), Sch 11 Pt 2(7)*].

The above provisions can be applied in combination with those at 27.11 below.

27.11 **Rollover of degrouping charge into new business assets.** Where, after 31 March 2002, a company ceases to be a member of a group such that a gain arises under *TCGA*

1992, s 179 (see 27.9 above) on a deemed sale and reacquisition of an asset, and the asset is a qualifying asset for rollover relief purposes, the company may claim ROLLOVER RELIEF (55) if it acquires a new qualifying asset. The normal rollover relief rules apply in the modified form described below. Where the degrouping charge arises under *TCGA 1992, s 179(5)–(8)*, rollover relief is available only where the 'relevant time' (see 27.9(2)(i) above) falls after 31 March 2002. [*TCGA 1992, s 179B(1)(2); FA 2002, s 43(1)(2)(4)*].

Interaction with TCGA 1992, s 179A. These provisions can be applied in combination with those at 27.10 above. Thus, where a joint election has been made under *TCGA 1992, s 179A* by Company A and Company C at 27.10 above to allocate the whole of the degrouping charge to Company C, and that company acquires a new qualifying asset and takes it into use for the purpose of its trade, a rollover relief claim can by made by Company C (but cannot then be made by Company A). In these circumstances, references below to Company A should be read as references to Company C where appropriate. Where the *section 179A* election covers only part of the gain, rollover relief is potentially available to each company, in relation to its proportion of the gain, as if the deemed sale under *TCGA 1992, s 179* had been of two separate assets. [*TCGA 1992, s 179B(3)–(6); FA 2002, s 43(1)*].

The relief. Relief under *TCGA 1992, s 152* (see 55.1 ROLLOVER RELIEF) is available to the company leaving the group (Company A), where all of the following conditions are satisfied.

- Company A is deemed under 27.9 above to have sold and immediately reacquired an asset ('*the old asset*'), and the company from which the asset was transferred (Company B) was carrying on a trade at the time of transfer.
- Throughout its ownership by Company B, the asset was used, and used only, for the purposes of that trade.
- A gain (as opposed to a loss) accrues to Company A on the deemed sale.
- An amount equivalent to the deemed sale proceeds is applied by Company A in acquiring other assets or an interest in other assets ('*the new assets*') within the time limit below (but see below as regards partial relief).
- On acquisition, the new assets are taken into use, and used only, for the purposes of a trade carried on by Company A.
- Both the old and new assets are within the classes of assets listed in *TCGA 1992, s 155* (see under Qualifying assets below).

On a claim by Company A to that effect, the deemed sale proceeds (if otherwise of a greater amount) are reduced by the amount necessary to secure that neither a gain nor a loss accrues on the deemed sale. The consideration given by Company A for the new assets is treated as reduced by the same amount. This does not affect the treatment for the purposes of *TCGA 1992* of the other party to the transaction involving the new assets. There is no reduction in the amount for which Company A is deemed to have reacquired the old asset.

The acquisition of the new assets must take place **within one year before, or three years after**, the 'time of accrual' (though as in 55.1 ROLLOVER RELIEF, HMRC have discretion to extend the specified period in either direction). It is sufficient if an unconditional contract for acquisition is entered into within the specified period, but adjustments can be made to the tax position, without time limit, if the contract is not completed.

The '*time of accrual*' is the time at which the gain on the deemed sale is treated as accruing under 27.9 above (and not, if earlier, the time at which the deemed sale is treated as taking place). Where the degrouping charge arises under *TCGA 1992, s 179(5)–(8)*, the time of accrual is the latest time that Company A satisfies the conditions at 27.9(2)(i) above.

The other provisions of *TCGA 1992, s 152* at 55.1 ROLLOVER RELIEF are suitably adapted; see also the case law and practice there. This applies equally to the provisions of *section 152(6)(7)(9)(11)* (partial non-trade use) at 55.6 ROLLOVER RELIEF; in particular, references there to the 'period of ownership', insofar as they relate to the old asset, are to be taken as references to the period during which that asset was owned by Company B.

[*TCGA 1992, ss 152, 179B, Sch 7AB paras 1, 2; FA 2002, s 43, Sch 7*].

Partial relief. Where the above conditions are satisfied except that the amount applied by Company A in acquiring the new assets is less than the deemed sale proceeds, the provisions of *TCGA 1992, s 153* (see 55.6 ROLLOVER RELIEF) apply with similar modifications as above. The part of the deemed proceeds not so applied must be less than the amount of the gain on the deemed sale; the relief then operates by reducing the gain *to* the amount of the said part and treating the consideration given for the new assets as reduced *by* the same amount. [*TCGA 1992, ss 153, 179B, Sch 7AB paras 1, 3*].

Claims for relief. By virtue of *FA 1998, Sch 18 para 55* (previously *TMA 1970, s 43*) (see 12.5 CLAIMS), the time allowed for making a claim under *TCGA 1992, s 152* or *s 153* above is six years after the *later* of:

(*a*) the end of the accounting period of Company A in which falls the time of accrual (as defined above); and

(*b*) the end of the accounting period of Company A in which the new assets are acquired.

It is considered that (*a*) above applies by reference to an accounting period of Company A even if it is Company C (see above) that claims the relief.

The procedure in *TCGA 1992, s 153A* for making *provisional claims* (see 55.2 ROLLOVER RELIEF) applies (with appropriate modifications). The 'relevant day' for the purpose of such claims is the fourth anniversary of the last day of the accounting period of Company A (not of Company C, see above, even if it is that company that provisionally claims the relief), in which falls the time of accrual (as defined above). [*TCGA 1992, ss 153, 179B, Sch 7AB paras 1, 4*].

Qualifying assets. The classes of assets qualifying for the relief are as listed in 55.3 ROLLOVER RELIEF. Note that certain of the classes listed are of no relevance to companies where the post-31 March 2002 intangible assets regime has effect. As regards class 1(*a*) (land, buildings etc.), the trade there referred to is, in relation to the old asset, the trade carried on by Company B and, in relation to the new asset, the trade carried on by Company A. [*TCGA 1992, ss 155, 179B, Sch 7AB paras 1, 5*].

Qualifying activities. The provisions of *TCGA 1992, s 158* (see 55.4 ROLLOVER RELIEF) have effect to the extent that these are relevant to companies.

New assets acquired by another group member. The provisions of *TCGA 1992, s 175* (see 55.5 ROLLOVER RELIEF) are adapted to make the above relief available where Company A is a member of a group at the time of accrual (as defined above), the acquisition of the new assets is made by another member of that group (judged at the time of acquisition) and the claim is made by both companies. The conditions to be met are that:

- *either* Company A is UK-resident at the time of accrual *or* the old asset (or, where relevant, the replacement property referred to in 27.9 above) is a chargeable asset in relation to that company immediately before that time; *and*

- *either* the acquiring company is UK-resident at the time of acquisition *or* the new assets are chargeable assets in relation to that company immediately after that time.

The relief is also available where

(i) Company B was not carrying on a trade when it transferred the old asset to Company A but was a member of a group at that time; and

(ii) immediately before that time, the old asset was used, and used only, for the purposes of the trade treated by *TCGA 1992, s 179(1)* as a single trade carried on by all the trading members of the group.

The relief can similarly be claimed where the acquiring company is a non-trading company but the new assets are taken into use, and used only, for the purposes mentioned in (ii) above. In no case is relief available where the acquisition of new assets results from a no gain/no loss disposal, e.g. where the assets are acquired from another group member. [*TCGA 1992, ss 175, 179B, Sch 7AB paras 1, 7; FA 2003, Sch 27 para 2*].

Wasting assets. The depreciating asset provisions of *TCGA 1992, s 154* (see 55.7 ROLLOVER RELIEF) apply equally in relation to the relief described above.

Overseas matters. Under a modified version of *TCGA 1992, s 159* (see 45.3 OVERSEAS MATTERS under Rollover relief), the above rollover relief is not available if the old asset (or, where relevant, the replacement property referred to in 27.9 above) is a chargeable asset in relation to Company A at the time of accrual (as defined above) unless the new assets are chargeable assets in relation to Company A immediately after they are acquired. This does not, however, apply where Company A acquires the new assets after the time of accrual and is UK-resident immediately after acquiring them (unless it is then dual resident and the assets are prescribed assets, as defined at 45.3 OVERSEAS MATTERS). The exclusion of rollover relief at 45.12(*b*) OVERSEAS MATTERS (where a company becomes non-UK resident between the time of accrual and the acquisition of the new assets) also applies in suitably adapted form. [*TCGA 1992, ss 159, 179B, 185, Sch 7AB paras 1, 6, 8; FA 2003, Sch 27 para 2*].

Intangible assets. The following applies where the time at which the gain on the deemed sale by Company A is treated as accruing under 27.9 above is after 31 March 2002 and the asset in question is an intangible fixed asset but is excluded from the corporation tax intangible assets regime by virtue of its commencement rules (see 14.13 COMPANIES—CORPORATE FINANCE AND INTANGIBLES). The degrouping charge may qualify for relief under the intangible asset rollover relief provisions of *FA 2002, Sch 29 Pt 7*, which are modified for this purpose by *FA 2002, Sch 29 para 131*. Where relief is claimed in such a case, then in calculating the gain arising (for the purposes of corporation tax on chargeable gains), the consideration for the deemed disposal is treated as reduced by the 'amount available for relief' (as defined in *FA 2002, Sch 29 para 41*). [*FA 2002, s 84(1), Sch 29 para 131*].

Note that intangible asset rollover relief is an entirely separate relief from capital gains rollover relief; for details of the former, see Tolley's Corporation Tax under Intangible Assets. See 55.1 ROLLOVER RELIEF for the interaction between capital gains rollover relief and the intangible assets regime, and for transitional rules.

27.12 **Degrouping charge — exemption for substantial shareholdings.** Where a company ceases to be a member of a group and is deemed under *TCGA 1992, s 179* to have sold and immediately reacquired at market value an asset transferred to it by another group member, then normally the time of the deemed sale is immediately after the transfer (see 27.9 above). However, where

- a company ceases to be a member of a group at any time (the '*time of degrouping*') after 31 March 2002, and
- a degrouping charge (as in 27.9 above) arises in relation to an asset, and
- a gain on a disposal of that asset (by the company then owning it) immediately before the time of degrouping would have been exempt under the provisions at 60 SUBSTANTIAL SHAREHOLDINGS OF COMPANIES,

the deemed sale and reacquisition is instead treated as taking place immediately before the time of degrouping.

A comparable rule applies where the degrouping charge arises under *TCGA 1992, s 179(5)–(8)* and the 'relevant time' (see 27.9(2)(i) above) falls after 31 March 2002. In this case, the rule applies by reference to the 'relevant time' rather than the 'time of degrouping'.

[*TCGA 1992, Sch 7AC para 38; FA 2002, s 44(2)(4), Sch 8 para 1*].

27.13 **Exemption from degrouping charge.** *TCGA 1992, s 179* in 27.9 above does not apply, subject to conditions, where, as part of a 'merger', a company (Company A) ceases to be a member of a group ('the A group'), and it is shown that the merger was carried out for bona fide reasons and that the avoidance of a liability to tax was not the main or one of the main purposes of the merger.

'*Merger*', in broad terms, means an arrangement whereby one or more companies ('the acquiring compan(y)(ies)') not in the A group acquire interests in the business previously carried on by Company A, and one or more members of the A group acquire interests in the business or businesses previously carried on either by the acquiring company or companies or by a company at least 90% of the ordinary share capital of which is owned by two or more of the acquiring companies. For this purpose a group member is treated as carrying on as one business the activities of that group. 25% of the value of the interests acquired must take the form of ordinary share capital, whilst the remainder of the interests acquired by the A group must consist of share capital or debentures or both. The value of the interests acquired must be substantially the same, and the consideration for the interests acquired by the acquiring companies must substantially consist of the interests acquired by the A group.

For these purposes, references to a company include a non-UK resident company, and this applied even before the change in the residence requirement in 27.1 above.

[*TCGA 1992, s 181; FA 2000, Sch 29 para 28*].

See HMRC Capital Gains Manual CG 45605 for examples on the operation of these provisions. See also 13.16 COMPANIES regarding demergers.

27.14 COMPANY BECOMING AN INVESTMENT TRUST AFTER ACQUIRING ASSET INTRA-GROUP

Similar treatment as in 27.9 above (company leaving group) applies where a company (the '*acquiring company*') becomes an investment trust (within *ICTA 1988, s 842* — see 65.3 UNIT TRUSTS ETC.) for an accounting period beginning after 16 March 1998 and not more than six years after the company acquired an asset from another company in its group, the disposal by which it acquired the asset (the corresponding disposal) having been treated by virtue of *TCGA 1992, s 171* (intra-group transfers — see 27.2 above) as a no gain/no loss disposal. The provisions apply where at the beginning of the said accounting period, the acquiring company owns, otherwise than as trading stock, either the asset itself or replacement property, i.e. property into which a chargeable gain on disposal of the asset has been rolled over as in 55 ROLLOVER RELIEF, whether directly (i.e. as a result of a single rollover relief claim) or indirectly (where two or more such claims have been made). For the purposes of these provisions, an asset acquired is deemed to be the same as an asset owned subsequently if the value of the latter asset is derived, wholly or partly, from the original asset (in particular where the original was a leasehold and the lessee has acquired the freehold reversion). The provisions do not apply if the acquiring company was an investment trust at the time of the corresponding disposal (in which case the no gain/no loss treatment would not have applied — see 27.2(vi) above) nor if it has been an investment trust for any intervening accounting period.

The acquiring company is treated as if, immediately after the corresponding disposal, it had sold and immediately reacquired the asset at its market value at that time. The resulting chargeable gain or allowable loss is treated as accruing immediately before the end of the acquiring company's accounting period which immediately preceded that in which it became an investment trust. Notwithstanding normal time limits, any consequential corporation tax assessment may be made at any time within six years after the end of the accounting period in which the company became an investment trust. These provisions are disapplied if, prior to the company becoming an investment trust, the above treatment has already applied to the asset by virtue either of 27.9 above or 27.15 below (company becoming a venture capital trust).

[*TCGA 1992, s 101A; FA 1998, s 133*(*1*)(*3*)].

27.15 COMPANY BECOMING A VENTURE CAPITAL TRUST AFTER ACQUIRING ASSET INTRA-GROUP

The same treatment as in 27.14 above (company becoming an investment trust) applies where the acquiring company becomes a venture capital trust (VCT) (within *ICTA 1988, s 842AA* — see 66 VENTURE CAPITAL TRUSTS) after 16 March 1998 and not more than six years after it acquired the asset intra-group by means of a no gain/no loss disposal under *TCGA 1992, s 171* (see 27.2 above). For this purpose, a company becomes a VCT at the time of the coming into effect of HMRC's approval for the purposes of *section 842AA* (the time of approval). The provisions apply where, at the time of approval, the acquiring company owns, otherwise than as trading stock, either the asset itself (with the same rules as in 27.14 above as to derivation of assets) or replacement property (as in 27.14 above). The provisions do not apply if the acquiring company was a VCT at the time of the intra-group disposal (in which case the no gain/no loss treatment would have applied only if that disposal occurred before 17 March 1998— see 27.2(via) above) and do not apply if it has been a VCT at any time in the intervening period. Nor do they apply if, prior to the company becoming a VCT, the said treatment has already applied to the asset by virtue either of 27.14 above or 27.9 above (company leaving group).

The chargeable gain or allowable loss resulting from the deemed disposal at market value immediately after the intra-group transfer is treated as accruing to the acquiring company immediately before the time of approval. Notwithstanding normal time limits, any consequential corporation tax assessment may, in a case in which HMRC's approval has effect as from the beginning of an accounting period, be made at any time within six years after the end of that accounting period.

[*TCGA 1992, s 101C; FA 1998, s 135*(*2*)(*5*)].

27.16 VALUE SHIFTING TO GIVE TAX-FREE BENEFIT, DEPRECIATORY TRANSACTIONS AND DIVIDEND STRIPPING

See 3.7–3.14 ANTI-AVOIDANCE for value shifting to give a tax-free benefit where groups may be involved. See 3.21 ANTI-AVOIDANCE for depreciatory transactions within a group. See 3.22 ANTI-AVOIDANCE for dividend stripping.

27.17 COMPANIES BUYING GAINS OR LOSSES

Over the years, governments have introduced three sets of anti-avoidance provisions designed to prevent groups of companies buying and selling companies in order to make use of capital losses suffered by another company or group.

The first set of provisions, introduced in 1993 and described at 27.20–27.30 below, applies to prevent 'loss buying' where a group of companies with unrealised gains would acquire a company with realised or unrealised losses. The assets in question would then be transferred to the new group company at no gain/no loss as in 27.2 above, and the gain would then be realised by that company, thus enabling the losses to be utilised against the gain. The provisions operate by restricting the deduction of losses accruing to a company before the time it becomes a member of a group or which accrue on assets held by it at such a time.

These provisions were supplemented in 1998 by provisions, described at 27.31 onwards below, countering 'gain buying', where a group of companies with unrealised capital losses would acquire a company with a realised gain. The assets in question would then be transferred to the new group company, and the losses then realised by that company in the same accounting period as it realised the gain, thus enabling the losses to be utilised against the gain. Under the 1998 provisions the losses that can be set against a gain realised before a company joins a group are restricted to those that arose before it joined the group and those that arise after it joins the group on assets which that company held at the time of its joining the group.

The final set of provisions was introduced in *FA 2006* as part of a package of anti-avoidance provisions relating to capital losses of companies (see 13.4 COMPANIES). The provisions restrict the use of losses in both loss buying and gain buying situations where there is a change of ownership of a company as a result of arrangements with a tax avoidance purpose and are described at 27.18, 27.19 below. The provisions apply in priority to the original loss buying provisions and replace the original gain buying provisions, which are repealed (with effect as indicated at 27.31 below). The provisions are wide in scope and can apply in certain cases where there is no group of companies involved (see 27.18(*c*) below).The stated intention of the provisions is to ensure that relief for a company's capital losses should only be available against its own capital gains or those of companies that were under the same economic ownership both when the capital loss was realised and when the loss is used to reduce other gains. (Treasury Explanatory Notes to the Finance Bill 2006).

27.18 RESTRICTION ON BUYING GAINS AND LOSSES: TAX AVOIDANCE SCHEMES

Subject to the commencement provisions below, the loss buying and gain buying provisions described below apply where

(A) there is a 'qualifying change of ownership' of a company (the '*relevant company*'), and

(B) the change occurs directly or indirectly in consequence of, or otherwise in connection with, any 'arrangements' the main purpose, or one of the main purposes, of which is to secure a 'tax advantage'.

For this purpose, there is a '*qualifying change of ownership*' of a company if any of the following occur.

(*a*) The company joins a group of companies. Whether a company is a member of a group is determined as in 27.1 above except that nothing in *TCGA 1992, s 170*(*10*) or (*10A*) is treated as preventing all the companies of one group from being regarded as joining another group when the principal company of the first group becomes a member of the other group at any time unless:

(i) the same persons own the 'shares' of the principal company of the first group immediately before that time and the shares of the principal company of the other group immediately after that time;

(ii) the principal company of the other group was not the principal company of any group immediately before that time; and

(iii) immediately after that time the principal company of the other group had assets consisting entirely (or almost entirely) of shares of the principal company of the first group.

References above to '*shares*' of a company are to the shares comprised in the company's issued share capital.

(*b*) The company ceases to be a member of a group.

(*c*) The company becomes subject to different control, i.e. one or more of the following occur:

(I) a person who did not previously have control (within *ICTA 1988, s 416*) of the company comes to have control (whether alone or together with one or more others);

(II) a person who previously had control of the company alone comes to have control of the company together with one or more others; or

(III) a person ceases to have control of the company (whether the person had control alone or together with one or more others).

A company is not, however, treated as becoming subject to different control where it joins a group of companies in circumstances in which (*a*)(i)–(iii) above apply or where, although there is a change in the direct ownership of the company, it continues to be a 75% subsidiary of the same company.

'*Arrangements*' include any agreement, understanding, scheme, transaction or series of transactions, whether or not legally enforceable. '*Tax advantage*' means relief or increased relief from, or repayment or increased repayment of, corporation tax or the avoidance or reduction of a charge or assessment to corporation tax or the avoidance of a possible assessment to corporation tax.

[*TCGA 1992, ss 184A(1)(4), 184B(1)(4), 184C, 184D, 288(1); FA 2006, s 70(2)*].

For HMRC's views on the application of the terms 'arrangements', 'tax advantage' and 'main purpose', see 13.4 COMPANIES and HMRC Guidance 'Avoidance through the creation and use of capital losses by companies', 22 March 2006, available on their website (www.hmrc.gov.uk).

Loss buying. The loss buying provisions apply where conditions (A) and (B) above are met and the tax advantage under the arrangements involves the deduction from any chargeable gains of a loss (a '*qualifying loss*') accruing to the relevant company on a disposal of a 'pre-change asset' (see 27.19 below). In these circumstances, the qualifying loss is not deductible from a company's chargeable gains except where the gains arise on the disposal of a pre-change asset. It is immaterial whether the loss accrues before, after or at the time of the qualifying change of ownership, whether the loss accrues at a time when there are no gains from which it could be deducted, whether the tax advantage also involves something other than the deduction of a qualifying loss or whether the advantage would be secured for the company to which the loss accrues or any other company. [*TCGA 1992, s 184A(1)(2)(5); FA 2006, s 70(2)*].

Gain buying. The gain buying provisions apply where conditions (A) and (B) above are met and the tax advantage under the arrangements involves the deduction of a loss from a gain (a '*qualifying gain*') accruing to the relevant company or any other company on a disposal of a pre-change asset. In these circumstances, only a loss arising on a disposal of a pre-change asset can be deducted from a qualifying gain. It is immaterial whether the gain accrues before, after or at the time of the qualifying change of ownership, whether the gain accrues at a time when there are no losses which could be deducted from it, whether the tax advantage also involves something other than the deduction of a loss from a qualifying gain or whether the advantage would be secured for the company to which the gain accrues or any other company. [*TCGA 1992, s 184B(1)(2)(5); FA 2006, s 70(2)*].

For HMRC examples of the operation of the provisions see HMRC Guidance 'Avoidance through the creation and use of capital losses by companies', 22 March 2006, available on their website (www.hmrc.gov.uk).

Commencement. The above provisions apply for the purpose of determining the chargeable gains to be included in a company's total profits for accounting periods ending on or after 5 December 2005. The provisions do not, however, apply to the deduction of a loss from gains accruing on disposals before that date unless the loss accrues on a disposal on or after that date.

The provisions can apply whether the qualifying change of ownership occurs before, on, or after 5 December 2005. Where, however, the change does occur before that date and

- the change occurs because the relevant company ceases to be a member of a group (whether or not it also occurs for any other reason);
- the principal company of the group continues to have control of the relevant company;
- the principal company does not, at or after the time of the change, join another group other than in circumstances in which (*a*)(i)–(iii) above apply; and
- a qualifying loss or qualifying gain accrues to the relevant company or any other company on a pre-5 December 2005 disposal,

the provisions apply to that loss or gain as if any asset held before the time of the change of ownership by any company which was a member of the relevant company's group immediately before that time were a pre-change asset.

[*FA 2006, s 70(6)–(11)*].

27.19 **Pre-change assets.** For the purposes of the provisions at 27.18 above, a '*pre-change asset*' is an asset held by the relevant company before the qualifying change of ownership occurs.

An asset ceases to be a pre-change asset on disposal by a company other than the relevant company if, after the qualifying change of ownership, it has been disposed of otherwise than by an intra-group no gain/no loss transfer within 27.2 above. If the company making the latter disposal retains an interest in or over the asset, that interest continues to be a pre-change asset.

If the relevant company or any other company holds an asset at or after the time of the qualifying change of ownership the value of which derives in whole or in part from a pre-change asset, the new asset is also treated as a pre-change asset provided that the company concerned did not acquire the asset as a result of a transfer other than an intra-group no gain/no loss transfer. For this purpose, the cases in which the value of an asset is derived from another asset include cases where assets have been merged or divided or have changed their nature and cases where rights or interests in or over assets have been created or extinguished.

Where a pre-change asset is the 'old asset' for the purposes of *TCGA 1992, s 116*, (reorganisation of share capital involving QUALIFYING CORPORATE BONDS (50.3)) the 'new asset' under that section is also a pre-change asset. Where a pre-change asset is the 'original shares' for the purposes of *TCGA 1992, ss 127–131* (reorganisation of share capital — see 58.1 SHARES AND SECURITIES), the 'new holding' under those provisions is also a pre-change asset.

Where one of the deferral provisions listed below applies to defer a gain on the disposal of a pre-change asset, so much of any gain or loss accruing on a subsequent occasion as accrues in consequence of the application of the deferral provision is treated as a gain or loss on the disposal of a pre-change asset. The provisions are:

- *TCGA 1992, s 139* (reconstruction involving transfer of business — see 13.10 COMPANIES);
- *TCGA 1992, s 140* (transfer of assets to non-resident company — see 45.9 OVERSEAS MATTERS);
- *TCGA 1992, s 140A* (transfer of UK trade between companies in different EC member states — see 45.10 OVERSEAS MATTERS);
- *TCGA 1992, s 140E* (formation of SE by merger leaving assets within UK tax charge — see 13.18 COMPANIES);
- *TCGA 1992, ss 152, 153* (ROLLOVER RELIEF—REPLACEMENT OF BUSINESS ASSETS (55)); and

- *TCGA 1992, s 187* (postponement of charge on deemed disposal on company ceasing to be UK resident — see 45.12 OVERSEAS MATTERS).

If a pre-change asset is transferred by the relevant company to another company directly or indirectly in consequence of, or in connection with the arrangements in 27.18(A), and any of *TCGA 1992, ss 139, 140A* or *140E* apply to the transfer, the asset is a pre-change asset in the hands of the transferee company. The above provisions for determining when an asset ceases to be a pre-change asset then apply as if the transferee company were the relevant company.

Pooled assets. Special identification rules apply where a pre-change asset (whether held by the relevant company or, as a consequence of an intra-group no gain/no loss transfer, by another company) consists of a 'section 104 holding' or '1982 holding' (see 59.2 SHARES AND SECURITIES — IDENTIFICATION RULES) of shares, securities or other assets dealt in without identifying the particular asset disposed of or acquired. Such a holding (a '*pre-change pooled asset*') cannot be added to as a result of any disposal or acquisition taking place after the qualifying change of ownership. Any shares etc. that would otherwise be added to the pre-change pooled asset instead form or are added to a separate section 104 holding (the '*other pooled asset*').

Shares etc. of the same class as those comprised in the other pooled asset which are disposed of at or after the time of the qualifying change of ownership are identified

- first with shares etc. forming part of the other pooled asset;
- next with shares etc. forming part of the pre-change pooled asset; and
- finally, in accordance with the normal identification rules described at 59.2 SHARES AND SECURITIES — IDENTIFICATION RULES).

These identification rules apply even if some or all of the assets disposed of are separately identified by the disposal or by a transfer or delivery giving effect to it.

Shares etc. disposed of by a company in one capacity are not identified with shares etc. which are held, or which can only be disposed of, in some other capacity. Shares or securities of a company are not treated as being of the same class unless they are so treated by the practice of a recognised stock exchange (see 58.23 SHARES AND SECURITIES) or would be if dealt with on such an exchange.

[*TCGA 1992, ss 184A(3), 184B(3), 184E, 184F; FA 2006, s 70(2)*].

27.20 RESTRICTION ON SET-OFF OF PRE-ENTRY LOSSES WHERE A COMPANY JOINS A GROUP

Where the loss buying provisions at 27.18 above do not apply, *TCGA 1992, Sch 7A* restricts the deduction of allowable losses ('pre-entry losses') which accrue to a company before the time it becomes a member of a group of companies (the '*relevant group*') or which accrue on assets held by it at such a time. The restriction is described in detail at 27.21–27.30 below. For HMRC comment on this legislation, see HMRC Capital Gains Manual CG 47500–47989.

The restriction applies for the calculation of the amount to be included in respect of chargeable gains in a company's total profits for any accounting period ending after 15 March 1993. However, the restriction applies only in relation to the deduction from chargeable gains accruing after 16 March 1993 of amounts in respect of, or of amounts carried forward in respect of:

(*a*) pre-entry losses accruing before it became a member of a UK CGT group to a company whose membership of that group began or begins after 31 March 1987; and (*b*) losses accruing on the disposal of any assets so far as it is by reference to such a company that the assets fall to be treated as being or having been 'pre-entry assets' or assets incorporating a part referable to pre-entry assets.

The restriction does not apply where the loss buying provisions at 27.18 above apply.

[*TCGA 1992, s 177A, Sch 7A para 1*(*1*); *FA 1993, s 88, Sch 8; FA 2006, s 70*(*3*)].

The restriction is widely drawn, and whilst its stated principal intention is to prevent the fiscal effectiveness of an acquisition of a 'capital loss' company (i.e. a company that has a *realised* allowable loss as its only commercial feature), it may also impinge on an acquisition of a company solely for commercial reasons where it becomes a member of a group whilst holding an asset which is later disposed of (whether by the company or another group member to whom the asset has been transferred) outside the group at a loss. Further restrictions were imposed by *FA 1994, s 94* in relation to the deduction of a loss from a chargeable gain where either the gain or the loss accrues after 10 March 1994. After 20 March 2000, the change in the residence requirement (see 27.1 above) as regards groups of companies is applied to these provisions.

For a worked example on pre-entry losses, see Tolley's Corporation Tax under Capital Gains.

27.21 **Definitions.** A '*pre-entry loss*', in relation to a company, means any allowable loss that accrued to it at a time before it became a member of the relevant group or the 'pre-entry proportion' (see 27.22–27.25 below) of any allowable loss accruing to it on the disposal of any 'pre-entry asset'. [*TCGA 1992, Sch 7A para 1*(*2*)].

A '*pre-entry asset*', in relation to any disposal, means any asset that was held, at the time immediately before the 'relevant event' occurred in relation to it, by any company (whether or not the one which makes the disposal) which is or has at any time been a member of the relevant group.

The '*relevant event*' occurs in relation to a company when it becomes a member of the relevant group provided that either the company is UK-resident at that time or the asset is then a 'chargeable asset' in relation to it. If the company is an SE (see 13.18 COMPANIES) resident in the UK and the asset was transferred to the SE as part of the process of its formation on or after 1 April 2005 by the merger by acquisition of two or more companies in accordance with *Council Regulation* (*EC*) *No 2157/2001, Arts 2*(*1*) and *17*(*2*), the relevant event occurs when the asset becomes a chargeable asset in relation to the SE or, if at the time of the formation of the SE the asset was a chargeable asset in relation to a company which ceased to exist as part of the process of the formation of the SE, when the asset became a chargeable asset in relation to that company. In any other case, a relevant event subsequently occurs when the company becomes UK-resident or the asset becomes a chargeable asset in relation to it (whichever is the earlier).

Originally, the '*relevant event*' occurred in relation to a company only when it became a member of the relevant group. The amendment to the definition was a consequence of the change in the residence requirement for groups of companies (see 27.1 above) and has effect in computing chargeable gains for accounting periods ending after 20 March 2000, but the question of whether a company is a member of a group at any time on or before that date is to be determined by reference to the residence requirement before *FA 2000*. If a company becomes a member of a group on 21 March 2000 purely as a result of the change in the residence requirement, *Sch 7A* is not thereby brought into effect.

For these purposes, an asset is a '*chargeable asset*' in relation to a company at a particular time if, on a disposal by that company at that time, any gain would be a chargeable gain and would be within the charge to corporation tax by virtue of *TCGA 1992, s 10* or *s 10B* (non-UK resident company trading in the UK through a permanent establishment (previously a branch or agency) — see 45.3 OVERSEAS MATTERS) or, if the company is an SE formed on or after 1 April 2005, by virtue of the asset having been transferred to the SE on its formation.

[*TCGA 1992, Sch 7A para 1(3)(3A); FA 2000, Sch 29 para 7(2)(3)(6)–(9); FA 2003, Sch 27 para 2; F(No 2)A 2005, s 65(2)(3)(6)*].

Subject to 27.23 below, an asset is not, however, a pre-entry asset if the company which held the asset at the time the relevant event occurred in relation to it is not the company which makes the disposal and since that time the asset has been disposed of otherwise than on the no gain/no loss basis of *TCGA 1992, s 171* (general provisions for transfers within a group; see 27.2 above) except where the company making the disposal retains an interest in or over the asset (when the interest is treated as a pre-entry asset). [*TCGA 1992, Sch 7A para 1(4); FA 2000, Sch 29 para 7(4)(6)–(8)*].

Subject to 27.23 below, an asset ('*the second asset*') which derives wholly or partly its value from another asset ('*the first asset*') acquired or held by a company at any time, is treated as the same asset if the second asset is held subsequently by the same company, or by any company which is or has been a member of the same group of companies as that company (e.g. a freehold derived from a leasehold where the lessee acquires the reversion). Where this treatment applies, whether under this provision or not (*TCGA 1992, s 43* is similar; see 15.7 COMPUTATION OF GAINS AND LOSSES), the second asset is treated as a pre-entry asset in relation to a company if the first asset would have been. [*TCGA 1992, Sch 7A para 1(8)*].

In relation to a pre-entry asset, references to '*the relevant time*' are references to the time when the relevant event occurred in relation to the company by reference to which that asset is a pre-entry asset. Where a relevant event has occurred in relation to a company more than once, an asset is a pre-entry asset in relation to that company if it would be a pre-entry asset in relation to that company in respect of any of those occasions, but in these circumstances any reference to the time when a relevant event occurred in relation to the company is a reference to the last such occasion. [*TCGA 1992, Sch 7A para 1(5); FA 2000, Sch 29 para 7(5)–(8)*].

Subject to so much of *Sch 7A para 9(6)* (see 27.29 below) as requires groups of companies to be treated as separate groups for the purposes of *Sch 7A para 9*, if

(*a*) the principal company of a group of companies ('*the first group*') has at any time become a member of another group ('*the second group*') so that the two groups are treated as the same under *TCGA 1992, s 170(10)* or *(10A)* (see 27.1 above), and

(*b*) the second group, together in pursuance of *TCGA 1992, s 170(10)* or *(10A)* with the first group, is the relevant group,

then, except where the circumstances are as listed below, the members of the first group are treated for the purposes of *Sch 7A* as having become members of the relevant group at that time, and not by virtue of *TCGA 1992, s 170(10)* or *(10A)* at the times when they became members of the first group. The circumstances are where:

(1) the persons who immediately before the time when the principal company of the first group became a member of the second group owned the shares comprised in the issued share capital of the principal company of the first group are the same as the persons who, immediately after that time, owned the shares comprised in the issued share capital of the principal company of the relevant group; and

(2) the company which is the principal company of the relevant group immediately after that time

   (i) was not the principal company of any group immediately before that time; and

   (ii) immediately after that time had assets consisting entirely, or almost entirely, of shares comprised in the issued share capital of the principal company of the first group.

[*TCGA 1992, Sch 7A para 1(6)(7); F(No 2)A 2005, s 65(4)*].

Where an allowable loss accrues to a company under *TCGA 1992, s 116(10)(b)* (gain or loss on shares exchanged on reorganisation, conversion or reconstruction for qualifying corporate bonds to crystallise when bonds sold; see 50.3 QUALIFYING CORPORATE BONDS and 27.27 below), that loss is deemed to accrue at the time of the reorganisation etc. for the purposes of deciding whether a loss accrues before a company becomes a member of the relevant group. [*TCGA 1992, Sch 7A para 1(9)*]. Likewise, the annual deemed disposals of unit trust etc. holdings of a life assurance company's long-term insurance fund under *TCGA 1992, s 212* (see Tolley's Corporation Tax under Life Insurance Companies) are deemed to occur for this purpose without regard to the 'spreading' provisions of *TCGA 1992, s 213*. [*TCGA 1992, Sch 7A para 1(10)*].

27.22 **Pre-entry proportion of losses on pre-entry assets.** Subject to 27.23–27.25 below, the '*pre-entry proportion*' of an allowable loss accruing on the disposal of a pre-entry asset is the allowable loss that would accrue on that disposal if that loss were the sum of the amounts determined, for every item of relevant allowable expenditure (within *TCGA 1992, s 38(1)(a)* or *(b)*; see 15.4 COMPUTATION OF GAINS AND LOSSES), according to the following formula:

$$A \times \frac{B}{C} \times \frac{D}{E}$$

where

A is the total amount of the allowable loss;

B is the sum of the amount of the item of relevant allowable expenditure concerned and, for disposals before 30 November 1993, the '*indexed rise*' (as in *TCGA 1992, s 54* (see 34.1 INDEXATION) but ignoring the effect of *TCGA 1992, s 110* (see 59.4 SHARES AND SECURITIES—IDENTIFICATION RULES)) where the above formula is applied for the purposes of 27.23 below) in that item;

C is the sum of the total amount of all such expenditure and, for disposals before 30 November 1993, the indexed rises in each of the items comprised in that expenditure;

D is the length of the period beginning with 'the relevant pre-entry date' and ending with the relevant time or, if that date is after that time, nil (i.e. there is no pre-entry proportion if the relevant time precedes the relevant pre-entry date); and

E is the length of the period beginning with the relevant pre-entry date and ending with the day of disposal.

[*TCGA 1992, Sch 7A para 2(1)(9); FA 1994, s 93(8)(a)(d), (11), Sch 26 Pt V*].

'*The relevant pre-entry date*', in relation to any item referred to above, is the later of 1 April 1982 and the date the asset was acquired or provided or, as the case may be, improvement expenditure became due and payable (such date being subject to the assumptions provided for by *Sch 7A para 2(4)(5)(6A)(6B)* below in relation to the deduction of a loss from a chargeable gain where either the gain or the loss accrues after 10 March 1994 and subject to the assumptions provided for by *Sch 7A para 2(4)(5)* in relation to the deduction of a loss from a chargeable gain, where both the gain and loss accrue before 11 March 1994). [*TCGA 1992, Sch 7A para 2(3); FA 1994, s 94(1)(2)(4)*].

Where any 'original shares' are treated as the same asset as a 'new holding' (within *TCGA 1992, s 127*; see 58.1 SHARES AND SECURITIES), the above formula and (where applicable) the provisions in 27.23 below are applied (except, for disposals before 30 November 1993, in relation to the calculation of any indexed rise):

(*a*) as if any item referred to above consisting in consideration given for the acquisition of the new holding had been incurred at the time the original shares were acquired; and (*b*) where there is more than one such time as if that item were incurred at those different times in the same proportions as the consideration for the acquisition of the original shares.

[*TCGA 1992, Sch 7A para 2*(*4*); *FA 1994, s 93*(*8*)(*b*)(*d*), (*11*), *Sch 26 Pt V*].

Without prejudice to (*a*) and (*b*) above, the formula is applied to any asset which

(A) was held by a company at the time when it became a member of the relevant group, and

(B) is treated as having been acquired by that company on *any* no gain/no loss corresponding disposal,

as if the company and every person who acquired that asset or 'the equivalent asset' (see below) at a 'material time' had been the same person and, accordingly, as if the asset had been acquired by the company when it or the equivalent asset was acquired by the first of those persons to have acquired it at a material time and the time at which any expenditure had been incurred were to be determined accordingly. [*TCGA 1992, Sch 7A para 2*(*5*)].

A '*material time*' is any time before an acquisition of an asset in circumstances as in (B) above and is, or is after, the last occasion before the occasion on which any person acquired that asset or the equivalent asset otherwise than on an acquisition which is within (B) above or is an acquisition by virtue of which any asset is treated as the equivalent asset; and the formula is applied in relation to any asset within (A) and (B) above without regard to *TCGA 1992, s 56*(*2*) (consideration on no gain/no loss disposal deemed to include indexation allowance; see 34.3 INDEXATION). [*TCGA 1992, Sch 7A para 2*(*6*)].

In relation to the deduction of a loss from a chargeable gain where either the gain or the loss accrues after 10 March 1994, and notwithstanding anything in *TCGA 1992, s 56*(*2*) (see above), where in the case of the disposal of any pre-entry asset any company has, between the relevant time and the time of the disposal, acquired that asset or the equivalent asset, and the acquisition was either an acquisition in pursuance of a no gain/no loss disposal under *TCGA 1992, s 171* (general provisions for no gain/no loss transfers within a group; see 27.12 above) or an acquisition by virtue of which an asset is treated as the equivalent asset, the items of relevant allowable expenditure in the above formula, and the times they are treated as having been incurred, are determined on the assumption that the company by reference to which the asset in question is a pre-entry asset, and the company which acquired the asset or the equivalent asset as above (and every other company which has made such an acquisition), were the same person and, accordingly, that the pre-entry asset had been acquired by the company disposing of it at the time when it or the equivalent asset would have been treated as acquired by the company by reference to which the asset is a pre-entry asset. [*TCGA 1992, Sch 7A para 2*(*6A*)(*6B*); *FA 1994, s 94*(*1*)(*2*)(*4*)].

In relation to the deduction of a loss from a chargeable gain where either the gain or the loss accrues after 10 March 1994, for the purposes of the provisions in *Sch 7A para 2*(*5*)(*6*)(*6A*)(*6B*) above, '*the equivalent asset*', in relation to another asset acquired or disposed of by any company, is any asset which falls in relation to that company to be treated (whether under *Sch 7A para 1*(*8*) in 27.21 or otherwise) as the same as the other asset or which would fall to be so treated after applying, as respects other assets, the assumptions for which those provisions provide. In relation to the deduction of a loss from a chargeable gain where both the gain and the loss accrue before 11 March 1994, for the purposes of the provisions in *Sch 7A para 2*(*5*)(*6*) above, '*the equivalent asset*', in relation to the acquisition of any asset by any company, is any asset which (whether under *Sch 7A para 1*(*8*) or otherwise) would be treated in relation to that company as the same as the asset in question. [*TCGA 1992, Sch 7A para 2*(*7*); *FA 1994, s 94*(*1*)(*2*)(*4*)].

The above provisions and (where applicable) those in 27.23 below have effect where a loss accrues to a company under *TCGA 1992, s 116*(*10*)(*b*) (see *Sch 7A para 1*(*9*) in 27.21 above), and the shares exchanged for qualifying corporate bonds are treated under 27.23 below as including pre-entry assets, as if the disposal on which the loss accrues were the disposal of the shares assumed to be made by *s 116(10)(a)* at the time of reorganisation etc. [*TCGA 1992, Sch 7A para 2(8)*].

In relation to disposals on or after 30 November 1993, where, under *TCGA 1992, s 55(8)* (rolled-up indexation on no gain/no loss disposals after 31 March 1982 and before 30 November 1993; see 8.7 ASSETS HELD ON 31 MARCH 1982), the allowable loss (or part) accruing on the disposal of a pre-entry asset is attributable to an amount of rolled-up indexation, the total relevant allowable expenditure is treated for the purposes of *Sch 7A para 2* above as increased by that rolled-up amount, each item of expenditure being treated as increased by the attributable proportion of the total. [*TCGA 1992, Sch 7A para 2(8A); FA 1994, s 93(8)(c), (11)*].

Also in relation to disposals on or after 30 November 1993, where *TCGA 1992, s 56(3)* (disapplication of *TCGA 1992, s 56(2)* on any no gain/no loss disposal on or after 30 November 1993; see 34.3 INDEXATION) applies to reduce the total allowable expenditure on the disposal of a pre-entry asset on which an allowable loss accrues, the amount of each item of relevant allowable expenditure is treated for the purposes of *Sch 7A para 2* as reduced by so much of that reduction as is attributable to it. [*TCGA 1992, Sch 7A para 2(8B); FA 1994, s 93(8)(c), (11)*].

27.23 **Disposals of pooled assets.** Subject to 27.24 and 27.25 below, the provisions below apply where any assets acquired by a company fall to be treated with other assets as indistinguishable parts of the same asset ('*a pooled asset*') and the whole or part of that asset is referable to pre-entry assets.

For the purposes of *Sch 7A*, where a pooled asset has at any time contained a pre-entry asset, the pooled asset is treated, until on the assumptions below all the pre-entry assets included in the asset have been disposed of, as incorporating a part which is referable to pre-entry assets, the size of that part being determined as below. [*TCGA 1992, Sch 7A para 3(1)(2)*].

Where there is a disposal of any part of a pooled asset and the proportion of the asset which is disposed of does not exceed the proportion of that asset which is represented by any part of it which is not, at the time of disposal, referable to pre-entry assets, that disposal is treated as confined to assets which are not pre-entry assets. Consequently, no part of any loss accruing on that disposal is treated as a pre-entry loss (except where *Sch 7A para 4(2)* in 27.24 below applies), and the part of the pooled asset which after the disposal is treated as referable to pre-entry assets is correspondingly increased (without prejudice to the effect of any subsequent acquisition of assets to be added to the pool in determining whether, and to what extent, any part of the pooled asset is to be treated as referable to pre-entry assets). [*TCGA 1992, Sch 7A para 3(3)(11)*].

Where there is such an excess as postulated above, the disposal is treated as relating to pre-entry assets only so far as required for the purposes of the excess. Consequently

(*a*) any loss accruing on that disposal is treated for the same purposes as an allowable loss on a pre-entry asset,

(*b*) the pre-entry proportion of that loss is deemed (except where *Sch 7A para 4(3)* in 27.24 below applies) to be the amount (insofar as it does not exceed the amount of the loss actually accruing) which would have been the pre-entry proportion under 27.22 above of any loss accruing on the disposal of the excess if the excess were a separate asset, and

(*c*) the pooled asset is treated after the disposal as referable entirely to pre-entry assets (with the same qualification as appears in parentheses at the end of the previous paragraph regarding any subsequent acquisition).

[*TCGA 1992, Sch 7A para 3(4)(11)*].

Where there is a disposal of the whole or part of a pooled asset at a time when the asset is referable entirely to pre-entry assets, (*a*) and (*b*) above apply to the disposal of the asset or the part as they apply in relation to the assumed disposal of the excess mentioned in the preamble to (*a*) and (*b*) but, where the whole of an asset only part of which is referable to pre-entry assets is disposed of, the reference in (*b*) above to the excess is taken as a reference to that part. [*TCGA 1992, Sch 7A para 3(5)*].

In applying (*b*) above, it is assumed that none of the assets treated as comprised in the separate asset mentioned in (*b*) has ever been comprised in a pooled asset with any assets other than those which are taken to constitute that separate asset for the purposes of determining what would have been the pre-entry proportion of any loss accruing on the disposal of any assets as that separate asset. [*TCGA 1992, Sch 7A para 3(6)*].

Assets comprised in any asset which is treated as separate are identified on the following assumptions:

(A) that assets are disposed of in the order of the relevant pre-entry dates for the acquisition consideration as under 27.22 above;

(B) subject to (A), that assets with earlier relevant times are disposed of before those with later ones;

(C) that disposals made when a company was not a member of the relevant group are made according to the provisions in *Sch 7A para 3(1)–(6)* and (A) and (B) above, as they have effect in relation to the group of companies of which the company was a member at the time of disposal or, as the case may be, of which it had most recently been a member before that time; and

(D) subject to (A)–(C) above, that a company disposes of assets in the order in which it acquires them.

[*TCGA 1992, Sch 7A para 3(7)*].

Where there is more than one pre-entry date in relation to acquisition consideration, the date in (A) above is the earlier or earliest of those dates if any such date relating to an option to acquire the asset is disregarded. [*TCGA 1992, Sch 7A para 3(8)*].

Where a second asset falls to be treated as acquired at the same time as a first asset was earlier acquired (whether under *Sch 7A para 1(8)* in 27.21 above or otherwise), and the second asset is either comprised in a pooled asset partly referable to pre-entry assets or is, or includes, an asset which is to be treated as so comprised, (A)–(D) above apply not only in relation to the second asset as if it were the first asset but also, in the first place, for identifying the asset which is to be treated as the first asset under the above provisions. [*TCGA 1992, Sch 7A para 3(10)*].

Where the formula in 27.22 above is applied to an asset treated as above as a separate asset, the amount or value of the asset's acquisition or disposal consideration and any related incidental costs are determined not under *TCGA 1992, s 129* or *s 130* (see 58.1 SHARES AND SECURITIES), but by apportioning the consideration or costs relating to both that asset and other assets acquired or disposed of at the same time according to the proportion that is borne by that asset to all the assets to which the consideration or costs related. [*TCGA 1992, Sch 7A para 3(9)*].

27.24 *Rules to prevent pre-entry losses on pooled assets being treated as post-entry losses.* The provisions below apply if:

(*a*) there is a disposal of any part of a pooled asset which under 27.23 above is treated as including a part referable to pre-entry assets;

(*b*) the assets disposed of are or include assets ('*the post-entry element of the disposal*') which, for the purposes of 24A.20, are treated as having been included in the part of the pooled asset which is not referable to pre-entry assets;

(*c*) an allowable loss ('*the actual loss*') accrues on the disposal; and

(*d*) the amount which in computing the allowable loss is allowed as a deduction of relevant allowable expenditure ('*the expenditure actually allowed*') exceeds such expenditure attributable to the post-entry element of the disposal.

[*TCGA 1992, Sch 7A para 4*(*1*)].

Subject to *Sch 7A para 4*(*6*) below, where the post-entry element of the disposal comprises all of the assets disposed of, the actual loss is treated for *Sch 7A* purposes as a loss accruing on the disposal of a pre-entry asset, and the pre-entry proportion of that loss is treated as being the amount (insofar as it does not exceed the amount of the actual loss) of the excess referred to in (*d*) above. [*TCGA 1992, Sch 7A para 4*(*2*)].

Subject to *Sch 7A para 4*(*6*) below, where the actual loss is treated under 27.23 above as a loss accruing on a pre-entry asset, and the expenditure actually allowed exceeds the actual cost of the assets to which the disposal is treated as relating, the pre-entry proportion of the loss is treated as being the amount which (insofar as it does not exceed the amount of the actual loss) is equal to the sum of that excess and what would, apart from the provisions in 27.25 below and these provisions, be the pre-entry proportion of the loss accruing on the disposal. [*TCGA 1992, Sch 7A para 4*(*3*)].

For the purposes of *Sch 7A para 4*(*3*) above, the actual cost of the assets to which the disposal is treated as relating is taken to be the sum of

(A) the relevant allowable expenditure attributable to the post-entry element of the disposal; and

(B) the amount which, in computing the pre-entry proportion of the loss under *Sch 7A para 3*(*4*)(*b*) (27.23(*b*) above) and *Sch 7A para 3*(*6*) (27.23 above), would be treated for the purposes of 'C' in the formula in 27.22 above as the total amount allowable as a deduction of relevant allowable expenditure in respect of such of the assets disposed of as are treated as having been incorporated in the part of the pooled asset referable to pre-entry assets.

[*TCGA 1992, Sch 7A para 4*(*4*)].

Without prejudice to *Sch 7A para 4*(*6*) below, where *Sch 7A para 4*(*2*) or (*3*) above applies for the purpose of determining the pre-entry proportion of any loss, no election can be made under 27.25 below for the purpose of enabling a different amount to be taken as the pre-entry proportion of that loss. [*TCGA 1992, Sch 7A para 4*(*5*)].

Where

(*aa*) the pre-entry proportion of the loss accruing to any company on the disposal of any part of a pooled asset falls to be determined under *Sch 7A para 4*(*2*) or (*3*) above,

(*bb*) the amount determined thereunder exceeds the amount determined under *Sch 7A para 4*(*7*) below ('*the alternative pre-entry loss*'), and

(*cc*) the company makes an election for the purpose,

the pre-entry proportion of the loss determined as specified in (*aa*) above is reduced to the amount of the alternative pre-entry loss. [*TCGA 1992, Sch 7A para 4*(*6*)]. For this purpose '*the alternative pre-entry loss*' is whatever apart from these provisions would have been the pre-entry proportion of the loss on the disposal in question, if for the purposes of *Sch 7A* the identification of the assets disposed of were to be made disregarding the part of the pooled asset which was not referable to pre-entry assets, except to the extent (if any) by which the part referable to pre-entry assets fell short of what was disposed of. [*TCGA 1992, Sch 7A para 4*(*7*)].

The election mentioned in (*cc*) above must be made by the company incurring the loss by notice to the inspector given within the period of two years beginning with the end of its accounting period in which the disposal giving rise to the loss is made, or within such longer period as HMRC may by notice allow. The provisions in 27.25 below may be taken into account under *Sch 7A para 4(7)* above in determining the amount of the alternative pre-entry loss as if an election had been made under 27.25 below, but only if the election under (*cc*) above contains an election corresponding to the election that otherwise might have been made under 27.25 below. [*TCGA 1992, Sch 7A para 4(8)*].

As the rules for pre-entry losses can operate in relation to losses which arise on disposals of assets by companies which became members of the relevant group after 31 March 1987, they may apply in situations where elections would be beneficial but the normal two-year time limit had already passed. The Revenue extended the period for elections for these cases, and others where the time limit would have expired less than two years after 27 July 1993. Elections were accepted as made in time in all cases where made by 27 July 1995.

For the purposes of the above the relevant allowable expenditure attributable to the post-entry element of the disposal is the amount which, in computing any allowable loss accruing on a disposal of that element as a separate asset, would have been allowed as a deduction of relevant allowable expenditure if none of the assets comprised in that element had ever been comprised in a pooled asset with any assets other than those which are taken to constitute that separate asset for the purposes of this provision. [*TCGA 1992, Sch 7A para 4(9)*]. To identify the assets which are to be treated for this purpose as comprised in the post-entry element of the disposal, a company is taken to dispose of assets in the order in which it acquired them. [*TCGA 1992, Sch 7A para 4(10)*].

Sch 7A para 3(9) in 27.23 above is applied *mutatis mutandis* for the purposes of *Sch 7A para 4(9)* above, as is *Sch 7A para 3(10)* in 27.23 for the purposes of this provision in relation to *Sch 7A para 4(10)* above. [*TCGA 1992, Sch 7A para 4(11)*].

In the above references to an amount allowed as a deduction of relevant allowable expenditure are references to the amount falling to be so allowed in accordance with *TCGA 1992, s 38(1)(a)* and (*b*) and (so far as applicable) *TCGA 1992, s 42*, together (for disposals before 30 November 1993) with the indexed rises (as in 27.22 above) in the items comprised in that expenditure or, as the case may be, in the appropriate portions of those items. Nothing in the above provisions affects the operation of the rules contained in 27.23 above for determining, for any purposes other than those of *Sch 7A para 4(7)* above, how much of any pooled asset at any time consists of a part which is referable to pre-entry assets. [*TCGA 1992, Sch 7A para 4(12)–(14); FA 1994, s 93(9)(11), Sch 26 Pt V*].

27.25 **Alternative calculation by reference to market value.** Subject to *Sch 7A para 4(5)* in 27.24 above and the following provisions, if an otherwise allowable loss accrues on the disposal by any company of any pre-entry asset, and that company makes an election accordingly, the pre-entry proportion of that loss (instead of being any amount arrived at under the above provisions of *Sch 7A*) is whichever is the smaller of

(*a*) the amount of any loss which would have accrued if that asset had been disposed of at the relevant time at its market value at that time; and

(*b*) the amount of the otherwise allowable loss accruing on the actual disposal of that asset.

[*TCGA 1992, Sch 7A para 5(1)(2)*].

In relation to disposals on or after 30 November 1993, in determining the amount of any notional loss under (*a*) above, it is assumed that the prohibition (and its consequences) of indexation allowance creating or increasing a loss introduced by *FA 1994, s 93(1)–(5)* with effect generally in relation to disposals on or after 30 November 1993 (see 8.7 ASSETS HELD ON 31 MARCH 1982 and 34.1 and 34.3 INDEXATION) has effect for disposals on or after the day on which the relevant time falls. [*TCGA 1992, Sch 7A para 5(2A); FA 1994, s 93(10)(11)*].

Where no loss would have accrued on the deemed disposal in (*a*) above, the loss mentioned in (*b*) above is deemed not to have a pre-entry proportion. [*TCGA 1992, Sch 7A para 5*(*3*)]. The election mentioned above must be made by the company incurring the loss by notice to the inspector given within the period of two years beginning with the end of its accounting period in which the disposal giving rise to the loss is made, or within such longer period as HMRC may by notice allow. [*TCGA 1992, Sch 7A para 5*(*8*)]. See 27.24 above regarding comments made about adherence to the similar two-year time limit mentioned there which apply equally here.

The provisions in *Sch 7A para 5*(*5*) below apply where an election as above is made in relation to any loss accruing on the disposal ('*the real disposal*') of the whole or any part of a pooled asset, and the case is one in which (but for the election) the provisions in 27.23 above would apply for determining the pre-entry proportion of a loss accruing on the real disposal. [*TCGA 1992, Sch 7A para 5*(*4*)]. In these circumstances, these provisions have effect as if the amount specified in (*a*) above were to be calculated

(A) on the basis that the disposal which is assumed to have taken place was a disposal of all the assets falling within (*aa*)–(*cc*) below; and

(B) by apportioning any loss that would have accrued on that disposal between

  (i) such of the assets falling within (*aa*)–(*cc*) below as are assets to which the real disposal is treated as relating, and

  (ii) the remainder of the assets so falling,

 according to the proportions of any pooled asset whose disposal is assumed which would have been, respectively, represented by assets mentioned in (i) above and by assets mentioned in (ii) above.

Where assets falling within (*aa*)–(*cc*) below have different relevant times there is assumed to have been a different disposal at each of those times. [*TCGA 1992, Sch 7A para 5*(*5*)].

Assets fall to be included within (A) and (B) above if

(*aa*) immediately before the time which is the relevant time in relation to those assets, they were comprised in a pooled asset which consisted of or included assets which fall to be treated for the purposes of 27.23 above as

  (i) comprised in the part of the pooled asset referable to pre-entry assets; and

  (ii) disposed of on the real disposal;

(*bb*) they were also comprised in such a pooled asset immediately after that time; and

(*cc*) the pooled asset in which they were so comprised immediately after that time was held by a member of the relevant group.

[*TCGA 1992, Sch 7A para 5*(*6*)].

Where

(AA) an election is made under *Sch 7A para 4*(*6*) (see 27.24(*cc*) above) requiring the determination by reference to these provisions of the alternative pre-entry loss accruing on the disposal of any assets comprised in a pooled asset, and

(BB) under that election any amount of the loss that would have accrued on an assumed disposal is apportioned in accordance with (A) and (B) above to assets ('*the relevant assets*') which

  (i) are treated for the purposes of that determination as assets to which the disposal related, but

(ii) otherwise continue after the disposal to be treated as incorporated in the part of that pooled asset which is referable to pre-entry assets,

then, on any further application of these provisions for the purpose of determining the pre-entry proportion of the loss accruing on a subsequent disposal of assets comprised in that pooled asset, that amount (without being apportioned elsewhere) is deducted from so much of the loss accruing on the same assumed disposal as, apart from the deduction, would be apportioned to the relevant assets on that further application of these provisions. [*TCGA 1992, Sch 7A para 5*(*7*)].

27.26 **Restrictions on the deduction of pre-entry losses.** In the calculation of the amount to be included in respect of chargeable gains in any company's total profits for any accounting period:

(*a*) if in that period there is any chargeable gain from which the whole or any part of any pre-entry loss accruing in that period is deductible in accordance with the provisions in 27.27 below, the loss or, as the case may be, that part of it is deducted from that gain;

(*b*) if, after all the deductions in (*a*) above have been made, there is in that period any chargeable gain from which the whole or any part of any pre-entry loss carried forward from a previous accounting period is deductible in accordance with the provisions in 27.27, the loss or, as the case may be, that part of it is deducted from that gain;

(*c*) the total of chargeable gains (if any) remaining after all the deductions in (*a*) or (*b*) above is subject to deductions in accordance with *TCGA 1992, s 8*(*1*) (chargeable gains less allowable losses of company to be included in chargeable profits; see 13.3 COMPANIES) in respect of any allowable losses that are not pre-entry losses; and

(*d*) any pre-entry loss which has not been the subject of a deduction under (*a*) or (*b*) above (as well as any other losses falling to be carried forward under *section 8*(*1*)) are carried forward to the following accounting period of that company.

[*TCGA 1992, Sch 7A para 6*(*1*)].

Subject to (*a*)–(*d*) above, any question as to which or what part of any pre-entry loss has been deducted from any particular chargeable gain is decided

(A) where it falls to be decided in respect of the setting of losses against gains in any accounting period ending before 16 March 1993 as if:

(i) pre-entry losses accruing in any such period had been set against chargeable gains before any other allowable losses accruing in that period were set against those gains;

(ii) pre-entry losses carried forward to any such period had been set against chargeable gains before any other allowable losses carried forward to that period were set against those gains; and

(iii) subject to (i) and (ii) above, the pre-entry losses carried forward to any accounting period ending after 15 March 1993 were identified with those losses which are determined in accordance with elections made by the company to which they accrued;

and

(B) in any other case, in accordance with such elections as may be made by the company to which the loss accrued;

and any question as to which or what part of any pre-entry loss has been carried forward from one accounting period to another is decided accordingly. [*TCGA 1992, Sch 7A para 6*(*2*)].

An election under (A)(iii) above must be made by the company by notice to the inspector given before the end of the period of two years beginning with the end of its accounting period which was current on 16 March 1993. An election under (B) above must similarly be made before the end of the period of two years beginning with the end of the company's accounting period in which the gain in question accrued. [*TCGA 1992, Sch 7A para 6(3)*].

For the purposes of *Sch 7A* where any matter falls to be determined under the above provisions by reference to an election but no election is made, it is assumed, so far as consistent with any elections that have been made that losses are set against gains in the order in which the losses accrued, and that the gains against which they are set are also determined according to the order in which they accrued with losses being set against earlier gains before they are set against later ones. [*TCGA 1992, Sch 7A para 6(4)*].

27.27 **Gains from which pre-entry losses are to be deductible.** A pre-entry loss that accrued to a company before it became a member of the relevant group is deductible from a chargeable gain accruing to that company if the gain is one accruing

(*a*) on a disposal made by that company before the date on which it became a member of the relevant group ('*the entry date*');

(*b*) on the disposal of an asset which was held by that company immediately before the entry date; or

(*c*) on the disposal of any asset which

(i) was acquired by that company on or after the entry date from a person who was not a member of the relevant group at the time of the acquisition; and

(ii) since its acquisition from that person has not been used or held for any purposes other than those of a trade which was being carried on by that company at the time immediately before the entry date and which continued to be carried on by that company until the disposal.

[*TCGA 1992, Sch 7A para 7(1)*].

The pre-entry proportion of an allowable loss accruing to any company on the disposal of a pre-entry asset is deductible from a chargeable gain accruing to that company if

(A) the gain is one accruing on a disposal made, before the date on which it became a member of the relevant group, by that company and that company is the one ('*the initial company*') by reference to which the asset on the disposal of which the loss accrues is a pre-entry asset;

(B) the pre-entry asset and the asset on the disposal of which the gain accrues were each held by the same company at a time immediately before it became a member of the relevant group; or

(C) the gain is one accruing on the disposal of an asset which

(i) was acquired by the initial company (whether before or after it became a member of the relevant group) from a person who, at the time of the acquisition, was not a member of that group; and

(ii) since its acquisition from that person has not been used or held for any purposes other than those of a trade which was being carried on, immediately before it became a member of the relevant group, by the initial company and which continued to be carried on by the initial company until the disposal.

[*TCGA 1992, Sch 7A para 7(2)*].

Where two or more companies become members of the relevant group at the same time and those companies were all members of the same group of companies immediately before they became members of the relevant group, then, without prejudice to the provisions in 27.29 below

(*aa*) an asset is treated for the purposes of (*b*) above as held, immediately before it became a member of the relevant group, by the company to which the pre-entry loss in question accrued if that company is one of those companies and the asset was in fact so held by another of those companies;

(*bb*) two or more assets are treated for the purposes (B) above as assets held by the same company immediately before it became a member of the relevant group wherever they would be so treated if all those companies were treated as a single company; and

(*cc*) the acquisition of an asset is treated for the purposes of (*c*) and (C) above as an acquisition by the company to which the pre-entry loss in question accrued if that company is one of those companies and the asset was in fact acquired (whether before or after they became members of the relevant group) by another of those companies.

[*TCGA 1992, Sch 7A para 7(3)*].

TCGA 1992, Sch 7A para 1(4) in 27.21 above is applied *mutatis mutandis* for determining for the purposes of the above provisions whether an asset on the disposal of which a chargeable gain accrues was held at the time when a company became a member of the relevant group. [*TCGA 1992, Sch 7A para 7(4)*].

Subject to *Sch 7A para 7(6)* below, where a gain accrues on the disposal of the whole or any part of

(1) any asset treated as a single asset but comprising assets only some of which were held at the time mentioned in (*b*) or (B) above, or

(2) an asset which is treated as held at that time by virtue of a provision requiring an asset which was not held at that time to be treated as the same as an asset which was so held (see 27.21 above),

a pre-entry loss is deductible under (*b*) or (B) above from the amount of that gain to the extent only of such proportion of that gain as is attributable to assets held at that time or, as the case may be, represents the gain that would have accrued on the asset so held. [*TCGA 1992, Sch 7A para 7(5)*].

Where

(AA) a chargeable gain accrues under *TCGA 1992, s 116(10)* on the disposal of a qualifying corporate bond which has been exchanged for shares etc. (see 50.3 QUALIFYING CORPORATE BONDS and 27.21 above),

(BB) that bond was not held as required by (*b*) or (B) above at the time mentioned respectively in (*b*) or (B), and

(CC) the whole or any part of the asset which is the 'old asset' for the purposes of *TCGA 1992, s 116* was so held,

the question whether that gain is one accruing on the disposal of an asset, the whole or any part of which was held by a particular company at that time, is determined for the purposes of *Sch 7A para 7* as if the bond were deemed to have been so held to the same extent as the old asset. [*TCGA 1992, Sch 7A para 7(6)*].

27.28 *Change of a company's nature.* If

(*a*) within any period of three years, a company becomes a member of a group of companies and there is (either earlier or later in that period, or at the same time) 'a major change in the nature or conduct of a trade' carried on by that company, or (*b*) at any time the scale of the activities in a trade carried on by a company has become small or negligible, and before any considerable revival of the trade, that company becomes a member of a group of companies,

the trade carried on before that change, or which has become small or negligible, is disregarded for the purposes of 27.27(*c*) and (C) above in relation to any time before the company became a member of the group in question.

'*A major change in the conduct of a trade*' includes a reference to a major change in services or facilities provided in the trade or a major change in customers of the trade or a change in the nature of investments held. Regard will also be had to appropriate changes in other factors such as the location of the company's business premises, the identity of the company's suppliers, management or staff, the company's methods of manufacture, or the company's pricing or purchasing policies to the extent that these factors indicate that a major change has occurred. Efficiency changes and technological advancements would not in themselves indicate that a major change in the nature or conduct of a trade has occurred.

HMRC will compare any two points in three years which include the date of change of ownership of the company. This applies even if the change is the result of a gradual process which began outside the period of three years mentioned in (*a*) above. HMRC take note of both qualitative and quantitative issues as discussed in the cases *Willis v Peeters Picture Frames Ltd CA (NI) 1982, 56 TC 436* and *Purchase v Tesco Stores Ltd Ch D 1984, 58 TC 46* respectively. (HMRC Statement of Practice 10/91).

Where the operation of the above provisions depends on circumstances or events at a time after the company becomes a member of any group of companies (but not more than three years after), an assessment to give effect to the provisions may be made within six years from that time or the latest such time. [*TCGA 1992, Sch 7A para 8*].

The above provisions are identical *mutatis mutandis* with those in *ICTA 1988, s 768* regarding the disallowance of trading losses on a change in ownership of a company. See Tolley's Corporation Tax under Losses for the appropriate case law and HMRC practice applying to that provision which may apply to the above.

27.29 **Identification of the 'relevant group' and application of Sch 7A to every connected group.** The provisions below apply where there is more than one group of companies which would be the relevant group in relation to any company.

Where any loss has accrued on the disposal by any company of any asset, *Sch 7A* does not apply by reference to any group of companies in relation to any loss accruing on that disposal unless

(*a*) that group is a group in relation to which that loss is a pre-entry loss because it is an allowable loss that accrued to that company at a time before it became a member of the group or, if there is more than one such group, the one of which that company most recently became a member;

(*b*) that group, in a case where there is no group falling within (*a*) above, is either

(i) the group of which that company is a member at the time of the disposal, or

(ii) if it is not a member of a group of companies at that time, the group of which that company was last a member before that time;

(*c*) that group, in a case where there is a group falling within paragraph (*a*) or, in relation to the deduction of a loss from a chargeable gain where either the gain or the loss accrues after 10 March 1994, paragraph (*b*) above, is a group of which that company was a member at any time in the accounting period of that company in which it became a member of the group falling within that paragraph;

(*d*) that group is a group the principal company (see 27.1 above) of which is or has been, or has been under the control (within *ICTA 1988, s 416*) of

(i) the company by which the disposal is made, or

(ii) another company which is or has been a member of a group by reference to which *Sch 7A* applies in relation to the loss in question under (*a*), (*b*) or (*c*) above; or

(*e*) that group is a group of which either

(i) the principal company of a group by reference to which *Sch 7A* applies, or

(ii) a company which has had that principal company under its control,

is or has been a member.

In the case of a loss accruing on the disposal of an asset where, under (*a*)–(*e*) above there are two or more groups ('*connected groups*') by reference to which *Sch 7A* applies, the further provisions in *Sch 7A para 9(3)–(5)* below apply. [*TCGA 1992, Sch 7A para 9(1)(2); FA 1994, s 94(1)(3)(4)*].

Schedule 7A is applied separately in relation to each of the connected groups (so far as they are not groups in relation to which the loss is a pre-entry loss because it is a loss that accrued to a company at a time before it became a member of the group) for the purpose of determining whether the loss on the disposal of an asset is a loss on the disposal of a pre-entry asset, and calculating the pre-entry proportion of that loss. [*TCGA 1992, Sch 7A para 9(3)*].

Subject to *Sch 7A para 9(5)* below, the provisions in 27.26 above have effect

(A) as if the pre-entry proportion of any loss accruing on the disposal of an asset which is a pre-entry asset in the case of more than one of the connected groups were the largest pre-entry proportion of that loss as calculated under *Sch 7A para 9(3)* above; and

(B) so that, where the loss accruing on the disposal of an asset is a pre-entry loss because it is an allowable loss that accrued to a company at a time before it became a member of a group in the case of any of the connected groups, that loss is the pre-entry loss for the purposes of 27.26 above, and not any amount which is the pre-entry proportion of that loss in relation to any of the other groups.

[*TCGA 1992, Sch 7A para 9(4)*].

Where, on the separate application of *Sch 7A* in the case of each of the groups by reference to which *Sch 7A* applies, there is, in the case of the disposal of any asset, a pre-entry loss by reference to each of two or more of the connected groups, no amount in respect of the loss accruing on the disposal is to be deductible under the provisions in 27.27 above from any chargeable gain if any of the connected groups is a group in the case of which, on separate applications of those provisions in relation to each group, the amount deductible from that gain in respect of that loss is nil. [*TCGA 1992, Sch 7A para 9(5)*].

Notwithstanding that the principal company of one group ('*the first group*') has become a member of another ('*the second group*'), those two groups are not under *TCGA 1992, s 170(10)* or *(10A)* (see 27.1 above) treated for the purposes of the above provisions as the same group if the principal company of the first group was under the control, immediately before it became a member of the second group, of a company which at that time was already a member of the second group. In addition, in relation to accounting periods ending after 16 March 1998, again where the principal company of the first group has become a member of the second group, the two groups are not for those purposes treated, in relation to any company that is (or has become) a member of the second group, as the same group if the time at which that company became a member of the first group falls in the same accounting period as that in which the principal company of the first group became a member of the second group. [*TCGA 1992, Sch 7A para 9(6); FA 1998, s 138; F(No 2)A 2005, s 65(5)*]. For an example, see HMRC Capital Gains Manual CG 47944.

Where, in the case of the disposal of any asset

(*aa*) two or more groups which, but for *Sch 7A para 9*(*6*) above, would be treated as the same group are treated as separate groups because of that provision; and

(*bb*) one of those groups is a group of which either

(i) the principal company of a group by reference to which *Sch 7A* applies by virtue of (*a*), (*b*) or (*c*) above in relation to any loss accruing on the disposal, or

(ii) a company which has had that principal company under its control,

is or has been a member,

the above provisions have effect as if that principal company had been a member of each of the groups mentioned in (*aa*) above. [*TCGA 1992, Sch 7A para 9*(*7*)].

27.30 **Miscellaneous.** Where, but for an election under *TCGA 1992, s 161*(*3*) (appropriation of asset to trading stock; see 6.3 ASSETS), there would be deemed to have been a disposal at any time by a company of an asset the amount by which the market value of it may be treated as increased under the election does not include the amount of any pre-entry loss that would have accrued on that disposal, and *Sch 7A* has effect as if the pre-entry loss of the last mentioned amount had accrued to the company at that time. [*TCGA 1992, Sch 7A para 10*].

The provisions of *Sch 7A* are prevented from applying where a loss arises, or a company joins a group, as a result of any enactment under which transfers of property etc. are made from a statutory body, a subsidiary of such a body or a company wholly owned by the Crown. [*TCGA 1992, Sch 7A para 11*].

For the purposes of *Sch 7A*, and without prejudice to the provisions in *Sch 7A para 11* above, where

(*a*) a company which is a member of a group of companies becomes at any time a member of another group of companies as the result of a disposal of shares in or other securities of that company or any other company; and

(*b*) that disposal is one of the no gain/no loss disposals mentioned in *TCGA 1992, s 35*(*3*)(*d*) (see 8.7 ASSETS HELD ON 31 MARCH 1982),

Sch 7A has effect in relation to the losses that accrued to that company before that time and the assets held by that company at that time as if any time when it was a member of the first group were included in the period during which it is treated as having been a member of the second group. [*TCGA 1992, Sch 7A para 12*].

27.31 RESTRICTION ON SET-OFF OF LOSSES AGAINST PRE-ENTRY GAINS WHERE A COMPANY JOINS A GROUP

The provisions of *TCGA 1992, s 177B, Sch 7AA* (added by *FA 1998, s 137, Sch 24*), as described at 27.32–27.35 below, were introduced to prevent 'gain buying'. The provisions are **repealed** with effect from the time that the provisions at 27.18 above, which prevent gain buying where there is a tax avoidance motive, take effect.

Under these provisions, the losses that can be set against a gain realised before a company joins a group are restricted to those that arose before it joined the group and those that arise after it joins the group on assets which that company held at the time of its joining the group. This also applies, with the appropriate modifications, where two or more companies leave one group and join another. These restrictions do not extend to the set-off of losses realised in an accounting period later than that in which the company or companies enter the gain-buying group, in view of the fact that losses cannot normally be carried back to preceding accounting periods. There is an exception under *TCGA 1992, s 213* for losses on certain deemed disposals by life assurance companies, for which see Tolley's Corporation Tax.

The provisions have effect in relation to accounting periods ending after 16 March 1998 where a company joins a group after that date and cease to have effect from the time that the provisions at 27.18 above take effect (see 27.18 above under Commencement). [*TCGA 1992, Sch 7AA para 1(3)(b); FA 1998, s 137(1)(2)(5), Sch 24; FA 2006, s 70(4)(6)–(11), Sch 26 Pt 3(9)*].

The legislation contains no motive test and thus applies wherever the necessary conditions are satisfied, with the result that innocent transactions are caught.

The change in the residence requirement in 27.1 above is taken into account in determining for the purposes of these provisions whether a company is a member of a group at any time after 20 March 2000. [*FA 2000, Sch 29 para 8; FA 2006, Sch 26 Pt 3(9)*].

Certain provisions, namely *TCGA 1992, s 213(1)(c)* and *s 214A(2)(b)*, deem gains and losses (on deemed disposals of certain holdings in unit trusts or offshore funds) to have arisen at the end of an accounting period of a life assurance company. For the purposes of the pre-entry gain provisions outlined above, such gains/losses are treated as having accrued *before* any time at which the company concerned joined a group in the accounting period in question (or before the earliest such time). [*TCGA 1992, Sch 7AA para 7*]. See Tolley's Corporation Tax for details.

For a worked example on set-off of losses against pre-entry gains, see Tolley's Corporation Tax under Capital Gains. For HMRC's commentary on the provisions, see HMRC Capital Gains Manual CG 48200–48224.

27.32 **The detailed provisions.** Subject to the repeal of the provisions noted at 27.31 above, the provisions apply in the case of any company (the '*relevant company*') in relation to any accounting period (the '*gain period*') in which a 'pre-entry gain' has accrued to that company. A '*pre-entry gain*' is a chargeable gain accruing to a company in an accounting period in which it becomes a member of a group of companies after 16 March 1998 and after the gain has accrued to it. When the principal company of a group becomes a member of another group, *TCGA 1992, s 170(10)* (see 27.1 above) does not prevent all the members of the first-mentioned group from being treated for these purposes as having become members of the second-mentioned group. [*TCGA 1992, Sch 7AA para 1*].

The relevant company's total chargeable gains for the gain period are split between pre-entry gains (X) and gains that arose after the company joined the group (Y). To the extent that current year and brought-forward capital losses can be set against X in accordance with the following rules, they cannot additionally be set against Y nor can they be carried forward to a succeeding accounting period. [*TCGA 1992, Sch 7AA para 2*].

Only so much of any allowable capital loss as is a 'qualifying loss' (see 27.33 below) in relation to a pre-entry gain can be set against it (to the extent that it has not been set against another pre-entry gain). If a loss is precluded by the pre-entry losses rules or the connected persons rule at *TCGA 1992, s 18(3)* from being set against a particular gain (see, respectively, 27.27 above and 40.5 LOSSES), those rules override these provisions. [*TCGA 1992, Sch 7AA para 3*]. Losses which are not qualifying losses can be set against post-entry gains of the same accounting period, with any balance being carried forward to subsequent accounting periods, under general principles.

27.33 *Qualifying losses*. The following allowable capital losses are '*qualifying losses*' (for the purposes of 27.32 above) in relation to a pre-entry gain accruing to the relevant company in the gain period (see 27.32 above):

- any loss brought forward from an earlier accounting period.
- any loss accruing in the gain period and accruing before, or at the same time as, the gain accrues.

- any loss accruing in the gain period and accruing after the gain accrues but before the company joined the group;
- any loss accruing in the gain period and accruing after the gain accrues and after the company joined a group of companies but which is a loss on the disposal of an asset which was owned, immediately before the relevant company joined the group, either by the relevant company itself or by another company which joined the group at the same time as the relevant company *and* which immediately before that time had been a member of the same group as the relevant company.

[*TCGA 1992, Sch 7AA para 4*].

As regards the final category above, see 27.34 below for pooled assets and 27.35 below for other cases where an asset is acquired over a period of time or derived from another asset.

27.34 *Pooled assets.* Where a loss-producing disposal is made of (or out of) a pool of shares or securities or similar assets (see 59.3–59.5 SHARES AND SECURITIES—IDENTIFICATION RULES), globally described below as '*securities*', special rules apply to determine to what extent the securities disposed of (or part disposed of) were held at the time the relevant company (or a member of its group) joined the new group (the entry time) (see 27.33 above). The rules apply in respect of any such disposal made in the gain period (see 27.32 above) and at or after the '*relevant entry time*' (being the entry time or, if there is more than one such time in the gain period, the earliest entry time). In practice, the rules need only be applied where the pool has been added to at or after the relevant entry time.

As regards any holding of securities, a 'notional net pre-entry loss' is computed. Actual losses on the disposals referred to above are matched with the notional net pre-entry loss in the order in which the actual losses accrued. The actual aggregate loss is regarded as a loss on disposal of securities held at the entry time to the extent that there is (or, in the case of a second or subsequent entry time, that there remains) an amount with which it can be so matched.

The notional net pre-entry loss is computed as follows. *For these purposes only* (actual losses still being computed under normal pooling rules), securities acquired at or after the relevant entry time ('*post-entry securities*') are not added to the pool existing immediately before the relevant entry time, which thus continues to consist only of securities acquired (and not disposed of) before that time ('*pre-entry securities*'). Disposals within these provisions (see above) are matched with the pool of pre-entry securities in preference to post-entry securities. Gains and losses on those disposals matched with pre-entry securities are computed and aggregated. If the net result of that aggregation is a loss, the amount of that loss is the notional net pre-entry loss. If the net result is a gain, there is no notional net pre-entry loss. See example at HMRC Capital Gains Manual CG 48214.

For the purposes of determining whether securities are pre-entry or post-entry securities, the rules of *TCGA 1992, s 127* applying on a reorganisation of share capital, i.e. the equation of a 'new holding' with the securities originally held (see 58.1 SHARES AND SECURITIES), are to be disregarded in as much as they would treat the 'new holding' as having been acquired at the same time as the original holding. So, for example, securities acquired by means of a bonus or rights issue must be taken as having been acquired at the time they were, in reality, acquired.

There are provisions to ensure that securities held by the relevant company, or by any 'associated company' at the relevant entry time, are taken to be pre-entry securities if, since the relevant entry time, but prior to the disposal in question, they have been disposed of by way of intra-group disposal. For this purpose, an '*associated company*' is one which was a member of the same group as the relevant company immediately before the relevant entry time and which joined the new group, along with the relevant company, at that time.

[*TCGA 1992, Sch 7AA para 5*].

27.35 *Rules for an asset acquired over a period of time or derived from another asset.* An apportionment is necessary if an asset within either of the two categories below (other than a pooled asset as in 27.34 above) is disposed of (or part disposed of) by the relevant company (at a loss) in the gain period (see 27.32 above) and at or after the time that the relevant company (or a member of its group) joined the new group (the entry time) (see 27.33 above). These rules apply (by reference to any entry time) to:

- an asset which is treated as a single asset but comprises assets only some of which were held at the entry time by the relevant company or an associated company; or
- an asset which is treated as held at the entry time by the relevant company or an associated company by virtue of any provision which treats an asset not held at that time as one which was so held.

An example of an asset within these rules is a leasehold interest in property held by a company which subsequently acquires the freehold. The proportion of the allowable loss treated as relating to a pre-entry asset and thus a qualifying loss (see 27.33 above) is made up of

(*a*) the proportion of the loss which, on a just and reasonable apportionment, is properly attributable to assets in fact held at the entry time; and

(*b*) such proportion of the loss not within (*a*) above as represents the loss that would have accrued if the asset disposed of had been the asset in fact held at that time.

For the above purposes, an '*associated company*' is one which was a member of the same group as the relevant company immediately before the entry time and which joined the new group, along with the relevant company, at that time.

[*TCGA 1992, Sch 7AA para 6*].

28 HMRC: Administration

28.1 From 18 April 2005, the collection and management of capital gains tax and corporation tax is administered by the **Commissioners for Her Majesty's Revenue and Customs**. [*TMA 1970, s 1; CRCA 2005, Sch 4 para 12*]. Previously, the taxes were administered by the Commissioners of Inland Revenue (normally referred to as 'the Board'). [*TMA 1970, s 1(1) as originally enacted*]. All the functions vested in the Board before that date (with the exception of prosecutions for tax offences, see below) are now vested in the Commissioners for HMRC. [*CRCA 2005, s 5; SI 2005 No 1126*].

Under the Commissioners for HMRC are officers of Revenue and Customs who are civil servants. Such officers may undertake the functions previously vested in either Inland Revenue officers or Customs and Excise officers, but not both at the same time. In relation to capital gains tax and corporation tax, officers of Revenue and Customs have broadly taken over the functions previously vested in officers of the Board of Inland Revenue, inspectors of taxes and collectors of taxes. [*CRCA 2005, ss 6, 7, Sch 1*]. As such they are responsible for processing returns, making assessments, dealing with claims, allowances and appeals, carrying out enquiries and collection and recovery of tax.

Criminal prosecutions of tax offences in England and Wales are conducted by an independent Revenue and Customs Prosecutions Office, whose director is appointed by the Attorney General. [*CRCA 2005, ss 34–42, Sch 3*]. Before 18 April 2005, the Inland Revenue was itself a prosecuting authority in England and Wales (see 28.3 below) and conducted its own prosecutions. See 23.13 FRAUDULENT OR NEGLIGENT CONDUCT and 48.26 PENALTIES for the Inland Revenue's practice in relation to prosecutions.

In this publication, 'HMRC' is generally used to mean both Her Majesty's Revenue and Customs, and, before 18 April 2005, the Inland Revenue. Where the context requires, however, 'the Revenue' is used to refer to the Inland Revenue.

28.2 **Appeal Commissioners.** Except as otherwise provided, assessments are made by officers of Revenue and Customs (or, before 18 April 2005, by officers of the Board) [*TMA 1970, s 30A; FA 1994, Sch 19 para 5; CRCA 2005, s 7, Sch 1*] and appeals against such assessments are heard by

(*a*) the *General Commissioners* (local people appointed on a voluntary basis by the Lord Chancellor for divisions in England and Wales and, from 3 April 1989, Northern Ireland or, for divisions in Scotland, by the Secretary of State) [*TMA 1970, s 2; FA 1975, s 57; FA 1988, s 125*], or

(*b*) the *Special Commissioners* (full-time civil servants, being barristers, advocates or solicitors of at least ten years' standing) [*TMA 1970, s 4; FA 1984, s 127, Sch 22 para 1*].

The Lord Chancellor has powers, by regulation, to change the appellations 'General Commissioners' and 'Special Commissioners' to something different. [*F(No 2)A 1992, s 75*].

See 4.6 and 4.9–4.19 APPEALS as regards jurisdiction of Appeal Commissioners and the conduct of appeals before them.

28.3 **'Care and management' powers.** As noted at 28.1 above, the Commissioners for HMRC have responsibility for the 'collection and management' of taxes, including capital gains tax and corporation tax. Before 18 April 2005, the Board of Inland Revenue had responsibility for the 'care and management' of direct taxes. The extent and limits of these care and management powers were considered before the Courts on a number of occasions.

For the validity of amnesties by the Board, see *R v CIR (ex p. National Federation of Self-Employed and Small Businesses Ltd) HL 1981, 55 TC 133.* HMRC EXTRA-STATUTORY

CONCESSIONS (24D) have been the subject of frequent judicial criticism but their validity has never been directly challenged in the Courts. In *R v CIR (ex p. Fulford-Dobson) QB 1987, 60 TC 168*, it was held that there had been no unfair treatment by the Revenue when it failed to apply a published extra-statutory concession because it was clear from the facts of the case that it was one of tax avoidance and this was a clearly stated general circumstance in which concessions would not be applied (cf. *R v Inspector of Taxes, Hull, ex p. Brumfield and others QB 1988, 61 TC 589* at 4.26 APPEALS). For a general discussion of the Board's care and management powers and an example of a ruling by the Court that the Board had acted reasonably, see *R v CIR (ex p. Preston) HL 1985, 59 TC 1*. See also *R v Attorney-General (ex p. ICI plc) CA 1986, 60 TC 1*, *R v CIR (ex p. MFK Underwriting Agencies Ltd and others) QB 1989, 62 TC 607* and *R v CIR (ex p. Matrix-Securities Ltd) HL 1994, 66 TC 587*. See also 4.26 APPEALS regarding judicial review of Revenue powers.

The Inland Revenue had a common law power to prosecute, which is ancillary to, supportive of and limited by their duty to collect taxes (*R v Criminal Cases Review Commission (ex p. Hunt) QB 2000, 73 TC 406*).

The Inland Revenue policy of selective prosecution for criminal offences (see 48.26 PENALTIES) in connection with tax evasion did not render a decision in a particular case unlawful or *ultra vires*, provided that the case was considered on its merits fairly and dispassionately to see whether the criteria for prosecution were satisfied, and that the decision to prosecute was then taken in good faith for the purpose of collecting taxes and not for some ulterior, extraneous or improper purpose (*R v CIR (ex p. Mead and Cook) QB 1992, 65 TC 1*).

The making of a 'forward tax agreement' with a non-UK domiciled individual (see 51.1 REMITTANCE BASIS) was held to be 'not a proper exercise' of the Inland Revenue's 'duties of care and management' (*Fayed and Others v Advocate-General for Scotland (representing CIR) SCS, [2002] STC 910*).

See 47.15 PAYMENT OF TAX for HMRC's practice as regards reduced payments under 'equitable liability'.

28.4 **Mistake or delay by HMRC.** Where the taxpayer complains, HMRC will reimburse any 'reasonable costs' incurred by him as a direct result of their mistake or 'unreasonable' delay. They may also pay non-taxable compensation of usually between £25 and £500 for worry and distress caused by the mistake or delay and/or for further delays or errors in handling the complaint itself. They will not compensate for time spent by the taxpayer sorting things out, unless he can show lost earnings as a direct result, nor for a difference of opinion where they are proved wrong but had not taken an unreasonable view of the law. These practices are embodied in HMRC's Code of Practice 1 (COP 1) 'Putting things right when we make mistakes'.

See also 37.7 INTEREST AND SURCHARGES ON UNPAID TAX and 47.10 PAYMENT OF TAX.

28.5 **Taxpayer's Charter.** The Board of Inland Revenue and HM Customs and Excise jointly produced a Taxpayer's Charter setting out the principles they try to meet in their dealings with taxpayers, the standards they believe the taxpayer has a right to expect, and what people can do if they wish to appeal or complain. Copies are available from local tax or collection offices and from local VAT offices. The Inland Revenue version is contained in Pamphlet IR 167.

HMRC have published a series of codes of practice, available from local tax offices, setting out the standards of service people can expect in relation to specific aspects of HMRC's work (see 30 HMRC EXPLANATORY PUBLICATIONS). The codes are not meant to represent any change of practice although some practices mentioned in them were not previously publicly available.

28.6 **Adjudicator.** A taxpayer who is not satisfied with the HMRC response to a complaint has the option of putting the case to an Adjudicator. The Adjudicator's office considers complaints about HMRC's handling of a taxpayer's affairs, e.g. excessive delays, errors, discourtesy or the exercise of HMRC discretion. Matters subject to existing rights of appeal are excluded.

Complaints will normally go to the Adjudicator only after they have been considered by the Director of the relevant HMRC office, and where the taxpayer is still not satisfied with the response received. The alternatives of pursuing the complaint to HMRC's Head Office, to an MP, or (through an MP) to the Parliamentary Ombudsman continue to be available. The Adjudicator will review all the facts, consider whether the complaint is justified, and, if so, make recommendations as to what should be done.

The Adjudicator publishes annual reports summarising the outcome of complaints made. Recent reports can be viewed on the Adjudicator's website (at www.adjudicatorsoffice.gov.uk). To date, HMRC have accepted all the Adjudicator's recommendations (see Adjudicator's leaflet AO 1 and Annual Report 2005). Contact should be made with the Adjudicator's Office, 3rd Floor, Haymarket House, 28 Haymarket, London SW1Y 4SP. Tel: 020–7930 2292. Fax: 020–7930 2298. An explanatory leaflet is available from the Adjudicator which describes the actions a taxpayer should take and how the Adjudicator will respond to complaints.

28.7 **Open Government.** Under the Government's 'Code of Practice on Access to Government Information', HMRC (in common with other Government departments) is to make information about its policies and decisions more widely available. Revenue Pamphlet IR 141 ('Open Government') set out the information to be made available, and how it could be obtained, and the basis on which a fee could be charged in certain circumstances to offset the cost of providing the information. The pamphlet was withdrawn in January 2005. Copies of the Code of Practice may be obtained by writing to Open Government, Room 417b, Office of Public Service and Science, 70 Whitehall, London SW1A 2AS (tel. 0345 223242).

28.8 **Use of electronic communications.** The Commissioners of Inland Revenue (and Customs & Excise) are given broad powers (which now vest in the Commissioners for HMRC) to make regulations, by statutory instrument (see *SI 2003 No 282* (previously *SI 2000 No 945*)), to facilitate two-way electronic communication in the delivery of information, e.g. tax returns and the making of tax payments. The regulations may allow or require the use of intermediaries such as Internet Service Providers. They will have effect notwithstanding any pre-existing legislation requiring delivery or payment in a manner which would otherwise preclude the use of electronic communications or intermediaries. [*FA 1999, ss 132, 133*].

The two departments are given further regulatory powers (see now *SI 2001 No 56*) to provide tax-free incentives to use electronic communications as above or otherwise in connection with tax matters. These may, in particular, take the form of discounts, the allowing of additional time for compliance or for payment of tax, or the facility to deliver information or make payments at more convenient intervals. [*FA 2000, s 143, Sch 38, ITTOIA 2005, s 778, Sch 1 para 518*]. In this connection, for one year from April 2000, individual taxpayers who personally filed their self-assessment tax return via the internet and paid any tax due electronically received a discount of £10 (Revenue Press Release 16 February 2000).

After 20 August 2001, agents are authorised to file individual clients' personal tax returns over the internet, subject to conditions as to authorisation of the agent by the client, authentication of the information by the client and use of Revenue approved software (Revenue Directions under *SI 2000 No 945, Reg 3*, 21 August 2001). After 4 March 2003, agents are likewise authorised to file companies' tax returns over the internet, subject to similar conditions (Revenue Directions under *SI 2003 No 282, Reg 3*, 4 March 2003).

For notes on electronic filing and payment, see Revenue Tax Bulletin June 2000 pp 757, 758. For payment by debit card over the internet, see Revenue Press Release 10 January

2001. For internet filing of returns and the Internet Corporation Tax Service (which allows companies and authorised agents to view details of liabilities and payments online), see the HMRC website at www.hmrc.gov.uk, which includes links to 'Frequently Asked Questions'. For the pre-existing system of electronic lodgement of returns, normally by agents, see 54.22 RETURNS.

28.9 **Revenue functions carried out by the Assets Recovery Agency.** Under *Proceeds of Crime Act 2002, Pt 6*, the Director of the Assets Recovery Agency is empowered, after 23 February 2003, to carry out the functions vested in the Board and its officers in relation to (amongst other matters) capital gains tax and corporation tax. The Director must have reasonable grounds to suspect either that

(*a*) a gain accruing to a person in respect of a chargeable period is a chargeable gain and accrues as a result (whether wholly or partly, directly or indirectly) of the 'criminal conduct' of that person or another, or

(*b*) a company is chargeable to corporation tax on its profits arising in a chargeable period and the profits arise as a result (whether wholly or partly, directly or indirectly) of the criminal conduct of the company or another person,

and must serve a notice on the Board specifying the person or company, the period or periods concerned, and the functions which he intends to carry out. The periods involved may include periods beginning before the *Act* was passed.

The Director may cease carrying out the functions specified in the notice at any time (by notifying the Board), but *must* so cease where the conditions allowing the notice to be made are no longer satisfied.

For the above purposes, '*criminal conduct*' is conduct which constitutes an offence anywhere in the UK or which would do so if it occurred there, but does not include conduct constituting an offence relating to a matter under the care and management of the Board.

It should be noted that the vesting of a function in the Director under these provisions does not divest the Board or its officers of the function (so that, for example, the Revenue can continue to carry out routine work). Certain functions, as listed in *Proceeds of Crime Act 2002, s 323*(*3*) cannot be carried out by the Director.

Appeals in respect of actions carried out by the Director in the exercise of Revenue functions are to the Special Commissioners. In hearing such appeals, the Special Commissioners may be assisted by one or more assessors selected for their special knowledge and experience of the matter to which the appeal relates from a panel appointed for the purpose by the Lord Chancellor.

[*Proceeds of Crime Act 2002, ss 317, 320*(*1*)–(*3*), *323*(*1*)(*3*), *326*(*1*)(*2*)].

The Assets Recovery Agency issued guidance on 1 November 2004 setting out the general principles which the Director will apply in carrying out Revenue functions in individual cases. Note that the Director will depart from those principles if she considers it appropriate in achieving her statutory objective. The guidance can be viewed on the Agency's website (www.assetsrecovery.gov.uk).

29 HMRC: Confidentiality of Information

29.1 Subject to certain specified exceptions relating to the functions of HMRC (and those at 29.2 below), officials of HMRC may not disclose information held by HMRC. All Commissioners and officers of HMRC must make a declaration acknowledging their duty of confidentiality as soon as reasonably practicable following their appointment. [CRCA 2005, ss 3, 18]. Officers of the Inland Revenue were required to make similar declarations. [*TMA 1970, s 6, Sch 1*].

As to production in Court proceedings of documents in the possession of HMRC or copies of documents previously submitted to HMRC which are held by a party to the proceedings, see *Brown's Trustees v Hay SCS 1897, 3 TC 598*; *In re Joseph Hargreaves Ltd CA 1900, 4 TC 173*; *Shaw v Kay SCS 1904, 5 TC 74*; *Soul v Irving CA 1963, 41 TC 517*; *H v H Fam D 1980, 52 TC 454*; *R v CIR (ex p. J Rothschild Holdings plc) CA 1987, 61 TC 178*; *Lonrho plc v Fayed and Others (No 4) CA 1993, 66 TC 220*.

29.2 By virtue of the vesting of the functions of the Board of Inland Revenue in the Commissioners for HMRC, HMRC are authorised to disclose information to the following (as were the Inland Revenue; and see also written reply in HC Official Report, 20 February 1990, col 685).

(*a*) **Charity Commissioners for England and Wales.** HMRC are authorised to disclose certain information to the Charity Commissioners regarding bodies which are or have been charities. Similar provisions apply in Scotland as regards disclosure to the Lord Advocate. [*Charities Act 1993, s 10; Law Reform (Miscellaneous Provisions) (Scotland) Act 1990, s 1*].

(*b*) **Department of Trade and Industry, Department of Employment or Office for National Statistics.** HMRC are authorised to disclose, for the purposes of statistical surveys, the names and addresses of employers and information concerning the number of persons employed by individual concerns. [*FA 1969, s 58; F(No 2)A 1987, s 69; ITEPA 2003, Sch 6 para 122*].

(*c*) **Tax authorities of other countries.** HMRC are authorised to disclose information concerning individual taxpayers where it is necessary to the administration or enforcement of double taxation agreements and may be required to disclose information to an advisory commission set up under the Arbitration Convention (*90/436/EEC*). [*ICTA 1988, s 816(1)(2A)–(5); TCGA 1992, s 277(4); F(No 2)A 1992, s 51(2); CRCA 2005, Sch 4 para 37*].

Disclosure may also be made to the tax authorities of other member states of the EU which observe similar confidentiality and use the information only for taxation purposes. [*FA 1978, s 77; EEC Directive 19 December 1977 No 77/799 EEC; FA 2003, s 197(1)–(5), Sch 43 Pt 5(1)*].

With effect from 19 July 2006, the UK may enter into agreements with other countries for mutual assistance in the enforcement of taxes. Such agreements may include provision for the exchange of information forseeably relevant to the administration, enforcement or recovery of any UK tax or foreign tax. HMRC may disclose information under such agreements only if satisfied that the confidentiality rules applied by the foreign authorities concerned with respect to the information are no less strict than the equivalent UK rules. [*FA 2006, s 173*]. This provision replaces similar powers to enter into tax information exchange agreements with other countries, which applied with effect from 28 July 2000 and were limited to income tax, capital gains tax and corporation tax, and foreign equivalents. Agreements made under those powers in force on 18 July 2006 are after that date treated as if made under the *FA 2006* powers. [*ICTA 1988, ss 815C, 816(2)(2ZA); FA 2000, s 146(1)(2); FA 2002, s 88(2)(3); FA 2003, s 198; FA 2006, s 173(8)–(10), Sch 26*

Pt 8(*2*)].The *FA 2006* powers also replace provisions for double taxation agreements to include arrangements for the exchange of information relating to the taxes covered by the agreement. Again, such arrangements in force under an agreement on 18 July 2006 are treated after that date as if made under the *FA 2006* powers. [*ICTA1988, ss 788*(*2*), *816*(*2*); *FA 2002, s 88*(*2*)(*3*); *FA 2003, s 198; FA 2006, s 173*(*8*)–(*10*), *Sch 26 Pt 8*(*2*)]. For agreements in connection with the EU Savings Directive and special withholding tax, see 19.9 DOUBLE TAX RELIEF.

See also 47.8 PAYMENT OF TAX.

(*d*) **Occupational Pensions Board.** HMRC are authorised to disclose information about pension schemes. [*Social Security Act 1973, s 89*(*2*)].

(*e*) **Social Security Departments.** HMRC may disclose information obtained in connection with the assessment or collection of income tax but for self-employed persons they may only disclose the fact that a person has commenced or ceased self-employment together with the identity of that person and information relating to earners employed by that person. [*Social Security Administration Act 1992, s 122*]. Information under this authority will be disclosed in connection with the tracing of absent parents liable to maintain lone-parent families receiving income support (Revenue Press Release 9 May 1990).

From 5 October 1999, HMRC may, and *must* if an authorised social security officer so requires, supply to the social security authorities information held for the purposes of tax credit functions (see Tolley's Income Tax under Social Security and National Insurance) (extended from 1 August 2002 to functions relating to child benefit or guardian's allowance) for use by those authorities for the purposes of functions relating to social security benefits, child support, tax credits, war pensions or prescribed evaluation or statistical studies. [*Tax Credits Act 1999, Sch 5 para 2; Tax Credits Act 2002, Sch 5 para 4; SI 2002 Nos 1727, 3036*].

From 2 July 1997, social security authorities are permitted to supply information to HMRC for investigative purposes. [*FA 1997, s 110; Tax Credits Act 1999, Sch 5 para 7; SI 1997 No 1603; Tax Credits Act 2002, Sch 5 para 13; SI 2002 No 1727*].

(*f*) After 13 December 2001 (but including information obtained before then),

- **organisations,** such as **the police, the National Criminal Intelligence Service and the National Crime Squad**, having a legitimate interest in, and capable of carrying out, criminal investigations and/or bringing proceedings for criminal offences: for the purposes of assisting criminal investigations or proceedings in the UK or elsewhere, including whether such investigations or proceedings should be initiated or brought to an end; and
- **the intelligence services**: for the purposes of facilitating the carrying out of their functions.

[*Anti-terrorism, Crime and Security Act 2001, ss 19, 20*]. See also Revenue Press Release 11 February 2002 and related voluntary Code of Practice on the Disclosure of Information.

Also, **the police**; to assist investigation into suspected murder or treason (*Royal Commission on Standards of Conduct in Public Life 1976, para 93*).

(*g*) **Non-UK resident entertainers and sportsmen.** In connection with the deduction of sums representing income tax from certain payments to such persons after 5 April 1987, HMRC may disclose relevant matters to any person who appears to HMRC to have an interest. [*ICTA 1988, s 558*(*4*)].

(*h*) (From 5 October 1999) as regards information held for the purposes of tax credit functions (see Tolley's Income Tax under Social Security) (extended from 1 August

2002 to functions relating to child benefit or guardian's allowance), a **local authority** (or authorised delegate) for use in the administration of housing benefit or council tax benefit. Information must also be provided in the opposite direction if the Board so require but only for use for purposes relating to tax credits etc. [*Tax Credits Act 1999, Sch 5 paras 4, 5; Tax Credits Act 2002, Sch 5 paras 7, 8; SI 2002 No 1727*].

(From 1 August 2002) as regards information held for the above-mentioned purposes, **Health Departments** for use for purposes of prescribed functions relating to health, relevant Government Departments for purposes of prescribed functions relating to **employment** or **training** (with provision also for certain information to pass in the opposite direction) and (as regards information held for child benefit and guardian's allowance functions only) any civil servant or other person for purposes of prescribed functions relating to provision of specified services concerning participation by young persons in **education and training**. [*Tax Credits Act 2002, Sch 5 paras 5, 6, 9, 10; SI 2002 No 1727*].

(*j*) **Financial Services Authority.** HMRC may authorise the disclosure of information to the Financial Services Authority or the Secretary of State for the purposes of investigations under *Financial Services and Markets Act 2000, s 168*. [*Financial Services and Markets Act 2000, s 350*]. Note that HMRC may only disclose information in this way if it was obtained or is held in the exercise of a function previously vested in the Inland Revenue. [*CRCA 2005, Sch 2 para 18*].

(*k*) **Assets Recovery Agency.** On or after 24 February 2003, HMRC may disclose information (including information obtained before that date) to the Director of the Assets Recovery Agency for the purpose of the exercise of his functions. [*Proceeds of Crime Act 2002, s 436; SI 2003 No 120*]. HMRC may also disclose information to the Lord Advocate and the Scottish Ministers in connection with the exercise of their functions in Scotland under *Proceeds of Crime Act 2002, Pt 3* and *Pt 5* respectively. [*Proceeds of Crime Act 2002, s 439*].

(*l*) From 6 April 2005, the **Financial Reporting Review Panel** or other person authorised under *Companies Act 1985, s 245C* (or NI equivalent) to apply to the court for a declaration that the annual accounts of a company do not comply with the requirements of that Act (or NI equivalent). HMRC may disclose information to such persons for the purpose of facilitating the taking of steps by that person to discover whether there are grounds for such an application or a determination by that person as to whether or not to make such an application. [*Companies Act, 1985, s 245C; Companies (Audit, Investigations and Community Enterprise) Act 2004, s 11; SI 2005 No 699*]. HMRC and the Financial Reporting Review Panel have entered into a memorandum of understanding governing the disclosure of information under these provisions. HMRC will only disclose information relating to accounting periods ending after 6 April 2005. See HMRC Internet Statement, 28 June 2005 and 2005 STI 1197.

(*m*) **Serious Organised Crime Agency**. From 1 April 2006, HMRC may disclose information to the Serious Organised Crime Agency for the purpose of the exercise of the Agency's functions. [*Serious Organised Crime and Police Act 2005, s 34; SI 2006 No 378*].

(*n*) **Certification of British films.** In relation to films commencing principal photography on or after 1 April 2006, HMRC may disclose information to the Secretary of State for the purposes of his functions under *Films Act 1985, Sch 1* (certification of films as British films for the purposes of film tax relief). Information so disclosed may be disclosed to the UK Film Council. [*FA 2006, Sch 5 para 24*].

Customs and Excise. Before the creation of HMRC on 18 April 2005, the Inland Revenue and Customs and Excise were authorised to disclose information to each other for the purpose of their respective duties. [*FA 1972, s 127*]. Following the merger, information acquired by HMRC in connection with one function may be used by them in connection with any other function. [*CRCA 2005, s 17*(*1*)].

Prosecutions. From 18 April 2005, HMRC are permitted to disclose information to the Revenue and Customs Prosecutions Office for the purpose of enabling the Office to consider whether to institute criminal proceedings in respect of a matter considered in the course of an investigation by HMRC or to give advice in connection with a criminal investigation. In relation to Scotland, HMRC are similarly authorised to disclose information to the Lord Advocate or a procurator fiscal. In Northern Ireland disclosures to the Director of Public Prosecutions for Northern Ireland are likewise permitted. [*CRCA 2005, s 21*].

29.3 From 5 October 1999, consequent upon the introduction of working families' tax credit and disabled person's tax credit (for which see Tolley's Income Tax under Social Security and National Insurance), the Board of Inland Revenue may pool the information they hold for the purposes of their functions relating to those tax credits and to tax, national insurance contributions, statutory sick pay, statutory maternity pay and certain functions under *Pension Schemes Act 1993* (and corresponding NI legislation). There is also provision for the exchange of information held for the purposes of functions relating to the aforementioned tax credits between the Board and persons providing services to the Board, for use in the exercise of those functions. [*Tax Credits Act 1999, Sch 5 para 1*]. From 1 August 2002, these provisions are extended to include functions relating to the working tax credit and child tax credit (see Tolley's Income Tax under Social Security and National Insurance), child benefit and guardian's allowance. [*Tax Credits Act 2002, Sch 5 paras 1, 2; CRCA 2005, Sch 4 para 91; SI 2002 No 1727*].

From 28 July 2000, information obtained by officers of the Board of Inland Revenue for the purposes of enforcing the *National Minimum Wage Act 1998* may be used for the purpose of any of the Board's other functions. Information obtained by other officers for similar purposes may likewise be supplied to the Board. [*FA 2000, s 148; CRCA 2005, Sch 4 para 80*].

From 18 April 2005, the above provisions are replaced by the general provision permitting HMRC to use information held or acquired in connection with one function in connection with any other function. [*CRCA 2005, s 17*(*1*)].

29.4 It is a criminal offence for a person to disclose tax information relating to an 'identifiable person' (as defined) held by him in the exercise of 'tax functions' or as a member of an advisory commission set up under the Arbitration Convention (*90/436/EEC*). '*Tax functions*' include functions relating to the General and Special Commissioners, HMRC, and the Board of Inland Revenue and its officers. This applies equally as regards HMRC's tax credit functions and social security functions. It does not apply if the person has (or believes he has) lawful authority or the information has lawfully been made available to the public, or if the person involved has consented. The maximum penalty for an offence is imprisonment for up to two years, a fine, or both. The above applies equally as regards national insurance contributions, statutory sick pay, statutory maternity pay and tax credits. [*FA 1989, ss 182, 182A; F*(*No 2*)*A 1992, s 51*(*3*); *FA 1995, Sch 29 Pt VIII*(*16*); *Government of Wales Act 1998, Sch 12 para 31; Social Security Contributions* (*Transfer of Functions, etc*) *Act 1999, Sch 6 para 9; Tax Credits Act 1999, s 12; SI 1999 No 527; Tax Credits Act 2002, Sch 5 para 11; SI 2002 No 1727; CRCA 2005, s 19, Sch 4 para 39*].

30 HMRC Explanatory Publications

30.1 HMRC EXPLANATORY PAMPHLETS

HMRC publish explanatory pamphlets (with supplements from time to time) on what were formerly Inland Revenue taxes. Those having a bearing on capital gains tax and corporation tax on chargeable gains are listed below, with the date of the latest edition in brackets, and are obtainable free of charge (except where otherwise stated) from local tax offices or from the internet (at www.hmrc.gov.uk). Alternatively, many can be ordered from the HMRC Orderline on 08459 000404 (or by fax on 08459 000604) or by post from PO Box 37, St. Austell, Cornwall PL25 5YN. HMRC have now withdrawn a substantial number of pamphlets and the information formerly contained in them is now available from their website.

CGT 1	Capital Gains Tax — An Introduction (December 2003).
CGT/FS1	Capital Gains Tax — A Quick Guide (July 2004).
IR 20	Residents and Non-residents: Liability to Tax in the United Kingdom (December 1999).
IR 46	Clubs, Societies and Voluntary Associations (January 2000).
IR 64	Giving to Charity by Business (September 2000).
IR 65	Giving to Charity by Individuals (November 2005).
IR 120	You and the Inland Revenue: Tax, Collection, NICs and Accounts Offices (September 2001).
IR 126	Corporation Tax Pay and File: A General Guide (July 1995).
IR 160	Inland Revenue enquiries under self-assessment (August 2004).
SA/BK4	Self-Assessment — A General Guide to Keeping Records (June 2003).
SA/BK8	Self-Assessment — Your Guide (June 2004).
CTSA/BK3	A Modern System for Corporation Tax Payments (September 2000).
CTSA/BK4	A General Guide to Corporation Tax Self-Assessment (October 2000).
SV1	Shares Valuation: An Introduction (March 2004).
COP 1	Putting things right when we make mistakes (June 2003).
COP 9 (2005)	Civil investigation of fraud (November 2005).
COP 10	Information and advice (April 1999).
COP 11	Self-Assessment — Local Office Enquiries (October 2004).
COP 14	Enquiries into company tax returns (April 2003).
AO1	How to complain about the Inland Revenue and the Valuation Office Agency (August 2001).

30.2 HMRC GUIDANCE MANUALS

The HMRC Guidance Manuals provide guidance to HMRC staff on the operation and application of tax law and the tax system and are also available to the public by inspection at any HMRC Enquiry Centre or on the internet (at www.hmrc.gov.uk).

References to the Capital Gains Manual are made throughout this book.

30.3 HMRC TAX BULLETIN

HMRC publish a bi-monthly Tax Bulletin aimed at tax practitioners and giving the views of HMRC technical specialists on various issues. The annual subscription is £22, and applications should be made to HMRC, Finance Division, Barrington Road, Worthing, West Sussex, BN12 4XH. Telephone enquiries can be made on 020–7147 2317. Tax Bulletin is also available on HMRC's website (free of charge).

30.4 HMRC HELPSHEETS

HMRC produce a number of free helpsheets designed to explain different aspects of the tax system and to assist in the completion of self-assessment tax returns. These can be ordered via the HMRC Orderline (Tel. 08459 000404, fax 08459 000604, between 8 a.m. and 10 p.m. seven days a week). Those concerned with capital gains tax are listed below.

IR 261*	Tax credit relief: capital gains (i.e. double tax relief).
IR 276	Incorporation relief
IR 277	Trusts with settlor interest: taper and losses
IR 278	Temporary non-residents and capital gains tax.
IR 279	Taper relief.
IR 280	Re-basing — assets held at 31 March 1982.
IR 281	Husband and wife, divorce and separation.
IR 282	Death, personal representatives and legatees.
IR 283	Private residence relief.
IR 284	Shares and capital gains tax.
IR 285	Share reorganisations, company takeovers and capital gains tax.
IR 286	Negligible value claims and income tax losses for shares you have subscribed for in unlisted trading companies.
IR 287	Employee share schemes and capital gains tax.
IR 288	Partnerships and capital gains tax.
IR 290	Business asset rollover relief.
IR 292	Land and leases, the valuation of land and capital gains tax.
IR 293	Chattels and capital gains tax.
IR 294	Trusts and capital gains tax.
IR 295	Relief for gifts and similar transactions.
IR 296	Debts and capital gains tax.
IR 297	Enterprise Investment Scheme and capital gains tax.
IR 298	Venture Capital Trusts and capital gains tax.
IR 299	Non-resident trusts and capital gains tax.
IR 301	Capital gains on benefits from non-resident and dual resident trusts.

* Supports foreign supplementary pages of self-assessment tax return; the remaining helpsheets support the capital gains supplementary pages.

HMRC have indicated that example 11 in the 2005/06 version of helpsheet IR 279 is incorrect. A corrected version has been published in HMRC Working Together Bulletin 25, May 2006.

30.5 HMRC WEBSITE

The HMRC website (at www.hmrc.gov.uk) has copies of, *inter alia*, recent press releases, extra-statutory concessions, statements of practice, consultative documents, HMRC Manuals, Tax Bulletins, explanatory pamphlets and helpsheets, as well as internet-only guidance.

30.6 TAX LAW REWRITE PROJECT

Tax law is being rewritten over a number of years in 'clearer and simpler language'. So far, the project has produced the following legislation: *CAA 2001*, *ITEPA 2003* and *ITTOIA 2005*.

31 HMRC Extra-Statutory Concessions

Below are summarised the concessions relating to tax on capital gains published by HMRC. Any concessions not yet designated by a formal prefix (see below) are summarised in date order at the end of the chapter. The full text of current extra-statutory concessions (at 31 August 2004) is published in an internet-only document on the HMRC website (www.hmrc.gov.uk). Copies of recently announced concessions are also available (with the relevant press release) on the website. In HMRC's document it is stated: 'The concessions described within are of general application, but it should be borne in mind that in a particular case there may be special circumstances which will need to be taken into account in considering the application of the concession. A concession will not be given in any case where an attempt is made to use it for tax avoidance'. See also 28.3 HMRC: ADMINISTRATION. Fuller coverage in context is normally given in the appropriate chapter referred to below. Except where the context otherwise requires, each concession relates to both individuals and companies. The full text of all current Extra-Statutory Concessions is reproduced in Tolley's Yellow Tax Handbook and Tolley's Tax Link.

See 3.25 ANTI-AVOIDANCE for the charge arising where concessions involving deferral of gains are abused.

D2 **Residence in the UK: year of commencement or cessation of residence.** Subject to conditions based on previous residence status, split year treatment is available to an individual becoming or ceasing to be UK resident partway through a tax year. See 52.3 RESIDENCE AND DOMICILE.

D3 **Private residence exemption: periods of absence (a).** Periods of absence are ignored where husband and wife are living together and the conditions are satisfied by the spouse who is not the owner. See 49.2 PRIVATE RESIDENCES.

D4 **Private residence exemption: periods of absence (b).** Resumption of occupation after certain periods of absence will not be necessary if the terms of his employment require the taxpayer to work elsewhere. See 49.2 PRIVATE RESIDENCES.

D5 **Private residence exemption** is extended to cover a residence disposed of by personal representatives and occupied before and after the death of the deceased as an only or main residence by an individual entitled to the whole or a substantial part of the proceeds of sale either absolutely or for life. Superseded by statutory provision for disposals after 9 December 2003. See 49.5 PRIVATE RESIDENCES.

D6 **Private residence exemption: separated couples.** If, as the result of a breakdown of the marriage, one spouse ceases to occupy the matrimonial home and later transfers it (or part of it) as part of a financial settlement to the other spouse who has continued in occupation, no gain will be chargeable unless election has been made for some other house to be the main residence of the transferring spouse. See 49.2 PRIVATE RESIDENCES.

D10 **Unquoted shares acquired before 6 April 1965: disposals following reorganisation of share capital.** Tax is not charged on a disposal of the entire new shareholding on more than the actual gains realised. See 7.10 ASSETS HELD ON 6 APRIL 1965.

D15 **Rollover relief: unincorporated associations.** Where property is held via the medium of a company in which at least 90% of the shares are held by the association or its members, the relief is available provided the other conditions are satisfied. See 55.5 ROLLOVER RELIEF.

D16 **Rollover relief: repurchase of the same asset.** An asset which is repurchased for purely commercial reasons after having been sold may be treated as the 'new asset' for the purposes of the relief. See 55.3 ROLLOVER RELIEF.

D17 **Unit trusts for exempt unit holders.** The exemption available to the unit trust is not withdrawn by reason of units being temporarily held by the trust's managers under the ordinary arrangements of the trust for the issue and redemption of units. Superseded by statutory provision for 2005/06 onwards. See 65.5 UNIT TRUSTS ETC..

D18 **Mortgage granted by vendor: subsequent default by purchaser as mortgagor.** In such circumstances and where the vendor regains beneficial ownership of the asset and so elects, the original sale is ignored and the chargeable gain arising is limited to the net proceeds obtained from the transactions. See 15.2 COMPUTATION OF GAINS AND LOSSES.

D21 **Private residence exemption: late elections in dual residence cases.** The two-year time limit will be extended in cases where the capital value of each of the residential interests, or each of them except one, is negligible and the individual was unaware of the possibility of electing. See 49.4 PRIVATE RESIDENCES.

D22 **Rollover relief: expenditure on improvements to existing assets.** Such expenditure is treated as incurred in acquiring other assets provided certain conditions are met. See 55.3 ROLLOVER RELIEF.

D23 **Rollover relief: partition of land and other assets on the dissolution of a partnership.** Partitioned assets are treated as 'new assets' for the purposes of the relief provided that the partnership is dissolved immediately thereafter. See 55.1 ROLLOVER RELIEF.

D24 **Rollover relief: assets not brought immediately into trading use.** The 'new asset' will qualify for relief even if not immediately taken into use for the purposes of the trade provided certain conditions are met. Land to be used for the site of a qualifying building will also qualify as the 'new asset' for the purposes of this concession subject to conditions. See 55.3 ROLLOVER RELIEF.

D25 **Rollover relief: acquisition of a further interest in an existing asset.** The further interest is treated as a 'new asset' for the purposes of the relief. See 55.3 ROLLOVER RELIEF.

D26 **Exchange of joint interests in land: form of rollover relief.** A form of rollover relief as on the compulsory purchase of land (see 38.11 LAND) is allowed on a disposal caused by the exchange of interests in land which is in the joint beneficial ownership of two or more persons. This relief is not confined to traders. The relief applies also to certain exchanges of milk or potato quota associated with such land. See 38.12 LAND.

D27 **Earn-outs.** *TCGA 1992, s 135* may be applied to a takeover which includes an 'earn-out' element. Superseded by *FA 1997, s 89*. See 58.5 SHARES AND SECURITIES.

D31 **Retirement relief: date of disposal.** If business activities continue beyond the date an unconditional contract is made, the date of completion will be accepted as the date of disposal. See 53.2 RETIREMENT RELIEF. Note that retirement relief is abolished for disposals in 2003/04 and subsequent years.

D32 **Transfer of a business to a company**. For the purposes of *TCGA 1992, s 162*, liabilities taken over by a company on the transfer are not treated as consideration so that no gain arises. See 33.10 HOLD-OVER RELIEFS.

D33 **Compensation and damages.** These are treated as derived from any underlying asset, and exempt or taxable accordingly, and as exempt if there is no underlying asset. See 6.1 ASSETS and 22.23 EXEMPTIONS AND RELIEFS.

D34 **Rebasing and indexation: shares held on 31 March 1982.** A single holding treatment will apply even if the shares were acquired on or before 6 April 1965. See 8.2 ASSETS HELD ON 31 MARCH 1982.

D35 **Employee trusts.** Concessional treatment will apply where an asset is transferred to a beneficiary who as a result suffers a Schedule E income tax charge. See 22.85 EXEMPTIONS AND RELIEFS.

D37 **Relocation of employees.** The exemption for a gain arising on the disposal of an employee's private residence is extended similarly to his right to share in any profits made by a relocation business or his employer to whom he sells property and which later sells it to a third party. See 49.2 PRIVATE RESIDENCES.

D38 **Loans to traders evidenced by qualifying corporate bonds.** A further concessional relief will apply in certain circumstances where the bonds concerned only became qualifying corporate bonds because of a change in definition, even though they are not evidenced by a qualifying loan. Obsolete as regards loans made on or after 17 March 1998. See 40.12 LOSSES.

D39 **Extension of leases.** No capital gains tax is payable where a lessee surrenders an existing lease and is granted, in an arm's length transaction (or equivalent), a new, longer lease on the same property at a different rent, but otherwise on the same terms. See 38.14 LAND.

D40 **Non-resident trusts.** The definition of 'participator' in *ICTA 1988, s 417(1)* is concessionally restricted for the purposes of *TCGA 1992, s 96* and specified provisions of *TCGA 1992, Sch 5*. See 44.9, 44.14 OFFSHORE SETTLEMENTS.

D42 **Mergers of leases.** Where a superior interest in leasehold land is acquired (being either a superior lease or the reversion of freehold), and the land is disposed of after 28 June 1992, indexation allowance on the expenditure incurred on the inferior lease will be calculated by reference to the date of its acquisition. See 38.13 LAND.

D44 **Re-basing and indexation: shares derived from larger holdings held at 31 March 1982.** In certain circumstances a valuation of a shareholding held or treated as having been held at 31 March 1982 can be calculated by reference to the size of the shareholding held by a spouse or group member at that date. See 8.7 ASSETS HELD ON 31 MARCH 1982.

D45 **Rollover into depreciating assets.** Where an asset employed in a trade carried on by a claimant to rollover relief ceases to be used due to the claimant's death, no charge to tax will arise under *TCGA 1992, s 154(2)(b)*. See 55.7 ROLLOVER RELIEF.

D47 **Temporary loss of charitable status due to reverter of school and other sites.** A temporary loss of charitable status will in general be ignored for tax purposes. See 10.3 CHARITIES.

D49 **Private residence exemption: short delay by owner occupier in taking up residence.** Restriction of relief is removed in certain circumstances where an individual acquires a property but does not immediately use it as his only or main residence. See 49.2 PRIVATE RESIDENCES. This replaces SP D4.

D50 **Compensation for loss or deprivation of property situated outside the UK** does not give rise to a chargeable gain in specified circumstances. See 9.1 CAPITAL SUMS DERIVED FROM ASSETS.

D51 **Close company transferring asset at undervalue.** An anti-avoidance provision is not applied in two sets of circumstances. See 3.17 ANTI-AVOIDANCE.

D52 **Share exchanges and company reconstructions: incidental costs of acquisition and disposal and warranty payments in respect of contingent liabilities.** Any such costs or payments are treated as allowable expenditure referable to the new holding of shares. See 58.4 and 58.6 SHARES AND SECURITIES.

D53 **TCGA 1992, s 50; Grants repaid.** Where a grant is repaid, and acquisition cost has been restricted by the amount of the grant, the consideration on disposal may be reduced by the amount repaid. See 15.6(*c*) COMPUTATION OF GAINS AND LOSSES.

The following income tax and corporation tax concessions are also relevant for the purposes of capital gains tax or corporation tax on chargeable gains.

A11 **Residence in the UK: year of commencement or cessation of residence.** Although there is no provision for splitting a tax year in relation to residence, liability to UK tax which is affected by residence is computed by reference to the period of actual residence in the UK during the year. See also D2 above. See Tolley's Income Tax.

A17 **Death of taxpayer before due date for payment of tax.** Personal representatives unable to pay tax before obtaining probate may have concessional treatment so that interest on tax falling due after the date of death runs from the later of the expiration of thirty days after the grant of probate and the statutory date for interest to run. See 37.7 INTEREST AND SURCHARGES ON UNPAID TAX.

A19 **Arrears of tax arising through HMRC delay.** Arrears of tax arising due to the HMRC's failure to make proper and timely use of information supplied will be waived in certain cases. See 47.10 PAYMENT OF TAX.

A78 **Residence in the UK — accompanying spouse.** Where an employee leaving the UK to work abroad satisfies the conditions of A11 above, the residence treatment of the employee may be extended to an accompanying spouse in certain circumstances. See 52.3–52.5 RESIDENCE AND DOMICILE.

A82 **Repayment supplement paid to individuals etc. resident in EC member states.** Residents of EC member states other than the UK will be treated on the same basis as UK residents in relation to a repayment supplement on a repayment of income tax. It is understood that this concession also applies to repayments of capital gains tax.

A94 **Profits and losses of theatre backers (angels).** Profits and losses of UK resident non-trading angels may be assessed and relieved under Schedule D, Case VI. See 40.17 LOSSES.

A99 **Tax treatment of compensation for mis-sold free standing additional voluntary contribution schemes.** Certain capital sums received by way of compensation are not regarded for capital gains tax purposes as the disposal of an asset. See 22.56 EXEMPTIONS AND RELIEFS.

B41 **Claims to repayment of tax.** Where an overpayment of tax arises because of an error by HMRC or another Government Department and where there is no dispute or doubt as to the facts, late claims to repayment of the tax overpaid will be allowed. See 47.10 PAYMENT OF TAX.

B46 **Late filing of company tax returns.** No flat-rate penalty will be charged if a return is received no later than the last business day within the seven days following the statutory filing date. See 48.4 PENALTIES.

C31 **Scientific research associations (SRAs).** Following changes announced on 4 September 1998 to the criteria for granting Government approval to SRAs, and to allow existing SRAs time to restructure accordingly, tax exemption is temporarily extended to SRAs which were approved or would have obtained approval under earlier criteria. See 22.57 EXEMPTIONS AND RELIEFS.

32 HMRC Statements of Practice

The following is a summary of those current Statements of Practice published by HMRC, which are referred to in this work.

Statements are divided into those originally published before 18 July 1978 (which are given a reference letter (according to the subject matter) and consecutive number, e.g. E11) and later Statements (which are numbered consecutively in each year, e.g. SP 5/02).

The full text of current statements of practice (at 31 August 2004) is published in an internet-only document on HMRC's website (www.hmrc.gov.uk). Copies of recently announced concessions are also available (with the relevant press release) on the website. The full text of all current statements is reproduced in Tolley's Yellow Tax Handbook and Tolley's Tax Link.

A8 **Stock dividends.** The interpretation of *ICTA 1988, s 251*(*2*) is clarified. See 58.9 SHARES AND SECURITIES.

A13 **Completion of return forms by attorneys.** In cases of age and infirmity of the taxpayer HMRC will accept the signature of an attorney who has full knowledge of the taxpayer's affairs. See 54.3 RETURNS.

B1 **Treatment of VAT.** The position of partly exempt persons is considered. See 35.3 INTERACTION WITH OTHER TAXES.

D1 **Part disposals of land.** Where part of an estate is disposed of, HMRC will accept that that part can be treated as a separate asset and the total cost apportioned accordingly (i.e. on an alternative basis to the usual part disposal formula). See 38.7 LAND.

D3 **Company liquidations: shareholders' capital gains tax.** Special rules can be applied where a shareholder receives more than one distribution in the liquidation. See 7.10 ASSETS HELD ON 6 APRIL 1965 and 58.11 SHARES AND SECURITIES.

D4 **Short delay by owner-occupier in taking up residence.** The period of occupation of a house will, in certain circumstances, include one year prior to taking up residence. This statement was replaced by ESC D49 on 18 October 1994. See 49.2 PRIVATE RESIDENCES.

D6 **Replacement of business assets: time limit.** Where land is acquired under a compulsory purchase order and leased back to the vendor, HMRC will, under certain conditions, extend the time limit for replacement. See 38.11 LAND.

D7 **Treatment of VAT.** See 35.3 INTERACTION WITH OTHER TAXES.

D10 **Termination of interest in possession in part of settled property.** HMRC will agree with the trustees what assets are to be identified with the termination. See 57.15 SETTLEMENTS.

D11 **Partnership: assets owned by a partner.** Rollover relief may be available. See 55.1 ROLLOVER RELIEF.

D12 **Partnerships.** This statement sets out a number of points on the capital gains tax treatment of partnerships (including limited liability partnerships) and of dealings between partners. It was revised in October 2002. See 46 PARTNERSHIPS.

D18 **Value-shifting: TCGA 1992, s 30, Sch 11 para 10(1).** These provisions do not apply when a farmer retires, leases the farm to his son, and sells the freehold, subject to the lease, to an outside investor. See 3.7 ANTI-AVOIDANCE.

D19 **Replacement of business assets in groups of companies.** To obtain rollover relief, HMRC do not insist that a company be a member of the group at the time of the transaction carried out by the other company. See 55.5 ROLLOVER RELIEF.

D21 **Time limit for an election for valuation on 6 April 1965 under TCGA 1992, Sch 2 para 17: company leaving a group: TCGA 1992, s 179.** See 27.9 GROUPS OF COMPANIES.

D23 **Overseas resident company.** The appropriate proportion of any overseas tax payable by a non-resident company is deductible in computing the gain chargeable on a UK participator under *TCGA 1992, s 13*. See 45.6 OVERSEAS MATTERS.

D24 **Initial repairs to property.** Such expense, including the cost of decorating, not allowable for Schedule A purposes, is regarded as allowable for capital gains tax purposes. See 15.4(*b*) COMPUTATION OF GAINS AND LOSSES.

SP 1/79 **Partnerships: extension of SP D12 above.** The practice whereby the capitalised value of an annuity paid to a retired partner is not treated as consideration for the disposal of his share in the partnership assets in certain circumstances is extended to cases where a lump sum is paid in addition. See 46.12 PARTNERSHIPS.

SP 8/79 **Compensation for acquisition of property under compulsory powers.** Any compensation for temporary loss of profits is taxable under Schedule D, Case I or II. See 9.1 CAPITAL SUMS DERIVED FROM ASSETS.

SP 10/79 **Power for trustees to allow a beneficiary to occupy a dwelling-house.** Depending upon the circumstances, this may be treated as giving rise to an interest in possession. See 57.13 SETTLEMENTS.

SP 14/79 **Unquoted shares or securities held on 6 April 1965: computation of chargeable gains where there has been a reorganisation of share capital.** See 7.10 ASSETS HELD ON 6 APRIL 1965.

SP 14/80 **Relief for owner-occupiers.** This statement explains the relief for owner-occupiers who let living accommodation in their homes. See 49.3, 49.8 PRIVATE RESIDENCES.

SP 18/80 **Securities dealt in on The Stock Exchange Unlisted Securities Market: status and valuation for tax purposes** (now obsolete). Such securities are not regarded as 'quoted' or 'listed' but are 'authorised to be dealt in'. See 41.5 MARKET VALUE.

SP 3/81 **Individuals coming to the UK: ordinary residence.** The ordinary residence position is further explained, regarding individuals coming to, or leaving, the UK who have, or acquire, accommodation for their use in the UK. See 52.4 RESIDENCE AND DOMICILE.

SP 8/81 **Rollover relief for replacement of business assets: trades carried on successively.** The Board's practice in deciding whether trades are carried on successively, how acquisitions in the interval between trades are to be regarded, and how this treatment is to be applied to groups of companies, is explained. See 55.4, 55.5 ROLLOVER RELIEF.

SP 5/83 **Use of schedules in making personal tax returns** (now obsolete). Schedules supporting a return are acceptable provided the taxpayer signs the official declaration and all material in the schedules is clearly linked to the official return form.

SP 1/84 **Trade unions: provident benefits** include legal expenses in connection with a member's accident or injury claim or unfair dismissal. See 22.60 EXEMPTIONS AND RELIEFS.

SP 6/84 **Leasing of mobile drilling rigs etc. by overseas residents.** HMRC indicate their practice. See 45.14 OVERSEAS MATTERS.

SP 7/84 **Exercise of a power of appointment or advancement over settled property.** HMRC indicate how they will decide whether a new settlement has been created. See 57.12 SETTLEMENTS.

SP 10/84 **Foreign bank accounts.** HMRC give their practice regarding direct transfers from one foreign bank account to another. See 22.5 EXEMPTIONS AND RELIEFS.

SP 5/85	**Division of a company on a share for share basis.** The special treatment accorded to a company reconstruction under *TCGA 1992, s 136* and *s 139* is extended to cover a division, for *bona fide* commercial reasons, of a company's undertakings into two or more companies owned by different sets of shareholders. For shares or debentures issued after 16 April 2002, a new definition of 'scheme of reconstruction' is introduced, partly to give statutory effect to this SP, which consequently no longer applies. See 3.18 ANTI-AVOIDANCE, 13.10 COMPANIES and 58.6 SHARES AND SECURITIES.
SP 5/86	**Rollover relief for employees and office-holders.** In certain circumstances relief is available to such persons where the land or building owned is in general use in the trade carried on by the employer. See 55.4 ROLLOVER RELIEF.
SP 5/87	**Tax returns: use of substitute forms.** HMRC states its requirements. See 54.3 RETURNS.
SP 2/88	**Civil tax penalties and criminal prosecution cases.** The Revenue explained a change of practice on seeking civil money penalties from certain taxpayers whom they have prosecuted. Statement withdrawn February 2006. See 48.26 PENALTIES.
SP 6/88	**Double taxation relief.** HMRC describe some situations where double taxation relief is available. See 19.7 DOUBLE TAX RELIEF.
SP 1/89	**Partnerships.** The practice concerning changes in partnership sharing ratios (see D12 above) is extended to cover the 1988 re-basing provisions. See 46.7 PARTNERSHIPS.
SP 4/89	**Company purchasing own shares.** HMRC's practice where a purchase gives rise to a distribution is explained. See 58.14 SHARES AND SECURITIES.
SP 5/89	**Capital gains re-basing and indexation: shares held at 31 March 1982.** A single holding treatment will apply if some shares were held on 31 March 1982 and the remainder are treated as held on that date. See 8.7 ASSETS HELD ON 31 MARCH 1982.
SP 6/89	**Delay in rendering tax returns: interest on unpaid tax.** The Revenue's practice is explained.
SP 1/90	**Company residence.** The Revenue's approach to the determination of a company's residence is explained. See 52.6 RESIDENCE AND DOMICILE.
SP 2/90	**Company migration: notice and arrangements under FA 1988, s 130.** Guidance is given on the procedure, information and arrangements HMRC will require under the provision. See 45.13 OVERSEAS MATTERS.
SP 5/90	**Accountants' working papers.** HMRC's investigatory powers as regards the disclosure of accountants' working papers are explained. See 23.8 FRAUDULENT OR NEGLIGENT CONDUCT.
SP 8/90	**Loans to traders evidenced by qualifying corporate bonds.** Loss relief will still be available where the security concerned ceases to have any value because it is redeemed early. See 40.11 LOSSES.
SP 2/91	**Residence in the UK: visits extended because of exceptional circumstances.** In deciding a person's residence status, days spent in the UK because of exceptional circumstances beyond the person's control will be ignored in certain cases. See 52.3 RESIDENCE AND DOMICILE.
SP 4/91	**Tax returns** (now obsolete). The principles adopted by the Revenue are explained.
SP 7/91	**Double taxation: business profits: unilateral relief.** The practice as regards admission of foreign taxes for unilateral relief is revised. See 19.4 DOUBLE TAX RELIEF.
SP 8/91	**Discovery assessments** (pre-self-assessment). The Revenue practice as regards the making of further assessments following 'discovery' is explained.

SP 10/91 **Corporation tax: a major change in the nature or conduct of a trade or business.** HMRC set out some of the circumstances which may amount to a major change in the nature or conduct of a trade for the purposes of, *inter alia*, *TCGA 1992, Sch 7A* (restriction of set-off of pre-entry losses where a company joins a group). See 27.28 GROUPS OF COMPANIES.

SP 17/91 **Ordinary residence in the UK.** The practice regarding the commencement of ordinary residence where the period to be spent in the UK is less than three years is explained. See 52.4 RESIDENCE AND DOMICILE.

SP 3/92 **Double taxation agreement with the USSR.** The Revenue clarified the position following the disintegration of the old Soviet Union. Superseded by SP 4/01. See 19.2 DOUBLE TAX RELIEF.

SP 4/92 **Capital gains tax re-basing elections.** HMRC describe the three kinds of disposal which will not be treated as the first relevant disposal for a re-basing election. See 8.3 ASSETS HELD ON 31 MARCH 1982.

SP 5/92 **Non-resident trusts.** HMRC give their views on a number of detailed matters in connection with: the residence of trustees; past trustees' liabilities; the settlor's right to repayment from the trustees; trusts created before 19 March 1991; transactions entered into at arm's length; close companies; transactions with wholly-owned companies; loans made to settlements; loans made by trustees; failure to exercise rights to reimbursement; administrative expenses; life tenants; indemnities and guarantees; variations; *ultra vires* payments; and intra-group transfers. See 44 OFFSHORE SETTLEMENTS.

SP 8/92 **Hold-over relief: valuation of assets.** The circumstances in which HMRC will require a valuation of assets in respect of which a claim to hold-over relief is made are described. See 33.1 HOLD-OVER RELIEFS and 53.2 RETIREMENT RELIEF.

SP 5/93 **Double taxation agreement with Czechoslovakia.** The Revenue clarified the position following the split of Czechoslovakia into separate Czech and Slovak republics. See 19.2 DOUBLE TAX RELIEF.

SP 6/93 **Double taxation agreement with Yugoslavia.** The Revenue clarified the position following the disintegration of the former Yugoslavia into separate republics. Superseded by SP 3/04. See 19.2 DOUBLE TAX RELIEF.

SP 9/93 **Corporation tax Pay and File: corporation tax returns** (now obsolete). The Revenue explain how its statutory powers were exercised in relation to corporation tax returns under Pay and File. See 54.18 RETURNS.

SP 10/93 **Corporation tax Pay and File: special arrangement for groups of companies** (now obsolete). For companies dealt with mainly in one tax district simplified procedures could operate regarding claims to group relief and giving consents to surrender such relief. Superseded by *Regulations* for accounting periods ending on or after 1 July 1999. See 54.18 RETURNS.

SP 11/93 **Corporation tax Pay and File: claims to capital allowances and group relief made outside the normal time limit** (now obsolete). The Revenue's power to exercise a discretion with regard to such late claims is explained. See now SP 5/01 for the position under self-assessment. See 54.18 RETURNS.

SP 13/93 **Compulsory acquisition of freehold by tenant.** HMRC will accept a rollover relief claim from a landlord whose tenant has exercised certain statutory rights to acquire the freehold reversion or extension of the lease. See 38.11 LAND.

SP 15/93 **Incidental costs of acquisition and disposal.** In certain cases, large companies may round these costs to the nearest £1,000. See 15.4 COMPUTATION OF GAINS AND LOSSES.

SP 4/94 **Enhanced stock dividends received by trustees of interest in possession trusts.** HMRC set out their view on tax treatment. See 58.9 SHARES AND SECURITIES.

SP 8/94 **Allowable expenditure: expenses incurred by personal representatives and corporate trustees under TCGA 1992, s 38(1)(b).** For deaths after 5 April 1993, a revised scale of expenditure is allowable for costs of establishing title in computing gains or losses of personal representatives on the sale of assets in a deceased person's estate. Now superseded by SP 2/04. See 18.8 DEATH.

SP 8/95 **Venture capital trusts: default terms in loan agreements.** Certain standard terms will be ignored in deciding whether a loan qualifies as a security. See 66.2 VENTURE CAPITAL TRUSTS.

SP 1/97 **The electronic lodgement service.** The Revenue provide details and procedures for filing self-assessment returns electronically. See 54.22 RETURNS.

SP 3/97 **Investment trusts investing in authorised unit trusts or open-ended investment companies.** HMRC express their views of the tax implications of such investment. Replaces SP 7/94 with effect from 18 July 1997. See 65.3 UNIT TRUSTS ETC.

SP 4/97 **Taxation of commissions, cashbacks and discounts.** No chargeable gain arises on receipt of a cashback. See 22.21 EXEMPTIONS AND RELIEFS. See Tolley's Income Tax for income tax consequences of the receipt of commissions, cashbacks and discounts.

SP 6/98 **EIS, reinvestment relief and venture capital trusts: loans to investors.** HMRC explain how they apply the rules which deny or withdraw the above reliefs where investors receive loans linked to their investments. Replaces SP 3/94. See 21.2(*g*) ENTERPRISE INVESTMENT SCHEME, 22.81 EXEMPTIONS AND RELIEFS and 66.7(*d*) VENTURE CAPITAL TRUSTS.

SP 1/99 **Self-assessment enquiries.** Where an enquiry into a personal, partnership or trust return remains open pending agreement of a CGT valuation, HMRC will not use the open enquiry to raise new issues which they would not otherwise have been able to raise. See 54.9 RETURNS.

SP 2/99 **Authorised unit trusts, approved investment trusts and open-ended investment companies — monthly savings schemes.** A simplified method of calculating the chargeable gain arising on a disposal can be used as regards acquisitions in accounting years of funds ending before 6 April 1999 where savings commenced before 6 April 1998. Replaces SP 2/97 which itself replaced SP 3/89. See 65.2, 65.3, 65.6 UNIT TRUSTS ETC.

SP 1/00 **Corporate venturing scheme: applications for advance clearance.** HMRC give guidance to potential qualifying issuing companies seeking advance clearance under the scheme. See 17.9 CORPORATE VENTURING SCHEME.

SP 2/00 **Venture capital trusts, EIS and corporate venturing scheme: value of gross assets.** HMRC set out their approach in applying the 'gross assets test'. Replaces SP 5/98. See 17.6 CORPORATE VENTURING SCHEME, 21.5 ENTERPRISE INVESTMENT SCHEME, and 66.3 VENTURE CAPITAL TRUSTS.

SP 3/00 **EIS, venture capital trusts, corporate venturing scheme and reinvestment relief: location of activity.** HMRC's interpretation of the requirement that qualifying trades for the purposes of the above reliefs must be carried on wholly or mainly in the UK. Replaces SP 7/98. See 17.7 CORPORATE VENTURING SCHEME, 21.6 ENTERPRISE INVESTMENT SCHEME, and 66.5 VENTURE CAPITAL TRUSTS.

SP 4/00 **Tonnage tax regime.** HMRC guidance on the practical operation of the regime. See 22.16 EXEMPTIONS AND RELIEFS.

SP 4/01 **Double taxation conventions with the former USSR and with newly independent states.** The position is updated, superseding SP 3/92 above. See 19.2 DOUBLE TAX RELIEF.

SP 5/01 **Corporation tax self-assessment: claims to loss relief, capital allowances and group relief made outside the normal time limit.** The circumstances in which HMRC will exercise their discretion with regard to such late claims are explained. See 54.18 RETURNS.

SP 1/02 **Corporation tax self-assessment enquiries.** Where an enquiry into a corporation tax return remains open pending agreement of a chargeable gains valuation, HMRC will not use the open enquiry to raise new issues which they would not otherwise have been able to raise. See 54.18 RETURNS.

SP 3/02 **Financial futures and options.** HMRC's views on the tax treatment of transactions in certain financial futures and options, with particular reference to whether such transactions are to be regarded as profits or losses of a trade or taxed under the chargeable gains rules. Replaces SP 14/91. See 6.7, 6.8 ASSETS.

SP 5/02 **Exemption for substantial shareholdings of companies.** HMRC guidance on the application of the anti-avoidance rule at 60.7 SUBSTANTIAL SHAREHOLDINGS OF COMPANIES.

SP 2/04 **Allowable expenditure: expenses incurred by personal representatives and corporate trustees under TCGA 1992, s 38(1)(b).** For deaths after 5 April 2004, a revised scale of expenditure is allowable for costs of establishing title in computing gains or losses of personal representatives on the sale of assets in a deceased person's estate. See 18.8 DEATH.

SP 3/04 **Double taxation convention with the former Yugoslavia.** The position is updated, superseding SP 6/93 above. See 19.2 DOUBLE TAX RELIEF.

SP 1/06 **Self-assessment — finality and discovery.** HMRC set out their views on finality of self-assessments and discovery following the decision in *Veltema v Langham*. See 5.2 ASSESSMENTS.

33 Hold-Over Reliefs

Cross-references. See 8.12 ASSETS HELD ON 31 MARCH 1982 for 50% relief etc. on held-over gains relating to an asset acquired before 31 March 1982; 9.2, 9.3 CAPITAL SUMS DERIVED FROM ASSETS for reliefs available where capital sums received as compensation are expended on restoration or replacement; 13.10 COMPANIES for the relief available on a scheme of reconstruction; 22 EXEMPTIONS AND RELIEFS generally; 22.81 EXEMPTIONS AND RELIEFS for reinvestment relief which could be used as an alternative to the reliefs in this chapter where a qualifying investment is made before 6 April 1998; 25.3 GIFTS for summary of special reliefs relating to gifts; 27.2 GROUPS OF COMPANIES for relief on disposals within a group; 38.8, 38.10, 38.11 LAND for reliefs available on small part disposals and compulsory purchase of land; 45.3 OVERSEAS MATTERS for transfer of UK branch or agency to UK resident company, 45.9 for transfers of assets to a non-UK resident company, 45.10 for transfer of trade between companies in different EC member states and 45.11 for transfer of non-UK trade between companies in different EC member states; 55 ROLLOVER RELIEF; 61.16 TAPER RELIEF.

33.1 RELIEF FOR GIFTS OF BUSINESS ASSETS AFTER 13 MARCH 1989

Where, after 13 March 1989,

(*a*) an individual ('*the transferor*') makes a disposal not at arm's length (e.g. a gift) of an asset specified below, and

(*b*) a joint claim for relief is made by him and the transferee, or, where the transferee is a trustee of a settlement, by him alone,

then, subject to *TCGA 1992, s 165(3)* below and the provisions in 33.5 below, the hold-over relief described below is to apply. [*TCGA 1992, s 165(1); FA 2000, s 90(1)*]. Note that the transferee need not be an individual and may, for example, be a company. See also 33.2 below re agricultural property and 33.3 below re settled property.

An asset is within (*a*) above if

(i) it is, or is an interest in, an asset used for the purposes of a trade, profession or vocation carried on by the transferor, his 'personal company' or a member of a 'trading group' of which the 'holding company' is his personal company), or

(ii) it consists of shares or securities of a 'trading company', or of the holding company of a trading group, where *either* the shares etc. are neither listed on a recognised stock exchange (within *ICTA 1988, s 841*—see 58.23 SHARES AND SECURITIES) nor dealt in on the Unlisted Securities Market (now closed) *or* the trading company or holding company is the transferor's personal company.

[*TCGA 1992, s 165(2); FA 1993, s 87, Sch 7 para 1, Sch 23 Pt III; FA 1996, Sch 38 para 10(1)–(3); FA 2000, s 90(3)*].

For these purposes, an individual's '*personal company*' is a company the voting rights in which are 'exercisable', as to not less than 5%, by that individual. ('*Exercisable*' means capable of being exercised, whether in fact exercised (*Hepworth v Smith Ch D 1981, 54 TC 396*).)

For 2003/04 onwards, '*trading group*', '*holding company*' and '*trading company*' have the same meanings for these purposes as they do for the purposes of taper relief. For 2002/03 and earlier years, they have the same meanings as they do for the purposes of RETIREMENT RELIEF (53.3). It should be noted that the taper relief definitions of 'trading group' and 'trading company' are more restrictive than were the retirement relief definitions in that the activities of the group or company must not include to a 'substantial' extent activities other than trading activities (as defined). In interpreting this, HMRC take '*substantial*' to mean 'more than 20%'. See 61.5 TAPER RELIEF for the full definitions and supporting notes.

'*Trade*', '*profession*' and '*vocation*' generally have the same meanings as in the *Income Tax Acts* but any UK property business or Schedule A business which consists of, or so far as it consist of, the commercial letting of FURNISHED HOLIDAY ACCOMMODATION (24) in the UK is treated as a trade for relief purposes; and, in determining whether for these purposes a company is a trading company, a '*trade*' includes the occupation of woodlands managed on a commercial basis by the occupier with a view to profit.

[*TCGA 1992, s 165(8)(9), s 241(3)(3A); FA 1993, s 87, Sch 7 para 1, Sch 23 Pt III; FA 1998, s 140(4)(6), Sch 5 para 62; FA 2002, Sch 8 para 3; ITTOIA 2005, Sch 1 para 441(3)*].

Nature of relief. Where there is no actual consideration for the disposal (as opposed to a deemed MARKET VALUE (41.1) consideration under *TCGA 1992, s 17(1)*), or where an actual consideration does not exceed the allowable expenditure within *TCGA 1992, s 38* (see 15.4 COMPUTATION OF GAINS AND LOSSES) relating to the asset, the effect of a claim is that the gain otherwise chargeable on the transferor and the transferee's acquisition cost are each reduced by the '*held-over gain*', i.e. the gain otherwise chargeable apart from taper relief and, where relevant, retirement relief (termed the '*unrelieved gain*') but subject to the reductions described below. Where actual consideration exceeds the allowable expenditure, the held-over gain is the unrelieved gain less that excess (see *Example 1* at 33.4 below) but again subject to the reductions below. (*Note.* Indexation allowance is deductible in arriving at the gain otherwise chargeable but it is not allowable expenditure within *TCGA 1992, s 38*.) [*TCGA 1992, s 165(4)(6)(7); FA 1998, Sch 27 Pt III(31)*]. See also 61.16 TAPER RELIEF.

HMRC consider that where assets are transferred between divorcing spouses under the terms of certain court orders, the spouse to whom the assets are transferred does not give actual consideration for the above purposes. The court orders concerned are orders for ancillary relief under the *Matrimonial Causes Act 1973* or similar orders under the *Family Law (Scotland) Act 1985* and orders formally ratifying an agreement reached by the divorcing parties dealing with the transfer of assets. This approach represents a change of view, and HMRC will apply it to claims made on or after, and claims unsettled on, 31 July 2002. (HMRC Capital Gains Manual CG 67192; Tax Bulletin August 2003 pp 1051, 1052).

Hold-over relief does not apply on a disposal if

- the disposal is a transfer of shares or securities after 8 November 1999 and before 6 April 2003 or after 20 October 2003 (see below), and the transferee is a company; or
- (for 2002/03 and earlier years) the gain arising is wholly relieved by RETIREMENT RELIEF (53); or
- (for 2002/03 and earlier years) the disposal is of shares or securities, and the 'appropriate proportion' of the gain is wholly relieved by retirement relief (see 53.8 RETIREMENT RELIEF); or
- the gain arises by virtue of *TCGA 1992, s 116(10)(b)* (disposal of qualifying corporate bonds derived from shares giving rise to deferred gain, see 50.3 QUALIFYING CORPORATE BONDS); or
- hold-over relief is available (or would be if a claim were made) under *TCGA 1992, s 260* in 33.7 below for gifts after 13 March 1989 on which inheritance tax is chargeable etc.

[*TCGA 1992, s 165(3); FA 1998, Sch 27 Pt III(31); FA 2000, s 90(4)(5); FA 2004, s 116, Sch 21 paras 3(3), 10(5)*].

The first exclusion above was inadvertently repealed for disposals after 5 April 2003, but was restored by *FA 2004*. It is confirmed by Revenue Tax Bulletin December 2000 p 815 that the exclusion does not apply to a transfer to a trust with a corporate trustee.

Hold-over relief claims must be made on a standard claim form (which can be found attached to HMRC Helpsheet IR 295). As they are usually bilateral claims, they cannot be made in the self-assessment tax return itself and will fall within the provisions of *TMA 1970, Sch 1A* (claims not included in returns — see 12.3 CLAIMS). A unilateral claim by a settlor will usually form part of his tax return. (Revenue Tax Bulletin April 1997 pp 417, 418).

In most circumstances, HMRC will admit a hold-over relief claim without requiring a computation of the gain, which would involve ascertaining the market value of the asset at the date of the transfer. Transferor and transferee must jointly request this in writing (for 1996/97 onwards, in the standard claim form — see above) and must provide, in particular, a calculation incorporating informally estimated valuations and a statement that the claimants are satisfied that the value of the asset exceeds the allowable expenditure plus any indexation allowance due. Once accepted by HMRC, a claim made on this basis cannot be withdrawn. In many cases, a formal valuation will never become necessary; in others, for example where the gain partially attracts retirement relief, valuation may still be deferred until a subsequent disposal of the asset by the transferee (or, in a retirement relief case, if and when the transferor makes a further gain attracting retirement relief). This practice applies equally to valuations on dates other than the date of transfer, where these are relevant to the computation of the gain. Where the asset was held by the transferor on 31 March 1982, then unless the transferee has paid *some* consideration, it will normally be necessary to agree a 31 March 1982 valuation only when the transferee disposes of the asset. (HMRC Statement of Practice 8/92). The informal valuations referred to above need not be made by an expert and are non-binding. (Revenue Tax Bulletin April 1997 pp 417, 418).

There is nothing in the legislation to deny relief if consideration for the use of the asset passes between an individual and a company, e.g. under a lease or tenancy agreement, and similarly there is no requirement that the individual need be a 'full-time working officer or employee' (see 53.3 RETIREMENT RELIEF). It is understood that HMRC will apply SP D11 (see 55 ROLLOVER RELIEF) *mutatis mutandis* for this hold-over relief as it applies to rollover relief (Tolley's Practical Tax 1990 p 143). As a claim applies separately to each asset, the comments made about the general relief for gifts from 1980 to 1989 in 33.9 below regarding the treatment of property as separate assets would seem also to apply to the above relief.

Where hold-over relief applies to a disposal the transferee may deduct for capital gains tax purposes on a subsequent disposal made by him any inheritance tax attributable to the value of the asset on the transfer to him which qualified for relief and which is either a chargeable transfer or a potentially exempt transfer which proves to be a chargeable transfer. The tax deductible may be varied on the subsequent death of the transferor within seven years or otherwise but it cannot in any circumstances give rise to an allowable loss on the subsequent disposal. [*TCGA 1992, s 165(10)(11); FA 2004, Sch 21 para 3(5)*]. See also 35.2 INTERACTION WITH OTHER TAXES.

Reductions in the held-over gain. If the qualifying asset disposed of was not used for the purposes of the trade, profession or vocation concerned throughout the period of its ownership by the transferor, the held-over gain is reduced by multiplying it by the fraction of which the denominator is the total period of ownership and the numerator the number of days in the period during which the asset was so used. (*Note.* In the determination of the period of ownership there is no exclusion of any period before 31 March 1982, cf. 55.6 ROLLOVER RELIEF.) Where the qualifying asset disposed of is a building or structure part only of which has been used for the trade etc. concerned over all or a 'substantial' part of the period of its ownership, the held-over gain is reduced as is 'just and reasonable'. [*TCGA 1992, Sch 7 para 4, para 5(1), para 6(1)*].

If the disposal of shares or securities of a company qualifies for relief and the company or group (as appropriate) then has 'chargeable assets' which are not 'business assets' and *either* at any time in the twelve months before the disposal the transferor could exercise 25% or more of the company's voting rights (as exercisable in general meeting) *or* the company is the personal company (see above) of an individual transferor at any time within that period of twelve months, the held-over gain is reduced by multiplying it by the fraction of which the denominator is the then market value of all of the company's or group's chargeable assets and the numerator is the then market value of the company's or group's business assets. In considering a group, a holding in the ordinary share capital of one group member by another is ignored, and if a 51% subsidiary is not wholly owned directly or indirectly by the holding company the values of its chargeable and business assets are reduced in proportion to the share capital owned; and for both purposes the expressions used are as in *ICTA 1988, s 838*. An asset is a '*business asset*' if it is or is an interest in an asset used for the purposes of a trade etc. carried on by the company or another group member, and an asset is a '*chargeable asset*' if a gain accruing on its disposal by the company or another group member would be a chargeable gain. [*TCGA 1992, Sch 7 paras 4, 7; FA 1993, s 87, Sch 7 para 1, Sch 23 Pt III*].

If, for 2002/03 and earlier years, the asset disposed of is a 'chargeable business asset' for the purposes of retirement relief (see 53.8 RETIREMENT RELIEF) and the held-over gain (as reduced under the above) would exceed the gain otherwise chargeable (ignoring hold-over relief itself but allowing for any deduction of retirement relief), the held-over gain is reduced by the amount of the excess. In the case of a disposal of shares or securities qualifying for retirement relief where the held-over gain (as reduced under the above) would exceed an amount equal to the 'appropriate proportion' of the gain otherwise chargeable (ignoring hold-over relief itself but allowing for any deduction of retirement relief), the held-over gain is reduced by the amount of the excess. [*TCGA 1992, Sch 7 paras 4, 8; FA 1998, Sch 27 Pt III(31)*].

33.2 **Agricultural property.** If an asset, or an interest in an asset,

(*a*) is 'agricultural property' within the inheritance tax provisions of *IHTA 1984, Pt V Ch II* and *either* qualifies for an inheritance tax reduction in value in relation to a chargeable transfer made simultaneously with the disposal *or* would so qualify if there were a chargeable transfer on the disposal *or* would so qualify but for *IHTA 1984, s 124A* (additional conditions for transfers within seven years before death of transferor) (assuming, where there is no chargeable transfer, that there were); but

(*b*) it fails to qualify for hold-over relief solely because the agricultural property is not used for the purposes of a trade etc. carried on as in 33.1(i) above,

then, notwithstanding (*b*) above, hold-over relief is granted to the individual transferor. Hold-over relief is also granted *mutatis mutandis* to trustees (see under settled property below) where the agricultural property would not otherwise qualify for relief solely because it is not used for the purposes of a trade etc. carried on as in 33.3(i) below. In these circumstances *TCGA 1992, Sch 7 para 4, para 5(1), para 6(1)* in 33.1 above do not apply. [*TCGA 1992, s 165(5), Sch 7 para 1, para 3, para 5(2), para 6(2)*]. Where development value over and above the agricultural value of the land is inherent in the property transferred, hold-over relief is available in respect of the whole of the gain, i.e. not just that part which reflects the land's agricultural value (Revenue Tax Bulletin November 1991 p 5).

33.3 **Settled property.** If

(*a*) trustees of a settlement make a non-arm's length disposal of an asset specified below, and

(*b*) a claim for relief under *TCGA 1992, s 165* is made by the trustees and the transferee or, if trustees are also the transferee, by the trustees making the disposal alone,

then, subject to *TCGA 1992, s 165(3)* (see 33.1 above) and the provisions in 33.5 below, hold-over relief given by *TCGA 1992, s 165(4)* (see 33.1 above) applies to the disposal.

An asset is within (*a*) above if

(i) it is, or is an interest in, an asset used for the purposes of a trade, profession or vocation carried on by the trustees making the disposal or a beneficiary who had an interest in possession in the settled property immediately before the disposal, or

(ii) it consists of shares or securities of a trading company, or of the holding company of a trading group, where *either* the shares etc. are neither listed on a recognised stock exchange (see 58.23 SHARES AND SECURITIES) nor dealt in on the Unlisted Securities Market (now closed) *or* not less than 25% of the voting rights as exercisable in general meeting are held by the trustees at the time of disposal.

Where hold-over relief is granted to trustees in this way, references to the trustees are substituted for references to the transferor in *TCGA 1992, s 165(4)(a)* above and *CGTA 1979, s 126C* in 33.5 below; and where hold-over relief is granted on a disposal deemed to occur by virtue of *TCGA 1992, s 71(1)* or *s 72(1)* (see 57.15–57.17 SETTLEMENTS and 33.5 below), no reduction in the held-over gain is made under *TCGA 1992, s 165(7)* in 33.1 above (reduction by excess of actual consideration over allowable expenditure). [*TCGA 1992, s 165(5), Sch 7 para 2; CGTA 1979, Sch 4 para 2; FA 1989, Sch 14 para 3(3); FA 1996, Sch 38 para 10(1)–(3); FA 2000, s 90(3); FA 2004, Sch 21 para 9*]. See also 33.2 above re agricultural property.

33.4 *Example 1 — partial consideration*

Zoë owns a freehold property which she lets to the family trading company, Sphere Ltd, in which she and her father each own half the shares and voting rights. Zoë inherited the property in April 1990 at a probate value of £50,000, and since then the whole of the property has been used for the purposes of the company's trade. In November 2006, Zoë transfers the property to her boyfriend. Its market value at that time is £115,000. The intention is that he should give sufficient consideration to leave Zoë with a chargeable gain exactly equal to the annual exempt amount (there being no other disposals in 2006/07). The indexation factor for the period April 1990 to April 1998 is 0.300.

Actual consideration should be £85,200 as shown by the following computation

		£	£
Deemed consideration			115,000
Deduct:	Cost	50,000	
	Indexation allowance £50,000 × 0.300	15,000	65,000
Unrelieved gain			50,000
Held-over gain (see below)			14,800
Pre-tapered gain			35,200
Taper relief £35,200 × 75% (business asset held at least 2 years)			26,400
Chargeable gain covered by annual exemption			£8,800

Computation of held-over gain

	£	£
Unrelieved gain		50,000
Actual consideration	85,200	
Less allowable expenditure (excluding indexation)	50,000	35,200
Held-over gain		£14,800

Notes to the example

(*a*) On a subsequent disposal of the property, the allowable expenditure would be £100,200 (deemed proceeds of £115,000 less held-over gain of £14,800). The actual consideration given does not enter into this calculation. No indexation allowance will be due as the expenditure was incurred after March 1998 (see 34.1 INDEXATION).

(*b*) If no part of the unrelieved gain were held over, business asset taper relief of 75% (see 61 TAPER RELIEF) would have been available on the full amount. As a result of the hold-over claim, taper relief is forgone on the amount held over; the transferee does not inherit the transferor's period of ownership. The availability and quantum of taper relief need to be taken into account in the decision-making. One consideration is whether the transferee's period of ownership and use of the asset are expected to be such as to obtain the maximum potential taper relief.

Example 2 — transfer of assets to a company, interaction with retirement relief

S has carried on his antique dealing business for 10 years. The assets of the business are valued as follows

	£
Freehold shop and office	140,000
Goodwill	40,000
Stocks	50,000
Debtors	9,500
Cash	4,500

Before the business began, S let the shop premises for one year. In October 2002, S transfers the business as a going concern to a company which he has formed with share capital of £1,000, held wholly by him. The transfer consideration is £1. At the time of the transfer S is 51. The gain arising in respect of the freehold is £55,000 and on goodwill it is £15,000 (both after deducting indexation allowance to April 1998).

		£	£
Gains eligible for retirement relief			
(£55,000 + £15,000)			70,000
Relief	£50,000 × 100%	50,000	
	£20,000 × 50%	10,000	60,000
Chargeable gain			£10,000

If S and the company jointly claim relief under *TCGA 1992, s 165*, part of the chargeable gain may be rolled over, as follows

	Freehold	Goodwill	
	£	£	£
Total gain	55,000	15,000	
Reduction for non-trade use [*TCGA 1992, Sch 7 para 5*] ($\frac{1}{11}$)	5,000		
	£50,000	£15,000	
Held-over gain before adjustment			65,000
Chargeable gain after retirement relief [*TCGA 1992, Sch 7 para 8*]			10,000
Excess			£55,000
Held-over gain (£65,000 – £55,000)			£10,000
Chargeable gain			Nil

Notes to the example

(*a*) There is no statutory formula for apportioning the held-over gain after retirement relief between different assets. The following is one possible method of computing the revised base costs in the hands of the company.

Freehold

Gain held over $\frac{55,000}{70,000} \times £10,000$	£7,857
Revised base cost (£140,000 – £7,857)	£132,143

Goodwill

Gain held over $\frac{15,000}{70,000} \times £10,000$	£2,143
Revised base cost (£40,000 – £2,143)	£37,857

(*b*) If S had transferred the business to the company in consideration for the issue of shares, *TCGA 1992, s 162* would have applied (see 33.10 below), but business assets relief under *TCGA 1992, s 165* would not. Retirement relief would still have applied in priority, so that the chargeable gain would have been £10,000. This gain would then have been rolled over against the base cost of the shares acquired by S. Alternatively, the *section 162* treatment could have been disapplied by election (see 33.11 below).

(*c*) If the chargeable gain, after retirement relief, of £10,000 were not held over, business asset taper relief of 75% would have reduced it to £2,500. As a result of the hold-over claim, taper relief is forgone. The availability and quantum of taper relief need to be taken into account in the decision-making.

(*d*) Retirement relief is abolished for disposals in 2003/04 and subsequent years (see 53.1 RETIREMENT RELIEF).

(*e*) In the hands of the company, the goodwill will not qualify for the special treatment of intangible assets of companies introduced by *FA 2002*, because it was acquired from a related party and was created before 1 April 2002 (by virtue of the business having been carried on before that date). See 14.13 COMPANIES—CORPORATE FINANCE AND INTANGIBLES.

33.5 **Restrictions on, and clawback of, hold-over relief under TCGA 1992, s 165, Sch 7 as applicable to disposals after 13 March 1989** *Gifts to non-residents.* The hold-over relief of *TCGA 1992, s 165(4)* in 33.1–33.3 above is not to apply where the transferee is neither resident nor ordinarily resident in the UK. It also does not apply where the transferee is an individual or, for disposals before 30 November 1993 (this date being the date of the coming into force of *FA 1994, s 249*; companies otherwise regarded as UK resident but under double tax relief arrangements already regarded as non-UK resident to be treated as non-UK resident for *Taxes Acts* purposes after 29 November 1993; see 52.6 RESIDENCE AND DOMICILE), a company if that individual or, for disposals before 30 November 1993, company, though resident or ordinarily resident in the UK, is regarded as resident elsewhere by virtue of DOUBLE TAX RELIEF (19.2) arrangements such that it would not under those arrangements be taxable in the UK on a gain arising on a disposal of the asset immediately after its acquisition. [*TCGA 1992, s 166; FA 1994, s 251(1)(7), Sch 26 Pt VIII*].

Gifts to foreign-controlled companies. Relief under *TCGA 1992, s 165(4)* is also denied where the transferee is a company which is controlled by a person who, or by persons each of whom, is neither UK-resident nor ordinarily resident and is connected (see 16 CONNECTED PERSONS) with the person making the disposal; and in determining a person's residence status, a person who either alone or with others controls a company by virtue of holding assets relating to that or any other company and who is UK-resident or ordinarily resident is regarded as neither UK-resident nor ordinarily resident if he is regarded under a double tax agreement as resident overseas in circumstances in which he would not be liable to a UK tax charge on a gain arising on a disposal of the assets. [*TCGA 1992, s 167*]. See *Foulser and another v MacDougall Ch D 2005, [2006] STC 311*, in which a complex avoidance scheme failed because of the application of this provision. The taxpayers' contention that the application of *section 167* to their case was incompatible with the EC Treaty was rejected by the Court.

Emigration of controlling trustees before 19 March 1991. If relief under *TCGA 1992, s 165* (formerly *CGTA 1979, s 126*) was given on a disposal of an asset to a company which was controlled by trustees of a settlement ('the relevant disposal') at a time when the person making the disposal was connected with the trustees, and at a time when the company had not disposed of the asset and the trustees still controlled the company the trustees became before 19 March 1991 neither UK-resident nor ordinarily resident (determined as above for *TCGA 1992, s 167*), then a gain equal to the held-over gain was deemed to accrue to the trustees immediately before the change in residence status. Provision was made for a corresponding reduction in the gain deemed to accrue to the trustees where before the change in residence status some of the held-over gain had been brought into charge on a disposal within the UK tax charge, e.g. on a part disposal, but this did not include a disposal under *TCGA 1992, s 171* (transfers within a group, see 27.2 GROUPS OF COMPANIES) or *TCGA 1992, s 172* (transfer of UK branch or agency, see 45.3 OVERSEAS MATTERS) although the first subsequent disposal of the asset to which neither of these provisions applied was taken into account as if it had been made by the company. If tax assessed on the trustees as a result of the above was not paid within twelve months of the date when it became payable, the transferor could be assessed, within six years after the end of the year of assessment in which the relevant disposal was made, and he was then given a right of recovery against the trustees. Where an amount was assessed in this way, the consideration deemed to have been given for the asset in question was no longer deemed to have been reduced by the amount of the held-over gain. [*CGTA 1979, s 126C: FA 1989, Sch 14 para 2; FA 1990, s 70(5)(9); FA 1991, s 92(1)(5)*]. For changes in residence status after 18 April 1991, see 44.2 OFFSHORE SETTLEMENTS.

Gifts into dual resident trusts. Hold-over relief under *TCGA 1992, s 165* is not available where the transferees are trustees who:

- for disposals on or after 6 April 2007, are resident and ordinarily resident in the UK; or

- for disposals before that date, fall to be treated as resident and ordinarily resident in the UK although the general administration of the trust is carried on overseas,

where, on a notional disposal of the asset by the trustees immediately after the disposal of it to them, the trustees would be regarded for double tax relief arrangements as resident overseas and as not liable to UK tax arising on the notional disposal. [*TCGA 1992, s 169; FA 2006, Sch 12 para 37*].

Where relief has been allowed under *TCGA 1992, s 165* in respect of a disposal made after 13 March 1989 and subsequently the trustees' circumstances become before 19 March 1991 such that a disposal to them would not then qualify for relief in view of the above, a clawback of relief under *TCGA 1992, s 168* (formerly *FA 1981, s 79*) (see under emigration of transferee below) is to have effect (subject to any previous clawback under that provision) as if the trustees had become neither resident nor ordinarily resident in the UK. [*FA 1986, s 58; FA 1989, Sch 14 para 6(4); FA 1991, s 92(4)(7)*]. For trustees becoming dual resident after 18 March 1991, see 44.2 OFFSHORE SETTLEMENTS.

Emigration of transferee. Subject to the exception mentioned below, a gain held over under *TCGA 1992, s 165* will be clawed back if the individual transferee concerned becomes neither resident nor ordinarily resident in the UK or if the transferee trustees concerned become neither resident nor ordinarily resident in the UK before 19 March 1991. If the transferee is an individual the clawback may be made within six years after the end of the year of assessment in which the disposal for which hold-over relief was claimed was made; otherwise (e.g. where trustees are the transferee) no time limit is specified. The charge, which is on a gain deemed to have accrued just prior to the cessation of UK residence and ordinary residence, is reduced to the extent that the held-over gain has already been taken into account in a disposal by the transferee (e.g. on a part disposal). For the latter purpose, a disposal does not include a no gain/no loss disposal between married persons or civil partners (see 42.4 MARRIED PERSONS AND CIVIL PARTNERS) under *TCGA 1992, s 58*. If such a transfer occurs, a disposal by the acquiring spouse or civil partner is treated as made by the spouse or partner who originally acquired the asset to which the held-over gain related. If not paid within twelve months from the due date of payment, tax on the deemed gain assessed on the transferee can be assessed on the transferor within six years after the end of the year of assessment in which the disposal for which hold-over relief was claimed was made, although the transferor then has the right to recover any tax so paid from the transferee.

Where a deemed gain relating to a previously held-over gain has been assessed under the above, then on a subsequent disposal of the asset in question the allowable expenditure relating to it is not reduced by the held-over gain.

An exception to the above clawback applies where the disposal for which relief was claimed was made to an individual, and

(*a*) the reason for his becoming neither resident nor ordinarily resident in the UK is that he works in an employment or office, all of the duties of which are performed abroad, and

(*b*) he again becomes UK-resident or ordinarily resident within three years of ceasing to be so, and

(*c*) in the meantime, the asset which is the subject of the hold-over relief has not been subject to a disposal by him in connection with which the allowable expenditure attaching to the asset, if the individual had been UK-resident, would have been reduced by the held-over gain; for this purpose the same provisions as above for inter-spouse transfers apply.

Where (*a*) applies, and (*b*) and (*c*) *may* apply, no assessment under the main provisions outlined above will be made before the end of the three-year period.

[*TCGA 1992, s 168; FA 1991, s 92(2)(6); SI 2005 No 3229, Reg 112*].

For changes of residence of trustees after 18 March 1991, see 44.2 OFFSHORE SETTLEMENTS.

Clawback of relief on life tenant's death. The exemption otherwise available for gains arising on deemed disposals under *TCGA 1992, s 71*(*1*) or *s 72*(*1*)(*a*) on the death of a life tenant etc. (see 57.15–57.17 SETTLEMENTS) does not apply to an asset (or part asset) where a claim for hold-over relief was made under *TCGA 1992, s 165* in relation to an original disposal of that asset after 13 March 1989 to the trustees. Any chargeable gain accruing to the trustees will, however, be restricted to the held-over gain (or corresponding part) on the original disposal of the asset. Where the life tenant's interest was in part only of the settled property, and that property is subject to a deemed disposal under *TCGA 1992, s 71(1)*, the clawback is proportional to the life tenant's interest. [*TCGA 1992, s 74*]. By analogy with the position when *FA 1980, s 79* (general relief for gifts) was extant before 14 March 1989, it seems to be possible for the trustees to claim hold-over relief under *TCGA 1992, s 165* (provided all the conditions are met) in respect of any gain arising from this clawback provision (Tolley's Practical Tax 1983 p 142). Alternatively, if the termination of the life interest is a chargeable transfer for inheritance tax purposes, hold-over relief can be claimed under 33.7 below (HMRC Capital Gains Manual CG 33552).

Limited liability partnerships (*LLPs*). Where, at a time after 2 May 2001 when the transparency treatment afforded by *TCGA 1992, s 59A*(*1*) ceases to apply to an LLP (see 46.19 PARTNERSHIPS) (for example, by virtue of its going into liquidation), a member of the LLP holds an asset whose CGT acquisition cost is reduced by a gain held over under *TCGA 1992, s 165* on a disposal to a partnership, a chargeable gain equal to the amount of the reduction is treated as accruing to the member immediately before that time. [*TCGA 1992, s 169A; FA 2001, s 75*(*3*)(*5*)]. In the absence of such a rule, the held-over gain would have fallen out of charge as a result of the tax treatment of an LLP in liquidation.

Exemptions relating to substantial shareholdings of companies. Where a company disposes of an asset whose CGT acquisition cost is reduced by a gain previously held over under *TCGA 1992, s 165*, and, by virtue of the provisions of *TCGA 1992, Sch 7AC*, any gain on the disposal would otherwise be exempt, the held-over gain, or an appropriate proportion of it, is treated as accruing to the company at that time (see 60.22 SUBSTANTIAL SHAREHOLDINGS OF COMPANIES).

Gifts to settlor-interested settlements. Hold-over relief under *TCGA 1992, s 165* is not available in the case of a disposal (the '*relevant disposal*') to the trustees of a settlement after 9 December 2003 if either

(*a*) there is a 'settlor' who has an interest in the settlement (or an 'arrangement' subsists under which such an interest will or may be acquired by a settlor) immediately after the making of the relevant disposal or at any time in the 'clawback period', or

(*b*) the following conditions are met:

- disregarding any hold-over relief, a chargeable gain would accrue to the transferor on the relevant disposal,
- in computing that gain, the allowable expenditure would be reduced in consequence, directly or indirectly, of a claim under *TCGA 1992, s 165* or *TCGA 1992, s 260* (see 33.7 below) in respect of an earlier disposal by an individual (whether or not to the transferor), and

- that individual has an interest in the settlement (or an arrangement subsists under which such an interest will or may be acquired by him) immediately after the making of the relevant disposal or at any time in the 'clawback period'.

Where neither of the above conditions are met immediately after the relevant disposal and relief under *section 165* is claimed (and the claim is not revoked), if either of the conditions are subsequently met at a time during the clawback period, then a chargeable gain is treated as accruing to the transferor at the first such time (the '*material time*') of an amount equal to the held-over gain under *section 165*. This does not apply if the transferor is an individual who has died before the material time. Where the relief is clawed back in this way, the chargeable gains and allowable losses of the trustees or of any person whose title to any property derives to any extent from them (whether directly or indirectly) are determined on the basis that *section 165* never applied to the relevant disposal. Any necessary adjustments can be made to give effect to these provisions, whether by assessment, discharge or repayment of tax or otherwise, notwithstanding any time limits for the making of such adjustments.

For these purposes, a person is a '*settlor*' in relation to a settlement if he is an individual and the settled property consists of or includes property originating from him. Property originates from a settlor where he provides it directly or indirectly for the purposes of the settlement (including property provided by another person under reciprocal 'arrangements') and where property represents such property (or a part thereof) or accumulated income from such property. '*Arrangements*' include any scheme, agreement or understanding, whether or not legally enforceable.

A settlor has an interest in a settlement if

(i) any property which may at any time be comprised in the settlement or any 'derived property' is, or will or may become, payable to or applicable for the benefit of the settlor or his spouse or civil partner in any circumstances whatsoever, or

(ii) the settlor, or his spouse or civil partner, enjoys a benefit deriving directly or indirectly from any property which is comprised in the settlement or any derived property.

At any time after 5 April 2006 (but see below), a settlor also has an interest in a settlement if

(iii) any property which is or may at any time be comprised in the settlement or any derived property is, or will or may become, payable to or applicable for the benefit of a child of the settlor at any time when that child is a 'dependent child' of his, in any circumstances whatsoever, or

(iv) a dependent child of the settlor enjoys a benefit deriving directly or indirectly from any property which is comprised in the settlement or any derived property.

Where the relevant disposal is made before 6 April 2006, a settlement is not, however, treated as becoming settlor-interested during the clawback period by virtue of (iii) or (iv) above.

A '*dependent child*' of the settlor is, for this purpose, a child or stepchild under the age of 18 who is unmarried and does not have a civil partner.

References to the spouse or civil partner of the settlor in (i) and (ii) above do not include a spouse or civil partner from whom the settlor is separated under a court order, separation agreement or in circumstances such that the separation is likely to be permanent, or the widow, widower or surviving civil partner of the settlor. No account is taken of a term of the settlement relating to dependent children of the settlor at any time when he has no such children.

A settlor does not have an interest under (i) above if and so long as none of the property which may at any time be comprised in the settlement and no derived property can become applicable or payable as mentioned in (i) above except in the event of:

- in the case of a marriage settlement or civil partnership settlement, the death of both the parties to the marriage or partnership and all or any of the children of one or both of the parities to the marriage or partnership (for disposals before 5 December 2005, all or any of the children of the marriage); or
- the death of a child of the settlor who had become beneficially entitled to the property or any derived property at an age not exceeding 25.

For these purposes, 'derived property' in relation to any property means income from that property or any property directly or indirectly representing proceeds of, or proceeds of income from, that property or income therefrom.

The above provisions do not apply to a disposal to trustees of a maintenance fund for an historic building if they have elected under *ICTA 1988, s 691(2)* that income arising under the settlement or part of the settlement involved is not to be treated as income of the settlor for the tax year in which the disposal is made.

The above provisions also do not apply if, immediately after the making of the relevant disposal,

(A) the settled property is held on trusts which secure that, during the lifetime of a 'disabled person',

- not less than half of the property which is applied, is applied for the benefit of the person concerned, and
- that person is entitled to not less than half of the income arising from the property, or no such income may be applied for the benefit of any other person, or no interest in possession subsists in the settled property; and

(B) if one or more settlors has an interest in the settlement (disregarding any interest arising because of a spouse, civil partner or dependent child) or will or may acquire such an interest under subsisting arrangements, each such settlor is a disabled person and a beneficiary (or would be a beneficiary if he had the interest acquirable under the arrangements).

A '*disabled person*' is either a 'mentally disabled person' or a person in receipt of 'attendance allowance' or of a 'disability living allowance' by virtue of entitlement to the care component at the highest or middle rate. '*Mentally disabled person*' means a person who, by reason of mental disorder within the meaning of *Mental Health Act 1983*, is incapable of administering his property or managing his affairs.

'*Attendance allowance*' means an allowance under *Social Security Contributions and Benefits Act 1992, s 64* or *Social Security Contributions and Benefits (Northern Ireland) Act 1992, s 64*.

'*Disability living allowance*' means a disability living allowance under *Social Security Contributions and Benefits Act 1992, s 71* or *Social Security Contributions and Benefits (Northern Ireland) Act 1992, s 71*.

Condition (A) above is not treated as not met by reason only of powers of advancement conferred on the trustees under *Trustee Act 1925, s 32* or *Trustee Act (Northern Ireland) 1958, s 33*. Where the income from the settled property is held for the benefit of a person on protective trusts, as under *Trustee Act 1925, s 33*, the reference in (A) above to the lifetime of a person is to be construed as a reference to the period during which the income is so held.

An HMRC officer may require by notice a trustee, a beneficiary or a settlor (or the spouse or civil partner of a settlor or a person who has been the spouse or civil partner of a settlor at any time after the making of the relevant disposal) to give him such particulars as he thinks necessary for the purposes of the above provisions within such time as he may direct, not being less than 28 days.

[*TCGA 1992, ss 169B–169G; FA 2004, s 116, Sch 21 paras 4, 10(4); FA 2006, Sch 12 paras 4, 19; SI 2005 No 3229, Regs 113–115*].

See also 25.4 GIFTS for the recovery by the trustees from the transferor of tax paid in respect of the deemed chargeable gain arising under the clawback provisions above, 47.6 PAYMENT OF TAX for payment of tax on such a gain by instalments and 61.15 regarding TAPER RELIEF.

33.6 RELIEF FOR GIFTS OF BUSINESS ASSETS BEFORE 14 MARCH 1989

If an individual ('*the transferor*') made a disposal before 14 March 1989 not at arm's length (e.g. a gift) to a person resident or ordinarily resident in the UK ('*the transferee*') of

(*a*) an asset which was, or was an interest in, an asset which was used for the purposes of a trade, profession or vocation carried on by the transferor or by a company which was his 'family company' (as defined), or

(*b*) shares or securities of a 'trading company' (as defined) which was the transferor's family company,

then, subject to certain exceptions, hold-over relief applied on a joint claim made by the transferor and transferee. The relief operated, as with other hold-over reliefs, by reducing the gain otherwise chargeable on the transferor and the transferee's acquisition cost by the held-over gain. Hold-over relief could also be claimed in certain circumstances where a trustee was deemed under *TCGA 1992, s 71(1)* (see 57.15 and 57.17 SETTLEMENTS) after 5 April 1982 to have disposed of, and immediately reacquired a business asset.

As a result of the availability of the general relief for gifts in 33.9 below, the rules relating specifically to gifts of business assets were of restricted application for gifts after 5 April 1980 and before 14 March 1989. None of the provisions in 33.5 above applied to the hold-over relief described above.

[*CGTA 1979, s 126, Sch 4*].

33.7 GIFTS ON WHICH INHERITANCE TAX IS CHARGEABLE ETC. AFTER 13 MARCH 1989

After 13 March 1989, if

(*a*) an individual or trustees ('the transferor') make a disposal within (i)–(vii) below of an asset,

(*b*) the asset is acquired by an individual or trustees ('the transferee'), and

(*c*) a claim for relief is made by the transferor and transferee or, where trustees are the transferee, by the transferor alone,

then, subject to the conditions below and in 33.8 below, hold-over relief is available as under *TCGA 1992, s 260(3)* below. [*TCGA 1992, s 260(1); FA 2000, s 90(2); FA 2004, Sch 21 para 5(2)*].

A disposal is within (*a*) above if it is made otherwise than under a bargain at arm's length (e.g. a gift) and it

(i) is a chargeable transfer within *IHTA 1984* (or would be but for annual exemptions under *IHTA 1984, s 19*) and is not a potentially exempt transfer within the meaning of *IHTA 1984*, or

(ii) is an exempt transfer by virtue of *IHTA 1984, s 24, s 27* or *s 30* (political parties, maintenance funds for historic buildings (see also 22.78 EXEMPTIONS AND RELIEFS) and designated property), or, for gifts before 16 March 1998, *IHTA 1984, s 26* (gifts for public benefit — see also 22.28 EXEMPTIONS AND RELIEFS), or

(iii) is a disposition to which *IHTA 1984, s 57A* applies and by which the property disposed of becomes held on trusts referred to in *IHTA 1984, s 57A(1)(b)* (maintenance funds for historic buildings), or

(iv) by virtue of *IHTA 1984, s 71(4)* (accumulation and maintenance trusts where property settled before 22 March 2006) does not constitute an occasion on which tax is chargeable under that provision, or

(v) by virtue of *IHTA 1984, s 71B(2)* (trusts for bereaved minors) does not constitute an occasion on which tax is chargeable under that provision, or

(vi) by virtue of *IHTA 1984, s 71E(2)* (age 18 to 25 trusts) does not constitute an occasion on which tax is chargeable under that provision, or

(vii) by virtue of *IHTA 1984, s 78(1)* (works of art etc., see also 22.37 and 22.80 EXEMPTIONS AND RELIEFS) does not constitute an occasion on which tax is chargeable under *IHTA 1984, Pt III Ch III*, or

(viii) is a disposal of an asset comprised in a settlement where, as a result of the asset or part of it becoming comprised in another settlement, there is no charge, or a reduced charge, to inheritance tax by virtue of *IHTA 1984, Sch 4 para 9, para 16* or *para 17* (maintenance funds for historic buildings).

[*TCGA 1992, s 260(2); FA 1998, Sch 27 Pt IV; FA 2006, Sch 20 para 32*].

The '*held-over gain*' on a disposal is the chargeable gain otherwise accruing and relief is given by deducting this amount from the gain otherwise accruing to the transferor and from the consideration otherwise regarded as being given by the transferee. [*TCGA 1992, s 260(3)(4)*].

Hold-over relief is reduced or eliminated to nil on a disposal where there is actual consideration (as opposed to any deemed MARKET VALUE (41) consideration) which exceeds the allowable expenditure under *TCGA 1992, s 38* (see 15.4 COMPUTATION OF GAINS AND LOSSES), any such excess being deducted from the held-over gain; but no deduction is made of any such excess where *TCGA 1992, s 260(3)* above applies to a deemed disposal under *TCGA 1992, s 71(1)* or *s 72(1)* (see 57.15–57.17 SETTLEMENTS). (*Note.* Indexation allowance is deductible in arriving at the gain otherwise chargeable but it is not allowable expenditure within *TCGA 1992, s 38.*) Before 2003/04, where part of a gain is relieved by RETIREMENT RELIEF (53), the held-over gain is reduced by so much, if any, of the excess of actual consideration over allowable expenditure as exceeds the part so relieved. [*TCGA 1992, s 260(5)(9); FA 1998, Sch 27 Pt III(31)*].

Hold-over relief does not apply to a disposal if it arises by virtue of *TCGA 1992, s 116(10)(b)* (disposal of qualifying corporate bonds derived from shares giving rise to deferred gain, see 50.3 QUALIFYING CORPORATE BONDS). [*TCGA 1992, s 260(6)*].

Before 6 April 2004, *section 260* included provisions denying hold-over relief for any gain accruing in accordance with *TCGA 1992, Sch 5B paras 4, 5* (crystallisation of a deferred gain on the happening of a chargeable event in relation to enterprise investment scheme shares, see 21 ENTERPRISE INVESTMENT SCHEME) or *TCGA 1992, Sch 5C paras 4, 5* (crystallisation of a deferred gain on the happening of a chargeable event in relation to venture capital trust shares, see 66.12 VENTURE CAPITAL TRUSTS). These provisions were considered to be unnecessary, as such gains were not gains accruing on the disposal of an asset as required by *section 260(1)* (see above) and were accordingly repealed by *FA 2004*. [*TCGA 1992, s 260(6A)(6B); FA 1995, s 72(6)(8), Sch 13 para 4(2); FA 2004, Sch 21 paras 5(3)(4), 10(8)*].

Where hold-over relief is claimed, or could have been claimed, on a transfer within (i) above, the transferee may deduct for capital gains tax purposes on a subsequent disposal made by him any inheritance tax attributable to the value of the asset on the transfer to him which qualified for hold-over relief. The tax deductible may be varied if the inheritance tax itself is varied but it cannot in any circumstances give rise to an allowable loss. [*TCGA 1992, s 260(7)(8); FA 2004, Sch 21 para 5(5)*]. See also 35.2 INTERACTION WITH OTHER TAXES.

Where a disposal is only partly within (i)–(vii) above, or is a disposal within (viii) above on which there is a reduced charge as mentioned therein, the foregoing provisions apply to an appropriate part of the disposal. [*TCGA 1992, s 260(10)*].

As a claim applies separately to each asset, the comments made about the general relief for gifts from 1980 to 1989 in 33.9 below regarding the treatment of property as separate assets would seem also to apply to the above relief.

See 49.7 PRIVATE RESIDENCES for the exclusion from relief under *TCGA 1992, s 223* where relief is claimed under the above provisions.

33.8 **Restrictions on, and clawback of, hold-over relief under TCGA 1992, s 260** *Gifts to non-residents.* Relief is denied under *TCGA 1992, s 260* where the transferee is neither UK-resident nor ordinarily resident. Relief is also denied where the transferee is an individual who though UK-resident or ordinarily resident is regarded under a double tax agreement as resident overseas in circumstances where he would not be liable to a UK tax charge on a gain arising on a disposal of an asset immediately after its acquisition. [*TCGA 1992, s 261*].

Gifts into dual resident trusts. TCGA 1992, s 169 (see 33.5 above) operates, with appropriate modifications, for hold-over relief claimed under *TCGA 1992, s 260* in respect of gifts after 13 March 1989 as it does for hold-over relief under *TCGA 1992, s 165* in respect of gifts made after that date. [*TCGA 1992, s 169*].

Emigration of transferee. TCGA 1992, s 168 (see 33.5 above) operates, with appropriate modifications, for hold-over relief claimed under *TCGA 1992, s 260* in respect of gifts after 13 March 1989 as it does for hold-over relief under *TCGA 1992, s 165* in respect of gifts made after that date. [*TCGA 1992, s 168*].

Clawback of relief on life tenant's death. TCGA 1992, s 74 (see 33.5 above) operates, with appropriate modifications, for hold-over relief claimed under *TCGA 1992, s 260* in respect of gifts after 13 March 1989 as it does for hold-over relief under *TCGA 1992, s 165* in respect of gifts made after that date. [*TCGA 1992, s 74*].

Limited liability partnerships (LLPs). Clawback under *TCGA 1992, s 169A* (see 33.5 above) applies in relation to hold-over relief under *TCGA 1992, s 260* as it does in relation to hold-over relief under *TCGA 1992, s 165.*

Gifts to settlor-interested settlements. TCGA 1992, ss 169B–169G (see 33.5 above) apply to hold-over relief under *TCGA 1992, s 260* as they apply to relief under *TCGA 1992, s 165.*

33.9 GENERAL RELIEF FOR GIFTS FROM 1980 TO 1989

A general relief for gifts by individuals applied after 5 April 1980 and before 14 March 1989. It applied also for gifts by trustees after 5 April 1982.

The effect of the relief was that the gain otherwise chargeable (less any RETIREMENT RELIEF (53)), and the transferee's acquisition cost, were each reduced by the '*held-over gain*', i.e. the gain otherwise chargeable (less any retirement relief) less any excess of actual consideration over the aggregate of allowable expenditure within *TCGA 1992, s 38* and any retirement relief.

In computing any chargeable gain accruing on the subsequent disposal of the asset, the transferee may deduct any inheritance tax (or capital transfer tax) attributable to the value of the asset on the original transfer, being either a chargeable transfer or a potentially exempt transfer which proves to be a chargeable transfer. The tax deductible may be varied on the subsequent death of the original transferor or otherwise but cannot create an allowable loss on the subsequent disposal. See also 35.2 INTERACTION WITH OTHER TAXES.

Emigration of transferee. TCGA 1992, s 168 (see 33.5 above) operated (and continues to operate after 13 March 1989) *mutatis mutandis* for hold-over relief claimed under the above provisions in respect of gifts made after 5 April 1981 and before 14 March 1989 as it does to hold-over relief under *TCGA 1992, s 165* in respect of gifts made after 13 March 1989.

Clawback of relief on life tenant's death. TCGA 1992, s 74 (see 33.5 above) operated (and continues to operate after 13 March 1989) *mutatis mutandis* for hold-over relief claimed under the above provisions in respect of interests terminating after 5 April 1982 and where the original gift to the trustees was after 5 April 1981 and before 14 March 1989 as it does to hold-over relief under *TCGA 1992, s 165* in respect of gifts made after 13 March 1989. See 8.12 ASSETS HELD ON 31 MARCH 1982 for the treatment by HMRC of the clawback in relevant cases occurring after 5 April 1988.

[*TCGA 1992, ss 67, 74, 168, 169; CGTA 1979, s 56A; FA 1980, s 79; FA 1981, ss 78, 79; FA 1982, s 82, s 84(3); FA 1986, s 58, s 101(2); FA 1989, s 124(1)(3), Sch 17 Pt VII; FA 1991, s 92(2)(4)(6)(7); SI 2005 No 3229, Reg 111*].

33.10 TRANSFER OF BUSINESS TO A COMPANY— INCORPORATION RELIEF

[*TCGA 1992, s 162*]

Where a person who is not a company transfers to a company a business as a going concern, together with the *whole* of the assets of the business (or together with the whole of those assets other than cash) ('the old assets') and the transfer is made wholly or partly in exchange for shares issued by the company to the transferor ('the new assets'), the chargeable gain on the disposal of the old assets is deferred by reducing the amount otherwise chargeable, by the fraction A/B, where 'A' is the 'cost of the new assets' and 'B' is the value of the overall consideration received by the transferor in exchange for the business. For transfers after 5 April 2002, an election can be made to disapply this treatment (see 33.11 below).

'*The cost of the new assets*' means the total allowable expenditure under *TCGA 1992, s 38(1)(a)* if the new assets were disposed of as a whole in circumstances giving rise to a chargeable gain. (See 15.4 COMPUTATION OF GAINS AND LOSSES.) The total expenditure otherwise allowable on the new assets is reduced by the amount of the chargeable gain deferred, and if the new assets comprise different classes of share, the reduction is apportioned by reference to the market value of each class of share at the time of their acquisition by the transferor. Deferment on part of the gain on the old assets therefore remains until the new assets are disposed of.

The only point of time at which the test should be made as to whether a business is being transferred 'as a going concern' is at the time of transfer, so that if the business continues without interruption past that time relief will be available notwithstanding the existence of a planned move of the entire assets of the business from one place to another (*Gordon v CIR (and cross-appeal) CS 1991, 64 TC 173*). For HMRC's interpretation of 'business' and 'going concern', see HMRC Capital Gains Manual CG 65712–65718.

HMRC are prepared not to treat the assumption of business liabilities by the transferee company as consideration for the transfer; the relief is not precluded if some or all of the liabilities of the business are not taken over by the company. However, the assumption of *personal* liabilities, which includes tax liabilities pertaining to the unincorporated business, is treated as part of the consideration. (HMRC Extra-Statutory Concession D32 and see also HMRC Capital Gains Manual CG 65746–65749). (See 3.25 ANTI-AVOIDANCE for the charge arising where concessions involving deferral of gains are abused.)

If some of the assets are retained by the original owner, relief under *TCGA 1992, s 162* above is not available and liability to capital gains tax arises by reference to the market value of any chargeable assets transferred. Where *section 162* relief is not available, it is likely that a business asset hold-over relief claim under *TCGA 1992, s 165* (see 33.1 above) will prevail, provided that the transfer is by way of a non-arm's length bargain, including a transaction deemed to be such because it is between connected persons (see 3.15 ANTI-AVOIDANCE) (see HMRC Capital Gains Manual CG 66973–66979).

Relief under *TCGA 1992, s 162* is available to individuals who are members of a partnership (even if one of the partners is a company) where the whole of the partnership business is transferred to a company. The relief is computed separately for each individual partner and is not precluded by virtue of any other partner receiving all or part of his consideration otherwise than in shares. (HMRC Capital Gains Manual CG 65757).

For further commentary and examples, see HMRC Capital Gains Manual CG 65700–65848.

Interaction with other reliefs. Subject to 33.11 below, incorporation relief under *TCGA 1992, s 162* is mandatory, although a claim for ROLLOVER RELIEF (55) takes precedence (HMRC Capital Gains Manual CG 61560–61562) as does RETIREMENT RELIEF (53) where available for 2002/03 and earlier years (HMRC Capital Gains Manual CG 60212, 60213). Although *section 162* relief cannot be restricted so as to leave sufficient gains in charge to make use of the annual exemption or allowable losses, the same result can effectively be achieved by arranging for an appropriate part of the total consideration to be payable other than in the form of shares in the company, for example in cash or by way of amount left to the credit of the transferor on loan account (as in the Example below), so that a sufficient chargeable gain arises.

Where part of the aggregate chargeable gain on the old assets remains in charge, after giving relief under *TCGA 1992, s 162*, HMRC will accept a computation of TAPER RELIEF (61) on this amount by reference to the holding period(s) of *any* of the chargeable assets transferred (HMRC Capital Gains Manual CG 65821, 65826).

Example

W has carried on an antiquarian bookselling business for many years. He decides to form an unquoted company, P Ltd, to carry on the business. He transfers, in August 2006, the whole of the business undertaking, assets and liabilities to P Ltd, in consideration for the issue of shares, plus an amount left outstanding on interest-free loan. The business assets and liabilities transferred are valued as follows

		Value	Chargeable gain (after indexation to April 1998)
		£	£
Freehold shop premises (acquired in 1990)		80,000	52,000
Goodwill		36,000	26,000
Fixtures and fittings		4,000	—
Trading stock		52,000	—
Debtors		28,000	—
		200,000	
Mortgage on shop	50,000		
Trade creditors	20,000	70,000	—
		£130,000	£78,000

The company issues 100,000 £1 ordinary shares, valued at par, to W in August 2006, and the amount left outstanding is £30,000. For illustration purposes only, it is assumed that W does not elect to disapply *TCGA 1992, s 162* treatment (see 33.11 below). In March 2007, W sells 20,000 of his shares for £45,000 to X. W's remaining shareholding is then worth, say, £155,000.

(i) Amount of chargeable gain rolled over on transfer of the business

$$\frac{100{,}000}{130{,}000} \times £78{,}000 \qquad £60{,}000$$

Of the chargeable gain, £18,000 (£78,000 – £60,000) remains taxable but is subject to TAPER RELIEF (61) at 75%, reducing it to £4,500.

The allowable cost of W's shares is £40,000 (£100,000 – £60,000).

(ii) On the sale of shares to X, W realises a chargeable gain

	£
Disposal consideration	45,000
Allowable cost $\dfrac{45{,}000}{45{,}000 + 155{,}000} \times £40{,}000$	9,000
Chargeable gain*	£36,000

*No indexation due as shares acquired after March 1998 and no taper relief due as shares held for less than 12 months

Note to the example

(*a*) In the hands of the company, the goodwill will not qualify for the special treatment of intangible assets of companies introduced by *FA 2002*, because it was acquired from a related party and was created before 1 April 2002 (by virtue of the business having been carried on before that date). See 14.13 COMPANIES—CORPORATE FINANCE AND INTANGIBLES.

Simon's Direct Tax Service. See Division C3.4.

33.11 **Election to disapply incorporation relief.** On a transfer (of a business) that is within 33.10 above and takes place after 5 April 2002, the transferor may make an election to the effect that the incorporation relief under *TCGA 1992, s 162* should not apply. The election must be made by notice in writing to HMRC. The deadline for making it is normally the second anniversary of 31 January following the tax year in which the transfer takes place. If, however, by the end of the tax year following that in which the transfer takes place, the transferor has disposed of *all* the 'new assets' (see below), the deadline is brought forward by one year. For this purpose, a transfer within *TCGA 1992, s 58* (see 42.4 MARRIED PERSONS AND CIVIL PARTNERS) is not counted as a disposal, but a subsequent disposal by the recipient spouse or civil partner (other than a transfer back to the original spouse or partner) counts as a disposal by the original spouse or partner.

As in 33.10 above, the '*new assets*' are the shares received by the transferor in exchange for the business, but in this case the expression also includes any shares or debentures treated by virtue of *TCGA 1992, s 127* (reorganisations of share capital — see 58.1 SHARES AND SECURITIES) as the same asset as the shares received in exchange for the business. The reference to *section 127* includes that *section* as applied by any other chargeable gains enactment (see, for example, 58.4, 58.6, 58.7 SHARES AND SECURITIES).

Where, immediately before the transfer of the business, it was owned by two or more persons (e.g. by a partnership, including a Scottish partnership), each person has a separate right to make the election in respect of his own entitlement to incorporation relief under *TCGA 1992, s 162* and by reference to his own share of the 'new assets'.

[*TCGA 1992, s 162A; FA 2002, s 49; SI 2005 No 3229, Reg 111*].

Whilst the detailed calculations must be undertaken in each case, the election is most likely to be beneficial in a case where the gain on the chargeable assets transferred to the company would qualify for TAPER RELIEF (61) at the maximum rate, but the shares are disposed of too soon to qualify for taper relief at that rate. The cost of obtaining incorporation relief is the taper relief forgone.

Example

The facts are as in the example at 33.10 above, except that W elects under *TCGA 1992, s 162A* to disapply *TCGA 1992, s 162*.

(i) Chargeable gain on transfer of the business

	£
Gain after indexation but before taper relief	78,000
Less Taper relief £78,000 @ 75% (asset held at least 2 years)	58,500
Chargeable gain	19,500

(ii) Chargeable gain on sale of shares

	£
Disposal consideration	45,000
Allowable cost $\frac{45,000}{45,000+155,000} \times £100,000$	22,500
Chargeable gain*	22,500

* No indexation due as shares acquired after March 1998 and no taper relief due as shares held for less than 12 months

Note to the example

(*a*) On the face of it, the election is not beneficial, producing aggregate gains of £42,000 as against £40,500 (£4,500 + £36,000) in 33.10 above. If, however, W sells his remaining 80,000 shares for £155,000 in, say, May 2007, he will have a chargeable gain for 2007/08 of £124,000 without the election or £77,500 with the election, giving a considerable overall saving if the election is made.

If instead of making these early sales, W had retained all 100,000 shares until, say, September 2008, such that the gain on eventual disposal would have qualified for 75% business asset taper relief, the election would have been neutral, the taper relief forgone on incorporation having been fully recovered. This does assume that the shares retain their status as business assets for taper relief throughout W's ownership.

34 Indexation

Cross-references. See 7 ASSETS HELD ON 6 APRIL 1965; 8 ASSETS HELD ON 31 MARCH 1982; 15 COMPUTATION OF GAINS AND LOSSES; 38.13 LAND for concessionary treatment of indexation allowance on the merger of leases; 59 SHARES AND SECURITIES—IDENTIFICATION RULES; 65.2, 65.3, 65.6 UNIT TRUSTS ETC. for HMRC practice in the case of unit trust units, investment trust shares and open-ended investment company shares acquired under monthly savings schemes.

Simon's Direct Tax Service. See Division C2.3.

34.1 INDEXATION ALLOWANCE

For the purposes of both capital gains tax and corporation tax on chargeable gains, an indexation allowance is deductible in certain circumstances from the unindexed gain.

For the purposes of capital gains tax, though *not* those of corporation tax on chargeable gains, no indexation allowance is available in respect of expenditure incurred after 31 March 1998. For expenditure incurred on or before that date and falling to be deducted on a disposal after 5 April 1998, indexation allowance is computed up to and including April 1998 only.

The gain (if any) arrived at by deducting an amount of allowable expenditure from the amount of consideration realised (see 15 COMPUTATION OF GAINS AND LOSSES), or deemed to be realised, on a disposal is termed an '*unindexed gain*'. In arriving at the chargeable gain, there is to be allowed against the unindexed gain an 'indexation allowance', which is the aggregate of the 'indexed rise' in each item of 'relevant allowable expenditure' (see below).

For disposals on or after 30 November 1993 (in contrast to the previous position), an indexation allowance is given *only* against an unindexed gain. If the disposal gives rise to a loss, no indexation allowance is given, notwithstanding anything in *TCGA 1992, s 16* (computation of losses — see 40.2 LOSSES), and if the indexation allowance equals or exceeds the unindexed gain on a disposal so as to extinguish it, the disposal is regarded as one on which, after taking account of the indexation allowance, neither a gain nor a loss accrues. See the 1999/2000 and earlier editions for details of a transitional relief available only for 1993/94 and 1994/95 in respect of 'indexation losses' (as defined) realised by individuals and by trustees of pre-30 November 1993 settlements.

'*Relevant allowable expenditure*' is allowable expenditure within *TCGA 1992, s 38*(*1*)(*a*) and *s 38*(*1*)(*b*), i.e. basically acquisition cost or value, taken for these purposes as incurred when the asset is acquired or provided, and expenditure on enhancement and on establishing, preserving and defending title and rights to the asset, such expenditure being taken for these purposes as incurred when it becomes due and payable (see 15.4(*a*)–(*c*) COMPUTATION OF GAINS AND LOSSES). Disposal costs are excluded. In determining relevant allowable expenditure, account is taken of any provision of any enactment which, for the purpose of computing gains, increases, excludes or reduces any item of expenditure, or provides for it to be written down. For the purposes of capital gains tax, though not those of corporation tax on chargeable gains, 'relevant allowable expenditure' *excludes* any item of expenditure incurred **after 31 March 1998**.

The '*indexed rise*' in each item of relevant allowable expenditure is computed by multiplying that item by a figure (rounded to the nearest third decimal place) calculated by the formula

$$\frac{RD - RI}{RI}$$

where

RD = retail prices index for the month in which the disposal occurs or, if earlier and for capital gains tax (not corporation tax) purposes, April 1998; and

RI = retail prices index for March 1982 or the month in which the expenditure was incurred, whichever is the later.

If, in relation to any item of expenditure, RD in the formula is equal to, or less than, RI, there is no indexed rise for that item.

The freezing of indexation allowance at its April 1998 level for capital gains tax (not corporation tax) disposals after 5 April 1998 does not affect the computation of a gain which arose on an actual or deemed disposal on or before that date but by virtue of any CGT enactment does not come into charge until after that date. An example might be the coming into charge of a gain previously deferred by reinvestment in an EIS company (see 21.9 ENTERPRISE INVESTMENT SCHEME) or a VCT (see 66.12 VENTURE CAPITAL TRUSTS).

[*TCGA 1992, s 53, s 54, s 288(1); ICTA 1988, s 833(2); FA 1994, s 93(1)–(3)(11); FA 1998, s 122(1)–(3)(6)(7), s 123(3)–(5)*].

The above rules do not apply to 'section 104 holdings' (i.e. single asset pools) of shares or securities, for which see 59.4 SHARES AND SECURITIES—IDENTIFICATION RULES.

For disposals after 5 April 1998 by individuals, trustees and personal representatives, indexation allowance, where still available, is deducted before applying TAPER RELIEF (61) to the gain.

Special provisions apply to the calculation of indexation allowance in relation to disposals involving ASSETS HELD ON 31 MARCH 1982 (8).

The rules outlined above are subject to the special provisions in 34.2–34.7 below.

Disposals before 30 November 1993. See the 1999/2000 and earlier editions for full commentary.

Indexation factors. The figure given by the above formula is commonly called the '*indexation factor*'. The consistent calculation of the indexation factor to more than three decimal places is generally accepted.

HMRC publishes the retail prices index and the associated indexation factors on its website. Yearly tables of indexation factors are contained in Tolley's Tax Data. Both the retail prices index and the April 1998 indexation factors are reproduced below.

Values of the retail prices index (*RPI*) for March 1982 and subsequent months are as follows.

	1982	1983	1984	1985	1986	1987	1988	1989	1990	1991
January	—	82.61	86.84	91.20	96.25	100.0	103.3	111.0	119.5	130.2
February	—	82.97	87.20	91.94	96.60	100.4	103.7	111.8	120.2	130.9
March	79.44	83.12	87.48	92.80	96.73	100.6	104.1	112.3	121.4	131.4
April	81.04	84.28	88.64	94.78	97.67	101.8	105.8	114.3	125.1	133.1
May	81.62	84.64	88.97	95.21	97.85	101.9	106.2	115.0	126.2	133.5
June	81.85	84.84	89.20	95.41	97.79	101.9	106.6	115.4	126.7	134.1
July	81.88	85.30	89.10	95.23	97.52	101.8	106.7	115.5	126.8	133.8
August	81.90	85.68	89.94	95.49	97.82	102.1	107.9	115.8	128.1	134.1
September	81.85	86.06	90.11	95.44	98.30	102.4	108.4	116.6	129.3	134.6
October	82.26	86.36	90.67	95.59	98.45	102.9	109.5	117.5	130.3	135.1
November	82.66	86.67	90.95	95.92	99.29	103.4	110.0	118.5	130.0	135.6
December	82.51	86.89	90.87	96.05	99.62	103.3	110.3	118.8	129.9	135.7

	1992	1993	1994	1995	1996	1997	1998	1999	2000	2001
January	135.6	137.9	141.3	146.0	150.2	154.4	159.5	163.4	166.6	171.1
February	136.3	138.8	142.1	146.9	150.9	155.0	160.3	163.7	167.5	172.0
March	136.7	139.3	142.5	147.5	151.5	155.4	160.8	164.1	168.4	172.2
April	138.8	140.6	144.2	149.0	152.6	156.3	162.6	165.2	170.1	173.1
May	139.3	141.1	144.7	149.6	152.9	156.9	163.5	165.6	170.7	174.2
June	139.3	141.0	144.7	149.8	153.0	157.5	163.4	165.6	171.1	174.4
July	138.8	140.7	144.0	149.1	152.4	157.5	163.0	165.1	170.5	173.3
August	138.9	141.3	144.7	149.9	153.1	158.5	163.7	165.5	170.5	174.0
September	139.4	141.9	145.0	150.6	153.8	159.3	164.4	166.2	171.7	174.6
October	139.9	141.8	145.2	149.8	153.8	159.5	164.5	166.5	171.6	174.3
November	139.7	141.6	145.3	149.8	153.9	159.6	164.4	166.7	172.1	173.6
December	139.2	141.9	146.0	150.7	154.4	160.0	164.4	167.3	172.2	173.4

	2002	2003	2004	2005	2006
January	173.3	178.4	183.1	188.9	193.4
February	173.8	179.3	183.8	189.6	194.2
March	174.5	179.9	184.6	190.5	195.0
April	175.7	181.2	185.7	191.6	196.5
May	176.2	181.5	186.5	192.0	197.7
June	176.2	181.3	186.8	192.2	
July	175.9	181.3	186.8	192.2	
August	176.4	181.6	187.4	192.6	
September	177.7	182.5	188.1	193.1	
October	177.9	182.6	188.6	193.3	
November	178.2	182.7	189.0	193.6	
December	178.5	183.5	189.9	194.1	

Re-referencing of retail prices index. The index is calculated by the Office for National Statistics and was re-referenced so as to make January 1987 = 100.0 and equivalent to 394.5 on the former index where January 1974 = 100.0. In the above table, all the index figures for months before January 1987 have been re-indexed to the January 1987 base. This has been done by dividing the index on the January 1974 base for such a month by 3.945 (i.e. 394.5 divided by 100.0) and rounding to two places of decimals (e.g. the index for December 1985 is 393.0 on the January 1974 base, which would have been the figure announced at the time, and is 96.05 on the January 1987 base). By so rounding the re-indexed figures, the same level of accuracy (to 1 in 10,000) is maintained compared with the figures quoted for months after December 1986.

The Revenue originally announced an incorrect RPI figure of 144.7 for September 1994. (Revenue Press Release 13 August 1997). Also, some incorrect indexation factors (not RPI figures) were included in tables appearing on the Revenue website before 21 September 2002 and covering disposals in February to July 2002 inclusive; see Revenue Internet Statement 1 October 2002 or Revenue Tax Bulletin December 2002 pp 991–993 for details of the inaccuracies and their plans to rectify consequential errors in returns.

The indexation factors for disposals in April 1998 are also relevant (other than for corporation tax purposes) for disposals after April 1998 of assets acquired before April 1998 (see above). In view of their added importance, those indexation factors are set out in full below.

Indexation factors for CGT disposals in or after April 1998 (per Revenue Press Release 20 May 1998)

	1982	1983	1984	1985	1986	1987	1988	1989	1990
January	—	0.968	0.872	0.783	0.689	0.626	0.574	0.465	0.361
February	—	0.960	0.865	0.769	0.683	0.620	0.568	0.454	0.353
March	1.047	0.956	0.859	0.752	0.681	0.616	0.562	0.448	0.339
April	1.006	0.929	0.834	0.716	0.665	0.597	0.537	0.423	0.300
May	0.992	0.921	0.828	0.708	0.662	0.596	0.531	0.414	0.288
June	0.987	0.917	0.823	0.704	0.663	0.596	0.525	0.409	0.283
July	0.986	0.906	0.825	0.707	0.667	0.597	0.524	0.408	0.282
August	0.985	0.898	0.808	0.703	0.662	0.593	0.507	0.404	0.269
September	0.987	0.889	0.804	0.704	0.654	0.588	0.500	0.395	0.258
October	0.977	0.883	0.793	0.701	0.652	0.580	0.485	0.384	0.248
November	0.967	0.876	0.788	0.695	0.638	0.573	0.478	0.372	0.251
December	0.971	0.871	0.789	0.693	0.632	0.574	0.474	0.369	0.252

	1991	1992	1993	1994	1995	1996	1997	1998
January	0.249	0.199	0.179	0.151	0.114	0.083	0.053	0.019
February	0.242	0.193	0.171	0.144	0.107	0.078	0.049	0.014
March	0.237	0.189	0.167	0.141	0.102	0.073	0.046	0.011
April	0.222	0.171	0.156	0.128	0.091	0.066	0.040	—
May	0.218	0.167	0.152	0.124	0.087	0.063	0.036	—
June	0.213	0.167	0.153	0.124	0.085	0.063	0.032	—
July	0.215	0.171	0.156	0.129	0.091	0.067	0.032	—
August	0.213	0.171	0.151	0.124	0.085	0.062	0.026	—
September	0.208	0.166	0.146	0.121	0.080	0.057	0.021	—
October	0.204	0.162	0.147	0.120	0.085	0.057	0.019	—
November	0.199	0.164	0.148	0.119	0.085	0.057	0.019	—
December	0.198	0.168	0.146	0.114	0.079	0.053	0.016	—

Examples

(1) X acquired an asset in November 1985 for £28,000. He disposes of the asset on 11 April 2006 for £99,000. The retail prices index for November 1985 is 95.92 and for April 1998 it is 162.6.

	£
Sale consideration	99,000
Cost of asset	28,000
Unindexed gain	71,000
Indexation allowance	
(162.6 – 95.92)/95.92 = 0.695	
0.695 × £28,000	19,460
Chargeable gain (subject to TAPER RELIEF (61))	£51,540

(2) Facts as in (1) above except that X receives consideration of £18,000.

	£
Sale consideration	18,000
Cost of asset	28,000
Allowable loss (no indexation allowance available)	£10,000

(3) Facts as in (1) above except that X received consideration of £40,000.

	£
Sale consideration	40,000
Cost of asset	28,000
Unindexed gain	£12,000

Indexation allowance is as in (1) above (£19,460) but as this exceeds the amount of the unindexed gain, the disposal gives rise neither to a gain nor to a loss.

(4) Facts as in (1) above except that the acquisition and disposal are by a company, X Ltd. The retail prices index for April 2006 is 196.5.

	£
Sale consideration	99,000
Cost of asset	28,000
Unindexed gain	71,000
Indexation allowance	
(196.5 – 95.92)/95.92 = 1.002	
1.049 × £28,000	29,372
Chargeable gain	£41,628

34.2 **Part disposals.** Apportionment of relevant allowable expenditure is to take place before computing the indexation allowance. The allowance is then only calculated for relevant allowable expenditure attributable to the part disposed of. [*TCGA 1992, s 56(1); FA 1994, Sch 26 Pt V*].

Example

X sells part of a plot of land on 18 January 2007 for £100,000. The then market value of the remaining part of the plot is £30,000. The cost, in September 1984, of the whole plot was £25,000. The retail prices index at September 1984 is 90.11 and for April 1998 it is 162.6.

	£
Allowable expenditure attributable to the part disposed of	
$\frac{100,000}{100,000+30,000} \times £25,000$	£19,231
Unindexed gain: £100,000 – £19,231	80,769
Indexation allowance	
(162.6 – 90.11)/90.11 = 0.804	
0.804 × £19,231	15,462
Chargeable gain (subject to TAPER RELIEF (61))	£65,307

Notes to the example

(*a*) Indexation allowance cannot be computed to a month later than April 1998 (other than for the purposes of corporation tax on chargeable gains). See 34.1 above.

(*b*) No indexation allowance is computed at this stage on the balance of expenditure to be carried forward of £5,769 (£25,000 – £19,231).

34.3 **Disposals on a no gain/no loss basis.** *Disposals on or after 30 November 1993.* On a 'no gain/no loss disposal' on or after 30 November 1993, both the disposal consideration of the transferor and the corresponding acquisition consideration of the transferee are calculated for the purposes of *TCGA 1992* on the assumption that, on the disposal, an unindexed gain accrues to the transferor which is equal to the indexation allowance on that disposal, and so that after taking account of the indexation allowance the disposal is one on which neither a gain nor a loss accrues.

For the purposes of calculating indexation allowance under *TCGA 1992, ss 53, 54* (see 34.1 above), any enactment is disregarded to the extent to which it provides that, on a subsequent disposal of an asset by the transferee which was acquired by him on a no gain/no loss disposal as above, the transferor's acquisition of the asset is to be treated as the transferee's acquisition of it. [*TCGA 1992, s 56(2); FA 1994, s 93(5)(11)*]. For further applications of this provision, see 8.7 ASSETS HELD ON 31 MARCH 1982 and 59.4 SHARES AND SECURITIES—IDENTIFICATION RULES.

Where otherwise a loss would accrue on the disposal of an asset, and the sums allowable as a deduction in computing the loss would include an amount attributable to the application of the assumption contained in *TCGA 1992, s 56(2)* above on any no gain/no loss disposal on or after 30 November 1993, those sums are determined as if *TCGA 1992, s 56(2)* had not applied on any such disposal made on or after that date and the loss is reduced accordingly or, if those sums are then equal to or less than the consideration for the disposal, the disposal is to be one on which neither a gain nor a loss accrues. [*TCGA 1992, s 56(3); FA 1994, s 93(5)(11)*].

For the purposes of *TCGA 1992, s 56(1)* (part disposals; see 34.2 above) and *TCGA 1992, s 56(2)(3)* above, a '*no gain/no loss disposal*' is one which, by virtue of any enactment other than *TCGA 1992, s 35(4)* (no gain/no loss disposal where the general re-basing rule of *TCGA 1992, s 35(1)(2)* would otherwise convert a gain into a loss and vice versa; see 8.2 ASSETS HELD ON 31 MARCH 1982), *s 53(1)* (no gain/no loss disposal where indexation allowance equals or exceeds indexation allowance; see 34.1 above) or *s 56* itself, is treated as a disposal on which neither a gain nor a loss accrues. [*TCGA 1992, s 56(4); FA 1994, s 93(5)(11)*]. For these purposes the definition is not therefore confined to those no gain/no loss disposals mentioned in *TCGA 1992, s 35(3)(d)* (see 8.7 ASSETS HELD ON 31 MARCH 1982), being disposals to which the general re-basing rule of *TCGA 1992, s 35(1)(2)* does not apply.

Disposals on or after the '1985 date' and before 30 November 1993. On a 'no gain/no loss disposal' on or after the '1985 date' and before 30 November 1993, the provisions of *TCGA 1992, s 56(2)* applied similarly as above but *TCGA 1992, s 56(3)(4)* did not apply. A '*no gain/no loss disposal*' was, in effect, a disposal which, by virtue of any enactment (other than, in practice, *TCGA 1992, s 35(4)* (as above), *s 53(1)* (*as originally enacted*) (indexation allowance equal to unindexed gain so as to produce neither gain nor loss) or *s 56* itself) was treated as one on which neither a gain nor a loss accrued. [*TCGA 1992, s 56(2)*]. The '*1985 date*' is 6 April 1985 for capital gains tax purposes and 1 April 1985 for the purposes of corporation tax on chargeable gains.

Examples

(1) In January 1993, Y gives his wife X an asset which is worth £170,000. The asset was purchased from a third party in May 1983 for £80,000. The retail prices index for May 1983 is 84.64 and for January 1993 it is 137.9.

	£
Cost of asset	80,000
Indexation allowance	
(137.9– 84.64)/84.64 = 0.629	
0.629 × £80,000	50,320
Deemed consideration	£130,320

X is deemed to acquire the asset for a consideration of £130,320.

(2) Facts in (1) above but Y and X subsequently divorce, with X retaining the asset. X later marries Z to whom the asset is transferred in February 1998 when it is worth £120,000. In May 2006 the asset is sold by Z to a third party for £130,000. The retail prices index for February 1998 is 160.3.

	£
Cost of asset	130,320
Indexation allowance	
(160.3 – 137.9)/137.9 = 0.162	
0.162 × £130,320	21,112
Deemed consideration (X to Z)	£151,432

	£
Sale consideration	130,000
Cost of asset	151,432
Loss (indexation allowance unavailable)	21,432
Less: Reduction under *TCGA 1992, s 56(3)* of £21,112 which was the indexation uplift on the no gain/no loss disposal of February 1998	21,112
Allowable loss accruing to Z	£320

Disposals on or after the '1982 date' and before the '1985 date'. On any no gain/no loss disposal (other than one occurring only by reason of the indexation provisions on the disposal of an asset outside the twelve month qualifying period) the consideration (and corresponding base cost) was adjusted so that after such adjustment, the transaction still gave rise to neither a gain nor a loss. In effect the disposal consideration (and corresponding base cost) was uplifted by the indexation allowance.

Except as provided below, for indexation purposes, any enactment was disregarded which provided that, on the subsequent disposal by the transferee of an asset acquired by him on a no gain/no loss disposal, the transferor's acquisition of the asset was imputed to the transferee.

If a *loss* accrued on a subsequent disposal of the same asset (a 'subsequent disposal'), the loss was to be reduced by the lesser of

(*a*) the indexation allowance on the initial disposal; and

(*b*) the amount required to secure that, on the subsequent disposal, neither a gain nor a loss accrued.

If a *gain* accrued on a subsequent disposal, the indexation allowance (if any) was calculated in the normal way, unless the no gain/no loss position on the initial disposal arose only by reason of any of the following enactments, viz. *TCGA 1992, s 139* (transfer of assets on reconstruction, see 13.10 COMPANIES); *TCGA 1992, s 171* (intra-group asset transfers, see 27.2 GROUPS OF COMPANIES); *TCGA 1992, s 58* (inter-spouse transfers, see 42.4 MARRIED PERSONS AND CIVIL PARTNERS); *FA 1982, s 148* (certain transfers of assets of the Hops Marketing Board, see 22.75 EXEMPTIONS AND RELIEFS); or *TCGA 1992, s 264* (certain transactions by local constituency associations, see 22.67 EXEMPTIONS AND RELIEFS). In those circumstances, if the transferor on the initial disposal had held the asset for at least the usual twelve month qualifying period, the requirement that the transferee must have held the asset for twelve months was removed, and the indexed rise in the deemed acquisition cost was taken from the month in which the expenditure was incurred (or March 1982 if later), and not the twelfth month thereafter. This provision applied both where the initial disposal took place on or after the '1982 date' and, in the Revenue's view, where it took place before that date (Revenue Statement of Practice 3/82). If the initial no gain/no loss disposal was within the above enactments, and was within the usual twelve-month qualifying period and thus ineligible for indexation allowance, the original transferor's acquisition was imputed to the second or subsequent transferee on further no gain/no loss disposals occurring within the twelve months of the initial no gain/no loss disposal. [*FA 1982, Sch 13 paras 2, 3*]. The '*1982 date*' is 6 April 1982 for capital gains tax purposes and 1 April 1982 for the purposes of corporation tax on chargeable gains. The '*1985 date*' is 6 April 1985 for capital gains tax purposes and 1 April 1985 for the purposes of corporation tax on chargeable gains.

34.4 **Receipts affecting allowable expenditure.** Where account is to be taken, in determining relevant allowable expenditure (see 34.1 above) of any provision which, for the purposes of computing gains, reduces such expenditure by reference to a '*relevant event*' (i.e. any event which is not treated as a capital gains tax disposal), the computation of the indexation allowance proceeds in three stages.

(i) The 'indexed rise' (see 34.1 above) is calculated for each item of expenditure ignoring the reduction.

(ii) The 'indexed rise' is calculated of a notional item of expenditure equal to the amount of the reduction, as if that notional amount had actually been incurred on the date of the 'relevant event'.

(iii) The figure calculated in (ii) above is deducted from that in (i) above.

[*TCGA 1992, s 57*]. Examples of such 'relevant events' are small part disposals of land as in 38.8 LAND and the sale of rights nil paid where the consideration received is small as in 58.1 SHARES AND SECURITIES.

For disposals on or after the '1982 date' and before the '1985 date', the above provisions also applied, subject to the twelve month qualifying period, i.e. no adjustment under (ii) above was required if the asset was sold within twelve months of the 'relevant event'. [*FA 1982, Sch 13 para 4*]. See 34.3 above for the meaning of the '1982 date' and the '1985 date'.

Example

Z purchases a large area of land in April 1990 for £800,000. In June 1993, he sells a small part of that land at arm's length for £2,000. In May 2006, he sells all the remaining land for £4,500,000. The retail prices index for April 1990 is 125.1, for June 1993 it is 141.0 and for April 1998 it is 162.6.

		£
Sale consideration		4,500,000
Cost	800,000	
Small sale not treated as a disposal	2,000	798,000
Unindexed gain		£3,702,000
Indexation allowance on cost		£
(162.6 – 125.1)/125.1 = 0.300		
0.300 × £800,000		240,000
Indexation allowance on notional expenditure equal to small sale consideration		
(162.6 – 141.0)/141.0 = 0.153		
0.153 × £2,000		306
Reduced indexation allowance		£239,694
Chargeable gain = £(3,702,000 – 239,694)		£3,462,306

Notes to the example

(*a*) Indexation allowance cannot be computed to a month later than April 1998 (other than for the purposes of corporation tax on chargeable gains). See 34.1 above.

(*b*) The chargeable gain is subject to TAPER RELIEF (61).

34.5 **Reorganisation, reconstructions etc.** In computing indexation allowance, any consideration given for 'the new holding' (treated under *TCGA 1992, s 127* as the same asset as 'the original shares' on a reorganisation or reduction of a company's share capital) is to be treated as an item of relevant allowable expenditure incurred when the consideration was, or was liable to be, given, i.e. not related back to the acquisition date of 'the original shares', as would normally be the case under *TCGA 1992, s 128*(*1*).

'*Reorganisation*', the '*original shares*' and '*the new holding*' are as defined in *TCGA 1992, s 126*(*1*). In addition the above provisions also apply where the treatment under *TCGA 1992, s 127* is adapted for a conversion of securities and for company reconstructions. See 58.1–58.7 SHARES AND SECURITIES. [*TCGA 1992, s 131, s 132*(*1*), *s 135*(*3*)].

Example

In November 1989, Y purchases 5,000 shares in A plc for £3,500. In June 1991, he acquires, for £960, 1,000 further shares by way of a 1 for 5 rights issue. In January 2007, he sells all his holding for £8,000. The retail prices index for November 1989 is 118.5, for June 1991 it is 134.1 and for April 1998 it is 162.6.

		£
Sale consideration		8,000
Original cost	3,500	
Cost of rights	960	
		4,460
Unindexed gain		£3,540

	£
Indexation allowance on original cost (162.6 – 118.5)/118.5 = 0.372 0.372 × £3,500	1,302
Indexation allowance on cost of taking up rights (162.6 – 134.1)/134.1 = 0.213 0.213 × £960	204
Total indexation allowance	£1,506
Chargeable gain = £(3,540 – 1,506)	£2,034

Notes to the example

(*a*) Technically, the pooling provisions in 59.4 SHARES AND SECURITIES—IDENTIFICATION RULES apply, as the acquisition in November 1989 is a 'section 104 holding'. For practical purposes, where, as in this example, there is a single acquisition and disposal, the above computation gives essentially the same result.

(*b*) Indexation allowance cannot be computed to a month later than April 1998 (other than for the purposes of corporation tax on chargeable gains). See 34.1 above.

(*c*) The chargeable gain is subject to TAPER RELIEF (61).

34.6 **Calls on shares.** Where the whole or part of the consideration for the issue of shares, securities or debentures is given after the period of twelve months beginning on the date of the issue of the shares etc., that consideration (or part) is treated as a separate item of expenditure for indexation purposes, incurred at the time it is given and not at the time at which the shares etc. were acquired or provided. [*TCGA 1992, s 113*]. Any calls paid within the twelve-month period are thus treated as incurred at the time the shares etc. were acquired or provided.

The above does not apply to privatisation issues, for which see 58.13 SHARES AND SECURITIES.

34.7 **Options.** Where, on a disposal, relevant allowable expenditure includes both

(*a*) the cost of acquiring an option binding the grantor to sell ('*the option consideration*'); and

(*b*) the cost of acquiring what was sold as a result of the exercise of the option ('*the sale consideration*')

the option consideration and sale consideration are regarded as separate items of expenditure incurred when the option was acquired and when the sale took place respectively. An option binding the grantor both to sell and to buy is treated for these purposes as two separate options with one half of the consideration attributable to each. These provisions do not apply where those at 59.4 SHARES AND SECURITIES—IDENTIFICATION RULES (under 'Consideration for options') apply. Where the whole of the option consideration is incurred after 31 March 1998, the above provisions apply only for corporation tax purposes, this being in consequence of the freezing of indexation allowance for CGT purposes at its April 1998 level (see 34.1 above). [*TCGA 1992, s 145; FA 1998, s 122(5)*].

As in 6.7 ASSETS, the reference above to an 'option' includes a reference to an option binding the grantor to grant a lease for a premium, or enter into any other transaction which is not a sale. [*TCGA 1992, s 144(6), s 145(3)*].

34.7 Indexation

In the case of the grantee of a 'cash-settled' option granted after 29 November 1993 (see 6.7 ASSETS), the cost of the option is treated as incurred when the option was acquired for the purposes of calculating any indexation allowance. [*TCGA 1992, s 144A*(*3*)(*c*); *FA 1994, s 96*].

35 Interaction with Other Taxes

Cross-references. See 2 ANNUAL RATES AND EXEMPTIONS for rates applicable to gains by reference to income tax rates; 15 COMPUTATION OF GAINS AND LOSSES for acquisition and disposal consideration taken into account for capital gains tax purposes generally; 33.7 HOLD-OVER RELIEFS for relief given to gifts after 13 March 1989 on which inheritance tax is chargeable etc; 38.15–38.18 LAND for premiums on leases of land charged to income tax; 58 SHARES AND SECURITIES for interaction with income tax provisions; 64.1 UNDERWRITERS AT LLOYD'S for treatment of assets in premium trust funds.

35.1 GENERAL AND INCOME TAX

Any money or money's worth charged to income tax as income of, or taken into account as a receipt in computing income or profits or gains or losses of (except, for accounting periods beginning before 1 April 2004, in relation to the computation under *ICTA 1988, s 76(2)* of management expenses of life assurance companies), the person making the disposal is excluded from the consideration for the disposal of the asset for capital gains tax purposes. However,

(*a*) this is not to be taken as excluding any money or money's worth

- taken into account in making a balancing charge for the purposes of capital allowances (other than assured tenancy allowances) (see *Hirsch v Crowthers Cloth Ltd Ch D 1989, 62 TC 759*), or
- brought into account as the disposal value of plant or machinery for capital allowances purposes, or
- brought into account as the disposal value of an asset representing qualifying expenditure under *CAA 2001, Pt 6* (research and development allowances);

(*b*) the capitalised value of a rentcharge (as in the case where a rentcharge is exchanged for another asset), ground annual or feu duty, or of a right of any other description to income or to payments in the nature of income over a period, or to a series of payments in the nature of income may be taken into account for capital gains tax purposes; and

(*c*) amounts chargeable to tax under *ICTA 1988, s 348* or *s 349* (deduction of basic rate income tax from annual payments) are not excluded from the disposal consideration for capital gains tax purposes.

[*TCGA 1992, s 37, s 52(2)(3)(5), Sch 8 para 5(6); CAA 2001, Sch 2 para 77; SI 2004 No 2310, Art 1, Sch para 48*].

For income tax matters relating to know-how and patents (and which have a capital gains tax effect), see 6.4, 6.5 ASSETS). See also 45.8 OVERSEAS MATTERS for offshore funds.

Expenditure which is deductible in computing profits or losses for income tax purposes (or would be so deductible if the asset were held as a fixed asset of a trade) is excluded from being allowable expenditure for capital gains tax purposes. [*TCGA 1992, s 39(1)(2)*]. See 15.6 COMPUTATION OF GAINS AND LOSSES.

Any assessment to income tax or decision on a claim under the *Income Tax Acts*, and any decision on an appeal in connection therewith, is conclusive for capital gains tax purposes where liability to tax depends on the provisions of the *Income Tax Acts*. [*TCGA 1992, s 284*]. Where *alternative* income tax and capital gains tax assessments are made in respect of the same transactions, the fact that the capital gains tax assessment becomes final does not preclude the income tax assessment taking effect instead (*Bye v Coren CA 1986, 60 TC 116*). See also *Lord Advocate v McKenna CS 1989, 61 TC 688* and *CIR v Wilkinson CA 1992, 65 TC 28*.

Income or capital? Whether the gain arising on the disposal of an asset is of income or capital nature has been tested in the courts on numerous occasions and the outcome is likely to be one of fact and degree. In particular, see 38.3 LAND for isolated and speculative transactions in land. 'No part of our law of taxation presents such almost insoluble conundrums as the decision whether a receipt or outgoing is capital or income for tax purposes' (Lord Upjohn in *Strick v Regent Oil Co Ltd HL 1965, 43 TC 1* which see for a comprehensive review of the law). A widely used test is the 'enduring benefit' one given by Viscount Cave in *Atherton v British Insulated & Helsby Cables Ltd HL 1925, 10 TC 155*.

Investment trusts and the tax treatment of forward currency transactions. See 65.3 UNIT TRUSTS ETC.

Transactions in certain options and futures by certain taxpayers. See 6.7 and 6.8 ASSETS.

35.2 **INHERITANCE TAX**

A lifetime disposal which contains an element of gift may incur liability to inheritance tax (IHT) as well as capital gains tax. For the purposes of IHT, no account is taken of any capital gains tax borne by the transferor in determining the reduction in value in his estate. [*IHTA 1984, s 164*].

Example

A makes a gift of land, to a non-UK resident discretionary trustee, B, which is valued at £20,000 and on which there is a capital gains tax liability of £3,000. The value for IHT purposes (subject to grossing-up for the IHT payable) is £20,000 (i.e. the same as if A had sold the land and given the £20,000 proceeds to B).

Relief for CGT against IHT

Capital gains tax paid will be taken into account for IHT purposes in the following instances.

(*a*) If the transferor fails to pay all or part of the capital gains tax within twelve months of the due date, an assessment may be made on the donee (see 25.4 GIFTS) and the amount of such tax borne by the donee is treated as reducing the value transferred. There is a similar effect when the transfer is from a settlement but, after 8 March 1982, this only applies if the capital gains tax is borne by a person who becomes absolutely entitled to the settled property concerned. [*IHTA 1984, s 165*(*1*)(*2*)].

Example

In the *Example* above, if A fails to pay the £3,000 capital gains tax and it is borne by B, the value transferred by A is £17,000 for the purposes of IHT (again subject to grossing-up for the IHT payable).

(*b*) Where a person sells, or is treated as having sold, national heritage property on the breach or termination of an undertaking (see 22.80 EXEMPTIONS AND RELIEFS) any capital gains tax payable is deductible in determining the value of the asset for IHT purposes. [*TCGA 1992, s 258*(*8*)].

Relief for IHT against CGT.

Where hold-over relief is granted under

(i) *TCGA 1992, s 165* in relation to gifts made after 13 March 1989 (see 33.1 HOLD-OVER RELIEFS),

(ii) *TCGA 1992, s 260* in relation to gifts after 13 March 1989 (see 33.7 HOLD-OVER RELIEFS), or

(iii) *FA 1980, s 79* in relation to gifts after 5 April 1980 and before 14 March 1989 (see 33.9 HOLD-OVER RELIEFS),

the transferee may deduct on a subsequent disposal any IHT attributable to the value of the asset on the original transfer (being either a chargeable transfer or a potentially exempt transfer which proves to be a chargeable transfer). The tax deductible may be varied on the subsequent death of the transferor or otherwise but it cannot in any circumstances create an allowable loss on the subsequent disposal. [*TCGA 1992, s 67(1)–(3), s 165(10)(11), s 260(7)(8)*]. In the case of (ii) above, the same treatment applies if a hold-over relief claim *could have been made* (HMRC Capital Gains Manual CG 67050).

There is no relief for IHT under (i) and (iii) above if hold-over relief is *not* claimed, so that even where the gain otherwise arising is negligible or covered by reliefs a hold-over relief claim may still be beneficial overall (Tolley's Practical Tax 1984 p 198). A hold-over relief claim can be made even if an allowable loss arises on the original gift and so give rise to an IHT deduction on a subsequent disposal by the donee whilst not affecting the loss relief position of the donor. Where only part of the asset gifted is subsequently disposed of, HMRC accept that any IHT paid on the original gift can still be deducted in full on the part disposal (subject to the size of the gain arising) and there is no need to apportion IHT paid between the part disposed of and the part retained (Taxation 5 October 1989 pp 12, 14). There is no provision for indexation allowance to be calculated by reference to the IHT that can be deducted.

Valuation of assets. Valuations of assets made *at death* for the purpose of an IHT charge on the value of a person's estate immediately before death are binding for capital gains tax purposes. [*TCGA 1992, s 274; IHTA 1984, s 168*]. See also Revenue Tax Bulletin April 1995 p 209. In practice (see HMRC Pamphlet IHT 15 p 15), unless there are special circumstances, quoted shares and securities are valued in the same way as for capital gains tax (see 41.3 MARKET VALUE). In the case of land and quoted shares and securities, proceeds of certain post-death sales within a specified period may be substituted for values at date of death for IHT purposes. The value of related property (as defined for IHT purposes) may also be revised in the event of a post-death sale. If such substitutions/revisions are made for IHT purposes, they must be made for CGT purposes also (but see *Stonor and Another (Executors of Dickinson deceased) v CIR (Sp C 288), [2001] SSCD 199* in which the executors failed in an attempt to use this rule to upgrade values of freehold properties for CGT purposes where there was no IHT liability). See Tolley's Inheritance Tax for details and also HMRC Capital Gains Manual CG 32290–32310.

35.3 VALUE ADDED TAX

If VAT is suffered on the purchase of an asset, but is available for set-off in full in the purchaser's VAT account (e.g. a capital asset purchased by a trader who is registered for VAT), then the cost of the asset for capital gains tax purposes is the cost exclusive of VAT. Where no VAT set-off is available, the cost is inclusive of VAT borne. On the disposal of an asset, VAT chargeable is disregarded in computing the disposal consideration for capital gains tax purposes (HMRC Statement of Practice D7).

A person whose output is partly exempt and partly taxable may set off only part of his VAT on inputs against his VAT on outputs. In such a case, although the computation of disposal proceeds is as above, it will be necessary to allocate the VAT ultimately suffered to the various expense payments made. Inspectors will be prepared to consider any reasonable arrangements made to carry out this apportionment. A taxable person making both taxable and exempt supplies may therefore treat as part of the capital gains tax cost of an asset the input tax that was not available for credit in respect of the acquisition (HMRC Statement of Practice B1).

The above practices should be read in the light of a Revenue Press Release of 20 March 1990 which mentioned that VAT on certain inputs (broadly land, buildings and computers with values above certain levels) after 31 March 1990 may require annual adjustment for a period of up to ten years after the input concerned under the VAT capital goods scheme. In certain circumstances a VAT adjustment may reduce the amount of expenditure on an asset qualifying for ROLLOVER RELIEF (55). Where a VAT adjustment is made after a claim to rollover relief has been determined, HMRC will not normally seek to reopen the claim.

36 Interest on Overpaid Tax

Cross-reference. See 47 PAYMENT OF TAX.

36.1 PERSONS OTHER THAN COMPANIES

Under self-assessment **for 1996/97 and subsequent years**, a repayment by HMRC of capital gains tax paid by or on behalf of an individual (or trustees of a settlement or personal representatives of a deceased person) carries interest at the rate(s) listed below. The amount by which the repayment is so increased is known as a **repayment supplement**. The interest runs from the date the tax is paid until the date on which the order for the repayment is issued by HMRC. [*TCGA 1992, s 283(1)(2)(4); FA 1994, s 196, s 199(2), Sch 19 para 46, Sch 26 Pt V(23); FA 1997, s 92(5)(6); FA 2006, Sch 12 para 24*]. A repayment supplement is not taxable in the hands of the recipient. [*ITTOIA 2005, s 749; ICTA 1988, s 824(8)*].

Rates of interest are:

2.25% p.a. from 6 September 2005

3.00% p.a. from 6 September 2004 to 5 September 2005

2.25% p.a. from 6 December 2003 to 5 September 2004

1.50% p.a. from 6 August 2003 to 5 December 2003

2.25% p.a. from 6 November 2001 to 5 August 2003

3.00% p.a. from 6 May 2001 to 5 November 2001

4.00% p.a. from 6 February 2000 to 5 May 2001

3.00% p.a. from 6 March 1999 to 5 February 2000

4.00% p.a. from 6 January 1999 to 5 March 1999

4.75% p.a. from 6 August 1997 to 5 January 1999

4.00% p.a. from 31 January 1997 to 5 August 1997

HMRC announced on 6 September 2005 that the interest rates that they had previously used for the period 6 May 2001 to 5 September 2005 were incorrect. The above rates are the corrected rates published on 6 September 2005. The incorrect rates used were higher than those above but HMRC will not make any attempt to recover any amounts overpaid. Where, however, a repayment is reviewed for other reasons, the correct amount of interest will be calculated. (HMRC News Release 6 September 2005).

It will be noted that the rates are considerably lower than those by reference to which interest is charged on late paid tax (see 37.1 INTEREST AND SURCHARGES ON UNPAID TAX). The rates are adjusted automatically by reference to changes in the average of base lending rates of certain clearing banks, and are announced by HMRC Press Release. For the relationship to base rates, see *SI 1989 No 1297, Reg 3AB* as inserted from 31 January 1997 by *SI 1996 No 3187*.

In contrast to the position prior to 1996/97, there is no requirement that the taxpayer be resident in the UK or European Community.

Although repayment supplement runs from the date the tax was paid, even if this falls before the due date, HMRC have stated that they will not pay repayment supplement on any amount deliberately overpaid (Revenue Press Release 12 November 1996). This is intended to deter taxpayers from using HMRC as a source of tax-free interest. Where a payment of tax is not set against any liability and repayment is not claimed, the payment remains on record until the next liability arises, but no repayment supplement will be given. (Revenue Tax Bulletin June 1999 p 674). As regards the date on which payment is treated as made, see 47.5 PAYMENT OF TAX. Interest is not payable on repayments made by order or judgement of a court having power to allow interest (for which see 47.4 PAYMENT OF TAX). [*TCGA 1992, s 283(3)*].

Repayment supplement is added in similar fashion to any repayment of a penalty imposed under any provision of *TMA 1970* (see 48 PENALTIES) or of a surcharge imposed under *TMA 1970, s 59C* (see 37.4 INTEREST AND SURCHARGES ON UNPAID TAX). [*ICTA 1988, s 824*]. For full details of repayment supplement under *section 824*, see Tolley's Income Tax.

See 12.2 CLAIMS for special rule where a claim affects two or more years, e.g. a loss carry-back claim.

For provisions applying where the tax repayable relates to 1995/96 and/or earlier years, see the 2005/06 and earlier editions.

36.2 **COMPANIES**

Accounting periods ending on or after 1 July 1999. Where a repayment of corporation tax falls to be made to a company for an accounting period ending on or after 1 July 1999 (self-assessment), the repayment carries interest (under *ICTA 1988, s 826*) from the 'material date' until the order for repayment is issued.

The '*material date*' is the later of the date the corporation tax was paid and the date on which it became (or would have become) due and payable, i.e. subject to the payment of tax in quarterly instalments where applicable, the day following the expiry of nine months from the end of the accounting period (see 47.2 PAYMENT OF TAX).

The interest rate is determined by criteria contained in Treasury regulations made by statutory instrument so that when such criteria change so as to alter the rate, HMRC must specify in an order the new rate and the day from which it has effect. For the criteria, see *SI 1989 No 1297, Reg 3B* and, as regards accounting periods ending on or after 1 July 1999, *Regs 3BA, 3BB* as inserted by *SI 1998 No 3176* and amended by *SI 1999 No 1928.*

The rates of interest for amounts overpaid **on or after the normal due date** for payment of corporation tax (see above) are:

3.00% p.a. from 6 September 2005

4.00% p.a. from 6 September 2004 to 5 September 2005

3.00% p.a. from 6 December 2003 to 5 September 2004

2.00% p.a. from 6 August 2003 to 5 December 2003

3.00% p.a. from 6 November 2001 to 5 August 2003

4.00% p.a. from 6 May 2001 to 5 November 2001

5.00% p.a. previously

The rates for amounts overpaid **before the due date, for example under the quarterly accounting rules for large companies** (see 47.2 PAYMENT OF TAX), are:

4.25% p.a. from 15 August 2005

4.50% p.a. from 16 August 2004 to 14 August 2005

4.25% p.a. from 21 June 2004 to 15 August 2004

4.00% p.a. from 17 May 2004 to 20 June 2004

3.75% p.a. from 16 February 2004 to 16 May 2004

3.50% p.a. from 17 November 2003 to 15 February 2004

3.25% p.a. from 21 July 2003 to 16 November 2003

3.5% p.a. from 17 February 2003 to 20 July 2003

3.75% p.a. from 19 November 2001 to 16 February 2003

4.25% p.a. from 15 October 2001 to 18 November 2001

4.50% p.a. from 1 October 2001 to 14 October 2001

4.75% p.a. from 13 August 2001 to 30 September 2001

5.00% p.a. from 21 May 2001 to 12 August 2001

5.25% p.a. from 16 April 2001 to 20 May 2001

5.50% p.a. from 19 February 2001 to 15 April 2001

5.75% p.a. from 21 February 2000 to 18 February 2001

5.50% p.a. from 24 January 2000 to 20 February 2000

5.25% p.a. from 15 November 1999 to 23 January 2000

5.00% p.a. from 20 September 1999 to 14 November 1999

4.75% p.a. from 21 June 1999 to 19 September 1999

5.00% p.a. from 19 April 1999 to 20 June 1999

5.25% p.a. from 15 February 1999 to 18 April 1999

5.75% p.a. from 18 January 1999 to 14 February 1999

6.00% p.a. from 7 January 1999 to 17 January 1999

The latter set of rates applies up to the earlier of the date of repayment and the normal due date (whereafter the normal rates apply).

There are restrictions on the amount of the interest where surplus advance corporation tax of a later accounting period displaces mainstream corporation tax paid in respect of an earlier accounting period, or trading losses or non-trading deficits of a later accounting period are offset against profits of an earlier period or there is a combination of such events.

Interest is paid without deduction of income tax and is chargeable to corporation tax as a non-trading credit under the loan relationship rules (see 14.2–14.6 COMPANIES—CORPORATE FINANCE AND INTANGIBLES and Tolley's Corporation Tax). Corporation tax repayments are as far as possible treated as repayments of tax paid on a later date rather than an earlier date.

Interest on overpaid tax paid to a company which becomes recoverable because of a change in the company's assessed corporation tax liability and not because of HMRC error can be recovered without an assessment.

[*ICTA 1988, ss 826, 826A; FA 1989, s 178, s 179(1)(c)(ii), s 180(6); FA 1991, Sch 15 para 23; FA 1993, ss 120, 170, Sch 14 para 10, Sch 18 para 5; SI 1989 No 1297; SI 1993 No 2212; FA 1996, s 100(4A) as previously enacted, s 100(7), Sch 18 para 13; FA 1998, ss 34, 35, Sch 4 paras 1–3, 5, 7; SI 1998 No 3175, Reg 8; FA 2002, s 79, Sch 23 para 6, Sch 40 Pt 3(10)*].

Accounting periods ending after 30 September 1993 and before 1 July 1999. Under Pay and File (i.e. for accounting periods ending after 30 September 1993 and before 1 July 1999), similar provisions to those described above in relation to self-assessment accounting periods apply, but with the following differences:

- interest on overpaid tax is not chargeable to corporation tax;
- the special rates for instalment payments for 'large' companies do not apply; and

- HMRC are not able to recover interest without assessment.

[*ICTA 1988, ss 826, 826A*].

Rates of interest are:

2.00% p.a. from 6 September 2005

2.75% p.a. from 6 September 2004 to 5 September 2005

2.00% p.a. from 6 December 2003 to 5 September 2004

1.25% p.a. from 6 August 2003 to 5 December 2003

2.00% p.a. from 6 November 2001 to 5 August 2003

2.75% p.a. from 6 May 2001 to 5 November 2001

3.50% p.a. from 6 February 2000 to 5 May 2001

2.75% p.a. from 6 March 1999 to 5 February 2000

3.25% p.a. from 6 January 1999 to 5 March 1999

4.00% p.a. from 6 August 1997 to 5 January 1999

3.25% p.a. from 6 February 1996 to 5 August 1997

4.00% p.a. from 6 March 1995 to 5 February 1996

3.25% p.a. from 6 October 1994 to 5 March 1995

2.50% p.a. from 6 January 1994 to 5 October 1994

3.25% p.a. from 1 October 1993 to 5 January 1994

36.3 OVER-PAYMENTS

See 47.12 PAYMENT OF TAX as regards assessment of repayment supplement or interest overpaid.

36.4 MISCELLANEOUS

Unauthorised demands for tax. There is a general right to interest under *Supreme Court Act 1981, s 35A* in a case where the taxpayer submits to an unauthorised demand for tax, provided that the payment is not made voluntarily to close a transaction (*Woolwich Equitable Building Society v CIR HL 1992, 65 TC 265*).

37 Interest and Surcharges on Unpaid Tax

Cross-references. See 5 ASSESSMENTS; 23 FRAUDULENT OR NEGLIGENT CONDUCT; 47 PAYMENT OF TAX; 48 PENALTIES.

37.1 PERSONS OTHER THAN COMPANIES

The provisions of *TMA 1970, s 86* as amended for self-assessment and described below apply in respect of capital gains tax **for 1996/97 and subsequent years,** i.e. under self-assessment, **and also** in respect of capital gains tax for an earlier year which is charged by an assessment first raised after 5 April 1998. [*FA 1995, s 110(2)*]. Where these provisions have effect, *TMA 1970, s 88* (interest on tax recovered to make good loss of tax due to taxpayer's fault) does not have effect. Capital gains tax paid more than 28 days after the due date is also subject to a surcharge, with an additional surcharge where payment is more than six months late (see 37.4 below).

Interest is charged by HMRC on late payments of capital gains tax, whether payable under a self-assessment or an assessment made by HMRC or as a result of an HMRC amendment to a self-assessment following an enquiry. (For details of interest charged on late payment of income tax, including interim payments, see Tolley's Income Tax.) Interest at the rates listed below accrues from the 'relevant date' (even if a non-business day) to the date of payment. The '*relevant date*' is, with one statutory exception, 31 January following the year of assessment. This applies equally to liabilities under pre-1996/97 assessments raised after 5 April 1998. The exception is that where the due date for payment of tax is deferred until three months after notice is given to deliver a self-assessment tax return (see 47.1 PAYMENT OF TAX), the relevant date is identically deferred. Where the due date of payment is *later* than the relevant date, either under the circumstances in 56.6 SELF-ASSESSMENT or because a successful application is made to postpone tax (see 47.3 PAYMENT OF TAX), this does *not* alter the relevant date for interest purposes.

[*TMA 1970, s 86(1)–(3); FA 1995, s 110; FA 1996, s 131(2)*].

In practice, where a self-assessment return is submitted by 30 September for calculation by HMRC of the tax due (see 54.5 RETURNS), the relevant date is deferred until 30 days after notification of the liability to the taxpayer if this occurs later than 31 December following the tax year (HMRC Self-Assessment Manual — Interest, penalties and surcharge section). This is of no significance where returns are filed over the internet (see 54.3 RETURNS) as the tax due is automatically computed during the filing process. See 37.7 below for a point concerning personal representatives.

As regards the date on which payment of tax is treated as made, see 47.5 PAYMENT OF TAX.

Rates of interest are:

6.50% p.a. from 6 September 2005

7.50% p.a. from 6 September 2004 to 5 September 2005

6.50% p.a. from 6 December 2003 to 5 September 2004

5.50% p.a. from 6 August 2003 to 5 December 2003

6.50% p.a. from 6 November 2001 to 5 August 2003

7.50% p.a. from 6 May 2001 to 5 November 2001

8.50% p.a. from 6 February 2000 to 5 May 2001

7.50% p.a. from 6 March 1999 to 5 February 2000

8.50% p.a. from 6 January 1999 to 5 March 1999

9.50% p.a. from 6 August 1997 to 5 January 1999

8.50% p.a. from 31 January 1997 to 5 August 1997

Interest charges are calculated automatically and, however small, will appear on taxpayer statements of account under self-assessment. There is no de minimis limit for charging interest. It will be noted that the above rates are greater than those by reference to which interest is paid by HMRC (see 36.1 INTEREST ON OVERPAID TAX). The rates are adjusted automatically by reference to changes in the average of base lending rates of certain clearing banks, and are announced by HMRC Press Release. For the relationship to base rates, see *SI 1989 No 1297, Reg 3* as substituted from 31 January 1997 by *SI 1996 No 3187*.

Interest is also chargeable at the above rates from 9 March 1998 on late payment of surcharges (see 37.4 below) and penalties (see 48.14 PENALTIES). [*TMA 1970, s 59C(6), s 103A; SI 1989 No 1297, Reg 3; SI 1998 Nos 310, 311*].

Interest is payable gross and recoverable, as if it were tax charged, as a Crown debt; it is *not deductible from profits or income* [*ITTOIA 2005, ss 54, 272, 869, Sch 1 para 378; TMA 1970, ss 69, 90; FA 1994, Sch 19 para 20; FA 1998, s 33; FA 2001, s 89(2)*] and is refundable to the extent that the tax concerned is subsequently cancelled. [*TMA 1970, s 91; ITEPA 2003, Sch 6 para 136*].

For the provisions applicable where the capital gains tax payable relates to 1995/96 and earlier years, see the 2005/06 and earlier editions.

37.2 TAX BECOMING DUE WHERE NOTICE OF APPEAL GIVEN

The rules for determining the due and payable date where an assessment etc. is under appeal are explained at 47.3, 47.4 PAYMENT OF TAX. For right of appeal, see 4.1 APPEALS. Under self-assessment for 1996/97 onwards, the giving of notice of appeal, whether or not accompanied by a postponement application, does not affect the date from which interest accrues, which remains as in 37.1 above. The same applies as regards assessments for 1995/96 and earlier years where these are first raised *after 5 April 1998*. (A similar situation applies for corporation tax purposes.)

37.3 TAX BECOMING DUE AFTER DETERMINATION OF AN APPEAL BY THE COURTS

The rules for determining the due and payable date where further tax is found to be chargeable on determination by the courts of an appeal against an assessment etc. are explained at 47.4 PAYMENT OF TAX. Under self-assessment for 1996/97 onwards, these rules do *not* affect the date from which interest accrues, which remains as in 37.1 above. The same applies as regards assessments for 1995/96 and earlier years where these are first raised *after 5 April 1998*. (A similar situation applies for corporation tax.)

37.4 SURCHARGES ON UNPAID TAX

The provisions described below apply in respect of capital gains tax (and income tax) **for 1996/97 and subsequent years** and **also apply** in respect of assessments for 1995/96 and/or earlier years which are raised after 5 April 1998. [*FA 1995, s 109(2)*].

An initial surcharge is payable where an amount of CGT (and/or income tax), whether payable under a self-assessment or an assessment made by HMRC or as a result of an HMRC amendment to a self-assessment following an enquiry, remains unpaid more than 28 days after the due date for payment. The due date for payment of CGT is normally 31 January following the year of assessment, but see 47.1 PAYMENT OF TAX, 56.6 SELF-ASSESSMENT for exceptions (and note also the postponement rules at 47.3, 47.4 PAYMENT OF TAX). As regards a pre-1996/97 assessment first raised after 5 April 1998, the due date is 30 days after the issue of the notice of assessment, though this is deferred to the extent that any tax is postponed on appeal (see 47.1, 47.3, 47.4 PAYMENT OF TAX). The surcharge is equal to 5% of the amount of tax unpaid. **An additional 5%** surcharge is payable on any of that tax which remains unpaid more than six months after the due date. Interest accrues on an unpaid surcharge with effect from the expiry of 30 days beginning with the date of the notice imposing the surcharge. An appeal may be made, within the same 30-day period, against the imposition of a surcharge as if it were an assessment to tax, and the surcharge may be set aside if it appears that, *throughout* the period from the due date until payment of the tax, the taxpayer had a 'reasonable excuse' for non-payment. Inability to pay the tax, i.e. due to insufficient funds, is not to be regarded as a reasonable excuse. The decision as to whether a taxpayer meets these criteria rests ultimately with the Appeal Commissioners (see the National Association of Tax Commissioners website at www.natax.org.uk). See also Revenue Tax Bulletin April 1998 pp 527–529.

There are provisions to prevent a double charge where tax has been taken into account in determining the tax-geared penalties of *TMA 1970, s 7* (see 48.1 PENALTIES), *s 93(5)* (tax-geared penalty for failure to make return for income tax and capital gains tax; see 48.2 PENALTIES), *s 95* (incorrect return etc. for income tax or capital gains tax; see 48.6 PENALTIES) and *s 95A* (incorrect return etc. for partnerships; see 48.7 PENALTIES). Any such tax will not be subject to a surcharge. HMRC have discretion to mitigate, or to stay or compound proceedings for recovery of, a surcharge and may also, after judgment, entirely remit the surcharge.

[*TMA 1970, s 59C; FA 1994, s 194, s 199(2); FA 1995, s 109*].

Where the due date is 31 January, it is HMRC's view that surcharge can only be avoided by full payment of the tax on or before 28 February. However, pending clarification by the courts, no surcharge was to be levied on payments due on 31 January 2001 if payment was received on 1 March 2001 (or, in the case of the additional surcharge, 1 August 2001). (Revenue Tax Bulletin February 2001 p 826). HMRC's view was confirmed by *Thompson v Minzly Ch D 2001, 74 TC 340* and the relaxation withdrawn for 2002 onwards (Revenue Tax Bulletin December 2001 p 904). See 47.5 PAYMENT OF TAX as regards effective dates of payment.

In practice, where a self-assessment return is submitted by 30 September for calculation by HMRC of the tax due (see 54.5 RETURNS), the due date by reference to which any surcharge is triggered is delayed until 30 days after notification by the Revenue of the amount due, where this occurs after 31 December following the tax year (ICAEW Technical Release TAX 9/94, June 1994).

No surcharge will be imposed where a taxpayer has entered into a 'Time to Pay' arrangement (see 47.6 PAYMENT OF TAX), provided that the payment proposals are received by HMRC before the relevant surcharge date, they lead to an acceptable agreement to settle the full liability for the self-assessment year, and the terms of the arrangement are adhered to, such that it is not cancelled. (HMRC Self-Assessment Manual — Payments section).

37.5 COMPANIES

Accounting periods ending on or after 1 July 1999. Corporation tax carries interest (under *TMA 1970, s 87A*) from the due and payable date (see 47.2 PAYMENT OF TAX), even if it is a non-business day, until payment. Where corporation tax assessed on a company may be assessed on other persons in certain circumstances, the due and payable date is that which refers to the company's liability.

The interest rate is determined by criteria contained in Treasury regulations made by statutory instrument so that when such criteria change so as to alter the rate, HMRC must specify in an order the new rate and the day from which it has effect. For the criteria, see *SI 1989 No 1297, Reg 3A* and, as regards accounting periods ending on or after 1 July 1999, *Regs 3ZA, 3ZB* as inserted by *SI 1998 No 3176* and amended by *SI 2000 No 893*.

37.5 Interest and Surcharges on Unpaid Tax

The rates of interest (such interest being deductible for tax purposes — see below) as regards corporation tax becoming due **on or after the normal due date** (nine months and one day after the end of the accounting period) are:

6.50% p.a. from 6 September 2005

7.50% p.a. from 6 September 2004 to 5 September 2005

6.50% p.a. from 6 December 2003 to 5 September 2004

5.50% p.a. from 6 August 2003 to 5 December 2003

6.50% p.a. from 6 November 2001 to 5 August 2003

7.50% p.a. from 6 May 2001 to 5 November 2001

8.50% p.a. previously

The rates for corporation tax payable by earlier **instalments**, under the quarterly accounting rules for large companies (see 47.2 PAYMENT OF TAX), are:

5.5% p.a. from 15 August 2005

5.75% p.a. from 16 August 2004 to 14 August 2005

5.50% p.a. from 21 June 2004 to 15 August 2004

5.25% p.a. from 17 May 2004 to 20 June 2004

5.00% p.a. from 16 February 2004 to 16 May 2004

4.75% from 17 November 2003 to 15 February 2004

4.50% p.a. from 21 July 2003 to 16 November 2003

4.75% p.a. from 17 February 2003 to 20 July 2003

5.00% p.a. from 19 November 2001 to 16 February 2003

5.50% p.a. from 15 October 2001 to 18 November 2001

5.75% p.a. from 1 October 2001 to 14 October 2001

6.00% p.a. from 13 August 2001 to 30 September 2001

6.25% p.a. from 21 May 2001 to 12 August 2001

6.50% p.a. from 16 April 2001 to 20 May 2001

6.75% p.a. from 19 February 2001 to 15 April 2001

7.00% p.a. from 20 April 2000 to 18 February 2001

8.00% p.a. from 21 February 2000 to 19 April 2000

7.75% p.a. from 24 January 2000 to 20 February 2000

7.50% p.a. from 15 November 1999 to 23 January 2000

7.25% p.a. from 20 September 1999 to 14 November 1999

7.00% p.a. from 21 June 1999 to 19 September 1999

7.25% p.a. from 19 April 1999 to 20 June 1999

7.50% p.a. from 15 February 1999 to 18 April 1999

8.00% p.a. from 18 January 1999 to 14 February 1999

8.25% p.a. from 7 January 1999 to 17 January 1999

The latter set of rates applies up to the earlier of the date of payment and the normal due date (whereafter the normal rates apply).

Interest on tax subsequently discharged is adjusted or repaid so as to secure that the total is as it would have been had the tax discharged never been charged. However, where surplus advance corporation tax of a later accounting period displaces mainstream corporation tax paid in respect of an earlier accounting period, or trading losses or non-trading deficits of a later accounting period are offset against profits of an earlier period, or there is a combination of such events, any such adjustment or repayment of interest is restricted. In considering an adjustment or repayment of interest, then, where relief for tax paid for an accounting period is given by way of repayment of tax, the amount repaid is, as far as possible, treated as if it were a discharge of the corporation tax charged for that period.

Interest is paid without deduction of income tax and is deductible in computing profits (as a non-trading debit under the loan relationship rules — see 14.2–14.6 COMPANIES—CORPORATE FINANCE AND INTANGIBLES and Tolley's Corporation Tax). It is recoverable (as if it were tax charged and due and payable under an assessment) as a Crown debt.

[*TMA 1970, ss 69, 87A, 90, s 91(1A)(2A); F(No 2)A 1987, s 85, s 86(5)(6); FA 1989, s 178; FA 1991, Sch 15 para 2; FA 1993, ss 120, 170, Sch 14 paras 4, 5, Sch 18 para 1; SI 1989 No 1297; SI 1993 No 2212; FA 1994, Sch 19 para 20; FA 1996, s 100(4A) as previously enacted, s 100(7), Sch 18 para 13; FA 1998, ss 33, 35, Sch 4 paras 4, 7; SI 1998 No 3175, Reg 7; FA 2000, Sch 29 para 9(2)(3), Sch 40 Pt II(12); FA 2001, s 89(2); FA 2002, s 79, Sch 23 para 6, Sch 40 Pt 3(10); ITTOIA 2005, Sch 1 para 378*].

Accounting periods ending after 30 September 1993 and before 1 July 1999. In relation to such accounting periods (Pay and File), the provisions described above in relation to self-assessment accounting periods apply, but with the following differences:

- interest is not deductible in computing income, profits or losses;
- the special rates for instalment payments for 'large' companies do not apply.

[*TMA 1970, ss 87A, 90, 91(1A)(1B)(2A), 109(3A)–(5); FA 1998, Sch 3 para 4, Sch 4 para 4*].

Rates of interest are:

5.25% p.a. from 6 September 2005

6.00% p.a. from 6 September 2004 to 5 September 2005

5.25% p.a. from 6 December 2003 to 5 September 2004

4.25% p.a. from 6 August 2003 to 5 December 2003

5.00% p.a. from 6 November 2001 to 5 August 2003

6.00% p.a. from 6 May 2001 to 5 November 2001

6.75% p.a. from 6 February 2000 to 5 May 2001

5.75% p.a. from 6 March 1999 to 5 February 2000

6.50% p.a. from 6 January 1999 to 5 March 1999

7.50% p.a. from 6 August 1997 to 5 January 1999

6.25% p.a. from 6 February 1996 to 5 August 1997

7.00% p.a. from 6 March 1995 to 5 February 1996

6.25% p.a. from 6 October 1994 to 5 March 1995

5.50% p.a. from 6 January 1994 to 5 October 1994

6.25% p.a. from 1 October 1993 to 5 January 1994

HMRC announced on 6 September 2005 that the interest rate that they had previously used for the period 6 December 2003 to 5 September 2004 was incorrect. The rate for that period shown above is the corrected rate published on 6 September 2005. The incorrect rate used was lower than that above but HMRC will not make any attempt to recover any further interest due. Where, however, a liability is reviewed for other reasons, the correct amount of interest will be calculated. (HMRC News Release 6 September 2005).

37.6 EXCHANGE RESTRICTIONS AND DELAYED REMITTANCES

Where gains arising overseas cannot be remitted to the UK due to government action in the country of origin etc., and HMRC agree to defer collection of the tax, interest ceases to run from the date on which HMRC were first in possession of information necessary to enable them to agree to deferment. If that date is three months or less from the due and payable date, no interest is payable. But where a demand is later made for payment of the deferred tax, interest (from the date of demand) is only assessable if the tax is not paid within three months of that demand. [*TMA 1970, s 92; F(No 2)A 1987, s 86(2)(a)*]. HMRC may defer collection indefinitely. See 45.5 OVERSEAS MATTERS for an alternative relief under *TCGA 1992, s 279*.

37.7 MISCELLANEOUS

Unreasonable delay by HMRC. Where the taxpayer complains, HMRC may remit or reimburse any interest on unpaid tax incurred during a period of unreasonable delay by HMRC in dealing with his affairs (HMRC Code of Practice 1 (COP 1)).

Personal representatives. Personal representatives unable to pay tax before obtaining probate may have concessional treatment so that interest on tax falling due after the date of death runs from the expiration of 30 days after the date of grant of probate or letters of administration (if this is later than the date arrived at under 34.2 or 37.2 above). (HMRC Extra-Statutory Concession A17). This concession continues to apply under self-assessment (HMRC Self-Assessment Manual — Interest, penalties and surcharges section).

Foot and mouth disease. Where the Revenue agreed that tax could be deferred owing to severe disruption or financial distress suffered by a business as a result of the 2001 outbreak of foot and mouth disease in the UK, no interest was chargeable for a certain period on the amount deferred. This interest pause commenced on 31 January 2001 or on such later date as the Revenue directed in any particular case (being the date that the agreement for deferred payment took effect) and ended with the date on which the agreement for deferred payment ceased to have effect (subject to any extension granted). The power to remit interest will cease from a date to be specified by Treasury order, but this will not affect the position as regards deferment agreements made before that date. [*FA 2001, s 107*]. See Revenue Press Release 4 May 2001 for further detail, including Helpline telephone numbers, and see generally Revenue Tax Bulletin, Special Foot and Mouth Disease Edition, May 2001.

The Revenue also announced that surcharges (see 37.4 above) would not be payable for an agreed period of deferral, as above, of payment of tax (Revenue Tax Bulletin, Special Foot and Mouth Disease Edition, May 2001 p 3).

38 Land

Cross-references. See 6.7 ASSETS for granting of options and 6.9 re milk quota; 7.6 ASSETS HELD ON 6 APRIL 1965 for land reflecting development value and 7.7–7.12 for other land held at that date; 9.1 CAPITAL SUMS DERIVED FROM ASSETS for treatment of statutory compensation received by tenants of land and 9.3 for buildings destroyed and replaced out of compensation; 22.18 EXEMPTIONS AND RELIEFS for certain agricultural grants; 22.36 for woodlands, 22.49 for housing associations, 22.58 for self-build societies and 22.80 for disposal by gift of national heritage property; 40.9 LOSSES for buildings becoming of negligible value; 41.7 MARKET VALUE; 43 MINERAL ROYALTIES; 47.6 PAYMENT OF TAX for payment by instalments on gifts of land; 49 PRIVATE RESIDENCES with land attached; 55 ROLLOVER RELIEF for a claim on disposal of land occupied for trade purposes.

Simon's Direct Tax Service. See Division C2.11.

The headings in this chapter are as follows.

38.1 INTRODUCTION

There are a number of special provisions in the capital gains tax legislation relating to land. For disposals of land generally, see 38.2–38.12 below. For provisions relating to leases of land, see 38.13–38.23 below. For contingent liabilities on the disposal of land, see 38.24 below.

38.2 GENERAL

The general principles of capital gains tax apply to disposals of land. There are, however, particular problems concerning land transactions.

(*a*) An isolated or speculative transaction may be liable to income tax rather than to capital gains tax as amounting to an adventure or concern in the nature of trade (see 38.3 below).

(*b*) Even where (*a*) above does not apply, capital gains from certain transactions in land may be treated as income (see 38.4 and 38.5 below).

(*c*) The definition of 'land' for the purposes of *TCGA 1992* is not exclusive and may lead to difficulties of interpretation, especially where property derives its existence from the existence of the physical land. '*Land*' includes for such purposes, except where the context otherwise requires, messuages, tenements and hereditaments, houses and buildings of any tenure. [*TCGA 1992, s 288*(*1*)]. This is the original 1851 definition and should be compared with the current *Interpretation Act 1978* definition which is that '*land*' includes buildings and other structures, land covered with water, and any estate, interest, easement, servitude or right in or over land. (Apart from the specific definition for certain transactions in land under *ICTA 1988, ss 776–778* in 38.4 below, it is not entirely clear which of the above definitions applies for purposes of *ICTA 1988*.) That said, many provisions in *TCGA 1992* refer to 'land' as including any interest in or right over land or to an interest in an asset which can include land or buildings etc. (e.g. *TCGA 1992, s 152* (ROLLOVER RELIEF (55), although *TCGA 1992, s 155* treats buildings and the underlying land as separate) and *TCGA 1992, s 247* (38.11 below)). Deciding whether property is an interest or right over land can thus depend on general legal principles and the surrounding facts. Milk quota does not constitute such an interest or right (see 6.9 ASSETS).

38.3 ISOLATED OR SPECULATIVE TRANSACTIONS

A line is drawn between realisations of property held as investment or as a residence and transactions amounting to an adventure or concern in the nature of a trade. Whether the surplus on the purchase and resale of land, otherwise than in the course of an established commercial enterprise, is derived from an adventure or concern in the nature of trade depends upon the facts.

Para. 116 of the Final Report of the Royal Commission on the Taxation of Profits and Income (1955 HMSO Cmd. 9474) lists six 'badges of trade'.

(*a*) The subject matter of the realisation.

(*b*) The length of period of ownership.

(*c*) The frequency or number of similar transactions.

(*d*) Supplementary work on assets sold.

(*e*) Reason for the sale.

(*f*) Motive.

Other relevant factors may be the degree of organisation, whether the taxpayer is or has been associated with a recognised business dealing in similar assets and how the purchases were financed.

In *Leeming v Jones HL 1930, 15 TC 333* an income tax assessment on the acquisitions and disposal of options over rubber estates was confirmed by Commissioners. The Crown had defended the assessment under both Schedule D, Case I and Case VI. In a Supplementary Case the Commissioners found there had been no concern in the nature of trade. The Court held there was no liability. Per Lawrence LJ 'in the case of an isolated transaction ... there is really no middle course open. It is either an adventure in the nature of trade, or else it is simply a case of sale and resale of property.' See also *Pearn v Miller KB 1927, 11 TC 610* and *Williams v Davies* below.

Property transactions by companies were held to be trading in *Californian Copper Syndicate v Harris CES 1904, 5 TC 159* (purchase of copper bearing land shortly afterwards resold); *Thew v South West Africa Co CA 1924, 9 TC 141* (numerous sales of land acquired by concession for exploitation); *Cayzer, Irvine & Co v CIR CS 1942, 24 TC 491* (exploitation of landed estate acquired by shipping company); *Emro Investments v Aller and Webb* (Lance) *Estates v Aller Ch D 1954, 35 TC 305* (profits carried to capital reserve on numerous purchases and sales); *Orchard Parks v Pogson Ch D 1964, 42 TC 442* (land compulsorily purchased after development plan dropped); *Parkstone Estates v Blair Ch D 1966, 43 TC 246* (industrial estate developed—land disposed of by sub-leases for premiums); *Eames v Stepnell Properties Ltd CA 1966, 43 TC 678* (sale of land acquired from associated company while resale being negotiated). See also *Bath & West Counties Property Trust Ltd v Thomas Ch D 1977, 52 TC 20*. Realisations were held to be capital in *Hudson's Bay Co v Stevens CA 1909, 5 TC 424* (numerous sales of land acquired under Royal

Charter—contrast *South West Africa Co* above); *Tebrau (Johore) Rubber Syndicate v Farmer CES 1910, 5 TC 658* (purchase and resale of rubber estates—contrast *Californian Copper* above); *Mamor Sendirian Berhad v Director-General of Inland Revenue PC, [1985] STC 801* (sales of timber in the course of developing forest land into an oil palm plantation). See also *Lim Foo Yong Sendirian Berhad v Comptroller-General of Inland Revenue PC, [1986] STC 255* where it was held that a company may hold property on both trading and capital account and the fact that acquisitions and disposals have taken place on the former does not automatically determine for all time the company's intention in acquiring, holding and developing other property; and contrast *Richfield International Land and Investment Co Ltd v Inland Revenue Commissioner PC, [1989] STC 820* where an initial finding that a property sale had been on trading account was upheld, such finding only being inferred from previous property sales which had either been taxed or accounted for as trading transactions.

In *Rand v Alberni Land Co Ltd KB 1920, 7 TC 629* sales of land held in trust were held not to be trading but contrast *Alabama Coal etc. Co Ltd v Mylam KB 1926, 11 TC 232*; *Balgownie Land Trust v CIR CS 1929, 14 TC 684*; *St Aubyn Estates v Strick KB 1932, 17 TC 412*; *Tempest Estates Ltd v Walmsley Ch D 1975, 51 TC 305*. Sales of property after a period of letting were held to be realisations of investments or not trading in *CIR v Hyndland Investment Co Ltd CS 1929, 14 TC 694*; *Glasgow Heritable Trust v CIR CS 1954, 35 TC 196*; *Lucy & Sunderland Ltd v Hunt Ch D 1961, 40 TC 132* but were held to be trading in *Rellim Ltd v Vise CA 1951, 32 TC 254* (notwithstanding that the company was previously admitted as an investment company); *CIR v Toll Property Co CS 1952, 34 TC 13*; *Forest Side Properties (Chingford) v Pearce CA 1961, 39 TC 665*. But sales by the liquidator of property owned by companies following the abandonment of a plan for their public flotation were held to be not trading in *Simmons v CIR HL 1980, 53 TC 461* (reversing Commissioners' decision). In *Rosemoor Investments v Inspector of Taxes (Sp C 320), [2002] SSCD 325*, it was not open to the Commissioners to recharacterise as trading a complex transaction routed via an investment company subsidiary and structured to produce capital.

Property transactions by individuals and partnerships. Profits were held assessable as income in *Reynold's Exors v Bennett KB 1943, 25 TC 401*; *Broadbridge v Beattie KB 1944, 26 TC 63*; *Gray & Gillitt v Tiley KB 1944, 26 TC 80*; *Laver v Wilkinson KB 1944, 26 TC 105*; *Foulds v Clayton Ch D 1953, 34 TC 382*; *Kirkby v Hughes Ch D 1992, 65 TC 532*; *Lynch v Edmondson (Sp C 164), [1998] SSCD 185* in all of which the taxpayers were or had been associated with building or estate development, and contrast *Williams v Davies KB 1945, 26 TC 371* in which the taxpayers were closely associated with land development but a profit on transactions in undeveloped land belonging to their wives was held not assessable as income. The acquisition and resale of land for which planning permission had been or was obtained was held as trading in *Cooke v Haddock Ch D 1960, 39 TC 64*; *Turner v Last Ch D 1965, 42 TC 517* and *Pilkington v Randall CA 1966, 42 TC 662* (and cf. *Iswera v Ceylon Commr PC 1965, 44 ATC 157*), but contrast *Taylor v Good CA 1974, 49 TC 277* (in which a house bought as a residence was found unsuitable and resold to a developer after obtaining planning permission) and *Kirkham v Williams CA 1991, 64 TC 253* (in which a site was acquired principally as a capital asset to be used in the taxpayer's trade but which was later developed and sold), in both of which cases it was held that there had not been an adventure. In *Burrell v Davis Ch D 1948, 38 TC 307*; *Johnston v Heath Ch D 1970, 46 TC 463*; *Reeves v Evans, Boyce & Northcott Ch D 1971, 48 TC 495* and *Clark v Follett Ch D 1973, 48 TC 677* the short period of ownership or other evidence showed an intention to purchase for resale at a profit and not for investment, and contrast *CIR v Reinhold CS 1953, 34 TC 389*, *Taylor v Good* above and *Marson v Morton Ch D 1986, 59 TC 381*. For other cases in which profits were held assessable as income see *Hudson v Wrightson KB 1934, 26 TC 55*, *MacMahon v CIR CS 1951, 32 TC 311* and *Eckel v Board of Inland Revenue PC 1989, 62 TC 331*.

38.4 **TRANSACTIONS IN LAND** [*ICTA 1988, ss 776–778; ITTOIA 2005, Sch 1 paras 312, 313*]

The following provisions apply to all persons, whether UK residents or not, if all or any part of the 'land' in question is in the UK.

Where

(*a*) land (or any 'property deriving its value from land') is acquired with the sole or main object of realising a gain from disposing of it, or

(*b*) land is held as trading stock, or

(*c*) land is developed with the sole or main object of realising a gain from disposing of it when developed,

any capital gain from 'disposal' of the land or any part of it (i.e. any amount not otherwise able to be included in any computation of income for tax purposes) which is realised (for himself or for any other person) by the person acquiring, holding or developing it (or by CONNECTED PERSONS (16), or a person party to, or concerned in, any arrangement or scheme to realise the gain indirectly or by a series of transactions) is, subject as below, treated for all tax purposes as income of the person realising the gain (or the person who transmitted to him, directly or indirectly, the opportunity of making that gain) assessable to income tax (under Schedule D, Case VI before *ITTOIA 2005* came into effect) or to corporation tax under Schedule D, Case VI, for the chargeable period in which the gain is realised. See *Yuill v Wilson HL 1980, 52 TC 674* and its sequel *Yuill v Fletcher CA 1984, 58 TC 145*, *Winterton v Edwards Ch D 1979, 52 TC 655* and *Sugarwhite v Budd CA 1988, 60 TC 679*. Bona fide transactions, not entered into with tax avoidance in view, may be caught by the legislation. See *Page v Lowther and Another CA 1983, 57 TC 199*.

'*Land*' includes buildings, and any estate or interest in land or buildings.

'*Property deriving its value from land*' includes any shareholding in a company, partnership interest, or interest in settled property, deriving its value, directly or indirectly, from land, and any option, consent or embargo affecting the disposition of land. But see 'Exemptions' below.

'*Disposal*' of land occurs for the above purposes if, by any one or more transactions or by any arrangement or scheme (whether concerning the land or any property deriving its value therefrom), the property in, or control over, the land is effectively disposed of. Any number of transactions may be treated as a single arrangement or scheme if they have, or there is evidence of, a common purpose. For the date of disposal where instalments are involved see *Yuill v Fletcher* above. See also under 'General' below.

Exemptions

(i) An individual's gain made from the sale, etc., of his residence exempted from capital gains tax under *TCGA 1992, ss 222–226* or which would be so exempt but for *TCGA 1992, s 224(3)* (acquired for purpose of making a gain, see 49.7 PRIVATE RESIDENCES).

(ii) A gain on the sale of shares in a company holding land as trading stock (or a company owning, directly or indirectly, 90% of the ordinary share capital of such a company) *provided that* the company disposes of the land by normal trade and makes all possible profit from it, and the share sale is not part of an arrangement or scheme to realise a land gain indirectly. See *Chilcott v CIR Ch D 1981, 55 TC 446*.

(iii) If the liability arises solely under (*c*) above, any part of the gain fairly attributable to a period before the intention was formed to develop the land.

Gains are to be computed 'as is just and reasonable in the circumstances', allowance being given only for expenses attributable to the land disposed of, and the following may be taken into account.

(A) If a leasehold interest is disposed of out of a freehold, the way in which the taxable trading profits of a person dealing in land are computed.

(B) Any adjustment under *ICTA 1988, s 99(2)(3)* or *ITTOIA 2005, s 158* for the amount of any lease premium treated as a receipt of a property business (see Tolley's Income Tax).

Where the computation of a gain in respect of the development of land (as under (*c*) above) is made on the footing that the land or property was appropriated as trading stock, that land, etc., is also to be treated for purposes of capital gains tax (under *TCGA 1992, s 161*; see 6.3 ASSETS) as having been transferred to stock.

Where, under *ICTA 1988, s 776,* tax is assessed on, and paid by, a person other than the one who actually realised the gain, the person paying the tax may recover it from the other party (for which purpose HMRC will, on request, supply a certificate of income in respect of which tax has been paid).

Clearance. The person who made or would make the gain may (if he considers that (*a*) or (*c*) above may apply), submit to his inspector particulars of any completed or proposed transactions. If he does so, the inspector must, within 30 days of receiving those particulars, notify the taxpayer whether or not he is satisfied that liability under above does not arise. If the inspector is so satisfied no assessment can thereafter be made on that gain under the provisions above, provided that all material facts and considerations have been fully and accurately disclosed.

General. There are also provisions to prevent avoidance by the use of indirect means to transfer any property or right, or enhance or diminish its value, e.g., by sales at less, or more, than full consideration, assigning share capital or rights in a company or partnership or an interest in settled property, disposal on the winding-up of any company, partnership or trust etc. For ascertaining whether, and to what extent, the value of any property or right is derived from any other property or right, value may be traced through any number of companies, partnerships and trusts, at each stage attributing property held by the company etc. to its shareholders etc., 'in such manner as is appropriate to the circumstances'.

For the above purposes HMRC may require, under penalty, any person to supply them with any particulars thought necessary, including particulars of

(I) transactions, etc., in which he acts, or acted, on behalf of others, and

(II) transactions, etc., which in the opinion of HMRC should be investigated, and

(III) what part, if any, he has taken, or is taking, in specified transactions, etc. (Under this heading a *solicitor* who has merely acted as professional adviser is not compelled to do more than state that he acted and give his client's name and address.)

The transactions of which particulars are required need not be identified transactions (*Essex v CIR CA 1980, 53 TC 720*).

The Valuation Office Agency has published its internal guidance manuals on the valuation of property (Revenue Press Release 19 February 1996).

38.5 LAND SOLD WITH RIGHT OF RECONVEYANCE

Where an interest in land is sold on terms requiring it to be subsequently *reconveyed* at a future date after the sale (or leased back one month or more after the sale) *to the vendor*, or a person connected with him, and the price at which the interest is sold exceeds that at which it is to be reconveyed (or, in the case of a lease-back, the value of the reversionary interest plus any premium for the lease), the excess less 1/50th for each full year (minus one) between the sale and the date of the earliest possible reconveyance (or lease-back) is treated as a receipt of the vendor's property business. [*ICTA 1988, s 36; FA 1998, Sch 5 para 17; ITTOIA 2005, ss 284–286, Sch 1 para 19*].

Any amount (as adjusted under *ICTA 1988, s 36(2)(b)* or *ITTOIA 2005, ss 301, 302*; price on reconveyance varying with time) brought into account as a receipt of a property business under these provisions is excluded from the consideration brought into account in the computation for capital gains tax purposes *except* in the denominator of the part disposal fraction (A/(A+B); see 15.7 COMPUTATION OF GAINS AND LOSSES). This does not apply where what is disposed of is the remainder of a lease or a sub-lease out of a lease the duration of which does not exceed 50 years. See 38.17 below for the alternative provisions which apply. [*TCGA 1992, Sch 8 para 5(3)(4), para 6(3); FA 1998, Sch 5 para 63(2); ITTOIA 2005, Sch 1 para 451(2)*].

38.6 BETTERMENT LEVY

Betterment levy paid in respect of certain development land is deductible as expenditure wholly and exclusively incurred in enhancing the value of the asset in the CGT computation arising on the disposal or part disposal of that land. [*TCGA 1992, Sch 11 para 17*].

38.7 PART DISPOSALS

The general provisions for part disposals in *TCGA 1992, s 42* apply to disposals of land. See 15.7 COMPUTATION OF GAINS AND LOSSES. These require the use of the market value of the part retained. HMRC will, however, accept an alternative basis of calculation in the case of land. Under this, the part disposed of will be treated as a separate asset and any fair and reasonable method of apportioning part of the total cost to it will be accepted — e.g. a reasonable valuation of that part at the acquisition date. Where the market value at 6 April 1965 is to be taken as the cost, a reasonable valuation of the part at that date will similarly be accepted.

The cost of the part disposed of will be deducted from the total cost of the estate (or the balance of total cost) to determine the cost of the remainder of the estate; thus the total of the separate amounts adopted for the parts will not exceed the total cost. The cost attributed to each part must also be realistic in itself and HMRC reserve the right to apply the general rule if not satisfied that apportionments are fair and reasonable. The taxpayer can always require that the general rule should be applied (except in cases already settled on the alternative basis). If he chooses the general rule it will normally be necessary to apply this rule to all subsequent disposals out of the estate; but where the general rule has been applied for a part disposal before the introduction of the alternative basis and it produced a result broadly the same as under the alternative basis, the alternative basis may be used for subsequent part disposals out of the estate.

So long as disposals out of an estate acquired before 6 April 1965 are dealt with on the alternative basis, each part disposal will carry a separate right to elect for acquisition at market value on 6 April 1965. Similarly, where part is sold with development value, the mandatory valuation at 6 April 1965 will apply only to that part. Even where the part is to be treated as acquired at market value on 6 April 1965, however, it will still be necessary to agree how much of the actual cost should be attributed to the part disposed of: first, to ensure that any allowable loss does not exceed the actual loss, and second, to produce a balance of total cost for subsequent disposals.

Adoption of the alternative basis is without prejudice to the treatment of small disposals set out in 38.8 below (HMRC Statement of Practice D1).

For provisions which apply to land held on 6 April 1965 generally, see 7.6–7.12 ASSETS HELD ON 6 APRIL 1965. Although HMRC have yet to confirm it, it seems the above practice could be applied to land held on 31 March 1982 with suitable modifications. See generally, 8 ASSETS HELD ON 31 MARCH 1982.

38.8 **Small part disposals.** Where there is a transfer of land forming part only of a holding of land (or an estate or interest therein) and the amount or value of the consideration does not exceed one-fifth of the market value of the holding as it existed immediately before the disposal, the transferor may claim under *TCGA 1992, s 242(2)* that the transfer is not treated as a disposal. The consideration which would have been brought into account in the capital gains tax computation is then treated as a reduction of allowable expenditure in relation to any subsequent disposal of the remaining holding.

The consideration for the transfer or, if the transfer is not for full consideration, the market value of the land transferred, must not exceed a limit of £20,000. Where the transferor has made other disposals of land in the year of assessment, the total amount or value of the consideration for all such disposals of land (other than those within 38.10 below) must not exceed the limit.

The provisions do not apply to

(*a*) transfers treated as giving rise to neither a gain nor a loss between spouses or civil partners (see 42.4 MARRIED PERSONS AND CIVIL PARTNERS) or between companies in the same group (see 27.1 GROUPS OF COMPANIES); or

(*b*) an estate or interest in land which is a wasting asset (e.g. a short lease under 38.14 below).

A claim for small part disposals must be made for the purposes of capital gains tax on or before the first anniversary of 31 January following the year of assessment in which the transfer is made. For corporation tax purposes, for accounting periods ending after 30 June 1999, the claim must be made within two years after the end of the accounting period in which the transfer is made. For earlier accounting periods the time limit is six years after the end of the accounting period in question.

Where the allowable expenditure is less than the consideration for the part disposal (or is nil) the claim referred to above cannot be made but, if the recipient elects under *TCGA 1992, s 244(2)* and there is allowable expenditure, the consideration for the part disposal is reduced by the amount of the allowable expenditure. None of that expenditure is then allowable as a deduction in computing the gain accruing on the part disposal or any subsequent disposal.

[*TCGA 1992, ss 242, 244; FA 1996, Sch 21 para 37*].

Example

C owns farmland which cost £134,000 in May 1988 and which is a business asset for the purposes of TAPER RELIEF (61). In February 1996, a small plot of land is exchanged with an adjoining landowner for another piece of land. The value placed on the transaction is £18,000. The value of the remaining estate excluding the new piece of land is estimated at £250,000. In March 2007, C sells the whole estate for £300,000. He makes no other disposals in 2006/07.

Indexation factors	May 1988 to February 1996	0.421
	February 1996 to April 1998	0.078
	May 1988 to April 1998	0.531

(i) No claim made under *TCGA 1992, s 242(2)*

		£	£
(*a*)	*Disposal in February 1996*		
	Disposal proceeds		18,000
	Allowable cost		
	$\dfrac{18{,}000}{18{,}000+250{,}000} \times \pounds\,134{,}000$		9,000
	Unindexed gain		9,000
	Indexation allowance £9,000 × 0.421		3,789
	Chargeable gain 1995/96		£5,211
(*b*)	*Disposal in March 2007*		
	Disposal proceeds		300,000
	Allowable cost		
	Original land £(134,000 – 9,000)	125,000	
	Exchanged land	18,000	143,000
	Unindexed gain		157,000
	Indexation allowance		
	Original land £125,000 × 0.531	66,375	
	Exchanged land £18,000 × 0.078	1,404	67,779
	Pre-tapered gain		89,221
	Business asset taper relief @ 75%		66,916
	Chargeable gain 2006/07		£22,305

(ii) Claim made under *TCGA 1992, s 242(2)*

		£	£
(*a*)	*No disposal in February 1996*		
	Allowable cost of original land		134,000
	Deduct disposal proceeds		18,000
	Adjusted allowable cost		£116,000
	Allowable cost of additional land		£18,000
(*b*)	*Disposal in March 2007*		
	Disposal proceeds		300,000
	Allowable cost		
	Original land	116,000	
	Additional land	18,000	134,000
	Unindexed gain		166,000

	£	£
Indexation allowance		
Original land £134,000 × 0.531	71,154	
Additional land £18,000 × 0.078	1,404	
	72,558	
Receipt set-off £18,000 × 0.078	1,404	71,154
Pre-tapered gain		94,846
Business asset taper relief @ 75%		71,135
Chargeable gain 2006/07		£23,711

Note to the example

(*a*) Although (ii) above gives the lower overall gain, (i) above would be preferable if there are little or no other gains for 1995/96, such that the 1995/96 gain in (i) above is fully covered by the annual exemption for that year.

38.9 COMPULSORY PURCHASE

The transfer of an interest in land to an 'authority exercising or having compulsory powers' (see 38.10 below) is a disposal for capital gains tax purposes. If the land is acquired under a contract, the date of disposal is the time the contract is made (and not, if different, the time at which the asset is conveyed or transferred). If the contract is conditional, the date of disposal is the time when the condition is satisfied. See also 15.3 COMPUTATION OF GAINS AND LOSSES. Otherwise, the disposal and acquisition are made at the time at which compensation for the acquisition is agreed or otherwise determined (any variation on appeal against the original determination being disregarded). For 1995/96 and earlier years, the time when the local authority entered on the land in pursuance of its powers, if earlier than the time given by the aforementioned rule, was taken instead. This continues to be the case as regards interests owned by companies as respects accounting periods ending before 1 July 1999, i.e. the appointed day for corporation tax self-assessment (see 13.2 COMPANIES).

[*TCGA 1992, ss 28, 246; FA 1996, s 121(8), s 141(4), Sch 41 Pt V(6)*].

Relief is available for small part disposals (see 38.10 below). Rollover relief may be claimed in certain circumstances (see 38.11 below). In addition, where land or an interest in or right over land is acquired and the acquisition is (or could have been) made under compulsory powers, then the existence of the compulsory powers and any statutory provision treating the purchase price, compensation or other consideration as exclusively paid in respect of the land itself is disregarded in considering whether, under *TCGA 1992, s 52(4)* (just and reasonable apportionments), the purchase price etc. should be apportioned on a just and reasonable basis and treated in part as a capital sum within *TCGA 1992, s 22(1)(a)* (whether as compensation for loss of goodwill, for disturbance or otherwise) or should be apportioned in any other way. [*TCGA 1992, s 245(1)*]. The effect of this is that, where it is just and reasonable, part of the proceeds may be treated as a capital sum derived from an asset. See 9.1(*a*) CAPITAL SUMS DERIVED FROM ASSETS.

The receipt of severance compensation or compensation for injurious affection where part of a holding of land is or could have been compulsorily purchased is treated as a part disposal of the remaining land. [*TCGA 1992, s 245(2)*]. Where the conditions are satisfied, a claim for rollover relief may be made (see 38.11 below) in which case the consideration rolled over will include such compensation and there will be no deemed disposal of the remaining land. [*TCGA 1992, s 247(6)*].

Example

(i) Rollover not claimed

D owns freehold land purchased for £77,000 in 1978. Part of the land is made the subject of a compulsory purchase order. The compensation of £70,000 is agreed on 10 August 2006. The market value of the remaining land is £175,000. The value of the total freehold land at 31 March 1982 was £98,000. The indexation factor for the period March 1982 to April 1998 is 1.047.

	£	£
Disposal consideration	70,000	70,000
Cost $£77,000 \times \dfrac{70,000}{70,000 + 175,000}$	22,000	
Market value 31.3.82		
$£98,000 \times \dfrac{70,000}{70,000 + 175,000}$		28,000
Unindexed gain	48,000	42,000
Indexation allowance £28,000 × 1.047	29,316	29,316
Gain after indexation	£18,684	£12,684
Chargeable gain (subject to TAPER RELIEF (61))		£12,684

(ii) Rollover claimed under *TCGA 1992, s 247*

If, in (i), D acquires new land costing, say, £80,000 in, say, December 2006, relief may be claimed as follows.

	£
Allowable cost of land compulsorily purchased	28,000
Indexation allowance	29,316
Deemed consideration for disposal	57,316
Actual consideration	70,000
Chargeable gain rolled over	£12,684
Allowable cost of new land (£80,000 – £12,684)	£67,316

38.10 **Small part disposals.** Where a part of a holding of land (or an interest therein) is transferred to an 'authority exercising or having compulsory powers', the transferor may claim under *TCGA 1992, s 243(2)* that the transfer is not treated as a disposal, in which case the consideration which would have been brought into account is treated as a reduction of allowable expenditure in relation to any subsequent disposal of the remaining holding. A claim must be made for the purposes of capital gains tax on or before the first anniversary of 31 January following the year of assessment in which the transfer is made. For corporation tax purposes, for accounting periods ending after 30 June 1999, the claim must be made within two years after the end of the accounting period in which the transfer is made. For earlier accounting periods the time limit is six years after the end of the accounting period in question. [*TCGA 1992, s 243(2A); FA 1996, Sch 21 para 38*]. A holding of land for these purposes comprises only the land in respect of which allowable expenditure would be apportioned under *TCGA 1992, s 42* if the transfer had been treated as a part disposal. The consideration for the transfer (or, if the transfer is not for full consideration, the market value of the land transferred) must be 'small' as compared with the market value of the holding immediately before the transfer. For this purpose, HMRC have regarded 'small' as meaning 5% or less (see HMRC Capital Gains Manual CG 57836, 72201). With effect from **24 February 1997**, they additionally regard an amount of £3,000 or less as 'small', regardless of whether or not it would pass the 5% test (Revenue Tax Bulletin February 1997 p 397).

The transferor must not have taken any steps, by advertising or otherwise, to dispose of any part of the holding or to make his willingness to dispose of it known to anyone. The provisions do not apply to wasting interests in land (e.g. a short lease under 38.14 below) but subject to this any estate or interest in land is included as a holding.

Where the allowable expenditure is less than the consideration for the part disposal (or is nil) the claim referred to above cannot be made but, if the recipient elects under *TCGA 1992, s 244(2)* and there is allowable expenditure, the consideration for the part disposal is reduced by the amount of the allowable expenditure. An election shall be made for the purposes of capital gains tax on or before the first anniversary of the 31 January next following the year of assessment in which part disposal is made; and in the case of corporation tax within two years after the end of the accounting period in which the part disposal is made. None of that expenditure is then allowable as a deduction in computing the gain accruing on the part disposal or any subsequent disposal.

'*Authority exercising or having compulsory powers*' means, in relation to the land transferred, a person or body of persons acquiring it compulsorily or who has or have been, or could be, authorised to acquire it compulsorily for the purposes for which it is acquired, or for whom another person or body of persons has or have been, or could be, authorised so to acquire it.

[*TCGA 1992, ss 243, 244; FA 1996, Sch 21 para 39*].

Example

(i) No rollover relief claimed

T inherited land in June 1988 at a probate value of £290,000. Under a compulsory purchase order, a part of the land is acquired for highway improvements. Compensation of £32,000 and a further £10,000 for severance, neither sum including any amount in respect of loss of profits, is agreed on 14 May 2006. The value of the remaining land is £900,000. Prior to the compulsory purchase, the value of all the land had been £950,000. The indexation factor for the period June 1988 to April 1998 is 0.525.

	£
Total consideration for disposal (£32,000 + £10,000)	42,000
Deduct allowable cost $\frac{42,000}{42,000+900,000} \times$ £290,000	12,930
Unindexed gain	29,070
Indexation allowance £12,930 × 0.525	6,788
Chargeable gain (subject to TAPER RELIEF (61))	£22,282

(ii) Rollover relief claimed under *TCGA 1992, s 243*

Total consideration for disposal is £42,000, less than 5% of the value of the estate before the disposal (£950,000). T may therefore claim that the consideration be deducted from the allowable cost of the estate.

Revised allowable cost (£290,000 – £42,000)	£248,000

38.11 **Rollover relief.** ROLLOVER RELIEF (55) is extended to *any landowner* (i.e. not confined to land (or any interest in or right over land) which is used and occupied for the purposes of a trade) who disposes of land to an 'authority exercising or having compulsory powers' (see 38.10 above) where the landowner reinvests part or the whole of the proceeds in acquiring new land. Any land which is a dwelling-house or part of one and on which the whole or part of the gain on a subsequent disposal within six years would be covered by the exemptions for PRIVATE RESIDENCES (49) is excluded. Where any land is not so excluded at the time of its acquisition, but becomes so within six years, relief is withdrawn notwithstanding time limits for the making of assessments.

The effect of a claim (under *TCGA 1992, s 247(2)*) is to defer capital gains tax by deducting the otherwise chargeable gain on the original land from the acquisition cost of the newly acquired land. Relief is restricted where part only of the proceeds is reinvested in qualifying land. See 55.6 ROLLOVER RELIEF.

The following further matters should be noted.

(*a*) The landowner must not have taken any steps, by advertising or otherwise, to dispose of the old land or to make his willingness to dispose of it known. In practice, any event which occurred more than three years before the date of disposal is ignored. (CCAB Statements TR 476 and 477, May and June 1982 and HMRC Capital Gains Manual CG 61902, 72202).

(*b*) The new land must be acquired in the period beginning twelve months before and ending three years after the disposal or such longer period as HMRC may allow e.g. where it has not been practical to acquire new land within the time limit.

New town corporations and similar authorities may purchase land for development and then grant the previous owner a lease or tenancy of the land until they are ready to commence building. Where land is so acquired under a compulsory purchase order or under the threat of such an order and is immediately leased back to the previous owner HMRC are prepared, so long as there is a clear continuing intention that the sale proceeds will be used to acquire assets qualifying for rollover relief, to extend the time limit to a date three years after the land ceases to be used by him for his trade. An assurance to this effect will be given in appropriate cases subject to the reservation that it would be necessary to raise a protective assessment on the gain arising if exceptionally the lease or tenancy continued so long as to extend beyond the statutory time limit for making assessments (HMRC Statement of Practice D6). See HMRC Capital Gains Manual CG 60660–60665.

(*c*) Where the new land is a depreciating asset, similar provisions apply as in 55.7 ROLLOVER RELIEF except that the gain is held over for ten years or until the new asset is disposed of, whichever is the sooner. A gain previously held over is never deemed to accrue in consequence of an event occurring after 5 April 1988 if the application of this provision would be directly attributable to the disposal of an asset before 1 April 1982.

(*d*) The normal treatment of severance compensation as a part disposal (see 38.9 above) is expressly excluded. Such compensation is treated as additional consideration for the old land.

(*e*) Claims under these provisions and under *TCGA 1992, s 243* (see 38.10 above) are mutually exclusive.

(*f*) Subject to all other conditions for the granting of relief being met, HMRC will accept a claim from a landlord whose leasehold tenant has exercised the following statutory rights:

- his right under the *Leasehold Reform Act 1967* or the *Leasehold Reform, Housing and Urban Development Act 1993* to acquire the freehold reversion of a property or an extension of the lease,
- his right to buy or to acquire the freehold or an extension of the lease under the *Housing Acts 1985* to *1996* (which covers the situation where a tenant's right to buy is preserved following a transfer of housing stock into the private sector) or the right to purchase tenanted property under the *Housing* (*Scotland*) *Act 1987*, or
- the right of a crofting community body to purchase croft land under *Land Reform* (*Scotland*) *Act 2003, Part 3*.

(HMRC Statement of Practice 13/93; HMRC Tax Bulletin June 2005, pp 1212, 1213).

(*g*) In relation to a group of companies, where there is a compulsory purchase from one group member and acquisition of land by another, ROLLOVER RELIEF (55) is available where the compulsory purchase or the acquisition is after 28 November 1994. The previous ability to 'frank' a compulsory purchase from one group member to another by an intra-group acquisition was ended with effect to acquisitions after 28 November 1994.

[*TCGA 1992, ss 247, 248, Sch 4 para 4*(*5*); *FA 1995, s 48*(*2*)(*6*); *FA 1996, s 121*(*8*), *s 141*(*5*)].

For a concessionary application of this relief to the exchange of joint interests in land, see 38.12 below.

Provisional claims are permitted under self-assessment, in much the same way as for ROLLOVER RELIEF (55.2), for disposals after 5 April 1996 for capital gains tax purposes and in company accounting periods ending on or after 1 July 1999 (the commencement date for corporation tax self-assessment — see 13.2 COMPANIES).

The claimant may make a declaration in his tax return for a tax year or company accounting period in which he has made a qualifying disposal of land that the whole or a specified part of the consideration will be invested, within the requisite time limits (see (*b*) above), in new land (or an interest in or right over land) and that the new land is not excluded by virtue of the availability of the private residence exemption (see above). As long as the declaration continues to have effect, the same consequences ensue as if both an acquisition and a valid rollover relief claim had been made. The declaration ceases to have effect on the day, and to the extent that, it is withdrawn or is superseded by a valid claim, if either occurs before the 'relevant day'. It otherwise ceases to have effect on the relevant day itself. On its ceasing to have effect, all necessary adjustments will be made to the claimant's tax position, even if they would otherwise be out of time.

The '*relevant day*' means

- in relation to capital gains tax, the third anniversary of 31 January following the tax year of disposal, e.g. 31 January 2003 for disposals in 1998/99; and
- in relation to corporation tax, the fourth anniversary of the last day of the accounting period of disposal.

[*TCGA 1992, s 247A; FA 1996, s 121*(*8*), *s 141*(*6*)].

To the extent that a provisional claim is withdrawn or lapses, interest on unpaid tax is chargeable as if no such claim had been made.

38.12 CONCESSIONARY ROLLOVER RELIEF FOR EXCHANGE OF JOINT INTERESTS IN LAND

A form of rollover relief is available by concession for exchanges made after 19 December 1984 on the lines provided in 38.11 above (i.e. not confined to land which is used and occupied for the purposes of a trade) where

(*a*) a 'holding of land' is held jointly and as a result of the exchange each joint owner becomes sole owner of part of the 'land' formerly owned jointly; or

(*b*) a number of separate holdings of land are held jointly and as a result of the exchange each joint owner becomes sole owner of one or more holdings.

The interest relinquished will be treated as the 'old land' and the interest acquired as the 'new land'. '*Land*' includes any interest or right over land and '*holding of land*' includes an estate or interest in a holding of land and is to be construed in accordance with *TCGA 1992, s 243*(*3*) (see 38.10 above).

Relief will be denied under the concession to the extent that the new land is, or becomes, a dwelling-house (or part) within the meaning of *TCGA 1992, ss 222–226* (see 49 PRIVATE RESIDENCES) but subject to this, relief will be restricted as in 38.11 above where there is only part re-investment or only part of the gain is chargeable because of time apportionment.

However, where individuals who are joint beneficial owners of dwelling-houses which are their respective residences become sole owners of those houses in consequence of an exchange of interests, an alternative concessionary relief may be claimed if the gain accruing on the disposal of each dwelling-house immediately after the exchange would be exempt under the provisions contained in 49.1–49.4 PRIVATE RESIDENCES. Each individual must undertake to accept that he is deemed to have acquired the other's interest in the dwelling-house at the original base cost and at the time at which that joint interest was acquired.

For the purposes of this concession, a married couple is treated as an individual, so that an exchange of interests which results in a married couple alone becoming joint owners of land or of a dwelling house will meet the terms of the concession.

Where

(i) the concession applies to an exchange of interests in land after 29 October 1987,

(ii) there is a parallel exchange of interests in milk or potato quota associated with the land, and

(iii) each joint owner becomes sole owner of the part of the quota relating to the land he now owns,

the concession applies also to the exchange of interests in quota. (HMRC Extra-Statutory Concession D26).

The operation of the concession should be read in the light of the decision of *Warrington v Brown and related appeals Ch D 1989, 62 TC 226.*

38.13 LEASES

For capital gains tax purposes, a '*lease*' in relation to land includes an underlease, sub-lease or any tenancy or licence, and any agreement for a lease, underlease, sub-lease or tenancy or licence. In the case of land outside the UK, any interest corresponding to a lease as so defined is included. '*Lessor*', '*lessee*' and '*rent*' are construed accordingly. [*TCGA 1992, s 240, Sch 8 para 10*(*1*)].

Where a leaseholder of land acquires a superior interest in that land (whether a superior lease or the freehold reversion) so that the first lease is extinguished, the two interests are merged within the meaning of *TCGA 1992, s 43* (assets derived from other assets). On a subsequent disposal the allowable expenditure relating to the merged interest will include the cost of the first lease, after exclusion, in the case of a lease with less than 50 years to run, of the part which was wasted under *TCGA 1992, Sch 8* to the date of the acquisition of the superior interest (see 38.14 below) and the cost of the superior interest. Where the superior interest is itself a lease with less than 50 years to run, the total of these two amounts will also be wasted under *TCGA 1992, Sch 8* down to the date of disposal. Strictly, indexation allowance should be calculated on the total of these two amounts by reference to the date of acquisition of the superior interest, but, by concession, for disposals after 28 June 1992, indexation on the expenditure on the earlier, inferior lease, will be calculated by reference to the date of its acquisition. For disposals before 29 June 1992, indexation allowance for the total of the two amounts is, by concession, calculated by reference to the date of acquisition of the inferior interest. (HMRC Extra-Statutory Concession D42).

Where a lease is surrendered on terms which include the release of the tenant from a liability under the lease to make good any dilapidations or from any other onerous liability, the value attributable to the release is consideration for the surrender (HMRC Capital Gains Manual CG 71260).

38.14 LEASES AS WASTING ASSETS

A lease of land is not a wasting asset until the time when its duration does not exceed fifty years. [*TCGA 1992, Sch 8 para 1*(*1*)]. The **duration** of a lease is to be decided by reference to the facts known or ascertainable at the time when the lease was acquired or created. In determining the duration, the following provisions apply.

(*a*) Where the terms of the lease include provision for the determination of the lease by notice given by the landlord, the lease is not to be treated as granted for a term longer than one ending at the earliest date on which it could be determined by notice given by the landlord.

(*b*) Where any of the terms of the lease or any other circumstances render it unlikely that the lease will continue beyond a date earlier than the expiration of the terms of the lease, the lease is not to be treated as having been granted for a longer term than one ending on that date. This applies in particular where the lease provides for rent to go up after a given date, or for the tenant's obligation to become more onerous after a given date, but includes provision for the determination of the lease on that date, by notice given by the tenant, and those provisions render it unlikely that the lease will continue beyond that date.

(*c*) Where the terms of the lease include provision for the extension of the lease beyond a given date by notice given by the tenant, the duration of the lease applies as if the term of the lease extended for as long as it could be extended by the tenant, but subject to any right of the landlord to determine the lease by notice.

[*TCGA 1992, Sch 8 para 8*].

A lease granted under *Landlord and Tenant Act 1954* to follow on from another is not a continuation of the old lease and is to be treated as having been acquired on the date it was granted (*Bayley v Rogers Ch D 1980, 53 TC 420*).

A similar view was taken in *Lewis v Walters Ch D 1992, 64 TC 489* regarding the right of a tenant to be granted a lease under *Leasehold Reform Act 1967* to follow on from another and where it was also held that (*c*) above did not apply since such a right was not included in the terms of the original lease.

Where a lease is 'extended' by the surrender of an old lease and the grant of a new one for a longer term, a disposal of the old lease will in strictness occur, the consideration for it normally being the value, if any, of the new lease. By concession, a disposal is not treated as arising in these circumstances provided that

- the parties are not connected and the transaction is at arm's length (or the parties *are* connected but the terms of the transaction are equivalent to those to be expected in an arm's length transaction between unconnected parties);
- the transaction is not part of or connected with a larger scheme or series of transactions;
- no capital sum is received by the lessee;
- the extent of the property in which the lessee has an interest is unchanged; and
- the terms of the leases remain the same except as regards the duration and amount of rent payable. For this purpose, trivial differences will be ignored.

(HMRC Extra-Statutory Concession D39). (See 3.25 ANTI-AVOIDANCE for the charge arising where concessions involving deferral of gains are abused.)

Computation. If a lease of land is a wasting asset, its original cost and any enhancement expenditure are not written off on a straight line basis (as would otherwise be required under *TCGA 1992, s 46*) but on a reducing basis as set out in the table below.

Table for depreciation of leases

Years	*Percentage*	*Years*	*Percentage*	*Years*	*Percentage*
50 (or more)	100.000	33	90.280	16	64.116
49	99.657	32	89.354	15	61.617
48	99.289	31	88.371	14	58.971
47	98.902	30	87.330	13	56.167
46	98.490	29	86.226	12	53.191
45	98.059	28	85.053	11	50.038
44	97.595	27	83.816	10	46.695
43	97.107	26	82.496	9	43.154
42	96.593	25	81.100	8	39.399
41	96.041	24	79.622	7	35.414
40	95.457	23	78.055	6	31.195
39	94.842	22	76.399	5	26.722
38	94.189	21	74.635	4	21.983
37	93.497	20	72.770	3	16.959
36	92.761	19	70.791	2	11.629
35	91.981	18	68.697	1	5.983
34	91.156	17	66.470	0	0

The fraction of the *original cost* which is not allowed is given by the fraction

$$\frac{P(1) - P(3)}{P(1)}$$

where

P(1) = the percentage derived from the table for the duration of the lease at acquisition

P(3) = the percentage derived from the table for the duration of the lease at the time of disposal

The fraction of any *enhancement expenditure* which is not allowed is given by the fraction

$$\frac{P(2) - P(3)}{P(2)}$$

where

P(2) = the percentage derived from the table for the duration of the lease at the time when the item of expenditure is first reflected in the nature of the lease

P(3) = as above

If the duration of the lease is not an exact number of years, the percentage is that for the whole number of years plus one twelfth of the difference between that and the percentage of the next higher number of years for each odd month, counting an odd 14 days or more as one month.

[*TCGA 1992, Sch 8 para 1(3)(4)*].

The provisions above apply even if the period of ownership of the lease exceeds 50 years. Accordingly, in such a case, any cost or enhancement expenditure incurred before the lease becomes a wasting asset is not reduced until the lease does become a wasting asset. [*TCGA 1992, Sch 8 para 1(5)*]. In these circumstances P(1) and P(2) will each be 100 in the fractions given above.

Example

X purchases a 30-year lease of business premises in 2000 for £250,000. In 2003, when 27 years of the lease remain, he spends £25,000 on improvements which are at once reflected in the value of the lease and continue to be so until he disposes of it with 24 years remaining in 2006. His allowable expenditure is reduced as follows

$$\text{Original cost } (£250{,}000) \times \frac{(87.330 - 79.622)}{87.330} = £22{,}066$$

$$\text{Additional cost } (£25{,}000) \times \frac{(83.816 - 79.622)}{83.816} = £1{,}251$$

£23,317

The total allowable expenditure is then (£275,000 – £23,317) = £251,683

Exceptions. The above provisions do not apply in the following circumstances.

(i) If at the beginning of the period of ownership of a lease, it is subject to a *sub-lease not at a rackrent* and the value of the lease at the end of the sub-lease (estimated at the beginning of the period of ownership) exceeds the expenditure allowable in computing the gain accruing on the disposal of the lease (see 15.4(*a*) COMPUTATION OF GAINS AND LOSSES), the lease is *not* a wasting asset until the end of the duration of the sub-lease. [*TCGA 1992, Sch 8 para 1(2)*].

(ii) Where the land, throughout the ownership of the person making the disposal, is used solely for the purposes of a trade, profession or vocation, and capital allowances have, or could have, been claimed in respect of its cost, or in respect of any enhancement expenditure. This also applies where the cost of land has otherwise qualified in full for any capital allowances. Where, however, the land disposed of has been used partly for non-business purposes, or has only partly qualified for capital allowances, the expenditure and consideration are apportioned and the restriction of allowable expenditure as above applies only to that portion of expenditure which has not qualified for capital allowances, or which relates to the period of non-business use. [*TCGA 1992, s 47, Sch 8 para 1(6)*].

38.15 PREMIUMS FOR LEASES

Where the payment of a ‘premium’ is required under a lease (or otherwise under the terms subject to which the lease is granted) there is a part disposal of the freehold or other interest out of which that lease is granted. [*TCGA 1992, Sch 8 para 2(1)*].

In the part disposal computation (which follows the normal rules in *TCGA 1992, s 42*, see 15.7 COMPUTATION OF GAINS AND LOSSES) the property which remains undisposed of includes a right to any rent or other payments (other than a premium) payable under the lease, and that right is valued at the time of the part disposal. [*TCGA 1992, Sch 8 para 2(2)*].

'*Premium*' includes any like sum, whether payable to the intermediate or superior landlord and includes any sum (other than rent) paid on or in connection with the granting of a tenancy except when the other sufficient consideration for the payment can be shown to have been given. In Scotland, '*premium*' includes in particular a *grassum* payable to any landlord or intermediate landlord on the creation of a sub-lease. [*TCGA 1992, Sch 8 para 10(2)(3); FA 1996, Sch 20 para 67*].

Capital sums treated as premiums. The legislation provides for other capital amounts payable under leases to be treated as if they were premiums. Where the landlord is a freeholder, or is a leaseholder and that lease has more than 50 years to run, and

(*a*) *under the terms of a lease*, a sum becomes payable by the tenant in lieu of the whole or part of the rent for any period ('commutation of rent'), or as consideration for the surrender of the lease, or

(*b*) a sum becomes payable by the tenant (otherwise than by way of rent) as consideration for the variation or waiver of any of the terms of the lease,

the lease is deemed to have required payment of a premium to the landlord (in addition to any actual premium) of the amount of that sum. This premium is treated as being due when the sum is payable by the tenant and as being in respect of, where (*a*) applies, the period in relation to which it is payable or, where (*b*) applies, the period from the time the variation or waiver takes effect to the time it ceases to have effect. The deemed receipt of the premium does not require a chargeable gain arising from the receipt of any other premium to be recomputed. Instead, it is regarded as a separate transaction effected at the time the premium is deemed to be due and as a part disposal (or further part disposal) of the freehold (or other asset out of which the lease is granted) or, in the case of a payment for surrender, as a disposal by the landlord of his interest in the lease.

Where a sum falls within (*b*) above and the transaction is not at arm's length and/or is entered into gratuitously, the amount actually payable is replaced in the tax computation by such sum as might have been required of the tenant in an arm's length transaction.

The above provisions apply as regards sums payable after 5 April 1996, having been changed to facilitate self-assessment. The previous rules were broadly similar but with the fundamental difference that, except in the case of consideration for the surrender of a lease, the premium was deemed to have been received by the landlord at the time the lease was originally granted. Any capital gains computation relating to a premium actually received on the grant of the lease had to be reworked to take the additional premium into account, and the requisite assessment could if necessary be made outside the normal six-year time limit then applicable.

The rules are modified (both before and after 5 April 1996 but not where the payment is consideration for the surrender of a lease) if the landlord is himself a tenant under a lease with 50 years or less to run at the time the capital sum is paid. The premium is deemed to have been given by way of consideration for the grant of the part of the sub-lease covered by the period in respect of which the premium is treated as having been paid. It is *not* thereby treated as having been received at the time the sub-lease was granted; the date of disposal is determined under general principles — see 15.3 COMPUTATION OF GAINS AND LOSSES. See the worked example at HMRC Capital Gains Manual CG 71371. As far as the sub-lessee is concerned, the payment is treated as allowable enhancement expenditure (see 15.4(*b*) COMPUTATION OF GAINS AND LOSSES) incurred by him and attributable to the aforementioned part of the sub-lease.

[*TCGA 1992, Sch 8 para 3; FA 1996, s 142*].

See HMRC Capital Gains Manual CG 71350–71371 for further commentary on the above and worked examples.

If a capital sum is paid by a tenant for commutation of rent and the terms of the lease do *not* provide for such a payment, the above rules do not apply. The transaction is treated as a part disposal within *TCGA 1992, s 22* (see 9.1 CAPITAL SUMS DERIVED FROM ASSETS). (HMRC Capital Gains Manual CG 71351, 71372).

Reverse premiums. In a New Zealand case, a substantial lump sum received by an accountancy firm as an inducement to enter into a lease of premises at a rent above the market rent, i.e. a payment *by* a lessor *to* a lessee (known as a reverse premium), was held to be a capital receipt (*New Zealand Commissioner of Inland Revenue v Wattie and another PC 1998, 72 TC 639*). As a result of this case, legislation was introduced in the UK to ensure that a reverse premium (as defined therein) is chargeable to income tax or corporation tax as a *revenue* receipt. This applies to a premium received on or after 9 March 1999 unless, disregarding any arrangements made on or after that date, the recipient was entitled to it immediately before that date. As regards earlier premiums, HMRC are guided by the decision in *Wattie*, although a reverse premium could still be a revenue receipt if, on the evidence, it is a contribution to revenue expenditure, e.g. relocation costs, although the linkage of the premium to an increased rental does not of itself give it the character of a revenue receipt. Where a reverse premium is a capital receipt, it gives rise to a chargeable gain *only* if derived from an asset held by the tenant. If the premium was paid before the tenant entered into the lease, this could be the case only if it were derived from some other asset, for example if it is a payment to induce the tenant to surrender an existing lease. See *FA 1999, s 54, Sch 6, ITTOIA 2005, ss 99–106*, and Revenue Tax Bulletin April 1999 p 641, and see Tolley's Income Tax for full coverage.

General. In *Clarke v United Real (Moorgate) Ltd Ch D 1987, 61 TC 353*, the taxpayer company contracted for a freehold site which it owned to be developed by a third party. Subsequently it entered into an 'agreement for a lease' with another third party ('A') under which A agreed to reimburse the company's development costs and the company was to grant him a long lease of the developed site at a rent below market value, which was to be ascertained by reference to his reimbursement payments to the company. The granting of the lease was agreed to be a part disposal. The reimbursement payments were held to be a premium within *TCGA 1992, Sch 8 para 2(1), para 10(2)*, because they were made to the company in its capacity as landlord, and not to meet an obligation incurred by the company on behalf of A.

38.16 **Premiums taxed as receipts of property business.** Where a premium is received for a lease not exceeding 50 years and part of it is liable to tax under *ICTA 1988, s 34* or *ITTOIA 2005, ss 277–281* as a receipt of a property business, that part is excluded from the computation for capital gains tax purposes *except* in the denominator of the part disposal fraction of A/(A+B) given by *TCGA 1992, s 42*. '*Premium*' includes a deemed premium under (*a*) or (*b*) in 38.15 above. [*TCGA 1992, Sch 8 para 5(1)(5); FA 1998, Sch 5 para 63(2); ITTOIA 2005, Sch 1 para 451(2)*].

Where the terms of a lease impose an obligation on the tenant to carry out work on the premises concerned, an amount equal to the increase in value of the landlord's interest occasioned by the work is treated as a premium under *ICTA 1988, s 34* or *ITTOIA 2005, s 277* above except insofar as the obligation relates to work which, had it been carried out by the landlord, would have been deductible as an expense of any property business carried on by the landlord. [*ICTA 1988, s 34(2)(3); FA 1998, Sch 5 para 15(3); ITTOIA 2005, s 278, Sch 1 para 17*]. For capital gains tax purposes the consequential effect is that the landlord is treated as incurring enhancement expenditure of that amount on the premises at the time of the grant of the lease. [*TCGA 1992, Sch 8 paras 7, 7A; FA 1995, s 41(4); FA 1998, Sch 5 para 63(4)(5); ITTOIA 2005, Sch 1 para 451(4)(5)*].

Example

X grants a 14-year lease of premises for a premium of £5,000 in 2006/07 and retains the freehold interest. The amount chargeable to income tax for that year is

	£
Premium	5,000
Deduct $\frac{14-1}{50} \times £5,000$	1,300
Chargeable to income tax	£3,700

If the allowable expenditure on the original unencumbered freehold (acquired in 1999) is £30,000 and the value of the reversion £47,000, the unindexed gain is computed as follows

	£
Consideration received (i.e. the premium)	5,000
Deduct amount chargeable to income tax	3,700
	£1,300
Allowable expenditure attributable to the part disposal	
$\frac{1,300}{(5,000+47,000)} \times £30,000 =$	£750
Unindexed gain: £1,300 – £750 =	£550

38.17 **Sub-leases granted out of short leases.** Where a sub-lease is granted out of a head-lease with less than 50 years to run, the normal part disposal rules do not apply. Instead, subject to below, a proportion of the cost and enhancement expenditure attributable to the lease is apportioned to the part disposed of as follows

$$\frac{P(1) - P(3)}{P(2)}$$

where

P(1) = the percentage derived from the table in 38.14 above for the duration of the lease at the date of granting the sub-lease

P(3) = the percentage for the duration of the lease at the date of termination of the sub-lease

P(2) = the percentage for the duration of the lease at the date of acquisition (for apportionment of cost) *or* the date when expenditure is first reflected in the nature of the lease (for apportionment of enhancement expenditure)

If the amount of the premium is less than what would be obtainable by way of premium for the sub-lease if the rent payable under the sub-lease were the same as the rent payable under the lease, the percentage attributable to the sub-lease as calculated above must be multiplied by the premium received over the premium so obtainable before being applied to cost or enhancement expenditure. [*TCGA 1992, Sch 8 para 4*(*1*)(*2*)].

Example

X purchases a 40-year lease of a flat in 2001 for £15,000. In 2006, he sub-lets the flat to Y for 20 years for a premium of £8,000. The premium obtainable on the basis of the rent paid under the head-lease is £10,000. X's original expenditure of £15,000 is apportioned as follows

$$\frac{91.981 - 61.617}{95.457} = 0.3180908 \times \frac{8,000}{10,000} = 0.2544726$$

0.2544726 × £15,000 = £3,817

The expenditure attributable to the part disposal is therefore £3,817 as against £4,771 (£15,000 × 0.3180908) if the premium had been the maximum obtainable, £10,000.

Where the sub-lease is a sub-lease of part only of the land comprised in the lease, the cost and enhancement expenditure of the head-lease must be apportioned between the sub-lease and the remainder in proportion to their respective values. [*TCGA 1992, Sch 8 para 4*(*3*)].

Where a premium (including a deemed premium as in 38.16 above) is paid for the sub-lease, an amount of which is liable to tax under *ICTA 1988, s 34* or *ITTOIA 2005, ss 277–281* as a receipt of a property business, that amount is deducted from any *gain* accruing on the disposal for which the premium is consideration but not so as to convert the gain into a loss or to increase any loss. [*TCGA 1992, Sch 8 para 5*(*2*)(*5*)*; FA 1998, Sch 5 para 63*(*2*)*; ITTOIA 2005, Sch 1 para 451*(*2*)]. Similar provisions apply where, under *ICTA 1988, s 36* or *ITTOIA 2005, ss 284–286* (see 38.5 above) what is disposed of is the remainder of a lease or a sub-lease out of a lease the duration of which does not exceed 50 years. [*TCGA 1992, Sch 8 para 5*(*4*)].

38.18 **Allowances to payer for premiums paid.** Where a premium paid on the grant of a lease falls to be included in computing the property business profits of the recipient (see 38.16 above and 38.20 below), or would have done but for exemption, the tenant is treated as incurring an expense of a revenue nature (referred to in the *ICTA 1988* provisions as 'additional rent') at a rate equivalent to the amount so included spread over the period to which it relates. Where the lease is sub-let, this expense is an allowable deduction in computing the property business profits of the intermediate landlord. [*ICTA 1988, s 37*(*4*)*; FA 1998, Sch 5 para 18; ITTOIA 2005, s 292, Sch 1 para 20*(*5*)]. If the sub-lease is granted for a premium, however, the deduction is restricted under *ICTA 1988, ss 37*(*5*)*, 37A or ITTOIA 2005, s 293*. See Tolley's Income Tax under Property Income for full details.

Where a person is treated in consequence of having granted a sub-lease as paying additional rent under *ICTA 1988, s 37*(*4*) or as incurring revenue expenses under *ITTOIA 2005, s 292*, the amount of any *loss* accruing for capital gains purposes to that person on the disposal by way of the grant of the sub-lease is reduced by the total amount of the additional rent or expenses, but not so as to convert the loss into a gain. Any adjustment under *ICTA 1988, s 36*(*2*)(*b*) or *ITTOIA 2005, ss 301, 302* (see 38.5 above) is taken into account. [*TCGA 1992, Sch 8 para 6*(*1*)(*3*)*; ITTOIA 2005, Sch 1 para 451*(*3*)].

Example

On 21 January 2000 C is granted a lease of a shop for 21 years for a rent and a premium of £12,800. On 21 January 2007 he grants a sub-lease for a period of 7 years for a premium of £1,000 and a rent equal to that payable under the terms of the head-lease. C is treated under *ITTOIA 2005, s 292* as incurring deductible expenses of £1,680. C's capital gains tax position is as follows.

		£
Premium received		1,000
Consideration given for lease	£12,800	
Percentage applicable to lease of 21 years	74.635	
Percentage applicable to lease of 14 years	58.971	
Percentage applicable to lease of 7 years	35.414	
Amount allowable		
$\frac{58.971 - 35.414}{74.635} \times £12{,}800$		4,040
Loss		3,040
Deduct amount allowable in computing profits		1,680
Allowable loss		£1,360

38.19 Where a premium is paid for the acquisition of a short lease, and the person acquiring the lease uses the property for the purposes of his trade, profession or vocation, such that income tax relief under *ICTA 1988, s 87* or *ITTOIA 2005, ss 60–67* is available (see Tolley's Income Tax), then on a subsequent disposal of the lease, the allowable expenditure is reduced by the income tax relief actually given. This reduction is made *before* the depreciation fraction at 38.14 above is applied, so that only the net expenditure is depreciated. (HMRC Capital Gains Manual CG 71200–71202).

38.20 **Anti-avoidance provisions.** Where a lease not exceeding 50 years granted at *less than market value* is assigned for a consideration exceeding any premium for which it was granted (or the consideration on any previous assignment) the excess, up to the limit of the amount of any premium, or additional premium, which the grantor forwent when granting the lease, is treated as a receipt of the assignor's property business to the same extent that an additional premium would have been so treated (see 38.16 above). [*ICTA 1988, s 35; FA 1998, Sch 5 para 16; ITTOIA 2005, s 282, Sch 1 para 18*].

Any assessment to income or corporation tax under these provisions is not taken into account in any capital gains computation. [*TCGA 1992, Sch 8 para 6*(*2*)*; FA 1998, Sch 5 para 63*(*3*)*; ITTOIA 2005, Sch 1 para 451*(*3*)]. There may, therefore, be a double charge to tax.

38.21 LAND SOLD AND LEASED BACK — PROPORTION OF CAPITAL SUM RECEIVED TO BE TAXED AS INCOME IN CERTAIN CIRCUMSTANCES

As regards arrangements within *ICTA 1988, s 779* (land sold and leased back), where the lease when sold has no more than 50 years still to run and the period for which the premises are leased back is *15 years or less*, any increased rent payable, so far as it does not exceed a commercial rent, is allowable as a deduction from profits, but of the consideration received by the lessee for giving up the original lease (or undertaking to pay an increased rent) a proportion equivalent to one-fifteenth of that consideration multiplied by the number of years by which the term of the lease-back falls short of 16 years will be treated as an income receipt instead of a capital one. Appropriate adjustment is made where the lease-back is of part only of the property previously leased. For the above purposes the term of the new lease is deemed to end on any date whereafter the rent payable is reduced, or, if the lessor or lessee has power to determine the lease or the lessee has power to vary its terms, on the earliest date on which the lease can be so determined or varied. [*ICTA 1988, s 780; ITTOIA 2005, Sch 1 para 315*].

38.22 INSURANCE RECOVERIES: SHORT LEASES

Where property is held on a lease which has 50 years or less to run, insurance payments received by the lessee before 6 April 1996 in respect of the property will not be treated as a capital sum derived from the lease within the meaning of *TCGA 1992, s 22(1)* to the extent that they are applied by the lessee in discharging an obligation to restore any damage to the property. (HMRC Extra-Statutory Concession D1). See generally 9.1(*a*) CAPITAL SUMS DERIVED FROM ASSETS. Subsequent legislation at 9.2 CAPITAL SUMS DERIVED FROM ASSETS has superseded this concessionary treatment.

38.23 VALUE SHIFTING — ADJUSTMENT OF LEASEHOLD RIGHTS

Where an owner of land (or of any other description of property) enters into a transaction whereby he becomes the lessee of that property (e.g. a sale and lease-back) and there is a subsequent adjustment of rights and liabilities under the lease (whether or not involving the grant of a new lease) which is on the whole favourable to the lessor, such an adjustment is a disposal by the lessee of an interest in the property. [*TCGA 1992, s 29(4)*]. See 3.5 ANTI-AVOIDANCE for full coverage.

38.24 CONTINGENT LIABILITIES

In the first instance, no allowance is made in a capital gains tax computation for

(*a*) in the case of a disposal by way of assigning a lease of land or other property, any liability remaining with, or assumed by, the person making the disposal which is contingent on a default in respect of liabilities thereby or subsequently assumed by the assignee under the terms and conditions of the lease; and

(*b*) any contingent liability of the person making the disposal in respect of any covenant for quiet enjoyment or other obligation assumed as vendor of land, or of any estate or interest in land, or as a lessor.

If it is subsequently shown to the satisfaction of the inspector that any such contingent liability has become enforceable, and is being or has been enforced, such adjustment is made as is required in consequence. [*TCGA 1992, s 49(1)(a)(b), (2)(3)*].

The receipt of a contingently repayable deposit in return for the grant of an option to purchase land was valued subject to the contingency because on the facts the contingency was not within (*b*) above (*Randall v Plumb Ch D 1974, 50 TC 392*).

39 Life Insurance Policies and Deferred Annuities

39.1 A gain on the disposal after 8 April 2003 of, or of an interest in, rights under a life insurance policy or contract for a deferred annuity is not a chargeable gain unless, in the case of a disposal of the rights, the rights or any interest in the rights, or, in the case of a disposal of an interest in the rights, the rights, the interest or any interest from which all or part of the interest directly or indirectly derives, have at any time been acquired by any person for 'actual consideration'.

A gain on such a disposal made before 9 April 2003 is not a chargeable gain unless it is made by a person other than the original beneficial owner who has acquired the rights or interest for money or money's worth.

For the above purposes, '*actual consideration*' is consideration other than consideration deemed to be given under any provision relating to tax on chargeable gains. Amounts paid under the policy or contract by way of premiums or as lump sum consideration are not actual consideration. Actual consideration given for a disposal made by one spouse or civil partner to the other, an 'approved post-marriage disposal', an 'approved post-civil partnership disposal', or an intra-group transfer to which *TCGA 1992, s 171(1)* (see 27.2 GROUPS OF COMPANIES) applies, is treated as not being actual consideration. A disposal is an '*approved post-marriage disposal*' or an '*approved post-civil partnership disposal*' if it is one made in consequence of the dissolution or annulment of a marriage or civil partnership by one party to the marriage or partnership to the other, with the approval, agreement or authority of, or pursuant to an order of, a court (or other person or body) having jurisdiction under the law of any country or territory, where the rights or interest disposed of were held by the person making the disposal immediately before the marriage or partnership was dissolved or annulled. An '*interest*' in relation to any rights is an interest as co-owner of the rights, whether the rights are owned jointly or in common and whether or not the interests of the co-owners are equal.

Where an allowable loss would otherwise accrue on a disposal after 8 April 2003 of, or of an interest in, the rights under a life insurance policy or contract for a deferred annuity but if *TCGA 1992, s 37* (exclusion from consideration of amounts charged to income tax — see 35.1 INTERACTION WITH OTHER TAXES) and *TCGA 1992, s 39* (exclusion from allowable expenditure of amounts deductible in computing profits or losses for income tax purposes — see 35.1 INTERACTION WITH OTHER TAXES) were disregarded there would be a loss of a smaller amount, that smaller amount is taken to be the loss on the disposal. Where, disregarding those provisions, either a gain or neither a gain nor a loss would accrue, the disposal is taken to be one on which neither a gain nor a loss accrue.

In the case of a life insurance policy, the receipt of the sum assured by the policy, the transfer of investments or other assets to the owner in accordance with the policy and the surrender of the policy are each treated as a disposal of the rights (or of all of the interests in the rights) under the policy. In the case of a contract for a deferred annuity, the receipt of the first instalment of the deferred annuity and the surrender of the rights under the contract are treated as a disposal of the rights (or of all the interests in the rights) under the contract. Where there is a disposal of (or of an interest in) the rights under a contract for a deferred annuity on receipt of the first instalment, the amount of the consideration for the disposal is deemed to be the aggregate of the amount or value of the first instalment and the then market value of the outstanding instalments (or, in the case of a disposal of an interest, such proportion of that aggregate as is just and reasonable), and no gain accruing on any subsequent disposal of the rights or any interest in them is a chargeable gain.

[*TCGA 1992, s 210; FA 2003, s 157; SI 2005 No 3229, Reg 116*].

Where a policy-holder receives compensation for mis-selling of the policy, no chargeable gain arises in respect of that compensation provided that the exemption in *TCGA 1992, s 210(2)* above applies to the policy. In such circumstances, HMRC Extra-Statutory Concession D33 (see 6.1 ASSETS) applies (HMRC Capital Gains Manual CG 69071).

Any transfer of investments or other assets to a policy-holder in accordance with a policy is deemed to be made at market value. [*TCGA 1992, s 204(3)(6); FA 2006, s 73(2)*].

Subject to the restriction noted above in relation to losses accruing after 8 April 2003, in computing any chargeable gain or allowable loss under the above provisions, allowable expenditure will be

(*a*) the base cost of the policy to the person to whom the gain accrues (this will be either market value or what that person paid for the policy), and

(*b*) any premiums paid by that person.

39.2 *ITTOIA 2005, ss 461–546* provide for income tax to be charged on the profits arising on certain life policies and life annuity contracts. Before 26 June 1982, where such policies or contracts were assigned for money or money's worth, any profit subsequently arising was taken out of charge to income tax and was subject instead to capital gains tax. To counter the tax advantages previously gained by the use of such policies and contracts, any profit on policies etc. taken out after 25 June 1982 cease to escape the charge to income tax. The former provisions also cease to apply to policies etc. issued and assigned for money or money's worth before 26 June 1982 if, after 23 August 1982,

(i) the rights under the policy etc. are again assigned for money or money's worth; or

(ii) further capital is injected; or

(iii) subject to certain conditions, loans are taken against the security of the policy etc.

[*ICTA 1988, s 540(3), s 542(3), s 544; ITTOIA 2005, Sch 1 para 213, Sch 2 para 102; SI 2005 No 3229, Reg 76*].

For full details, see Tolley's Income Tax.

39.3 For gains made in connection with life insurance policies which are assessable to income tax or corporation tax, not capital gains tax, see Tolley's Income Tax or Tolley's Corporation Tax respectively.

39.4 For the treatment of other kinds of policy, see 22.10 EXEMPTIONS AND RELIEFS.

40 Losses

Cross-references. See also 13.4 COMPANIES; 17.19, 17.20 CORPORATE VENTURING SCHEME; 21.8 ENTERPRISE INVESTMENT SCHEME; 57.15, 57.20 SETTLEMENTS; 60.4–60.6 SUBSTANTIAL SHAREHOLDINGS OF COMPANIES.

The headings in this chapter are as follows.

40.1 SET-OFF OF CAPITAL LOSSES AGAINST CHARGEABLE GAINS

Main rules. Subject to the annual exempt amount (see 2.3 ANNUAL RATES AND EXEMPTIONS) and TAPER RELIEF (61), the charge to capital gains tax is on all chargeable gains accruing to the taxpayer in the year of assessment, less any allowable losses accruing to him in that year and, so far as not allowed as a deduction from chargeable gains accruing in any previous year of assessment, any allowable losses accruing to him in any previous year (but not earlier than 1965/66), subject to 40.8 below (interaction with annual exempt amount). [*TCGA 1992, s 2(2)*].

A person's allowable capital losses, whether of the tax year under review or brought forward from previous years (or brought back from the year of death — see 18.5 DEATH), cannot be set off against any of the following that might be attributed to him:

(*a*) (in relation to gains accruing in 1998/99 to 2002/03 inclusive but subject to the election below for 2000/01 onwards) gains treated under *TCGA 1992, s 77* as accruing to him as settlor from a UK resident settlement in which he has an interest (see 57.5 SETTLEMENTS);

(*b*) (in relation to gains accruing in 1998/99 to 2002/03 inclusive but subject to the election below for 2000/01 onwards) gains treated under *TCGA 1992, s 86* as accruing to him as settlor from a non-UK resident settlement in which he has an interest (see 44.5 OFFSHORE SETTLEMENTS);

(*c*) (in relation to gains accruing in 1998/99 onwards) gains treated under *TCGA 1992, s 87* or *s 89(2)* as accruing to him as a beneficiary of a non-UK resident settlement (see 44.14 OFFSHORE SETTLEMENTS).

In relation to gains accruing in 1997/98 or an earlier year, none of these restrictions applied. In relation to gains accruing in 2003/04 or a subsequent year, only the restriction at (*c*) above continues to apply. In relation to gains accruing in 2000/01, 2001/02 and/or 2002/03, the taxpayer may elect (under *FA 2002, Sch 11 para 8*) to disapply the restrictions at (*a*) and (*b*) above. An election in respect of any one or more of these years must be made by notice in writing to the Revenue no later than 31 January 2005. Where gains are treated as accruing to the taxpayer from more than one settlement, the election can be limited so as to apply only in relation to a specified settlement or settlements. If the overall effect of an election for one, two or all three of these years (taken together) is that the trustees of an affected settlement would be required to reimburse a larger amount of tax to the settlor under the 'right of recovery' rule at 57.5 SETTLEMENTS or 44.12 OFFSHORE SETTLEMENTS, the trustees of that settlement must join in the election(s).

Where personal losses are set against attributed gains under (*a*) or (*b*) above (either for 2003/04 or a later year or, by election, for 2000/01, 2001/02 and/or 2002/03), the amount of an attributed gain is computed without regard to TAPER RELIEF (61) (subject to the exception below). After offsetting the losses, the net attributed gain is then tapered by reference to the rate of taper relief that would have applied if taper relief were deductible in computing the gain to be attributed, i.e. by reference to the period the asset was held by the trustees and its status in their hands. Personal losses must be set against personal gains for any particular tax year in priority to attributed gains treated as accruing in that year. Subject to that, in accordance with *TCGA 1992, s 2A* (see 61.2 TAPER RELIEF), losses may be set against attributed gains (where there is more than one) in such order as gives the maximum taper relief. Where two or more attributed gains from different settlements attract the same rate of taper relief, or are not eligible for taper relief, and any personal losses set against those gains are insufficient to fully extinguish them, a proportion of those losses is deducted from each of those gains on a pro rata basis; this rule will affect the amount recoverable by the settlor from the trustees in respect of tax on the attributed gains (see 57.5 SETTLEMENTS and 44.12 OFFSHORE SETTLEMENTS).

[*TCGA 1992, s 2(4)–(8); FA 1998, s 121(3)(4), Sch 21 para 2; FA 2002, s 51, Sch 11 paras 2, 7, 8*].

Exception to the above. Where the attributed gain arises, under (*b*) above, by virtue of the charge under *TCGA 1992, s 10A* (temporary non-UK residence — see 45.4 OVERSEAS MATTERS), and the gain is subject to limitation under *TCGA 1992, s 86A*, the attributed gain is computed *after* applying taper relief but is then regarded as falling within (*c*) above and not (*b*) above (so that personal losses cannot be set against it). See 44.13 OFFSHORE SETTLEMENTS.

Miscellaneous. Short-term losses which accrued before 1971/72 but which were not relieved under Schedule D, Case VII may be brought forward against gains chargeable to capital gains tax. [*TCGA 1992, Sch 11 para 12*]. This is the only instance where losses incurred before 6 April 1965 can be carried forward.

A person may be able to enjoy the benefit of unutilised losses of trustees which have accrued to them in respect of property to which the person has become absolutely entitled. However, where a person becomes so entitled after 15 June 1999, the previously unfettered right to utilise such losses is significantly restricted. See 57.15 SETTLEMENTS. This facility to transfer losses does not apply as regards personal representatives and legatees (see 18.7 DEATH).

Where a loss accrues on the disposal of an asset held on 6 April 1965 there are provisions (e.g. time apportionment), which may restrict the loss allowable. See 7 ASSETS HELD ON 6 APRIL 1965. Similar observations may apply to disposals after 5 April 1988 of assets held on 31 March 1982. See 8 ASSETS HELD ON 31 MARCH 1982. See also 15.6(*j*) COMPUTATION OF GAINS AND LOSSES where an asset has qualified for capital allowances.

A loss accruing to a person in a year of assessment during no part of which he is resident or ordinarily resident in the UK is not allowable unless

- if there had been a gain instead of a loss, he would have been chargeable under *TCGA 1992, s 10* or, for accounting periods ending after 15 March 2005, *TCGA 1992, s 10B* (see 45.3 OVERSEAS MATTERS), in respect of that gain; or
- it is a loss accruing to trustees in a year of assessment for which *CGTA 1979, s 17* or *TCGA 1992, s 87* (see 44 OFFSHORE SETTLEMENTS) applies to the settlement.

[*TCGA 1992, s 16(3), s 97(6); F(No 2)A 2005, Sch 4 paras 7, 10(2)*].

A loss arising to an individual not domiciled in the UK but resident or ordinarily resident here in respect of the disposal of an asset overseas is not allowable. See 45.2 OVERSEAS MATTERS. [*TCGA 1992, s 16(4)*].

For provisions relating to losses of companies see 13.4 COMPANIES.

40.2 **Computation of loss.** Losses are computed as for gains (see 15 COMPUTATION OF GAINS AND LOSSES) except as in *FA 1991, s 72* (see 40.7 below) and where expressly provided otherwise (e.g. as in 34.1 INDEXATION). Wherever an exemption is given under *TCGA 1992* (or under any provision which is to be construed as one with it) so as to make a gain not a chargeable gain, that exemption applies similarly to losses so that they are not to be allowable losses. [*TCGA 1992, s 16(1)(2); ICTA 1988, s 834(1)*].

Losses are not deductible if, and so far as, other tax relief can be claimed in respect of them and may only be deducted once for capital gains tax purposes. They may not be deducted at all if already given relief for income tax (see 40.13 and 40.15 below regarding an election for capital losses arising on the disposal of certain shares in unquoted trading companies to be set off against general income). [*TCGA 1992, s 2(3)*]. For restrictions on the use of losses by companies see 13.4 COMPANIES.

Example

On 30 April 2006 Q sells for £40,000 a part of the land which he owns. The market value of the remaining estate is £160,000. Q bought the land for £250,000 in March 1993.

	£
Disposal consideration	40,000
Allowable cost $\dfrac{40{,}000}{40{,}000+160{,}000} \times £250{,}000$	50,000
Allowable loss	£10,000

40.3 **Notification of capital losses.** Under self-assessment, for 1996/97 and subsequent years for capital gains tax and for accounting periods ending on or after 1 July 1999 (see 13.2 COMPANIES) for corporation tax, a capital loss is not an allowable loss unless its amount is quantified and notified to HMRC, such notice being subject to the provisions of *TMA 1970, s 42*, and to the enquiry regime (see 54.8 RETURNS, 12.3 CLAIMS), as if it were a claim for relief (see 12.2 CLAIMS). For capital gains tax purposes, losses must, if possible, be notified on the self-assessment tax return or in an amendment thereto, or failing that may be notified separately in writing on or before the fifth anniversary of 31 January following the year of assessment in which they arose (regardless of whether they are utilised within that period — there is no time limit on the utilisation of losses brought forward). The equivalent time limit for corporation tax purposes is six years after the end of the accounting period in which the loss arose. [*TCGA 1992, s 16(2A); FA 1995, s 103(7), s 113(1)*].

No notification time limit applies to capital losses arising in 1995/96 and earlier years or in company accounting periods ending before 1 July 1999. In *Tod v South Essex Motors (Basildon) Ltd Ch D 1987, 60 TC 598*, the absence of any statutory machinery before 1996/97 for claiming capital losses, other than to the extent that there were gains against which they could be set, meant that an agreement under *TMA 1970, s 54* (see 4.7 APPEALS) allied to the existence of a loss for a chargeable period did not preclude the Revenue from challenging its size or existence in a later chargeable period in which gains arose.

Order of set-off. Losses arising to individuals, trustees and personal representatives in the year 1996/97 and subsequent years are to be treated as utilised before losses arising in earlier years. Similarly, losses accruing to companies for accounting periods ending on or after 1 July 1999 (see 13.2 COMPANIES) will have preference to losses arising in accounting periods ending before that date. [*FA 1995, s 113*(*2*)].

40.4 **Carry-back prohibited.** Losses may not be carried back against the gains of an earlier year (except from the year of death, see 18.5 DEATH). [*TCGA 1992, s 2*(*3*)]. See also 40.18 below for the election to treat a loss on a right to unascertainable consideration as accruing in an earlier year.

40.5 **Connected persons.** A loss on a disposal to a CONNECTED PERSON (16) is deductible only from chargeable gains arising on other disposals to that same person while he is still connected. A disposal, whereby capital and income are settled wholly or primarily for educational, cultural or recreational purposes, the beneficiaries being 'an association of persons' most of whom are *not* connected persons, is not subject to this restriction on losses. [*TCGA 1992, s 18*(*3*)(*4*)]. The restriction does not apply where a person becomes absolutely entitled as against the trustee to property in a settlement (see 57.15 SETTLEMENTS).

Where the disposal is of an option to enter into a transaction with the disposer, no loss accruing to a connected person who acquires the option is allowable unless it accrues on the disposal of the option at arm's length to a person unconnected with the acquirer. [*TCGA 1992, s 18*(*5*)].

See 3.15 ANTI-AVOIDANCE for special market value provisions for disposals between connected persons.

Debts. A loss accruing on the disposal of a debt by a person making the disposal (the 'subsequent creditor') who acquired it from the 'original creditor' at a time when the original creditor or his personal representative or legatee was connected with the subsequent creditor, is not an allowable loss. Purchases through persons all of whom are connected with the subsequent creditor are also included as are acquisitions from the original creditor's personal representative or legatee. Where trustees of a settlement are the original creditor (or, for debts created before 6 April 2006, where the original creditor is a trustee and the debt, when created, is settled property), any loss accruing to the subsequent creditor is not allowable if he is connected with any person (or his personal representative or legatee) who becomes absolutely entitled to the debt on its ceasing to be settled property. [*TCGA 1992, s 251*(*4*)(*5*); *FA 2006, Sch 12 para 23*]. HMRC takes the view that these provisions do not apply to debts on a security (HMRC Capital Gains Manual CG 53451). For debts generally, see 22.5 EXEMPTIONS AND RELIEFS.

40.6 **Anti-avoidance.** Where a deemed disposal arises under *TCGA 1992, s 29*(*2*) on the transfer of value between different shares or rights in a company by the person controlling it, no loss is allowable on such a disposal. See 3.5 ANTI-AVOIDANCE. Value-shifting to give a tax free benefit may result in losses being allowable only to such extent as is just and reasonable. See 3.7–3.14 ANTI-AVOIDANCE.

Where there are depreciatory transactions within a group of companies or where there is 'dividend stripping' by one company holding 10% or more of a class of shares in another company, any related loss is only allowable to the extent that it is just and reasonable. See 3.21, 3.22 ANTI-AVOIDANCE.

A restriction of a loss accruing to a company which is a member of a group of companies may occur where the loss is wholly or partly referable to a time before it joined the group or the disposal of an asset which was held by another group member when that member company joined the group. See 27.20 GROUPS OF COMPANIES.

Trading losses effectively converted into allowable capital losses under *FA 1991, s 72* in 40.7 below cannot be carried forward as a deduction against chargeable gains after the time the trade concerned ceases.

40.7 SET-OFF OF TRADING LOSSES ETC. AGAINST CHARGEABLE GAINS

General. A person other than a company cannot normally set off his allowable losses for capital gains tax purposes against his income. A company, also, cannot normally set off its allowable losses for the purposes of corporation tax on chargeable gains against income but trading losses or management expenses of a company can, in certain cases, be set off against profits chargeable to corporation tax, such profits including chargeable gains. See 13.3, 13.4 COMPANIES. See, however, 40.13 and 40.15 below for the allowance of capital losses arising on the disposal of certain shares in unquoted trading companies against general income of *individuals* and *investment companies* respectively.

There are specific provisions enabling trading losses and certain other expenditure for income tax purposes to be set off against chargeable gains to the extent that they cannot be relieved against income (due to an insufficiency of income) for the year of assessment in question. These are described below.

Set-off of trading losses against chargeable gains of a person other than a company. Where trading losses arise, and a person makes a claim for relief under *ICTA 1988, s 380* (set-off for income tax purposes of trading losses against general income — see Tolley's Income Tax under Losses) for a year of assessment in respect of an amount ('the trading loss') which is available for relief under that provision, he may, in the notice by which the claim is made, make a further claim (under *FA 1991, s 72(1)*) for 'the relevant amount for the year' to be determined. Where such a claim is finally determined (see below), the relevant amount for the year (or the 'maximum amount' if lower) is treated as an allowable loss for capital gains tax purposes accruing to the claimant in the year. (This means that in effect capital losses flowing from a claim are treated as current year losses rather than losses brought forward from prior years; see 40.1 above and 40.8 below.) However, an amount treated as an allowable loss under the foregoing is not allowed as a deduction from chargeable gains accruing to a person in any year of assessment beginning after he has ceased to carry on the trade, profession etc. in which the relevant trading loss was sustained. For the purpose of applying this rule, any such losses brought forward are treated as set against gains in priority to genuine capital losses (HMRC Capital Gains Manual CG 3519).

'*The relevant amount for the year*' is so much of the trading loss as

(*a*) cannot be set off against the claimant's income for the year, and

(*b*) has not already been taken into account for the purposes of giving relief (under *ICTA 1988, s 380*, this relief provision or otherwise) for any year.

'*The maximum amount*' is the amount on which the claimant would be chargeable to capital gains tax for the year, disregarding the annual exemption available under *TCGA 1992, s 3(1)* and the effect of this relief provision. In relation to claims in respect of trading losses sustained in 2004/05 and subsequent years, TAPER RELIEF (61) is also disregarded (so that the 'maximum amount' is pre-tapered). A person may elect under *FA 2002, s 48* to apply this amendment in relation to trading losses sustained in 2002/03 and to so apply it in relation to chargeable gains of 2001/02 or 2002/03 or both. Similarly, he may elect to apply it in relation to losses sustained in 2003/04 and to so apply it in relation to gains of 2002/03 or 2003/04 or both. The election must be made in writing to HMRC within the time allowed for making the *FA 1991, s 72* claim itself (see below) for the year in question.

In ascertaining the maximum amount, no account is taken of any event occurring after the date on which the claim for relief is finally determined, and in consequence of which the maximum amount is reduced by virtue of any capital gains tax provision (e.g. a claim for rollover relief in a later year having the effect of reducing the amount chargeable for the year for which this relief provision is claimed; in such a case the allowable capital losses flowing from a claim under this provision would be displaced by the effect of the rollover claim but would be available for carry forward to subsequent years). A claim for relief is not deemed finally to be determined until the relevant amount for the year can no longer be varied, whether by the Commissioners on appeal or on the order of any court.

Trading losses relieved under the above are treated similarly to losses relieved under *ICTA 1988, s 380* as regards *ICTA 1988, s 382(3)* (prevention of double allowances) and *s 385(1)* (carry-forward of trading losses against subsequent profits reduced by other set-offs claimed).

[*FA 1991, s 72; FA 1994, s 209(1), s 211(2), s 215(4)(5), s 218(1)(5), Sch 20 para 8, Sch 26 Pt V; FA 2002, s 48*].

The tax years for which relief may be claimed under *ICTA 1988, s 380* against income, and consequently under *FA 1991, s 72* against gains, are the year in which the trading loss is incurred or the preceding year. The relief must be claimed no later than the first anniversary of 31 January following the tax year in which the loss is incurred.

A claim under *FA 1991, s 72* may be made even though there is no income for the year in question to justify making a claim under *ICTA 1988, s 380* alone (HMRC Business Income Manual BIM 75425).

Although in strictness the two claims should be made in the same notice, HMRC are prepared to accept a separate claim under *FA 1991, s 72* where: the trader has previously made a claim under *ICTA 1988, s 380* to which a *section 72* claim could have been added; a separate *section 72* claim is made within the time limits for the original *section 380* claim; after giving relief under *section 380* there is a balance of trading losses which have not otherwise been relieved; and all the other conditions for the relief are satisfied (Revenue Tax Bulletin August 1993 p 87).

Example

M has carried on a trade for some years, preparing accounts to 30 June each year. For the year ended 30 June 2006 he makes a trading loss of £17,000. His taxable profit for 2005/06 is £5,000, and his other income for both 2005/06 and 2006/07 amounts to £2,000. He makes a capital gain of £13,000 and a capital loss of £1,000 for 2006/07 and has capital losses brought forward of £6,800. The gain is after indexation allowance to April 1998 and qualifies for a 35% deduction for TAPER RELIEF (61). M makes claims for loss relief, against income of 2005/06 and income and gains of 2006/07, under *ICTA 1988, s 380(1)(b), ICTA 1988, s 380(1)(a)* and *FA 1991, s 72* respectively.

Calculation of 'relevant amount'

	£
Trading loss — year ended 30.6.06	17,000
Relieved against other income for 2006/07 (*ICTA 1988, s 380(1)(a)*)	(2,000)
Relieved against income for 2005/06 (*ICTA 1988, s 380(1)(b)*)	(7,000)
Relevant amount	£8,000

Calculation of 'maximum amount'

		£
Gains for 2006/07		13,000
Deduct	Losses for 2006/07	(1,000)
	Unrelieved losses brought forward	(6,800)
Maximum amount		£5,200

Relief under *FA 1991, s 72*

	£	£
Gains for the year		13,000
Losses for the year	1,000	
Relief under *FA 1991, s 72*	5,200	
		6,200
Gain (covered by annual exemption)		£6,800
Capital losses brought forward and carried forward		£6,800

Loss memorandum

	£
Trading loss	17,000
Claimed under *ICTA 1988, s 380(1)(a)*	(2,000)
Claimed under *ICTA 1988, s 380(1)(b)*	(7,000)
Claimed under *FA 1991, s 72*	(5,200)
Unutilised loss	£2,800

Note to the example

(*a*) In this example, £2,000 of the capital gains tax annual exemption of £8,800 is wasted, but the brought forward capital losses are preserved for carry-forward against gains of future years. If M had *not* made the claim under *FA 1991, s 72*, his net gains for the year of £12,000 would have been reduced to the annual exempt amount by deducting £3,200 of the losses brought forward. (Taper relief would be irrelevant as the untapered net gains would be exempt in any case.) Only £3,600 of capital losses would remain available for carry-forward against future gains and a further £5,200 of trading losses would have been available for carry-forward against future trading profits. So the effect of the claim is to preserve capital losses at the expense of trading losses.

Set-off of post-cessation expenditure of a trade against capital gains. Relief is available against both income and capital gains for individuals who incur qualifying business expenditure in connection with a trade or profession which has ceased within seven years of its ceasing. Broadly, qualifying expenditure includes costs of remedying defective work or services rendered and damages in respect thereof, insurance premiums paid to insure against such costs and legal and other professional expenses incurred in connection therewith. Relief is also given for bad debts which prove to be bad or which are released in whole or in part, and for the costs of collecting debts which have been taken into account in the final accounts. The relief is reduced by accruals for costs in the final accounting period which remain unpaid. On a claim, the relief may be set against income and then against capital gains of the tax year in which the qualifying expenditure is incurred, otherwise it will have to be carried forward to be set only against any post-cessation receipts under *ITTOIA 2005, s 254*. Claims must be made within twelve months after 31 January following the tax year in which the expenditure was incurred. A claim for relief cannot exceed the capital gains available, disregarding losses brought forward, the annual exemption and trading losses set against gains under *FA 1991, s 72*. For full details of the provisions see Tolley's Income Tax under Post-Cessation Etc. Receipts and

Expenditure. [*ICTA 1988, s 109A; FA 1995, s 90; FA 1996, Sch 20 para 5; ITTOIA 2005, Sch 1 para 89; FA 2005, Sch 4 para 6; F(No 2)A 2005, Sch 6 para 4(1), Sch 11 Pt 2(6)*].

Set-off of post-employment deductions against capital gains. Relief against income or capital gains is available to former employees who bear the costs of indemnity insurance or certain work-related uninsured liabilities relating to their former employment where such costs are incurred by them up to six years after the year in which the employment ended. On a claim, the relief may be set against income and then against capital gains of the year of assessment in which the qualifying expenditure is incurred, otherwise it will be lost. Claims must be made within five years after 31 January following the year of assessment to which the claim relates. A claim for relief cannot exceed the capital gains available, disregarding losses brought forward, the annual exemption, trading losses set against gains under *FA 1991, s 72* and post-cessation expenditure set against gains under *FA 1995, s 90*. For full details of the provisions see Tolley's Income Tax under Schedule E — Employment Income. [*TCGA 1992, s 263ZA; ICTA 1988, s 201AA; FA 1995, ss 91, 92; ITEPA 2003, ss 555–564, Sch 6 paras 28, 217*].

40.8 INTERACTION WITH ANNUAL EXEMPTION

In giving relief for capital losses brought forward from earlier years (or carried back from a subsequent year in which the taxpayer dies — see 18.5 DEATH), such losses are deducted from the net chargeable gains (i.e. chargeable gains less allowable losses) for the year only to the extent necessary to reduce those net gains to the amount of the annual exemption for the year, thus avoiding any wastage of losses brought forward (or back). Any balance of losses remains available to carry forward (or back). For 1998/99 and subsequent years, the deduction is made from, and by reference to, the 'adjusted net gains' rather than the net chargeable gains, the '*adjusted net gains*' being the net chargeable gains before applying TAPER RELIEF (61). [*TCGA 1992, s 3(5)–(5C); FA 1998, s 121(3)(4), Sch 21 para 3*]. See also 2.3 ANNUAL RATES AND EXEMPTIONS (including worked examples) and 61.3 TAPER RELIEF.

40.9 ASSETS OF NEGLIGIBLE VALUE

Where the owner of an asset which has become of 'negligible value' makes a claim under *TCGA 1992, s 24(2)* to that effect he is treated as if he had sold, and immediately reacquired, the asset at the time of the claim or (subject to the following) at any earlier time specified in the claim for a consideration of an amount equal to the value specified in the claim. An earlier time can be specified in the claim if the claimant owned the asset at that time, the asset had become of negligible value at that time and that time is not more than two years before the beginning of the year of assessment in which the claim is made or, for corporation tax, is on or after the first day of the earliest accounting period ending not more than two years before the time of the claim. [*TCGA 1992, s 24(2); FA 1996, Sch 39 para 4*].

For the purposes of a claim under *TCGA 1992, s 24(2)*, a building may be regarded as a separate asset from the land on which it stands, but where there is a deemed sale of a building, the land comprising the site of the building (including any land occupied for purposes ancillary to the use of the building) is likewise treated as if it was sold, and immediately reacquired, at its then market value. [*TCGA 1992, s 24(3)*].

'*Negligible value*' is not defined but is taken by HMRC to mean 'worth next to nothing' (HMRC Capital Gains Manual CG 13124).

In *Director v Inspector of Taxes (Sp C 161), [1998] SSCD 172*, a negligible value claim was refused on the grounds that the shares in question had a nil acquisition cost by virtue of *TCGA 1992, s 17* (see 41.1 MARKET VALUE) and thus could not *become* of negligible value.

For certain qualifying corporate bonds becoming of negligible value where evidencing a 'qualifying loan', see 40.11 below.

The backdating facility above cannot be used by a company to obtain relief for a loss that would otherwise be non-allowable under the provisions for SUBSTANTIAL SHAREHOLDINGS OF COMPANIES (see 60.19).

For HMRC practice and procedure, see HMRC Capital Gains Manual CG 13128–13133. HMRC have extended their post-transaction valuation checking service (see 54.4 RETURNS) to negligible value claims. Form CG34 must be submitted at the same time or after the claim is made. Acceptance by HMRC of the value submitted does not mean that they necessarily accept that all the conditions for the claim are met or that any allowable loss arises. (HMRC Internet Statement 31 January 2006).

Quoted securities. HMRC have accepted that certain quoted securities have become of negligible value within the meaning of *TCGA 1992, s 24(2)*. For securities so accepted in recent years, see the HMRC website (at www.hmrc.gov.uk).

40.10 LOANS TO TRADERS

Relief for lender on loan becoming irrecoverable. Provided that, at the time of the claim, the claimant and borrower were neither spouses or civil partners living together nor companies in the same 'group' when the loan was made or at any subsequent time, and that the claimant has not assigned his right of recovery, loss relief is available to the extent that any outstanding amount of the principal of a 'qualifying loan' made by the claimant after 11 April 1978 has become irrecoverable otherwise than under the express terms of the loan or related arrangements, or by reason of any act or omission by the lender (or, as appropriate, the guarantor of a loan claiming the relief below). The loss is treated as accruing either when the claim under *TCGA 1992, s 253(3)* is made or, within limits (see below), at an earlier specified time. As regards loans the principal on which became irrecoverable on or after 1 April 1996 the amount of the loss cannot include any amount falling to be relieved by way of a debit under the loan relationship provisions in 14.2–14.6 COMPANIES—CORPORATE FINANCE AND INTANGIBLES. [*TCGA 1992, s 253(3)(12)(14)(a)(aa), (15); FA 1996, Sch 14 para 65, Sch 15 para 7(a), Sch 39 para 8; SI 2005 No 3229, Reg 120*]. For cases in which the Revenue failed in contending that the loans became irrecoverable by reason of acts of the lender, see *Cann v Woods (Sp C 183), [1999] SSCD 77*, and *Crosby and Others (Crosby's Trustees) v Broadhurst (Sp C 416), [2004] SSCD 348*.

The allowable loss accrues at the time of the claim or at whatever earlier time is specified in the claim, so long as the amount claimed was also irrecoverable at that earlier time. For capital gains tax purposes, the time specified cannot be earlier than two years before the beginning of the tax year in which the claim is made. For corporation tax purposes, the time specified must fall on or after the first day of the earliest accounting period ending within the two years ending with the date of claim. [*TCGA 1992, s 253(3)(3A); FA 1996, Sch 39 para 8*].

Relief is not available and nor is a clawback of relief made (see below) if the amount in question is taken into account for computing income for the purposes of income tax or corporation tax. [*TCGA 1992, s 253(10)*].

Qualifying loan. A '*qualifying loan*' is a loan to a UK resident borrower in the case of which the money lent is used by him wholly for the purposes of a trade, profession or vocation (not being a trade which consists of or includes the lending of money) carried on by him (and for this purpose money used by a borrower for setting up a trade which is subsequently carried on by him is treated as used for the purposes of that trade), and which is not a 'debt on a security'. However, for guarantees see below, and for loans evidenced by securities which are qualifying corporate bonds, see 40.11 below.

The 'commercial letting' of 'furnished holiday accommodation' in the UK is treated as a trade. See 24 FURNISHED HOLIDAY ACCOMMODATION.

A '*debt on security*' is defined by reference to *TCGA 1992, s 132,* security thereby embracing any loan stock or similar security of any government or public or local authority in the UK or elsewhere, or of any company, and whether secured or unsecured. See further 22.5 EXEMPTIONS AND RELIEFS.

Where a company re-lends money to a 'trading company' in the same group, the original loan is treated as having been used by the first company as it is used by the second while the second remains a member of the group. For the purposes of these provisions, a group of companies is construed in accordance with 27.1 GROUPS OF COMPANIES, with the change in the residence requirement there mentioned having effect in relation to loans made (and guarantees given — see below) on or after 1 April 2000. For 2002/03 and earlier years, '*trading company*' has the same meaning for this purpose as it does for the purposes of RETIREMENT RELIEF (53.3). For 2003/04 onwards, it has the more restrictive meaning that it has for the purposes of TAPER RELIEF (61.5).

[*TCGA 1992, s 253(1)(2)(14)(b)(c); FA 1989, Sch 12 para 6; FA 1998, s 140(5)(6); FA 2000, Sch 29 para 34*].

A loan was held not to be a qualifying loan in *Robson v Mitchell CA, [2005] STC 893.*

Relief for payment made under guarantee. The relief given above to a lender also applies (with the exception of the backdating facility) to a guarantor of a qualifying loan who makes a claim under *TCGA 1992, s 253(4)* and who must additionally have made a payment under the guarantee to the lender or a co-guarantor. The claimant is treated as if an allowable loss of the amount of the payment had accrued to him when the payment was made. Where loss relief is given, no allowable loss and no chargeable gain (otherwise than on a clawback of relief as below) will accrue on the disposal of rights consequent on his having made a payment (which may include a payment in respect of interest as well as principal) under the guarantee. The guarantee must have been given after 11 April 1978. Relief is available to a guarantor even though the original loan is a 'debt on a security' (see above and 40.11 below). Relief is reduced to the extent that any contribution is 'payable' to the claimant by any co-guarantor. [*TCGA 1992, s 253(4)(11)(15); FA 1996, Sch 39 para 8; SI 2005 No 3229, Reg 120*].

A claim shall be made for the purposes of capital gains tax on or before the fifth anniversary of 31 January following the year of assessment in which the payment was made; and in the case of corporation tax within six years after the end of the accounting period in which the payment was made. [*TCGA 1992, s 253(4A); FA 1996, Sch 21 para 40*].

'*Payable*' has its ordinary meaning, so that if under general legal principles the claimant could have made a recovery against one or more co-guarantors of part of a sum paid by him under a guarantee but chose not to do so, the relief given to him is reduced proportionately (*Leisureking Ltd v Cushing Ch D 1992, 65 TC 400*).

'*Guarantee*' covers the case where a person's property is charged as security for a qualifying loan. It does not include an indemnity, which creates a primary liability. A guarantee can apply to the repayment of an overdraft but not a hire purchase agreement. (CCAB Memorandum TR 308, 4 October 1978).

HMRC ignore voluntary payments, only those being made as a consequence of the formal calling in of a guarantee being covered by the relief. (Tolley's Practical Tax 1987 p 147). The Revenue confirmed that a trading debt arising from the supply of stock to a trading company was considered capable of being treated as a qualifying loan as regards a guarantee made in respect of the debt. (Tolley's Practical Tax 1988 p 40).

Clawback of relief. Where loss relief has been obtained by the person who made the loan or a guarantor of it, and all or part of the outstanding amount of, or of interest in respect of (in the case of a guarantor), the principal of the loan is recovered, a chargeable gain is deemed to accrue to him at the time of recovery equal to so much of the allowable loss (for which relief was claimed) as corresponds to the amount recovered. Where a claimant has obtained loss relief in respect of a payment under a guarantee and recovers the whole or any part of that payment, he will be treated as if there had accrued to him at that time a chargeable gain equal to so much of the allowable loss as corresponds to the amount recovered. A similar treatment will apply to a company ('the second company') which recovers the whole or any part of the outstanding amount of the principal of a loan which has become irrecoverable in circumstances where a company ('the first company'), which made the loan originally and is in the same group as the second company when the loan was made or at any subsequent time, has obtained loss relief in respect of that loan becoming irrecoverable. Where the first company has obtained loss relief in relation to a payment made under a guarantee in respect of a loan which has become irrecoverable, a similar treatment of the second company applies if it recovers the whole or any part of the outstanding amount of, or of interest in respect of, the principal of the loan, or the whole or any part of the guarantee payment made by the first company. An amount is treated as recovered if money or money's worth is received in satisfaction of the right of recovery. If this right is assigned otherwise than at arm's length, its full market value at that time is deemed to have been received. [*TCGA 1992, s 253(5)–(9)(13)*].

40.11 LOANS TO TRADERS EVIDENCED BY QUALIFYING CORPORATE BONDS

Relief to lender on loan becoming irrecoverable etc. A loss incurred on a qualifying corporate bond is not an allowable loss (see 50.1 QUALIFYING CORPORATE BONDS). However, special provisions apply whereby if, at the time of a claim under *TCGA 1992, s 254* by a person who has made a 'qualifying loan' **before 17 March 1998**, one of the three conditions given below is fulfilled, the claimant is treated as if an allowable loss equal to the 'allowable amount' had accrued to him either at the time of the claim or, within limits (see below), at an earlier specified time. For accounting periods ending after 31 March 1996, to which the regime in 14.2–14.6 COMPANIES—CORPORATE FINANCE AND INTANGIBLES applies, these provisions do not apply for the purposes of corporation tax, but, by virtue of *FA 1996, Sch 15 para 7(b)*, this does not prevent a company making a claim in respect of any security whose value became negligible before 1 April 1996. The provisions are **repealed** for capital gains tax purposes in relation to loans made after 16 March 1998.

A '*qualifying loan*' means a loan in the case of which

(*a*) the borrower's debt is a debt on a security within *TCGA 1992, s 132* (see 40.10 above) which was issued after 14 March 1989, or issued before 15 March 1989 but held on 15 March 1989 by the person who made the loan,

(*b*) but for the borrower's debt being a debt on a security, the loan would be a qualifying loan within *TCGA 1992, s 253* (see 40.10 above), and

(*c*) the security is a QUALIFYING CORPORATE BOND (50), other than a deeply discounted security (see 58.16 SHARES AND SECURITIES) and with certain other modifications (see *TCGA 1992, s 117(13)*), in particular so as to exclude building society permanent interest bearing shares).

The first condition is that

(i) the value of the security has become negligible (but relief will still be available where the security ceases to have any value because it is redeemed early; HMRC Statement of Practice 8/90 and see (1) below for 'redemption date'),

(ii) the claimant has not assigned his right to recover any outstanding amount of the principal of the loan, and

(iii) the claimant and the borrower are not companies which have been in the same group (within *TCGA 1992, s 170*, see 27.1 GROUPS OF COMPANIES) at any time after the loan was made.

The second condition is that

(1) the security's 'redemption date' (i.e. the latest date on which, under the terms under which the security was issued, the company or body which issued it can be required to redeem it) has passed,

(2) all the outstanding amount of the principal of the loan was irrecoverable (taking the facts existing on that date) or proved to be irrecoverable (taking the facts existing on a later date), and

(3) the requirements in (ii) and (iii) above are fulfilled.

The third condition is that

(A) the security's redemption date (as at (1) above) has passed,

(B) sub-condition (2) of the second condition above was fulfilled on a similar basis as regards part (rather than the whole) of the outstanding principal of the loan, and

(C) the requirements in (ii) and (iii) above are fulfilled.

Where the first or second condition is fulfilled, '*the allowable amount*' is the lesser of the outstanding amount of the principal of the loan and the amount of the security's acquisition cost (i.e. the amount or value of the consideration in money or money's worth given, by or on behalf of the person who made the loan, wholly and exclusively for the acquisition of the security, together with the incidental costs to him of the acquisition). However, if any amount of the principal of the loan has been recovered the amount of the security's acquisition cost is for this purpose reduced (but not beyond nil) by the amount recovered. An amount is treated as recovered if money or money's worth is received in satisfaction of the right of recovery. If this right is assigned otherwise than at arm's length, its full market value at that time is deemed to have been received.

Where the third condition is fulfilled, then '*the allowable amount*' is an amount equal to the excess (if any) of the security's acquisition cost over the 'relevant amount' or nil (if there is no such excess). The '*relevant amount*' is the aggregate of the amount (if any) of the principal of the loan which has been recovered (as above) and the amount (if any) of the principal of the loan which has not been recovered but which is recoverable.

The allowable loss accrues at the time of the claim or at whatever earlier time is specified in the claim, so long as the relevant condition was also fulfilled at that earlier time. The time specified cannot be earlier than two years before the beginning of the tax year in which the claim is made. For corporation tax purposes, the time specified cannot be 1 April 1996 or later (see above) and, subject to that, must fall on or after the first day of the earliest accounting period ending within the two years ending with the date of claim.

Relief is not available and nor is a clawback of relief made (see below) if the amount in question is taken into account for computing income for the purposes of income tax or corporation tax. An amount is not treated as irrecoverable for the purposes of the relief if it becomes irrecoverable under the express terms of the loan or related arrangements, or by reason of any act or omission by the lender.

[*TCGA 1992, s 254(1)–(8)(12), s 255(1)(2)(4)(5); FA 1996, Sch 14 para 66, Sch 39 para 9; FA 1998, s 141(1)(b), (2)(b), Sch 27 Pt III(32); ITTOIA 2005, Sch 1 para 443*].

Clawback of relief. Where an allowable loss has been treated under the above as accruing to any person and the whole or any part of the 'relevant outstanding amount' is at any time recovered (as above) by him, he is treated as if there had accrued to him at that time a chargeable gain equal to so much of the allowable loss as corresponds to the amount recovered. A similar treatment applies to a company ('the second company') where an allowable loss has been treated under the above as accruing to a company ('the first company'), and the whole or any part of the relevant outstanding amount is at any time recovered by the second company which is in the same group (as above) as the first company at any time after the loan was made. The '*relevant outstanding amount*' means, in a case where the first or second condition was fulfilled, the amount of the principal of the loan outstanding when the claim was allowed or, in a case where the third condition was fulfilled, the amount of the part (or the greater or greatest part) arrived at by the inspector under sub-condition (B) of the third condition above.

[*TCGA 1992, s 254(9)–(11), s 255(3)–(5); FA 1996, Sch 39 para 9; FA 1998, s 141(1)(b), (2)(b), Sch 27 Pt III(32)*].

40.12 **Qualifying corporate bonds: reorganisations etc. thereof and relief under 40.11 above.** *TCGA 1992, s 116(10)(11)* deals with the situation where, on a reorganisation etc. of shares (which are not qualifying corporate bonds), such shares ('the old asset') are replaced by securities ('the new asset') which are qualifying corporate bonds (and thus exempt from capital gains tax). The broad effect is to defer the chargeable gain or allowable loss that would have accrued on a disposal of the old asset at its market value immediately before the reorganisation until such time as a part or the whole of the new asset is disposed of, at which time the corresponding part or the whole of the deferred gain or loss is deemed to accrue. See 50.3 QUALIFYING CORPORATE BONDS for full details. In such a case and where the new asset is a qualifying corporate bond in respect of which an allowable loss is treated as accruing under *TCGA 1992, s 254(2)* in 40.11 above, and the loss is treated as so accruing at a time falling after the reorganisation but before any actual disposal of the new asset subsequent to the reorganisation, then, for the purposes of *TCGA 1992, s 116(10)(11)*, a disposal of the new asset is deemed to have occurred at (and only at) the time the loss is deemed to have accrued. This applies whatever the time the reorganisation occurs. [*TCGA 1992, s 116(15)*]. The effect is that the deferred gain or loss relating to the old asset will be deemed to accrue at the same time as the loss arising on a claim under *TCGA 1992, s 254(2)* above in respect of the new asset is deemed to accrue, and any later disposal of the new asset is ignored for the purposes of ascertaining when and in what amount the deferred gain or loss is treated as arising.

A concessional practice, contained in HMRC Extra-Statutory Concession D38, applies as follows. Where a person acquired corporate bonds in respect of shares and securities and those bonds became, or would fall to be treated as, qualifying corporate bonds by virtue only of *FA 1989, s 139* (extension of definition to include a wider range of sterling bonds; see 50.2 and 50.3 QUALIFYING CORPORATE BONDS), an allowable loss, computed in accordance with the rules in *TCGA 1992, s 116* (see 40.11 above), will accrue if

(*a*) the qualifying corporate bonds were issued in respect of shares or other securities before 14 March 1989 and were still retained at that date by the person to whom they were issued;

(*b*) the bonds were acquired in a transaction within *TCGA 1992, s 116(10)(11)* (see above) and on disposal after 13 March 1989 fall to be treated as qualifying corporate bonds as a result of *FA 1989, s 139*;

(*c*) relief under *TCGA 1992, s 254* would have been available had the loan been a qualifying loan within *TCGA 1992, s 254(1)*;

(*d*) the taxpayer claiming the concessional relief agrees that if all or part of the amount relieved is subsequently recovered the relief will be clawed back in the same way as if *TCGA 1992, s 254* had applied, save that in all cases the chargeable gain will be treated as accruing to the claimant; and

(*e*) when this concession applies, any gain or loss on the original shares or securities will be treated as accruing at the same time as the loss on the bonds in accordance with *TCGA 1992, s 116(15)* (see above and also 50.3 QUALIFYING CORPORATE BONDS for an additional relief which may apply in such circumstances where the bonds are gifted to a charity).

Under the concession the allowable loss will be treated as arising when a claim is made but it will be treated as arising in an earlier year of assessment or accounting period provided the claim is made not later than two years after the end of that year of assessment or accounting period, all the conditions for relief are satisfied at the date of claim, and the relief would have been available at the end of the year of assessment or accounting period for which relief is claimed.

40.13 LOSSES ON SHARES IN UNLISTED TRADING COMPANIES: INDIVIDUALS

Where an individual who has 'subscribed' for 'shares' in a 'qualifying trading company' incurs an allowable loss (for capital gains tax purposes) on the disposal of the shares in any year of assessment, he may, by written notice given on or before the first anniversary of 31 January following that year, make a claim for relief from income tax on

(1) so much of his income for that year as is equal to the amount of the loss or, where it is less than that amount, the whole of that income; or

(2) so much of his income for the last preceding year as is equal to the amount of the loss as remains after deducting any part of the loss utilised under (1) above or, where it is less than that remaining amount, the whole of that income.

See generally HMRC Venture Capital Schemes Manual VCM 10000 *et seq.* and 45000 *et seq.*

Where relief as above is given in respect of the loss or any part of it, no deduction from chargeable gains is available in respect of the loss or (as the case may be) that part. Relief claimed under (1) above in respect of any income is given in priority to any relief claimed under (2) in respect of that income; and relief claimed under either (1) or (2) in respect of any income is given in priority to relief claimed under *ICTA 1988, s 380* (trading losses set against general income) or *ICTA 1988, s 381* (further relief for trading losses to be set against general income in early years of a trade) in respect of that income.

Relief for a loss of a particular year may be claimed either for that year or the preceding year or both years; the taxpayer may choose which year takes priority and should make this clear in his claim (HMRC Helpsheet IR 286). Any part of the loss remaining unrelieved against income reverts to being a capital loss for the year of disposal.

Relief is available only if

(*a*) the disposal is at arm's length for full consideration, or

(*b*) it is by way of a distribution on a winding-up or dissolution, or

(*c*) the value of the shares has become negligible and a claim to that effect made under *TCGA 1992, s 24(2)* (see 40.9 above and note there the application of ESC D28 as regards claims before 6 April 1996, which also applies to this relief), or

(*d*) a deemed disposal occurs after 5 April 2000 under *TCGA 1992, s 24(1)* (which deems the entire loss, destruction, dissipation or extinction of an asset to be a disposal — see 9.1 CAPITAL SUMS DERIVED FROM ASSETS).

An individual '*subscribes*' for shares if they are issued to him by the company for money or money's worth, or if they were so issued to his 'spouse' or 'civil partner', who transferred them to him by a transaction inter vivos. '*Spouse*' refers to one of two spouses who are living together and '*civil partner*' refers to one of two civil partners who are living together (see 42.3 MARRIED PERSONS AND CIVIL PARTNERS).

As regards shares issued **after 5 April 1998**, a '*qualifying trading company*' is a company which

- either

  (i) is an 'eligible trading company' at the date of disposal, or

(ii) has ceased to be an eligible trading company within three years before that date and has not since that cessation been an 'excluded company', an 'investment company' or a non-eligible trading company, *and*

- either

  (i) has been an eligible trading company for a continuous period of at least six years prior to the disposal (or prior to the cessation, as the case may be), or

  (ii) has been an eligible trading company for a shorter continuous period ending with the disposal or cessation and has not previously been an excluded company, an investment company or a non-eligible trading company, *and*

- has carried on its business wholly or mainly in the UK throughout the 'relevant period'.

For shares issued before 7 March 2001, it was also a condition that the company be an 'unquoted' company (as defined for the purposes of the EIS — see 21.5 ENTERPRISE INVESTMENT SCHEME) throughout that part of the 'relevant period' that falls before 7 March 2001 (and see now below in the definition of 'eligible trading company').

As regards shares issued **before 6 April 1998**, a '*qualifying trading company*' is a company none of the shares in which have at any time in the 'relevant period' been listed on a recognised stock exchange (within *ICTA 1988, s 841* — see 58.23 SHARES AND SECURITIES) and which

- either

  (i) is a 'trading company' at the date of disposal, or

  (ii) has ceased to be a trading company within three years before that date and has not since that cessation been an 'excluded company' or an 'investment company', *and*

- either

  (i) has been a trading company for a continuous period of at least six years prior to the disposal (or prior to the cessation, as the case may be), or

  (ii) has been a trading company for a shorter continuous period ending with the disposal or cessation and has not previously been an excluded company or an investment company, *and*

- has been resident in the UK throughout the period from incorporation to the date of disposal.

The '*relevant period*' is the period ending with the disposal of the shares and beginning with the incorporation of the company or, if later, one year before the date on which the shares were issued (one year before they were subscribed for as regards shares issued before 6 April 1998).

An '*eligible trading company*' is a company which is, or would be, a qualifying company for the purposes of the EIS (see 21.5, 21.6 ENTERPRISE INVESTMENT SCHEME). For this purpose, the EIS legislation is applied (by *ICTA 1988, s 576(4A)(4B)*) with appropriate minor modifications; for example, certain references to the relevant period for EIS purposes are replaced with references to the date of disposal or ceasing to be an eligible trading company (whichever is relevant) or whichever is the relevant continuous period (see definition of 'qualifying trading company' above). In relation to shares issued on or after 7 March 2001, in line with a change to the EIS rules, the company must be unquoted at the time of issue and no arrangements must then exist for it to cease to be unquoted (see 21.5 ENTERPRISE INVESTMENT SCHEME for further detail). However, there is no requirement that the company *remain* unquoted, and this applies equally on and after 7 March

2001 in relation to shares issued before that date and after 5 April 1998. A winding-up does not prevent a company being an eligible trading company but only for so long as it continues to be a 'trading company'; the condition now applies in relation to shares issued after 5 April 2001 (but did originally apply up to and including 20 March 2000, after which a drafting error inadvertently altered the law).

The above represents a narrowing of the loss relief against income rules as regards shares issued after 5 April 1998 in that the company which issued the shares must satisfy the EIS requirements as to, inter alia, qualifying activities, qualifying trades, gross assets and, where applicable, group structure. However, it is not a condition that the company issued the shares under the EIS, that the shares be held for a minimum period, or that any EIS income tax relief has been, or could have been, claimed in respect of them.

'*Trading company*' is any company (other than an excluded company — see below) whose business consists wholly or mainly of the carrying on of a trade or trades. The 'holding company' of a 'trading group' is also within this definition.

'*Excluded company*' means a company the trade of which consists wholly or mainly of dealing in land, in commodities or futures or in shares, securities or other financial instruments (as regards shares issued before 6 April 1998, dealing in shares, securities, land, trades or commodity futures). A company which does not carry on its trade on a commercial basis and with a reasonable expectation of profit is within this definition, as are the holding company of a non-trading group, a building society or a registered industrial and provident society.

'*Trading group*' means a 'group' the business of the members of which, taken together, consists wholly or mainly in the carrying on of a trade or trades. Any trade carried on by a subsidiary which is an excluded company (or, as regards shares issued before 6 April 1998, which is non-UK resident) is disregarded.

'*Group*' means a company and its 51% subsidiary or subsidiaries, and a '*holding company*' is one the business of which consists wholly or mainly in the holding of shares or securities in its 51% subsidiary or subsidiaries. 51% subsidiaries are as defined by *ICTA 1988, s 838*.

'*Investment company*' has the meaning given by *ICTA 1988, s 130* (i.e. any company the business of which consists wholly or mainly in the making of investments and the principal part of the income of which is derived therefrom but including savings banks and other banks for savings (except trustee savings banks)) except that it does not include the holding company of a trading group. In *Tintern Close Residents Society Ltd v Winter (Sp C 7), [1995] SSCD 57*, it was decided that property management companies which collect income from residents for the upkeep of relevant properties are not investment companies within the meaning of *ICTA 1988, s 130*.

'*Shares*' (except in the definition of 'excluded company', when all shares and stock are covered) means 'ordinary share capital' as defined in *ICTA 1988, s 832(1)* (see 58.4 SHARES AND SECURITIES).

Identification rules. Where an individual who has subscribed for shares in a company has also acquired shares of the same class in the same company by other means, and both the subscription shares and the other shares form part of the same holding (i.e. a number of shares of the same class held by one person in one capacity, whether or not pooled for CGT purposes), then in determining the extent (if any) to which a disposal relates to shares subscribed for (qualifying shares), disposals are to be identified with acquisitions on a last in/first out (LIFO) basis.

For disposals after 5 April 1998, there is an exception to the above rule where the holding includes any of the following:

- Shares in respect of which Business Expansion Scheme (BES) relief has been given and not withdrawn (see 22.20 EXEMPTIONS AND RELIEFS);

- Shares to which Enterprise Investment Scheme (EIS) income tax relief is attributable (see 21.2 ENTERPRISE INVESTMENT SCHEME);
- Shares to which EIS capital gains deferral relief is attributable (see 21.9 ENTERPRISE INVESTMENT SCHEME).

In such a case, disposals are identified in accordance with the identification rules generally applicable to EIS and BES shares (first in/first out (FIFO), subject to certain special rules — see 21.8 ENTERPRISE INVESTMENT SCHEME, 22.20 EXEMPTIONS AND RELIEFS). (See below as regards the application of these loss relief provisions to EIS and BES shares.)

Loss relief under these provisions on the disposal of qualifying shares forming part of a larger holding is restricted to the sums that would have been allowable as deductions in computing the loss if the qualifying shares had been acquired and disposed of as a separate holding (see Step 4 in the example at 40.14 below).

HMRC Venture Capital Schemes Manual VCM 47150 identifies four steps in the computation of loss relief under these provisions where a holding does not entirely consist of qualifying shares. Step 1 is to compute the allowable loss for CGT purposes under normal CGT principles and identification rules (see 59 SHARES AND SECURITIES—IDENTIFICATION RULES). Step 2 is to identify the qualifying and non-qualifying shares included in the disposal (using the special identification rules described above). If it is found that the disposal comprises both, Step 3 is to apportion the loss, on a just and reasonable basis, between qualifying and non-qualifying shares. Step 4 is to compare the loss so attributed to the qualifying shares with the actual allowable expenditure incurred on those shares and to apply, if necessary, the restriction mentioned above. See the example at 40.14 below.

Miscellaneous. Relief is not available in respect of a 'new holding' (within *TCGA 1992, s 127*) unless relief could have been given (assuming the legislation to have been in force) on the disposal which would have occurred on the reorganisation but for *TCGA 1992, s 127 or* unless the claimant gave 'new consideration' for the new holding, in which latter case the relief is restricted to such amount or value of the new consideration as represents allowable expenditure. See, generally, 58.1 SHARES AND SECURITIES and see HMRC Venture Capital Schemes Manual VCM 48000 *et seq.*

'*New consideration*' means consideration in money or money's worth (other than the surrender of rights etc. and that met out of the company's assets).

A scheme of reconstruction which is undertaken for tax avoidance purposes or other than for *bona fide* commercial reasons, and therefore gives rise to a chargeable disposal under *TCGA 1992, s 137*, cannot support a claim under these provisions. See 3.18 ANTI-AVOIDANCE.

Where a claim is made under these provisions, *TCGA 1992, s 30* (value shifting to give tax-free benefit, see 3.7 ANTI-AVOIDANCE) has effect in relation to the disposal if *any* benefit is conferred, whether tax-free or not.

[*ICTA 1988, ss 574–576; FA 1988, Sch 14 Pt VIII; FA 1989, Sch 12 para 14; FA 1994, s 146, s 210, s 218(5), Sch 17 para 6, Sch 20 para 8; FA 1995, s 119; FA 1996, Sch 38 para 6(1)(2)(h), (9); FA 1998, s 80, Sch 27 Pt III(16); FA 2000, s 63(2)(3), Sch 16 para 3(3); FA 2001, Sch 15 para 38, Sch 33 Pt II(3); SI 2005 No 3229, Regs 77, 78*].

Application to EIS shares. It is formally provided that the provisions described above apply to a loss on the disposal by an individual of shares to which EIS income tax relief is attributable (see 21 ENTERPRISE INVESTMENT SCHEME), except that the above-mentioned LIFO identification rules do not apply to such disposals (whether made before or on or after 6 April 1998). [*ICTA 1988, s 305A; FA 1994, s 137, Sch 15 para 20; FA 1998, Sch 13 para 18*].

Application to BES shares. There is no equivalent to *ICTA 1988, s 305A* in respect of a loss arising on shares issued after 18 March 1986 and before 1 January 1994 in respect of which BES relief (see 22.20 EXEMPTIONS AND RELIEFS) has been given and not withdrawn, because any loss so arising was not allowable for capital gains tax purposes. A complete withdrawal of relief would mean that any loss was allowable for such purposes and, all conditions being met, there seems nothing to prevent the above relief from applying. The position would appear to be the same in respect of a loss arising on shares issued before 19 March 1986 in respect of which BES relief has been given but completely withdrawn. A loss arising on shares issued before 19 March 1986 in respect of which BES relief has been given and not withdrawn, could give rise to an allowable (albeit reduced) loss so that, again, there seems nothing to prevent the reduced loss from being similarly set against income if all conditions are met.

40.14 *Example*

P subscribed for 3,000 £1 ordinary shares at par in W Ltd, a qualifying trading company, in June 1988. In September 1995, P acquired a further 2,200 shares at £3 per share from another shareholder. In December 2006, P sold 3,900 shares at 40p per share.

Indexation factors	June 1988 to September 1995	0.413
	September 1995 to April 1998	0.080

Establish 'section 104 holding' pool.

	Shares	Qualifying expenditure	Indexed pool
		£	£
June 1988 subscription	3,000	3,000	3,000
Indexation to September 1995 £3,000 × 0.413			1,239
September 1995 acquisition	2,200	6,600	6,600
	5,200	9,600	10,839
Indexed rise: September 1995 to April 1998 £10,839 × 0.080			867
	5,200	9,600	11,706
December 2006 disposal	(3,900)	(7,200)	(8,780)
Pool carried forward	1,300	£2,400	£2,926

Step 1. Calculate the CGT loss in the normal way, as follows

	£
Disposal consideration 3,900 × £0.40	1,560
Allowable cost $\frac{3,900}{5,200} \times$ £9,600	7,200
Allowable loss	£5,640

Step 2. Applying a LIFO basis, identify the qualifying shares (1,700) and the non-qualifying shares (2,200) comprised in the disposal.

Step 3. Calculate the proportion of the loss attributable to the qualifying shares.

Loss referable to 1,700 qualifying shares	$\frac{1{,}700}{3{,}900} \times £5{,}640$	£2,458

Step 4. Compare the loss in *Step 3* with the actual cost of the qualifying shares, *viz.*

Cost of 1,700 qualifying shares	$\frac{1{,}700}{3{,}000} \times £3{,}000$	£1,700

The loss available against income is restricted to £1,700 (being lower than £2,458).

The loss not relieved against income remains an allowable loss for CGT purposes.

£5,640 – £1,700 =	£3,940

40.15 LOSSES ON SHARES IN UNLISTED TRADING COMPANIES: INVESTMENT COMPANIES

Where an 'investment company' disposes of shares in a 'qualifying trading company' for which it has subscribed (i.e. not purchased in the open market), and thereby incurs an allowable capital loss in an accounting period, it may claim relief for the loss against income of that accounting period, instead of against gains chargeable to corporation tax. Additionally, if it was an investment company at that earlier time, it may claim to set off any balance of the loss remaining, after relief above, against income of the twelve months immediately preceding the accounting period in which the loss was incurred (income of the relevant accounting periods being time apportioned for this purpose).

The investment company must have been such on the date of the relevant disposal and must either

(*a*) have been an investment company for a continuous period of six years ending on that date; or

(*b*) have been an investment company for a shorter continuous period ending on that date, and must not have been, before the beginning of that period, a 'trading company' or an 'excluded company'.

It must also not have been 'associated' with, or have been a member of the same 'group' as, the qualifying trading company, at any time in the period beginning with the date of its (the investment company's) subscription for the shares, and ending with the date of disposal.

Companies are '*associated*' with each other, for this purpose, if one controls the other, or both are under the control of the same person or persons. The general definitions of *ICTA 1988, s 416*(*2*)(*6*) (meaning of 'control') apply for this purpose. See Tolley's Corporation Tax under Close Companies.

Subject to the above, the definitions of '*excluded company*', '*group*', '*investment company*', '*qualifying trading company*', '*eligible trading company*', '*trading company*', and the other general definitions and provisions (including identification rules and concessionary treatment under ESCs D28 and D46) relating to the similar relief for individuals outlined in 40.13 above, apply, *mutatis mutandis*, to this relief. Note that 40.13(*d*) above applies in this case to deemed disposals on or after 1 April 2000. Just as the normal identification rule for this relief is disapplied in the case of EIS and BES shares held by individuals, so is it disapplied where the investment company's holding includes shares issued on or after 1 April 2000 to which investment relief under the Corporate Venturing Scheme is attributable and which have been held continuously (see 17.20 CORPORATE VENTURING SCHEME) by the company; the identification rules at 17.17 CORPORATE VENTURING SCHEME (generally first in/first out) apply instead.

Relief must be claimed within two years of the end of the accounting period in which the loss arises and is given before any deduction for charges on income, expenses of management or other deductions, except that a claim for a loss on a Corporate Venturing Scheme investment to be relieved against income does take priority (see 17.20 CORPORATE VENTURING SCHEME).

[*ICTA 1988, ss 573, 575, 576; FA 1989, Sch 12 para 14; FA 1994, s 146, Sch 17 para 6; FA 1998, s 80, Sch 27 Pt III(16); FA 2000, s 63(2)(3), Sch 16 para 3(2)–(4)*].

40.16 WRITE-OFF OF GOVERNMENT INVESTMENT

Where any amount of an investment, by the Government, in a *corporate body*, is written off, an equal amount is to be set off against the body's tax 'losses', starting with losses available at the end of the accounting period ended before the write-off, and continuing for subsequent periods, until the investment is covered. The definition of '*losses*', for this purpose, includes, inter alia, unrelieved allowable losses under *TCGA 1992, s 8* (capital losses of companies). It should be noted, however, that the investment is only written off against capital losses as a last resort, i.e. after the extinction of other losses, unrelieved capital allowances, management expenses and charges. The investment can also be written off against the losses of any member of the same 51% group within *ICTA 1988, s 838*. An investment is written off if the liability to repay any money lent is extinguished; if any shares subscribed for out of public funds are cancelled; or if 'commencing capital debts' (as defined) or 'public dividend capital' (as defined) is reduced otherwise than by being paid off or repaid. These provisions do not apply where the investment written off is replaced in some other form. [*ICTA 1988, s 400*]. See Tolley's Corporation Tax under Losses for further details.

40.17 PROFIT AND LOSSES OF THEATRE BACKERS (ANGELS)

Angels are theatrical backers who invest in productions. An investment which occurs in the normal course of a backer's trade falls within the trading income or Schedule D, Case I rules (see Tolley's Income Tax). Special tax treatment applies to non-trading backers.

HMRC's view is that the profits of non-trading theatre angels are assessable as income whilst a loss forms an allowable loss for capital gains tax.

A '*profit*' for these purposes is the return the angel receives over and above the original investment. A '*loss*' arises where there is no further prospect of a return from the investment. The contract is viewed in normal circumstances as an asset for capital gains purposes (although most certainly this would have to be established on the facts of each case).

However, by concession HMRC will allow the profits and losses of non-trading theatre angels resident in the UK to be assessed and relieved accordingly under income tax rules. Where this treatment applies, any loss cannot also be treated as an allowable loss for capital gains tax purposes.
(HMRC Extra-Statutory Concession A94).

40.18 DEFERRED UNASCERTAINABLE CONSIDERATION: ELECTION FOR TREATMENT OF LOSS AS ACCRUING IN EARLIER YEAR

Where a person within the charge to capital gains tax makes a disposal on or after 10 April 2003 of a right to future unascertainable consideration (see below) acquired as consideration for the disposal of another asset, and a loss accrues, he may, subject to conditions, make an election for the loss to be treated as arising in the year in which that other asset was disposed of. Accordingly, where the election is made, the loss on disposal of the right can be set against the gain arising on the disposal of the original asset. The detailed provisions are described below.

Conditions for making election. The election is available where a person (the '*taxpayer*') disposes of a right on or after 10 April 2003 and the following conditions are satisfied.

(1) An allowable loss (the '*relevant loss*') accrues on the disposal.

(2) The tax year in which the relevant loss actually accrues (the '*year of the loss*') is one in which the taxpayer is chargeable to capital gains tax in respect of chargeable gains accruing to him in that year, or would be so chargeable (apart from the deduction of any allowable losses and the annual exempt amount) were there any such gains.

(3) The right was, in whole or part, acquired by the taxpayer as the whole or part of the consideration for a disposal (the '*original disposal*') by him of another asset (the '*original asset*').

(4) The original disposal was made in a tax year earlier than that in which the disposal of the right is made. Where the right was acquired as consideration for two or more disposals, this condition must be satisfied with respect to all those disposals.

(5) On the taxpayer's acquisition of the right, there was no corresponding disposal of it.

(6) The right is a 'right to unascertainable consideration' (see below).

(7) A chargeable gain accrued to the taxpayer, or would have so accrued but for the deferral provisions of *TCGA 1992, Sch 5B para 2(2)(a)* (see 21.10 ENTERPRISE INVESTMENT SCHEME) or *Sch 5C para 2(2)(a)* (see 66.12 VENTURE CAPITAL TRUSTS), on one or more of the following events:

   (*a*) the original disposal,

   (*b*) an earlier disposal of the original asset by the taxpayer in the tax year of the original disposal, or

   (*c*) a later disposal of the original asset by the taxpayer in a tax year earlier than the actual year of the disposal of the right.

   Where the right was acquired as consideration for two or more original disposals, any reference in (*a*) to (*c*) above to the original disposal should be read as a reference to any of the original disposals, any reference to the original asset as a reference to the original asset in relation to that original disposal, and any reference to the tax year of the original disposal should be construed accordingly.

(8) There is a tax year (an '*eligible year*'), which is earlier than the year of the loss but not earlier than 1992/93, in which a chargeable gain within (7) above accrued to the taxpayer and for which there remains a relevant amount on which capital gains tax is chargeable immediately before the election. Where the deferral provisions mentioned in (7) above applied to prevent a gain within (7) above from accruing, a tax year in which a chargeable gain is treated as accruing to the taxpayer in respect of that gain under *TCGA 1992, Sch 5B paras 4, 5* or *Sch 5C paras 4, 5* (chargeable events — see 21.10 ENTERPRISE INVESTMENT SCHEME and 66.12 VENTURE CAPITAL TRUSTS) will be an eligible year.

   For these purposes, a tax year is one for which there remains a relevant amount on which capital gains tax is chargeable immediately before an election if, immediately before the making of the election, there remains for that year an amount in respect of which the taxpayer is chargeable to capital gains tax, after taking account of any previous elections under these provisions, after excluding any gains attributed under *TCGA 1992, ss 77, 86, 87* or *89(2)* (see 2.3 ANNUAL RATES AND EXEMPTIONS), and on the assumption that no losses fall to be deducted in consequence of any election under these provisions which could be, but has not been, made.

For the above purposes, any question as to whether a chargeable gain or loss is one that accrues (or would accrue but for any particular provision) on a particular disposal or a disposal of any particular description, or the time at which, or year in which, any particular disposal takes place, is determined without regard to *TCGA 1992, s 10A* (gains and losses accruing during period of temporary non-residence treated as accruing in year of return — see 45.4 OVERSEAS MATTERS). This provision does not, however, affect the determination of any question as to the tax year in which, by virtue of *TCGA 1992, s 10A(2)*, the gain or loss is treated as accruing (apart from the effect of an election under these provisions), nor does it prevent a loss accruing during a period of temporary non-residence from being an allowable loss.

Losses treated by virtue of *TCGA 1992, s 10A* as accruing in 2003/04 are, for the purposes of these provisions, treated as accruing after 9 April 2003 (so that, where the other conditions are satisfied, an election can be made).

[*TCGA 1992, ss 279A, 279B(1)(7)(8); FA 2003, s 162(1)(3)*].

Effect of election. Where an election is made under the above provisions, the relevant loss is treated for capital gains tax purposes as if it were a loss accruing in the earliest tax year which is an eligible year. The amount of the relevant loss that can be deducted from chargeable gains of that year is limited to the amount (the '*first year limit*') found by taking the following steps.

Step 1. Take the total amount of chargeable gains accruing to the taxpayer in the year.

Step 2. Exclude from that amount any amounts attributed to the taxpayer under *TCGA 1992, ss 77, 86, 87* or *89(2)* (see 2.3 ANNUAL RATES AND EXEMPTIONS).

Step 3. Deduct from the remaining amount any amounts in respect of allowable losses except for any losses falling to be set against gains attributed to the taxpayer under *TCGA 1992, ss 77* or *86* (see 40.1 above). Account must be taken of any previous elections made under these provisions, but no account must be taken of the relevant loss.

Where the earliest eligible year is 2003/04 or a later year, or where it is a year in respect of which an election under *FA 2002, Sch 11 para 8* (see 40.1 above) has been made, two further steps must be taken to arrive at the first year limit, as follows.

Step 4. Add to the remaining amount every amount attributed to the taxpayer as a chargeable gain under *TCGA 1992, ss 77* or *86*.

Step 5. Deduct any losses falling to be set against such attributed gains.

To the extent that the relevant loss exceeds the first year limit (and so is not utilised in the first eligible year), it may be carried forward for set-off against gains of later years. In the case of tax years falling between the first eligible year and the year of the loss, any remaining part of the relevant loss can only be deducted if the year is an eligible year. For such years, the amount of the loss which may be deducted is limited to the amount (the '*later year limit*') in respect of which the taxpayer would be chargeable to capital gains tax for the year

- on the assumption that no part of the relevant loss, or any other loss in respect of which an election under these provisions could be made but which, immediately after the making of the election in question, has not been made, falls to be deducted from the gains for the year;
- taking account of any previous elections under these provisions; and
- apart from any available taper relief and any gains from which the taxpayer's personal losses are not deductible (see 40.1 above).

[*TCGA 1992, s 279C; FA 2003, s 162(1)*].

Where the right in respect of which an election is made is an earn-out right within the meaning of *TCGA 1992, s 138A* (see 58.5 SHARES AND SECURITIES) conferred before

10 April 2003, no election can be made under that section for the right to be treated as a security, whether at the same time as the election under these provisions or subsequently. [*FA 2003, s 162*(*2*)(*4*)].

Meaning of 'right to unascertainable consideration'. A right is a '*right to unascertainable consideration*' if, and only if, it is a right to consideration the amount or value of which is unascertainable when the right is conferred because it is referable, in whole or part, to matters which are uncertain at that time because they have not yet occurred.

The amount or value of any consideration is not regarded as unascertainable by reason only

(i) that the right to receive all or part of the consideration is postponed or contingent, to the extent that the consideration is brought into account in accordance with *TCGA 1992, s 48* (see 15.6(g) COMPUTATION OF GAINS AND LOSSES) in the computation of a gain accruing to the taxpayer on the disposal of an asset;

(ii) in a case where the right to receive all or part of the consideration is postponed and may be to any extent satisfied by the receipt of alternative types of property, that some person has the right to select the property or type of property that is to be received; or

(iii) that either the amount or the value of the consideration has not been fixed, if either the amount will be fixed by reference to the value, and the value is ascertainable, or the value will be fixed by reference to the amount, and the amount is ascertainable.

An earn-out right treated as a security by virtue of *TCGA 1992, s 138A* (see 58.5 SHARES AND SECURITIES) is not regarded as a right to unascertainable consideration for the purposes of these provisions.

[*TCGA 1992, s 279B*(*2*)–(*6*); *FA 2003, s 162*(*1*)].

Making of election. An election under the above provisions is irrevocable and must be made by notice in writing to HMRC on or before the first anniversary of 31 January following the year of the loss. The notice must specify the following:

- the amount of the relevant loss,
- the right disposed of,
- the tax year of the right's disposal, and, if different, the year of the loss,
- the tax year in which the right was acquired,
- the original asset or assets,
- the eligible year in which the relevant loss is to be treated as accruing,
- the first year limit, and
- the amount to be deducted from gains of that year.

If any part of the relevant loss is to be carried forward to later eligible years, the notice must also specify each such year and the later year limit and amount to be deducted for each such year.

A separate notice is required for each loss in respect of which an election is being made. Where two or more elections are made on the same day, the notices must specify the order in which they are to be treated as made. [*TCGA 1992, s 279D; FA 2003, s 162*(*1*)].

41 Market Value

Cross-references. See 3.15 and 3.16 ANTI-AVOIDANCE for anti-avoidance provisions which may override or amend the general rules given below; 4.3 and 4.6 APPEALS for appeals relating to market values; 7.2 ASSETS HELD ON 6 APRIL 1965 for valuation of quoted shares and securities held on 6 April 1965; 15.4 COMPUTATION OF GAINS AND LOSSES for allowable expenditure relating to acquisition of assets at market value; 18.3 DEATH for valuation at death; 40.9 LOSSES for loss relief where the market value of an asset has become negligible; 46 PARTNERSHIPS for further valuation rules which apply to partnership assets.

41.1 **Market value** is the price which assets might reasonably fetch in the open market, sold individually, with no allowance being made for any reduction in market value arising out of the whole of the assets being placed on the market at one and the same time. [*TCGA 1992, s 272(1)(2)*]. This provision applies subject to special rules applying under *TCGA 1992, s 25A* (deemed disposals of plant or machinery on commencement or termination of long funding lease — see 6.6 ASSETS) and *TCGA 1992, s 41A* (restriction on loss on disposal of fixture used for leasing under long funding lease — see 15.6(*k*) COMPUTATION OF GAINS AND LOSSES). [*TCGA 1992, s 272(6); FA 2006, Sch 9 para 6*].

After 9 March 1981, acquisition and disposal are treated as being made at market value (subject to any other provision and the exception below) if the transaction is

(*a*) not at arm's length (which includes, in particular, any transaction between connected persons — see 3.15 ANTI-AVOIDANCE), or

(*b*) by way of gift, or

(*c*) on a transfer into settlement by a settlor, or

(*d*) a distribution from a company in respect of shares in that company, or

(*e*) wholly or partly for a consideration that cannot be valued (see *Fielder v Vedlynn Ltd Ch D 1992, 65 TC 145*), or

(*f*) in connection with his own or another's loss of office or employment, diminution of emoluments (see *Whitehouse v Ellam Ch D, [1995] STC 503*), or in consideration for or recognition of his or another's services (in any office, employment or otherwise), past or future.

Exception. The market value provisions in (*a*)–(*f*) above do not apply to the *acquisition* of an asset if there is no corresponding disposal of it *and* there is no consideration in money or money's worth (or the consideration is of an amount or value lower than the market value of the asset).

[*TCGA 1992, s 17*].

An attempt by a taxpayer to substitute market value for actual price paid in a transaction between unconnected persons failed in *Bullivant Holdings Ltd v CIR Ch D 1998, 71 TC 22*. For the application of the market value rule to shares acquired by reason of employment, see 20.3, 20.5, 20.15, 20.25, 20.26, 20.27, 20.30 EMPLOYEE SHARE SCHEMES.

Special rules applied to disposals by 'excluded persons' after 9 March 1981 and before 6 April 1985. See the 2005/06 and earlier editions of this work.

41.2 **Chargeable intangible assets.** Where, after 31 March 2002, there is a transfer of an intangible asset between 'related parties' (see below), at least one of which is a company, and the asset is a 'chargeable intangible asset' in the hands of the transferor or transferee (or both), the transfer is treated for *all* direct tax purposes (as regards both transferor and transferee) as being at 'market value'. For this purpose, the '*market value*' of an asset is the price it might reasonably be expected to fetch on a sale in the open market. An asset is a '*chargeable intangible asset*' if a gain on its realisation would give rise to a credit falling to be brought into account under the intangible assets regime summarised at 14.13 COMPANIES—CORPORATE FINANCE AND INTANGIBLES and covered in detail in Tolley's Corporation Tax under Intangible Assets.

There are four exceptions to the above rule, as follows.

1. Where the consideration for the transfer falls to be adjusted under the transfer pricing rules in *ICTA 1988, Sch 28AA* or, in certain circumstances, *would* fall to be so adjusted were it not for the fact that the consideration is an arm's length amount.

2. Where the transfer is 'tax-neutral' under any provision of the intangible assets regime; this applies mainly in connection with intra-group transfers and certain transfers of a business.

3. For transfers on or after 16 March 2005, where the asset is transferred to the company and a reduction is made under *TCGA 1992, s 165(4)(a)* (reduction of chargeable gain on gift of business asset — see 33.1 HOLD-OVER RELIEFS). In this case, for the purposes of the intangible assets regime, the transfer is treated as being at market value less the amount of the reduction.

4. For transfers on or after 16 March 2005, where

   - the asset is transferred from the company at less than its market value or to the company at more than market value,
   - the related party is not a company or, if it is a company, the asset is not a chargeable intangible asset in its hands, and
   - the transfer gives rise (or would but for the above rule) to an amount to be taken into account in computing any person's income, profits or losses for tax purposes under *ICTA 1988, s 209* (company distributions) or *ITEPA 2003, Pt 3* (earnings and benefits treated as employment income).

   In this case, the market value rule above is disapplied only for the purposes of the computation mentioned above.

[*FA 2002, Sch 29 para 92; FA 2004, Sch 5 para 16(3); F(No 2)A 2005, s 41(2)(6)*].

Parties are '*related parties*' in any of the following circumstances.

- Both are companies, and one has 'control' of, or holds a 'major interest' in, the other (both terms being as defined in *FA 2002, Sch 29 para 96*).
- Both are companies, and both are under the 'control' of the same person (except, broadly, where that person is a state, a government or an international organisation).
- One is a close company (within the meaning given by *ICTA 1988, ss 414, 415*) and the other is, or is an 'associate' (within *ICTA 1988, s 417(3)*) of, a 'participator' (within *FA 2002, Sch 29 para 100(1)*) in that company.
- One is a close company and the other is, or is an associate of, a participator in a company that has control of, or holds a major interest in, that company. For the purposes of *FA 2002, Sch 29 para 92* above as it applies otherwise than for the purpose of determining the debits or credits to be brought into account under the intangible assets regime, this provision applies in relation to the transfer of an asset on or after 16 March 2005. For all other purposes of the intangible assets regime the provision applies in relation to debits and credits to be brought into account for accounting periods beginning on or after 16 March 2005. In relation to such accounting periods, it is deemed always to have had effect. For this purpose, an accounting period beginning before, and ending on or after, 16 March 2005 is treated as two separate accounting periods, the first ending on 15 March 2005 and the second beginning on 16 March 2005.

- In relation to debits and credits to be brought into account for accounting periods beginning on or after 20 June 2003, both are companies within the same 'group' (as defined in *FA 2002,Sch 29 paras 47–54*). In relation to such accounting periods, this provision is deemed always to have had effect. For this purpose, an accounting period beginning before, and ending on or after, 20 June 2003 is treated as two separate accounting periods, the first ending on 19 June 2003 and the second beginning on 20 June 2003.

[*FA 2002, Sch 29 para 95; FA 2003, s 184(3)–(5); F(No 2)A 2005, s 41(3)(7)–(9)*].

41.3 QUOTED SHARES AND SECURITIES

The market value of shares and securities quoted in The Stock Exchange Daily Official List is the lesser of

(*a*) the lower of the two prices quoted in The Stock Exchange Daily Official List for the relevant date, plus a quarter of the difference between those prices (*'the quarter-up rule'*), and

(*b*) the average of the highest and lowest prices for normal bargains recorded on that date, if any.

If the London trading floor is closed on the relevant date, the prices are to be taken by reference to the latest previous date or to the earliest subsequent date, whichever produces the lower figure.

The above method of valuation does not apply for computing the value of shares as at 6 April 1965 (see 7.2 ASSETS HELD ON 6 APRIL 1965), nor where special circumstances may affect the value. [*TCGA 1992, s 272(3)(4)(6), Sch 11 para 6(1)(2)(4), para 7(1); FA 1996, Sch 38 para 12*]. See *Hinchcliffe v Crabtree HL 1971, 47 TC 419*.

HMRC may make regulations extending, inter alia, provisions relating to tax on chargeable gains and referring to The Stock Exchange to any or all other investment exchanges within the meaning given by *Financial Services and Markets Act 2000, s 285(1)(a)*. [*TCGA 1992, ss 285, 287; SI 2001 No 3629, Art 69*].

Units in unit trusts, subject to similar valuation rules at 6 April 1965 (as above), are valued at the lower of the two prices published by the managers on the relevant date or if no price is published at that time, on the latest date before the relevant date. [*TCGA 1992, s 272(5)(6), Sch 11 para 6(1)(3)*].

Simon's Direct Tax Service. See C2.122.

41.4 UNQUOTED SHARES

Market value of unquoted shares is determined on the assumption that all information is available which a prudent prospective purchaser might reasonably require before purchase by private treaty at arm's length from a willing vendor. [*TCGA 1992, s 273*]. This counteracts *In re Lynall HL 1971, 47 TC 375*.

This provision applies to disposals after 5 July 1973 and valuations are made on the present basis in connection both with acquisition (even if before 6 July 1973, or 6 April 1965) and disposal. Otherwise, the chargeable gain on a part disposal before 6 July 1973 is not itself affected but it is re-computed on the present basis for the purpose of calculating the gain on a subsequent disposal after 5 July 1973. As regards deemed acquisitions on death after 30 March 1971 and before 6 July 1973, the present basis does not apply if the shares constituted a controlling holding and were valued on the assets basis for estate duty purposes. [*TCGA 1992, Sch 11 paras 3–5*].

In arriving at a valuation, unpublished information concerning the company's profits may be taken into account (*Caton's Administrators v Couch (Sp C 6), [1995] SSCD 34*; *Clark (Clark's Executor) v Green & CIR (Sp C 5), [1995] SSCD 99*).

Other cases concerning disputes as to the value of unquoted shares include *Hawkings-Byass v Sassen (and related appeals) (Sp C 88), [1996] SSCD 319*; *Denekamp v Pearce Ch D 1998, 71 TC 213*; *Billows v Hammond (Sp C 252), [2000] SSCD 430*; *Marks v Sherred (Sp C 418), [2004] SSCD 362*; *Shinebond Ltd v Carrol (Sp C 522), [2006] SSCD 147*.

Simon's Direct Tax Service. See C2.124.

41.5 UNLISTED SECURITIES MARKET (USM) (NOW CLOSED)

Securities dealt in on the USM were not treated as 'listed' or 'quoted' for those provisions of the *Taxes Acts* which use such terms in relation to securities. Evidence of the open-market value of such securities would have been suggested, initially, by details of the bargains done at, or near, the relevant date. Where other factors needed to be weighed, the Shares Valuation Division of the Capital Taxes Office would consider whether a value offered on the basis of those bargains could be accepted as an adequate reflection of the open-market value. The Revenue stated that securities dealt in on the USM would satisfy the tests of being 'authorised to be dealt in' and 'dealt in (regularly or from time to time)' on a recognised stock exchange (SP 18/80 — now obsolete). It appears that the Revenue applied similar criteria to securities covered by Rule 4.2 of The Stock Exchange. This may also have been the position as regards the Third Market of The Stock Exchange which closed on 31 December 1990.

The USM is now closed.

41.6 ALTERNATIVE INVESTMENT MARKET (AIM)

Companies not wishing to apply for a full listing have access to the Alternative Investment Market (AIM) launched on 19 June 1995. AIM replaced the existing Rule 4.2 (of the Stock Exchange) dealing facility, and transitional provisions were available to assist companies already under Rule 4.2 to migrate to the AIM at minimum cost. AIM companies are not treated as 'quoted' or 'listed' for those provisions of the Taxes Acts which use such terms in relation to securities. (HMRC Press Releases 20 February 1995, 28 November 2001).

41.7 LAND

Where, at a certain date, freehold land was subject to a tenancy by a company controlled by the freeholder, the valuation had to be of the reversion in the land expectant on the determination of the tenancy and not of the unencumbered freehold (*Henderson v Karmel's Exors Ch D 1984, 58 TC 201*).

41.8 EXCHANGE CONTROL

In relation to assets of a kind the sale of which was subject to restrictions imposed under the *Exchange Control Act 1947*, a determination of market value at any time before 13 December 1979 is subject to adjustment for the premium which would have been payable by a purchaser but not receivable by a seller. [*TCGA 1992, Sch 11 para 7*(*2*)].

42 Married Persons and Civil Partners

Cross-references. See 2 ANNUAL RATES AND EXEMPTIONS; 7.1 and 7.3 ASSETS HELD ON 6 APRIL 1965; 8.5 ASSETS HELD ON 31 MARCH 1982; 33 HOLD-OVER RELIEFS; 34.3 INDEXATION for certain transfers between spouses before 6 April 1985 and after 5 April 1982; 40.10 LOSSES for loss relief restrictions on qualifying loans between spouses; 49.1 and 49.2 PRIVATE RESIDENCES; 52 RESIDENCE AND DOMICILE for treatment of spouses; 53.9 RETIREMENT RELIEF for reliefs applicable to spouses before 6 April 2003; 61.14 TAPER RELIEF.

42.1 MARRIED PERSONS

For 1990/91 and subsequent years of assessment, the spouses, whether or not 'living together' (see 42.3 below), are each treated as separate individuals so that

(*a*) each spouse is assessed and charged by reference only to their own gains and circumstances (e.g. the rate of tax applicable);

(*b*) losses of one spouse are not deductible from the gains of the other; and

(*c*) each spouse has a separate right to the whole of the annual exempt amount available to individuals generally.

Where a husband and wife have made a declaration under *ICTA 1988, s 282B* in respect of their individual beneficial interests in, and in the income from, jointly held property (see Tolley's Income Tax under Married Persons) and the declaration is still effective at the time of disposal of the property, there is a presumption that the declared split of interests is effective for capital gains tax purposes. Where there is no declaration which has effect at the time of disposal but it is clear that there is a particular split of ownership (e.g. a separate agreement may provide for the spouses' respective rights or that one spouse is merely a nominee and has no beneficial interest in the property) any gain on a disposal should be reported to HMRC on that basis. In other cases where the split of ownership is not clear HMRC will normally accept that the spouses hold the property in equal shares (Revenue Press Release 21 November 1990).

Transfers of assets between spouses living together are treated as made on a 'no gain/no loss basis' as in 42.4 below.

Where

(i) the husband makes a claim under *TCGA 1992, s 279* (previously *CGTA 1979, s 13*; enforced delay in remitting gains from disposals of overseas assets, see 45.5 OVERSEAS MATTERS) in respect of gains accruing to the wife before 6 April 1990 (when gains of the wife were, with certain exceptions, assessed on the husband), and

(ii) under that provision the amount of the gains falls to be assessed as if it were an amount of gains accruing after 5 April 1990,

the assessment is to be made on the wife (or her personal representatives). [*TCGA 1992, s 279(7)*].

Gains accruing to one spouse as trustee or personal representative cannot affect the position of the other spouse. [*TCGA 1992, s 65(2)*].

Spouses living together may claim exemption in respect of only one main residence. See 49.1 PRIVATE RESIDENCES.

See 59.2 SHARES AND SECURITIES—IDENTIFICATION RULES as regards joint husband and wife shareholdings.

42.2 CIVIL PARTNERS

FA 2005 includes provisions enabling the Treasury to make regulations providing for same-sex partners in a 'civil partnership' to be treated for tax purposes in the same way as married persons. For this purpose a '*civil partnership*' is one which exists under or by virtue of the *Civil Partnerships Act 2004* and '*civil partner*' is to be construed accordingly. [*FA 2005, s 103*]. The regulations, the *Tax and Civil Partnership Regulations 2005 SI 2005 No 3229*, take effect from 5 December 2005, the date from which the *Civil Partnership Act 2004* comes into effect.

Transfers of assets between civil partners who are living together are treated as made on a 'no gain/no loss basis' as in 42.4 below.

Civil partners living together may claim exemption in respect of only one main residence. See 49.1 PRIVATE RESIDENCES.

42.3 'LIVING TOGETHER'

Individuals who are married to, or are civil partners of, each other are treated as living together unless they are

(*a*) separated under a court order or separation deed, or

(*b*) in fact separated in circumstances which render permanent separation likely.

[*ICTA 1988, s 282; TCGA 1992, s 288(3); SI 2005 No 3229, Regs 62, 122*].

Both (*a*) and (*b*) above require the marriage or civil partnership to have broken down (HMRC Capital Gains Manual CG 22074). As regards (*b*), HMRC give further guidance in their Relief Manual at RE 1060–1065.

42.4 TRANSFERS BETWEEN SPOUSES OR CIVIL PARTNERS

Transfers of assets, in a year of assessment, between spouses or civil partners who are living together (see 42.3 above) in any part of that year are regarded as made on a 'no gain/no loss' basis. This treatment also applies to transfers between spouses or civil partners in the part of a year following the start of the marriage or civil partnership and in the whole of the year in which separation takes place, even though the spouses or civil partners may not be 'living together' at the time of transfer (but does not apply following a decree absolute). The no gain/no loss treatment does not apply to transfers (i) by way of *donatio mortis causa* (see 18.4 DEATH); or (ii) to or from trading stock of either spouse or civil partner. [*TCGA 1992, s 58; SI 2005 No 3229, Reg 107*].

The deemed consideration for a no gain/no loss transfer between spouses or civil partners is thus equal to the transferor's acquisition cost for CGT purposes, including any enhancement expenditure, plus indexation allowance if applicable (see 34 INDEXATION). The no gain/no loss rule cannot be disapplied, and any *actual* consideration given for the transfer is ignored. It should be noted that the transaction is still a disposal by the transferor spouse or partner and an acquisition by the transferee as at the date of transfer; the legislation does not operate by deeming no disposal to have taken place (though see 61.14 TAPER RELIEF which combines the periods for which the asset is held by each spouse or partner but which applies only for the purpose of computing that relief).

Where either spouse or civil partner is non-UK resident, but the definition at 42.3 above nevertheless treats them as 'living together', there is no authority for disapplying the no gain/no loss treatment even if the transfer results in an asset leaving the UK tax net (see HMRC Capital Gains Manual CG 22304 and see *Gubay v Kington HL 1984, 57 TC 601*).

See 15.7 COMPUTATION OF GAINS AND LOSSES for part disposals between spouses or civil partners and 38.8 LAND for small part disposals of land.

Example

(*A*) *No inter-spouse transfer*

Paul and Heidi are a married couple with total income of £32,800 and £38,800 respectively for 2006/07. On 4 April 2007, Heidi sells a painting which she had acquired in June 1994 at a cost of £5,000. Net sale proceeds amount to £23,000 and the indexation factor for the period June 1994 to April 1998 is 0.124. Neither spouse disposed of any other chargeable assets during 2006/07.

Chargeable gain — Heidi

	£
Net proceeds	23,000.00
Cost	5,000.00
Unindexed gain	18,000.00
Indexation allowance £5,000 × 0.124	620.00
Pre-tapered gain	17,380.00
Taper relief @ 35%	6,083.00
	11,297.00
Annual exemption	8,800.00
Taxable gain	£2,497.00

	£
Total income	38,800.00
Personal allowance	5,035.00
Taxable income	£33,465.00
Basic rate limit = £33,300, so gain of £2,497 is all taxed at 40%.	
Tax payable £2,497 × 40%	£998.80

(*B*) *Inter-spouse transfer*

The facts are as in (A) above except that in January 2007, Heidi gives the painting to Paul who then makes the sale on 4 April 2007.

Chargeable gain — Heidi

	£
Deemed consideration (January 2007) note (*a*)	5,620
Cost	5,000
Unindexed gain	620
Indexation allowance (to April 1998) £5,000 × 0.124	620
Chargeable gain	Nil

Chargeable gain — Paul

	£
Net proceeds (4.4.07)	23,000
Cost (January 2007)	5,620
Pre-tapered gain	17,380
Taper relief @ 35% (note (*b*))	6,083
	11,297
Annual exemption	8,800
Taxable gain	£2,497

	£
Total income	32,800
Personal allowance	5,035
Taxable income	£27,765

Taxable income falls short of the basic rate limit (£33,300) by £5,535, so gain of £2,497 is all taxed at 20%.

Tax payable £2,497 × 20%	£499.40
Tax saving compared with (A) above	£499.40

Notes to the example

(*a*) The inter-spouse transfer is deemed to be for such consideration as to ensure that no gain or loss accrues. Effectively, the consideration is equal to cost plus indexation to April 1998 (see 34.1 INDEXATION).

(*b*) Taper relief is computed by reference to the combined period of ownership after 5 April 1998 (see 61.14 TAPER RELIEF). In this instance, relief is at the non-business asset rate of 35% by reference to a qualifying holding period of nine complete years (including the bonus year for assets acquired before 17 March 1998).

(*c*) The fact that transfers of assets between husband and wife are no gain/no loss transfers enables savings to be made by ensuring that disposals are made by a spouse with an unused annual exemption and/or basic rate band.

(*d*) An inter-spouse transfer followed by a sale could be attacked by HMRC as an anti-avoidance device. To minimise the risk, there should be a clear time interval between the two transactions and no arrangements made to effect the ultimate sale until after the transfer. The gift should be outright with no strings attached and with no 'arrangement' for eventual proceeds to be passed to the transferor.

A transfer of shares or securities between spouses or civil partners under the no gain/no loss rule can cause conflict between the rules at 59.2 SHARES AND SECURITIES — IDENTIFICATION RULES which treat the shares as acquired by the transferee at the date of transfer and those at 61.14 TAPER RELIEF which treat them for taper relief purposes as acquired by the transferee at the time they were acquired by the transferor. In practice, this is a problem only if the transferor acquired the shares at different times *and* the transferee's disposal is a part disposal. An article in Revenue Tax Bulletin August 2001 pp 876, 877, with worked example, explains HMRC's pragmatic approach, and is also a useful illustration of how the no gain/no loss rule, the share identification rules and the taper relief rules generally interact.

Transfers whilst spouses separated or treated as separated. In a case in which spouses, after several years of separation, were divorced and the court order (by consent) on the decree nisi provided for the transfer of certain property (which was not otherwise exempt) it was held that the property had been disposed of at the time of the decree nisi. As the divorce was not then absolute, the spouses were still connected persons and the consideration was to be taken as the market value. See 16.1 CONNECTED PERSONS and 41.1 MARKET VALUE and HMRC Capital Gains Manual CG 22400–22510. The normal 'no gain/no loss' basis did not apply as the spouses were not living together. (*Aspden v Hildesley Ch D 1981, 55 TC 609*).

Unmarried couples. The no gain/no loss rule applies only to transfers between persons legally recognised as married or as civil partners under English or Scottish law. Polygamous marriages may be so recognised in limited circumstances (see HMRC Capital Gains Manual CG 22072). The rule does not apply to a transfer to a so-called 'common-law' husband or wife. An unmarried couple or a couple who are not civil partners are not CONNECTED PERSONS (16) by reason of their relationship alone (though they may be for other reasons, for example if they are also business partners). However, a transfer of an asset between them is likely to be treated as taking place at MARKET VALUE (see 41.1) unless made at arm's length in any case.

43 Mineral Royalties

Cross-reference. See 38 LAND.

43.1 Where a person resident or ordinarily resident in the UK is entitled to receive mineral royalties (i.e. so much of any rents, tolls, royalties or periodical payments as relates to the winning and working of minerals other than water, peat, topsoil, etc.) under a lease, licence or agreement conferring a right to win and work minerals in the UK or under a sale or conveyance of such minerals, only one-half of any such royalties receivable in any tax year or accounting period is treated as income for the purposes of income tax or for corporation tax on profits other than chargeable gains. The other half of the royalties is treated as a chargeable gain to which no allowable expenditure attaches.

A 'terminal loss' which accrues on a 'relevant event' may (if the taxpayer so claims within six years of the event) be carried back and set against chargeable gains accruing in the years of assessment or accounting periods falling wholly or partly within a period of 15 years before the relevant event, taking later years first.

A '*relevant event*' occurs on the expiry or termination of the mineral lease or the disposal (or deemed disposal under any provision) of the interest held in the land to which the lease relates ('*the relevant interest*'). The taxpayer must have been entitled to receive mineral royalties under the mineral lease and held the interest immediately before the relevant event.

A '*terminal loss*' is an allowable loss for capital gains tax purposes which arises

(*a*) on the expiry or termination of the mineral lease, and on an additional claim within the same time limit as above, by which the taxpayer is treated as if he had disposed of and immediately re-acquired the relevant interest at its market value; or

(*b*) on the actual disposal (or any other deemed disposal under any provision) of the relevant interest.

Relief in any one tax year or accounting period is restricted to the chargeable gains previously assessed by reason of the treatment above in respect of the mineral lease in question, except that any unrelieved balance is treated as accruing at the date of the relevant event and as allowable against general gains. If no claim is made for the terminal loss to be treated as above, the whole of such loss is treated as accruing at the date of the relevant event and as an allowable loss against general gains. Repayments of tax are made as may be necessary.

Regulations may be made by HMRC to facilitate the above provisions. [*SI 1971, No 1035*]. These deal with apportionments of payments where they relate to other matters as well as mineral royalties.

Where, on the last disposal (before 23 July 1970) affecting a mineral lease, betterment levy was chargeable under Case B (as defined by *Land Commission Act 1967, Pt III*) the chargeable gain was limited to a fraction (base value of that disposition/consideration received) of one half of the royalties received. After 5 April 1988, this limitation applies only if it applied in a chargeable period ending before 6 April 1988. But if such a lease has been renewed, extended or varied after 22 July 1970, one half of any subsequent royalty receipt is treated as a chargeable gain.

[*TCGA 1992, ss 201–203; ICTA 1988, s 122(1)(5)–(7); FA 1995, Sch 29 Pt VIII(22); ITTOIA 2005, ss 157, 319, 340–343, Sch 1 para 106*].

Example

L Ltd, which prepares accounts to 31 December, is the holder of a lease of land acquired in 1993 for £66,000, when the lease had an unexpired term of 65 years. In January 2001,

L Ltd grants a 10-year licence to a mining company to search for and exploit minerals beneath the land. The licence is granted for £60,000 plus a mineral royalty calculated on the basis of the value of any minerals won by the licensee. The market value of the retained land (exclusive of the mineral rights) is then £10,000. L Ltd receives mineral royalties as follows

		£
Year ended	31 December 2001	12,000
	31 December 2002	19,000
	31 December 2003	29,000
	31 December 2004	38,000
	31 December 2005	17,000
	31 December 2006	10,000

On 2 January 2007, L Ltd relinquishes its rights under the lease and receives no consideration from the lessor.

(i) Chargeable gains 2001

		£
(*a*)	Disposal proceeds	60,000
	Allowable cost $\dfrac{60{,}000}{60{,}000+10{,}000} \times £66{,}000$	56,571
	Chargeable gain subject to indexation	£3,429
(*b*)	½ × £12,000	£6,000

(ii) Chargeable gains 2002 to 2006

	£
2002 ½ × £19,000	9,500
2003 ½ × £29,000	14,500
2004 ½ × £38,000	19,000
2005 ½ × £17,000	8,500
2006 ½ × £10,000	5,000

(iii) Loss 2007

Proceeds of disposal of lease	Nil
Allowable cost £66,000 – £56,571	9,429
Allowable loss	£9,429

(iv) The loss may be set off against the chargeable gains arising on the mineral royalties as follows

	£
2006 (whole)	5,000
2005 (part)	4,429
	£9,429

44 Offshore Settlements

Cross-references. See 45.3 OVERSEAS MATTERS for non-UK residents trading in the UK through branch or agency or permanent establishment; 52 RESIDENCE AND DOMICILE for the determination of a person's residence, ordinary residence and domicile status; and 57 SETTLEMENTS for settlements generally and provisions relating to UK resident settlements.

Simon's Direct Tax Service. See Division C4.4.

44.1 INTRODUCTION

The provisions set out in this chapter apply generally in relation to settlements whose trustees are, or become, not resident and not ordinarily resident in the United Kingdom or where the trustees are regarded for the purposes of DOUBLE TAX RELIEF (19) arrangements as resident outside the UK. Such trustees are not, in general, chargeable to capital gains tax (see 45.1 and 45.3 OVERSEAS MATTERS) but trustees becoming non-resident are subject to an 'exit charge', and charges arise in certain circumstances on settlors and beneficiaries of such offshore settlements.

Residence of trustees. The trustees of a settlement are treated as if they were a single person (distinct from the persons who may from time to time be trustees). For 2005/06 and earlier years, the legislation treated the trustees as a single and continuing body of persons. [*TCGA 1992, s 69(1); FA 2006, Sch 12 para 2*].

For 2007/08 onwards (irrespective of when the settlement was created), the deemed single person is treated as resident and ordinarily resident in the UK at any time when either all the trustees are resident in the UK or:

(*a*) at least one trustee is resident in the UK and at least one is not so resident; and

(*b*) a settlor of the settlement was resident, ordinarily resident or domiciled in the UK at a time when he made the settlement (or was treated as making the settlement — see below) or, where the settlement arose on his death, immediately before his death.

For the circumstances in which a settlor makes a settlement or is treated as making a settlement, see 57.3 SETTLEMENTS. In the case of a transfer of property between two settlements to which *TCGA 1992, s 68B* (identification of settlor on transfer of property between settlements — see 57.3 SETTLEMENTS) applies, (*b*) above is satisfied in relation to the transferee settlement if a settlor of the transferred property satisfied the condition in relation to the transferor settlement before the transfer.

For these purposes, a trustee who is not resident in the UK is treated as if he were so resident at any time when he acts as trustee in the course of a business he carries on in the UK through a branch, agency or permanent establishment.

A deemed person not treated as resident and ordinarily resident in the UK under the above provisions is treated as neither resident nor ordinarily resident in the UK.

[*TCGA 1992, s 69(2)–(2E); FA 2006, Sch 12 para 2*].

For 2006/07 and earlier years, the deemed person or body is treated as resident and ordinarily resident in the UK unless the administration of the settlement is ordinarily carried on outside the UK and the trustees or a majority of them for the time being are not resident or not ordinarily resident in the UK. A person carrying on the business of managing settlements (and acting as trustee in the course of that business) is treated as not resident in relation to a settlement if the entire settled property consists of, or is derived from, property provided by a person not at the time (or, in the case of a will trust, at death) domiciled, resident or ordinarily resident in the UK. If, in such a case, the trustees or a majority of them are, or are treated as, not resident in the UK, the administration of the settlement is treated as ordinarily carried on outside the UK. [*TCGA 1992, s 69(1)(2) as originally enacted*].

See also 52.3 and 52.4 RESIDENCE AND DOMICILE for the meaning of resident and ordinarily resident.

All non-UK resident settlements, and settlements not administered or created under UK law, are dealt with by HMRC at Centre for Non-Residents, Non-Resident Trusts, St John's House, Merton Road, Bootle, Merseyside L69 9BB. Tel. 0151–472 6001.

The remainder of this chapter is set out under the following headings.

44.2 CHARGE ON TRUSTEES CEASING TO BE RESIDENT IN THE UK

Where, at any time ('*the relevant time*') after 18 March 1991, trustees of a settlement become neither resident nor ordinarily resident in the UK (see 44.1 above), they are deemed for capital gains tax purposes to have disposed of 'the defined assets' immediately before the relevant time, and immediately to have reacquired them, at their market value at that time.

'*The defined assets*' are all assets constituting settled property of the settlement immediately before the relevant time. However, if immediately after the relevant time the trustees carry on a trade in the UK through a branch or agency, or, in the case of corporate trustees for accounting periods beginning after 31 December 2002, through a permanent establishment, and any assets are situated in the UK and either used in or for the purposes of the trade or used or held for the purposes of the branch or agency or permanent establishment, those assets are not defined assets (see also 45.3 OVERSEAS MATTERS). In addition, assets are not defined assets if they are of a description specified in any DOUBLE TAX RELIEF (19.2) arrangements, and were the trustees to dispose of them immediately before the relevant time, the trustees would fall to be regarded for the purposes of those arrangements as not liable in the UK to tax on gains accruing to them on the disposal (but see below under Dual resident trustees).

TCGA 1992, s 152 (55 ROLLOVER RELIEF) is not to apply where the trustees have disposed of, or their interest in, 'the old assets' before the relevant time, and acquire 'the new assets', or their interest in them, after that time. However, this denial of relief does not apply to new assets if, at the time they are acquired, the trustees carry on a trade in the UK through a branch or agency or permanent establishment, and any new assets are situated in the UK and either used in or for the purposes of the trade or used or held for the purposes of the branch or agency or permanent establishment. '*The old assets*' and '*the new assets*' have the same meanings as in *TCGA 1992, s 152*.

[*TCGA 1992, s 80; FA 2003, s 153*(*2*)(*b*)(*4*)].

For HMRC's practice in this area, see HMRC Statement of Practice 5/92, paras 2 and 3. Revenue Tax Bulletin April 2001 p 840 illustrated a perceived method of circumventing the above rules, using the 30-day matching rule at 59.2 SHARES AND SECURITIES — IDENTIFICATION RULES; whilst the Revenue concluded that this method does not work, others may be far less certain.

For 1996/97 onwards, the normal rules for assessment of trustees (see 5.8 ASSESSMENTS) are disapplied so that no assessment to CGT payable under *TCGA 1992, s 80* by the migrating trustees can be made on a person who ceased to be a trustee of the settlement before the relevant time and who shows that, when he did so cease, there was no proposal that the trustees might migrate. [*TCGA 1992, s 65*(*3*)(*4*)*; FA 1995, s 103*(*7*)*, s 114*].

Death of trustee: special rules. Special rules apply where *TCGA 1992, s 80* above applies as a result of the death of a trustee of the settlement, and within the period of six months beginning with the death, the trustees of the settlement become resident and ordinarily resident in the UK. In such circumstances, *TCGA 1992, s 80* is to apply as if the defined assets were restricted to such assets (if any) as would, apart from this special rule, be defined assets and which either:

- are disposed of by the trustees in the period which begins with the death and ends when the trustees become resident and ordinarily resident in the UK, or
- are of a description specified in any double tax relief arrangements; constitute settled property of the settlement immediately after the trustees become resident and ordinarily resident in the UK; and, were the trustees to dispose of them at that time, the trustees would fall to be regarded for the purposes of the arrangements as not liable in the UK to tax on gains accruing to them on the disposal.

Further special rules apply where at any time the trustees of a settlement become resident and ordinarily resident in the UK as a result of the death of a trustee of the settlement, and *TCGA 1992, s 80* above applies as regards the trustees of the settlement in circumstances where the relevant time (within the meaning of that provision) falls within the period of six months beginning with the death. In such circumstances, *TCGA 1992, s 80* is to apply as if the defined assets were restricted to such assets (if any) as would, apart from this special rule, be defined assets and which the trustees acquired in the period beginning with the death and ending with the relevant time as a result of a disposal in respect of which relief is given under *TCGA 1992, s 165* (hold-over relief for gifts of business assets; see 33.1 HOLD-OVER RELIEFS) or in relation to which *TCGA 1992, s 260(3)* (hold-over relief for gifts on which inheritance tax is chargeable etc; see 33.7 HOLD-OVER RELIEFS) applies. [*TCGA 1992, s 81*].

Past trustees: liability for tax. Where *TCGA 1992, s 80* above applies as regards the trustees of a settlement ('*the migrating trustees*'), and any resulting capital gains tax which is payable by the migrating trustees is not paid within six months from the time when it became payable, HMRC may act as below.

HMRC may, at any time before the end of the period of three years beginning with the time when the amount of tax is finally determined, serve on any person who, at any time within the 'relevant period', was a trustee of the settlement (but not so as to include a person ceasing to be a trustee before the end of the relevant period who can show that at the time he ceased to be a trustee there was no proposal that the trustees might become neither resident nor ordinarily resident in the UK), a notice requiring the payment of outstanding tax and interest within 30 days from the service of the notice. The notified amount can be recovered from the person concerned as if it were tax due and payable; and he may recover from the migrating trustees any amount paid by him. No tax relief is given on any such payment in computing taxable profits etc.

The '*relevant period*' is the period of twelve months ending with the relevant time. (Where the relevant time for the purposes of *TCGA 1992, s 80* above was within the period of twelve months beginning with 19 March 1991, the relevant period was restricted to the period beginning with that date and ending with that time.) [*TCGA 1992, s 82*].

For HMRC's practice in this area, see HMRC Statement of Practice 5/92, paras 4–6.

Dual resident trustees. *Charge on becoming dual resident.* Where, at any time, the trustees of a settlement, while continuing to be resident and ordinarily resident in the UK, become trustees who fall to be regarded for the purposes of any DOUBLE TAX RELIEF (19.2) arrangements as resident overseas and as not liable in the UK to tax on gains accruing on disposals of assets ('*relevant assets*') which constitute settled property of the settlement and fall within descriptions specified in the arrangements, they are deemed for capital gains tax purposes to have disposed of the relevant assets immediately before that time, and immediately to have reacquired them, at their market value at that time. [*TCGA 1992, s 83*].

Disapplication of rollover relief provision. TCGA 1992, s 152 (55.1 ROLLOVER RELIEF) is not to apply where

- the new assets (as in 55.1 ROLLOVER RELIEF) are, or the interest in them is, acquired after 18 March 1991 by the trustees of a settlement;
- at the time of acquisition the trustees are resident and ordinarily resident in the UK and fall to be regarded for the purposes of any double tax relief arrangements as resident overseas;
- the assets are of a description specified in the arrangements; and
- were the trustees to dispose of the assets immediately after the acquisition, the trustees would fall to be regarded for the purposes of the arrangements as not liable in the UK to tax on gains accruing to them on the disposal.

[*TCGA 1992, s 84*].

44.3 TRUSTEES BOTH RESIDENT AND NON-RESIDENT IN TAX YEAR

The following applies where a chargeable gain accrues to trustees of a settlement on a disposal of an asset on or after 16 March 2005 in a tax year in which they are within the charge to capital gains tax but at a time when they are 'non-UK resident'.

Nothing in any DOUBLE TAX RELIEF (19) arrangements is to be read as preventing the trustees from being chargeable to capital gains tax (or as preventing a charge to tax arising, whether or not on the trustees) in respect of the gain.

For these purposes, trustees are within the charge to capital gains tax for a tax year if, during any part of the year they are resident and, for 2007/08 onwards, ordinarily resident in the UK and not 'treaty non-resident' or, for 2006/07 and earlier years, if during the year they are ordinarily resident in the UK and not treaty non-resident. Trustees are '*non-UK resident*' at a particular time if they are then neither resident nor ordinarily resident in the UK or:

- for 2007/08 onwards, they are then resident and ordinarily resident in the UK but are treaty non-resident; or
- for 2006/07 and earlier years, they are then resident or ordinarily resident in the UK but are treaty non-resident.

Trustees are '*treaty non-resident*' if they fall to be regarded as resident in a territory outside the UK for the purposes of DOUBLE TAX RELIEF (19) arrangements. For the meaning of 'resident' and 'ordinarily resident' see 52 RESIDENCE AND DOMICILE.

[*TCGA 1992, ss 83A, 288(7B); F(No 2)A 2005, s 33; FA 2006, s 74(3)(4)(6), Sch 12 paras 32, 33, 34(1)–(3)*].

44.4 DISPOSAL OF SETTLED INTEREST

The exemption in *TCGA 1992, s 76(1)* (see 57.14 SETTLEMENTS) by virtue of which no chargeable gain accrues in certain circumstances on the disposal of an interest created by or arising under a settlement does not apply to such disposals in either of the following circumstances.

(*a*) At the time of disposal, the trustees are neither resident nor ordinarily resident in the UK (see 44.1 above) and the disposal is not one which arises on a person becoming absolutely entitled to settled property as against the trustees and accordingly treated under *TCGA 1992, s 76(2)* (see 57.14 SETTLEMENTS) as made in consideration of his obtaining the settled property. [*TCGA 1992, s 85(1)*].

(*b*) Subject to the same exclusion as in (*a*) above, the disposal is made **after 5 March 1998** and there has ever been a time (whether before, on or after that date) when the trustees of the settlement were neither resident nor ordinarily resident in the UK or fell to be treated under a double tax agreement as resident in a territory outside the UK. Nor does the exemption apply if any property comprised in the settlement in question derives directly or indirectly from a settlement which is caught by this provision. [*TCGA 1992, s 76(1A)(1B)(3); FA 1998, s 128; FA 2006, Sch 12 para 30(1)(2)(4)*].

Calculation of gain on disposal of interest after trustees becoming non-resident. Subject to the exceptions below, for the purpose only of calculating any chargeable gain accruing to a person on the disposal of an interest created by or arising under a settlement, where

(i) *TCGA 1992, s 80* at 44.2 above (charge on trustees becoming non-resident) applies as regards the trustees of the settlement;

(ii) the disposal is made after the 'relevant time' (see 44.2 above) and the circumstances are such that the exemption for disposal of an interest in a settlement is prevented from applying by (*a*) above; and

(iii) the interest was created for his benefit, or he otherwise acquired it, before the relevant time, he is treated as if he had disposed of the interest immediately before the relevant time, and immediately reacquired it, at its market value at that time.

This treatment does not apply where

- *TCGA 1992, s 83* at 44.2 above (charge on trustees ceasing to be liable to UK tax under double tax relief arrangements) applied as regards the trustees in circumstances where 'the time concerned' (see 44.2 above) fell before the time when the interest was created for the benefit of the person disposing of it or when he otherwise acquired it; or
- the relevant time fell after 20 March 2000 and the settlement had 'relevant offshore gains' at that time.

A settlement has '*relevant offshore gains*' at any time if, were the tax year to end at that time, there would be an amount of trust gains which by virtue of *TCGA 1992, s 89(2)* (see 44.14 below) or *TCGA 1992, Sch 4C para 8(3)* (see 44.19 below) would be available to be treated as chargeable gains accruing to any beneficiaries of the settlement receiving capital payments in the following tax year.

The above treatment is also disapplied where conditions (i)–(iii) above apply but, in addition, *TCGA 1992, s 83* at 44.2 above applied as regards the trustees in circumstances where 'the time concerned' (see 44.2 above) fell in the 'relevant period' (see below). In these circumstances, for the purposes only of calculating any chargeable gain accruing on the disposal of the interest, the person disposing of it is instead treated as if he had disposed of it immediately before the time concerned (where there is only one such time) or the earliest time concerned (where there is more than one because *TCGA 1992, s 83* applied more than once), and had immediately reacquired it, at its market value at that time. This treatment does not apply where the time concerned or, as the case may be, the earliest time concerned, fell after 20 March 2000 and the settlement had relevant offshore gains (as defined above) at that time.

For this purpose, the '*relevant period*' is the period which begins when the interest was created for the benefit of the person disposing of it or when he otherwise acquired it, and ends with the relevant time (within the meaning of *TCGA 1992, s 80* at 44.2 above).

[*TCGA 1992, s 85(2)–(11); FA 2000, s 95*].

44.5 CHARGE ON SETTLOR WITH INTEREST IN SETTLEMENT

Where all the conditions listed below are fulfilled, chargeable gains of an amount equal to that referred to in (*e*) below are treated as accruing in a particular year of assessment to 'the settlor' (see 44.9 below) of a settlement such that they are treated as forming the highest part of the amount on which he is chargeable to capital gains tax for the year. See also 44.13 below.

The conditions are

(*a*) the settlement is a 'qualifying settlement' (see 44.10 below) in a particular year of assessment;

(*b*) *either*

(i) the trustees are neither resident nor ordinarily resident in the UK during any part of the year (see 44.1 above); or

(ii) the trustees are resident and ordinarily resident during any part of the year (for 2006/07 and earlier years, resident in the UK during any part of the year or ordinarily resident in the UK during the year), but at any time of such residence and/or ordinary residence they fall to be regarded for the purposes of any DOUBLE TAX RELIEF (19.2) arrangements as resident overseas;

(*c*) the person who is the settlor in relation to the settlement is domiciled in the UK at some time in the year and is either resident in the UK during any part of the year or ordinarily resident in the UK during the year (and see 45.4 OVERSEAS MATTERS re 'temporary' non-residence);

(*d*) at any time during the year the settlor has an 'interest' (see 44.6 below) in the settlement;

(*e*) by virtue of disposals of any of the settled property 'originating' from the settlor (see 44.9 below), there is an amount on which the trustees would be chargeable to tax for the year under *TCGA 1992, s 2(2)* (i.e. an amount of chargeable gains less current and brought forward allowable losses — see 40.1 LOSSES) if the assumption as to residence below were made; and

(*f*) the provisions in 44.8 below do not preclude a charge.

Where the residence condition specified in (*b*)(i) above applies, the assumption as to residence in (*e*) above is that the trustees are resident and ordinarily resident (for 2006/07 and earlier years, resident or ordinarily resident) in the UK throughout the year; and where the residence condition specified in (*b*)(ii) above applies, the assumption as to residence in (*e*) above is that the double tax relief arrangements do not apply.

In arriving at the amount to be charged on the settlor for a particular year of assessment, the effects of *TCGA 1992, s 3* (annual exempt amount — see 57.10 and 57.11 SETTLEMENTS) and *TCGA 1992, ss 77–79* (settlor having interest in UK resident settlement chargeable instead of trustees in certain circumstances — see 57.5 SETTLEMENTS) are ignored. In addition, any deductions provided for by *TCGA 1992, s 2(2)* (current and brought forward allowable losses) are to be made in respect of disposals of any of the settled property originating from the settlor, and *TCGA 1992, s 16(3)* (losses of non-resident not to be allowable — see 45.3 OVERSEAS MATTERS) is to be assumed not to prevent losses accruing to trustees in one year of assessment from being allowed as a deduction from chargeable gains in a later year (so far as not previously set against gains).

Where trustees are participators in a company in respect of property which originates from the settlor, and under *TCGA 1992, s 13* (gains of non-resident close company assessable on shareholder — see 45.6 OVERSEAS MATTERS) gains or losses would be treated as accruing to the trustees in a particular year of assessment by virtue of so much of their interest as participators as arises from that property if the assumption as to residence in (*e*) above were made, the gains or losses are taken into account in arriving at the amount charged on the settlor as regards that year as if they had accrued by virtue of disposals of settled property originating from the settlor.

Where the trustees fall within the residence condition specified in (*b*)(i) above, further rules apply to arrive at the amount to be charged on the settlor as regards a particular year of assessment ('*the year concerned*'). If the conditions for the charge to apply are not fulfilled as regards the settlement in any year of assessment falling before the year concerned, no deductions are made for losses accruing before the year concerned. If those conditions are fulfilled as regards the settlement in any year or years of assessment falling before the year concerned, no deductions are made for losses accruing before that year (or the first of the years) so falling. However, these two prohibitions on deductions being made for losses are not to prevent deductions being made in respect of losses accruing in a year of assessment in which the conditions in (*a*) to (*d*) and (*f*) above are fulfilled as regards the settlement. As regards a particular year of assessment and in relation to a settlement created before 19 March 1991, no account is taken of disposals made before 19 March 1991 (whether for the purpose of arriving at gains or losses).

Where, as regards a particular year of assessment, there would otherwise be an amount to be charged on the settlor and the trustees fall within the residence condition specified in (*b*)(ii) above, the following assumptions and adjustments to the amount are made. It is to be assumed that references in the foregoing to settled property originating from the settlor were to such of it as constitutes 'protected assets' and that references in the foregoing to shares originating from the settlor were to such of them as constitute protected assets. The amount (if any) to be charged on the settlor is found on those assumptions, and if there is no amount found there is deemed to be no amount to be charged on the settlor, and if an amount is found on these assumptions it is compared with the amount which would otherwise be charged on the settlor, and the smaller of the two is taken to be the amount to be charged on the settlor.

Assets are '*protected assets*' if they are of a description specified in the double tax relief arrangements mentioned in connection with the residence condition specified in (*b*)(ii) above, and were the trustees to dispose of them at any 'relevant time', the trustees would fall to be regarded for the purposes of the arrangements as not liable in the UK to tax on gains accruing to them on the disposal. For this purpose, the alternative assumptions as to residence in (*e*) above are ignored, the '*relevant time*' is any time, in the year of assessment concerned, when the trustees fall to be regarded for the purposes of the arrangements as resident overseas, and if different assets are identified by reference to different relevant times, all of them are protected assets.

[*TCGA 1992, s 86(1)–(4)(5), Sch 5 para 1; FA 1996, s 174(10)(11); FA 2006, Sch 12 paras 30(1)(2)(4), 34(1)–(3), 35(1)(2), 41*].

44.6 **Test whether settlor has an interest.** A settlor has an interest in a settlement if

(*a*) any property originating from the settlor ('*relevant property*') which is or may at any time be comprised in the settlement is, or will or may become, applicable for the benefit of or payable to a 'defined person' in any circumstances whatever;

(*b*) any income originating from the settlor ('*relevant income*') which arises or may arise under the settlement is, or will or may become, applicable for the benefit of or payable to a defined person in any circumstances whatever; or

(*c*) any defined person enjoys a benefit directly or indirectly from any relevant property which is comprised in the settlement or any relevant income arising under the settlement.

Each of the following is a '*defined person*':

- the settlor;
- the settlor's spouse;
- the settlor's civil partner;
- any child (which term includes stepchild) of the settlor or of the settlor's spouse or civil partner;
- the spouse or civil partner of any such child;
- any grandchild of the settlor or of the settlor's spouse or civil partner (see 44.7 below as regards the addition of grandchildren to the list of defined persons); ('*grandchild*' includes a child of a stepchild or a stepchild of a child or stepchild);
- the spouse or civil partner of any such grandchild (see 44.7 below as regards the addition of grandchildren and their spouses or civil partners to the list of defined persons);
- a company controlled by a person or persons mentioned in the foregoing (see 44.7 below as regards the addition of grandchildren and their spouses or civil partners to the fore-mentioned categories); ('*control*' is construed as in *ICTA 1988, s 416* but for these purposes no rights or powers of (or attributed to) an associate or associates of a person are attributed to him under *ICTA 1988, s 416(6)* if he is not a participator (within *ICTA 1988, s 417(1)*, but subject to ESC D40 (see 44.9 below)) in the company);

- a company associated with any such company; ('*associated*' is construed as in *ICTA 1988, s 416* but for these purposes where it falls to be decided whether a company is controlled by a person or persons, a similar relaxation to that for 'control' applies as above).

A settlor does not have an interest in a settlement at any time when none of the property or income concerned can become applicable or payable as mentioned above except in the event of:

- the bankruptcy of some person who is or may become beneficially entitled to that property or income;
- any assignment of or charge on the property or income being made or given by some such person;
- in the case of a marriage settlement or civil partnership settlement, the death of both parties to the marriage or civil partnership and of all or any of the children of one or both of the parties to the marriage or civil partnership (before 5 December, all or any of the children of the marriage); or
- the death under the age of 25 or some lower age of some person who would be beneficially entitled to the property or income on attaining that age.

He also does not have an interest in a settlement under (*a*) above at any time when some person is alive and under the age of 25 if during that person's life none of the property or income concerned can become applicable or payable as mentioned in (*a*) above except in the event of that person becoming bankrupt or assigning or charging his interest in the property or income concerned.

[*TCGA 1992, Sch 5 para 2; FA 1998, s 131, Sch 22 para 2; SI 2005 No 3229, Reg 126*(*2*)].

44.7 **Addition of grandchildren to list of defined persons.** Grandchildren and their spouses or civil partners (and companies which they control or which are associated with such companies) are included in the list of defined persons in 44.6 above **in relation to disposals made on or after 17 March 1998**. Their inclusion applies as regards all disposals by settlements created on or after that date. As regards **settlements created before that date**, post-16 March 1998 disposals (whether giving rise to gains or losses) to which the 'charge on settlor' provisions would not apply if the addition of the said categories to the above-mentioned list were disregarded are left out of account (i.e. are regarded as not falling within 44.5(*e*) above) unless they are made in a tax year in which one of the following events occurs or in a subsequent tax year. (Where the tax year in question is 1997/98, only post-16 March 1998 events are taken into account.)

(*a*) Property or income is provided directly or indirectly for the purposes of the settlement (i.e. is added to the settlement) otherwise than under an arm's length transaction and otherwise than in pursuance of a liability incurred by any person before 17 March 1998. Property or income provided towards (and not beyond) an excess for a tax year of trust expenses (relating to administration and taxation) over trust income is ignored.

(*b*) The trustees become neither resident nor ordinarily resident in the UK or begin to fall to be regarded under a double tax agreement as resident in a territory outside the UK.

(*c*) The terms of the settlement are varied so as to enable for the first time any one or more of the persons mentioned below to benefit from the settlement.

(*d*) Any one or more of the persons mentioned below does enjoy a benefit for the first time but would not have been capable of doing so by reference to the terms of the settlement as they stood immediately before 17 March 1998.

The persons mentioned in (*c*) and (*d*) above are: any grandchild (as in 44.6 above) of the settlor or of the settlor's spouse or civil partner, the spouse or civil partner of any such grandchild, a company controlled by any such grandchildren and/or their spouses or civil partners (with or without other defined persons — see 44.6 above) and a company associated with any such company. (For these purposes, '*control*' and '*associated*' are to be construed as in 44.6 above.)

[*TCGA 1992, Sch 5 para 2A; FA 1998, Sch 22 para 2; SI 2005 No 3229, Reg 126*(*3*)].

44.8 **Exceptions to charge.** There is no charge on the settlor if he dies in the year.

There is also no charge on the settlor where **both** (*a*) and (*b*) below apply.

(*a*) The settlor has no interest in the settlement at any time in the year except for one (or, where they are satisfied by reference to the same person, for two or all) of the following reasons:

- property is, or will or may become, applicable for the benefit of or payable to a person, being the settlor's spouse or civil partner, any child (which term includes stepchild) or grandchild (defined as in 44.6 above, and see below for the addition of grandchildren to this list) of the settlor or of the settlor's spouse or civil partner, or the spouse or civil partner of any such child or grandchild;
- income is, or will or may become applicable for the benefit of or payable to such a person; or
- such a person enjoys a benefit from property or income.

(*b*) Either

- the person referred to in (*a*) above dies in the year; or
- where the person referred to in (*a*) above is the settlor's spouse or civil partner or the spouse or civil partner of any child or grandchild of the settlor or of the settlor's spouse or civil partner, that person ceases to be married to, or to be a civil partner of, the settlor, the child or the grandchild concerned (as the case may be) during the year.

Again no charge arises on the settlor in the following circumstances:

(i) the settlor has no interest in the settlement at any time in the year except for the reason that there are two or more persons, each of whom is one of the following: the settlor's spouse or civil partner, any child (which term includes stepchild) or grandchild (defined as in 44.6 above, and see below for the addition of grandchildren to this list) of the settlor or of the settlor's spouse or civil partner, or the spouse or civil partner of any such child or grandchild and stands to gain for one or more of the following reasons:

- property is, or will or may become, applicable for his benefit or payable to him;
- the income is, or will or may become, applicable for his benefit or payable to him; or
- he enjoys a benefit from property or income, *and*

(ii) each of the persons referred to in (i) dies in the year.

References above to grandchildren apply only in relation to disposals made **on or after 17 March 1998** to which the 'charge on settlor' provisions would otherwise apply by reference to grandchildren (see 44.6 and 44.7 above).

[*TCGA 1992, Sch 5 paras 3–5; FA 1998, Sch 22 para 3; SI 2005 No 3229, Reg 126*(*4*)].

44.9 **Meaning of 'settlor'.** For the purposes of these provisions, a person is a '*settlor*' in relation to a settlement if the settled property consists of or includes property originating from him. [*TCGA 1992, Sch 5 para 7*].

Meaning of 'originating'. References to property originating from a person are taken as references to property provided by that person, property representing property provided by that person, and so much of any property provided by that person and other property as, on a just apportionment, can be taken to represent property provided by that person. References to income originating from a person are taken as references to income from property originating from that person and income provided by that person.

Where a person who is a settlor in relation to a settlement makes reciprocal arrangements with another person for the provision of property or income, then the property or income provided by the other person under the arrangements is treated as provided by the settlor, but property or income provided by the settlor under the arrangements is treated as provided by the other person (and not by the settlor).

Where property is provided by a '*qualifying company*' (i.e. a company which is a close company within *ICTA 1988, ss 414, 415* or which would be a close company if it were resident in the UK) controlled (construed as in *ICTA 1988, s 416* but with the same relaxation as in 44.6 above) by one person alone at the time it is provided, that person is taken to provide it. Where property is provided by a qualifying company controlled by two or more persons (taking each one separately) at the time it is provided, those persons are taken to provide the property in equal shares. Where property is provided by a qualifying company controlled by two or more persons (taking them together) at the time it is provided, the persons who are participators (construed as in *ICTA 1988, s 417(1)*) in the company at the time it is provided are taken to provide it in just proportions (save that where a person would otherwise be treated under this last provision as providing less than 5% of any property, he is not taken as providing any property). By concession, a beneficiary in the settlement is not to be regarded as a participator in the company solely by virtue of his status as beneficiary (HMRC Extra-Statutory Concession D40).

References to property representing other property include references to property representing accumulated income from that other property. A person is treated as providing property or income if he provides it directly or indirectly. For gains accruing before 28 November 1995, the above provisions for determining whether property of any kind originates from a person apply equally to determine whether shares held by the trustees of a company whose gains and losses are taken into account in arriving at the amount to be charged on the settlor (see 44.5 above) originate from the settlor.

[*TCGA 1992, Sch 5 para 8; FA 1996, Sch 41 Pt V(30)*].

44.10 **Qualifying settlements, and commencement.** A settlement **created on or after 19 March 1991** is a '*qualifying settlement*' for the purposes of 44.5(*a*) above in the year of assessment in which it is created and subsequent years of assessment.

A settlement **created before 19 March 1991** which was not previously a qualifying settlement (see also below) becomes a qualifying settlement with effect **in and after the tax year 1999/2000**. (Subject to the transitional provisions at 44.11 below, disposals made before 6 April 1999, whether giving rise to gains or losses, are left out of account in arriving at any figure within 44.5(*e*) above.) The above does **not** apply if the settlement is a 'protected settlement' immediately after the beginning of 6 April 1999 in which case it becomes a qualifying settlement with effect in and after any tax year in which *either* the settlement ceases to be a protected settlement *or* any of the four conditions set out below becomes fulfilled. See 44.11 below for provisions bringing into charge certain **gains realised in the transitional period** between the announcement of these rules on 17 March 1998 and their first coming into effect in 1999/2000.

A settlement is a '*protected settlement*' at any time if at that time the 'beneficiaries' are confined to persons falling within some or all of the following categories:

- children of a settlor or of a spouse or civil partner of a settlor who are under 18 either at that time or at the end of the immediately preceding tax year;
- unborn children of a settlor, of a spouse or civil partner of a settlor, or of a future spouse or civil partner of a settlor;
- future spouses or civil partners of any children or future children of a settlor, a spouse or civil partner of a settlor or any future spouse or civil partner of a settlor;
- a future spouse or civil partner of a settlor;
- persons who are not at that time defined persons (see 44.6 above) in relation to the settlement and by reference to any current settlor.

  Despite the addition of grandchildren to the list of defined persons (see 44.7 above), HMRC do *not* regard the existence as beneficiaries of the settlor's (or his spouse's) grandchildren (of whatever age) as denying protected settlement status (Revenue Tax Bulletin December 1998 p 620).

The term 'children' includes stepchildren. For these purposes, a person is a '*beneficiary*' of a settlement if

- there are any circumstances whatever in which

  (*a*) 'relevant property' which is, or may become, comprised in the settlement, or

  (*b*) 'relevant income' which arises, or may arise, under the settlement,

  is, or will or may become, applicable for his benefit or payable to him; or
- he enjoys a benefit directly or indirectly from any 'relevant property' comprised in, or 'relevant income' arising under, the settlement.

  '*Relevant property*' and '*relevant income*' mean, respectively, property and income originating (see 44.9 above) from a settlor.

A settlement created **before 19 March 1991** is also a qualifying settlement **in any year of assessment before 1999/2000** in which any of the four conditions set out below becomes fulfilled and in subsequent years of assessment.

The **four conditions** twice referred to above are as follows.

- The first condition is that after 18 March 1991 property or income is provided directly or indirectly for the purposes of the settlement otherwise than under a transaction entered into at arm's length and otherwise than in pursuance of a liability incurred by any person before 19 March 1991. However, if the settlement's expenses relating to administration and taxation for a year of assessment exceed its income for the year, property or income provided towards meeting those expenses is ignored for the purposes of this condition if the value of the property or income so provided does not exceed the difference between the amount of those expenses and the amount of the settlement's income for the year. By concession, a repayable on demand loan which was made to a relevant trust on non-commercial terms before 19 March 1991 was not caught by this condition provided that, before 31 July 1992, it was either repaid in full with any outstanding interest or made subject to fully commercial terms (HMRC Extra-Statutory Concession D41 — this concession contained further detailed notes on the treatment of amounts paid where the loan was put on a commercial basis. See also Revenue Tax Bulletin August 1993 p 83).
- The second condition is that the trustees become after 18 March 1991 neither resident nor ordinarily resident in the UK, or the trustees, while continuing to be resident and ordinarily resident in the UK, become after 18 March 1991 trustees who fall to be regarded for the purposes of any double tax relief arrangements as resident overseas.

- The third condition is that after 18 March 1991 the terms of the settlement are varied so that a defined person (see 44.6 above) becomes for the first time a person who will or might benefit from the settlement.
- The fourth condition is that after 18 March 1991 a defined person enjoys a benefit from the settlement for the first time and the person concerned is not one who (looking only at the terms of the settlement immediately before 19 March 1991) would be capable of enjoying a benefit from the settlement on or after that date.

For the purposes of the third and fourth conditions above, grandchildren (as in 44.6 above) and their spouses (and companies which they control or which are associated with such companies) are not defined persons in relation to events before 17 March 1998 (see also 44.7 above).

[*TCGA 1992, Sch 5 para 9; FA 1998, s 132, Sch 22 para 4, Sch 27 Pt III(30); SI 2005 No 3229, Reg 126(5)*].

For HMRC's practice in this area, see HMRC Statement of Practice 5/92, paras 11–37, Revenue Tax Bulletin August 1993 p 82 and April 1995 pp 204, 205, and ICAEW guidance note TAX 20/92, 14 December 1992, paras 7–23.

44.11 **Pre-19 March 1991 settlements in the transitional period 17 March 1998 to 5 April 1999.** The decision to bring remaining non-qualifying pre-19 March 1991 settlements (except for protected settlements) within the 'charge on settlor' provisions (see 44.10 above) was announced on 17 March 1998 but its coming into effect was delayed until 1999/2000 in order to allow time for those affected to reorganise their affairs if they so wished. However, the rules in (*a*)–(*c*) below were introduced to prevent certain gains in the **transitional period (17 March 1998 to 5 April 1999 inclusive)** from escaping tax.

(*a*) *Settlements that become qualified in 1999/2000.* Where a pre-19 March 1991 settlement was not a qualifying settlement (see 44.10 above) in 1998/99 but becomes one in 1999/2000 (without having been a 'protected settlement' immediately after the beginning of 6 April 1999), then, in the case of any settlor of the settlement, gains and losses actually accruing to the trustees in the transitional period are deemed to have accrued on 6 April 1999, with the result that the 'charge on settlor' provisions apply in relation to such gains etc. in the year 1999/2000. Any gains/losses realised in a tax year in which the residence condition in 44.5(*b*) above is not fulfilled (broadly, a year in which the trustees are UK-resident) are left out of account. If the trustees do not fulfil the residence condition in 1999/2000, they are treated (only for the purpose of applying this transitional provision) as having done so. For these purposes, a '*protected settlement*' is defined as in 44.10 above but also includes a settlement which would be within that definition if the settlor under consideration were the only settlor of the settlement.

HMRC have altered their interpretation of the above provisions. Their revised view is that, in computing the amount chargeable on the settlor for 1999/2000, a net loss from disposals in the transitional period is available for offset against gains on actual disposals in 1999/2000 (with any excess loss being available for carry-forward as normal) and a net gain from disposals in the transitional period can be covered by losses on actual disposals in 1999/2000. Any 1999/2000 liability settled on the basis of their earlier, unduly restrictive, interpretation can be revised under the normal procedure for amending self-assessment tax returns (see 54.6 RETURNS). (Revenue Tax Bulletin October 2001 pp 888–890).

(*b*) *Transfers to another settlement.* The treatment described below applies where

- a gain or loss accrues on the disposal of an asset in the transitional period by the trustees of a pre-19 March 1991 settlement (the '*transferor settlement*');
- the disposal is made in a tax year in which the trustees fulfil the residence condition in 44.5(*b*) above (broadly a year in which they are non-UK resident) but the settlement is not a qualifying settlement;

- a person who is a settlor in relation to the transferor settlement (the '*chargeable settlor*') is UK-domiciled at some time in both 1999/2000 and the tax year of disposal, is either UK-resident during any part of each of those years or ordinarily resident during each of those years *and* is alive at the end of the tax year 1999/2000;
- the asset disposed of is property originating (see 44.9 above) from the chargeable settlor;
- there is property comprised in another settlement (the '*transferee settlement*') at some time after the said disposal and *before 6 April 1999* which is or includes (whether or not in consequence of the disposal) the asset disposed of or any 'relevant property';
- the transferor settlement has a 'relevant connection' with the transferee settlement;
- the said gain/loss is not one treated under (*a*) above as accruing on 6 April 1999 to the trustees of the transferor settlement.

The 'charge on settlor' provisions are applied for the tax year 1999/2000 in relation to the *transferee* settlement as if the above-mentioned gain/loss had accrued on 6 April 1999 to the trustees of that settlement on a disposal by them of property originating from the chargeable settlor. Where those provisions would not otherwise have applied in relation to that settlement in the case of the chargeable settlor, they are treated as if they did apply, but only for the purpose of so taking into account the said gain/loss. Where the same gain/loss would be treated as accruing to trustees of more than one settlement, it is to be apportioned between them in a just and reasonable manner. These provisions are disapplied if, for the tax year of disposal, the exceptions in 44.8 above would have prevented the 'charge on settlor' provisions from applying (on the assumption that they would otherwise have applied) in the case of the chargeable settlor in relation to the transferor settlement or from so applying in relation to the transferee settlement.

'*Relevant property*', in relation to a disposal by the trustees of the transferor settlement, means any property (other than the asset disposed of) which is (or represents) property or income originating from the chargeable settlor, has been comprised in (or has arisen to) the transferor settlement at any time after the disposal *and* is property or income of the trustees of the transferee settlement acquired or otherwise deriving (directly or indirectly) from the trustees of the transferor settlement.

A transferor settlement has, in relation to a disposal by its trustees, a '*relevant connection*' with a transferee settlement if

- immediately before the disposal, the 'beneficiaries' (as very broadly defined by *FA 1998, Sch 23 para 6*(*5*)) of the transferor settlement are, or include, defined persons (as in 44.6 above and by reference to the chargeable settlor) in relation to that settlement at that time;
- the transferor settlement is not a 'protected settlement' at that time in relation to the chargeable settlor; ('*protected settlement*' is defined as in 44.10 above but on the assumption that the chargeable settlor is the only settlor and with the omission of the reference to children under 18 at the end of the immediately preceding tax year);
- at the beginning of 6 April 1999 the beneficiaries of the transferee settlement are, or include, persons aged 18 or over who have been defined persons in relation to the transferor settlement; and
- the property comprised in the transferee settlement in respect of which some or all of the persons mentioned immediately above are beneficiaries at the beginning of 6 April 1999 is, or includes, anything which, in relation to either the transferee settlement or the transferor settlement, is property or income originating from the chargeable settlor.

(*c*) *Transfers to a foreign institution.* Provisions broadly similar to those in (*b*) above apply, with appropriate modifications, where the effective transfer of property by the pre-

19 March 1991 settlement is not to another settlement but to a '*foreign institution*', meaning a company or other institution resident outside the UK, with which the transferor settlement has a 'relevant connection'. In this case, the gain/loss is treated as accruing on 6 April 1999 to the trustees of the *transferor* settlement, and for this purpose the transferor settlement is deemed to exist in 1999/2000 even if it does not actually do so. The gain/loss is not brought into account under this provision if it falls to be brought into account under (*a*) or (*b*) above. The transferor settlement has, in relation to a disposal by its trustees, a '*relevant connection*' with the transferee institution if

- immediately before the disposal, the beneficiaries of the transferor settlement are, or include, defined persons (as in 44.6 above and by reference to the chargeable settlor) in relation to that settlement at that time;
- the transferor settlement is not a 'protected settlement' (defined as in (*b*) above) at that time in relation to the chargeable settlor; and
- the transferee institution is one
  - (i) in which a 'relevant defined person' is a participator (within *ICTA 1988, s 417*(*1*)) at the beginning of 6 April 1999; or
  - (ii) which is under the control of a company in which (or two or more companies in any of which) a relevant defined person is a participator at that time; or
  - (iii) whose 'relevant property' or 'relevant income' includes property or income in which a relevant defined person has an interest (as very broadly defined by *FA 1998, Sch 23 para 3*(*10*)) at that time.

A person is a '*relevant defined person*' at any time if he is 18 or over and has been, by reference to the chargeable settlor, a defined person in relation to the transferor settlement. '*Relevant property*' and '*relevant income*', in relation to a foreign institution, mean, respectively, property or income of that institution which, if the institution were a settlement, would be treated for the purposes of the 'charge on settlor' provisions as originating from the chargeable settlor.

Prevention of double charge. There are provisions (*FA 1998, Sch 23 paras 4, 5*) to ensure that gains realised in the transitional period, and falling to be brought into account under (*a*), (*b*) or (*c*) above, are not charged twice, i.e. on the settlor and also on beneficiaries under the provisions of *TCGA 1992, s 87* or *s 89*(*2*) (the 'charge on beneficiaries' provisions — see 44.14 below). The provisions are applied separately as regards each settlor of the settlement. Broadly, any excess of capital payments to beneficiaries over trust gains unattributed at 17 March 1998 is regarded as referable to trust gains on disposals in the transitional period and is deducted from the amount that would otherwise fall to be treated as gains of the settlor for 1999/2000 under (*a*)–(*c*) above. Only so much of any capital payment or trust gains as is properly referable to property originating from the settlor in question is to be taken into account for this purpose, any necessary apportionments being made on a just and reasonable basis. These provisions interact with those of *TCGA 1992, s 87*(*3*) (see 44.14 below) under which trust gains potentially chargeable on beneficiaries are reduced by amounts chargeable on settlors of the settlement.
[*FA 1998, s 132*(*6*)*, Sch 23*].

44.12 **Right of recovery.** Where a charge is made on a settlor, any tax he pays as a result may be recovered by him from any person who is a trustee of the settlement. For this purpose, the settlor may require certificated proof from HMRC of the amount of the gains concerned and the amount of tax paid. [*TCGA 1992, Sch 5 para 6*].

For HMRC's practice in this area, see HMRC Statement of Practice 5/92, paras 7–10 and ICAEW guidance note TAX 20/92, 14 December 1992, paras 5, 6 and 24–26.

HMRC information powers. HMRC can by notice require a trustee, beneficiary or settlor to provide, within a specified time limit of at least 28 days beginning with the day the notice is given, particulars they think necessary for the purposes of these provisions. Penalties under *TMA 1970, s 98* apply for failure. [*TCGA 1992, Sch 5 para 10*].

44.13 **Interaction with other provisions.** 'The trust gains for the year' of *TCGA 1992, s 87(2)* (gains of overseas resident settlements chargeable on beneficiaries — see 44.14 below) and the 'Schedule 4B trust gains' of *TCGA 1992, Sch 4C* (gains chargeable on beneficiaries accruing on transfer of value linked with borrowing by trustees of overseas resident settlement — see 44.19 below) are reduced by the amount or the aggregate of the amounts chargeable on the settlor, under the provisions in 44.5 above, net of any available taper relief (irrespective of whether taper relief did, in fact, fall to be applied by the trustees — see below). [*TCGA 1992, s 87(3), Sch 4C paras 3, 6; FA 2000, s 92(4)(5), Sch 26 para 1; FA 2002, Sch 11 paras 6–8*]. Where amounts chargeable on the settlor are so chargeable by virtue of *TCGA 1992, s 10A* (charge on temporary non-residents — see 45.4 OVERSEAS MATTERS), there are provisions (see below) to prevent a double tax charge where gains have been charged on beneficiaries.

Both the 'charge on settlor' provisions at 44.5 above and the provisions of *TCGA 1992, ss 77–79* (charge on settlor with interest in UK resident settlement) contain a direction that the charge on the settlor is to be treated as the highest part of the amount on which he is chargeable to capital gains tax for a year of assessment. Where charges under both provisions apply to the same person in the same year, then the direction under *TCGA 1992, ss 77–79* takes effect subject to the similar direction under the provisions at 44.5 above. [*TCGA 1992, s 78(3)*].

Offset of losses and application of taper relief. For 2003/04 and subsequent years, and for any of the years 2000/01, 2001/02 or 2002/03 for which an election is made by the settlor under *FA 2002, Sch 11 para 8* (see 40.1 LOSSES), the amount treated as accruing to him under the above provisions is computed without applying TAPER RELIEF (61). However, trust losses are set against trust gains in such order as would give the maximum entitlement to taper relief if such relief were available to the trustees; this establishes the rate of taper relief to be applied to the gains in the settlor's hands after deducting any personal losses (see 40.1 LOSSES).

For years prior to 2003/04, other than any of the years 2000/01, 2001/02 or 2002/03 for which an election is made by the settlor under *FA 2002, Sch 11 para 8* (see 40.1 LOSSES), the amount treated as accruing to him will be net of taper relief where this is available. No further taper relief is available to the settlor. In addition, for 1998/99 onwards, the settlor's own, untapered, losses, whether of the current tax year or brought forward from previous years, cannot be set off against gains treated as accruing to him as above (see 40.1 LOSSES).

[*TCGA 1992, s 2(4)–(8), s 86(1)(e), (4A); FA 1998, s 121(3)(4), Sch 21 paras 2, 6(2); FA 2002, Sch 11 paras 4, 7, 8, Sch 40 Pt 3(4)*].

Settlor temporarily non-resident. Where a charge on a settlor arises under the provisions in 44.5 above by virtue of the charge under *TCGA 1992, s 10A* (the charge on individuals temporarily non-resident in the UK — see 45.4 OVERSEAS MATTERS) in the year of his return to the UK, there is a limitation on the amount to be so charged. The limitation applies if for any intervening year (i.e. any complete tax year between the 'year of departure' and the 'year of return' — see 45.4 OVERSEAS MATTERS), beneficiaries of the settlement were charged to tax in respect of any capital payments received by them from the settlement under *TCGA 1992, s 87* or *s 89(2)* (see 44.14 below) or *TCGA 1992, Sch 4C* (see 44.19 below).

Where the beneficiaries were charged to tax under *TCGA 1992, s 87* or *s 89(2)*, the limitation applies by reducing the amount falling within the charge on the settlor under these provisions for the intervening year (or years), and to be attributed to the settlor for the year of return, by the excess (if any) of the 'relevant chargeable amounts for the non-residence period' over the amount of the 'section 87 pool' at the end of the 'year of departure' (as defined in 45.4 OVERSEAS MATTERS and which must be 1997/98 or a subsequent year of assessment).

Where the above limitation has effect, i.e. where there *is* such an excess as is referred to above, the amount falling within the charge on the settlor is first reduced by applying any available taper relief. No further taper relief is available to the settlor, and the settlor's personal losses, whether of the current tax year or brought forward from previous years, cannot be set off against these attributed gains. This continues to be the position for 2003/04 and subsequent years, in contrast to the normal position under the heading 'Offset of losses and application of taper relief' above, and is not affected by an election by the settlor under *FA 2002, Sch 11 para 8* for any of the years 2000/01, 2001/02 or 2002/03.

The '*relevant chargeable amounts for the non-residence period*' is the aggregate of the amounts on which beneficiaries of the settlement are charged to capital gains tax in respect of any capital payments received by them from the settlement under *TCGA 1992, s 87* or *s 89(2)* for the intervening year or years. The '*section 87 pool*' at the end of a year of assessment is the amount (if any), under that section, of 'the trust gains for the year' (see 44.14 below) which are to be carried forward from that year to be included in the amount of the trust gains for the immediately following year of assessment. In calculating the above amounts, where the settlement property has at any time included property not originating from the settlor, only so much (if any) of any capital payment or amount of trust gains for the year carried forward as, on a just and reasonable apportionment, is properly referable to property originating from the settlor (see 44.9 above) is taken into account.

These provisions interact with those of *TCGA 1992, s 87(3)* (see 44.14 below) under which trust gains potentially chargeable on beneficiaries are reduced by amounts chargeable on settlors of the settlement. The reduction is equal to the gains attributable to settlors *after* applying taper relief (regardless of whether taper relief did, in fact, fall to be applied by the trustees).

[*TCGA 1992, s 86A; FA 1998, s 129(1)(3); FA 2002, Sch 11 paras 5, 7, 8, Sch 40 Pt 3(4)*].

Where the beneficiaries were charged to tax under *TCGA 1992, Sch 4C*, the provisions of *TCGA 1992, s 86A* above do not apply. Instead, the limitation applies by taking the amount of the gains included in the settlement's Schedule 4C pool (see 44.19 below) (or, for capital payments made before 9 April 2003, the amount of the gains accruing under *TCGA 1992, Sch 4B* (see 57.19 SETTLEMENTS)) which fall within the charge on the settlor under these provisions for the intervening years, and which are to be attributed to the settlor for the year of return, and reducing it by the total of the amounts on which beneficiaries of any relevant settlements (see 44.19 below) were charged to tax under *TCGA 1992, Sch 4C* in respect of those gains for all the intervening years. In calculating the amount on which the beneficiaries have been so charged to tax, where the property comprised in the transferor settlement has at any time included property not originating from the settlor, only so much (if any) of any capital payment taken into account for the purposes of *TCGA 1992, Sch 4C* as, on a just and reasonable apportionment, is properly referable to property originating from the settlor (see 44.9 above) is taken into account.

[*TCGA 1992, Sch 4C paras 1, 12; FA 2000, Sch 26 para 1; FA 2003, Sch 29 para 6(2)*].

44.14 CHARGE ON BENEFICIARY IN RESPECT OF CAPITAL PAYMENTS RECEIVED FROM SETTLEMENT

The following provisions apply to a settlement for a tax year if

(*a*) the 'trustees' are neither resident nor ordinarily resident in the UK (see 44.1 above) during any part of the year; and

(*b*) for 1996/97 and earlier years, and also for any subsequent year as regards gains and losses accruing to the trustees **before 17 March 1998** and capital payments received by beneficiaries before that date, the 'settlor', or one of the settlors, either at some time during the tax year or when the settlement was made, was domiciled and either resident or ordinarily resident in the UK. (A settlement arising under a will or intestacy is treated as made by the testator or intestate at the time of his death.)

Where the above conditions are satisfied, a 'beneficiary' of the settlement is liable to capital gains tax on the gains of the settlement in the following circumstances.

- The beneficiary must be domiciled in the UK at some time during the year of assessment.
- There must be 'trust gains for the year'.
- The beneficiary must have received 'capital payments' from the trustees.

[*TCGA 1992, s 87(1)(2)(4)(7)(9)(10); FA 1998, s 130(1)(3)(4), Sch 27 Pt III(30); FA 2006, Sch 12 paras 36(1)(2), 41*].

Note that these provisions have effect subject to the provisions of *TCGA 1992, Sch 4C* (transfers of value linked with trustee borrowing: attribution of gains to beneficiaries — see 44.19 below). [*TCGA 1992, s 85A(2), Sch 4C para 1(2); FA 2000, s 92(4)(5), Sch 26 para 1; FA 2003, s 163(1)*].

After 5 April 2006, in relation to settlements whenever created, '*settlor*' is defined as at 57.3 SETTLEMENTS. Previously, '*settlor*' was defined as in *ITTOIA 2005, s 620* (see 16.7 CONNECTED PERSONS) but included, in the case of a settlement arising under a will or intestacy, the testator or intestate. '*Settlement*' is defined as in *ITTOIA 2005, s 620* (see 16.7 CONNECTED PERSONS) and 'settled property' and references to property comprised in a settlement are construed accordingly. [*TCGA 1992, s 97(7); FA 1995, Sch 17 para 30; ITTOIA 2005, Sch 1 para 432; FA 2006, Sch 12 para 15(1)(3)*]. In a case where a residuary legatee (who was domiciled, resident and ordinarily resident in the UK) settled the unadministered residue of the estate of a testator (who was domiciled, resident and ordinarily resident outside the UK) under a deed of family arrangement within *TCGA 1992, s 62(6)* (see 18.6 DEATH), it was held that the legatee was the settlor for the purposes of *TCGA 1992, s 87* (*Marshall v Kerr HL 1994, 67 TC 56*).

After 5 April 2006, '*trustee*' is specifically expressed to include, where a settlement would otherwise have no trustees, any person in whom the settled property or its management is vested. [*TCGA 1992, s 97(7A); FA 2006, Sch 12 para 15(2)(3)*].

'*Beneficiary*' is not otherwise defined, but in any case where:

(1) at any time after 18 March 1991 a capital payment is received from the trustees of a settlement or is treated as so received by virtue of *TCGA 1992, s 96(1)* (see below under Payments by and to companies);

(2) it is received by a person, or treated as received by a person by virtue of *TCGA 1992, s 96(2)–(5)* (see below under Payments by and to companies);

(3) at the time it is received or treated as received, the person is not otherwise a beneficiary of the settlement; and

(4) certain exceptions do not apply;

then for the purposes of *TCGA 1992, ss 87–90* (for which see further below) and *TCGA 1992, Sch 4C* (see 44.19 below) the person is treated as a beneficiary of the settlement as regards events occurring on or after that time. The first exception is where a payment within (1) above is made in circumstances where it is treated (otherwise than under the provision in the last sentence) as received by a beneficiary. The second exception is where the trustees of the settlement concerned or trustees of any other settlement are beneficiaries of the settlement concerned. [*TCGA 1992, s 97(8)–(10); FA 2000, s 92(4)(5), Sch 26 para 4*].

The trust gains for a year of assessment are treated as chargeable gains accruing in that year to beneficiaries of the settlement who receive capital payments from the trustees in that year or have received such payments in any earlier year, such attribution being made in proportion to, but not exceeding, the amounts of capital payments received by them. A capital payment is left out of account for these purposes to the extent that chargeable gains have by reason of the payment been treated as accruing to the recipient in an earlier year. [*TCGA 1992, s 87(4)–(6)*].

'*Trust gains for the year*'. This is an amount which is the aggregate of

(i) an amount computed for the current year, being the amount which would have been chargeable on the trustees under *TCGA 1992, s 2(2)* (i.e. chargeable gains less current year and brought forward losses), had they been resident and ordinarily resident (for 2006/07 and earlier years, resident or ordinarily resident) in the UK in that year; and

(ii) the corresponding amount for any earlier year(s) (1981/82 onwards) which has not yet been attributed under *TCGA 1992, s 87(4)* (see above) or *TCGA 1992, s 89(2)* (see below under Migrant settlements) to beneficiaries.

[*TCGA 1992, s 87(2); FA 2006, Sch 12 para 34(1)–(3)*].

See 44.19 below for the interaction of these provisions with those of *TCGA 1992, Sch 4C* (transfers of value linked with trustee borrowing: attribution of gains to beneficiaries).

Example

T and M are the only beneficiaries under a Jersey settlement set up by their grandfather.

T is resident in the UK but M is neither resident nor ordinarily resident in the UK. Both beneficiaries have a UK domicile. In 2005/06, the trustees sell shares realising a chargeable gain of £102,000. No disposals are made in 2006/07.

The trustees make capital payments of £60,000 to M in 2005/06. In 2006/07 they make capital payments of £60,000 to T and £10,000 to M.

2005/06	£
Trust gains	102,000
Capital payment	60,000
Trust gains carried forward	£42,000

M has chargeable gains of £60,000 but is not subject to CGT.

2006/07	£
Trust gains (brought forward)	42,000
Capital payments (£60,000 + £10,000)	70,000
Balance of capital payments carried forward	£28,000

The chargeable gains are apportioned as follows

	£
T $\frac{60,000}{70,000} \times$ £42,000	36,000
M $\frac{10,000}{70,000} \times$ £42,000 (not assessable)	6,000
	£42,000

The capital payments carried forward are apportioned as follows

	£
T £60,000 – £36,000	24,000
M £10,000 – £6,000	4,000
	£28,000

Where as regards the same settlement and for the same year of assessment chargeable gains, whether of one amount or of two or more amounts, are treated as accruing by virtue of *TCGA 1992, s 86(4)* (offshore settlement where settlor has interest — see 44.5 above), and an amount falls to be computed under *TCGA 1992, s 87(2)* above, the amount so computed is treated as reduced by the amount, or aggregate of the amounts, mentioned in 44.5 above, net of any available taper relief (irrespective of whether taper relief did, in fact, fall to be applied by the trustees — see 44.13 above). [*TCGA 1992, s 87(3); FA 2002, Sch 11 paras 6–8*]. In addition, in computing an amount under *TCGA 1992, s 87(2)* for years of assessment after 1990/91, the effect of *TCGA 1992, ss 77–79* (charge on settlor with interest in UK resident settlement — see 57.5 SETTLEMENTS) is ignored. (The interaction between these two charging provisions is not explicitly stated for 1988/89, 1989/90 and 1990/91 but in *De Rothschild v Lawrenson CA 1995, 67 TC 300*, it was held that a practically similar position applied for those years.) [*TCGA 1992, s 87(8)*].

Where a loss accrues to the trustees in a year of assessment for which these provisions apply, or *CGTA 1979, s 17* applied, the loss is allowable against gains accruing to the trustees in any later year (1981/82 onwards) insofar as it has not previously been set against gains for the purpose of a computation under these provisions, those of *CGTA 1979, s 17* or otherwise. [*TCGA 1992, s 97(6)*].

'*Capital payments*'. These are any 'payments' received after 9 March 1981 which either are not chargeable to income tax on the 'recipient' (formerly 'beneficiary' for payments etc. before 19 March 1991), or, in the case of a recipient neither resident nor ordinarily resident in the UK, are payments received otherwise than as income. However, payments received *after 9 March 1981 and before 6 April 1984* and which represent chargeable gains accruing to the trustees *before 6 April 1981* are dealt with under the previous legislation, subject to provisions which avoid double taxation. For payments received after 18 March 1991, a capital payment does not include a payment under a transaction entered into at arm's length. [*TCGA 1992, s 87(10), s 97(1); FA 1995, Sch 17 para 30*].

A beneficiary is regarded as having received a capital payment from the trustees where

- the beneficiary receives the payment from them, whether directly or indirectly;
- the trustees, directly or indirectly, apply the payment in settlement of any of the beneficiary's debts, or it is otherwise paid or applied for his benefit; or

- a third party receives it at the beneficiary's direction.

[*TCGA 1992, s 97(5)*].

'*Payment*' includes the transfer of an asset and the conferring of any other benefit. It also includes any occasion where settled property becomes property to which *TCGA 1992, s 60* applies (e.g. property held by nominees or on bare trusts for persons absolutely entitled). [*TCGA 1992, s 97(2)*]. A benefit treated (in whole or in part), under *ICTA 1988, s 740(2)(b)* (transfer of assets abroad: liability of non-transferors on benefits received — see Tolley's Income Tax under Anti-Avoidance), as the recipient's income for a year of assessment *later* than the year of receipt, is not precluded from being treated as a capital payment in relation to any year *prior* to the year of assessment for which it is treated as income. It cannot, however, be treated as a capital payment in relation to the year for which it is treated as income, or in relation to any *subsequent* year. [*TCGA 1992, s 97(3)*].

The amount of capital payment made by way of loan, and of any other capital payment which is not an outright payment of money, is to be taken as the value of the benefit conferred by it. [*TCGA 1992, s 97(4)*]. Where trustees made loans which were repayable on demand they conferred a continuing benefit on the borrower by leaving the loans outstanding for any period, and were thus making annual capital payments, which were taken in this case to be equal to the interest that would have been payable had the loans (interest-free in this case) been made on a commercial basis (*Cooper v Billingham; Fisher v Edwards CA 2001, 74 TC 139*).

A beneficiary would not be chargeable if he was neither resident nor ordinarily resident (despite being domiciled) in the UK for the year of assessment in question under the general rules of *TCGA 1992, s 2(1)* (see 45.1 OVERSEAS MATTERS). Thus, in respect of capital payments received by a beneficiary in these circumstances, whilst trust gains are attributed to those capital payments, no charge to tax can be made in respect of them.

As regards capital payments received by UK charities as beneficiaries, see 10.3 CHARITIES.

For allowable expenditure on a subsequent disposal of an asset transferred to a beneficiary, see 41.1 MARKET VALUE. Where beneficiaries resident or ordinarily resident in the UK became absolutely entitled to settled property (see 57.15 SETTLEMENTS) after 5 April 1982 and before 14 March 1989 hold-over relief was available as in 33.9 HOLD-OVER RELIEFS (Tolley's Practical Tax 1984 p 25). By analogy, the other current HOLD-OVER RELIEFS (33) would be available in such circumstances (provided all the conditions for the relief in question are met).

Offset of losses and application of taper relief. The amount treated as accruing to the beneficiary under the above provisions will be net of TAPER RELIEF (61) where this is available. No further taper relief is available to the beneficiary. In addition, for 1998/99 and subsequent years of assessment, the beneficiary's own, untapered, losses, whether of the current year of assessment or brought forward from previous years, cannot be set off against gains treated as accruing to him as above. [*TCGA 1992, s 2(4)(5), s 87(6A); FA 1998, s 121(3)(4), Sch 21 paras 2, 6(3)*].

Dual resident settlements. *TCGA 1992, s 87* above also applies to a settlement for years of assessment beginning after 1990/91 if the trustees are resident and ordinarily resident in the UK during any part of the year (for 2006/07 and earlier years, resident in the UK during any part of the year or ordinarily resident in the UK during the year) *and* at any time of such residence and/or ordinary residence they fall to be regarded for the purposes of a double tax agreement as resident overseas. For 1996/97 and earlier years, and also for any subsequent year as regards gains and losses accruing to the trustees **before 17 March 1998** and capital payments received by beneficiaries before that date, these provisions applied **only** if (in addition to the above conditions being satisfied) the settlor, or one of the settlors, either at some time during the tax year in question or when the settlement was made, was domiciled and either resident or ordinarily resident in the UK.

In the above circumstances, *TCGA 1992, s 87* is to have effect for every year of assessment as if the amount to be computed under *TCGA 1992, s 87(2)* (see (i) above) were 'the assumed chargeable amount'; and the reference in *TCGA 1992, s 87(2)* to 'the corresponding amount' in respect of any earlier year(s) (see (ii) above) is to be construed as a reference to the amount computed under *TCGA 1992, s 87(2)* apart from this provision (*TCGA 1992, s 88*) or (as the case may be) the amount computed under *TCGA 1992, s 87(2)* by virtue of this provision.

'*The assumed chargeable amount*' in respect of a year of assessment is the lesser of: the amount on which the trustees would be chargeable to tax for the year under *TCGA 1992, s 2(2)* on the assumption that the double tax relief arrangements did not apply; and the amount on which, by virtue of disposals of protected assets, the trustees would be chargeable to tax for the year under *TCGA 1992, s 2(2)* on the assumption that those arrangements did not apply. Assets are '*protected assets*' if they are of a description specified in the double tax relief arrangements, and were the trustees to dispose of them at any 'relevant time', the trustees would fall to be regarded for the purposes of the arrangements as not liable in the UK to tax on gains accruing to them on the disposal. For the purposes of this definition of protected assets: the second assumption in the first sentence of this paragraph is ignored; '*the relevant time*' is any time, in the year of assessment concerned, when the trustees fall to be regarded for the purposes of the arrangements as resident overseas; and if different assets are identified by reference to different relevant times, all of them are protected assets. In computing the assumed chargeable amount in respect of a particular year of assessment, the effect of *TCGA 1992, ss 77–79* (charge on settlor with interest in UK resident settlement — see 57.5 SETTLEMENTS) is ignored. For the purposes of *TCGA 1992, s 87* as it applies by virtue of this provision, capital payments received before 6 April 1991 are disregarded.

[*TCGA 1992, s 88; FA 1998, s 130(2)–(4), Sch 27 Pt III(30); FA 2006, Sch 12 para 35(1)(2)*].

Migrant settlements. A capital payment (see above) made to a beneficiary in a period of one or more years of assessment 'for each of which *TCGA 1992, s 87* above does not apply to the settlement' (before 25 July 1991 'in each of which the trustees were at some time resident or ordinarily resident in the UK') (a '*resident period*') is disregarded provided that the payment is not anticipatory of a disposal by the trustees in a succeeding period of one or more years of assessment for which *TCGA 1992, s 87* applies to the settlement (a '*non-resident period*'). Where a resident period follows a non-resident period and part or whole of the trust gains for the last year of the non-resident period have not yet been apportioned and charged to beneficiaries, the outstanding trust gains are, to the extent, each year, that the beneficiaries receive capital payments, apportioned and charged to them for the first year of the resident period and so on for successive years, until the outstanding gains are exhausted. [*TCGA 1992, s 89(2)*]. *TCGA 1992, s 87(5)(7)* is applied to *TCGA 1992, s 89(2)* as it applies to *TCGA 1992, s 87(4)*. [*TCGA 1992, s 89(3)*].

Offset of losses and application of taper relief. The amount treated as accruing to the beneficiary under the above provisions will be net of TAPER RELIEF (61) where this is available. No further taper relief is available to the beneficiary. In addition, for 1998/99 and subsequent years of assessment, the beneficiary's own, untapered, losses, whether of the current year of assessment or brought forward from previous years, cannot be set off against gains treated as accruing to him as above. [*TCGA 1992, s 2(4)(5), s 87(6A), s 89(3); FA 1998, s 121(3)(4), Sch 21 paras 2, 6(4)*].

Transfers between settlements. There are provisions for the carry-over of unattributed trust gains under *TCGA 1992, s 87* or *s 89(2)* (apportioned where necessary), in cases where transfers of settled property are made from one settlement to another other than for consideration in money or money's worth. If neither of the last mentioned provisions would otherwise apply to the transferee settlement for the year of transfer, *TCGA 1992, s 89(2)* is deemed to apply to it as if the year were the first year of a resident period following a non-resident period, and the trust gains equal to the trust gains for the last year of the non-resident period. These provisions do not apply to a transfer to which *TCGA 1992, Sch 4B* (transfers of value by trustees linked with trustee borrowing — see 57.19 SETTLEMENTS) applies, or to 'Schedule 4C gains' within 44.19 below. [*TCGA 1992, s 90; FA 2000, s 92(4)(5), Sch 26 para 2; FA 2003, s 162(3)*].

Payments by and to companies. By virtue of *TCGA 1992, s 96(1)*, where a capital payment is received after 18 March 1991 from a 'qualifying company' which is 'controlled' by the trustees of a settlement at the time it is received, it is treated for the purposes of *TCGA 1992, ss 87–90* above and (for capital payments received after 20 March 2000) *TCGA 1992, Sch 4C* (see 44.19 below) as received from the trustees. A '*qualifying company*' is a close company within *ICTA 1988, ss 414, 415* or a company which would be a close company if it were UK resident. For this purpose, a company is 'controlled' by the trustees of a settlement if it is 'controlled' by the trustees alone or by the trustees together with a person who (or persons each of whom) is a settlor in relation to the settlement or is connected (see 16 CONNECTED PERSONS) with such a settlor. '*Control*' is to be construed in accordance with *ICTA 1988, s 416* except that for this purpose no rights or powers of (or attributed to) an associate or associates of a person are attributed to him under *ICTA 1988, s 416(6)* if he is not a participator (within *ICTA 1988, s 417(1)*) in the company. By concession, a beneficiary in the settlement is not to be regarded as a participator in the company solely by virtue of his status as beneficiary (HMRC Extra-Statutory Concession D40).

By virtue of *TCGA 1992, s 96(2)–(5)*, where a capital payment is received after 18 March 1991 from trustees of a settlement (or treated as so received under the foregoing) and it is received by a '*non-resident qualifying company*' (i.e. a company which is not resident in the UK and would be a close company if it were so resident), the following provisions apply for the purposes of *TCGA 1992, ss 87–90* above and (for capital payments received after 20 March 2000) *TCGA 1992, Sch 4C* (see 44.19 below).

If the company is 'controlled' (construed as above) by one person alone at the time the payment is received, and that person is (or is deemed to be) then resident or ordinarily resident in the UK, it is treated as a capital payment received by that person.

If the company is controlled by two or more persons (taking each one separately) at the time the payment is received, then: if one of them is (or is deemed to be) then resident or ordinarily resident in the UK, it is treated as a capital payment received by that person; and if two or more persons are (or are deemed to be) then resident or ordinarily resident in the UK ('*the residents*') it is treated as being as many equal capital payments as there are residents and each of them is treated as receiving one of the payments.

If the company is controlled by two or more persons (taking them together) at the time the payment is received and, where the payment is received before 21 March 2000, each of them is (or is deemed to be) then resident or ordinarily resident in the UK: it is treated as being as many capital payments as there are participators in the company at the time it is received; and each such participator (whatever his residence or ordinary residence) is treated as receiving one of the payments, quantified on the basis of just and reasonable apportionment. But where a participator would otherwise be treated as receiving less than 5% of the payment actually received by the company, he is not treated as receiving anything by virtue of the foregoing.

For HMRC's practice in this area, see SP 5/92, paras 38–40.

For the above purposes, an *individual* is deemed to be resident in the UK at any time in any year of assessment which is an intervening year for the purposes of the charge to capital gains tax on temporary non-residents (see 45.4 OVERSEAS MATTERS). Where it appears after the end of a year of assessment that this does apply to an individual and consequential adjustments are required to the amounts of tax chargeable on any person under the above provisions, no time limits for making any assessment or claim prevent the making of those adjustments (whether by assessment, amended assessment, tax repayment or otherwise).

[*TCGA 1992, s 96; FA 1998, s 127(3); FA 2000, s 92(4)(5), s 95, Sch 26 para 3*].

HMRC information powers. HMRC may, by notice in writing, require any person, within such time as it directs (not less than 28 days), to furnish them with such particulars as they think necessary for the purposes of *TCGA 1992, ss 87–90* above and *TCGA 1992, Sch 4C* (see 44.19 below). The very wide information powers of *ICTA 1988, s 745(2)–(6)*, suitably adapted, are also expressly stated to apply. [*TCGA 1992, s 98; FA 2000, s 92(4)(5), s 95, Sch 26 para 5; FA 2006, Sch 12 para 16*].

44.15 FURTHER CHARGE ON BENEFICIARY IN RESPECT OF CAPITAL PAYMENTS RECEIVED FROM SETTLEMENT

Further provisions apply as regards the regime of provisions in 44.14 above for taxing beneficiaries of overseas resident settlements. They provide for an increased tax charge on the beneficiary in certain cases.

The provisions apply where

(*a*) a 'capital payment' (see 44.14 above) is made by the trustees of a settlement after 5 April 1992;

(*b*) the payment is made in a year of assessment for which *TCGA 1992, s 87* applies to the settlement or in circumstances where *TCGA 1992, s 89(2)* treats chargeable gains as accruing in respect of the payment;

(*c*) the whole payment is matched with a 'qualifying amount' of the settlement for a year of assessment falling at some time before that immediately preceding the one in which the payment is made (but see 44.16 below for the application of the provisions where a capital payment is matched with more than one qualifying amount, only part of a capital payment is matched with a qualifying amount, or a payment or part of a payment is matched with part of a qualifying amount); and

(*d*) a beneficiary is charged to tax in respect of the payment by virtue of *TCGA 1992, s 87* or *s 89(2)*.

In the above circumstances the tax payable by the beneficiary in respect of the payment is increased by the amount found below, except that it cannot be increased beyond the amount of the payment.

The amount is equal to the interest that would be yielded if an amount equal to the tax which would be otherwise payable by him in respect of the payment carried interest for 'the chargeable period' at the rate of 10% per annum. The percentage may be amended by Treasury Order.

'*The chargeable period*' is the period which begins with the later of 1 December in the year of assessment following that for which the qualifying amount mentioned in (*c*) above is the qualifying amount and 1 December falling six years before 1 December in the year of assessment following that in which the capital payment is made, and ends with 30 November in the year of assessment following that in which the capital payment is made.

In arriving, for the above purposes, at the amount of CGT payable by the beneficiary in respect of the capital payment, that payment is deemed to form the lowest slice of the beneficiary's total gains (HMRC Helpsheet IR 301 p 1). Therefore, it may, for example, be reduced by the annual exemption.

Qualifying amounts. If *TCGA 1992, s 87* applies to a settlement for the year 1991/92 or a subsequent year of assessment, the settlement has a qualifying amount for the year, and that amount is the amount computed for the settlement in respect of the year concerned under *TCGA 1992, s 87(2)* (i.e. the amount in 44.14(i) above).

If *TCGA 1992, s 87* applied to a settlement for the year 1990/91, the settlement had a '*qualifying amount*' for the year, and that amount was the amount constituting the 'trust gains for the year' (see 44.14 above) less so much of them as were by virtue of *TCGA 1992, s 87* treated as chargeable gains accruing in that year to the beneficiaries.

A qualifying amount for 1990/91 is also determined where

(i) there was a period ('*a non-resident period*') of one or more years of assessment for each of which *TCGA 1992, s 87* applied to a settlement and each of which fell before the year 1990/91;

(ii) *TCGA 1992, s 87* did not apply to the settlement for the year 1990/91; and

(iii) there were trust gains for the last year of the non-resident period which were not (or were not wholly) treated by virtue of *TCGA 1992, s 87* or *s 89(2)* as chargeable gains accruing to beneficiaries before the year 1990/91.

In such a case the settlement had a qualifying amount for the year 1990/91 of the amount constituting the trust gains mentioned in (iii) above (or the outstanding part of them) less so much of them as were by virtue of *TCGA 1992, s 87(2)* treated as chargeable gains accruing in that year to beneficiaries.

Matching capital payments. Where capital payments are made by the trustees of a settlement after 5 April 1991 and the payments are made in a year or years of assessment for which *TCGA 1992, s 87* applies to the settlement or in circumstances where *TCGA 1992, s 89(2)* treats chargeable gains as accruing in respect of the payments, the payments are matched with qualifying amounts of the settlement for the year 1990/91 and subsequent years of assessment (so far as the amounts are not already matched with payments by virtue of this provision). Payments are matched with qualifying amounts so that: earlier payments are matched with earlier amounts; payments are carried forward to be matched with future amounts (so far as not matched with past amounts); a payment which is less than an unmatched amount (or part) is matched to the extent of the payment; and a payment which is more than an unmatched amount (or part) is matched, as to the excess, with other unmatched amounts.

Where part only of a capital payment is taxable, the part which is not taxable does not fall to be matched until taxable parts of other capital payments (if any) made in the same year of assessment have been matched, and the provisions in the paragraph above have effect accordingly. For this purpose a part of a capital payment is taxable if the part results in chargeable gains accruing under *TCGA 1992, s 87* or *s 89(2)*.

See 44.16 and 44.17 below for matching in certain special cases. For an example of matching, see Tolley's Tax Computations or Tolley's Capital Gains Tax Workbook. [*TCGA 1992, ss 91, 92*].

44.16 **Matching: special cases.** Where, applying the matching rules in 44.15 above, a capital payment is matched with more than one qualifying amount, only part of the capital payment is matched with a qualifying amount, or a payment or part of a payment is matched with part of a qualifying amount (so that condition (*c*) at 44.15 above is not strictly met), the further charge in 44.15 above applies as follows.

More than one qualifying amount. Where the whole capital payment is matched with qualifying amounts of the settlement for different years of assessment, each falling at some time before that immediately preceding the one in which the payment is made, the capital payment ('*the main payment*') is treated as being as many payments ('*subsidiary payments*') as there are qualifying amounts. A qualifying amount is attributed to each subsidiary payment and each payment is quantified accordingly, and the tax in respect of the main payment is divided up and attributed to the subsidiary payment on the basis of a just and reasonable apportionment. The provisions in 44.15 above then apply in the case of each subsidiary payment, the qualifying amount attributed to it and the tax attributed to it.

Payment partly ignored. Where part of the capital payment is matched with a qualifying amount of the settlement for a year of assessment falling at some time before that immediately preceding the one in which the payment is made, or with qualifying amounts of the settlement for different years of assessment each so falling, only the tax in respect of so much of the payment as is so matched is taken into account, and references below to the tax are to be construed accordingly. The capital payment is divided into two, the first part representing so much as is matched as mentioned above and the second so much as is not. The second part is ignored, and the first part is treated as a capital payment, the whole of which is matched with the qualifying amount or amounts mentioned above, and the whole of which is charged to tax. The provisions in 44.15 above and the above provisions relating to the matching of a payment with more than one qualifying amount (as the case may be) are then applied in the case of the capital payment divided as above, the qualifying amount or amounts, and the tax.

Parts of amounts matched. The above provisions and the provisions in 44.15 above apply (with suitable modifications) where a payment or part of a payment is to any extent matched with part of an amount.

[*TCGA 1992, s 93*].

44.17 **Transfers between settlements.** For the purposes of the provisions at 44.15 and 44.16 above, the following applies if: in the year 1990/91 or a subsequent year of assessment the trustees of a settlement ('*the transferor settlement*') transfer all or part of the settled property to the trustees of another settlement ('*the transferee settlement*'), and looking at the state of affairs at the end of the year of assessment in which the transfer is made, there is a qualifying amount of the transferor settlement for a particular year of assessment ('*the year concerned*') and the amount is not (or not wholly) matched with capital payments.

In the above circumstances, if the whole of the settled property is transferred, the transferor settlement's qualifying amount for the year concerned is treated as reduced by so much of it as is not matched, and so much of that amount as is not matched is treated as (or as an addition to) the transferee settlement's qualifying amount for the year concerned.

If, in the above circumstances, only part of the settled property is transferred, so much of the transferor settlement's qualifying amount for the year concerned as is not matched is apportioned on a just and reasonable basis, part being attributed to the transferred property and part to the property not transferred. The transferor settlement's qualifying amount for the year concerned is treated as reduced by the part attributed to the transferred property; and that part is treated as (or as an addition to) the transferee settlement's qualifying amount for the year concerned.

If the transferee settlement did not in fact exist in the year concerned, then it is treated as having been made at the beginning of that year. If the transferee settlement did in fact exist in the year concerned, the foregoing provisions are to apply whether or not *TCGA 1992, s 87* applies to the settlement for that year or for any year of assessment falling before that year.

Matching after transfer. In the case of a transferee settlement, matching is to be made in accordance with the provisions in 44.15 and 44.16 above by reference to the state of affairs existing immediately before the beginning of the year of assessment in which the transfer is made, and the transfer is not to affect matching so made. Subject to this, payments are matched with amounts in accordance with the provisions in 44.15 and 44.16 above and by reference to amounts arrived at under the 'transfer between settlements' provisions above.

[*TCGA 1992, ss 94, 95*].

44.18 ANTI-AVOIDANCE: TRANSFERS OF VALUE BY TRUSTEES LINKED WITH TRUSTEE BORROWING

See 57.19 SETTLEMENTS for provisions deeming chargeable gains to arise to trustees of a settlement where they make a 'transfer of value' (as defined). Where the trustees are not UK resident or they are treated as non-resident under double tax relief arrangements, the resulting gains are, in certain circumstances, chargeable either on the settlor (see 44.5 above) or on beneficiaries who receive capital payments under *TCGA 1992, Sch 4C* (see 44.19 below).

44.19 TRANSFERS OF VALUE: ATTRIBUTION OF GAINS TO BENEFICIARIES

The provisions charging beneficiaries receiving capital payments from trustees in respect of gains within *TCGA 1992, Sch 4B* (see 44.18 above) were amended by *FA 2003* to prevent their exploitation for tax avoidance purposes. The avoidance schemes at which the amendments are aimed typically relied on the transferor settlement (see below) having realised gains but few, if any, assets. Both the original and the revised provisions apply in respect of 'transfers of value' (within 57.19 SETTLEMENTS) made after 20 March 2000, but the latter broadly apply only where capital payments are made after 8 April 2003. The detailed provisions are described below.

Post *FA 2003* provisions. Subject to the transitional rules below, the following provisions apply where the trustees of a 'settlement' (the 'transferor settlement') make a 'transfer of value' to which *TCGA 1992, Sch 4B* (see 57.19 SETTLEMENTS) applies, whether or not any chargeable gain or allowable loss accrues in respect of the transfer under that Schedule. Where the provisions apply, *TCGA 1992, s 86A* (limitation on amount chargeable on temporarily non-resident settlor following transfer of value — see 44.13 above) and *ss 87–95* (the normal provisions attributing gains to beneficiaries receiving capital payments from offshore settlements — see 44.14 above) have effect subject to them. Accordingly,

- in computing trust gains for a year in accordance with *TCGA 1992, ss 87–89*, no account is taken of any chargeable gains or allowable losses accruing by virtue of *TCGA 1992, Sch 4B* (except in computing the 'outstanding section 87/89 gains' of a settlement (see below)); and
- in computing the gains or losses accruing by virtue of *TCGA 1992, Sch 4B*, no account is taken of any chargeable gains or allowable losses to which *TCGA 1992, ss 87–89* apply.

For the purpose of attributing them to beneficiaries who receive capital payments, the following gains (the '*Schedule 4C gains*') are pooled

- any 'Schedule 4B trust gains' (see below) accruing by virtue of the transfer of value; and
- any 'outstanding section 87/89 gains' (see below) of the transferor settlement at the end of the tax year in which the transfer is made,

thereby creating the '*Schedule 4C pool*'.

In the event of a further transfer of value, further gains will be added to the pool as follows. If the further transfer takes place in the same tax year as the original transfer, any Schedule 4B trust gains accruing are added to the pool at the end of the year. If the further transfer takes place in a later tax year, at the beginning of which there are unattributed gains in the pool, any Schedule 4B trust gains and any outstanding section 87/89 gains of the settlement at the end of that year are added to the pool at the end of the year. If there is no pool at the beginning of the year of the further transfer (because all the gains have been attributed to beneficiaries) a new pool is created.

The gains in a settlement's Schedule 4C pool at the end of any tax year are treated as chargeable gains accruing in that year to 'beneficiaries' who receive in that year, or have received in an earlier year, 'capital payments' (as defined by *TCGA 1992, s 97(1)* — see 44.14 above) from the trustees of any settlement which is a 'relevant settlement' in relation to the pool. The attribution of chargeable gains to beneficiaries is made in proportion to, but not exceeding, the amounts of the capital payments received by them. A chargeable gain is not attributed to a beneficiary unless he is 'chargeable to tax' for that year (but see below re beneficiaries temporarily non-resident in the UK). Any gains in the pool not so attributed to beneficiaries are carried forward to the next tax year for attribution to beneficiaries receiving capital payments that year, and so on.

The following rules apply in attributing gains to beneficiaries.

- Gains of earlier years are attributed to beneficiaries before gains of later years.
- Gains of the same year are matched with capital payments made at any time by trustees of any relevant settlement.
- If gains of one year are wholly matched, gains of the next year are then matched, and so on.

For this purpose, a Schedule 4B trust gain is a gain of the tax year in which the transfer of value took place, and a section 87/89 gain is a gain of the year in which it first forms part of the settlement's 'trust gains for the year' (see 44.14 above).

Where in a particular tax year gains in a settlement's Schedule 4C pool are to be attributed to beneficiaries of relevant settlements and one or more of those settlements also have gains that are to be attributed to beneficiaries under *TCGA 1992, s 87(4)* or *s 89(2)* (see 44.14 above), the above rules apply in relation to all those gains, and, as between gains of the same year, Schedule 4C gains are attributed to beneficiaries in priority to other gains.

A capital payment is left out of account to the extent that chargeable gains have, by reason of it, been treated as accruing to the recipient in an earlier tax year under these provisions or under those at 44.14 above. Capital payments received before 21 March 2000 or before the tax year preceding that in which the transfer of value is made are also disregarded.

Attribution of gains to temporarily non-resident beneficiaries. Where, by virtue of *TCGA 1992, s 10A* (the charge on individuals temporarily non-resident in the UK — see 45.4 OVERSEAS MATTERS) an amount of gains would be treated as accruing to a beneficiary under *TCGA 1992, s 87* in the year of his return to the UK in respect of a capital payment made to him in an intervening year (i.e. any complete tax year between the 'year of departure' and the 'year of return' — see 45.4 OVERSEAS MATTERS), so much of that capital payment as exceeds the amount of such gains (or any gains attributed to him under *TCGA 1992, s 89(2)*) is treated as a capital payment for the purposes of these provisions, made to the beneficiary in the year of return. For the purposes of the provisions at 44.20 below only, the deemed capital payment is treated as made at the time of the actual capital payment.

Effect of settlement ceasing to exist after transfer of value. Where a settlement ceases to exist at any time after the trustees have made a transfer of value to which *TCGA 1992, Sch 4B* applies, the above provisions apply as if a tax year ended immediately before that time (and the Schedule 4C pool is calculated on that basis).

[*TCGA 1992, s 85A, Sch 4C paras 1, 7B, 8, 8B–9, 12A, 13A; FA 2003, s 163(1)(2), Sch 29 paras 1–4; FA 2006, Sch 12 para 34(1)–(3)*].

Transitional rules. Where there was a transfer of value to which *TCGA 1992, Sch 4B* applies after 20 March 2000 but before 9 April 2003, the transferor settlement is treated as having a Schedule 4C pool as from the latter date, containing such Schedule 4C gains as would fall to be included if the tax year in which the transfer of value was made had ended on 8 April 2003. For this purpose, where a transferor settlement ceased to exist after 20 March 2000 but before 9 April 2003, it is treated as if it had ceased to exist on 8 April 2003. So much of the amended provisions as provide that gains treated as accruing to beneficiaries not chargeable to tax are treated as outstanding section 87/89 gains and that gains in a Schedule 4C pool are not treated as accruing to such beneficiaries apply only in relation to capital payments made after 8 April 2003. Outstanding section 87/89 gains included in a Schedule 4C pool are only attributed under that Schedule to beneficiaries receiving capital payments after that date. [*FA 2003, s 163(4)(6)*].

Pre-*FA 2003* provisions. In respect of capital payments made before 9 April 2003 and subject to the above transitional rules, the provisions described below apply where in any tax year a chargeable gain or allowable loss accrues under *TCGA 1992, Sch 4B* to trustees of a settlement 'within *TCGA 1992, s 87*' in respect of a transfer of value made after 20 March 2000. They apply in place of the provisions of *TCGA 1992, ss 87–95* (the normal provisions attributing gains to beneficiaries receiving capital payments from offshore settlements — see 44.14 above), so that

- in computing the trust gains for a tax year in accordance with *TCGA 1992, ss 87–89* no account is taken of any such chargeable gain or allowable loss; and
- in computing the Schedule 4B trust gains in accordance with these provisions, no account is taken of any chargeable gain or allowable loss to which *TCGA 1992, ss 87–89* apply.

Schedule 4B trust gains computed as below and relating to a transfer of value by trustees of such a settlement are treated as chargeable gains accruing to beneficiaries of the transferor settlement or of any transferee settlement, who

- receive capital payments from the trustees in the tax year in which the transfer of value is made, or
- have received such payments in any earlier year,

to the extent that such payments exceed the amount of any gains attributed to the beneficiaries under *TCGA 1992, s 87(4)* or *s 89(2)* (see 44.14 above). Any Schedule 4B trust gains remaining are carried forward to the following tax year and treated as if they were gains from a transfer of value made in that year.

A capital payment is left out of account to the extent that chargeable gains have, by reason of it, been treated as accruing to the recipient in an earlier year of assessment. Capital payments received before 21 March 2000 or before the tax year preceding that in which the transfer of value is made are also disregarded.

The attribution of chargeable gains to beneficiaries is made in proportion to, but not exceeding, the amounts of the capital payments received by them. A beneficiary is not charged to tax on chargeable gains so treated as accruing to him in any year unless he is domiciled in the UK at some time in that year.

To the extent that chargeable gains have, by reason of a capital payment, been treated as accruing to the recipient under these provisions, the payment is left out of account for the purposes of *TCGA 1992, s 87(4)(5)* and *s 89(2)* (see 44.14 above).

[*TCGA 1992, s 85A, Sch 4C paras 1, 2, 8, 9; FA 2000, s 92(3)–(5), Sch 26 para 1*].

Payments by and to companies. See 44.14 above for the application of these provisions where capital payments are made by or to certain companies.

Residence of trustees from whom capital payment received. Subject to the following exception, it is immaterial for the purposes of the above provisions that the trustees of any relevant settlement are or have at any time been resident and ordinarily resident (for 2006/07 and earlier years, resident or ordinarily resident) in the UK. A capital payment received by a beneficiary of a settlement from the trustees in a tax year

- for 2006/07 and earlier years, during the whole of which the trustees are resident in the UK, or in which the trustees are ordinarily resident in the UK, or
- for 2007/08 onwards, during the whole of which the trustees are resident and ordinarily resident in the UK,

is disregarded for the purposes of the above provisions if it was made before, but was not made in anticipation of, chargeable gains accruing under the provisions of *TCGA 1992, Sch 4B* or of a transfer of value being made to which those provisions apply. For these purposes, trustees are not regarded as resident and ordinarily resident in the UK (or, for 2006/07 and earlier years, as resident or ordinarily resident) in the UK at any time when they fall to be treated as resident outside the UK for the purposes of any double tax relief arrangements. [*TCGA 1992, Sch 4C para 10; FA 2003, Sch 29 para 6(1); FA 2006, Sch 12 paras 34(1)–(3), 40, 41*].

Application of taper relief. The amount treated as accruing to the beneficiary under the above provisions will be net of TAPER RELIEF (61) where this is available. No further taper relief is available to the beneficiary. [*TCGA 1992, Sch 4C para 11*].

HMRC information powers. See 44.14 above for details of HMRC's information powers in relation to the above provisions.

Definitions. '*Settlement*' is defined by the references in *ITTOIA 2005, s 620* — see 16.7 CONNECTED PERSONS.

The following are '*relevant settlements*' in relation to a Schedule 4C pool:

- the '*transferor settlement*' (being the settlement the trustees of which made the transfer of value);
- any '*transferee settlement*' (i.e. any settlement of which the settled property includes property representing, directly or indirectly, the proceeds of the transfer of value); and
- where the trustees of a relevant settlement make, after 8 April 2003, a transfer of value to which *TCGA 1992, Sch 4B* applies or a transfer of settled property to which *TCGA 1992, s 90* applies (see 44.14 above under 'Transfers between settlements'), any transferee settlement in relation to that transfer.

Where the trustees of a settlement which is a relevant settlement in relation to a Schedule 4C pool make a transfer, after 8 April 2003, of value to which *TCGA 1992, Sch 4B* applies, any other settlement which is a relevant settlement in relation to that pool is also a relevant settlement in relation to the Schedule 4C pool arising from the further transfer.

A settlement is '*within TCGA 1992, s 87*' for a tax year if in that year the trustees are at no time resident or ordinarily resident in the UK or they fall to be regarded for the purpose of any DOUBLE TAX RELIEF (19) arrangements as resident outside the UK.

A beneficiary is '*chargeable to tax*' for a tax year if he is resident in the UK for any part of the year or is ordinarily resident in the UK for the year and he is domiciled in the UK at some time in the year.

'*Beneficiaries*' include

- persons who have ceased to be beneficiaries by the time the chargeable gains accrue, and
- persons who were beneficiaries of the settlement before it ceased to exist (where this is the case),

but who were beneficiaries of the settlement at a time in a previous tax year when a capital payment was made to them. See 44.14 above for a further circumstance in which, by virtue of *TCGA 1992, s 97(8)–(10)*, a person is treated as a beneficiary.

[*TCGA 1992, s 97(7), Sch 4C paras 1, 8(4), 8A, 14; FA 2000, Sch 26 paras 1, 4; FA 2003, s 163(4)–(6), Sch 29 para 4; ITTOIA 2005, Sch 1 para 432*].

Computation of Schedule 4B trust gains. The amount of the '*Schedule 4B trust gains*', which is to be computed for the above purposes in relation to each transfer of value, is given by

CA – SG – AL, where

CA = the 'chargeable amount' (see below),

SG = the amount of any gains attributed to the settlor (within the meaning below), and

AL = the amount of any allowable losses that may be deducted as described below.

Chargeable amount. If the transfer of value is made in a tax year during which the trustees of the transferor settlement are at no time resident and ordinarily resident (for 2006/07 and earlier years, resident or ordinarily resident) in the UK, the '*chargeable amount*' is the amount on which the trustees would have been chargeable to CGT by virtue of *TCGA 1992, Sch 4B* (i.e. the chargeable gains, net of allowable losses, on the disposals deemed to occur at the time of the transfer of value — see 57.19 SETTLEMENTS) if they had been resident and/or ordinarily resident in the UK in the year.

If the transfer of value is made in a tax year where the trustees of the transferor settlement are treated as resident outside the UK for the purposes of any double tax relief arrangements at a time when they are, in fact, UK-resident and ordinarily resident (for 2006/07 and earlier years, UK-resident or ordinarily resident), the chargeable amount is the lesser of

- the amount on which the trustees would be chargeable to CGT by virtue of *TCGA 1992, Sch 4B* on the assumption that the double tax relief arrangements did not apply, and
- the amount on which the trustees would be so chargeable to CGT by virtue of disposals of 'protected assets' (as defined by *TCGA 1992, s 88(4)* — see 44.14 above under Dual resident settlements).

In computing the chargeable amount the effect of *TCGA 1992, ss 77–79* (under which a settlor having an interest in a UK-resident settlement is chargeable on gains of the trustees in certain circumstances — see 57.5 SETTLEMENTS) is ignored.

Gains attributed to the settlor means the tapered amount of any chargeable gains (i.e. the amount after deducting taper relief at the rate which would apply if such relief were available to the trustees — see 44.13 above) arising by virtue of the transfer of value that

(*a*) are treated as accruing to the settlor under *TCGA 1992, s 86(4)* (see 44.5 above), disregarding any losses arising otherwise than under *TCGA 1992, Sch 4B*, or

(*b*) where *TCGA 1992, s 10A* applies (charge on individuals temporarily non-resident in the UK — see 45.4 OVERSEAS MATTERS and also 44.13 above), are treated as accruing to the settlor in the year of his return to the UK.

Allowable losses. The allowable losses that may be deducted in arriving at the Schedule 4B trust gains in relation to a transfer of value by the trustees of a settlement are losses arising under *TCGA 1992, Sch 4B* in relation to other transfers of value by those trustees, and any such loss is deductible *only* in accordance with the following rules.

- The loss is deducted first from chargeable amounts arising from other transfers of value made in the same tax year.
- If there is more than one chargeable amount and the aggregate allowable losses is less than the aggregate chargeable amounts, each of the chargeable amounts is reduced proportionately.
- If in any tax year the aggregate allowable losses exceeds the aggregate chargeable amounts, the excess is carried forward to the following tax year and treated as if it were an allowable loss arising in relation to a transfer of value made in that following year.

Losses are deducted from chargeable amounts after any deduction for gains attributed to the settlor as above.

[*TCGA 1992, Sch 4C paras 3–7; FA 2003, s 163(2)(4), Sch 29 para 5; FA 2006, Sch 12 paras 34(1)–(3), 35, 36*].

Computation of outstanding section 87/89 gains. The amount of '*outstanding section 87/89 gains*' of a settlement at the end of a tax year is given by

G – B + NC, where

G = the amount of the settlement's section 87/89 gains for the year (see below);

B = the amount of the gains treated as accruing in that year to beneficiaries under *TCGA 1992, s 87(4)* or *s 89(2)*; and

NC = the amount of gains so treated as accruing in that year to beneficiaries who were not chargeable to tax for that year.

For the above purposes, a settlement's section 87/89 gains for a year are the amount of the 'trust gains for the year' within 44.14 above (but including any chargeable gains or allowable losses accruing by virtue of *TCGA 1992, Sch 4B*) plus any amount treated as such under *TCGA 1992, s 90* (see 43.13 above under 'Transfers between settlements').

[*TCGA 1992, s 85A(3), Sch 4C para 7A; FA 2003, s 163(1)(2)(4), Sch 29 para 3*].

44.20 **Increase in tax payable by beneficiary receiving capital payments.** Where

- a capital payment is made by the trustees of a settlement;
- chargeable gains are treated as accruing in respect of the payment under 44.19 above; and
- a beneficiary is accordingly charged to tax in respect of the payment,

the tax payable is increased by an amount equal to the interest that would be yielded if an amount equal to that tax carried interest for the 'chargeable period' at the rate specified in *TCGA 1992, s 91(3)* (i.e. 10% per annum — see 44.15 above), except that it cannot be increased beyond the amount of the payment.

The '*chargeable period*' is the period which

(*a*) begins with the later of

(i) 1 December in the tax year following the 'year of the gain', and

(ii) 1 December falling 6 years before 1 December in the tax year following that in which the capital payment is made; and

(*b*) ends with 30 November in the tax year following that in which the capital payment is made.

For this purpose, the '*year of the gain*' is, in the case of a Schedule 4B trust gain, the tax year in which the transfer of value took place, or, in the case of a section 87/89 gain, the year in which it first forms part of the settlement's 'trust gains for the year' (see 44.14 above).

[*TCGA 1992, Sch 4C paras 8B(3), 13; FA 2003, Sch 29 paras 4, 6(3)*].

44.21 INFORMATION REQUIRED TO BE RETURNED IN RESPECT OF SETTLEMENTS WITH A FOREIGN ELEMENT

There are extensive requirements for information relating to 'settlements with a foreign element' to be returned to HMRC within certain time limits *without a notice to make a return having to be given by HMRC*. Penalties under *TMA 1970, s 98* apply for failure to comply although no failure will arise where information already has been returned or will be returned later under any other provision. In particular, the following requirements should be observed.

(*a*) Where property is transferred after 16 March 1998, otherwise than by way of an arm's length transaction or in pursuance of a liability incurred on or before that date, to a settlement created before 17 March 1998 which is non-UK resident at the time of transfer, a return of certain particulars must be made by the transferor within twelve months of the day ('the relevant day') of the transfer if he knows, or has reason to believe, the residence status of the settlement. (Before 17 March 1998, this requirement operated only in relation to transfers to settlements created before 19 March 1991.)

(*b*) Where a settlement is created at a time after 18 March 1991 which, at that time, is either non-UK resident or both UK resident and, under double tax relief arrangements, resident elsewhere, a return of certain particulars must be made by the settlor within twelve months of the day ('*the relevant day*') he first fulfils after 2 May 1994 the condition that he is UK domiciled and UK resident or ordinarily resident, not having met that condition at the time of the settlement's creation. Similarly, where such a settlement is created after 2 May 1994, a return of certain particulars must be made by the settlor who meets the above condition at the time of the settlement's creation within *three months* of the day ('*the relevant day*') on which the settlement was created.

(*c*) Where a settlement becomes at any time ('*the relevant time*') after 2 May 1994 non-UK resident or, whilst continuing to be UK resident becomes at any time ('*the relevant time*') after 2 May 1994, under double tax relief arrangements, resident elsewhere, a return of certain particulars must be made by a person who was a trustee immediately before the relevant time within *twelve months* of the day ('*the relevant day*') when the relevant time falls.

[*TCGA 1992, s 98A, Sch 5A; FA 1994, s 97(1)–(3)(6); FA 1998, Sch 22 para 5; FA 2006, Sch 12 paras 30, 34*].

Returns of information should be made to Centre for Non-Residents, Non-Resident Trusts, St John's House, Merton Road, Bootle, Merseyside L69 9BB. Tel. 0151–472 6265.

45 Overseas Matters

Cross-references. See 6.2 ASSETS for location of assets; 13.18 COMPANIES for European Companies (SEs); 15.5 COMPUTATION OF GAINS AND LOSSES for acquisitions from persons neither resident nor ordinarily resident in the UK after 9 March 1981 and before 6 April 1985; 19 DOUBLE TAX RELIEF for relief which may be claimable and for double tax agreements which may override or amend statutory provisions; 33 HOLD-OVER RELIEFS for clawback of relief where transferee becomes before 19 March 1991 neither resident nor ordinarily resident in the UK; 41.1 MARKET VALUE for special market value rules which apply to disposals by persons neither resident nor ordinarily resident in the UK after 9 March 1981 and before 6 April 1985; 44 OFFSHORE SETTLEMENTS for provisions dealing with settlements whose trustees are, or become, neither resident nor ordinarily resident in the UK; 46.4 PARTNERSHIPS for partnerships controlled and managed abroad; 52 RESIDENCE AND DOMICILE for the determination of a person's residence, ordinary residence and domicile status; 57.4 SETTLEMENTS for the residence status of settlements; and 64.4 UNDERWRITERS AT LLOYD'S for overseas resident underwriters.

Simon's Direct Tax Service. See Division C1.6.

The headings in this chapter are as follows.

45.1 INTRODUCTION

As a general rule a person is chargeable to capital gains tax in respect of chargeable gains accruing to him in a year of assessment during any part of which he is resident in the UK, or during which he is ordinarily resident in the UK. [*TCGA 1992, s 2(1)*]. However, where an individual is not domiciled in the UK but resident or ordinarily resident here, and where a person neither resident nor ordinarily resident in the UK trades etc. in the UK through a branch or agency or permanent establishment, alternative rules apply. See 45.2 and 45.3 below. See 45.3 also for the relief applying when a non-UK resident company transfers the trade of a UK branch or agency before 1 April 2000 to a UK resident company. Gains on assets acquired by an individual whilst UK resident and disposed of during a period of temporary non-residence (less than five full tax years) beginning after 16 March 1998 are charged in the tax year of his resuming UK residence — see 45.4 below.

Where a person is within the ambit of *TCGA 1992, s 2(1)* he may be unable to remit overseas gains to the UK. See 45.5 below for the special relief available in such circumstances.

Persons within *TCGA 1992, s 2(1)* may also be assessed by reference to chargeable gains accruing to non-UK resident persons with whom they have certain specified relationships. See 45.6 below for circumstances where a UK resident is a participator in a closely-held overseas resident company; and see 44 OFFSHORE SETTLEMENTS where a UK domiciled individual is a beneficiary of an overseas resident settlement and where a UK domiciled settlor has an interest in an overseas resident settlement.

Where a UK resident company has an interest in a 'controlled foreign company' and where a UK resident has 'offshore income gains' arising out of certain interests in 'offshore funds', there may be a capital gains tax effect. See 45.7 and 45.8 below.

A special relief is available where a UK resident company transfers the assets of an overseas trading branch or agency to an overseas resident company in exchange for shares in that company. See 45.9 below.

See 45.10 below for the special relief claimable where a UK trade is transferred between companies in different EC member states and 45.11 for the claim and double taxation relief available where a non-UK trade is transferred between companies in different EC member states.

There are 'exit charges' and provisions for the recovery of unpaid tax where a company ceases to be UK resident etc., is a dual resident company (before 30 November 1993) or is not resident in the UK. See 45.12 and 45.13 below. See also 44.2 OFFSHORE SETTLEMENTS for the 'exit charge' where trustees of a settlement cease to be UK-resident etc.

For exploration and exploitation rights to the UK territorial sea-bed, see 45.14 below.

For European Economic Interest Groupings, see 45.15 below.

For the collection of tax where an overseas element is involved, see 45.16 below.

Regulations (*SI 1998 No 3177*) have been made to modify the application of the Taxes Acts on the introduction of the European single currency in certain countries other than the UK on 1 January 1999. The regulations are meant to prevent unintended tax consequences arising as a result of the conversion of the currencies of participating EU member states into euros. Broadly, they provide for continuity of treatment for assets, contracts, financial instruments etc. redenominated in euros, and grant tax relief, by means of a deduction from profits, for the costs of converting a company's shares or other securities into euros. (Revenue Press Release 17 December 1998). See 6.1 ASSETS, 22.5 EXEMPTIONS AND RELIEFS and 58.7 SHARES AND SECURITIES for specific CGT measures included.

45.2 INDIVIDUALS NOT DOMICILED IN THE UK DISPOSING OF OVERSEAS ASSETS

Individuals not domiciled in the UK, but resident or ordinarily resident here, are liable on gains arising in the UK, but gains accruing after 5 April 1965 from disposals of assets abroad are chargeable if, and only so far as, remitted here (with no allowance for losses arising abroad). [*TCGA 1992, s 12(1), s 16(4)*]. For this purpose, gains effectively transferred to the UK through loan, etc. transactions as under the REMITTANCE BASIS (51) are treated as if remitted here. [*TCGA 1992, s 12(2); ITTOIA 2005, Sch 1 para 429*].

45.3 NON-UK RESIDENT TRADING ETC. IN THE UK THROUGH PERMANENT ESTABLISHMENT OR BRANCH OR AGENCY

Disposals and other events after 13 March 1989. Subject to transitional provisions and any other exceptions in the legislation, for disposals after 13 March 1989 a person is chargeable to capital gains tax in respect of chargeable gains accruing to him in a year of assessment in which he is not resident and not ordinarily resident in the UK and which are made at a time when he is carrying on a trade, profession or vocation in the UK through a 'branch or agency', and is so chargeable on chargeable gains accruing on the disposal

(*a*) of assets situated in the UK and used in or for the purposes of the trade, profession or vocation at or before the time when the gain accrued, or (*b*) of assets situated in the UK and used or held for the purposes of the branch or agency at or before that time, or assets acquired for use by or for the purposes of the branch or agency.

The commercial letting of FURNISHED HOLIDAY ACCOMMODATION (24.2) in the UK, although treated as a trade for certain capital gains tax provisions, is not so treated for the purposes of *TCGA 1992, s 10*.

Companies. These provisions are applied for accounting periods beginning before 1 January 2003 to companies not resident in the UK carrying on a trade or vocation through a UK branch or agency as for individuals not resident and not ordinarily resident in the UK in arriving at their chargeable profits for an accounting period. [*TCGA 1992, s 10(1)–(3)(5)*]. For accounting periods of non-resident companies beginning after 31 December 2002, the above provisions apply with the substitution of the term 'permanent establishment' for 'branch or agency'. [*TCGA 1992, s 10B; FA 2003, s 149(4)(6)*]. For this purpose, and for chargeable gains purposes generally, a company has a '*permanent establishment*' in a territory if

(i) it has a 'fixed place of business' there through which the business of the company is wholly or partly carried on, or

(ii) an agent (other than one of independent status acting in the ordinary course of his business) acting on behalf of the company has and habitually exercises there authority to do business on behalf of the company,

unless the activities carried on there are only of a 'preparatory or auxiliary character'. A '*fixed place of business*' includes a place of management, a branch, an office, a factory, a workshop, an installation or structure for the exploration of natural resources, a mine, an oil or gas well, a quarry or other place of extraction of natural resources, or a building, construction or installation project. Activities of a '*preparatory or auxiliary character*' include the use of facilities for the purpose of storage, display or delivery of goods or merchandise belonging to the company; the maintenance of a stock of goods or merchandise belonging to the company for the purpose of storage, display, delivery or processing by another person; or purchasing goods or merchandise, or collecting information, for the company. Where 'alternative finance return' within *FA 2005, s 47* or 'profit share return' within *FA 2005, s 49A* (alternative finance arrangements; see Tolley's Corporation Tax) is paid to a non-UK resident company, the company is not regarded as having a permanent establishment in the UK merely by virtue of anything done for the purposes of the arrangements by the other party or any other person acting for the company. [*TCGA 1992, s 288(1); FA 2003, s 148; FA 2005, s 48(2); FA 2006, s 95(9)*].

1989 transitional provisions. Under transitional provisions, a person was chargeable under *TCGA 1992, s 10(1)* (formerly *CGTA 1979, s 12(1)*) above for 1988/89 in respect of a disposal made after 13 March 1989 if he ceased to carry on a *trade* (but not a *profession or vocation*) in the UK through a branch or agency before 14 March 1989 but a person is not to be chargeable under *TCGA 1992, s 10(1)* for 1988/89 and later years of assessment where he carries on a profession or vocation in the UK through a branch or agency in respect of chargeable gains accruing on the disposal of assets only used in or for the purposes of the profession or vocation before 14 March 1989 or only used or held for the purposes of the branch or agency before that date. [*TCGA 1992, s 10(5)*].

As a further transitional measure, where immediately before 14 March 1989 a person was not resident and not ordinarily resident in the UK but was carrying on a *profession* or *vocation* (but not a *trade*) in the UK through a branch or agency, he was deemed to have disposed immediately before 14 March 1989 of every specified asset and to have immediately reacquired every such asset, all such deemed transactions being treated as made at market value at that time. An asset was specified for this purpose if it was held by the person concerned immediately before 14 March 1989 and if at the beginning of 14 March 1989 it was a 'chargeable asset' in relation to him by virtue of his carrying on the profession or vocation. For this purpose an asset was at the beginning of 14 March 1989 a '*chargeable asset*' in relation to the person if, had it been disposed of at that time, any chargeable gains accruing would have been chargeable under *TCGA 1992, s 10(1)* above. [*FA 1989, s 126(3)–(5)*]. (No chargeable gain actually arose on the deemed disposal immediately before 14 March 1989 as professions and vocations were not then within the charge of *TCGA 1992, s 10(1)* and the broad effect was that the assets of a person carrying on a profession or vocation which became within the charge of *TCGA 1992, s 10(1)* were re-based to their market value on that date.)

Deemed disposals. Where an asset ceases after 13 March 1989 by virtue of becoming situated outside the UK to be a 'chargeable asset' (as below) in relation to a person, he is deemed to have disposed of the asset immediately before the time when the asset becomes situated outside the UK and immediately to have reacquired it, both such transactions being treated as made at market value. This does not apply where the asset becomes situated outside the UK contemporaneously with the person involved ceasing to carry on a trade, profession or vocation in the UK through a branch or agency (see below), or, in the case of a non-resident company in an accounting period beginning after 31 December 2002, through a permanent establishment (see above), or where the asset is an '*exploration or exploitation asset*' (i.e. an asset used in connection with 'exploration or exploitation activities' carried on in the UK or a 'designated area' as defined by *TCGA 1992, s 276* in 45.14 below; in this case comparable provisions apply). [*TCGA 1992, s 25(1)(2)(8); FA 2003, s 153(2)(b)(4)*].

Where an asset ceases to be a chargeable asset in relation to a person by virtue of his ceasing after 13 March 1989 to carry on a trade, profession or vocation in the UK through a branch or agency, or, in the case of a non-resident company in an accounting period beginning after 31 December 2002, through a permanent establishment, he is deemed to have disposed of the asset immediately before the time when he ceased to carry on the trade, profession or vocation in the UK through the branch or agency or permanent establishment and immediately to have reacquired it, both such transactions being treated as made at market value. The deemed disposal and reacquisition does not apply to an asset which is a chargeable asset in relation to the person concerned at any time after he ceases to carry on the trade, profession or vocation in the UK through a branch or agency or permanent establishment and before the end of the chargeable period in which he does so. There is no deemed disposal and reacquisition of an asset to which a claim for relief under *TCGA 1992, s 172* applies (see below under transfer of UK branch or agency before 1 April 2000). HMRC take a similar view as regards relief under *TCGA 1992, s 162* (see 33.10 HOLD-OVER RELIEFS) (Taxation Practitioner May 1990 p 232). Similarly, there is no deemed disposal and reacquisition on a transfer within *TCGA 1992, s 140A* of a UK trade between companies in different EC member states (see 45.10 below).

There is no deemed disposal and reacquisition of an asset by reason of the transfer of the trade by a company to another company in circumstances such that the assets transferred are transferred on or after 1 April 2000 at no gain/no loss by virtue of *TCGA 1992, s 139* or *s 171* (see, respectively, 13.10 COMPANIES and 27.2 GROUPS OF COMPANIES). Previously, there was no deemed disposal and reacquisition of an asset by reason of a transfer of the whole or part of the long term business of an insurance company to another company if *TCGA 1992, s 139* had effect in relation to the asset by virtue of *TCGA 1992, s 211* (see Tolley's Corporation Tax under Life Insurance Companies).

[*TCGA 1992, s 25(3)–(6)(8), s 140A(4)(b), s 172(2)(b); F(No 2)A 1992, s 44; FA 2000, Sch 29 para 6; FA 2003, s 153(2)(b)(4)*].

For the purposes of *TCGA 1992, s 25* above, an asset is at any time a '*chargeable asset*' in relation to a person if, were it to be disposed of at that time, any chargeable gains accruing to him on the disposal either would be chargeable under *TCGA 1992, s 10(1)* or would form part of his chargeable profits for corporation tax purposes by virtue of *TCGA 1992, s 10(3)* or *s 10B*. [*TCGA 1992, s 25(7); FA 2003, Sch 27 para 2*].

Rollover relief. Where the disposal of the 'old assets' or the acquisition of the 'new assets' (or both) (within the meaning of *TCGA 1992, s 152*, see 55 ROLLOVER RELIEF) takes place after 13 March 1989, rollover relief under that provision is not to apply if the old assets are 'chargeable assets' (having the same meaning as in *TCGA 1992, s 25* above) in relation to the person concerned at the time of disposal unless the new assets are chargeable assets in relation to him immediately after the time they are acquired.

References to acquisition of the new assets include references to acquisition of an interest in them or to entering into an unconditional contract for the acquisition of them. However, rollover relief may apply where the acquisition of the new assets occurs before 14 March 1989 and the disposal of the old assets is after 13 March 1989 but within twelve months (or such longer period as is allowed by written notice given by HMRC) of the acquisition of the new assets.

Rollover relief will, however, apply, where the acquisition of the new assets takes place after the disposal of the old assets and immediately after the time of acquisition the person concerned is resident or ordinarily resident in the UK, unless he is also then a 'dual resident' and the new assets are 'prescribed assets'. A '*dual resident*' is a person who is resident or ordinarily resident in the UK and falls to be regarded under any DOUBLE TAX RELIEF (19.2) arrangements as resident overseas. A '*prescribed asset*', in relation to a dual resident, is one which under any double tax relief arrangements would not give rise to a UK tax charge on him in respect of a gain accruing to him on a disposal of it.

[*TCGA 1992, s 159; FA 2003, Sch 27 para 2*].

Non-payment of tax attributable to TCGA 1992, s 10(3) by non-resident company. See 45.13 below.

General provisions for disposals. No charge to tax under *TCGA 1992, s 10* or *s 10B* applies to a person who, by virtue of any relevant double tax agreement, is exempt from income tax or corporation tax for the particular period in respect of profits or gains from the permanent establishment or branch or agency. [*TCGA 1992, ss 10(4), 10B(3); FA 2003, ss 149(4), 155, Sch 27 para 2*].

'*Branch or agency*' means, for *TCGA 1992, s 10* and capital gains tax provisions generally, any factorship, agency, receivership, branch or management but excludes any general agents or brokers carrying on *bona fide* business as such who act for non-residents and are exempt under *TMA 1970, s 82*. [*TCGA 1992, s 10(6)*]. For consideration of this definition in relation to a partnership where two of the partners were resident outside the UK at the time of disposal of a partnership asset but the third partner was UK resident at that time, see *White v Carline (Sp C 33), [1995] SSCD 186*. See also *Puddu v Doleman (Sp C 38), [1995] SSCD 236* (where a non-UK resident sole trader employed a supervisor to manage the UK trading activity) and *Willson v Hooker Ch D 1995, 67 TC 585* (where a UK resident individual was held to be an agent, not exempted by *TMA 1970, s 82*, of a non-UK resident company in relation to the company's purchase and subsequent sale of UK land, being transactions in which the individual was closely involved). (*TMA 1970, s 82* was repealed for 1996/97 and subsequent years and for company accounting periods beginning after 31 March 1996. See now UK representatives of non-residents below.)

Losses accruing to a person in a year of assessment during no part of which he is resident or ordinarily resident in the UK are not allowable unless, under *TCGA 1992, s 10* or, for accounting periods ending after 15 March 2005, *TCGA 1992, s 10B* above, he would be chargeable in respect of a chargeable gain if there had been a gain instead of a loss on that occasion. [*TCGA 1992, s 16(3); F(No 2)A 2005, Sch 4 paras 7, 10(2)*].

See 52.3 RESIDENCE AND DOMICILE for the exclusion, after 5 April 1989, of extra-statutory concession D2 in respect of the period from the cessation of UK residence to the end of the year of assessment.

UK representatives of non-residents. For 1996/97 and subsequent years and for company accounting periods beginning after 31 March 1996 and before 1 January 2003, certain obligations and liabilities fall upon UK representatives of non-residents carrying on a trade in the UK through a branch or agency. Provided detailed conditions are satisfied, certain persons, e.g. casual agents, brokers, investment managers and persons acting in relation to alternative finance arrangements within *FA 2005, s 47* or *s 49A*, are not treated as UK representatives for these purposes. Subject to this, a branch or agency in the UK through which a non-resident carries on (solely or in partnership) a trade, profession or vocation is his UK representative in relation to capital gains arising in connection with the branch or agency and chargeable under *TCGA 1992, s 10*. Where the non-resident ceases to carry on the trade etc. through the branch or agency, it continues to be his UK representative for tax purposes in relation to amounts arising during the period of the agency.

For accounting periods beginning after 31 December 2002 for corporation tax purposes only, references in the legislation to a 'branch or agency' are replaced by references to a 'permanent establishment' (see above). Consequently, for such accounting periods, a UK permanent establishment through which a non-resident company carries on a trade is its UK representative in relation to chargeable gains within *TCGA 1992, s 10B* arising in connection with the permanent establishment. Where the company ceases to carry on the trade through the permanent establishment, it continues to be the UK representative for tax purposes in relation to amounts arising during the period of trading. Subject to detailed conditions, certain brokers, investment managers and Lloyd's agents in relation to certain transactions are not regarded as UK representatives of non-resident companies.

A UK representative is regarded as a legal entity distinct from the non-resident.

As regards the taxation of any amounts in relation to which a non-UK resident has a UK representative, legislation making provision for, or in connection with, the assessment, collection and recovery of income tax, corporation tax and capital gains tax, and interest on tax, has effect as if the obligations and liabilities of the non-resident were *also* obligations and liabilities of the UK representative.

[*FA 1995, ss 126, 127, Sch 23; FA 2003, ss 150, 152, 155, Schs 26, 27 paras 4, 5; ITTOIA 2005, Sch 1 para 479; FA 2005, s 48(3); FA 2006, s 95(10)*]. For the full provisions, see Tolley's Income Tax under Non-Residents and Tolley's Corporation Tax under Residence.

Transfer of UK branch or agency before 1 April 2000. For disposals after 19 March 1990 and before 1 April 2000 a relief for the purposes of corporation tax on chargeable gains applies where

(*a*) there is a scheme for the transfer by a non-UK resident 'company' ('company A') which carries on a trade in the UK through a branch or agency of the whole or part of the trade to a UK resident company ('company B'),

(*b*) company A disposes of an asset to company B in accordance with the scheme at a time when both companies are members of the same 'group', and

(*c*) a claim under *TCGA 1992, s 172(1)* relating to the asset is made by both companies within two years after the end of the accounting period of company B during which the disposal is made.

'*Company*' and '*group*' have the same meanings as in *TCGA 1992, s 170* but ignoring *subsections (2)(a)* and *(9)* thereof (references to company only to include UK resident companies etc. incorporated under UK and overseas legislation etc.). For disposals on or after 1 April 2000, the relief is made redundant by the change in the residence requirement as regards groups of companies. See 27.1 GROUPS OF COMPANIES.

The relief given is that, firstly, the asset is treated as disposed of by company A and acquired by company B for a no gain, no loss consideration and, secondly, *TCGA 1992, s 25(3)* (deemed disposal by non-resident on ceasing to trade in the UK through a branch or agency; see above under disposals and other events after 13 March 1989) is not to apply to the asset by reason of the transfer.

The relief did not apply on a disposal before 30 November 1993 where company B was UK resident but under any double tax relief arrangements was regarded as resident elsewhere and would not have been liable to UK tax on a gain arising on the disposal of the asset occurring immediately after its acquisition. Relief is also denied if company B is a 'dual resident investing company' within *ICTA 1988, s 404* or an 'investment trust' within *ICTA 1988, s 842*. No relief is given unless any gain accruing to company A on the disposal of the asset in accordance with the scheme, or, where that disposal occurs after the transfer has taken place, on a disposal of the asset immediately before the transfer, would be a chargeable gain and would, under *TCGA 1992, s 10(3)* above, form part of its profits for corporation tax purposes.

[*TCGA 1992, s 172; FA 1994, s 251(1)(7), Sch 26 Pt VIII; FA 2000, Sch 29 para 3*].

FOREX. The following applies where there is a disposal or acquisition of currency; a 'qualifying asset' consisting of the right to settlement under a debt which is not a debt on a security (within *TCGA 1992, s 132*; see 22.5 EXEMPTIONS AND RELIEFS); a 'qualifying asset' consisting of the right to settlement under a debt on a security; or an obligation which by virtue of *TCGA 1992, s 143* (futures contracts; see 6.8 ASSETS) is regarded as an asset to the disposal of which *TCGA 1992* applies and which is a duty under a currency contract. Where the disposal or acquisition is by a 'qualifying company' and is made on or after the company's 'commencement day', and immediately before the disposal or after the acquisition, as the case may be, the asset is held wholly for 'qualifying purposes', and *TCGA 1992, s 172* (now repealed — see above) would otherwise apply, that provision does not apply as regards the disposal or acquisition and the corresponding acquisition or disposal. '*Qualifying purposes*' are purposes of long-term or mutual insurance business. [*FA 1993, s 169, Sch 17 para 7; FA 2000, Sch 29 para 43; FA 2002, Sch 40 Pt 3(10); SI 2001 No 3629, Art 81*]. See 14.15 COMPANIES—CORPORATE FINANCE AND INTANGIBLES for a note of the terms quoted and not otherwise defined.

45.4 INDIVIDUALS TEMPORARILY NON-RESIDENT IN THE UK

Conditions. The following provisions apply where an individual leaves the UK **after 16 March 1998** for a period of temporary residence outside the UK, and

- four out of the seven years of assessment immediately preceding the 'year of departure' were years for which the individual satisfied 'the residence requirements', and
- there are fewer than five years of assessment (the '*intervening years*') falling between (and not including) the 'year of departure' and the 'year of return'.

For the purposes of these provisions, the '*year of departure*' means the last year of assessment before the year of return for which the taxpayer satisfied the 'residence requirements'. The '*year of return*' is any year of assessment for which the individual satisfies the 'residence requirements' and which immediately follows one or more years of assessment for which he did not satisfy those requirements.

An individual satisfies the '*residence requirements*' for a tax year if during any part of the year he is resident in the UK and not 'treaty non-resident' or if during the year he is ordinarily resident in the UK and not treaty non-resident. This definition is as amended by *F(No 2)A 2005, s 32* and applies where the year of departure is, or (on the assumption that the definition as amended had always had effect) would be, 2005/06 or a subsequent year and also applies where the year of departure is (or on the same assumption would be) 2004/05 if at a time in that year on or after 16 March 2005 the individual was resident or ordinarily resident in the UK and not treaty non-resident.

Previously, an individual satisfied the '*residence requirements*' for a tax year if that year was one during any part of which he was resident in the UK or during which he was ordinarily resident in the UK.

For the meaning of 'resident' and 'ordinarily resident' see 52 RESIDENCE AND DOMICILE. An individual is '*treaty non-resident*' at any time if he falls at that time to be regarded for the purposes of DOUBLE TAX RELIEF (19) arrangements as resident in a territory outside the UK.

The charge. Where the above conditions apply, and subject to the exclusions below, the individual is chargeable to capital gains tax as if all the chargeable gains and losses which accrued to him in the intervening years were gains or losses accruing to him in the year of return. Any gains or losses accruing in the year of departure (whether accruing before or after the date of departure), and any gains or losses accruing in the year of return (whether accruing before or after the date of return) are chargeable to capital gains tax in the year of departure or return under general principles (*TCGA 1992, s 2(1)* — see 45.1 above). The treatment otherwise available under ESC D2 (whereby, subject to certain conditions, an individual is charged to capital gains tax in respect of gains accruing in a year in which his residence status changes only to the extent that the gains accrued from disposals made before his departure or, as the case may be, after his return) does not apply where the above conditions are satisfied. See 52.3 RESIDENCE AND DOMICILE.

The chargeable gains to be treated as accruing in the year of return include any chargeable gains which would have been treated as having accrued to him in any intervening year, if he had been resident in the UK throughout that year, under

(i) *TCGA 1992, s 13* (gains of non-resident companies attributed to members — see 45.6 below); or

(ii) *TCGA 1992, s 86* (attribution of gains to settlers with an interest in non-resident or dual-resident settlements — see 44.5 OFFSHORE SETTLEMENTS).

Where (i) above applies, any losses accruing to the non-resident company in an intervening year which, under 45.6 below, would have been allowable to the individual if he had been UK-resident throughout that year are treated as accruing in the year of return but only to the extent that such losses do not exceed the amount of the gains of the company (or another non-resident company) attributed to the individual for that same year and similarly treated.

Where (ii) above applies, see 44.13 OFFSHORE SETTLEMENTS for details of the limitation on the amount to be brought into charge where beneficiaries of the settlement have been charged in respect of capital payments from the settlement.

Where a tax year is an intervening year only because the taxpayer is at some time in that year treaty non-resident, gains attributed to him under *TCGA 1992, ss 87 or 89(2)* (attribution of gains to beneficiaries of OFFSHORE SETTLEMENTS (44.14)) for that year are not chargeable in the year of return under these provisions. The year is treated as not being an intervening year for the purpose of attributing gains under (i) and (ii) above.

Where these provisions apply, any assessment to capital gains tax may be made for the year of departure at any time before the second anniversary of 31st January following the year of return.

Where the amended definition of the residence requirements above applies, nothing in any DOUBLE TAX RELIEF (19) arrangements is to be read as preventing the taxpayer from being chargeable to capital gains tax under the above provisions in respect of gains other than those attributed under (i) and (ii) above. Previously, the provisions did not prejudice any right to claim double tax relief under a bilateral agreement.

Exclusions from the charge. The gains or losses treated as accruing in the year of return do not include a gain or loss on the disposal of an asset in the intervening years if it was acquired by the taxpayer at a time either in the year of departure or in an intervening year when he was neither resident nor ordinarily resident in the UK or, where the amended definition of the residence requirements above applies, when he was resident or ordinarily resident in the UK but was treaty non-resident, provided that

(*a*) the asset was not acquired by means of a 'relevant disposal' (see below) which is treated as having been a disposal on which neither a gain nor a loss accrued, by virtue of *TCGA 1992, s 58* (transfer between husband and wife — see 42.4 MARRIED PERSONS AND CIVIL PARTNERS), *TCGA 1992, s 73* (reversion of settled property to settlor on death of person entitled to interest in possession — see 57.17 SETTLEMENTS) or *TCGA 1992, s 258(4)* (gifts of national heritage property — see 22.80 EXEMPTIONS AND RELIEFS);

(*b*) that asset is not an interest created by or arising under a settlement; and

(*c*) the acquisition cost of the asset to the taxpayer does not fall, by reference to any 'relevant disposal' (see below), to be treated as reduced under any of the following provisions:

- *TCGA 1992, s 23(4)(b)* or *(5)(b)* (rollover where the replacement asset is acquired after receipt of compensation or insurance money — see 9.3 CAPITAL SUMS DERIVED FROM ASSETS);
- *TCGA 1992, s 152(1)(b)* (ROLLOVER RELIEF (55) on business assets);
- (in relation to relevant disposals made on or after 16 March 2005) *TCGA 1992, s 153(1)(b)* (ROLLOVER RELIEF (55) on business assets where assets only partly replaced);
- *TCGA 1992, s 162(3)(b)* (hold-over relief where shares are acquired on the disposal of a business to a company — see 33.10 HOLD-OVER RELIEFS);
- *TCGA 1992, s 247(2)(b)* or *(3)(b)* (rollover relief where replacement land is acquired on the compulsory acquisition of other land — see 38.11 LAND).

For the purposes of (*a*) and (*c*) above, a '*relevant disposal*' is a disposal of an asset acquired by the person making the disposal at a time when that person was resident or ordinarily resident in the UK and was not treaty non-resident. Where the acquisition by the person making the disposal was before 16 March 2005, the requirement was simply that the acquisition had to be made at a time when that person was resident or ordinarily resident in the UK.

Note that this exclusion does not apply to assets acquired within a non-resident trust to which the provisions of *TCGA 1992, ss 86, 87* (see 44.5, 44.14 OFFSHORE SETTLEMENTS) apply or a non-resident company to which *TCGA 1992, s 13* (see 45.6 below) applies.

Where a chargeable gain has accrued on the disposal of an asset which is not within (*a*)–(*c*) above, but the gain falls to be postponed by virtue of one of the following CGT deferral provisions and treated as accruing on the disposal of the whole or part of another asset which *is* within (*a*)–(*c*) above, the above exclusion from the charge does not apply. The said provisions are:

- *TCGA 1992, s 116(10)* or *(11)* (deferral of gain arising on a company reconstruction where the new asset is a QUALIFYING CORPORATE BOND (see 50.3));
- *TCGA 1992, s 134* (deferral of gain arising where gilts are acquired as compensation for compulsory acquisition of SHARES AND SECURITIES (see 58.7);
- *TCGA 1992, s 154(2)* or *(4)* (deferral of gain on a business asset where a depreciating asset is acquired as replacement — see 55.7 ROLLOVER RELIEF).

Also excluded from the charge is any chargeable gain or allowable loss accruing to the taxpayer in an intervening year which is brought into account for that year under *TCGA 1992, s 10, s 16(3)* (non-residents carrying on a trade etc. in the UK through a branch or agency — see 45.3 above).

[*TCGA 1992, ss 10A, 288(7B); FA 1998, s 127(1)(4); F(No 2)A 2005, s 32; FA 2006, s 74(3)(4)(6)*].

45.5 RELIEF FOR UNREMITTABLE OVERSEAS GAINS

Where chargeable gains accrue from assets situated abroad and the taxpayer is unable with reasonable endeavour to transfer those gains to the UK due to the laws of the territory where the assets were situated at the time of disposal, or to the executive action of its government, or to the impossibility of obtaining foreign currency in that territory, he may claim under *TCGA 1992, s 279(1)* that they be left out of account. No claim shall be made for the purposes of capital gains tax later than the fifth anniversary of 31 January following the year of assessment in which the gains arose; or in the case of corporation tax more than six years after the end of the accounting period in which the gains arose. The gains are then treated as gains of the year, if any, in which the conditions cease to apply. The claim is open to personal representatives.

For capital gains tax purposes, the gain to be left out of account in the first instance is the untapered gain. The availability of taper relief when the gain is brought into charge is determined by reference to the original disposal date (see 61.15 TAPER RELIEF).

[*TCGA 1992, s 279(1)–(3)(5)(6)(8); FA 1996, Sch 20 para 64, Sch 21 para 41; FA 1998, s 121(3)(4), Sch 21 para 9*].

These provisions cannot be relied upon as a defence against an assessment under *TCGA 1992, s 13* (see 45.6 below) if the taxpayer's inability to transfer the gain to the UK is owing to the company's failure to distribute the gain. Relief can only be given if the gain is represented by money, or money's worth, in the hands of the taxpayer (*Van Arkadie v Plunket, Ch D 1982, 56 TC 310*).

See 37.6 INTEREST AND SURCHARGES ON UNPAID TAX for an alternative relief given to interest on tax overdue, where collection of tax is deferred in similar circumstances. See also 42.1 MARRIED PERSONS AND CIVIL PARTNERS where a claim for the relief above has effect before 1990/91 in respect of a wife's gains which would otherwise have been assessed on the husband.

Gains which are subject to payments made by the Export Credits Guarantee Department under statutory arrangements for export guarantees do not qualify for the relief above to the extent of such payments. [*TCGA 1992, s 279(4)*].

45.6 UK RESIDENT PARTICIPATOR IN OVERSEAS RESIDENT COMPANY

The following provisions apply where chargeable gains accrue after 27 November 1995 to a company which is not resident in the UK but which would be a close company (within *ICTA 1988, ss 414, 415* — see Tolley's Corporation Tax under Close Companies) if it were so resident. Subject to the following, every person who at the time when the gain accrues to the company is resident or ordinarily resident in the UK, who, if an individual, is domiciled in the UK, and who is a participator (within *ICTA 1988, s 417(1)*) in the company, is treated for the purposes of capital gains tax (or corporation tax on chargeable gains) as if part of the chargeable gain had accrued to him. The amount of the gain accruing to the non-resident company is computed (where it is not the case) as if the company were within the charge to UK corporation tax on chargeable gains. The gain is not eligible for taper relief.

The part that is taken as accruing to the participator is equal to the proportion of the gain that corresponds to the extent of the participator's interest as a participator in the company. However, there is **no charge** on the participator where the aggregate amount otherwise falling to be apportioned to him and to persons connected (see 16 CONNECTED PERSONS) with him does not exceed **one-tenth** of the gain (one-twentieth as regards gains accruing to the company before 7 March 2001).

References to a person's interest as a participator in a company are references to the interest in the company which is represented by all the factors by reference to which he falls to be treated as such a participator. References to the extent of such an interest are references to the proportion of the interests as participators of all the participators in the company (including any who are not resident or ordinarily resident in the UK) which on a just and reasonable apportionment is represented by that interest. Any appeal involving any question as to the extent of a person's interest as a participator is made to the Special Commissioners.

These provisions do *not* apply in relation to

- a gain accruing after 6 March 2001 on the disposal of an asset used only for the purposes of a trade carried on by the company wholly outside the UK;
- a gain accruing after 6 March 2001 on the disposal of an asset used only for the purposes of the part carried on outside the UK of a trade carried on by the company partly within and partly outside the UK;
- a gain accruing before 7 March 2001 on the disposal of *tangible property* (or a lease thereof) used only for the purposes of a trade carried on by the company wholly outside the UK;
- a gain on which the company is chargeable to UK tax by virtue of *TCGA 1992, s 10*(*3*) or *s 10B* (trade carried on via UK permanent establishment (previously branch or agency) — see 45.3 above); or
- a gain on the disposal of foreign currency or of a debt within *TCGA 1992, s 252*(*1*) (see 22.5 EXEMPTIONS AND RELIEFS) which in either case is or represents money used for the purposes of a trade carried on by the company wholly outside the UK.

Where any amount of tax (i.e. capital gains tax or corporation tax on chargeable gains) is paid by a participator as a result of the charge above and an amount in respect of the gain charged is distributed (either by way of dividend or distribution of capital or on the dissolution of the company) within a specified period, that amount of tax (so far as neither reimbursed by the company nor applied as a deduction under the further provisions below) is applied for reducing or extinguishing any liability of his to income tax, capital gains tax or corporation tax in respect of the distribution. For gains accruing after 6 March 2001, the specified period is whichever of the following ends earlier:

- the period ending three years after the end of the period of account of the non-resident company in which the gain accrued; or
- the period of four years beginning with the date the gain accrued.

For gains accruing before 7 March 2001, the specified period is the two years beginning with the date the gain accrued.

Any tax paid by the participator resulting from the above treatment (so far as neither reimbursed by the company nor applied as above for reducing any liability to tax) is treated as allowable expenditure in the computation of the gain arising on his disposal of any asset representing his interest as a participator in the company (e.g. shares in the company by reference to which he is a participator). (This applies also to tax paid under *TCGA 1992, s 13* as it applied to gains accruing before 28 November 1995.)

In ascertaining for the purposes above the amount of capital gains tax or income tax chargeable on a participator for any year on or in respect of any chargeable gain or distribution (*a*) any distribution as is mentioned above which falls to be treated as his income for that year is regarded as forming the highest part of the income on which he is chargeable to tax for the year;

(*b*) any gain accruing in that year on the disposal of any asset representing his interest as a participator in the company is regarded as forming the highest part of the gains on which he is chargeable to tax for that year;

(*c*) where any distribution as is mentioned above falls to be treated as a disposal on which a gain accrues on which he is so chargeable, that gain is regarded as forming the next highest part of the gains on which he is so chargeable, after any gains falling within (*b*) above; and

(*d*) any gain treated as accruing as above to him in that year by virtue of a chargeable gain accruing to a company is regarded as the next highest part of the gains on which he is so chargeable, after any gains falling within (*c*) above.

Any loss arising on the disposal of assets by the company can be similarly treated as accruing to the participator concerned, but only insofar as it reduces or extinguishes gains accruing in the same year of assessment which are charged on him by reference to that company.

If a person who is a participator in the company at the time when the chargeable gain accrues to the company is itself a company which is not resident in the UK but which would be a close company if it were resident in the UK, an amount equal to the amount which would otherwise have been apportioned as above out of the chargeable gain to the participating company's interest as a participator in the company to which the gain accrues is further apportioned among the participators in the participating company according to the extent of their respective interests as participators, and an amount is apportioned to them as above accordingly in relation to the amounts further apportioned, and so on through any number of companies.

The person treated by these provisions as if a part of a chargeable gain accruing to a company had accrued to them expressly include the trustees of a settlement who are participators in the company, or in any company amongst the participators in which the gain is apportioned as above, if when the gain accrues to the company the trustees are neither resident nor ordinarily resident in the UK. See further in 44 OFFSHORE SETTLEMENTS. For anti-avoidance provisions concerning the attribution of gains under these provisions to trustees of a UK-resident trust, see 57.21 SETTLEMENTS. An interest held by trustees (other than bare trustees) is treated as the beneficial interest in determining if and how the gain of the non-resident company should be attributed to participators; the interests of the beneficiaries are disregarded.

A gain accruing to a non-resident company after 6 March 2001 is not attributed under these provisions to a pension scheme or superannuation fund which is exempt from capital gains tax on disposals of assets forming part of the scheme etc. (see 22.56, 22.59 EXEMPTIONS AND RELIEFS) if it would otherwise be attributed only if such exempt assets were taken into account in determining the extent of the scheme's interest as a participator.

If any tax payable by a participator as a result of a gain accruing to a non-resident company is paid by that company, or in a case where there are other intervening non-UK resident companies as above is paid by any such other company, the amount so paid is left out of account in relation to that person for income tax, capital gains tax and corporation tax purposes.

[*TCGA 1992, ss 13, 288(1); FA 1996, s 174(1)–(9); FA 1998, s 121(3)(4), s 120(4), Sch 21 para 4; FA 2001, s 80; FA 2002, s 103(3), Sch 40 Pt 3(16); FA 2003, Sch 27 para 2; FA 2004, Sch 35 para 39; FA 2006, Sch 12 para 8*].

The appropriate proportion of any overseas tax in respect of its gain which the company pays in its country of residence is deductible, by way of double tax relief, against UK capital gains tax payable by the participator. To the extent that the overseas tax cannot be relieved in this way, the deduction may be made in arriving at the amount of the gain chargeable on the participator. (HMRC Statement of Practice D23).

An individual who is 'temporarily' non-UK resident, such as to be within the charge to tax under *TCGA 1992, s 10A* on his return to the UK, is chargeable for the tax year of return on gains that would have been attributed to him under the above provisions had he remained UK-resident. See 45.4 above.

General. For the purposes of the above, the provisions at 27.2, 27.4, 27.6, 27.9 GROUPS OF COMPANIES, *TCGA 1992, s 172* (now repealed) at 45.3 above, and *TCGA 1992, s 175(1)* at 55.5 ROLLOVER RELIEF apply, with appropriate modifications, in relation to non-UK resident companies which are members of a non-UK resident group of companies as they apply in relation to members of a CGT group as in 27.1 GROUPS OF COMPANIES. [*TCGA 1992, s 14; FA 2000, Sch 29 para 16*]. The provisions mentioned in *section 14* are so applied not only where the UK-resident participator or shareholder on whom gains fall to be assessed is subject to corporation tax on chargeable gains but also where he is within the charge to capital gains tax (Revenue Tax Bulletin May 1993 p 74).

A person who holds shares in an overseas resident company can be required by notice from HMRC to provide sufficient information to give effect to the above provisions. [*TMA 1970, s 28; TCGA 1992, Sch 10 para 2(5)*].

The appropriate proportion of any overseas tax in respect of its gain which the company pays in its country of residence is deductible in computing the gain chargeable on the shareholder; alternatively, tax credit relief may be allowable for the overseas tax (HMRC Statement of Practice D23). HMRC has confirmed that where the overseas resident company is a subsidiary of a UK resident parent company and the relevant double taxation agreement has an article exempting residents of the overseas territory from a charge to UK capital gains tax, then such an article may prevent the imposition of a charge under the above provisions (CCAB Statement TR 500 March 1983).

The relief for unremittable overseas gains (see 45.5 above) is not a defence to an assessment under the above provisions. See also 45.7 below for a UK resident company having an interest in a 'controlled foreign company'.

45.7 UK RESIDENT COMPANY HAVING AN INTEREST IN A CONTROLLED FOREIGN COMPANY

Legislation relating to controlled foreign companies ('CFC's') is contained in *ICTA 1988, ss 747–756, Schs 24–26* (as amended). For full coverage of these provisions see Tolley's Corporation Tax under Controlled Foreign Companies. Broadly, the Board of Inland Revenue used to be able to direct that the provisions should apply in relation to an accounting period of a 'CFC'. For accounting periods ending on or after the appointed day for corporation tax self-assessment (1 July 1999), the provisions (as significantly amended by *FA 1998, Sch 17* and *FA 2000, Sch 31*) apply automatically whenever the conditions are met, and the Board are no longer required to make a direction. The Revenue have published guidance notes on the CFC legislation, which include the position under self-assessment and details of a comprehensive CFC clearance procedure introduced on 1 January 1999 (Revenue Press Release 18 June 1999).

A '*CFC*' is a company which is

(i) resident outside the UK for the purposes of the provisions;

(ii) 'controlled' by persons resident in the UK; and

(iii) subject to a 'lower level of taxation' in the territory in which it is 'resident'.

Where the provisions apply, a UK resident company which has an 'interest' in the CFC at any time in the accounting period is then liable to a sum as if it were corporation tax. Such sum is computed by multiplying the part of the 'chargeable profits' arising in an accounting period of the CFC that is proportionate to the interest held by the UK resident company and the 'appropriate rate' of UK corporation tax. The foregoing is subject to further detailed rules. See Tolley's Corporation Tax for these and the definitions assigned to the terms given above. Rules specifically relating to corporation tax on chargeable gains are given below.

(*a*) **Gains on disposal of shares.** Relief may be claimed where

(i) an apportionment falls to be made (before self-assessment, a direction is given) in respect of a CFC's accounting period;

(ii) a UK resident company (the '*claimant company*') disposes of shares, acquired before the end of that accounting period, in either the CFC or another company whose shares give rise to the claimant company's interest in the CFC; and

(iii) chargeable profits of the CFC are apportioned to the claimant company, and a sum is accordingly chargeable on it as if it were corporation tax.

Where a claim is made, in the computation of the chargeable gain accruing on the disposal in (ii) above, a deduction is allowed of the sum assessed as in (iii) above, reduced to the proportion thereof that the average market value, in the period for which the apportionment falls to be made, of the interest in the CFC in respect of which the charge as in (iii) above arose bears to the average market value in that period of the shares disposed of. A sum assessed as at (iii) above may only be relieved once in this way.

Relief may, however, be restricted where, before the disposal, a dividend is paid by the CFC out of profits from which the chargeable profits in (iii) above derived. If either

(1) the effect of the payment of the dividend is to reduce the value of the shares disposed of as in (ii) above; or

(2) the claimant company obtains relief (see (*b*) below) in respect of a dividend paid on the shares disposed of as in (ii) above, by reference to sums including that referred to in (iii) above,

then relief is denied in respect of so much of the sum chargeable as corresponds to the part of the chargeable profits in (iii) above corresponding to the profits which the dividend represents.

Claims for relief must be made within three months of the later of the end of the accounting period in which the disposal occurs and the date the assessment in (iii) above becomes final and conclusive. Such claims are outside the main provisions governing claims under corporation tax self-assessment (included in returns or otherwise).

Identification of shares disposed of for this purpose is with those acquired earlier before those acquired later.

[*ICTA 1988, Sch 26 para 3; FA 1998, Sch 17 paras 35, 37*].

(*b*) **Dividends from the CFC.** The total of assessments on UK resident companies under the provisions in respect of a CFC's chargeable profits (the '*gross attributed tax*') is treated as underlying tax for double taxation relief purposes (see Tolley's Corporation Tax under Double Taxation Relief) where a dividend is paid by the CFC wholly or partly out of profits from which those chargeable profits derive. The gross attributed tax is *not*, however, treated as increasing the amount of the dividend income in determining liability on that income.

If *ICTA 1988, s 796* or *s 797(1)* act to limit the foreign tax credit by reference to the UK tax on the dividends concerned, the amount so debarred from relief, insofar as it does not exceed the foreign tax *other than* underlying tax attributable to the dividend, is set against the gross attributed tax chargeable on UK resident companies. On a claim by any of those companies, the tax so chargeable on it is reduced and, if appropriate, repaid.

Any condition for double tax relief under *ICTA 1988, s 788* or *s 789* (by agreement with other countries) or *s 790* (unilateral relief) (see 19 DOUBLE TAX RELIEF) requiring a particular degree of control of the company paying the dividend is treated as satisfied for these purposes.

Where the CFC dividend is paid out of unspecified profits, and any part of its chargeable profits is apportioned other than to UK resident companies, the gross attributed tax is attributed to the proportion of the chargeable profits apportioned to UK resident companies (the '*taxed profits*'). So much of the dividend as is received by, or by a 'successor in title' of, any such company is regarded as paid primarily out of the taxed profits. '*Successor in title*' for this purpose refers to a successor in respect of the whole or part of the interest in the CFC giving rise to a charge under these provisions.

If

(i) relief has been allowed for the purposes of corporation tax on chargeable gains, on a disposal of shares, in respect of a sum chargeable under these provisions (see (*a*) above); and

(ii) that sum forms part of the gross attributed tax in relation to a dividend, as above; and

(iii) a person receiving the dividend in respect of the shares referred to in (i) above (the '*primary dividend*'), or any other dividend in respect of shares in a company resident outside the UK representing profits consisting directly or indirectly of or including the primary dividend, is entitled to relief by way of underlying tax (as above) by reference to the whole or part of the gross attributed tax,

then the relief available as in (iii) above is reduced or extinguished by deducting therefrom the amount allowed by way of relief as in (i) above.

[*ICTA 1988, Sch 26 paras 4–6; FA 1998, Sch 17 paras 36, 37*].

Simon's Direct Tax Service. See Division D4.12.

45.8 OFFSHORE FUNDS

For disposals after 31 December 1983 'offshore income gains' arising out of certain interests in 'offshore funds' which are considered not to distribute sufficient income are charged to income tax or corporation tax as income rather than to capital gains tax or corporation tax in respect of chargeable gains. Broadly, a capital gains tax treatment applies to any part of such a gain accruing before 1 January 1984 but the whole of the gain arising thereafter (without indexation allowance) is taxed as income. [*ICTA 1988, s 437(2)(a), s 441, s 660B(4), s 686A, ss 756A–764, Schs 27, 28; FA 1990, Sch 7 para 3; FA 1995, Sch 17 para 1; FA 2004, s 145, Sch 26; ITTOIA 2005, s 632, Sch 1 paras 271, 308, 309, 350; F(No 2)A 2005, s 23; FA 2006, Sch 13 paras 3, 23; SI 2004 No 2572*]. Interests held were identified under the rules applicable to securities generally before 6 April 1985 (1 April 1985 for companies). After 5 April 1985 (31 March 1985 for companies) interests are designated 'relevant securities' and amended identification rules apply. See 59.6 SHARES AND SECURITIES—IDENTIFICATION RULES. See Tolley's Income Tax under Overseas

Matters for general coverage and definitions assigned to terms used in the provisions. Rules relating to capital gains tax are given below.

Deduction of offshore income gain in determining capital gain. There are provisions in substitution of *TCGA 1992, s 37(1)* (deduction of consideration chargeable to tax on income) to prevent a double charge to tax when a disposal gives rise to both an offshore income gain and a chargeable gain for capital gains tax purposes.

(i) Where an offshore income gain arises on a 'material disposal' that gain is deducted from the sum which would otherwise constitute the amount or value of the consideration in the calculation of the capital gain arising under *TCGA 1992* although the offshore gain is not to be deducted in calculating the figure 'A' in the A/(A + B) fraction under the rules relating to part disposal. See 15.7 COMPUTATION OF GAINS AND LOSSES.

(ii) Where a capital gains tax disposal forms part of a transfer within *TCGA 1992, s 162* (see 33.10 HOLD-OVER RELIEFS) the offshore income gain is taken into account to reduce 'B' in the A/B fraction determined under those provisions.

(iii) Where, by virtue of *TCGA 1992, ss 127, 135* or *136* (reorganisation of shares or securities etc. (see 58.1, 58.4 and 58.6 SHARES AND SECURITIES respectively), a transaction does not constitute a disposal for capital gains purposes, but does constitute a disposal for the purposes of the offshore fund provisions, the amount of any offshore income gain to which the disposal gives rise is treated as consideration for the 'new holding' (within *TCGA 1992, s 128* — see 58.1 SHARES AND SECURITIES).

(iv) Where, by virtue of *TCGA 1992, s 127* or *s 132* (see 58.1 and 58.7 SHARES AND SECURITIES) an exchange of interests of different classes in an offshore fund does not constitute a disposal for capital gains purposes, but does constitute a disposal of an interest in an offshore fund, the amount of any offshore income gain to which the disposal gives rise is treated as consideration for the new holding.

[*ICTA 1988, s 763(1)–(6A); FA 2004, s 145, Sch 26 paras 15(2), 16*].

45.9 UK RESIDENT COMPANY TRANSFERRING ASSETS TO OVERSEAS RESIDENT COMPANY

Where a UK resident company carrying on a trade (which includes vocations, offices and employments) outside the UK through a permanent establishment (or, for accounting periods beginning before 1 January 2003, through a branch or agency) transfers the whole or part of that trade together with its assets, or its assets other than cash, to a company not resident in the UK in exchange, wholly or partly, for shares (or shares and loan stock) in that company, so that thereafter it holds one quarter or more of the transferee company's ordinary share capital, and the chargeable gains on the transfer exceed the allowable losses, a proportion of the resulting net chargeable gains relating to the shares (in the proportion that the market value of the shares at the time of the transfer bears to the market value of the whole consideration received) may be claimed by the transferor company as being deferred and not treated as arising until the happening of one of the following events.

(i) The transferor company disposes of all or any of the shares received. The 'appropriate proportion' of the deferred gain (insofar as not already charged under this specific provision or under (ii) below) is then added to the consideration received on the disposal. The '*appropriate proportion*' is the proportion which the market value of the shares disposed of bears to the market value of the shares held immediately before the disposal. However, where the disposal of the shares received occurs after 5 April 1988 no addition to the consideration is made under this provision if its application would be directly attributable to the disposal of an asset before 1 April 1982.

(ii) The transferee company disposes, within six years of the transfer, of the whole or part of the assets on which chargeable gains were deferred. The gain chargeable (insofar as it has not already been charged under this provision, or under (i) above) is the proportion which the deferred gain on the assets disposed of bears to the total deferred gain on assets held immediately before the disposal.

The following disposals are disregarded.

- For the purposes of (i) above, intra-group transfers within *TCGA 1992, s 171* (see 27.2 GROUPS OF COMPANIES). A charge will arise when a subsequent group company makes a disposal outside the group.
- For the purposes of (i) above, transfers to an SE in the process of forming it in circumstances in which *TCGA 1992, s 140E* applies (see 13.18 COMPANIES). In relation to a subsequent disposal of the shares or disposal by the transferee company of assets within (ii) above, the SE is treated as if it were the transferor company.
- For the purposes of (ii) above, intra-group transfers which would be within *TCGA 1992, s 171* if for those purposes a group included (without qualification) non-UK resident companies. A charge will arise when a subsequent group company makes a disposal outside the group.

A claim under *TCGA 1992, s 140C* (transfer of non-UK trade between different EC member states; see 45.11 below) as regards a transfer precludes a claim under the above.

[*TCGA 1992, s 140, Sch 4 para 4(5); F(No 2)A 1992, s 46(4); FA 2000, Sch 29 para 23; FA 2003, s 153(1)(b)(4); F(No 2)A 2005, s 64(2)*].

For interaction between (i) above and the exemptions relating to SUBSTANTIAL SHAREHOLDINGS OF COMPANIES, see 60.21.

Insurance companies. Where a UK resident insurance company (i.e. not confined to life insurance companies) transfers its foreign permanent establishment (or, for accounting periods beginning before 1 January 2003, branch or agency) business and assets to an overseas company in exchange wholly or partly for shares in that company in circumstances corresponding to those set out above any profit or loss on the assets transferred which would otherwise be included in the computation of profits or losses under Schedule D, Case I will be disregarded for that purpose (otherwise than in restricting management expenses under *ICTA 1988, s 76(2)*) and treated as chargeable gains or allowable losses. Any net chargeable gain may then be deferred as given above. [*ICTA 1988, s 442(1)–(3); FA 2003, s 153(1)(a)(4)*]. *ICTA 1988, s 442(3)* is ignored in calculating any relief given under *TCGA 1992, s 140C* (transfer of non-UK trade between different EC member states; see 45.11 below). [*TCGA 1992, s 140C(8); F(No 2)A 1992, s 45*].

45.10 TRANSFER OF UK TRADE BETWEEN COMPANIES IN DIFFERENT EC MEMBER STATES

A special relief may be claimed where, **after 31 December 1991**, a 'qualifying company' resident in one EC member state transfers the whole or part of a trade carried on by it in the UK to a qualifying company resident in another member state wholly in exchange for shares or debentures (for issues effected before 1 April 2005, securities (including shares)) in the latter company, provided that certain conditions (see below) are met. On such a claim made by both companies (under *TCGA 1992, s 140A*), any assets included in the transfer are treated for the purposes of corporation tax on chargeable gains as transferred for a no gain/no loss consideration, and *TCGA 1992, s 25(3)* (deemed disposal by non-resident on ceasing to trade in the UK through a permanent establishment or a branch or agency, see 45.3 above) does not apply to the assets by reason of the transfer.

A '*qualifying company*' is a body incorporated under the law of a member state.

A company is regarded for the above purposes as resident in a member state under the laws of which it is chargeable to tax because it is regarded as so resident (unless it is regarded under DOUBLE TAX RELIEF (19.2) arrangements entered into by the member state as resident in a territory not within any of the member states).

The conditions referred to above are:

(*a*)

(i) if the transferee company is non-UK resident immediately after the transfer, any chargeable gain accruing to it on a disposal of the assets included in the transfer would form part of its corporation tax profits under *TCGA 1992, s 10*(*3*) or *s 10B*, or

(ii) if it is UK resident at that time, none of the assets included in the transfer is exempt from UK tax on disposal under double tax relief arrangements; and

(*b*) the transfer is effected for *bona fide* commercial reasons and not as part of a scheme or arrangement a main purpose of which is avoidance of income, corporation or capital gains taxes.

Advance clearance in relation to (*b*) above may be obtained from HMRC on the application of the companies, to the same address and subject to the same conditions and appeal procedures as apply to clearances under *TCGA 1992, s 138* (see 3.18 ANTI-AVOIDANCE). [*TCGA 1992, ss 140A, 140B; F(No 2)A 1992, s 44; FA 2003, Sch 27 para 2; F(No 2)A 2005, s 59*(*3*)(*7*)].

The above provisions were introduced to comply with EEC Directive No 90/434/EEC.

45.11 TRANSFER OF NON-UK TRADE BETWEEN COMPANIES IN DIFFERENT EC MEMBER STATES

Where, **after 31 December 1991**,

(*a*) a 'qualifying company' resident in the UK transfers to a qualifying company resident in another member state the whole or part of a trade carried on by the UK company immediately before the transfer through a permanent establishment (or, for accounting periods beginning before 1 January 2003, through a branch or agency) in a member state other than the UK,

(*b*) the transfer includes all the UK company's assets used in that trade or part (with the possible exception of cash),

(*c*) the transfer is wholly or partly in exchange for shares or debentures (for issues effected before 1 April 2005, securities (including shares)) in the non-UK company,

(*d*) the aggregate of the chargeable gains accruing to the UK company on the transfer exceeds the aggregate of the allowable losses so accruing, and

(*e*) the transfer is effected for *bona fide* commercial reasons and not as part of a scheme or arrangement a main purpose of which is avoidance of income, corporation or capital gains taxes,

the UK company may claim that the transfer be treated as giving rise to a single chargeable gain of the excess at (*d*) above. No claim may, however, be made where a claim is made under *TCGA 1992, s 140* at 45.9 above in relation to the same transfer. As regards insurance companies, *ICTA 1988, s 442*(*3*) (also see 45.9 above) is ignored in arriving at the chargeable gains and allowable losses accruing on the transfer.

A '*qualifying company*' is a body incorporated under the law of a member state.

For the purposes of (*a*) above, a company is not regarded as resident in the UK if it is regarded under any DOUBLE TAX RELIEF (19.2) arrangements to which the UK is a party as resident in a territory not within any of the member states. A company is regarded as resident in another member State under the laws of which it is chargeable to tax because it is regarded as so resident (unless it is regarded under a double tax relief arrangement entered into by the member state as resident in a territory not within any of the member states).

Advance clearance in relation to (*e*) above may be obtained from HMRC on the application of the UK company, to the same address and subject to the same conditions and appeal procedures as apply to clearances under *TCGA 1992, s 138* (see 3.18 ANTI-AVOIDANCE).

[*TCGA 1992, ss 140C, 140D; F(No 2)A 1992, s 4; FA 2003, s 153(1)(b)(4); F(No 2)A 2005, s 59(4)(7)*].

The above provisions were introduced to comply with EEC Directive No 90/434/EEC (the 'Mergers Directive').

Double tax relief. Where the above provisions apply, where gains accruing to the UK company would have been chargeable to tax under the law of the member state in which the trade was carried on immediately before the transfer but for the Mergers Directive, the amount of tax is treated for double tax relief purposes as tax paid in that other member state. In calculating the amount of the tax so treated it is assumed that, so far as permitted under the law of the member state, any losses arising on the transfer are set against the gains, and that the UK company claims any available reliefs.

These provisions apply also where *TCGA 1992, s 140F* (formation of SE by merger: assets not left within UK tax charge — see 13.18 COMPANIES) applies.

[*ICTA 1988, s 815A(3); F(No 2)A 1992, s 50; FA 1996, Sch 20 para 39; FA 2003, s 153(1)(4); F(No 2)A 2005, s 59(1)*].

45.12 COMPANY CEASING TO BE UK RESIDENT ETC., DUAL RESIDENT COMPANIES (BEFORE 30 NOVEMBER 1993) AND NON-RESIDENT COMPANIES

Company ceasing to be UK resident etc. If, at any time ('*the relevant time*') after 14 March 1988, a company ceases to be resident in the UK, except with Treasury consent under *ICTA 1988, s 765(1)(a)* on an application made before 15 March 1988, and does not cease to exist,

(*a*) it is deemed to dispose of immediately before the relevant time, and immediately reacquire, all its 'assets' at market value at that time, and

(*b*) ROLLOVER RELIEF (55) under *TCGA 1992, s 152* is not subsequently available by reference to disposals of old assets made before that time and acquisitions of new assets after that time.

If at any later time the company carries on a trade in the UK through a permanent establishment, or, for accounting periods beginning before 1 January 2003, through a branch or agency (both terms as defined in 45.3 above), the foregoing does not apply

(i) for (*a*) above, to any assets which, immediately after the relevant time, or

(ii) for (*b*) above, to any new assets which, after the relevant time,

are situated in the UK and are used in or for a trade, or are used or held for the permanent establishment or branch or agency. '*Assets*' include various assets and rights relating to exploration or exploitation activities in the UK or a designated area of the sea, within *TCGA 1992, s 276* in 45.14 below. [*TCGA 1992, s 185; FA 2003, s 153(1)(b)(4)*].

HMRC takes the view that any gain resulting from a deemed disposal within paragraph (*a*) above cannot be the subject of a rollover relief claim by reference to a deemed acquisition within that paragraph because only the same and not a different asset is being acquired (HMRC International Tax Handbook ITH 408).

Where the company concerned ceases to be resident in the UK on 30 November 1993 solely by virtue of the coming into force of *FA 1994, s 249* (companies otherwise regarded as UK resident but under double tax relief arrangements already regarded as non-UK resident to be treated as non-UK resident for *Taxes Acts* purposes after 29 November 1993; see 52.6 RESIDENCE AND DOMICILE) and a deemed disposal under (*a*) above occurs, further provisions apply. Where an actual disposal of the assets is made on or before the day when corporation tax would otherwise be due and payable in respect of the deemed disposal, the tax is due and payable on that day; otherwise the tax is due and payable on the earlier of the day the assets are actually disposed of and 30 November 1999. Interest on unpaid tax in respect of the deemed disposal will only run from the due and payable date as determined above. If an actual part disposal of the assets is made, these further provisions are applied separately to the different parts, and the tax apportioned (and carrying interest) accordingly. [*FA 1994, s 250(3)–(6)*].

Where, at any time after 14 March 1988 and before 30 November 1993 (the latter date being the date of the coming into force of *FA 1994, s 249* above), a company, while continuing to be UK resident, commenced to be regarded, for the purposes of any DOUBLE TAX RELIEF (19.2) arrangements, as resident in a territory outside the UK, and as not liable to UK tax on gains on disposals of assets specified in those arrangements, (*a*) and (*b*) above applied to those assets. [*TCGA 1992, s 186; FA 1994, s 251(1)(9), Sch 26 Pt VIII*].

If the deemed disposal described in paragraph (*a*) above includes any '*foreign assets*' (i.e. assets which are situated, and are used in or for a trade carried on, outside the UK), any charge to tax will be postponed, as described below, if

(A) immediately after the relevant time the company was a '75% subsidiary' (see below) of a company ('*the principal company*') which was resident in the UK, and

(B) both companies elect in writing within two years after that time.

The excess of gains over losses arising on the foreign assets included in the deemed disposal is treated as a single chargeable gain not accruing to the company on the disposal. An equal amount ('*the postponed gain*') is instead treated as follows.

If within six years after the relevant time the company disposes of any assets (the '*relevant assets*') capital gains on which were taken into account in arriving at the postponed gain, a chargeable gain equal to the whole, or 'the appropriate proportion', of the postponed gain, so far as this has not already been treated as a chargeable gain under these provisions, is deemed to accrue to the principal company. '*The appropriate proportion*' is the proportion which the chargeable gain taken into account in arriving at the postponed gain in respect of the part of the relevant assets disposed of bears to the aggregate of the chargeable gains so taken into account in respect of the relevant assets held immediately before the time of the disposal.

If at any time

(I) the company ceases to be a 75% subsidiary of the principal company on a disposal by the principal company of ordinary shares in it, or

(II) after the company otherwise ceases to be a 75% subsidiary, the principal company disposes of ordinary shares in it, or

(III) the principal company ceases to be resident in the UK,

a chargeable gain, equal to so much of the postponed gain as has not previously been charged under these provisions, is deemed to arise.

If any part of the postponed gain becomes chargeable, and the subsidiary has unrelieved capital losses, the companies can elect within two years for part or all of the losses to be set against the amount chargeable.

For the purposes of the above provisions a company is a '*75% subsidiary*' of another company if and so long as not less than 75% of its ordinary share capital is owned *directly* by that other company. [*TCGA 1992, s 187; FA 1994, s 251(1)*(9), *Sch 26 Pt VIII*].

Dual resident companies. Where, at any time after 14 March 1988 and before 30 November 1993 (the latter date being the date of the coming into force of *FA 1994, s 249* above), an asset of a 'dual resident company' became a 'prescribed asset', the company was deemed immediately before that time to have disposed of and immediately reacquired it, both transactions being treated as carried out at the then market value. No deemed disposal and acquisition was to take place under this provision, however, where the asset became a prescribed asset on the company becoming to be regarded as a dual resident company as this already took place on such an event under *TCGA 1992, s 186* above. A company was a '*dual resident company*' if it was UK resident and fell to be regarded under any double tax relief arrangements as resident in another territory elsewhere. A '*prescribed asset*', in relation to a dual resident company, was an asset treated under any double tax relief arrangements as not giving rise to a UK tax charge on the company in respect of a gain arising on its disposal. [*TCGA 1992, s 188; FA 1994, s 251(1)*(*10*), *Sch 26 Pt VIII*].

Where either the disposal of the 'old assets' (or of the interest in them) or the acquisition of the 'new assets' is made (or the acquisition of the interest in them is made or the unconditional contract for their acquisition is entered into) (or both such events) occurred after 13 March 1989, then, if either such event occurred before 30 November 1993 (the latter date being the date of the coming into force of *FA 1994, s 249* above), ROLLOVER RELIEF (55) under *TCGA 1992, s 152* (the above quoted terms having the same meaning as in that provision) did not apply where a company was a 'dual resident company' (having the same meaning as in *TCGA 1992, s 188* above) at the time of disposal and at the time of acquisition, and the old assets were not 'prescribed assets' (defined as for in *TCGA 1992, s 188* above) at the time of disposal, unless the new assets were not prescribed assets immediately after the time of acquisition. However, rollover relief could apply where the acquisition of the new assets occurred before 14 March 1989 and the disposal of the old assets was after 13 March 1989 but within twelve months (or such longer period as is allowed by written notice given by HMRC) of the acquisition of the new assets. [*TCGA 1992, s 160; FA 1994, s 251(1)*(*6*), *Sch 26 Pt VIII*].

45.13 **Company ceasing to be UK resident etc: compliance.** Before a company, after 14 March 1988, ceases to be resident in the UK, otherwise than with Treasury consent under *ICTA 1988, s 765(1)*(*a*), it must give HMRC

(*a*) notice of its intention to cease to be resident, specifying the time when it intends to do so,

(*b*) a statement of the amount of tax which it considers payable for periods beginning before that time, and

(*c*) particulars of the arrangements which it proposes to make to secure the payment of that tax.

It must also make arrangements to secure the payment of that tax; and the arrangements must be approved by HMRC.

References to tax payable are not defined but include specified liabilities such as certain income tax payments, sub-contractors' deductions and amounts payable under *FA 1973, Sch 15 para 4* (territorial extension of charge of tax as in 45.14 below). Interest on unpaid tax is included in certain circumstances.

Any question as to the amount of tax payable is to be determined by the Special Commissioners. If any information provided by the company does not fully and accurately disclose all the material facts and considerations, any resulting approval is void. [*FA 1988, s 130; FA 2004, Sch 12 para 12*].

A person who is, or is deemed to be, involved in a failure to comply with the foregoing provisions is liable to a penalty not exceeding the amount of unpaid tax for periods beginning before the failure occurred. [*FA 1988, s 131*].

The requirements of *FA 1988, s 130* and the penalty that can be exacted under *FA 1988, s 131* above do not apply where the company concerned ceases to be resident in the UK on 30 November 1993 solely by virtue of the coming into force of *FA 1994, s 249* (companies otherwise regarded as UK resident but under double tax relief arrangements already regarded as non-UK resident to be treated as non-UK resident for *Taxes Acts* purposes after 29 November 1993; see 52.6 RESIDENCE AND DOMICILE). [*FA 1994, s 250*(*1*)].

Any tax in respect of accounting periods beginning before the cessation of UK residence which is still unpaid six months after the time when it became payable can (see also 45.12 above), within three years of final determination of the tax due, be recovered from a person who is, or in the twelve months before the cessation of UK residence (or, if less, the period after 14 March 1988) was, a member of the same group of companies (as in *TCGA 1992, s 170* (see 27.1 GROUPS OF COMPANIES) but disregarding the pre-FA 2000 UK residence requirement and substituting 51 per cent subsidiary for '75 per cent subsidiary') or a controlling director (as defined). [*FA 1988, s 132; FA 2000, Sch 29 para 15*].

Guidance on the procedure to be followed under these provisions is given in HMRC Statement of Practice 2/90. In particular, notice under (*a*) above should be sent to HMRC, International Division (Company Migrations), Room 312, Melbourne House, Aldwych, London, WC2B 4LL.

Non-resident companies. Where a non-UK resident company makes a gain on the disposal after 13 March 1989 and before 1 April 2000 of an asset, the gain forms part of its chargeable profits for corporation tax purposes under *TCGA 1992, s 10*(*3*) (non-UK resident trading etc. in the UK, see 45.3 above), and any of the corporation tax assessed relating to the accounting period in which the gain accrued remains unpaid after six months from it becoming payable, then the unpaid tax (or an amount equal to corporation tax on the amount of the gain at the rate in force at the time when the gain accrued if lower) can be recovered by HMRC within three years from the amount being determined from a person who is, or in the twelve months before the disposal occurred (or, if less, the period after 13 March 1989) was, a member of the same group of companies (as in *TCGA 1992, s 170* but excluding any references to UK residence and substituting '51 per cent subsidiary' for '75 per cent subsidiary') or a controlling director (as defined). For gains accruing after 31 March 2000, these provisions are superseded by those at 27.8 GROUPS OF COMPANIES. [*TCGA 1992, s 191; FA 2000, Sch 29 para 9*(*1*)(*3*)(*4*)].

45.14 EXPLORATION AND EXPLOITATION RIGHTS TO TERRITORIAL SEA-BED AND CONTINENTAL SHELF

Any gains accruing on the disposal of 'exploration or exploitation rights' are treated for the purposes of *TCGA 1992* as gains accruing on the disposal of assets situated in the UK. For this and all other purposes of the taxation of chargeable gains, the territorial sea of the UK is deemed to be part of the UK. (Under the *Territorial Sea Act 1987, s 1*, the breadth of the territorial sea adjacent to the UK is 12 nautical miles, a nautical mile being approximately 1,852 metres.)

Gains accruing on the disposal of 'exploration or exploitation assets' which are situated in a 'designated area', or 'unquoted shares' (i.e. not listed on a recognised stock exchange — see 58.23 SHARES AND SECURITIES) deriving their value or the greater part of their value directly or indirectly from exploration or exploitation assets situated in the UK or a designated area or from such assets and exploration or exploitation rights taken together, are treated for the purposes of *TCGA 1992* as gains accruing on the disposal of assets situated in the UK. Gains accruing to a person not resident in the UK on the disposal of such rights or of such assets (the latter including for this purpose unquoted shares of the description above) are treated for the same purposes as gains accruing on the disposal of assets used for the purposes of a trade carried on by that person in the UK through a branch or agency or, in the case of a non-resident company for accounting periods beginning after 31 December 2002, through a permanent establishment (for which see 45.3 above).

If exploration or exploitation rights or exploration or exploitation assets (the latter including for this purpose unquoted shares of the description above) are disposed of by a company resident in an overseas territory to either a company resident in the same territory or a UK-resident company, or by one UK-resident company to another, the provisions at 27.2, 27.4, 27.6, 27.9, 27.13 GROUPS OF COMPANIES, and *TCGA 1992, s 172* (now repealed) at 45.3 above apply, with appropriate modifications.

'*Exploration or exploitation rights*' means rights to assets to be produced by 'exploration or exploitation activities' or to interests in or to the benefit of such assets. '*Exploration or exploitation activities*' means activities carried on in connection with the exploration or exploitation of so much of the seabed and subsoil and their natural resources as is situated in the UK or a designated area.

References in the above to the disposal of exploration or exploitation rights include references to the disposal of shares deriving their value or the greater part of their value directly or indirectly from such rights, other than shares listed on a recognised stock exchange. '*Shares*' includes stock and any security as defined in *ICTA 1988, s 254(1)*. '*Designated area*' means an area designated by Order in Council under the *Continental Shelf Act 1964, s 1(7)*.

For the above purposes, an asset disposed of is an '*exploration or exploitation asset*' if either

(*a*) it is not a mobile asset and it is being or has at some time (for disposals before 14 March 1989, being a time within the period of two years ending at the date of disposal) been used in connection with exploration or exploitation activities carried on in the UK or a designated area; or

(*b*) it is a mobile asset which has at some time (for disposals before 14 March 1989, being a time within the period of two years ending at the date of disposal) been used in connection with exploration or exploitation activities so carried on and is dedicated to an oil field in which the person making the disposal, or a person connected with him, is or has been a participator;

and expressions used in (*a*) and (*b*) above have the same meanings there as if those paragraphs were included in *Oil Taxation Act 1975, Pt I*.

[*TCGA 1992, s 276; FA 1989, s 130, Sch 17 Pt VII; FA 1996, Sch 38 para 10(2)(d); FA 2000, Sch 29 para 35; FA 2003, s 153(2)(b)(4)*].

There are comprehensive information and enforcement powers in relation to tax assessed by virtue of *TCGA 1992, s 276* above. In particular, unpaid tax so assessed on an overseas resident person may be recovered together with interest thereon from the holder of a licence granted under *Petroleum (Production) Act 1934* in respect of chargeable gains accruing on the disposal of exploration or exploitation rights connected with activities authorised, or carried on in connection with activities authorised, by the licence. An overseas resident liable to charge and who HMRC are satisfied will meet his obligations under the *Taxes Acts* may apply for a certificate to be issued to the licence holder exempting him (subject to detailed conditions) from a charge on the default of the applicant. [*FA 1973, s 38(2)(8), Sch 15; ITTOIA 2005, Sch 1 para 388*].

Where an 'exploration or exploitation asset' (for this purpose, an asset used in connection with 'exploration or exploitation activities' carried on in the UK or a 'designated area', both expressions having the same meanings as in *TCGA 1992, s 276* above) ceases to be 'chargeable' in relation to a person by virtue of ceasing after 13 March 1989 to be 'dedicated to an oil field' in which he, or a person connected with him, is or has been a 'participator' (these last two expressions having the same meanings as in *Oil Taxation Act 1975, Pt I*), he is deemed for all purposes of *TCGA 1992* to have disposed of the asset immediately before the time when it ceased to be so dedicated, and immediately to have reacquired it, at its market value at that time.

An asset is a '*chargeable*' asset at any time in relation to a person if, were it to be disposed of at that time, any chargeable gains accruing to him on the disposal would be brought into charge for capital gains tax or corporation tax by virtue of *TCGA 1992, s 10(1)* or *s 10(3)* or *s 10B* respectively.

A similar deemed disposal and acquisition takes place where a person who is not resident or ordinarily resident ceases after 13 March 1989 to carry on a trade through a branch or agency, or, in the case of a non-resident company in an accounting period beginning after 31 December 2002, through a permanent establishment, in respect of any exploration or exploitation asset, other than a mobile asset, used in or for the purposes of the trade at or before the time of the deemed disposal. No such deemed disposal and reacquisition takes place if, immediately after the cessation of the trade carried on through the UK branch or agency, the asset is used in or for the purposes of exploration or exploitation activities carried on by him in the UK or a designated area. However, on a person ceasing after 13 March 1989 so to use the asset, there will be a deemed disposal and reacquisition. [*TCGA 1992, s 199; FA 2003, s 153(2)(b)(4), s 155, Sch 27 para 2(3)*].

As regards leasing of mobile drilling rigs and other assets by overseas resident companies, see HMRC Statement of Practice 6/84.

See also 52.9 RESIDENCE AND DOMICILE for the territorial extent of the UK.

45.15 EUROPEAN ECONOMIC INTEREST GROUPINGS

With retrospective effect after 30 June 1989, provisions were introduced governing the tax treatment of European Economic Interest Groupings ('groupings'), wherever registered, within *EEC Council Regulation No 2137/85* dated 25 July 1985. For the purposes of charging tax in respect of chargeable gains and subject to exceptions as below, a grouping is regarded as acting as the agent of its members. Its activities are regarded for such purposes as those of its members acting jointly, each member being regarded as having a share of its property, rights and liabilities, and a person is regarded as acquiring or disposing of a share of its assets not only where there is an acquisition or disposal by it while he is a member but also where he becomes or ceases to be a member or there is a change in his share of its property. A member's share in a grouping's property, rights or liabilities is that determined under the contract establishing the grouping or, if there is no provision determining such shares, it will correspond to the profit share to which he is entitled under the provisions of the contract (or if the contract makes no such provision, members are regarded as having equal shares). Where the grouping carries on a trade or profession, the members are regarded for the purposes of tax on gains as carrying on that trade or profession in partnership.

[*ICTA 1988, s 510A; FA 1990, s 69, Sch 11; FA 1995, Sch 29 Pt VIII(16); FA 2002, s 82, Sch 25 para 49*].

The EEC provision of 25 July 1985 mentioned above covers all groupings established within the European Economic Area on the coming into force of the European Economic Area Agreement on 1 January 1994 (Revenue Press Release 9 February 1994).

See also 54.19 RETURNS, and 48.5, 48.9 PENALTIES as regards non-compliance.

45.16 COLLECTION OF TAX

Although tax is legally assessable by notice served abroad, there are difficulties in collection. The UK courts will not enforce the revenue laws of other countries, see *Government of India v Taylor (re Delhi Electric Supply & Traction Co. Ltd) HL, [1955] AC*

491 and *Brokaw v Seatrain UK Ltd, CA, [1971] 2 All ER 98*. See, however, 29.2(c) HMRC: CONFIDENTIALITY OF INFORMATION for agreements for mutual assistance in the collection of taxes. See also 45.3 above for the assessment of UK resident agents of overseas resident traders and 45.13 above for arrangements required to secure payment of tax by a company ceasing to be UK resident or by a non-UK resident company. See also 44.2 OFFSHORE SETTLEMENTS for the arrangements where trustees become non-resident.

46 Partnerships

Cross-references. See 45.15 OVERSEAS MATTERS for European Economic Interest Groupings deemed to carry on a trade in partnership; 53 RETIREMENT RELIEF; 55 ROLLOVER RELIEF and 56 SELF-ASSESSMENT.

Simon's Direct Tax Service. See Division C3.2.

See also Tolley's Partnership Taxation.

46.1 A partnership is defined in *Partnership Act 1890, s 1* as 'the relation which subsists between persons carrying on a business in common with a view of profit'. This does not include purely capital transactions, e.g. the sale of a house by joint tenants.

46.2 An English partnership or firm is not a legal entity distinct from the partners themselves, but a collection of separate persons (which may be companies or individuals). In Scotland a firm is a legal person, but in general this does not affect the application of the *Taxes Acts.* A partnership cannot be a company for the purposes of *TCGA 1992*. [*TCGA 1992, s 288*(*1*)]. See 46.19 below as regards limited liability partnerships from 6 April 2001 onwards.

46.3 The taxation of partnership gains is based on a body of HMRC practice superimposed on the general capital gains rules. There are few specific references to partnerships in the capital gains legislation. For a useful codification of HMRC practice, reference should be made to HMRC Statements of Practice D12 (revised October 2002), 1/79 and 1/89 on which much of this chapter is based. The Statements of Practice are supplemented by the HMRC Capital Gains Manual at CG 27000–27902.

For details of **returns under self-assessment** for 1996/97 and subsequent years, see 54.15–54.17 RETURNS.

46.4 TREATMENT AND ASSESSMENT GENERALLY

Where two or more persons carry on a trade or business in partnership, tax is assessed and charged on them separately in respect of chargeable gains accruing to them on the disposal of any partnership assets. (The treatment of partnerships in Scotland as a legal person is ignored for this purpose.) Any partnership dealings are treated as dealings by the partners and not by the firm as such. [*TCGA 1992, s 59*(*1*)(*a*)(*b*); *ITTOIA 2005, Sch 1 para 431*].

In general terms, because of the separate assessment and charging procedure of capital gains tax (and the charge to corporation tax in respect of chargeable gains), it will be the residence and domicile circumstances of each partner (whether an individual or company) that will dictate the basis of charge on him (although prior to the introduction of self-assessment this was not made explicitly clear; see *TCGA 1992, s 59*(*c*) applying *ICTA 1988, s 112*(*1*)(*2*) (*as originally enacted*) (partnerships controlled abroad). For example, an individual partner who is resident or ordinarily resident in the UK and domiciled there will be assessable wherever partnership gains arise and whether remitted to the UK or not. An individual partner neither resident nor ordinarily resident in the UK would only be liable in respect of partnership assets under *TCGA 1992, s 10* (UK branch or agency; see 45.3 OVERSEAS MATTERS). However, it is specifically provided that, if, under a double tax agreement, any capital gains of a partnership which resides outside the UK or which carries on any trade, profession or business the control or management of which is situated outside the UK is relieved from tax in the UK, such relief is not to affect the liability of any UK resident partner's share of the capital gains. Such treatment is always deemed to have applied (thus overruling *Padmore v CIR CA 1989, 62 TC 352* (and see *Padmore v CIR (No 2) Ch D 2001,73 TC 470*)) except as regards cases where proceedings had before 17 March 1987 been determined by Commissioners or had a judgement given in court in respect of them before that date. [*ICTA 1988, s 112*(*4*), *s 115*(*5*)(*5A*); *TCGA 1992, s 59*(*2*)(*3*); *ITTOIA 2005, Sch 1 paras 93, 95, 431*].

46.5 PARTNERS' FRACTIONAL SHARES

Each partner is regarded as owning a fractional share of each asset, which is calculated by reference to his asset-surplus-sharing ratio. Where no such ratio is specified, the share will follow the treatment in the accounts, subject to any external agreement. Failing that, regard will be had to the normal profit-sharing ratios. For appeals regarding apportionments of amounts etc., see 4 APPEALS and *White v Carline (Sp C 33), [1995] SSCD 186.*

The fraction is applied to the value of the total partnership interest in the asset disposed of, and no discount is allowed against market value for the size of an individual partner's share.

Expenditure on the acquisition of partnership assets will be allocated for capital gains tax purposes, in similar fashion to gains/losses, at the time of acquisition, subject to adjustment on any subsequent change in partnership sharing ratios.

(SP D12 (revised October 2002) introduction and paras 1, 2).

Examples

Each of the following partnerships disposes of its offices to outside parties at arm's length at a chargeable gain of £30,000. The gain is apportioned among the partners in the manner shown.

(*a*) *A & Co.* The partnership agreement states that each of the three partners shall be entitled to share equally in any surplus arising from assets disposed of by the partnership. Each partner is therefore treated as if he had made a gain of £10,000.

(*b*) *B & Co.* The three partners in B & Co have no formal agreement, but interest on capital contributed to the partnership is shown in the accounts at the same sum for each. The inference is that the capital has been equally contributed and can be equally withdrawn, so that the apportioned gain is £10,000 to each partner.

(*c*) *C & Co.* The three partners in C & Co, X, Y, and Z, have no formal agreement and the capital is shown in the accounts as a global sum. The profit-sharing ratio is 3:2:1, so that the apportioned gain is X–£15,000, Y–£10,000, and Z–£5,000.

A partner makes a disposal (or part disposal) of his fractional share of a partnership asset not only when the partnership disposes (or part disposes) of the asset as above but also when his share is extinguished (or reduced) for which see 46.6–46.11 below.

46.6 CHANGES IN SHARING RATIOS

Where changes occur in partnership sharing ratios (including partners joining or leaving the firm), each partner is treated as acquiring or disposing of part or the whole of a share in each of the partnership assets, insofar as his share increases or decreases. Subject to (*a*) and (*b*) below, the disposal consideration of each chargeable asset is equal to the relevant fraction (i.e. the fractional share changing hands) of the current balance sheet value. Where there have been no accounting adjustments (for which see 46.10 below), the disposal is thus treated as a *no gain/no loss disposal.* A partner whose share decreases will carry forward a smaller proportion of cost to set against any future disposal (including a disposal of one or more of the assets outside the partnership), and a partner whose share increases will carry forward a larger proportion of cost than before. An incoming partner will thereby take over a proportion of the cost of existing assets in accordance with his fractional entitlement. The *cost* of any part disposal under these provisions is calculated as a corresponding fraction of the total acquisition cost, and *not* by way of apportionment under *TCGA 1992, s 42* as in 15.7 COMPUTATION OF GAINS AND LOSSES. (SP D12 para 4). See the *Example* at 46.8 below.

A different disposal consideration figure may have to be used in the following cases.

(*a*) Where a direct payment is made in connection with the change in sharing ratios (see 46.11 below).

(*b*) Where the change in sharing ratios results from a transaction made otherwise than at arm's length or made between CONNECTED PERSONS (16). The meaning of connected persons for these purposes is narrowed. See 46.14 below.

46.7 **Re-basing to 1982 and indexation allowance (SP 1/89).** HMRC have agreed that a disposal of a share of partnership assets which is treated under SP D12 para 4 above as on a no gain/no loss basis (before indexation, for disposals before 6 April 1988) may be treated as if it were a no gain/no loss disposal within *TCGA 1992, s 35(3)(d)* (see 8.7 ASSETS HELD ON 31 MARCH 1982). Such a disposal may also be treated as if it were a no gain/no loss disposal within that provision for the purposes of *TCGA 1992, s 36, Sch 4* (deferred charges — see 8.12 ASSETS HELD ON 31 MARCH 1982).

Where such a disposal occurs after 5 April 1988, the amount of the consideration is calculated on the assumption that an unindexed gain accrues to the transferor equal to the indexation allowance, so that after taking into account the indexation allowance due, neither a gain nor a loss accrues. Where under the above a partner is treated as having owned the asset on 31 March 1982 in relation to a disposal after 5 April 1988 of all or part of his share of partnership assets, the indexation allowance on the disposal may be calculated as if he had acquired the share on 31 March 1982. A disposal of a share in a partnership asset on or after 31 March 1982 which is treated under SP D12 para 4 above as on a no gain/no loss basis may be treated for the purposes of *TCGA 1992, s 55(5)(6)* as if it were a no gain/no loss disposal within those provisions (see 8.7 ASSETS HELD ON 31 MARCH 1982). A special rule applies, however, where the share changed hands after 5 April 1985 (31 March 1985 in the case of an acquisition from a company) and before 6 April 1988: in these circumstances the indexation allowance is calculated by reference to the 31 March 1982 value *but* from the date of the last disposal of the share before 6 April 1988.

(HMRC Statement of Practice 1/89).

For indexation allowance in relation to no gain/no loss disposals generally, see 34.3 INDEXATION. Note that, other than for companies, indexation allowance is frozen at its April 1998 level — see 34.1 INDEXATION.

For further commentary, see HMRC Capital Gains Manual CG 27450–27570.

46.8 *Example*

J and K have traded in partnership for many years, sharing capital and income equally. The acquisition costs and 31 March 1982 values of the chargeable assets of the firm are as follows

	Cost	31.3.82 value
	£	£
Premises	60,000	150,000
Goodwill	10,000	50,000

The assets have not been revalued in the firm's balance sheet. On 1 June 2006, J and K admit L to the partnership, and the sharing ratio is J 35%, K 45% and L 20%. The indexation factor for March 1982 to April 1998 is 1.047.

J and K are regarded as disposing of part of their interest in the firm's assets to L as follows

	£	£
J		
Premises		
Deemed consideration		
£60,000 × (50% – 35%)	9,000	
Add indexation allowance (see below)	23,558	
Total deemed consideration	32,558	
Allowable cost	9,000	
Unindexed gain	23,558	
Indexation allowance (50% – 35%) × £150,000 × 1.047	23,558	—
Goodwill		
Deemed consideration		
£10,000 × (50% – 35%)	1,500	
Add indexation allowance (see below)	7,853	
Total deemed consideration	9,353	
Allowable cost	1,500	
Unindexed gain	7,853	
Indexation allowance (50% – 35%) × £50,000 × 1.047	7,853	—
Chargeable gain/allowable loss		Nil
K		
Premises		
Deemed consideration		
£60,000 × (50% – 45%)	3,000	
Add indexation allowance (see below)	7,853	
Total deemed consideration	10,853	
Allowable cost	3,000	
Unindexed gain	7,853	
Indexation allowance (50% – 45%) × £150,000 × 1.047	7,853	—

Goodwill

	£	£
Deemed consideration		
£10,000 × (50% – 45%)	500	
Add indexation allowance (see below)	2,618	
Total deemed consideration	3,118	
Allowable cost	500	
Unindexed gain	2,618	
Indexation allowance (50% – 45%) × £50,000 × 1.047	2,618	—
Chargeable gain/allowable loss		Nil

The allowable costs (inclusive, in L's case, of indexation allowance to April 1998) of the three partners are now

	Freehold land	Goodwill
	£	£
J	21,000	3,500
K	27,000	4,500
L (note (*b*))	43,411	12,471

Notes to the example

(*a*) The treatment illustrated above is taken from SP D12 para 4 as extended by SP 1/89. Each partner's disposal consideration is equal to his share of current balance sheet value of the asset concerned plus indexation allowance (to April 1998), and each disposal treated as producing no gain and no loss.

(*b*) L's allowable costs comprise 20% of original cost, plus indexation allowance to April 1998 (see 34.1 INDEXATION) based on 20% of 31 March 1982 value.

46.9 **Application of reliefs.** Where a partner is treated as making a disposal it may also qualify for HOLD-OVER RELIEFS (33), RETIREMENT RELIEF (53) (if made before 6 April 2003) or ROLLOVER RELIEF (55). As regards a partner's acquisition, this may be used to cover a chargeable gain as in ROLLOVER RELIEF (55). A partner treated as disposing of a partnership asset (or share) can roll over any chargeable gain arising against an acquisition in another trade carried on, whether as sole trader or in another partnership trade, and *vice versa*. See 55.1 ROLLOVER RELIEF as regards assets owned personally by a partner and let to the partnership. As regards RETIREMENT RELIEF, see, in particular, 53.4(*a*).

Where SP D12 treats a disposal of a fractional share in the partnership assets, say by A to B, as a no gain/no loss disposal, it follows that TAPER RELIEF (61) is unavailable. On a subsequent disposal of that share by B for consideration, such that a chargeable gain arises, no part of the period prior to the no gain/no loss disposal forms part of B's qualifying holding period for taper relief purposes. See 46.13 below as regards taper relief on the disposal of a fractional share acquired in stages, and see HMRC Capital Gains Manual CG 27610–27645.

46.10 ACCOUNTING ADJUSTMENTS

An upward revaluation of a partnership asset with the consequent credit to a partner's current or capital account does not give rise to a chargeable gain, but if after such a revaluation, a change occurs in a partner's sharing ratio (see 46.6 above), the disposal which he is thereby treated as making takes place at the increased value and may therefore give rise to a chargeable gain. Any acquisition is similarly treated.

Examples (ignoring indexation)

(*a*) X, Y and Z are partners in D & Co and share both capital and income profits and losses in the ratio 3:2:1. X wishes to take a less active part in the business, and Z to devote more time to it. The asset-surplus-sharing ratio is amended to 2:2:2. X is treated as having disposed of a one-sixth interest in each chargeable asset belonging to the partnership for a consideration equal to one-sixth of their respective book values, and Z as having acquired that interest for the same consideration.

(*b*) The facts are as (*a*) above, save that before the ratio is altered, the partnership premises are written up in the books from £120,000 to £180,000. No charge arises on this occasion. On the change in sharing ratio, however, X is treated as having made a gain of £10,000 (one-sixth of the book gain), subject to indexation and taper relief, and this forms part of Z's acquisition cost on a future disposal.

A downward revaluation, even if following an upward revaluation, is similarly not treated as giving rise to an allowable loss, but a change in partnership shares following such a revaluation may do so.

(SP D12 (revised October 2002) para 5).

46.11 CONSIDERATION OUTSIDE THE ACCOUNTS

Where actual consideration is given in connection with an alteration in partnership sharing ratios (see 46.6 above), it is added to the consideration deemed to have been received under the rules in 46.6 and 46.10 above, and may therefore give rise to a chargeable gain or increased gain, the payer's acquisition cost being adjusted accordingly. Where such an extraneous payment is expressed to be in respect of goodwill not included in the balance sheet, it is only deductible by the payer from a subsequent disposal (including a reduction in his share) of the goodwill, or on the payer's leaving the partnership. (SP D12 para 6). It is understood that HMRC do not accept that the writing down to nil of the value of goodwill by a professional partnership is able to form the basis of a 'negligible value' loss claim (see 40.9 LOSSES) by a partner who has previously given consideration for goodwill (see further HMRC Capital Gains Manual CG 27700–27733).

Example

D, E and F are partners in a firm of accountants who share all profits in the ratio 7:7:6. G is admitted as a partner in May 2006 and pays the other partners £10,000 for goodwill. The new partnership shares are D 3/10, E 3/10, F 1/4 and G 3/20. The book value of goodwill is £18,000, its cost on acquisition of the practice from the predecessor in 1991.

The partners are treated as having disposed of shares in goodwill as follows

D	£	£
7/20 – 3/10 = 1/20		
Disposal consideration		
Notional 1/20 × £18,000	900	
Actual 7/20 × £10,000	3,500	
		4,400
Allowable cost 1/20 × £18,000		900
Unindexed gain		£3,500

E

$7/20 - 3/10 = 1/20$

Disposal consideration (as for D)		4,400
Allowable cost (as for D)		900
Unindexed gain		£3,500

F

$6/20 - 1/4 = 1/20$

Disposal consideration		
Notional 1/20 × £18,000	900	
Actual 6/20 × £10,000	3,000	
		3,900
Allowable cost		900
Unindexed gain		£3,000

G's allowable cost of his share of goodwill is therefore		
Actual consideration paid		10,000
Notional consideration paid 3/20 × £18,000		2,700
		£12,700

Note to the example

(*a*) In practice, the above calculations must be adjusted for indexation allowance to April 1998 (see 34.1 INDEXATION) which is added to the notional consideration and deducted from the unindexed gain (see *Example* at 46.8 above). Any chargeable gains remaining after indexation are reduced by TAPER RELIEF (61).

46.12 Insofar as **annual payments** (whether under covenant or not) **to a retired partner** exceed an amount regarded as reasonable in view of the partner's past work for the firm, the capitalised value of the annuity is treated as consideration for the disposal of his partnership share (and as allowable expenditure by the remaining partners). If he had been a partner for at least ten years, the maximum 'reasonable' annuity is two-thirds of his average share of the partnership profits (before capital allowances or charges on income) in the best three of the last seven years in which he was required to devote substantially the whole of his time to the partnership. The ten-year period includes any period during which the partner was a member of another firm which has been merged with the existing firm. For periods less than ten years, the relevant fractions are as follows (instead of two-thirds).

Complete years	Fraction
1–5	1/60 for each year
6	8/60
7	16/60
8	24/60
9	32/60

This treatment applies to certain cases in which a lump sum is paid as well as the annuity. (SP D12 para 8). Where the aggregate of the annuity and one-ninth of the lump sum does not exceed the appropriate fraction of the retired partner's average share of the profits (as above), the capitalised value is not treated as consideration in his hands. The lump sum continues to be treated as consideration. (HMRC Statement of Practice 1/79).

46.13 FRACTIONAL SHARES ACQUIRED IN STAGES

Where a partner's fractional share in one or more partnership assets is built up in stages, i.e. acquired at different times as a result of different transactions, such acquisitions are pooled for capital gains tax purposes. A subsequent part disposal is then regarded as a part disposal of a single asset and the pooled acquisition cost is apportioned accordingly (as in 46.6 above). However, pooling does not apply to any part of the fractional share that was acquired before 6 April 1965; part disposals are to be identified with each such acquisition separately, on a first in/first out basis, in priority to the post-5 April 1965 pool (unless this produces an unreasonable result when applied to purely temporary changes in partners' shares, for example when a partner's departure and a replacement partner's admission are out of step by a few months). (SP D12 para 10).

Fungible assets. In consequence of the capital gains tax identification rules applicable after 5 April 1998 to *fungible* assets (see 59.2 SHARES AND SECURITIES —IDENTIFICATION RULES), pooling does not apply to acquisitions after that date of non-corporate partners' fractional shares of such assets. Examples of such assets are the goodwill generated by the activities of the partnership (but see below under Taper Relief) and milk quota (see 6.9 ASSETS). To the extent that part disposals relate to such assets, they are identified with acquisitions in accordance with the rules at 59.2 SHARES AND SECURITIES —IDENTIFICATION RULES. See HMRC Capital Gains Manual CG 27640–27645. It is arguable that a partner's fractional share in partnership assets generally is itself a fungible asset and that, whatever the nature of the underlying assets, pooling should not apply after 5 April 1998, but HMRC do not appear to take this view.

Taper relief. Where a partner's fractional share of a partnership asset has been acquired in stages, the effect of pooling is that the qualifying holding period (see 61.2 TAPER RELIEF) begins on the date he originally acquired his fractional share (or on 6 April 1998 if later). See HMRC Capital Gains Manual CG 27610–27628. However, where the partnership asset is a fungible asset (see above), disapplication of pooling means that for each post-5 April 1998 acquisition falling to be identified with a particular disposal, the qualifying holding period for taper relief begins on the date of acquisition (HMRC Capital Gains Manual CG 27643).

Goodwill. In the October 2002 revision to their Statement of Practice SP D12, HMRC state that goodwill will *not* be regarded as a fungible asset for taper relief purposes in either of the following circumstances:

- where the value of goodwill generated in the conduct of the partnership business ('self-generated goodwill') is not recognised in the balance sheet and, as a matter of consistent practice, no value is placed on that goodwill in dealings between the partners; or
- where goodwill has been acquired by the partnership for consideration ('purchased goodwill') but has never been recognised in the balance sheet at a value exceeding cost nor otherwise taken into account in dealings between the partners.

For taper relief purposes, self-generated goodwill and purchased goodwill must be considered separately and not pooled with each other; where a disposal involves both types of goodwill and the taper relief percentage would be different for each, proceeds will need to be split on a just and reasonable basis. For purchased goodwill, the qualifying holding period begins on the later of the date of purchase by the partnership, the date the disposing partner first became entitled to a share in it and 6 April 1998.

As the revised practice was published before the deadline for amending 2000/01 tax returns, partners *may* (if they wish and within the normal time limits for doing so — see 54.6 RETURNS) amend those returns (and/or, if already filed, their 2001/02 returns) to take account of it.

(SP D12 (revised October 2002) para 12 and Revenue Tax Bulletin October 2002 pp 971–973).

Example

Q is a partner in a medical practice. The partnership's only chargeable asset is a freehold house used as a surgery. The cost of the house to the partnership was £3,600 in 1962 and it was revalued in the partnership accounts to £50,000 in 1990. Q was admitted to the partnership in June 1964 with a share of 1/6 of all profits. As a result of partnership changes, Q's profit share altered as follows

1970 1/5

1981 1/4

2002 3/10

For capital gains tax, Q's allowable cost of his share of the freehold house is calculated as follows

	£	
1964 1/6 × £3,600		£600
1970 (1/5 – 1/6) × £3,600	120	
1981 (1/4 – 1/5) × £3,600	180	
2002 (3/10 – 1/4) × £50,000	2,500	£2,800

Notes to the example

(*a*) The pre-6.4.65 costs are not pooled.

(*b*) On Q's acquisition of an increased share of the property in 2002 (subsequent to the revaluation in 1990), any partner with a reduced share will be treated as having made a disposal and thus a gain or loss (see 46.10 above). The re-basing rules will apply to the disposal (subject to the usual comparison with the gain or loss without re-basing).

46.14 TRANSACTIONS BETWEEN PERSONS NOT AT ARM'S LENGTH

Transactions within the partnership are not treated as made between CONNECTED PERSONS (16), provided they are pursuant to genuine commercial arrangements, unless the partners are otherwise connected. Market value will be substituted for actual consideration only if the consideration would have been different had the parties been at arm's length. Where market value is applied, the deemed disposal proceeds are treated as in 46.11 above. (SP D12 (revised October 2002) para 7).

46.15 PARTNERSHIP ASSETS DISTRIBUTED IN KIND

The disposal of a partnership asset to one or more of the partners is treated as being made at market value which is apportioned among all the partners as in 46.6 above. Chargeable gains thus attributable to partners receiving no asset are taxed at the time of the disposal. Any gain notionally accruing to a receiving partner is treated as reducing his allowable expenditure on a subsequent disposal of the asset. The same principle applies where a loss arises. (SP D12 para 3).

Example

R, S and T are partners sharing all profits in the ratio 4:3:3. Farmland owned by the firm is transferred in November 2006 to T for future use by him as a market gardening enterprise separate from the partnership business. No payment is made by T to the other partners but a reduction is made in T's future share of income profits. The book value of the farmland is £5,000, its cost in 1992, but the present market value is £15,000.

		£
R		
Deemed disposal consideration	4/10 × £15,000	6,000
Allowable cost	4/10 × £5,000	2,000
Gain (subject to indexation allowance to April 1998 and TAPER RELIEF (61))		£4,000
S		
Deemed disposal consideration	3/10 × £15,000	4,500
Allowable cost	3/10 × £5,000	1,500
Gain (subject to indexation allowance to April 1998 and TAPER RELIEF (61))		£3,000
T		
Partnership share	3/10 × £5,000	1,500
Market value of R's share		6,000
Market value of S's share		4,500
Allowable cost of land for future disposal		£12,000

46.16 MERGERS

Mergers of existing partnerships are treated as in 46.6–46.11 above. If gains arise for reasons similar to 46.10 and 46.11 above, a continuing partner may claim ROLLOVER RELIEF (55) insofar as he disposes of his share of assets of the old firm and acquires a share in other assets of the new firm. (SP D12 para 9).

46.17 6 APRIL 1965 AND 31 MARCH 1982 ELECTIONS

The election under *TCGA 1992, Sch 2 para 4* for quoted securities, whereby 6 April 1965 market value is substituted for acquisition cost and the securities form part of the '1982 holding' for identification purposes (see 7.3, 7.4 ASSETS HELD ON 6 APRIL 1965) is available separately to each partner as regards his share of partnership assets. Each partner's right to elect is distinct from his right to elect in respect of securities held by him in his personal capacity. The time limit for making the election in respect of a particular partner's share of partnership securities operates by reference to the earlier of the first relevant disposal by the partnership and the first post-19 March 1968 reduction of his share of partnership assets. (SP D12 para 11).

A universal re-basing election made under *TCGA 1992, s 35(5)* (see 8.3 ASSETS HELD ON 31 MARCH 1982) by a person in one capacity does not cover disposals made by him in a different capacity. [*TCGA 1992, s 35(7)*]. HMRC have confirmed that an election for assets held privately will not apply to assets held in the capacity of partner, and *vice versa*. As regards partnership assets, the election is available separately to each partner in respect of his share. (Revenue Tax Bulletin November 1991 p 5).

46.18 CORPORATE PARTNERS

The above rules apply, with appropriate modifications, to company partners, but bearing in mind the differences listed at 13.1 COMPANIES between capital gains tax and corporation tax on chargeable gains and in particular the non-application of taper relief to companies. See also 14.3 COMPANIES—CORPORATE FINANCE AND INTANGIBLES.

Anti-avoidance: withdrawal of capital from partnership. *FA 2004* introduced provisions to prevent companies using an avoidance scheme to shelter taxable profits through a partnership. Under the scheme, profits of the partnership are allocated out of proportion to the capital contributed by each partner: income is allocated to a non-UK partner, and capital is allocated to the UK company which then realises untaxed profits as capital. The *FA 2004* measures deem profits to accrue to the UK company in line with its partnership share, and taxes those profits under Schedule D Case VI, when the company realises capital. The provisions apply to capital realisations comprising untaxed profits arising after 16 March 2004. [*FA 2004, ss 131, 132*]. See Tolley's Corporation Tax for full details.

Where such a tax charge applies as a result of the receipt on or after 17 March 2004 by a company of any consideration for a disposal (the '*section 131 disposal*') on or after that date of all or any of its interest in the partnership and a chargeable gain accrues to the company on a 'relevant disposal', the following provisions apply to prevent a double charge to tax. For this purpose, a '*relevant disposal*' is any disposal of an asset that, alone or together with other disposals of assets, constitutes a section 131 disposal.

If the total chargeable gains accruing to the company on relevant disposals exceed the total allowable losses on such disposals, those gains and losses are excluded from the company's profits chargeable to corporation tax for the accounting period in which they accrue.

Instead, the 'relevant net gain' is treated as a chargeable gain for the accounting period in which the receipt of consideration for the section 131 disposal occurs. The '*relevant net gain*' is the total of chargeable gains less allowable losses accruing to the company on relevant disposals, reduced (but not below nil) by the '*chargeable amount*' (i.e. the amount chargeable to tax under *FA 2004, s 131* in relation to the receipt of consideration for the section 131 disposal). Where there are two or more receipts of consideration by a company in relation to the same section 131 disposal, this provision applies only in relation to the first receipt, but in computing the net relevant gain all of the chargeable amounts relating to the receipts are deducted.

In computing a chargeable gain or allowable loss on a relevant disposal *TCGA 1992, s 37(1)* (exclusion from consideration of amounts charged to income tax etc. — see 35.1 INTERACTION WITH OTHER TAXES) does not apply to exclude the chargeable amount or any amount taken into account in computing it from the consideration and *TCGA 1992, s 39(1)* (exclusion from allowable deductions of amounts deductible in computing profits or losses for income tax purposes — see 35.1 INTERACTION WITH OTHER TAXES) does not apply to exclude from the allowable deductions any amount taken into account in computing the chargeable amount.

If the above provisions prevent an allowable loss that accrued otherwise than on a relevant disposal from being deductible from a chargeable gain accruing on a relevant disposal, the loss (to the extent that it has not been deducted from any other gains) is deductible from the total chargeable gains of the company in the accounting period in which the receipt of consideration for the section 131 disposal occurs (so that it may be set against the relevant net gain). If the loss (or losses) arose on a disposal to a connected person so that *TCGA 1992, s 18(3)* applies (see 40.5 LOSSES), the total amount so deductible in respect of the loss (or losses) is restricted to the amount of the relevant net gain.

[*FA 2004, s 133*].

46.19 LIMITED LIABILITY PARTNERSHIPS

A limited liability partnership (LLP) is in law a body corporate (with legal personality separate from that of its members) incorporated under *Limited Liability Partnerships Act 2000* which came into force on 6 April 2001. [*LLPA 2000, ss 1, 19(1); SI 2000 No 3316*]. But, for the purposes of income tax and corporation tax, a trade, profession or business carried on by an LLP with a view to profit is treated as if carried on instead by its members in partnership, and the property of the LLP is treated for those purposes as partnership property. [*ICTA 1988, s 118ZA; LLPA 2000, s 10(1); FA 2001, s 75(1)(6); ITTOIA 2005, s 863, Sch 1 para 97*]. The essential feature of an LLP is that it combines the organisational flexibility and tax status of a partnership with limited liability for its members. LLPs are likely to be used mainly by professional partnerships.

Similarly, for the purposes of taxing chargeable gains, assets held by an LLP carrying on a trade or business with a view to profit are treated as held by its members as partners, and dealings by an LLP are treated as dealings by its members in partnership. As in 46.4 above, tax is assessed and charged on the members separately in respect of chargeable gains accruing to them on the disposal of LLP assets. [*TCGA 1992, s 59A(1); LLPA 2000, s 10(3); FA 2001, s 75(2)(6)*].

All references to partnerships and partnership members in the legislation on taxation of chargeable gains are to be taken as including LLPs within *section 59A(1)* and members of such LLPs. [*TCGA 1992, s 59A(2); LLPA 2000, s 10(3); FA 2001, s 75(2)(6)*]. Thus, the preceding paragraphs of this chapter generally apply as if an LLP were an ordinary partnership.

If an LLP *temporarily* ceases to carry on a trade or business with a view to profit, the treatment under *TCGA 1992, s 59A(1)* above continues. In the case of a permanent cessation, *section 59A(1)* treatment continues during an informal winding-up, provided the winding-up is not wholly or partly for tax avoidance reasons and is not unreasonably prolonged. *Section 59A(1)* treatment does, however, cease upon the appointment of a liquidator or (if earlier) the making of a winding-up order by the court (or upon the equivalent in each case under non-UK law). Neither the commencement of *section 59A(1)* treatment nor its ceasing to apply is to be taken as giving rise to the disposal of any assets by the LLP itself or by any of its members. During a liquidation period, an LLP is itself taxable (through its liquidator) on disposals of assets, under the normal corporate insolvency rules. Chargeable gains on assets disposed of in the liquidation period are taxed as if *section 59A(1)* tax treatment had never applied, and the only capital asset which a member then holds for tax purposes is his interest in the LLP. The proceeds of disposal of that interest is based on the amount of the liquidator's capital distributions (if any). In calculating the chargeable gain or allowable loss on that disposal, the member's interest is to be taken as acquired on the date he originally joined the LLP and by reference to the capital cost of his becoming a member. [*TCGA 1992, s 59A(3)–(6); LLPA 2000, s 10(3); FA 2001, s 75(2)(6)*]. See 33.5, 33.8 HOLD-OVER RELIEFS, 55.1 ROLLOVER RELIEF for other implications.

Revenue Tax Bulletin December 2000 pp 801–805 set out the Revenue's views on matters concerning LLPs. In particular: the transfer of the business of an ordinary partnership to an LLP does not of itself constitute a disposal by the partners of their interests in the underlying assets and does not affect the availability of INDEXATION (34) allowance, the holding period for TAPER RELIEF (61) or the ownership period for RETIREMENT RELIEF (53); the transfer from an ordinary partnership to an LLP of a partner's annuity rights and/or annuity obligations to former members or the agreement by an annuitant to the substitution (as payer) of the LLP for the old partnership is not regarded as a chargeable disposal, provided that the rights/terms remain substantially the same; HMRC Statement of Practice SP D12 (revised October 2002 and referred to throughout this chapter) applies equally to the members of an LLP for as long as it remains within *TCGA 1992, s 59A(1)*; the above treatment of an LLP in liquidation and of its members does not affect the tax treatment of pre-liquidation disposals, which will remain undisturbed.

Property investment LLPs. The normal exemptions for income and gains of pension funds, life insurance companies in respect of their pension business, and friendly societies in respect of their tax-exempt business do not apply where the income or gains accrue to the fund etc. in its capacity as a member of a 'property investment LLP'. See, for example, 22.56, 22.59 EXEMPTIONS AND RELIEFS. A '*property investment LLP*' is an LLP whose business consists wholly or mainly in the making of investments in land and the principal part of whose income is derived therefrom. Whether or not an LLP is within this definition must be judged for each period of account separately. [*TCGA 1992, s 288(1); ICTA 1988, s 842B; FA 2001, s 76, Sch 25 para 1*].

47 Payment of Tax

Cross-references. See 4 APPEALS; 5 ASSESSMENTS; 10.7 CHARITIES for gifts of tax repayments to charities via the tax return; 23 FRAUDULENT OR NEGLIGENT CONDUCT; 37 INTEREST AND SURCHARGES ON UNPAID TAX; 44.2 OFFSHORE SETTLEMENTS as regards the liability of migrating trustees of a settlement; 45.5 OVERSEAS MATTERS for relief for unremittable overseas gains and 45.13 for companies ceasing to be UK resident and non-resident companies; 56 SELF-ASSESSMENT.

47.1 CAPITAL GAINS TAX

For 1996/97 and subsequent years, capital gains tax becomes due and payable as part of a taxpayer's self-assessment. The due date for payment (or repayment) is 31 January following the year of assessment. The one exception is where the taxpayer gave notice of chargeability under *TMA 1970, s 7* (see 48.1 PENALTIES) within six months after the end of the year of assessment, but was not given notice under *TMA 1970, s 8* or *s 8A* (personal and trustee's return; see 54.2 RETURNS) until after 31 October following the year of assessment; in such case, the due date is the last day of the three months beginning with the date of the said notice. The tax payable is reduced by any income tax overpayment for the year. [*TMA 1970, s 59B(1)–(4)(7)(8); FA 1994, s 193, s 196, s 199(2), Sch 19 para 45; FA 1996, s 122(2), s 126(2); ITEPA 2003, Sch 6 para 131; ITTOIA 2005, Sch 1 para 377*].

See 56.6 SELF-ASSESSMENT for deferral of the due date for payment (repayment) of an amount of tax as a result of an amendment or correction to an individual's or trustees' self-assessment or a consequential amendment arising from an amendment or correction to a partnership return or partnership statement. Note, however, that those rules do *not* defer the date from which interest accrues, which is as in 37.1 INTEREST AND SURCHARGES ON UNPAID TAX (36.1 INTEREST ON OVERPAID TAX), although they do determine the due date for surcharge purposes — see 37.4 INTEREST AND SURCHARGES ON UNPAID TAX.

Where an HMRC officer enquires into the return (see 54.8 RETURNS) and a repayment is otherwise due, the repayment is not required to be made until the enquiry is completed (see 54.11 RETURNS) although the officer may make a provisional repayment at his discretion.

Subject to the appeal and postponement provisions in 4.1 APPEALS and 47.3 below, the due date for payment of tax charged by assessment otherwise than by self-assessment, e.g. a discovery assessment under *TMA 1970, s 29* (see 5.2 ASSESSMENTS), is 30 days after the date of the assessment (but see also 37.1 INTEREST AND SURCHARGES ON UNPAID TAX).

[*TMA 1970, s 59B(4A)(6); FA 1994, s 193, s 199(2)(3); FA 1995, s 103(7), s 115(6); FA 1996, s 127; FA 2001, s 88, Sch 29 paras 14(2), 16*].

47.2 CORPORATION TAX (ON CHARGEABLE GAINS)

Accounting periods ending after 30 September 1993. Corporation tax (including that in respect of chargeable gains) is due and payable without assessment on the day following the expiry of nine months from the end of the period. The amount shown in the return for the period under *TMA 1970, s 11* (see 54.18 RETURNS) as the corporation tax due for the period is treated for collection purposes as tax charged and due and payable under an assessment on the company.

If the company subsequently has grounds for believing that a change in circumstances has rendered payment for a period excessive, it may, by notice to the inspector stating the grounds and the amount it considers should be repaid, claim repayment of the excess. Such notice may not be given before the date on which the tax became (or would have become) due and payable as above, or after an assessment for the period has become final. If the company wishes to claim repayment at a time when an assessment for the period is under appeal, the company must apply to the Appeal Commissioners concerned for a determination of the amount to be repaid pending determination of the appeal. Such an application may be combined with an application for postponement of tax pending an appeal (see 47.3 below). [*ICTA 1988, s 10; FA 1990, s 106; FA 1998, s 117, Sch 19 para 1, Sch 27 Pt III(28); SI 1992 No 3066*].

Corporation tax self-assessment. Under corporation tax self-assessment for accounting periods ending on or after 1 July 1999 (see 56.2 SELF-ASSESSMENT), comparable provisions generally apply (except that assessments are replaced by self-assessments). [*TMA 1970, ss 59D, 59DA; FA 1998, s 117, Sch 19 para 29; FA 2004, Sch 12 paras 2, 3*]. For 'large' companies, however, this is subject to the rules outlined below for payment of corporation tax by quarterly instalments.

Quarterly accounting by large companies. A system of *quarterly accounting* for corporation tax (i.e. payment by instalments) by 'large' companies is introduced for accounting periods ending on or after 1 July 1999 (to coincide with the introduction of corporation tax self-assessment). [*TMA 1970, s 59E; FA 1998, s 30*]. Under the *Corporation Tax (Instalment Payments) Regulations 1998*, '*large*' companies are those liable to the full rate of corporation tax, i.e. those with profits (including UK dividend income, other than intra-group dividends, plus tax credits) exceeding £1,500,000 in a year, divided by one plus the number of active associated companies if any. However, such a company is not treated as 'large' in respect of an accounting period if its total corporation tax liability for that period does not exceed £10,000 (£5,000 for accounting periods ending before 1 July 2000), which might be the case if it would otherwise be large only by reference to the number of its associates or the level of its dividend income. A company is also exempt from payment by instalments for an accounting period if it was not 'large' in the 12 months preceding the accounting period and its profits for the accounting period do not exceed £10 million, divided by one plus the number of active associated companies as at the end of the preceding accounting period. Each of these monetary limits is proportionately reduced for accounting periods of less than 12 months.

The switch to full payment by instalments was achieved over a transitional period ending on 30 June 2002. For accounting periods ending before 1 July 2000, 60% of the total liability was payable by a maximum of four instalments, increasing to 72% for those ending in the year to 30 June 2001, 88% for those ending in the year to 30 June 2002 and finally to 100% for all subsequent accounting periods. During the transitional period, the balance not payable by instalments was payable by the normal due date (see above). The first instalment is due 6 months and 14 days into the accounting period and the last is due 3 months and 14 days after the end of the accounting period. Interim instalments are due at quarterly intervals. Except for accounting periods of less than 12 months, the amount of each instalment should be one quarter of the total payable by instalments. Interest on tax underpaid by any instalment will run from the due date of that instalment. In cases of deliberate or reckless non-payment or underpayment, a penalty of up to twice the amount of interest may be charged. Subject to similar penalty for fraud or negligence, a company may claim repayment of tax paid by instalments if its circumstances change such that the total liability is likely to be less than previously calculated. See Revenue Tax Bulletins February 2000 pp 723–726 and April 2001 pp 831–836 for practical articles on the operation of the system. HMRC are given extensive powers to require information and records to ascertain reasons for non-payment of an instalment, the validity of a repayment claim or whether the amount of an instalment is consistent with the quality and quantity of information available as to the company's likely corporation tax liability. See below re HMRC guidance on use of their information and penalty powers.

In the absence of counteraction, companies could delay the commencement of instalments or obtain excessive benefit from the transition (by, for example, arranging that more than one year's corporation tax liability fell in the first year of the transition); they could do so by changing their accounting date and/or transferring profitable activities to companies in the same group but with different accounting dates. There are anti-forestalling provisions to counteract this. Changes of accounting date decided upon, or based on facts in existence, before 25 November 1997 or occasioned by the company being taken over and aligning its accounting date with that of its new ultimate parent company are exempted, as are transfers of profits not exceeding £5 million, reduced proportionately for accounting periods of less than 12 months.

[*SI 1998 No 3175; SI 1999 No 1929; SI 2000 No 892*].

HMRC have published guidance outlining the way in which they will use their information and penalty powers under the above regulations; the information powers are not intended for routine use, and the majority of cases of late or inadequate payment will attract only an interest charge, not a penalty. A penalty will be sought in only the most serious cases involving flagrant abuse of the regulations. (Revenue Press Release 8 June 1999). Further guidance on 'acceptable' methods of estimating quarterly instalments has been published on HMRC's website (Revenue Internet Statement 28 June 2002).

Penalties are also chargeable for non-compliance with a notice to produce information, records etc. [*TMA 1970, s 98; FA 1999, s 89(1)(3)*].

Groups of companies. Under corporation tax self-assessment, HMRC are given power to enter into arrangements ('Group Payment Arrangements') with some or all of the members of a group of companies (defined to include all 51% subsidiaries) for one of them to discharge any liability of each of them for the accounting period to which the arrangements relate. [*FA 1998, s 36*]. This facility was put in place for accounting periods ending on or after 31 December 1999 (Revenue Press Release 26 February 1999). See Revenue Tax Bulletins April 1999 pp 647–650 and April 2001 pp 831–836.

There are continuing provisions to allow two companies within a group (as defined for group relief purposes under *ICTA 1988, Pt X Ch IV*) to jointly give notice to the inspector that a 'tax refund relating to an accounting period' which falls to be made to one of them should be surrendered in whole or part to the other. The surrendering company is then treated as having received on the 'relevant date' a payment equal to the refund (or part), and the recipient company as having paid on that date corporation tax equal to the amount of the refund (or part). [*FA 1989, s 102; FA 1993, Sch 14 para 11; FA 1999, s 89(2)(3), s 93, Sch 11 para 3; F(No 2)A 2005, Sch 11 Pt 2(7); SI 1998 No 3175, Reg 9; SI 1999 No 1929, Reg 3*]. These provisions are designed to enable group members to rearrange their tax liabilities without suffering a disadvantage because of the higher rates for interest on unpaid tax as compared with those for interest on overpaid tax. See Tolley's Corporation Tax under Groups of Companies for full coverage of the provisions. For the interaction between these provisions and the Group Payment Arrangements referred to above, see Revenue Tax Bulletin April 2001 pp 834, 835.

47.3 POSTPONEMENT OF TAX PENDING APPEAL

The following applies under self-assessment for 1996/97 onwards as regards CGT (and income tax) and for corporation tax accounting periods ending on or after 1 July 1999, and applies in the case of APPEALS (4) against

(*a*) (for enquiries completed on or after 11 May 2001) a conclusion stated or amendment made by a closure notice on completion of enquiry into a personal, trustee or partnership tax return (see 54.11, 54.17 RETURNS);

(*b*) (for enquiries completed before 11 May 2001) a Revenue amendment of a personal, trustee or partnership self-assessment following enquiry (see 54.12 RETURNS);

(*c*) an HMRC amendment of a company tax return following enquiry (see *FA 1998, Sch 18 para 34*);

(*d*) an HMRC amendment to a self-assessment during enquiry to prevent potential loss of tax (see 54.12 RETURNS and, for companies, *FA 1998, Sch 18 para 30*); and (*e*) an assessment other than a self-assessment.

In the absence of any application for postponement of tax as below, tax is **due and payable** as if there had been no appeal.

If the appellant has grounds for believing that he is overcharged to tax by the amendment or assessment or as a result of the conclusion stated (as the case may be), he (or his agent) may, by notice in writing stating those grounds and given to the HMRC officer in question within 30 days after the 'relevant date', apply to the Appeal Commissioners for postponement of a specified amount of tax pending determination of the appeal. The '*relevant date*' is the date of issue of the notice of amendment or assessment or, in the case of an appeal within (*a*) above, the date of issue of the closure notice.

The taxpayer and the HMRC officer may then come to an agreement in writing as to the amount of tax to be postponed (if any), and the giving by either party to the other of written notice, confirming the existence of an agreement and the terms thereof, is treated as a written agreement for this purpose. Where the parties cannot (or do not attempt to) come to an agreement, the matter is referred to the Appeal Commissioners, who, if they consider that there are reasonable grounds for believing that an amount of tax has been overcharged, must postpone that amount pending determination of the substantive appeal.

On the determination of (or agreement on) the amount of tax to be postponed, the balance of tax *not postponed* (if any) becomes **due and payable** as if it had been charged by an amendment or assessment issued on the date of that determination or agreement (or on the date of notice of confirmation of the latter) and in respect of which there had been no appeal.

Application for postponement may be made outside the normal 30-day time limit if there is a change in circumstances which gives grounds for belief that the appellant is overcharged by the amendment etc. The Revenue indicated that a 'change in circumstances' is not just a change of mind but a change in the circumstances in which the original decision not to apply for postponement was made. Two examples cited by the Revenue (prior to the self-assessment regime) are (*a*) where further work on the preparation of accounts indicates that an estimated assessment is 'wide of the mark' and (*b*) where it has become apparent that further relief (e.g. loss or group relief) is due (CCAB Statement TR 477, 28 June 1982). A late application does not, however, defer the due date of any balance of tax *not postponed*.

If, after the determination of an amount of tax to be postponed and as a result of a change in the circumstances of the case, either the appellant or the HMRC officer has grounds for believing that the amount postponed is excessive or insufficient, he may apply to the Appeal Commissioners for a further determination of the amount to be postponed. Such application may be made by notice in writing to the other party at any time before the determination of the substantive appeal. The notice must state the amount of the supposed excess or insufficiency and the grounds for that supposition. If, on this further determination, an amount of tax ceases to be postponed, that amount is treated as charged by an assessment issued on the date of the further determination and in respect of which no appeal is pending. If, on the other hand, an amount of tax has been overpaid, that amount becomes repayable.

A postponement application is to be heard in the same way as the appeal, and consideration of the application does not preclude the same Commissioners from hearing and determining the appeal or from considering a further application as above. Any transfer of proceedings from one body of Commissioners to another does not affect the validity of a postponement determination.

[*TMA 1970, s 55(1)–(3)(3A)(4)–(6)(7)(8)(10)(10A)(10B)(11); F(No 2)A 1975, s 45(1); FA 1982, s 68; FA 1989, s 156(2)(4); FA 1990, s 104(2)(4); FA 1994, ss 196, 199, Sch 19 para 18; FA 1998, Sch 19 para 28; FA 2001, s 88, Sch 29 para 31*].

Under self-assessment of CGT (and income tax) for 1996/97 onwards, the giving of notice of appeal, whether or not accompanied by a postponement application, does *not* affect the date from which interest accrues, for which see 37.1 INTEREST AND SURCHARGES ON UNPAID TAX. The same applies as regards assessments for 1995/96 and earlier years where first raised after 5 April 1998. A similar situation applies for corporation tax under 'Pay and File' for accounting periods ending after 30 September 1993, and continues under self-assessment for accounting periods ending after 30 June 1999. For interest implications as regards CGT (and income tax) assessments for 1995/96 and earlier years raised before 6 April 1998, see 37.2 INTEREST AND SURCHARGES ON UNPAID TAX.

47.4 PAYMENT OF TAX ON DETERMINATION OF APPEAL

The following applies where tax is payable in accordance with the determination of an appeal within 47.3(*a*)–(*e*) above and it is either tax postponed in accordance with 47.3 above or an addition to the tax charged by the amendment or assessment before appeal. Such tax becomes **due and payable** as if it were charged by an amendment or assessment issued on the date on which the inspector or other HMRC officer issued to the taxpayer a notice of the total amount payable in accordance with the determination and in respect of which there had been no appeal. Any tax found to be overpaid on determination of the appeal becomes repayable. [*TMA 1970, s 55(9); F(No 2)A 1975, s 45(1); FA 1989, s 156(2)(4); FA 1994, ss 196, 199, Sch 19 para 18*].

Any tax charged in accordance with the Commissioners' determination in an appeal against an assessment must be paid as above, notwithstanding any pending appeal to the courts. If, on determination of the appeal by the court, further tax is found to be chargeable, it becomes due and payable 30 days after the date on which the inspector issues to the taxpayer a notice of the total amount payable in accordance with the order or judgment of the court. Tax overpaid consequent on the decision of the court is repaid (with, at the court's discretion, interest) even though further appeal is possible (*T & E Homes Ltd v Robinson CA 1979, 52 TC 567*). [*TMA 1970, ss 56(9), 56A(8)(9); F(No 2)A 1975, s 45(3); FA 1989, s 156(3)(4); SI 1994 No 1813*].

For interest implications as regards CGT (and income tax) assessments for 1995/96 and earlier years raised before 6 April 1998, see 37.2, 37.3 INTEREST AND SURCHARGES ON UNPAID TAX.

47.5 EFFECTIVE DATES OF PAYMENT

HMRC take the date of payment in respect of each payment method to be as follows.

- Cheques, cash, postal orders handed in at HMRC offices or received by post (except as below): the day of receipt by HMRC.
- Cheques, cash, postal orders received by post following a day when the office has been closed for whatever reason (including a weekend): the day the office was first closed.
- Electronic Funds Transfer — payment by BACS (transfer over two days) or CHAPS (same day transfer): one day prior to receipt by the Revenue.
- Bank Giro or Girobank: the date on which payment was made at the bank or Post Office.

(Revenue 'Working Together' Bulletin July 2000 p 3).

For the purposes of *TMA 1970* generally and also of the statutory provisions dealing specifically with INTEREST ON OVERPAID TAX (36), it is provided by law that where any payment to HMRC is received by cheque after 5 April 1996 and the cheque is paid on its first presentation to the bank on which it is drawn, the payment is treated as made on the date of receipt of the cheque by HMRC. [*TMA 1970, s 70A; FA 1994, s 196, Sch 19 para 22*].

47.6 PAYMENT BY INSTALMENTS ETC.

Where the whole or part of the consideration for a disposal is receivable by instalments over a period exceeding 18 months, beginning not earlier than the date of disposal, the tax arising may at the option of the person making the disposal be paid by such instalments as HMRC allows, over a period not exceeding eight years (and ending not later than the time at which the last of the instalments of the consideration is payable). [*TCGA 1992, s 280; FA 1996, Sch 20 para 65*]. For guidance given to inspectors on the practical operation of this relief, see HMRC Capital Gains Manual CG 14910–14922.

Interest on unpaid tax will be charged only if an instalment is paid late. It will be charged on that instalment, and will run from the date when the instalment was due (Tolley's Practical Tax 1988, p 176 and 1989, p 5).

For postponed or contingent future consideration, see 9.1 CAPITAL SUMS DERIVED FROM ASSETS and 15.6 COMPUTATION OF GAINS AND LOSSES.

Gifts etc. Subject to the conditions below, capital gains tax chargeable on a gift may, on election in writing, be paid by ten equal yearly instalments. The first instalment is due on the ordinary due date and the unpaid tax will attract interest on unpaid tax in the usual way and which will be payable with each instalment. The outstanding balance together with accrued interest may be paid at any time. The deferral of payment is available where the whole or any part of specified assets is disposed of by way of gift or is deemed to be disposed of by trustees under *TCGA 1992, s 71*(*1*) or *s 72*(*1*) (see 57.15–57.17 SETTLEMENTS) and the disposal is *either* one to which neither *TCGA 1992, s 165*(*4*) nor *s 260*(*3*) (see 33.1 and 33.7 HOLD-OVER RELIEFS) applies (or would apply if a claim was made) *or* one to which either of those *sections* does apply but on which the held-over gain only partly reduces the gain otherwise arising or is nil. The assets specified for this purpose are: land or any interest or estate in land; any shares or securities of a company which, immediately before the disposal, gave control to the person making or deemed to be making the disposal; and any shares or securities of a company not falling within the foregoing and not listed on a recognised stock exchange (see 58.23 SHARES AND SECURITIES) nor dealt in on the Unlisted Securities Market (now closed). Tax and any accrued interest is payable immediately if the disposal was by way of a gift to a person connected (see 16 CONNECTED PERSONS) with the donor or was deemed to be made under *TCGA 1992, s 71*(*1*) or *s 72*(*1*) and the assets are disposed of for a valuable consideration under a subsequent disposal (whether or not made by the original donee). Interest on unpaid tax is chargeable on each instalment as if no election to pay by instalments had been made. Instalments and interest may be paid at any time with the interest calculation adjusted accordingly.

These provisions apply in relation to a chargeable gain accruing under *TCGA 1992, s 169C*(*7*) (clawback of relief under *TCGA 1992, s 165* or *s 260* if settlement becomes settlor-interested — see 33.5 HOLD-OVER RELIEFS) as they apply to a gain accruing on a disposal if

- the 'relevant disposal' (see 33.5 HOLD-OVER RELIEFS) in question was a disposal of the whole or part of any asset of a type specified above, and
- at the time that the chargeable gain is deemed to accrue, no part of the subject-matter of the relevant disposal has been disposed of for valuable consideration under a subsequent disposal (whether or not by the trustees to whom the relevant disposal was made).

Tax and accrued interest are payable immediately if any part of the subject-matter of the relevant disposal is disposed of for valuable consideration under a subsequent disposal (whether or not by the trustees to whom the relevant disposal was made).

[*TCGA 1992, s 281; FA 1996, Sch 18 para 15, para 17*(*3*)*, Sch 38 para 10*(*1*)*–*(*3*)*; FA 2004, Sch 21 para 6, Sch 42 Pt 2*(*13*)].

For a summary of other reliefs available to disposals by way of gift etc., see 25.3 GIFTS.

'Time to Pay' arrangements. By concession, under a 'time to pay' arrangement, a taxpayer enters into a negotiated agreement with HMRC, which takes full account of his circumstances (e.g. illness, unemployment, unforeseen short-term business difficulties), and thereby commits to settle his tax liabilities by regular instalments. Clear reasons for allowing settlement over an extended period that runs beyond the due date must be established during negotiations and any such arrangement is normally subject to adequate provision being made to settle future liabilities on time. Interest on unpaid tax is chargeable in the normal way on the full amount unpaid at the due date and not just on overdue instalments. However, a surcharge may be avoided where a 'Time to Pay' arrangement is in force (see 37.4 INTEREST AND SURCHARGES ON UNPAID TAX). (HMRC Self-Assessment Manual — Payments section, Personal Contact Manual para 4.8).

47.7 COLLECTION AND GENERALLY

The Collector of Taxes may distrain (poind in Scotland). [*TMA 1970, ss 61–64; FA 1989, ss 152–155; FA 2004, Sch 12 paras 4–6; SI 1994, Nos 87, 236; SI 1995 No 2151*]. See also *Herbert Berry Associates Ltd v CIR HL 1977, 52 TC 113.* Where an amount of CGT or corporation tax due is less than £2,000 (£1,000 prior to the self-assessment regime), the Collector may within one year after the due date take summary magistrates' court proceedings. The Collector may also recover the tax by proceedings in the county court. [*TMA 1970, ss 65, 66; FA 1984, s 57; FA 1994, Sch 19 para 19; FA 1998, Sch 19 para 30; FA 2001, s 89(1); SI 1991 Nos 724, 1877*]. But for limitations in Scotland and NI see *TMA 1970, s 65(4), s 66(3)(4), s 67; FA 1976, s 58; FA 1995, s 156; FA 2001, s 89(1)*, and see *Mann v Cleaver KB 1930, 15 TC 367*. Unpaid tax (and arrears) may also be recovered (with full costs) as a Crown debt in the High Court. [*TMA 1970, s 68*]. The amount of an assessment which has become final cannot be re-opened in proceedings to collect the tax (*CIR v Pearlberg CA 1953, 34 TC 57*; *CIR v Soul CA 1976, 51 TC 86*), and it is not open to the taxpayer to raise the defence that the Revenue acted *ultra vires* in raising the assessment (*CIR v Aken CA 1990, 63 TC 395*).

For whether unpaid tax is a business liability for commercial etc. purposes, see *Conway v Wingate CA, [1952] 1 All ER 782*; *Stevens v Britten CA, [1954] 3 All ER 385*; *R v Vaccari CCA, [1958] 1 All ER 468*; *In re Hollebone's Agreement CA, [1959] 2 All ER 152*.

For the limited priority given to payment of corporation tax in a winding-up of a company, see 13.8 COMPANIES.

47.8 RECOVERY OF FOREIGN TAXES ETC.

EU member states. Provision is made for the recovery in the UK of direct taxes (and interest and penalties) in respect of which a request for enforcement has been made in accordance with the Mutual Assistance Recovery Directive (*Directive 76/308/EEC as amended*) by an authority in another EU member state. Disclosure of information by a UK tax authority (e.g. HMRC) for these purposes (or for the purposes of a request by the UK for enforcement elsewhere) is not generally precluded by any obligation of secrecy.

Broadly, the UK tax authority has the same powers it would have for a corresponding claim in the UK, in particular in relation to interest and penalties. Treasury regulations may make provision as to what UK claim corresponds to a foreign claim, and for other procedural and supplementary matters (see now *SI 2004 No 674*). Regulations may also be made by the UK tax authority for the application, non-application or adaptation of the law applicable to corresponding UK claims, without prejudice to its application when not dealt with by such regulations.

No proceedings may be taken against a person under these provisions if he shows that proceedings relevant to the liability in question are pending (i.e. still subject to appeal), or are about to be instituted, before a competent body in the relevant member state. This does not apply if the foreign proceedings are not prosecuted or instituted with reasonable expedition. If a final decision on the foreign claim (i.e. one no longer appealable) (or a part of it) has been given in the taxpayer's favour by a competent body in the relevant member state, no proceedings may be taken under these provisions in relation to the claim (or part).

The Treasury may, by regulations, amend, replace or repeal any of the above provisions for the purpose of giving effect to future amendments to the Directive.

[*FA 2002, s 134, Sch 39; SI 2005 No 1479*].

Tax enforcement agreements. Provision is made for the Treasury to make regulations for the recovery in the UK of foreign taxes covered by a tax enforcement agreement with another country (see 29.2(*c*) HMRC: CONFIDENTIALITY OF INFORMATION). [*FA 2006, s 175*].

47.9 RECOVERY OF TAX FROM OFFICERS

Tax which has fallen due may be recovered from the treasurer or acting treasurer (the 'proper officer') of a company which is not a body corporate or not incorporated under a UK enactment or by charter. That officer then has a right of reimbursement out of moneys coming into his hands on behalf of that company, and to be indemnified by the company for any balance. [*TMA 1970, s 108*(*2*)(*3*)].

47.10 REMISSION OF TAX IN CASES OF HMRC DELAY

Arrears of income tax or capital gains tax may be given up if they result from HMRC's failure to make proper and timely use of information supplied by:

- a taxpayer about his or her own income, gains or personal circumstances;
- an employer where the information affects a taxpayer's coding; or
- the Department for Work and Pensions (previously the DSS) about a taxpayer's State retirement, disability or widow's pension.

Tax will normally be given up only where the taxpayer could reasonably have believed that his or her tax affairs were in order; and

- was notified of the arrears more than twelve months after the end of the tax year in which HMRC received the information in question; or
- was notified of an over-repayment after the end of the tax year following the year in which the repayment was made.

In exceptional circumstances arrears of tax notified twelve months or less after the end of the relevant tax year may be given up if HMRC either failed more than once to make proper use of the facts they had been given about one source of income or allowed the arrears of tax to build up over two whole tax years in succession by failing to make proper and timely use of information they had been given.

(HMRC Extra-Statutory Concession A19).

Under *TMA 1970*, unless a longer or shorter period is prescribed, no statutory claim for relief is allowed unless it is made on or before the fifth anniversary of 31 January following the tax year to which it relates. However, repayments of tax will be made in respect of claims made outside the statutory time limit where an overpayment of tax has arisen because of an error by HMRC or another Government Department, and where there is no dispute or doubt as to the facts (HMRC Extra-Statutory Concession B41).

47.11 OVERPAYMENTS OF TAX

For an article on HMRC practice re allocations of overpayments under SELF-ASSESSMENT (56), see Revenue Tax Bulletin June 1999 pp 673, 674.

47.12 OVER-REPAYMENTS OF TAX

If not otherwise assessable under *TMA 1970, s 29* (discovery assessments — see 5.2 ASSESSMENTS), capital gains tax repaid in error, or over-repaid, by HMRC may be assessed and recovered as if it were unpaid tax. For this purpose, a repayment includes an amount allowed by way of set-off. For 1996/97 and subsequent years under self-assessment, HMRC's right to assess under these provisions is subject to the same exceptions (modified as appropriate) as apply to discovery assessments. Excess repayment supplement (see 36 INTEREST ON OVERPAID TAX) may be similarly assessed or may be included in an assessment of over-repaid tax. The normal deadline for raising assessments is extended in the above cases to the later of

- the end of the tax year following that in which the repayment was made, and
- (for 1996/97 onwards) in the event of an HMRC enquiry into a return, the day on which the enquiry is statutorily completed (see 54.11 RETURNS),

but remains subject to the normal extensions in cases of FRAUDULENT OR NEGLIGENT CONDUCT (see 23.3).

Comparable provisions apply for the purposes of corporation tax (and interest on overpaid corporation tax). The normal deadline for raising assessments is extended to the later of

- the end of the accounting period following that in which the repayment was made, and
- (for accounting periods ending on or after 1 July 1999) in the event of an HMRC enquiry into a relevant company tax return, the end of the period of three months following the day on which the enquiry is completed (in accordance with *FA 1998, Sch 18 para 32*),

subject to extension in cases of fraudulent or negligent conduct.

[*TMA 1970, s 30; FA 1982, s 149; F(No 2)A 1987, s 88; FA 1989, s 149(3); FA 1990, s 105; FA 1994, ss 196, 199(2)(3), Sch 19 para 4; FA 1998, s 117, Sch 18 paras 52, 53, Sch 19 para 13; FA 2001, s 88, Sch 29 para 23; ITTOIA 2005, Sch 1 para 369*].

The exercise by HMRC of their discretion to raise an assessment under *TMA 1970, s 30* can be challenged only by way of judicial review (see 4.24 APPEALS) and not by appeal to the Appeal Commissioners (*Guthrie v Twickenham Film Studios Ltd Ch D, [2002] STC 1374*).

47.13 CERTIFICATES OF TAX DEPOSIT

Such certificates, which enable money to be set aside for payment of future tax liability, may be used in payment of capital gains tax. Interest is received on these certificates from the date of purchase until the date on which the tax in respect of which they are surrendered falls due. Certificates may also be encashed (with interest to the date of encashment) but a lower rate of interest is then paid. Certificates for use against corporation tax liabilities ceased to be available for purchase after 30 September 1993 as a result of the introduction of Pay and File procedures. For further details, see Tolley's Income Tax.

47.14 RECOVERY OF TAX IN RESPECT OF DISPOSALS BY OTHERS

There are instances in the legislation whereby HMRC can assess, and/or recover tax from, persons other than the person actually making the disposal which gives rise to the liability. This right usually follows from the non-payment of tax by the person originally assessed in respect of the chargeable disposal by him but may also arise because of specific legislation (e.g. UK residents charged in respect of disposals made by certain overseas resident companies, see 45.6 OVERSEAS MATTERS). The person from whom tax is recovered is normally given a right of recovery from any person originally assessed.

Specific occurrences of the foregoing are to be found at: 3.18 ANTI-AVOIDANCE; 11.3 and 11.4 CHILDREN; 13.9, 13.10 COMPANIES; 25.4 GIFTS; 27.8, 27.9 and 27.13 GROUPS OF COMPANIES; 33.5, 33.8 and 33.9 HOLD-OVER RELIEFS; 38.4 LAND; 44.2 and 44.12 OFFSHORE SETTLEMENTS; 45.13 and 45.14 OVERSEAS MATTERS; and 57.5, 57.6 and 57.14 SETTLEMENTS.

47.15 REDUCED PAYMENTS UNDER 'EQUITABLE LIABILITY'

An assessment not appealed against or for which a late appeal application is refused becomes final and conclusive and HMRC is able to take recovery proceedings accordingly for the full amount charged even though this may be in excess of the actual liability. Whilst there is no legal right to adjustment of the liability, where the taxpayer has exhausted all other possible remedies, HMRC may, depending on the circumstances, be prepared not to pursue its legal right to recover the full amount due where it would be unscrupulous to do so.

HMRC may be prepared to operate the practice of 'equitable liability' where, depending on the circumstances and in the light of all the evidence, it is clearly demonstrated that the liability assessed is greater than the amount which would have been charged had the returns etc. required been submitted at the proper time, and acceptable evidence (not an estimate) is provided of what the correct liability should have been. This treatment is conditional on the taxpayer's affairs being brought fully up to date and full payment of the reduced tax being made, and only most unusually will it be applied more than once in favour of the same taxpayer.

Under self-assessment procedures, there is in most cases no need for HMRC to operate the above practice because of the ability of the taxpayer to displace an HMRC determination of tax liability by a self-assessment made within the later of the first anniversary of the date of determination and the fifth anniversary of the statutory filing date for the year of assessment concerned. Where exceptionally a determination can no longer be displaced and the conditions of the practice described above are fulfilled, HMRC will be prepared to consider extending its practice to meet this situation.

Cases are dealt with in HMRC's Enforcement and Insolvency Services in Worthing, Belfast and Edinburgh but local officers will be involved in considering the quantum of any claims for reduction in liability and the acceptability of the supporting evidence (HMRC Recovery Manual REC 4828, 4831; Revenue Tax Bulletin August 1995 p 245).

47.16 PAYMENT OF TAX IN EUROS

From 1 January 1999, British businesses may, if they wish, pay tax in euros (the European single currency). The taxpayer will be credited with the sterling value actually received by HMRC after conversion at the prevailing rate. There is no facility for making tax repayments in euros. (Revenue Press Release 31 July 1998). See also HMRC Pamphlet IR 166.

48 Penalties

Cross-references. See 23 FRAUDULENT OR NEGLIGENT CONDUCT; 37 INTEREST AND SURCHARGES ON UNPAID TAX; 45.13 OVERSEAS MATTERS for companies ceasing to be UK resident; 47 PAYMENT OF TAX; 54 RETURNS.

The headings in this chapter are as follows.

48.1 NOTIFICATION OF CHARGEABILITY

Capital gains tax (and income tax). For 1995/96 and subsequent tax years, a person chargeable to income tax or capital gains tax for a particular tax year who has not received a notice under *TMA 1970, s 8* (see 54.2) to deliver a return for that year of his total income and chargeable gains has until 5 October following that tax year to notify HMRC that he is so chargeable. A person is excepted from this requirement if his total income is fully taxed at source (see Tolley's Income Tax for the detailed provisions) *and* he has no chargeable gains for the year; in practice, this is taken to mean no chargeable gains in excess of the annual exempt amount — see HMRC Self Assessment Legal Framework Manual SALF 210 para 2.91. The maximum penalty for non-compliance is equal to the amount of tax payable for the year that remains unpaid after 31 January following that year.

The above applies equally to 'relevant trustees' of settlements (see 57.5 SETTLEMENTS) by reference to a notice under *TMA 1970, s 8A* (see 54.2) to deliver a tax return.

[*TMA 1970, s 7; FA 1994, ss 196, 199*(*2*), *Sch 19 para 1; FA 1995, s 103*(*1*)(*2*)(*7*), *s 115*(*1*), *Sch 21 para 1; ITEPA 2003, Sch 6 para 124; ITTOIA 2005, Sch 1 para 358*].

The trustees of occupational pension schemes which have income or capital gains are also within these provisions (see Revenue Press Release 29 August 1997, Pension Schemes Office Update 30, 5 September 1997 and see generally Revenue Tax Bulletin February 1999 pp 628, 629).

Corporation tax. A company chargeable to corporation tax for a particular accounting period which has not received a notice to deliver a company tax return has 12 months after the end of the accounting period in which to notify HMRC that it is so chargeable. The maximum penalty for non-compliance is equal to the amount of tax payable for the accounting period that remains unpaid 12 months after the end of the period. Tax payable is computed in accordance with *FA 1998, Sch 18 para 8* (but disregarding any deferred relief arising from the repayment of loans made to close company participators). [*FA 1998, s 117, Sch 18 para 2*].

The above has effect for accounting periods ending on or after 1 July 1999 (i.e. under corporation tax self-assessment), but virtually identical provisions applied for earlier accounting periods (ending after 30 September 1993) under Pay and File. In arriving at tax payable for this purpose, no account was taken of any advance corporation tax (now abolished) carried back from a subsequent accounting period. [*TMA 1970, s 10; FA 1988, s 121; FA 1993, s 120, Sch 14 para 1; FA 1998, ss 31, 117, Sch 3 para 2, Sch 19 para 1*].

See also 54.18 RETURNS for the requirement to give notice of coming within the charge to corporation tax within three months of the *beginning* of an accounting period, subject to penalties under *TMA 1970, s 98* (see 48.15 below).

48.2 **FAILURE TO DELIVER TAX RETURN ON OR BEFORE FILING DATE**

Capital gains tax (and income tax). A person (the taxpayer) who fails to deliver a return for 1996/97 or a subsequent year on or before the 'filing date' when required to do so by notice under *TMA 1970, s 8* or *s 8A* (personal or trustees' return — see 54.2 RETURNS) is liable to an automatic penalty of £100. The '*filing date*' is 31 January following the tax year in question or, if later, the last day of the period of three months beginning with the day on which the said notice is given.

For continuing failure, a further penalty of up to £60 per day may be imposed by the Appeal Commissioners (but not at any time after the failure has been remedied) on application by an HMRC officer, such daily penalty to start from the day after the taxpayer is notified of the Commissioners' direction (but not for any day for which such a daily penalty has already been imposed). HMRC have formed specialist teams to take daily penalty proceedings where there is persistent delay in submitting returns. However, they have indicated that they will not seek to charge daily penalties unless they believe that the tax at risk is high so that fixed penalties may be an insufficient deterrent (Revenue Working Together Bulletin Issue 15, January 2004).

If the failure continues for more than six months beginning with the filing date, and no application for a daily penalty was made within those six months, the taxpayer is liable to a further automatic penalty of £100. If failure continues after the anniversary of the filing date, and there would have been a liability under *TMA 1970, s 59B* (final payment of income tax and capital gains tax — see 56.5 SELF-ASSESSMENT), based on a proper return promptly delivered, the taxpayer is liable to a further penalty of an amount not exceeding that liability.

If the taxpayer's outstanding liability to income tax and capital gains tax under *TMA 1970, s 59B*, based on a proper return promptly delivered, would not have exceeded a particular amount, his total liability to the two automatic penalties above is reduced to that amount. For example, a payment on account, made under *TMA 1970, s 59A* or otherwise, which reduces the liability outstanding after 31 January to, say, £50 will similarly reduce the total automatic penalties otherwise chargeable (see HMRC Enquiry Manual EM 4562). Similarly, if there is no outstanding liability there can be no automatic penalty, though HMRC could use their power of determination (see 54.14 RETURNS) in order to encourage the delivery of a return. Where a number of tax years are being finalised together following late returns, HMRC will not regard earlier years' overpayments as set against later years' underpayments so as to reduce or extinguish fixed penalties for the later years (Tolley's Practical Tax 2002 p 152).

On an appeal against either of the automatic fixed penalties (reduced where appropriate), the Commissioners may either confirm the penalty or, if it appears to them that *throughout* the period of failure the taxpayer had a reasonable excuse for not delivering the return, set it aside. In practice, HMRC allow 14 days for the return to be filed after the excuse has ended (Revenue Tax Bulletin April 1998 p 529). See HMRC booklet SA/BK6 'Self-assessment: penalties for late tax returns', and see also Revenue Tax Bulletin April 1998 pp 527–529 for HMRC's views on what does and does not constitute a 'reasonable excuse', although it is important to note that the decision rests ultimately with the Commissioners.

[*TMA 1970, s 93; FA 1994, ss 196, 199(2), Sch 19 para 25*].

By concession, HMRC do not charge a fixed late-filing penalty where

- they reject a return as being 'unsatisfactory',
- they consequently send it back (to whoever submitted it — taxpayer or agent) with an explanatory letter no earlier than the 13th day before the filing date (e.g. 18 January where the filing date is 31 January), and
- they then receive a satisfactory return within 14 days from the date of the said letter.

An 'unsatisfactory' return is not the same as an incomplete return (for example, a return omitting income) for which the correct redress would be an enquiry (see 54.8 RETURNS) rather than rejection. A return is '*unsatisfactory*' if, for example, it is unsigned or incorrectly signed, it is not on the standard HMRC form (or agreed alternative) or supplementary pages are missing. See 54.3 RETURNS as regards each of these items. The 14-day period of grace will not be given where the original return is itself late or where the taxpayer appears to be using deliberate delaying tactics. This concession applies for 2000/01 returns and will be kept under review. A similar concession applied to earlier years' self-assessment returns. (Revenue Tax Bulletins June 2001 pp 848, 849 and February 2002 p 916).

See also *Steeden v Carver (Sp C 212), [1999] SSCD 283*, in which reliance on the Revenue's advice as to the practical extension of a deadline, unequivocally given, was held to be 'as reasonable an excuse as could be found'. Following the decision in this case, HMRC's practice for 1999/2000 returns onwards is as follows. They regard a return due on 31 January as delivered on time if found in a tax office post box when first opened on 1 February (or if delivered before midnight on 31 January by hand, courier or electronically). They do not charge a late filing penalty for returns subsequently delivered to the post box no later than first opening on 2 February (or delivered any time on 1 February by other means); however, such returns are nevertheless late, and the enquiry window is automatically extended as in 54.8(*b*) RETURNS (though in practice the Revenue did not take that point for 1998/99 returns — see Revenue 'Working Together' Bulletin April 2000 p 8). The same approach applies to later filing dates where the return is issued after 31 October (see 54.2 RETURNS). (HMRC Enquiry Manual EM 4563). This practice also applied, but in a slightly different form, for 1998/99 returns (Revenue Tax Bulletin December 1999 pp 705, 706).

48.3 **Partnership returns.** The same automatic penalties and daily penalties as in *TMA 1970, s 93* (see 48.2 above) apply in the case of failure to submit a partnership return on or before the filing date as required by a notice under *TMA 1970, s 12AA* (see 54.15 RETURNS) for 1996/97 and subsequent years. However, there is no tax-related penalty and no provision for reducing the £100 penalties. Each person who was a partner at any time during the period in respect of which the return was required is separately liable to the fixed and daily penalties. The penalties apply by reference to failure by the representative partner, i.e. the partner required by the notice under *TMA 1970, s 12AA* to deliver the return or his successor (see 54.15 RETURNS). Where penalties are imposed on two or more partners, an appeal cannot be made otherwise than by way of composite appeal by the representative partner (or successor). The same reasonable excuse provisions apply as under *TMA 1970, s 93* but by reference to the representative partner (or successor). [*TMA 1970, s 93A; FA 1994, ss 196, 199(2)(3), Sch 19 para 26; FA 1996, s 123(8)–(11)*].

48.4 **Company returns.** A company which fails to deliver a company tax return for an accounting period ending on or after 1 July 1999 on or before the 'filing date' when required to do so by notice under *FA 1998, Sch 18 para 3* is liable to a flat-rate penalty of

- £100, if the return is delivered within three months after the filing date; or
- £200, if the return is delivered more than three months after the filing date.

The '*filing date*' is the last day of whichever of the periods at 54.18(*a*)–(*c*) RETURNS is the last to end (see *FA 1998, Sch 18 para 14*). In the straightforward case, it will be the last day of the 12 months following the accounting period in question.

For a third successive failure, the above amounts are increased to £500 and £1,000 respectively. Such a failure occurs where a company is within the charge to corporation tax throughout three successive accounting periods, is required to deliver a return for each such period, is liable to a flat-rate penalty in respect of each of the first two such periods, and is again liable in respect of the third such period. The first two such periods may be periods ending before 1 July 1999, in which case the reference to a flat-rate penalty is to a corresponding penalty under the pre-self-assessment provisions referred to below. See *Lessex Ltd v Spence Sp C 2003, [2004] SSCD 79, Sp C 391*.

The flat-rate penalty does not apply if the period for which the return is required (the 'return period') is one for which accounts are required under *Companies Act 1985* (or NI equivalent) and the return is delivered to HMRC no later than the last day for delivery of the accounts to the Registrar of Companies.

By concession, no flat-rate penalty is charged if the return is received by HMRC no later than the last business day within the seven days following the filing date (HMRC Extra-Statutory Concession B46).

If a failure to deliver a return continues beyond the 18 months following the end of the accounting period in question (or beyond the filing date if, exceptionally, it falls later than that), then, in addition to a flat-rate penalty, the company is liable to a tax-related penalty. This is equal to 10% of the 'unpaid tax', increasing to 20% if the return is still not delivered within two years after the end of the return period. The '*unpaid tax*' is so much of the tax payable for the accounting period in question as remains unpaid beyond the 18-month period referred to above (or beyond the filing date if later). Tax payable is computed for this purpose in accordance with *FA 1998, Sch 18 para 8* (but disregarding any deferred relief arising from the repayment of loans made to close company participators). [*FA 1998, s 117, Sch 18 paras 17–19*].

Pre-self-assessment. Provisions virtually identical to those above applied in respect of returns for accounting periods ending before 1 July 1999 (and after 30 September 1993) where the notice under *TMA 1970, s 11* requiring delivery of the return (see 54.18 RETURNS) was served after 31 December 1993. In arriving at tax payable for these purposes, no account was taken of any advance corporation tax (now abolished) carried back from a subsequent accounting period ending more than two years after the accounting period in question. [*TMA 1970, s 94; F(No 2)A 1987, s 83; FA 1993, s 120, Sch 14 para 6; FA 1998, s 117, Sch 19 para 33*].

48.5 **European Economic Interest Grouping returns.** For income tax and capital gains tax purposes, a failure by a European Economic Interest Grouping (see 45.15 OVERSEAS MATTERS) or a member thereof to deliver a return under *TMA 1970, s 12A* (see 54.19 RETURNS) for 1996/97 or a subsequent year is subject to a fixed penalty of £300 multiplied by the number of members of the grouping at the time of failure. For continuing failure, there is a further daily penalty of up to £60 multiplied by the number of members of the grouping at the end of the day on which the grouping or member is notified of a direction to impose such a penalty by the Appeal Commissioners on an application by an HMRC officer, such daily penalty to start from the day after the taxpayer is so notified (but not for any day for which such a daily penalty has already been imposed). Neither the fixed nor the daily penalty can be imposed after the failure is remedied, and the aggregate of any fixed and daily penalties cannot exceed £100 if there is no income or chargeable gain to be included in the return. [*TMA 1970, s 98B(1)–(4); FA 1990, Sch 11 paras 3, 5; FA 1994, ss 196, 199(2)(3), Sch 19 para 30*]. For 1995/96 and earlier years, the same fixed and daily penalties applied as above except that these were not multipliable by the number of members of the grouping. For corporation tax purposes, the revised rules above apply for accounting periods ending on or after 1 July 1999.

48.6 **NEGLIGENCE OR FRAUD IN CONNECTION WITH RETURN OR ACCOUNTS**

Capital gains tax (and income tax). Where a person fraudulently or negligently

- delivers an incorrect tax return under *TMA 1970, s 8* or *s 8A* (personal or trustees' return — see 54.2 RETURNS);
- makes any incorrect return, statement or declaration in connection with any claim for an allowance, deduction or relief; or
- submits to HMRC or the Appeal Commissioners any incorrect accounts;

he is liable to a maximum penalty of an amount equal to the resulting tax underpayment. In arriving at the latter, one takes into account the tax year *in which* the return is delivered etc., the following tax year and any previous tax year. [*TMA 1970, s 95; FA 1988, Sch 14 Pt VIII; FA 1989, s 163; FA 1994, ss 196, 199(2), Sch 19 para 27*]. Liability to a penalty is supplementary to the liability to make good the tax underpayment itself.

For the above purposes, an innocent error is attributed to negligence unless it is rectified without unreasonable delay after its discovery by the taxpayer (or, following his death, by his personal representatives). Accounts submitted on a person's behalf are deemed to have been submitted by him unless he proves that they were submitted without his consent or connivance. [*TMA 1970, s 97*].

Use of a provisional or estimated figure in a return (see also 54.3 RETURNS) may result in its being incorrect, and subject to a penalty, if the figure was calculated without reasonable care or if the final figure could have been obtained before the return was filed (Revenue Tax Bulletin February 2002 p 916).

48.7 **Partnerships.** In relation to 1996/97 and subsequent years, provisions similar to those at 48.6 above apply as regards partnership returns under *TMA 1970, s 12AA* (see 54.15 RETURNS). They apply where a partner (the representative partner) delivers an incorrect partnership return, or, in connection with such a return, makes an incorrect statement or declaration or submits incorrect accounts, and either he does so fraudulently or negligently or his doing so is attributable to fraudulent or negligent conduct on the part of a 'relevant partner' (i.e. any person who was a partner at any time in the period covered by the return). Each relevant partner is liable to a penalty not exceeding the income tax (or corporation tax) underpaid by him as a result of the incorrectness. Where penalties are imposed on two or more partners, an appeal cannot be made otherwise than by way of composite appeal by the representative partner or his successor (see 54.15 RETURNS).

As regards corporate partners, these provisions have effect for accounting periods ending on or after 1 July 1999.

[*TMA 1970, s 95A; FA 1994, ss 196, 199(2)(3), Sch 19 para 28; FA 1996, s 123(12)(13); FA 2001, s 88, Sch 29 para 32*].

Note that there is no capital gains tax-related penalty under these provisions; however, there is nothing to prevent such a penalty arising under 48.6 above in relation to an individual's share of partnership chargeable gains.

Pre-self-assessment. In relation to 1995/96 and earlier years, penalties in connection with partnership returns were exigible under the provisions at 48.6 above.

48.8 **Companies.** Where a company fraudulently or negligently delivers an incorrect company tax return under *FA 1998, Sch 18 para 3* for an accounting period ended on or after 1 July 1999, it is liable to a maximum penalty of an amount equal to the resulting tax underpayment for the accounting period in question. The penalty is also chargeable if the return is delivered neither fraudulently or negligently but the company discovers it is incorrect and fails to remedy the error without unreasonable delay. [*FA 1998, s 117, Sch 18 para 20*].

A similar penalty applies where a company fraudulently or negligently makes an incorrect return, statement or declaration in connection with a claim for any allowance, deduction or relief, or submits to HMRC or the Appeal Commissioners any incorrect accounts. Accounts submitted on a company's behalf are deemed to have been submitted by it unless it proves that they were submitted without its consent or connivance. [*FA 1998, Sch 18 para 89*].

Pre-self-assessment. For accounting periods ending before 1 July 1999, provisions virtually identical to those above applied under *TMA 1970, ss 96, 97*.

48.9 **European Economic Interest Groupings.** If a European Economic Interest Grouping (see 45.15 OVERSEAS MATTERS) or a member thereof fraudulently or negligently delivers an incorrect return, accounts or statement under *TMA 1970, s 12A* (see 54.19 RETURNS) or makes an incorrect declaration in such a return, the grouping or member is liable to a maximum penalty of £3,000 multiplied by the number of members of the grouping at the time of delivery. [*TMA 1970, s 98B(5); FA 1990, Sch 11 paras 3, 5*].

48.10 FAILURE TO KEEP AND PRESERVE RECORDS

The maximum penalty for non-compliance with *TMA 1970, s 12B* (records to be kept and preserved for the purposes of self-assessment tax returns — see 54.7 RETURNS) in relation to any tax year is £3,000. [*TMA 1970, s 12B(5)–(5B); FA 1994, ss 196, 199(2)(3), Sch 19 para 3; FA 1995, s 103(7), s 105(6)(7); FA 1996, s 124(4)(5); FA 1998, Sch 19 para 6*]. The same applies for companies under corporation tax self-assessment. [*FA 1998, s 117, Sch 18 para 23*].

A separate maximum £3,000 penalty applies in relation to records relating to a claim made otherwise than in a self-assessment tax return (see 12.3 CLAIMS). [*TMA 1970, Sch 1A para 2A(4)(5); FA 1994, ss 196, 199, Sch 19 para 35; FA 1995, s 107(11), Sch 20 para 2; FA 1996, s 124(6)–(8); FA 1998, s 117, Sch 19 para 42*]. This also applies in relation to certain claims by companies under corporation tax self-assessment. [*FA 1998, s 117, Sch 18 para 57(4), para 58(3), para 59*].

48.11 FAILURE TO PRODUCE DOCUMENTS

Where, under self-assessment for 1996/97 and subsequent years, a person fails to comply with a notice or requirement under *TMA 1970, s 19A* (notice requiring production of documents etc. for purposes of HMRC enquiry into a return — see 54.10 RETURNS), he is liable to a fixed penalty of £50 and, for each subsequent day of continuing failure (but not for any day for which such a daily penalty has already been imposed), a further penalty not exceeding the 'relevant amount'. Neither the fixed nor the daily penalty may be imposed after the failure has been remedied. The '*relevant amount*' is £30 per day if the daily penalty is determined by an HMRC officer under *TMA 1970, s 100* (see 48.19 below) or £150 per day if it is determined by the Appeal Commissioners under *TMA 1970, s 100C* (see 48.21 below).

The above provisions apply equally in relation to an enquiry into a claim made otherwise than in a tax return (see 12.3 CLAIMS). For accounting periods ending on or after 1 July 1999, the same provisions apply to companies in relation to returns and claims.

[*TMA 1970, s 97AA; FA 1994, ss 196, 199(2)(3), Sch 19 para 29; FA 1996, Sch 19 para 3; FA 1998, s 117, Sch 18 para 29, Sch 19 para 36*].

The Revenue decided to discharge any penalty charged after 14 December 1998 as a result of a failure to comply with a *TMA 1970, s 19A* notice that was invalid because it required compliance in less than the necessary 30 days from receipt (see 54.10 RETURNS) (Revenue 'Working Together' Bulletin April 2000 p 8).

48.12 TWO OR MORE TAX-RELATED PENALTIES IN RESPECT OF SAME TAX

Where two or more tax-related penalties are determined by reference to the same income tax, capital gains tax or corporation tax liability, the aggregate penalty is reduced to the greater or greatest of those separate penalties. [*TMA 1970, s 97A; FA 1988, s 129; FA 1998, s 117, Sch 18 para 90, Sch 19 para 37*]. See 48.17 below for mitigation of penalties.

48.13 ASSISTING IN PREPARATION OF INCORRECT RETURN ETC.

Assisting in or inducing the preparation or delivery of any information, return, accounts or other document known to be incorrect and to be, or to be likely to be, used for any tax purpose carries a maximum penalty of £3,000. [*TMA 1970, s 99; FA 1989, s 166*]. For the taxpayer's position where an agent has been negligent or fraudulent, see *Mankowitz v Special Commrs & CIR Ch D 1971, 46 TC 707* and cf. *Clixby v Pountney Ch D 1967, 44 TC 515* and *Pleasants v Atkinson Ch D 1987, 60 TC 228*.

48.14 INTEREST ON PENALTIES

From 9 March 1998, as regards 1996/97 and subsequent tax years and for company accounting periods ending on or after 1 July 1999, all of the above penalties carry interest, calculated from the due date (broadly, 30 days after issue of a notice of determination by an HMRC officer — see 48.19 below, or immediately upon determination by Appeal Commissioners or judgement of the High Court — see 48.21, 48.22 below) to the date of payment. [*TMA 1970, s 103A; FA 1994, ss 196, 199(2)(3), Sch 19 para 33; FA 1995, s 103(7), s 115(8); FA 1998, s 117, Sch 19 para 40; SI 1998 No 311*]. For income tax and capital gains tax, rates of interest on penalties are synonymous with those on unpaid tax — see 37.1 INTEREST AND SURCHARGES ON UNPAID TAX.

48.15 SPECIAL RETURNS ETC.

Failure to render any information or particulars or any return, certificate, statement or other document which is required, whether by notice or otherwise, under the provisions listed in *TMA 1970, s 98* is the subject of a maximum penalty of £300, plus £60 for each day the failure continues after that penalty is imposed (but not for any day for which such a daily penalty has already been imposed). These penalties are increased by a factor of ten in the case of a failure under *ICTA 1988, s 765A* (movements of capital between residents of EC member states). The maximum penalty for an incorrect return etc. given fraudulently or negligently is £3,000. Penalties for failure to render information etc. required by notice cannot be imposed after the failure is rectified, and daily penalties can similarly not be imposed where the information etc. was required other than by notice. [*TMA 1970, s 98; FA 1980, s 121; FA 1989, s 164(1)–(4)(7); FA 1990, s 68(3)(4); FA 2004, s 105(1)–(3)*].

Failure to allow access to computers renders a person liable to a maximum £500 penalty. [*FA 1988, s 127*].

48.16 FAILURE TO DISCLOSE TAX AVOIDANCE SCHEME

Failure by a promoter or, where the promoter is not UK-resident or there is no promoter, by a taxpayer to notify HMRC of notifiable proposals or arrangements within the disclosure provisions at 3.2 ANTI-AVOIDANCE, renders the promoter etc. liable to a penalty of up to £5,000. A further penalty or penalties of up to £600 applies for each day on which the failure continues after the above penalty is imposed. Similar penalties apply for failure by a promoter to inform a client of the reference number allocated by HMRC to notifiable proposals or arrangements which the promoter has disclosed.

Parties to notifiable arrangements who fail to notify HMRC of the scheme reference number etc. are liable to a penalty of £100 in respect of each scheme to which the failure relates. The penalty is increased for a second failure, occurring within three years from the date on which the first failure began, to £500 in respect of each scheme to which the failure relates (whether or not the same as the scheme to which the first failure relates). Any further such failures occurring within three years from the date on which the previous failure began, result in a penalty of £1,000 in respect of each scheme to which the failure relates (whether or not the same as the schemes to which any of the previous failures relates).

[*TMA 1970, s 98C; FA 2004, s 315*].

48.17 MITIGATION OF PENALTIES

The Commissioners for HMRC (or, before 18 April 2005, the Board of Inland Revenue) may mitigate penalties before or after judgment. [*TMA 1970, s 102; FA 1989, s 168*(*1*)(*4*); *CRCA 2005, s 5*]. A binding agreement by a taxpayer to pay an amount in composition cannot be repudiated afterwards by him or his personal representatives (*A-G v Johnstone KB 1926, 10 TC 758*; *A-G v Midland Bank Executor and Trustee Co Ltd KB 1934, 19 TC 136*; *CIR v Richards KB 1950, 33 TC 1*).

Negotiated settlements. In the case of tax-based penalties where a maximum penalty of 100% is in strict law exigible, HMRC will start with the maximum figure and then take into account the following factors in arriving at the penalty element which they will expect to be included in any offer in settlement.

- Disclosure. A reduction of up to 20% (or 30% in cases of full voluntary disclosure), depending on how much information was provided, how soon, and how that contributed to settling the enquiry.
- Co-operation. A reduction of up to 40%, depending upon a comparison of the extent of co-operation given with the co-operation which the inspector believes would have been possible.
- Gravity. A reduction of up to 40%, depending upon the nature of the offence, how long it continued and the amounts involved.

(HMRC Pamphlet IR 160). See, for example, *Caesar v Inspector of Taxes 1997 (Sp C 142), [1998] SSCD 1*.

See also 54.23 RETURNS as regards *TMA 1970, s 118*(*2*) (reasonable excuse for failure etc.).

For the validity of tax amnesties, see *R v CIR (ex p. National Federation of Self-Employed and Small Businesses Ltd) HL 1981, 55 TC 133*.

48.18 COMMISSIONERS' PRECEPTS

Summary penalties (to be treated as tax assessed and due and payable) may be determined by Commissioners against any party to proceedings before them who fails to comply with a precept, order for inspection etc. (see 4.12 APPEALS). The maximum penalty is £300 in the case of the General Commissioners, £10,000 in the case of the Special Commissioners (and in the case of the General Commissioners, a daily penalty up to £60 may also be imposed for continuing failure). A penalty up to £10,000 may similarly be imposed for failure to comply with any other direction of the Special Commissioners (including in relation to a preliminary hearing). [*SI 1994 No 1811, Reg 24*(*1*)(*3*); *SI 1994 No 1812, Reg 10*(*1*)(*3*)(*4*)]. If a person on whom a witness summons is served (see 4.11 APPEALS) fails to attend in obedience thereto, or attends but refuses to be sworn or to affirm, or refuses to answer any lawful question, or refuses to produce any document required by the summons, the Commissioners may summarily determine a penalty against that person, to be treated as tax assessed and due and payable. The maximum penalty is £1,000 in the case of the General Commissioners, £10,000 in the case of the Special Commissioners. [*SI 1994 No 1811, Reg 24*(*2*)(*3*); *SI 1994 No 1812, Reg 4*(*12*)(*13*)].

Appeal against such summary penalties lies to the High Court (or Court of Session). [*TMA 1970, s 53; SI 1994 No 1813*]. For the procedure on such appeals, see *QT Discount Foodstores Ltd v Warley Commrs Ch D 1981, 57 TC 268* and, for a case in which penalties were quashed because the taxpayer's evidence that he was unable to supply the information in question was not properly tested, *Boulton v Poole Commrs Ch D 1988, 60 TC 718*.

For appeals against penalties for non-compliance with precepts etc., see *Shah v Hampstead Commrs Ch D 1974, 49 TC 651*; *Chapman v Sheaf Commrs Ch D 1975, 49 TC 689*; *Toogood v Bristol Commrs Ch D 1976, 51 TC 634 and [1977] STC 116*; *Campbell v Rochdale Commrs Ch D 1975, 50 TC 411*; *B & S Displays Ltd v Special Commrs Ch D 1978, 52 TC 318*; *Galleri v Wirral Commrs Ch D 1978, [1979] STC 216*; *Beach v Willesden Commrs Ch D 1981, 55 TC 663*; *Stoll v High Wycombe Commrs and CIR Ch D 1992, 64 TC 587*; *Wilson v Leek Commrs and CIR Ch D 1993, 66 TC 537*.

48.19 PROCEDURE

The following applies in relation to events occurring after 26 July 1989. For the procedure as respects events occurring on or before that date, see the 1999/2000 and earlier editions. *Except* in the case of

(*a*) penalty proceedings instituted before the courts in cases of suspected fraud (see 48.22 below); or

(*b*) penalties under

- *TMA 1970, s 93(1)(a)* as it applied before self-assessment (£300 late filing penalty — see 48.2 above);
- *TMA 1979, s 94* as it had effect for notices served before 1 January 1994 (late company tax return filing penalty for pre-Pay and File accounting periods, i.e. those ended before 1 October 1993);
- *TMA 1970, s 98(1)(i)* (£300 penalty for non-filing of returns etc. under the provisions listed in *TMA 1970, s 98* — see 48.15 above); or
- *TMA 1970, s 98B(2)(a)* as it applied before self-assessment (£300 late filing penalty for European Economic Interest Groupings — see 48.5 above); or

(*c*) penalties in respect of which application to the Commissioners is specifically required, as mentioned where relevant in the preceding paragraphs of this chapter (for example, the daily penalty for late income tax and capital gains tax returns as in 48.2 above),

an authorised HMRC officer may make a determination imposing a penalty under any tax provision and setting it at such amount as, in his opinion, is correct or appropriate.

The notice of determination must state the date of issue and the time within which an appeal can be made. It cannot be altered unless

- there is an appeal (see 48.20 below), or
- an authorised HMRC officer discovers that the penalty is or has become insufficient (in which case he may make a further determination), or
- the penalty is an automatic or tax-related penalty under *TMA 1970, s 93* (late delivery of personal or trustees' tax returns — see 48.2 above) or arises under *TMA 1970, s 94(6)* or *FA 1998, Sch 18 para 18(2)* (tax-related penalty for late filing of company tax returns — see 48.4 above), and an authorised HMRC officer subsequently discovers that the amount of tax is or has become excessive (in which case it is to be revised accordingly).

A penalty under these provisions is due for payment 30 days after the issue of the notice of determination, and is treated as tax charged in an assessment which is due and payable. A determination which could have been made on a person who has died can be made on his personal representatives, and is then payable out of his estate.

[*TMA 1970, ss 100, 100A; FA 1989, s 167; FA 1990, Sch 11 para 3(2), para 5; FA 1998, s 117, Sch 19 para 38; FA 2001, s 91; SI 1994 No 1813*].

Note that self-assessment has effect for 1996/97 and subsequent years as regards income tax and capital gains tax and for company accounting periods ending on or after 1 July 1999.

48.20 **Appeals.** Subject to the following points, the general APPEALS (4) provisions apply to an appeal against a determination of a penalty as in 48.19 above.

TMA 1970, s 50(6)–(8) (see 4.13 APPEALS) do not apply. Instead (subject to below), on appeal the Commissioners can

- in the case of a penalty which is required to be of a particular amount, set the determination aside, confirm it, or alter it to the correct amount, and
- in any other case, set the determination aside, confirm it if it seems appropriate, or reduce it (including to nil) or increase it as seems appropriate (but not beyond the permitted maximum).

Neither *TMA 1970, s 50(6)–(8)* nor the above apply on an appeal against a determination of an automatic late filing penalty for personal or partnership tax returns (see 48.2, 48.3 above), where the 'reasonable excuse' let-out may have effect (see 48.2 above for the options open to the Commissioners in those cases).

Without prejudice to any right to have a case stated by the General Commissioners for the opinion of the High Court, or to appeal against a Special Commissioners' decision (see 4.21, 4.25 APPEALS), an appeal lies to the High Court (in Scotland, the Court of Session).

[*TMA 1970, s 100B; FA 1989, s 167; FA 1994, ss 196, 199, Sch 19 para 31; FA 1995, s 115(7); SI 1994 No 1813*].

48.21 **Proceedings before Commissioners.** For a penalty within 48.19(*b*) above or the higher daily penalty within 48.11 above (failure to produce documents), an authorised HMRC officer can commence proceedings before the General or Special Commissioners. The proceedings are by way of information in writing to the Commissioners, upon summons to the defendant (or defender); and they are heard and decided in a summary way. An appeal lies to the High Court (or Court of Session) on a question of law, or by the defendant (defender) against the amount. The court can set the determination aside, confirm it if it seems appropriate, or reduce it (including to nil) or increase it as seems appropriate (but not beyond the permitted maximum). The penalty is treated as tax charged in an assessment and due and payable. [*TMA 1970, s 100C; FA 1989, s 167*].

48.22 **Proceedings before court.** If the Commissioners for HMRC (or, before 18 April 2005, the Board of Inland Revenue) consider that liability for a penalty arises from fraud by any person, proceedings can be brought in the High Court (or Court of Session). If the court does not find fraud proved, it can nevertheless impose a penalty to which it considers the person liable. [*TMA 1970, s 100D; FA 1989, s 167*].

48.23 **General matters.** Non-receipt of notice of the hearing at which the Commissioners awarded penalties is not a ground of appeal to the courts (*Kenny v Wirral Commrs Ch D 1974, 50 TC 405*; *Campbell v Rochdale Commrs Ch D 1975, 50 TC 411*).

A mere denial of liability to penalties implies an intention by the taxpayer to set up a case in refutation, and details must be supplied (*CIR v Jackson CA 1960, 39 TC 357*).

For the validity of penalty proceedings while assessments remain open, see *A-G for Irish Free State v White SC (RI) 1931, 38 TC 666* and *R v Havering Commrs (ex p. Knight) CA 1973, 49 TC 161*. For other procedural matters, see *Collins v Croydon Commrs Ch D 1969, 45 TC 566*; *Bales v Rochford Commrs Ch D 1964, 42 TC 17*; *Sparks v West Brixton Commrs Ch D, [1977] STC 212*; *Moschi v Kensington Commrs Ch D 1979, 54 TC 403*; and for other appeals against penalties for failure to make returns, see *Dunk v Havant Commrs Ch D*

1976, 51 TC 519; *Napier v Farnham Commrs CA, [1978] TR 403*; *Garnham v Haywards Heath Commrs Ch D 1977, [1978] TR 303*; *Cox v Poole Commrs and CIR (No 1) Ch D 1987, 60 TC 445*; *Montague v Hampstead Commrs & Others Ch D 1989, 63 TC 145*; *Cox v Poole Commrs (No 2) Ch D 1989, 63 TC 277*.

For variation etc. of penalties by the court, see *Dawes v Wallington Commrs Ch D 1964, 42 TC 200*; *Salmon v Havering Commrs CA 1968, 45 TC 77*; *Williams v Special Commrs Ch D 1974, 49 TC 670*; *Wells v Croydon Commrs Ch D 1968, 47 ATC 356*; *Taylor v Bethnal Green Commrs Ch D 1976, [1977] STC 44*; *Stableford v Liverpool Commrs Ch D 1982, [1983] STC 162*; *Sen v St. Anne, Westminster Commrs Ch D, [1983] STC 415*; *Jolley v Bolton Commrs Ch D 1986, 65 TC 242*; *Lear v Leek Commrs Ch D 1986, 59 TC 247*; *Walsh v Croydon Commrs Ch D 1987, 60 TC 442*; *Fox v Uxbridge Commrs & CIR Ch D 2001, [2002] STC 455*.

For the test used by the court in considering whether penalties are excessive, see *Brodt v Wells Commrs Ch D 1987, 60 TC 436*. Per Scott LJ, penalties awarded by different bodies of Commissioners 'should, in relation to similar cases, bear some resemblance to one another'.

Statements made or documents produced by or on behalf of a taxpayer are admissible evidence in proceedings against him, notwithstanding that reliance on the Board's practice in cases of full disclosure may have induced him to make or produce them. [*TMA 1970, s 105; FA 1989, s 149(5), s 168(1)(5)*].

48.24 **Time limits.** The following applies in relation to events occurring after 26 July 1989. For the position as respects events occurring on or before that date, see the 1999/2000 and earlier editions.

The time within which a penalty can be determined, or proceedings can be commenced, depends on the penalty, as follows.

(*a*) If the penalty is ascertainable by reference to tax payable, the time is

- (i) six years after the date the penalty was incurred, or
- (ii) (subject to below) a later time within three years after the final determination of the amount of tax.

(*b*) If the penalty arises under *TMA 1970, s 99* (assisting in preparation of incorrect return etc. — see 48.13 above) the time is twenty years after the date it was incurred.

(*c*) In any other case, the time is six years from the time when the penalty was, or began to be, incurred.

Where the person liable has died, and the determination falls to be made in relation to his personal representatives, the extension in (*a*)(ii) above does not apply if the tax is charged in an assessment made more than six years after 31 January following the chargeable period for which it is charged. For 1995/96 and earlier years, this applied by reference to tax charged in an assessment made more than six years after the chargeable period for which it is charged.

[*TMA 1970, s 103; FA 1989, s 169; FA 1994, ss 196, 199, Sch 19 para 32*].

Final determination of tax. Provisional agreement of the amount due subject to the inspector being satisfied later with statements of assets, etc. is not final determination (*Carco Accessories Ltd v CIR CS 1985, 59 TC 45*).

48.25 BANKRUPTS

Penalties awarded after a bankruptcy are provable debts, but in practice HMRC does not proceed for penalties during a bankruptcy where there are other creditors. The trustee may agree to compromise any penalties awarded but the compromise must also be agreed by the bankrupt (*Re Hurren Ch D 1982, 56 TC 494*).

48.26 LIABILITY UNDER CRIMINAL LAW

'False statements to the prejudice of the Crown and public revenue' are criminal offences (*R v Hudson CCA 1956, 36 TC 561*). False statements in income tax returns, or for obtaining any allowance, reduction or repayment may involve liability to imprisonment for up to two years, under *Perjury Act 1911, s 5,* for 'knowingly and wilfully' making materially false statements or returns for tax purposes. Also, in Scotland, summary proceedings may be taken under *TMA 1970, s 107*.

From 18 April 2005, criminal prosecutions for tax fraud in England and Wales are conducted by the Revenue and Customs Prosecution Office, which is independent of HMRC. Previously, the Inland Revenue was itself a prosecuting authority. For HMRC and the Revenue's practice in considering whether to accept a money settlement or institute criminal proceedings for fraud, see 23.13 FRAUDULENT OR NEGLIGENT CONDUCT.

In relation to any criminal prosecution case, the Revenue's practice, now withdrawn, was to

- (*a*) refrain from taking steps to recover civil money penalties on the basis of fraud in respect of an offence which has been before the criminal courts;
- (*b*) seek appropriate civil money penalties in respect of any offence which has not been brought before the courts; and
- (*c*) reserve the right to seek, where there are grounds to do so, a civil penalty in respect of negligence by a taxpayer who has been acquitted of criminal intent in respect of a prosecution for fraud.

(Revenue Statement of Practice 2/88). See also 28.3 HMRC: ADMINISTRATION.

Falsification etc. of documents which are required to be produced as in 23.8 FRAUDULENT OR NEGLIGENT CONDUCT is a criminal offence punishable, on summary conviction, by a fine of the statutory maximum or, on indictment, by a fine or imprisonment for up to two years or both. [*TMA 1970, s 20BB; FA 1989, s 145*].

From 1 January 2001, the fraudulent evasion of *income tax* (not capital gains tax or corporation tax) on behalf of oneself or another person is itself a criminal offence. [*FA 2000, s 144*].

49 Private Residences

Cross-references. See 38 LAND generally; 20.22, 20.36 EMPLOYEE SHARE SCHEMES for restriction on rollover relief arising from disposal of shares to, respectively, an approved share incentive plan and, before 6 April 2001, an employee share ownership trust, where replacement asset is or becomes exempt as a private residence.

Simon's Direct Tax Service. See Division C2.13.

49.1 EXEMPTION GENERALLY

Where a gain accrues to an individual so far as attributable to the disposal of, or of an interest in,

(*a*) a dwelling-house or part of a dwelling-house which is, or has at any time in his period of ownership been, his only or main residence, or

(*b*) land which he has for his own occupation and enjoyment with that residence as its garden or grounds up to the 'permitted area',

then either the whole or a fraction of the gain is exempt as below. [*TCGA 1992, s 222(1)*].

Any loss accruing is similarly treated as being wholly or partly a non-allowable loss. [*TCGA 1992, s 16(2)*].

The '*permitted area*' in (*b*) above means an area (inclusive of the house itself) of 0.5 hectares (i.e. 5,980 sq. yards or 5,000 sq. metres) or larger area if required for the reasonable enjoyment of the whole or part of the dwelling-house as a residence having regards to its size and character.

Where part of the land occupied with a residence is and part is not within (*b*) above, then (up to the permitted area) the part that is to be taken within (*b*) is that part which would be most suitable for occupation and enjoyment with the residence if the remainder were separately occupied.

[*TCGA 1992, s 222(2)–(4); FA 1991, s 93*].

Note that the exemption is *not* restricted to dwelling-houses situate in the UK.

See below for case law on the 'permitted area' and the extent to which subsidiary buildings may form part of the residence.

There can only be one main residence in the case of an individual and his spouse or civil partner living with him, so long as they are 'living together' (see 42.3 MARRIED PERSONS AND CIVIL PARTNERS). [*TCGA 1992, s 222(6); SI 2005 No 3229, Reg 117(2)*]. As regards separation or divorce, see 49.2(*c*) below.

Total exemption (under *TCGA 1992, s 223(1)*) applies to a gain within *TCGA 1992, s 222(1)* above if the dwelling-house or part of a dwelling-house has been the individual's only or main residence throughout the period of ownership, or throughout the period of ownership except for all or any part of the last 36 months of that period. The Treasury has the power, to be exercised by statutory instrument, to reduce this set period to 24 months, and again to increase it to 36 months, and so on down or up to these levels. The power cannot be used retrospectively and in practice reasonable notice of any variation will be given (HC Official Report Standing Committee B 7th sitting col 312, 13 June 1991).

Fractional exemption (under *TCGA 1992, s 223(2)*) applies where total exemption does not apply to a gain within *TCGA 1992, s 222(1)*. The fraction of the gain that is exempt is given by

(i) the length of the part or parts of the period of ownership during which the dwelling-house (or part) was the individual's only or main residence, but inclusive of the last 36 months of the period of ownership in any event, divided by

(ii) the length of the period of ownership.

In considering 'period of ownership' for the purposes of the total or fractional exemption (but *not* for determining for the purposes of *TCGA 1992, s 222(1)* above whether the dwelling-house (or part) has at any time in the period of ownership been the only or main residence), any period before 31 March 1982 (6 April 1965 for disposals before 6 April 1988) is ignored, and if time apportionment applies (see 7.7 ASSETS HELD ON 6 APRIL 1965 but subject to the rules in 8 ASSETS HELD ON 31 MARCH 1982), the resulting fraction is applied only to that part of the gain that would otherwise be chargeable after the time apportionment. [*TCGA 1992, s 223(1)(2)(5)–(7), Sch 2 para 16(10); FA 1988, Sch 8 para 8; FA 1991, s 94*].

See 49.2 below for certain periods of ownership that additionally qualify for the purposes of total and fractional exemption.

Where the individual has had different interests at different times, the period of ownership is taken for the purposes of *TCGA 1992, ss 222–226* generally (i.e. all the provisions contained in this chapter) to begin from the first acquisition taken into account in arriving at the amount of the allowable expenditure deductible in the computation of the gain to which *TCGA 1992, s 222(1)* above applies. In the case of an individual living with his spouse or civil partner

(A) if one disposes of, or of his interest in, the dwelling-house (or part) which is their only or main residence to the other, and in particular if it passes on death to the other as legatee, the other's period of ownership is treated as beginning with the beginning of the period of ownership of the one making the disposal, and

(B) if (A) above applies, but the dwelling-house (or part) was not the only or main residence of both throughout the period of ownership of the one making the disposal, account is taken of any part of that period during which it was his only or main residence as if it was also that of the other.

[*TCGA 1992, s 222(7); SI 2005 NO 3229, Reg 117(3)*].

For the purposes of *TCGA 1992, ss 222–226*, apportionments of consideration are to be made wherever required, and, in particular, where a person disposes of a dwelling-house only part of which is his only or main residence. [*TCGA 1992, s 222(10)*].

See 49.3 to 49.8 below for provisions supplementary to the above.

TCGA 1992, s 222(10) seems to override *TCGA 1992, s 52(4)* (apportionments to be on just and reasonable basis; see 15.7 COMPUTATION OF GAINS AND LOSSES) so that, because of the absence of the 'just and reasonable' criterion, there may be an argument that a different basis of apportionment may apply, e.g. where the residence and the permitted area of land block access to other land outside the permitted area but sold together with the residence etc. it may fall that the value of the other land should reflect the situation as if the two areas were in separate ownership (*Taxation 7 December 1995 p 256* and HMRC Capital Gains Manual CG 64900, 64901 and 74162).

An immobilised caravan with main services installed has been held to be a dwelling-house (*Makins v Elson Ch D 1976, 51 TC 437*) but one still on wheels and with no services installed was not so held (*Moore v Thompson Ch D 1986, 61 TC 15*). A houseboat will often be an exempt asset in its own right (see 22.4 EXEMPTIONS AND RELIEFS regarding tangible movable wasting assets). If this is not the case, it may qualify as a dwelling-house if it is permanently located on a site and connected to all mains services. Such a houseboat *will* be regarded as a dwelling-house if it has been used as an immobile residence for a period of six months or more and has had its engines removed. Other cases will be considered on their merits. (HMRC Capital Gains Manual CG 64329).

A lodge built for occupation rent-free by a caretaker/gardener and his wife, the housekeeper, and separated from the main house by the width of a tennis court (around nine yards) with the total area of land involved being around 1.1 acres, was held to be within the exemption (*Batey v Wakefield CA 1981, 55 TC 550*). A residence for exemption purposes was declared to be a dwelling-house and all of those buildings which are part and parcel of the whole, where each part is appurtenant to and occupied for the purposes of the building occupied by the taxpayer. However, this is a question of fact and degree.

Whereas *Batey v Wakefield* was concerned with buildings physically separate from the main dwelling-house, *Green v CIR CS 1982, 56 TC 10*, in contrast, involved the disposal of a mansion (occupied by the taxpayer) and its two wings. The Commissioners' finding that the wings were not part of his dwelling-house was upheld.

In *Markey v Sanders Ch D 1987, 60 TC 245*, a finding by Commissioners that a staff bungalow situated 130 metres away from the main dwelling-house and screened from it by a belt of trees, formed part of the taxpayer's residence was not accepted. It was held that *Batey v Wakefield* laid down two tests:

(1) the occupation of the building must increase the taxpayer's enjoyment of the main dwelling-house, and

(2) the building must be 'very closely adjacent to' the main dwelling-house.

Each of these was held to be a necessary, but not by itself sufficient, test and in the present case the first test was satisfied but not the second. The total area of land involved was around twelve acres.

However, *Markey v Sanders* was expressly not followed in *Williams v Merrylees Ch D 1987, 60 TC 297*, so that a finding by Commissioners that a lodge situated 200 metres from the main dwelling-house formed part of the taxpayer's residence during his occupation of the latter was upheld. The total area of the property was around four acres. In the latter case doubt was expressed whether the *Batey v Wakefield* decision did require the satisfaction of two distinct conditions and it was concluded that all the circumstances should be looked at to see whether there is 'an entity which could sensibly be described as being a dwelling-house though split up into different buildings performing different functions'.

The *Williams v Merrylees* decision was itself disapproved by the Court of Appeal in *Lewis v Rook CA 1992, 64 TC 567*. A finding by Commissioners that a gardener's cottage some 170 metres from the main dwelling-house formed part of the taxpayer's residence was initially upheld in the High Court, but was rejected in the Court of Appeal. The true test was declared to be whether the cottage was 'within the curtilage of, and appurtenant to [the main house], so as to be part of the entity which, together with [the main house], constituted the dwelling-house occupied by the taxpayer as her residence'. The curtilage concept was derived from a non-tax case, *Methuen-Campbell v Walters CA, [1979] QB 525* (and see also *Dyer v Dorset County Council CA, [1989] QB 346*), in which Buckley LJ stated that 'for one corporeal hereditament to fall within the curtilage of another, the former must be so intimately associated with the latter as to lead to the conclusion that the former in truth forms part and parcel of the latter'. The cottage in *Lewis v Rook* was not 'intimately associated' with the main house as it was some way off and separated from it by a large garden. The total area of land involved was around 10.5 acres and Balcombe LJ remarked that as 'the "permitted area" of garden and grounds which is exempt from capital gains tax is limited to one acre [now 0.5 hectares] or such larger area as the [Appeal] Commissioners may determine as required for the reasonable enjoyment of the dwelling-house as a residence, it does seem to me to be remarkable that a separate lodge or cottage which by any reasonable measurement must be outside the permitted area can nevertheless be part of the entity of the dwelling-house'. It should also be noted that Counsel for the Revenue reserved the right to argue in the House of Lords, had the case proceeded that far, that the reference in *TCGA 1992, s 222(1)(a)* to a 'dwelling-house' in the singular meant that buildings which are separate from the main house cannot be included within the exemption if they form separate, self-contained dwelling-houses in their own right. See Revenue Tax Bulletin, August 1994, p 148 for further discussion of this matter.

In *Honour v Norris Ch D 1992, 64 TC 599*, the taxpayer owned four separate, self-contained flats in a London square. Two of these were adjacent and were converted to form a single property, the other two being some way off and not adjacent to each other. Although the taxpayer and his wife had occasionally used the non-adjacent flats themselves, their main function was to provide sleeping accommodation for guests and a nanny. The Commissioners upheld the taxpayer's contention that one of the distant flats, which had been sold, was part of his main residence. However, the Revenue's appeal was upheld in the High Court, Vinelott J remarking that the proposition that the flat which had been sold formed part of the taxpayer's main residence was 'an affront to common sense'.

In *Varty v Lynes Ch D 1976, 51 TC 419*, the taxpayer owned and occupied a house and garden (together comprising an area less than one acre, the latter being the then 'maximum' permitted area subject to an appeal Commissioners' determination). He sold the house and part of the garden in June 1971. In May 1972, he sold at a substantial profit the rest of the garden for which he had meanwhile obtained planning permission. An assessment on the gain accruing on the disposal of the remainder of the garden was upheld. The exemption provided by (*b*) above related only to the actual moment of disposal of the land, and in relation to land formerly used as garden and grounds did not apply to a disposal subsequent to the disposal of the residence. The judgment of Brightman J pointed to anomalies in the legislation. In particular, he stated 'The anomaly which I find most striking [is] the disregard for the purposes of [the provisions providing for total exemption] of the last twelve months [this period being the then period disregarded above] of the period of ownership in respect of the dwelling-house. On the construction advanced by the Crown it must follow, I am disposed to think, that if the taxpayer goes out of occupation of the dwelling-house a month before he sells it, the exemption will be lost in respect of the garden. That, however, is merely my impression, and I do not intend so to decide because it is not a matter for decision before me'. The Revenue did say that they would not take this point unless the garden had development value (CCAB Statements TR 211 December 1976 and TR 233 June 1977). However, HMRC no longer seek to apply arguments based on the dicta in this case, but will apply the decision itself, so that no relief is due on any sale of a garden taking place after a prior sale of the dwelling-house (Revenue Tax Bulletin August 1994 pp 148, 149 and see HMRC Capital Gains Manual CG 64377–64387).

For a useful summary of the considerations made by HMRC in arriving at the 'permitted area' and whether a subsidiary building forms part of the residence as a whole, see Revenue Tax Bulletin, February 1992, p 10. The Revenue made the point that land, other than that taken by the site of the dwelling-house, must be 'garden or grounds' at the time of sale if it is to be within the permitted area. In deciding whether an area of garden or grounds larger than 0.5 hectares is 'required for the reasonable enjoyment' of the dwelling-house as a residence, it considers the following words of Du Parcq J in the compulsory purchase case of *In Re Newhill Compulsory Purchase Order 1937, Payne's Application KB 1937, [1938] 2 All ER 163* to be useful guidance: ' "Required", I think, in this Section does not mean merely that the occupiers of the house would like to have it, or that they would miss it if they lost it, or that anyone proposing to buy the house would think less of the house without it than he would if it was preserved to it. "Required" means, I suppose that without it there will be such a substantial deprivation of amenities or convenience that a real injury would be done to the property owner.'

In *Longson v Baker Ch D 2000, 73 TC 415*, in which a permitted area of 7.56 hectares was unsuccessfully claimed and in which the taxpayer stressed the equestrian aspect of the property, it was held that the reasonable enjoyment test is an objective one. It was not objectively *required*, in other words necessary, to keep horses at a house to enjoy it *as a residence*. An individual taxpayer may subjectively wish to do so but that was not the same thing.

It should be noted that HMRC considers that a separate disposal of part of the garden or grounds of a residence may be prima facie evidence that the part disposed of was not required for the reasonable enjoyment of the dwelling-house as a residence although this only becomes of relevance where the area of the garden or grounds exceeds 0.5 hectares. It states that in practice any land disposed of separately is likely to be from that part of the garden or grounds which can be disposed of while detracting least from the enjoyment of the residence. In such circumstances it believes the disposal itself presents strong evidence that the land could not have been required for the reasonable enjoyment of the residence so that the permitted area should exclude the area disposed of. However, it accepts that there are two common circumstances where this inference may be incorrect. The first is where the owner of the land makes a disposal to a member of his family where he may be prepared to tolerate some curtailment of the reasonable enjoyment of the residence. The second is where financial necessity may force the owner to sell land which would be regarded as part of the most suitable area of garden or grounds to be included in the permitted area (HMRC Capital Gains Manual CG 64832–64834).

As regards the exemption granted by (*b*) above, there is no requirement that the land occupied and used with the residence as garden or grounds at the time of disposal has to adjoin the land on which the dwelling-house stands. See *Wakeling v Pearce (Sp C 32), [1995] SSCD 96* where the distance between the garden (which was disposed of) and the land including the dwelling-house (which was retained) was less than 10 metres. However, HMRC consider the facts of the case and the decision do not affect its interpretation of the underlying provisions and that it will be rare for exemption to be given to land (even if used as a garden) separated from the residence by other land which is not in the same ownership as the residence (see Revenue Tax Bulletin August 1995 p 239).

See *Taxation 5 January 1989, p 311* for a case where the Ombudsman considered the District Valuer to have been wrong in taking the view that the presence of a tennis court and swimming pool must be regarded as irrelevant in deciding what was the permitted area.

For the question of whether or not a dwelling-house is a 'main residence', see *Frost v Feltham Ch D 1980, 55 TC 10* which concerned mortgage interest relief for income tax purposes but note that that question may be determined, for capital gains tax purposes only, by election as in 49.4 below.

49.2 PERIODS OF OWNERSHIP QUALIFYING FOR EXEMPTION

For the purposes of the total or fractional exemption of a gain to which *TCGA 1992, s 222*(*1*) in 49.1 above applies the following provisions apply.

(*a*) **Periods of absence.** A '*period of absence*' means a period during which the dwelling-house (or part) was not the individual's only or main residence and throughout which he had no residence or main residence eligible for relief under the provisions of *TCGA 1992, s 223* in 49.1 above. In applying the total or fractional exemption provided by *TCGA 1992, s 223*(*1*) and (*2*) respectively in 49.1 above (i.e. ignoring periods of ownership before 31 March 1982 (6 April 1965 for disposals before 6 April 1988))

(i) a period of absence not exceeding three years (or periods of absence which together did not exceed three years), and in addition

(ii) any period of absence throughout which the individual worked in an employment or office all the duties of which were performed outside the UK (holidays spent in the UK are ignored but any duties, even incidental ones, carried out in the UK will not be; HMRC Capital Gains Manual CG 65042), and in addition

(iii) any period of absence not exceeding four years (or periods of absence which together did not exceed four years) throughout which the individual was prevented from residing in the dwelling-house (or part) in consequence of the situation of his place of work or in consequence of any condition imposed by his employer requiring him to reside elsewhere, being a condition reasonably imposed to secure the effective performance by the employee of his duties (the individual may be self-employed or the holder of an office or employment for these purposes; see HMRC Capital Gains Manual CG 65043, 65044),

is treated as if in that period of absence the dwelling-house (or part) was the individual's only or main residence *provided* both before and after the period there was a time when the dwelling-house (or part) was the individual's only or main residence. [*TCGA 1992, s 223(3)(7)*].

HMRC will view residence as a question of fact. A minimum period is not specified and HMRC do not attempt to impose one. They take the view that it is quality of occupation rather than length of occupation which determines whether a dwelling-house is its owner's residence. Miller J in *Moore v Thompson Ch D 1986, 61 TC 15* commented that 'the Commissioners were alive to the fact that even occasional and short residence in a place can make that a residence; but the question was one of fact and degree' (Revenue Tax Bulletin, August 1994, p 149). In *Goodwin v Curtis CA 1998, 70 TC 478*, it was held that the nature, quality, length and circumstances of the taxpayer's 32-day occupation of a farmhouse was such that he had moved into it on a temporary basis and his occupation did not qualify as residence. *Dicta* of Viscount Cave in *Levene v CIR* (see 52.4 RESIDENCE AND DOMICILE) applied.

Where the periods of absence exceed the three or four years mentioned in (i) and (iii) above, it is only the excess which does not qualify for the exemption treatment (CCAB Statement TR 500, 10 March 1983). Where in the case of a husband and wife who are living together the conditions in (i) to (iii) above are satisfied as regards the spouse who is not the owner of the dwelling-house, they are deemed satisfied as regards the spouse who is the owner. Also, the condition requiring the dwelling-house to be the only or main residence after absence under (ii) and (iii) above will be treated as satisfied if the individual is unable to resume residence because the terms of his employment require him to work elsewhere (HMRC Extra-Statutory Concessions D3, D4).

The requirement that the period of absence is a period throughout which the individual has no residence or main residence eligible for relief under *TCGA 1992, s 223* may be difficult to meet in practice given the view (see commentary in 49.4 below) of HMRC that any residence in which the individual has a legal or equitable interest or, broadly before 17 October 1994, which the individual occupies under licence can constitute an individual's residence eligible for relief, albeit that it may only have a negligible capital value. However, HMRC will accept a main residence election as in 49.4 below nominating the residence from which the taxpayer is absent even though he is not using it as a residence. No other residence is then eligible for relief, so the requirement is satisfied. See HMRC Capital Gains Manual CG 65048.

Example

T purchased a house on 1 August 1981 from which date it was used as her only residence until 10 February 1982 when she moved to France to live in rent-free accommodation provided by her employer whilst she carried out all the duties of the employment there. She returned from France on 4 August 1990 when she again occupied the house as her only residence. On 30 November 1996 she left the house empty and moved to live with her elderly father in a residence owned by him, intending to sell her own house. In the event, the house was not sold until 1 November 2006 when an otherwise chargeable gain (before taper relief) of £36,000 was realised.

		£
Gain on sale		36,000
	Deduct $\dfrac{8y\ 4m + 6y\ 4m + 3y}{24y\ 7m} \times £36{,}000$	25,871
Chargeable gain (subject to TAPER RELIEF (61))		£10,129

Notes to the example

(1) The period of ownership for the exemption calculation does not include any period before 31 March 1982. This applies regardless of whether the gain has been calculated by reference to cost or 31 March 1982 value under the re-basing rules.

(2) All of the period spent in France (ignoring the period before 31 March 1982) counts as a period of residence under (ii) above. It is assumed that the supply of accommodation to T in France was such that it was not eligible for relief under *TCGA 1992, s 223* (e.g. a licence; see 49.4 below for HMRC comment). None of the period from 30 November 1996 to 1 November 2006 can count as a period of residence under (i) above as there was not a time afterwards that the house was T's only or main residence. However, under *TCGA 1992, s 223(1)* the last 36 months of ownership are exempt provided the house has at some time during the period of ownership (not restricted to periods after 31 March 1982) been the only or main residence.

(3) For the purposes of taper relief, the gain to be tapered is the gain *after* applying the private residence exemption, i.e. the gain of £10,129.

(*b*) **Delay in taking up residence.** The treatment as the individual's only or main residence applies during the twelve months (or longer period up to a maximum of two years if a good reason can be shown) prior to taking up residence during which the dwelling-house was built, alterations etc. were made to it or the necessary steps were being taken to dispose of the individual's previous residence. (HMRC Extra-Statutory Concession D49 replacing Statement of Practice D4). The period will not be extended beyond twenty-four months. If the twelve-month or longer period allowed is exceeded, none of the period of ownership prior to taking up residence is treated as a period of residence. No main residence election (see 49.4 below) is required if the effect of this concession is to treat an individual as having two residences for a period since relief will be available for both residences for that period (HMRC Capital Gains Manual CG 65009–65014).

(*c*) **Separation or divorce of married persons.** Where a married couple separate or are divorced and one partner ceases to occupy the matrimonial home and subsequently, as part of a financial settlement, disposes of the home, or an interest in it, to the other partner, the home may be regarded for the purposes of the exemption as continuing to be a residence of the transferring partner from the date his or her occupation ceases until the date of transfer, provided that it has throughout this period been the other partner's only or main residence. Thus where a husband leaves the matrimonial home while still owning it, the exemption for the only or main residence would be given on the subsequent transfer to the wife, provided she has continued to live in the house and the husband has not elected that some other house should be treated as his main residence for this period (HMRC Extra-Statutory Concession D6). See also 42.4 MARRIED PERSONS AND CIVIL PARTNERS.

(*d*) **'Job-related' accommodation.** If at any time during an individual's period of ownership (as for *TCGA 1992, s 222(1)* in 49.1 above so that a period before 31 March 1982 is *not* ignored) of part or the whole of a dwelling-house he resides in 'job-related' living accommodation and he intends in due course to occupy the dwelling-house (or part) as his only or main residence, he is deemed at that time to occupy the dwelling-house (or part) as a residence for the purposes of *TCGA 1992, ss 222–226* (i.e. all the provisions contained in this chapter). Living accommodation is 'job-related' for these purposes if it is provided for a taxpayer by reason of his (or for his spouse or civil partner by reason of their) employment, in any of the following cases.

(i) Where it is necessary for the proper performance of the duties of the employment that the employee should reside in that accommodation.

(ii) Where the provision of such accommodation is customary and it is provided for the better performance of the duties of employment.

(iii) Where there is a special threat to the employee's security, special security arrangements are in force, and the employee resides in the accommodation as part of those arrangements.

With certain exceptions, (i) and (ii) above do not apply to accommodation provided to its directors by a company (or associated company).

In respect of residence after 5 April 1983, living accommodation is also job-related if either the person claiming the relief or his or her spouse or civil partner is carrying on a trade, profession or vocation on premises or other land provided by another person, under tenancy or otherwise, and is bound under an arm's length contract to live in those premises or on other premises provided. Relief is not given if the accommodation is provided, in whole or in part, by a company in which the borrower, or his or her spouse or civil partner, has a material interest (as defined) or by any person or persons with whom he or she carries on a business in partnership. [*TCGA 1992, s 222(8)(8A)–(8D)(9); ICTA 1988, s 356; FA 1999, Sch 4 para 17, para 18(4); ITEPA 2003, Sch 6 para 213; SI 2005 No 3229, Reg 117(4)(5)*].

The above treatment still applies if the dwelling-house is disposed of without having been occupied by the individual (but subject to the test of intention to occupy being satisfied previously) or if the property has been let (see 49.8 below). It appears that the above provisions do not obviate the need to consider, subject to HMRC's views there mentioned, a main residence election as in 49.4 below.

(*e*) **Relocation of employees.** HMRC are prepared concessionally to extend the exemption for a private residence where an employee sells his home to a relocation business or his employer and is given the right to share in any profits made when that business or his employer later sells the home, with the result that the right will generally be exempt to the same extent as the home itself. Relocation arrangements must be set up under arm's length agreements whereby the employee moves home because of the requirements of his place of work or employer and the right to a profit share by the employee must not endure for more than three years. The concession applies equally to office holders and any other joint owners of the home provided the employee qualifies for his interest in it (HMRC Extra-Statutory Concession D37). Where the concession does not apply, the eventual disposal of the right cannot itself attract any private residence relief as it is not a disposal of an interest in a residence (HMRC Capital Gains Manual CG 14970, 64611).

49.3 PART-BUSINESS USE, CHANGES OF USE ETC.

If a gain accrues on the disposal of a dwelling-house or part of a dwelling-house part of which is used *exclusively* for the purposes of a trade or business, or of a profession or vocation, the gain is apportioned and *TCGA 1992, s 223* applied in relation to the part of the gain apportioned to the part which is not exclusively used for those purposes. [*TCGA 1992, s 224(1); FA 2004, s 117, Sch 22 para 3*].

It will be noted that the apportionment required by *TCGA 1992, s 224*(*1*) applies only where part of the house is used *exclusively* for business purposes. A room used partly for business and partly for residential purposes does not give rise to any restriction. However, in determining exclusivity, occasional and very minor residential use of a business room, for example its use for the keeping of private possessions, is disregarded (HMRC Capital Gains Manual CG 64666). An apportionment based on the number of rooms used respectively for business and residential purposes will often suffice in cases of relatively small business use. It may not produce a result acceptable to the Revenue if the residential part of a mixed property is likely to have a disproportionately lower value than the business part, as is probable in the case of, for example, accommodation above a public house (see the worked example at HMRC Capital Gains Manual CG 64674). An apportionment fraction already in use for income tax purposes under Schedule D is not necessarily appropriate for CGT purposes (HMRC Capital Gains Manual CG 64666 and, as regards farmhouses, CG 64680, 64681).

The legislation does not specifically address the question of part of a residence used for the purposes of an employment, though it is arguable that the reference in *TCGA 1992, s 224*(*1*) to a 'business' includes the business carried on by the individual's employer. In practice, HMRC do not require a restriction to be made for the use (exclusive or otherwise) for employment purposes of a small part of a residence, for example a room used as a study, and this remains the case even if an expenses allowance has been given against employment income. If, however, a 'substantial part' of the property is used exclusively in connection with the employment, they will insist on a restriction of the CGT exemption on the more general grounds that relief is available only for a dwelling-house (or part) which has been the individual's only or main *residence* (see 49.1 above). (HMRC Capital Gains Manual CG 64690, 64691).

Although, where *TCGA 1992, s 224*(*1*) applies, the pre-tapered gain arguably relates entirely to the part of the dwelling-house used exclusively for business purposes, *TCGA 1992, Sch A1 para 9* (see 61.13 TAPER RELIEF) requires the gain to be apportioned for taper relief purposes (i.e. between business and non-business asset) by reference to the use to which the entire asset (i.e. the whole house) has been put during its period of ownership since 6 April 1998. This arguably inequitable interpretation has apparently been confirmed by HMRC (see *Taxation 12 December 2002 p 271*).

If at any time in the period of ownership there is a change in what is occupied as the individual's residence, whether on account of a reconstruction or conversion of a building or for any other reason, or there have been changes as regards the use of part of the dwelling-house for the purpose of a trade etc. or for any other purpose, the relief given under *TCGA 1992, s 223* may be adjusted in such manner as is just and reasonable. [*TCGA 1992, s 224*(*2*)*; FA 1996, Sch 20 para 60*].

HMRC's approach in cases falling within *TCGA 1992, s 224*(*2*) is to deal with each case on its merits, and to require an adjustment which as far as possible reflects the extent to which, and the length of time over which, each part of the dwelling-house has been used as part of residence. It is not normally considered appropriate to take into account intervening market values when apportioning gains to different periods in such cases since *TCGA 1992, s 223* clearly provides for time apportionment as the appropriate method (Revenue Tax Bulletin August 1994 p 149). Where part of a residence has been used for part of the period of ownership for other (e.g. business) purposes, but has *at some time* during the period of ownership been used as part of the main residence, the last 36 months of ownership is an exempt period by virtue of the rule at 49.1(i) above, and this applies regardless of actual use during those last 36 months (HMRC Capital Gains Manual CG 64765, 64988, 64989).

ROLLOVER RELIEF (55) may be available in respect of any chargeable gain arising on the business portion of a dwelling-house if a new dwelling-house is acquired, part of which will also be used *exclusively* for the purposes of a trade etc. The rolled over gain will be set against the acquisition cost of the business part of the new property.

Letting the dwelling-house may restrict the exemption given by 49.1 and 49.2 above (subject to the relief at 49.8 below) but there is no restriction where a lodger (but a restriction is applied if there are two or more lodgers — see HMRC Capital Gains Manual CG 64702) lives as part of a family, sharing their living accommodation and taking meals with them (HMRC Statement of Practice 14/80). Participation in the 'rent a room' income tax relief scheme of *ITTOIA 2005, ss 784–802* will not normally lead to any capital gains tax liability (HL Written Answers, 27 January 1993, Vol 514 col 94).

49.4 ELECTION FOR MAIN RESIDENCE

So far as it is necessary for the purposes of *TCGA 1992, s 222* to determine which of two or more residences is an individual's main residence for 'any period' (see below), the individual may conclude that question by written notice to an HMRC officer given within two years from the beginning of that period but subject to a right to vary that notice by a further written notice to an HMRC officer as respects any period beginning not earlier than two years before the giving of the further notice. [*TCGA 1992, s 222(5); FA 1996, Sch 20 para 59(3); FA 2004, s 117, Sch 22 para 1*].

In the case of a man and his wife living with him or of civil partners, there can only be one residence or main residence for both, so long as 'living together' (see 42.3 MARRIED PERSONS AND CIVIL PARTNERS) and, where a notice specifying the main residence affects both spouses or civil partners, it must be given by both. [*TCGA 1992, s 222(6); FA 1996, Sch 20 para 59(4); SI 2005 No 3229, Reg 117(2)*]. If when a couple marry they each have a residence and they continue to use both, the two-year period for jointly nominating the main residence begins on the date of marriage (HMRC Capital Gains Manual CG 64525). See Revenue Tax Bulletin, August 1994, pp 149, 150 for further discussion on elections by married couples.

The nomination of a residence as the main residence has effect until the earlier of, if any, the date from which the original notice is varied and the date on which the taxpayer's combination of residences changes (such that a new nomination becomes possible) (HMRC Capital Gains Manual CG 64522). In the absence of a nomination covering any particular period of time, the question of which is the main residence is decided on the facts. The main residence will not necessarily be the one at which the taxpayer spends most of his time, although it commonly will be; for other criteria taken into account by HMRC, see HMRC Capital Gains Manual CG 64552, 64554.

It is worth noting that the choice is not between two or more properties but between two or more *residences*. A property never occupied by the taxpayer as a residence cannot enter the equation. A nomination given more than two years after the *acquisition* of a property will not be late if made within two years after the property is first occupied as a residence (see further below).

The case of *Griffin v Craig-Harvey Ch D 1993, 66 TC 396* upheld the Revenue's long-standing view (see HMRC Capital Gains Manual CG 64495) that, broadly and subject to the following, initial notice nominating the main residence *must* be given within two years after the individual first begins to have two or more residences if it is to be effective. Notice(s) of variation can then be made subsequently but not so as to vary the nomination of the main residence more than two years before the giving of the further notice.

The *ratio decidendi* (supported by certain words in the original *FA 1965* legislation and the *CGTA 1979* consolidation and, under principles established in *Pepper v Hart* (see 4.24 APPEALS), by a Minister's statement in the HC Official Report relevant to the enactment of the *FA 1965* legislation) of the judgment of Vinelott J in *Griffin v Craig-Harvey* appears to be that 'the reference to "any period" in the opening part of [*TCGA 1992, s 222(5)* as above] and to "that period" [as above] are most naturally read as referring to "the whole or any part of the period of ownership in question" that being the period in relation to which in default of agreement or of any notice under [*section 222(5)*] the inspector's determination is to be made'. However, in the judgment the following hypothetical situations were put forward.

(1) The taxpayer owns two houses, each of which he occupies as a residence. More than two years have elapsed since he began to have two residences. He then begins to use a third house as a residence. A new two-year period begins to run at that time so that he can make an election as between all three residences during that two-year period.

(2) If on the same facts the taxpayer ceased, after acquiring a third residence, to use one of them as a residence a new period will begin at the time of cesser so that, again, he will have a period of two years during which he can elect between the remaining residences.

(3) The taxpayer owns two houses which he occupies as residences. The taxpayer conveys one of the houses to the trustees of the settlement under which he has a beneficial interest and the trustees have power which they exercise to permit him to continue to reside in the residence. A new two-year period begins at the time when he creates the settlement and again an election can be made (jointly by the taxpayer and the trustees; see 49.5 below) within the subsequent two years.

(4) The taxpayer has two residences, one owned by him and the other by the trustees of a settlement under which the trustees have power to permit the taxpayer to occupy it as a residence. No election is made during the two years following the inception of this state of affairs. If the trustees have and exercise a power to transfer the residence which they own to the taxpayer he can elect that that residence is to be his main residence at any time during the subsequent two years.

In *obiter dicta* comment on these examples, Vinelott J said (1) and (2) 'do no more than illustrate the inevitable consequence of [*TCGA 1992, s 222(5)*], namely that it becomes necessary to determine which of two or more residences is an individual's main residence whenever there is a change in the number of properties which he occupies as a residence; apart from an election ... that question has to be determined afresh by the inspector (unless, of course, the disposal of one property occupied as a residence leaves him with only one residence)'. However, although not stated but crucial in the instant case, it appears implicit in the overall judgement that, in relation to examples similar to (1) and (2) above, an initial notice and a further notice ... can only affect the position since the last change of circumstances in which the individual has two or more residences; they cannot change the main residence nomination for a previous combination of two or more residences which existed before that change even though such notices are made within the time limits. Vinelott J found it unnecessary to comment on a submission given in evidence that the taxpayer can give a initial notice of election and so preserve a right to vary an election even if at the time he has only one residence.

As regards the examples at (3) and (4) above, Vinelott J said they 'seem to be altogether unsurprising consequences of the legislation. If [there is a transfer as in (3) and (4) above], the transfer of the house to the trustees or from the trustees to the taxpayer is a disposal giving rise to a charge to capital gains tax on any gain so far as not exempt under [*TCGA 1992, s 222*]. The position is the same as if he had bought the house from or sold it to a stranger'.

The decision in *Griffin v Craig-Harvey* also led to doubt as to when an election under *TCGA 1992, s 222(5)* was necessary where, for example, the individual used one or more residences with a minimal capital value. With effect after 16 October 1994, HMRC takes the view that any election or inspector's determination made or given under *TCGA 1992, s 222(5)* cannot be valid if it relies on the existence of a residence which is occupied under a licence so that after that date such an election or determination can only be valid where there is a legal or equitable interest (which includes all forms of ownership, from that of the sole owner of the fee simple absolute in possession to that of the co-owner of a minimal tenancy) in the residence. Job-related accommodation (see 49.2 above) may be occupied under either a service occupancy (i.e. under a licence) or a tenancy.

An election made before 17 October 1994 in favour of a residence in which there is a legal or equitable interest continued to be regarded as valid even if it relied on the existence of a residence occupied under licence for its effect. An election made before 17 October 1994 in favour of a residence occupied under licence was regarded as ceasing to have effect after 16 October 1994. Where there is only one other residence in which a legal or equitable interest is held that residence after 16 October 1994 becomes the only or main residence subject to the rules for total or fractional exemption in 49.1 above. Where an election was made before 17 October 1994 in favour of a residence occupied under licence and there are two (or, presumably, more) residences in which a legal or equitable interest is held, a new two-year period for making an election between them was regarded as beginning when the existing election ceased to take effect after 16 October 1994. Only this cessation is regarded as giving rise to a change in the combination of residences held so that any new election made within two years after 16 October 1994 cannot be backdated to before 17 October 1994. However, this does not mean that an election made after 16 October 1994 cannot be backdated to before 17 October 1994 if there was an earlier change of residences giving rise to a two-year period which has not expired. Finally, the Revenue stated that where an assessment was still open an individual could choose to disregard an election made before 17 October 1994 which relied for its effect on the existence of a residence occupied under licence, in which case the strict statutory rules would be applied in accordance with its new view to the whole of the period affected although this might mean, for example, that an election was out of time as regards two residences in which a legal or equitable interest was held (Revenue Tax Bulletin October 1994 p 167).

Prior to the above change of view regarding the validity of an election where a licence to occupy a residence is held, the Revenue had announced on 17 May 1985 a concessional practice which is presumably only applicable after 16 October 1994 to interests in residences which are not licences. Under the concession, where for any period an individual has, or is treated by the *Taxes Acts* as having, more than one residence but his interest in each of them, or in each of them except one, is such as to have no more than a negligible capital value on the open market (e.g. a weekly rented flat or accommodation provided by an employer), the two-year time limit laid down by *TCGA 1992, s 222(5)* for nominating one of those residences as the individual's main residence will be extended where the individual was unaware that such a nomination could be made. In such cases the nomination may be made within a reasonable time of the individual becoming aware of the possibility of so doing, and it will be regarded as effective from the date on which the individual first had more than one residence (HMRC Extra-Statutory Concession D21).

Example 1

S purchased the long lease of a London flat on 1 June 1998. He occupied the flat as his sole residence until 31 July 2000 when he acquired a property in Shropshire. Both properties were thereafter occupied as residences by S until the lease of the London flat was sold on 28 February 2007, realising an otherwise chargeable gain of £75,000.

The possibilities open to S are

(i) Election for London flat to be treated as main residence throughout

Exempt gain	£75,000

(ii) Election for Shropshire property to be treated as main residence from 31.7.00 onwards

Exempt gain	$£75{,}000 \times \dfrac{2y\ 2m + 3y}{8y\ 9m}$	£44,286

(iii) Election for London flat to be treated as main residence up to 28 February 2004, with election for the Shropshire property to be so treated thereafter

Exempt gain	$£75{,}000 \times \dfrac{5y\ 9m + 3y}{8y\ 9m}$	£75,000

Note to the example

(*a*) The elections in (iii) are the most favourable, provided they could have been made by 31 July 2002 in respect of the London flat, and by 28 February 2006 in respect of the Shropshire property. Note that the last three years' ownership of the London flat is an exempt period in any case (see 49.1 above). The advantage of (iii) over (i) is that the period of ownership 1 March 2004 to 28 February 2007 of the Shropshire property will be treated as a period of residence as regards any future disposal of that property.

Example 2

HMRC themselves give the example of an individual with two residences, X and Y. He has long since nominated X as his main residence but on, say, 15 January 2007 he disposes of Y at a substantial gain. On, say, 1 March 2007, he gives notice of variation nominating Y as his main residence from, say, 1 March 2005. On 8 March 2007, he gives further notice of variation renominating X as his main residence from, say, 8 March 2005.

The outcome is that Y has been the individual's main residence at some time during the period of ownership, albeit for only one week at the beginning of March 2005. This is enough to give the individual the benefit of the 'final 36 months' exemption at 49.1 above, so he has secured three years relief on Y at a cost of just one week's relief on X.

(HMRC Capital Gains Manual CG 64512).

49.5 OCCUPATION UNDER TERMS OF SETTLEMENT OR BY WILL OR INTESTACY

The provisions of *TCGA 1992, ss 222–224* (see 49.1–49.4 above) also apply in relation to a gain accruing to the trustees of a settlement on a disposal of settled property being an asset within *TCGA 1992, s 222*(*1*) (see 49.1 above) where, during the period of ownership of the trustees, the dwelling-house (or part) has been the only or main residence of a person entitled to occupy it under the terms of the settlement. In the application of those provisions, references to the individual are taken as references to the trustees except in relation to the occupation of the dwelling-house. Any election for main residence treatment under 49.4 above is to be a joint notice by the trustees and the person entitled to occupy. In relation to disposals after 9 December 2003, the trustees must make a claim for *section 223* to apply in this way. [*TCGA 1992, s 225; FA 2004, s 117, Sch 22 paras 4, 7*(*1*)(*2*)].

A person is 'entitled' to occupy if he does so by permission of the trustees of a discretionary trust of which he is a beneficiary (*Sansom v Peay Ch D 1976, 52 TC 1*). See 57.13 SETTLEMENTS as to HMRC's views on whether an 'interest in possession' is created in such circumstances.

TCGA 1992, ss 222–224 (see 49.1–49.4 above) similarly apply in relation to a gain accruing to personal representatives on a disposal after 9 December 2003 of an asset within *TCGA 1992, s 222*(*1*) (see 49.1 above) provided that

- *immediately before and after* the deceased's death the dwelling-house (or part) was the only or main residence of one or more individuals, one or more of whom have a 'relevant entitlement', and
- the aggregate relevant entitlements of those individuals account for at least 75% of the 'net proceeds of disposal' of the property.

For this purpose, '*relevant entitlement*' means an entitlement as legatee of the deceased to, or to an interest in possession in, the whole or any part of the net proceeds of disposal. The '*net proceeds of disposal*' are the disposal proceeds realised by the personal representatives less any incidental costs allowable as a deduction under *TCGA 1992, s 38*(*1*)(*c*) (see 15.4 COMPUTATION OF GAINS AND LOSSES) but on the assumption that none of the proceeds is needed to meet the liabilities of the estate, including any inheritance tax liability.

In the application of *sections 222–224*, references to the individual are taken as references to the personal representatives except in relation to the occupation of the dwelling-house (or part). Any election for main residence treatment under 49.4 above is to be a joint notice by the personal representatives and the individuals entitled to occupy.

The personal representatives must make a claim for *section 223* to apply in this way.

[*TCGA 1992, s 225A; FA 2004, s 117, Sch 22 paras 5, 7*(*2*)].

For disposals before 10 December 2003, relief is available to personal representatives as above by virtue of Extra-Statutory Concession D5. Note, however, that there are certain differences between the concession and the statutory provisions, including that the concession refers only to the disposal of a dwelling-house, and does not require a claim by the personal representatives. See Revenue Tax Bulletin, August 1994, pp 150, 151 for further discussion on the concession.

49.6 OCCUPATION BY DEPENDENT RELATIVE

If an individual so claims, relief as in 49.1–49.4 above is given to a gain accruing to him so far as attributable to the disposal of, or of an interest in, a dwelling-house (or part) which, on 5 April 1988 or at any earlier time in his period of ownership, was the *sole* residence of a 'dependent relative' of the individual, provided 'rent-free and without any other consideration'. Such relief is given in respect of the dwelling-house and its garden and grounds as would be given under *TCGA 1992, ss 222–224* if the dwelling-house had been the individual's only or main residence in the period of residence by the dependent relative; and any such relief is to be in addition to any relief already available under those provisions. Not more than one dwelling-house (or part) may qualify for relief as the residence of a dependent relative at any one time. In the case of an individual and his spouse or civil partner living with him, no more than one dwelling-house may qualify as the residence of a dependent relative of the claimant or of the claimant's spouse or civil partner at any one time. [*TCGA 1992, s 226*(*1*)(*2*)(*4*); *SI 2005 No 3229, Reg 118*].

If in a case within *TCGA 1992, s 226*(*1*) above the dwelling-house (or part) ceases, whether before 6 April 1988 or later, to be the sole residence (provided as mentioned above) of the dependent relative, any subsequent period of residence beginning after 5 April 1988 by that or any other dependent relative is disregarded for the purposes of the above relief. [*TCGA 1992, s 226*(*3*)]. If a dependent relative is obliged temporarily to live elsewhere (e.g. in a nursing home), the absence will not normally be treated as bringing this provision into play (ICAEW Statement TR 739, 13 February 1989).

For disposals before 6 April 1988, the dwelling-house (or part) merely had to be, or had to have been at some time in the period of ownership, the sole residence; and *TCGA 1992, s 226*(*3*) did not apply. [*FA 1988, s 111*].

The condition that the dwelling-house must have been provided 'rent-free and without any other consideration' will be regarded as satisfied where the dependent relative paid all or part of the occupier's rates or council tax and the cost of repairs to the dwelling-house attributable to normal wear and tear. In addition, the exemption will not be lost where the dependent relative made other payments in respect of the property either to the individual claiming the exemption or to a third party, provided that no net income was receivable by the individual, taking one year with another. For this purpose, the income receivable and allowable deductions will be computed in accordance with normal property business income tax rules, except that account will be taken of mortgage payments (including both income and capital elements) and of other payments made by the dependent relative as consideration for the provision of the property, whether such payments were made directly to the mortgagee or other recipient or indirectly via the individual (HMRC Extra-Statutory Concession D20).

'*Dependent relative*' means, in relation to an individual

(*a*) any 'relative' of the individual or of his spouse who is incapacitated by old age or infirmity from maintaining himself, or

(*b*) the mother of the individual or of his spouse who, whether or not incapacitated, is widowed, separated, or a single woman in consequence of dissolution or annulment of marriage.

[*TCGA 1992, s 226(5)(6); FA 1996, Sch 20 para 61*].

This definition seems to exclude the mother of a child born out of wedlock (unless the mother either is incapacitated or has married subsequent to the child's birth and then become widowed etc.) but HMRC have confirmed that such persons will in practice be included (Tolley's Practical Tax 1986 p 143). Also included, it seems in (*a*), is the incapacitated widowed stepmother of an individual, or of an individual's spouse, where the father has remarried and subsequently died. (Tolley's Practical Tax 1981 p 171 and 1984 p 198). '*Relative*' is undefined but may be compared with a specific meaning for other provisions as in 16.7 CONNECTED PERSONS i.e. brother, sister, ancestor or lineal descendant.

Old age, according to HMRC, is reached at an age of 65 years in any case, and can be reached at an age greater than 54 years if the individual becomes, only because of age, not capable of working again 'in his own industry' (i.e. a man aged 57 years is not considered to have reached old age if he chooses not to work again or is unemployed because of a general lack of jobs). An individual is regarded as infirm if he is prevented by physical or mental illness from supporting himself by working. (HMRC Capital Gains Manual CG 65575–65577).

Where a property qualifies for the main private residence exemption only by virtue of these provisions, it is HMRC's view that the residential lettings exemption at 49.8 below is *not* available. (HMRC Capital Gains Manual CG 65562, 64718).

49.7 EXCLUSIONS FROM EXEMPTIONS

Dwelling-house acquired for profit. The exemptions given by *TCGA 1992, s 223* do not apply in relation to a gain if the acquisition of, or of the interest in, the dwelling-house (or part) was made wholly or partly for the purpose of realising a gain from the disposal of it, and does not apply in relation to a gain *so far as attributable to* any expenditure which was incurred after the beginning of the period of ownership and was incurred wholly or partly for the purpose of realising a gain from the disposal. [*TCGA 1992, s 224(3)*]. HMRC's practice is not to take into account expenditure incurred in obtaining planning permission or in removing restrictive covenants when considering whether to apply the second leg of *TCGA 1992, s 224(3)* (Revenue Tax Bulletin, August 1994, p 150). The three most common applications of the second leg are

- acquisition by a leaseholder of a superior interest in the property,
- conversion of an undivided house into self-contained flats, and

- redevelopment of part of the garden or grounds, e.g. barn conversions.

(HMRC Capital Gains Manual CG 65245, 65274).

In *Jones v Wilcock (Sp C 92), [1996] SSCD 389*, a married couple incurred a loss on the sale of their house. They contended that the house had been purchased 'wholly or partly for the purpose of realising a gain'. However, from the facts of the case it was decided that the house was purchased to use as the couple's home.

Relief obtained under *TCGA 1992, s 260* on earlier disposal. Anti-avoidance provisions were introduced in *FA 2004* to prevent perceived exploitation of the interaction between the exemption for private residences and hold-over relief under *TCGA 1992, s 260* (see 33.7 HOLD-OVER RELIEFS). Subject to the transitional rules below, the provisions apply where

- exemption under *section 223* would otherwise be available in relation to a gain (or part of a gain) accruing after 9 December 2003 to an individual or the trustees of a settlement on a disposal (the '*later disposal*'), and
- in computing the chargeable gain which would (apart from *section 223*) accrue on that disposal, the allowable expenditure falls to be reduced to any extent in consequence, directly or indirectly, of a claim or claims under *section 260* in respect of one or more earlier disposals (whether or not made to the person making the later disposal).

Where the claim to relief under *section 260* in respect of the earlier disposal (or, if there is more than one earlier disposal, any of them) is made on or before the making of the later disposal (or, in the case of trustees, on or before the making of a claim for relief under *section 223*), the exemption given by *TCGA 1992, s 223* does not apply in relation to the gain (or part of the gain) on the later disposal. Where the claim (or any of the claims) is made after the later disposal (or claim for relief under *section 223*), *section 223* is treated as never having applied to the gain (or part of the gain) on the later disposal and any adjustments required, whether by assessment, discharge or repayment of tax or otherwise, can be made notwithstanding any time limit for the making of adjustments.

Where a claim under *section 260* is revoked, it is treated for the purposes of these provisions as having never been made.

The above provisions do not apply to a later disposal made by the trustees of a settlement if they have elected for *ICTA 1988, s 691(2)* (certain income of maintenance funds for historic buildings not to be income of settlor — see Tolley's Income Tax) to apply in relation to each tax year in which there is a '*relevant earlier disposal*' (i.e. an earlier disposal in respect of which a claim under *section 260* is made).

Transitional provisions. The above provisions are modified where the relevant earlier disposal, or, if more than one, each of the relevant earlier disposals, is made before 10 December 2003. Total exemption (under *section 223(1)*) is excluded as above, but fractional exemption (under *section 223(2)*) can be obtained. In calculating the fractional exemption, the dwelling-house (or part thereof) in question is taken not to have been the individual's only or main residence at any time after 9 December 2003, and the period of ownership after that date is taken not to form part of the last 36 months of the period of ownership.

[*TCGA 1992, ss 226A, 226B: FA 2004, s 117, Sch 22 paras 6, 7(3)(4), 8*].

49.8 EXEMPTION FOR LETTING AS RESIDENTIAL ACCOMMODATION

Where a gain to which *TCGA 1992, s 222* (see 49.1 above) applies accrues to an individual and the dwelling-house in question, or any part of it, is or has at any time in his 'period of ownership' been wholly or partly let (thus including any tenancy or licence or agreement for a lease, tenancy or licence; see *TCGA 1992, Sch 8 para 10*) by him as residential accommodation, the part of the gain, if any, which otherwise would be a chargeable gain by reason of the letting is exempt to the extent of the lower of

(*a*) £40,000 (£20,000 for disposals before 19 March 1991); and

(*b*) the amount of the gain otherwise exempt under *TCGA 1992, s 222(1)*–*(3)* (see 49.1 and 49.2 above).

[*TCGA 1992, s 223(4); FA 2004, s 117, Sch 22 para 2(2)*].

'*Period of ownership*' does not include any period before 31 March 1982. [*TCGA 1992, s 223(7)*].

Note that the exemption applies to gains arising both from a residential letting of the entire residence whilst the owner is not occupying the property and to a partial residential letting whilst the owner is in residence.

The length of a letting is not determinative and the words 'residential accommodation' do not limit the above relief to accommodation which is used by a tenant etc. as his home (*Owen v Elliott CA 1990, 63 TC 319*). (In this case the taxpayer let short- and long-term accommodation in private hotel premises which he also occupied different parts of at different times of the year as his main residence in such a way that every part of the premises had at some time in his period of ownership been his main residence and it was agreed that on a disposal of the premises one-third of the gain arising was exempt under *TCGA 1992, ss 222–224*. The CA held that the above relief was also available in respect of the remaining non-exempt gain but Leggatt LJ indicated that it would not be available 'to a taxpayer the whole or part of whose dwelling-house is exclusively used as an hotel or boarding house. It will apply only where a dwelling-house has at any time been used wholly or partly for that or a like purpose by a person whose only or main residence it is'. Cf. HMRC's practice below as to whether let accommodation forms part of the dwelling-house.)

Whether the let accommodation is part of the owner's dwelling-house, or is itself a separate dwelling-house, will depend on the facts of particular cases. In HMRC's view, the relief will apply to the common case where the owner of a house, which was previously occupied as his or the family home, lets part as a flat or set of rooms without structural alteration, or with only minor adaptations. Whether or not the tenants have separate washing or cooking facilities will not affect the relief. Where a property, although part of the same building, forms a dwelling-house separate from that which is, or has been, the owner's dwelling-house, e.g. a fully self-contained flat with its own access from the road, relief will not be granted. (HMRC Statement of Practice 14/80).

The maximum gain that can be relieved under these provisions is the gain arising by reason of the letting. In a simple case in which a dwelling-house has at all times either been used as the owner's only or main residence or been let as residential accommodation, the gain remaining after the main private residence relief can be taken to be the gain arising by reason of the letting. See also *Example 2* below.

Where husband and wife are joint owners, they are treated like any other joint owners for the purposes of this exemption, with the result that relief of up to £80,000 is potentially available to the couple. However, HMRC officers have instructions to investigate the fact of a property being in joint ownership of husband and wife where the tax is significant. (HMRC Capital Gains Manual CG 64716, 64738).

The availability of the residential lettings exemption extends to gains accruing to trustees and qualifying for the main private residence exemption under *TCGA 1992, s 225* (see 49.5 above). (HMRC Capital Gains Manual CG 64717).

Where a dwelling-house qualifies for the main private residence exemption due only to its having been occupied by a dependent relative on or before 5 April 1988 (see 49.6 above), it is HMRC's view that the residential lettings exemption is *not* available. (HMRC Capital Gains Manual CG 64718).

These provisions do not apply to restrict an allowable loss.

For the capital gains tax consequences of eligibility for 'rent a room' income tax relief, see 49.3 above.

For reliefs applicable to the commercial letting of furnished holiday accommodation in the UK, see 24 FURNISHED HOLIDAY ACCOMMODATION.

Example 1

P sold a house on 1 July 2006 realising an otherwise chargeable gain (before taper relief) of £50,540. The house was originally purchased by P on 1 February 1981 and was occupied as a residence until 30 June 1989 when P moved to another residence, letting the house as residential accommodation. He did not re-occupy the house prior to its sale.

	£
Gain on sale	50,540
Deduct Exempt amount under main residence rules	
$\dfrac{7y\ 3m + 3y}{24y\ 3m} \times £50{,}540$	21,362
	29,178
Deduct Let property exemption (see note (2))	21,362
Net chargeable gain 2006/07 (subject to TAPER RELIEF (61))	£7,816

Notes to the example

(1) The period of ownership for the exemption calculation does not include any period before 31 March 1982. This applies regardless of whether the gain has been calculated by reference to cost or to 31 March 1982 value under the re-basing rules.

(2) The gain attributable to the letting (£29,178) is exempt to the extent that it does not exceed the lesser of £40,000 and the gain otherwise exempt (£21,362 in this example).

Example 2

Q purchased a house on 1 February 1995, moved in immediately and occupied it as his main residence until 31 January 1996. It was let as residential accommodation from 1 February 1996 to 31 January 1997, was then empty until 31 January 2000, was again let as residential accommodation until 31 January 2002 and was subsequently let as office accommodation until being sold on 31 January 2007 at an otherwise chargeable gain (before taper relief) of £72,000.

			£
Gain on sale			72,000
Deduct Exempt amount under main residence rules			
$\frac{1y + \text{last } 3y}{12y} \times £72{,}000$			24,000
			48,000
Deduct Let property exemption:			
Lowest of:	main residence relief	£24,000	
	statutory limit	£40,000	
	gain attributable to residential letting*	£18,000	18,000
Chargeable gain 2006/07 (subject to TAPER RELIEF (61))			£30,000

$$* \frac{1y + 2y}{12y} \times £72{,}000 = £18{,}000$$

50 Qualifying Corporate Bonds

Simon's Direct Tax Service. See Division C2.8.

50.1 EXEMPTION RULES

A gain on the disposal of a qualifying corporate bond (as defined in 50.2 below) is not a chargeable gain, and a loss is not an allowable loss. [*TCGA 1992, s 115*(*1*)(*a*)].

The same applies to disposals of options or contracts to acquire or dispose of qualifying corporate bonds (see 6.7, 6.8 ASSETS).

See 50.3 below re share capital reorganisations involving qualifying corporate bonds.

See 40.11 LOSSES for allowable loss relief in respect of certain qualifying corporate bonds evidencing loans made before 17 March 1998 which become irrecoverable etc.

See 13.13 COMPANIES for appropriations of qualifying corporate bonds to and from trading stock by companies.

50.2 DEFINITIONS

Position for companies after 31 March 1996. For corporation tax purposes as regards disposals after 31 March 1996, with certain exceptions (see below), the definition of 'qualifying corporate bond' is extended so as to include *any* asset representing a loan relationship of a company (see 14.5 COMPANIES—CORPORATE FINANCE AND INTANGIBLES). Exceptions are as follows:

- (before the repeal of *FA 1996, s 92* by *FA 2004*) convertible securities held as non-trading assets (see 14.6(i) COMPANIES—CORPORATE FINANCE AND INTANGIBLES, and in particular the detailed repeal provisions there);
- (before the repeal of *FA 1996, s 93* by *FA 2004*) certain debts linked to the value of non-trading chargeable assets (see 14.6(ii) COMPANIES—CORPORATE FINANCE AND INTANGIBLES, and in particular the detailed repeal provisions there);
- (for accounting periods beginning before 1 October 2002) an asset held in 'exempt circumstances' (defined by reference to *FA 1993, Sch 17 para 3* — see 22.8 EXEMPTIONS AND RELIEFS) where the debt to which it relates is not a debt on a security (see 22.5 EXEMPTIONS AND RELIEFS) and its settlement currency is not sterling or is a debt on a security and is 'a debt in a foreign currency' (as defined) (see *TCGA 1992, s 117A* — now repealed);
- (for accounting periods beginning before 1 October 2002) certain rights under a unit trust scheme or interests in an offshore fund which fall to be treated under *FA 1996, Sch 10 para 4* as rights under a creditor relationship of a company and which are denominated in a currency other than sterling and held in 'exempt circumstances' (as defined by reference to *FA 1993, Sch 17 para 3* — see 22.8 EXEMPTIONS AND RELIEFS) (see *TCGA 1992, s 117B* — now repealed).

[*TCGA 1992, s 117*(*A1*), *s 117A, s 117B; FA 1996, s 92*(*4*), *s 93*(*4*), *s 104, s 105, Sch 14 paras 61, 62, Sch 15 para 7*(*c*); *FA 2000, Sch 29 paras 20, 21; FA 2002, Sch 40 Pt 3*(*10*); *FA 2004, Sch 10 paras 9, 11*].

Definition of corporate bond. The following is subject to the overriding rule for company disposals after 31 March 1996 (as above). Before defining a 'qualifying corporate bond', it is first necessary to define a 'corporate bond'. Subject to the specific inclusion of certain securities within this definition (see below) and the exclusion of some (again, see below), a '*corporate bond*' is a 'security' which fulfils both the following conditions.

(*a*) The debt on the security represents, and has at all times represented, a 'normal commercial loan'.

'*Normal commercial loan*' is as would be defined by *ICTA 1988, Sch 18 para 1*(*5*) if, for *para* (*a*)(*i*)–(*iii*) of *sub-para* (*5*), there were substituted the words 'corporate bonds (within the meaning of *TCGA 1992, s 117*)'. The broad effect of the modification is that securities can be treated as corporate bonds if they carry conversion rights into other corporate bonds but not if the conversion rights relate to securities other than corporate bonds. Securities carrying an indirect right of conversion into ordinary shares were held not to be corporate bonds in *Weston v Garnett CA, [2005] STC 1134.*

(*b*) The security is expressed in sterling and no provision is made for its conversion into, or redemption in, a currency other than sterling.

A security is *not* treated as expressed in sterling if the amount of sterling falls to be determined by reference to the value at any time of any other currency or asset. A provision for redemption in a currency other than sterling is disregarded provided the rate of exchange to be used is that prevailing at redemption.

[*TCGA 1992, s 117*(*1*)(*2*)].

'*Security*' includes any loan stock or similar security of any government or public or local authority in the UK or elsewhere, or of any company, and whether secured or unsecured. [*TCGA 1992, s 117*(*1*), *s 132*(*3*)(*b*)].

Inclusion of other securities within the definition of corporate bond. For 1996/97 onwards, a **deeply discounted security** (within 58.16 SHARES AND SECURITIES) is a corporate bond (and is also a qualifying corporate bond — see below). [*TCGA 1992, s 117*(*2AA*)*; FA 1996, Sch 14 para 61; ITTOIA 2005, Sch 1 para 433*(*2*)]. For this purpose, the widened definition of 'deeply discounted security' (i.e. taking further account of potential redemptions before maturity) applies as regards any disposal or part disposal of an asset after 14 February 1999. [*FA 1999, s 65*(*11*)*; ITTOIA 2005, Sch 1 para 507*].

Save in relation to the application of this definition for the purposes of *TCGA 1992, s 254* (loss relief for irrecoverable loans made before 17 March 1998 to traders and evidenced by qualifying corporate bonds — see 40.11 LOSSES), 'corporate bond' also includes a **share in a building society** (within *Building Societies Act 1986*) which meets the condition in (*b*) above and which is a 'qualifying share' (i.e. a share which is either a 'permanent interest bearing share', as defined, or is of a description specified in Treasury regulations for this purpose). [*TCGA 1992, s 117*(*4*)–(*6*)(*11*)(*b*), (*12*)(*13*)*; SI 1999 No 1953; SI 2001 No 3629, Arts 63, 109, Sch*].

In relation to chargeable periods ended after 15 March 1993, 'corporate bond' also includes any debenture issued after that date which is not a 'security' as defined above but would fall to be treated as such under *TCGA 1992, s 251*(*6*) (see 22.5 EXEMPTIONS AND RELIEFS). This does not apply to debentures acquired by a person following a prior disposal of a qualifying corporate bond derived from shares giving rise to a deferred gain (where the general exemption in *TCGA 1992, s 115* has had effect in accordance with *TCGA 1992, s 116*(*10*)(*c*) — see 50.3 below). (This provision and *TCGA 1992, s 251*(*6*) prevent, in certain circumstances, the issue of a debenture which neither represents a debt on a security nor is a qualifying corporate bond.) [*TCGA 1992, s 117*(*6A*)*; FA 1993, s 84*(*1*)(*3*)].

Securities excluded from being corporate bonds. An **excluded indexed security** (as defined by *ITTOIA 2005, s 433* and meaning broadly a security the amount payable on redemption of which is linked to the value of chargeable assets) issued **after 5 April 1996** is *not* a corporate bond. An excluded indexed security issued before that date is a corporate bond only if it satisfies the general conditions above and if the question of whether or not it is a corporate bond arises only for the purposes of *TCGA 1992, s 116*(*10*) (reorganisation of share capital involving the issue of a qualifying corporate bond — see 50.3 below). [*TCGA 1992, s 117(6B)(6C); FA 1996, Sch 14 para 61; ITTOIA 2005, Sch 1 para 433(3)*].

Definition of qualifying corporate bond. The following is subject to the overriding rule for company disposals after 31 March 1996 (as above). A corporate bond

(A) is a '*qualifying corporate bond*' if it is issued after 13 March 1984; and

(B) becomes a '*qualifying corporate bond*' if, having been issued before 14 March 1984, it is acquired by any person after 13 March 1984 unless

- (i) the acquisition is as the result of *any* disposal treated as a no gain/no loss transaction or a disposal where the consideration is reduced by an amount of held-over gain under *TCGA 1992, s 165* or *s 260* (see 33.1–33.9 HOLD-OVER RELIEFS); and

- (ii) the bond was not a qualifying corporate bond before the disposal.

[*TCGA 1992, s 117(7)(8)*].

See the example below.

Where a right to a security is comprised in a provisional letter of allotment or similar instrument, the security is not deemed to be issued until acceptance has been made. [*TCGA 1992, s 117(11)(a)*].

A security which is a corporate bond due to its being a **relevant discounted security** (see above) is a qualifying corporate bond whatever its date of issue. [*TCGA 1992, s 117(8A); FA 1996, Sch 14 para 61*].

Example

B has the following transactions in 5% unsecured loan stock issued in 1983 by F Ltd.

		£
11.11.83	Purchase £2,000	1,800
10.7.89	Gift from wife £1,000 (original cost £800)	—
30.9.97	Purchase £2,000	2,100
5.6.06	Sale £4,000	(3,300)

Apart from the gift on 10.7.89, all acquisitions were arm's length purchases. B's wife acquired her £1,000 holding on 11.11.83. Indexation allowance of £266 arose on the transfer from wife to husband.

For the purposes of the accrued income scheme, the sale is without accrued interest and the rebate amount is £20. The stock is a corporate bond as defined by *TCGA 1992, s 117(1)* and a 'relevant security' as defined by *TCGA 1992, s 108(1)*.

Under the rules for matching relevant securities in *TCGA 1992, s 106A* (see 59.2 SHARES AND SECURITIES—IDENTIFICATION RULES), the stock disposed of is identified with acquisitions as follows.

(i) Identify £2,000 with purchase on 30.9.97 (LIFO)

		£
Disposal consideration	$£3,300 \times \frac{2,000}{4,000}$	1,650
Add rebate amount	$£20 \times \frac{2,000}{4,000}$	10
		1,660
Allowable cost		2,100
Loss		£440

The loss is *not* allowable as the £2,000 stock purchased on 30.9.97 is a qualifying corporate bond (note (*a*)). [*TCGA 1992, s 115*].

(ii) Identify £1,000 with acquisition on 10.7.89

		£
Disposal consideration	$£3,300 \times \frac{1,000}{4,000}$	825
Add rebate amount	$£20 \times \frac{1,000}{4,000}$	5
		830
Allowable cost (including indexation to 10.7.89)		1,066
Allowable loss		£236

The loss is allowable as the stock acquired on 10.7.89 is not a qualifying corporate bond (note (*b*)).

(iii) Identify £1,000 with part of purchase on 11.11.83

		£
Disposal consideration	$£3,300 \times \frac{1,000}{4,000}$	825
Add rebate amount	$£20 \times \frac{1,000}{4,000}$	5
		830
Allowable cost	$£1,800 \times \frac{1,000}{2,000}$	900
Allowable loss		£70

The loss is allowable as the stock acquired on 11.11.83 is not a qualifying corporate bond (note (*c*)).

Notes to the example

(*a*) The acquisition on 30.9.97 is a qualifying corporate bond as it was acquired after 13 March 1984 otherwise than as a result of an excluded disposal.

(*b*) The acquisition on 10.7.89 was the result of an excluded disposal, being a no gain/no loss transfer between spouses where the first spouse had acquired the stock before 14 March 1984. It is therefore not a qualifying corporate bond.

(*c*) Securities acquired before 14 March 1984 cannot be qualifying corporate bonds in the hands of the person who so acquired them.

50.3 REORGANISATION OF SHARE CAPITAL

Special provisions apply to a transaction ('*relevant transaction*') where otherwise *TCGA 1992, ss 127–130* (share reorganisation rules for 'original shares' and 'new holding'; see 58.1 SHARES AND SECURITIES) would apply under any provision contained in *TCGA 1992, Pt IV Ch II* (reorganisation of share capital, conversion of securities etc.), and either the original shares would consist of or include a qualifying corporate bond and the new holding would not, or the original shares would not and the new holding would consist of or include such a bond. In relation to any disposal after 25 November 1996, the provisions apply equally to a conversion of securities occurring before or after that date and effected other than by means of a transaction, for example in consequence of the terms of the security. Where the qualifying corporate bond would constitute the original shares it is referred to as '*the old asset*', the shares and securities constituting the new holding being referred to as '*the new asset*'. Where the qualifying corporate bond would constitute the new holding it is referred to as '*the new asset*', the shares and securities constituting the original shares being referred to as '*the old asset*'.

TCGA 1992, ss 127–130 do not apply to the relevant transaction so far as the latter relates to the old asset and the new asset. (HMRC has stated that where shares (or other chargeable securities) are exchanged, converted etc. for a new holding consisting partly of qualifying corporate bonds and partly of shares etc., then *TCGA 1992, ss 127–130* are only disapplied to the extent that the consideration takes the form of qualifying corporate bonds, any apportionment of the base cost of the original shares being on a just and reasonable basis under *TCGA 1992, s 52(4)* by reference to the respective market values at the time of exchange etc. of the shares etc. and qualifying corporate bonds received in exchange etc. (Revenue Tax Bulletin February 1993 p 57).)

Where the qualifying corporate bond would constitute the old asset, the shares or securities which constitute the new asset are to be treated as being acquired on the date of the relevant transaction and for a consideration of the market value of the old asset immediately before the relevant transaction. Similar provisions apply where the qualifying corporate bond constitutes the new asset. Where a sum of money by way of consideration for the old asset is received, in addition to the new asset, that sum is to be deducted from the deemed market value consideration and where a sum of money is paid by way of consideration, in addition to the old asset, that sum is to be added to the deemed market value consideration. See also (ii) below.

Where the old asset consists of a qualifying corporate bond, then so far as it relates to the old and the new asset, the relevant transaction is to be treated as a disposal of the old asset and an acquisition of the new asset. [*TCGA 1992, s 116*(*9*)].

In all other cases (e.g. **where the new asset consists of a qualifying corporate bond**) then so far as it relates to the old asset and to the new asset the relevant transaction is *not* to be treated as a disposal of the old asset but

(*a*) the chargeable gain or allowable loss is calculated that would have accrued had the old asset been disposed of at the time of the relevant transaction at its market value immediately before that time, and

(*b*) subject to the exclusions below, the whole or a corresponding part of the calculated chargeable gain or allowable loss at (*a*) above is to be deemed to accrue on a subsequent disposal of the whole or part of the new asset. The exemption provided by 50.1 above applies only to the gain or loss that actually accrues on that disposal and not to the gain or loss that is deemed to accrue. [*TCGA 1992, s 116*(*10*)].

The following exclusions are made to the above provisions.

(i) The provisions in (*b*) above do not apply to disposals falling within: *TCGA 1992, s 58*(*1*) (see 42.4 MARRIED PERSONS AND CIVIL PARTNERS); *s 62*(*4*) (see 18.9 DEATH); *s 139* in respect of disposals after 13 March 1989 (see 13.10 COMPANIES); *s 140A* (see 45.10 OVERSEAS MATTERS); *s 140E* (see 13.18 COMPANIES); *s 171*(*1*) (see 27.2 GROUPS OF COMPANIES); or *s 172* (now repealed — see 45.3 OVERSEAS MATTERS). Where there is such a disposal (and without there having been a previous disposal other than such a disposal or a devolution on death) the person who has acquired the new asset is treated for the purposes of (*b*) above as if the new asset had been acquired by him at the same time and for the same consideration as it was acquired by the person making the disposal.

(ii) Where a chargeable gain arises under (*a*) above *and* part of the consideration for the old asset is received as money, a proportion of the chargeable gain is deemed to accrue at that time. The proportion is the ratio which the sum of money bears to the market value of the old asset immediately before the relevant transaction. On a later disposal of a part or the whole of the new asset, the proportion already deemed to have accrued is to be deducted from the gain accruing under (*b*) above. However, if the sum of money is 'small' in comparison with the market value of the old asset immediately before the relevant transaction, HMRC may direct that no chargeable gain accrues at that time. The money consideration is then deducted from allowable expenditure on any subsequent disposal (see 9.2 CAPITAL SUMS DERIVED FROM ASSETS).

For the purpose of the above, HMRC have regarded 'small' as meaning 5% or less (see HMRC Capital Gains Manual CG 53857, 57836). With effect from **24 February 1997**, they additionally regard an amount of £3,000 or less as 'small', regardless of whether or not it would pass the 5% test (Revenue Tax Bulletin February 1997 p 397).

(iii) The treatment at (*a*) and (*b*) above) is disapplied in certain circumstances (with the result that the transaction is treated as a disposal of the old asset and an acquisition of the new asset) where the old asset consists of shares or securities that have qualified for tax relief under the corporate venturing scheme or the community investment tax credit scheme. See 17.22 CORPORATE VENTURING SCHEME and Tolley's Income Tax under Community Investment Tax Relief. See also 60.14 SUBSTANTIAL SHAREHOLDINGS OF COMPANIES.

[*TCGA 1992, s 116(1)–(14); FA 1985, s 67(2)(c), Sch 27 Part VII; FA 1989, s 139(6); FA 1990, s 70(6)(9); F(No 2)A 1992, s 46(1)(3); FA 1997, s 88(4)(6); FA 2000, Sch 29 para 19; F(No 2)A 2005, s 64(1)*].

See also 60.20 SUBSTANTIAL SHAREHOLDINGS OF COMPANIES.

In relation to disposals after 13 March 1989, the changes made by *FA 1989, s 139* are to be regarded as always having had effect. [*TCGA 1992, Sch 11 para 16*].

Where the new asset is a qualifying corporate bond which is subsequently gifted to a charity (within 10.5 CHARITIES), HMRC take the view that no deferred gain or loss will arise to the donor (or the charity) under (*b*) above (Revenue Tax Bulletin May 1992 p 21 and HMRC Capital Gains Manual CG 66646).

A special rule has effect where, before 15 February 1999, there occurred a transaction (the original transaction) to which *TCGA 1992, ss 127–130* applied and the new holding consisted of or included something (the new asset) which becomes a 'relevant discounted security' (and thus a qualifying corporate bond — see 50.2 above) by virtue of the widening of the definition of that term to take further account of potential redemptions before maturity (see 58.16 SHARES AND SECURITIES). In relation to any disposal or part disposal of the new asset after 14 February 1999, there is deemed to have been a transaction subsequent to the original transaction whereby the holder of the new asset disposed of it and immediately re-acquired it. The re-acquired asset is deemed to consist of a qualifying corporate bond and the subsequent transaction is deemed to be one to which *TCGA 1992, s 116* applies, with the same consequences as in (*a*) and (*b*) above. The subsequent transaction is deemed to have occurred immediately after the original transaction, except that where the original transaction occurred before 5 April 1996 the subsequent transaction is deemed to have occurred on that date. [*FA 1999, s 66*].

See 20.35 EMPLOYEE SHARE SCHEMES for the interaction of the provisions above with those relating to certain disposals to employee share ownership trusts.

See 61.15 TAPER RELIEF for the application of that relief to the postponed gain where the new asset is a qualifying corporate bond.

See 40.11 LOSSES for the interaction of the provisions above with the now repealed provisions relating to loss relief by reference to certain qualifying corporate bonds evidencing loans which become irrecoverable etc.

Example

D holds 5,000 £1 ordinary shares in H Ltd. He acquired the shares in April 1992 by subscription at par. On 1 August 1995, he accepted an offer for the shares from J plc. The terms of the offer were one 25p ordinary share of J plc and £10 J plc 10% unsecured loan stock (a qualifying corporate bond) for each H Ltd ordinary share. Both the shares and the loan stock are listed on the Stock Exchange. In December 2006, D sells £20,000 loan stock at its quoted price of £105 per cent.

The value of J plc ordinary shares at 1 August 1995 was £3.52 per share and the loan stock was £99.20 per cent. The indexation factor for April 1992 to August 1995 is 0.080.

The cost of the H Ltd shares must be apportioned between the J plc ordinary shares and loan stock.

	£
Value of J plc shares	
5,000 × £3.52	17,600
Value of J plc loan stock	
£50,000 × 99.2%	49,600
	£67,200

Allowable cost of J plc shares

$$\frac{17,600}{67,200} \times £5,000 \qquad £1,310$$

Allowable cost of J plc loan stock

$$\frac{49,600}{67,200} \times £5,000 \qquad £3,690$$

Chargeable gain on H Ltd shares attributable to J plc loan stock to date of exchange

	£
Deemed disposal consideration	49,600
Allowable cost	3,690
Unindexed gain	45,910
Indexation allowance £3,690 × 0.080	295
Deferred chargeable gain	£45,615

Deferred chargeable gain accruing on disposal of loan stock in December 2006

Loan stock sold (nominal)	£20,000
Total holding of loan stock before disposal (nominal)	£50,000

Deferred chargeable gain accruing in 2006/07

$$\frac{20,000}{50,000} \times £45,615 \qquad £18,246$$

Notes to the example

(*a*) The gain on the sale of J plc loan stock is exempt (as the stock is a qualifying corporate bond) except for that part which relates to the gain on the previous holding of H Ltd shares. [*TCGA 1992, s 115, s 116*(*10*)]. There will also be income tax consequences under the accrued income scheme.

(*b*) For taper relief purposes, the deferred gain is deemed to arise in August 1995 (and not in December 2006)—see 61.15 TAPER RELIEF. Thus, there can be no taper relief due in this example.

(*c*) The qualifying corporate bond is treated as acquired at the date of the reorganisation, so even if the original shares had been held at 31 March 1982, re-basing could *not* apply on the subsequent disposal, after 5 April 1988, of the loan stock. However, where the original shares were acquired before 31 March 1982, the reorganisation took place before 6 April 1988, and the qualifying corporate bonds are disposed of after 5 April 1988, the deferred chargeable gain is halved (under the provisions at 8.12 ASSETS HELD ON 31 MARCH 1982).

(*d*) The exchange of J plc ordinary shares for H Ltd shares is dealt with under *TCGA 1992, ss 127–130* (see 58.1 SHARES AND SECURITIES), and no gain or loss will arise until the J plc shares are disposed of.

51 Remittance Basis

Cross-references. See 6.2 ASSETS for the location of assets; 19.6 DOUBLE TAX RELIEF for relief available where remittance basis applies; 45.5 OVERSEAS MATTERS for relief available where overseas gains are unremittable to the UK; 52 RESIDENCE AND DOMICILE.

Simon's Direct Tax Service. See C1.603, E1.323.

51.1 The remittance basis implies that assessments to UK capital gains tax on gains arising abroad are restricted to sums actually remitted (or deemed to have been remitted) into the UK out of those gains, such remittances being treated as gains accruing when received in the UK. Subject to any relevant double taxation agreement, it applies to disposals by individuals *resident or ordinarily resident but not domiciled* in the UK of assets situated abroad (with no allowance for losses arising abroad). [*TCGA 1992, s 12*(*1*), *s 16*(*4*)].

HMRC practice appears to be to leave out of account remittances made out of the proceeds of disposals made whilst a non-UK domiciled individual was neither resident nor ordinarily resident in the UK and, subject to this, to treat a remittance as taxable to the extent given by the proportion which represents chargeable gain on normal disposal principles (see 15.4 COMPUTATION OF GAINS AND LOSSES for allowable expenditure and proceeds in foreign currency). This practice even seems to extend to the case where the taxpayer divides the proceeds of disposal but only makes remittances from that part which represents the original allowable expenditure and indexation allowance.

In an appeal to General Commissioners, the Revenue were successful in applying the provisions where the individual was at all material times resident and ordinarily resident in the UK but acquired a UK domicile between the realisation of the gains in question and the time, in a later year of assessment, when the proceeds of the gains were remitted to the UK (Taxation, 6 June 1991, p 257).

Taper relief is computed by reference to actual time of disposal and not time of remittance (see 61.15 TAPER RELIEF).

For the situation where an individual becomes, or ceases to be, resident or ordinarily resident in the UK, see 52.3 RESIDENCE AND DOMICILE.

HMRC's views on the practical operation of the remittance basis are contained in HMRC Capital Gains Manual CG 25301–25440.

Forward agreements. It is known that it was Revenue practice in the past to make 'forward tax agreements' with certain wealthy non-UK domiciled individuals, under which the individual would pay a set amount each year, agreed in advance, 'in full and final settlement' of his UK income tax and CGT liability. Such agreements have now been held to be illegal (*Fayed and Others v Advocate-General for Scotland (representing CIR) SCS, [2002] STC 910*).

51.2 REMITTANCES GENERALLY

By analogy with cases relating to income tax, a taxable remittance may include the repatriation of reinvested gains, provided those gains were made whilst the disposer was resident or ordinarily resident in the UK (*Scottish Provident Institution v Farmer CS 1912, 6 TC 34* and *Kneen v Martin CA 1934, 19 TC 33*). Similarly, a remittance from a foreign bank account into which overseas gains have been paid may be assessable, depending on the circumstances, see *Walsh v Randall KB 1940, 23 TC 55* (sterling draft on foreign bank received by UK resident drawer before handing to UK payee) and *Thomson v Moyse HL 1960, 39 TC 291* (dollar cheques on US bank sold to the Bank of England held to be remitted) but cf. *Carter v Sharon KB 1936, 20 TC 229* (drafts on foreign bank posted abroad by UK drawer for daughter's maintenance; held no remittance as, under relevant foreign law, gift to daughter complete on posting of draft). In *Harmel v Wright Ch D 1973,*

49 TC 149 an amount received via two South African companies, ending as a loan from one of them, was held to be a remittance. An erroneous remittance by a bank, contrary to the customer's instructions, was held not liable in *Duke of Roxburghe's Exors v CIR CS 1936, 20 TC 711*. In *Grimm v Newman & Another CA, [2002] STC 1388* (a negligence case in which the Revenue were not a party), an absolute inter-spousal gift, perfected abroad, of overseas assets subsequently used to purchase a matrimonial home in the UK was held not to be a remittance.

51.3 CONSTRUCTIVE REMITTANCES

Gains arising abroad to a person ordinarily resident in the UK and which he applies abroad towards the satisfaction of

(*a*) a debt (or interest thereon) for money lent to him in the UK, or

(*b*) a debt for money lent to him abroad and brought here, or

(*c*) a loan incurred to satisfy such debts,

are treated as received by him in the UK.

For this purpose, if any of the money lent is used to satisfy a debt, the debt for the money so used is treated as incurred for satisfying that other debt, and a debt incurred to satisfy, wholly or in part, a debt within (*c*) above is itself treated as falling within (*c*) above.

In the case of a debt for money lent abroad (within (*b*) or (*c*) above), it is immaterial whether the money lent is received in or brought to the UK before or after the gain is used to satisfy the debt, except that, if the money lent is received in or brought to the UK at a time *after* the gain is so used, the gain is treated as received in the UK at that later time.

Gains available in any form to the 'lender' so that the amount of a loan debt, or the time of its repayment, depends directly or indirectly on the amount of property so available to the lender, are treated as having been applied towards satisfaction of the loan. '*Lender*' includes any person for the time being entitled to repayment.

[*TCGA 1992, s 12(2); ICTA 1988, s 65(6)–(9); ITTOIA 2005, ss 833, 834, Sch 1 paras 38, 429*].

Example

X, ordinarily resident but not domiciled in the UK, borrows £28,000 in the UK in order to buy a residence here. Out of a later loan of US $50,000 raised abroad, he uses $40,000 to repay the loan incurred in the UK. He repays the $50,000 loan out of the disposal proceeds of assets situated abroad but he uses the balance ($10,000) of the actual dollars borrowed in improving his UK residence. The disposal proceeds of the overseas assets were $140,000 and the disposal would have given rise to a chargeable gain of £60,000 on normal disposal principles. Subject to double taxation arrangements the gain arising abroad will be liable to UK capital gains tax as follows.

(i) $40,000 under (*c*) above, treated as remitted on the repayment of the dollar loan.

(ii) $10,000 treated as remitted at the date of importation, representing money lent abroad.

Thus, for example, in (i) above the chargeable gain arising is

$$\pounds 60,000 \times \frac{40,000}{140,000} = \pounds 17,143$$

The balance of the disposal proceeds $(140,000 – 50,000) will remain exempt unless and until it is remitted (or deemed remitted) to the UK.

(*Note.* Foreign currency and bank balances denominated therein are themselves chargeable assets in certain cases. See 6.2 ASSETS and 22.5, 22.8 EXEMPTIONS AND RELIEFS.)

52 Residence and Domicile

Cross-references. See 18.7 DEATH for residence etc. status of personal representatives; 19 DOUBLE TAX RELIEF for double tax agreements which may override or amend statutory provisions or HMRC practice for the purposes of such agreements; 44 OFFSHORE SETTLEMENTS; 45 OVERSEAS MATTERS; 46.4 PARTNERSHIPS for overseas resident partners and partnerships; and 57.4 SETTLEMENTS for residence etc. status of trustees.

Simon's Direct Tax Service. See C1.201, Division C1.6.

52.1 The legislation contains few specific directions as to the ascertainment of a person's 'residence' and 'ordinary residence' status in a particular year of assessment for general tax purposes and this is especially so of capital gains tax. Consequently, it is a body of case law that has brought about the view that these terms are to be interpreted according to their normal meanings and that each case must rest on its own facts and particular circumstances. HMRC have taken case decisions, *inter alia*, in formulating their own practice as to the determination of residence and ordinary residence (see 52.3–52.5 below for individuals and 52.6 for companies). The term 'domicile' is governed by the general legal meaning rather than any specific definitions for tax purposes but again, each case rests on its own facts. See 52.7 below. For appeals relating to residence and domicile generally, see 52.8 below.

The extent of the UK for tax purposes is given in 52.9 below and special rules relating to residence status in connection with the double taxation agreement between the UK and Ireland are in 52.10 below.

52.2 **HMRC administrative procedures.** Individuals who come to the UK to take up employment are asked to complete Form P86 to enable their residence status to be considered. This form also now includes a section on domicile so that, in straightforward cases (where, e.g., a person never domiciled in the UK comes here only to work and with the intention of leaving the UK when the employment ceases) the two matters may be dealt with together. In less straightforward cases, Form DOM1 was introduced to obtain the information necessary to the determination of domicile. On leaving the UK, a shortened form P85 (Form P85(S)) was introduced to enable any repayment to be claimed in straightforward cases. Otherwise, Form P85 continues to be used.

Under self-assessment from 1996/97 onwards, Forms P85, P85(S), P86 and DOM 1 continue in operation, but individuals who regard themselves as not resident, not ordinarily resident or not domiciled in the UK are required to self-certify their status in the self-assessment tax return and to complete the 'NON-RESIDENCE ETC.' supplementary pages to the return. HMRC no longer provide residence 'rulings' but will give specific advice in limited circumstances. HMRC queries on residence status and domicile aspects may be made as part of an enquiry into the self-assessment return or into an initial claim made outside the return (see 54.8 RETURNS, 12.3 CLAIMS). See Revenue Tax Bulletin June 1997 pp 425–427.

From 1 April 2001, a new HMRC office, the Centre for Non-Residents, provides, *inter alia*, advice on the residence and domicile status of individuals (Revenue Tax Bulletin October 2000 p 788).

52.3 **RESIDENCE**

An individual can be resident for a particular year of assessment in one or more countries for tax purposes so that a claim not to be UK resident merely because of resident status in another country will usually fail. Unusually, an individual may be regarded as not resident in any country.

Subject to the foregoing an individual is resident in the UK for a year of assessment if any one of the following applies.

(*a*) He is in the UK for some temporary purpose only and not with any view or intent to establish his residence in the UK and if, and only if, the period (or the sum of the periods) for which he is resident (i.e. physically present) in the UK in the year of assessment exceeds six months. [*TCGA 1992, s 9(3); FA 1998, s 127(2)*]. After 1992/93, the question whether for the purposes of this provision an individual is in the UK for some temporary purpose only and not with any view or intent to establish his residence in the UK is decided without regard to any living accommodation available in the UK for his use. [*TCGA 1992, s 9(4); FA 1993, s 208(2)(4)*].

The six months' rule is rigidly applied, even in cases of force majeure, and in border-line cases hours may be significant. See *Wilkie v CIR Ch D 1951, 32 TC 495* where 'six months' was held to mean six calendar months. Otherwise, to be regarded by HMRC as UK resident for a year of assessment an individual would normally have to be physically present in the UK at some time in the tax year and would also depend on the circumstances. See, for example, *Shepherd v HMRC Ch D, 2006 STI 1518*, in which an airline pilot who was in the UK for only 80 days in a tax year was nevertheless held to be resident in the UK for that year. HMRC treat, *with no exceptions* (including years after 1992/93), an individual as resident if he is in the UK for six months or more during the year. Six months are regarded as 183 days and days of arrival and departure are normally ignored (HMRC Pamphlet IR 20, December 1999 edition, para 1.2).

(*b*) He *visits the UK year after year* (so that his visits become in effect 'part of his habit of life') and the annual visits are for a substantial period or periods of time. HMRC would normally regard an average annual period or periods which amount to 91 days or more as substantial. Where, after four years, the individual's visits average 91 days or more per year, he is treated as resident from the beginning of the fifth year. However, he will be treated as resident from the beginning of the first year if it is clear at the time of his first visit that he intends to make such visits. Also, if the individual decides that he will make such visits before the beginning of the fifth year, he will be treated as resident from the beginning of the year in which that decision is made (HMRC Pamphlet IR 20, para 3.3). For an example of the averaging calculation, see HMRC Pamphlet IR 20, para 2.10.

Where HMRC apply the above averaging treatment it will exclude any days spent in the UK because of exceptional circumstances beyond the individual's control (e.g. illness of the individual or a member of his immediate family) although each case will be examined on its facts and the exclusion will not apply for the purposes of the six months' rule in (*a*) above (HMRC Statement of Practice 2/91 and HMRC Pamphlet IR 20, para 3.3).

For further discussion on the position of visitors to the UK see Revenue Tax Bulletin, May 1994, p 130.

(*c*) For years prior to 1993/94, he has *accommodation* (e.g. a house or flat) available for his use in the UK and makes one visit to the UK, however short, in the tax year.

After 1992/93, the enactment of *TCGA 1992, s 9(4)* in (*a*) above (no regard to be had for the purposes of *TCGA 1992, s 9(3)* to any living accommodation available in the UK for an individual's use) means that this Inland Revenue practice (which is based on case law prior to 1993/94) ceases. However, HMRC have said that there will be no change in the practice of treating as resident and ordinarily resident an individual who comes to and remains in the UK where he owns or acquires on a lease of three years or more accommodation in the UK. Similarly, where an individual leaves the

UK, the retention of a home here will continue to be a factor in considering whether he has left the UK permanently (HMRC Pamphlet IR 20, paras 2.8, 3.11 and Revenue Press Release 16 March 1993).

Subject to the above, if an individual works full-time in a trade, profession or vocation which does not have a branch or place of business in the UK, or in an office or employment the whole of the duties under which (apart from mere 'incidental' duties) are performed outside the UK, or in a combination of such activities, any accommodation maintained in the UK for his use is disregarded in determining whether or not he is resident in the UK (although the legislation is unclear whether this provision applies equally to capital gains tax as well as income tax). [*TCGA 1992, s 9(1); ICTA 1988, s 335*]. As to whether duties are 'incidental', see *Robson v Dixon Ch D 1972, 48 TC 527* where an airline pilot was employed abroad but occasionally landed in the UK where the family home was maintained. Held, the UK duties were more than incidental. See also HMRC Pamphlet IR 20, paras 5.7 and 5.8. In deciding whether an individual works full-time in the activities mentioned, HMRC will consider the particular facts of the case, such as whether there is a standard or irregular number of hours to be worked, a formal job structure, concurrent part-time appointments or a mix of employments and self-employments (Revenue Tax Bulletin February 1993 p 57).

Where available accommodation in the UK is to be taken into account for the determination of an individual's residence or ordinary residence status, it does not depend on ownership, but on whether any accommodation is in fact available for use. Accommodation may be treated as not available for an individual's use if it is:

(i) let on a lease which denies his right to stay in the property;

(ii) left unfurnished so that it is not possible to live in it;

(iii) only available for the individual's use when he is not in the UK;

(iv) too far away from the place visited to be reasonably used when the individual makes one brief business visit to the UK during the tax year;

(v) owned purely for investment purposes and is neither used nor usable by the individual when he is in the UK;

(vi) rented furnished for the individual's use for a period of less than two years;

(vii) rented unfurnished for the individual's use for a period of less than one year.

A house owned or rented by one spouse would (subject to the above) normally be considered available for the use of the other.

(*d*) He is a *Commonwealth* or *Republic of Ireland* citizen, having been ordinarily resident (see 52.4 below) in the UK, who has left the UK for the purpose only of 'occasional residence' abroad (although the legislation is unclear whether the provisions apply equally to capital gains tax as well as income tax). [*TCGA 1992, s 9(1); ICTA 1988, s 334*].

For a discussion of the meaning of 'occasional residence', see *Reed v Clark Ch D 1985, 58 TC 528.*

Change in residence status. In general, residence status in the UK for part of a year is taken to apply for a whole year (see *Neubergh v CIR Ch D 1977, 52 TC 79* and *Gubay v Kington HL 1984, 57 TC 601*) and, for capital gains tax in particular, disposals are chargeable where they accrue to a person in a year of assessment *during any part of which* he is resident in the UK. [*TCGA 1992, s 2(1)*]. Concessional split year treatment for a year in which an individual's residence status changes is, however, available in the following circumstances.

- Where an individual comes to live in the UK and is treated as resident in the UK for any year of assessment from the date of arrival, he or she is charged to capital gains tax only in respect of chargeable gains from disposals made after arrival, provided that,
  - where the individual arrives on or after 6 April 1998, he or she has not been resident or ordinarily resident in the UK at any time during the five years of assessment immediately preceding the year of assessment in which he or she arrived in the UK; or
  - where the individual arrived before 6 April 1998, he or she had not been regarded at any time within the period of 36 months immediately preceding the date of arrival as resident or ordinarily resident in the UK.
- Where an individual leaves the UK and is treated on departure as not resident and not ordinarily resident in the UK, he or she is not charged to capital gains tax on gains from disposals made after the date of departure, provided that, where the date of departure is after 16 March 1998, the individual was not resident and not ordinarily resident in the UK for the whole of at least four out of the seven years of assessment immediately preceding the tax year of departure.

(HMRC Extra-Statutory Concession D2).

The more stringent conditions which apply for arrivals on or after 6 April 1998 and departures after 16 March 1998 result from the introduction of the charge on individuals who become temporarily non-resident in the UK — see 45.4 OVERSEAS MATTERS. In its original form, the concession applied also to companies but ceased to so apply as regards disposals after 5 April 1998 (HMRC Capital Gains Manual CG 42370).

The circumstances in which an individual will be treated by HMRC on departure as not resident and not ordinarily resident in the UK or on arrival as resident and ordinarily resident are those set out in HMRC Extra-Statutory Concession A11 (see HMRC Pamphlet IR 20, paras 1.5–1.7, and Tolley's Income Tax).

ESC D2 does not apply to

- any person in relation to gains accruing to him on the disposal of assets in the UK which, at any time between his departure and the end of the year, are used for a trade, profession or vocation carried on by him in the UK through a branch or agency, or are used for or acquired for use by or for such a branch or agency (see also 45.3 OVERSEAS MATTERS);
- trustees who commence or cease residence in the UK (see 44.2, 44.4 OFFSHORE SETTLEMENTS);
- a settlor who commences or ceases UK residence during a year in relation to gains of a settlement which are assessed on him as in 57.5 SETTLEMENTS; or
- a settlor on whom gains are taxed under *TCGA 1992, s 86, Sch 5* (see 44.5 OFFSHORE SETTLEMENTS).

As with all published extra-statutory concessions, ESC D2 will not be applied in cases where it would have been part of a tax avoidance arrangement (see 31 HMRC EXTRA-STATUTORY CONCESSIONS and *R v CIR (ex p. Fulford-Dobson) QB 1987, 60 TC 168*). In straightforward cases where the terms of a disposal are negotiated before emigration but the contract is not signed until after the date of departure from the UK, HMRC will not withhold the concession merely on the grounds that the disposal was arranged to take place after departure. On its own, a genuine postponement of the disposal is not regarded as an attempt to use the concession for tax avoidance, but where coupled with other arrangements it might be so regarded. (HMRC Capital Gains Manual CG 25982).

Where this split year basis is applied, the day of departure from, or arrival in, the UK is treated as falling into the period of UK residence or ordinary residence (HMRC Pamphlet IR 20, para 1.6).

For visits to the UK for educational purposes, see 52.4 below. For visits abroad generally, see 52.5 below.

Temporary employment in the UK. An individual coming to the UK to work for a period of *at least two years* is treated as resident for the whole period from the day of arrival to the day of departure. Otherwise the normal rules are applied e.g. the six months' or, before 1993/94, the accommodation available rule. (HMRC Pamphlet IR 20, para 3.7).

Examples

(*Note*. After 1992/93, the case law decisions below, which all predate 1993/94, should be read in the light of the enactment of *TCGA 1992, s 9(4)* mentioned in (*a*) and (*c*) above (no regard to be had for the purposes of *TCGA 1992, s 9(3)* to any living accommodation available in the UK for an individual's use).)

A resident of the Republic of Ireland making monthly visits here as director of a British company, having no place of abode here, but a permanent one in Ireland, was held to be resident and ordinarily resident (*Lysaght v CIR HL 1928, 13 TC 511*). However, compare *CIR v Combe CS 1932, 17 TC 405*. An officer succeeding to an Irish estate, intending to return there permanently but prevented by military duties in the UK, was held, on the facts, to be resident in both countries (*Inchiquin v CIR CA 1948, 31 TC 125*).

In *CIR v Brown KB 1926, 11 TC 292*, and *CIR v Zorab KB 1926, 11 TC 289*, it was held that retired Indian civil servants making periodical visits to, but having no business interests in, the UK, were not resident.

An American holding a lease of a shooting box in Scotland and spending two months there every year (*Cooper v Cadwalader CES 1904, 5 TC 101*), and a merchant physically present and carrying on business in Italy, but owning a house in the UK where he resided for less than six months (*Lloyd v Sulley CES 1884, 2 TC 37*) have both been held to be resident.

A Belgian who had at his disposal for the visits he paid here a house owned not by him but by a company which he controlled, so that it was in fact available whenever he chose to come, was held to be taxable as a resident (*Loewenstein v De Salis KB 1926, 10 TC 424*). But in *Withers v Wynyard KB 1938, 21 TC 724*, an actress (after 18 months abroad) performing in the UK and occupying for 3½ months in 1933/34 a leasehold flat (unable to be disposed of and sub-let when possible), was held not to be UK resident for that year.

A husband and wife who were not actually physically present during the year, although their children were in the UK, were held not to be UK resident (*Turnbull v Foster CES 1904, 6 TC 206*). In *Reed v Clark Ch D 1985, 58 TC 528* the taxpayer had left the UK with the intention to remain abroad throughout a year of assessment and, in the event, did so remain abroad. He was held not to be resident in the UK for the year of absence since his purpose was not only of 'occasional residence' abroad (see (*d*) above).

The taxpayer's presence in the UK need not be voluntary, see *In re Mackenzie decd Ch D 1940, 19 ATC 399* (taxpayer confined in a lunatic asylum).

52.4 ORDINARY RESIDENCE

The term 'ordinary residence' is not defined in the *Taxes Acts*. Broadly, it denotes greater permanence than the term 'residence' (see 52.3 above), and is equivalent to habitual residence; if an individual is resident year after year, he is ordinarily resident. An individual, whose home has been abroad, coming to the UK to live here permanently or intending to stay here for three years or more is treated as resident and ordinarily resident here from the date of his arrival (HMRC Pamphlet IR 20, para 3.1). An individual may be resident in the UK under the six months' rule of *TCGA 1992, s 9(3)* (see 52.3(*a*) above) without becoming ordinarily resident. Equally, he may be ordinarily resident without being resident in a particular year, e.g. because he usually lives in the UK but is absent on an extended holiday throughout a tax year. (HMRC Pamphlet IR 20, para 1.3).

Accommodation. The availability of accommodation (see 52.3(*c*) above) in the UK for the use of an individual has an important bearing on the determination of ordinary residence status. An individual who has accommodation available and who visits the UK regularly for only limited periods in one or more tax years is regarded as ordinarily resident for each of those years. If such accommodation is not available, he will only be so regarded after such visits have averaged 91 days or more per tax year for four consecutive years (although if he intends such visits from the start of the period, ordinary residence may commence earlier on the same basis as in 52.3(*b*) above). (HMRC Statement of Practice 3/81 and HMRC Pamphlet IR 20, paras 3.4, 3.5, 3.11).

If an individual regarded as ordinarily resident solely because of the availability of accommodation disposes of it and leaves the UK within three years of arrival, he is normally treated as not ordinarily resident for the duration of his stay (assuming this is to his advantage). (HMRC Statement of Practice 3/81 and HMRC Pamphlet IR 20, para 3.12).

Longer term visitors—commencement of ordinary residence. HMRC practice is to treat an individual coming to the UK but not intending to stay more than three years (and not buying or leasing for three years or more accommodation for use in the UK), as ordinarily resident from the beginning of the tax year following the third anniversary of arrival. If, before the beginning of that tax year, either there is a change in the individual's intention (i.e. to an intention to stay in the UK for three years or more in all) or accommodation for use in the UK is bought (or leased for three years or more), ordinary residence is treated as commencing at the beginning of the tax year in which either of those events happens (or from the date of arrival in the UK if later). (HMRC Statement of Practice 17/91 and HMRC Pamphlet IR 20, paras 3.1 and 3.8–3.11).

Education. An individual who comes to the UK for a period of study or education which is not expected to exceed four years will be treated as not ordinarily resident provided that

(i) he does not own or buy accommodation here, or acquire it on a lease of three years or more; or

(ii) on leaving the UK he will not be returning regularly for visits which average 91 days or more in each tax year.

(HMRC Pamphlet IR 20, para 3.13).

Spouse accompanying employee working overseas. See 52.5(*b*) below.

Averaging of visits to UK over a period. Where this applies in the foregoing, see 52.3(*b*) above for HMRC's practice in applying averaging treatment.

Examples

(*Note.* After 1992/93, the case law decisions below, all of which predate 1993/94, should be read in the light of the enactment of *TCGA 1992, s 9(4)* mentioned in 52.3(*a*) and (*c*) above (no regard to be had for the purposes of *TCGA 1992, s 9(3)* to any living accommodation available in the UK for an individual's use).)

In *Reid v CIR CS 1926, 10 TC 673*, a British subject was held ordinarily resident in the UK although she had no fixed residence either here or abroad and was regularly absent abroad for 8½ months every year. She had here an address, family ties, bank account and furniture in store. *Levene v CIR HL 1928, 13 TC 486*, was decided similarly (British subject abroad for health reasons since 1918, no fixed residence here since (or abroad until 1925), but having ties with this country and in the usual ordering of his life making habitual visits to the UK for 20 weeks yearly for definite purposes). The judgements in this case interpreted the meaning of 'ordinarily resident' by the following phrases: 'habitually resident', 'residence in a place with some degree of continuity' and 'according to the way a man's life is usually ordered'. In *Peel v CIR CS 1927, 13 TC 443*, although the taxpayer had his business and house in Egypt, he was held ordinarily resident in the UK because he also had a house here, and spent an average of 139 days of each year in the UK.

In *Kinloch v CIR KB 1929, 14 TC 736*, a widow living mainly abroad with a son at school in the UK, who had won an appeal in previous years but continued regular annual visits, was held to be resident and ordinarily resident. In *Elmhirst v CIR KB 1937, 21 TC 381* the taxpayer was held to have been ordinarily resident although denying any intention at the time of becoming so. See *Miesegaes v CIR CA 1957, 37 TC 493* (minor at school here for five years, spending the occasional vacation with his father in Switzerland, held ordinarily resident).

In *R v Barnet London Borough Council, ex p. Nilish Shah HL 1982, [1983] 1 All E R 226*, a non-tax case, the words 'ordinarily resident' were held to refer to a man's abode in a particular place or country which he has adopted voluntarily and for settled purposes (i.e. with a sufficient degree of continuity) as part of the regular order of his life for the time being, whether of short or long duration. In *Reed v Clark Ch D 1985, 58 TC 528*, ordinary residence was held to be the converse of 'occasional residence' (see 52.3(*d*) above).

See also the cases under 52.3 above.

52.5 VISITS ABROAD AND CLAIMS TO NON-UK RESIDENCE AND TO NON-UK ORDINARY RESIDENCE

Visits abroad are broadly differentiated by HMRC as follows.

(*a*) **Visits abroad for short periods.** An individual who has been ordinarily resident in the UK is regarded as remaining resident and ordinarily resident in the UK if he only makes short visits abroad, i.e. for less than a complete tax year. (HMRC Pamphlet IR 20, para 2.1). See also 52.3(*d*) above.

HMRC will not usually accept that *mobile workers,* i.e. those who live in the UK but make frequent and regular trips abroad in the course of their employment or business (e.g. lorry or coach drivers driving to and from the Continent and those working on cross-Channel transport), are anything other than resident and ordinarily resident in the UK (Revenue Tax Bulletin April 2001 pp 836–838).

(*b*) **Going abroad for full-time service under a contract of employment.** In such circumstances, where specified conditions are satisfied, the employee is normally regarded as not resident and not ordinarily resident in the UK from the day following the date of his departure until the day preceding the day of return. On his return (if at all), the individual is treated as a new permanent resident. On both occasions (going abroad and eventual return) the year of assessment will be 'split' because of the change in ordinary residence as in 52.3 above (HMRC Extra-Statutory Concession A11; see also HMRC Pamphlet IR 20, paras 2.2, 2.3).

Although the residence status of each spouse is determined independently, the following concessional treatment applies where an individual going abroad for full-time employment meets the specified conditions and is accompanied, or later joined, by his or her spouse who is not in full-time employment. Where the accompanying spouse is abroad for a complete tax year and interim visits to the UK do not amount to 183 days or more in any tax year, or an average of 91 days or more in a tax year over the period of absence (up to a maximum of four years), then the accompanying spouse's liability to UK tax which is affected by residence, for the years of departure and return at the beginning and end of the period spent abroad, is determined by reference to the period of his or her residence in the UK during the year. However, for this treatment to apply for years before 1993/94 in circumstances where accommodation in the UK was available for use by the accompanying spouse, the latter had to ensure that there were no visits to the UK between the date of departure and the following 5 April or, for the year of return, between 6 April and the date of return. In addition, for years before 1993/94, an accompanying spouse who had available accommodation in the UK was regarded as not ordinarily resident in the UK from the day after leaving the UK to the day before the date of return, provided that the absence was for three years or more and visits to the UK averaged less than 91 days in a tax year over the period of absence. If the absence abroad was expected to be for three years or more but was cut short because the period of the spouse's employment was terminated unexpectedly, the shorter absence 'might' (HMRC do not specify further conditions so presumably 'would normally' is intended) qualify for this treatment provided that it included a complete tax year and any visits to the UK averaged less than 91 days in a tax year over the period of absence (HMRC Extra-Statutory Concession A78; see also HMRC Pamphlet IR 20, para 2.6). For HMRC's practice in applying averaging treatment, see 52.3(*b*) above.

(*c*) **Permanent emigration for reasons other than a full-time service contract abroad.** Despite *actual* permanent residence abroad, the taxpayer may still fall into one of the *tax* residence traps in 52.3(*a*)–(*c*) above. If, e.g. on retirement abroad, he claims that he has ceased residence and ordinary residence, and requires an immediate provisional HMRC ruling to that effect, he must show, in general terms, that he has completely cut his ties with the UK (e.g. that he has taken steps to acquire accommodation abroad to live in as a permanent home, and if he continues to own property in the UK, the reason is consistent with his stated aim of permanent residence abroad; see the comments made about available accommodation in the UK at 52.3(*c*) above). If he can do this, the claim is usually provisionally admitted with effect from the day after departure and the ruling is confirmed after absence for a period including a complete fiscal year during which any visits to this country have been for an annual average of less than 91 days (for HMRC's practice in applying this averaging treatment, see 52.3(*b*) above). If the individual cannot produce sufficient evidence to HMRC to obtain a ruling at the start of his absence, HMRC adopt a 'wait and see' approach for a period of three years, during which the individual's tax liabilities are computed provisionally on the basis that the individual is UK resident. That liability is adjusted, if necessary, when a final HMRC decision is made at the end of the three-year period. Again a tax year may be split as in 52.3 above if a claim for a change of status is sustained (HMRC Pamphlet IR 20, paras 2.7–2.9). See *Shepherd v HMRC (Sp C 484). [2005] SSCD 644*, in which an airline pilot was held to have remained resident in the UK for a tax year in which he had been physically in the UK for only 80 days.

52.6 COMPANIES

Subject to transitional provisions in *FA 1988, Sch 7* (under which certain companies could remain non-UK resident up to 14 March 1993), after 14 March 1988, a company incorporated in the UK is regarded for the purposes of the *Taxes Acts* as resident there, irrespective of any rule of law giving a different place of residence. [*FA 1988, s 66*(*1*)]. See the 2004/05 and earlier editions for details of the transitional provisions.

After 29 November 1993, a company which would otherwise be regarded as resident in the UK for the purposes of the *Taxes Acts*, and is regarded for the purposes of any double tax relief arrangements within *ICTA 1988, s 788* as resident in a territory outside the UK and not resident in the UK (on the assumption that a claim for relief under those arrangements has been made and under the claim it falls to be decided whether the company is to be so regarded for the purposes of those arrangements), is treated for the purposes of the *Taxes Acts* as resident outside the UK and not resident in the UK. This treatment applies whether the company would otherwise be regarded as resident in the UK for the purposes of the *Taxes Acts* under the 'incorporation test' above, the test for SEs below or by virtue of some other rule of law (see below). [*FA 1994, s 249; F(No 2)A 2005, s 60*(*2*)].

For companies incorporated outside the UK there is no statutory definition of residence. The courts have determined that such a company resides where its real business is carried on, i.e. '*where its central management and control actually abide*'. This was the criterion applied to all companies prior to the introduction of the above provisions.

A company doing business abroad but controlled from the UK is therefore resident in the UK (subject to any overriding provisions contained in relevant double taxation agreements). In the following cases, the company was held to be managed and controlled from, and hence resident in, the UK:

- *Calcutta Jute Mills Co Ltd v Nicholson Ex D 1876, 1 TC 83* (UK company operating abroad but directors and shareholders meeting in UK);
- *De Beers Consolidated Mines Ltd v Howe HL 1906, 5 TC 198* (South African company operating there but important affairs controlled from UK where majority of directors resided);
- *New Zealand Shipping Co Ltd v Thew HL 1922, 8 TC 208* (New Zealand company with New Zealand directors, but overall control lay with separate London board);
- *American Thread Co v Joyce HL 1913, 6 TC 163* (UK company operating in USA with US directors in charge of current business, but overall control in London);
- *John Hood & Co Ltd v Magee KB (I) 1918, 7 TC 327* (company registered in both UK and USA, with the only director resident in USA, but general meetings and material trading activities in UK);

But in *A-G v Alexander Ex D, [1874] 10 Ex 20,* a foreign state bank with a UK branch was held resident abroad, notwithstanding that shareholders' meetings were held in London. See also *Wood and another v Holden CA, [2006] STC 443* (company registered in Netherlands with Netherlands director, held non-resident).

HMRC's approach to applying the basic test of the place of central management and control is first to ascertain whether the directors in fact themselves exercise central management and control; if so, to determine where that central management and control is exercised (not necessarily where they meet); if not, to establish where and by whom it is exercised. The concept of the place of central management and control is directed at the highest level of control of the company's business, rather than the place where the main business operations are to be found. This must always be a question of fact in any particular case, but the place of directors' meetings will usually be of significance if they are the medium through which central management and control is exercised. If, however, central management and control is in reality exercised by, for example, a single individual, the company's residence will be where that individual exercises his powers. With regard to the particular problem of residence of a subsidiary, HMRC would not normally seek to impute to the subsidiary the residence of its parent unless the parent in effect usurps the functions of the Board of the subsidiary. Matters taken into account would include the extent to which the directors of the subsidiary take decisions on their own authority as to investment, production, marketing and procurement without reference to the parent (and see below).

In all cases, HMRC will seek to determine whether a major objective of the existence of any particular factors bearing on residence is the obtaining of tax benefits from residence or non-residence, and to establish the reality of the central management and control (HMRC Statement of Practice 1/90).

Incorporation in the UK and compliance with the requirements of the *Companies Act 1985* did not in themselves render a company resident there before 15 March 1988. See *Todd v Egyptian Delta Land and Investment Co Ltd HL 1928, 14 TC 119* and cf. *Eccott v Aramayo Francke Mines Ltd HL 1925, 9 TC 445*. A company may be resident in more than one country. See *Swedish Central Railway Co Ltd v Thompson HL 1925, 9 TC 342,* and for an authoritative discussion of dual residence, *Union Corporation Ltd v CIR HL 1953, 34 TC 207*.

A company may have a domicile (see *Gasque v CIR KB 1940, 23 TC 210*), but it would seem from the *Union Corporation* case above that, for a company, ordinary residence and residence are synonymous. In the light of *ICTA 1988, s 11* and *TCGA 1992, ss 10* and *10B* it would seem, anyway, that ordinary residence is not relevant to the chargeable gains of companies.

European Companies (SEs). An SE (a European Company — see 13.18 COMPANIES) which transfers its registered office to the UK on or after 1 April 2005 in accordance with *Council Regulation (EC) 2157/2001, Art 8* is regarded upon registration in the UK as resident in the UK for tax purposes. If a different place of residence is given by any rule of law, that place is not taken into account for tax purposes. Where this rule applies, the SE is not treated as ceasing to be UK-resident by reason only of the subsequent transfer from the UK of its registered office. [*FA 1988, s 66A; F(No 2)A 2005, s 60(1)(3)*]. This provision is subject to *FA 1994, s 249* above.

52.7 DOMICILE

An individual may have only one domicile at any given time, denoting the country or state considered his natural home. Domicile does not necessarily correspond with either residence or nationality and is essentially a question of fact (*Earl of Iveagh v Revenue Commissioners SC (RI), [1930] IR 431*). A *domicile of origin* is acquired at birth (normally that of the taxpayer's father, see below), but may be replaced by a *domicile of choice* (to be proved by subsequent conduct). A domicile of choice may be replaced by another domicile of choice (if the necessary proof is forthcoming), but if a domicile of choice is lost without another being acquired, the domicile of origin immediately revives (*Fielden v CIR Ch D 1965, 42 TC 501*).

It is normally more difficult to show the displacement of a domicile of origin than that of a domicile of choice. See *CIR v Bullock CA 1976, 51 TC 522* where a taxpayer with a domicile of origin in Canada lived in England and intended to remain here during his wife's lifetime. He was held not to have acquired an English domicile of choice (the judgements in this case give a useful review of the law relating to domicile). In *Buswell v CIR CA 1974, 49 TC 334*, the taxpayer had a domicile of origin in South Africa. He came to England to school in 1928, and was called up into the British Army during the Second World War, serving in India. On his return, he signed a written declaration that he intended to remain permanently in the UK. In 1955, he took out a South African passport. In 1961, he married an English lady and their children were brought up in the UK, though registered as South African nationals. In 1968, he and his wife visited South Africa for the first time for 40 years and, with the intention of eventually settling there permanently, bought property there in which they spent three months in each year. He was held never to have abandoned his domicile of origin. In *Re Clore (decd.) (No 2), Official Solicitor v Clore and Others Ch D, [1984] STC 609*, it was held that an English domicile of origin was never lost as, on the evidence, the taxpayer never formed a settled intention to reside permanently elsewhere. Contrast *Qureshi v Qureshi Fam D, [1972] Fam D 173*, and *In re Lawton Ch D 1958, 37 ATC 216*. Actual settlement abroad is necessary as well as intention; see *Plummer v CIR Ch D 1987, 60 TC 452*.

In *Steiner v CIR CA 1973, 49 TC 13*, a Jew who had acquired a German domicile of choice, but who fled to England in 1939 and obtained British naturalisation was held to have acquired an English domicile of choice. In *F and Another (Personal Representatives of F deceased) v CIR 1999 (Sp C 219), [2000] SSCD 1*, an Iranian who had obtained British naturalisation following the 1979 Islamic Revolution was held on the facts to have had a settled intention to return to Iran permanently and thus not to have abandoned his domicile of origin. See also *Moore's Executors v CIR (Sp C 335), [2002] SSCD 463*, *Surveyor v CIR (Sp C 339), [2002] SSCD 501* and *Johnson's Executors v HMRC (Sp C 481), [2005] SSCD 614*.

In determining domicile for capital gains tax on or after 6 April 1996, relevant action taken by a person in connection with electoral rights is disregarded unless otherwise requested by the person whose liability is in question. Relevant action refers to prospective or actual registration as an overseas elector or use of such vote. [*FA 1996, s 200*].

Married women. Up to 31 December 1973, a woman automatically acquired the domicile of her husband on marriage. From 1 January 1974 onwards, the domicile of a married woman is ascertained in the same way as any other individual capable of having an independent domicile, except that a woman already married on that date will retain her husband's domicile until it is changed by acquisition or revival of another domicile. [*Domicile and Matrimonial Proceedings Act 1973, ss 1, 17*(*5*)]. See *CIR v Duchess of Portland Ch D 1981, 54 TC 648*. But a woman who is a national of the USA and who married a man with UK domicile before 1974 will be treated (after 5 April 1976) in determining her domicile, as if the marriage had taken place in 1974. See Article 4(4) of the US/UK Double Tax Agreement and any similar provisions in double tax agreements with other countries. A widow retains her late husband's domicile unless she later acquires a domicile of choice (or reverts to a domicile of origin) (*In re Wallach PDA 1949, [1950] 1 All E R 199*).

Minors. The domicile of a minor follows that of a person on whom he is legally dependent (usually his father). Under *Domicile and Matrimonial Proceedings Act 1973, s 3* (which does not extend to Scotland), a person first becomes capable of having an independent domicile when he attains 16 (in Scotland, 14 for boys and 12 for girls) or marries under that age. Under *section 4* thereof, where a child's father and mother are living apart, his domicile is that of his mother if he has his home with her and has no home with his father.

52.8 APPEALS

Ordinary residence and domicile in relation to capital gains tax are determined by the Commissioners for HMRC (or, before 18 April 2005, by the Board of Inland Revenue). Any appeal from a decision of the Commissioners or Board is to the Special Commissioners and the normal time limit of thirty days from the receipt of written notice of the decision is extended to three months if the appeal concerns ordinary residence or domicile. [*TCGA 1992, s 9*(*2*)*; ICTA 1988, s 207; ITEPA 2003, ss 42, 43, Sch 6 paras 33, 208; CRCA 2005, s 5*]. Other disputes regarding residence are settled by appeal against the relevant assessment in the ordinary way. See generally, 4 APPEALS.

52.9 UNITED KINGDOM

The United Kingdom for tax purposes comprises England, Scotland, Wales and Northern Ireland. The Channel Islands (Jersey, Guernsey, Alderney, Sark, Herm and Jethou) and the Isle of Man are excluded. Great Britain comprises England, Scotland and Wales only.

See 45.14 OVERSEAS MATTERS for the territorial extension of the UK in certain circumstances.

52.10 IRELAND

For double taxation relief purposes a person cannot be resident in both the UK and Ireland. The residence of an *individual* is first determined under normal tax rules relating to abode, domicile etc. If this results in him being technically resident in both States the question is decided by reference successively to permanent home, personal and economic ties, habitual abode, and nationality, and if necessary is decided by agreement between the States. A *company or body of persons* is deemed to be resident where its place of effective management is situated. [*SI 1976 Nos 2151, 2152*]. See also 19.3 DOUBLE TAXATION RELIEF.

53 Retirement Relief

Cross-references. See 24.2 FURNISHED HOLIDAY ACCOMMODATION for application of retirement relief to such accommodation in the UK; 33 HOLD-OVER RELIEFS for interaction of retirement relief and those reliefs.

Simon's Direct Tax Service. See Division C3.6.

53.1 ABOLITION OF RETIREMENT RELIEF

Retirement relief is **abolished for disposals in 2003/04 and subsequent years**. *TCGA 1992, ss 163, 164, Sch 6* are repealed accordingly. Prior to abolition, the maximum relief available was reduced annually in equal stages for disposals in the years 1999/2000 to 2002/03 inclusive (see 53.9 below for the figures). [*FA 1998, s 140*(*2*), *Sch 27 Pt III*(*31*)]. See Revenue Tax Bulletin April 1999 pp 653, 654 for examples of situations in which disposals do not qualify for retirement relief, because the requisite associated event occurs after 5 April 2003.

53.2 RELIEF FOR DISPOSALS BEFORE 6 APRIL 2003

Relief is given for material disposals of business assets by individuals on retirement from their own, partnership or incorporated business provided the necessary conditions are met (see 53.4 below). In addition, relief may also be given for disposals, associated with retirement, of

(*a*) assets used in an office or employment (see 53.5 below);

(*b*) assets owned by a partner, or by an officer or employee of a company, and used in the business of the partnership or, as the case may be, the company (see 53.6 below); and

(*c*) settled property consisting of shares or assets used for business purposes if a beneficiary has an interest in possession in the settled property (see 53.7 below).

Except in the case of a disposal made by an individual who has attained the age of 50, relief is subject to a claim being made (under *TCGA 1992, Sch 6 para 5*(*2*)) on or before the first anniversary of 31 January following the tax year in which the disposal occurred. In the case of a trustees' disposal, the claim (under *TCGA 1992, Sch 6 para 5*(*3*)) must be made jointly by the trustees and the beneficiary concerned. Where a claim is dependent upon an individual having retired on ill-health grounds below the age of 50, the claim must be made to the Board. [*TCGA 1992, Sch 6 para 5*(*2*)–(*4*); *FA 1996, s 176, Sch 21 para 44*(*3*)].

Husband and wife. A husband and wife are each eligible for the relief if they individually meet the qualifying conditions. See also 53.9 below.

Date of disposal. For an unconditional contract this is strictly the date the contract is made but if business activities continue beyond that date pending completion of the contract, the date of completion will be accepted as the date of disposal, but *solely* for the purposes of calculating the relief (HMRC Extra-Statutory Concession D31). This treatment applies even to the extent of allowing relief where the individual's 50th birthday falls in the intervening period. It cannot, however, shift the disposal into a later tax year. (HMRC Capital Gains Manual CG 63290, 63291). Where the concession is claimed, the completion date applies to all aspects of retirement relief including the limit of relief available (see 53.9(*a*) & (*b*) below) in the tax year of completion. For example, where the unconditional contract date is on or before 5 April 2003 and completion is after that date, the concession will not give access to retirement relief, as the relief is abolished after that date (see 53.1 above). (Revenue Tax Bulletin April 1999 p 653).

Valuation where hold-over relief also claimed. Where the gain arising on the disposal of an asset is partly relieved by retirement relief and partly by hold-over relief, HMRC require a valuation of the asset. However, unless the claimants request otherwise, the valuation may be deferred until either:

(*a*) it is necessary to determine the amount of retirement relief due, for example where the transferor makes another disposal which attracts retirement relief; or

(*b*) it is necessary to determine the transferee's cost of the asset.

(HMRC Statement of Practice 8/92). For further details, see 33.1 HOLD-OVER RELIEFS.

53.3 **Definitions.** The following definitions apply for the purposes of 53.4–53.9 below.

'*Business*' is not defined but is effectively limited to trades (which includes for retirement relief purposes commercial letting of FURNISHED HOLIDAY ACCOMMODATION (24) in the UK and the activities of both parties to a share farming agreement, provided the landowner takes an active part in the venture (see Country Landowners Association statement of 19 December 1991 reproduced at 1992 STI 189)), professions, vocations, offices or employments as in 53.8 below. Except as regards holiday lettings as mentioned above, retirement relief does not extend to furnished lettings (*Hatt v Newman Ch D 2000, 72 TC 462*).

'*Commercial association of companies*' means a company together with such associated companies (within *ICTA 1988, s 416*, see Tolley's Corporation Tax under Close Companies) as carry on businesses of such a nature that the businesses of all the companies together may be reasonably considered to make up a single composite undertaking.

'*Full-time working officer or employee*', in relation to one or more companies, is an officer or employee required to devote substantially the whole of his time (the Revenue suggested at least 75% of the company's full normal working hours where there are other full-time employees; see HMRC Capital Gains Manual CG 63621) to the service of the company or companies in question in a managerial or technical capacity. In *Palmer v Maloney and Shipleys CA 1999, 71 TC 502*, a case to which the Revenue were not a party, it was held by the CA, reversing the decision of the lower court, that a person who worked for a company for 42½ hours each week qualified as a 'full-time working officer or employee'. The fact that he also spent 7½ hours each week conducting a business as a sole trader was not material. The Revenue had already stated that, pending the final outcome of this case, they would abide by their above-mentioned published guidance (Revenue Tax Bulletin April 1999 p 653).

'*Group of companies*' means a company which has one or more '51% subsidiaries' within *ICTA 1988, s 838(1)* together with those subsidiaries.

'*Holding company*' means a company whose business (disregarding any trade carried on by it) consists wholly or mainly of the holding of shares or securities of one or more companies which are its 51% subsidiaries (within *ICTA 1988, s 838*).

'*Ill-health grounds*'. A person is treated as having retired on ill-health grounds if he has ceased to be engaged in the work previously undertaken, is incapable of engaging in that kind of work by reason of ill-health and is likely to remain permanently so incapable.

Under the rules of self-assessment HMRC has general powers within *TMA 1970* to enquire into any return, claim or election (see 56 SELF-ASSESSMENT). If an enquiry is made into a taxpayer's claim on the grounds of ill-health, HMRC has specific power to request that such evidence be produced. In practice, they will in all cases require claimants to provide a medical certificate (on form CG85), signed by a qualified medical practitioner. They will themselves take advice from their medical adviser and in some cases a further medical examination will be required (HMRC Helpsheet IR 289). A claim for relief on these grounds must be due to the ill-health of the claimant: the ill-health of one party cannot force the retirement of another (Revenue Tax Bulletin November 1991 p 5). For cases in which relief was refused, see *Mayes v Woods (Sp C 126), [1997] SSCD 206* and *Palmer v Richardson (Sp C 467), [2005] SSCD 418*.

'*Permitted period*' is a period of one year or such longer period as the Board may, in any particular case, by notice allow.

'*Personal company*', in relation to an individual, is a company where not less than 5% of the voting rights are 'exercisable' by the individual. '*Exercisable*' means capable of being exercised, whether in fact exercised (*Hepworth v Smith Ch D 1981, 54 TC 396*).

'*Trading company*' and '*trading group*' mean a company or group whose business consists wholly or mainly of the carrying on of a trade or trades, i.e. including every trade, manufacture, adventure or concern in the nature of trade.

[*TCGA 1992, s 163(9), Sch 6 paras 1, 3, 5; FA 1993, s 87, Sch 7 paras 1, 2, Sch 23 Pt III; FA 1996, Sch 20 para 66(2)*].

53.4 **Disposals by individuals on retirement from their own or partnership business or from personal company.** Relief is given where an individual who has attained the age of 50 or has retired below that age on 'ill-health grounds' makes a 'material disposal of business assets'.

A '*material disposal of business assets*' is one of the following.

(*a*) A disposal of the whole or part of a business (including an interest in the assets of a partnership carrying on a business — see further below) where throughout a period of at least one year ending with the date of disposal (the '*qualifying period*') the business is owned by

(i) the individual making the disposal; or

(ii) a 'trading company' which is either the individual's 'personal company' or a member of a 'trading group' of which the 'holding company' is that individual's personal company. The individual must be a 'full-time working officer or employee' of that company or, if that company is a member of a 'group of companies' or 'commercial association of companies', of one or more companies which are members of the group or association.

Where the business is carried on by a partnership, it is treated as owned by each partner who is, at that time, a member of the partnership.

[*TCGA 1992, s 163(1)–(3)(8), Sch 6 para 4(1)(2); FA 1993, s 87, Sch 7 paras 1, 2, Sch 23 Pt III; FA 1996, s 176*].

Disposal of 'part of a business', which qualifies for relief as above, must be distinguished from the disposal of assets of the business. Where an asset is disposed of prior to cessation of a business, HMRC consider relief to be due only if that disposal 'directly and immediately causes the whole or part of that business to cease' (HMRC Capital Gains Manual CG 63536). In this connection, a number of cases have been heard by the courts, particularly relating to farming. See *McGregor v Adcock Ch D 1977, 51 TC 692* where a farmer sold part of his land for which outline planning permission had been obtained and was refused relief. This decision was followed in *Atkinson v Dancer; Mannion v Johnston Ch D 1988, 61 TC 598*, and see also *Pepper v Daffurn Ch D 1993, 66 TC 68* and *Wase v Bourke Ch D 1995, 68 TC 109*. In *Jarmin v Rawlings Ch D 1994, 67 TC 130*, in which relief was allowed, it was held that the taxpayer had disposed of a dairy farming business, which was 'a separate and distinguishable part' of his business. In *Barrett v Powell Ch D 1998, 70 TC 432*, it was held that a disposal of a tenancy to farm land which the taxpayer then continued to farm under a temporary licence did not qualify for relief; the taxpayer had continued to carry on exactly the same business as before, albeit more precariously; see also *Purves v Harrison Ch D 2000, 73 TC 390*. For a discussion of this topic, see HMRC Capital Gains Manual CG 63530–63543.

As regards partnerships, retirement relief can be available on a reduction of a partner's fractional share of the partnership assets (see 46.5 PARTNERSHIPS) by virtue of his having thereby disposed of part of a business. HMRC also accept that, for retirement relief purposes, where a sole trader takes on a partner, such that the incoming partner is granted a share in the business assets, the sole trader has thereby disposed of part of his business. (HMRC Capital Gains Manual CG 63551, 63553).

(*b*) A disposal of one or more assets used for the purposes of a business at the time when the business ceased to be carried on, where throughout a period of at least one year ending with the date of cessation of business (the '*qualifying period*') either the business was owned by the individual making the disposal or by a company where the conditions in (*a*)(ii) above applied. The individual must have attained the age of 50, or retired below that age on 'ill-health grounds', on or before the date of cessation of business and the asset(s) must be disposed of within the '*permitted period*' (defined as a period of one year or such longer period as is allowed in a written notice by the Board) after that date. Where the business is carried on by a partnership, it is treated as owned by each partner who is, at the time, a member of the partnership. [*TCGA 1992, s 163(1)(2)(4)(8), Sch 6 para 4(1)(2); FA 1993, s 87, Sch 7 paras 1, 2, Sch 23 Pt III; FA 1996, s 176*].

Retirement relief was granted on the sale by an individual of land which he had rented to his family company for use for the purposes of its business (*which was discontinued at the time of the sale*). The CA did not consider it essential that the business for the purposes of which the asset was used had to have been the business of the individual making the disposal as opposed to its being that of a company within (*a*)(ii) above. (*Plumbly & Others (Harbour's Personal Representatives) v Spencer CA 1999, 71 TC 399*). (The references in the legislation to a 'family company' have since been replaced by references to a 'personal company'.) Following *Plumbly*, HMRC accept that, in these circumstances, relief may be due *either* under *TCGA 1992, s 163 or* as an associated disposal under *TCGA 1992, s 164(6)* (see 53.6 below) (HMRC Capital Gains Manual CG 63572, 63739).

In practice, the period permitted after cessation will be up to three years provided the asset or, in the case of a company, any chargeable business asset retained by it at the date of cessation, is not used or leased for any purpose beyond the first anniversary of cessation (HMRC Capital Gains Manual CG 63582). See also *Taxation 27 July 1989 p 516* and HMRC Capital Gains Manual CG 63583 *et seq.* for a possible further relaxation in certain cases where assets are retained for reasons beyond the control of the individual concerned. If a business is closed down on a basis intended to be only temporary but that becomes, in the event, permanent, the date, for the purposes of *TCGA 1992, s 163*, when the business ceases to be carried on is the date on which the business is closed down (*Marriott v Lane Ch D 1996, 69 TC 157*).

A disposal of assets after 5 April 2003 will not attract retirement relief (following its abolition — see 53.1 above), even if cessation of business took place on or before that date (Revenue Tax Bulletin April 1999 p 654).

(*c*) A disposal of shares or securities of a company (including a deemed disposal of an interest in shares under *TCGA 1992, s 122* as a result of a capital distribution (see 58.10 SHARES AND SECURITIES), or a distribution treated as such under ESC C16 (see Tolley's Corporation Tax under Distributions) — HMRC Capital Gains Manual CG 63670) where throughout a period of at least one year ending with the 'operative date' (the '*qualifying period*') either

(i) the individual owns the business which, at the date of disposal, is owned by the company, or, if the company is the 'holding company' of a 'trading group', by any member of the group; or

(ii) the company is the individual's 'personal company' and is either a 'trading company' or the 'holding company' of a 'trading group'. The individual must be a 'full-time working officer or employee' of the company or, in the case of a member of a 'group of companies' or 'commercial association of companies', of one or more companies which are members of the group or association.

The '*operative date*' is normally the date of disposal but there are two exceptions.

(A) If within the permitted period (as in (*b*) above) before disposal the company concerned ceased to be either a trading company or a member of a trading group (without becoming the other), and on or before the cessation, the individual making the disposal attained the age of 50 or retired earlier on 'ill-health grounds', then, subject to (B) below, the operative date is the date of cessation. In consequence, the reference in (*c*)(i) above to the date of disposal is to be read as referring to the date of cessation of trading.

(B) If the individual ceased to be a full-time working officer or employee of the company (or, in the case of a member of a group or commercial association of companies, of one or more companies which are members of the group or association) but remained an officer or employee of the company concerned (or one or more members of the group or association) and worked an average of at least ten hours per week in a technical or managerial capacity until either the date of disposal or the date of cessation of trading where (A) above applies, the operative date is the date on which he ceased to be a full-time working officer or employee.

Where under *TCGA 1992, s 127* a new holding would be treated as the same asset as a previous holding after a reorganisation under *TCGA 1992, s 126* (including an exchange of shares or securities treated as such a reorganisation under *TCGA 1992, s 135* or *s 136*) the individual may elect by notice in writing on or before the first anniversary of 31 January following the tax year in which the disposal occurs for *TCGA 1992, s 127* not to apply.

[*TCGA 1992, s 163(1)(2)(5)–(7), Sch 6 para 1, para 2, para 4(1)(2); FA 1993, s 87, Sch 7 paras 1, 2, Sch 23 Pt III; FA 1996, s 176, Sch 21 para 44(2); FA 2002, Sch 9 paras 5(14), 7*].

For reorganisation and exchanges of shares etc., see 58.1, 58.4 SHARES AND SECURITIES. In HMRC's opinion an election cannot be made in respect of part only of the shares held before and concerned in the reorganisation (Tolley's Practical Tax 1986 p 166). On a reorganisation of shares into QUALIFYING CORPORATE BONDS (50.3) no such election is available as *TCGA 1992, s 127* is disapplied. However, retirement relief can be taken into account in arriving at the gain otherwise chargeable on the disposal deemed to occur on the reorganisation. Any gain remaining after deduction of retirement relief is deferred under *TCGA 1992, s 116(10)(b)* until disposal of the bonds. (HMRC Capital Gains Manual CG 53867–53869).

53.5 **Assets used in an office or employment.** Relief is given where an individual who has attained the age of 50 or has retired below that age on 'ill-health grounds' makes a 'relevant disposal' of the whole or part of the assets provided or held for the purposes of his office or employment.

A disposal is a '*relevant disposal*' if

(*a*) the office or employment was the individual's full-time occupation throughout a period of at least one year ending with the date of disposal (the '*qualifying period*'), or if the office etc. ceased earlier, before the cessation date; and

(*b*) the office or employment was not as officer or employee of his 'personal company' or a member of a 'trading group' of which the 'holding company' was his personal company (as this situation is covered by 53.4 above); and

(*c*) where the individual ceased office or employment before the disposal

(i) he either attained 50 on or before the date of cessation or retired on ill-health grounds on that date; and

(ii) the disposal took place within one year of ceasing office or employment (or such longer period as is allowed by the Board; see 53.4(*b*) above).

[*TCGA 1992, s 164(1)(2), Sch 6 para 1, para 4(1)(2); FA 1993, s 87, Sch 7 paras 1, 2, Sch 23 Pt III; FA 1996, s 176*].

53.6 **Associated disposals of assets owned by a partner, or by an officer or employee of a company, and used in the business of the partnership or company.** Where relief is available to partners, or to officers or employees of personal companies, for a 'material disposal of business assets' (see 53.4 above) consisting of an interest in the assets of a partnership, or of shares etc. in a personal company, relief is also available where the individual concerned makes an 'associated disposal' of assets.

A disposal is an '*associated disposal*' if

(*a*) it takes place as part of a withdrawal of the individual from the business carried on by the partnership or company concerned;

(*b*) the asset was in use for the purposes of the partnership or company business until immediately before the material disposal or, if earlier, the cessation of the business; and

(*c*) the asset has been used for all or part of the period in which it has been owned by the individual for business purposes (including other previous businesses carried on by the individual whether alone or in partnership or by a personal company).

The '*qualifying period*' in the case of an associated disposal is the same as that for the material disposal of business assets with which it is associated.

[*TCGA 1992, s 164(6)–(8), Sch 6 para 4(1)(2); FA 1993, s 87, Sch 7 paras 1, 2, Sch 23 Pt III*].

See 53.8 below for circumstances, including the charging of rent for the asset, in which only part of the gain on an associated disposal qualifies for relief.

In *Clarke v Mayo Ch D 1994, 66 TC 728*, Evans-Lombe J held that the words 'immediately before ... the cessation of the business' should not be construed in isolation, but in the context of *TCGA 1992, ss 163, 164* as a whole. The words 'immediately before' could be construed as meaning 'sufficiently proximate in time to the material disposal or cessation so as to justify the conclusion that the transaction formed part of it'.

A withdrawal may be partial and is a disposal of an interest in the partnership, or of shares in the company, concerned (HMRC Helpsheet IR 289 p 2). There is no requirement that a member of a partnership should dispose of the whole of his interest in the partnership (Tolley's Practical Tax 1986 p 40). It is not necessary for the individual to reduce the amount of working time spent on the partnership's or company's business (HMRC Capital Gains Manual CG 63729).

Abolition of retirement relief. If the material disposal occurs before 6 April 2003 and the associated disposal on or after that date, the associated disposal will fall into 2003/04 and will not attract relief (due to the abolition of retirement relief — see 53.1 above), though relief remains available for the material disposal. If, however, the associated disposal takes place before 6 April 2003 and the material disposal on or after that date, no retirement relief can be due on *either* disposal. (Revenue Tax Bulletin April 1999 p 654).

53.7 **Disposal of assets by trustees.** Relief is given where trustees dispose of settled property consisting of shares or securities of a company, or of an asset used or previously used for business purposes, if a beneficiary has an interest in possession (excluding one for a fixed term) in the settled property and certain conditions are met. For consideration of the meaning of 'interest in possession', see 57.13 SETTLEMENTS.

In relation to a disposal of shares or securities of a company (including a deemed disposal of an interest in shares under *TCGA 1992, s 122* as a result of a capital distribution; see 58.10 SHARES AND SECURITIES), the conditions are that

(*a*) the company was the beneficiary's 'personal company' and either a 'trading company' or the 'holding company' of a 'trading group' throughout a period of at least one year (the '*qualifying period*') ending not earlier than one year (or longer if the Board allow; see 53.4(*b*) above) before the date of disposal; and

(*b*) the beneficiary was a 'full-time working officer or employee' of the company (or, if the company is a member of a 'group of companies' or 'commercial association of companies', of one or more companies which are members of the group or association) throughout a period of at least one year ending as in (*a*) above; and

(*c*) the beneficiary ceased to be a full-time working officer or employee on or within one year (longer if the Board allow; see 53.4(*b*) above) before the date of disposal, having attained the age of 50 or retired earlier on 'ill-health grounds'.

Where under *TCGA 1992, s 127* a new holding would be treated as the same asset as a previous holding after a reorganisation under *TCGA 1992, s 126* (including an exchange of shares or securities treated as such a reorganisation under *TCGA 1992, s 135* or *s 136*) the trustees and the individual may jointly elect in writing, on or before the first anniversary of 31 January following the year of assessment in which the disposal occurred, for *TCGA 1992, s 127* not to apply. For reorganisation and exchanges of shares etc., see 58.1, 58.4 SHARES AND SECURITIES.

In relation to a disposal of an asset, the conditions are that

(i) the asset was used for the purposes of a business carried on by the beneficiary throughout a period of at least one year (the '*qualifying period*') ending not earlier than one year (or longer if the Board allow, see 53.4(*b*) above) before the disposal;

(ii) the beneficiary ceased to carry on that business on or within one year (or longer if the Board allow) before the date of disposal; and

(iii) the beneficiary attained the age of 50 or retired earlier on 'ill-health grounds' on or before the date of disposal or, if earlier, the date he ceased to carry on the business.

[*TCGA 1992, s 164(3)–(5), Sch 6 para 1, para 2, para 4(1)(2); FA 1993, s 87, Sch 7 paras 1, 2, Sch 23 Pt III; FA 1996, s 176, Sch 21 para 44; FA 2002, Sch 9 paras 5(14), 7*].

53.8 **GAINS QUALIFYING FOR RELIEF**

Subject to the provisions below relating to trustees' disposals, associated disposals and capital distributions

(*a*) in the case of a qualifying disposal within 53.4–53.7 above, other than one of shares or securities of a company, the gains accruing on the disposal of 'chargeable business assets' comprised in the qualifying disposal are aggregated and only the excess of those gains over 'the amount available for relief' (see 53.9 below) is a chargeable gain [*TCGA 1992, Sch 6 para 6*]; and (*b*) where the qualifying disposal is of shares or securities of a company, the gains accruing are aggregated, and of the 'appropriate proportion' of the aggregated gains, only the excess of that proportion over 'the amount available for relief' is a chargeable gain (but not so as to affect liability in respect of gains representing the balance of the aggregated gains).

The '*appropriate proportion*' is a proportion given as follows.

(i) *For a trading company which is not a holding company*, the proportion is that which the value of the company's 'chargeable business assets' bears to the value of all its 'chargeable assets' immediately before the end of the qualifying period.

(ii) *For a holding company*, the proportion is that which the value of the trading group's 'chargeable business assets' bears to the value of all the group's 'chargeable assets' immediately before the end of the qualifying period. If a 51% subsidiary of a holding company is not wholly owned, the values of its chargeable assets and chargeable business assets are reduced in proportion to the share capital owned.

See 53.4–53.7 above as appropriate for the qualifying period.

A '*chargeable asset*' is every asset except one where a gain accruing on a disposal immediately before the end of the qualifying period would not be a chargeable gain, but a holding by one member of a trading group of the ordinary share capital of another is not a chargeable asset.

If the company or group has no chargeable assets, the appropriate proportion is the whole. [*TCGA 1992, Sch 6 paras 7, 8*].

Where the qualifying disposal is a disposal which the individual is (or trustees are) treated as making under *TCGA 1992, s 122* (see 58.10 SHARES AND SECURITIES) in consideration of a capital distribution, the recipient of the distribution can elect, by notice in writing on or before the first anniversary of 31 January following the end of the year of assessment in which he received the capital distribution for any asset sold not more than six months before the end of the qualifying period to be treated as remaining the property of the company and in use for the purposes for which it was used before the sale. The proceeds of disposal are treated as not forming part of the assets of the company. [*TCGA 1992, Sch 6 para 12(5)(6); FA 1996, Sch 21 para 44(4)*].

A '*chargeable business asset*' is an asset which is, or is an interest in, an asset used for the purposes of a trade, profession, vocation, office or employment carried on by the individual or beneficiary concerned, his personal company, a member of a trading group of which the holding company is his personal company or a partnership of which he is a member. Goodwill is included but not shares or securities or other assets held as investments. An asset is not a chargeable business asset if, on the disposal of it, any gain which might accrue would not be a chargeable gain. [*TCGA 1992, Sch 6 para 12(2)–(4); FA 1993, s 87, Sch 7 paras 1, 2, Sch 23 Pt III*].

In *Durrant v CIR (Sp C 24), [1995] SSCD 145*, it was held that all shares or securities are excluded from being chargeable business assets within *TCGA 1992, Sch 6 para 12(2)*, regardless of whether they are held as investments.

In arriving at the aggregate gains, the normal capital gains tax provisions fixing the amount of chargeable gains apply, and any allowable loss accruing on the qualifying disposal concerned is deducted. The retirement relief provisions do not affect the computation of the amount of any allowable loss. [*TCGA 1992, Sch 6 para 12(1)*].

Example

P Ltd carries on a trade of printing and bookbinding. Its directors include C who owns 10% of the issued share capital and of the voting rights. In December 2002, on reaching the age of 63, C gives his shares to his sister. At the date of transfer, the company's assets are valued as follows.

				Market value	Cost
		£	£	£	£
Leasehold printing works				190,000	50,000
Goodwill				60,000	—
Stocks of materials				80,000	75,000
Plant					
Printing presses	No 1	8,000			3,000
	No 2	8,500			3,500
	No 3	6,500	23,000		2,000
Typesetter			10,500		15,000
Binding machine			16,500		12,000
Small tools, type etc.			7,000		10,000
Motor cars			20,000		30,000
Office fixtures and fittings (items under £6,000)			9,000	86,000	15,000
Shares in associated publishing company				60,000	40,000
Cash at bank and in hand				7,500	—
Debtors				11,500	—

The pre-tapered chargeable gain arising on the shares given to C's sister is £75,000.

The value of the company's chargeable assets is as follows

	Business	Non-business
	£	£
Leasehold	190,000	—
Goodwill	60,000	—
Plant (£23,000 + £10,500 + £16,500)	50,000	—
Shares	—	60,000
	£300,000	£60,000

Gain eligible for retirement relief is therefore

$$£75,000 \times \frac{300,000}{300,000 + 60,000} \qquad £62,500$$

Note to the example

(*a*) Chargeable assets are all assets other than those on which any gain accruing on a disposal immediately before the end of the qualifying period would not be a chargeable gain.

Trustees' disposals. Where the disposal is a trustees' disposal under 53.7 above, and at least one beneficiary other than the one carrying on the business etc. (the '*qualifying beneficiary*') also has an interest in possession in the same property at the end of the qualifying period, only the 'relevant proportion' of the gain accruing to the trustees on disposal qualifies for relief, and the remainder is a chargeable gain. The '*relevant proportion*' is the proportion which the qualifying beneficiary's interest in the income from the settled property comprising the shares, securities or asset in question bears to the interests in the income of all the beneficiaries (including the qualifying beneficiary) who then have interests in possession in that part. [*TCGA 1992, Sch 6 para 9*].

Associated disposals. Where the disposal is an associated disposal under 53.6 above, only part of the gain qualifies for relief if (i) the asset was not used for business purposes throughout the individual's period of ownership (*Note.* In the determination of the period of ownership there is no exclusion of any period before 31 March 1982, cf. 55.6 ROLLOVER RELIEF); or (ii) during part of the period of use in a business the individual was not concerned in the carrying on of that business (whether personally, in partnership or as a full-time working officer or employee); or (iii) rent (including consideration in any form) was paid for use of the asset. The part which qualifies for relief is that which is just and reasonable having regard to the lengths of the periods in question and the extent to which any rent paid was less than the open market rent. [*TCGA 1992, Sch 6 para 10; FA 1996, Sch 20 para 66(4)*]. See HMRC Capital Gains Manual CG 63836 for an example of HMRC's interpretation of this provision. Note that the CA decision in *Plumbly* (see 53.4(*b*) above) offers a way around the restriction in (iii) (charging of rent) in a case involving cessation of the business of a company in which the asset was used.

Capital distributions. Where a material disposal of business assets (see 53.4 above) or a trustees' disposal (see 53.7 above) is a disposal deemed to be made under *TCGA 1992, s 122* in consideration of a capital distribution, the gain on which relief may be given is restricted if the capital distribution consists wholly or partly of chargeable business assets. If the distribution consists wholly of such assets, no relief is available. If the distribution consists partly of chargeable business assets, the aggregated gains are proportionately reduced and the appropriate proportion then applied to the reduced amount. Any question as to whether a capital distribution consists of chargeable business assets is determined by reference to the status of the assets immediately before the end of the qualifying period. [*TCGA 1992, Sch 6 para 11*].

53.9 AMOUNT OF RELIEF

The basic rule. For disposals after 5 April 1988 (and before 6 April 2003 — see 53.1 above), 'the amount available for relief' (or more simply, the amount of relief) is the aggregate of

(*a*) so much of the 'gains qualifying for relief' as does not exceed the 'appropriate percentage' of

£50,000 for disposals after 5 April 2002 and before 6 April 2003;

£100,000 for disposals after 5 April 2001 and before 6 April 2002;

£150,000 for disposals after 5 April 2000 and before 6 April 2001;

£200,000 for disposals after 5 April 1999 and before 6 April 2000;

£250,000 for disposals after 29 November 1993 and before 6 April 1999;

£150,000 for disposals after 18 March 1991 and before 30 November 1993;

£125,000 for disposals after 5 April 1988 and before 19 March 1991;

and

(*b*) one half of any excess of such gains, up to a maximum excess equal to the appropriate percentage of

£150,000 for disposals after 5 April 2002 and before 6 April 2003;

£300,000 for disposals after 5 April 2001 and before 6 April 2002;

£450,000 for disposals after 5 April 2000 and before 6 April 2001;

£600,000 for disposals after 5 April 1999 and before 6 April 2000;

£750,000 for disposals after 29 November 1993 and before 6 April 1999;

£450,000 for disposals after 18 March 1991 and before 30 November 1993;

£375,000 for disposals after 5 April 1988 and before 19 March 1991.

No relief is available for disposals after 5 April 2003 (see 53.1 above).

'*Gains qualifying for relief*' is the aggregate amount of gains described in 53.8 above, after the application of the provisions mentioned there but before deduction of any retirement relief.

The '*appropriate percentage*' is a percentage determined according to the length of the qualifying period, rising arithmetically from 10% (the minimum) where the period is one year to 100% (the maximum) where it is ten years.

For the purposes of the above a trustees' disposal under 53.7 above is regarded as a qualifying disposal by the beneficiary. However, if, on the same day, an individual makes a material disposal of business assets under 53.4 above and is also the beneficiary in relation to a trustees' disposal, the amount available for relief is applied to the former disposal in priority to the latter.

For disposals after 5 April 1998, retirement relief is given in priority to TAPER RELIEF (61), which is thus applied to the balance of the gain after retirement relief. Where there is more than one qualifying gain and they are not wholly covered by retirement relief, that relief is to be applied in the way that then provides the maximum possible benefit from taper relief (Revenue Press Release IR 17, 17 March 1998).

For disposals before 6 April 1988, the amount of relief was a percentage of £125,000 (£100,000 before 6 April 1987), determined in the same way as the appropriate percentage described above.

[*TCGA 1992, Sch 6 para 4(3), para 13; FA 1988, s 110(1)(2)(8); FA 1991, s 100(1)(3)(4); FA 1994, s 92; FA 1998, s 140(1)(2)*].

Example

X, who is aged 51, disposes in June 2002 of a business which he has owned for 6 years, and realises gains qualifying for retirement relief amounting to £250,000. His entitlement to relief is calculated as follows.

		£
Appropriate percentage of £50,000: 60% of £50,000		30,000
Excess of gains over £30,000:	£220,000	
Appropriate percentage of £150,000: 60%	£90,000	
Relief is available on £90,000		
Half thereof		45,000
Total relief		£75,000

Aggregation of earlier business periods. The amount available for relief may be increased where the qualifying period appropriate to a qualifying disposal (the '*original qualifying period*') would be less than ten years but the individual or beneficiary was 'concerned in the carrying on of another' business ('*the previous business*') in some earlier part (the '*earlier business period*') of the ten-year period up to the end of the original qualifying period. There must be no more than a two-year gap between the end of the earlier business period and the beginning of the original qualifying period. For the purposes of calculating the increase, the previous business is assumed to be the same business as the 'business at retirement', and, in the first instance, any gap between the two businesses is ignored so that the two periods are assumed to be one continuous extended qualifying period. However, this extended qualifying period is not to begin earlier than the beginning of the ten-year period ending at the end of the original qualifying period, and is then to be reduced by the gap between the businesses. Where there is more than one earlier business (and, therefore, more than one earlier business period) the provisions are to be first applied to the latest of the earlier business periods and the original qualifying period, and then to the extended qualifying period so resulting and the next latest of the earlier business periods, and so on.

The reference to a person being '*concerned in the carrying on of another business*' above is a reference to his being so concerned personally or as a member of a partnership or, if the business was owned by a company, then as a 'full-time working officer or employee' of that company or, as the case may be, of any member of the 'group' or 'commercial association of companies' of which it is a member.

The '*business at retirement*' is a reference to the business giving rise to the qualifying disposal being one within 53.4, 53.6 and 53.7 above (i.e. the length of an original qualifying period relating to employee disposals within 53.5 above cannot be the subject of an increase). [*TCGA 1992, Sch 6 para 4(3), para 14; FA 1993, s 87, Sch 7 para 2(1)*].

In strictness, the original qualifying period must be a period of at least one year as in 53.4–53.7 above. However, HMRC treat as a qualifying disposal a disposal which was not a qualifying disposal by reason only that the original qualifying period was less than one year. Hence any final business period can be aggregated with earlier business periods (presumably subject to the two-year gap limit mentioned above) irrespective of the length of the final business period. This does not mean that a final business period of less than one year is treated as a period of one year in calculating the length of the extended qualifying period. (HMRC Extra-Statutory Concession D48). For disposals occurring after 5 April 1996, this concession is given statutory effect in *TCGA 1992, Sch 6 para 14*.

However, although the original qualifying period may be aggregated with previous business periods of any length, the extension will only apply if the total aggregate period exceeds one year. [*TCGA 1992, Sch 6 para 14; FA 1996, Sch 39 para 7*].

There is no specific requirement for there to have been a material disposal of business assets, a trustees' disposal or an associated disposal in connection with the previous business. If a business is owned for some period by a company which is not the individual's 'personal company', the qualifying period cannot be extended by that period (see *Fraser v HMRC (Sp C 530), [2006] SSCD 285*). (Revenue Tax Bulletin February 1997 pp 397, 398).

Example

A owned a business for 7 years before disposing of it in 1996 when he was 48 and in good health. After a break of exactly 2 years he buys another business and runs it for 5 years before disposing of it in 2002/03. The percentage of the maximum relief available on the 2002/03 disposal is $^{8}/_{10}$ = 80% (and not $^{12}/_{14}$ = 86%).

Relief given on earlier disposals. Where qualifying disposals are made at different times, the relief available on a later disposal is restricted by reference to the relief given on any earlier disposals (including relief given under the provisions of pre-*TCGA 1992* legislation).

Relief on the later disposal is restricted to the excess of

(A) the amount of relief which would otherwise have been available if

 (i) the gains qualifying for relief on the disposal were increased by the amount of the 'underlying gains' relieved on earlier disposals, and

 (ii) the qualifying period appropriate to this disposal (redetermined as above for aggregation of earlier business periods) were extended by the addition of periods equal to so much (if any) of previous qualifying periods appropriate to earlier disposals not already falling within the qualifying period appropriate to this disposal;

over

(B) the aggregate amount of relief given on all earlier disposals.

The amount of the 'underlying gains' is determined in one of the following ways, according to what disposal(s) occurred.

(I) If the earlier disposal or all of the earlier disposals occurred before 6 April 1988, the amount of the underlying gains is the total relief obtained on that disposal or those disposals.

(II) If there has only been one earlier disposal and it occurred after 5 April 1988, the amount of the underlying gains is the aggregate of the relief obtained by reference to the appropriate percentage of whichever is the appropriate figure of those listed at (*a*) above (under 'The basic rule') and twice the relief obtained by reference to any excess.

(III) In cases not within (I) and (II) above, the amount of the underlying gains is calculated as in (II) above, but on the assumption that

 (i) the previous disposal was the only earlier disposal, and

 (ii) the totals calculated for (A)(i) and (A)(ii) above on that disposal were the gains qualifying for relief on that disposal, and the qualifying period appropriate to that disposal, respectively.

General. Where earlier disposals took place before 12 April 1978, the reference in (A)(ii) above to the qualifying period appropriate to the later disposal is to be taken as the period of ten years ending with that disposal. [*TCGA 1992, Sch 6 para 4(3), para 15; FA 1988, s 110(3)–(6)(8)*].

Example

P, who was born in May 1941, carried on the following businesses, and made gains qualifying for retirement relief on disposals of them at cessation, as follows.

Business A	1.4.84 – 30.6.96	£100,000
Business B	1.4.98 – 30.6.02	£125,000

His entitlement to retirement relief is calculated as follows.

Business A

Gains qualifying for relief		£100,000
Qualifying period		10 years
Maximum available for 100% relief:		£
10/10 × £250,000 × 100% = £250,000		
Relief given £100,000 × 100%		£100,000
Chargeable gain 1996/97		Nil
Underlying gains (see (II) above)		£100,000

Business B

(1) Before restriction applied:		
Gains qualifying for relief		£125,000
Qualifying period (extended under *TCGA 1992, Sch 6 para 14* as gap between businesses less than 2 years — see above — 10 years (maximum) less 1.75 years from 1.7.96 to 31.3.98)		8.25 years
Maximum available for 100% relief:		£
8.25/10 × £50,000 × 100%		41,250
Maximum available for 50% relief:		
8.25/10 × £150,000 =	£123,750	
Excess of gains £125,000 – 41,250 =	£83,750	
£83,750 × 50%		41,875
Relief due subject to (2) below		£83,125
(2) Applying *TCGA 1992, Sch 6 para 15* restriction:		£
Gains qualifying for relief		125,000
Add underlying gains on earlier disposal		100,000
		£225,000
Qualifying period for later disposal (as above)	8.25 years	
Extended by qualifying period for earlier disposal up to a maximum of 10 years	1.75 years	10 years

		£
Maximum available for 100% relief:		
10/10 × £50,000 × 100%		50,000
Maximum available for 50% relief:		
10/10 × £150,000 =	£150,000	
Excess of gains £225,000 – 50,000 =	£175,000	
£150,000 × 50%		75,000
		125,000
Less relief given on disposal of Business A		100,000
Relief due (as less than £83,125 in (1) above)		£25,000
Chargeable gain 2002/03 (£125,000 – £25,000)		£100,000

For further commentary and examples, see HMRC Capital Gains Manual CG 63880–63888.

Aggregation of spouse's interest in the business. Where an individual makes a material disposal of business assets (within 53.4 above) which, in whole or in part, he acquired either under the will or intestacy of his spouse or by way of lifetime gift from her, he may make a written election, on or before the first anniversary of 31 January following the end of the year of assessment in which the material disposal occurs for his qualifying period (which must be at least one year as in 53.4–53.7 above) to be extended by what would have been his spouse's qualifying period if the relevant conditions of ownership etc. had applied to the spouse. The individual and spouse must have been living together at the time of the spouse's death or lifetime gift and the whole of the spouse's interest in the business, assets, shares or securities concerned immediately before the acquisition or, as the case may be, the spouse's death, must be acquired.

Example

R acquired her late husband's 30% shareholding in X Ltd on his death in June 1998. She took over the office he had held for 15 years as a full-time working officer until, at the age of 63, she sold her shares in June 2002 incurring an otherwise chargeable gain of £66,000 (after indexation and before taper relief).

	£
The chargeable gain is calculated as follows	
Gain eligible for relief	66,000
Maximum available for 100% relief:	
$\frac{4+6}{10} \times £50{,}000 \times 100\%$	(50,000)
Maximum available for 50% relief:	
$\frac{4+6}{10} \times £200{,}000 = £200{,}000 - £50{,}000 = £150{,}000$	
£66,000 – £50,000 = £16,000 × 50%	(8,000)
Chargeable gain 2002/03 (subject to TAPER RELIEF (61))	£8,000

For disposals after 5 April 1988, where the acquisition was by way of lifetime gift, the amount available for relief is not to exceed the amount that would be available for relief on the assumption that the lifetime transfer had not taken place and the material disposal had been made by the spouse (to whom is attributed anything done by the individual in relation to the business concerned after the lifetime gift). *For disposals before 6 April 1988*, an alternative restriction applied if lower: namely, £125,000 (£100,000 before 6 April 1987) less any relief (including relief under earlier legislation) given on the spouse's own disposals, or on trustees' disposals where the spouse was a beneficiary, up to and including the lifetime transfer. [*TCGA 1992, Sch 6 para 16; FA 1988, s 110(7)(8); FA 1996, Sch 21 para 44(5)*].

54 Returns

Cross-references. See 48 PENALTIES as regards late or incorrect returns; 48.1 PENALTIES as regards duty to notify chargeability to tax.

The headings in this chapter are as follows.

54.1 SELF-ASSESSMENT

The obligations under self-assessment of individuals and others within the charge to capital gains tax are covered at 54.2–54.14 below. For convenience, these also cover income tax obligations to some extent, but see Tolley's Income Tax for full coverage of those. As regards companies, see 54.18 below. For provisions applicable before pre-self-assessment, see the 2005/06 and earlier editions.

54.2 **Annual tax returns.** For the purposes of establishing the amounts in which a person is chargeable to income tax and capital gains tax for 1996/97 and subsequent years of assessment, an officer of Revenue and Customs (or, before 18 April 2005, an officer of the Board of Inland Revenue) may by notice require that person to deliver a return (i.e. a self-assessment tax return) on or before 31 January following the year of assessment or, if later, within three months beginning with the date of the notice. The return must contain such information and be accompanied by such accounts, statements and documents as may reasonably be required. The return must include a declaration that, to the best of the knowledge of the person making it, it is complete and correct. The information, accounts and statements required by the notice may differ in relation to different periods, or different sources of income, or different descriptions of person. [*TMA 1970, s 8; FA 1994, s 178(1), s 199(2), Sch 26 Pt V; FA 1995, s 103(7), s 104(1)–(3); FA 1996, s 121(1)–(3)(8); ITTOIA 2005, Sch 1 para 359; CRCA 2005, s 7*]. Similar provisions apply in relation to returns by trustees. [*TMA 1970, ss 8A, 12; FA 1994, s 178(2), s 199(2), Sch 26 Pt V; FA 1995, s 103(3)(4)(7), s 104(1); FA 1996, s 121(1)–(3)(8); ITTOIA 2005, Sch 1 para 360*]. See 48.2 PENALTIES as regards automatic and possible daily penalties for non-compliance (i.e. late returns).

The Government has announced that it is considering changing the tax return filing deadline for paper returns with effect from 2008. It is proposed that the deadline for such returns will be 31 October following the end of the tax year for which the return is made where that return is made on paper. The deadline for returns filed via the internet (see 54.22 below) will continue to be 31 January following the tax year. The period within which HMRC may make enquiries into a return will be linked to the filing date rather than the deadline, to encourage earlier filing. (HMRC Budget Document 'Progress towards a new relationship: How HMRC is working to make life easier for business' 22 March 2006; HMRC Internet Statement 18 July 2006).

Reporting limits. Where an individual's chargeable gains for 2003/04 or any subsequent year do not exceed the annual exempt amount (see 2.3 ANNUAL RATES AND EXEMPTIONS) *and* the aggregate amount or value of the consideration for all disposals of chargeable assets other than those treated under *TCGA 1992, s 58* as giving rise to neither a gain nor a loss (see 42.4 MARRIED PERSONS AND CIVIL PARTNERS) does not exceed *four times* the annual exempt amount, a statement in the self-assessment tax return to that effect complies with the above obligations so far as they relate to chargeable gains (though not so as to prejudice HMRC's right to more detailed information). For this purpose, the amount of an individual's chargeable gains is, where there are no allowable losses to be deducted, the amount after taper relief. Where allowable losses are to be deducted, the amount to be taken is before the deduction of such losses and taper relief. For returns for 2002/03 and earlier years, these reduced reporting requirements apply where the individual's chargeable gains for the year (before deducting losses or taper relief) do not exceed the annual exempt amount *and* the aggregate amount of the consideration for all disposals of chargeable assets (without excluding inter-spouse transfers) does not exceed *twice* the annual exempt amount. [*TCGA 1992, ss 3(6), 3A(1)–(3); FA 2003, s 159, Sch 28 paras 1, 3(1)(2), 7, Sch 43 Pt 3(7); SI 2005 No 3229, Reg 106*]. These provisions apply to personal representatives as they apply to individuals but only for the year of assessment in which the individual concerned dies and the next two tax years. [*TCGA 1992, ss 3(7), 3A(4); FA 2003, Sch 28 paras 1, 3(3)*]. Similar provisions apply to the trustees of settlements, but apply to returns for 2002/03 and earlier years only in the case of certain settlements for the disabled (as in 57.11 SETTLEMENTS) and other settlements made before 7 June 1978. For such years, the limits apply, except in the case of settlements for the disabled, by reference to reduced annual exempt amounts (see 57.10 SETTLEMENTS). For 2003/04 onwards, the total gains limit continues to apply by reference to such reduced amounts where applicable, but the aggregate consideration limit is four times the annual exempt amount *for an individual.* [*TCGA 1992, ss 3(8), 3A(5), Sch 1 para 1(1)(5A), para 2(1)(3)(6A); FA 2003, Sch 28 paras 1,4,5, Sch 43 Pt 3(7)*].

The above-mentioned statement should *not*, however, be made if a net capital loss has been incurred: a claim has to be made for such a loss to be allowable (see 40.3 LOSSES) and this requires full disclosure.

Acquisitions of chargeable assets. The notice under *TMA 1970, s 8* (or *s 8A* for trustees) may also require particulars of chargeable assets acquired in the tax year including the consideration given for them and possibly even details of the person from whom an asset was acquired. [*TMA 1970, s 12(2)(3)(5); CGTA 1979, s 157(2)–(4), Sch 7 para 1(2)(9); ICTA 1988, Sch 29 para 32; FA 1989, s 123(1)(2); FA 1990, s 90(2)(5); TCGA 1992, Sch 10 para 2(1)(3)*]. In practice though, the standard self-assessment tax return does *not* ask for this information.

Informal procedure for personal representatives of deceased estates. In respect of income tax and capital gains tax liabilities arising during the administration period of a deceased estate, HMRC operate an informal procedure under which self-assessment tax returns are not required. For deaths occurring after 5 April 2003, HMRC will normally operate the procedure where the estate is not complex and the tax arising during the whole of the administration period is less than £10,000. Where this procedure is used, only a simple computation of the estate's liability need be submitted to HMRC, who in turn provide the personal representative with a payslip to enable payment of the tax due. Self-assessment returns are required in all cases not meeting the above conditions. For these purposes, HMRC consider an estate to be complex where there is a very high probate or confirmation value, generally in excess of £2.5 million, the administration of the estate is continuing and has entered the third tax year from the date of death, or the personal representatives have disposed of a chargeable asset and the sale proceeds exceed £250,000. For deaths occurring before 6 April 2003, the Revenue operated the procedure where the probate value of the estate was less than £400,000. (Revenue Tax Bulletin August 2003 p 1043).

See 54.6 below for amendments of returns and self-assessments. See 54.7 below for record-keeping requirements and 54.8 below for enquiries into returns. See 54.14 below for determination of tax liability where no return delivered.

54.3 **Form and delivery of returns.** The power of the Commissioners for HMRC (or, before 18 April 2005, the Board of Inland Revenue) to prescribe the form of returns is given by *TMA 1970, s 113(1)*. The basic self-assessment tax return does not include a space to enter details of chargeable gains and allowable losses. These must be entered on supplementary pages, which form part of the return and which may come attached to it if the taxpayer has a history of making taxable gains and/or allowable losses but must otherwise be ordered, along with any required Helpsheets (see 30.4 HMRC EXPLANATORY PUBLICATIONS), via the HMRC Orderline on 0845 9000404, fax 0845 9000604, between 8am and 10pm seven days a week. If the statement mentioned in 54.2 above under 'Reporting limits' can be made, it is made in the basic return, and the supplementary pages are not then required. Similarly, if the only gain arises from the disposal of the taxpayer's main residence and it is wholly exempt under the provisions in 49 PRIVATE RESIDENCES, a statement in the basic return to this effect is sufficient. Following submission of the return, HMRC have the power, under the enquiry provisions at 54.8 below, to require full details of gains and losses.

HMRC accept schedules which mimic the capital gains supplementary pages as an alternative to completion of the pages themselves. These may include computer generated schedules, but they must follow the *form* of the actual supplementary pages. (Revenue 'Working Together' Bulletin July 2000 p 4).

HMRC do not require detailed calculations or supporting documents to be submitted with the return, although the taxpayer *may* provide these if he feels it necessary in a particular case to indicate how a gain or loss entered on the return is arrived at, bearing in mind HMRC's 'discovery' powers (see 5.2 ASSESSMENTS). It is necessary in any case to indicate on the return that a valuation (for which see also 54.4 below) or an estimate has been used in calculating a gain or loss, and the return also includes space for additional information to be entered.

Provisional figures. A return containing a provisional figure will be accepted provided that the figure is reasonable, taking account of all available information, and is clearly identified as such. An explanation should be given as to why the final figure is not available, all reasonable steps having been taken to obtain it, and when it is expected to be available (at which time it should be notified without unreasonable delay). The absence of such explanation and expected date will influence HMRC in selecting returns for enquiry (see 54.8 below). Before 23 October 2001, Revenue practice in such cases was to reject the return as unsatisfactory (see also 48.2 PENALTIES) and send it back to whoever submitted it (taxpayer or agent). Pressures of work and complexity of tax affairs are not regarded as acceptable explanations. If the provisional figure is accepted but the final figure is not provided by the expected date, HMRC will take appropriate action to obtain it, which may mean opening an enquiry. See HMRC Tax Return Guide, Revenue Tax Bulletins October 1998 pp 593–596, December 1999 p 705, June 2001 p 848 and February 2002 p 916, and Revenue 'Working Together' Bulletin July 2000 p 5. Note that a provisional figure is different in concept to an estimate that is not intended to be superseded by a more accurate figure. See also the point on provisional and estimated figures at 48.6 PENALTIES.

Where the replacement of a provisional figure by a final figure leads to a *decrease* in the self-assessment, and the time limit for making amendments (see 54.6 below) has passed, the amendment may be made by way of error or mistake relief claim (see 12.7 CLAIMS) where the conditions for such relief are otherwise met. Where such replacement leads to an *increase* in the self-assessment, a discovery assessment (see 5.2 ASSESSMENTS) may be made to collect the additional tax due. (Revenue Tax Bulletin December 2000 p 817).

Signing of returns. Returns (or claims) may, in cases of physical inability to sign, be signed by an attorney acting under a general or enduring power. The attorney must have full knowledge of the taxpayer's affairs and a copy of the original power or a certified copy will need to be provided when the return (or claim) is first made. The attorney will need to be appointed under an enduring power registered with the Court of Protection (except in Scotland, where there is no such registration, and a signature of an attorney or curator bonis will be accepted) where he acts in the case of a mentally incapacitated person, for whom any receiver or committee appointed by the Court may also sign. These criteria apply similarly to any other declaration required for tax purposes. An attorney cannot sign in any case where the taxpayer is physically capable of signing, even if he is unavailable abroad. (HMRC Statement of Practice A13 and Revenue Tax Bulletin February 1993 p 51).

Although the above practice pre-dates self-assessment, HMRC have published further information in their Tax Bulletin, which confirms that the only exceptions to the personal signature requirement are where, due to his age, physical infirmity or mental incapacity, the taxpayer is unable to cope adequately with the management of his affairs or where his general health might suffer if he were troubled for a personal signature. In all other cases, HMRC expect the return to be signed personally and will reject the return as unsatisfactory, and send it back to whoever submitted it (taxpayer or agent), if it is not (see also 48.2 PENALTIES). In the case of a return submitted via the internet (see below), the taxpayer's personal authentication (password and User ID) takes the place of his signature. Where a return is lodged electronically by an agent (see 54.22 below), the taxpayer must sign a copy before the electronic version is sent. (Revenue Tax Bulletin June 2001 pp 847, 848).

Substitute returns. HMRC has also stated its practice concerning the acceptability of facsimile and photocopied tax returns. Whenever such a substitute form is used, it is important to ensure that it bears the correct taxpayer's reference. A facsimile must satisfactorily present to the taxpayer the information which HMRC have determined shall be before him when he signs the declaration that the return is correct and complete to the best of his knowledge. It should be readily recognisable as a return when received in the HMRC office, and the entries of taxpayers' details should be distinguishable from the background text. Copies of the return forms for which a facsimile is to be produced together with an information sheet on the production of substitute forms are available from HMRC, Corporate Communications Office, 6th Floor (KB), North West Wing, Bush House, London WC2B 4PP. Approval must be obtained from HMRC, Corporate Communications Office, Room 9/3A, 9th Floor, North West Wing, Bush House, London WC2B 4PP before a facsimile return is used, and the facsimile must bear an agreed unique imprint for identification purposes.

Photocopies must bear the actual, not photocopied, signature of the relevant person. They are acceptable provided that they are identical (except as regards use of colour) to the official form. Where double-sided copies are not available, it is sufficient that all pages are present and attached in the correct order. Although the copying of official forms is, in strictness, a breach of HMSO copyright, action will be taken only where forms are copied on a large scale for commercial gain.

(HMRC Statement of Practice 5/87).

Electronic filing. For one year from April 2000, individual taxpayers who personally file their self-assessment tax return via the internet and pay any tax due electronically were entitled to a discount of £10 (Revenue Press Release 16 February 2000). After 20 August 2001, agents are authorised to file individual clients' personal tax returns over the internet, subject to conditions as to authorisation of the agent by the client, authentication of the information by the client and use of HMRC approved software (Revenue Directions under *SI 2000 No 945, Reg 3*, 21 August 2001). For notes on electronic filing and payment, see Revenue Tax Bulletin June 2000 pp 757, 758. For internet filing of returns, see the HMRC website (www.hmrc.gov.uk). For payment by debit card over the internet, see Revenue Press Release 10 January 2001.

For the pre-existing and continuing system of electronic lodgement of returns, normally by agents, see 54.22 below.

54.4 **Post-transaction valuation checks and rulings.** From April 1997 individuals and trustees may submit asset valuations used in their capital gains tax calculations to their Tax Office for checking before they make their returns (**post-transaction valuation checks**). The service is free of charge, but valuations will be considered only *after* the relevant transaction has occurred. Full information about the transactions to which they relate together with any relevant tax computations must be submitted to the Tax Office with the valuations using Form CG34. From 31 January 2006, the service is extended to valuations of assets that are the subject of a negligible value claim (see 40.9 LOSSES).

If HMRC agree the valuations they will not be challenged when the return is submitted unless information affecting the valuation was not provided. If HMRC disagree with the valuations they will suggest alternatives. HMRC should be allowed a minimum of 56 days to agree a valuation or suggest an alternative. The due date for filing the return cannot be deferred.

(Revenue Press Release 4 February 1997).

Under the principles at 15.4(*d*) COMPUTATION OF GAINS AND LOSSES, costs reasonably incurred in making a valuation or apportionment submitted for a post-transaction valuation check are deductible in arriving at the gain, but any costs incurred in making the submission or in subsequent negotiations cannot be so deducted (HMRC Capital Gains Manual CG 15261, 16615). The service is extended to companies from January 2000 (see 54.18 below).

On written request to a person's own tax office, and free of charge, HMRC will also give a ruling (a **post-transaction ruling**) on the application of tax law to a specific transaction. They will deal with such a request only after the transaction has been completed but whether before or (with exceptions) after the self-assessment return has been filed. Rulings can cover matters concerning income tax, corporation tax or capital gains tax. HMRC will usually consider themselves bound by a post-transaction ruling they have given to a particular person on a particular transaction unless the information provided to them proves to be incomplete or incorrect. A taxpayer is not bound to accept HMRC's ruling and may choose to treat the transaction differently in his tax return (subject to HMRC's right to amend on enquiry and the taxpayer's right of appeal). The due date for filing a return cannot be deferred whilst a ruling is awaited. There are copious information requirements. Full details, including circumstances in which HMRC will not give a ruling and issues they will not rule on, are in HMRC Code of Practice booklet COP 10.

54.5 **Self-assessments.** For 1996/97 and subsequent years of assessment, every return under *TMA 1970, s 8* or *s 8A* (see 54.2 above) must include, subject to the exception below, an assessment (a self-assessment) of the liability, based on the information in the return and taking into account all reliefs, allowances, tax credits, tax at source and tax repayments, of the person making the return to income tax and capital gains tax for the year of assessment. HMRC's Tax Calculation Guide, which is supplied with the annual tax return, is designed to assist in the calculation of the tax liability, a separate version of the Guide being available for individuals with capital gains.

A person need not comply with this requirement if he makes and delivers his return on or before 30 September following the year of assessment or, if later, within two months beginning with the date of the notice to deliver the return. In such cases, HMRC will compute the tax due. For returns submitted outside these time limits, HMRC will calculate the tax and make the assessment if the taxpayer fails to do so, but will not guarantee to do so before the due date for payment of tax.

Assessments made as above by an HMRC officer are treated as self-assessments by the person making the return and as included in the return.

[*TMA 1970, ss 8, 8A, s 9(1)–(3A); FA 1994, ss 179, 199(2); FA 1995, s 103(7), s 104(4), s 115(2); FA 1996, s 121(1)–(4), s 122(1); FA 2001, s 88, Sch 29 para 1; ITEPA 2003, Sch 6 para 125; ITTOIA 2005, Sch 1 paras 359–361*].

The 30 September deadline is of no significance where returns are filed over the internet (see 54.3 above) as the tax due is automatically computed during the filing process.

54.6 **Amendments of returns other than where enquiries made.** At any time within twelve months after the filing date (i.e. the date by which the return must be delivered, as in 54.2 above), a person may by notice to an HMRC officer amend his return.

At any time within nine months after the delivery of a person's return, an HMRC officer may by notice to that person amend his return to correct obvious errors and omissions (whether of principle, arithmetical or otherwise). Where the correction is required in consequence of an amendment by the taxpayer as above, then as from 11 May 2001 the nine-month period begins immediately after the date of the taxpayer's amendment. Also as from 11 May 2001 the taxpayer has a legal right to reject an officer's correction, by notice within 30 days beginning with the date of the notice of correction. In practice HMRC will reverse a correction regardless of this 30-day limit, unless they are no longer empowered to do so, i.e. if all deadlines for corrections and amendments (by HMRC or taxpayer) have passed and the HMRC enquiry window (see 54.8 below) has closed (Revenue Tax Bulletin June 2001 pp 850, 851).

[*TMA 1970, s 9(4)(6), ss 9ZA, 9ZB; FA 1994, ss 179, 199(2); FA 2001, s 88, Sch 29 para 2*].

The amending of a return by the taxpayer under these provisions does not preclude HMRC from taking penalty action under *TMA 1970, s 95* (see 48.6 PENALTIES) in relation to the original incorrect figures in cases where the taxpayer has acted fraudulently or negligently (Revenue Tax Bulletin October 1998 p 597).

For amendments to returns subject to an HMRC enquiry, see 54.11, 54.12 below.

54.7 RECORD-KEEPING

For 1996/97 and subsequent years, for capital gains tax and income tax, any person who may be required to make and deliver a personal or trustee tax return (see 54.2 above) for a tax year or a partnership tax return (see 54.15 below) for any period is required by law to keep all records necessary for the preparation of a complete and correct return *and* to preserve them until the end of the 'relevant day'. The 'relevant day' is initially

(*a*) in the case of a person carrying on a trade (including for these purposes any letting of property), profession or business, whether alone or in partnership, the fifth anniversary of 31 January following the year of assessment or, for partnership returns, the sixth anniversary of the end of the period covered by the return; and

(*b*) in any other case, the first anniversary of 31 January following the year of assessment.

Where, as is normal, notice to deliver the return is given before the day given by whichever is the applicable of (*a*) and (*b*) above, the '*relevant day*' is the *later* of that day and whichever of the following applies:

(i) where HMRC enquiries are made into the return, the day on which the enquiries are statutorily completed (see 54.11 below);

(ii) where no such enquiries are made, the day on which HMRC no longer have power to enquire (see 54.8 below).

Where notice to deliver a return is given *after* the day given by whichever is the applicable of (*a*) and (*b*) above, (i) and (ii) above still apply to determine the relevant day but only in relation to such records as the taxpayer has in his possession at the time the notice is given.

In the case of a person within (*a*) above, the records in question include records concerning business receipts and expenditure and, in the case of a trade involving dealing in goods, all sales and purchases of goods. All supporting documents (including accounts, books, deeds, contracts, vouchers and receipts) relating to such items must also be preserved. Generally, copies of documents may be preserved instead of the originals and are admissible in evidence in proceedings before the Appeal Commissioners. Exceptions to this are vouchers, certificates etc. which show tax credits or deductions at source of UK or foreign tax, e.g. dividend vouchers, interest vouchers (including those issued by banks and building societies) and evidence of tax deducted from payments to sub-contractors under the construction industry tax deduction scheme, which after 28 April 1996 must be preserved in their original form.

The maximum penalty for non-compliance in relation to any year of assessment or accounting period is £3,000. This does not apply to records only required for claims, elections or notices not included in the return, as there are separate record-keeping requirements (and a separate penalty) for those (see 12.3 CLAIMS) nor does it apply in respect of original dividend vouchers and interest certificates where HMRC are satisfied that other documentary evidence supplied to them proves any facts they reasonably require to be proved and which such vouchers etc. would have proved.

[*TMA 1970, s 12B; FA 1994, ss 196, 199(2)(3), Sch 19 para 3; FA 1995, s 103(7), s 105; FA 1996, s 124(2)–(5)(9); FA 1998, s 117, Sch 19 para 6; FA 2001, s 88, Sch 29 para 20; FA 2004, Sch 12 para 1*].

HMRC have given guidance as to the type of records to be kept. The above-mentioned penalty will not be charged for any failure before 6 April 1996 to keep records in accordance with that guidance. For capital gains tax, it is recommended that the following records be kept:

- contracts for the purchase, sale, lease or exchange of assets;
- documentation relating to assets acquired other than by purchase;
- details of assets gifted to others (including a trust);
- copies of valuations used in a computation of chargeable gains or losses;
- bills, invoices or other evidence of payment records such as bank statements and cheque stubs for costs claimed for the purchase, improvement or sale of assets;
- any correspondence with a purchaser or vendor leading up to the sale or acquisition of an asset;
- details supporting any apportionment (e.g. where home is partly let or partly used for business purposes).

(HMRC Pamphlet SA/BK4).

54.8 ENQUIRIES INTO RETURNS

Notice of enquiry. For 1996/97 and subsequent years, an HMRC officer may enquire into a personal or trustees' return, and anything (including any claim or election) contained (or required to be contained) in it. Under the post-*FA 2004* transfer pricing provisions, an enquiry can also extend to consideration by HMRC of whether to give the taxpayer a transfer pricing notice under *ICTA 1988, Sch 28AA para 5C*. An enquiry can also extend to consideration of whether to give the taxpayer a notice under *ICTA 1988, s 804ZA* (schemes and arrangements designed to increase DOUBLE TAX RELIEF (19.8)).

The officer must give notice that he intends to carry out an enquiry (notice of enquiry) within whichever of the following periods is appropriate:

(*a*) in the case of a return delivered on or before the filing date (i.e. the date on or before which the return must be delivered — see 54.2 above), the twelve months after the filing date (the twelve months beginning with that date as regards returns for 2000/01 and earlier years);

(*b*) in the case of a return delivered after the filing date, the period ending with the 'quarter day' next following the first anniversary of the delivery date;

(*c*) in the case of a return amended by the taxpayer under 54.6 above, the period ending with the 'quarter day' next following the first anniversary of the date of amendment.

For these purposes, the '*quarter days*' are 31 January, 30 April etc. A return cannot be enquired into more than once, except in consequence of an amendment (or further amendment). If notice under (*c*) above is given at a time when the deadline in (*a*) or (*b*) above, as the case may be, has expired or after a previous enquiry into the return has been completed, the enquiry is limited to matters affected by the amendment.

[*TMA 1970, s 9A; FA 1994, ss 180, 199(2); FA 1996, Sch 19 para 2; FA 2001, s 88, Sch 29 para 4; FA 2004, Sch 5 para 1; FA 2005, s 88(1)*].

The 'giving' of notice under *TMA 1970, s 9A* is effected not when the notice is issued or posted but at the time it would be received in the ordinary course of post (generally taken to be four working days for second class mail) or, if proved, the time of actual receipt (*Holly and another v Inspector of Taxes 1999 (Sp C 225), [2000] SSCD 50*, and see also *Wing Hung Lai v Bale (Sp C 203), [1999] SSCD 238*). HMRC now accept this to be the case; for their views on the implications for 1996/97 enquiry notices issued shortly before the 30 January 1999 deadline, see Revenue 'Working Together' Bulletin April 2000 p 8.

In *R (oao Spring Salmon and Seafood Ltd) v CIR CS, [2004] STC 444* it was held that, under the corporation tax self-assessment enquiry powers of *FA 1998, Sch 18 para 24*, a notice of enquiry need not be in writing. Furthermore, it need not be sent to a company's registered office but is valid if sent to a company's place of business.

54.9 **Conduct of enquiry.** A Code of Practice (COP 11 for individuals etc., COP 14 for companies, or in certain simple cases a short, single-page version of whichever is relevant) will be issued at the start of every enquiry. This sets out the rules under which enquiries are made into returns and explains how taxpayers can expect HMRC to conduct enquiries. It describes what HMRC do when they receive a return and how they select cases for enquiry, how they open and carry out enquiries, and what happens if they find something wrong.

HMRC have also published an Enquiry Manual as part of their series of internal guidance manuals (see 30.2 HMRC EXPLANATORY PUBLICATIONS) and, as an extended introduction to the material on operational aspects of the enquiry regime covered in the manual, a special edition of their Tax Bulletin (Special Edition 2, August 1997). The following points are selected from the Bulletin.

- Early submission of a tax return will not increase the likelihood of selection for enquiry.
- HMRC do not have to give reasons for opening an enquiry — and they *will not do so*.
- Enquiries may be full enquiries or 'aspect enquiries'. An aspect enquiry will fall short of an in-depth examination of the return (though it may develop into one), but will instead concentrate on one or more aspects of it.
- Greater emphasis than before is placed on examination of underlying records. HMRC will make an informal request for information before, if necessary, using their powers under *TMA 1970, s 19A* (see 54.10 below).
- Where penalties are being sought, HMRC will aim to conclude the enquiry by means of a contract settlement (as was the case with pre-self-assessment investigations — see 23.12 FRAUDULENT OR NEGLIGENT CONDUCT) rather than issue a closure notice under *TMA 1970, s 28A* (see 54.11 below).

In March 2002, the Revenue published a framework within which enquiries will be worked and to which professional advisers will be encouraged to adhere. Particular topics covered are the opening enquiry letter, requests for and conduct of interviews and meetings, and requests for non-business bank and building society accounts (plus credit/charge/store card details). (Revenue 'Working Together' Bulletin March 2002 pp 1–6).

Where an enquiry remains open beyond the period during which notice of intention to enquire had to be given (see above) and solely because of an unagreed valuation for capital gains tax purposes, HMRC will not take advantage of the open enquiry to raise further enquiries into matters unrelated to the valuation or the CGT computation except in circumstances where a 'discovery' (see 5.2 ASSESSMENTS) could in any case have been made if the enquiry had been completed (HMRC Statement of Practice 1/99).

See also HMRC Pamphlet IR 160 (Inland Revenue Enquiries under Self-Assessment).

54.10 **Power to call for documents.** At the same time as giving notice of enquiry under 54.8 above to any person, or at any subsequent time, an HMRC officer may by notice in writing require that person, within a specified period of at least 30 days, to produce to the officer such documents (as are in the person's possession or power) and such accounts or particulars as the officer may reasonably require to check the validity of the return (or, where applicable, the amendment to the return). Copies of documents may be produced but the officer has power to call for originals, and may himself take copies of, or make extracts from, any document produced. A person is not obliged under these provisions to produce documents etc. relating to the conduct of any pending appeal by him or any pending referral (see 54.13 below) to which he is a party. There is provision for a person to appeal, within 30 days of the giving of the notice, against any requirement imposed by a notice as above. [*TMA 1970, s 19A; FA 1994, ss 187, 199(2)(3); FA 1996, Sch 22 para 2; FA 1998, s 117, Sch 19 para 7; FA 2001, s 88, Sch 29 para 21*].

The minimum 30 days notice required from HMRC begins with the date of receipt of the *section 19A* notice by the taxpayer (*Self-assessed v Inspector of Taxes (Sp C 207), [1999] SSCD 253*). HMRC have altered their practice to comply with this ruling, but consider they are entitled still to make use of information previously obtained where insufficient notice was given (Revenue 'Working Together' Bulletin April 2000 p 8).

For a case in which the taxpayer failed in an attempt to limit the documentation to be supplied, see *Mother v Inspector of Taxes (Sp C 211), [1999] SSCD 279*. 'Documents' are not limited to those covered by *TMA 1970, s 12B* (records to be kept — see 54.7 above) and in particular may include a balance sheet where none has previously been prepared (*Accountant v Inspector of Taxes (Sp C 258), [2000] SSCD 522*).

The provisions of *TMA 1970, s 19A* 'override the contractual duty of confidence owed by a solicitor to his clients', and 'the rule of legal professional privilege is excluded because it is not expressly preserved by *section 19A*' (*Guyer v Walton (Sp C 274), [2001] SSCD 75*). See also Revenue Tax Bulletin April 2000 pp 743–746. However, in *R (oao Morgan Grenfell & Co Ltd) v Special Commr HL, [2002] STC 786*, the HL quashed a notice under *TMA 1970, s 20(1)* (see 23.8(*a*) FRAUDULENT OR NEGLIGENT CONDUCT) on the grounds that the inspector was not entitled to require delivery of documents subject to legal professional privilege (of the person under enquiry), a fundamental human right not expressly overridden by that *subsection*; HMRC accept that the same reasoning applies as regards their power under *section 19A* (Revenue Tax Bulletin December 2002 p 993).

The fact that a taxpayer has already supplied documents to HMRC in the course of a working families tax credit enquiry does not prevent HMRC from including those documents in a notice under *TMA 1970, s 19A* (*Low v HMRC Sp C 2005 (Sp C 510), [2006] SSCD 21*).

See 48.11 PENALTIES as regards penalties for non-compliance.

54.11 **Completion of enquiry.** An enquiry is completed when an HMRC officer gives the taxpayer notice (closure notice) that he has completed his enquiries and states his conclusions. The closure notice takes effect when it is issued and must either make the necessary amendments to the return to give effect to the stated conclusions or state that no amendment of the return is required. Before the enquiry is complete, the taxpayer may apply to the Commissioners for a direction requiring HMRC to give closure notice within a specified period, such application to be heard and determined in the same way as an appeal. The Commissioners must give the direction unless satisfied that there are reasonable grounds for not giving closure notice within a specified period. These provisions apply to enquiries commenced (i.e. where notice of enquiry has been given) on or after 11 May 2001 or in progress at that date. Largely similar provisions applied previously (and see also 54.12 below). [*TMA 1970, s 28A; FA 1994, s 188; FA 1996, Sch 19 paras 2, 4(1)(2); FA 2001, s 88, Sch 29 para 8*].

For enquiries completed before 11 May 2001, the *date* of completion was the day the taxpayer *received* the closure notice (Revenue Tax Bulletin August 2000 p 769).

See 4.1 APPEALS for right of appeal against any conclusion stated or amendment made by a closure notice.

Where an enquiry is to be concluded by means of a contract settlement (see 23.12 FRAUDULENT OR NEGLIGENT CONDUCT) HMRC do not normally issue a closure notice. A notice will be issued only if the taxpayer or agent insist. (HMRC Enquiry Manual EM 6001).

54.12 **Amendments of returns where enquiries made.** As from 11 May 2001, if a return is amended by the taxpayer under 54.6 above while an enquiry into it is in progress (i.e. during the inclusive period between notice of enquiry and closure notice), the amendment does not restrict the scope of the enquiry but may itself be taken into account in the enquiry. The amendment does not take effect to alter the tax payable until the enquiry is completed and closure notice is issued (see 54.11 above). It may then be taken into account separately or, if the officer so states in the closure notice, in arriving at the amendments contained in the notice. It does not take effect if the officer concludes in the closure notice that the amendment is incorrect. [*TMA 1970, s 9B; FA 2001, s 88, Sch 29 para 4(1)*]. Before 11 May 2001, no amendment could be made by a taxpayer to a return while an enquiry was in progress. [*TMA 1970, s 9(5); FA 1994, ss 179, 199; FA 2001, s 88, Sch 29 para 2(1)*].

If in his opinion there is otherwise likely to be a loss of tax to the Crown, an officer may amend a self-assessment contained in the return while an enquiry is still in progress. If the enquiry is itself limited to an amendment to the return (see 54.8 above), the officer's power in this respect is limited accordingly. [*TMA 1970, s 9C, s 28A(2) as previously enacted; FA 1994, ss 188, 199; FA 2001, s 88, Sch 29 para 4(1)*].

For enquiries completed before 11 May 2001, a set procedure applied for amending a self-assessment following completion of an enquiry into the return. This is in part replaced by the procedure at 54.11 above and in part rendered unnecessary by the rules above on taxpayer amendments to returns during an enquiry. The earlier procedure is as follows.

The taxpayer is given 30 days beginning with the date of completion of the officer's enquiries to amend his self-assessment in accordance with the officer's conclusions. Where the enquiry was into a return rather than an amendment, and the return was made before the expiry of twelve months beginning with the due date for delivery (see 54.2 above), the taxpayer also has this 30-day period to amend his self-assessment in accordance with any amendments to the return which he has notified to the officer. The officer then has a further 30 days in which to amend the self-assessment himself. In both cases, the date of *receipt* of the amendment determines whether or not the 30-day limit is met (Revenue Tax Bulletin August 2000 pp 769, 770). [*TMA 1970, s 28A(3)(4) as previously enacted; FA 1994, ss 188, 199; FA 1996, Sch 19 para 4(1)*].

54.13 **Referral of questions during enquiry.** For enquiries commenced (i.e. where notice of enquiry has been given) on or after 11 May 2001 or in progress at that date, provisions are introduced to enable specific contentious points to be litigated while the enquiry is still open, instead of waiting until it is completed.

At any time whilst the enquiry is in progress (i.e. during the inclusive period between notice of enquiry as in 54.8 above and closure notice as in 54.11 above), any one or more questions arising out of it may be referred, jointly by the taxpayer and an HMRC officer and by written notice, to the Special Commissioners for their determination. More than one notice of referral may be given in relation to the enquiry. Either party may withdraw a notice of referral before the first hearing, by giving written notice to the other party and to the Special Commissioners. Until the questions referred have been finally determined (or the referral withdrawn), no closure notice may be given or applied for in relation to the enquiry. The Lord Chancellor is given power to make regulations by statutory instrument to govern the operation of the referral process. See now *SI 2001 No 4024* which, after 30 January 2002 and with appropriate modifications, applies to referrals the provisions of *TMA 1970, s 56A* (appeals to the High Court etc.) and *s 58* (proceedings in NI) at 4.25 APPEALS. Specified pre-existing regulations and regulatory powers relating to appeals are adapted so as also to relate to referrals.

The determination of the question(s) by the Special Commissioners is binding on both parties in the same way, and to the same extent, as a decision on a preliminary issue in an appeal. HMRC must take account of it in concluding their enquiry. Following completion of the enquiry, the question concerned may not be reopened on appeal except to the extent (if any) that it could have been reopened had it been determined on appeal following the enquiry rather than on referral during the enquiry.

[*TMA 1970, ss 28ZA–28ZE; FA 2001, s 88, Sch 29 para 6*].

54.14 DETERMINATION OF TAX WHERE NO RETURN DELIVERED

Where a notice has been given under *TMA 1970, s 8* or *s 8A* (notice requiring an individual or trustee to deliver a return — see 54.2 above) for 1996/97 and subsequent years of assessment and the return is not delivered by the due date (the filing date), an HMRC officer may make a determination of the amounts of taxable income, capital gains and income tax payable which, to the best of his information and belief, he estimates for the year of assessment. The officer must serve notice of the determination on the person concerned. Tax is payable as if the determination were a self-assessment, with no right of appeal. No determination may be made after the expiry of five years beginning with the filing date.

A determination is automatically superseded by any self-assessment made (whether by the taxpayer or HMRC), based on information contained in a return. Such self-assessment must be made within the five years beginning with the filing date or, if later, within twelve months beginning with the date of the determination. Any tax payable or repayable as a result of the supersession is deemed to have fallen due for payment or repayment on the normal due date, usually 31 January following the tax year (see 56.5 SELF-ASSESSMENT). Any recovery proceedings commenced (restricted for proceedings commenced before 11 May 2001 to those commenced by a Revenue officer) before the making of such a self-assessment may be continued in respect of so much of the tax charged by the self-assessment as is due and payable and has not been paid.

[*TMA 1970, ss 28C, 59B(5A); FA 1994, ss 190, 199(2)(3); FA 1996, s 125; FA 2001, s 88, Sch 29 para 17(1)(3)*].

54.15 PARTNERSHIP RETURNS

The following provisions apply for 1996/97 and subsequent years of assessment and, where relevant, for company accounting periods ending on or after 1 July 1999 (see 13.2 COMPANIES).

Any partner may be required by notice to complete and deliver a return of the partnership profits (a partnership return) together with accounts, statements etc. The return must include the names, addresses and tax references of all persons (including companies) who were partners during the period specified in the notice and such other information as may reasonably be required by the notice, which may include information relating to disposals of partnership property and to acquisitions (see 54.2 above). The general requirements are similar to those for personal returns under *TMA 1970, s 8* (see 54.2 above). The notice will specify the period (the relevant period — normally a period of account of the partnership) to be covered by the return and the date by which the return should be delivered (the filing date). For a partnership including at least one individual, the filing date will be no earlier than 31 January following the year of assessment concerned (normally that in which the period of account ends). For a partnership including at least one company, the filing date will be no earlier than the first anniversary of the end of the relevant period. In both cases, the filing date will be deferred until, at the earliest, the last day of the three-month period beginning with the date of the notice, if this is a later date than that given above.

Where the partner responsible for dealing with the return ceases to be available, a successor may be nominated for this purpose by a majority of the persons (or their personal representatives) who were partners at any time in the period covered by the return. A nomination (or revocation of a nomination) does not have effect until notified to HMRC. Failing a nomination, a successor will be determined according to rules on the return form or will be nominated by HMRC.

[*TMA 1970, s 12AA; FA 1994, ss 184, 199(2)(3); FA 1995, s 103(7), s 104(6), s 115(4); FA 1996, s 121(6)(7), s 123(1)–(4); FA 1998, s 117, Sch 19 para 3; FA 2001, s 88, Sch 29 para 18; ITTOIA 2005, Sch 1 para 363*].

See 48.3 PENALTIES re penalties for non-compliance. For the capital gains tax position as regards partnership transactions, see 46 PARTNERSHIPS.

54.16 **Partnership statements.** Each partnership return must include a statement (a partnership statement) showing, in respect of the period covered by the return and (if that period is not a single period of account) each period of account ending within that period,

- the amount of the partnership income or loss from each source,
- the amount of each charge on partnership income,
- the amounts of tax deducted at source from or tax credits on partnership income,
- the amount of consideration for each disposal of partnership property,

and each partner's share of each of those amounts. [*TMA 1970, s 12AB(1)(5); ICTA 1988, s 832(1); FA 1994, ss 185, 199(2); FA 1995, s 103(7), s 104(7)(8); FA 1996, s 123(5); FA 2001, s 88, Sch 29 para 19; FA 2002, s 103(1), Sch 40 Pt 3(16)*].

Where a company carries on a trade etc. in partnership the company tax return (see 54.18 below) for any period must include amounts in respect of the company's share of any income, loss, consideration, tax credit or charge stated in any relevant statement falling to be made by the partnership for a period which includes, or includes any part of, the period in respect of which the return is required. [*FA 1998, s 117, Sch 18 para 12*]. In the case of an individual carrying on a trade etc. in partnership, a return under *TMA 1970, s 8* (see 54.2 above) must include each amount, which according to any 'relevant partnership statement' is his share of any income, loss, tax, credit or charge for the period covered by the statement. A '*relevant partnership statement*' is a statement falling to be made, as respects the partnership, under the above provisions for a period which includes, or includes any part of, the year of assessment or its basis period. [*TMA 1970, s 8(1B)(1C); FA 1994, s 178(1), s 199(2); FA 1995, s 103(7), s 104(2)*].

Amendments to partnership returns. Provisions similar to those in 54.6 above apply as regards amendments and corrections to partnership returns. Where a partnership return is so amended or corrected (and the correction is not rejected by the taxpayer), the partners' returns will be amended by HMRC accordingly, by notice to each partner concerned. [*TMA 1970, s 12AB(2)–(5), ss 12ABA, 12ABB; FA 1994, ss 185, 199(2); FA 1996, s 123(6); FA 1998, s 117, Sch 19 para 4; FA 2001, s 88, Sch 29 para 3; ITTOIA 2005, Sch 1 para 364*].

54.17 **Enquiries into returns.** Provisions similar to those at 54.8 above apply as regards enquiries into a partnership return. The notice of enquiry may be given to a successor (as defined) of the person who made the return (see 54.15 above). The giving of such notice is deemed to include the giving of notice under *TMA 1970, s 9A* (see 54.8 above) (or, where applicable, the equivalent corporation tax provision of *FA 1998, Sch 18 para 24*) to each partner affected. [*TMA 1970, ss 12AC, 118(1)(3); FA 1994, ss 186, 196, 199(2)(3), Sch 19 para 34, Sch 26 Pt V; FA 1996, s 123(7), Sch 19 para 2; FA 1998, s 117, Sch 19 para 5; FA 2001, s 88, Sch 29 para 5*]. HMRC's power to call for documents at 54.10 above also applies here.

Similar provisions to those at 54.11–54.13 above apply in the case of an enquiry into a partnership return. However, there is no equivalent provision to *TMA 1970, s 9C* in 54.12 above (amendment by HMRC while enquiry in progress). Where a partnership return is amended under the relevant provisions in 54.11, 54.12 above, HMRC will, by notice, make any necessary consequential amendments to the partners' returns (including those of company partners). [*TMA 1970, ss 12AD, 28ZA–28ZE, 28B; FA 1994, ss 189, 199(2)(3); FA 1996, Sch 19 paras 2, 5(1); FA 2001, s 88, Sch 29 paras 5(1), 6, 9*].

54.18 COMPANY TAX RETURNS

Notification of coming within charge to corporation tax. A company must give notice to HMRC of the beginning of its first accounting period and of the beginning of any subsequent accounting period that does not immediately follow the end of a previous accounting period (i.e. the first accounting period following a period of dormancy). This requirement applies in respect of accounting periods beginning on or after 22 July 2004. The notice must be given in writing to an HMRC officer not later than three months after the beginning of the accounting period. It must state when the accounting period began and include the following information:

- the company's name, registered number, registered office and principal place of business;
- the nature of the business carried on;
- the date to which accounts are to be drawn up;
- the full name and home address of each of the directors;
- if the company has taken over a business, the name and address of that former business and the name and address of the person from whom it was acquired;
- the name of any parent company and its registered office; and
- if the company then has any PAYE obligations, the date on which those obligations first arose.

Penalties under *TMA 1970, s 98* (see 48.15 PENALTIES) apply for failure to meet this requirement, but a company which has a reasonable excuse for failing to give the required notice is not regarded as failing to comply until the excuse ceases and, after the excuse ceases, is not so regarded if the notice is given without unreasonable delay. The requirement does not apply to unincorporated associations or partnerships. [*FA 2004, s 55; SI 2004 No 2502*].

Notification of chargeability. A company chargeable to corporation tax for any accounting period which has neither made a return of its profits for that period nor received a notice requiring such a return (see below) must give notice of its chargeability to

HMRC within 12 months after the end of that accounting period. [*TMA 1970, s 10(1); FA 1988, s 121; FA 1998, s 117, Sch 18 para 2, Sch 19 para 2*]. See 48.1 PENALTIES regarding failure to meet the requirement.

Self-assessment returns. Corporation tax self-assessment applies to accounting periods ending on or after 1 July 1999. If so required by notice, a company must make a return of such information, relevant to its corporation tax liabilities, as is required under the notice. Supporting accounts, statements and reports may also be required, although the accounts required of companies resident in the UK throughout the period to which the return relates ('*the return period*'), and required to prepare accounts under the *Companies Act 1985* (or NI equivalent) for any period consisting of or including the return period, are only those it is so required to prepare. A notice requiring a return *may* require details of chargeable assets acquired, with certain specified exceptions.

The return must include a declaration to the effect that, to the best of the knowledge of the person making it, it is correct and complete. *TMA 1970, s 108(1)* requires that person to be '*the proper officer of the company*' (i.e. the secretary of a corporate body, except where a liquidator (or, where a company enters administration on or after 15 September 2003, an administrator) has been appointed when the latter is the proper officer, or the treasurer of a non-corporate body) or, except where a liquidator has been appointed, any authorised person.

Similar self-assessment provisions as in 54.5, 54.6 above apply, except that a company does not have the option of requiring HMRC to compute the tax liability.

[*FA 1998, s 117, Sch 18 paras 3, 7, 8, 11, 13, 15, 16; SI 2001 No 3629, Art 103*].

The return must be made by the later of

(*a*) twelve months after the end of the period to which it relates,

(*b*) twelve months after the end of the period for which the company makes up accounts ('*period of account*') in which falls the last day of the accounting period to which it relates (except that periods of account in excess of 18 months are treated as ending after 18 months for this purpose), and

(*c*) three months after service of the notice requiring the return.

If the period specified by the notice for the making of a return ('*the specified period*') is not an accounting period of the company, but the company is within the charge to corporation tax for some part of the specified period, the notice is to be taken as referring to all company accounting period(s) ending in or at the end of the specified period. If there is no such accounting period, but there is a part of the specified period which does not fall within an accounting period, the notice is to be treated as requiring a return for that part of the period. Otherwise, the notice is of no effect, and the company is not required to make any return pursuant to it. For the determination of a company's accounting period, see Tolley's Corporation Tax under Accounting Periods. See also 54.16 above where a company carries on a trade in partnership

[*ICTA 1988, s 832(1); FA 1998, s 117, Sch 18 paras 5, 14; FA 2002, s 103(1)(6), s 141, Sch 40 Pt 3(16)*].

In the absence of a return, HMRC have power to determine the corporation tax liability. [*FA 1998, s 117, Sch 18 paras 36–40*].

An enquiry regime analogous to that in 54.8–54.13 above applies to companies. Note that in addition to the matters mentioned at 54.8 above in respect of which an enquiry can be made, for corporation tax purposes an enquiry can also extend to consideration of whether to give the taxpayer a notice under *F(No 2)A 2005, s 24* or *s 26* (tax arbitrage — see 3.26 ANTI-AVOIDANCE) or *TCGA 1992, s 184G* or *s 184H* (avoidance utilising losses — see 13.5 COMPANIES). [*FA 1998, Sch 18 paras 24–35; FA 2001, Sch 29 paras 7, 38(4); FA 2004, Sch 5 para 10; F(No 2)A 2005, s 29(1); FA 2006, s 71(2)*].

Simplified procedures for group relief can be operated under *SI 1999 No 2975* as amended. SP 5/01 explains the criteria HMRC adopt in exercising their power to admit claims to loss relief, capital allowances and group relief which are made outside the normal time limits.

Similar record-keeping requirements as in 54.7 above apply to companies under corporation tax self-assessment. A company must preserve its records for six years from the end of its return period. [*FA 1998, s 117, Sch 18 paras 21–23; FA 2004, Sch 12 para 16*]. For an article on the record-keeping requirements for corporation tax purposes, see Revenue Tax Bulletin October 1998 pp 587–589.

Corporation tax self-assessment is covered in full in Tolley's Corporation Tax.

From 10 January 2000, HMRC offer post-transaction (pre-return) valuation checks to companies (in relation to their chargeable gains) as they do to individuals (see 54.4 above). Form CG34 should be sent to the company's tax office together with full information about the transactions to which the valuations relate and any relevant computations. (Revenue Press Release 10 January 2000).

Where an enquiry remains open beyond the period during which notice of intention to enquire had to be given and solely because of an unagreed valuation for chargeable gains purposes, HMRC will not take advantage of the open enquiry to raise further enquiries into matters unrelated to the valuation or the chargeable gains computation except in circumstances where a 'discovery' (see 5.2 ASSESSMENTS) could in any case have been made if the enquiry had been completed (HMRC Statement of Practice 1/02).

Returns will also incorporate claims for group relief, capital allowances, payments of tax credits and repayments of income tax deducted from payments received. Such claims are covered in detail in Tolley's Corporation Tax under the appropriate subject heading.

See 48.4 PENALTIES regarding non-compliance. See also 13.18 COMPANIES regarding the application of these provisions where a company ceases to be UK-resident in the course of the formation of an SE and where an SE becomes non-UK resident.

Returns under Pay and File. For accounting periods ending after 30 September 1993 and before 1 July 1999 companies were required to make returns and pay corporation tax under the 'Pay and File' system. The requirements and deadlines relating to the making of returns under Pay and File were broadly the same as under self-assessment, except, of course, that the company was not required to include a self-assessment in the return. Details of assets acquired on which chargeable gains or allowable losses may arise could also be required under *TMA 1970, s 12(2)(3)* (see 54.2 above). Amendments to returns had to be in such form, and accompanied by such information etc., as the Revenue required. [*TMA 1970, s 11; F(No 2)A 1987, s 82; FA 1990, s 91; SI 1992 No 3066*].

Useful background information on the making of returns under Pay and File is contained in a Revenue consultative document published on 28 February 1991 and a Revenue Press Release of 7 December 1992. Reference should also be made to Revenue Pamphlets IR 126 and 128 and Revenue Tax Bulletin August 1993 pp 83–85. In addition, three substantive Revenue Statements of Practice have been issued as follows (all dated 8 October 1993).

- Revenue Statement of Practice 9/93 (now obsolete under self-assessment) explained that, under Pay and File, an amended corporation tax return for an accounting period could be made by completing and delivering to the inspector an official corporation tax amended return form. Alternatively, a form or letter could be substituted provided that it gave clear and sufficient information about the change, showed the tax effect of the change and included a declaration that the information was correct and complete.
- Revenue Statement of Practice 10/93 (replaced by the statutory provisions mentioned above for accounting periods ending on or after 1 July 1999) provided an opportunity for companies to use a simpler procedure under Pay and File for making

or revising claims to group relief, and for giving and receiving notices of consent to surrender relief, where a group of companies was dealt with mainly in one tax district.

- Revenue Statement of Practice 11/93 (see now SP 5/01 under self-assessment) explained the criteria the Revenue adopted in exercising their power to admit claims to capital allowances or group relief which were made outside the normal time limit.

HMRC give post-transaction rulings on corporation tax matters (see 54.4 above) but, in the case of a Pay and File return, did so only *before* the return was filed.

54.19 EUROPEAN ECONOMIC INTEREST GROUPINGS

A European Economic Interest Grouping (see 45.15 OVERSEAS MATTERS) registered in the UK or having an establishment there must make and deliver a return (through its manager or the individual representative of its manager) containing such information and accompanied by such accounts and statements as may be required by a notice given by the inspector. In the case of any other grouping, a return is required from any member of it resident in the UK, or, if none is, from any member. [*TMA 1970, s 12A; FA 1990, Sch 11 paras 2, 5; FA 1994, ss 196, 199, Sch 19 para 2*]. See 48.5 PENALTIES as regards non-compliance.

54.20 HOTELS AND BOARDING HOUSES

Certain details of all lodgers and persons resident in any dwelling-house, hostel, hotel, etc. must be given by the proprietor, if required by notice from the inspector. [*TMA 1970, s 14*].

54.21 ISSUING HOUSES, STOCKBROKERS, AUCTIONEERS, NOMINEE SHAREHOLDERS ETC.

Certain details of assets dealt with from issuing houses, members of stock exchanges (but not jobbers or market makers), commodity clearing houses and auctioneers must be given together with a return of the parties to the transaction, if required by notice from the inspector. [*TMA 1970, s 25; FA 1986, s 63, Sch 18 para 8; FA 1989, s 123(1)(c)(2)*]. HMRC have published spreadsheet templates for making returns under this provision on their website (www.hmrc.gov.uk).

In respect of shares, securities and loan capital registered in the name of a person, that person must, if required by notice from the inspector issued for the purpose of obtaining particulars of chargeable gains, state whether he is the beneficial owner thereof or otherwise provide the name and address of the persons on whose behalf he acts as nominee. [*TMA 1970, s 26*].

54.22 ELECTRONIC FILING OF RETURNS

Individuals and companies can file tax returns electronically via HMRC's website.

After 20 August 2001, agents are authorised to file individual clients' personal tax returns over the internet subject to certain conditions (see 28.8 HMRC: ADMINISTRATION). Initially, this facility was available in addition to the electronic lodgement service described below and did not displace it until 31 March 2006. After 4 March 2003, agents are likewise authorised to file companies' tax returns over the internet, subject to similar conditions.

Electronic lodgement service. Subject to the conditions detailed below, returns under *TMA 1970, s 8, s 8A* and *s 12AA* (see 54.2, 54.15 above) may be lodged using HMRC's electronic lodgement service at any time before 31 March 2006. Any supporting documentation (including accounts, statements or reports) required to be delivered with a return may similarly be lodged electronically if the return is so lodged (or may instead be delivered by the last day for submission of the return).

The normal powers and rights applicable in relation to returns etc. delivered by post are applied to information transmitted electronically. A properly made and authenticated hard copy (see (*c*) below) is treated in any proceedings as if it were the return or other document in question, but if no such copy is shown to have been made, a hard copy certified by an HMRC officer to be a true copy of the information transmitted is so treated instead.

There are four conditions for electronic lodgement.

(*a*) A person seeking approval must be given notice of the grant or refusal of approval, which may be granted for the transmission of information on the person's own behalf or on behalf of another person or persons. Approval may be withdrawn by notice from a given date, and any notice refusing or withdrawing approval must state the grounds. An appeal against refusal or withdrawal must be made within 30 days of such notice having been given, and lies to the Special Commissioners, who may grant approval from a specified date if they consider the refusal or withdrawal to have been unreasonable in all the circumstances.

(*b*) The transmission must comply with any requirements notified by HMRC to the person making it, including in particular any relating to the hardware or software to be used.

(*c*) The transmission must signify, in an approved manner, that a hard copy was made under arrangements designed to ensure that the information contained in it is the information in fact transmitted.

(*d*) The information transmitted must be accepted under a procedure selected by HMRC for this purpose, which may in particular consist of or include the use of specifically designed software.

As regards (*c*) above, the hard copy must have been authenticated by the person required to make the return:

(i) in the case of a return required by notice, by endorsement with a declaration that it is to the best of his knowledge correct and complete; or

(ii) otherwise by signature.

[*TMA 1970, s 115A, Sch 3A; FA 1995, s 153, Sch 28; FA 1998, s 117, Sch 19 para 43; FA 1999, s 133(3)(4); ITEPA 2003, Sch 6 para 143; ITTOIA 2005, Sch 1 para 384*].

HMRC Statement of Practice 1/97 describes how HMRC operates the electronic lodgement service and covers the detailed requirements.

The electronic lodgement service is to be withdrawn with effect from 31 March 2006. (HMRC News Release 29 September 2005).

54.23 REASONABLE EXCUSE (GENERAL)

It is generally provided for the purposes of *TMA 1970* that a person is deemed not to have failed to do anything required to be done where there was a reasonable excuse for the failure and, if the excuse ceased, provided that the failure was remedied without unreasonable delay after the excuse had ceased. Similarly, a person is deemed not to have failed to do anything required to be done within a limited time if he did it within such further time as HMRC, or the Commissioners or officer concerned, may have allowed. [*TMA 1970, s 118(2); F(No 2)A 1987, s 94*]. Consideration of what constitutes a reasonable excuse was made in *R v Sevenoaks Commrs, ex p. Thorne*; *Thorne v Sevenoaks Commrs & CIR, Ch D & QB 1989, 62 TC 341*.

Under self-assessment of income tax and capital gains tax, there are separate 'reasonable excuse' let-outs as regards penalties for late returns (see 48.2 PENALTIES) and surcharges for late payment of tax (see 37.4 INTEREST AND SURCHARGES ON UNPAID TAX).

55 Rollover Relief—Replacement of Business Assets

Cross-references. See 8.12 ASSETS HELD ON 31 MARCH 1982 for 50% relief on rolled over gains relating to an asset acquired before 31 March 1982; 20.34 EMPLOYEE SHARE SCHEMES for application of rollover relief in relation to certain disposals to employee share ownership trusts; 24.2 FURNISHED HOLIDAY ACCOMMODATION for application of rollover relief to such accommodation in the UK; 27.11 GROUPS OF COMPANIES for rollover of degrouping charge where a company leaves a group; 33 HOLD-OVER RELIEFS generally; 38.11 and 38.12 LAND for rollover relief on compulsory purchase of land and exchanges of joint interests in land (including milk and potato quotas in certain cases) respectively; 44.2 OFFSHORE SETTLEMENTS for disapplication of rollover relief where trustees cease to be UK-resident or liable to UK tax; 45.3, 45.12 and 45.14 OVERSEAS MATTERS for restriction on rollover relief in certain cases; 61.17 TAPER RELIEF.

Simon's Direct Tax Service. See Division C3.3.

55.1 NATURE OF RELIEF

If the consideration which a person carrying on a trade obtains for the disposal of, or of his interest in, assets ('*the old assets*') used, and used only, for the purposes of the trade throughout the 'period of ownership' (which, for disposals after 5 April 1988, excludes any period before 31 March 1982) is applied by him, within a specified period — see below, in acquiring other assets, or an interest in other assets ('*the new assets*') which on the acquisition are taken into use, and used only, for the purposes of the trade, and the old assets and the new assets are within the classes of assets listed in *TCGA 1992, s 155* (see 55.3 below), then the person carrying on the trade is, on making a claim as respects the consideration which has been so applied, treated for the purposes of *TCGA 1992*

(*a*) as if the consideration for the disposal of, or of the interest in, the old assets were (if otherwise of a greater amount or value) of such an amount as would secure that on the disposal neither a gain nor a loss accrues to him, and

(*b*) as if the amount or value of the consideration for the acquisition of, or of the interest in, the new assets were reduced by the excess of the amount or value of the actual consideration for the disposal of, or of the interest in, the old assets over the amount of the consideration which he is treated as receiving under (*a*) above.

The treatment in (*a*) and (*b*) above does not affect the treatment for the purposes of *TCGA 1992* of the other party to the transaction involving the old assets, or of the other party to the transaction involving the new assets. [*TCGA 1992, s 152*(*1*)(*9*)].

The relief given under (*a*) and (*b*) above applies in relation to a person who, either successively or at the same time, carries on two or more trades as if both or all of them were a single trade. [*TCGA 1992, s 152*(*8*)]. For consideration of this provision and activities other than trades, see 55.4 below.

Partial relief is available in certain circumstances. See 55.6 below.

Where (*a*) above applies to exclude a gain which, in consequence of *TCGA 1992, Sch 2* (ASSETS HELD ON 6 APRIL 1965 (7)), is not all chargeable gain, the amount of the reduction to be made under (*b*) above is the amount of the chargeable gain, and not the whole amount of the gain. [*TCGA 1992, s 152*(*2*)].

The old assets must actually be used for the trade in question, any original intention for such use being ignored. Relief was refused where land was purchased on which it was proposed to build a factory for use in the taxpayer's trade but was sold without the factory being built (*Temperley v Visibell Ltd Ch D 1973, 49 TC 129*). Subject to concessionary treatment as in 55.3 below, the new assets must be taken into trading use immediately on acquisition, and not as soon as reasonably practicable after acquisition, again any original intention to attempt at immediate use being ignored (*Campbell Connelly & Co. Ltd v*

Barnett CA 1993,66 TC 380). In this case the taxpayer company (C Ltd) claimed relief in respect of a gain accruing from the sale in 1984 of its trading premises, the sale taking place shortly after C Ltd had become a wholly-owned subsidiary of M Ltd. C Ltd and M Ltd henceforth traded from premises already occupied by M Ltd. In January 1986 C Ltd acquired the freehold interest in a new property but it was not until September 1986 that C Ltd and M Ltd were able to occupy and use it for trading purposes because the property was subject to both a headlease and an underlease to two third parties. Occupation and use was only possible after M Ltd had acquired in September 1986 the underlease for a capital sum. During the period from January 1986 to September 1986 C Ltd received rent from the lessee whilst from September 1986 to November 1987, when the headlease was itself surrendered, M Ltd paid a slightly higher rent to the lessee. Although it had been the intention to acquire the freehold interest in, and vacant possession of, the new property at the same time, relief was refused in relation to C Ltd's claim to roll over the gain into the freehold interest acquisition. It was held that the words 'which on the acquisition are taken into use, and used only for the purposes of the trade' referred to the acquisition of the assets (and *not* to an interest in them) mentioned in the phrase which occurs earlier in *TCGA 1992, s 152*(*1*) 'If the consideration ... is applied by him in acquiring other assets'. In addition *TCGA 1992, s 152* only covered one acquisition by one person; it could not be extended to cover two different interests in the same asset being acquired by two different legal persons at different times. *Obiter dicta* of Knox J in the Ch D suggests that the time of acquisition and disposal for the purposes of *TCGA 1992, s 152* is the date of transfer or conveyance, and not the date of the contract (cf. *TCGA 1992, s 28* at 15.3 COMPUTATION OF GAINS AND LOSSES).

For convenience, references in the rest of this chapter to the acquisition or disposal of an asset can be taken to include references to the acquisition or disposal of an interest in that asset except where the context requires otherwise.

HMRC has indicated that in its view the wording of *TCGA 1992, s 152*(*1*), which states that 'if the consideration which a person ... obtains for the disposal of ... assets ... is applied by him in acquiring other assets', simply requires the taxpayer to reinvest an amount equal to the proceeds received. It also sees no reason why in principle relief should not be available where the acquisition consideration is satisfied by the issue of shares by a company (Institute of Taxation TIR/11/91, 1991 STI 1097). See also HMRC Capital Gains Manual CG 60770–60773.

In *Watton v Tippett CA 1997, 69 TC 491*, a trader made a part disposal of some business premises and attempted unsuccessfully to roll over the gain against the previous acquisition of the part of those premises still retained. It was held that the premises had been acquired as, and until the part disposal continued to be, a single asset, and that the acquisition cost could not be divided between the part of the premises sold and the part retained and treated as having been given for two separate assets.

HMRC have confirmed the relief is available where assets are exchanged (CCAB Statement TR 508 9 June 1983). Where land or other assets used for the purposes of a trade carried on in partnership are partitioned by the partners, the asset acquired is treated as a newly acquired asset provided the partnership is dissolved immediately thereafter (HMRC Extra-Statutory Concession D23).

Relief is denied if the acquisition of the new assets was made wholly or partly for the purpose of realising a gain from their subsequent disposal. [*TCGA 1992, s 152*(*5*)].

Time limit for replacement of assets. The acquisition of the new assets must take place **within one year before, or three years after**, the disposal of the old assets, though HMRC may allow further time where the trader can show that there was a firm intention to acquire new assets within the time limit but was prevented from doing so by circumstances outside his control (Revenue Tax Bulletin November 1991 p 5 and see HMRC Capital Gains Manual CG 60640). HMRC seems prepared to extend this treatment even though an asset qualifying for rollover relief is acquired within the statutory time limit but which the taxpayer chooses not to make the subject of a claim (Institute of Taxation TIR/11/91, 1991 STI 1097). It is sufficient if an unconditional contract for acquisition is entered into within the specified periods; but adjustments are made, without time limit, if the contract is not completed. [*TCGA 1992, s 152(3)(4)*]. See also the *obiter dicta* of Knox J in *Campbell Connelly & Co. Ltd v Barnett* above. The non-exercise of HMRC's statutory discretion to extend the time limit may be challenged by judicial review but cannot be reviewed by the Appeal Commissioners (*Steibelt v Paling Ch D 1999, 71 TC 376*). Such a challenge was unsuccessful in *R (oao Barnett) v CIR QB 2003, [2004] STC 763*.

For corporation tax purposes, where the disposal occurs after 31 March 2002 and is of an asset within Classes 4 to 7 at 55.3 below, the acquisition of the new asset must be made before that date (and within 12 months before the disposal). [*FA 2002, s 84(1), Sch 29 para 132(1)*].

Example

L Ltd carries on a vehicle repair business. In December 2003 it sells a workshop for £90,000 net of costs. The workshop had cost £45,000 inclusive in April 1995. A new workshop is purchased for £144,000 (including incidental costs of acquisition) in January 2004 and is sold for £168,000 in January 2007.

Indexation factors:	April 1995 to December 2003	0.232
	January 2004 to January 2007 (estimated)	0.050

L Ltd claims rollover of the chargeable gain.

	£
Allowable cost of original workshop	45,000
Indexation allowance £45,000 × 0.232	10,440
	55,440
Actual disposal consideration	90,000
Chargeable gain rolled over	£34,560
Cost of new workshop	144,000
Deduct amount rolled over	34,560
Deemed allowable cost	£109,440
Disposal consideration, replacement workshop	168,000
Allowable cost	109,440
Unindexed gain	58,560
Indexation allowance £109,440 × 0.050	5,472
Chargeable gain	£53,088

Trade carried on by individual's personal company etc. In relation to a case where

(i) the person disposing of the old assets and acquiring the new assets is an individual, and

(ii) the trade or trades in question are carried on not by that individual but by a company, which, both at the time of disposal and at the time of the acquisition referred to in (i) above, is his 'personal company',

any reference in *TCGA 1992, ss 152–156* (see 55.3, 55.4, 55.6 and 55.7 below) to the person carrying on the trade includes a reference to that individual.

For this purpose, an individual's '*personal company*' is a company the voting rights in which are 'exercisable', as to not less than 5%, by that individual. ('*Exercisable*' means capable of being exercised, whether in fact exercised (*Hepworth v Smith Ch D 1981, 54 TC 396*).) [*TCGA 1992, s 157; FA 1993, s 87, Sch 7 para 1, Sch 23 Pt III; FA 1998, s 140(3)(6)*].

In correspondence the Revenue expressed the view that *TCGA 1992, s 157* does not extend to the acquisition of a new asset for use by a subsidiary of a personal company carrying on a trade or trades where the old asset was disposed of by the personal company (and vice versa). Assets must be disposed of and acquired by the individual for use by the same personal company (although relief in relation to use by such a company may not be precluded if contemporaneous use is made by one or more subsidiaries of the company) and the provisions of *TCGA 1992, s 175(1)* (see 55.5 below) do not extend to the position of regarding all companies within a group as one taxable entity. The payment of rent to the individual by the company concerned for the use of property will not debar relief under *TCGA 1992, s 157*. In addition, the occupancy test of *TCGA 1992, s 155* for land and buildings (see 55.3 below) may be met by either the individual or the company concerned, so the existence of a lease or tenancy (whether or not with consideration passing), or consideration passing, will not prevent relief under *TCGA 1992, s 157*. The position here should be contrasted with a claim under *TCGA 1992, s 158(1)(c)* by an employee to which HMRC Statement of Practice 5/86 applies (see 55.4 below). It is not possible to 'mix' claims under *TCGA 1992, s 157* and *s 158(1)(c)* (e.g. the disposal of land owned by an individual but occupied and used exclusively for the purposes of a trade carried on by his personal company cannot be rolled over into his acquisition of land which is to be occupied and used by him exclusively as an employee of the same company). See also Institute of Taxation TIR/11/91, 1991 STI 1097, for confirmation of these points.

It is worth noting that *TCGA 1992, s 157* does not require the individual to be a full-time working officer or employee of the company.

Partnerships. Relief is available to the owner of assets let to a trading or professional partnership of which he is a member, provided they are used for the purposes of the partnership's trade or profession (HMRC Statement of Practice D11). See also 46.9 PARTNERSHIPS as regards disposals by partners and 46.16 as regards mergers of partnerships and 55.5 below for partnerships involving a member of a group of companies.

Interaction with other provisions. Any provision which fixes the amount of consideration deemed to be given for the acquisition or disposal of assets is applied before operating the relief. [*TCGA 1992, s 152(10)*]. However, the relief is not affected by the fact that the new asset may have attracted a grant such as to reduce the expenditure allowable on a subsequent disposal — see 17.5(*c*) DISPOSAL (*Wardhaugh v Penrith Rugby Union Football Club Ch D 2002, 74 TC 499*). The Revenue was asked its views on whether relief could be claimed where a gain arises on a simple gift and where an asset is appropriated from 'capital' to 'trading stock' within *TCGA 1992, s 161(1)*. It replied that in its view gifts of assets were within *TCGA 1992, s 152(10)*. Where the other conditions for relief were met, relief will be available based on the amount of the consideration deemed to have been received under other provisions of *TCGA 1992*. It does not, however, regard relief as available where there is a deemed disposal and reacquisition of the same asset (Institute of Taxation TIR/11/91, 1991 STI 1097).

Although relief under *TCGA 1992, s 162* (**transfer of a business to a company** — see 33.10 HOLD-OVER RELIEFS) is mandatory (unless disapplied by election — see 33.11), a valid claim for rollover relief takes precedence (HMRC Capital Gains Manual CG 61560–61562).

Where rollover relief is claimed, the gain to be deducted from the cost of the new asset is the *untapered* gain arising on the old asset; **taper relief** is given only on gains left in charge after all reliefs other than the annual exempt amount have been taken into account. Taper relief operates on the ultimate disposal of the new asset by reference only to the period for which that asset has been held. See 61.17 TAPER RELIEF. Where the period of ownership of the new asset is insufficient to obtain the maximum taper relief, the claim for rollover relief can be found to have increased, perhaps substantially, the overall tax liability on the disposals of the old and the new asset. The potential loss of taper relief should not be ignored when considering a rollover relief claim. (Note that taper relief is not available to companies.)

For the application of the relief to **groups of companies**, see 55.5 below. Rollover relief is not available where one company makes a disposal and an *associated* company makes an acquisition (*Joseph Carter & Sons Ltd v Baird; Wear Ironmongers & Sons Ltd v Baird Ch D 1998, 72 TC 303*). Where, after 31 March 2002, a company ceases to be a member of a group such that a gain (a 'degrouping charge') arises under *TCGA 1992, s 179* (see 27.9 GROUPS OF COMPANIES) on a deemed sale and reacquisition of an asset, and the asset is a qualifying asset for rollover relief purposes, the company may claim rollover relief if it acquires a new qualifying asset. The rollover relief rules described in this chapter apply in modified form. Where the degrouping charge arises under *TCGA 1992, s 179(5)–(8)*, rollover relief is available only where the 'relevant time' (see 27.9(2)(i) GROUPS OF COMPANIES) falls after 31 March 2002. See 27.1 GROUPS OF COMPANIES.

Where a member of a **limited liability partnership (LLP)** (see 46.19 PARTNERSHIPS) has rolled over a gain into an LLP asset and, at a later time but before any disposal of the asset, the transparency treatment afforded by *TCGA 1992, s 59A(1)* ceases to apply to the LLP (for example, by virtue of its going into liquidation), a chargeable gain equal to the amount rolled over is treated as accruing to the member immediately before that later time. Similarly, a postponed gain under 55.7 below (where the LLP asset is a depreciating asset) is brought back into charge immediately before that time. [*TCGA 1992, s 156A; LLPA 2000, s 10(4), s 19*]. In the absence of such a rule, the rolled over or postponed gain would have fallen out of charge as a result of the tax treatment of an LLP in liquidation. A previously rolled over gain accruing as above does not attract taper relief (Revenue Tax Bulletin December 2000 p 804) (presumably because no disposal is deemed to take place).

Corporation tax: intangible fixed assets. Following the introduction of the intangible assets regime in *FA 2002* (see 14.13 COMPANIES—CORPORATE FINANCE AND INTANGIBLES), the rollover relief provisions are amended *for corporation tax purposes only*.

Disposals. A gain on the disposal on or after 1 April 2002 of an asset that is both an intangible fixed asset and within one of the classes of qualifying assets at 55.3 below may qualify for rollover relief only where the acquisition of the new asset occurs before that date (and within twelve months before the disposal). As a result, rollover relief normally ceases to be available for disposals of intangible fixed assets after 31 March 2003, whether or not the asset falls within the intangible assets regime. After that time, the acquisition of the new asset cannot be made both within twelve months prior to the disposal and before 1 April 2002.

Disposals of intangible fixed assets (whether or not within one of the classes of qualifying assets) excluded from the intangible assets regime by virtue of its commencement rules do, however, qualify for relief under the intangible fixed assets rollover relief provisions of *FA 2002, Sch 29 Pt 7,* which are modified for this purpose by *FA 2002, Sch 29 para 130*. Where relief is claimed in such a case, then in calculating the chargeable gain on the disposal of the asset, the consideration is treated as reduced by the amount available for relief. Note that intangible asset rollover relief is an entirely separate relief from the capital gains relief; for details of the relief see Tolley's Corporation Tax under Intangible Assets.

A gain on a disposal on or after 1 April 2002 but before 1 April 2003 of an intangible fixed asset which is also within one of the classes of qualifying assets may potentially qualify for both capital gains rollover relief (where a new asset is acquired before 1 April 2002) and intangible asset rollover relief (where a 'new asset' is acquired on or after 1 April 2002) (provided in either case that all the appropriate conditions are met). Where this is the case, the company may claim relief under either set of provisions or partly under one and partly under the other.

Acquisitions. Assets within Classes 4 to 7 and 9 at 55.3 below and acquired on or after 1 April 2002 are not qualifying assets for corporation tax purposes if they are 'chargeable intangible assets'. An asset is a '*chargeable intangible asset*' if a gain on its realisation would give rise to a credit falling to be brought into account under the intangible assets regime.

[*FA 2002, Sch 29 paras 130, 132, 137(1); F(No 2)A 2005, s 41(4)*].

55.2 CLAIMS FOR RELIEF

A claim for rollover relief relates to both a disposal and an acquisition of assets and so cannot be made until both have occurred (but see below re provisional claims under self-assessment).

Form of claim. A claim for relief must be made in writing and must specify:

- the identity of the claimant;
- the assets which have been disposed of;
- the date of disposal of each of those assets;
- the consideration received for the disposal of each of those assets;
- the assets which have been acquired;
- the date of acquisition of each of those assets or the dates on which unconditional contracts for the acquisition of each of those assets were entered into;
- the consideration given for each of those assets; and
- the amount of the consideration received for the disposal of each of the specified assets which has been applied in the acquisition of each replacement asset.

(HMRC Helpsheet IR 290).

HMRC Helpsheet IR 290 contains a form on which an individual may make a claim. The completed form can be attached to the Capital Gains supplementary pages of the self-assessment tax return.

Where the disposal is made by one group company and the acquisition made by another (see 55.5 below), a rollover relief claim made on or after 29 November 1994 must be made by both companies. [*TCGA 1992, s 175(2A); FA 1995, s 48(1)(3)(4)*].

Time limits for claims. As no time limit is specified, the general time limits in *TMA 1970, s 43* and *FA 1998, Sch 18 para 55* apply (see 12.5 CLAIMS). For rollover relief purposes, the period of time allowed for the making of a claim (six years for companies and approximately five years ten months for other persons from 1996/97) begins with the *later* of

- the end of the year of assessment or company accounting period in which the disposal takes place, and
- the end of the year of assessment or company accounting period in which the new assets are acquired.

A claim to relief is not prevented by the finality of an assessment on chargeable gains.

(HMRC Capital Gains Manual CG 60600).

Provisional claims. It would have been anomalous to require a taxpayer, who intended to roll over gains, to pay the tax on those gains under self-assessment and thus reduce the funds available to invest in the new assets. Provisional rollover relief claims were therefore made possible for disposals after 5 April 1996 for capital gains tax purposes and in company accounting periods ending on or after 1 July 1999 (the commencement date for corporation tax self-assessment — see 13.2 COMPANIES) as outlined below.

The claimant may make a declaration in his tax return for a tax year or company accounting period in which he has made a disposal of qualifying assets (see 55.3 below) that the whole or a specified part of the consideration will be invested, within the requisite time limits (see 55.1 above), in qualifying assets which on acquisition will be taken into use exclusively for the purposes of the trade. The form in HMRC Helpsheet IR 290 referred to above may be used by an individual for this purpose. As long as the declaration continues to have effect, the same consequences ensue as if both an acquisition and a valid rollover relief claim had been made. The declaration ceases to have effect on the day, and to the extent that, it is withdrawn or is superseded by a valid claim, if either occurs before the 'relevant day'. It otherwise ceases to have effect on the relevant day itself. On its ceasing to have effect, all necessary adjustments will be made to the claimant's tax position, even if they would otherwise be out of time.

The '*relevant day*' means

- in relation to capital gains tax, the third anniversary of 31 January following the tax year of disposal, e.g. 31 January 2003 for disposals in 1998/99; and
- in relation to corporation tax, the fourth anniversary of the last day of the accounting period of disposal.

[*TCGA 1992, s 153A; FA 1996, s 121*(*8*), *s 141*(*2*)].

To the extent that a provisional claim is withdrawn or lapses, interest on unpaid tax is chargeable as if no such claim had been made. There is nothing to prevent a valid claim subsequently being made if new assets are acquired either within the normal time limit or within such further time as may be allowed by HMRC (see 55.1 above). However, no application for postponement of tax will be allowed (HMRC Capital Gains Manual CG 60707).

55.3 QUALIFYING ASSETS

Subject to the overriding requirement of use for the purposes of a trade as specified in *TCGA 1992, s 152*(*1*) in 55.1 above, qualifying assets, for the purpose of relief under that provision, are divided into the classes listed below (the Treasury having power to specify additional classes). Both the old and the new assets must fall within these classes though not necessarily within the same class. For capital gains tax purposes, and for corporation tax purposes for acquisitions before 1 April 2002, the classes are as follows.

1.

(*a*) Land, buildings (including parts thereof) and any permanent or semi-permanent structures in the nature of buildings, all such assets being occupied (as well as used) only for the purposes of the trade. A lessor of tied premises, within *ICTA 1988, s 98* or *ITTOIA 2005, s 19*, is treated as occupying (as well as using) those premises for the purposes of the trade (to the extent that the conditions of *ICTA 1988, s 98*(*1*) or *ITTOIA 2005, s 19*(*1*) are met in relation to the premises). See also 55.4 below where the trade involves dealing in or developing land, etc.

(*b*) Fixed plant or machinery (see *Williams v Evans Ch D, 1982, 59 TC 509*, and Tolley's Practical Tax 1983 p 211) which does not form part of a building or of a permanent or semi-permanent structure in the nature of a building.

2. Ships, aircraft and hovercraft.
3. Satellites, space stations and spacecraft (including launch vehicles).

4. Goodwill. See HMRC Capital Gains Manual CG 68000–68976 for consideration of what constitutes goodwill. Note, however, that in *Balloon Promotions Ltd v Wilson (Sp C 524) [2006] SSCD 167* the Special Commissioner questioned the applicability of HMRC's approach to goodwill. HMRC have subsequently published their view on the implications of this case in HMRC Tax Bulletin June 2006 pp 1291, 1292. See also *Kirby v Thorn EMI plc CA 1987, 60 TC 519*.

5.

   (*a*) 'Milk quotas'; i.e. rights to sell dairy produce without liability to pay milk levy, or to deliver dairy produce without liability to pay a milk levy contribution (see also 6.9 ASSETS).

   (*b*) 'Potato quotas'; i.e. rights to produce potatoes without liability to pay more than the ordinary contribution to the Potato Marketing Board's fund.

6. 'Ewe and suckler cow premium quotas', i.e. rights in respect of any ewes or suckler cows to receive payments by way of any subsidy entitlement to which is determined by reference to limits contained in a European Community instrument.

7. Fish quota, i.e. an allocation of quota to catch fish stocks, which derives from the Total Allowable Catches set in pursuance of specified European Community instruments (see also below). This class qualifies where the old asset is fish quota and the disposal date is after 28 March 1999, where the new asset is fish quota and the acquisition date is after 28 March 1999 and where both old and new assets are fish quota and both disposal and acquisition take place after 28 March 1999. See also below for earlier concessional treatment.

8.

   (*a*) Syndicate rights of an individual (i.e. non-corporate) underwriting member of Lloyd's (see 64.5 UNDERWRITERS AT LLOYD'S) acquired or disposed of after 5 April 1999.

   (*b*) Syndicate rights of an individual (i.e. non-corporate) underwriting member of Lloyd's held through a Members' Agent Pooling Arrangement (MAPA) and treated by *FA 1999, s 82* as a single asset (see 64.6 UNDERWRITERS AT LLOYD'S). Assets under this heading qualify where acquired or disposed of after 5 April 1999: (it is thought that post-5 April 1999 enhancement expenditure must also qualify — by virtue of ESC D22 (see below)).

9. Payment entitlements under the single payment scheme, i.e. the scheme of income support for farmers under Title III of EC Council Regulation 1782/2003. This class qualifies where the old asset is a payment entitlement and the disposal date is after 21 March 2005, where the new asset is a payment entitlement and the acquisition date is after 21 March 2005 and where both old and new assets are payment entitlements and both disposal and acquisition take place after 21 March 2005.

For corporation tax purposes, Classes 4 to 7 and 9 do not apply as regards the acquisition on or after 1 April 2002 of new assets that are 'chargeable intangible assets' for the purposes of the intangible fixed assets regime (see 55.1 above).

[*TCGA 1992, s 155, s 156(1)(4); FA 1993, s 86; FA 1998, s 41(2); FA 1999, s 84; FA 2002, Sch 29 para 132(5); ITTOIA 2005, Sch 1 para 439; F(No 2)A 2005, s 41(4)(5); SI 1999 No 564; SI 2005 No 409*].

As regards disposals and acquisitions thereof before 1 July 1999, except as affects the determination of any Commissioners or the judgement of any court made or given before 14 May 1987, a UK oil licence under *Petroleum Act 1998, Pt I* (or earlier corresponding legislation) or under *Petroleum (Production) Act (Northern Ireland) 1964* was not (and was assumed never to have been) an asset falling within any of the classes above. [*TCGA 1992, s 193; Petroleum Act 1998, Sch 4 para 32; FA 1999, s 103*].

Fish quota (see Class 7 above) are amounts of various types of fish that are allocated by the EU to the UK and sub-allocated to UK fishermen according to rules prescribed by the Fisheries Departments. They are one of a number of items that may be involved in a disposal of a fishing vessel (and may be disposed of separately in certain circumstances). The vessel itself is a qualifying asset for rollover relief. A fishing vessel licence and a 'track record' (being the amount of particular stocks of fish caught in previous years) are separate chargeable assets; each is treated as constituting goodwill and thus eligible for rollover relief in its own right. Fish quota is also a separate chargeable asset but is not regarded as goodwill. However, prior to the addition of fish quota to the above classes of qualifying assets, the Revenue concession treated sales of fish quota as qualifying for rollover relief on a similar basis as a licence and track record. (Revenue Press Release 2 March 1999).

See HMRC Tax Bulletin, Special Edition June 2005 as regards the single payment scheme (see Class 9 above).

Where a building is rebuilt after having been destroyed by fire, gains on other assets may be rolled over into the cost of rebuilding (subject to any claim made under *TCGA 1992, s 23* in respect of insurance proceeds, see 9.2 and 9.3 CAPITAL SUMS DERIVED FROM ASSETS and CCAB Statement TR 508 9 June 1983). Capital expenditure to enhance the value of other assets already held is treated for rollover relief purposes as incurred in *acquiring* other assets provided the other assets are used only for the purposes of the trade or, on completion of the enhancement work, the assets are immediately taken into use and used only for the purposes of the trade. An extension to this treatment was announced in a Revenue Press Release of 12 May 1995 so that it is also applied for the purposes of *TCGA 1992, Sch 4* (deferred charges on gains before 31 March 1982; see 8.12 ASSETS HELD ON 31 MARCH 1982) (HMRC Extra-Statutory Concession D22). Similar treatment is given where a *further* interest is acquired in another asset which is already in use for the purposes of the trade (HMRC Extra-Statutory Concession D25). An asset which is repurchased for purely commercial reasons after having been sold will be treated as the 'new asset' for the purposes of the relief (HMRC Extra-Statutory Concession D16). (See 3.25 ANTI-AVOIDANCE for the charge arising where concessions involving deferral of gains are abused.)

Where a new asset is not, on acquisition, immediately taken into use for the purposes of a trade it will nevertheless qualify for relief by concession provided

(*a*) the owner proposes to incur capital expenditure for the purpose of enhancing its value;

(*b*) any work arising from such capital expenditure begins as soon as possible after acquisition, and is completed within a reasonable time;

(*c*) on completion of the work the asset is taken into use for the purpose of the trade and for no other purpose; and

(*d*) the asset is not let or used for any non-trading purpose in the period between acquisition and the time it is taken into use for the purposes of the trade.

Where a person acquires land with a building on it, or with the intention to construct a building on it, the land is treated as qualifying for the above concession provided that the building itself qualifies for relief whether under the above concession or otherwise and provided that the land is not let or used for any non-trading purpose between its acquisition and the time that both it and the building are taken into use for the purposes of the trade.

(HMRC Extra-Statutory Concession D24).

HMRC have stated that, in some circumstances, relief would not be denied, where the asset is not ready to be taken into use immediately, solely on the grounds that it was not brought into use as soon as acquired, provided that all reasonable steps are taken to make it ready and that it is then brought into use without unnecessary delay (Revenue Tax Bulletin November 1991 p 5). It is not clear to what extent, if any, this last statement extends the scope of ESC D24. It is difficult too, to reconcile both treatments with the Revenue's arguments in the case of *Campbell Connelly & Co Ltd v Barnett CA 1993, 66 TC 380* mentioned at 55.1 above. In *Steibelt v Paling Ch D 1999, 71 TC 376*, Sir Richard Scott V-C commented that on the facts of the case the taxpayer had failed to comply with condition (*b*) above.

Buildings and structures (but not normally including dwelling-houses) provided by a trader for the welfare of employees, though qualifying for industrial building allowances are technically outside the scope of rollover relief, not being used exclusively for the purposes of the trade. Similar observations can be made in respect of agricultural buildings (which may include dwellings) and agricultural building allowances. It is understood that HMRC may not always, in practice, take this point. (In *Anderton v Lamb Ch D 1980, 55 TC 1*, it was held that houses occupied by farm employees were not *occupied for the purposes of the business,* and, therefore, were not qualifying assets. The taxpayer appealed to the CA where the appeal was stayed on agreed terms: see *1982 STI 179*.)

Acquisitions of fixed plant and machinery under hire purchase agreements will qualify for relief as regards the capital element but lease purchase agreements are not considered by HMRC to be equivalent to the rights which accrue under the former so that acquisitions under the latter will not be eligible for relief (Tolley's Practical Tax 1986 p 136).

Provided relief would be due on the disposal of the underlying land which is the subject of the grant of an option, HMRC are prepared to ignore the separate disposal treatment of *TCGA 1992, s 144(1)* so that any gain arising on the grant of the option can be the subject of a rollover relief claim. HMRC point out that relief will only be obtained if the land continues to be occupied and used for the claimant's trade (Revenue Tax Bulletin, February 1992, p 13). Presumably this treatment applies regardless of whether an option is exercised (such an event bringing into play the single transaction treatment of *TCGA 1992, s 144(2)*). HMRC make no comment whether the cost of the option and the exercise price under it could frank a rollover relief claim where the grantee of an option subsequently exercises it (such an event bringing into play the single transaction treatment of *TCGA 1992, s 144(3)*) and brings the underlying land into trading use and occupation immediately on exercise. For options generally, see 6.7 ASSETS.

A 1995 assignment, for a capital sum, of the right to receive rental income for a fixed period (a 'rent factoring' transaction) was held to be a part disposal of the property in question, producing a chargeable gain, in this case eligible for rollover relief (*CIR v John Lewis Properties plc CA, [2003] STC 117*), but note that, under subsequent legislation, rent factoring receipts are now chargeable as income (see Tolley's Corporation Tax under Property Income).

Rollover relief is not available to the extent that the new asset is used wholly and exclusively for the purposes of a shipping company's activities within the tonnage tax regime (see 22.16 EXEMPTIONS AND RELIEFS). If a new asset begins to be used for such purposes after rollover relief has been given, the rolled over gain becomes a chargeable gain, which is, however, deferred until the new asset is disposed of. [*FA 2000, Sch 22 para 67*].

55.4 QUALIFYING UNDERTAKINGS

TCGA 1992, ss 152–157 (see 55.1 and 55.3 above and 55.6 and 55.7 below) apply with necessary modifications in relation to the following activities as they apply in relation to a trade.

(*a*) The discharge of the functions of a public authority.

(*b*) The occupation of woodlands where the woodlands are managed by the occupier on a commercial basis and with a view to the realisation of profits.

(*c*) A profession, vocation, office or employment.

(*d*) Such of the activities of a body of persons whose activities are carried on otherwise than for profit and are wholly or mainly directed to the protection or promotion of the interests of its members in the carrying on of their trade or profession as are so directed.

(*e*) The activities of an unincorporated association or other body chargeable to corporation tax, being a body not established for profit whose activities are wholly or mainly carried on otherwise than for profit, but in the case of assets within 1.(*a*) in 55.3 above only if they are both occupied and used by the body, and in the case of other assets only if they are used by the body.

'Trade', 'profession', 'vocation', 'office' and 'employment' have the same meanings as in the *Income Tax Acts* for the purposes of the above and *TCGA 1992, ss 152–157*, but not so as to apply the provisions of the *Income Tax Acts* as to the circumstances in which, on a change in the persons carrying on a trade, a trade is to be regarded as discontinued, or as set up and commenced. These provisions and *TCGA 1992, ss 152–157* are construed as one. [*TCGA 1992, s 158*]. '*Trade*' includes every trade, manufacture, adventure or concern in the nature of trade, but the other expressions are not directly defined. [*ICTA 1988, s 832(1)*]. For discussion of the meaning of 'trade' for rollover relief purposes, see *CIR v Richmond and Jones (Re Loquitur Ltd) Ch D 2003, 75 TC 77*.

Commercial letting of 'furnished holiday accommodation' in the UK is treated as a trade for the purposes of the relief. See 24 FURNISHED HOLIDAY ACCOMMODATION.

HMRC have indicated that both parties to a share farming agreement may be considered to be carrying on a farming business for taxation purposes provided that the landowner takes an active part in the venture, e.g. by concerning himself with details of farming policy, etc. (1992 STI 189 reproducing statement of 19 December 1991 issued by Country Landowners Association).

If land or a building is owned by an employee or office-holder but is made available to the employer for general use in his trade, the employee etc. may nonetheless satisfy the occupation test of *TCGA 1992, s 155* (see 55.3 above at 1.) provided the employer does not make any payment (or give other consideration) for his use of the property nor otherwise occupy it under a lease or tenancy. The qualifying use of assets by an employee etc. for the purposes of *TCGA 1992, s 152* (see 55.1 above) will include any use or operation of those assets by him, in the course of performing the duties of his employment or office, as directed by the employer (HMRC Statement of Practice 5/86). The practice may be compared with the relief available under *TCGA 1992, s 157* (see 55.1 above) where the trade is carried on by the individual's personal company, although in relation to SP 5/86 consideration passing or the existence of a lease or tenancy would deny relief but would not under *TCGA 1992, s 157*. Where relief under *TCGA 1992, s 157* is unavailable (e.g. where the individual as a partner disposes of an asset which has been used by the partnership and acquires an asset which is to be used by his personal company or, possibly, where different such companies are involved) then, provided the factors mentioned previously are absent, relief may still be claimed (Tolley's Practical Tax 1986 p 183 and subsequent correspondence with the Revenue).

Lessors of tied premises are treated as occupying and using them solely for the purposes of a relevant trade. [*TCGA 1992, s 156(4); ITTOIA 2005, Sch 1 para 439*]. Where the trade is one of dealing in or developing land or of providing services for the occupier of land in which the trader has an interest, the trader's disposal of the land does not qualify for relief. However, this does not apply where a profit on the sale of any land held for the purposes of a trade of dealing in or developing land would not form part of the trading profits. [*TCGA 1992, s 156(1)–(3)*]. However, it appears that HMRC may allow relief on the disposal of a caravan site where the disposer's occupation of that site amounts to the carrying on of a trade, notwithstanding that that trade is one of providing services for the occupier(s). See also 24 FURNISHED HOLIDAY ACCOMMODATION for such accommodation in the UK.

The application of the relief in relation to a person who, either successively or at the same time, carries on two or more trades as if both or all of them were a single trade (see *TCGA 1992, s 152(8)* in 55.1 above) is not further qualified, so that one or all the trades could be situated outside the UK and outside the scope of UK taxation because the taxpayer is neither resident nor ordinarily resident in the UK (see also Tolley's Practical Tax 1981 p 126 but note the restrictions in 44.2 OFFSHORE SETTLEMENTS and 45.3, 45.12 and 45.14 OVERSEAS MATTERS in certain cases and note that 'furnished holiday accommodation' must be in the UK).

Where a trader ceases carrying on one trade and, within three years, commences carrying on another, HMRC will treat the trades as carried on 'successively'. If the disposal or acquisition takes place in the intervening period, relief will be restricted in respect of the period during which the assets disposed of were not used for trade purposes, and will be conditional on the replacement assets not being used or leased for any purpose prior to commencement of the new trade, and on their being taken into use for the purposes of the new trade on its commencement (HMRC Statement of Practice 8/81). HMRC generally has no difficulty in regarding a second or subsequent new trade as the successor trade for the purposes of *TCGA 1992, s 152(8)*. This means relief will be available where a gain arises from the old trade and new assets are acquired in the second or subsequent new trade, provided that the other conditions for the relief are met and the gap between the cessation of the old trade and the commencement of the new trade in question is within the limits of SP 8/81 (Institute of Taxation TIR/11/91, 1991 STI 1097). In *Steibelt v Paling Ch D 1999, 71 TC 376*, a nine-year gap between trades meant that they could not be said to be carried on successively.

55.5 GROUPS OF COMPANIES

Cross-reference. See 27.11 GROUPS OF COMPANIES for rollover of degrouping charge where a company leaves a group.

For the purposes of *TCGA 1992, ss 152–158* (see 55.1–55.4 above and 55.6 and 55.7 below) all the trades carried on by members of a group of companies (within 27.1 GROUPS OF COMPANIES) are, for the purposes of corporation tax on chargeable gains treated as a single trade (unless, for cases where the acquisition of the new assets was before 29 November 1994, it was a case of one member of the group acquiring the new assets from another or disposing of the old assets to another). Where the disposal or the acquisition, or both, occurs on or after 1 April 2000, the change in the residence requirement as regards groups of companies (see 27.1 GROUPS OF COMPANIES) applies in determining whether a company is a member of a group, but the reference above to 'all the trades' does not include any trade carried on by a non-UK resident company otherwise than in the UK through a permanent establishment or, for accounting periods beginning before 1 January 2003, through a branch or agency. [*TCGA 1992, s 175(1)(1A); FA 1995, Sch 29 Pt VIII(4); FA 2000, Sch 29 para 10(1)–(3)(7)(8); FA 2003, s 153(1)(b)(4)*].

TCGA 1992, s 154(2) (see 55.7 below) applies where the company making the claim is a member of a group of companies as if all members of the group for the time being carrying on trades within these provisions (see above) were the same person (and, in accordance with *TCGA 1992, s 175(1)* above, as if all those trades were the same trade) and so that the gain accrues to the member of the group holding the asset concerned on the occurrence of the event mentioned in *TCGA 1992, s 154(2)* (i.e. the earlier of the disposal of the depreciating asset, cessation of its trading use or the expiry of ten years from its acquisition). [*TCGA 1992, s 175(3); FA 2000, Sch 29 para 10(6)*].

Acquisitions as a group member by a 'dual resident investing company' within *ICTA 1988, s 404* are excluded from the treatment given by *TCGA 1992, s 175(1)* above. [*TCGA 1992, s 175(2); FA 1994, s 251(1)(8), Sch 26 Pt VIII*].

In *Campbell Connelly & Co Ltd v Barnett CA 1993, 66 TC 380* (see 55.1 above), an argument that *TCGA 1992, s 175(1)* should be construed such that not only should the trades carried on by members of a group of companies be treated as a single trade and thereby the same trade but that members of a group of companies should be treated as a single person and thereby the same person was rejected. It was pointed out that the wording of *TCGA 1992, s 175(3)* was an instructive contrast to that in *TCGA 1992, s 175(1)*. The words in parentheses at the end of *section 175(1)* 'unless it is a case ... the old assets to another' were described *obiter* by Knox J in the Ch D as 'an anti-avoidance provision to prevent the shuffling of assets within a group of companies to postpone liability to ... tax when a member of a group disposes of an asset outside the group'. Subject to this, one interpretation of *section 175(1)* would allow relief to a group member disposing of an asset outside the group at a gain if that member acquired an asset from another group member provided all other conditions for relief are fulfilled. By virtue of *TCGA 1992, s 171(1)* the acquisition cost to the group member would be limited to the cost to the group plus improvement costs, expenses of transfer (but less any reduction in respect of previous rollover relief claims) and any indexation allowance. This interpretation would not allow a claim for relief where one group member disposes of an asset outside the group and another group member acquires an asset from a third group member. In addition to this, the 'normal' use of *section 175(1)* has been accepted as being to frank the disposal of old assets by one group member outside the group by the acquisition of new assets by another group member from outside the group. However, the Revenue indicated that, if necessary, steps would be taken to ensure that the established practice (see below) in relation to rollover relief and groups of companies would continue whatever the outcome of the *Campbell Connelly* case. This practice allowed 'one trading company in a group to obtain rollover relief even though the replacement asset was acquired by another trading member of the same group'. (Revenue Press Release, 15 September 1992).

Provisions were introduced by *FA 1995* to put into effect the established Revenue practice (see below) in order that rollover relief would apply in the following circumstances:

(*a*) where there is a disposal by a member of a group of companies and an acquisition by another member of the same group and both companies claim rollover relief after 28 November 1994 as if they were the same person (giving effect to part of the Revenue's concessionary practice in Revenue Statement of Practice 8/81, see below); or

(*b*) where a non-trading member of a group makes a disposal or acquisition of assets after 28 November 1994 used only for trading purposes by other members of the same group (giving effect to Revenue Extra-Statutory Concession D30 which applied up to that date, see below).

With regard to (*a*) above, this is deemed always to have had effect.

However, rollover relief will not apply where there is an acquisition of new assets after 28 November 1994 by a member of a group from another member of that group resulting from a no gain/no loss disposal (see 8.7 ASSETS HELD ON 31 MARCH 1982 above).

Where the disposal or the acquisition, or both, occurs on or after 1 April 2000, then, in consequence of the change in the residence requirement in 27.1 GROUPS OF COMPANIES, the following conditions must be met for (*a*) above to apply:

- *either* the company making the disposal is UK-resident at the time of disposal *or* the assets in question are 'chargeable assets' in relation to that company immediately before that time; *and*
- *either* the acquiring company is UK-resident at the time of acquisition *or* the assets are 'chargeable assets' in relation to that company immediately after that time.

For these purposes, an asset is a '*chargeable asset*' in relation to a company at a particular time if, on a disposal by that company at that time, any gain would be a chargeable gain and would be within the charge to corporation tax by virtue of *TCGA 1992, s 10* or *s 10B* (non-UK resident company trading in the UK through a permanent establishment (previously a branch or agency) — see 45.3 OVERSEAS MATTERS).

[*TCGA 1992, s 175(2A)–(2C); FA 1995, s 48(1)(3)–(5); FA 1996, s 121(8), s 141(3); FA 2000, Sch 29 para 10(4)(5)(7)(8); FA 2003, Sch 27 para 2*].

The remaining part of this section on groups should be read in the light of the *FA 1995* provisions.

The disposing company must be a member of a group at the time of disposal, and the acquiring company must be a member of the same group at the time of acquisition, but HMRC does not insist that either company be a member of that group at the time of the transaction carried out by the other (HMRC Statement of Practice D19). Where this applies in a case where one member of a group makes the disposal and a second the acquisition, it may happen that the disposal takes place after the first company has ceased to trade, or the acquisition takes place before the second company commences trading. Relief will then be restricted in respect of the period during which the assets disposed of were not used for business purposes, and will be conditional on the replacement assets not being used or leased for any purpose prior to the second company's commencing trading, and being taken into use for the purposes of the trade on its commencement (HMRC Statement of Practice SP 8/81, and see also 55.4 above). If an asset is sold by a member of a sub-group and a replacement asset is acquired by another member of that sub-group, but in the interval before replacement the sub-group leaves the main group and becomes part of a second main group, HMRC take the view that rollover relief is not available (CCAB Statement TR 508, 9 June 1983).

HMRC have confirmed that where an asset is transferred to another group company prior to disposal outside the group, entitlement to relief depends on its use during the final period of ownership (CCAB Statement TR 425, 3 April 1981).

If a qualifying unincorporated association uses property owned by a company in which at least 90% of the shares are held by or on behalf of the association or its members, rollover relief can be claimed subject to the usual conditions. (HMRC Extra-Statutory Concession D15). (See 3.25 ANTI-AVOIDANCE for the charge arising where concessions involving deferral of gains are abused.)

See 38.11(*g*) LAND above with regard to rollover relief in cases of compulsory purchase of land.

55.6 PARTIAL RELIEF

A modification of the relief under *TCGA 1992, s 152(1)* (see 55.1 above) is available where not all of the amount or value of the consideration received for the disposal of the old assets is applied in acquiring the new assets. Provided that the part of the disposal consideration *not* applied in acquiring the new assets is less than the amount of the gain (whether all chargeable gain or not; this presumably only applies when *TCGA 1992, Sch 2* is in point for ASSETS HELD ON 6 APRIL 1965 (7)) otherwise accruing on the disposal of the old assets, the person carrying on the trade, on making a claim as respects the consideration applied in acquiring the new assets, is treated for the purposes of *TCGA 1992*

(*a*) as if the gain accruing on the disposal of the old assets were reduced *to* the amount of the said part, and

(*b*) as if the amount or value of the consideration for the acquisition of the new assets were reduced *by* the amount by which the gain is reduced in (*a*) above.

If not all the gain accruing on the disposal of the old assets is a chargeable gain, (*a*) above applies but with a proportionate reduction in the amount of the chargeable gain, and in (*b*) above the reduction in consideration is the amount by which the chargeable gain is proportionately reduced. Neither (*a*) nor (*b*) above affects the treatment for the purposes of *TCGA 1992* of the other party to the transaction involving the old assets, or of the other party to the transaction involving the new assets. *TCGA 1992, s 152(3)–(11)* (see 55.1 above and also see further below) are applied to the above provisions. [*TCGA 1992, s 153*].

If, over the period of ownership (excluding any period before 31 March 1982) or any substantial part of the period of ownership, part of a building or structure is, and part is not, used for the purposes of a trade, *TCGA 1992, s 152* applies as if the part so used, with any land occupied for purposes ancillary to the occupation and use of that part of the building or structure, were a separate asset, and subject to any necessary apportionments of consideration for an acquisition or disposal of the building or structure and other land. [*TCGA 1992, s 152(6)(9)*].

See Revenue Tax Bulletin, October 1994, p 166 for further discussion on partial relief.

If the old assets were not used for the purposes of the trade throughout the period of ownership (excluding any period before 31 March 1982) *TCGA 1992, s 152* applies as if a part of the asset representing its use for the purposes of the trade having regard to the time and extent to which it was, and was not, used for those purposes, were a separate asset which had been wholly used for the purposes of the trade, and this treatment applies in relation to that part subject to any necessary apportionment of consideration for an acquisition or disposal of the asset. [*TCGA 1992, s 152(7)(9)*].

Without prejudice to *TCGA 1992, s 52(4)* (just and reasonable apportionments of consideration and expenditure; see 15.7 COMPUTATION OF GAINS AND LOSSES), where consideration is given for the acquisition or disposal of assets some or part of which are assets in relation to which a claim under *TCGA 1992, s 152* applies, and some or part of which are not, the consideration is apportioned in such manner as is just and reasonable. [*TCGA 1992, s 152(11)*].

Where the taxpayer acquires an undivided share in the new asset which is only partly used for trade purposes, relief is limited to the proportion so used of the individual's undivided share of the asset (*Tod v Mudd Ch D 1986, 60 TC 237*). Vinelott J noted in his judgement that a concession might be in existence as regards *TCGA 1992, s 156(6)(7)(9)(11)* above (although he was not required to consider the point further as it was not argued before him) because those provisions do not seem strictly to prevent relief being denied under *TCGA 1992, s 152(1)* in 55.1 above because the new asset is only partly used for trade purposes. For consideration of the difficulties that arise in such a case, see *Taxation 18 November 1993, p 141*.

Examples

(*a*) In 1995, X purchased a factory for £40,000. It was used and occupied entirely for carrying on his trade until sold for £100,000 in October 2006. In the same month X bought another factory for £120,000 which was immediately used and occupied for carrying on a new trade carried on by him. Assume indexation allowance (computed to April 1998) of £3,200 is available as regards the sale. He claimed rollover relief, computed as follows.

	£
Proceeds of sale of factory 1	100,000
Allowable expenditure on factory 1	40,000
Unindexed gain on sale of factory 1	60,000
Indexation allowance	3,200
Chargeable gain eligible to be rolled over	£56,800

Cost of factory 2	120,000
Rolled-over gain	56,800
Base cost for factory 2 on subsequent disposal	£63,200

Note that a gain does not qualify for taper relief to the extent that it is rolled over. See 61.17 TAPER RELIEF.

(*b*) Facts as in (*a*) above, except factory 2 is bought for £90,000. The part of the £100,000 disposal consideration of factory 1 which is not applied in acquiring factory 2 is £10,000. This is less than the gain otherwise arising on the disposal of factory 1 (£56,800). The gain deemed to arise on the disposal of factory 1 is therefore £10,000 (subject to taper relief). The gain so arising has therefore been reduced by £46,800, with the result that this amount is deducted from the £90,000 consideration given for factory 2, and so producing a base cost of £43,200 on a subsequent disposal.

(*c*) In September 2006, Y purchased a new factory for £100,000, having sold his old one in the same month for £52,000. The original factory had been bought in September 1996 for £20,000 but had only been used for his trade since September 1998. He claimed rollover relief. It is accepted that one-quarter of the new factory is not used for trade purposes. Assume indexation allowance (computed to April 1998) at 17%.

	£
Proceeds of sale of old factory	52,000
Cost of old factory	20,000
Unindexed gain	32,000
Indexation allowance: 17% × £20,000	3,400
Chargeable gain	£28,600

$$\frac{\text{Period of trading use of old asset}}{\text{Period of ownership}} = \frac{8\text{years}}{10\text{ years}}$$

Gain on old asset eligible for relief	
£28,600 × 8/10	£22,880
Cost of qualifying part of new factory	
(3/4 × £100,000)	75,000
Rolled-over gain	22,880
Base cost of qualifying part of new factory	£52,120

The unrelieved gain of £5,720 (£28,600 – £22,880) is brought into charge on the disposal of the old factory, but can be reduced by TAPER RELIEF (61). The base cost of the non-qualifying part of the new factory, treated as separate, is £25,000.

55.7 WASTING ASSETS

For the purpose of relief under *TCGA 1992, ss 152, 153* (see 55.1 and 55.6 above), if the new asset is at the time of acquisition a WASTING ASSET (67) or will become so within ten years beginning at that time, it is known as a '*depreciating asset*'. In such cases, the gain on the disposal of the old asset is not deducted from the acquisition consideration of the new asset, but held over until ten years after the time of acquisition of the new asset, or until the new asset is disposed of, or until the new asset ceases to be used for the trade, whichever is the sooner, upon which event the held-over gain becomes chargeable to capital gains tax; but the held-over gain is not brought into charge under this provision in consequence of an event after 5 April 1988 if its application would be directly attributable to the disposal of an asset before 1 April 1982. [*TCGA 1992, s 154(1)(2)(7), Sch 4 para 4(5)*].

However, if not later than the time when the held-over gain would be brought into charge a further asset is acquired which is not a depreciating asset, the trader may claim relief under *TCGA 1992, s 152* or *s 153* as if it had been acquired within the time limits of *TCGA 1992, s 152(3)* for the application of the proceeds of the disposal of the old asset, the depreciating asset being effectively disregarded. The trader may claim relief if only part of the proceeds can be treated in this way, the balance remaining held over until crystallisation by virtue of one of the events specified. [*TCGA 1992, s 154(4)–(6)*].

A transfer of the new asset or of shares in a company which holds the new asset to an SE does not bring the held-over gain into charge under the above provisions if the transfer is part of the process of merger by which the SE is formed and *TCGA 1992,s 140E* (formation of SE by merger: assets left within UK charge to tax — see 13.18 COMPANIES) applies to that merger. In such circumstances, if the SE holds the new asset it is treated as if it had claimed the rollover relief. If the SE holds shares in the company which holds the new asset, *TCGA 1992, s 175* (see 55.5 above) applies as if the SE's group were the same group as any group of which the company claiming the rollover relief was a member before the formation of the SE. [*TCGA 1992, s 154(2A); F(No 2)A 2005, s 64(3)*].

Where, as part of the process of merger by which an SE is formed in circumstances in which *TCGA 1992, s 140E* applies, the SE becomes a member of a group of which a company which has claimed rollover relief in respect of a wasting asset is a member, *TCGA 1992, s 175* (see 55.5 above) applies for the purposes of determining when the held-over gain is brought into charge as if the group of which the SE is a member were the same group as the group of which the claimant was a member before the formation of the SE. [*TCGA 1992, s 154(2B); F(No 2)A 2005, s 64(3)*].

By concession, where a held-over gain would otherwise be brought into charge on a cessation of trading use due to the trader's death, no charge to tax will arise (HMRC Extra-Statutory Concession D45).

A gain which has been held over under *TCGA 1992, s 154* will crystallise on a disposal even where the disposal concerned is within *TCGA 1992, s 162* (hold-over on a transfer of a business to a company; see 33.10 HOLD-OVER RELIEFS) (Tolley's Practical Tax 1985 p 139).

See 55.1 above for a special rule where the new asset is held by a limited liability partnership at the time of its going into liquidation.

See 61.15 TAPER RELIEF for the application of that relief where a gain is held over under these provisions.

A building constructed on leasehold land where the lease has less than 60 years to run at the time of construction is considered by HMRC to be a depreciating asset. This is despite the treatment in *TCGA 1992, s 155* (see 55.3 above) which treats land and buildings as separate assets (and contrary to the general rule for land as in 38.2 LAND). If, as contemplated by *TCGA 1992, s 155*, an item of fixed plant or machinery has effectively become a part of a building or structure, it will be so treated for rollover relief purposes, with the result that such assets acquired for installation in a building etc. then held freehold or on a lease with more than 60 years to run will not be treated as depreciating assets. Subject to this, because an item of plant and machinery is always to be treated as being a wasting asset (see 67.1 WASTING ASSETS), it will also be treated as a depreciating asset. Deciding whether an item of fixed plant or machinery has become part of a building etc. will normally be done by reference to the size and nature of the item in question, how it is attached to the building and whether damage to the fabric of the building would be caused if the item was removed (Revenue Tax Bulletin May 1993 p 73).

Milk quota (see 6.9 ASSETS) is not regarded by HMRC as a wasting asset (HMRC Capital Gains Manual CG 77940).

Example

In March 2002, a father and son partnership carrying on a car dealing trade sold a freehold showroom for £400,000 realising a chargeable gain (after indexation) of £190,000. On 30 June 2002, the firm purchased for £450,000 the remaining term of a lease due to expire on 30 June 2032 and used the premises as a new showroom. The whole of the gain on the old asset was held over under *TCGA 1992, s 154* on the acquisition of the new asset. In consequence of the father's decision to retire from the business and the resulting need to downsize the operation, the firm assigns the lease for £490,000 on 1 July 2006.

The chargeable gains to be apportioned between the two partners for 2006/07 are as follows

	£	£
Proceeds of assignment		490,000
Cost (see note (*a*))	450,000	
Deduct Wasted $\frac{87.330 - 82.496}{87.330} \times$ £450,000	24,909	425,091
Chargeable gain 2006/07 (see note (*b*))		£64,909
Held-over gain becoming chargeable under *TCGA 1992, s 154(2)(a)* (see note (*b*))		£190,000

Notes to the example

(*a*) The gain is deferred as opposed to being rolled over and does not reduce the cost of the new asset.

(*b*) Each of the partners will be entitled to taper relief on his share of the gain of £64,909 to the extent that it is not reduced by the offset of capital losses. Taper relief on the deferred gain operates by reference to the date of disposal and period of ownership of the old asset. See 61.15 TAPER RELIEF.

56 Self-Assessment

Simon's Direct Tax Service. See Division E1.8.

56.1 INTRODUCTION

Self-assessment for individuals, partnerships and trustees has effect generally for 1996/97 and subsequent years of assessment, although some aspects of the system came into effect earlier and some in 1997/98. The term 'self-assessment' refers to the system whereby the annual tax return includes a self-assessment of the taxpayer's liability for income tax and capital gains tax. Payment of tax is then due automatically, based on the self-assessment. The main body of legislation introducing self-assessment is contained in *Finance Act 1994*, with further provisions in subsequent Finance Acts. As regards corporation tax self-assessment, see 56.2 below.

Two detailed Revenue booklets, SAT 1 'The new current year basis of assessment' and SAT 2 'Self Assessment: the legal framework', both guides for Revenue officers and tax practitioners, were published in August/September 1995. Note that SAT 1 is no longer published, and SAT 2 has been replaced by the Revenue Self Assessment Legal Framework Manual, available on the Revenue's website.

Returns. The return for individuals consists of a basic ten pages to which are attached any supplementary pages relevant to the individual concerned, forming a single 'customised' tax return. The supplementary pages are colour-coded and cover employment, share schemes, self-employment, partnership income, land and property, foreign income, trust income, capital gains and non-residence etc. Each individual should also receive a tax return guide containing explanatory notes relevant to his circumstances. It is the individual's responsibility to obtain any supplementary pages he needs but has not received, which he may do by telephoning an HMRC Orderline, by which means he may also obtain the relevant explanatory notes and/or 'helpsheets' (see 30.4 HMRC EXPLANATORY PUBLICATIONS) on specific topics. Each return sent out is accompanied by a tax calculation guide designed to assist the individual in calculating his tax liability if he chooses to do so. See 54.2–54.6 RETURNS. Partnership returns follow a similar pattern (see 54.15, 54.16 RETURNS).

Returns must normally be filed by 31 January following the year of assessment (see 54.2 RETURNS). Taxpayers who would prefer not to compute their own liabilities do not have to do so providing they file their return early, normally by 30 September following the year of assessment, though this date is of no significance where returns are filed over the internet (see 54.5 RETURNS). Penalties are imposed for late submission of returns, subject to appeal on the grounds of reasonable excuse (see 48.2 PENALTIES). There are provisions for making amendments to returns (see 54.6 RETURNS). The Revenue are given broadly one year from the filing date to give notice of their intention to enquire into the return (see 54.8 RETURNS). A formal procedure is laid down for such enquiries (see 54.8–54.13 RETURNS). If they do not give such notice, the return becomes final and conclusive, subject to any 'error or mistake' claim by the taxpayer (see 12.7 CLAIMS) or 'discovery' assessment by HMRC (see 5.2 ASSESSMENTS). In the event of non-submission of a return, HMRC are able to make a determination of the tax liability; there is no right of appeal but the determination may be superseded upon submission of the return (see 54.14 RETURNS). Capital losses must be quantified on a claim if they are to be allowable (see 40.3 LOSSES).

A different style of return has to be filed by partnerships. This must include a statement of the allocation of partnership income between the partners. See 54.15–54.17 RETURNS.

Payment of tax. Income tax (on all sources of taxable income) for a year of assessment is payable by means of two interim payments of equal amounts, based normally on the liability for the previous year of assessment and due on 31 January in the year of assessment and the following 31 July, and a final balancing payment due on the following 31 January which is also the due date for capital gains tax liability. Taxpayers have the right to reduce their interim payments if they believe their income tax liability will be less than that for the previous year of assessment or to dispense with interim payments if they believe they will have no liability. Interim payments are not in any case required where substantially all of a taxpayer's income is subject to deduction of tax at source, including PAYE, or where the amounts otherwise due are below de minimis limits. See 56.4–56.6 below.

Interest on overdue payments runs from the due date to the date of payment (see 37.1 INTEREST AND SURCHARGES ON UNPAID TAX). There is also a 5% surcharge on any tax unpaid by 28 February following the year of assessment and a further 5% surcharge on any tax unpaid by the following 31 July, such surcharges being subject to appeal on the grounds of reasonable excuse (see 37.4 INTEREST AND SURCHARGES ON UNPAID TAX). Interest on tax overpaid normally runs from the date of payment to the date of repayment (see 36.1 INTEREST ON OVERPAID TAX); the rate of interest is lower than that on overdue tax.

Miscellaneous. There is a statutory requirement for taxpayers to keep records for the purpose of making returns and to preserve such records for specified periods (see 54.7 RETURNS). A formal procedure applies to the making of claims, elections and notices (see 12.2 CLAIMS). For appeals under the self-assessment regime, see 4.1 APPEALS.

56.2 CORPORATION TAX SELF-ASSESSMENT

Similarly, there are provisions extending, for company accounting periods ending on or after an appointed day, the principles of self-assessment to the pre-existing Pay and File system for corporation tax payment and returns. The appointed day for corporation tax self-assessment is 1 July 1999. [*SI 1998 No 3173*]. The main body of corporation tax self-assessment provisions is contained in *FA 1998, Sch 18*. Corporation tax self-assessment is fully covered in Tolley's Corporation Tax. See also Revenue booklet 'A Guide to Corporation Tax Self-Assessment — for Tax Practitioners and Inland Revenue Officers (April 1999)' and Simon's Direct Tax Service, Division D2.8.

56.3 INTERPRETATION OF REFERENCES TO ASSESSMENTS ETC.

Following the introduction of self-assessment, references to a person being assessed to tax, or being charged to tax by an assessment, are to be construed as including a reference to his being so assessed, or being so charged, by a self-assessment under *TMA 1970, s 9* (see 54.5 RETURNS) or by a determination under *TMA 1970, s 28C* (see 54.14 RETURNS) which has not been superseded by a self-assessment. [*FA 1994, ss 197, 199*].

56.4 INTERIM PAYMENTS OF TAX ON ACCOUNT

For 1997/98 and subsequent years of assessment, where, as regards the year immediately preceding the year of assessment in question,

(*a*) a person is assessed to income tax (including Class 4 national insurance contributions treated as income tax under *Social Security Contributions and Benefits Act 1992, s 16*) under *TMA 1970, s 9* (self-assessment in personal or trustee's return — see 54.5 RETURNS),

(*b*) the assessed amount exceeds any income tax deducted at source (including tax deducted under PAYE, taking in any deduction in respect of that year but to be made in a subsequent year but subtracting any amount paid in that year but in respect of a previous year, tax treated as deducted from, or as paid on, any income, and tax credits on dividends), and

(*c*) the said excess (the 'relevant amount') and the proportion which the relevant amount bears to the assessed amount are not less than, respectively, £500 and 20%, the person must make two interim payments on account of his income tax liability (but not his capital gains tax liability) for the year of assessment in question, each payment being equal to 50% of the relevant amount (see (*c*) above), the first such payment being due on or before 31 January in the year of assessment, the second being due on or before the following 31 July. If the preceding year's self-assessment is made late or is amended, the relevant amount is determined as if the liability as finally agreed had been shown in a timeous self-assessment, with further payments on account then being required as appropriate. If a discovery assessment (see 5.2 ASSESSMENTS) is made for the preceding year each payment on account due is deemed always to have been 50% of the relevant amount plus 50% of the tax charged by the discovery assessment as finally determined.

At any time before 31 January following the year of assessment, the taxpayer may make a claim stating his belief that he will have no liability for the year or that his liability will be fully covered by tax deducted at source, and his grounds for that belief, in which case each of the interim payments is not, and is deemed never to have been, required to be made. Within the same time limit, the taxpayer may make a claim stating his belief that his liability for the year after allowing for tax deducted at source will be a stated amount which is less than the amount otherwise due, and stating his grounds for that belief, in which case each of the interim payments required will be, and deemed always to have been, equal to 50% of the stated amount. Either claim should be made on form SA 303. The maximum penalty for an incorrect statement fraudulently or negligently made in connection with either claim is the amount or additional amount he would have paid on account if he had made a correct statement. Interim payments of tax are subject to the same recovery provisions as any other payments of tax. The Revenue may direct, prior to 31 January following the year of assessment, that payments on account are not required (see Revenue Tax Bulletin August 2001 p 875 for the very limited circumstances in which they will exercise this power). Any payments on account already made will be repaid. [*TMA 1970, s 59A; FA 1994, ss 192, 196, 199(2), Sch 19 para 45; FA 1995, s 103(7), s 108; FA 1996, s 126(1), Sch 18 para 17(1); ITEPA 2003, Sch 6 para 130; ITTOIA 2005, Sch 1 para 376; SI 1996 No 1654; SI 1997 No 2491*].

See Tolley's Income Tax for special transitional arrangements regarding payments on account for 1996/97. For an article on payments on account (including the 1996/97 arrangements), see Revenue Tax Bulletin October 1996 pp 353–356. For an article on HMRC practice on repayment, and allocations and reallocations of overpayments, see Revenue Tax Bulletin June 1999 pp 673, 674.

All self-assessment taxpayers sent a statement of account (see below) in August 1999 and/or December 1999 were for the first time given the opportunity to pay their tax by debit card over the telephone (Revenue Press Release 13 August 1999 and Revenue Tax Bulletin December 1999 p 704). From 10 January 2001, the Revenue introduced a facility to pay tax by debit card over the internet (see 28.8 HMRC: ADMINISTRATION).

Agents for whom HMRC hold the taxpayer's authority on form 64–8, for information to be copied, are automatically provided in June and December each year with Clients' Account Information, i.e. details (though not true copies) of their clients' taxpayer statements of account (advisory statements issued to taxpayers notifying them of payments due and outstanding). A customised payslip is attached to the agent statement. A taxpayer may also elect, again using form 64–8, for his statement of account to be sent to his agent instead of to him. Agents registered for electronic lodgement (see 54.22 RETURNS), and authorised to receive copy information, automatically receive electronic copies of statements of account. (Revenue Tax Bulletins December 1998 pp 618–620, December 1999 pp 703–705 and Revenue 'Working Together' Bulletins July 2000 p 4, November 2000 p 3).

Simon's Direct Tax Service. See E1.806.

56.5 FINAL PAYMENT (REPAYMENT) OF TAX

For 1996/97 and subsequent years of assessment, a final payment is due for a year of assessment if a person's combined income tax (including certain Class 4 national insurance contributions treated as income tax as in 56.4 above) and capital gains tax liabilities contained in his self-assessment (see 54.5 RETURNS) exceed the aggregate of any payments on account (whether under *TMA 1970, s 59A*, see 56.4 above, or otherwise) and any income tax deducted at source. If the second total exceeds the first, a repayment will be made. Tax deducted at source has the same meaning as in 56.4(*b*) above (but see below as regards partnership income tax for 1996/97).

Subject to 56.6 below, the due date for payment (or repayment) is 31 January following the year of assessment. The one exception is where the person gave notice of chargeability under *TMA 1970, s 7* (see 48.1 PENALTIES) within six months after the end of the year of assessment, but was not given notice under *TMA 1970, s 8* or *s 8A* (personal and trustee's return — see 54.2 RETURNS) until after 31 October following the year of assessment; in such case, the due date is the last day of the three months beginning with the date of the said notice. [*TMA 1970, s 59B(1)–(4)(7)(8); FA 1994, ss 193, 196, 199(2), Sch 19 para 45; FA 1996, s 122(2), s 126(2); ITEPA 2003, Sch 6 para 131; ITTOIA 2005, Sch 1 para 377*].

See 56.4 above re notification of taxpayer statement of account details to agents. Note that statements of account are not routinely issued to taxpayers for amounts of less than £32, the amount instead being carried forward to the next statement, though this practice does not prevent interest accruing as normal (Revenue 'Working Together' Bulletin December 2001 p 5).

56.6 **Due date: further provisions.** Where an amount of tax is payable (repayable) as a result of an amendment or correction to an individual's or trustees' self-assessment under any of (*a*)–(*e*) below, then, subject to the appeal and postponement provisions in, respectively, 4.1 APPEALS, 47.3 PAYMENT OF TAX, the due date for payment (repayment) is as stated below (if this is later than the date given under the general rules in 56.5 above). **Note** that these rules do *not* defer the date from which interest accrues, which is as in 37.1 INTEREST AND SURCHARGES ON UNPAID TAX (36.1 INTEREST ON OVERPAID TAX), although they do determine the due date for surcharge purposes — see 37.4 INTEREST AND SURCHARGES ON UNPAID TAX.

(*a*) Taxpayer amendment to return as in 54.6 RETURNS: 30 days after the date of the taxpayer's notice of amendment.

(*b*) HMRC correction to return as in 54.6 RETURNS: 30 days after the date of the officer's notice of correction.

(*c*) Taxpayer amendment to return whilst enquiry in progress as in 54.12 RETURNS, where accepted by HMRC: 30 days after the date of the closure notice (see 54.11 RETURNS).

(*d*) HMRC amendment to return where amendment made by closure notice following enquiry (see 54.11 RETURNS): 30 days after the date of the closure notice.

(*e*) HMRC amendment of self-assessment to prevent potential loss of tax to the Crown (see 54.12 RETURNS): 30 days after the date of the notice of amendment.

As regards amendments and corrections to partnership returns, (*e*) above is not relevant, and the equivalent date in each of (*a*)–(*d*) above as regards each partner is 30 days after the date of the officer's notice of consequential amendment to the partner's own tax return. The same applies in the case of a consequential amendment by virtue of any of the following: an amendment of a partnership return on discovery (see 5.3 ASSESSMENTS), a partnership error or mistake relief claim (see 12.7 CLAIMS), or a reduction or increase in the partnership tax liability made by the Appeal Commissioners.

These rules apply where the notice referred to in (*a*)–(*e*) above (or, for partnerships, the notice of consequential amendment) is given on or after 11 May 2001. Previously, where a self-assessment was amended under the relevant provisions in 54.6 RETURNS, 54.12 RETURNS (disregarding those provisions applying only as from 11 May 2001) or 5.3 ASSESSMENTS, then subject to the same point as above as regards interest (and subject to the appeal and postponement rules), the due date was 30 days after the date of the notice of amendment (if such due date was later than that given under 56.5 above).

[*TMA 1970, s 59B(5), Sch 3ZA; FA 1994, ss 193, 199(2); FA 2001, s 88, Sch 29 paras 14(3), 15, 16*].

Where HMRC enquire into the return (see 54.8 RETURNS) and a repayment is otherwise due, the repayment is not required to be made until the enquiry is completed (see 54.11 RETURNS) although the officer may make a provisional repayment at his discretion.

Subject to the appeal and postponement rules, the due date for payment of tax charged by an assessment other than a self-assessment, e.g. a discovery assessment under *TMA 1970, s 29* (see 5.2 ASSESSMENTS), is 30 days after the date of the assessment (but, for interest consequences, see 37.1 INTEREST AND SURCHARGES ON UNPAID TAX). [*TMA 1970, s 59B(4A)(6); FA 1994, ss 193, 199(2)(3); FA 1995, s 103(7), s 115(6); FA 1996, s 127; FA 2001, s 88, Sch 29 paras 14(2), 16*].

57 Settlements

Cross-references. See 2 ANNUAL RATES AND EXEMPTIONS; 5.8 ASSESSMENTS for assessments on trustees; 10 CHARITIES; 11.2 CHILDREN for bare trustees for children; 18 DEATH for provisions relating to death and to personal representatives; 20.32 EMPLOYEE SHARE SCHEMES for certain transfers of shares to employee share ownership trusts; 22.81 EXEMPTIONS AND RELIEFS for reinvestment relief available on disposals by trustees where proceeds reinvested before 6 April 1998; 22.85 EXEMPTIONS AND RELIEFS for settlements for the benefit of employees; 25 GIFTS and 33 HOLD-OVER RELIEFS for disposals not at arm's length and the availability of hold-over reliefs generally; 44 OFFSHORE SETTLEMENTS for overseas resident settlements etc.; 49.5 PRIVATE RESIDENCES for reliefs applicable to trustees; 53.7 RETIREMENT RELIEF for relief available on disposals by trustees before 6 April 2003; 54.3, 54.9 RETURNS for returns by trustees; 58.9 SHARES AND SECURITIES for stock dividends received by trustees; 61 TAPER RELIEF; 67.6 WASTING ASSETS for the situation where a disposal of a life interest in settled property gives rise to a chargeable event.

Simon's Direct Tax Service. See Part C4.

The headings in this chapter are as follows.

57.1 RATES OF TAX

For 1998/99 and subsequent years, the rate of capital gains tax applicable to the trustees of any settlement who are liable in respect of disposals of settled property (see 57.2 and 57.4 below) is equivalent to the 'rate applicable to trusts' under *ICTA 1988, s 686* (but subject to the charge on settlors with interests in settlements as in 57.5 below). The rate for 2004/05 to 2006/07 inclusive is **40%**. For 1998/99 to 2003/04 inclusive it is 34%.

[*TCGA 1992, s 4(1)(1AA), s 5; ICTA 1988, s 1, s 686(1)(1A), s 832(1); FA 1998, s 120, Sch 27 Pt III(29); FA 1999, s 26(3); ITTOIA 2005, Sch 1 para 277*].

57.2 MEANING OF 'SETTLED PROPERTY'

'*Settled property*' means any property held in trust other than property held by 'nominees' or 'bare trustees' (see below). After 5 April 2006 it is specifically provided that references in *TCGA 1992*, however expressed, to property comprised in a settlement are references to settled property. Property held by a trustee or assignee in bankruptcy or under a deed of arrangement (see below) is not settled property. Property under a unit trust scheme (as defined) is also excluded from being settled property. [*TCGA 1992, s 66(4), s 68, s 99; FA 2006, Sch 12 para 1(1)(3)*]. See also 65.2 UNIT TRUSTS ETC.

Nominees and bare trustees. Where property is held by a person

(i) as nominee for another or others, or

(ii) as trustee for a person (or persons) 'absolutely entitled' as against him,

capital gains tax is chargeable as if the property were held by that other person or persons and such property were not settled property.

A person is '*absolutely entitled*', for these purposes, if he has the exclusive right (subject only to satisfying any outstanding charge, lien or other right of the trustee to resort to the property for the payment of duty, tax, costs or other outgoings) to direct how that property shall be dealt with, or would have that right but for being an infant or under some other legal disability (e.g. a mentally handicapped person). (Note that before 6 April 2006, the legislation referred to 'assets' rather than 'property'.)

[*TCGA 1992, s 60; FA 2006, Sch 12 para 10*].

The disability must arise from the general law, and not from the wording of the trust deed (see *Tomlinson v Glyn's Exor and Trustee Co Ltd CA 1969, 45 TC 600* where the trustees were held assessable to capital gains tax because the beneficiary's interest was contingent on his attaining majority, and could not be deemed to be vested in him). In *Booth v Ellard CA 1980, 53 TC 393*, several taxpayers by agreement transferred their shares in a company to trustees. The trusts were determinable by a majority of the beneficiaries (who were also the settlors), each beneficiary had a right of pre-emption over the others' shares, and the income was to be distributed in proportion to the number of shares to which each beneficiary was entitled (which corresponded with the number which he had settled). It was held that each beneficiary retained his interest in the same number of shares as he had settled (albeit not the identical shares). Despite the restraints, it was within the beneficiaries' collective power to terminate the trusts, and each beneficiary was therefore absolutely entitled as against the trustees. See also *Jenkins v Brown, Warrington v Brown and related appeals Ch D, [1989] STC 577*.

Kidson v Macdonald Ch D 1973, 49 TC 503 laid down that tenants in common of land held on trust for sale were jointly absolutely entitled. It is not necessary that particular assets to which the beneficiaries are entitled should be identifiable (*Stephenson v Barclays Bank Trust Co Ltd Ch D 1974, 50 TC 374*), but see *Cochrane's Exors v CIR CS 1974, 49 TC 299* (entitlement to residue) and *Crowe v Appleby CA 1975, 51 TC 457*. See also *Newman v Pepper; Newman v Morgan (Sp C 243), [2000] SSCD 345*.

Trustees of bare trusts treated as such for tax purposes are not required to complete self-assessment tax returns or make tax payments, the 'beneficiaries' being liable to give details of the income and gains in their own tax returns. (Revenue Tax Bulletin February 1997 p 395). The trustees may, *if they wish*, make a self-assessment return of income, and account for basic or lower rate income tax thereon. Capital gains and capital losses *cannot* be included in any such return, these being the sole responsibility of the beneficiaries. (Revenue Tax Bulletin December 1997 pp 486, 487).

Insolvents' assets. Assets held by a trustee or assignee in bankruptcy or under a 'deed of arrangement' are treated as if still owned by the bankrupt or debtor (the trustee's acquisitions from, or disposals to, the bankrupt being disregarded) and as if the trustee's acts in relation to those assets were acts of the bankrupt. But tax on chargeable gains arising from such acts is assessable on, and payable by, the trustee, etc. '*Deed of arrangement*' means a deed to which the *Deeds of Arrangement Act 1914* (or any corresponding Act in Scotland or NI) applies. [*TCGA 1992, s 66(1)(5)*].

When the bankrupt etc. dies, the assets held by the trustee are deemed for the purposes of *TCGA 1992, s 62(1)* (see 18.1 DEATH) to have then been acquired by the trustee as if he were a personal representative. The provisions above do not then apply after death. But if the bankrupt is dead before the trustee is appointed, the provisions above also do not apply, the assets being regarded as held by the deceased's personal representative. [*TCGA 1992, s 66(2)–(4)*].

In re McMeekin QB (NI) 1973, 48 TC 725 it was held that capital gains tax is an administration cost of bankruptcy.

57.3 MEANING OF 'SETTLOR'

The following extended definition of 'settlor' applies for all capital gains purposes, unless the context otherwise requires, with effect from 6 April 2006. It applies from that date in relation to all settlements, whenever created and, in the case of the provisions dealing with the variation of a will or intestacy (see below), irrespective of the date on which the deceased person died. [*FA 2006, Sch 12 para 1(4)(5)*]. Previously, there was no general definition of the term, although there were definitions for the purposes of particular provisions (see, for example, 44.14 OFFSHORE SETTLEMENTS) and, in certain cases, those definitions continue to apply (see, for example, 57.5 below).

Subject to the above, a '*settlor*' of a settlement is the person, or any of the persons, who has made, or is treated as having made, the settlement. A person is a settlor of property which is settled property by reason of his having made the settlement or of an event which causes him to be treated as having made the settlement or which derives from such property (see below).

For these purposes, a person is treated as having made a settlement if he has, directly or indirectly, made or entered into the settlement. In particular, a person is so treated if he has provided, or undertaken to provide, property directly or indirectly for the purposes of the settlement. Where the settlement arises by will, intestacy or otherwise on a person's death, that person is treated as having made the settlement if the settled property, or property derived from it, is or includes property of which he was 'competent to dispose immediately before his death'. A person making or entering into a settlement in accordance with reciprocal 'arrangements' with another person is not treated as having made the settlement by reason only of those arrangements. Instead, the other person is treated as having made the settlement.

A settlor is treated as ceasing to be a settlor of a settlement if

- no property of which he is a settlor remains in the settlement;
- he has not undertaken to provide property directly or indirectly for the purposes of the settlement in the future; and
- he has not made reciprocal arrangements with another person to enter into the settlement in the future.

For the purposes of these provisions, 'arrangements' include a scheme, agreement or understanding, whether or not legally enforceable. Property is derived from other property if it derives, directly or indirectly, wholly or partly, from that property or any part of it or from income from that property or any part of it. Property of which a person was '*competent to dispose immediately before his death*' is any property which (otherwise than in right of a power of appointment or of the testamentary power conferred by statute to dispose of entailed interests) he could, if of full age and capacity, have disposed of by his will, assuming that all the property was situated in England and, if he was not domiciled in the United Kingdom, that he was domiciled in England, and include references to his severable share in any property to which, immediately before his death, he was beneficially entitled as joint tenant.

[*TCGA 1992, ss 62(10), 68A; FA 2006, Sch 12 para 1(2)*].

Transfers between settlements. Where there is a 'transfer of property' from the trustees of one settlement to the trustees of a second settlement otherwise than for full consideration or at arm's length, the settlor or settlors of the property so transferred are treated from the time of the transfer as settlors of the second settlement. If there is more than one settlor of the property transferred, each is treated in relation to the second settlement as the settlor of a proportionate part of the 'transferred property'.

There is a '*transfer of property*' for these purposes if there is a disposal of property by the trustees of one settlement and the acquisition by the trustees of the second settlement either of property disposed of by the trustees of the first settlement or property created by the disposal. References above and below to '*transferred property*' are to property acquired by the trustees of the second settlement on the disposal. Where a transfer of property is between trustees who are CONNECTED PERSONS (13) the transfer is not treated as being otherwise than at arm's length by reason of the connection.

If and to the extent that property disposed of by the trustees of the first settlement was provided for the purposes of that settlement or is derived from property so provided, the transferred property is treated from the time of the disposal as having been provided for the purposes of the second settlement by the person or persons who provided the property disposed of or the property from which it was derived (and hence those persons are treated as having made the second settlement). If there is more than one such person each of them is treated as having provided a proportionate part of the transferred property. This does not apply to a transfer of property

- occurring by reason of the assignment or assignation by a beneficiary of the first settlement of an interest in that settlement to the trustees of the second settlement;
- occurring by reason only of the exercise of a general power of appointment; or
- resulting from a variation of a will or intestacy within the provisions below such that property of which the deceased person is a settlor is comprised in a settlement immediately before the variation and immediately afterwards the property, or property derived from it, becomes comprised in another settlement.

[*TCGA 1992, s 68B; FA 2006, Sch 12 para 1(2)*].

Variation of will or intestacy. The following provisions apply where, within two years of a person's death, there is a variation in a disposition of property of which the deceased was competent to dispose to which *TCGA 1992, s 62(6)* (deeds of family arrangement etc. — see 18.6 DEATH) applies.

Where property becomes settled property as a result only of the variation, the following persons are treated as having made the settlement and as having provided property for the purposes of the settlement:

- a person who immediately before the variation was entitled absolutely as legatee to the property or property from which it derives, or who would have been so entitled but for being an infant or other person under a disability; and
- a person who would, but for the variation, have become absolutely entitled as legatee to the property or property from which it derives or who would have become so entitled but for being an infant or other person under a disability.

In determining for this purpose whether a person was, or would be entitled absolutely as legatee, property taken under a testamentary disposition or on an intestacy or partial intestacy includes any property appropriated by the personal representative in or towards satisfaction of a pecuniary legacy or any other interest or share in the property devolving.

Where property which would, but for the variation, have become comprised in an existing settlement (whether or not the deceased was the settlor) or a settlement arising on the death of the deceased person (by will, intestacy or otherwise) instead becomes comprised in another settlement as a result of the variation, the deceased person is treated as having made that other settlement. Unless that settlement arose on the deceased's death, he is treated as having made it immediately before his death.

Where property of which the deceased person is a settlor is comprised in a settlement immediately before the variation and immediately afterwards the property, or property derived from it, becomes comprised in another settlement, the deceased person is treated as having made that other settlement. Unless that settlement arose on the deceased's death, he is treated as having made it immediately before his death.
[*TCGA 1992, s 68C; FA 2006, Sch 12 para 1(2)*].

57.4 LIABILITY OF TRUSTEES, SETTLORS AND BENEFICIARIES

Trustees of a settlement are liable to capital gains tax, under provisions relating to the tax generally, on disposals or deemed disposals of settled property (but subject to the charge on settlors with interests in settlements at 57.5 below). The exempt amount for a year of assessment available to trustees is given in 57.10 and 57.11 below.

The trustees of a settlement are treated as if they were a single person (distinct from the persons who may from time to time be trustees). For 2005/06 and earlier years, the legislation treated the trustees as a single and continuing body of persons. [*TCGA 1992, s 69(1); FA 2006, Sch 12 para 2*]. For the residence etc. status of the deemed person or body, see 44.1 OFFSHORE SETTLEMENTS. See 57.8 below for the election available for the sub-fund of a settlement to be treated as a separate settlement.

Special rules apply to overseas resident settlements etc. See 44 OFFSHORE SETTLEMENTS.

Where part of the property comprised in a settlement is vested in one trustee or set of trustees and part in another (and in particular settled land within the meaning of the *Settled Land Act 1925* is vested in the tenant for life and investments representing capital money are vested in the trustees of the settlement), all the trustees are treated as together constituting and, insofar as they act separately, as acting on behalf of a single body of trustees. [*TCGA 1992, s 69(3)*].

HMRC may by notice in writing require a person who is a 'party' to a settlement (within *ITTOIA 2005, s 620*) to provide within not less than 28 days information they think necessary for the purposes of *TCGA 1992*. [*TMA 1970, s 27; ITTOIA 2005, Sch 1 para 368*].

57.5 **Charge on settlors with interests in settlements.** In certain circumstances gains accruing to trustees in a year after 1987/88 are not chargeable on them, but instead an equal amount of gains (as in (*b*) below) is treated as accruing to the settlor in the year. (See 44 OFFSHORE SETTLEMENTS for interaction between the provisions mentioned therein and those given below.) See 57.9 below for the operation of the provisions in the case of settlements with vulnerable beneficiaries.

The charge on the settlor arises if all of the following conditions are fulfilled.

(*a*) Chargeable gains (including those arising under *TCGA 1992, s 13* as in 45.6 OVERSEAS MATTERS) accrue in a year to the trustees of a settlement from the disposal of any or all of the settled property.

(*b*) The trustees would otherwise, after making deductions for losses (including those taken into account under *TCGA 1992, s 13*) under *TCGA 1992, s 2(2)* (see 40.1 LOSSES) but taking no account of the annual exemption under *TCGA 1992, s 3* (see 57.10 and 57.11 below), be chargeable to tax for the year in respect of those gains.

(*c*) For 2006/07 and earlier years, the settlor is, and the trustees are, either resident in the UK during any part of the year or ordinarily resident in the UK during the year.

(*d*) For 2007/08 and subsequent years, the settlor is either resident in the UK during any part of the year or ordinarily resident in the UK during the year and the trustees are resident and ordinarily resident in the UK during any part of the year.

(*e*) The settlor is alive at the end of the year.

(*f*) At any time during the year the settlor has an interest in the settlement.

(*g*) The settlor is not excepted from the charge as below.

A settlor has an interest in a settlement if

(i) any property which is or may at any time be comprised in the settlement or any 'derived property' is, or will or may become, payable to or applicable for the benefit of the settlor or his spouse, civil partner in any circumstances whatsoever, or

(ii) the settlor, or his spouse, civil partner, enjoys a benefit deriving directly or indirectly from any property which is comprised in the settlement or any derived property.

At any time after 5 April 2006, a settlor also has an interest in a settlement if

(iii) any property which is or may at any time be comprised in the settlement or any derived property is, or will or may become, payable to or applicable for the benefit of a child of the settlor at any time when that child is a 'dependent child' of his, in any circumstances whatsoever, or

(iv) a dependent child of the settlor enjoys a benefit deriving directly or indirectly from any property which is comprised in the settlement or any derived property.

A '*dependent child*' of the settlor is, for this purpose, a child or stepchild under the age of 18 who is unmarried and does not have a civil partner.

References to the spouse or civil partner of the settlor in (i) and (ii) above do not include a person to whom the settlor is not for the time being married but may marry later, a person of whom the settlor is not for the time being a civil partner but of whom he may later be a civil partner, or a spouse or civil partner from whom the settlor is separated under a court order or similar arrangement that is likely to be permanent, or the widow, widower or surviving civil partner of the settlor. No account is taken of a term of the settlement relating to dependent children of the settlor at any time when he has no such children.

A settlor does not have an interest under (i) above if and so long as

(A) none of the property which may at any time be comprised in the settlement and no derived property can become applicable or payable as mentioned in (i) above except in the event of:

- the bankruptcy of some person who is or may become beneficially entitled to that property or any derived property;
- any assignment of or charge on that property or any derived property being made or given by some such person;
- in the case of a marriage settlement or civil partnership settlement, the death of both the parties to the marriage or civil partnership and all or any of the children of one or both of the parties to the marriage or civil partnership (before 5 December 2005, all or any of the children of the marriage); or
- the death of a child of the settlor who had become beneficially entitled to the property or any derived property at an age not exceeding 25; or

(B) some person is alive and under the age of 25 during whose life the property or any derived property cannot become applicable or payable as mentioned in (i) above except in the event of that person becoming bankrupt or assigning or charging his interest in that property.

The settlor is excepted from the charge where either:

(I) he has an interest in a settlement only because property is, or will or may become, payable to or applicable for the benefit of his spouse or civil partner *or* his spouse or civil partner enjoys a benefit from property, or for both such reasons, and his spouse or civil partner dies, or he and his spouse or civil partner cease to be married to or to be civil partners of each other, during the year; or

(II) he has an interest in a settlement only because property is, or will or may become, payable to or applicable for the benefit of a dependent child of his *or* a dependent child of his enjoys a benefit from property, or for both such reasons, and he ceases during the year to have (and does not in that year subsequently come to have) any dependent children to whom (iii) or (iv) above applies.

For these purposes, '*derived property*' means income from that property or any other property directly or indirectly representing proceeds of that property or income therefrom. See, for example, *Trennery v West HL, [2005] STC 214, [2005] UKHL 5*.

Where the trustees of a maintenance fund for an historic building elect under *ICTA 1988, s 691(2)* that income arising under the settlement or part of the settlement involved is not to be treated as income of the settlor for a year of assessment, no charge arises under these provisions in relation to the settlement or part for the year.

For these provisions a person is a '*settlor*' in relation to a settlement if the settled property consists of or includes property originating from him. Property originates from a settlor where he provides it directly or indirectly for the purposes (see *Countess Fitzwilliam and others v CIR (and related appeals) HL 1993, 67 TC 614*) of the settlement (including property provided by another person under reciprocal 'arrangements') and where property (or a proper part thereof) represents that property. In general, references to settled property (and to property comprised in a settlement), in relation to a settlor, are references only to property originating from that settlor. In respect of property provided to a settlement after 9 December 2003, '*arrangements*' are defined to include any scheme, agreement or understanding, whether or not legally enforceable. Previously the term was undefined.

A settlor has a right of recovery against any trustee for the amount of tax he is charged under these provisions. Such amount is identified by treating the gains that are deemed to accrue to him as forming the highest part of his chargeable amount for the year.

An HMRC officer may require a settlor, trustee or former trustee to provide him with particulars for the purposes of these provisions. Failure to do so within a specified time (which cannot be less than 28 days) incurs penalties under *TMA 1970, s 98*.

[*TCGA 1992, s 77, s 78(1)(2), s 79; FA 1988, Sch 10 para 5(3)–(5), Sch 14 Pt VIII; FA 1995, Sch 17 paras 27–29; FA 2004, s 116, Sch 21 paras 2, 10(2)(3); FA 2006, Sch 12 paras 3, 13, 31, 33; SI 2005 No 3229, Reg 108*].

Offset of losses and application of taper relief. For 2003/04 and subsequent years, and for any of the years 2000/01, 2001/02 or 2002/03 for which an election is made by the settlor under *FA 2002, Sch 11 para 8* (see 40.1 LOSSES), the amount treated as accruing to him under the above provisions is computed without applying TAPER RELIEF (61). However, trust losses are set against trust gains in such order as would give the maximum entitlement to taper relief if such relief were available to the trustees; this establishes the rate of taper relief to be applied to the gains in the settlor's hands after deducting any personal losses (see 40.1 LOSSES).

For years prior to 2003/04, other than any of the years 2000/01, 2001/02 or 2002/03 for which an election is made by the settlor under *FA 2002, Sch 11 para 8* (see 40.1 LOSSES), the amount treated as accruing to him will be net of taper relief where this is available. No further taper relief is available to the settlor. In addition, for 1998/99 onwards, the settlor's own, untapered, losses, whether of the current year of assessment or brought forward from previous years, cannot be set off against gains treated as accruing to him as above (see 40.1 LOSSES).

[*TCGA 1992, s 2(4)–(8), s 77(1)(b), (6A); FA 1998, s 121(3)(4), Sch 21 para 2, para 6(1); FA 2002, Sch 11 paras 3, 7, 8, Sch 40 Pt 3(4)*].

57.6 **Collection of unpaid tax from beneficiaries etc.** If tax assessed on trustees in respect of a chargeable gain accruing to them is not paid within six months from the date when it becomes payable *and* before or after that date the asset in respect of which the gain accrued, or any part of the proceeds of sale of that asset, is transferred to a person who becomes absolutely entitled to it, or the proceeds etc., that person may be assessed and charged in the name of the trustees within two years from the time when the tax became payable. The tax chargeable is not to exceed the tax chargeable on an amount equal to the chargeable gain and, where only a part of the asset or of the proceeds was transferred, is not to exceed a proportionate part of that amount. [*TCGA 1992, s 69(4)*].

57.7 **Relevant trustees.** For 1996/97 onwards under self-assessment, the following has effect for the assessment and collection of tax on trust income and gains where there is more than one trustee. Anything done by a 'relevant trustee' is regarded as done by all the relevant trustees, including the making of returns and self-assessment. Liability for penalties, interest or surcharge may be recovered (but only once) from any one or more of the relevant trustees other than one who was not a relevant trustee at the relevant time (as defined by *TMA 1970, s 107A(3)*). In relation to chargeable gains, the '*relevant trustees*' of a settlement are the persons who are trustees in the tax year in which the gains accrue and any persons who subsequently become trustees. [*TMA 1970, s 7(2)(9), s 8A(1)(5), ss 107A, 118(1); FA 1995, s 103, Sch 29 Pt VIII(14)*].

For 1996/97 onwards, chargeable gains which accrue to a settlement can be assessed on any relevant trustee (see 5.8 ASSESSMENTS).

57.8 **SUB-FUND SETTLEMENTS**

For 2006/07 onwards, trustees of a settlement (the '*principal settlement*') may make an irrevocable election under which a specified part (a '*sub-fund*') of the settled property is treated for capital gains tax purposes as a separate settlement, known as a '*sub-fund settlement*'. [*TCGA 1992, s 69A, Sch 4ZA paras 1, 13; FA 2006, Sch 12 para 6*]. The election applies also for income tax purposes (see *ICTA 1988, s 685G* and Tolley's Income Tax).

For an election to be made, the principal settlement must not be itself a sub-fund settlement, and the following conditions must be satisfied when the election is made and throughout the period (if any) beginning with the time the election is treated as taking effect (see below) and ending immediately before it is made.

(i) The sub-fund must not be the whole of the property comprised in the principal settlement.

(ii) On the assumption that the election had then taken effect, the sub-fund settlement would not include an 'interest' in any asset in which an interest was retained by the principal settlement. The provisions of *TCGA 1992, s 104* and *s 109* treating certain holdings of shares etc. as a single asset (see 59.2, 59.5 shares and securities — identification rules) are ignored for this purpose. An '*interest*' in an asset means an interest as co-owner, whether the asset is owned jointly or in common and whether or not the interests of the co-owners are equal.

(iii) On the assumption that the election had then taken effect, nobody would be a beneficiary of both the sub-fund settlement and the principal settlement. A person is a beneficiary of a settlement for this purpose if any property which is or may at any time be comprised in the settlement, or any 'derived property', is or will or may be payable to him or applicable for his benefit in any circumstances whatsoever, or if he enjoys a benefit deriving directly or indirectly from any property comprised in the settlement or any derived property. '*Derived property*' means income from other property, property directly or indirectly representing proceeds of, or of income from, other property or income from property which is itself derived property.

A person is not treated as a beneficiary, however, if property comprised in the settlement or any derived property will or may become payable to him or applicable for his benefit by reason only of:

- his marrying or becoming a civil partner of a beneficiary;
- the death of a beneficiary;
- the exercise by the trustees of the principal settlement of a power of advancement within *Trustee Act 1925, s 32* (or Northern Ireland equivalent), a similar power conferred by the law of a jurisdiction other than England and Wales or Northern Ireland, or a power of advancement which is subject to the same restrictions as those specified in *Trustee Act 1925, s 32*(*1*)(*a*)(*c*) and which is conferred by either the instrument creating the settlement or another instrument made in accordance with the terms of the settlement; or
- the failure or determination of protective trusts within *Trustee Act 1925, s 33*.

[*TCGA 1992, Sch 4ZA paras 3–9; FA 2006, Sch 12 para 6*(*2*)].

Making an election. An election, which is irrevocable, must be made by notice in writing to HMRC in such form as HMRC may require. The notice must specify the date on which the election is to be treated as having taken effect, which must not be later than the date on which it is made. The election must be made within one year after 31 January following the tax year in which the date on which it is to be treated as taking effect falls. An election must include:

- a declaration of consent by each trustee of the principal settlement;
- a statement by those trustees that the conditions for making an election are satisfied;
- such information as HMRC may require in relation to the principal settlement including, in particular, information relating to the trustees, the trusts, property comprised in the settlement, the settlors and the beneficiaries;
- a declaration by the trustees of the principal settlement that the information given in the election is correct to the best of their knowledge and belief; and
- such other declarations as HMRC may require.

A penalty under *TMA 1970, s 98* applies for fraudulently or negligently providing incorrect information in an election.

Where an election is made, HMRC have the power to require, by notice in writing, a person who is or has been a trustee, beneficiary or settlor of either the principal settlement or the sub-fund settlement to supply information for the purpose of determining whether the conditions for making an election are satisfied. The notice must specify a period of not less than 60 days within which the information must be supplied and is subject to a penalty under *TMA 1970, s 98* for failure to comply or fraudulently or negligently providing incorrect information.

[*TCGA 1992, s 288*(*1*), *Sch 4ZA paras 10–16; FA 2006, Sch 12 paras 6*(*2*), *46*].

Consequences of an election. A sub-fund settlement election takes effect at the beginning of the day, not being before 6 April 2006, specified in the election. If there is a deemed disposal by the trustees of the principal settlement at the beginning of that day under the provisions below, the election is deemed to take effect on that day immediately after that disposal.

The sub-fund settlement is treated as having been created at the time the election takes effect. Each trustee of the trusts on which the property in the sub-fund settlement is held is treated as a trustee of the sub-fund settlement and, unless he is also a trustee of trusts on which property in the principal settlement is held, as ceasing to be a trustee of the principal settlement from the time the election takes effect. A trustee of the principal settlement is not treated as a trustee of the sub-fund settlement unless he is also a trustee of trusts on which property in that settlement is held.

The trustees of the sub-fund settlement are treated as becoming absolutely entitled to the property comprised in that settlement as against the trustees of the principal settlement at the time the election takes effect.

The taking effect of the election may trigger deemed disposals by the trustees of the principal settlement under:

(*a*) *TCGA 1992, s 71*(*1*) (person becoming absolutely entitled to settled property — see 57.15 below); and

(*b*) *TCGA 1992, s 80*(*2*) (see 44.2 OFFSHORE SETTLEMENTS) where the principal settlement becomes non-UK resident as a result of the trustees of the sub-fund settlement ceasing to be trustees of the principal settlement.

Such a deemed disposal is treated as being made at the beginning of the day on which the election takes effect. No deemed disposal of an asset is treated as being made by virtue of (*b*) above if there is a deemed disposal of the same asset by virtue of (*a*) above. Any assets acquired by the trustees of the sub-fund settlement in respect of which there is a deemed disposal are treated as acquired by them at the time the election takes effect.

If the trustees of the sub-fund settlement are treated as becoming absolutely entitled as above to money expressed in sterling they are treated as acquiring it at the time the election takes effect and the trustees of the principal settlement are treated as disposing of it at the beginning of the day on which the election takes effect.

In the case of non-resident settlements, if there is a deemed disposal of an asset within (*a*) above when the election takes effect, then for the purposes of the provisions charging beneficiaries to capital gains tax in respect of capital payments (see 44.14 OFFSHORE SETTLEMENTS) and the further charge on such beneficiaries (see 44.15–44.17 OFFSHORE SETTLEMENTS), the trustees of the principal settlement are treated as having transferred the asset to the sub-fund settlement trustees (so that the relevant provisions for transfers between settlements may apply). This applies also if there would have been such a deemed disposal at that time of money expressed in sterling if (*a*) above applied to such property.

[*TCGA 1992, Sch 4ZA paras 2, 17–22; FA 2006 para 6*(*2*)(*3*)].

57.9 TRUSTS WITH VULNERABLE BENEFICIARY

For 2004/05 and subsequent years, the trustees of a settlement may claim special tax treatment for a tax year if

- in that year they hold property on 'qualifying trusts' for the benefit of a 'vulnerable person', and
- a 'vulnerable person election' has effect for all or part of that year in relation to those trusts and that person.

[*FA 2005, ss 23, 24, 45; FA 2006, Sch 13 para 35*(*1*)(*2*)(*7*)].

The claim has effect for both income tax and capital gains tax purposes; for the income tax consequences see Tolley's Income Tax.

Definitions. A '*vulnerable person*' is a 'disabled person' or a 'relevant minor'. A '*disabled person*' is a person who

(*a*) by reason of mental disorder within the meaning of *Mental Health Act 1983*, is incapable of administering his property or managing his affairs;

(*b*) is in receipt of attendance allowance (i.e. an allowance under *Social Security Contributions and Benefits Act 1992, s 64* or *Social Security Contributions and Benefits* (*Northern Ireland*) *Act 1992, s 64*);

(*c*) is in receipt of a disability living allowance under *Social Security Contributions and Benefits Act 1992, s 71* or *Social Security Contributions and Benefits* (*Northern Ireland*) *Act 1992, s 71* by virtue of entitlement to the care component at the highest or middle rate; or

(*d*) satisfies HMRC that, if he were to meet the residence requirements for those allowances, he would be entitled to receive an allowance within (*b*) or (*c*) above.

A person who is a disabled person by virtue of (*b*)–(*d*) above does not cease to be a disabled person by reason of any provision made by regulations under *Social Security Contributions and Benefits Act 1992, s 67*(*1*)(*2*) or *Social Security Contributions and Benefits* (*Northern Ireland*) *Act 1992, s 67*(*1*)(*2*) (non-satisfaction of attendance allowance conditions where person undergoing hospital treatment for renal failure or where person provided with certain accommodation) or under *Social Security Contributions and Benefits Act 1992, s 72*(*8*) or *Social Security Contributions and Benefits* (*Northern Ireland*) *Act 1992, s 72*(*8*) (no payment of disability living allowance where person provided with certain accommodation).

A person under the age of 18 is a '*relevant minor*' if at least one of his parents has died.

Where property is held on trusts for the benefit of a disabled person, those trusts are '*qualifying trusts*' if they secure that, during the lifetime of the disabled person or until the termination of the trusts (if earlier),

- any property applied for the benefit of a beneficiary is applied for the benefit of the disabled person, and
- either the disabled person is entitled to all the income arising from any of the property or no such income may be applied for the benefit of any other person.

A power of advancement within *Trustee Act 1925, s 32* (or Northern Ireland equivalent), or, after 5 April 2006, a similar power conferred by the law of a jurisdiction other than England and Wales or Northern Ireland or a power of advancement which is subject to the same restrictions as those specified in *Trustee Act 1925, s 32*(*1*)(*a*)(*c*) and which is conferred by either the instrument creating the settlement or another instrument made in accordance with the terms of the settlement, does not disqualify the trusts. The reference above to the lifetime of the disabled person is, where property is held for his benefit on protective trusts within *Trustee Act, s 33*, to be construed as a reference to the period during which such property is held on trust for him.

Where property is held on trusts for the benefit of a relevant minor, those trusts are '*qualifying trusts*' if they are

(i) statutory trusts for the relevant minor under *Administration of Estates Act 1925, ss 46, 47*(*1*) (succession on intestacy and statutory trusts in favour of relatives of intestate),

(ii) trusts established under the will of a deceased parent of the relevant minor, or

(iii) trusts established under the Criminal Injuries Compensation Scheme (i.e. schemes established under *Criminal Injuries Compensation Act 1995*, arrangements made by the Secretary of State for compensation for criminal injuries in operation before the commencement of those schemes or the scheme established under the *Criminal Injuries* (*Northern Ireland*) *Order 2002 SI 2002 No 796*).

Trusts within (ii) or (iii) above must secure that

- when the relevant minor reaches 18 he will become absolutely entitled to the property, any income arising from it, and any income that has arisen from property held on the trusts for his benefit which has been accumulated before that time;

- until the relevant minor reaches 18 (so long as he is living), any property applied for the benefit of a beneficiary is applied for his benefit; and
- until the relevant minor reaches 18 (so long as he is living), either he is entitled to all the income arising from any of the property or no such income may be applied for the benefit of any other person.

A power of advancement within *Trustee Act 1925, s 32* (or Northern Ireland equivalent), or, after 5 April 2006, a similar power conferred by the law of a jurisdiction other than England and Wales or Northern Ireland or a power of advancement which is subject to the same restrictions as those specified in *Trustee Act 1925, s 32(1)(a)(c)* and which is conferred by either the instrument creating the settlement or another instrument made in accordance with the terms of the settlement, does not disqualify trusts within (ii) or (iii) above.

References in these provisions to property being held on trusts include references to a part of an asset being held on trusts if that part and any income arising (or treated as arising) from it can be identified for the purpose of determining whether the trusts are qualifying trusts.

[*FA 2005, ss 23(7), 34–36, 38, 39; FA 2006, Sch 12 para 48(2)(3)(5)*].

The above definitions apply in Scotland with certain modifications (see *FA 2005, s 42*).

Vulnerable person election. A '*vulnerable person election*' can be made jointly by the trustees and a beneficiary if the trusts are qualifying trusts and the beneficiary is a vulnerable person. The election is irrevocable and must be made by notice in writing to HMRC in such form as they may require. It must specify the date from which it will take effect and be made within twelve months of 31 January following the tax year in which that date falls or within such further time as HMRC may by notice allow. The notice of election must include a statement that the trusts are qualifying trusts, a declaration that all the information included is correct to the best of the knowledge and belief of the trustees and beneficiary, a declaration by the beneficiary that he authorises the trustees to make a claim under these provisions for any tax year as they consider appropriate, and any other information and declarations as HMRC may require.

An election is effective until the beneficiary ceases to be a vulnerable person or the trusts cease to be qualifying trusts or are terminated. Where the trustees become aware that one of these events has occurred, they must, subject to a penalty under *TMA 1970, s 98* for failure, notify HMRC that the election has ceased to have effect within 90 days beginning on the day on which they first became aware of the event.

Where property held on trusts in respect of which an election is in force is treated for tax purposes as comprised in a sub-fund settlement (see 57.8 above) and the election was not made by the trustees of that settlement, the election applies to those trusts as if it had been made by those trustees and the vulnerable person. This treatment does not relieve the trustees of the principal settlement (see 57.8 above) from their notification obligations under the above provisions in relation to matters arising before the sub-fund settlement election took effect.

HMRC have powers to require the trustees or the vulnerable person by notice in writing to provide any particulars that they may require to determine whether the requirements for an election were met at the time it was made or whether an event has occurred such that the election ceases to be effective. The notice must specify the time (at least 60 days) within which the information must be provided. If HMRC determine that the requirements were not so met or that such an event has occurred they may give notice in writing to the trustees and the vulnerable person that the election never had effect or, as appropriate, that it ceased to have effect from a specified date. This is subject to a right of appeal to the General Commissioners, which must be made within 30 days after the notice was given. The provisions above which treat an election as made by trustees of a sub-fund settlement do not prevent HMRC from issuing a notice to the trustees of the principal settlement in relation to matters arising before the sub-fund settlement election took effect.

[*FA 2005, ss 37, 40, 41*(*1*), *43; FA 2006, Sch 12 para 48*(*4*), *Sch 13 para 35*(*1*)(*2*)(*6*)(*7*)].

Capital gains tax. The special capital gains tax treatment described below applies for a tax year if

(1) chargeable gains (the '*qualifying trusts gains*') accrue in that year to the trustees of a settlement from the disposal of settled property (see 57.2 above) which is held on qualifying trusts for the benefit of a vulnerable person;

(2) the trustees would (apart from these provisions) be chargeable to capital gains tax in respect of those gains;

(3) the trustees are either resident in the UK during any part of the year or ordinarily resident in the UK during the year (see 57.4 above); and

(4) a claim for special tax treatment for the year is made by the trustees. (Note that a claim applies for income tax purposes also.)

The treatment does not apply for a tax year in which the vulnerable person dies.

The qualifying trusts gains in (1) above include attributed gains of non-resident companies within 45.6 OVERSEAS MATTERS.

Condition (2) above is not treated as not satisfied if the provisions at 57.5 above (charge on settlors with interests in settlements) would (but for these provisions) apply only because the settlor is treated as having an interest in the settlement under 57.5(iii) or (iv) above (dependent children).

Where the above conditions are satisfied, the provisions at 57.5 do not apply, except to the extent that they are applied as below in the case of a vulnerable person treated as the settlor.

[*FA 2005, s 30; FA 2006, Sch 12 para 48*(*1*)].

UK resident vulnerable person. If the vulnerable person is either resident in the UK during any part of the tax year or ordinarily resident in the UK during the tax year, then, for the purposes of the charge on settlors with interests in settlements at 57.5 above, he is treated as the settlor and as having an interest in the settlement during that year. The settled property disposed of, together with any other settled property disposed of at any time when it was 'relevant settled property' is treated as if it originated from the vulnerable person. For this purpose, property is '*relevant settled property*' at any time when it is held on qualifying trusts for the benefit of a vulnerable person and the trustees would (apart from these provisions) be chargeable to capital gains tax in respect of any gains accruing to them on a disposal of it. [*FA 2005, ss 31, 41*(*2*)(*a*)]. Broadly, the effect is that gains accruing to the trustees are chargeable on the vulnerable person, with the tax payable recoverable from the trustees.

Non-resident vulnerable person. If the vulnerable person is neither resident in the UK during any part of the tax year nor ordinarily resident in the UK during the tax year, the trustees' liability to capital gains tax for the year is reduced by an amount equal to

TQTG – (TVLA – TVLB)

where

TQTG = the amount of capital gains tax to which the trustees would, apart from these provisions, be liable for the tax year in respect of qualifying trust gains;

TVLB = the total amount of income tax and capital gains tax to which the vulnerable person would be liable for the tax year if his income for the tax year were equal to the sum of his 'actual income' and the 'trustees' specially taxed income' and his taxable amount for capital gains tax purposes (see 2.3 ANNUAL RATES AND EXEMPTIONS) for the tax year were equal to his 'deemed CGT taxable amount'; and

TVLA = what TVLB would be if his taxable amount for capital gains tax included his 'notional section 77 gains' for the tax year.

For this purpose, the vulnerable person's '*actual income*' for a tax year is the income which would be assessable to income tax for the year on the assumption that he was resident and domiciled in the UK throughout the year. The '*trustees' specially taxed income*' for a tax year is the income of the trustees for the year from property held on qualifying trusts for the benefit of the vulnerable person in connection with which special income tax treatment applies by virtue of a claim under these provisions.

The vulnerable person's '*deemed CGT taxable amount*' for a tax year is the total of his taxable amount for the year calculated by reference only to 'actual gains' and 'actual losses' and his taxable amount calculated only by reference to 'assumed gains' and 'assumed losses'. Any claims or elections made in relation to any assumed gains are disregarded. In calculating the taxable amount by reference to assumed gains and assumed losses, no deduction is made for losses brought forward or, on the death of the vulnerable person, for losses carried back.

The '*actual gains*' are any chargeable gains accruing to the vulnerable person in respect of which he is chargeable to capital gains tax for the tax year. '*Actual losses*' are allowable losses, including losses brought forward. '*Assumed gains*' are any chargeable gains, other than actual gains, in respect of which the vulnerable person would be chargeable to capital gains tax on the assumption that

(A) he is resident and domiciled in the UK throughout the tax year, and

(B) he has given a notice to HMRC quantifying the amount of any losses accruing in the tax year (see 40.3 LOSSES).

Note that assumption (A) above does not apply for the purposes of *TCGA 1992, s 10A* (temporary non-residents — see 45.4 OVERSEAS MATTERS).

'*Assumed losses*' are any allowable losses, other than actual losses, which would accrue to the vulnerable person for the tax year on the same assumptions as apply for calculating assumed gains. A vulnerable person's '*notional section 77 gains*' for a tax year are the chargeable gains that would be treated as accruing to him under *TCGA 1992, s 77* by virtue of the above provisions for UK resident beneficiaries on the same assumptions.

[*FA 2005, s 32, 33, 41(2), Sch 1*].

57.10 ANNUAL EXEMPTIONS

An annual exempt amount is allowed to trustees in the same way as it is to individuals, and the same rules apply as to the interaction between this amount, allowable losses and taper relief. See 2.3 ANNUAL RATES AND EXEMPTIONS.

The level and availability of the exemption are subject to conditions. These are given below or, in the case of settlements for the disabled etc., in 57.11 below.

Settlements made before 7 June 1978. An outright exemption of *one-half* of the full annual exemption for individuals is available to trustees of such settlements. The exemption limits are thus **£4,400** for 2006/07, £4,250 for 2005/06, £4,100 for 2004/05, £3,950 for 2003/04, £3,850 for 2002/03, £3,750 for 2001/02, £3,600 for 2000/01.

Settlements made after 6 June 1978. The same exemption is available as for settlements made before 7 June 1978 above with the addition of special provisions for 'groups' of settlements. Where a settlement is one of two or more 'qualifying settlements' comprised in a group, the annual exemption is the amount given by dividing one-half of the full annual exemption for individuals (see above) by the number of settlements in the group. However, there is a minimum exemption per settlement of one-tenth of the full annual exemption for individuals. These provisions apply without regard to any sub-fund settlement elections (see 57.8 above), so that a principal settlement and its sub-fund settlements count as only one settlement for the purpose of dividing up the exempt amount. See also below regarding sub-fund settlements.

A '*qualifying settlement*' is any settlement made after 6 June 1978 and which is not a settlement for the disabled, etc. (see 57.11 below) or an 'excluded settlement' (see below). A '*group*' of settlements constitutes all those qualifying settlements with the same 'settlor'. Where, in consequence of this, a settlement is comprised in two or more groups because that settlement was made by two or more settlors, then, in determining the level of annual exemption available as above, it is deemed to be in the group comprised of the greatest number of settlements.

After 5 April 2006, '*settlor*' is as in 57.3 SETTLEMENTS. Previously, '*settlor*' had the meaning given by *ITTOIA 2005, s 620* (see 16.7 CONNECTED PERSONS) and included, in the case of a settlement arising under a will or intestacy, the testator or intestate. Settlements created by a deed of variation within 18.6 DEATH do not 'arise under' a will so that in HMRC's view the testator is not the settlor of the settlements created (Tolley's Practical Tax 1986 p 48).

'*Excluded settlements*' are any of the following

(i) Settlements, the trustees of which are not for the whole or any part of the year of assessment resident and ordinarily resident in the UK (see 44.1 OFFSHORE SETTLEMENTS).

(ii) Settlements, the property in which is held solely for charitable purposes and cannot become applicable for other purposes. See also 10.1 CHARITIES.

(iii) Settlements, the property in which is held for the purposes of certain pension schemes and funds which are exempt from a charge on capital gains.

An HMRC officer may, by notice in writing, require any party to a settlement to provide, within a stipulated time (not less than 28 days), such information as the officer thinks necessary for the application of the above provisions.

[*TCGA 1992, s 3(1)–(5C), Sch 1 paras A1, 2; FA 1993, s 82; FA 1994, s 90; FA 1995, Sch 17 para 32; FA 1998, s 121(3)(4), Sch 21 para 3; FA 2003, s 159, Sch 28 paras 2(3), 5; FA 2004, Sch 35 para 42, Sch 42 Pt 3; ITTOIA 2005, Sch 1 para 449; FA 2006, Sch 12 paras 28(2)(3), 38, 44(1); SI 1992 No 626; SI 1994 No 3008; SI 1995 No 3033; SI 1996 No 2957; SI 1998 No 757; SI 1999 No 591; SI 2000 No 808; SI 2001 No 636; SI 2002 No 702; SI 2003 No 840; SI 2004 No 774; SI 2005 No 721*].

Sub-fund settlements. Where a settlement has been divided for tax purposes into a principal settlement and one or more sub-fund settlements (see 57.8 above), the exempt amount available to the trustees of each deemed settlement is, initially, the amount that would be available to the trustees of the principal settlement under the provisions above or those at 57.11 below if no sub-fund settlement elections had been made. The amount available to each set of trustees is reduced, however, where the deemed settlements include two or more non-excluded settlements (i.e. settlements which are not excluded settlements (see above)). In such circumstances, the exempt amount available to each set of trustees is equal to the amount otherwise available divided by the number of non-excluded settlements. [*TCGA 1992, Sch 1 para 3; FA 2006, Sch 12 para 44(2)*].

57.11 **Settlements for the disabled etc.** Subject to the 'grouping' provisions below the same annual exemption as for individuals (e.g. **£8,800** for 2006/07) (applied, in general, as for individuals: see 2.3 ANNUAL RATES AND EXEMPTIONS for this and for exemptions for earlier years) is available to trustees of such settlements, provided that, during the whole or part of the year of assessment concerned, the settled property is held on trusts which secure that, during the lifetime of a 'mentally disabled person' or a person in receipt of 'attendance allowance' or of a 'disability living allowance' by virtue of entitlement to the care component at the highest or middle rate, (*a*) not less than half of the property which is applied, is applied for the benefit of the person concerned, and

(*b*) that person is entitled to not less than half of the income arising from the property, or no such income may be applied for the benefit of any other person.

'*Mentally disabled person*' means a person who, by reason of mental disorder within the meaning of *Mental Health Act 1983,* is incapable of administering his property or managing his affairs.

'*Attendance allowance*' means an allowance under *Social Security Contributions and Benefits Act 1992, s 64* or *Social Security Contributions and Benefits (Northern Ireland) Act 1992, s 64*.

'*Disability living allowance*' means a disability living allowance under *Social Security Contributions and Benefits Act 1992, s 71* or *Social Security Contributions and Benefits (Northern Ireland) Act 1992, s 71*.

For the purposes of (*a*) and (*b*) above, powers of advancement conferred on the trustees under *Trustee Act 1925, s 32* or *Trustee Act (Northern Ireland) 1958, s 33* will not, as such, disqualify the trust from the relief, and requirements that income be applied for qualifying purposes 'during the lifetime' of a person are deemed satisfied if income is applied for such purposes, during a period where it is held for that person on protective trusts, as under *Trustee Act 1925, s 33*.

Groups. Where a settlement is one of two or more 'qualifying settlements' made after 9 March 1981 comprised in a 'group', the annual exemption is the full annual exemption for individuals divided by the number of settlements in the 'group'. However, there is a minimum exemption of one-tenth of the full annual exemption. These provisions apply without regard to any sub-fund settlement elections (see 57.8 above), so that a principal settlement and its sub-fund settlements count as only one settlement for the purpose of dividing up the exempt amount. See also 57.10 above.

A '*qualifying settlement*' is any settlement for a disabled person, etc. within the provisions above made after 9 March 1981 and which is not an 'excluded settlement'. A '*group*' of settlements constitutes all those qualifying settlements with the same 'settlor'. Where in consequence of this, a settlement is comprised in two or more groups because that settlement was made by two or more settlors, then, in determining the level of annual exemption available as above, it is deemed to be in the group comprised of the greatest number of settlements.

'*Settlor*' and '*excluded settlement*' are as defined in 57.10 above in relation to other settlements made after 6 June 1978 and there are similar powers to call for information.

[*TCGA 1992, s 3(1)–(5C), Sch 1 paras A1, 1; FA 1993, s 82; FA 1994, s 90; FA 1998, s 121(3)(4), Sch 21 para 3; FA 2003, s 159, Sch 28 paras 2(2), 4; FA 2006, Sch 12 paras 28(1)(3), 44(1); SI 1992 No 626; SI 1994 No 3008; SI 1995 No 3033; SI 1996 No 2957; SI 1998 No 757; SI 1999 No 591; SI 2000 No 808; SI 2001 No 636; SI 2002 No 702; SI 2003 No 840; SI 2004 No 774; SI 2005 No 721*].

57.12 CREATION OF A SETTLEMENT

A transfer into settlement, whether revocable or irrevocable, is a disposal of the entire property settled even if the transferor is a beneficiary or trustee of the settlement. [*TCGA 1992, s 70*]. The acquisition and disposal are treated as being made at MARKET VALUE (41) subject to the exclusion therein mentioned. HOLD-OVER RELIEFS (33) may be available in respect of chargeable gains that would otherwise arise to the settlor. The settlor of a settlement and the trustees of that settlement are CONNECTED PERSONS (16) and further rules may operate as to valuation and losses (in particular see 3.15 and 3.16 ANTI-AVOIDANCE, 41.1 MARKET VALUE and 40.5 LOSSES).

Example

In December 2006, C transfers to trustees of a settlement for the benefit of his disabled daughter 10,000 shares in W plc, a quoted company. The value of the gift is £85,000. C bought the shares in 1981 for £20,000 and their value at 31 March 1982 was £35,000. The indexation factor for March 1982 to April 1998 is 1.047.

	£	£
Deemed disposal consideration	85,000	85,000
Cost	20,000	
Market value 31.3.82		35,000
Unindexed gain	65,000	50,000
Indexation allowance £35,000 × 1.047	36,645	36,645
Gain after indexation	£28,355	£13,355
Chargeable gain (subject to TAPER RELIEF (61))		£13,355
Trustees' allowable cost		£85,000

Note to the example

(*a*) If the transfer is a chargeable lifetime transfer for inheritance tax purposes, or would be one but for the annual inheritance tax exemption and C does not have an interest in the settlement within *TCGA 1992, s 169F* (see 33.5 HOLD-OVER RELIEFS), C could elect under *TCGA 1992, s 260* to hold the gain over against the trustees' base cost of the shares. The trustees do not join in any such election. Where taper relief is otherwise available, it is the untapered gain that is held over (see 61.16 TAPER RELIEF).

Exercise of power of appointment or advancement. For the consequences of the exercise of such a power see *Hoare Trustees v Gardner*; *Hart v Briscoe Ch D 1977, 52 TC 53*; *Chinn v Collins HL 1980, 54 TC 311*; *Roome v Edwards HL 1981, 54 TC 359*; *Eilbeck v Rawling HL 1981, 54 TC 101*; *Bond v Pickford CA 1983, 57 TC 301*; *Swires v Renton Ch D 1991, 64 TC 315*. Following the decision in *Bond v Pickford* above, the Revenue issued Statement of Practice 7/84 to set out their views on the capital gains tax implications of the exercise of a power of appointment or advancement when continuing trusts are declared. This Statement modified the earlier SP 9/81 which was issued for a similar purpose following the decision in *Roome v Edwards* above and accordingly SP 9/81 was withdrawn from 11 October 1984.

The Revenue stated in SP 7/84 that the judgments in *Roome v Edwards* emphasised that, in deciding whether or not a new settlement has been created by the exercise of a power of appointment or advancement, each case must be considered on its own facts, and by applying established legal doctrine to the facts in a practical and commonsense manner. The Court of Appeal judgements in *Bond v Pickford* explained that the consideration of the facts must include examination of the powers which the trustees purported to exercise, and the determination of the intention of the parties, viewed objectively.

HMRC consider it now clear that a deemed disposal under *TCGA 1992, s 71*(*1*) (see 57.15 below) cannot arise unless the power exercised by the trustees, or the instrument conferring the power, expressly or by necessary implication, confers on the trustees authority to remove assets from the original settlement by subjecting them to trusts of a different settlement. Such powers (which may be powers of advancement or appointment) were referred to by the Court of Appeal in *Bond v Pickford* as 'powers in the wider form'. HMRC consider that a deemed disposal will not arise when such powers are exercised and trusts are declared in circumstances such that (*a*) the appointment is revocable, or

(*b*) the trusts declared of the advanced or appointed funds are not exhaustive so that there exists a possibility at the time when the advancement or appointment is made that the funds covered by it will, on the occasion of some event, cease to be held upon such trusts and once again come to be held upon the original trusts of the settlement.

HMRC also consider it unlikely a deemed disposal will occur when trusts are declared following the exercise of such a power if the duties of trusteeship as regards the appointed assets fall to the trustees of the original settlement. This follows from the provision in *TCGA 1992, s 69(1)* that the trustees of a settlement form a single and continuing body (see 57.4 above).

In conclusion, HMRC accept that a power of appointment or advancement can be exercised over only a part of settled property and that the foregoing would apply to that part.

See *Begg-McBrearty v Stilwell Ch D 1996, 68 TC 426* for interpretation of *Family Law Reform Act 1969*.

HMRC practice regarding validity of trust deeds for general and tax law purposes. New trust deeds (other than those for special types of trust such as unit trusts, charitable trusts and employee trusts) are not examined individually by HMRC for their validity under general law as well as tax law. HMRC normally rely on the information shown in returns etc. made by the settlors, trustees and beneficiaries and only seek further information where necessary, and only exceptionally will they ask to see deeds or other documents. Trustees are asked to supply information about themselves and the settlor and whether the trustees have power to accumulate income or to distribute it at their discretion (Revenue Press Release 19 December 1990).

57.13 INTERESTS IN SETTLED PROPERTY

Interests in settled property take a variety of forms as outlined below. Their treatment for capital gains tax purposes is given in 57.14 to 57.17 below. See 57.2 above as regards bare trusts.

Interests created by or arising under a settlement. These include, in particular, an annuity or life interest (see below), and the reversion to an annuity or life interest, but are otherwise not specifically defined. [*TCGA 1992, s 76*].

Life interests in relation to a settlement. The meaning of 'life interest' includes a right under the settlement to the income of, or the use or occupation of, settled property for the life of a person other than the person entitled to the right, or for lives. [*TCGA 1992, s 72(3)(a)*]. Any right which is contingent on the exercise of the discretion of the trustee or some other person is not a life interest. [*TCGA 1992, s 72(3)(b)*]. The ordinary meaning of 'life interest' (i.e. the right of a person to income etc. during his life) is also accepted as applying. Interests which are not primarily defined by reference to a life are not considered to be life interests, so that a beneficiary with an interest in possession (see below) in settled property which will come to an end on obtaining a specified age does not have a life interest (HMRC Extra-Statutory Concession D43). However, concessional treatment is available for such non-life interests which cease on the death of a beneficiary as in 57.16 and 57.17 below.

An annuity created by the settlement is included as a life interest if

(i) some or all of the settled property is appropriated by the trustees as a fund out of which the annuity is payable and

(ii) there is no right of recourse to settled property not so appropriated or to the income thereof.

While such an annuity is payable, and on the occasion of the death of the annuitant, the appropriated part of the settled property is treated as being settled property under a separate settlement. Annuities, other than those above, are not life interests notwithstanding that they are payable out of, or charged on, settled property or the income thereof. [*TCGA 1992, s 72(3)(c), (4)*]. However, where an annuity which is not a life interest is terminated by the death of the annuitant, certain provisions in 57.16 and 57.17 below apply as on the termination of a life interest by the death of the person entitled thereto.

Life interest in possession in all or part of settled property. The legislation gives no meaning to the term 'life interest in possession' although it seems regard must be made to the meaning of 'life interest' (as above) and to judicial interpretation of the term 'interest in possession'. Such interpretation arose in *Pearson and Others v CIR HL, [1980] STC 318* where the point at issue was the meaning of the term 'interest in possession' as used in certain capital transfer tax legislation dealing with settled property. The majority opinions of the HL indicated the following.

(*a*) There must be a *present right to the present enjoyment* of something for there to be an interest in possession in settled property. So a person with an interest in possession will have an immediate right to trust income as it arises.

(*b*) If the trustees have *any power to withhold income* as it arises there is no interest in possession. There is a distinction between a power to terminate a present right to present enjoyment and a power which prevents a present right of present enjoyment arising. It follows that

(i) a power to accumulate income is sufficient to prevent a beneficiary from having an interest in possession. The position is the same if there is a trust to accumulate. Whether or not income is in fact accumulated is irrelevant;

(ii) an overriding power of appointment which could be used to defeat the interest of a beneficiary does not prevent that interest from being in possession if it does not affect the right of the beneficiary to the income which has already arisen;

(iii) the possibility of future defeasance of an interest does not prevent it from being in possession until the occurrence of the relevant event; and

(iv) a power of revocation does not prevent an interest from being in possession until it is exercised.

(*c*) There is a distinction between trustees' *administrative powers,* such as those to pay duties, taxes etc., and their *dispositive powers* to dispose of the net income of the trust. The existence of the former does not prevent an interest from being in possession. Any interest in possession will be in the net income of the trust after deduction of administrative expenses.

(*d*) The fact that an interest in settled property is not in remainder or reversion or contingent does not automatically make it an interest in possession.

The Revenue had published their views on the meaning of 'interest in possession' prior to the HL decision in *Pearson* above. Their statement, although now withdrawn, was reproduced in Revenue Pamphlet IHT 1 (1991), p 88 and the Revenue regarded the views expressed therein as 'not inconsistent' with the opinions given in *Pearson.*

If, in exercise of their powers under the settlement, the trustees grant a beneficiary an exclusive or joint right to occupy a dwelling-house which forms part of the settled property with the intention of providing the beneficiary with a permanent home, HMRC regard this as creating an interest in possession, even if the right is revocable or for a limited period. A right granted for non-exclusive occupation or for full consideration is not so regarded

(HMRC Statement of Practice 10/79). See 49.5 PRIVATE RESIDENCES for the exemption available on the disposal of a dwelling-house which has been occupied in the above circumstances.

57.14 DISPOSAL OF AN INTEREST IN SETTLED PROPERTY

Subject to the exclusions below for settlements which are, or have ever been, non-resident settlements, no chargeable gain accrues on the disposal of an interest created by or arising under a settlement (see 57.13 above) if the disposal was made

(*a*) by the person for whose benefit the interest was created by the terms of the settlement; or

(*b*) by any other person except one who acquired, or derives his title from one who acquired, the interest for a consideration in money or money's worth, other than consideration consisting of another interest under the settlement.

Subject to the above, where a person who has acquired an interest in settled property becomes, as the holder of that interest, absolutely entitled (see 57.2 above) as against the trustee to any settled property, he is treated as disposing of the interest in consideration of obtaining the property so received (but without prejudice to any gain accruing to the trustee on the deemed disposal by the trustee under *TCGA 1992, s 71*(*1*) (see 57.15 below)).

[*TCGA 1992, s 76*(*1*)(*2*); *FA 1998, s 128*(*1*)].

Where the disposal of a life interest in settled property does give rise to a chargeable event, the interest may be treated as a wasting asset in certain circumstances. See 67.6 WASTING ASSETS.

See 57.18 below for anti-avoidance provisions deeming there to be, in specified circumstances, a disposal of underlying assets at the same time as an actual disposal of an interest in settled property for consideration.

Exclusion for certain non-resident settlements. The exemption above does not apply to disposals of interests in settlements which are, or have ever been, non-resident. See 44.4 OFFSHORE SETTLEMENTS.

57.15 PERSON BECOMING ABSOLUTELY ENTITLED TO SETTLED PROPERTY

General rule. Subject to the exception below, where a person becomes absolutely entitled to any settled property as against the trustee, all the assets forming part of the settled property to which he becomes so entitled are deemed to have been disposed of by the trustee and immediately reacquired by him in the capacity of bare trustee or nominee within *TCGA 1992, s 60*(*1*) (see 57.2 above) for a consideration equal to the market value of the assets. [*TCGA 1992, s 71*(*1*)]. See *Figg v Clarke Ch D 1996, 68 TC 645* for interpretation of date of absolute entitlement.

Where an interest in possession in part of settled property terminates (whether voluntarily or involuntarily) and the part can properly be identified with one or more specific assets, or where within a reasonable time, normally three months, of the termination, the trustees appropriate specific assets to give effect to the termination, HMRC will treat the deemed disposal and reacquisition as applying to those assets, and not to any part of the other assets comprised in the settlement. In particular, agreement will be made of lists of assets properly identifiable with the termination, and any such agreement will be regarded as binding on HMRC and the trustees (HMRC Statement of Practice D10).

Any resulting net chargeable gain is assessed on the trustee in the usual way (subject to a claim for HOLD-OVER RELIEFS (33) but note the general relief for gifts in 33.9 was only extant after 5 April 1982 and before 14 March 1989).

Losses. Where, **after 15 June 1999**, a person (the beneficiary) becomes absolutely entitled to any settled property as against the trustee and a loss accrues to the trustee on the resulting deemed disposal under *TCGA 1992, s 71(1)* (see above) of an asset comprised in that property, then, subject to the restrictions below, the loss is treated as a loss accruing to the beneficiary instead of to the trustee. Such treatment is mandatory, but applies only to the extent that the loss cannot be deducted from gains accruing to the trustee either on the deemed disposal of other assets on that occasion or on disposals made earlier in the same year of assessment, and for this purpose only (and not, for example, for taper relief purposes) such a loss is treated as deductible in priority to any other allowable losses accruing to the trustee in that year. Where a loss is so treated as accruing to the beneficiary, it is allowable *only* against chargeable gains accruing to him on disposal by him of the same asset, i.e. the asset on the deemed disposal of which the loss occurred, or, where the asset is land, any asset which is 'derived' from it (as defined). The loss can be carried forward to subsequent years of assessment until such time as it has been fully allowed against such gains. Where there is such a gain, the loss in question is treated as deductible in priority to any other allowable losses accruing to the beneficiary in the year of assessment concerned and, where it is brought forward, is deductible as if it were a loss accruing in that year (see 40.1 LOSSES for set-off of losses generally). For a worked example, see Tolley's Tax Computations or Tolley's Capital Gains Tax Workbook. These provisions are equally applicable where it is another set of trustees who become absolutely entitled as against the trustees with the losses (HMRC Capital Gains Manual CG 37209).

Where the occasion on which a person became absolutely entitled to any settled property as against the trustee occurred **before 16 June 1999**, *any* allowable loss which had accrued to the trustees in respect of property which was, or was represented by, the property to which the beneficiary became so entitled (including allowable losses on *actual* disposals by the trustees and any such losses brought forward from previous years of assessment) was treated (to the extent that it could not be set against other chargeable gains arising to the trustee in that year of assessment but before that occasion) as an allowable loss accruing to the beneficiary at the time he became entitled. The beneficiary can utilise that loss without restriction.

[*TCGA 1992, s 71(2)–(2D); FA 1999, s 75*].

The position should be contrasted with that of allowable losses made by personal representatives as in 18.7 DEATH.

Where trust losses are transferable to a beneficiary as above, HMRC do not restrict those losses under *TCGA 1992, s 18(3)* (see 40.5 LOSSES) where the trustees and the person becoming absolutely entitled are CONNECTED PERSONS (16) (Revenue Tax Bulletin February 1993 p 57).

No loss accruing after 5 April 1996 is transferable to beneficiaries unless it has been notified by the trustees under the normal self-assessment rules at 40.3 LOSSES (HMRC Capital Gains Manual CG 37210).

Miscellaneous. References in the foregoing to the case where a person becomes absolutely entitled to settled property as against the trustee include references to the case where a person would become so entitled but for being an infant or other person under disability. [*TCGA 1992, s 71(3)*].

Where a person disposes of an asset held by another person as trustee to which he became absolutely entitled as against the trustee, any incidental expenditure incurred by that person or the trustee in relation to the transfer of the asset to him is allowable as a deduction in the computation of the gain arising on the disposal. [*TCGA 1992, s 64(1); FA 2006, Sch 12 para 12*]. The expenditure incurred by the person concerned, but not that incurred by the trustees, may qualify for indexation allowance (HMRC Capital Gains Manual CG 31192).

Exception where a life interest is terminated by the death of the person entitled thereto. Where, as above, a person becomes absolutely entitled as against the trustee to assets forming part of settled property and that occasion is the termination of a life interest by the death of the person entitled to that interest then, where that interest meets certain conditions (and, subject to exceptions), *no* chargeable gain arises on the deemed disposal. See 57.17(*a*) below for full details.

57.16 TERMINATION OF LIFE INTEREST IN POSSESSION ON DEATH OF PERSON ENTITLED: ASSETS REMAINING SETTLED PROPERTY

Where an interest in possession in all or part (see SP D10 in 57.15 above) of settled property is terminated on the death of the person entitled to it (e.g. a life tenant), the whole or a corresponding part of each of the assets forming part of the settled property and not at that time ceasing to be settled property is deemed to be disposed of and immediately reacquired by the trustee at that time for a consideration equal to the whole or a corresponding part of the market value of the asset. However, any gain arising on such a deemed disposal is not a chargeable gain. Where the deceased became entitled to the interest in possession on or after 22 March 2006, this applies only if:

(i) the deceased died under the age of 18 and, immediately before his death, *IHTA 1984, s 71D* (age 18 to 25 trusts) applies to the property in which the interest subsists; or

(ii) immediately before his death,

(*a*) the interest in possession is an immediate post-death interest within *IHTA 1984, s 49A*;

(*b*) the interest is a transitional serial interest within *IHTA 1984, s 49B*;

(*c*) the interest is a disabled person's interest within *IHTA 1984, s 89B*(*1*)(*c*)(*d*); or

(*d*) *IHTA 1984, s 71A* (trusts for bereaved minors) applies to the property in which the interest subsists.

[*TCGA 1992, s 72(1)–(1C); FA 1996, Sch 39 para 5(2)(4); FA 2006, Sch 20 para 30(2)*]. (See the exception below as regards previously held-over gains.)

The above provisions also apply where the person entitled to an interest in possession in all or part of the settled property dies but the interest does not then terminate. Again, where the deceased became entitled to the interest in possession on or after 22 March 2006, this applies only if, immediately before his death, one of (ii)(*a*) to (*c*) above applies. [*TCGA 1992, s 72(2)(2A); FA 1996, Sch 39 para 5(2)(4); FA 2006, Sch 20 para 30(3)*].

Annuities. For deaths after 5 April 1996, the above provisions apply on the death of the person entitled to any annuity payable out of, or charged on, settled property or the income of settled property as it applies on the death of a person whose interest in possession in the whole or any part of settled property terminates on his death. Where, in the case of any entitlement to an annuity created by a settlement some of the settled property is appropriated by the trustees as a fund out of which the annuity is payable, and there is no right of recourse to, or to the income of, settled property not so appropriated, then without prejudice to *TCGA 1992, s 72(5)* below, the settled property so appropriated is, while the annuity is payable, and on the occasion of the death of the person entitled to the annuity, treated for the purposes of *TCGA 1992, s 72* as being settled property under a separate settlement. [*TCGA 1992, s 72(3)(4); FA 1996, Sch 39 para 5(3)(4)*]. For deaths before 6 April 1996 broadly similar provisions applied. [*TCGA 1992, s 75; FA 1996, Sch 41 Pt VIII(4)*]. In the case where the annuity is not paid out of specified funds, HMRC treats the corresponding part (see above) of the assets forming the settled property as being given by the proportion which the amount of the annuity bears to the whole of the settlement income arising in the year prior to the date of death.

Part interests and income interests. For the purposes of the above provisions, an interest which is a right to part of the income of settled property is treated as such an interest in a corresponding part of the settled property. [*TCGA 1992, s 72*(*1*); *FA 1996, Sch 39 para 5*(*2*)(*4*)].

If there is an interest in income in a part of settled property such that there is no right of recourse to, or to the income from, the remainder of the settled property, then the part of the settled property in which such interest subsists is similarly treated as being settled property under a separate settlement for so long as such an interest subsists. [*TCGA 1992, s 72*(*5*); *FA 1996, Sch 39 para 5*(*2*)(*4*)].

Exception where hold-over relief under TCGA 1992, s 165 or s 260 or FA 1980, s 79 claimed previously. In certain circumstances where a claim has been made for hold-over relief in respect of the disposal of an asset to the trustee and, subsequently, the trustee is deemed to dispose of and immediately reacquire the asset so that under *TCGA 1992, s 72* above there would otherwise be no chargeable gain arising, it is specifically provided by *TCGA 1992, s 67* or *s 74* that a chargeable gain, restricted to the amount of the held-over gain, is to accrue to the trustee. See 33.5, 33.8 and 33.9 HOLD-OVER RELIEFS.

57.17 TERMINATION OF LIFE INTEREST ON DEATH OF PERSON ENTITLED: PERSON BECOMING ABSOLUTELY ENTITLED

(*a*) Where, under *TCGA 1992, s 71*(*1*) in 57.15 above, the assets forming part of any settled property are deemed to be disposed of and reacquired at market value by the trustee on the occasion when a person becomes, or would but for a disability become, absolutely entitled thereto as against the trustee, then, if that occasion is the death of a person entitled to an interest in possession in the settled property (e.g. the death of a life tenant)

- (i) no chargeable gain accrues on the deemed disposal; and
- (ii) if on the death the property reverts to the disponer (e.g. the original settlor), the disposal and reacquisition by the trustee is treated as taking place on a no gain/no loss basis, and if the acquisition by the trustee was at a time prior to 6 April 1965, the reversion is related back to that date.

In relation to a sub-fund settlement (see 57.8 above), (ii) above is treated as applying if the property does not revert to the trustees of the principal settlement (see 57.8 above) only because it becomes comprised in another sub-fund of the principal settlement in respect of which a sub-fund settlement election is in force.

(*b*) Where the interest is an interest in part (see SP D10 in 57.15 above) only of the settled property to which the person becomes absolutely entitled, (*a*)(i) above does not apply but although a chargeable gain will accordingly arise as under *TCGA 1992, s 71*(*1*) in 57.15 above it is reduced by a proportion corresponding to that represented by the part in which the interest subsisted. Any remaining chargeable gain may be the subject of a claim for one of the HOLD-OVER RELIEFS (33).

Where the deceased became entitled to the interest in possession on or after 22 March 2006, these provisions apply only if either 57.16(i) or (ii) above applies.

[*TCGA 1992, s 73*(*1*)(*2*); *FA 1996, Sch 39 para 6*(*2*)(*3*)(*5*); *FA 2006, Sch 12 para 42, Sch 20 para 31*].

(See the exception below as regards previously held-over gains.)

Annuities. For deaths after 5 April 1996, (*a*) and (*b*) above apply on the death of the person entitled to any annuity payable out of, or charged on, settled property or the income of settled property as it applies on the death of a person whose interest in possession in the whole or any part of settled property terminates on his death. Where, in the case of any entitlement to an annuity created by a settlement some of the settled property is appropriated by the trustees as a fund out of which the annuity is payable, and there is no right of recourse to, or to the income of, settled property not so appropriated, then without prejudice to *TCGA 1992, s 72(5)* below, the settled property so appropriated is, while the annuity is payable, and on the occasion of the death of the person entitled to the annuity, treated for the purposes of *TCGA 1992, s 72* as being settled property under a separate settlement. [*TCGA 1992, s 72(3)(4), s 73(3); FA 1996, Sch 39 para 5(3)(4), para 6(4)(5)*]. For deaths before 6 April 1996 broadly similar provisions applied. [*TCGA 1992, s 75; FA 1996, Sch 41 Pt VIII(4)*]. In the case where the annuity is not paid out of specified funds, HMRC treats the 'proportion corresponding to that represented by the part in which the interest subsisted' (see (*b*) above) of the assets forming the settled property as being given by the proportion which the amount of the annuity bears to the whole of the settlement income arising in the year prior to the date of death.

Part interests and income interests. For the purposes of (*a*) and (*b*) above, an interest which is a right to part of the income of settled property is treated as such an interest in a corresponding part of the settled property. [*TCGA 1992, s 72(1), s 73(3); FA 1996, Sch 39 para 5(2)(4), para 6(4)(5)*].

If there is an interest in income in a part of settled property such that there is no right of recourse to, or to the income from, the remainder of the settled property, then the part of the settled property in which such interest subsists is similarly treated as being settled property under a separate settlement for so long as such an interest subsists. [*TCGA 1992, s 72(5), s 73(3); FA 1996, Sch 39 para 5(2)(4), para 6(4)(5)*].

Exception where hold-over relief under TCGA 1992, s 165 or s 260 or FA 1980, s 79 claimed previously. In certain circumstances where a claim has been made for hold-over relief in respect of the disposal of an asset to the trustee and, subsequently, the trustee is deemed to dispose of and immediately reacquire the asset so that under *TCGA 1992, s 73* above there would otherwise be no chargeable gain arising, it is specifically provided by *TCGA 1992, s 67* or *s 74* that a chargeable gain, restricted to the amount of the held-over gain, is to accrue to the trustee. See 33.5, 33.8 and 33.9 HOLD-OVER RELIEFS.

57.18 ANTI-AVOIDANCE: DEEMED DISPOSAL OF UNDERLYING ASSETS ON CERTAIN DISPOSALS OF INTERESTS IN SETTLED PROPERTY

Cross-reference. See 57.14 above for the general exemption from CGT on a disposal of an interest in settled property.

Deemed disposal. Where

- a disposal of an 'interest in settled property' is made, or is effectively completed (see below under Time lapse before effective completion), after 20 March 2000,
- the disposal is 'for consideration', and
- specified conditions are present as detailed below (as to UK residence of trustees and settlor and as to settlor interest in the settlement),

the trustees of the settlement are deemed for all CGT purposes to have disposed of and immediately reacquired the underlying assets (see below) at market value. The deemed disposal takes place at the same time as the actual disposal of the interest in settled property. It is regarded as made under a bargain at arm's length (which effectively precludes a claim for the gain to be deferred as in 33.1 or 33.7 HOLD-OVER RELIEFS). [*TCGA 1992, s 76A, Sch 4A paras 1, 4(1)(3), para 9; FA 2000, s 91, Sch 24*]. Where applicable, any gain on the deemed disposal is chargeable on the settlor under the relevant provisions in 57.5 above.

See below for modifications to the above where there is a time lapse before effective completion of the actual disposal.

Where the trust is a maintenance fund for an historic building, the same exception applies as under the charge on settlor rules in 57.5 above. [*TCGA 1992, Sch 4A para 14*].

For these purposes, an '*interest in settled property*' is any interest created by or arising under the settlement. This includes the right to enjoy any benefit arising from the exercise of a discretion or power by the trustees of a settlement or by any person in relation to a settlement. A disposal is '*for consideration*' if actual consideration is given or received by any person for, or in connection with, any transaction by which the disposal is effected. Consideration deemed to have been given under any CGT provision is disregarded for these purposes. Consideration in the form of another interest under the same settlement is also disregarded, as long as that interest has not previously been disposed of by any person for consideration. [*TCGA 1992, Sch 4A paras 2, 3*]. HMRC consider that consideration for these purposes does not include incidental costs, in particular reasonable fees charged by professional advisers for legal and tax advice as to the effects of the transaction or for drafting and executing the relevant paperwork. Where there are no payments other than in respect of such costs, the transaction does not fall within these provisions. (Revenue Tax Bulletin August 2003 p 1048).

Underlying assets. Where the interest disposed of is in the whole of the settled property, the deemed disposal is of each of the assets comprised in that property. Where the interest disposed of is in a specific fund or other defined part of the settled property, the deemed disposal is of each of the assets comprised in that fund or part. In either case, the deemed disposal is of the whole of each of the assets concerned, unless the interest disposed of is an interest in a specified fraction or amount of the income or capital, in which case the deemed disposal is of a corresponding part of each of the assets concerned. Where part only of an asset is comprised in a specific fund or other defined part of the settled property, that part of the asset is treated as a separate asset for the purposes of these provisions. [*TCGA 1992, Sch 4A para 8*]. See also below under Time lapse before effective completion.

Conditions. All the following conditions must be present for the disposal of underlying assets to be deemed to take place (and see also the modifications below under Time lapse before effective completion).

UK residence of trustees. The trustees must have been

- for 2007/08 onwards, resident and ordinarily resident in the UK during any part of the tax year of disposal, or
- for 2006/07 and earlier years, either resident in the UK during all or part of the tax year of disposal or ordinarily resident in the UK during that tax year,

and, in either case, not regarded under a double tax agreement as resident elsewhere.

UK residence of settlor. In the tax year of disposal or in any of the previous five tax years (not counting years before 1999/2000), a person who is a settlor (defined as in 57.5 above) in relation to the settlement must have been either resident in the UK during all or part of the year or ordinarily resident in the UK during the year.

Settlor interest in the settlement. At some time during the 'relevant period', either

- a person who is a settlor (defined as in 57.5 above) in relation to the settlement must have had an interest in the settlement (for which see 57.5 above), or
- the settlement must have comprised property derived, directly or indirectly, from another settlement in which a settlor had an interest at any time in the relevant period.

The '*relevant period*' is the period beginning two years before the beginning of the tax year of disposal (or beginning on 6 April 1999 if later) and ending with the date of the disposal of the interest in settled property.

Where the settlor dies or the exceptions from the charge on settlor in 57.5 above on death of spouse or civil partner, end of marriage or civil partnership or ceasing to have any dependent children would apply, the above condition is treated as not present in the tax year of death or in which those events occur.

[*TCGA 1992, Sch 4A para 4(2), paras 5–7, 12; FA 2006, Sch 12 paras 5, 29, 34(1)–(3), 39, 41; SI 2005 No 3229, Reg 125*].

Prevention of double charge. Where there would be a deemed disposal as above and the actual disposal of the interest in settled property is not itself exempt by virtue of *TCGA 1992, s 76* (see 57.14 above), the following provisions apply to ensure that there is no double charge or double allowance of a loss.

- If both the deemed disposal and the actual disposal give rise to a chargeable gain (or in the case of the deemed disposal a net chargeable gain by reference to all the assets involved), the lower gain is disregarded.
- If both disposals give rise to an allowable loss (or net allowable loss), the lower loss is disregarded.
- If one disposal gives rise to a (net) chargeable gain and the other a (net) allowable loss, the loss is disregarded.
- If the actual disposal gives rise to neither a chargeable gain nor an allowable loss, any net chargeable gain on the deemed disposal is taken as accruing instead.

[*TCGA 1992, Sch 4A para 10*].

Trustees' right of recovery. Where tax becomes chargeable in respect of a deemed disposal as above and either it is chargeable on the trustees or it is chargeable on the settlor and recovered by him from the trustees as in 57.5 above, the trustees have the right to recover the tax from the person who made the actual disposal (i.e. of an interest in the settlement) giving rise to the deemed disposal. For this purpose, they may require an inspector to certify the gain and the tax paid.

[*TCGA 1992, Sch 4A para 11*].

Time lapse before effective completion. The above provisions are subject to the modifications below where there is a period between the beginning of the disposal of the interest in settled property and the effective completion of that disposal. For these purposes, the disposal begins when a contract is entered into or, where relevant, an option is granted. It is effectively completed when the person acquiring the interest becomes for all practical purposes unconditionally entitled to the whole of the intended subject matter of the disposal.

Where the beginning of the disposal and the effective completion take place in different tax years:

- the deemed disposal is treated as taking place in the tax year of effective completion;
- the conditions as to UK residence of trustees and settlor are treated as present if they are present by reference to either of those tax years or any intervening year;
- the '*relevant period*' for the purpose of the condition as to settlor interest in the settlement is the period beginning two years before the beginning of the first of those tax years (or beginning on 6 April 1999 if later) and ending with the effective completion.

If the identity or value of the underlying assets changes during the period between the beginning of the disposal and its effective completion, an asset is subject to the deemed disposal rules if it was comprised in the settled property (or specific fund or other defined part) at any time during that period, unless it was disposed of (and not reacquired) by the trustees during that period under a bargain at arm's length. The market value of an asset for the purposes of the deemed disposal is its highest market value at any time in that period.

[*TCGA 1992, Sch 4A para 13*].

HMRC have given examples of circumstances in which they would consider that the person acquiring the asset is for all practical purposes unconditionally entitled to the intended subject matter of the disposal (as above). These are where the buyer has the power to compel the trustees to transfer the property to him on giving due notice, and where the buyer has a right to enjoy the property now, but is not entitled to it until a particular contingency is fulfilled, and there is no real likelihood of its not being fulfilled. (Revenue Tax Bulletin August 2003 p 1049).

57.19 ANTI-AVOIDANCE: TRANSFERS OF VALUE BY TRUSTEES LINKED WITH TRUSTEE BORROWING

The following provisions were introduced to counter a particular avoidance scheme (known as the 'flip-flop' scheme), although they apply in any case where the conditions are met without regard to any avoidance motive. The scheme was considered in *Trennery v West HL 2005, [2005] STC 214, [2005] UKHL 5*.

See Revenue Tax Bulletin August 2003 pp 1048–1051, for HMRC's views on various terms used in the provisions.

Deemed disposal. Where

- the trustees of a settlement make a 'transfer of value' after 20 March 2000;
- the transfer is treated as 'linked with trustee borrowing'; and
- it takes place in a tax year in which the settlement is within *TCGA 1992, s 77, s 86* or *s 87* (see below)

the trustees are deemed for all CGT purposes to have disposed of and immediately reacquired the whole or a proportion (see below) of each of the 'chargeable assets' that continue to form part of the settled property immediately after the transfer ('*the remaining chargeable assets*'). The deemed disposal takes place at the time of the transfer of value and is treated as made under a bargain at arm's length and for a consideration equal to the whole or, as the case may be, a proportion of the market value of each asset. Where applicable, gains (less losses) on the deemed disposals are then chargeable on the settlor under *TCGA 1992, s 77* (see 57.5 above) or, in the case of an offshore settlement, on the settlor under *TCGA 1992, s 86* (see 44.5 OFFSHORE SETTLEMENTS) or on beneficiaries receiving capital payments under *TCGA 1992, Sch 4C* (see 44.18 OFFSHORE SETTLEMENTS).

The significance of the deemed disposal being treated as an arm's length disposal is that the provisions at 33.1 and 33.7 HOLD-OVER RELIEFS are thereby disapplied.

For these purposes, an asset is a '*chargeable asset*' if a gain on a disposal of the asset by the trustees at the time of the transfer of value would be a chargeable gain. A settlement is within *TCGA 1992, s 77* (see 57.5 above) in a tax year if, assuming that there were net chargeable gains (after deducting losses) accruing to the trustees from the disposal of settled property, chargeable gains would be treated as accruing to the settlor in that year under that *section* (otherwise than by virtue of *FA 2005, s 31* (trust with vulnerable beneficiaries — see 57.9 above). A settlement is within *TCGA 1992, s 86* (see 44.5 OFFSHORE SETTLEMENTS) in a tax year if, assuming that there were net gains (after deducting losses) accruing to the trustees from disposals of any of the settled property originating from the settlor, chargeable gains would be treated as accruing to the settlor in that year under that *section*. A settlement is within *TCGA 1992, s 87* (see 44.14 OFFSHORE SETTLEMENTS) in a tax year if, assuming there were 'trust gains for the year' (within the meaning of that *section*) and that beneficiaries of the settlement received capital payments from the trustees in that or an earlier year, chargeable gains would be treated as accruing to the beneficiaries in that year under that *section* or *TCGA 1992, s 89(2)* (see 44.14 OFFSHORE SETTLEMENTS).

[*TCGA 1992, s 76B, Sch 4B paras 1, 3, 10; FA 2000, s 92(1)(2)(5), Sch 25*].

Transfer of value. Trustees of a settlement make a '*transfer of value*' if they

- lend money or any other 'asset' to any person;
- 'transfer an asset' to any person and receive either no consideration or a consideration lower than the market value of the asset transferred; or
- issue a security of any description to any person and receive either no consideration or a consideration lower than the value of the security.

For the purposes of these provisions, an '*asset*' includes money expressed in sterling. References below to the value or market value of such an asset are to its amount. The '*transfer of an asset*' includes anything that is, or is treated as, a disposal of the asset for capital gains tax purposes, or would be if money expressed in sterling were an asset for capital gains tax purposes. Part disposals are not excluded. However, a transfer of an asset does not include a transfer of an asset that is itself created by the part disposal of another asset. For example, the grant of a leasehold interest in freehold land is for these purposes a transfer of the freehold (and not of the leasehold).

The transfer of value is treated as made at the time when the loan is made, the transfer is 'effectively completed' or the security is issued. A transfer is '*effectively completed*' at the point at which the person acquiring the asset becomes for practical purposes unconditionally entitled to the whole of the intended subject matter of the transfer.

The amount of value transferred is taken to be

- in the case of a loan, the market value of the asset;
- in the case of a transfer of an asset:
  - (i) if any part of the value of the asset is 'attributable to trustee borrowing' (see below), the market value of the asset; or
  - (ii) if no part of the value of the asset is attributable to trustee borrowing, the market value of the asset reduced by any consideration received for it; and
- in the case of the issue of a security, the value of the security reduced by any consideration received for it.

For this purpose, the value of an asset is its value immediately before the time the transfer of value is treated as made, unless the asset does not exist before that time in which case its value immediately after that time is taken.

[*TCGA 1992, Sch 4B paras 2, 13*].

HMRC consider that a distribution made by the trustees of a discretionary trust which is income of the recipient for UK tax purposes is not a transfer of value for the purposes of these provisions. Likewise, where a beneficiary occupies property under rights arising as a consequence of the trust deed or the will, the Revenue consider that the occupation does not give rise to a transfer of value. They may not take this view where the rights arise as a consequence of the exercise of a power of appointment or advancement. 'Lending money' does not include putting money into a conventional current or deposit account at a bank or building society. (Revenue Tax Bulletin August 2003 pp 1049, 1050).

Transfer of value linked with trustee borrowing. Trustees of a settlement are treated as borrowing if

- money or any other asset is lent to them; or
- an asset is transferred to them and, in connection with the transfer, the trustees assume a contractual obligation (whether absolute or conditional) to restore or transfer to any person that or any other asset.

References below to a '*loan obligation*' include any such obligation as is mentioned above.

The amount borrowed (the '*proceeds*' of the borrowing) is taken to be

- in the case of a loan, the market value of the asset;
- in the case of a transfer, the market value of the asset reduced by any consideration received for it.

For this purpose, the market value of an asset is its market value immediately before the loan is made, or the transfer is effectively completed (see above under Transfer of value), unless the asset does not exist before that event in which case its market value immediately after that event is taken.

A transfer of value by trustees is treated as '*linked with trustee borrowing*' if at the time of the transfer there is 'outstanding trustee borrowing'. There is '*outstanding trustee borrowing*' at any time to the extent that

- any loan obligation is outstanding, and
- there are proceeds of trustee borrowing that have not been either
  - 'applied for normal trust purposes', or
  - taken into account under these provisions in relation to an earlier transfer of value which was treated as linked with trustee borrowing.

For the purposes of these provisions, the proceeds of trustee borrowing are '*applied for normal trust purposes*' if and only if

(*a*) they are applied by the trustees in making a payment in respect of an 'ordinary trust asset' and the following conditions are met:

(i) the payment is made under a transaction at arm's length or is not more than the payment that would be made if the transaction were at arm's length;

(ii) the asset forms part of the settled property immediately after the transfer of value or, if it (or part of it) does not do so, the alternative condition described below is met; and

(iii) the sum paid is allowable under *TCGA 1992, s 38* (see 15.4 and 15.6 COMPUTATION OF GAINS AND LOSSES) as a deduction in computing a gain accruing to the trustees on a disposal of the asset (or would be so allowable were it not for the application of *TCGA 1992, s 17*, see 41.1 MARKET VALUE, or *TCGA 1992, s 39*, see 15.6(*a*) COMPUTATION OF GAINS AND LOSSES); or

(*b*) they are applied by the trustees in wholly or partly discharging a loan obligation, and the whole of the proceeds of the borrowing connected with that obligation (or all but an insignificant amount) have been applied by the trustees for normal trust purposes; or

(*c*) they are applied by the trustees in making payments to meet *bona fide* current expenses incurred by them in administering the settlement or any of the settled property.

The following are '*ordinary trust assets*':

(1) shares or securities (the latter as defined in *TCGA 1992, s 132* — see 58.7 SHARES AND SECURITIES);

(2) tangible property, whether movable or immovable, or a lease of such property;

(3) property not within (1) or (2) above which is used for the purposes of a trade, profession or vocation carried on by the trustees or by a beneficiary who has an interest in possession in the settled property; and

(4) any right in or over, or any interest in, property of a description within (2) or (3) above.

The alternative condition mentioned in (*a*)(ii) above in relation to an asset (or part of an asset) which no longer forms part of the settled property is that

- the asset (or part) is treated as having been disposed of by virtue of *TCGA 1992, s 24(1)* (entire loss or destruction of an asset — see 9.1 CAPITAL SUMS DERIVED FROM ASSETS), or
- one or more ordinary trust assets which taken together directly or indirectly represent the asset (or part)
  - form part of the settled property immediately after the transfer of value, or
  - are treated as having been disposed of by virtue of *TCGA 1992, s 24(1)*.

Where there has been a part disposal of the asset, the main condition in (*a*)(ii) above and the alternative condition above may be applied in any combination in relation to the subject matter of the part disposal and what remains.

The Treasury has the power to make regulations to add to, amend or repeal any of the provisions defining the circumstances in which the proceeds of trustee borrowing are treated as applied for normal trust purposes.

[*TCGA 1992, Sch 4B paras 4–9*].

HMRC consider that 'borrowing' for these purposes includes borrowing from a company controlled by the trustees or their associates, and that outstanding trustee borrowing can include money borrowed before 21 March 2000. *Bona fide* delay in payment of a bill, for example for repairs to trust property, is not borrowing for these purposes. A futures contract relating to commodities is not an ordinary trust asset. (Revenue Tax Bulletin August 2003 pp 1049, 1050). See this article also for HMRC's views on whether the proceeds of borrowing are applied for normal trust purposes.

Whether deemed disposal is of the whole or a proportion of the assets. If the amount of value transferred

- is less than the amount of outstanding trustee borrowing immediately after the transfer of value, and
- is also less than the 'effective value' of the remaining chargeable assets,

the deemed disposal and reacquisition is of the proportion of each of the remaining chargeable assets given by:

$$\frac{VT}{EV}$$

where

VT = the amount of value transferred, and

EV = the effective value of the remaining chargeable assets.

If the amount of value transferred

- is not less than the amount of outstanding trustee borrowing immediately after the transfer of value, but
- is less than the effective value of the remaining chargeable assets,

the deemed disposal and reacquisition is of the proportion of each of the remaining chargeable assets given by:

$$\frac{TB}{EV}$$

where

TB = the amount of outstanding trustee borrowing immediately after the transfer of value, and

EV = the effective value of the remaining chargeable assets.

In any other case the deemed disposal and reacquisition is of the whole of each of the remaining chargeable assets.

The '*effective value*' of the remaining chargeable assets is the aggregate market value of those assets immediately after the transfer of value, reduced by so much of that value as is attributable to trustee borrowing (see below).

[*TCGA 1992, Sch 4B para 11*].

Value attributable to trustee borrowing. The value of any asset is '*attributable to trustee borrowing*' to the extent that

- the trustees have applied the proceeds of trustee borrowing in acquiring or enhancing the value of the asset, or
- the asset represents directly or indirectly an asset whose value was attributable to the trustees having so applied the proceeds of trustee borrowing.

Where the asset itself has been borrowed by trustees, in addition to any extent to which the value of the asset may be attributable to trustee borrowing by virtue of the above, the value of the asset is attributable to trustee borrowing to the extent that the proceeds of that borrowing have not been applied for normal trust purposes (see above).

For these purposes, an amount is treated as applied by the trustees in acquiring or enhancing the value of an asset if it is applied by them wholly and exclusively

- as consideration in money or money's worth for the acquisition of the asset;
- for the purpose of enhancing the value of the asset in a way that is reflected in the state or nature of the asset;
- in establishing, preserving or defending their title to, or to a right over, the asset; or
- where the asset is a holding of shares or securities (the latter as defined in *TCGA 1992, s 132* — see 58.7 SHARES AND SECURITIES) that is treated as a single asset, by way of consideration in money or money's worth for additional shares or securities forming part of the same holding;

at a time when, and to the extent that, there is outstanding trustee borrowing.

[*TCGA 1992, Sch 4B para 12*].

57.20 ANTI-AVOIDANCE: RESTRICTION ON SET-OFF OF SETTLEMENT LOSSES

Cross-reference. See 57.15 above for restrictions on transfer of settlement losses to beneficiary becoming absolutely entitled to settled property.

Where the circumstances set out below apply in relation to a chargeable gain accruing after 20 March 2000 to the trustees of a settlement, no allowable losses accruing to the trustees (whether in the same year of assessment or brought forward from an earlier year) may be set against any part of that gain.

The circumstances are as follows.

- In computing the gain in question, the allowable expenditure would be greater if it were not for a claim having been made for gifts hold-over relief under *TCGA 1992, s 165* or *s 260* (see 33.1, 33.7 HOLD-OVER RELIEFS) in respect of an earlier disposal (not necessarily of the same asset) to the trustees; and
- the person who made that earlier disposal, or a person connected with him (within *TCGA 1992, s 286* — see 16 CONNECTED PERSONS), has at any time acquired an 'interest in the settled property' (defined as in 57.18 above), or entered into an arrangement to acquire such an interest, as a result of which any person has at any time received (or become entitled to receive) any consideration.

[*TCGA 1992, s 79A; FA 2000, s 93*].

57.21 ANTI-AVOIDANCE: ATTRIBUTION TO TRUSTEES OF GAINS OF NON-RESIDENT COMPANIES

The following apply where the trustees of a settlement are participators (within *ICTA 1988, s 417(1)*) in a close company (within *ICTA 1988, ss 414, 415* — broadly a company under the control of five or fewer participators or of directors who are participators, see Tolley's Corporation Tax under Close Companies) or in a non-UK resident company which would otherwise be a close company.

Where, by reason of such participation by the trustees, any part of a chargeable gain accruing after 20 March 2000 to a non-UK resident company falls to be attributed to them under *TCGA 1992, s 13* (see 45.6 OVERSEAS MATTERS), nothing in any double tax agreement (see 19.2 DOUBLE TAX RELIEF) is to be taken as averting the tax charge otherwise arising.

Where

(*a*) a chargeable gain accrues after 20 March 2000 to a non-UK resident company which would otherwise be a close company;

(*b*) all or part of the gain is attributed under *TCGA 1992, s 13* to a close company which, by reason of a double tax agreement, is not chargeable to corporation tax on the gain; and

(*c*) had that close company been a non-UK resident company, all or part of the chargeable gain would have been attributed to the trustees by reason of such participation as is mentioned above;

then, for the purposes of the provisions in 45.6 OVERSEAS MATTERS which enable a gain to be attributed through a chain of companies, the company in (*b*) above is treated as a non-UK resident company, with the result that the gain can be attributed to the trustees. This treatment also applies to any other company which, if it were non-UK resident, would have been part of the chain, such that all or part of the gain in question would have been attributed as in (*c*) above.

[*TCGA 1992, s 79B; FA 2000, s 94; FA 2006, Sch 12 para 14*].

58 Shares and Securities

Cross-references. See 3 ANTI-AVOIDANCE for certain provisions which apply to share disposals; 4.6 APPEALS for appeals regarding values of unquoted shares; 6.2 ASSETS for location of shares; 6.7 ASSETS for options to acquire shares; 7 ASSETS HELD ON 6 APRIL 1965; 8 ASSETS HELD ON 31 MARCH 1982; 13 COMPANIES; 14.2–14.6 COMPANIES—CORPORATE FINANCE AND INTANGIBLES; 17 CORPORATE VENTURING SCHEME; 20 EMPLOYEE SHARE SCHEMES; 21 ENTERPRISE INVESTMENT SCHEME; 22.5 EXEMPTIONS AND RELIEFS for meaning of 'debt on a security'; 22.20 EXEMPTIONS AND RELIEFS for business expansion scheme shares; 26 GOVERNMENT SECURITIES; 33 HOLD-OVER RELIEFS for relief in respect of gifts of shares in certain cases and transfers to companies in exchange for shares; 40 LOSSES for reliefs available for losses arising from certain share disposals and for negligible value claims; 41 MARKET VALUE; 43 MINERAL ROYALTIES for shares in companies deriving their value from exploration etc. rights; 45 OVERSEAS MATTERS for shares in certain overseas resident companies and funds; 50 QUALIFYING CORPORATE BONDS; 53 RETIREMENT RELIEF and 55 ROLLOVER RELIEF for relief where shares etc. are held in certain companies; 59 SHARES AND SECURITIES—IDENTIFICATION RULES; 60 SUBSTANTIAL SHAREHOLDINGS OF COMPANIES; 61.2, 61.18 TAPER RELIEF; 65 UNIT TRUSTS ETC.; 66 VENTURE CAPITAL TRUSTS.

Simon's Direct Tax Service. See C2.7.

The headings in this chapter are as follows.

For the rules for matching part disposals of shares and securities with multiple acquisitions, see 59 SHARES AND SECURITIES—IDENTIFICATION RULES.

58.1 REORGANISATION OF SHARE CAPITAL

By virtue of *TCGA 1992, s 127*, a '*reorganisation*' (i.e. a 'reorganisation' or 'reduction' of a company's share capital) does not normally constitute a disposal, the 'new holding' being treated as the same asset, acquired at the same date, as the 'original shares', any additional consideration given by the shareholder at the time of reorganisation (e.g. as a subscription for a rights issue — see 58.3 below) being added to the cost of the original holding for the purpose of computing the unindexed gain on a subsequent disposal. See 34.5 INDEXATION for the calculation of indexation allowance in respect of the additional consideration.

For this purpose

(*a*) '*original shares*' means shares held before, and concerned in, the reorganisation, and (*b*) '*new holding*' means, in relation to any original shares, the shares in and debentures of the company which, following the reorganisation, represent the original shares, and any remaining original shares.

[*TCGA 1992, s 126*(*1*), *s 127*].

The surrender, cancellation or alteration of the original holding or the rights attached thereto; and any consideration met out of the assets of the company (e.g. on a bonus issue) or represented by a dividend or other distribution declared but not paid are not regarded as 'additional consideration' for the above purpose. Similarly, in the case of a reorganisation occurring after 9 March 1981, any consideration given, otherwise than by way of a bargain made at arm's length, for part or all of the new holding will be disregarded, to the extent that its amount or value exceeds the amount by which the market value of the new holding, immediately after the reorganisation, exceeds the market value of the original shares immediately before the reorganisation. (See also *CIR v Burmah Oil Co. Ltd HL 1981, 54 TC 200*.) [*TCGA 1992, s 128*(*1*)(*2*)].

HMRC have expressed their views on 'open offers' and 'vendor placings'. An open offer is where a company invites its shareholders to subscribe for shares subject to a minimum entitlement based on their existing holdings, and possibly enabling them to also subscribe for shares which other shareholders do not want. For capital gains tax purposes HMRC will treat any subscription for shares, which is equal to or less than the shareholder's minimum entitlement, as a share reorganisation. Any shares subscribed for in excess of the minimum entitlement will be treated as a separate acquisition. In addition, a vendor placing is where company shares, which have previously been allotted to a vendor as consideration for an asset disposed of by the vendor to the company, are offered by the company to its existing shareholders on the vendor's behalf. No part of any acquisition by existing shareholders can be treated as a share reorganisation because the shares have already been allotted to the vendor. (HMRC Capital Gains Manual CG 51760–51766).

For HMRC's views on the treatment of rights to acquire shares in other companies, see HMRC Capital Gains Manual CG 52065–52070.

Where, on a reorganisation, a person receives (or is deemed to receive), or becomes entitled to receive, any consideration, other than the new holding, for the disposal of an interest in the original shares, and in particular

(i) where under *TCGA 1992, s 122* he is to be treated as if he had in consideration of a capital distribution disposed of an interest in the original shares (see 58.10 below and note the procedure where the amount of the capital distribution is small or exceeds the allowable expenditure attaching to the original shares),

(ii) where he receives (or is deemed to receive) consideration from other shareholders in respect of a surrender of rights derived from the original shares,

he is treated as if the new holding resulted from his having for that consideration disposed of an interest (but without prejudice to the original shares and the new holding being treated in accordance with *TCGA 1992, s 127* above as the same asset. [*TCGA 1992, s 128*(*3*)].

For transactions between companies in the same group, see 27.2 GROUPS OF COMPANIES.

Reorganisations covered by the provisions. '*Reorganisation*' for the purposes above includes the making of bonus and rights issues of shares or debentures in proportion to the original holdings, the reduction of share capital and the alteration of rights attaching to the original shares. [*TCGA 1992, s 126*(*1*)(*2*)]. See also *Dunstan v Young Austen Young Ltd CA 1988, 61 TC 448* and *Unilever (UK) Holdings Ltd v Smith CA, 2002 STI 1806*. Unit trust schemes are treated similarly to companies. [*TCGA 1992, s 99*]. See 65.1 UNIT TRUSTS ETC. for the disapplication of the above provisions as regards collective investment schemes entitling participants to exchange rights in one part of a scheme property for rights in another.

'*Reduction*' of share capital for the purposes above does not include the paying off of redeemable share capital, and where shares in a company are redeemed by the company otherwise than by the issue of shares or debentures (with or without other consideration) and otherwise than in a liquidation, the shareholder is treated as disposing of the shares at the time of the redemption. [*TCGA 1992, s 126(3)*].

Separate rules apply to a reorganisation of share capital involving qualifying corporate bonds. See 50.3 QUALIFYING CORPORATE BONDS.

In certain cases involving RETIREMENT RELIEF (53.4), an election may be made for the reorganisation to be treated as an actual disposal and reacquisition.

Valuation of different classes of share on subsequent disposal. Where the new holding consists of more than one class of share, security, debenture, etc. none of which is quoted on a recognised stock exchange within three months of the reorganisation, the allowable acquisition cost is arrived at on the basis of the market value of the various classes at the date of a chargeable disposal of the new holding or part thereof. This also applies where consideration, other than the new holding, is received as in *TCGA 1992, s 128(3)* above. [*TCGA 1992, s 128(4), s 129*].

However, in the case of shares and securities any one class or more of which is or are quoted on a recognised stock exchange (within *ICTA 1988, s 841* — see 58.23 below) in the UK or elsewhere (or, in the case of unit trust rights, of which the prices were published daily by the managers) within three months after the reorganisation takes effect (or such longer time as HMRC may allow), the base value is determined *once and for all* by reference to the respective market value, on the first day on which the market values or prices of the shares are quoted or published (whether published before or after the actual reorganisation). The provisions apply, *mutatis mutandis*, to the reorganisation of rights under unit trusts. See 65 UNIT TRUSTS ETC.. A reorganisation which involves the allotment of holdings is deemed to take effect on the day following the day on which the right to renounce any allotment expires. [*TCGA 1992, ss 130, 288(1)*].

For the application of the indexation provisions to holdings of shares arising out of these rules, see 34.5 INDEXATION and 59.4, 59.5 SHARES AND SECURITIES—IDENTIFICATION RULES.

Assets held on 6 April 1965. See 7.5 and 7.10 ASSETS HELD ON 6 APRIL 1965 for certain situations that may still arise in relation to reorganisations.

Example

A Ltd, an unquoted company, was incorporated in 1996 with an authorised share capital of £50 million denominated into 500 million Ordinary Shares of 10p each, of which 300 million were issued at par on incorporation. In 1999, the directors decide to reorganise the company's share capital by issuing the balance of the authorised share capital in the form of a bonus issue of 200 million Ordinary Shares of 10p so that two such shares are issued for every three of such shares already held. The 500 million Ordinary Shares of 10p each in issue are then consolidated into 50 million New Ordinary Shares of £1 each. A rights issue is then made on the basis of one 7% Cumulative Preference Share of £1 issued at par for every five New Ordinary Shares of £1 already held.

X was issued 90,000 Ordinary Shares of 10p on incorporation and has held them continually since then. Assuming he takes up the rights issue, his new holding after the reorganisation is as follows.

	No. of shares	Par value	Cost
			£
Original holding: 10p Ords	90,000	10p	9,000
Bonus issue: 10p Ords	60,000	10p	Nil
	150,000		£9,000
Consolidation: 10p Ords to £1 New Ords	15,000	£1	9,000
Rights issue: £1 Prefs	3,000	£1	3,000
Cost of complete new holding			£12,000

X disposes of 1,500 £1 Prefs in 2006 when each such share is worth £3 and each £1 New Ord is worth £1.80. The apportionment is as follows

		£
Total value of £1 Prefs: (£3 × 3,000)	=	9,000
Total value of £1 New Ords: (£1.80 × 15,000)	=	27,000
		£36,000
Proportional value of £1 Prefs × original cost		
9/36 × £12,000	=	£3,000
Allowable cost of 1,500 £1 Prefs (£3,000 × 2)	=	£1,500

Note. If X later disposes of the remainder (1,500) of the £1 Prefs when their value is £4 each and that of the £1 Ords is £2 each, the calculation will be made as follows

		£
Total value of £1 Prefs: (£4 × 1,500)	=	6,000
Total value of £1 Ords: (£2 × 15,000)	=	30,000
		£36,000
Original cost (as reduced by previous disposal)	=	£10,500
Proportional value of £1 Prefs × original cost		
6/36 × £10,500	=	£1,750
Allowable cost of 1,500 £1 Prefs	=	£1,750

58.2 **Bonus issues (aka scrip issues).** These are treated as a reorganisation within 58.1 above, but see 58.9 below for stock dividends.

Where a company has acquired its own shares and holds them as treasury shares (see 58.14 below) a bonus issue in respect of shares of the same class can be a reorganisation whether or not bonus shares are issued in respect of the treasury shares (HMRC Capital Gains Manual CG 51750).

In practice, where a bonus issue follows a repayment of share capital (e.g. under *ICTA 1988, s 210*), and is treated as income of the recipient, the amount of that income net of basic rate tax is treated as the acquisition cost of the new shares (CCAB Statement June 1968).

Example

X plc, a quoted company, makes a bonus issue in September 2006 of one preference share for every eight ordinary shares held. On first trading after issue, the preference shares were valued at £10 and the ordinary shares at £6.

Mr A had purchased 1,000 ordinary shares in December 2004 for £7,000. After the issue of preference shares, the allowable expenditure on a subsequent disposal of the ordinary and preference shares is computed as follows.

	£
Initial value of preference shares (125 × £10)	1,250
Initial value of ordinary shares (1,000 × £6)	6,000
Total	£7,250

Allowable cost of 1,000 ordinary shares

$$\frac{6{,}000}{7{,}250} \times 7{,}000 \quad = \quad £5{,}790$$

Allowable cost of 125 preference shares

$$\frac{1{,}250}{7{,}250} \times 7{,}000 \quad = \quad £1{,}210$$

These rules do not apply to loyalty bonus shares issued to subscribers to privatisation issues, for which see 58.13 below.

58.3 **Rights issues.** A rights issue of shares or debentures in respect of shares already held in a company is treated as a reorganisation within 58.1 above. A company cannot grant rights in respect of treasury shares, but this will not in itself prevent the rights issue being a reorganisation (HMRC Capital Gains Manual CG 51750).

Disposal of rights. Where a person receives or becomes entitled to receive in respect of any shares in a company a provisional allotment or shares in or debentures of the company and he disposes of his rights, *TCGA 1992, s 122* applies as if the amount of consideration for the disposal were a capital distribution received by him from the company in respect of the first-mentioned shares, and as if he had, instead of disposing of the rights, disposed of an interest in those shares. This rule also applies to rights obtained in respect of any debentures of a company. [*TCGA 1992, s 123*].

See 58.10 below for *TCGA 1992, s 122* and note the procedure where the amount of the capital distribution is small or exceeds the allowable expenditure attaching to the original shares etc.

Example

W plc is a quoted company which in June 1992 made a rights issue of one £1 ordinary share for every eight £1 ordinary shares held, at £1.35 payable on allotment. V, who held 16,000 £1 ordinary shares purchased in May 1984 for £15,000, took up his entitlement in full, and was allotted 2,000 shares. In December 2006, he sells 6,000 of his shares for £12,000.

Indexation factors May 1984 to April 1985	0.065
April 1985 to June 1992	0.470
June 1992 to April 1998	0.167

'Section 104 holding'	Shares	Qualifying expenditure £	Indexed pool £
May 1984 acquisition	16,000	15,000	15,000
Indexed rise: May 1984 – April 1985			
£15,000 × 0.065			975
Pool at 6.4.85	16,000	15,000	15,975
Indexed rise: April 1985 – June 1992			
£15,975 × 0.470			7,508
June 1992 rights issue	2,000	2,700	2,700
	18,000	17,700	26,183
Indexed rise: June 1992 – April 1998			
£26,183 × 0.167			4,373
			30,556
December 2006 disposal	(6,000)	(5,900)	(10,185)
Pool carried forward	12,000	£11,800	£20,371

Calculation of chargeable gain	£
Disposal consideration	12,000
Allowable cost $\frac{6,000}{18,000} \times £17,700$	5,900
Unindexed gain	6,100
Indexation allowance $\frac{6,000}{18,000} \times £30,556 = £10,185$	
£10,185 – £5,900	4,285
Chargeable gain 2006/07 (subject to TAPER RELIEF (61))	£1,815

58.4 **Exchange of securities for those in another company.** (See also 13.10 COMPANIES). The same treatment as in 58.1 above is applied to shares or debentures issued in exchange for the shares or debentures of a company (Company A) by another company (Company B) which in consequence of the exchange will hold more than 25% of the 'ordinary share capital' of, or more than 50% of the voting power in, Company A. Similar treatment applies where Company B issues the shares etc. in exchange for those of Company A as the result of a general offer made to the members of company A (or any class of them), provided that the offer was initially made on a condition which, if satisfied, would give Company B control of Company A. (This covers abortive takeover bids which become unconditional, but which do not succeed.)

For this purpose, the '*ordinary share capital*' of a company is all its issued share capital (by whatever name called), other than shares carrying only a right to fixed rate dividends and no other right to participate in profits. [*ICTA 1988, s 832(1)*]. In relation to shares or debentures issued after 16 April 2002, 'ordinary share capital' also includes units in a unit trust and, in relation to a company with no share capital, interests in the company possessed by its members. In relation to such a company, references above to shares or debentures include any such interests.

These provisions are subject to the anti-avoidance rule below.

[*TCGA 1992, s 135; FA 2002, s 45, Sch 9 paras 1, 7* replacing *TCGA 1992, s 135(1)(3) as previously enacted; F(No 2)A 1992, s 35*].

See 65.1 UNIT TRUSTS ETC. for the application of *TCGA 1992, s 135* as regards collective investment schemes entitling participants to exchange rights in one part of a scheme for rights in another.

For the tax consequences of a share exchange before 14 March 1988 within a group of companies, see *Westcott v Woolcombers Ltd CA 1987, 60 TC 575* and *NAP Holdings UK Ltd v Whittles HL 1994, 67 TC 166* at 27.2 GROUPS OF COMPANIES.

Treasury shares. Where company A has acquired its own shares and is holding them as treasury shares (see 58.14 below) at the time of the exchange, no issue of shares by Company B can be made in respect of the treasury shares. The treasury shares do not count as issued share capital in determining whether the conditions for the above treatment are met. A disposal of its treasury shares by Company B is treated as the company issuing those shares. (HMRC Capital Gains Manual CG 52521–52523).

Incidental costs of acquisition and disposal and warranty payments in respect of contingent liabilities. Any such costs or payments attributable to the new holding of shares or debentures are by concession treated as consideration given for that holding. In the case of warranty payments, relief under this concession and *TCGA 1992, s 49(1)(c)* (see 15.6 COMPUTATION OF GAINS AND LOSSES) will in total be restricted to what would have been allowed under *TCGA 1992, s 49(1)(c)* had *TCGA 1992, s 135* not applied (HMRC Extra-Statutory Concession D52).

Anti-avoidance. TCGA 1992, s 135 does not apply unless the exchange is made for bona fide commercial reasons and does not form part of a scheme or arrangements of which the main purpose, or one of the main purposes, is the avoidance of capital gains tax or corporation tax. In such cases, a chargeable disposal is treated as taking place except where a person to whom the new shares are issued owns (or he and persons connected with him together own) less than 5% of, or any class of, the shares or debentures of the acquired company. There are provisions for advance clearance of an exchange by HMRC. [*TCGA 1992, ss 137, 138*]. For full coverage, see 3.18 ANTI-AVOIDANCE.

Where *TCGA 1992, s 135* is disapplied, then under general principles the disposal proceeds will be the value in money's worth of the shares or debentures issued by the acquiring company or, if the transaction is not a bargain made at arm's length, the market value of the shares or debentures sold (if different).

Miscellaneous. TCGA 1992, s 135 is disapplied in certain circumstances (with the result that an exchange of securities is treated as a disposal of the original holding and an acquisition of a new holding) in relation to shares and securities that have qualified for tax relief under one of the various venture capital tax schemes or the community investment tax credit scheme. See 17.23 CORPORATE VENTURING SCHEME, 21.8, 21.12 ENTERPRISE INVESTMENT SCHEME, 22.20 EXEMPTIONS AND RELIEFS (as regards the Business Expansion Scheme), 66.11 VENTURE CAPITAL TRUSTS and Tolley's Income Tax under Community Investment Tax Relief. See also 60.14 SUBSTANTIAL SHAREHOLDINGS OF COMPANIES.

HMRC have confirmed that it is possible for a Delaware Limited Liability Company that issues shares to be a party to share exchanges within *TCGA 1992, s 135* (Revenue Tax Bulletin February 2001 p 827).

58.5 **Earn-out rights.** An agreement for the sale of shares in a company may include the right to receive deferred consideration which is itself unascertainable at the time of the agreement, usually because it depends on the future profit performance of the company. Such a right was held to be a separate asset in *Marren v Ingles HL 1980, 54 TC 76* (see 9.1 CAPITAL SUMS DERIVED FROM ASSETS). From 26 April 1988, an extra-statutory concession (D27) (see below) provided that, in certain circumstances, this right (known as the 'earn-out right') could itself be treated as a security so that the deferral rules for capital gains on the shares could apply. Finance Act 1997 placed this concession on a statutory footing. Originally, an election was required for treatment as a security to apply, but Finance Act 2003 made such treatment mandatory for rights conferred after 9 April 2003 (subject to the option to disapply the treatment by election).

Statutory rules. Where a person ('the seller') transfers securities (i.e. shares or debentures) of a company and, as all or part of the consideration for the transfer, has conferred upon him a right to receive securities ('the new securities') of another company ('the acquiring company'), the value or quantity of which is 'unascertainable' (see below) at that time, such right is known as an '*earn-out right*'. It is a further condition that the terms of the right are such that it cannot be discharged otherwise than by the issue of the new securities. Any right to receive cash and/or an ascertainable amount of securities as part of the total consideration does not fall within these provisions and must be distinguished from the earn-out right.

Provided that *TCGA 1992, s 135* (exchange of securities — see 58.4 above) would have applied if the earn-out right were an ascertainable amount of securities of the acquiring company, the right is treated for CGT purposes as if it were itself a security of the acquiring company (so that *section 135* may apply).This treatment does not apply if the seller so elects. For rights conferred before 10 April 2003, the seller must make an election in order for treatment as a security to apply.

An election (whether to apply or disapply the rules) is irrevocable and must be made by written notice to an HMRC officer by the first anniversary of 31 January following the tax year in which the earn-out right is conferred, or, where made by a company, within two years after the end of the accounting period in which the right is conferred.

Where security treatment applies, it is then assumed, as regards the seller and any subsequent owner of the earn-out right, that

(*a*) the earn-out right is a security within the definition in *TCGA 1992, s 132* (see 58.7 below);

(*b*) the notional security represented by the earn-out right is not a QUALIFYING CORPORATE BOND (50);

(*c*) all references in *TCGA 1992* to a debenture include references to such a notional security; and

(*d*) the eventual issue of actual securities in pursuance of the earn-out right constitutes a conversion of the right, insofar as it is discharged by the issue, into those securities (see 58.7 below re conversion of securities).

Where an earn-out right is treated as a notional security of a company as above and it is extinguished and replaced with a new right to be issued with securities of the same company, the value or quantity of which is 'unascertainable' (see below) at that time, the new right is treated for CGT purposes as if it were a security of the company, with the same consequences as above. The person on whom the new right is conferred may make an election to disapply this treatment. For rights conferred before 10 April 2003, however, the person on whom the new right is conferred must make an election for treatment as a security to apply. The time limits for election (whether to apply or disapply the rules) operate by reference to the tax year or accounting period in which the new right is conferred.

An election to apply treatment as a security cannot be made in respect of a right conferred before 10 April 2003 if an election under *TCGA 1992, s 279A* (loss on right to unascertainable consideration treated as accruing in earlier year — see 40.18 LOSSES) has previously been made in respect of the right, and an election made at the same time as a *section 279A* election has no effect. [*FA 2003, s 162(2)(4)*].

Meaning of 'unascertainable'.

1. The value or quantity of securities to be issued in pursuance of an earn-out right is unascertainable at a particular time if, and only if it is made referable to matters relating to any business or assets of one or more 'relevant companies' and those matters are then uncertain on account of future business or future assets being included in the business or assets to which they relate. A '*relevant company*' is either the acquiring company or the acquired company or any company in the same group of companies as either of those. A group of companies is construed in accordance with 27.1 GROUPS OF COMPANIES, and the change in the residence requirement there mentioned applies for these purposes in relation to rights conferred on or after 1 April 2000.

2. The value or quantity of securities to be issued in pursuance of an earn-out right is *not* to be taken as unascertainable merely by reason of any part of the consideration for the transaction being contingent or of any risk of its being irrecoverable. In such cases, *TCGA 1992, s 48* (consideration due after time of disposal — see 15.6 COMPUTATION OF GAINS AND LOSSES) applies in computing the gain.

3. The existence of an option to choose between shares in and debentures of the acquiring company does not in itself render unascertainable the value or quantity of such securities. However, neither does such option prevent the above provisions from applying.

4. If the value of securities to be issued in pursuance of an earn-out right is ascertainable and the quantity is to be fixed by reference thereto, or *vice versa*, this does not in itself render the value or quantity unascertainable.

[*TCGA 1992, s 138A; FA 1997, s 89(1); FA 2000, Sch 29 para 22; FA 2003, ss 161, 162(2)(4)*].

Note that an earn-out right treated as a security by virtue of *TCGA 1992, s 138A* is not regarded as a right to unascertainable consideration for the purposes of *TCGA 1992, ss 279A–279D* (loss on right to unascertainable consideration treated as accruing in earlier year — see 40.18 LOSSES).[*TCGA 1992, s 279B(6); FA 2003, s 162(1)*].

For HMRC's views on earn-outs, see HMRC Capital Gains Manual CG 58000–58102.

Example

K owns 10,000 ordinary shares in M Ltd, which he acquired for £12,000 in December 1998. In July 2005, the whole of the issued share capital of M Ltd was acquired by P plc. Under the terms of the takeover, K receives £2 per share plus the right to further consideration up to a maximum of £1.50 per share depending on future profit performance. The initial consideration is receivable in cash, but the deferred consideration is to be satisfied by the issue of shares in P plc. In December 2006, K duly receives 2,000 ordinary shares valued at £6 per share in full settlement of his entitlement. The right to future consideration is valued at £1.40 per share in July 2005.

If K elects to disapply TCGA 1992, s 138A the position would be
2005/06

	£	£
Disposal proceeds 10,000 × £2	20,000	
Value of rights 10,000 × £1.40	14,000	34,000
Cost		12,000
Chargeable gain (subject to TAPER RELIEF (61))		£22,000

2006/07

	£
Disposal of rights to deferred consideration:	
Proceeds — 2,000 P plc shares @ £6	12,000
Deemed cost of acquiring rights	14,000
Allowable loss	£2,000
Cost for CGT purposes of 2,000 P plc shares	£12,000

Without an election, the position would be
2005/06

	£
Proceeds (cash) (as above)	20,000
Cost $\pounds 12,000 \times \dfrac{20,000}{20,000 + 14,000}$	7,059
Chargeable gain (subject to TAPER RELIEF (61))	£12,941
Cost of earn-out right for CGT purposes (£12,000 – £7,059)	£4,941

2006/07

The shares in P plc stand in the place of the earn-out right and will be regarded as having been acquired in December 1998 for £4,941. No further gain or loss arises until a disposal of the shares takes place.

An extension to the above concession (announced in a Revenue Press Release of 25 July 1990 and available in all cases where the liability for the relevant chargeable period had not then been finally determined) applies to financial concerns who hold shares or securities as trading stocks rather than as capital assets. (Such concerns cannot benefit from the unextended concession because any profits they make on the disposal of shares would be liable to tax as part of their trading profits rather than as a capital gain.) Where *ICTA 1988, s 473* (conversion etc. of securities held as circulating capital not to be treated as disposal of original holding) does not apply to an exchange of shares only because *TCGA 1992, ss 126–136* would not have applied, then, if the taxpayer so claims, it may apply by concession if *TCGA 1992, ss 126–136* would have applied by virtue of the unextended concession above, if it had been claimed. The vendor must claim the benefit of the extension to the concession before his trading profit or loss for the relevant chargeable period is finally determined, and must agree to accept this treatment for all tax purposes (Revenue Extra-Statutory Concession D27).

58.6 **'Scheme of reconstruction' involving issue of securities.** Where, under an arrangement entered into for the purposes of such a scheme between a company (Company A) and its share- or debenture-holders (or any class of them), another company (Company B) issues shares or debentures to those holders in respect of, or in proportion to (or as nearly as may be in proportion to), their original holdings, which latter are then retained, cancelled or otherwise extinguished, the treatment in 58.1 above applies, as if the holders had exchanged their holdings in Company A for the shares or debentures held by them as a consequence of the arrangement and as if the exchange were a reorganisation of share capital. Any shares in or debentures of Company A that are of a class involved in the scheme and that are retained are treated as if they had been cancelled and replaced by a new issue. Where Company A reorganises its share capital as a prelude to a scheme of reconstruction, then, for shares or debentures issued after 16 April 2002, it is made clear that the above provisions apply to the position after the preliminary reorganisation has been carried out.

References above to shares or debentures being retained include their being retained in altered form, whether as a result of reduction, consolidation, division or otherwise. In relation to a company with no share capital, references to shares or debentures include any interests in the company possessed by its members.

[*TCGA 1992, s 136; FA 2002, s 45, Sch 9 paras 2, 7* replacing *TCGA 1992, s 135(2)(3), s 136 as previously enacted*].

Meaning of 'scheme of reconstruction'. For shares or debentures issued after 16 April 2002, a '*scheme of reconstruction*' is a scheme of merger, division or other restructuring that meets the following conditions.

(1) The scheme must involve the issue of 'ordinary share capital' of a company or companies (the '*successor company(ies)*') to holders of 'ordinary share capital' of another company (the '*original company*') (or, where relevant, to the holders of one or more particular classes of 'ordinary share capital' involved in the scheme). Where there is more than one original company involved in the scheme, the issue must be to holders of 'ordinary share capital' of (or of one or more particular classes of 'ordinary share capital' of) any of those companies. The scheme must *not* involve the issue of ordinary share capital of the successor company(ies) to anyone else. For this purpose a transfer of treasury shares (i.e. of the company's own shares acquired and held by it — see 58.14 below) is treated as an issue of shares (HMRC Capital Gains Manual CG 52707a).

(2) Holders of a class of ordinary share capital (of the original company(ies)) involved in the scheme must each have the same proportionate entitlement to acquire ordinary share capital of the successor company(ies) (see example at HMRC Capital Gains Manual CG 52707b). This does not apply to treasury shares because such shares are treated as if they had been cancelled (HMRC Capital Gains Manual CG 52707b).

(3) Unless condition (4) below is satisfied, the effect of the restructuring must be that the business or substantially the whole of the business carried on by the original company is carried on either by a successor company which is not the original company or by two or more successor companies (which may include the original company). Where there is more than one original company, the effect must be that all or part of the business(es) carried on by one or more of the original companies is carried on by a different company *and* the whole or substantially the whole of the businesses carried on by the original companies is carried on

- by the successor company (which may be one of the original companies) where there is only one such company, or
- by the successor companies (which may be the same as the original companies or include any of them) where there are two or more such companies.

For the above purposes, the whole or substantially the whole of a business (or businesses) is carried on by two or more successor companies if, inter alia, the activities of those companies taken together embrace the whole or substantially the whole of that business (or those businesses). A business carried on by a company that is under the control (within *ICTA 1988, s 840*) of another company is treated as carried on by each of them. This enables a holding company with no business of its own to meet condition (3) by reference to the business of its subsidiary. See HMRC Capital Gains Manual CG 52709 for the meaning of 'business' for these purposes.

For the purposes of this condition, there are disregarded any assets retained by an original company in order to make a capital distribution within *TCGA 1992, s 122* (see 58.10 below), for example to any significant minority of shareholders who indicated their unwillingness to maintain their investment in the business following the reconstruction.

(4) If condition (3) above is not satisfied, the scheme must be carried out in pursuance of a compromise or arrangement under *Companies Act 1985, s 425* (or NI or foreign equivalent) without involving any transfer of the business of the original company(ies).

For these purposes, '*ordinary share capital*' is as defined in 58.4 above, including the extension to units in a unit trust and, in relation to a company with no share capital, interests in the company possessed by its members.

Where any of the original companies 'reorganise' (within 58.1 above) their share capital as a prelude to a scheme of reconstruction, conditions (1) and (2) above apply to the position after the preliminary reorganisation has been carried out. For the purposes of those two conditions, there is disregarded any issue of shares in or debentures of any of the successor companies which is made after the latest date on which any of the successor companies issues shares or debentures

- in consideration of the transfer of any business (or part of a business) under the scheme, or
- (where applicable) in pursuance of the compromise or arrangement mentioned in condition (4) above.

[*TCGA 1992, s 136(4), Sch 5AA; FA 2002, s 45, Sch 9 paras 3, 7*].

For practical illustrations of schemes of reconstruction, see HMRC Capital Gains Manual CG 52720–52729.

For shares or debentures issued on or before 16 April 2002, the legislation referred instead to a '*scheme of reconstruction or amalgamation*', which was defined only very briefly as 'a scheme for the reconstruction of any company or companies or the amalgamation of any two or more companies'. [*TCGA 1992, s 136(2) as previously enacted*]. For further detail, see HMRC Capital Gains Manual CG 52730–52733. The new definition is intended partly to give statutory effect to HMRC Statement of Practice SP 5/85 (which is covered at 3.18 ANTI-AVOIDANCE and 13.10 COMPANIES) (Revenue Budget Note BN 7, 17 April 2002).

For a case in which the taxpayer argued successfully that no scheme of reconstruction had taken place, see *Fallon and Another (Executors of Morgan deceased) v Fellows Ch D 2001, 74 TC 232*. For shares or debentures issued after 16 April 2002, the new definition above of 'scheme of reconstruction' is intended to reverse the effect of the decision in this case (Treasury Explanatory Notes to Finance Bill 2002).

Anti-avoidance. The same anti-avoidance rule applies as in 58.4 above [*TCGA 1992, s 136(6)*]. For full coverage see 3.18 ANTI-AVOIDANCE.

Incidental costs of acquisition and disposal and warranty payments in respect of contingent liabilities. Any such costs or payments attributable to the new holding of shares or debentures are by concession treated as consideration given for that holding. In the case of warranty payments, relief under this concession and *TCGA 1992, s 49(1)(c)* (see 15.6 COMPUTATION OF GAINS AND LOSSES) will in total be restricted to what would have been allowed under *TCGA 1992, s 49(1)(c)* had *TCGA 1992, s 136* not applied (HMRC Extra-Statutory Concession D52).

Miscellaneous. TCGA 1992, s 136 is disapplied in certain circumstances (with the result that a scheme of reconstruction is treated as a disposal of the original holding and an acquisition of a new holding) in relation to shares and securities that have qualified for tax relief under one of the various venture capital tax schemes or the community investment tax credit scheme. See 17.23 CORPORATE VENTURING SCHEME, 21.8, 21.12 ENTERPRISE INVESTMENT SCHEME, 22.20 EXEMPTIONS AND RELIEFS (as regards the Business Expansion Scheme), 66.11 VENTURE CAPITAL TRUSTS and Tolley's Income Tax under Community Investment Tax Relief. See also 60.14 SUBSTANTIAL SHAREHOLDINGS OF COMPANIES.

Merger to form European Company (SE). The following applies where an SE is formed on or after 1 April 2005 by the merger of two or more companies in accordance with *Council Regulation (EC) No 2157/2001, Arts 2(1), 17(2)* (see 13.18 COMPANIES) and each merging company is resident in a member State but not all of them are resident in the same member State. If it does not constitute or form part of a scheme of reconstruction within the meaning of *TCGA 1992, s 136*, the merger is nevertheless treated as if it were a scheme of reconstruction for the purposes of that section, but the anti-avoidance provision above does not apply (and neither does *section 137* (restrictions on company reconstructions — see 3.18 ANTI-AVOIDANCE)). See, however, the anti-avoidance provisions at 13.18 COMPANIES. [*TCGA 1992, s 140G; F(No 2)A, s 51*].

Example

N Ltd carries on a manufacturing and wholesaling business. In 1994, it was decided that the wholesaling business should be carried on by a separate company. Revenue clearance under *TCGA 1992, s 138* was obtained, and a company, R Ltd, was formed which, in consideration for the transfer to it by N Ltd of the latter's wholesaling undertaking, issued shares to the shareholders of N Ltd. Each holder of ordinary shares in N Ltd received one ordinary share in R Ltd for each N Ltd share he held. W, who purchased his 2,500 N shares for £10,000 in December 1991, received 2,500 R shares. None of the shares involved is quoted. In August 2006, W sells 1,500 of his N shares for £6 each, a total of £9,000, agreed to be their market value. The value of W's remaining N shares is also £6 per share, and the value of his R shares is £4.50 per share. The indexation factor for the period December 1991 to April 1998 is 0.198.

	£
Disposal consideration	9,000
Allowable cost $£10,000 \times \dfrac{9{,}000}{9{,}000 + (1{,}000 \times £6) + (2{,}500 \times £4.50)}$	3,429
Unindexed gain	5,571
Indexation allowance £3,429 × 0.198	679
Chargeable gain 2006/07 (subject to TAPER RELIEF (61))	£4,892

Note to the example

(*a*) If the original shares had been held on 31 March 1982, the above fraction would be applied to their 31 March 1982 value for the purposes of the re-basing calculation under *TCGA 1992, s 35*.

58.7 **Conversion of securities.** The provisions outlined in 58.1 above apply *mutatis mutandis* to the '*conversion of securities*', which phrase includes

(*a*) a conversion of securities of a company into shares in that company;

(*b*) in relation to any disposal after 25 November 1996 (whenever the conversion itself occurred), a conversion of a security which is not a qualifying corporate bond (QCB) (see 50 QUALIFYING CORPORATE BONDS) into a security of the same company which is a QCB;

(*c*) in relation to any disposal after 25 November 1996 (whenever the conversion itself occurred), a conversion of a QCB into a security of the same company which is not a QCB;

(*d*) a conversion in lieu of redemption at the option of the holder of the securities; and

(*e*) any exchange of securities in pursuance of compulsory purchase powers.

In relation to disposals after 25 November 1996, even where the conversion took place before then, any of the above is a conversion of securities regardless of whether effected by a transaction or occurring as a result of the operation of the terms of any security or debenture.

'*Security*' includes any loan stock or similar security issued by national or local government or public authority in the UK or elsewhere, or by a company, and whether secured or unsecured. Certain company debentures are deemed under *TCGA 1992, s 251* to be securities for the purposes of that section (see 22.5 EXEMPTIONS AND RELIEFS). There are provisions to ensure that (*b*) and (*c*) above operate in relation to such debentures.

[*TCGA 1992, s 132; FA 1997, s 88(1)–(3)(6)*].

A premium in money (in addition to a new holding) on a conversion of securities is treated in virtually identical terms as under *TCGA 1992, s 122* for a capital distribution in 58.10 below. (It would appear that the case of *O'Rourke v Binks CA 1992, 65 TC 165* mentioned therein applies equally to premiums on conversion within this provision as it does to capital distributions within *TCGA 1992, s 122*.) Similar rules as in *section 122* apply if the premium is 'small' (which is as defined in 58.10 below). [*TCGA 1992, s 133; FA 1996, Sch 20 para 53*].

Alternative rules apply to the conversion of securities of a company involving qualifying corporate bonds. See 50.3 QUALIFYING CORPORATE BONDS.

See also 65.1 UNIT TRUSTS ETC. for the disapplication of *TCGA 1992, s 132* as regards collective investment schemes entitling participants to exchange rights in one part of a scheme for rights in another.

Example

N bought £10,000 8% convertible loan stock in S plc, a quoted company, in June 1991. The cost was £9,800. In August 1995, N exercised his right to convert the loan stock into 'B' ordinary shares of the company, on the basis of 50 shares for £100 loan stock, and acquired 5,000 shares. In June 2006, N sells 3,000 of the shares for £5.00 each. The indexation factor for June 1991 to April 1998 is 0.213.

	£
Disposal consideration	15,000
Cost $\frac{3,000}{5,000} \times £9,800$	5,880
Unindexed gain	9,120
Indexation allowance £5,880 × 0.213	1,252
Chargeable gain 2006/07 (subject to TAPER RELIEF (61))	£7,868

Notes to the example

(*a*) The shares acquired on the conversion in 1995 stand in the shoes of the original loan stock. [*TCGA 1992, s 132*].

(*b*) The loan stock cannot be a corporate bond (and thus cannot be a qualifying corporate bond) as it is convertible into securities other than corporate bonds, i.e. into ordinary shares. [*ICTA 1988, Sch 18 para 1(5); TCGA 1992, s 117(1)*].

Compensation stock. Instead of *TCGA 1992, s 132* above applying, gilt-edged securities issued on the compulsory acquisition after 6 April 1976 of shares or securities are treated as acquired on the date of issue (or, if earlier, of compulsory acquisition) at a cost equal to the value of the shares etc. as determined for the purposes of the exchange, which transaction is treated as not involving any disposal of the shares or securities. The gain that would have accrued had the shares or securities been disposed of at that value at that time is not treated as arising until the gilt-edged securities are disposed of, so that it is added to any actual chargeable gain (or deducted from any actual allowable loss) which may, before 2 July 1986, accrue at that time. However, where the gilt-edged securities received are disposed of after 5 April 1988 no addition or deduction is made under this provision if its application would be directly attributable to the disposal of an asset before 1 April 1982.

Before 2 July 1986 disposals were identified as far as possible with similar securities acquired within the preceding twelve months (otherwise than under the above provisions) and thereafter with securities so acquired, taking earlier issues before later ones. The then rules for identifying gilt-edged securities were disregarded for this latter purpose.

After 1 July 1986 (when disposals of gilt-edged securities are exempt *in all cases*) disposals are, so far as possible, identified with gilts issued under the above provisions rather than with other gilts of the same kind and subject to this, with gilts issued at an earlier time rather than with those issued at a later time.

The deferment of the gain otherwise arising on the issue of the gilt-edged securities is extended to the recipient where their later disposal is within *TCGA 1992, s 58(1)* (spouses), *s 62(4)* (legatee acquiring asset from personal representatives) and *s 171(1)* (groups of companies).

[*TCGA 1992, s 134, Sch 4 para 4(5); CGTA 1979, s 84; FA 1985, s 67(2)(b), Sch 27 Pt VII*].

See 61.15 TAPER RELIEF for the application of that relief to the deferred gain.

Euroconversion of securities. A 'small' cash payment received on a 'euroconversion' of a security, not involving a disposal of the security and therefore not within *TCGA 1992, s 132* (see above), is treated in virtually identical terms as a 'small' capital distribution under *TCGA 1992, s 122* (see 58.10 below). '*Euroconversion*' for these purposes refers to the redenomination into euros of a security expressed in the currency of an EU Member State participating in the European single currency. [*TCGA 1992, s 133A; SI 1998 No 3177, regs 3, 39*].

58.8 **Quoted option granted following reorganisation.** If a quoted option (within *TCGA 1992, s 144(8)* — see 6.7 ASSETS) to subscribe for shares in a company is dealt in (on the stock exchange where it is quoted) within three months after (or such longer period after as may be allowed in written notice by HMRC) a reorganisation, reduction, conversion, exchange or scheme of reconstruction (within the provisions in 58.1–58.7 above) relating to the company granting the option, then

(*a*) the option is regarded for those provisions as the shares which could be acquired following the reorganisation etc. by exercising the option, and

(*b*) the ordinary market value rules for quoted securities apply (see 41.3 MARKET VALUE).

[*TCGA 1992, s 147; FA 2002, Sch 9 paras 5(8), 7*].

58.9 **STOCK DIVIDENDS (AKA SCRIP DIVIDENDS)**

Individuals. Issues of shares in lieu of dividend on or before 5 April 1975 were treated as bonus issues, and no allowance for capital gains tax purposes was made for the cash dividend forgone. This continues to be the case as regards issues made by a non-UK resident company. Issues made by a UK resident company after 5 April 1975 are subject to income tax (see Tolley's Income Tax under Stock Dividends), and the 'appropriate amount in cash' is treated as allowable expenditure for capital gains tax purposes. An issue before 6 April 1998 was then treated as a reorganisation within 58.1 above in respect of which additional consideration was given. [*TCGA 1992, s 141*].

An issue of shares by a UK resident company **after 5 April 1998** in lieu of dividend does not constitute a reorganisation but is treated in the hands of the recipient shareholder as a free-standing acquisition made at the time of the issue for a consideration equal to the 'cash equivalent of the share capital'. [*TCGA 1992, s 142; FA 1998, s 126; ITTOIA 2005, Sch 1 para 434*].

The above provisions apply not only where the shares are issued as a consequence of an option to receive additional shares instead of a cash dividend but also where they are issued as a bonus issue in a case where the existing shares carry the right under the original terms of issue (or original terms as extended or varied) to receive bonus share capital of the same or a different class. [*ICTA 1988, s 249(1)(2); ITTOIA 2005, s 410(1)*].

The '*cash equivalent of the share capital*' in the case of an issue of shares in lieu of dividend is the amount of the cash dividend alternative, except where the difference between that amount and the market value of the shares issued is 15% or more of the market value, in which case, the cash equivalent is the market value. In the case of a bonus issue of share capital, the cash equivalent is the market value of the shares issued. [*ICTA 1988, s 251(2)–(4); ITTOIA 2005, s 412, Sch 1 para 121*]. Note that, before *ITTOIA 2005* came into effect the legislation referred to a 'substantial' difference between the cash dividend alternative and the market value. The 15% rule applied under Revenue Statement of Practice A8.

If two or more persons are entitled to the shares issued, those shares (and the appropriate amount in cash) are apportioned among them by reference to their interests in the shares at the date of issue. [*ICTA 1988, s 249(3); ITTOIA 2005, s 413(3)*].

Settlements and personal representatives. The position above applies equally to personal representatives, to trustees of discretionary and accumulation trusts where the dividend would have been chargeable at the rate applicable to trusts if received in cash, and, as regards the position after 5 April 1998, to trustees of interest in possession trusts. [*TCGA 1992, ss 141, 142; ICTA 1988, s 249(4)–(6); FA 1996, Sch 6 para 6; F(No 2)A 1997, Sch 4 para 10; FA 1998, s 126; ITTOIA 2005, s 410(2)–(4), Sch 1 paras 119(3), 434*]. Where, before 6 April 1998, shares were issued in lieu of dividend to trustees of an interest in possession trust where one or more beneficiaries were absolutely entitled as against the trustees (or would have been but for infancy or disability), the issue did not constitute a reorganisation. (The changes made by Finance Act 1998 do not affect that position.) The trustees' acquisition cost of the original shareholding remains unaltered and the beneficiaries are regarded as acquiring the stock dividend shares as at the dividend date for the appropriate amount in cash. However, see SP 4/94 below re enhanced stock dividends.

The beneficiaries of a bare trust are treated in the same way as individuals, the trust being ignored for this purpose (HMRC Capital Gains Manual CG 33811(a)).

In the case of a discretionary or accumulation trust where the dividend would have been chargeable at the rate applicable to trusts if received in cash, the appropriate amount in cash forms part of the trustees' allowable expenditure. Any subsequent distribution of the stock dividend shares to the beneficiaries is a part disposal at market value by the trustees, with the normal identification rules applying (see 59 SHARES AND SECURITIES—IDENTIFICATION RULES).

In the case of an *enhanced stock dividend*, i.e. one which is worth significantly more than the cash dividend forgone, there was some doubt as to whether the position for interest in possession trusts outlined above could apply, the point being that the stock dividend may under trust law be capital rather than income. It is up to the trustees to decide in the light of the trust deed whether the enhanced stock dividend should properly be regarded as income or as capital. The Revenue issued Statement of Practice 4/94 setting out their views. They are prepared to accept whichever of the three approaches listed below the trustees conclude that they should adopt, provided that their conclusion is supportable on the facts of the case.

- If the trustees treat the dividend as income, the beneficiary is chargeable to income tax under *ITTOIA 2005, s 410* and is treated as acquiring the shares for the 'appropriate amount in cash'. The issue is not treated as a reorganisation (whether before or on or after 6 April 1998).
- If the trustees treat the dividend as capital, the issue is a reorganisation within *TCGA 1992, s 126* (see 58.1 above) and the trustees are not regarded as having made any payment for the shares.
- If the trustees treat the dividend as capital but pay compensation to a beneficiary in the form of shares for forgoing the cash dividend alternative, the transfer constitutes a part disposal of the new holding.

See HMRC Capital Gains Manual CG 33810–33817 for a full discussion of the above.

Close companies. The appropriate amount in cash relating to shares issued in lieu of a dividend made by a UK resident company to a close company in accounting periods ending before 1 April 1989 was treated as part of its apportionable income for income tax purposes, and any income tax in respect of such income apportioned (but not paid) to a participator can be added to his allowable expenditure, for capital gains tax purposes, on a disposal of shares in the close company. The close company's allowable expenditure in respect of the shares was increased by the cash equivalent of the share capital. [*CGTA 1979, s 89; TCGA 1992, s 124; ICTA 1988, Sch 19 para 12; FA 1989, Sch 17 Pt V*]. See further in 58.19 below. There is no addition to allowable expenditure of the shares held for later accounting periods or, for any accounting period, where the shares are held by a non-close company.

Example

D holds ordinary 20p shares in PLC, a quoted company. The company operates a scrip dividend policy whereby shareholders are given the option to take dividends in cash or in new fully-paid ordinary 20p shares, the option being exercisable separately in relation to each dividend. D purchased 2,000 shares for £1,500 in March 1980 and a further 3,000 shares for £8,100 in May 1992 and up until the end of 1997 he had always taken cash dividends. In January 1998, he opts for a scrip dividend and receives 25 shares instead of a cash dividend of £100. On 20 April 1998, he purchases a further 1,000 shares for £3,950. In July 1998, he opts for a scrip dividend of 44 shares instead of a cash dividend of £180. He opts for cash dividends thereafter. In May 2006, he sells 2,069 shares for £8,550 (ex div), leaving himself with a holding of 4,000.

In the case of both scrip dividends taken by D, the market value of the new shares is equivalent to the cash dividend forgone. The 'cash equivalent of the share capital' is thus the amount of that dividend. Relevant indexation factors are as follows.

May 1992 to January 1998	0.145
January 1998 to April 1998	0.019

The gain on the disposal in May 2006 is calculated as follows

(i) Identify 44 shares sold with those received by way of scrip dividend in July 1998 (LIFO)

	£
Proceeds £8,550 × 44/2,069	182
Cost (equal to 'appropriate amount in cash')	180
Chargeable gain	£2

(ii) Identify 1,000 shares sold with those acquired on 20 April 1998

	£
Proceeds £8,550 × 1,000/2,069	4,132
Cost	3,950
Chargeable gain	£182

(iii) Identify remaining 1,025 shares sold with 'section 104 holding' at 5 April 1998

Section 104 holding

	Shares	Qualifying expenditure	Indexed pool
		£	£
May 1992 acquisition	3,000	8,100	8,100
Indexed rise: May 1992 to Jan 1998 £8,100 × 0.145			1,175
	3,000	8,100	9,275
January 1998 scrip dividend 25 × 3,000/5,000	15	60	60
	3,015	8,160	9,335
Indexed rise: Jan 1998 to April 1998 (note (*a*)) £9,335 × 0.019			177
Pool at 5.4.98	3,015	8,160	9,512
May 2006 disposal	(1,025)	(2,775)	(3,234)
Pool carried forward	1,990	£5,385	£6,278

	£
Proceeds £8,550 × 1,025/2,069	4,236
Cost £8,160 × 1,025/3,015	2,775
Unindexed gain	1,461
Indexation allowance	
£9,512 × 1,025/3,015 = £3,234	
£3,234 – £2,775	459
Chargeable gain	£1,002
Total chargeable gain 2006/07 (subject to TAPER RELIEF (61)) (£2 + £182 + £1,002)	£1,186

The remaining holding of 4,000 shares consists of a 'section 104 holding' of 1,990 as illustrated above and a '1982 holding' of 2,010 (which was irrelevant to the May 2006 disposal) consisting of 2,000 purchased in March 1980 and 10 scrip dividend shares acquired in January 1998 and equated with the said purchase.

Note to the example

(*a*) The indexed pool is upgraded as if the entire holding had been disposed of at the end of 5 April 1998 but is not adjusted for any subsequent indexed rise in expenditure (see 59.2 SHARES AND SECURITIES—IDENTIFICATION RULES).

58.10 CAPITAL DISTRIBUTIONS

A capital distribution (other than of a new holding within 58.1 above), on liquidation or otherwise (defined as any distribution in money or money's worth by a company to a shareholder, which is not treated as income for tax purposes) is treated as accruing to the shareholder from the disposal of an interest in the shares. [*TCGA 1992, s 122*(*1*)(*5*)].

If the amount or value of the capital distribution is 'small' as compared with the value of the shares in respect of which it is made, the capital distribution shall not be treated as a disposal, in which case no immediate capital gains tax liability arises, but the proceeds are deducted from the acquisition cost of the shares on a subsequent disposal. [*TCGA 1992, s 122*(*2*)*; FA 1996, Sch 20 para 52*]. For this purpose, HMRC have regarded 'small' as meaning 5% or less (see HMRC Capital Gains Manual CG 57836 and Revenue Tax Bulletin November 1992 p 46). With effect from **24 February 1997**, they additionally regard an amount of £3,000 or less as 'small', regardless of whether or not it would pass the 5% test (Revenue Tax Bulletin February 1997 p 397).

Where the amount or value of the capital distribution exceeds any allowable expenditure on the shares, the taxpayer may elect to have *all* such expenditure set against the distribution with the balance of the distribution being treated as on a part disposal and the expenditure deducted not allowable on that or any subsequent disposal. [*TCGA 1992, s 122*(*4*)]. In *O'Rourke v Binks CA 1992, 65 TC 165*, it was held that the right to make the election under *TCGA 1992, s 122*(*4*) was constrained by the requirement of *TCGA 1992, s 122*(*2*) that the amount or value of the capital distribution be small as compared with the value of the shares in respect of which it was made.

Income tax charges under *ICTA 1988, s 186*(*3*) (approved profit sharing schemes — see 20.29 EMPLOYEE SHARE SCHEMES) are to be disregarded in determining whether a distribution is a capital distribution. [*TCGA 1992, s 238*(*2*)(*b*)].

Example 1

T holds 10,000 ordinary shares in a foreign company M SA. The shares were bought in April 1996 for £80,000. In February 2007, M SA has a capital reconstruction involving the cancellation of one-fifth of the existing ordinary shares in consideration of the repayment of £10 to each shareholder per share cancelled. T's holding is reduced to 8,000 shares, valued at £96,000. The indexation factor for April 1996 to April 1998 is 0.066.

	£
Disposal consideration (2,000 × £10)	20,000
Allowable cost $\frac{20,000}{20,000+96,000} \times £80,000$	13,793
Unindexed gain	6,207
Indexation allowance £13,793 × 0.066	910
Chargeable gain 2006/07 (subject to TAPER RELIEF (61))	£5,297

The allowable cost of the remaining shares is

£80,000 – £13,793	£66,207

Example 2 (Sale of rights)

X is a shareholder in K Ltd, owning 2,500 £1 ordinary shares which were purchased for £7,000 in October 1996. K Ltd makes a rights issue, but X sells his rights, without taking them up, for £700 in August 2006. The ex-rights value of X's 2,500 shares at the date of sale is £14,500. The indexation factor for the period October 1996 to April 1998 is 0.057.

'Section 104 holding' of K Ltd £1 ordinary shares

	Shares	Qualifying expenditure £	Indexed pool £
October 1996 acquisition	2,500	7,000	7,000
Indexed rise to April 1998 £7,000 × 0.057			399
	2,500	£7,000	£7,399

HMRC cannot require the capital distribution to be treated as a disposal, as the £700 received for the rights does not exceed 5% of (£700 + £14,500) and in any case does not exceed £3,000. If the transaction is not treated as a disposal, the £700 is deducted from both the acquisition cost of the shares and the indexed pool, leaving balances of, respectively, £6,300 and £6,699. If the transaction is treated as a disposal (possibly because X wishes to utilise part of his annual exemption), the computation is as follows

	£
Disposal proceeds	700
Allowable cost $\dfrac{700}{700+14{,}500} \times £7{,}000$	322
Unindexed gain	378
Indexation allowance $£7{,}399 \times \dfrac{700}{700+14{,}500} = £341$	
£341 – £322	19
Chargeable gain 2006/07 (subject to TAPER RELIEF (61))	£359

The allowable cost of the shares is then reduced to £6,678 (£7,000 – £322) and the indexed pool to £7,058 (£7,399 – £341).

58.11 **Distributions in a liquidation: unquoted shares.** Instead of requiring a strict valuation of unquoted shares for the purposes of the part disposal arising on a distribution, HMRC are prepared to accept a reasonable estimate of the residual value of the shares if the liquidation is expected to be completed within two years of the first distribution. If the distribution takes longer, the valuations may be reopened. Where time apportionment (see 7.7 *et seq.* ASSETS HELD ON 6 APRIL 1965) applies, HMRC are prepared to calculate the gain on each distribution by applying the time apportionment fraction as at the date of the first distribution (HMRC Statement of Practice D3).

58.12 **Distributions of assets in specie in a liquidation.** Where a company-owned asset, for example shares in a subsidiary, is distributed by the liquidator in specie to shareholders, *TCGA 1992, s 17* (see 41.1 MARKET VALUE) must be applied in determining the acquisition cost of an asset so received by a shareholder. For this purpose, each distribution to each shareholder is considered in isolation from the others. For example, if an asset is distributed equally to each of five shareholders, the acquisition cost for capital gains tax purposes of the part received by each (and also its disposal value from the point of view of the company) is the value of a 20% share, and not one-fifth of the value of a 100% share which may have produced a different (and almost certainly higher) figure. In a case in which the company is controlled by persons connected with each other, so that each such person is connected with the company (see 16.5 CONNECTED PERSONS), it is understood that the above nevertheless applies and that HMRC would not normally invoke the linked transactions provisions of *TCGA 1992, s 19* (see 3.16 ANTI-AVOIDANCE) so as to value each distribution as a percentage of the whole.

58.13 PRIVATISATIONS

The following is concerned with the privatisations of utilities previously in public ownership, e.g. power, water, telecommunications. For the de-mutualisation of building societies and other mutual organisations, e.g. insurance companies, see 58.22 below.

Payment by instalments. Most privatisation issues required payment of the subscription price by instalments. For the purposes of INDEXATION (34) allowance, the subscriber is deemed to have incurred, *at the time of acquisition of the shares*, relevant allowable expenditure equal to the full amount he is committed to paying (not just the amount of the first instalment). This applies only to privatisation issues — otherwise see 34.6 INDEXATION. If he disposes of the shares before all instalments are paid, the subscriber may choose to include the amount of the unpaid instalments in the cost of acquisition and add that same amount to the disposal proceeds (or, in the case of a non-arm's length disposal, to the MARKET VALUE (41) of the part-paid shares). Where indexation allowance is due, this choice is to his advantage as he thereby receives an allowance on instalments he has not paid. The new owner's allowable expenditure on a subsequent disposal of the shares fully-paid will in any case comprise the actual purchase price (or market value) and the instalments which he has had to pay on the shares. (HMRC Capital Gains Manual CG 50772, 50776, 50777).

Bonus shares. Many privatisations included the option of receiving bonus shares if the subscriber retained his original shares for a specified period. The issue of such bonus shares does not constitute a reorganisation as in 58.2 above. Instead, the subscriber is treated as acquiring the bonus shares at their date of issue at their then market value. (HMRC Capital Gains Manual CG 50773).

Vouchers. A subscriber to a privatisation issue may have been given the option of receiving vouchers which he can set against bills from the privatised company. No tax liability arises on receipt of such vouchers, but the acquisition cost of the shares for CGT purposes must be reduced by the value so received. (HMRC Capital Gains Manual CG 50774).

58.14 COMPANY PURCHASE OF OWN SHARES (AKA SHARE BUY-BACK)

Treasury shares. From 1 December 2003, the *Companies (Acquisition of Own Shares) (Treasury Shares) Regulations 2003 SI 2003 No 1116* permit listed companies (including those listed on the Alternative Investment Market) to purchase *and hold* their own shares. Such shares, often referred to as 'treasury shares' can then be sold, transferred to an employee share scheme or cancelled. The following provisions apply in relation to any acquisition of its shares by a company on or after the above date and ensure that for tax purposes own shares held without cancellation are treated as if cancelled, and as newly issued shares if they are subsequently sold.

Where a company acquires any of its shares, whether by purchase, bonus issue or otherwise, it is not treated for tax purposes as acquiring an asset. The company is not treated as a result of acquiring or holding the shares, or of being entered on its register of members in respect of any of them, as a member of itself. The company's issued share capital is treated as reduced by the nominal value of the shares acquired. Any shares not cancelled on acquisition are treated as cancelled, and any subsequent cancellation is disregarded (and is therefore not a disposal of an asset and does not give rise to an allowable loss). If the shares were issued to the company as bonus shares (i.e. share capital issued as paid up otherwise than by the receipt of new consideration within *ICTA 1988, s 254*) they are treated as if they had not been issued.

Where a company holds any treasury shares and it issues bonus shares in respect of those shares or any class of those shares, the above provisions do not prevent the existing shares being the company's 'holding' of shares for the purposes of the application of *TCGA 1992, s 126* (reorganisation of share capital — see 58.1 above) other than its application in modified form by virtue of any chargeable gains provision (see, for example, *TCGA 1992, s 192(2)* at 13.16 COMPANIES).

Where a company disposes of any of its treasury shares, the shares are not treated as having been disposed of by the company at the time of the disposal but are treated as having been issued as new shares by the company at that time. The person acquiring the shares is treated as having subscribed for them for an amount equal to any consideration payable for the disposal of the shares by the company. If that consideration does not exceed the nominal value of the shares, the share capital of the shares is treated for the purposes of *ICTA 1988, Pt VI* (company distributions etc.) as being the amount of the consideration. If the consideration exceeds the nominal value, the shares are treated as issued at a premium equal to that excess.

The above provisions do not apply to a company purchasing its own shares if the price payable by the company is taken into account in computing its Schedule D, Case I or II profits.

[*FA 2003, s 195; SI 2003 No 3077*].

Treatment of vendor on company purchasing own shares. Any consideration given by a company for the redemption, repayment or purchase of its own shares, *except* insofar as it represents repayment of share capital, is normally treated as a distribution, and hence as income in the hands of the recipient (see Tolley's Corporation Tax under Distributions). Such payments after 5 April 1982 in respect of shares in certain unquoted trading companies (or holding companies) are *not* treated as distributions, and thus give rise to liability to capital gains tax (or corporation tax on chargeable gains) on the recipient in the normal way. See Tolley's Corporation Tax under Company Purchasing Own Shares for detailed conditions. [*ICTA 1988, ss 219–229*].

In relation to purchases after 19 April 1989, if the purchase of its own shares by a UK resident company gives rise to a distribution, and the shareholder receiving such a distribution is itself a company, the HMRC's practice is to include the distribution in the consideration for the disposal of the shares for the purposes of the charge to corporation tax on chargeable gains. In HMRC's view the effect of *ICTA 1988, s 208* and *TCGA 1992, s 8(4)* is that the distribution does not suffer a tax charge as income within the terms of *TCGA 1992, s 37(1)* (see 35.1 INTERACTION WITH OTHER TAXES) (HMRC Statement of Practice 4/89). The legality of HMRC's practice in this respect was, however, rejected in *Strand Options and Futures Ltd v Vojak CA 2003, [2004] STC 64*. In that case, Carnwath LJ held that *ICTA 1988, s 208* should be construed as preventing the imposition of 'a tax which is directly charged on the dividends as such, rather than indirectly as part of the computation of a taxable amount'.

58.15 ACCRUED INCOME SCHEME

The accrued income scheme provisions of *ICTA 1988, ss 710–728* apply, broadly, to transfers of any government, public authority or company loan stock. (See further 59.6 SHARES AND SECURITIES—IDENTIFICATION RULES.)

The accrued income scheme does not apply for the purposes of corporation tax. [*ICTA 1988, s 710(1A); FA 1996, s 104, s 105(1), Sch 14 para 36, Sch 15 para 18*].

It also does not apply on a transfer to which *FA 1996, Sch 13* applies (charge to or relief from tax on the profit or loss realised from the discount on a relevant discounted security — see 58.16 below).

For deaths occurring after 5 April 1996 the accrued income scheme no longer applies to the transfer of securities on death to the deceased's personal representatives. [*ICTA 1988, s 710(5)(a), s 721; FA 1996, s 158*].

If a transfer is with accrued interest, the transferor is treated as entitled to the 'accrued amount' for income tax purposes, and the transferee is allowed similar relief for income tax purposes, for the interest period in which the settlement day falls. If the transfer is without accrued interest, the transferor is allowed relief on the 'rebate amount', and the transferee is treated as entitled to the same amount, for the relevant interest period.

Where a transfer within the accrued income provisions also constitutes a disposal for the purposes of *TCGA 1992*, neither *TCGA 1992, s 37* nor *s 39* applies (see 35.1 INTERACTION WITH OTHER TAXES). Instead, where a transfer is with accrued interest, an amount equal to the accrued amount is excluded for those purposes from the transferor's disposal consideration, and the same amount is excluded from the transferee's allowable expenditure when he makes a subsequent disposal. Where the transfer is without accrued interest, an amount equal to the rebate amount is added for those purposes to the transferor's disposal consideration, and the same amount is added to the transferee's allowable expenditure when he makes a subsequent disposal. Similar rules apply where there is a disposal (e.g. a deemed disposal) for the purposes of *TCGA 1992* without there being a contemporaneous transfer within the scope of the accrued income provisions. Where on a 'conversion' (being one within *TCGA 1992, s 132*; see 58.7 above) or an 'exchange' (being one which is not treated as a disposal: see generally 58.1 above) of securities, a person is treated as entitled to the accrued amount, an equal amount less any consideration received on the conversion or exchange (other than the new holding of securities) is treated for the purposes of *TCGA 1992* as consideration given on the conversion or exchange. Where the consideration received on the conversion or exchange (other than the new holding of securities) equals or exceeds an amount equal to the accrued amount, that consideration is treated for the purposes of *TCGA 1992* as reduced by that amount. If on a conversion or exchange of securities, a rebate amount is allowed for income tax purposes, an amount equal to the rebate amount is treated for the purposes of *TCGA 1992* as consideration received on the conversion or exchange.

Where a transfer of securities is made with the right to receive interest ('unrealised interest') payable on them on an interest payment date falling before the settlement day, neither *TCGA 1992, s 37* nor *s 39* applies. Instead, an amount equal to any such unrealised interest charged to income tax on the transferor is excluded for the purposes of *TCGA 1992* from the transferor's disposal consideration. Where such a transfer is made, an amount equal to the unrealised interest left out of account in charging income tax on the transferee is excluded for those purposes from the transferee's allowable expenditure when he makes a subsequent disposal.

[*TCGA 1992, s 119*].

See Tolley's Income Tax for full details of the accrued income scheme.

The above procedures will not be required for the purposes of computing a chargeable gain where the security is otherwise exempt. See 26 GOVERNMENT SECURITIES and 50 QUALIFYING CORPORATE BONDS.

58.16 DEEPLY DISCOUNTED SECURITIES

For 1996/97 and subsequent years, when a person transfers a 'deeply discounted security', or becomes entitled, as holder, to any payment on its redemption, he is chargeable to **income tax** on the excess of the amount payable on the transfer or redemption over the amount paid for its acquisition. In the event of a loss on a transfer or redemption before 27 March 2003, a claim may be made for relief against income of the tax year of transfer or redemption. Loss relief is abolished from that date except in the case of listed securities held on 26 March 2003 and strips of government securities. There are anti-avoidance provisions denying loss relief in respect of strips of government securities where there is a scheme for the manipulation of the acquisition, sale or redemption price. The provisions are extended to prevent an allowable loss arising for capital gains tax purposes after 16 March 2004 as a result of the making of a payment under such a scheme otherwise than in respect of the acquisition or disposal of a strip (see now *TCGA 1992, s 151C*). Similar provisions prevent an allowable loss arising for capital gains tax as a result of the making of a payment under a scheme for the manipulation of the acquisition, sale or redemption price of a 'corporate strip' (see below) acquired after 1 December 2004 (see now *TCGA 1992, s 151D*).

See Tolley's Income Tax for the detailed provisions. The provisions do **not** apply for corporation tax purposes.

A '*deeply discounted security*' is, except as excluded below, any security such that the amount payable on redemption (excluding interest) is or might be an amount involving a '*deep gain*', i.e. the issue price is less than the amount payable on redemption by 15% of that amount or, if less, by ½% per annum of that amount (counting months and part months as 1/12th of a year) to the redemption date. This comparison is made as at the time of issue of the security and assuming redemption in accordance with the terms of issue. 'Redemption' for these purposes referred originally to redemption on maturity or, if the holder of the security could opt for earlier redemption, the earliest occasion on which the holder might require redemption. In relation to any transfer of a security after 14 February 1999 or any occasion after that date on which a holder of a security becomes entitled to payment on redemption, the definition is widened so that one must consider, in addition to redemption on maturity, possible earlier occasions on which a security might be redeemed. The security will be a deeply discounted security if it would be such by reference to at least one such occasion. One need not take into account any occasion on which there may be a redemption other than at the option of the holder *unless* issuer and holder are connected or the obtaining of a tax advantage (as defined) is a main benefit that might be expected to accrue from the redemption provision. Additionally, where the holder has an option entitling him to redeem only on the occurrence of an 'event adversely affecting the holder' (as defined) or of a person's default *and* such entitlement is unlikely, judged at time of issue, to arise, the potential redemption is disregarded.

Gilt strips and strips of overseas government securities acquired after 26 March 2003 are always deeply discounted securities regardless of their issue terms. Strips of interest-bearing corporate securities ('*corporate strips*') acquired after 1 December 2004 are likewise always deeply discounted securities regardless of their issue terms.

Special rules apply to determine the issue price of (and the amount paid for the acquisition of) securities issued to a person in accordance with the terms of a 'qualifying earn-out right' (as defined). See Tolley's Income Tax for details.

The following are not deeply discounted securities:

(i) shares in a company;

(ii) gilt-edged securities (but see above concerning gilt strips and strips of overseas government securities);

(iii) excluded indexed securities (as defined);

(iv) life assurance policies;

(v) capital redemption policies; and

(vi) (with exceptions) securities issued under the same prospectus as other securities issued previously but not themselves deeply discounted securities.

After 14 February 1999, securities within (iii) and (vi) above may, however, be treated as deeply discounted securities in certain circumstances involving their being held by a person connected with the issuer. *ICTA 1988, s 839* applies to determine whether persons are connected for the purposes of these provisions but without taking any account of the security under review or any security issued under the same prospectus.

[*ITTOIA 2005, ss 427–460; Sch 1 paras 438, 487, 490; TCGA 1992, ss 151C, 151D; FA 1996, s 102, s 105(1)(b), Sch 13; FA 1999, s 65(1)–(6)(8); FA 2002, s 104; FA 2003, s 182, Sch 39; FA 2004, s 138(6)(13); F(No 2)A 2005, Sch 7 paras 8, 21, 25; FA 2006, Sch 13 para 32*].

For the avoidance of a double charge, i.e. to both income tax and capital gains tax (and double relief for losses), any deeply discounted security, whatever its date of issue, is brought within the definition of a QUALIFYING CORPORATE BOND (50). [*TCGA 1992, s 117(2AA)(8A); FA 1996, s 104, s 105(1), Sch 14 para 61; FA 1999, s 65(11); ITTOIA 2005, Sch 1 para 433(2)*]. However, a deeply discounted security does not qualify for the relief at 40.11 LOSSES for irrecoverable pre-17 March 1998 loans on securities.

58.17 DEPOSITARY RECEIPTS

Depositary receipts are used as substitute instruments indicating ownership of shares and securities and designed primarily to enable investors to hold and deal in shares of companies located outside the investor's country. They are issued by a bank or other financial institution (the depositary), with whom the share certificate is deposited. For CGT purposes, the holder of a depositary receipt has two separate chargeable assets, i.e. the depositary receipt itself (being the document evidencing title, and comprising certain rights as against the depositary) and a beneficial interest in the underlying shares. In practice, however, the value of the depositary receipt is likely to relate entirely, or almost entirely, to the underlying shares, and, therefore, no apportionment is usually made, as regards either base cost or consideration received, on a disposal of shares in depositary receipt form. Likewise, there will normally be no chargeable gain or allowable loss on the 'conversion' of a depositary receipt back into shares, even though this does constitute a disposal of the second asset. (HMRC Capital Gains Manual CG 50240–50242). See 6.2 ASSETS as regards location of shares held in depositary receipt form.

58.18 PERSONAL EQUITY PLANS

From 1 January 1987 and before 6 April 1999, a 'qualifying individual' could subscribe a specified maximum to a Personal Equity Plan (PEP) (to which no-one else could subscribe). New regulations came into force on 6 April 1989 (*SI 1989 No 469* — subsequently amended). Plans under the earlier 1986 Regulations operated by reference to calendar years rather than tax years.

No further subscriptions to PEPs can be made after 5 April 1999, but existing PEPs may continue, and independently of individual savings accounts (ISAs) (see 22.29 EXEMPTIONS AND RELIEFS). A 10% tax credit is payable on dividends received from UK equities before 6 April 2004.

A '*qualifying individual*' had to be 18 years of age or over, and resident and ordinarily resident in the UK or a non-resident Crown employee serving overseas whose duties were treated as performed in the UK. Subscriptions up to specified limits could be made to one general plan and one 'single company plan' in any tax year. A '*single company plan*' allowed investment only in shares of one designated company and was often known as a corporate PEP. After 5 April 2001, the distinctions between general plans and single company plans are abolished, allowing such plans to be merged if the investor wishes. Plans, or (after 5 April 2001) parts of plans, may be transferred between plan managers.

After 5 April 2001, the range of qualifying investments that may be held under a plan is brought into line with that applicable to the stocks and shares component of an ISA (see 22.29 EXEMPTIONS AND RELIEFS), except that qualifying investments held immediately before 6 April 2001 may be retained in the plan even if they no longer otherwise qualify. For the range of qualifying investments applicable before 6 April 2001, see the 2000/01 and earlier editions.

Investments may not be purchased from the plan investor or spouse. Subscription to a plan had to be by payment of cash to the plan manager for investment by him, except that

- qualifying shares allotted to the investor under public offers, and
- (in relation to single company plans) shares acquired by him under certain approved employee share schemes,

could be transferred into plans before 6 April 1999. This also applied to shares issued by a building society on conversion to plc status and, from 20 March 1997, to shares in a mutual insurer transferring its business to a company limited by shares (see Revenue Tax Bulletins April 1997 p 418 and April 1998 pp 522, 523). Where such would not otherwise have been the case, any shares sold during the period allowed for transfer were identified first with shares which were ineligible for transfer so as to ensure that investors were able to transfer the maximum number of shares into a PEP. There was no deemed disposal for capital gains purposes when the plan investor transferred shares into a plan, the investor retaining his beneficial ownership of plan investments even though legal ownership is held by the plan manager.

Cash held for reinvestment within a plan must be held in sterling and invested in a designated account with a deposit taker or building society. Interest is paid gross and is exempt from tax. However, if interest exceeding £180 in a tax year is paid by the plan manager to or for the plan investor in respect of cash held within a plan, the plan manager must account for a sum representing lower rate tax on all such interest payments in the year; the interest payments are for all purposes treated as interest taxable in the year in which they arise.

Otherwise, for so long as the various conditions continue to be met, dividends and interest on securities are tax-free, and, as regards pre-6 April 2004 dividends on UK equities, the plan manager may reclaim the related tax credits, including (from 21 August 1998) those pertaining to investors who have ceased to be UK-resident since subscribing to the plan.

No chargeable gain or allowable loss arises on the disposal of an investment within the plan. Where plan investments are withdrawn *in specie*, the plan investor is deemed to have made a disposal and reacquisition at market value, thus exempting any gain or loss arising and establishing a CGT acquisition cost for future disposals. The plan investor is treated as holding securities within the plan in a capacity other than that in which he holds any other securities of the same class so that identification rules and, for acquisitions before 6 April 1998, share pooling rules are applied separately to plan investments. The normal share reorganisation rules are disapplied in respect of plan investments in the event of a reorganisation of share capital involving an allotment for payment, e.g. a rights issue.

[*TCGA 1992, ss 151, 287; ICTA 1988, ss 333, 333A, 828; FA 1988, s 116; FA 1991, s 70; FA 1993, s 85; FA 1995, s 64; ITTOIA 2005, ss 694–701, Sch 1 paras 141, 142, 334, 436; SI 1989, No 469; SI 1990, No 678; SI 1991 Nos 733, 2774; SI 1992 No 623; SI 1993 No 756; SI 1995 Nos 1539, 3287; SI 1996 Nos 846, 1355; SI 1997 Nos 511, 1716; SI 1998 No 1869; SI 2000 No 3109; SI 2001 No 923; SI 2001 No 3629, Arts 120–125; SI 2001 No 3777; SI 2003 No 2748; SI 2004 No 1676; SI 2005 Nos 2562, 3348*].

58.19 CLOSE COMPANIES

Income tax which has been charged on a participator as a result of an apportionment under *ICTA 1988, ss 423–430, Sch 19* (broadly only in relation to accounting periods ending before 1 April 1989; see Tolley's Corporation Tax under Close Companies) and paid by him in respect of income of a close company which has not subsequently been distributed (including stock dividends; see 58.9 above), may be deducted, pro rata, in computing a gain on the disposal of any of his shares in that company. Apportioned income is treated as the top slice of income and shares are identified on a first in, first out basis. [*TCGA 1992, s 124*].

Tax paid which is referable to gains of a non-resident company charged on a UK participator or shareholder under *TCGA 1992, s 13* (see 45.6 OVERSEAS MATTERS) is similarly deductible. See also 15.5 COMPUTATION OF GAINS AND LOSSES for an alternative concessional treatment.

58.20 LIFE ASSURANCE POLICIES

Investments or other assets transferred to a policy holder by an insurance company, in accordance with a life assurance policy, are deemed to be transferred at market value. [*TCGA 1992, s 204(3)(6); FA 2006, s 73(2)*].

58.21 STOCK LENDING AND AGREEMENTS FOR SALE AND REPURCHASE OF SECURITIES

The provisions of *TCGA 1992, ss 263B, 263C* come into force on **1 July 1997** (*SI 1997 No 991*) from which date the comparable provisions of *TCGA 1992, s 271(9)* are repealed.

Stock lending arrangements. *Definition.* A '*stock lending arrangement*' is an arrangement between two persons ('the borrower' and 'the lender') under which:

(*a*) the lender transfers 'securities' to the borrower otherwise than by way of sale; and

(*b*) a requirement is imposed on the borrower to transfer those securities back to the lender otherwise than by way of sale.

The disposals and acquisitions made in pursuance of any stock lending arrangement *are disregarded* for the purposes of capital gains tax. [*TCGA 1992, s 263B*(*1*)(*2*); *FA 1997, Sch 10 para 5*].

Disposals by the borrower. If the borrower under any stock lending arrangement disposes of any securities transferred to him under the arrangement such that that disposal is made otherwise than in the discharge of the requirement for the transfer of securities back to the lender, and that requirement, so far as it relates to the securities disposed of, has been or will be discharged by the transfer of securities other than those transferred to the borrower, any question relating to the acquisition of the securities disposed of shall be determined as if the securities disposed of were the securities with which that requirement (so far as relating to the securities disposed of) has been or will be discharged. [*TCGA 1992, s 263B*(*3*); *FA 1997, Sch 10 para 5*].

Transfer back to the lender not taking place. The ensuing consequences will occur in the case of any stock lending arrangement, where it becomes apparent, at any time after the making of the transfer by the lender, that the requirement for the borrower to make a transfer back to the lender will not be complied with.

(i) The lender shall be deemed to have made a disposal at that time of the securities transferred to the borrower;

(ii) The borrower shall be deemed to have acquired them at that time; and

(iii) *TCGA 1992, s 263B*(*3*) (above) shall have effect in relation to any disposal before that time by the borrower of securities transferred to him by the lender as if the securities deemed to have been acquired by the borrower were to be used for discharging a requirement to transfer securities back to the lender.

[*TCGA 1992, s 263B*(*4*); *FA 1997, Sch 10 para 5*].

References, in relation to a person to whom securities are transferred, to the transfer of those securities back to another person are to be construed as if the cases where those securities are taken to be transferred back to that other person included any case where securities of the same description as those securities are transferred to that other person either:

(*a*) in accordance with a requirement to transfer securities of the same description; or

(*b*) in exercise of a power to substitute securities of the same description for the securities that are required to be transferred back.

[*TCGA 1992, s 263B*(*5*); *FA 1997, Sch 10 para 5*].

Securities shall not be taken to be of the same description as other securities unless they are in the same quantities, give the same rights against the same persons and are of the same type and nominal value as the other securities. '*Securities*' means shares of any company resident in the United Kingdom (*United Kingdom equities*), securities of the government of the United Kingdom, any public or local authority in the United Kingdom or of any company or other body resident in the United Kingdom, but excluding quoted Eurobonds held in a recognised clearing system (*United Kingdom securities*) or shares, stock or other securities issued by a government or public or local authority of a territory outside the United Kingdom or by any other body of persons not resident in the United Kingdom and quoted Eurobonds (within *ICTA 1988, s 124*) held in a recognised clearing system (*overseas securities*). Reference to '*interest*' includes dividends. [*ICTA 1988, Sch 23A; TCGA 1992, s 263B*(*6*)(*7*); *FA 1997, Sch 10 para 5*].

Provisions to ensure continuity of treatment for stock lending arrangements involving securities redenominated in euros following the introduction on 1 January 1999 of the European single currency in certain EU member states other than the UK are contained in *SI 1998 No 3177, Regs 20–23*.

Stock lending involving redemption. A transfer back to a person of securities transferred by him shall be taken to include references to the payment to him, in pursuance of an obligation arising on any person's becoming entitled to receive an amount in respect of the redemption of those securities, of an amount equal to the amount of the entitlement. Where, in pursuance of any such obligation, the lender under any stock lending arrangement is paid any amount in respect of the redemption of any securities to which the arrangement relates:

(A) that lender shall be deemed to have disposed, for that amount, of the securities in respect of whose redemption it is paid ('*the relevant lent securities*');

(B) the borrower shall not, in respect of the redemption, be taken to have made any disposal of the relevant lent securities; and

(C) *TCGA 1992, s 263B(3)* (see above) shall have effect in relation to disposals of any of the relevant lent securities made by the borrower before the redemption as if:

   (i) the amount paid to the lender were an amount paid for the acquisition of securities, and

   (ii) the securities acquired were to be used by the borrower for discharging a requirement under the arrangement to transfer the relevant lent securities back to the lender.

[*TCGA 1992, s 263C; FA 1997, Sch 10 para 5*].

Pre-1 July 1997 provisions. A transfer of securities (including stocks and shares) under either of the following types of arrangement is ignored for the purposes of the charge to tax on capital gains.

(i) Where a person (A) enters into an arrangement under which another person (B) is to transfer securities to A or his nominee, and securities of the same kind and amount are to be transferred by someone to B or his nominee.

(ii) Where, to enable B to make such a transfer to A or his nominee, similar arrangements are made between B or his nominee and another person (C) or his nominee; and where a similar arrangement is entered into after 30 September 1993 as part of a chain of arrangements for overseas securities, all having the effect of enabling B to make the transfer to A or his nominee.

Transfers within (i) or (ii) are also left out of account in computing income for tax purposes of any trade carried on by the transferor or transferee. The Treasury may make regulations by statutory instrument imposing further conditions. Except in so far as those regulations otherwise provide, the above provisions only apply if A enters into the arrangement mentioned in (1) above to enable him to fulfil a contract under which he is required to sell securities. [*TCGA 1992, s 271(9); ICTA 1988, ss 129, 828; FA 1991, s 57; FA 1995, s 84; FA 1997, Sch 10 para 5(2); ITTOIA 2005, Sch 1 para 334; SI 1989 No 1299; SI 1992 No 572; SI 1993 No 2003; SI 1995 No 1283; SI 1997 No 991*].

Replacement loans. A loan of securities is also left out of account for income and capital gains tax purposes where it is made to enable a borrower to replace an existing loan of such securities rather than to meet a sale, provided the existing loan was within the above provisions (as extended by this concessional treatment if necessary) and the replacement loan would otherwise have been within them but for the requirement that it must be made to enable the transferee to fulfil a contract to sell securities (or to transfer the securities to a third party to enable him to fulfil a contract to sell securities). [*SI 1989 No 1299, Reg 3C; SI 1995 No 3219, Reg 4*]. This applies with effect from 2 January 1996, but previously applied under ESC B36.

Agreements for sale and repurchase of securities. Where *ICTA 1988, s 737A(1)* (treatment of price differential on sale and repurchase of securities as interest payment in certain cases; see Tolley's Income Tax under Anti-Avoidance) applies (or would apply were the sale and repurchase price different), the acquisition and disposal by the interim holder, and (except where the repurchaser is or may be different from the original owner) the disposal and acquisition (as repurchaser) by the original owner, are disregarded for capital gains tax purposes. This does not, however, apply

(*a*) where the repurchase price falls to be computed by reference to the provisions of *ICTA 1988, s 737C* ('manufactured' dividends and interest; see Tolley's Income Tax under Anti-Avoidance) which are not in force in relation to the securities when the repurchase price becomes due; or

(*b*) if the agreement(s) in question are non-arm's length agreements, or if all the benefits or risks arising from fluctuations in the market value of the securities accrue to, or fall on, the interim holder; or

(*c*) in relation to any disposal or acquisition of QUALIFYING CORPORATE BONDS (50) where the securities disposed of by the original owner, or those acquired by him or another person as repurchaser, are not such bonds.

[*TCGA 1992, s 263A; FA 1995, s 80(4)(5)*]. Where *ICTA 1988, s 730A(1)* applies but *TCGA 1992, s 263A* does not, the repurchase price is, as the case may be, either reduced by the excess of that price over the sale price or increased by the excess of the sale price over that price for CGT purposes. [*ICTA 1988, s 730A(2)(4); FA 1995, s 80(1)(5)*].

Provisions to ensure continuity of treatment for stock lending arrangements involving securities redenominated in euros following the introduction on 1 January 1999 of the European single currency in certain EU member states other than the UK are contained in *SI 1998 No 3177, Regs 20–23*.

Gain accruing to person paying manufactured dividend. Subject to the commencement rules below, the following provisions apply where a person resident in the UK, other than a company,

(*a*) disposes of 'UK equities' (as defined in *ICTA 1988, Sch 23A para 1(1)*)

  (i) transferred to him as the interim holder under a repurchase agreement which falls within *ICTA 1988, s 730A(1)* or which would fall within *section 730A(1)* if the sale and repurchase prices were different,

  (ii) transferred to him as the borrower under a stock lending arrangement (as above), or

  (iii) under a 'short sale transaction' (i.e. a contract or other arrangements for the transfer of the equities which is neither a repurchase agreement nor a stock lending arrangement) to which he is a party; and

(*b*) pays a 'manufactured dividend' under that agreement, arrangement or transaction, which is representative of a dividend on those equities.

If a chargeable gain accrues to that person on the disposal, an allowable loss is treated as accruing to him on the same date, deductible only from that gain. The amount of the loss is the lesser of the chargeable gain and the 'adjusted amount'. For this purpose the '*adjusted amount*' is equal to the lesser of the manufactured dividend and the dividend of which the manufactured dividend is representative less so much of the manufactured dividend as is allowable as a deduction for income tax purposes under *ICTA 1988, Sch 23A para 2A*.

A 'manufactured dividend' is as defined in *ICTA 1988, Sch 23A para 2*, and references above to a manufactured dividend being paid include deemed payment under *ICTA 1988, s 737A(5)* but do not include deemed payment under *ICTA 1988, s 736B(2)*. See Tolley's Income Tax under Anti-Avoidance.

The above provisions apply where the manufactured dividend is paid, or treated as paid, after 16 March 2004 or the chargeable gain accrues after that date.

[*TCGA 1992, s 263D; FA 2004, s 136 Sch 24 para 3*].

58.22 BUILDING SOCIETY AND OTHER DE-MUTUALISATIONS

Statutory rules. The following applies where there is a transfer of the whole of a building society's business to a successor company in accordance with the relevant provisions of the *Building Societies Act 1986*.

Subject to the operation of *TCGA 1992, s 217(1)* (rights to acquire shares in successor company treated as valueless options, see 6.7(*f*) ASSETS), shares issued to members by the successor company, or disposed of to members by the society, are regarded as acquired for any new consideration given and as having at the time of acquisition a value equal to such new consideration (if any). Where shares are so issued or disposed of to trustees of a settlement on terms providing for their transfer to members for no new consideration

(*a*) they are regarded as acquired by the trustees for no consideration;

(*b*) a member's interest in the shares is regarded as acquired for no consideration and as having no value at the time of acquisition;

(*c*) on the member becoming absolutely entitled to any shares, or where such entitlement would arise but for the member being an infant or otherwise under disability, the shares are treated as disposed of and reacquired by the trustees in a nominee capacity under *TCGA 1992, s 60(1)* and at a no gain/no loss price and *TCGA 1992, s 71* (see 57.15 SETTLEMENTS) does not then apply; and

(*d*) on the member disposing of his interest in the settled property, any gain is a chargeable gain and *TCGA 1992, s 76(1)* (see 57.14 SETTLEMENTS) does not then apply.

Any gain on the disposal by the society of shares in the successor company in connection with the transfer is not a chargeable gain. [*TCGA 1992, s 216(1), s 217(2)–(7); FA 2006, Sch 12 para 20*].

The conferring of any benefit under the above or *TCGA 1992, s 217(1)* on a member of a society in connection with a transfer, or any payment in lieu of such a benefit, or any distribution in pursuance of *Building Societies Act 1986, s 100(2)(b)*, is not regarded as either the making of a distribution for corporation tax purposes or the payment of a dividend by the society. However, any such disregarded benefit etc. may be taken into account as a capital distribution as in 58.10 above. [*FA 1988, Sch 12 para 6*].

Practice. It has become customary for building societies to offer their members cash bonuses or free shares as an inducement towards their voting in favour of de-mutualisation of the society, i.e. a takeover by a limited company or a unilateral conversion from mutual to corporate status. In *Foster v Williams; Horan v Williams (Sp C 113), [1997] SSCD 112*, concerning *cash payments* received by investors on the takeover of Cheltenham and Gloucester Building Society by Lloyds Bank plc in August 1995, a Special Commissioner, allowing the taxpayers' appeals, held that both share account and deposit account investors in the society had made a total disposal of their accounts, for which the consideration consisted of the opening balances on new accounts with the successor company plus the cash bonus payments. No chargeable gain arose on the disposal of a *deposit account*, this being the disposal of a debt (which was not a debt on a security) (see 22.5 EXEMPTIONS AND RELIEFS). On the disposal of a share account, a chargeable gain did arise, and the allowable expenditure was the amount of the closing credit balance on the account on the vesting day (plus INDEXATION (34) allowance, which could therefore reduce or eliminate the gain). The Revenue accepted the decision without further appeal and announced that it would also be applied to cash payments received as a result of the de-mutualisation of other building societies. (Revenue Press Release 27 March 1997 and Revenue Tax Bulletin April 1998 pp 517–523).

Where cash is received by a member on the de-mutualisation of a building society, the resulting gain is not eligible for TAPER RELIEF (see 61.25).

The treatment of *shares* issued to members on the de-mutualisation of a building society is governed by *TCGA 1992, s 217* (see above) and remains unchanged, the member realising no chargeable gain or allowable loss on receipt of the shares but, in the case of free shares, having no acquisition cost (and thus no indexation allowance) in computing the gain on a subsequent disposal. (Revenue Press Releases 21 March 1996, 27 March 1997 and Revenue Tax Bulletin April 1998 pp 517–523).

The Revenue Tax Bulletin article referred to above also comments on a number of specific points, *viz.* the treatment of multiple accounts (a separate calculation is required for each account in the case of cash bonuses; free shares acquired before 6 April 1998 are pooled), free shares sold immediately by successor company on investor's behalf (this is *not* equivalent to a cash bonus), statutory cash bonuses received by members ineligible to vote (treated like any other cash bonus), joint accounts (cash bonus/free shares treated as received/acquired equally between account holders), child, nominee and client accounts (cash bonus/free shares treated as received/acquired wholly by the beneficial owner of the account, i.e. the child etc.), partnership accounts (cash bonus/free shares treated as received/acquired by all the partners in accordance with their partnership sharing ratios), and accounts in the form of permanent interest bearing shares (PIBs) (cash bonuses are free of CGT as a PIB is a QUALIFYING CORPORATE BOND (50)).

There is also a detailed discussion in Tax Bulletin of the position, including that for inheritance tax, where an investor dies before de-mutualisation. Where death occurs after the de-mutualisation is announced and the entitlement to a cash bonus or free shares passes to the personal representatives/beneficiaries, the value of the right to receive the cash bonus or free shares may increase the value at death of a share account for both CGT and inheritance tax purposes (and see *Ward and others (Executors of Cook, deceased) v CIR 1998 (Sp C 175), [1999] SSCD 1*). A Table is provided to assist in valuations. The Bulletin also covers the position of a surviving holder of a joint account.

The CGT treatment of 'windfalls' received on the de-mutualisation of other organisations, e.g. insurance companies, sports clubs, depends on the facts of each particular case. The Tax Bulletin comments on the conversion of Norwich Union (where the position differs according to the date the free shares were unconditionally allotted to policy holders) and the takeover of Scottish Amicable, both in 1997.

(Revenue Tax Bulletin April 1998 pp 517–523).

The treatment of windfalls made to Scottish Widows policy holders is covered in Revenue 'Working Together' Bulletin August 2001 p 8.

Example

Mr C Bagger opened a share account with the Toytown Building Society in August 1993. The society was taken over by High Street Bank plc in December 1997 and Mr Bagger received in that month a cash distribution of £13,000 which comprised a fixed payment of £500 and a percentage payment based on the higher of the balances on the account at two stated dates but restricted to 12½% of £100,000. Mr Bagger's passbook showed the following account details.

Date		*Debit*	*Credit*	*Balance*
		£	£	£
4.8.93	Deposit		50,000	50,000
31.3.94	Net interest		1,500	51,500
16.6.94	Deposit		75,000	126,500
31.3.95	Net interest		5,000	131,500
1.5.95	Withdrawal	25,000		106,500
31.3.96	Net interest		4,800	111,300
31.3.97	Net interest		5,300	116,600
1.6.97	Withdrawal	8,000		108,600
12.12.97	Cash bonus on takeover		13,000	121,600
12.12.97	Closing interest		2,800	124,400
12.12.97	Balance transferred to new deposit account at High Street Bank plc	124,400		Nil

Relevant indexation factors are as follows:

August 1993 to March 1994	0.008
March 1994 to June 1994	0.015
June 1994 to March 1995	0.019
March 1995 to May 1995	0.014
May 1995 to March 1996	0.013
March 1996 to March 1997	0.026
March 1997 to June 1997	0.014
June 1997 to December 1997	0.016

The chargeable gain on the cash bonus is computed as follows:

	Qualifying expenditure	*Indexed pool*
	£	£
4.8.93 acquisition	50,000	50,000
Indexed rise: August 1993–March 1994		
£50,000 × 0.008		400
31.3.94 acquisition	1,500	1,500
	51,500	51,900
Indexed rise: March 1994–June 1994		
£51,900 × 0.015		779
16.6.94 acquisition	75,000	75,000
	126,500	127,679
Indexed rise: June 1994–March 1995		
£127,679 × 0.019		2,426
31.3.95 acquisition	5,000	5,000
	131,500	135,105

Indexed rise: March 1995–May 1995		
£135,105 × 0.014		1,890
	131,500	136,995
1.5.95 disposal (no gain/no loss)	(25,000)	(26,045)*
	106,500	110,950
Indexed rise: May 1995–March 1996		
£110,950 × 0.013		1,442
31.3.96 acquisition	4,800	4,800
	111,300	117,192
Indexed rise: March 1996–March 1997		
£117,192 × 0.026		3,047
31.3.97 acquisition	5,300	5,300
	116,600	125,539
Indexed rise: March 1997–June 1997		
£125,539 × 0.014		1,758
	116,600	127,297
1.6.97 disposal (no gain/no loss)	(8,000)	(8,734)**
	108,600	118,563
Indexed rise: June 1997–December 1997		
£118,563 × 0.016		1,897
12.12.97 acquisition	2,800	2,800
	111,400	123,260
12.12.97 disposal	(111,400)	(123,260)

$$* \; £136,995 \times \frac{25,000}{131,500} = \qquad £26,045$$

$$** \; £127,297 \times \frac{8,000}{116,600} = \qquad £8,734$$

	£
Proceeds:	
Cash bonus	13,000
Balance of account	111,400
Total proceeds	124,400
Allowable cost	111,400
Unindexed gain	13,000
Indexation allowance £123,260 – 111,400	11,860
Chargeable gain	£1,140

Note to the example

(*a*) For the purpose of calculating the indexation allowance, each £1 deposited or withdrawn is treated in the same way as an acquisition or disposal of a share in a company.

Mergers of building societies. Cash payments on the merger of two building societies are chargeable to income tax (Revenue Press Release 21 March 1996).

Cashbacks. Cashbacks paid by banks and building societies as an inducement to purchase goods or services, e.g. to take out a mortgage, are not chargeable to capital gains tax (HMRC Statement of Practice 4/97). See 22.21 EXEMPTIONS AND RELIEFS.

58.23 RECOGNISED STOCK EXCHANGES

Under *ICTA 1988, s 841* (applied for capital gains purposes by *TCGA 1992, s 288*(*1*)), the expression '*recognised stock exchange*' means the London Stock Exchange and any overseas stock exchange designated as such by Order. A list of designated overseas stock exchanges is available on the HMRC website (www.hmrc.gov.uk). A list of recognised stock exchanges also appears in Simon's Direct Tax Service, Binder 1, p 7521 *et seq*. In a Revenue policy statement published on the internet on 27 November 2002, a change to a more broadly based approach in designating overseas exchanges was announced.

After 27 November 2001, HMRC interpret the phrase 'listed on a recognised stock exchange', and similar phrases frequently used in tax legislation, as denoting,

(*a*) in the EU and other European Economic Area countries (Norway, Iceland and Liechtenstein): listing *by* a competent authority and admission to trading *on* a recognised stock exchange; and

(*b*) outside these countries: admission to trading *by* a recognised stock exchange.

The phrase 'listed in the Official List of the Stock Exchange' therefore denotes listing by the Financial Services Authority and admission to trading on the London Stock Exchange.

Under the previous interpretation, (*b*) above applied in all cases. Under the revised interpretation, the status of most securities, i.e. as listed or unlisted for tax purposes, does not change. However, the Revenue used to regard securities admitted to trading on most semi-official and junior markets of overseas exchanges as listed. Under the revised interpretation, securities traded on some such exchanges in the EU/EEA are no longer so regarded, as they are not listed by a competent authority.

HMRC have undertaken to apply the revised view in such a way as not to disadvantage those who had made investments now reclassified as unlisted. Alternatively, they will to some extent accept claims to certain unlisted/unquoted company reliefs on pre-existing investments so reclassified. Full details in each case are given in the press release. An investment cannot be treated as simultaneously continuing to be listed for some purposes and unlisted for others.

The change of interpretation does not affect shares admitted to trading on the UK Alternative Investment Market (AIM) (see 41.6 MARKET VALUE), which continue to count as unlisted.

(Revenue Press Release 28 November 2001).

59 Shares and Securities — Identification Rules

Cross-references. See 34 INDEXATION; 58 SHARES AND SECURITIES; 61 TAPER RELIEF.

Simon's Direct Tax Service. See Division C2.7.

59.1 INTRODUCTION

Prior to 6 April 1998, acquisitions by the same person of shares (and securities) of the same class in the same company were pooled and treated as a single asset, each subsequent disposal out of that shareholding being treated as a part disposal of the single asset and the chargeable gain or allowable loss calculated by reference to the average cost (or, where applicable, the average indexed cost) per share of the shares sold. As a consequence of the introduction of TAPER RELIEF (61) for disposals after 5 April 1998 by individuals, trustees and personal representatives, share pooling is abolished for such disposals. A share pool already established at 5 April 1998 continues to be treated as a single asset but acquisitions after that date are not pooled (see 59.2 below). **These changes do not apply for the purposes of corporation tax on chargeable gains**, as regards which share pooling continues after 5 April 1998 as before.

Summary of current identification rules. For capital gains tax purposes (but not corporation tax purposes — see above), disposals after 5 April 1998 are to be identified with acquisitions in the following order.

- acquisitions on the same day as the disposal;
- acquisitions within 30 days after the day of disposal (thus countering 'bed and breakfasting');
- previous acquisitions after 5 April 1998 on a last in/first out (LIFO) basis;
- shares acquired after 5 April 1982 and comprised in the pool at 5 April 1998 (i.e. the 'section 104 holding' in 59.4 below — previously known as the 'new holding');
- shares acquired before 6 April 1982 (the '1982 holding' in 59.5 below);
- shares acquired on or before 6 April 1965 on a LIFO basis;
- if the shares disposed of are still not exhausted, shares acquired subsequent to the disposal (and beyond the above-mentioned 30-day period).

The post-5 April 1998 rules for capital gains tax are covered in detail at 59.2 below. The rules applying for the purposes of corporation tax on chargeable gains are similarly covered at 59.3–59.6 below. Those rules also applied for capital gains tax purposes pre-6 April 1998.

See the 2005/06 and earlier editions for the identification rules for disposals in the period before the '1985 date' (see 59.3 below) but on or after the '1982 date' (i.e. 6 April 1982 (1 April 1982 for companies)) and for the period before the '1982 date'.

59.2 IDENTIFICATION RULES FOR SHARES AND SECURITIES AFTER 5 APRIL 1998 (OTHER THAN FOR CORPORATION TAX PURPOSES)

See 59.1 above for background and for a **summary** of the capital gains tax identification rules for disposals after 5 April 1998 as detailed below. **The provisions described below do not apply for the purposes of corporation tax on chargeable gains.**

Abolition of pooling and preservation of pools in existence at 5 April 1998. The share pooling rules at 59.3, 59.4 below are disapplied for capital gains tax purposes as regards any shares (or securities) acquired after 5 April 1998. Where, however, shares etc. are actually acquired after that date as a result of a reorganisation (e.g. a scrip or rights issue) but are regarded by virtue of *TCGA 1992, s 127* (see 58.1 SHARES AND SECURITIES) as equating to shares etc. acquired on or before that date and included in the 5 April 1998 single asset pool (the 'section 104 holding' — see below), the newly-acquired shares etc. are themselves added to the pool if they are of the same class as the original shares or form a new single asset pool if they are of a different class (see HMRC Capital Gains Manual CG 50572).

The single asset pool for shares acquired on or after 6 April 1982, previously referred to in the legislation as the 'new holding', is preserved and is renamed, for all purposes, the '*section 104 holding*'. This consists of shares etc. of the same class in the same company acquired by the same person in the same capacity. Such shares etc. are regarded as a single asset growing or diminishing as and when additional shares are acquired and shares are disposed of (see also 59.4 below). However, except as mentioned above as respects reorganisations, the 'section 104 holding' cannot grow for capital gains tax purposes by reference to acquisitions after 5 April 1998. Where appropriate, reference should be made to 59.3 and 59.4 below for the detailed rules on share pooling.

Shares etc. held by a person who acquired them as an employee of the company concerned or of anyone else and on terms which for the time being restrict his right to dispose of them (known as 'clogged shares') are treated as being of a different class from both

- shares etc. held by him in the same company and acquired otherwise than as an employee; and
- shares etc. held by him in the same company which are not, or are no longer, subject to the same restrictions.

Upon the removal of the restrictions, the clogged shares are identified in the same way as any other shares held of the same class in the same company and by reference to their actual acquisition date where this is after 5 April 1998 (HMRC Capital Gains Manual CG 56504). [*TCGA 1992, s 104; FA 1998, s 123(1)–(6), s 125(3)(4); FA 2006, Sch 12 para 17*].

Application of indexation allowance to section 104 holding. As stated at 34.1 INDEXATION, indexation allowance is frozen for capital gains tax (but not corporation tax) purposes at its April 1998 level and is not available at all in respect of expenditure incurred after 31 March 1998. The indexed pool of expenditure at 5 April 1998 is computed in accordance with the rules in 59.4 below as if the entire holding had been disposed of at the end of that day. Indexation allowance is thus given on the 'section 104 holding' up to and including April 1998. On a disposal after 5 April 1998 of, or out of, the 'section 104 holding' in accordance with the identification rules below, or on any other operative event, the indexed pool continues to be maintained as in 59.4 below and indexation allowance computed accordingly, except that the indexed pool is *not* to be increased by any indexed rise in expenditure after April 1998. [*TCGA 1992, s 110A; FA 1998, s 125(2)(4)(5)*].

Identification rules. The identification rules detailed below apply in relation to disposals after 5 April 1998 for the purposes of capital gains tax. They apply for the purpose of identifying a disposal of shares with an acquisition of shares etc. of the same class made by the person making the disposal and held by him in the same capacity as that in which he makes the disposal. For identification purposes, disposals are considered in the date order in which they take place. These rules override any identification purporting to be made by the disposal itself or by a transfer or delivery giving effect to it.

The rules below do not apply to shares (or securities) to which Enterprise Investment Scheme relief, venture capital trust scheme relief or community investment tax relief is attributable or to shares in respect of which relief has been given (and not withdrawn) under the Business Expansion Scheme (BES). Disposals of such shares retain their own identification rules — see 21.8, 21.10, 21.14 ENTERPRISE INVESTMENT SCHEME, 66.11, 66.12 VENTURE CAPITAL TRUSTS, 22.20 EXEMPTIONS AND RELIEFS (as regards the BES) and Tolley's Income Tax under Community Investment Tax Relief. The rules below *do* apply to the matching of share transactions carried out during a period of non-UK residence (Revenue Tax Bulletin April 2001 p 839).

HMRC take the view that shares etc. held in the name of an individual are held in the same capacity as his or her portion of any shares of the same class in the same company which are held in the joint names of that individual and his or her spouse (*Taxation 13 May 1999 p 170*). See 42.1 MARRIED PERSONS AND CIVIL PARTNER re jointly held assets generally.

These identification rules apply not only to shares but to securities of a company, to 'relevant securities' (see 59.6 below) and to any other assets of such nature as to be dealt in without identifying the particular assets disposed of or acquired, e.g. units in a unit trust and milk quota, such assets being known as *fungible* assets. Shares and securities are treated as being of the same class only if they are, or would be, so treated by the practice of a recognised stock exchange (as defined by *ICTA 1988, s 841* — see 58.23 SHARES AND SECURITIES). [*TCGA 1992, s 104(3)*].

The rules apply **in the order set out below**, so that each rule is taken into account only to the extent that the shares disposed of are not exhausted by the preceding rule(s).

(1) *Same day rule.* Where two or more acquisitions of shares etc. of a particular class are made on the same day by the same person in the same capacity, they are treated as a single acquisition. The same applies to disposals. A disposal is then identified first and foremost and as far as possible with an acquisition made on the same day. In certain limited circumstances, an election is available for alternative treatment of same-day acquisitions by individuals after 5 April 2002 (see below). Note that the same day rule does not apply to relevant securities (see 59.6 below).

(2) *30-day rule* (see also below under 'Bed and breakfasting'). If within the period of 30 days after a disposal, the person making it acquires shares of the same class, the disposal is identified with those acquisitions, taken in the order in which they occur within that period. For acquisitions on or after 22 March 2006, this rule does not require shares to be identified with shares which the person making the disposal acquires at a time when he is neither resident nor ordinarily resident in the UK or when he is '*treaty non-resident*' (i.e. at a time when he falls to be regarded as resident in a territory outside the UK for the purposes of DOUBLE TAX RELIEF (19) arrangements).

(3) *LIFO basis.* The disposal is then identified with acquisitions made after 5 April 1998 (or, in the case of relevant securities, at any time) on a last in/first out (LIFO) basis.

(4) *Share pool at 5 April 1998.* The disposal is then identified with the 'section 104 holding' (if any), i.e. the single asset pool for shares acquired after 5 April 1982 and before 6 April 1998 (see above and 59.4 below). (This is not applicable to disposals of 'relevant securities' (see 59.6 below), which were never included in a 'section 104 holding' and to which the LIFO basis (see (3) above) applies in respect of acquisitions made on or before 5 April 1998 as well as after that date.)

(5) '*1982 holding*'. The disposal is then identified with the '1982 holding' (if any), i.e. the single asset pool for shares held at 5 April 1982 (but treated as having been acquired at 31 March 1982 for these purposes) (see 59.5 below).

(6) *Shares acquired on or before 6 April 1965.* The disposal is then identified on a last in/first out (LIFO) basis with shares held on 6 April 1965 (see 7.4 and 7.9 ASSETS HELD ON 6 APRIL 1965 for quoted and unquoted securities respectively) to the extent, in the case of quoted shares, that these have not, by election, been included in the '1982 holding' (see 59.5(*a*) below).

(7) *Shares acquired subsequent to the disposal.* To the extent, if any, that the rules at (1)–(6) above have not exhausted the shares disposed of, the disposal is finally identified with shares acquired after the disposal (and after the expiry of the 30-day period in (2) above), taken in the order in which such acquisitions occur.

[*TCGA 1992, ss 105, 106A, 288(7B); FA 1998, s 124(1)(2)(7); FA 2006, s 74*].

Same-day rule: election for alternative treatment. For shares acquired by an individual after 5 April 2002, an election is available (under *TCGA 1992, s 105A*) to modify the application of the same-day rule at (1) above, as it relates to acquisitions, where

(*a*) an individual acquires shares of the same class on the same day in the same capacity; and

(*b*) some, but not all, of those shares are acquired on the exercise of an option under an enterprise management incentive scheme (see 20.24 EMPLOYEE SHARE SCHEMES), or under an approved employee share option scheme (see 20.26–20.28 EMPLOYEE SHARE SCHEMES) in circumstances such that no income tax charge arises.

Where the election is made,

(i) the shares in (*b*) above (the '*approved-scheme shares*') and the balance of the shares in (*a*) above (the '*remainder shares*') are treated as *separate* acquisitions; and

(ii) any disposal falling to be matched (under the identification rules above) with the shares acquired on the day in question is matched with the remainder shares in priority to the approved-scheme shares.

The election must be made by written notice to an HMRC officer on or before the first anniversary of 31 January following the tax year in which the individual first makes a disposal within (ii) above. It then has effect in relation to that disposal and all subsequent disposals within (ii) above. In determining, for these purposes, which is the first disposal, any capital distribution treated as a disposal by *TCGA 1992, s 122*(*1*) (see 58.10 SHARES AND SECURITIES) is disregarded, as is a receipt of consideration, on a capital reorganisation etc., treated as a disposal by virtue of any application of *TCGA 1992, s 128*(*3*) (see 58.1 SHARES AND SECURITIES).

Where the election is made, any 'clogged shares' (see above) acquired on the same day and in the same capacity as the shares in (*a*) above are automatically brought within the election from the time they cease to be treated as being of a different class from the shares in (*a*) above. Shares or securities received on a capital reorganisation etc. and treated by virtue of any application of *TCGA 1992, s 127* (see 58.1, 58.4, 58.6, 58.7 SHARES AND SECURITIES) as the same asset as the shares in (*a*) above are split proportionately between the approved scheme shares and the remainder shares and continue to be covered by the election.

The election cannot be made in respect of ordinary shares in VENTURE CAPITAL TRUSTS (66).

[*TCGA 1992, s 105A*(*1*)–(*3*)(*5*)(*6*), *s 105B; FA 2002, s 50*(*1*)(*2*); *F*(*No 2*)*A 2005, Sch 5 para 3*].

'Bed and breakfasting' after 16 March 1998. The 30-day rule at (2) above is designed to counter the previously common practice known as 'bed and breakfasting' whereby shares are sold and bought back the next day or very shortly afterwards, the purpose being to realise a gain by reference to historical cost (and upgrade the acquisition cost on a future disposal) or to similarly realise an allowable loss. This particular identification rule also applies for capital gains tax (not corporation tax) purposes to disposals made **after 16 March 1998** and before 6 April 1998. It applies to such disposals in priority to the identification rules in 59.3 below, except for the 'same-day rule' in *TCGA 1992, s 105*, and acquisitions so matched under the 30-day rule do not form part of the 'section 104 holding'. The 30-day rule applies equally to disposals of 'relevant securities' (see 59.6 below). [*FA 1998, s 124*(*8*)(*9*)]. 'Bed and breakfasting' remains feasible for couples where the disposal is by one partner and the acquisition is by the other.

It is confirmed by HMRC Capital Gains Manual CG 50566 that a disposal of rights attached to shares (see 58.3 SHARES AND SECURITIES) does not fall to be matched under the 30-day rule with a subsequent acquisition of shares of the same class but with no rights attached. Nor does a disposal of shares fall to be matched with shares of the same class subsequently acquired by a scrip or rights issue (as the reorganisation rules deem such shares to have been acquired at the same time as the original shares to which they attach — see below).

The amendment to the rule applying for acquisitions on or after 22 March 2006 was introduced following the decision in *Davies v Hicks, Ch D, [2005] STC 850*. In that case, trustees sold a holding of shares, became resident in Mauritius and then purchased shares of the same class within 30 days, thereby avoiding a capital gain on the shares sold under the 30-day rule as it then operated. Furthermore, it was held that the 30-day rule is simply an identification rule and does not deem shares to be owned by the taxpayer during the period after disposal and before acquisition of the replacement shares so that there was no deemed disposal under *TCGA 1992, s 80* (see 44.2 OFFSHORE SETTLEMENTS) on becoming non-resident, as the trustees did not then own the shares.

Scrips, rights issues etc. For the purpose of applying the above identification rules, shares and securities acquired as a result of a reorganisation, e.g. a scrip or bonus issue or a rights issue, and treated under *TCGA 1992, s 127* (see 58.1 SHARES AND SECURITIES) as equating to shares already held are regarded as having been acquired at the time the original shares were acquired. Where the original holding comprises a number of acquisitions (counting a 5 April 1998 share pool as a single acquisition), the new holding is apportioned pro rata between them. This does not apply to scrip dividends (aka stock dividends) after 5 April 1998 from a UK resident company; these are treated not as reorganisations but as free-standing acquisitions as at the dividend date (see 58.9 SHARES AND SECURITIES). See also 61.2 TAPER RELIEF.

Deemed disposals and reacquisitions. Where under any capital gains tax legislation shares are deemed to be disposed of and immediately reacquired by the same person (see, for example, 40.9 LOSSES as regards negligible value claims), it is HMRC's view that neither the same day rule at (1) above nor the 30-day rule at (2) above require the deemed disposal to be matched with the deemed reacquisition (Revenue Tax Bulletin April 2001 pp 839, 840).

Example

A, who is resident and ordinarily resident in the UK throughout, has the following acquisitions/disposals of ordinary 25p shares in QED plc. Throughout their period of ownership by A, these shares are non-business assets for the purposes of TAPER RELIEF (61). QED ordinary 25p shares were worth 210p per share at 31 March 1982, and A has not made the universal re-basing election in 8.3 ASSETS HELD ON 31 MARCH 1982. In 2006/07, A made no disposals of chargeable assets other than as shown below.

Date	*No. of shares bought/(sold)*	*Cost/ (proceeds)*
		£
1 May 1980	1,000	2,000
1 October 1983	2,000	4,500
1 December 1996	500	1,800
1 May 1999	(1,000)	(3,900)
25 May 1999	2,000	7,600
	4,500	
2 January 2000	(2,000)	(9,000)
1 July 2006	(2,000)	(12,000)
Remaining holding	500	

Relevant indexation factors are

March 1982 to April 1998	1.047
October 1983 to April 1985	0.097
April 1985 to December 1996	0.629
December 1996 to April 1998	0.053

The disposal on 1 May 1999 is matched with 1,000 of the shares acquired on 25 May 1999 (under the 30-day rule at (2) above). The resulting chargeable gain is as follows.

	£
Proceeds 1.5.99	3,900
Cost (£ 7,600 × 1,000/2,000)	3,800
Chargeable gain (no taper relief due)	£100

The disposal of 2,000 shares on 2 January 2000 is matched firstly with the remaining 1,000 acquired on 25 May 1999 (LIFO — see (3) above), and secondly with 1,000 of the 2,500 forming the 'section 104 holding' (see (4) above) as follows.

	No. of shares	*Qualifying expenditure*	*Indexed pool*
		£	£
Pool at 6.4.85	2,000	4,500	4,500
Indexation allowance to date			
October 1983–April 1985 £4,500 × 0.097			437
	2,000	4,500	4,937
Indexed rise to December 1996:			
April 1985–December 1996 £4,937 × 0.629			3,105
Additional shares 1 December 1996	500	1,800	1,800
	2,500	6,300	9,842
Indexed rise to April 1998:			
December 1996–April 1998 £9,842 × 0.053			522
	2,500	6,300	10,364
Disposal 2.1.2000	(1,000)	(2,520)	(4,146)
Pool carried forward	1,500	£3,780	£6,218

Chargeable gains are as follows.

	£	£
Proceeds 2.1.2000	4,500	4,500
Cost (£ 7,600 × 1,000/2,000)	3,800	
Cost (as above)		2,520
Unindexed gains	700	1,980
Indexation (£4,146 – £2,520)	—	1,626
Chargeable gains	£700	£354

Neither gain qualifies for taper relief. In each case, the shares acquired have been held for less than the requisite three complete years (for non-business asset taper relief) after 5 April 1998.

The disposal of 2,000 shares on 1 July 2006 is matched firstly with the remaining 1,500 in the 'section 104 holding' (see (4) above) and secondly with 500 of the 1,000 shares forming the '1982 holding' (see (5) above).

Chargeable gains are as follows.

	£
Proceeds of 1,500 shares on 1.7.06	9,000
Cost (as per pool above)	3,780
Unindexed gain	5,220
Indexation (£6,218 – £3,780)	2,438
Chargeable gain subject to taper relief	2,782
Taper relief £2,782 × 35% (see below)	974
Chargeable gain	£1,808

	£	£
Proceeds of 500 shares on 1.7.06	3,000	3,000
Cost (£2,000 × 500/1,000)	1,000	
Market value 31.3.82 500 × £2.10		1,050
Unindexed gain	2,000	1,950
Indexation to April 1998:		
£1,050 × 1.047	1,099	1,099
Gain after indexation	£901	£851
		£
Chargeable gain subject to taper relief		851
Taper relief £851 × 35% (see below)		298
Chargeable gain		£553

Taper relief is at 35% as the shares are non-business assets and have been held for eight plus one years since 5 April 1998, the one-year addition being by virtue of the fact that both the 'section 104 holding' and the '1982 holding' were acquired before 17 March 1998 (see 61.2 TAPER RELIEF).

Inter-spouse transfers. An article in Revenue Tax Bulletin August 2001 pp 876, 877, with worked example, illustrates how the share identification rules, the no gain/no loss rule at 42.4 MARRIED PERSONS AND CIVIL PARTNERS, and the rules at 61.14 TAPER RELIEF generally interact.

59.3 IDENTIFICATION RULES FOR SHARES AND SECURITIES FOR CORPORATION TAX PURPOSES ON OR AFTER THE '1985 DATE' (AND FOR CAPITAL GAINS TAX PURPOSES BEFORE 6 APRIL 1998)

For disposals for corporation tax purposes on or after 1 April 1985 (referred to as the '*1985 date*') the identification rules for securities are as set out below. These rules also apply for the purposes of capital gains tax, but by reference to a '1985 date' of 6 April 1985 and only before 6 April 1998.

Special rules apply to the following.

(*a*) Shares to which Enterprise Investment Scheme relief or venture capital trust scheme relief is attributable, shares in respect of which relief has been given (and not withdrawn) under the Business Expansion Scheme (BES) and shares or securities held by companies to which investment relief under the corporate venturing scheme or community investment tax relief is attributable. Disposals of such shares retain their own identification rules — see 21.8, 21.10, 21.14 ENTERPRISE INVESTMENT SCHEME, 66.11, 66.12 VENTURE CAPITAL TRUSTS, 22.20 EXEMPTIONS AND RELIEFS (as regards the BES), 17.17 CORPORATE VENTURING SCHEME and Tolley's Income Tax under Community Investment Tax Relief.

(*b*) '*Relevant securities*', i.e. securities within the accrued income ('bondwashing') provisions, QUALIFYING CORPORATE BONDS (50), deep discount securities (not applicable under current legislation) and securities which are, or have been, material interests in non-qualifying offshore funds. See 59.6 below for further details.

For shares and securities not falling within (*a*) and (*b*) above and any other assets dealt in without identifying the particular assets disposed of or acquired, then, subject to the rules for

(i) disposals on or before the day of acquisition (see below);

(ii) (before 5 December 2005) acquisitions and disposals of securities within a short period by companies (see 13.14 COMPANIES); and

(iii) acquisitions and disposals within a ten day period (see below)

securities disposed of are identified, in order of priority, with

(A) securities acquired on or after the '1982 date' (see 59.4 below) and forming part of a '*section 104 holding*' (see 59.4 below);

(B) securities forming part of a '*1982 holding*' (see 59.5 below); and then

(C) other securities on a 'last in, first out' basis. (Broadly, those held on 6 April 1965, see 7.4 and 7.9 ASSETS HELD ON 6 APRIL 1965 for quoted and unquoted securities respectively.)

Securities held by a person in one capacity cannot be identified with similar securities which he holds or can dispose of only in some other capacity (e.g. as a trustee).

[*TCGA 1992, s 104(1)–(3), s 107(1)(1A)(2)(7)–(9), s 150(5), s 150A(5); FA 1994, s 137, Sch 15 para 30; FA 1998, s 124(3)(7), s 125(3)(4); FA 2006, s 72(2)(a), Sch 12 para 17*].

Disposals and acquisitions on the same day. Securities disposed of on a particular day are matched with securities acquired on the same day by the same person in the same capacity and the pooling rules do not apply for this purpose. Where more securities are disposed of than are acquired, and the excess can neither be identified with previous acquisitions or a 'section 104 holding' (see 59.4 below), that excess is matched with a subsequent acquisition or acquisitions, taking the earliest first. [*TCGA 1992, s 105; FA 2006, s 72(2)(b)*].

Acquisitions and disposals within a ten-day period. Subject to the rules for disposals on or before the day of acquisition (see above) if, within a ten-day period, a number of securities are acquired which would otherwise increase or constitute a 'section 104 holding' (see 59.4 below) and subsequently a number of securities are disposed of, which would otherwise decrease or extinguish the same 'section 104 holding', then the securities disposed of are identified with those acquired and are not regarded as forming part of, or constituting, a 'section 104 holding'. If the number of securities acquired exceeds the number disposed of, the excess is regarded as forming part of, or constituting, a 'section 104 holding' and where securities were acquired at different times within the ten-day period, securities disposed of are first identified with those acquired at an earlier time (first in/first out). If the number of securities disposed of exceeds the number acquired, the excess is not identified under this rule. Any securities which are identified under this rule do not qualify for indexation allowance. [*TCGA 1992, s 107(3)–(6)*].

'*Bed and breakfasting*'. The Revenue stated, in connection with the application of the principles established in decided cases up to and including *Furniss v Dawson*, that the indexation provisions applying on and after the 1985 date were clearly not designed to make bed and breakfast share etc. transactions more difficult as compared to the position before the 1982 date, but it remained necessary to make sure that the transactions involved were effective in (for instance) transferring beneficial ownership of the shares. (ICAEW Guidance Note TR 588, 25 September 1985). **See 59.2 above as regards bed and breakfasting after 16 March 1998.**

59.4 **'Section 104 holdings' of securities acquired on or after the '1982 date'.** Securities acquired on or after 6 April 1982, or, for companies, 1 April 1982 (the '*1982 date*') are pooled. Thus any securities of the same class acquired on or after the '1982 date' and held by the same person in the same capacity immediately before the '1985 date' are pooled as a single asset which grows or diminishes as acquisitions and disposals are made on or after that date. Securities of the same class acquired for the first time on or after the '1985 date' are pooled as a single asset in the same way. This treatment has no effect on any market value that has to be ascertained. Pooling is abolished for capital gains tax purposes (not for those of corporation tax) for acquisitions after 5 April 1998 — see 59.1 above.

Shares and securities of a company are not to be treated as being of the same class unless they are so treated by the practice of the Stock Exchange or would be so treated if dealt with on the Stock Exchange.

The single asset is referred to as the '*section 104 holding*' (previously known as 'the new holding') and the part disposal rules apply on any disposal other than one of the whole holding.

A separate 'section 104 holding' applies in relation to any securities held by a person to whom they were issued as an employee of the company or of any other person on terms which restrict his rights to dispose of them, so long as those terms are in force (known as 'clogged shares'). While such a separate 'section 104 holding' exists the owner of it is treated as holding it in a different capacity to that in which he holds any other securities of the same class. Upon the removal of restrictions, two such separate 'section 104 holdings' merge. If restrictions are removed from only some of the clogged shares, they are transferred from the clogged share pool to the normal share pool at average cost (HMRC Capital Gains Manual CG 56503).

Indexation allowance. On any disposal from a 'section 104 holding' (other than the whole of it) the 'qualifying expenditure' and the 'indexed pool of expenditure' are apportioned between the part disposed of and the remainder in the same proportions as, under the normal capital gains tax rules for part disposals, the relevant allowable expenditure is apportioned (see 15.7 COMPUTATION OF GAINS AND LOSSES). The indexation allowance on the disposal is the amount by which the part of the indexed pool of expenditure apportioned to the part disposed of exceeds the equivalent part of the qualifying expenditure. On a disposal of the whole of the 'section 104 holding', the indexation allowance is the amount by which the indexed pool of expenditure at the time of disposal exceeds the qualifying expenditure at that time.

The '*qualifying expenditure*' is, at any time, the amount which would be the aggregate of the 'relevant allowable expenditure' in relation to a disposal of the whole of the holding at that time. See 34.1 INDEXATION for '*relevant allowable expenditure*'.

The '*indexed pool of expenditure*' in the case of a 'section 104 holding' in existence immediately before the '1985 date' comes into existence immediately before that date. It consists of the aggregate of the qualifying expenditure at that time and the indexation allowance which would have been available if all the securities in the holding were disposed of at that time on the assumption that the twelve month qualifying period and restrictions on loss-making disposals (which applied before the '1985 date') had never applied. In the case of any other 'section 104 holding', the indexed pool of expenditure is created at the same time as the holding (or, if earlier, when any of the qualifying expenditure is incurred) and is equal, at that time, to the qualifying expenditure.

Where a disposal on or after 30 November 1993 to a person acquiring or adding to a 'section 104 holding' is treated under any enactment as one on which neither a gain nor a loss accrues to the person making the disposal, *TCGA 1992, s 56*(*2*) (general treatment on no gain/no loss disposal; see 34.3 INDEXATION) does not apply to the disposal (so that the amount of the consideration on the disposal is not calculated on the assumption that an unindexed gain of an amount equal to the indexation allowance accrues to the person making the disposal). However, an amount equal to the indexation allowance on the disposal is added to the indexed pool of expenditure for the holding acquired or, as the case may be, held by the person to whom the disposal is made, and in such a case where there is an addition to the indexed pool of a 'section 104 holding' already held, the addition is made after any increase required by (*a*) below.

Whenever there is an event, called an '*operative event*', which has the effect of increasing or reducing the qualifying expenditure, a change is made to the indexed pool of expenditure.

(*a*) The indexed pool of expenditure is increased by the 'indexed rise' since the last operative event or, if none, since the pool came into being. This is done before the calculation of the indexation allowance on a disposal.

(*b*) If the operative event increases the qualifying expenditure, the indexed pool of expenditure is increased by the same amount.

(*c*) If there is a disposal resulting in a deduction in the qualifying expenditure, the indexed pool of expenditure is reduced in the same proportion. This is done after the calculation of the indexation allowance on the disposal.

(*d*) If the qualifying expenditure is reduced but there is no disposal, the indexed pool of expenditure is reduced by the same amount.

The '*indexed rise*' is the sum obtained by multiplying the value of the indexed pool of expenditure immediately before the operative event by a figure (expressed as a decimal but with no express requirement as to the number of decimal places to be calculated) calculated by the formula

$$\frac{RE - RL}{RL}$$

where

RE = the retail prices index for the month in which the operative event occurs; and

RL = the retail prices index for the month of the immediately preceding operative event or, if none, that in which the indexed pool of expenditure came into being.

If RE is equal to or less than RL, the indexed rise is nil.

See 34.1 INDEXATION for values of the retail price index for March 1982 and subsequent months.

Note. Reorganisations of shares do not normally constitute disposals or acquisitions but they may constitute an operative event as above; e.g. an issue of shares of the same class for payment under a rights issue would be an operative event as the qualifying expenditure is increased, but a bonus issue of shares of the same class would not be. Where the reorganisation involves shares of a different class this automatically gives rise to an operative event as the qualifying expenditure attributable to the 'section 104 holding' consisting of the original class of shares is decreased. An additional 'section 104 holding' is created as only shares of the same class can be pooled in the original 'section 104 holding'. The rules in 58.1 SHARES AND SECURITIES determine the proportions of qualifying expenditure to be attributed to holdings of shares following a reorganisation and these also apply to the indexed pool of expenditure.

Consideration for options. Where an increase in qualifying expenditure under (*b*) above is wholly or partly attributable to the cost of acquiring an option binding the grantor to sell, then the indexed pool of expenditure is additionally increased by a sum obtained by multiplying the consideration for the option by a figure (expressed as a decimal but without any clarification as to the number of decimal places to be calculated) calculated by the formula

$$\frac{RO - RA}{RA}$$

where

RO = the retail prices index for the month in which the option is exercised; and

RA = the retail prices index for the month in which the option was acquired, or March 1982 if later.

If RO is equal or less than RA, the indexed rise is nil.

[*TCGA 1992, s 104(1)(3)–(6), s 110, s 114; FA 1994, s 93(6)(11); FA 1998, s 125(1)(3)–(5); FA 2006, s 72(2)(d), Sch 12 para 17*].

The above rules do not apply for capital gains tax purposes where the option, but not the shares, was acquired before 6 April 1998. Indexation allowance to April 1998 on the cost of the option is given under the rules at 34.7 INDEXATION (HMRC Capital Gains Manual CG 50761).

For disposals before 30 November 1993, it was possible in practice not to keep a running total of the amount of qualifying expenditure because the chargeable gain or allowable loss on a disposal was the difference (positive or negative respectively) between the disposal proceeds and the amount by which the indexed pool was reduced. The denial of indexation allowance creating or increasing a loss on a disposal after 29 November 1993 required the ascertainment of such a running total.

Example

At 6 April 1985, B owned 5,000 shares in REG plc purchased at a cost of £7,500 in June 1983. Subsequently B carried out the following transactions in those shares.

Date	*No. of shares bought/(sold)*	*Cost/(proceeds)*
		£
May 1985	1,000	1,250
October 1985	400	500
December 1986	(2,000)	(5,000)
December 1992	(440)	(900)
January 1997	(2,000)	(4,700)

In addition, in January 1994 B acquired from a spouse (i.e. a gain/no loss disposal) 1,000 further such shares which had hitherto comprised the total holding of the spouse and been purchased originally in July 1985 at a cost of £1,500.

Relevant values of the retail prices index are

June 1983	84.84	December 1986	99.62
April 1985	94.78	December 1992	139.20

May 1985	95.21	January 1994	141.30
July 1985	95.23	January 1997	154.40
October 1985	95.59		

	No. of shares	*Qualifying expenditure*	*Indexed pool*
		£	£
Pool at 6.4.85	5,000	7,500	7,500
Indexation allowance to initial pool: June 1983–April 1985			
$\frac{94.78 - 84.84}{84.84} \times £7{,}500$			878
			8,378
May 1985			
Indexed rise: April 1985–May 1985			
$\frac{95.21 - 94.78}{94.78} \times £8{,}378$			38
			8,416
Additional shares	1,000	1,250	1,250
	6,000	8,750	9,666
October 1985			
Indexed rise: May 1985–Oct 1985			
$\frac{95.59 - 95.21}{95.21} \times £9{,}666$			39
			9,705
Additional shares	400	500	500
	6,400	9,250	10,205
December 1986			
Indexed rise: Oct 1985–Dec 1986			430
$\frac{99.62 - 95.59}{95.59} \times £10{,}205$			
			10,635
Disposal	(2,000)	(i) (2,891)	(ii) (3,323)
	4,400	6,359	7,312

December 1992			
Indexed rise: Dec 1986–Dec 1992			2,905
$\dfrac{139.2 - 99.62}{99.62} \times £7,312$			
			10,217
Disposal	(440)	(636)	(1,022)
	3,960	5,723	9,195
January 1994			
Indexed rise: Dec 1992–Jan 1994			
$\dfrac{141.3 - 139.2}{139.2} \times £9,195$			139
Additional shares from spouse	1,000	1,500	1,500
Indexation allowance on such shares: Jul 1985–Jan 1994			
$\dfrac{141.3 - 95.23}{95.23} \times £1,500$			725
	4,960	7,223	11,559
January 1997			
Indexed rise: Jan 1994–Jan 1997			
$\dfrac{154.4 - 141.3}{141.3} \times £11,559$			1,072
	4,960	7,223	12,631
Disposal	(2,000)	(2,912)	(5,093)
Pool carried forward	2,960	£4,311	£7,538

Computation

		£
Disposal December 1986		
Proceeds		5,000
Cost	(i) 2,891	
Indexation allowance	(iii) 432	
		(ii) 3,323
Chargeable gain		£1,677

Disposal December 1992		
Proceeds		900
Cost	636	
Indexation allowance	386	
		1,022
Allowable loss		£122

Disposal January 1997

Proceeds of £4,700, although greater than the qualifying expenditure attributable to the shares disposed of (£2,912) and so producing an unindexed gain of the excess (£1,788), are less than the indexed pool of expenditure attributable to the shares disposed of (£5,093). The indexation allowance on the disposal of £2,181 (i.e. £5,093 – £2,912) therefore extinguishes the unindexed gain with the result that the disposal is one on which neither a gain nor a loss accrues (see 34.1 INDEXATION).

Notes to the example

(*a*) The figure at (i) is given by

$$\frac{2,000}{6,400} \times \pounds 9,250 = \pounds 2,891$$

The figure at (ii) is given by

$$\frac{2,000}{6,400} \times \pounds 10,635 = \pounds 3,323$$

The figure at (iii) is given by the difference between (ii) and (i) i.e. £432.

The corresponding figures for the disposals in December 1992 and January 1997 are arrived at in a similar way.

(*b*) On the freezing of indexation for capital gains tax (but not corporation tax) purposes, the indexed pool is updated to 5 April 1998 as if the entire holding had been disposed of at the end of that day (not illustrated here). Indexation allowance is thus given on the section 104 holding up to and including April 1998. On a disposal after 5 April 1998 of, or out of, the section 104 holding in accordance with the identification rules at 59.2 above, or on any other operative event, the indexed pool continues to be maintained and indexation allowance computed accordingly, except that the indexed pool is *not* to be increased by any indexed rise in expenditure after April 1998.

59.5 **'1982 holding'**. On the introduction of indexation, pools of securities in existence before the '1982 date' continued to be treated as pools which were to be reduced where subsequent disposals were identified with them but which could not grow by acquisitions of additional securities of the same class. There were, however, special rules for adjustments to such pools where the relevant allowable expenditure at the '1982 date' exceeded such expenditure one year previously. All securities acquired between those dates were excluded from the pool in so far as they were not identified with disposals before the '1982 date'.

The '1982 holding' comprises the following.

(*a*) Any pooled holding of securities under the above provisions which is retained at the '1985 date'. The pooled holding includes quoted securities held on 6 April 1965 where an election had been made that their actual cost be ignored and computations made by reference to their market value at 6 April 1965 only. A further opportunity is available for an election to be made where the original time limit has expired by extending the time limit so as to apply by reference to the first relevant disposal on or after the '1985 date'. See 7.3 and 7.4 ASSETS HELD ON 6 APRIL 1965.

(*b*) Any securities treated as separate assets under the special rules outlined above which have not been disposed of before the '1985 date'.

The '1982 holding', as determined above, continues, or starts, to be a single asset but one which cannot grow by the acquisition of additional securities of the same class. The relevant allowable expenditure attributable to it for capital gains tax purposes is the aggregate of that for the assets of which it is comprised.

Where securities forming part of a 1982 holding were acquired between 1 and 5 April 1982 inclusive, they are treated for the purposes of re-basing indexation allowance (for disposals before 6 April 1988) under 8.13 ASSETS HELD ON 31 MARCH 1982 as held on 31 March 1982. This treatment also applies for the general re-basing rules of 8 ASSETS HELD ON 31 MARCH 1982.

[*TCGA 1992, s 109; FA 2006, Sch 12 para 18*].

59.6 **Relevant securities.** The identification rules in 59.3–59.5 above do not apply to disposals of 'relevant securities'. Instead, the following rules apply for corporation tax purposes (and for capital gains tax purposes for disposals before 6 April 1998).

'*Relevant securities*' are as follows.

(*a*) Qualifying corporate bonds.

(*b*) Securities within the accrued income ('bondwashing') provisions (other than those within (a) or (b) above). These comprise any loan stock or similar security of any government, public or local authority in the UK or elsewhere or any company or other body other than

(i) shares in a company (except qualifying shares in a building society);

(ii) (for chargeable periods beginning before 1 April 2004) securities on which the whole of the return is a distribution by virtue of *ICTA 1988, s 209(2)(e)(iv)(v)*;

(iii) national savings and war savings certificates;

(iv) certificates of deposit;

(v) any security which is redeemable, for which the amount payable on redemption exceeds the issue price and in respect of which no return other than the amount of that excess is payable; and

(vi) any deeply discounted security within 58.16 SHARES AND SECURITIES transferred or redeemed after 26 March 2003.

(*c*) Deep discount securities. The legislation relating to deep discount securities was repealed for 1996/97 onwards and, subject to transitional provisions, for company accounting periods ending after 31 March 1996. See the 2001/02 and earlier editions under Shares and Securities.

(*d*) Securities which are, or at any time have been, material interests in a non-qualifying offshore fund.

Relevant securities are not subject to pooling. The identification rules direct how disposals of such securities are to be identified with acquisitions of securities of the same class held by the same person in the same capacity. Where relevant securities were held on 6 April 1965, special rules apply. See 7.4 and 7.9 ASSETS HELD ON 6 APRIL 1965 for quoted and unquoted securities respectively.

The general rules are subject to

(i) (for disposals before 5 December 2005) the special rules for acquisitions and disposals of securities within a short period by companies (see 13.14 COMPANIES), and

(ii) special rules for 'contangos' (see below).

The general rules, in order of priority, are as follows.

(*a*) For identification purposes, disposals are to be taken in chronological order. The identification of relevant securities comprised in an earlier disposal therefore determine (by elimination) which securities can be comprised in a later disposal.

(*b*) Securities disposed of for transfer or delivery on a particular date (e.g. a stock exchange settlement date) or in a particular period (e.g. a stock exchange account) are not to be identified with securities acquired for transfer or delivery on a later date or in a later period. They must be identified with acquisitions of securities for transfer or delivery on or before that date, or, in or before that period. However, subject to this, they have to be first identified with acquisitions for *transfer or delivery* on or after the contract disposal date. (The 'transfer or delivery', i.e. settlement, date is generally different from the contract date. See also *MacPherson v Hall Ch D 1972, 48 TC 210.*)

(*c*) Disposals are to be identified, on a 'first in, first out' basis, with acquisitions within the twelve months preceding the disposal. Otherwise, disposals are to be identified with acquisitions on a 'last in, first out' basis.

(*d*) Disposals are to be identified with acquisitions at different times on the same day in as nearly as may be equal proportions.

Contangos. Where, under arrangements designed to postpone the transfer or delivery of securities disposed of, a person by a *single bargain* acquires relevant securities for transfer or delivery on a particular date or in a particular period (the 'earlier date' or 'earlier period'), and disposes of them for transfer or delivery on a later date or in a later period, then the disposal and acquisition covered by the single bargain are matched. Any previous disposal which, apart from the above matching provisions, would have been identified with the acquisition under the contango arrangement must (subject to the general rule that disposals must be taken in chronological sequence) be identified with any 'available securities' acquired for transfer or delivery on the earlier date or in the earlier period. '*Available securities*' are securities which have not been matched under the above 'single bargain' rule, or under the general identification rules, with disposals for transfer or delivery on the earlier date or in the earlier period. Insofar as the previous disposal cannot be identified with 'available securities', the disposal is to be treated as being for transfer or delivery on the later date, or in the later period.

Where any of the securities within (*c*) or (*d*) above are disposed of on or after the '1985 date' and within a period of ten days beginning on the day on which the expenditure was incurred, no indexation allowance is due.

[*TCGA 1992, s 54(2), s 108; FA 1996, ss 104, 105, Sch 14 para 59, Sch 41 Pt V(3); FA 1998, s 124(4)(5)(7); FA 2006, s 72(2)(c)*].

'Bed and breakfasting' after 16 March 1998. For capital gains tax (not corporation tax) purposes, the above identification rules for disposals of relevant securities are superseded for disposals after 16 March 1998 and before 6 April 1998 (after which new identification rules apply in any case). See 59.2 above.

59.7 ELECTION FOR 'PARALLEL POOLING' BY COMPANIES FOR DISPOSALS AFTER 31 MARCH 1982 AND BEFORE 1 APRIL 1985

For companies, an alternative method was available, by election, to identify particular shares and securities which were disposed of after 31 March 1982 and before 1 April 1985 with shares etc. of the same kind which had been previously acquired. Following the abolition of the general twelve-month qualifying period for indexation allowance to apply and the general reintroduction of a form of pooling for disposals after 31 March 1985, any 'parallel pooling' election made ceased to apply to such disposals. An opportunity was given to revoke any election previously made, by written notice before 1 April 1987 (or within such longer period as the Revenue allowed), with the effect that the gains on all disposals which were subject to the election were recomputed under the normal rules for disposals after 31 March 1982 and before 1 April 1985. If an election was not so revoked, no adjustment was to be made to the gains on disposals which were subject to the election, and further provisions enable the rules given in 59.3–59.6 above to apply to the pooled holding in respect of disposals after 31 March 1985. [*TCGA 1992, s 112; FA 1983, s 34, Sch 6; FA 1985, Sch 19 Pt V; SI 1986 No 387*].

For full coverage of the above, see Tolley's Capital Gains Tax 1986/87.

60 Substantial Shareholdings of Companies

60.1 **INTRODUCTION**

As detailed in this chapter, a gain on a disposal by a company of shares **after 31 March 2002** is exempt (and a loss is not allowable) where, throughout a continuous twelve-month period beginning not more than two years before the disposal, the company (the '*investing company*') held a 'substantial shareholding' (broadly, at least a **10%** interest) in the company (the '*investee company*') whose shares are the subject of the disposal. The exemption extends to assets related to shares (as in 60.5 below). The investing company must be a trading company or a member of a trading group and the investee company must be a trading company or the holding company of a trading group (or subgroup). Shares held by members of a worldwide group are aggregated in determining whether a company holds a substantial shareholding. [*TCGA 1992, s 192A, Sch 7AC; FA 2002, s 44(1)–(3), Sch 8 para 1*].

For HMRC's own coverage of these provisions, see HMRC Capital Gains Manual CG 53000–53240.

60.2 For the purposes of these provisions, a '*company*' is as defined at 27.1 GROUPS OF COMPANIES. A '*group of companies*' is also as defined at 27.1 but as if each reference there to '75%' were a reference to '51%'. Thus, subject to the detailed rules there, a '*group*' comprises a company and its effective '51% subsidiaries' (within *ICTA 1988, s 838*), and may include non-UK resident companies. A '*holding company*' of a group is the principal company of the group (within the meaning given in 27.1). A '*subgroup*' is a number of companies that *would* form a group were it not for the fact that one of them (the '*holding company*' of the subgroup) is itself a 51% subsidiary. [*TCGA 1992, Sch 7AC para 26*].

60.3 The exemptions described in this chapter are of no application to a disposal the gain (or loss) on which would, by virtue of some other enactment, not be a chargeable gain (or an allowable loss). Neither do they apply to a disposal which, by virtue of any chargeable gains enactment, is a no gain/no loss disposal. [*TCGA 1992, Sch 7AC para 6(1)*].

60.4 **THE EXEMPTIONS**

Exemption for shares. A gain accruing to a company (the '*investing company*') on a disposal of shares (or an interest in shares — see 60.25 below) in another company (the '*investee company*') is not a chargeable gain if

(*a*) the investing company held a 'substantial shareholding' (see 60.8 below) in the investee company throughout any continuous period of twelve months beginning not more than two years prior to the disposal (see 60.9 below);

(*b*) the investing company meets the requirements at 60.10 below; and

(*c*) the requirements at 60.12 below are met in relation to the investee company.

See also the anti-avoidance rule at 60.7 below.

[*TCGA 1992, Sch 7AC paras 1, 7, 28*].

By virtue of *TCGA 1992, s 16(2)* (see 22.2 EXEMPTIONS AND RELIEFS), a loss on a disposal is not an allowable loss if a gain on that disposal would not have been a chargeable gain.

The nature of the condition at (*a*) above is such that part disposals out of a once-substantial shareholding can continue to attract the exemption for up to a year after the shareholding has ceased to be substantial.

Note that the exemption is available even where the shares disposed of are not the shares that meet the substantial shareholding requirement at (*a*) above. If (*a*) above is met in relation to ordinary shares (and (*b*) and (*c*) above are also met), a disposal of a holding of, say, fixed-rate preference shares in the investee company will qualify for the exemption, irrespective of the size and duration of that holding (HMRC Capital Gains Manual CG 53155).

The exemption is automatic and does not require the making of a claim.

60.5 **Exemption for assets related to shares.** A gain accruing to a company (Company A) on a disposal of an asset 'related to shares' in another company (Company B) is not a chargeable gain (and a loss is not an allowable loss) if,

- at the time of the disposal, Company A holds shares (or an interest in shares — see 60.25 below) in Company B, and
- any gain on a disposal at that time of those shares (or that interest) would be exempt under 60.4 above (disregarding 60.3 above).

This exemption also applies where

- the shares etc. are held not by Company A itself but by another member of a group of companies (see 60.2 above) of which Company A is a member, and
- any gain on a disposal at that time of those shares etc., on the assumption that they were held by Company A, would be exempt under 60.4 above (disregarding 60.3 above).

Where assets of a company are vested in a liquidator, the above applies as if they were vested in the company and as if the acts of the liquidator were the acts of the company (disposals by the company to the liquidator, and vice versa, being disregarded).

See also the anti-avoidance rule at 60.7 below.

[*TCGA 1992, Sch 7AC paras 2, 6(2)*].

The exemption is automatic and does not require the making of a claim.

For this purpose, an asset is '*related to shares*' in a company if it is

(*a*) an option to acquire or dispose of shares (or an interest in shares — see 60.25 below) in that company; or

(*b*) (broadly) a security that is convertible or exchangeable into shares (or an interest in shares) in that company, or into an option within (*a*) above, or into another security within this definition; or

(*c*) an option to acquire or dispose of a security within (*b*) above (or an interest in any such security); or

(*d*) an interest in, or option over, any option or security within (*a*)–(*c*) above; or

(*e*) an interest in, or option over, any interest or option within (*d*) above (or an interest in, or option over, any interest or option within this sub-paragraph).

As regards (*b*) above, a convertible or exchangeable security is not an asset related to shares if when the conversion etc. rights were granted there was no more than a negligible likelihood that they would be exercised to any significant extent. Therefore, it is not possible to bring a security within the scope of the exemption by attaching some spurious or extremely remote rights to convertibility in the event of some unlikely occurrence (HMRC Capital Gains Manual CG 53010).

Note that certain securities, options etc. are outside the scope of corporation tax on chargeable gains, and thus outside the exemptions in this chapter, due to their falling within the special rules for loan relationships, derivative contracts etc. (see HMRC Capital Gains Manual CG 53010).

An '*interest*' in a security or option has a similar meaning to an 'interest in shares' at 60.25 below.

[*TCGA 1992, Sch 7AC para 30*].

60.6 **Exemption where main conditions previously met.** A further possibility of exemption is provided, as detailed below, where the exemption at 60.4 or 60.5 above, whichever is relevant, does not apply because some of the conditions were not satisfied at the time of the disposal even though they *had been* satisfied at a time in the two years immediately preceding the disposal.

A gain accruing to a company (Company A) on a disposal of shares (or an interest in shares — see 60.25 below), or an asset related to shares (see 60.5 above), in another company (Company B) is not a chargeable gain (and a loss is not an allowable loss) if the conditions at 60.4 or 60.5 above, whichever is relevant, are not fully met (with the result that a chargeable gain or allowable loss would otherwise arise on the disposal) *but all* of the following conditions *are* met.

(*a*) At the time of disposal, Company A had held a 'substantial shareholding' (see 60.8 below) in Company B throughout any continuous period of twelve months beginning not more than two years prior to the disposal (see also 60.9 below).

(*b*) At the time of disposal, either Company A is UK-resident or any chargeable gain accruing to it on the disposal would form part of its corporation tax profits by virtue of *TCGA 1992, s 10B* (trade carried on via UK permanent establishment — see 45.3 OVERSEAS MATTERS) or, before 16 March 2005, *TCGA 1992, s 10(3)* (trade carried on via UK branch or agency — see 45.3 OVERSEAS MATTERS).

(*c*) There was a time within the two years ending with the disposal (the '*relevant period*') when a gain on a hypothetical disposal by

- Company A, or
- a company that at any time in the relevant period was a member of the same group (see 60.2 above) as Company A,

being a disposal of shares (or an interest in shares) in Company B that the disposing company then held, would have been exempt under 60.4 above (disregarding 60.3 above, and see also below).

(*d*) If, at the time of disposal, the requirements at 60.12 below as to the investee company are not met in relation to Company B, there was a time within the relevant period (as defined at (*c*) above) when Company B was controlled by

- Company A, or
- Company A together with any persons connected with it (within *TCGA 1992, s 286* — see 16 CONNECTED PERSONS), or
- a company that at any time in the relevant period was a member of the same group (see 60.2 above) as Company A, or
- any such company together with persons connected with it.

'Control' is to be construed in accordance with *ICTA 1988, s 416*.

If the exemption at 60.4 or 60.5 above is not available for the sole reason that the investing company fails to meet the requirement at 60.10(*b*) below (as to its status immediately after the time of the disposal), this further possibility of exemption is available only if the failure is due to the actual or imminent winding-up or dissolution of the investing company (provided that, in a case where this is imminent, it actually takes place as soon as is reasonably practicable in the circumstances).

For the purpose only of determining the 'relevant period' for the purposes of (*c*) or (*d*) above, the time of disposal is taken as the time the contract is made, notwithstanding that the contract may be conditional. In determining whether the gain on the hypothetical disposal in (*c*) above would have attracted the exemption at 60.4 above, the requirements at 60.10(*b*) and 60.12(*b*) below as to the status of the investing and investee companies immediately after the time of disposal are taken to be satisfied.

See also the anti-avoidance rule at 60.7 below.

[*TCGA 1992, s 288(1), Sch 7AC para 3(1)–(4)(7)(8), para 6(2); F(No 2)A 2005, Sch 4 paras 9, 10(4)*].

Thus, for example, where the investee company ceases to trade on being put into liquidation, so that it can no longer meet the requirements at 60.12 below, disposals by the investing company (including capital distributions — see 58.10 SHARES AND SECURITIES) can continue to attract the exemption for a further two years.

It should be noted, however, that the above exemption also contains an anti-avoidance element in that if, for example, the investee company's trade is transferred elsewhere (within a group, for instance) and the conditions above are all met, a loss on a disposal by the investing company within the two years following the transfer will not be an allowable loss.

A further anti-avoidance measure applies as follows to prevent the exemption from applying where value has been transferred into the investee company within the said two-year period. Where the above exemption would otherwise apply but

(i) immediately before the disposal by Company A, Company B holds an asset; and

(ii) the allowable expenditure attributable to that asset has been reduced by a claim for gifts hold-over relief under *TCGA 1992, s 165* (see 33.1 HOLD-OVER RELIEFS) on an earlier disposal of the asset within the relevant period (as defined above),

a gain on the disposal by Company A does not attract the exemption *but* a loss on the disposal is not an allowable loss. (Where assets of Company B are vested in a liquidator, (i) above applies as if they were vested in the company.)

[*TCGA 1992, Sch 7AC para 3(5)(6)*].

The exemption is automatic and does not require the making of a claim.

60.7 ANTI-AVOIDANCE

None of the exemptions in 60.4–60.6 above are available where

(*a*) an 'untaxed' gain accrues to an investing company (Company A) on a disposal of shares (or an interest in shares — see 60.25 below), or an asset related to shares (see 60.5 above), in another company (Company B); and

(*b*) before the accrual of that gain, either

- Company A acquired control of Company B, or the same person(s) acquired control of both companies; or
- there was a 'significant change of trading activities affecting Company B' at a time when it was controlled by Company A or when both companies were controlled by the same person(s);

and these circumstances occur in pursuance of arrangements (as very widely defined) from which the sole or main benefit that could be expected is that the gain would be exempt under any of 60.4–60.6 above.

For the above purposes,

(i) a gain is '*untaxed*' if it (or all but an insubstantial part of it) represents profits that have not been brought into account (in the UK or elsewhere and including profits apportioned to a UK resident company under the controlled foreign company rules — see 45.7 OVERSEAS MATTERS) for the purposes of tax on profits for a period ending on or before the date of the disposal; 'profits' means income or gains (including unrealised income or gains);

(ii) 'control' is to be construed in accordance with *ICTA 1988, s 416*; and

(iii) there is a '*significant change of trading activities affecting Company B*' if

- there is a 'major change in the nature or conduct of a trade' carried on by Company B or a 51% subsidiary of Company B; or
- there is a major change in the scale of the activities of a trade carried on by Company B or a 51% subsidiary; or
- Company B or a 51% subsidiary begins to carry on a trade.

By virtue of *ICTA 1988, s 768*, a '*major change in the nature or conduct of a trade*' includes a major change in the type of property dealt in or services or facilities provided, or in customers, outlets or markets. Some of the circumstances which may amount to a major change are set out in HMRC Statement of Practice 10/91 (covered at 27.28 GROUPS OF COMPANIES).

[*TCGA 1992, s 288(1), Sch 7AC para 5*].

HMRC expect cases where this anti-avoidance rule is in point to be unusual and infrequent. It is a question of fact as to whether a gain wholly (or wholly but for an insubstantial part of it — interpreted by them as 20% or less) represents untaxed profits; this involves looking at how the consideration obtained for the disposal by Company A is derived from assets held directly or indirectly by Company B. Profits are not 'untaxed' if they are simply covered by a specific relief or if they represent dividends which are themselves paid out of taxed profits. If a gain represents both taxed and untaxed profits, it should be taken as first representing taxed profits, with only the balance representing untaxed profits. See HMRC Statement of Practice SP 5/02, 29 October 2002.

60.8 'SUBSTANTIAL SHAREHOLDING' REQUIREMENT

Meaning of substantial shareholding. For the purposes of these provisions, a company holds a '*substantial shareholding*' in another company if it holds shares (or interests in shares — see 60.25 below) in that company by virtue of which

- it holds **at least 10%** of the company's ordinary share capital;
- it is beneficially entitled to at least 10% of the profits available for distribution to equity holders of the company; and
- it would be beneficially entitled on a winding-up to at least 10% of the assets of the company available for distribution to equity holders.

ICTA 1988, Sch 18 applies, with suitable modifications, to define an 'equity holder' and to determine the profits or assets available for distribution.

[*TCGA 1992, Sch 7AC para 8*].

For the purposes of deciding whether the 'substantial shareholding' test is satisfied, holdings of shares (and interests in shares) by members of the same group of companies (which may be a worldwide group — see 60.2 above) are aggregated. [*TCGA 1992, Sch 7AC para 9(1)*].

Where assets of the investing company, or of a member of the same group as the investing company, are vested in a liquidator, they are treated for the purposes of the substantial shareholding requirement (and those of 60.15, 60.16 below) as if they were vested in the company and as if the acts of the liquidator were the acts of the company (disposals by the company to the liquidator, and vice versa, being disregarded). [*TCGA 1992, Sch 7AC para 16*].

Special rules apply in relation to assets of long-term insurance funds where the investing company is an insurance company, or in certain cases a 51% subsidiary of an insurance company, or a member of the same group as an insurance company. [*TCGA 1992, Sch 7AC paras 9(2), 17*].

60.9 **Holding period.** As stated at 60.4(*a*) above, the investing company must have held a substantial shareholding in the investee company throughout a continuous period of twelve months beginning not more than two years prior to the disposal. Shares are treated as having been held for such a period if, for example, they were acquired at any time on 15 June 2002 and sold at any time on 14 June 2003; they do not have to be held on the anniversary of the acquisition (HMRC Capital Gains Manual CG 53008). The following special rules apply.

No gain/no loss transfers. Where the investing company acquired any shares from another company by means of a no gain/no loss transfer, i.e. under any chargeable gains enactment that states that a disposal is to be treated as made for such consideration that no gain or loss accrues, the period during which it is treated as holding those shares is extended to include the period during which the previous owner held them. The period is further extended back through any series of no gain/no loss transfers by which the shares arrived in the hands of the present owner. The present owner is treated as having had the same entitlements, to shares and to any rights enjoyed by virtue of holding shares, as the company or companies by which they were held at any earlier time in the extended period. These include any entitlements etc. arising from the aggregation rule for groups of companies in 60.8 above. These rules also cover interests in shares (see 60.25 below), and the extension also covers any period during which the asset held by any of the previous companies concerned in the no gain/no loss series consisted of shares (or an interest in shares) from which the current shares (or interest) are 'derived'.

For the above purposes, any transfer falling within 27.2(viii) GROUPS OF COMPANIES (intra-group share exchanges), and which would otherwise have been a no gain/no loss transfer within *TCGA 1992, s 171*, is treated as if it had been a no gain/no loss transfer.

Shares (or interests in shares) are '*derived*' from other shares (or interests) only where

- a company becomes co-owner of shares previously owned by it alone, or vice versa,
- a company's interest in shares as co-owner changes (but co-ownership continues),
- a shareholding is treated by virtue of *TCGA 1992, s 127* (including its application by virtue of another enactment — see, for example, 58.1, 58.4, 58.6, 58.7 SHARES AND SECURITIES) as the same asset as another shareholding, or
- there is a sequence of two or more of the above occurrences.

[*TCGA 1992, Sch 7AC para 10*].

Deemed disposals and reacquisitions. Where, under any corporation tax enactment, shares have been deemed to be disposed of and immediately reacquired by a company, the company is regarded as not having held the shares during any part of the holding period falling before the deemed disposal and reacquisition. This rule extends to interests in shares (see 60.25 below) and to shares (or interests) from which the current shares (or interest) are 'derived' (as above). [*TCGA 1992, Sch 7AC para 11*].

Sale and repurchase agreements (repos). Where the company that holds shares transfers them under a repo (as defined), such that, by virtue of *TCGA 1992, s 263A* (see 58.21 SHARES AND SECURITIES), the disposal falls to be disregarded, it is similarly disregarded for the purposes of the provisions in this chapter. Thus, during the period covered by the repo, the ownership of the shares, and the entitlement to any rights attached to them, rests with the original owner and not the interim holder. If, at any time during that period, the original owner, or a member of the same group (see 60.2 above) as the original owner, becomes the *actual* holder of any of the shares transferred (or any shares directly or indirectly representing them), this rule ceases to have effect at that time in relation to the shares concerned. [*TCGA 1992, Sch 7AC para 12; FA 2003, s 181, Sch 38 para 9*].

Stock lending arrangements. Rules identical to those above for repos apply where shares are transferred under a stock lending arrangement (as defined), such that, by virtue of *TCGA 1992, s 263B(2)* (see 58.21 SHARES AND SECURITIES), the disposal falls to be disregarded. [*TCGA 1992, Sch 7AC para 13*].

60.10 REQUIREMENTS TO BE MET BY INVESTING COMPANY

The requirements to be met by the investing company for the purposes of the exemption at 60.4 above are that

(*a*) it must have been a sole 'trading company' (see 60.11 below) or a member of a 'qualifying group' (see below) throughout the period

- beginning with the start of the latest twelve-month period (within the two years prior to disposal) for which the substantial shareholding requirement (see 60.4(*a*) above) was met, and
- ending with the time of the disposal; and

(*b*) it must be a sole 'trading company' or a member of a 'qualifying group' immediately after the time of the disposal.

A '*qualifying group*' is a 'trading group' (see 60.11 below) or a group that would be a trading group if the activities of any group member not established for profit were disregarded to the extent that they are carried on otherwise than for profit. In determining whether a company is established for profit, any object or power which is merely incidental to the company's main objects is to be ignored.

The requirement at (*a*) above is met if the company was a sole trading company for part of the said period and a member of a qualifying group for the rest of it.

Where the disposal is made under a contract and, by virtue of *TCGA 1992, s 28* (see 15.3 COMPUTATION OF GAINS AND LOSSES), the time of disposal for tax purposes precedes the conveyance or transfer of the asset disposed of, the requirements at both (*a*) and (*b*) above must be met by reference to the time of conveyance or transfer as well the time of the disposal.

The requirement at (*a*) above is treated as met if, at the time of the disposal (and, where relevant, the time of the conveyance or transfer),

- the investing company is a member of a group (as in 60.2 above), and
- the requirement is not met by that company but would have been met by another group member if, immediately before the disposal, the subject matter of the disposal had been transferred to that member under the no gain/no loss provisions of *TCGA 1992, s 171* (see 27.2 GROUPS OF COMPANIES) and that member had then made the disposal.

[*TCGA 1992, Sch 7AC para 18*].

60.11 For the purposes of this chapter, a '*trading company*' is a company whose activities do not include to a 'substantial' extent activities other than 'trading activities'. A '*trading group*' is a group (as in 60.2 above), one or more of whose members carry on 'trading activities' and the activities of whose members, taken together, do not include to a 'substantial' extent activities other than 'trading activities'. '*Substantial*', in this connection, is taken by

HMRC to mean 'more than 20%' (Revenue Tax Bulletin December 2002 p 985); see also the points made at 61.5 TAPER RELIEF, which apply equally here.

In relation to a single company, *'trading activities'* means 'activities' carried on by the company

(*a*) in the course of, or for the purposes of, a 'trade' being carried on by it; or

(*b*) for the purposes of a 'trade' that it is preparing to carry on; or

(*c*) with a view to its acquiring or starting to carry on a trade; or

(*d*) with a view to its acquiring a 'significant interest' in the share capital of another company that is itself a trading company or the holding company (as in 60.2 above) of a trading group or 'trading subgroup' (see 60.13 below) and that is not already a member of the same group as the acquiring company.

'Activities' is interpreted by HMRC to mean what a company does, and thus the expression in itself includes engaging in trading activities, making and holding investments, planning, holding meetings and so forth (Revenue Tax Bulletin December 2002 p 984). *Trade'* means any trade, profession or vocation conducted on a commercial basis with a view to profit. It also comprises the commercial letting of FURNISHED HOLIDAY ACCOMMODATION (24). Activities qualify under (*c*) or (*d*) above only if the acquisition is made, or the trade commenced, as soon as is reasonably practicable in the circumstances. A company acquires a *'significant interest'* (see (*d*) above) if it acquires sufficient ordinary share capital in the other company to make that company its 51% subsidiary (within *ICTA 1988, s 838*), or to give the acquiring company a qualifying shareholding in a joint venture company (see 60.17 below) without making the two companies members of the same group.

In relation to a group, *'trading activities'* means activities carried on by a member of the group, being activities that would fall within (*a*)–(*d*) above if these are interpreted by reference not only to that member but also to any other member of the group. The activities of group members are regarded as a single business, so that intra-group activities are disregarded. A group member acquires a *'significant interest'* (see (*d*) above) if it acquires sufficient ordinary share capital in the other company to make that company a member of the same group as the acquiring company, or to give the acquiring company a qualifying shareholding in a joint venture company.

[*TCGA 1992, Sch 7AC paras 20, 21, 26(4), 27*].

Many of the expressions used above are considered further in Revenue Tax Bulletin December 2002 pp 982–987. A company may ask its tax district to give a view on its status for the above purposes, but any opinion expressed will be subject to revision to the extent that it relates to a time for which the full facts are not yet available. The Tax Bulletin article lists (at p 987) the information the inspector will require to form a view.

See 60.17 below as regards the treatment of holdings in joint venture companies.

60.12 REQUIREMENTS RELATING TO INVESTEE COMPANY

The requirements to be met in relation to the investee company for the purposes of the exemption at 60.4 above are that

(*a*) it must have been a 'qualifying company' (see below) throughout the period

- beginning with the start of the latest twelve-month period (within the two years prior to disposal) for which the substantial shareholding requirement (see 60.4(*a*) above) was met, and
- ending with the time of the disposal; and

(*b*) it must be a 'qualifying company' immediately after the time of the disposal.

A '*qualifying company*' is a 'trading company' (see 60.11 above) or the holding company (as in 60.2 above) of a 'trading group' (see 60.11 above) or 'trading subgroup' (see 60.13 below).

Where the disposal is made under a contract and, by virtue of *TCGA 1992, s 28* (see 15.3 COMPUTATION OF GAINS AND LOSSES), the time of disposal for tax purposes precedes the conveyance or transfer of the asset disposed of, the requirements at both (*a*) and (*b*) above must be met by reference to the time of the conveyance or transfer as well as the time of the disposal.

[*TCGA 1992, Sch 7AC para 19*].

60.13 For the purposes of this chapter, a '*trading subgroup*' is a subgroup (as in 60.2 above), one or more of whose members carry on 'trading activities' and the activities of whose members, taken together, do not include to a 'substantial' extent (see 60.11 above) activities other than 'trading activities'. '*Trading activities*' are defined in relation to a subgroup as they are in relation to a group (for which see 60.11 above), with the appropriate modifications; the activities of subgroup members are regarded as a single business, so that intra-subgroup activities are disregarded, but this does not extend to activities between a member of the subgroup and a company that is a member of the main group but not the subgroup (Revenue Tax Bulletin December 2002 p 983).

[*TCGA 1992, Sch 7AC para 22*].

It is worth noting that it is possible to have a trading subgroup within an otherwise non-trading group. See 60.17 below as regards the treatment of holdings in joint venture companies.

60.14 SHARE REORGANISATIONS ETC.

Treatment of certain events as disposals. Without the special rules below, the exemptions at 60.4–60.6 above would be of no relevance to any of the following events (in relation to shares held by the investing company in the investee company).

(*a*) A reorganisation of share capital, company take-over/reconstruction or conversion of securities which, by virtue of *TCGA 1992, s 127*, does not constitute a disposal (see 58.1, 58.4, 58.6, 58.7 SHARES AND SECURITIES), the 'new holding' standing in the shoes of the original shares.

(*b*) An event which would have been within (*a*) above but for the fact that the 'new asset' consists of a qualifying corporate bond and which, by virtue of *TCGA 1992, s 116*(*10*), is not treated as a disposal (see 50.3 QUALIFYING CORPORATE BONDS).

(*c*) A tax-exempt distribution on a demerger which, by virtue of *TCGA 1992, s 192* (see 13.16 COMPANIES), does not constitute a capital distribution within 58.10 SHARES AND SECURITIES).

To the extent that a gain would thereby be exempt (or a loss non-allowable) under 60.4–60.6 above, the enactment mentioned in (*a*), (*b*) or (*c*) above, whichever is relevant, is disapplied, so that an event in (*a*) or (*b*) is treated as a disposal, a distribution in (*c*) is treated as a capital distribution and the new shares or securities are normally treated as acquired at market value. This disapplication does not, however, have effect if the result would be a withdrawal or reduction (under *FA 2000, Sch 15 para 46*) of investment relief under the CORPORATE VENTURING SCHEME (17.11). Where it does have effect, the provisions at 17.24 CORPORATE VENTURING SCHEME, where relevant, are modified accordingly.

[*TCGA 1992, Sch 7AC para 4*].

HMRC have provided illustrations of how these and related provisions operate in two different types of intra-group transaction and also in relation to a share exchange outside a group (Revenue Internet Statement 'The Substantial Shareholdings Exemption Regime and Share Reorganisations', 1 July 2004 (originally published 21 June 2002)).

60.15 **Effect of earlier company reconstruction etc.** The following applies where

(*a*) shares held by the investing company in the investee company were acquired as a result of either

(i) an exchange of securities within *TCGA 1992, s 135* (see 58.4 SHARES AND SECURITIES), or

(ii) a scheme of reconstruction within *TCGA 1992, s 136* (see 58.6 SHARES AND SECURITIES); and

(*b*) *TCGA 1992, s 127* (see 58.1 SHARES AND SECURITIES) applied, such that the event was not treated as a disposal and the 'new holding' stood in the shoes of the original shares; and

(*c*) *TCGA 1992, s 127* did not fall to be disapplied by 60.14 above (because, for example, the conditions for the exemptions at 60.4–60.6 above were not satisfied or the event took place before 1 April 2002).

The question of whether, at any time *before* the event in (*a*)(i) or (ii) above, the substantial shareholding requirement at 60.8 above was met, or the requirements relating to the investee company at 60.12 above were met, is determined by reference to the shares held by the investing company at that time. This rule can apply more than once, i.e. where there has been more than one event within (*a*)(i) or (ii) above, and it can apply in combination with the rule at 60.16 below where there have been one or more transfers within that paragraph as well as one or more events within (*a*)(i) or (ii) above.

[*TCGA 1992, Sch 7AC paras 14, 25*].

60.16 **Effect of earlier demerger.** The following applies where

- shares held by the investing company in the investee company were acquired as a result of a transfer by a parent company of shares in its subsidiary; and
- the demerger provisions of *TCGA 1992, s 192* applied (see 13.16 COMPANIES), such that the transfer was not treated as a capital distribution and the transferred shares in the subsidiary fell to be treated as received as a result of a reorganisation of share capital and thus (by virtue of *TCGA 1992, s 127*) as standing in the shoes of the shares previously held in the parent company.

The question of whether, at any time *before* the transfer, the substantial shareholding requirement at 60.8 above was met, or the requirements relating to the investee company at 60.12 above were met, is determined by reference to the shares held by the investing company at that time. This rule can apply more than once, i.e. where there has been more than one such transfer, and it can apply in combination with the rule at 60.15 above where there have been one or more events within that paragraph as well as one or more transfers within this paragraph.

[*TCGA 1992, Sch 7AC paras 15, 25*].

60.17 TREATMENT OF HOLDINGS IN JOINT VENTURE COMPANIES (JVCS)

For the following purposes, a company is a '*joint venture company*' (JVC) if (and only if)

(i) it is a 'trading company' (see 60.11 above) or the holding company (as in 60.2 above) of a 'trading group' (see 60.11 above) or 'trading subgroup' (see 60.13 below), *and*

(ii) there are five or fewer persons who between them hold **75% or more** of its ordinary share capital (within *ICTA 1988, s 832(1)*) (counting members of a group of companies, as in 60.2 above, as if they were a single company).

The following provisions apply only where a company has a 'qualifying shareholding' in a JVC. A company has a '*qualifying shareholding*' in a JVC if (and only if) (*a*) it is a sole company (i.e. not a member of a group) and it holds shares, or an interest in shares (see 60.25 below), in the JVC by virtue of which it holds **10% or more** of the JVC's ordinary share capital, or

(*b*) it is a member of a group, the group members between them hold 10% or more of the ordinary share capital of the JVC *and* the company itself holds part of that ordinary share capital.

Where the above conditions are satisfied, definitions of 'trading company', 'trading group' and 'trading subgroup' have effect with the modifications in (1)–(3) below. Where the JVC is itself a 'holding company' (as in 60.2 above), the references in (1), (2) and (3) below to its activities are to the activities (other than intra-group activities) of the JVC and its '51% subsidiaries' (within *ICTA 1988, s 838*). Each reference below to a holding of shares in a JVC includes securities of the JVC or an interest in shares in, or securities of, the JVC.

(1) In determining whether a company with a qualifying shareholding in a JVC is a 'trading company' (see 60.11 above), its holding of shares in the JVC is disregarded. It is treated as carrying on a share of the JVC's activities proportionate to its percentage shareholding in the JVC. This does not apply if the company and the JVC are members of the same group of companies.

(2) In determining whether a group, of which a company with a qualifying shareholding in a JVC is a member or is the holding company, is a 'trading group' (see 60.11 above), there is disregarded any holding of shares in the JVC by any member of the group which has a qualifying shareholding in the JVC. Each such member is treated as carrying on a share of the JVC's activities proportionate to its percentage shareholding in the JVC. This does not apply if the JVC is itself a member of the group.

(3) In determining whether a company with a qualifying shareholding in a JVC is the holding company of a 'trading subgroup' (see 60.13 above), there is disregarded any holding of shares in the JVC by the company and by any of its 51% subsidiaries which itself has a qualifying shareholding in the JVC. The company and each such subsidiary is treated as carrying on a share of the JVC's activities proportionate to its percentage shareholding in the JVC. This does not apply if the JVC is a member of the same group as the company.

[*TCGA 1992, Sch 7AC paras 23, 24, 26(4)*].

60.18 CONSEQUENTIAL RULES

Degrouping charge. See 27.12 GROUPS OF COMPANIES for interaction between the exemptions in this chapter and the charge where a company ceases to be a member of a 75% group of companies and has had an asset transferred to it by another group member within the preceding six years.

60.19 **Negligible value claims.** Where

- a company makes a negligible value claim under *TCGA 1992, s 24(2)* (see 40.9 LOSSES) in respect of an asset, and
- by virtue of the provisions in this chapter, a loss on a disposal of that asset at the time of the claim would not be an allowable loss,

the consequent deemed disposal and reacquisition is regarded as taking place at the time of the claim and cannot be backdated to an earlier time. Thus, in these circumstances, a negligible value claim cannot result in an allowable loss. [*TCGA 1992, Sch 7AC para 33*].

60.20 **Reorganisation involving qualifying corporate bond.** Where, on a reorganisation of share capital, the 'new asset' consists of a qualifying corporate bond (see 50.3 QUALIFYING CORPORATE BONDS), the exemptions in this chapter do not apply to or affect the chargeable gain or allowable loss deemed to accrue under *TCGA 1992, s 116(10)(b)* on a subsequent disposal of the whole or part of the new asset. This does not apply if the 'reorganisation' was, in fact, a deemed disposal and reacquisition within *FA 1996, s 92(7)* (asset ceasing to be a 'convertible security' but continuing to be a creditor relationship of the company — see 14.6(i) COMPANIES—CORPORATE FINANCE AND INTANGIBLES). [*TCGA 1992, Sch 7AC para 34*].

Note that the above is of no application where the reorganisation has itself been treated as an exempt disposal by virtue of 60.14 above.

60.21 **UK resident company transferring assets to overseas company.** Where in specified circumstances a UK resident company transfers its non-UK trade to a non-UK resident company in exchange (or part exchange) for securities, the whole (or part) of any resulting gain may be deferred under *TCGA 1992, s 140* (see 45.9 OVERSEAS MATTERS). If, subsequently,

(*a*) the UK resident company disposes of any securities received in exchange for the transfer, such that all or part of the deferred gain would normally become chargeable; but

(*b*) by virtue of the provisions in this chapter, any gain on the disposal would not be a chargeable gain,

the provisions at 45.9(i) OVERSEAS MATTERS are disapplied. Instead, the deferred gain, or the 'appropriate proportion' of it (as there defined), is treated as a gain accruing to the company at the time of the disposal in (*a*) above and as being a gain which is outside the exemptions in this chapter. Any gain on the disposal of the securities themselves may still attract the exemptions in this chapter (and, equally, any loss may be non-allowable). [*TCGA 1992, Sch 7AC para 35*].

60.22 **Held-over gains on gifts of business assets.** Where

(*a*) a company disposes of an asset;

(*b*) the allowable expenditure attributable to that asset would have been greater were it not for a claim for gifts hold-over relief under *TCGA 1992, s 165* (see 33.1 HOLD-OVER RELIEFS) having been made in respect of an earlier disposal; and

(*c*) by virtue of the provisions in this chapter, any gain on the disposal in (*a*) above would not be a chargeable gain,

the amount of the held-over gain is treated as a gain accruing to the company at the time of the disposal in (*a*) above and as being a gain which is outside the exemptions in this chapter. If the disposal in (*a*) above is a part disposal, only an appropriate proportion of the held-over gain becomes chargeable on that occasion. [*TCGA 1992, Sch 7AC para 37*].

60.23 **FOREX matching regulations.** No gain or loss is treated as arising under *SI 1994 No 3227* (matching of foreign exchange differences — see 14.15(*f*) COMPANIES—CORPORATE FINANCE AND INTANGIBLES) on a disposal on which any gain would be exempt under the provisions in this chapter. [*TCGA 1992, Sch 7AC para 39*].

60.24 MISCELLANEOUS

The question of whether an asset is a chargeable asset for the purposes of corporation tax on chargeable gains generally is to be determined without regard to the availability, or potential availability, of the exemptions covered in this chapter, and references throughout this book to 'chargeable assets' should be read accordingly. Similarly, the definition of 'chargeable shares' at 13.14 COMPANIES is to be read without regard to the exemptions in this chapter. [*TCGA 1992, Sch 7AC para 32*].

60.25 For the purposes of this chapter, an '*interest in shares*' is an interest as a co-owner of shares (whether they be owned jointly or in common and whether the interests of the co-owners are equal or disparate). [*TCGA 1992, Sch 7AC para 29*].

61 Taper Relief

Cross-references. See 6.7 ASSETS for taper relief on disposal of asset acquired in pursuance of an option; 20.24 EMPLOYEE SHARE SCHEMES for taper relief on disposal of shares acquired in pursuance of a qualifying option under the enterprise management incentives scheme; 46.9, 46.13 PARTNERSHIPS.

Simon's Direct Tax Service. See Division C2.14.

The headings in this chapter are as follows.

61.1 INTRODUCTION

For 1998/99 and subsequent years of assessment, chargeable gains realised by individuals, trustees and personal representatives (but not companies) are reduced (tapered) according to the length of time the asset has been held after 5 April 1998, with greater reductions for 'business assets'. Losses are not reduced as such, but they are set against gains before applying taper relief to the net gain so that the losses are effectively tapered. The provisions are described in detail in this chapter. These provisions start to have effect at the same time as the freezing of indexation allowance at its April 1998 level (see 34.1 INDEXATION), so that taper relief will eventually replace indexation allowance completely.

61.2 TAPER RELIEF

Taper relief applies where for 1998/99 or any subsequent year of assessment a person has an excess of chargeable gains over the aggregate of allowable losses for the year and losses brought forward and the excess is or includes the whole or a part of any chargeable gain that is eligible for the relief. It thus applies *after* the deduction of any INDEXATION (34) allowance available and after any other deductions due in arriving at the chargeable gain, except that the relief is deducted in priority to the annual exemption (see 2.3 ANNUAL RATES AND EXEMPTIONS). See 61.3 below for the interaction between losses brought forward, the annual exempt amount and taper relief. **Taper relief does not apply at all for the purposes of corporation tax on chargeable gains.**

In computing the extent, if any, to which a gain on a particular disposal is included in the above-mentioned excess of gains over losses, both current year losses and brought forward losses are set against gains in such order as gives the maximum taper relief. See *Example 2* below (and see also 61.12 below).

Qualifying holding period. A chargeable gain is eligible for taper relief if at the time of disposal the asset has been held for at least one year in the case of a 'business asset' (see 61.4 below) or at least three years otherwise. For these purposes, only so much of the period for which the asset is held as falls **after 5 April 1998** (called the '*qualifying holding period*') is taken into account.

61.2 Taper Relief

If the time of acquisition (see below) of an asset fell before 17 March 1998 and either the asset is a non-business asset or it is a business asset disposed of before 6 April 2000, **an additional one year (the 'bonus year') is added**, in arriving at the qualifying holding period, to the actual period for which the asset is held after 5 April 1998. For example, a non-business asset acquired in 1996/97 and disposed of in 2002/03 is treated as having been held for *five* complete years after 5 April 1998. The one-year addition does not apply if there is a period after 5 April 1998 which, under the anti-avoidance rules in 61.21, 61.22 below, does not count as a period of holding for the purposes of taper relief. See 61.18 below as regards shares. See 21.13 ENTERPRISE INVESTMENT SCHEME for special rules in cases of serial reinvestment in EIS companies.

The period for which an asset is held after 5 April 1998 is expressly defined as the period beginning with the acquisition of the asset by the person making the disposal or 6 April 1998, whichever is the later, and ending with the time of disposal (and see 61.14 below re assets transferred between spouses). Specified CGT provisions which otherwise effectively treat an asset as acquired at a time other than its actual acquisition date are disregarded for this purpose, *viz. TCGA 1992, s 73(1)(b)* (to the extent that it relates the acquisition date back to before 6 April 1965 — see 57.17(*a*)(ii) SETTLEMENTS), *s 239(2)(b)* (settlements for the benefit of employees — see 22.85 EXEMPTIONS AND RELIEFS), *s 257(2)(b)* (gifts to charities — see 10.5 CHARITIES) and *s 259(2)(b)* (housing associations — see 22.49 EXEMPTIONS AND RELIEFS). Where certain anti-avoidance provisions apply (see 61.19–61.22 below), periods which are thereby treated as not counting for taper relief purposes are left out of account in determining the qualifying holding period.

In the case of shares acquired by way of scrip issue (aka bonus issue) or rights issue or other reorganisation of share capital, such that *TCGA 1992, s 127* treats the new shares as the same asset as the original shares (see 58.1 SHARES AND SECURITIES), taper relief runs from the acquisition date of the original shares (or from 6 April 1998 if later). This does not apply to shares received by way of scrip *dividend* (aka stock dividend) from a UK-resident company after 5 April 1998, which are treated as a free-standing acquisition as at the dividend date and not as a reorganisation (see 58.9 SHARES AND SECURITIES); the taper period thus begins at the scrip dividend date.

The date of any enhancement expenditure is not relevant for taper relief purposes; it does not alter the qualifying holding period (HMRC Capital Gains Manual CG 17900).

Where an asset was created rather than acquired, for example goodwill, the date of acquisition is the date the asset was created, determined as a question of fact on the basis of the evidence available (HMRC Capital Gains Manual CG 17900).

Amount of reduction. Chargeable gains are tapered according to the Table below up to a maximum of 75% for 'business assets' (see 61.4 below) and 40% for non-business assets, the maximum reductions applying where the qualifying holding period is at least two years (for disposals after 5 April 2002) for business assets and ten years for non-business assets. So much of any chargeable gain accruing to any person on disposal of an asset as is not a gain on disposal of a business asset is to be taken to be a gain on disposal of a non-business asset (and see 61.12 below as regards an asset which has been a business asset for part only of its period of ownership and 61.13 below as regards an asset used at the same time for different purposes).

Gains on disposals of **business** assets
after 5 April 2002

No. of whole years in qualifying holding period	Percentage reduction available	Percentage of gain chargeable
0	—	100.0
1	50.0	50.0
2 or more	75.0	25.0

Gains on disposals of **business** assets
after 5 April 2000 and before 6 April 2002

No. of whole years in qualifying holding period	Percentage reduction available	Percentage of gain chargeable
0	—	100.0
1	12.5	87.5
2	25.0	75.0
3	50.0	50.0
4 or more	75.0	25.0

Gains on disposals of **business** assets
after 5 April 1998 and before 6 April 2000

No. of whole years in qualifying holding period*	Percentage reduction available	Percentage of gain chargeable
0	—	100.0
1	7.5	92.5
2	15.0	85.0
3	22.5	77.5
4	30.0	70.0
5	37.5	62.5
6	45.0	55.0
7	52.5	47.5
8	60.0	40.0
9	67.5	32.5
10 or more	75.0	25.0

Gains on disposals of **non-business** assets
after 5 April 1998

No. of whole years in qualifying holding period*	Percentage reduction available	Percentage of gain chargeable
0	—	100
1	—	100
2	—	100
3	5	95
4	10	90
5	15	85
6	20	80
7	25	75
8	30	70
9	35	65
10 or more	40	60

* Including bonus year added for assets held on 17 March 1998 (see main text)

An asset will have a qualifying holding period of six years, for example, if acquired after 5 April 1998 and disposed of at any time on the sixth anniversary of the date of acquisition (HMRC Capital Gains Manual CG 17900). An asset held on 5 April 1998 will have a qualifying holding period of six years (ignoring the bonus year where available) if it is disposed of at any time on 6 April 2004, but only five years if it is disposed of on 5 April 2004.

The amount on which capital gains tax is to be charged for the tax year, subject to the annual exempt amount and the provisions at 61.3 below re losses brought forward, is the above-mentioned excess of gains over current year and brought forward losses less any available taper relief computed as above by reference to the gains(s) included in that excess.

[*TCGA 1992, s 2A, Sch A1 para 1, para 2(1)(3)(4)(a), (5), para 3(4); FA 1998, s 121, Sch 20; FA 1999, s 72(3); FA 2000, s 66; FA 2002, s 46, Sch 40 Pt 3(3)*].

Example 1

Brett acquired an asset in 1996 for £20,000 and sells it in September 2006 for £37,000. He makes no other disposals in 2006/07. At no time after 5 April 1998 was the asset used as a business asset. The indexation factor from date of acquisition to April 1998 is, say, 0.060.

At the time of disposal the asset has been held for eight complete years after 5 April 1998. Because it was acquired before 17 March 1998, a further one year is added. Using the Table above, the taper relief for a non-business asset held for nine complete years after 5 April 1998 is 35%.

	£
Proceeds	37,000
Less Cost of acquisition	20,000
Unindexed gain	17,000
Indexation to April 1998 £20,000 × 0.060	1,200
Chargeable gain	15,800
Less Taper relief £15,800 × 35%	5,530
Taxable gain subject to annual exemption	£10,270

Example 2

Hannah made four disposals in 2006/07, as follows.

On Asset A, she realised a chargeable gain of £13,000 (after indexation to April 1998). This asset was acquired in 1995 and sold in May 2006 and was a non-business asset throughout its ownership.

On Asset B, she realised a chargeable gain of £2,000. This asset was acquired in December 2003 and sold in October 2006 and was a non-business asset throughout its ownership.

On Asset C, she realised a chargeable gain of £9,500. This asset was acquired in August 2003 and sold in December 2006 and was a business asset throughout its ownership.

On Asset D, she realised an allowable loss of £6,000.

Asset A was held for eight complete years after 5 April 1998 and qualifies for a one-year addition as it was acquired before 17 March 1998. It thus qualifies for 35% taper relief.

Asset B was held for less than the minimum period of ownership necessary for a gain on a non-business asset to qualify for taper relief (three complete years).

Asset C was held for three complete years. It thus qualifies for 75% taper relief.

It is beneficial to offset the loss on Asset D firstly against the gain attracting no taper relief, i.e. the gain on Asset B, with the balance against the gain attracting the lower rate of taper relief, i.e. the gain on Asset A.

	£
Asset A	
Chargeable gain	13,000
Less Allowable loss	4,000
	9,000
Less Taper relief £9,000 × 35%	3,150
Tapered gain	£5,850

	£
Asset B	
Chargeable gain	2,000
Less Allowable loss	2,000
	£
Asset C	
Chargeable gain	9,500
Less Taper relief £9,500 × 75%	7,125
Tapered gain	£2,375
Total taxable gains subject to annual exemption	£8,225

61.3 INTERACTION WITH ANNUAL EXEMPT AMOUNT AND LOSSES BROUGHT FORWARD ETC.

Taper relief is given in priority to deduction of the annual exempt amount (see 2.3 ANNUAL RATES AND EXEMPTIONS), but after deduction of any allowable losses (see 61.2 above).

Where for 1998/99 or any subsequent year of assessment a person's 'adjusted net gains' are equal to or less than the annual exempt amount, any allowable losses brought forward from a previous year or carried back from the year of an individual's death (see 18.5 DEATH) need not be deducted and are thus preserved for further carry-forward (or, if possible, carry-back). Where the 'adjusted net gains' exceed the annual exempt amount, such losses are deducted only to the extent necessary to wipe out the excess. The '*adjusted net gains*' are the chargeable gains for the year *before taper relief* less any allowable losses for the year. (An additional adjustment is necessary if any gains of a settlement fall to be charged on the person concerned as a settlor or any gains of a non-resident settlement fall to be attributed to him as a beneficiary — see 2.3 ANNUAL RATES AND EXEMPTIONS for details of this adjustment.)

[*TCGA 1992, s 3(5)–(5C)(7)(8); FA 1998, s 121(3)(4), Sch 21 para 3*].

It follows that whilst brought-forward or carried-back losses are preserved to the extent that the current year gains are covered by the annual exemption, any taper relief available will then reduce the gains to less than the annual exempt amount so that the taper relief is effectively wasted in this instance.

See the examples at 2.3 ANNUAL RATES AND EXEMPTIONS.

61.4 MEANING OF 'BUSINESS ASSET'

Amendments were made by *FA 2000* and *FA 2003* to the definition of a 'business asset' for taper relief purposes and these are fully covered below. The *FA 2003* amendments apply to disposals after 5 April 2004 and have effect in relation to periods of ownership after that date. They do not affect the status of an asset at any time before 6 April 2004 even if that status falls to be determined as a result of a disposal on or after that date. [*FA 2003, s 160(5)*]. The *FA 2000* amendments have effect for determining the status of an asset at any time after 5 April 2000. They do not affect the status of an asset at any time before 6 April 2000 even if that status falls to be determined as a result of a disposal on or after that date. [*FA 2000, s 67(7)*]. On the disposal of an asset which became a business asset on 6 April 2000 or 6 April 2004 as a result of the changes to the rules, the gain must be apportioned using the normal rules at 61.12 below.

Assets other than shares and securities. For the purposes of taper relief, an asset, other than shares or securities (for which see below) or an interest therein, is a '*business asset*' at any specified time before its disposal if at that time it satisfies whichever is the relevant of the conditions set out below. See 61.5 below for definitions, except where otherwise stated.

In the case of a disposal **after 5 April 2004**, whether by an individual, the trustees of a settlement or the personal representatives of a deceased individual, the asset is a business asset at any specified time, where that time is after that date, if at that time it was being used wholly or partly for the purposes of a trade carried on by any individual, the trustees of a settlement, the personal representatives of a deceased individual or a partnership whose members then included

- an individual,
- the trustees of a settlement or any one or more persons who are trustees of a settlement at that time and who are acting in their capacity as such, or
- an individual's personal representatives or any one or more persons who are personal representatives of a deceased individual at that time and who are acting in their capacity as such.

In the case of a disposal by an **individual** other than one satisfying the above conditions, the asset is a business asset at any specified time if at that time it was being used wholly or partly for one or more of the following purposes:

- where that time is before 6 April 2004, those of a 'trade' carried on at that time by the individual or by a partnership in which he is a partner;
- those of any trade carried on by a company which is at that time a 'qualifying company' (see 61.6 below) by reference to the individual;
- those of any trade carried on by a company which is at that time a member of a 'trading group' of which the 'holding company' is at that time a qualifying company by reference to the individual;
- where that time is after 5 April 2004, those of a trade carried on by a partnership whose members then included a company which at that time was a qualifying company by reference to the individual or a company which at that time was a member of a trading group whose holding company was a qualifying company by reference to the individual;
- where that time is before 6 April 2000, those of any 'qualifying office or employment' to which the individual is at that time required to devote 'substantially the whole of his time' (which HMRC take to mean at least 75% of normal working hours — see HMRC Capital Gains Manual CG 17954);
- where that time is before 6 April 2000, those of any office or employment not qualifying as above but with a 'trading company' in relation to which the individual falls to be treated as being, at that time, a 'full-time working officer or employee';
- where that time is after 5 April 2000, those of any office or employment (full-time or otherwise) held by the individual with a person carrying on a trade.

Where the individual acquired the asset as legatee (within *TCGA 1992, s 64* — see 18.9 DEATH), it is taken to be a business asset at any specified time, where such would not otherwise be the case, if at that time it was being held by the deceased's personal representatives and being used for one or more of the purposes specified below for disposals by personal representatives only.

The receipt by the owner of rent for the use of an asset by his partnership or company does not prevent the asset from being a business asset (HMRC Capital Gains Manual CG 17940a).

In the case of a disposal by **trustees of a settlement** other than one satisfying the post-5 April 2004 conditions above, the asset is a business asset at any specified time if at that time it was being used wholly or partly for one or more of the following purposes:

- where that time is before 6 April 2004, those of a 'trade' carried on by the trustees;
- where that time is after 5 April 2000 and before 6 April 2004, those of a trade carried on by a partnership whose members at that time include the trustees, or include any one or more persons who are trustees of the settlement at that time and are acting in their capacity as such;
- where that time is before 6 April 2004, those of a trade carried on at that time by an 'eligible beneficiary' (see 61.9 below) or by a partnership in which he is a partner;
- those of any trade carried on by a company which is at that time a 'qualifying company' (see 61.6 below) by reference to *either* the trustees *or* an eligible beneficiary;
- those of any trade carried on by a company which is at that time a member of a 'trading group' of which the 'holding company' is at that time a qualifying company by reference to the trustees *or* an eligible beneficiary;
- where that time is after 5 April 2004, those of a trade carried on by a partnership whose members then included a company which at that time was a qualifying company by reference to the trustees *or* an eligible beneficiary or a company which at that time was a member of a trading group whose holding company was a qualifying company by reference to the trustees *or* an eligible beneficiary;
- where that time is before 6 April 2000, those of any 'qualifying office or employment' to which an eligible beneficiary is at that time required to devote 'substantially the whole of his time' (see above);
- where that time is before 6 April 2000, those of any office or employment not qualifying as above but with a 'trading company' in relation to which an eligible beneficiary falls to be treated as being, at that time, a 'full-time working officer or employee';
- where that time is after 5 April 2000, those of any office or employment (full-time or otherwise) held by an eligible beneficiary with a person carrying on a trade.

In the case of a disposal by the **personal representatives** (PRs) of a deceased individual other than one satisfying the post-5 April 2004 conditions above, the asset is a business asset at any specified time if at that time it was being used wholly or partly for one or more of the following purposes:

- where that time is before 6 April 2004, those of a 'trade' carried on by the PRs;
- those of any trade carried on by a company which is at that time a 'qualifying company' (see 61.6 below) by reference to the PRs;
- those of any trade carried on by a company which is at that time a member of a 'trading group' of which the 'holding company' is at that time a qualifying company by reference to the PRs.
- where that time is after 5 April 2004, those of a trade carried on by a partnership whose members then included a company which at that time was a qualifying company by reference to the deceased's personal representatives or a company which at that time was a member of a trading group whose holding company was a qualifying company by reference to the personal representatives.

Shares, securities or an interest in shares etc. For the purposes of taper relief, an asset consisting of, or of an 'interest' in, any shares in or securities (see 61.5 below) of a company (the relevant company) is a '*business asset*' at any specified time before its disposal if at that time it satisfies whichever is the relevant of the conditions set out below. See 61.5 below for definitions, except where otherwise stated.

In the case of a disposal by an **individual** or by **trustees**, the asset is a business asset at any specified time if at that time the relevant company is a 'qualifying company' (see 61.6 below) by reference to the individual or, as the case may be, the trustees.

Where the individual acquired the asset as legatee (within *TCGA 1992, s 64* — see 18.9 DEATH), it is taken to be a business asset at any specified time, where such would not otherwise be the case, if at that time

- it was being held by the deceased's personal representatives and
- where that time is before 6 April 2000, the pre-6 April 2000 condition below for disposals by personal representatives is satisfied; or where that time is after 5 April 2000, the relevant company is a 'qualifying company' (see 61.6 below) by reference to the personal representatives.

In the case of a disposal by **personal representatives** (PRs), the asset is a business asset at any specified time before 6 April 2000 if at that time the relevant company is a 'trading company' or the 'holding company' of a 'trading group' and the PRs may exercise at least 25% of the voting rights. The asset is a business asset at any specified time after 5 April 2000 if at that time the relevant company is a 'qualifying company' (see 61.6 below) by reference to the personal representatives.

[*TCGA 1992, Sch A1 paras 4, 5; FA 1998, s 121(2)(4), Sch 20; FA 2000, s 67(2)(3)(5); FA 2001, s 78, Sch 26 paras 2, 5; FA 2003, s 160(1)–(3)(5)*].

61.5 **Definitions.** The expressions 'qualifying company' and 'eligible beneficiary' are defined at, respectively, 61.6 and 61.9 below. Otherwise, the definitions below apply for the purposes of 61.4 above and this chapter generally.

A '*trade*' means a trade, profession or vocation, as understood for income tax purposes, which is conducted on a commercial basis with a view to realisation of profits. The expression also expressly includes the commercial letting of FURNISHED HOLIDAY ACCOMMODATION (24), but other letting of furnished property is excluded (*Patel v Maidment Sp C 2003, [2004] SSCD 41, Sp C 384*).

A new definition of '*trading group*' is provided for disposals after 16 April 2002 in relation to periods of ownership after that date, although it is not intended to 'alter the substance' of the pre-existing definition (Treasury Explanatory Notes to Finance Bill 2002). Under the new definition, a trading group is a 'group of companies' (see below), one or more of whose members carry on 'trading activities' and the activities of whose members, taken together, do not include to a 'substantial' extent activities other than trading activities. '*Trading activities*' means activities carried on by a member of the group, being activities that would fall within (*a*)–(*d*) below if these are interpreted by reference not only to that member but also to any other member of the group. The activities of group members are regarded as a single business, so that intra-group activities are disregarded. A group member acquires a '*significant interest*' (see (*d*) below) if it acquires sufficient ordinary share capital in the other company to make that company a member of the same group as the acquiring company, or to give the acquiring company a qualifying shareholding in a joint venture company (see 61.8 below).

Under the old definition, a trading group means a 'group of companies' (see below) the activities of which, taken together, do not to any 'substantial' extent include activities carried on otherwise than in the course of, or for the purposes of, a trade.

The views expressed in HMRC's Capital Gains Manual on the meaning of 'trading company' (see below) are also of relevance to 'trading groups', but intra-group activities are disregarded in applying the various tests (HMRC Capital Gains Manual CG 17953f).

A '*non-trading group*' means a 'group of companies' which is not a trading group.

A '*group of companies*' means a company and its '51% subsidiary(ies)' (within *ICTA 1988, s 838*).

For disposals after 16 April 2002 in relation to periods of ownership after that date, a '*holding company*' is a company with one or more 51% subsidiaries. Previously, the definition was narrower, in that a '*holding company*' was a company whose business consisted wholly or mainly of the holding of shares in its 51% subsidiary(ies) (and for the purpose of this definition any trade carried on by the holding company itself was disregarded). It does not matter that such a company may be an investment company for corporation tax purposes. 'Wholly or mainly' means more than half of whatever measure is reasonable in the circumstances of the case. Intra-group transactions such as the letting of property to subsidiaries are disregarded. (HMRC Capital Gains Manual CG 17953f). See 61.8 below for treatment of investments in joint venture companies and joint enterprise companies (both as there defined).

'*Qualifying office or employment*' means an 'office' or 'employment' (as those expressions are understood for income tax purposes) with a person who at the time specified is carrying on a trade.

A new definition of '*trading company*' is provided for disposals after 16 April 2002 in relation to periods of ownership after that date, although it is not intended to 'alter the substance' of the pre-existing definition (Treasury Explanatory Notes to Finance Bill 2002). Under the new definition, a trading company is a company carrying on 'trading activities' whose activities do not include to a 'substantial' extent activities other than trading activities. '*Trading activities*' means 'activities' carried on by the company

(*a*) in the course of, or for the purposes of, a trade being carried on by it; or

(*b*) for the purposes of a trade that it is preparing to carry on; or

(*c*) with a view to its acquiring or starting to carry on a trade; or

(*d*) with a view to its acquiring a 'significant interest' in the share capital of another company that is itself a trading company or the holding company of a trading group and that is not already a member of the same group as the acquiring company (where applicable).

'*Activities*' is interpreted by HMRC to mean what a company does, and thus the expression in itself includes engaging in trading activities, making and holding investments, planning, holding meetings and so forth (HMRC Capital Gains Manual CG 17953). Activities qualify under (*c*) or (*d*) above only if the acquisition is made, or the trade commenced, as soon as reasonably practicable in the circumstances. A company acquires a '*significant interest*' (see (*d*) above) if it acquires sufficient ordinary share capital in the other company to make that company its 51% subsidiary (within *ICTA 1988, s 838*), or to give the acquiring company a qualifying shareholding in a joint venture company (see 61.8 below) without making the two companies members of the same group. For further interpretation of (*a*)–(*d*) above, see HMRC Capital Gains Manual CG 17953i–17953l.

Under the old definition, a trading company is a company which exists solely for the purpose of carrying on one or more trades, disregarding any purposes capable of having no substantial effect on the extent of the company's activities.

In interpreting the above, HMRC take '*substantial*' to mean 'more than 20%'. Depending on the facts of the case, this measure may be applied to turnover, expenditure and/or time spent by officers and employees where one or more of these items relate partly to non-trading activities, and/or to non-trading assets as a proportion of all assets (either of which may possibly include intangible assets such as goodwill). The fact that a company has investment income does not necessarily bring the 20% test into play. If it can be shown that holding the investment is integral to the conduct of the trade or is a short-term lodgement of surplus funds held to meet demonstrable trading liabilities, the investment is unlikely to be seen as evidence of a non-trading purpose. An investment outside these categories still has the safety net of the 20% test. As regards *property* owned by the company but surplus to immediate business requirements, HMRC do not *necessarily* regard any of the following as indicating a non-trading purpose:

- letting part of the trading premises;
- letting properties no longer required for the trade and intended to be sold eventually;
- subletting property where it would be impractical or uneconomic to assign or surrender the lease;
- acquiring property, whether vacant or already let, with the provable intention of bringing it into use for the purpose of the trade.

In establishing 'purposes' under the old definition, only those reflected in the company's actual, or seriously contemplated, activities are to be taken into account and not, for example, myriad activities theoretically available to the company under wide powers conferred by its articles of association.

A company may ask its tax district to give a view on its status in relation to any period that has ended, but any view given will be valid as regards that period only. HMRC Capital Gains Manual CG 17953r lists the information the inspector will require to form a view. It is possible for a company to move in and out of trading company status, with the potential result that an asset is a business asset for part only of the period of ownership, in which case any gain must be apportioned as in 61.12 below. A company in liquidation is not disqualified from being a trading company but in practice is unlikely to be able to meet the above tests.

For more on the above points, and for other points relevant to trading company status, see HMRC Capital Gains Manual CG 17953–17953r.

A '*non-trading company*' is a company which is not a trading company.

See 61.8 below for treatment of investments in joint venture companies and joint enterprise companies (both as there defined).

A '*full-time working officer or employee*', in relation to a company, is an individual who

- is an officer or employee of that company or of that company and any other company(ies) with which it has a 'relevant connection', and
- is required in that capacity to devote 'substantially the whole of his time' to the service of that company or of those companies taken together. HMRC take this to mean at least 75% of normal working hours — see HMRC Capital Gains Manual CG 17954.

A company has a '*relevant connection*' with another company at any time when they are both members of the same group of companies (as defined above) or of the same 'commercial association of companies'. The latter expression means a company and such of its associated companies (within *ICTA 1988, s 416*) as carry on businesses which are of such a nature as to be reasonably considered to form a single composite undertaking. See also 61.8 below as regards joint venture companies and joint enterprise companies (both as there defined).

An '*interest in shares*' means an interest as a co-owner of shares (whether they be owned jointly or in common and whether the interests of the co-owners are equal or disparate). This definition applies for disposals after 16 April 2002 in relation to periods of ownership after that date; previously, no definition was provided.

[*TCGA 1992, Sch A1 para 22(1)(2), paras 22A, 22B; FA 1998, s 121(2)(4), Sch 20; FA 2000, s 67(2)(3)(5); FA 2001, s 78, Sch 26 para 5; FA 2002, Sch 10 paras 4(1)(3), 5, 7, 9, 10*].

The term '*securities*' is not defined for taper relief purposes, but HMRC accept that any of the following fall within that description for those purposes:

- securities within *TCGA 1992, s 132(3)(b)* (see definition at 58.7 SHARES AND SECURITIES);
- earn-out rights treated as securities under *TCGA 1992, s 138A* (see 58.5 SHARES AND SECURITIES);
- any company debenture possessing the characteristics of a debt on a security (see 22.5 EXEMPTIONS AND RELIEFS).

(Revenue Tax Bulletin June 2001 p 858).

Debentures which are not securities but which, by virtue of *TCGA 1992, s 251(6)* (debentures issued on company reorganisations, takeovers etc.), are *deemed* to be securities for the purposes of *TCGA 1992, s 251* (see 22.5 EXEMPTIONS AND RELIEFS) are treated as securities for taper relief purposes. This applies only for disposals after 5 April 2001, although, as respects such disposals, it applies in relation to the full period for which the debenture was owned after 5 April 1998. The intention is that this treatment should have no retrospective effect to the taxpayer's detriment, so for the purposes of specified provisions in this chapter (as listed at HMRC Capital Gains Manual CG 17930) it applies only in relation to periods after 16 April 2002. [*TCGA 1992, Sch A1 para 22(1); FA 2002, Sch 10 para 8*]. In relation to disposals before 6 April 2001, HMRC's opinion, based on the law as it then stood, is that such a debenture is *not* a security for taper relief purposes (Revenue Tax Bulletin June 2001 p 858).

Many commentators felt that HMRC's published views on the meaning of 'security' created as much uncertainty as they dispelled, did not necessarily reflect the draftsman's intentions and were unduly harsh in their exclusion of *TCGA 1992, s 251(6)* debentures. For useful articles, see *Taxation 5 July 2001 p 335* and *Tax Journal 9 July 2001 p 5*.

61.6 **Meaning of 'qualifying company'**. For the purposes of 61.4 above, a company is a '*qualifying company*' by reference to an **individual** at any time **before 6 April 2000** when

- the company is a 'trading company' or the 'holding company' of a 'trading group' (all expressions as defined in 61.5 above); *and*
- at least 25% of the voting rights are exercisable by that individual;

or at any time when

- the company is a trading company or the holding company of a trading group;
- at least 5% of the voting rights are exercisable by that individual; *and*
- the individual is a 'full-time working officer or employee' (as defined in 61.5 above) of that company or of a company which at that time has a 'relevant connection' (see 61.5 above) with it.

A company is a '*qualifying company*' by reference to an **individual** at any time **after 5 April 2000** when the company is a 'trading company' or the 'holding company' of a 'trading group' (all expressions as defined in 61.5 above) and *one or more* of the following conditions is met:

- the company is 'unlisted' (see below); or
- the individual is an officer or employee (full-time or otherwise) of the company or of a company having a 'relevant connection' (see 61.5 above) with it; or
- at least 5% of the voting rights in the company are exercisable by the individual.

A company is **also** a '*qualifying company*' by reference to an **individual** at any time **after 5 April 2000** when

- the company is a 'non-trading company' or the 'holding company' of a 'non-trading group' (all expressions as defined in 61.5 above);
- the individual is an officer or employee (full-time or otherwise) of the company or of a company having a 'relevant connection' (see 61.5 above) with it; *and*
- the individual does not have a 'material interest' (see 61.7 below) in the company or in any company which at that time has control (within *ICTA 1988, s 416*) of the company.

A company is a '*qualifying company*' by reference to the **trustees of a settlement** at any time **before 6 April 2000** when

- the company is a 'trading company' or the 'holding company' of a 'trading group' (all expressions as defined in 61.5 above); *and*
- at least 25% of the voting rights are exercisable by the trustees;

or at any time when

- the company is a trading company or the holding company of a trading group;
- at least 5% of the voting rights are exercisable by the trustees; *and*
- an 'eligible beneficiary' (see 61.9 below) is a 'full-time working officer or employee' (as defined in 61.5 above) of that company or of a company which at that time has a 'relevant connection' (see 61.5 above) with it.

A company is a '*qualifying company*' by reference to the **trustees of a settlement** at any time **after 5 April 2000** when the company is a 'trading company' or the 'holding company' of a 'trading group' (all expressions as defined in 61.5 above) and *one or more* of the following conditions is met:

- the company is 'unlisted' (see below); or
- an 'eligible beneficiary' (see 61.9 below) is an officer or employee (full-time or otherwise) of the company or of a company having a 'relevant connection' (see 61.5 above) with it; or
- at least 5% of the voting rights in the company are exercisable by the trustees.

A company is **also** a '*qualifying company*' by reference to the **trustees of a settlement** at any time **after 5 April 2000** when

- the company is a 'non-trading company' or the 'holding company' of a 'non-trading group' (all expressions as defined in 61.5 above);
- an 'eligible beneficiary' (see 61.9 below) is an officer or employee (full-time or otherwise) of the company or of a company having a 'relevant connection' (see 61.5 above) with it; *and*
- the trustees do not have a 'material interest' (see 61.7 below) in the company or in any company which at that time has control (within *ICTA 1988, s 416*) of the company.

A company is a '*qualifying company*' by reference to the **personal representatives** (PRs) of a deceased individual at any time **before 6 April 2000** when

- the company is a 'trading company' or the 'holding company' of a 'trading group' (all expressions as defined in 61.5 above); *and*
- at least 25% of the voting rights are exercisable by the PRs.

A company is a '*qualifying company*' by reference to the **personal representatives** (PRs) of a deceased individual at any time **after 5 April 2000** when the company is a 'trading company' or the 'holding company' of a 'trading group' (all expressions as defined in 61.5 above) and *one or both* of the following conditions is met:

- the company is 'unlisted' (see below); or
- at least 5% of the voting rights are exercisable by the PRs.

An '*unlisted*' company is a company none of whose shares are listed on a recognised stock exchange (see 58.23 SHARES AND SECURITIES) and which is not a 51% subsidiary (within *ICTA 1988, s 838*) of a company whose shares (or any class of whose shares) are so listed. Note that shares traded on the Alternative Investment Market (see 41.6 MARKET VALUE) are treated as unlisted for these purposes.

Note that on the disposal of an asset which became a business asset on 6 April 2000 as a result of the changes to the definition of a qualifying company effective from that date, the gain must be apportioned using the normal rules at 61.12 below.

[*TCGA 1992, s 288(1), Sch A1 paras 6(1)–(3), 22(1); FA 1998, s 121(2)(4), Sch 20; FA 2000, s 67(4)(5)(7); FA 2001, s 78, Sch 26 para 3(2)(3)*].

61.7 **Meaning of 'material interest'.** The following applies for the purpose of ascertaining whether a *non-trading company* or the holding company of a *non-trading group* is a qualifying company at any time after 5 April 2000 by reference to an individual or trustees of a settlement (see 61.6 above). In determining whether the individual has a 'material interest' in the company, the interests of persons connected with him (see 16 CONNECTED PERSONS) are taken into account. The same applies as regards trustees. A '*material interest*' in a company means possession of, or ability to control (directly or indirectly),

- more than 10% of the issued shares of any particular class; or
- more than 10% of the voting rights; or
- rights giving entitlement to more than 10% of the income theoretically available for distribution among participators (disregarding anyone's entitlement as a loan creditor); or
- rights giving entitlement to more than 10% of the assets theoretically available for distribution among participators in a winding-up or in other circumstances.

A right to acquire shares or rights, including a future entitlement to acquire shares or rights or an entitlement to acquire shares or rights at a future date, is treated as a right to control them. Entitlement under a conditional contract is nonetheless taken into account from the contract date.

[*TCGA 1992, Sch A1 para 6(4)–(7), para 6A; FA 2001, s 78, Sch 26 para 3(4), para 4*].

Example

J is an employee of a non-trading company, JKL Ltd, and currently holds 70 ordinary shares out of an issued ordinary share capital of 1,000 shares. He holds options to acquire 15 (as yet unissued) ordinary shares. He has an existing contractual entitlement to a further 20 (as yet unissued) ordinary shares if certain profit targets are met.

For the purpose of the material interest test, J is treated as having an interest in 105 JKL Ltd ordinary shares (70 + 15 + 20). To the extent that unissued shares are included in this total, they must be added to the total shares of the same class currently in issue in order to determine J's deemed percentage holding [*TCGA 1992, Sch A1 para 6A(5)–(7)*]. JKL Ltd's issued ordinary share capital is thus treated as being 1,035 shares (1,000 + 15 + 20). J's percentage holding is thus 105/1,035 = 10.144%. As this is more than 10%, J does have a material interest in the company, and his 70 shares are not business assets for taper relief purposes.

61.8 **Joint venture companies (JVCs) and joint enterprise companies (JECs).** The following has effect for determining whether or not an asset is a business asset at any time after 5 April 2000. It does not affect the status of an asset at any time before 6 April 2000.

On the disposal of an asset which became a business asset on 6 April 2000 in consequence of these rules, the gain must be apportioned as in 61.12 below.

For the purposes of these provisions, a company is a *'joint venture company'* if (and *only* if)

(i) it is a 'trading company' or the 'holding company' of a 'trading group' (all expressions as defined in 61.5 above), *and*

(ii) at least 75% in aggregate of its ordinary share capital (within *ICTA 1988, s 832(1)*) is held by no more than five persons (counting shares held by different members of a 'group of companies', as in 61.5 above, as held by a single company).

For disposals before 17 April 2002 and for later disposals in relation to periods of ownership before that date, the test in (ii) above had to be satisfied by reference to five or fewer *companies* rather than persons generally.

The following provisions apply to a company (an *'investing company'*) only if it has a 'qualifying shareholding' in a JVC. A company has a *'qualifying shareholding'* in a JVC if

(*a*) it holds 10% or more of the ordinary share capital of the JVC, *or*

(*b*) it is a member of a 'group of companies' (as in 61.5 above) which between them hold 10% or more of the ordinary share capital of the JVC *and* the company itself holds part of that capital.

For disposals before 17 April 2002 and for later disposals in relation to periods of ownership before that date, the threshold in both (*a*) and (*b*) above was 'more than 30%' rather than '10% or more'.

Where the above conditions are satisfied, the definitions of 'trading group', 'holding company' and 'trading company' in 61.5 above (which are also of application in defining a 'qualifying company' for the purposes of business asset taper relief — see 61.6 above) have effect with the modifications in (1)–(3) below.

(1) In determining whether a group of companies is a *'trading group'*, there is disregarded any shareholding in a JVC by any member of the group which is an investing company within (*a*) or (*b*) above. Each such member is regarded as carrying on a share of the JVC's activities proportionate to its percentage shareholding in the JVC. This does not apply if the JVC is itself a member of the group.

(2) In determining whether an investing company within (*a*) or (*b*) above is a *'holding company'* (for disposals before 17 April 2002 and for later disposals in relation to periods of ownership before that date), there is disregarded any holding of shares by it in the JVC. It is regarded as carrying on a share of the JVC's activities proportionate to its percentage shareholding in the JVC. This does not apply if the JVC is a 51% subsidiary (within *ICTA 1988, s 838*) of the investing company.

(3) In determining whether an investing company within (*a*) or (*b*) above is a *'trading company'*, there is disregarded any holding of shares by it in the JVC. It is regarded as carrying on a share of the JVC's activities proportionate to its percentage shareholding in the JVC. For disposals before 17 April 2002 and for later disposals in relation to periods of ownership before that date, this did not apply if the investing company was a holding company.

Where the JVC is itself the holding company of a trading group, the references in (1), (2) and (3) above to its activities are to the activities of its group. For disposals after 16 April 2002 in relation to periods of ownership after that date, the activities of the JVC and its 51% subsidiaries are regarded as a single business, so that intra-group activities are disregarded.

A company is a *'joint enterprise company'* if it satisfies condition (ii) above, without necessarily satisfying condition (i) above. A JVC is therefore a type of JEC. Any other type of JEC is relevant only in determining whether a non-trading company or holding company of a non-trading group is a qualifying company for business asset taper relief at any time after 5 April 2000 (see 61.6 above). The rule below applies where an investing company satisfies the 'qualifying shareholding' condition at (*a*) or (*b*) above, but by reference to a JEC (including a JVC).

The following are treated as having a '*relevant connection*' (see 61.5 above) with each other, even if this would not otherwise be the case:

- the investing company;
- the JEC;
- any company having a 'relevant connection' with the investing company;
- any company having a 'relevant connection' with the JEC by virtue of its being a 51% subsidiary of the JEC or a member of the same commercial association of companies (see 61.5 above).

[*TCGA 1992, Sch A1 para 22(1)(2), para 23(1)–(7A)(10), para 24; FA 1998, s 121(2)(4), Sch 20; FA 2000, s 67(6)(7); FA 2001, s 78, Sch 26 paras 6, 7; FA 2002, Sch 10 paras 4(2)(3), 6, 7, 11, 12*].

Although ostensibly aimed at joint ventures, it should be noted that the above provisions may also be of application to company investments not regarded by the interested parties as investments in joint ventures (see *Taxation 4 April 2002 pp 5–7*).

61.9 **Eligible beneficiaries of a settlement.** For the purposes of 61.4 and 61.6 above, an '*eligible beneficiary*', in relation to an asset comprised in a settlement and a specified time, is any individual having at that time a 'relevant interest in possession' under the settlement in either the whole of the settled property or a part which includes that asset. A '*relevant interest in possession*' means any interest in possession in the settlement other than a right to receive an annuity or a 'fixed-term entitlement'. The latter expression means any interest under the settlement which is limited to a fixed term other than a term at the end of which the person concerned will become entitled to the property. The simplest example of an eligible beneficiary is one with a life interest in the whole of the settled property.

Where the settled property originates from more than one settlor, the taper relief provisions have effect, and references to an '*eligible beneficiary*' are to be construed, as if there were a separate and distinct settlement for the property originating from each settlor, and *TCGA 1992, s 79(1)–(5A)* (see 57.5 SETTLEMENTS) apply for these purposes.

[*TCGA 1992, Sch A1 paras 7, 20; FA 1998, s 121(2)(4), Sch 20; FA 2006, Sch 12 para 27(4)(6)*].

See 57.13 SETTLEMENTS re meaning of 'interest in possession'.

61.10 **Non-qualifying beneficiaries.** A special rule applies where the trustees of a settlement dispose of an asset and that asset's relevant period of ownership (see 61.11 below) is or includes a period (known as a sharing period) throughout which

- the asset is a business asset (see 61.4 above) by reference to one or more eligible beneficiaries (see 61.9 above) and would not otherwise have been so; and
- there is a 'non-qualifying part of the relevant income' or would be if there *were* any relevant income for the period.

The '*non-qualifying part of the relevant income*' for any period is so much of the '*relevant income*', i.e. the income for that period from the part of the settled property comprising the asset disposed of, as is, or would be, income to which no eligible beneficiary has any entitlement or to which a 'non-qualifying eligible beneficiary' has an entitlement. A '*non-qualifying eligible beneficiary*', in relation to any period, is an eligible beneficiary who is not a beneficiary by reference to whom (if he were the only beneficiary) the asset disposed of would be a business asset throughout that period.

Where the above applies, each sharing period is apportioned by reference to the proportion which the non-qualifying part of the relevant income bears, or *would* bear if there were any income, to the relevant income. The resulting part of each sharing period is then deemed to be a period for which the asset was not a business asset (see 61.12 below for ramifications). Where different proportions apply to different parts of a single sharing period, a separate apportionment must be made for each such part.

[*TCGA 1992, Sch A1 para 8; FA 1998, s 121(2)(4), Sch 20*].

For worked examples, see HMRC Capital Gains Manual CG 17968.

61.11 RELEVANT PERIOD OF OWNERSHIP

For the purposes of 61.10 above and 61.12, 61.13 below, an asset's '*relevant period of ownership*' is the period after 5 April 1998 for which the asset has been held at the time of its disposal or, if shorter, the period of ten years ending with that time. Where certain anti-avoidance provisions apply (see 61.19–61.22 below) or the special rule for serial investors in EIS companies applies (see 21.13 ENTERPRISE INVESTMENT SCHEME), periods which are thereby treated as not counting for taper relief purposes are left out of account in computing the said ten-year period and are treated as not comprised in the relevant period of ownership. [*TCGA 1992, Sch A1 para 2(2)(4)(b); FA 1998, s 121(2)(4), Sch 20; FA 1999, s 72(3)*]. Where a 'bonus year' falls to be added in arriving at the qualifying holding period (see 61.2 above), it is *not* added to the relevant period of ownership.

61.12 ASSETS WHICH ARE BUSINESS ASSETS FOR PART ONLY OF PERIOD OF OWNERSHIP

A chargeable gain on the disposal of an asset is a gain on the disposal of a business asset, and therefore qualifies for the more beneficial taper rates in 61.2 above, if the asset was a business asset (see 61.4 above) *throughout* its relevant period of ownership (see 61.11 above).

If the above is not the case, but the asset has been a business asset for one or more periods comprising part of its relevant period of ownership, part of the gain is taken to be a gain on disposal of a business asset and the remainder taken to be a gain on disposal of a non-business asset, with different rates of taper relief applying accordingly to each part by reference to the qualifying period of holding (see 61.2 above) as if they were two separate gains accruing on separate disposals of separate assets held for the same period of time. The part taken to relate to a business asset is the proportion of the gain which the period(s) comprised in the relevant period of ownership for which the asset was a business asset bears to the whole of the relevant period of ownership. Where appropriate, the provisions at 61.10 above and 61.13 below must be taken into account in ascertaining the numerator of the fraction.

[*TCGA 1992, Sch A1 para 3(1)–(3)(5); FA 1998, s 121(2)(4), Sch 20*].

The apportionment of the single gain into two *separate* gains can be of advantage when seeking to allocate allowable losses between multiple gains in the most tax-efficient manner (as in 61.2 above). See Example 4 at HMRC Capital Gains Manual CG 17976.

Example 1 — general

Penny acquired a freehold property in March 1991 and sold it on 30 September 2007, realising a chargeable gain (after indexation to April 1998) of £95,000. Between March 1991 and September 2001 inclusive, the property was used as business premises and qualifies as a business asset for taper relief purposes. From October 2001 to September 2007 inclusive, it was let to a private non-trading tenant and was not a business asset. Penny made no other disposal in 2007/08.

The relevant period of ownership (see 61.11 above) is the 9½ years from 6 April 1998 to 30 September 2007. During that period, the asset was a business asset for 3½ years (April 1998 to September 2001) and a non-business asset for the remaining six years. Therefore, 3.5/9.5 of the gain (£35,000) qualifies for the business assets taper and 6/9.5 of the gain (£60,000) qualifies for the non-business assets taper.

The number of complete years in the qualifying holding period is nine. However, there is a one-year addition in the case of the non-business asset proportion as the property was acquired before 17 March 1998.

	Business asset	*Non-business asset*	*Total*
	£	£	£
Chargeable gain	35,000	60,000	95,000
Less Taper relief 75% / 40%	26,250	24,000	50,250
Taxable gain subject to annual exemption	£8,750	£36,000	£44,750

Example 2 — shares becoming business asset on 6 April 2000 as a result of statutory changes

Titus inherited 40 ordinary shares in Oates Ltd, an unlisted trading company, on 2 April 1997 at a probate value of £30,000. His shares represent 4% of the issued ordinary share capital and of the voting rights. He does not work for the company. He sells his shares to another shareholder on 5 October 2006 for £47,450, and makes no other disposals in 2006/07. The indexation factor for the period April 1997 to April 1998 is 0.040.

The relevant period of ownership (see 61.11 above) is the 8½ years from 6 April 1998 to 5 October 2006. During that period, the asset was a non-business asset for the first 2 years (6 April 1998 to 5 April 2000) as Titus held insufficient voting rights, and a business asset for the remaining 6½ years (6 April 2000 to 5 October 2006) by virtue of the company's unlisted status — see 61.6 above. Therefore, 2/8.5 of the gain qualifies for non-business asset taper relief and 6.5/8.5 of the gain qualifies for business asset taper relief.

The number of complete years in the qualifying holding period is eight. However, there is a one-year addition in the case of the non-business asset proportion as the shares were acquired before 17 March 1998.

	£
Proceeds	47,450
Less Cost of acquisition	30,000
Unindexed gain	17,450
Indexation to April 1998 £30,000 × 0.040	1,200
Pre-tapered gain	£16,250

	Business asset	Non-business asset	Total
	£	£	£
Pre-tapered gain	12,427	3,823	16,250
Less Taper relief 75% / 35%	9,320	1,338	10,658
Taxable gain subject to annual exemption	£3,107	£2,485	£5,592

61.13 **ASSET USED AT SAME TIME FOR DIFFERENT PURPOSES**

An asset's relevant period of ownership (see 61.11 above) may be, or may include, a period (a mixed-use period) throughout which the asset (not being shares or securities or an interest therein) is a business asset by reference to its use for the purposes mentioned in 61.4 above but at the same time is used for other, i.e. non-qualifying, purposes. On the disposal at a gain of such an asset, a fraction of every mixed-use period is taken to be a period throughout which the asset was *not* a business asset (see 61.12 above for the ramifications). The fraction, in relation to any mixed-use period, is that which represents the proportion of non-qualifying use to total use during that period. Where that proportion has been different at different times within a mixed-use period, separate fractions must be applied to separate parts of the mixed-use period. For worked examples, see HMRC Capital Gains Manual CG 17960, 17962.

Where, on a trustees' disposal, both these provisions and those at 61.10 above apply to the whole or any part of a period, the last-mentioned provisions are applied first. These provisions are then applied, to the period(s) for which the asset is taken to have been a business asset, by reference only to the 'relevant part' of any non-qualifying use, being the proportion of that use which is not a use to which a 'non-qualifying part' of any 'relevant income' (see 61.10 above) is attributable. For a worked example, see HMRC Capital Gains Manual CG 17970. Where different attributions have to be made for different parts of a mixed-use period, separate fractions must be applied to separate parts of the mixed-use period.

[*TCGA 1992, Sch A1 para 9; FA 1998, s 121(2)(4), Sch 20; FA 2003, s 160(4)*].

See also HMRC Capital Gains Manual CG 17959 where there is a part disposal of an asset used for different purposes at the same time.

Note that these provisions apply only where there is non-qualifying use. Where part of an asset is a business asset and part is not used at all, for example unoccupied space in a building, there is *prima facie* no restriction of business asset taper relief. For further discussion of this, see *Taxation 17/24 December 1998 p 303*.

61.14 **ASSETS TRANSFERRED BETWEEN SPOUSES OR CIVIL PARTNERS**

On a disposal of an asset acquired from a spouse or civil partner under the no gain/no loss rule in *TCGA 1992, s 58* (see 42.4 MARRIED PERSONS AND CIVIL PARTNERS), taper relief applies as if the time when the transferee spouse or partner acquired the asset was the time when the transferor acquired it (or is treated as having acquired it, for example where there has been more than one inter-spouse or inter-partner transfer of the same asset). In other words, the combined period of holding of both spouses or civil partners is taken into account.

An article in Revenue Tax Bulletin August 2001 pp 876, 877, with worked example, illustrates how this rule, the no gain/no loss rule at 42.4 MARRIED PERSONS AND CIVIL PARTNERS and the matching rules at 59.2 SHARES AND SECURITIES generally interact.

As regards assets other than shares and securities, the question of whether the asset was a business asset (see 61.4 above) at any specified time in the combined period of holding is determined by reference to the use to which it was put by the spouse or civil partner holding it at that time. Thus, if a husband acquires a property on 1 April 1998 and holds it as an investment for four years after 5 April 1998 and then gives it to his wife who uses it in her business for five years before selling it, four-ninths of the gain on the ultimate disposal will attract nine years' taper relief at the non-business asset rate and five-ninths will attract nine years' taper relief at the business asset rate (see the rules at 61.12 above). During that part of the combined period of holding which falls *before* the inter-spouse or inter-partner transfer, the asset is also a business asset at any time if it then qualifies as such by reference to the spouse or civil partner to whom it is eventually transferred, i.e. where an asset owned by one spouse or partner is used in the other's business.

As regards shares and securities, the question of whether the asset was a business asset at any specified time in the combined period of holding is determined only by reference to the individual making the ultimate disposal. Say husband and wife each own 4% of the voting shares in a quoted trading company (acquired after 5 April 2000) but only the husband is an employee, and that this situation persists for five years at which point the wife gives her shareholding to her husband. After a further one year the husband sells the combined shareholding. The gain will attract six years' taper relief at the business asset rate, as the company has been a qualifying company by reference to the husband (see 61.6 above) throughout those six years. If, on the other hand, only the wife is an employee, only one-sixth of the ultimate gain will qualify for taper relief at the business asset rate. The company is a qualifying company by reference to the husband for only one of the six years; the fact that it is a qualifying company by reference to the wife for five of those years is irrelevant as it is not she who makes the ultimate disposal.

[*TCGA 1992, Sch A1 para 15; FA 1998, s 121(2)(4), Sch 20; FA 2003, s 160(4); SI 2005 No 3229, Reg 123*].

61.15 POSTPONED GAINS

A special rule applies where a gain would have accrued on an actual or deemed disposal (the 'charged disposal') of an asset at a particular time, but is treated on one or more occasions under any of the CGT provisions listed below as accruing at a later time (whether or not the time of a subsequent disposal) and after 5 April 1998. The said provisions are:

- *TCGA 1992, s 10A* (temporary non-UK residence — see 45.4 OVERSEAS MATTERS);
- *TCGA 1992, s 116(10)* (company reconstruction where new asset is a QUALIFYING CORPORATE BOND — see 50.3);
- *TCGA 1992, s 134* (issue of gilts as compensation for compulsory acquisition of shares or securities — see 58.7 SHARES AND SECURITIES);
- *TCGA 1992, s 154(2)(4)* (ROLLOVER RELIEF into a depreciating asset — see 55.7);
- *TCGA 1992, s 169C(7)* (clawback of relief under *TCGA 1992, s 165* or *s 260* if settlement becomes settlor-interested — see 33.5 HOLD-OVER RELIEFS);
- *TCGA 1992, Sch 5B* (deferral of gains on reinvestment into an EIS company — see 21.9 ENTERPRISE INVESTMENT SCHEME); (but special rules apply in cases of serial reinvestment — see 21.13 ENTERPRISE INVESTMENT SCHEME);
- *TCGA 1992, Sch 5C* (deferral of gains on reinvestment into a VCT — see 66.12 VENTURE CAPITAL TRUSTS);
- *FA 1996, Sch 15 para 27* (transitional rules for qualifying indexed securities);
- *SI 2006 No 964, Regs 67(4), 68(4)* (qualified investor schemes — see 65.7 UNIT TRUSTS, ETC.).

61.16 Taper Relief

Taper relief is applied to the postponed gain only at the time it becomes chargeable but is applied by reference to the time of the charged disposal and the asset which was disposed of, or would have been disposed of, by the charged disposal. Accordingly, the end of the period (if any) after 5 April 1998 for which the asset had been held at the time of the disposal on which the postponed gain accrued is deemed to be the time of the charged disposal.

Where under *TCGA 1992, s 12(1)* (gains charged on REMITTANCE BASIS — see 51.1) or *s 279(2)* (delayed remittances of overseas gains — see 45.5 OVERSEAS MATTERS), a gain is treated as accruing later than it actually accrued, those provisions are ignored for the purposes of taper relief.

[*TCGA 1992, Sch A1 para 16; FA 1998, s 121(2)(4), Sch 20; FA 2004, s 116, Sch 21 para 8; SI 2006 No 964, Reg 110*].

Example

Gordon disposes of shares in A Ltd, his family trading company, in August 2006, realising a chargeable gain (after indexation to April 1998) of £50,000. He had held the shares since 1989 and they qualified as a business asset for the purposes of taper relief. He acquires shares in an enterprise investment scheme company in March 2007 for £60,000 and makes a claim for deferral relief under *TCGA 1992, Sch 5B*. He makes no other disposals in 2006/07 and wishes to leave sufficient gains in charge to cover his annual exemption.

The A Ltd shares were held for eight complete years after 5 April 1998. The taper is therefore 75%.

	£
Gain before taper relief	50,000
Less Deferred on reinvestment in EIS company (optimum amount)	14,800*
	35,200
Less Taper relief £35,200 × 75%	26,400
Tapered gain covered by annual exemption	£8,800

*£8,800 × (100/(100 – 75)) = £35,200, £50,000 – 35,200 = £14,800

In June 2009, Gordon sells his EIS company shares. The deferred gain becomes chargeable in 2009/10 and is computed as follows.

	£
Deferred gain before taper relief	14,800
Less Taper relief £14,800 × 75% (April 1998 to August 2006)	11,100
Taxable gain subject to annual exemption	£3,700

See also 21.13 ENTERPRISE INVESTMENT SCHEME for special taper relief provisions for serial investments in EIS companies.

61.16 HOLD-OVER RELIEF

It is implicit in the legislation that the gain to be held over, where such a claim is made on the transfer of an asset within 33 HOLD-OVER RELIEFS, is the untapered gain; as stated in 61.2 above, taper relief is given only on gains left in charge after all reliefs other than the annual exempt amount have been taken into account.

On the ultimate disposal by the transferee of an asset which he acquired by way of a transfer on which hold-over relief was claimed, only the period for which he personally has held the asset will determine the taper relief available; there is no provision for combining the holding period of transferor and transferee as there is with inter-spouse transfers (see 61.14 above). (Revenue Press Release IR 16, 17 March 1998).

61.17 ROLLOVER RELIEF

Where rollover relief is claimed on the replacement of a qualifying business asset, taper relief operates on the ultimate disposal of the new asset by reference only to the period for which that asset has been held. (Revenue Press Release IR 16, 17 March 1998). Where the replacement is a wasting asset, so that the gain is postponed rather than rolled over against the cost of the new asset (see 55.7 ROLLOVER RELIEF), the rules at 61.15 above apply on the postponed gain being brought into charge.

It is implicit in the legislation that in the event of a rollover relief claim the gain to be deducted from the cost of the new asset is the *untapered* gain arising on the old asset; as stated in 61.2 above, taper relief is given only on gains left in charge after all reliefs other than the annual exempt amount have been taken into account.

See also 55.1 ROLLOVER RELIEF.

61.18 SHARES AND SECURITIES

In order to apply taper relief, it is clearly necessary to be able to match disposals with acquisitions of shares or securities where more than one acquisition and/or disposal is made of shares etc. of the same class in the same company. Consequently, the 'share pooling rules' which previously operated are abolished for acquisitions after 5 April 1998 and new identification rules introduced in their place. See 59 SHARES AND SECURITIES—IDENTIFICATION RULES.

Shares acquired on or after 17 March 1998 but before 6 April 1998 and added to a 'section 104 holding' (of shares of the same class in the same company) in existence before 17 March 1998 are themselves regarded as acquired before 17 March 1998 and thus may qualify for the 'bonus year' addition in 61.2 above. This follows from the pre-6 April 1998 rules at 59.3, 59.4 SHARES AND SECURITIES—IDENTIFICATION RULES. (HMRC Capital Gains Manual CG 17901).

61.19 ANTI-AVOIDANCE RULES

Periods of limited exposure to fluctuations in value of an asset. An anti-avoidance rule applies where the period after 5 April 1998 for which an asset has been held includes a period during which the person making the disposal (or a 'relevant predecessor' of his) had limited exposure to fluctuations in the value of the asset. Such a period does not count for the purposes of taper relief and is left out of account in determining the qualifying holding period (see 61.2 above) and treated as not comprised in the relevant period of ownership (see 61.11 above).

The times when a person is taken to have had such limited exposure are all times while he held the asset when a 'transaction' entered into at any time (whether or not after 5 April 1998) by him (or by a 'relevant predecessor' of his) had the effect that, without disposing of the asset, he had relinquished economic ownership of it; in other words that he was neither exposed to any 'substantial' extent to risk of loss from fluctuations in the asset's value nor able to enjoy to any 'substantial' extent any opportunities to benefit from such fluctuations. '*Transaction*' includes any agreement, arrangement or understanding, whether or not legally enforceable, and also includes a series of transactions. The following transactions are excluded from these provisions:

- any policy of insurance against loss and/or damage to the asset, being one which the person concerned might reasonably have been expected to enter into; and

- any transaction having effect in relation to fluctuations only insofar as they result from fluctuations in the value of foreign currencies.

A '*relevant predecessor*' of the person disposing of the asset, or of a relevant predecessor of his, is a person who held that asset at a time falling within the period which is taken to be the period (including for this purpose any time before 6 April 1998) for which the asset has been held at the time of disposal. Typically, it will be the spouse of the person making the disposal.

[*TCGA 1992, Sch A1 para 10, para 22(1); FA 1998, s 121(2)(4), Sch 20*].

For the purposes of the above provisions, '*substantial*' is taken by HMRC to mean greater than 20%, so that the provisions will apply where a person divests himself of at least 80% of the exposure to fluctuations in value. (HMRC Capital Gains Manual CG 17916).

Whilst reserving their position on complex or non-commercial arrangements, HMRC have stated that the above provisions will not be applied where loan notes (other than qualifying corporate bonds) are issued in exchange for shares as part of the normal commercial arrangements on a company takeover (to which *TCGA 1992, s 135* will normally apply — see 58.4 SHARES AND SECURITIES), even if the loan notes are underwritten by third party guarantee as part of those arrangements. (HMRC Capital Gains Manual CG 17916).

For a brief example of circumstances in which the above provisions would apply, involving put and call options, see HMRC Capital Gains Manual CG 17917.

61.20 **Close company share ownership: periods during which company not active.** The following provisions have effect in relation to disposals after 16 April 2002, replacing those at 61.21 below.

Where there is a disposal of an asset consisting of shares in (or securities of) a company, any period after 5 April 1998 during which

- the asset consisted of shares in (or securities of) a *close company* (as defined by *ICTA 1988, ss 414, 415*), *and*
- the company was not 'active',

does not count for taper relief purposes. For this purpose, a company is regarded as '*active*' at any time when it is carrying on, or preparing to carry on, a business of any description, or when a business that it has ceased to carry on is in the process of being wound up. There is no requirement that the business be conducted on a commercial basis or with a view to profit. An activity of holding and managing assets counts as a business for this purpose. However, a company is not regarded as '*active*' by reason only of its doing one or more of the following:

- holding money (in any currency) in cash or on deposit;
- holding other assets whose aggregate value is insignificant (see HMRC Capital Gains Manual CG 17921h);
- holding shares in, or debentures of, a company that is not itself 'active' (or holding interests in (see below), or options in respect of, any such shares or debentures);
- making loans to an associated company (within *ICTA 1988, s 416*) or to a participator or his associate (both within the meaning of *ICTA 1988, s 417*);
- carrying out administrative functions in order to comply with company law requirements.

Notwithstanding any of the above, a company is treated as '*active*' if

- it is the 'holding company' of a 'group of companies' (see in both cases 61.5 above) that includes at least one 'active' company; or

- it has a qualifying shareholding in a joint venture company (see 61.8 above) or is the holding company of a group any member of which has a qualifying shareholding in a joint venture company.

[*TCGA 1992, Sch A1 para 11A; FA 2002, Sch 10 para 3*].

See 61.5 above for the meaning of an 'interest in shares'; an '*interest in debentures*' has a corresponding meaning. [*TCGA 1992, Sch A1 para 22*(*1*)*; FA 2002, Sch 10 para 5*].

Note that where the above conditions are satisfied for any period, that period does not count in determining either the qualifying holding period (see 61.2 above) or the relevant period of ownership (see 61.11 above). This can be to a taxpayer's advantage in that the shares will not be classed as non-business assets during a period in which the company is dormant before commencing a trade; the period of dormancy is simply disregarded. Note also that, for the purposes of these provisions only, a 'business' is not restricted to a trade or profession and can include, for example, a Schedule A lettings business. For commentary, with examples, on these and other matters above, see HMRC Capital Gains Manual CG 17921–17921j.

61.21 **Close company share ownership: change of activity by the company.** The following provisions have effect in relation to disposals on or before 16 April 2002, after which they are replaced by those at 61.20 above.

Where there is a disposal of shares in (or securities of) a close company (as defined by *ICTA 1988, ss 414, 415*) and the inclusive period between the 'relevant time' and the time of disposal includes at least one 'relevant change of activity' involving that company, so much of the period after 5 April 1998 for which the shares have been held at the time of disposal as falls before that change, or the latest such change, does not count for the purposes of taper relief. It is left out of account in determining the qualifying holding period (see 61.2 above) and treated as not comprised in the relevant period of ownership (see 61.11 above). Where the shares were acquired before 17 March 1998, the one-year addition in computing the qualifying holding period (see 61.2 above) does not apply. The stated purpose of these provisions is to prevent any increase in taper relief that could otherwise be achieved by transferring to a close company an asset held for a shorter period than the shares in the company, and then selling those shares.

The '*relevant time*' is the beginning of the period after 5 April 1998 for which the shares have been held at the time of their disposal. A '*relevant change of activity*' occurs at either of the times given below.

(1) Where the close company or any of its '51% subsidiaries' begins at any time to carry on a 'trade' and neither it nor any of its 51% subsidiaries was carrying on a trade immediately before that time, there is a relevant change of activity at that time. For this purpose, a company's '*51% subsidiary*' is a company which, under *TCGA 1992, s 170*(*7*), is an effective 51% subsidiary of the first company for the purposes of *TCGA 1992, ss 170–181* (see 27.1 GROUPS OF COMPANIES and note that the change in the residence requirement therein mentioned has effect for this purpose after 31 March 2000). '*Trade*' is defined as in 61.5 above, but does not include a trade which is merely incidental to any non-trading activities carried on by the company in question or another company in the group.

(2) Where

- at the time of disposal of the shares the close company was carrying on a business of holding or making investments, and
- there has been any occasion falling either within the period of twelve months ending with the disposal or within any period of twelve months ending after the relevant time (see above) when it was not carrying on that business or when the size of that business was small (see below) by comparison with its size at the end of that period,

a relevant change of activity is to be taken to have occurred immediately after the latest such occasion before the time of the disposal. For this purpose, the size of a business at any time is determined by reference to aggregate acquisition costs for assets held at that time for the purposes of the business. In determining both whether a company is carrying on a business of holding or making investments (see also below) and the size of that business, the activities of the company and all its 51% subsidiaries (defined as above) are taken together, but the following activities (of any of those companies) are not to be regarded as included in such a business

- the holding of shares in a 51% subsidiary,
- the making of loans to an 'associated company' or to a participator (as defined by *ICTA 1988, s 417(1)* and whether in the company making the loan or in an associated company), or
- placing money on deposit.

For this purpose, two companies are '*associated companies*' at any time if at that time or at any time in the previous twelve months one has controlled the other or they have been under common control.

[*TCGA 1992, Sch A1 para 11; FA 1998, s 121(2)(4), Sch 20; FA 2000, Sch 29 para 36; FA 2002, Sch 10 para 2*].

The acquisition by a company of a shareholding in a 'joint venture company' (see 61.8 above), such that the acquiring company falls within 61.8(*a*) or (*b*) above, is not to be treated as a relevant change of activity. [*TCGA 1992, Sch A1 para 23(9); FA 2000, s 67(6); FA 2002, Sch 40 Pt 3(3)*].

For the purposes of (2) above, HMRC have issued guidance on the meaning of 'carrying on a business of holding … investments'. A 'business' is not necessarily a trade, but companies that trade may also carry on a business of holding investments. However, the mere existence of investments does not necessarily point to a separate investment-holding business. Where the holding of investments is to meet current trading liabilities, and forms capital of the trade, it is unlikely that those investments form part of such a business. However, there will be companies where the holding of investments forms no part of the trade or in any sense represents capital employed in the trade. Each case must be judged on its facts. HMRC confirm that a company that does no more than invest funds 'surplus to its immediate trading requirements' (i.e. where there is a foreseeable and demonstrable need for future use of those funds in the trade) will not be regarded for these purposes as carrying on a business of holding investments. Thus, neither the initial making of such an investment nor a subsequent change in the nature of that investment can constitute a relevant change of activity. HMRC do not regard any of the following activities carried out by a trading company as amounting in themselves to a business of holding investments

- letting part of the trading premises;
- letting properties no longer required for the trade and intended to be sold eventually;
- subletting property where it would be impractical or uneconomic to assign or surrender the lease;
- the acquisition of property which is let intra-group for use in the lessee company's trade.

A company in winding-up will not be regarded as commencing an investment-holding business by reason only of a temporary investment made by the liquidator pending a distribution.

It should be noted that the law is concerned with *increases in the size* of an investment-holding business and not with the continued existence of such a business at a constant level. HMRC regard an investment-holding business as being 'small' at any time, compared to its size at a later time, if its earlier size is less than 5% of its later size.

(Revenue Tax Bulletin June 2001 pp 856–858).

61.22 **Close company share ownership: value shifting.** Where there is a disposal of shares in (or securities of), or rights over, a close company (as defined by *ICTA 1988, ss 414, 415*) and the inclusive period between the relevant time (defined as above) and the time of disposal includes at least one 'relevant shift of value' involving those shares (or rights), so much of the period after 5 April 1998 for which the shares (or rights) have been held at the time of disposal as falls before that shift, or the latest such shift, does not count for the purposes of taper relief, with the same consequences as above.

A '*relevant shift of value*' involving any shares (or rights) is to be taken to have occurred whenever

- a person having control of the close company exercises his control so that value passed into the shares (or rights) out of a 'relevant holding'; or
- effect was given to any other 'transaction' by virtue of which value passed into the shares (or rights) out of a relevant holding.

A relevant shift of value is disregarded for these purposes if the value passing is insignificant or the shift of value took place at a time when the qualifying holding period (see 61.2 above) for the relevant holding was at least as long as that for the shares (or rights).

A '*relevant holding*', in relation to value passing into shares in (or rights over) a company, is any holding by

- the person who, following the exercise of control or other transaction, held the shares (or rights), or
- any person connected with that person (see 16 CONNECTED PERSONS),

of any shares in (or rights over) the company or in (or over) a company under the control of the same person(s) as that company.

'*Transaction*' includes any agreement, arrangement or understanding, whether or not legally enforceable, and also includes a series of transactions.

[*TCGA 1992, Sch A1 para 12, para 22(1); FA 1998, s 121(2)(4), Sch 20*].

See HMRC Capital Gains Manual CG 17923 for an example of the application of these provisions.

61.23 **MISCELLANEOUS**

Assets derived from other assets.

Where

- assets have merged,
- an asset has divided or otherwise changed its nature, or
- different rights or interests in or over any asset have been created or extinguished at different times,

and the value of any asset disposed of is thus derived from one or more other assets previously acquired into the same ownership, the asset disposed of is treated for the purposes of taper relief as having been acquired at the earliest time at which any asset from which its value is derived was acquired. For the purpose only of determining whether the asset disposed of was a business asset (see 61.4 above) at a time when another asset from which its value is derived was owned by the person making the disposal, that other asset is deemed to be, or to be comprised in, the asset disposed of.

[*TCGA 1992, Sch A1 para 14; FA 1998, s 121(2)(4), Sch 20*].

For taper relief rules for **options**, see 6.7 ASSETS. For rules concerning **Lloyd's ancillary trust funds**, see 64.1 UNDERWRITERS.

61.24 **Property settled by a company.** Where an asset is placed into trust by a company which has an interest in the trust, a gain on a disposal of that asset by the trustees would, in the absence of any special rule, qualify for taper relief, whereas if the asset had been retained by the company it would not so qualify (but would be reduced or extinguished by indexation relief computed beyond April 1998 — see 34.1 INDEXATION). As a compromise, such a disposal is kept within the taper relief provisions but the relief is restricted to the rate applicable to non-business assets.

The detailed rules prevent any part of a gain accruing to trustees on the disposal of an asset from being treated as a gain on disposal of a business asset (see 61.4 above) if the settlor is a company which has an interest in the settlement, i.e. may benefit from it (as defined), at the time of the disposal. The provisions apply equally if an associated company (as defined) may benefit from the trust, but do not apply at all unless the company or an associated company is within the charge to corporation tax on chargeable gains for the accounting period in which the chargeable gain accrues.

[*TCGA 1992, Sch A1 para 17; FA 1998, s 121(2)(4), Sch 20; ITTOIA 2005, Sch 1 para 448; FA 2006, Sch 12 para 27*].

61.25 **Shares acquired in reconstruction of mutual businesses etc.** Where shares are issued to members on the reconstruction of a 'mutual company' and otherwise fall, by virtue of *TCGA 1992, s 136* (see 58.6 SHARES AND SECURITIES), to be treated in the hands of a person to whom they are issued as having been acquired at the same time as the interest for which they are exchanged, the shares are treated for taper relief purposes as having been acquired at the time they were issued to the person concerned and not at any earlier time. A '*mutual company*' means a mutual insurance company (i.e. an insurance company, as defined, carrying on a business without having a share capital) or a company of another description carrying on a business on a mutual basis. A similar rule applies where, in consequence of the incorporation of a registered friendly society (see 22.47 EXEMPTIONS AND RELIEFS), a member of the registered society (or branch) becomes a member of the incorporated society (or branch).

[*TCGA 1992, Sch A1 para 18; FA 1998, s 121(2)(4), Sch 20; FA 2002, Sch 9 paras 5(13), 7; SI 2001 No 3629, Art 71*].

Gains in connection with reorganisations of mutual businesses. A gain is not eligible for taper relief if it accrues on a disposal in connection with a 'relevant reorganisation' or on anything which, in a case in which capital sums are received under or in connection with a relevant reorganisation, falls under *TCGA 1992, s 22* (see 9.1 CAPITAL SUMS DERIVED FROM ASSETS) to be treated as a disposal. A '*relevant reorganisation*' means

- any '*scheme of reconstruction*' (within *TCGA 1992, s 136* — see 58.6 SHARES AND SECURITIES) applying to a mutual company (defined as above);
- the transfer of the whole of a building society's business to a company (see 58.22 SHARES AND SECURITIES);
- the incorporation of a registered friendly society (see 22.47 EXEMPTIONS AND RELIEFS).

[*TCGA 1992, s 214C; FA 1998, s 121(3)(4), Sch 21 para 7; FA 2002, Sch 40 Pt 3(2); SI 2001 No 3629, Art 68*].

Thus where, for example, a cash bonus is received by a member on the occurrence of any of the above events, no taper relief can be applied to the resulting gain.

61.26 **Apportionments.** Any apportionment needed for the purposes of taper relief is to be made on a 'just and reasonable' basis and on the assumption that amounts accrue evenly over a period. [*TCGA 1992, Sch A1 para 21; FA 1998, s 121(2)(4), Sch 20*].

Provision of assets. References to the acquisition of an asset which was provided, rather than acquired, by the person making the disposal are references to its provision.

Part disposals. In relation to part disposals (see 15.7 COMPUTATION OF GAINS AND LOSSES), references to an asset disposed of are to be taken as references to an asset of which there is a part disposal.

[*TCGA 1992, Sch A1 para 22(3)(4); FA 1998, s 121(2)(4), Sch 20*].

62 Time Limits—Fixed Dates

Cross-references. See also 12.5 CLAIMS; 63 TIME LIMITS—MISCELLANEOUS.

Scope of chapter. This chapter lists fixed date time limits (for capital gains tax) falling in the **twelve months to 30 September 2007**. It also notes time limits for corporation tax on chargeable gains where these are dependent upon the company's accounting date (see also Tolley's Corporation Tax).

Exercise of HMRC discretion. The legislation dealing with certain claims and elections allows the time limit to be extended at the discretion of the Commissioners of HMRC (or, before 18 April 2005, the Board of Inland Revenue) but where this is not the case the Commissioners (or Board) may make an extension by exercising its collection and management powers. Cases in which they would do so are limited but there would be a presumption in favour of admitting a late claim where there had been a relevant error on the part of HMRC, and the claim is made shortly after the error has been drawn to the taxpayer's attention; where the taxpayer has given clear notice of his intention to claim, but before the time limit expires he has not completed any statutory requirement or specified the claim in sufficient detail; or where the reason for the delay in making the claim was clearly beyond the taxpayer's control (e.g. because he—or in the case of a company the only individual who had the relevant information and experience—was seriously ill and there was no-one else who could reasonably be expected to stand in his shoes). The same stance seems to be taken as regards the withdrawal of elections that are stated to be irrevocable. Claims that have not become final may be withdrawn (even after the time for making a claim has expired), and the same applies to elections that are not irrevocable (HMRC Capital Gains Manual CG 13800–13850).

62.1 TIME LIMITS OF ONE YEAR OR LESS

(*a*) **Three months from beginning of company accounting period.**

Coming within charge to corporation tax. For accounting periods beginning on or after 22 July 2004, a company must notify HMRC of the beginning of its first accounting period and of the beginning of any subsequent accounting period which follows a period of dormancy within three months after the beginning of that accounting period. See 54.18 RETURNS.

(*b*) **30 September 2006** for action in respect of **2005/06.**

Self-assessment. If a taxpayer does not wish to compute his own liability to income tax and/or CGT, he must file his tax return on or before 30 September following the year of assessment to which it relates. See 54.5 RETURNS.

(*c*) **5 October 2006** for action in respect of **2005/06.**

Chargeability to tax. A person chargeable to CGT for a year of assessment must, unless he has received a tax return for completion, notify HMRC, within six months after the end of that year, that he is so chargeable. See 48.1 PENALTIES.

(*d*) **Nine months from end of company accounting period.**

Payment of tax. Payment of corporation tax in respect of chargeable gains is normally required by the day following the expiry of nine months from the end of the accounting period if interest on unpaid tax is to be avoided. ('Large' companies must pay by instalments for accounting periods ending on or after 1 July 1999.) See 47.2 PAYMENT OF TAX.

(*e*) **31 January 2007** for action in respect of **2005/06.**

(i) *Returns.* A person other than a company who has received a self-assessment tax return for completion must generally file it on or before 31 January following the year of assessment to which it relates. See 54.2 RETURNS.

(ii) *Payment of tax.* CGT is normally due on or before 31 January following the year of assessment. See 47.1 PAYMENT OF TAX.

(*f*) **5 April 2007** for action in respect of **2005/06**.

(i) *Claims following late assessments.* A claim (including a supplementary claim) which could not have been allowed but for the making of an assessment to CGT after the year of assessment to which it relates or the making (after 10 July 2003) of an HMRC amendment to a self-assessment issued as part of an enquiry closure notice (see 54.11 RETURNS), may be made at any time before the end of the year of assessment following that in which the assessment or amendment was made. See 12.5 CLAIMS.

(ii) *Claims following discovery assessments.* Where a discovery assessment not involving fraudulent or negligent conduct is made, a relevant claim, election etc. can be made, revoked or varied within a year after the end of the year of assessment (or company accounting period) in which the assessment was made. The provisions apply also to an HMRC amendment to a self-assessment issued after 10 July 2003 as part of an enquiry closure notice (see 54.11 RETURNS). See 12.5 CLAIMS.

(iii) *Tax over-repaid.* This (and any associated excess repayment supplement) may be recovered by the end of the year of assessment (or company accounting period) following that in which the repayment was made, where the normal time limit for assessment has expired. This deadline is extended in the event of an HMRC enquiry into a self-assessment tax return. See 47.12 PAYMENT OF TAX.

(iv) *Capital payments made by an overseas resident settlement.* Broadly, trustees of overseas resident settlements must distribute capital gains no later than the end of the year of assessment following that in which the gains arose if a supplementary CGT charge under *TCGA 1992, s 91* on UK resident and domiciled beneficiaries is to be avoided. See 44.15 OFFSHORE SETTLEMENTS for the detailed rules, including those for matching capital payments with gains.

(*g*) **Twelve months from end of company accounting period.**

(i) *Chargeability to tax.* A company chargeable to corporation tax for an accounting period must, unless it has received notice to file a return for that period, notify HMRC, within twelve months after the end of that period, that it is so chargeable. See 54.18 RETURNS.

(ii) *Corporation tax returns.* A company must generally comply with a notice to make a corporation tax return within twelve months of the end of the relevant accounting period or, if later, within three months of service of the notice. See 54.18 RETURNS.

62.2 ONE-YEAR TEN-MONTH (APPROX.) TIME LIMITS (AND EQUIVALENT TWO-YEAR TIME LIMITS FOR COMPANIES)

That is, for CGT, action in respect of **2004/05** must be taken on or before **31 January 2007** (and for the purposes of corporation tax on chargeable gains, where applicable, action must be taken within two years after the end of the accounting period in question).

(*a*) **Quoted shares and securities held on 6 April 1965.** Election for adoption of 6 April 1965 values for quoted securities (within either of the two categories) that were held on that date, where the first relevant disposal since 19 March 1968 took place during a particular year of assessment (or company accounting period) must be made on or before the first anniversary of 31 January following that year of assessment (or within two years after the end of that accounting period). With respect to disposals after 5 April 1985 (31 March 1985 for companies) the foregoing is to be read as if '5 April 1985' or '31 March 1985' (as relevant) were substituted for '19 March 1968'. See 7.3 ASSETS HELD ON 6 APRIL 1965. An election is only relevant if the rules for ASSETS HELD ON 31 MARCH 1982 (8) do not apply.

(*b*) **Miscellaneous disposals of assets held on 6 April 1965.** Election for adoption of 6 April 1965 value of miscellaneous assets (apart from quoted investments and UK land disposed of for a consideration including development value) disposed of must be made on or before the first anniversary of 31 January following the year of assessment (or within two years after the end of the company accounting period) in which the disposal was made. See 7.8 ASSETS HELD ON 6 APRIL 1965. An election is only relevant if the rules for ASSETS HELD ON 31 MARCH 1982 (8) do not apply.

(*c*) **Assets held on, and gains arising before, 31 March 1982.** The latest time for making an irrevocable election for universal re-basing at 31 March 1982 is the first anniversary of 31 January following the year of assessment (or two years after the end of the company accounting period) in which 'the first relevant disposal' occurs. See 8.3 ASSETS HELD ON 31 MARCH 1982. A claim for 50% relief in taxing deferred charges on gains before 31 March 1982 must be made on or before the first anniversary of 31 January following the year of assessment (or within two years after the end of the company accounting period) in which the disposal or deferred gain in question occurs or accrues. See 8.12 ASSETS HELD ON 31 MARCH 1982.

(*d*) **Loss relief for subscribing individual shareholders.** A claim for a loss arising in a year of assessment on a disposal of qualifying unlisted shares by a subscriber to be set against his income of that year or the preceding year must be made on or before the first anniversary of 31 January following the year in which the loss is incurred. See 40.13 LOSSES.

(*e*) **Furnished holiday accommodation.** A claim for 'averaging' of let periods of holiday accommodation must be made on or before the first anniversary of 31 January following the relevant year of assessment (or within two years after the end of the relevant company accounting period). See 24.1 FURNISHED HOLIDAY ACCOMMODATION.

(*f*) **Loss on right to unascertainable consideration.** An election to treat a loss arising on disposal after 9 April 2003 of a right to unascertainable consideration as accruing in an earlier year, enabling the loss to be set against the gain on the disposal in respect of which the right was acquired must be made on or before the first anniversary of 31 January following the actual tax year of the loss. See 40.18 LOSSES.

(*g*) **Relief for trading losses to be set against chargeable gains of a person other than a company.** A claim to set off a trading loss against chargeable gains of the same or the preceding year of assessment, which can normally be made only in conjunction with a claim under *ICTA 1988, s 380* against income, must be made on or before the first anniversary of 31 January following the year of assessment in which the loss is incurred. See 40.7 LOSSES.

A separate election may be made, within the time limit above, to disregard taper relief in computing the amount of trading loss available to set off against gains for the same year of assessment and/or the preceding year. (For losses sustained in 2004/05 onwards, this applies automatically.) See 40.7 LOSSES.

(*h*) **Relief for post-cessation expenditure of a trade to be set against chargeable gains of a person other than a company.** A claim to set off excess post-cessation expenditure of a trade against chargeable gains, which can be made only in conjunction with a claim under *ICTA 1988, s 109A* against income, must be made on or before the first anniversary of 31 January following the year of assessment in which the expenditure is incurred. See 40.7 LOSSES.

(*j*) **Amendment of tax return.** A person other than a company has up to twelve months after the filing date (which itself is normally 31 January following the year of assessment) to notify an amendment to his tax return. See 54.6 RETURNS.

(*k*) **Appropriation of asset to trading stock.** An election may be made to treat the transfer as, effectively, taking place at cost instead of market value. See 6.3 ASSETS (and note that for companies, where the accounting period in question ends before 1 July 1999, a six-year time limit applies; thereafter, a two-year time limit applies).

(*l*) **Small part disposals of land (claim for disposal not to be treated as such).** See 38.8 and 38.10 LAND. Note that for companies, where the accounting period in question ends before 1 July 1999, a six-year time limit applies; thereafter a two-year time limit applies.

(*m*) **Earn-out rights.** An election for a right to receive securities of unascertainable value acquired in consideration for a transfer of securities not to be treated as a security itself for chargeable gains purposes must be made on or before the first anniversary of 31 January following the tax year in which the earn-out right is conferred (or within two years of the end of the accounting period in which it is conferred). See 58.5 SHARES AND SECURITIES.

(*n*) **Incorporation relief.** An election to disapply incorporation relief under *TCGA 1992, s 162* on a transfer of a business to a company must be made on or before the first anniversary of 31 January following the year of assessment in which the transfer takes place. This applies only if *all* the shares etc. received in exchange for the business transferred are disposed of by the end of the year of assessment following that in which the transfer takes place; in other cases, an extra one year is given to make the election (see 62.4 below). See 33.11 HOLD-OVER RELIEFS.

(*p*) **Same-day acquisitions of shares.** With regard to shares acquired by an individual on the same day, an election may be made to treat certain shares acquired under employee share options as acquired separately from other shares for the purpose of identifying the shares comprised in any subsequent part disposal. The election must be made on or before the first anniversary of 31 January following the year of assessment in which falls the first disposal falling to be matched with acquisitions on the day in question. See 59.2 SHARES AND SECURITIES — IDENTIFICATION RULES.

(*q*) **Trusts with vulnerable beneficiaries.** A vulnerable person election allowing claims to be made for special income tax and capital gains tax treatment must be made on or before the first anniversary of 31 January following the tax year in which the election is to take effect. See 57.9 SETTLEMENTS.

62.3 TWO-YEAR TIME LIMITS

That is, for CGT, where applicable, action in respect of **2004/05** must be taken by **5 April 2007** (and for the purposes of corporation tax on chargeable gains, action must be taken within two years after the end of the accounting period in question).

(*a*) **Relief for assets of negligible value, loans to traders becoming irrecoverable and loans to traders evidenced by qualifying corporate bonds.** Broadly, a claim to this effect may be made within two years after the end of the year of assessment (or company accounting period) in which the relevant date falls. See 40.9, 40.10, 40.11 LOSSES. (The last-mentioned relief is abolished for loans made after 16 March 1998 — see 40.11 LOSSES.)

(*b*) **Loss relief for subscribing investment companies.** A claim for a loss arising on a disposal of qualifying unlisted shares by a subscribing investment company to be set against income must be made within two years after the end of the accounting period in which the loss is incurred. See 40.15 LOSSES.

(*c*) **Loss relief for companies investing under the Corporate Venturing Scheme.** A claim for a loss arising on a disposal of shares to which corporate venturing scheme investment relief is attributable to be set against income must be made within two years after the end of the accounting period in which the loss is incurred. See 17.20 CORPORATE VENTURING SCHEME.

(*d*) **Amendment of company tax return.** A company has up to twelve months after the filing date (which itself is normally twelve months after the end of the relevant accounting period) to notify an amendment to its tax return. [*FA 1998, Sch 18 para 15*].

(*e*) **Groups of companies: pre-entry losses.** Certain elections have to be made within two years after the end of the accounting period in which a loss or gain (as appropriate) is made. See 27.24–27.26 GROUPS OF COMPANIES.

62.4 TWO-YEAR TEN-MONTH (APPROX.) TIME LIMITS

Therefore, action in respect of **2003/04** must be taken on or before **31 January 2007**.

Incorporation relief. An election to disapply incorporation relief under *TCGA 1992, s 162* on a transfer of a business to a company must be made on or before the second anniversary of 31 January following the year of assessment in which the transfer takes place. If, however, *all* the shares etc. received in exchange for the business transferred are disposed of by the end of the year of assessment following that in which the transfer takes place, the deadline is brought forward by one year as in 62.2(*n*) above. See 33.11 HOLD-OVER RELIEFS.

62.5 THREE-YEAR TIME LIMITS

Therefore, action in respect of **2003/04** must be taken by **5 April 2007**.

Charities. Where property ceases to be held on charitable trusts in circumstances giving rise to a deemed disposal by the trustees, an assessment on the cumulative gains must be made within three years after the end of the tax year in which the cessation occurred. See 10.3 CHARITIES.

62.6 THREE-YEAR TEN-MONTH (APPROX.) TIME LIMITS

Therefore, action in respect of **2002/03** must be taken on or before **31 January 2007**.

(*a*) **Deceased persons.** Assessments on gains arising or accruing before death must be made on the deceased's personal representatives on or before the third anniversary of 31 January following the year of assessment in which death occurred. Assessments to recoup loss of tax due to the deceased's fraudulent or negligent conduct can be made, on or before that date, for any year of assessment ending not earlier than six years before the death. See 5.7 ASSESSMENTS, 23.5 FRAUDULENT OR NEGLIGENT CONDUCT.

(*b*) **Rollover relief — provisional claims.** If not superseded by an actual claim or withdrawn, a provisional claim for rollover relief on replacement of business assets for capital gains tax (not corporation tax) purposes lapses on the third anniversary of 31 January following the year of assessment in which the disposal occurred. (This does not in itself prevent an actual claim being made at a later date.) See 55.2 ROLLOVER RELIEF.

62.7 FIVE-YEAR TEN-MONTH (APPROX.) TIME LIMITS

That is, for CGT, where applicable, action in respect of **2000/01** must be taken by **31 January 2007** (and for the purposes of corporation tax on chargeable gains, where applicable, action must be taken within six years after the end of the accounting period in question).

The more important of these time limits are as follows.

(*a*) **Error or mistake claims.** See 12.7 CLAIMS.

(*b*) **Raising assessments** other than in cases of fraudulent or negligent conduct. See 5.7 ASSESSMENTS.

(*c*) **Claim against double assessment** where the same person has been assessed 'for the same cause' in the same year. See 5.5 ASSESSMENTS.

(*d*) **Relief against double taxation.** See 19 DOUBLE TAX RELIEF.

(*e*) **Relief for unremittable overseas gains.** See 45.5 OVERSEAS MATTERS.

(*f*) **Disposals by way of gift etc. (election for tax to be paid by instalments).** See 47.6 PAYMENT OF TAX.

(*g*) **Capital distributions in respect of shares etc.** Where allowable expenditure on shares etc. is less than the amount of a capital distribution, the taxpayer may make an election to set off all that expenditure against the distribution. See 58.10 SHARES AND SECURITIES.

(*h*) **Extension of private residence exemption to a residence occupied by a dependent relative on or before 5 April 1988.** See 49.6 PRIVATE RESIDENCES.

(*j*) **Hold-over relief** for gifts of business assets and assets on which inheritance tax is chargeable etc. See 33.1–33.8 HOLD-OVER RELIEFS.

(*k*) **Rollover relief.** See 55.2 ROLLOVER RELIEF and note that the period for claiming relief starts with the later of the end of the year of assessment or company accounting period in which the disposal takes place and the end of the year of assessment or company accounting period in which the new assets are acquired.

(*l*) **Relief on compulsory acquisition of land.** See 38.11 LAND and note also that proceeds must not be invested in land which would be exempt from CGT under the private residence rules on a disposal of it within six years of acquisition.

(*m*) **EIS deferral relief.** See 21.14 ENTERPRISE INVESTMENT SCHEME and note that the period for claiming relief starts with the later of the end of the year of assessment in which the gain accrues and the end of the year of assessment in which the qualifying investment (i.e. a subscription for EIS shares) is acquired.

(*n*) **VCT deferral relief.** See 66.12 VENTURE CAPITAL TRUSTS and note that the period for claiming relief starts with the later of the end of the year of assessment in which the gain accrues and the end of the year of assessment in which the qualifying investment (i.e. a subscription for VCT shares) is acquired.

(*p*) **Relief for post-employment deductions to be set against chargeable gains.** A claim can be made only in conjunction with a claim under *ICTA 1988, s 201AA* (now *ITEPA 2003, ss 555–564*) against income. See 40.7 LOSSES.

(*q*) **Notification of capital losses.** See 40.3 LOSSES.

(*r*) **CVS investment relief.** See 17.4 CORPORATE VENTURING SCHEME.

(*s*) **CVS deferral relief.** See 17.21 CORPORATE VENTURING SCHEME.

62.8 OTHER ACTION BEFORE 6 APRIL 2007

Tax-loss selling. Appropriate disposals should be made if it is desired to realise capital losses to set off against chargeable gains in 2006/07. See 34 INDEXATION; 40 LOSSES; 61.2 TAPER RELIEF; and, with regard to companies, 13.14 COMPANIES.

Use of annual exemption. Action should be taken so as to utilise the CGT annual exemption for 2006/07. See 2.3 ANNUAL RATES AND EXEMPTIONS.

'Bed and breakfasting' of shares and securities, i.e. the sale and subsequent repurchase of shares etc. where the seller and buyer are *not* the same person, e.g. disposal by one spouse, repurchase by the other. See 59.2 SHARES AND SECURITIES — IDENTIFICATION RULES.

63 Time Limits—Miscellaneous

Cross-reference. See 62 TIME LIMITS—FIXED DATES (in particular, the head-note dealing with HMRC's practice regarding late claims and elections which apply equally here).

Note. Time limits other than by reference to the end of a year of assessment or company accounting period are set out below.

63.1 TIME LIMITS OF ONE YEAR OR LESS

(*a*) **Thirty days**

(i) For appeals against assessments, HMRC amendments to self-assessment tax returns and claims made outside returns, and HMRC conclusions on completion of enquiry, notice of appeal must be lodged within thirty days. See 4.1 APPEALS, 12.3 CLAIMS. For postponement of tax, see 37.2 INTEREST AND SURCHARGES ON UNPAID TAX, 47 PAYMENT OF TAX.

(ii) Rejections of HMRC corrections to self-assessment tax returns must be made within thirty days after the notice of correction. See 54.6 RETURNS.

(iii) For appeals to the High Court, written notice requiring the Commissioners to state and sign a case must be sent to their Clerk within thirty days of the determination. The case stated must be transmitted to the High Court within thirty days of its receipt. See 4.21, 4.23 APPEALS.

(iv) Returns of income and chargeable gains for 1995/96 and earlier years ought strictly to be completed within thirty days of issue.

(v) For 1995/96 and earlier years, capital gains tax generally becomes due and payable thirty days after the issue of the notice of assessment (if later than 1 December following the end of the year of assessment). Interest may run on tax which is yet to be due and payable. See 37.1–37.4 INTEREST AND SURCHARGES ON UNPAID TAX and 47 PAYMENT OF TAX.

(vi) A notice specifying the apportionment of a reduction in tax liability involving more than one period or person, in certain discovery cases, must be given within thirty days of the inspector issuing a notice apportioning it. See 12.5 CLAIMS.

(*b*) **Forty days**

Where a disqualifying event occurs in relation to a qualifying option granted under the Enterprise Management Incentives scheme, the option must be exercised within forty days after that event if the shares acquired by the exercise are to be qualifying shares and thus attract beneficial taper relief treatment on disposal. See 20.24 EMPLOYEE SHARE SCHEMES.

(*c*) **Ninety-two days**

The grant of an option under the Enterprise Management Incentives scheme must be notified to HMRC within ninety-two days after the option is granted (thirty days for options granted before 11 May 2001). See 20.24 EMPLOYEE SHARE SCHEMES.

(*d*) **Three months**

(i) Appeals against a decision of the Commissioners for HMRC (or, before 18 April 2005, the Board of Inland Revenue) relating to residence, ordinary residence or domicile. See 52.8 RESIDENCE AND DOMICILE.

(ii) Certain reliefs in relation to a disposal of shares in a 'controlled foreign company' must be claimed within three months of the later of the end of the relevant accounting period and the date that an assessment made on the claimant company in respect of the apportioned profits of the controlled foreign company becomes final and conclusive. See 45.7 OVERSEAS MATTERS.

(iii) Applications for judicial review must be made within three months of the date when the grounds for application arose. See 4.26 APPEALS.

(iv) Certain particulars of a settlement with a foreign element etc. must be supplied within three months of the creation of it. See 44.21 OFFSHORE SETTLEMENTS.

(*e*) **Six months**

In respect of the form of rollover relief available on a disposal of shares to an approved share incentive plan or, before 6 April 2001, to an employee share ownership trust, the disposal consideration must be used to acquire replacement assets within six months (or longer period in certain cases) of the disposal. See 20.20, 20.32 EMPLOYEE SHARE SCHEMES.

(*f*) **Twelve months**

(i) To qualify for rollover relief an acquisition must be made twelve months before the associated disposal (or three years after). See 55.1 ROLLOVER RELIEF. This applies also to the general relief for compulsory acquisition of land (see 38.11 LAND).

(ii) Where, within twelve months of receipt, a capital sum, received as compensation is applied in replacing an asset lost or destroyed, a claim may be made for the deemed disposal arising on the loss etc. to be treated as made for a 'no gain, no loss' consideration. See 9.3 CAPITAL SUMS DERIVED FROM ASSETS.

(iii) Certain particulars of a settlement with a foreign element etc. must be supplied within twelve months of certain events. See 44.21 OFFSHORE SETTLEMENTS.

(iv) Acquisition of ordinary shares of an approved venture capital trust, against which the deferral of a capital gain can be claimed, must take place within a qualifying period of twelve months before the disposal or other chargeable event giving rise to the gain and twelve months afterwards. Note that the relief is abolished for shares issued after 5 April 2004. See 66.12 VENTURE CAPITAL TRUSTS.

(v) Acquisition of EIS shares must, for the purpose of EIS capital gains deferral relief, take place within twelve months before the disposal or other chargeable event giving rise to the gain to be deferred (or three years after). See 21.10 ENTERPRISE INVESTMENT SCHEME.

(vi) Acquisition by a company of qualifying shares under the Corporate Venturing Scheme must, for the purposes of deferral relief, take place within twelve months before the disposal or other chargeable event giving rise to the gain to be deferred (or three years after). See 17.21 CORPORATE VENTURING SCHEME.

63.2 **TWO-YEAR TIME LIMITS**

(*a*) **Only or main residence**. The election by individuals with more than one private residence must be made within two years after the acquisition of the second residence. Subsequent notice of variation must be given within two years after the date from which it is to take effect. See 49.4 PRIVATE RESIDENCES.

(*b*) **Family arrangements and disclaimers after death** must be made within two years of the death. See 18.6 DEATH.

(*c*) **Unpaid corporation tax — certain capital distributions and reconstructions.** In a case where unpaid corporation tax falls to be recovered from a shareholder in receipt of a capital distribution, notice of liability must be served within two years after the later of the date on which the assessment was made on the company and the date on which the tax became due and payable. See 13.9 COMPANIES. Similar rules apply in a case where unpaid corporation tax falls to be recovered from a third party following a scheme of reconstruction involving the transfer of a company's business to another company. See 13.10 COMPANIES.

(*d*) **Unpaid corporation tax — groups of companies.** A group company can be liable for unpaid corporation tax on a chargeable gain arising from the disposal before 1 April 2000 by another group member of an asset owned by the first-mentioned company at any time in the two years preceding the time the gain accrued. See 27.8 GROUPS OF COMPANIES and see also 63.3(*g*) below.

The principal company of the group (and other group members in certain circumstances) can be held liable for unpaid corporation tax on a chargeable gain accruing before 1 April 2000 under the provisions for companies leaving a group within six years after acquiring an asset intra-group (see 63.5(*a*) below). Notice of liability must be served within two years after the later of the date on which the assessment was made on the chargeable company and the date on which the tax became due and payable. See 27.9 GROUPS OF COMPANIES and see also 63.3(*g*) below.

(*e*) **Know-how.** A joint election for know-how not to be treated as goodwill must be made within two years of the disposal. See 6.4 ASSETS.

(*f*) **Company ceasing to be UK resident etc: postponement of charge on deemed disposal.** Subject to certain conditions an election may be made by the company concerned and the principal company within two years of the cessation of UK residence etc. so that postponement is obtained. If any part of the postponed gain becomes chargeable on the principal company, it and the company concerned can elect within two years of the time the gain becomes chargeable that any unrelieved capital losses of the company be set against the gain. See 45.12 OVERSEAS MATTERS.

(*g*) **Share Incentive Plan: rollover relief.** In respect of the form of rollover relief available on a disposal of shares, other than by a company, to the trustees of an approved share incentive plan, the relief must be claimed within the two years beginning with the acquisition of the replacement assets. See 20.21 EMPLOYEE SHARE SCHEMES.

63.3 THREE-YEAR TIME LIMITS

(*a*) **Rollover relief** is only available if the acquisition is made within three years after the disposal (or twelve months before). See 55.1 ROLLOVER RELIEF. This applies also to the general relief for compulsory acquisition of land (see 38.11 LAND).

(*b*) **Acquisition of EIS shares** must, for the purpose of EIS capital gains deferral relief, take place within three years after the disposal or other chargeable event giving rise to the gain to be deferred (or twelve months before). See 21.10 ENTERPRISE INVESTMENT SCHEME.

(*c*) **Acquisition by a company of qualifying shares under the Corporate Venturing Scheme** must, for the purpose of corporate venturing deferral relief, take place within three years after the disposal or other chargeable event giving rise to the gain to be deferred (or twelve months before). See 17.21 CORPORATE VENTURING SCHEME.

(*d*) For shares issued after 5 April 2000, a gain deferred by means of **EIS capital gains deferral relief** becomes chargeable if the investor becomes neither resident nor ordinarily resident in the UK within the period ending immediately before the third anniversary of the issue date or, if later, the third anniversary of the date of commencement of the qualifying trade (except in certain cases of temporary working abroad). See 21.10 ENTERPRISE INVESTMENT SCHEME and see also 63.4(*a*) below.

(*e*) For shares issued after 5 April 2000, a gain deferred by means of **VCT capital gains deferral relief** becomes chargeable if the investor becomes neither resident nor ordinarily resident in the UK within the three years beginning with his acquisition of the VCT shares (except in certain cases of temporary working abroad). See 66.12 VENTURE CAPITAL TRUSTS and see also 63.4(*b*) below.

(*f*) **Unpaid corporation tax — groups and non-resident companies.** The principal company of the group (and other group members in certain circumstances) or a controlling director of a non-UK resident company trading in the UK through a permanent establishment (previously a branch or agency) can be held liable for unpaid corporation tax on a chargeable gain accruing after 31 March 2000 to a group company or to the non-resident company in question. Notice of liability must be served within three years beginning with the date on which the liability of the defaulting company is finally determined. See 27.8 GROUPS OF COMPANIES and see also 63.2(*e*) above and (*j*) below.

(*g*) **Unpaid corporation tax — company ceasing to be UK-resident.** Any tax due by a company ceasing to be UK resident and not paid within six months of becoming payable can, within three years of the amount being finally determined, be recovered from a person who is, or was in the twelve months before residence ceased, a member of the same group or a controlling director. See 45.13 OVERSEAS MATTERS.

(*h*) **Unpaid corporation tax — non-resident companies.** A member of the same group of companies or a controlling director can be held liable for unpaid corporation tax on a chargeable gain accruing before 1 April 2000 to a non-UK resident company trading in the UK through a branch or agency. Notice of liability must be served within three years beginning with the date on which the liability of the defaulting company is finally determined. See 45.13 OVERSEAS MATTERS and see also (*g*) above.

(*j*) **Distribution of gains by overseas companies.** Capital gains tax or corporation tax on chargeable gains paid by a participator on part of a gain accruing after 6 March 2001 which is apportioned to him can be used to offset income tax, capital gains tax or corporation tax in respect of the distribution if the gain is distributed within three years after the end of the period of account of the non-resident company in which it accrued or within four years beginning with the date it accrued, whichever gives the earlier date. For gains accruing before 7 March 2001, the distribution must be made within the two years beginning with the date the gain accrued. See 45.6 OVERSEAS MATTERS.

63.4 FIVE-YEAR TIME LIMITS

(*a*) For shares issued before 6 April 2000, a gain deferred by means of **EIS capital gains deferral relief** becomes chargeable if the investor becomes neither resident nor ordinarily resident in the UK within the five years beginning with the issue of the EIS shares (except in certain cases of temporary working abroad). See 21.10 ENTERPRISE INVESTMENT SCHEME and see also 63.3(*e*) above.

(*b*) For shares issued before 6 April 2000, a gain deferred by means of **VCT capital gains deferral relief** becomes chargeable if the investor becomes neither resident nor ordinarily resident in the UK within the five years beginning with his acquisition of the VCT shares (except in certain cases of temporary working abroad). See 66.12 VENTURE CAPITAL TRUSTS and see also 63.3(*f*) above.

63.5 SIX-YEAR TIME LIMITS

(*a*) **Intra-group transfers: company ceasing to be a member of a group.** If a company leaves a group within six years of the transfer to it of a capital asset by another member of the group, it will be liable on the market value of the asset at the time of transfer less the 'no gain/no loss' transfer price. See 27.9 GROUPS OF COMPANIES. Similar provisions apply where, after 16 March 1998, the company which acquired such an asset becomes an investment trust or venture capital trust. See 27.14, 27.15 GROUPS OF COMPANIES.

(*b*) **Company ceasing to be UK resident etc: postponement of charge on deemed disposal.** If within six years after the cessation of residence etc. the company disposes of assets held at that time, the whole or the appropriate part of the postponed gain (insofar as not already so treated) is deemed to accrue to the principal company. See 45.12 OVERSEAS MATTERS.

64 Underwriters at Lloyd's

64.1 **INDIVIDUALS**

Trust funds. Trust funds held by an underwriting member of Lloyd's are classified as to '*premium trust funds*' (defined by reference to the Lloyd's Sourcebook, part of the FSA Handbook, made by the Financial Services Authority under *Financial Services and Markets Act 2000*), 'new-style special reserve funds' (see below) and 'ancillary trust funds'. An '*ancillary trust fund*', in relation to the member, does not include his premium trust fund or new-style special reserve fund but otherwise means any trust fund (including an 'old-style special reserve fund' as below) required or authorised by Lloyd's rules, or required by a members' agent of his.

Use of an asset as part of an ancillary trust fund does not in itself make the asset a business asset for taper relief purposes, but neither does such use prevent the asset from being a business asset; such use is not regarded as non-qualifying use in relation to assets used for more than one purpose at the same time (see 61.13 TAPER RELIEF). [*TCGA 1992, Sch A1 para 19; FA 1998, s 121(2)(4), Sch 20; FA 2003, s 160(4)*].

Premium trust funds. In general terms, disposals of assets in a Lloyd's member's premium trust fund are now only taken into account for income tax purposes, consideration relating to acquisitions and disposals of those assets being left out of account for CGT purposes.

Basis of assessment of profits. For 1997/98 and subsequent years, the profits charged for a year of assessment are those which are *declared* in the corresponding underwriting year (an underwriting year and a year of assessment being deemed to correspond to each other if the underwriting year ends in the year of assessment). Profits for a particular underwriting year are declared in the underwriting year immediately following the underwriting year in which the particular year is closed. For example, the profits of the underwriting year 1999 are declared in 2002 and taxed in 2002/03, the 1999 year having closed at the end of 2001. This does not apply to ancillary trust funds, for which see below as regards the CGT position.

Gains from ancillary trust funds. Gains arising from the disposals of assets forming part of an ancillary trust fund are charged in the normal way to CGT (and losses are treated as allowable capital losses) on a fiscal year basis. See 64.7 below for rollover relief on disposal of ancillary trust fund assets to a successor company.

Entitlement of member. A member is treated for CGT purposes as absolutely entitled as against the trustees to the assets forming part of any of his premium trust fund or ancillary trust funds. From 1994/95, money deposits required to be paid out of a premium trust fund under overseas regulatory arrangements are still deemed to form part of the fund. Both such funds are therefore not 'settled property' as in 57.2 SETTLEMENTS.

[*FA 1993, ss 171, 172, s 174(1), ss 176, 184; FA 1994, s 228, Sch 21 para 1(1)(3)(a), paras 2, 3, 8, Sch 26 Pt V; F(No 2)A 1997, s 22(1)(7), s 36, Sch 6 para 20; ITTOIA 2005, Sch 1 para 464; SI 2001 No 3629, Arts 79, 82*].

Special reserve funds. The reference above to a '*new-style special reserve fund*' is to the 'new-style' funds authorised by *FA 1993, s 175(1)* to be set up in respect of 1992 and subsequent underwriting years although the capital of '*old-style special reserve funds*' authorised under *ICTA 1988, s 452(1)* for underwriting years prior to 1992 may be transferred to a new style fund within certain time limits, any asset so transferred being deemed for CGT purposes to be disposed of by the member at its market value at the time of transfer. [*FA 1993, s 175(4), Sch 20 para 14(1)*]. As regards a new-style special reserve fund, the member is treated for CGT purposes as absolutely entitled as against the trustees to the assets forming part of his fund but, for 1994/95 and later years, the transfer by the member of an asset to the trustees is a chargeable event for CGT purposes. Profits and losses arising from assets forming part of the fund are excluded for all CGT (and income tax) purposes. [*FA 1993, s 175, Sch 20 para 8, para 9(1); FA 1994, s 228, Sch 21 para 13; SI 1999 No 3308, Reg 4*].

On cessation of underwriting, whether on death or otherwise, the amount of a member's new style special reserve fund, so far as not required as cover for cash calls and syndicate losses, must be paid over to him. Where an asset is transferred by the trustees to the member or his personal representatives or assigns on or after 1 January 2000, whether on cessation or otherwise, the asset is treated as acquired by the member etc.,

- in a case where the asset was held by the trustees at the end of the 'penultimate underwriting year', at the end of that year at its market value at that time;
- in a case where it was acquired by the trustees after the end of the 'penultimate underwriting year', at the date on which, and for the consideration for which, it was acquired by the trustees; and
- in a case where it was both acquired by the trustees and transferred to the member etc. before the end of the 'penultimate underwriting year', at the date of transfer at its market value at that time.

Before 1 January 2000, an asset transferred to the member out of the special reserve fund on cessation was treated as acquired by him at its market value as at the end of the 'penultimate underwriting year' and there were no other special rules. The '*penultimate underwriting year*' is the underwriting year corresponding to the year of assessment immediately preceding the member's final year of assessment.

[*FA 1993, s 175, Sch 20 para 11(4)(5); FA 1994, s 228, Sch 21 para 15(2)(3); SI 1995 No 353, Reg 8; SI 1999 No 3308, Reg 6(5)*].

Syndicate capacity. From 1995 onwards, members have been able to buy and sell syndicate capacity, i.e. the right to underwrite on a particular syndicate, which is a chargeable asset for CGT purposes. For the CGT consequences, see 64.5 and 64.7 below, and as regards capacity held via a Members' Agent Pooling Arrangement (MAPA), see 64.6 below.

64.2 CORPORATE UNDERWRITERS

For accounting periods ending after 31 December 1993 or, as the case may require, for the underwriting year 1994 and subsequent years, *FA 1994, ss 219–227, 229, 230* (i.e. *FA 1994, Pt IV Ch V* except *s 228* and *Sch 21*) broadly apply the above provisions *mutatis mutandis* to corporate members of Lloyd's except that there is no provision for a corporate member to set up a new-style special reserve fund.

64.3 SCOTTISH LIMITED PARTNERSHIPS AND LIMITED LIABILITY PARTNERSHIPS

Regulations provide for the tax treatment of profits or losses arising to the partners of a Scottish limited partnership or a limited liability partnership from its business as a Lloyd's underwriting member. They apply to accounting periods of Scottish limited partnerships ending on or after 1 December 1997 and to accounting periods of limited liability partnerships ending on or after 14 February 2006. See *SI 1997 No 2681* as amended by *SI 2006 No 111*.

64.4 OVERSEAS RESIDENTS

Where a capital gains tax treatment, rather than an income tax, or corporation tax charging income, treatment, would apply to assets held as part of an individual underwriter's or corporate underwriter's trust funds, then if the individual or company is neither resident nor, in the case of an individual, ordinarily resident in the UK, he or the company is still liable to capital gains tax or corporation tax on chargeable gains on such assets which are situate in the UK. See 6.2 ASSETS and 45.3 OVERSEAS MATTERS. For this purpose, investments comprised in the Lloyd's American and Canadian Trust Funds are regarded as not situate in the UK. Investments held in the Lloyd's Sterling Trust Fund are situate in the UK, except for non-UK equities. The double taxation arrangements between the UK and the relevant countries should be consulted, as well as the relevant domestic legislation of the overseas countries concerned. For overseas matters generally and for the determination of residence and domicile, see 45 OVERSEAS MATTERS and 52 RESIDENCE AND DOMICILE.

64.5 TRANSACTIONS IN SYNDICATE CAPACITY

A Lloyd's member can participate in a particular underwriting syndicate only to the extent that he possesses the relevant rights to do so. From the 1995 Account onwards, a member is permitted to realise all or part of his rights in any particular syndicate (his syndicate capacity) by offering them for sale at one of the periodical syndicate capacity auctions or by entering into a bilateral agreement with a purchaser. Each member's right to participate in each syndicate of which he is a member is therefore a marketable asset. For capital gains tax purposes, and for corporation tax purposes for accounting periods ending before 1 April 2002, any gain arising on disposal is a chargeable gain. For corporation tax purposes for accounting periods ending after 31 March 2002, gains are dealt with under the intangible assets regime (see 14.13 COMPANIES—CORPORATE FINANCE AND INTANGIBLES) and are consequently removed from the charge to corporation tax on chargeable gains. In exceptional cases, transactions in syndicate capacity may be sufficiently frequent so as to constitute a trade of dealing, in which case income tax may apply in the case of an individual. The date of disposal in the case of an auction is normally the day after it takes place. Allowable costs of disposal include tendering and auction expenses. HMRC do not accept that rights in syndicates had any acquisition value for CGT purposes prior to the 1995 Account. The allowable expenditure on the disposal of rights acquired subsequently by purchase will be their acquisition cost plus any incidental expenditure. As regards a new syndicate set up for the 1996 Account onwards, the allowable expenditure is normally the price paid to the managing agent by the member to join that syndicate. The initial Lloyd's admission fee is also an allowable expense, which may be relieved once the member has resigned.

HMRC have confirmed that business asset taper relief is available on disposals after 5 April 1998 other than by corporate members. (Lloyd's Market Bulletin TAX/HAB/In/Y2122, 6 September 1999).

'Bespoke' capacity is the term given to rights held by a member in his own name. Bespoke capacity must be kept separate from MAPA (Members' Agent Pooling Arrangement) capacity, for which see 64.6 below.

As regards acquisitions and disposals of syndicate rights by non-corporate members after 5 April 1999, such rights are a qualifying asset for the purposes of ROLLOVER RELIEF (55) on replacement of business assets. [*TCGA 1992, s 155; FA 1999, s 84*].

Current HMRC practice is to treat all a member's bespoke capacity in one syndicate as a single asset. Further acquisitions are treated as enhancement expenditure, part disposals are dealt with under the normal rules at 15.7 COMPUTATION OF GAINS AND LOSSES, and taper relief is calculated by reference to the date of the initial acquisition. This represents a change of view: the Revenue previously considered that acquisitions and disposals of capacity should be treated similarly to those of shares and securities. (Lloyd's Market Bulletin TAX/HAB/In/Y2122, 6 September 1999).

A member's interest in a syndicate (though not his ancillary trust funds — see 64.1 above) is a business asset for the purposes of RETIREMENT RELIEF (53) (**abolished after 5 April 2003**). Where a member disposes of the whole of his syndicate capacity in any one year of account such that he does not underwrite in the following year of account, a 'material disposal of business assets' (see 53.4 RETIREMENT RELIEF) will have taken place. A disposal of part only of a member's syndicate capacity in any one year was regarded by the Revenue as being merely a reduction in the scale of the business, and retirement relief would not be granted. (Lloyd's Market Bulletin TAX/HAB/In/Y2122, 6 September 1999).

Conversion to corporate status. The transfer of syndicate capacity by an individual member to a corporate vehicle, whether by gift or in exchange for shares, is a disposal for CGT purposes. See 64.7 below for rollover relief on transfer of syndicate capacity in exchange for shares. Alternatively, where the necessary conditions are satisfied, retirement relief (before 6 April 2003 only) and/or the reliefs at 33.1, 33.10 HOLD-OVER RELIEFS are available. (Lloyd's Market Bulletin TAX/HAB/In/Y2122, 6 September 1999).

Example

Justin acquired a £1m line on Syndicate X for £60,000 on 30 April 2004. He acquired a further £250,000 line on the same Syndicate for £20,000 on 1 June 2005. The £1.25m line is a single asset for CGT purposes costing £80,000. On 1 May 2006, Justin sells a £500,000 line for £50,000. The remaining £750,000 line is therefore worth £75,000. Incidental costs of acquisition and disposal are ignored for the purposes of this example. Justin makes no other disposals in 2006/07.

	£
Proceeds	50,000
Deduct Cost:	
$\pounds 80{,}000 \times \dfrac{50{,}000}{50{,}000 + 75{,}000} =$	32,000
Untapered gain	18,000
Deduct Taper relief £18,000 @ 75%*	13,500
Chargeable gain (subject to annual exemption)	£4,500

* Business asset held for 2 whole years (30.4.04–1.5.06)

64.6 **Members' Agent Pooling Arrangements.** A Members' Agent Pooling Arrangement (MAPA), in relation to a member, is an arrangement under which

- a 'members' agent' arranges for the member's participation in Lloyd's syndicates,
- the member must participate in each syndicate to which the arrangement relates, and
- the extent of his participation is determined by the members' agent or in accordance with a formula provided for in the arrangement.

A '*members' agent*' is a person registered as such at Lloyd's and acting as such for the member concerned. [*FA 1999, s 83*(*1*)(*2*)].

MAPAs have been in existence since 1994 and allow a member access to a wide range of syndicates. It is understood that most individual members underwrite wholly or partly through a MAPA rather than solely through rights (capacity) held directly in individual syndicates. In the absence of special rules, there could be numerous transactions each year which should strictly count as a CGT disposal. For example, whenever a new participant joins a MAPA, the total syndicate rights held in the MAPA have to be re-divided between all participants, so that each existing participant will have disposed of a fraction of his capacity to the new participant. Sales of rights by the MAPA and changes in the syndicates in which it partakes likewise give rise to CGT disposals by its participants. The Revenue and Lloyd's negotiated a practice designed to avoid most of the complexity. For example, where a member transferred capacity into a MAPA (either from his bespoke capacity (see 64.5 above) or from another MAPA), no disposal was deemed to arise on any part of that capacity which was retained within his share of the MAPA capacity (Lloyd's Market Bulletin TAX/HAB/In/Y1082, 4 February 1999). Previous practice was replaced by the statutory provisions in *Finance Act 1999* described below. They do not apply to corporate members of Lloyd's. The provisions do apply, with appropriate modification, to Scottish limited partnerships which are Lloyd's members (see 64.3 above).

The statutory provisions apply where an individual (i.e. non-corporate) Lloyd's member has entered into a MAPA, and apply for the purpose of determining any CGT liabilities of his that may arise from transactions effected in pursuance of the MAPA. They apply in relation to any MAPA entered into on or after 6 April 1999 and also to any MAPA entered into earlier and still in existence on that date (see also below). Under these provisions, the syndicate rights held by the member under the MAPA are treated as a single asset acquired by him at the time of his entering into the MAPA. The member's initial acquisition cost is the amount paid by him on joining the MAPA. Any other amount paid by him under the MAPA is treated as allowable enhancement expenditure on the single asset. A disposal (or, as the case may be, a part disposal) of the single asset occurs *only* when an amount is paid to the member, the disposal proceeds being equal to that amount, or, by virtue of *TCGA 1992, s 24(1)* (see 9.1 CAPITAL SUMS DERIVED FROM ASSETS), where the asset is entirely extinguished.

If the MAPA was entered into before 6 April 1999, the time of acquisition is taken to be the earliest time that the member acquired any of the syndicate rights still held by him through the MAPA immediately before 6 April 1999, the initial acquisition cost is the amount paid for such of those rights as were acquired at that earlier time, and the amount paid for any additional rights acquired between that time and 6 April 1999 (and still held) qualifies as enhancement expenditure. The incidental costs of rights acquired before 6 April 1999 (and still held) are taken to be the incidental costs of acquiring the single asset.

References above to the payment of any amount include payments in money's worth, in which case the member's expenditure or disposal proceeds, as the case may be, is equivalent to the market value of the money's worth at the time of payment. This covers, for example, the transfer by a member into a MAPA of syndicate rights which he previously owned directly, and *vice versa*. On the other side of the coin, a transfer of rights by a member into a MAPA constitutes a disposal by him of those rights at market value, and similarly a transfer of rights from a MAPA to a member constitutes an acquisition by him at market value.

[*FA 1999, ss 82, 83*].

Note that where a member has two or more MAPAs, each is treated as a *separate* single asset.

As regards acquisitions and disposals after 5 April 1999 of syndicate rights held through a MAPA and treated as a single asset as above, such rights are a qualifying asset for the purposes of ROLLOVER RELIEF (55) on replacement of business assets. [*TCGA 1992, s 155; FA 1999, s 84*]. It is thought that additions on or after 6 April 1999 to a MAPA held on and before that date (which fall to be treated as expenditure on enhancing the single asset — see above) would qualify for rollover relief by virtue of ESC D22 which allows gains to be rolled over against enhancement expenditure in appropriate circumstances (see 55.3 ROLLOVER RELIEF).

Syndicate capacity, whether held through a MAPA or otherwise, is a business asset for the purposes of TAPER RELIEF (61). The treatment of further acquisitions as enhancement expenditure means that taper relief on a disposal or part disposal falls to be calculated by reference to the date of the initial acquisition. (Lloyd's Market Bulletin TAX/HAB/In/Y2122, 6 September 1999).

64.7 CONVERSION TO UNDERWRITING THROUGH SUCCESSOR COMPANY

Where an individual Lloyd's underwriter converts to underwriting through a company under Lloyd's rules, two reliefs are available to defer charges to CGT on certain assets transferred to the company. The provisions apply to disposals after 5 April 2004. To qualify for the reliefs the following conditions must be met.

(*a*) The member must give (and not withdraw) notice of his resignation from membership of Lloyd's in accordance with the rules or practice of Lloyd's, and in accordance with those rules must not undertake any new insurance business at Lloyd's after the end of his '*last underwriting year*' (i.e. the underwriting year in which, or at the end of which, he ceases to be an underwriting member and becomes a non-underwriting member).

(*b*) All of the member's 'outstanding syndicate capacity' must be disposed of by the member under a 'conversion arrangement' to a 'successor company' with effect from the beginning of the underwriting year next following the member's last underwriting year. For this purpose, a member's '*outstanding syndicate capacity*' consists of any of his syndicate capacity (see 64.5 above) which is not disposed of to a person other than a 'successor member' (as defined by the rules or practice of Lloyd's) at or before the end of his last underwriting year and which does not cease to exist with effect from the end of that year. A '*conversion arrangement*' is one made under the rules or practice of Lloyd's. A '*successor company*' is a corporate member (within *FA 1994, Pt IV Ch V*) which is a successor member.

(*c*) Immediately before the disposal of outstanding syndicate capacity, the member must control (within *ICTA 1988, s 416*) the successor company and beneficially own more than 50% of its ordinary share capital (as defined in *ICTA 1988, s 832(1)*).

(*d*) The disposal of outstanding syndicate capacity must be made in consideration only of the issue to the member of shares in the successor company.

(*e*) The successor company must start to carry on its underwriting business (as in *FA 1994, Pt IV Ch V*) in the underwriting year next following the member's last underwriting year.

For the purposes of these provisions, shares comprised in a letter of allotment are treated as issued unless the rights to the shares conferred by it remains provisional until accepted, and there has been no such acceptance.

Where a member has made a claim for one or more of the reliefs below and subsequently withdraws his notice of resignation from membership of Lloyd's, he must, subject to penalties for fraudulent or negligent failure, give notice in writing of such withdrawal to an HMRC officer within six months from the date of the withdrawal. All necessary adjustments can be made, whether by assessment, discharge or repayment of tax or otherwise, as a result of the withdrawal of the notice of resignation notwithstanding any time limits for making such adjustments.

[*FA 1993, s 179B, Sch 20A paras 1, 5, 9–11; FA 2004, s 144, Sch 25 para 2*].

Rollover relief on disposal of outstanding syndicate capacity. If, on the disposal of outstanding syndicate capacity in (*b*) above, the aggregate chargeable gains exceed the aggregate allowable losses and the member makes a claim to an HMRC officer, the amount of that excess is reduced for CGT purposes by 'the amount of the rolled-over gain'. For this purpose 'the amount of the rolled-over gain' is the lesser of the amount of the excess and the aggregate of any amounts which would be allowable as a deduction under *TCGA 1992, s 38(1)(a)* (cost of acquisition — see 15.4 COMPUTATION OF GAINS AND LOSSES) if the 'issued shares' were disposed of as a whole by the member in circumstances giving rise to a chargeable gain. (The '*issued shares*' are the shares in the successor company issued to the member in consideration for the disposal of outstanding syndicate capacity.)

The amount of the rolled-over gain is apportioned between the issued shares as a whole. If the issued shares are not all of the same class, the apportionment is made in accordance with their market values at the time of acquisition by the member. On a disposal by the member of an issued share (or any asset directly or indirectly derived from any issued share), the amount allowable as a deduction in computing the chargeable gain under *TCGA 1992, s 38(1)(a)* (cost of acquisition — see 15.4 COMPUTATION OF GAINS AND LOSSES) is reduced by the amount of the rolled-over gain apportioned to the share. In the case of a derived asset, the reduction is restricted to an appropriate proportion of the apportioned amount.

[*FA 1993, Sch 20A para 3; FA 2004, Sch 25 para 2*].

Rollover relief on disposal of assets of ancillary trust fund. Rollover relief is also available if at the time of, or after, the disposal of outstanding syndicate capacity in (*b*) above, assets forming some or all of the member's ancillary trust fund (ATF) are withdrawn from the fund and disposed of by him to the successor company without unreasonable delay in consideration solely of the issue to him of shares (the '*issued shares*') in that company. The member must make a claim to an HMRC officer for relief to apply, and must control the successor company and beneficially own more than 50% of its ordinary share capital throughout the period beginning with the outstanding syndicate capacity disposal and ending with the disposal of the ATF assets. Relief is not available if the member could have made a claim for rollover relief on the disposal of the outstanding syndicate capacity but has not done so. If such a claim has been made but is subsequently revoked, it is treated for this purpose as never having been made. Note that the relief is available only for the first qualifying disposal of ATF assets after 5 April 2004. Although the disposal of ATF assets must be made after 5 April 2004, it is not necessary for the disposal of the outstanding syndicate capacity to have been made after that date.

Where relief is available the excess of the aggregate chargeable gains on the disposal of the ATF assets over the aggregate allowable losses is reduced for CGT purposes by 'the amount of the rolled-over gain'.

For this purpose '*the amount of the rolled-over gain*' is the lesser of the amount of the excess (reduced, for this purpose only, in certain circumstances as indicated below) and the aggregate of any amounts which would be allowable as a deduction under *TCGA 1992, s 38(1)(a)* (cost of acquisition — see 15.4 COMPUTATION OF GAINS AND LOSSES) if the issued shares were disposed of as a whole by the member in circumstances giving rise to a chargeable gain. The excess is reduced where, immediately before the disposal of the ATF assets, the market value of those assets exceeds 'the amount of the ATF assets required'. The reduction is made by multiplying the excess by the amount of ATF assets required and dividing by the market value of the ATF assets disposed of immediately before the disposal. For this purpose, '*the amount of the ATF assets required*' is the lesser of

- the amount of security required to be provided by the member in respect of his underwriting business in his last underwriting year, and
- the amount of security required to be provided by the successor company in respect of its underwriting business in its first underwriting year.

The amount of the rolled-over gain is apportioned between the issued shares as a whole. If the issued shares are not all of the same class, the apportionment is made in accordance with their market values at the time of acquisition by the member. On a disposal by the member of an issued share (or any asset directly or indirectly derived from any issued share), the amount allowable as a deduction in computing the chargeable gain under *TCGA 1992, s 38(1)(a)* (cost of acquisition — see 15.4 COMPUTATION OF GAINS AND LOSSES) is reduced by the amount of the rolled-over gain apportioned to the share. In the case of a derived asset, the reduction is restricted to an appropriate proportion of the apportioned amount.

[*FA 1993, Sch 20A paras 4, 11(2); FA 2004, Sch 25 para 2*].

65 Unit Trusts and Other Investment Vehicles

Cross-references. See 7.2 ASSETS HELD ON 6 APRIL 1965 and 41.3 MARKET VALUE for valuation of units in unit trusts; 13.10 COMPANIES for transfers of businesses to authorised unit trusts and investment trusts; 27.2 GROUPS OF COMPANIES for intra-group disposals of assets by authorised unit trusts and investment trusts; 66.1 VENTURE CAPITAL TRUSTS.

Simon's Direct Tax Service. See Division D4.13.

65.1 COLLECTIVE INVESTMENT SCHEMES

A '*collective investment scheme*' is an arrangement with respect to property of any description, including money, the purpose or effect of which is to enable persons taking part in the arrangements (whether by becoming owners of all or part of the property or otherwise) to participate in or receive profits or income arising from the acquisition, holding, management or disposal of the property or sums paid out of such profits or income. [*TCGA 1992, s 288(1); Financial Services and Markets Act 2000, s 235; FA 2004, s 118(4); SI 2001 No 3629, Arts 62(2), 70; SI 2006 No 964, Reg 109(2)*]. The object of such a scheme is to enable a large number of investors to pool their money by investing in a professionally managed fund of investments, thus spreading risk. The most common forms of collective investment schemes are unit trusts (see 65.2 below) and open-ended investment companies (see 65.6 below). A body corporate (other than an open-ended investment company) is not regarded as a collective investment scheme, so that investment trusts (see 65.3 below), VENTURE CAPITAL TRUSTS (66), industrial and provident societies and friendly societies are not collective investment schemes. Certain limited liability partnerships may however meet the criteria. (HMRC Company Taxation Manual CTM 48070).

If under a collective investment scheme, contributions to it and profits arising from it are pooled in relation to separate parts of the property in the scheme and the participants are entitled to exchange rights in one part for rights in another, then for such exchanges after 13 March 1989 *TCGA 1992, s 127* (reorganisation etc. of shares etc.) is not to prevent the exchange constituting a disposal and acquisition for capital gains tax purposes. For this purpose *TCGA 1992, s 127* includes a reference to that provision as applied by *TCGA 1992, s 132* (conversion of securities) but does not include a reference to that provision as applied by *TCGA 1992, s 135* (exchange of securities for those in another company) or *s 136* (scheme of reconstruction); see 58.1, 58.4, 58.6 and 58.7 SHARES AND SECURITIES. [*TCGA 1992, s 102; FA 2002, Sch 9 paras 5(4), 7*].

For exchanges before 14 March 1989 and after 22 July 1987 any question as to whether arrangements of a multi-portfolio collective investment scheme which provided for pooling constituted a single collective investment scheme was determined for capital gains tax purposes without regard to any entitlement of the participants to exchange rights in one part of the property for rights in another. [*TCGA 1992, s 102; F(No 2)A 1987, s 78*]. As regards exchanges before 23 July 1987 the position was governed by *Arbuthnot Financial Services Ltd v CIR Ch D, [1985] STC 211* (a stamp duty case in which it was decided that a participant had transferred his units in one fund of a multi-fund unit trust scheme to the managers in consideration for units in another fund of the scheme). See Revenue Tax Bulletin April 1997 pp 419–421 for a summary of the legislative history.

65.2 AUTHORISED UNIT TRUSTS

These are 'unit trust schemes' in respect of which an order under *Financial Services and Markets Act 2000, s 243* is in force. A '*unit trust scheme*' is a collective investment scheme under which the property is held on trust for the participants, but the Treasury may by regulation provide for any scheme of a specified description not to be treated as a unit trust scheme for capital gains purposes. [*TCGA 1992, s 99(2)(3); ICTA 1988, s 468(6); Financial Services and Markets Act 2000, s 237(1), Sch 20 para 4(3); FA 2004, s 118(2); SI 1988*

No 266; SI 2000 No 2550; SI 2001 No 3629, Arts 62(1), 116]. Certain limited partnership schemes and employee share schemes have been excepted from treatment as unit trust schemes for such purposes.

For capital gains purposes, any unit trust scheme is treated as if the scheme were a company and the rights of the unit holders were shares in the company, and in the case of an authorised unit trust as if the company were resident and ordinarily resident in the UK. [*TCGA 1992, s 99(1)*]. A unit trust scheme other than an authorised unit trust is not within the charge to corporation tax so that the trustees are assessable to capital gains tax unless there is exemption under 65.5 below (HMRC Capital Gains Manual CG 41351).

Gains realised by authorised unit trusts (including umbrella schemes, see below) are not chargeable gains. [*TCGA 1992, s 100(1)*].

Monthly savings schemes. An individual acquiring units in authorised unit trusts under a monthly savings scheme can opt for a simplified arrangement for computing any chargeable gains arising. To do so, he must make a written request to his tax office no later than the first anniversary of 31 January following the first tax year in which he both disposes of such units and either his *total* gains for the year exceed the annual exemption or his total proceeds exceed twice the exemption or his disposals of other assets result in a net loss. The arrangement must cover all an individual's monthly schemes in the same unit trust. Under the arrangement, the individual will be treated in most cases as having made a single annual investment in the seventh month of the trust's accounting year. This will be made up of savings plus reinvested income less any small withdrawals in the year concerned. Following the freezing of indexation allowance to April 1998 (see 34.1 INDEXATION), the arrangement is withdrawn in all cases where savings commenced after 5 April 1998 and in other cases for acquisitions in any accounting year of a trust ending after 5 April 1999. Where the arrangement is in operation, it has effect in determining the availability or otherwise of the 'bonus year' addition for taper relief purposes (see 61.2 TAPER RELIEF). (HMRC Statement of Practice SP 2/99). (This Statement of Practice updates SP 2/97 which itself replaced SP 3/89).

Accumulation units. No distributions are made to holders of accumulation units. Instead the net amount that would normally be distributed is automatically reinvested in the fund. No new units are issued but the value of the existing holding of units is increased. Where the notional distribution is charged to income tax as income of the unit holder (or would be but for a relief) or is taken into account as a receipt in calculating the profits, gains or losses of the unit holder for income tax purposes, it is treated as allowable expenditure for CGT purposes. Where the trust is an authorised unit trust, the deemed expenditure is treated as having been incurred on the 'distribution date' for the 'distribution period' in respect of which the amount is reinvested. In the case of any other unit trust scheme, the expenditure is deemed to be incurred on the date on which the notional distribution is reinvested. For this purpose, a '*distribution period*' is a period by reference to which the total amount available for distribution to unit holders is ascertained, and the '*distribution date*' for a distribution period is the date specified under the terms of the trust for any distribution for that period or, if no such date is specified, the last day of the period. [*ICTA 1988, s 468H(3)(4); TCGA 1992, s 99B; F(No 2)A 2005, s 21; SI 2006 No 964, Regs 15(2)(4), 89*]. Note that this provision applies only to disposals on or after 16 March 2005: previously, however, the Revenue operated a broadly similar practice (see HMRC Capital Gains Manual CG 57707).

Umbrella schemes. An '*umbrella scheme*' is an authorised unit trust which has arrangements for separate pooling of investors' contributions and the profits or income out of which payments are to be made to them, and under which investors can exchange rights in one pool for rights in another. [*TCGA 1992, s 99A(1); FA 2004, s 118(3)*].

For 2004/05 and subsequent years, and for accounting periods beginning after 31 March 2004, each sub-fund of the umbrella scheme is treated for capital gains purposes as being itself an authorised unit trust and the umbrella scheme as a whole is treated as not being an authorised unit trust or any other form of collective investment scheme (so that *TCGA 1992, s 102* does not apply to it — see 65.1 above). Any person who has rights in a particular sub-fund is treated as a unit holder in the deemed authorised unit trust consisting of that sub-fund. An umbrella scheme continues effectively to be treated as itself being an authorised unit trust for the purposes of *TCGA 1992, s 100(1)* above, *TCGA 1992, s 139(4)* (reconstructions involving transfer of business — exclusion of transfers to authorised unit trusts etc. (see 13.10 COMPANIES) and *TCGA 1992, s 271(1)(j)* (exemption for 2005/06 and earlier years for disposal of units in an authorised unit trust which is also a personal pension scheme etc. — see 22.56 EXEMPTIONS AND RELIEFS). [*TCGA 1992, s 99A(2)–(4); FA 2004, s 118(3)(5), Sch 42 Pt 3*].

Previously, there were no specific capital gains provisions, but in practice HMRC apply substantially the same principles as above, so that each sub-fund is treated as a separate authorised unit trust and the scheme as a whole is transparent. Note that *TCGA 1992, s 102* at 65.1 above applies to umbrella schemes before the enactment of *TCGA 1992, s 99A*. See Revenue Tax Bulletin April 1997 pp 419–421.

65.3 INVESTMENT TRUSTS

See 65.4 below for real estate investment trusts.

Gains realised by investment trusts are not chargeable gains. [*TCGA 1992, s 100(1)*].

An investment trust is a 'company' fulfilling the following conditions.

(*a*) It is not a close company.

(*b*) It is resident in the UK.

(*c*) Its income consists 'wholly or mainly' of income deriving from shares or securities or, for accounting periods beginning before 19 July 2006, eligible rental income (within *ICTA 1988, s 508A*). In practice, 'wholly or mainly' is taken as 70% or more (50% or more in the case of the first accounting period of a newly-formed company) (HMRC Capital Gains Manual CG 41414).

(*d*) No 'holding' in any one company represents more than 15% of the value of its investments, unless that company is itself an investment trust or would be so but for being unquoted. This requirement is waived in respect of investments which, when acquired, represented no more than 15% of the value of the investments, and in respect of an investment held on 6 April 1965 provided that the holding represented not more than 25% of the overall value of the investments at that date. There is no waiver in either case where there has been an 'addition' to the holding.

(*e*) Its 'ordinary share capital' (and every class thereof, if there is more than one) is listed in the Official List of the Stock Exchange.

(*f*) Its Memorandum or Articles prohibit the distribution by way of dividend of gains arising from the sale of investments.

(*g*) It does not retain an amount greater than 15% of its income which is either derived from shares or securities or, for accounting periods beginning before 19 July 2006, consists of eligible rental income as in (*c*) above. However, this requirement does not apply if the excess over the 15% limit is less than £10,000 (or proportionately reduced amount if the period is less than twelve months) or the company is required by law to retain an amount of income for the period in excess of the 15% limit and in circumstances such that the aggregate of the excess of the amount of income retained for the period over the amount of income required to be retained for the period and any amount distributed in respect of the period is less than £10,000 (or proportionately reduced amount where the period is less than twelve months).

(*h*) It is approved by HMRC.

For the purposes of (*c*) and (*g*) above, for accounting periods beginning on or after 1 October 2002, a company's total income and the income which it derives from shares or securities is to be determined without reference to any debtor relationships within the loan relationship rules (i.e. relationships within 14.2–14.6 COMPANIES—CORPORATE FINANCE AND INTANGIBLES in the case of which the company stands in the position of debtor as regards the debt in question).

As regards (*c*) above, units in an authorised unit trust (see 65.2 above) or shares in an open-ended investment company (OEIC) incorporated in the UK (see 65.6 below) are for this purpose treated as shares in a company. Where the condition at (*d*) above is then relevant, it is regarded as being satisfied *provided that* during the period of time in the investment trust's accounting period during which it held investments in an authorised unit trust or OEIC, the authorised unit trust or OEIC itself satisfied the condition at (*c*) above. This condition will always be regarded as satisfied where the authorised unit trust is a 'securities fund' under *Financial Services Act 1986* or subsequent corresponding legislation or the OEIC is a 'securities company' under corresponding regulations. These practices are modified as necessary to embrace rights in a sub-fund of an umbrella scheme treated as an authorised unit trust for tax purposes and shares in an umbrella company which confer rights in a sub-fund treated as an OEIC for tax purposes. (HMRC Statement of Practice 3/97, replacing SP 7/94).

'*Company*' includes any body corporate or unincorporated association, but not a partnership. [*TCGA 1992, s 288*(*1*)].

'*Shares*' includes stock.

'*Holding*' means the shares or securities of whatever class or classes held in any one company. Where, in connection with a scheme of reconstruction (see 13.10 COMPANIES, 58.6 SHARES AND SECURITIES), a company issues shares or securities to persons holding shares or securities in another in respect of and in proportion to (or as nearly as may be in proportion to) such holdings, without the recipients becoming liable for any consideration, the old and the new holdings are treated as the same. In relation to share etc. issues made after 16 April 2002, 'scheme of reconstruction' is accorded the definition in *TCGA 1992, Sch 5AA* (see 58.6 SHARES AND SECURITIES).

For accounting periods ending after 5 April 1988, if the investing company is a member of a group (i.e. a company and its 51% subsidiaries), money owed to it by another group member is treated as a security and, as such, as part of its holding in that other group member. Holdings in companies which are members of a group (whether or not including the investing company) are treated as holdings in a single company.

An '*addition*' is made to a holding whenever the investing company acquires further shares or securities in any company in which it already has a holding, otherwise than by being allotted them without liability for consideration (e.g. a bonus issue). The holding is deemed to have been acquired at the date of the latest addition.

'*Ordinary share capital*' means all the issued share capital (by whatever name called) of a company, other than that which produces a fixed rate of dividend and is non-participating. [*ICTA 1988, s 832*(*1*)].

[*ICTA 1988, s 842; FA 1988, s 117; FA 1990, s 55; FA 1994, ss 146, 170, Sch 17 para 8; FA 1996, s 160, Sch 30 paras 2, 3, Sch 34 para 7; FA 2002, ss 82, 83, Sch 9 paras 4*(*7*), *8*(*4*), *Sch 25 para 56, Sch 40 Pt 3*(*2*)(*13*); *FA 2004, s 45*(*4*); *FA 2006, ss 143, 145*(*2*)].

See Tolley's Corporation Tax for the definition of a close company.

See HMRC Statement of Practice 2/99 (as in 65.2 above) re monthly savings schemes, which applies to investment trusts as it does to authorised unit trusts.

65.4 **REAL ESTATE INVESTMENT TRUSTS**

For accounting periods beginning on or after 1 January 2007, companies meeting the necessary conditions (see below) can elect to become real estate investment trusts. The 'property rental business' (as defined, and including both UK and overseas property) of such a trust is ring-fenced and treated as if it were a separate business carried on by a separate company. Profits and gains arising in respect of the business are exempt from corporation tax (although a tax charge may arise in certain tax avoidance cases and the Treasury has powers to make regulations under which an amount will be charged to tax where a company fails to meet certain debt funding requirements or where it pays a dividend to a person with a 10% or more interest in the company). Profits of the company which are not from the tax-exempt business are chargeable to corporation tax at the main rate (currently 30%). To the extent that dividends paid by the company derive from ring-fenced profits and gains they are taxed in the hands of the recipient as property income rather than as distributions. Companies wishing to enter the regime must pay an entry charge. Companies may exit the regime at any time by notice, and may be required to do so by HMRC notice where they repeatedly fail to meet certain conditions. Exit from the regime is automatic where one or more of conditions (1), (2), (5) or (6) below cease to be met. The provisions apply in modified form to enable groups of companies to become group real estate investment trusts. [*FA 2006, ss 103–145, Schs 16, 17*]. For full coverage of the provisions see Tolley's Corporation Tax.

Conditions. A company may make an election to become a real estate investment trust only if it meets the following conditions.

(1) It is resident in the UK and not resident in another place for the tax purposes of that other place.

(2) It is not an open-ended investment company (see 65.6 below).

(3) The shares forming its ordinary share capital are listed on a recognised stock exchange (see 58.23 SHARES AND SECURITIES).

For the special tax regime to apply for an accounting period, the company must meet the above conditions and the following conditions throughout the period.

(4) It is not a close company (defined, subject to certain modifications, as in *ICTA 1988, s 414*) or is a close company only by virtue of having a limited partnership which is a collective investment scheme (see 65.1 above) as a participator.

(5) Each share issued by the company either forms part of the company's ordinary share capital or is a non-voting fixed-rate preference share (within *ICTA 1988, Sch 25 para 2*).

(6) The company is not a party to any loans under which the creditor is entitled to interest which varies according to the results of the company's business, which depends on the value of the company's assets or which exceeds a reasonable commercial return or under which the creditor is entitled on repayment to an amount greater than the amount lent or an amount reasonably comparable with the amount that would generally be repayable under the terms of securities listed on a recognised stock exchange.

For the property rental business of the company to be '*tax-exempt business*', to which the special tax regime applies, for an accounting period, the following conditions must be met.

(i) Throughout the accounting period, the property rental business involves at least three properties.

(ii) Throughout the accounting period, no one property represents more than 40% of the total value (under international accounting standards) of the properties 'involved' in the property rental business.

(iii) Throughout the accounting period, the property rental business does not involve property falling to be treated under generally accepted accounting practice as owner-occupied (as further defined).

(iv) Subject to certain exceptions, at least 90% of the profits of the property rental business are distributed by way of dividend before the tax return filing date for the accounting period.

(v) At least 75% of the company's total profits (as defined) for the accounting period arise from the property rental business.

(vi) At the beginning of the accounting period, at least 75% of the company's assets by value are involved in the property rental business.

References above to property which is '*involved*' in a business are references to an estate, interest or right by the exploitation of which the business is conducted.

The Treasury has powers to make regulations for dealing with minor or inadvertent breaches of conditions (3), (4) and (i) to (vi) above as an alternative to requiring the company to leave the regime.

[*FA 2006, ss 106–108, 116*].

Capital gains. On entry into the regime the company's accounting period is deemed to come to an end, and a new one begins. 'Assets' held by the company which immediately before entry into the regime are involved (as above) in the property rental business are treated for corporation tax purposes as sold immediately before, and reacquired immediately after, entry at market value. Any gain arising on the deemed sale is not a chargeable gain (and a loss is not an allowable loss). [*FA 2006, s 111*].

A gain accruing to the company on the disposal of an asset which was used wholly and exclusively for the purposes of the tax-exempt business is not a chargeable gain and a loss is not an allowable loss (but see below where the disposal is in the course of non-exempt trade). Likewise, a gain accruing on disposal of an asset, which was so used but for an aggregate period of less than one year in which it was partly used for the purposes of the tax-exempt business and partly used for the purposes of a non-exempt business of the company, is not a chargeable gain (and a loss is not an allowable loss). Where the aggregate period of mixed use is one year or more, any gain or loss is apportioned and any part reasonably attributable to the tax-exempt business, having regard to the extent of and the length of the periods of use for the different purposes, is not a chargeable gain or allowable loss. Corporation tax on the non-exempt part of a gain is chargeable at the main rate (currently 30%).

Where an asset which has been used wholly and exclusively for the purposes of the tax-exempt business begins to be used (otherwise than by being disposed of in the course of trade), wholly and exclusively for other purposes, it is treated as disposed of and immediately reacquired at that time at market value. Any gain is not a chargeable gain (and a loss is not an allowable loss).

Where an asset which has been used wholly and exclusively for the purposes of the tax-exempt business is disposed of in the course of trade for the purposes of a non-exempt business of the company, the disposal is treated as made in the course of that business (so that the gain is brought into account as part of the business's trading profits) and any deemed disposal and reacquisition on entry into the regime is disregarded. Where the asset was held at the time of entry, the company may claim repayment of part of the entry charge. This provision applies in particular where a property has been developed since acquisition, the cost of that development exceeds 30% of the fair value (under international accounting standards) of the property at the time of entry into the regime or of acquisition, whichever is later, and the company disposes of the property within three years of completion of the development.

Where an asset which has been used wholly and exclusively for the purposes of a non-exempt business of the company begins to be used wholly and exclusively for the purposes of the tax-exempt business, it is treated as disposed of by the non-exempt business and immediately reacquired by the tax-exempt business at market value. Any gain arising is a chargeable gain, and any loss an allowable loss.

[*FA 2006, ss 124–127*].

On exit from the regime, any assets involved in the tax-exempt business immediately before exit are treated as being disposed of immediately before exit and reacquired immediately afterwards at market value. The above provisions then apply to determine whether, and to what extent, the gain is a chargeable gain or the loss is an allowable loss.

If a company which has chosen to leave the regime, having been within it for a continuous period of less than ten years, disposes of an asset which was involved in the tax-exempt business within two years of exit, its liability to corporation tax is determined disregarding any deemed disposals of the asset on exit from the regime, on transfer out of the tax-exempt business and, where a gain arose, on entry to the regime. Where a company is forced, by HMRC notice or automatically, to leave the regime within ten years of entry, HMRC may direct (subject to appeal to the Special Commissioners) that the above provisions and corporation tax provisions generally will apply with specified modifications.

[*FA 2006, ss 131–133*].

For the purposes of the above provisions, an '*asset*' includes part of an asset and an interest in, or right in relation to, an asset. References to assets used in a business include references to assets acquired for the purposes of the business and not in use in another business, assets available for use in the business and assets which are in any other way held in respect of, or associated or connected with, the business. Deemed disposals and reacquisitions of assets have effect for the purposes of all subsequent disposals, real or deemed, except where indicated above. [*FA 2006, ss 141, 142*].

65.5 UNIT TRUSTS FOR EXEMPT UNIT HOLDERS

If, for any reason other than non-residence, none of the holders of units in a unit trust scheme would be liable to capital gains tax (or to corporation tax on chargeable gains) on a disposal of units, gains accruing to the trust itself are not chargeable gains. In determining whether this rule applies, no account is taken of any units in a scheme which, having been disposed of by a unit holder, are held by the managers of the scheme, in their capacity as managers, pending disposal. For 2005/06 onwards, no account is taken of the possibility of a corporation tax charge on income in respect of a gain accruing to an insurance company (within *ICTA 1988, s 431*) or an incorporated or registered friendly society (within *ICTA 1988, s 466(2)*). [*TCGA 1992, s 100(2)–(2B); F(No 2)A 2005, s 20*]. Note that for 2004/05 and earlier years, the disregard for units held by the scheme managers was by virtue of Revenue Extra-Statutory Concession D17.

This exemption applies whenever the gains accrued, but is of practical importance only in relation to unit trust schemes which have not been designated as in 65.2 above.

65.6 OPEN-ENDED INVESTMENT COMPANIES

An '*open-ended investment company*' (OEIC) is a collective investment scheme under which the investments belong beneficially to, and are managed on behalf of, a body corporate having as its purpose the spreading of investment risk and giving its members the benefit of the results of management of those funds which is incorporated in the United Kingdom. [*ICTA 1988, s 468(10) treated as inserted by SI 1997 No 1154, Reg 10(4), s 468A(2); TCGA 1992, s 99(2)(c) treated as inserted by SI 1997 No 1154, Reg 20; s 288(1); Financial Services and Markets Act 2000, s 236; F(No 2)A 2005, s 16; SI 2001 No 3629, Art 166; SI 2006 No 964, Regs 4, 109(2)*]. It is a form of retail investment fund which can be set up in the UK from 1997. An OEIC is constituted as a company, with directors, and issues shares rather than units as with a unit trust. The Treasury are given power by *FA 1995, s 152* and *F(No 2)A 2005, s 17* to make the regulations necessary to establish a tax regime for UK incorporated OEICs (see now *SI 2006 No 964* and previously *SI 1997 No 1154*). The regime is broadly equivalent to that which applies to authorised unit trusts and their investors. See Tolley's Corporation Tax for information concerning dividend and interest distributions.

OEICs are chargeable to corporation tax at a rate equal to the lower rate of income tax. [*ICTA 1988, ss 468(1A), 468A; F(No 2)A 2005, s 16; SI 1997 No 1154, Reg 5*]. Gains accruing to an OEIC are not chargeable gains. [*TCGA 1992, s 100(1) as modified by SI 1997 No 1154, Reg 5; SI 1997 No 1715, Reg 4; SI 2006 No 964, Reg 100*]. Investors incur chargeable gains and allowable losses in the normal way on disposals of shares. Where shares of a given class consist of both smaller and larger denomination shares, and a person owns both, the shares are treated for CGT purposes as being securities of the same class. [*SI 1997 No 1154, Reg 24; SI 2006 No 964, Reg 76*]. The individual sub-funds of an umbrella company are treated as being separate OEICs in their own right and the umbrella company treated as if it were not a company. (An umbrella company is an OEIC whose investments are pooled separately in sub-funds, usually having different investment objectives, and whose shareholders are entitled to exchange their rights in one sub-fund for rights in another.) [*ICTA 1988, ss 468(11), 468A(3)(4); TCGA 1992, s 99AA treated as inserted by SI 2006 No 964, Reg 106; F(No 2)A 2005, s 16; SI 1997 No 1154, Reg 10(4)*]. For disposals on or after 6 April 2006 (1 April 2006 for companies), the provisions at 65.2 above, dealing with accumulation units of unit trusts, apply equally to accumulation shares in an OEIC (i.e. shares in respect of which income is credited periodically to the capital part of the scheme property of the OEIC). [*SI 2006 No 964, Reg 103*].

See HMRC Statement of Practice SP 2/99 (as in 65.2 above) re monthly savings schemes, which applies to OEICs as it does to authorised unit trusts.

Authorised unit trusts are able to convert to, or merge with, OEICs without the incurring of any significant direct tax charges. [*SI 1997 No 1154, Regs 25–27; SI 2006 No 964, Regs 78–85*]. As far as investors are concerned, the exchange of units in an authorised unit trust for shares in an OEIC is subject to the normal rules for reconstructions (see 58.6 SHARES AND SECURITIES) so that the new shares will normally stand in the shoes of the old units and have the same acquisition date and cost for CGT purposes. (Revenue Press Release 7 April 1997, para 6).

65.7 QUALIFIED INVESTOR SCHEMES

A '*qualified investor scheme*' (QIS) is a fund (either an open-ended investment company or a unit trust), authorised by the Financial Services Authority, in which a statement that the fund is a qualified investor scheme is included in the instrument constituting the scheme. [*SI 2006 No 964, Reg 53(3)*]. Only institutional and certain sophisticated investors are eligible to participate in such schemes, which can be set up from 2004.

A special tax regime applies to participants with a 'substantial holding' in a QIS with effect from 6 April 2006 (1 April 2006 for companies). Broadly, the regime operates as follows. The participant is required to ascertain the market value of his holding at specified measuring dates. The difference in value compared to the previous measuring date is then calculated, and the aggregate of those differences for a tax year or accounting period is taken. Where the aggregate is a positive amount, that amount is charged to tax under *ITTOA 2005, Pt 5 Ch 8* or under Schedule D, Case VI (and a negative amount is an income loss). The regime does not apply to participants which are charities, registered pension schemes, insurance companies (where the holding is held as an asset of its long-term insurance fund), friendly societies, persons in whose hands any profit on a sale of units in the QIS would be trading income, and other QISs. As increases in the value of a holding are taxed under the regime as income, no chargeable gain arises on disposals of all or part of the holding. A gain will arise at the time of the disposal, however, in respect of any increase in the value of the holding (or part) before entry into the regime. See below for full details.

For these purposes, a holding in a QIS is a '*substantial holding*' if the participant, either alone or together with associates (within *ICTA 1988, s 417*) or connected persons (within

ICTA 1988, s 839 — see 16 CONNECTED PERSONS), owns (otherwise than as a nominee or bare trustee) units which represent rights to 10% or more of the net asset value of the fund. [*SI 2006 No 964, Regs 53–69*].

See Tolley's Income Tax for full details of the regime.

Capital gains. On the 'first measuring date' in relation to a substantial holding in a QIS, the participant must calculate the chargeable gain or loss that would have accrued on a disposal of the holding at market value at that time.

The general rule is that the '*first measuring date*' in relation to a substantial holding is the first date on which a participant owns the substantial holding. Where the participant owns a substantial holding on 6 April 2006 (1 April 2006 for companies) that date is the first measuring date (but if the participant ceases to own a substantial holding by the measuring date first occurring after 30 June 2006 that holding does not enter the special tax regime and 1 or 6 April 2006 is not the first measuring date). Special rules apply where a participant acquires a substantial holding within the period of twelve months beginning with the date of issue of the first prospectus of a new QIS or comes to own a substantial holding in a QIS otherwise than as a result of acquiring units in it.

The gain calculated as above is not immediately chargeable (or the loss immediately allowable), but it becomes chargeable (or allowable) on disposal of all or part of the substantial holding. In the case of a disposal of part only of the holding, a corresponding part of the gain or loss is treated as accruing. On disposal of the whole of the holding, the whole gain or loss is treated as accruing or, where there was a previous part disposal, the remaining part of the gain or loss is treated as accruing.

The participant is treated as making the actual disposal of the whole or part of the substantial holding for such consideration as secures that neither a gain nor a loss accrues. This does not affect the acquisition cost of the person acquiring the holding.

Where the disposal would fall within one of the provisions listed below, the gain or loss calculated at the first measuring date is not deemed to accrue on the disposal. Instead, the transferee's holding in the QIS is treated as a substantial holding from the time of the disposal, and the gain or loss (or part thereof) is treated as accruing to the transferee on a disposal by him of all (or part) of the substantial holding. The provisions concerned are:

- *TCGA 1992, s 58(1)* (transfers between spouses or civil partners — see 42.4 MARRIED PERSONS AND CIVIL PARTNERS);
- *TCGA 1992, s 62(4)* (acquisition as legatee — see 18.9 DEATH);
- *TCGA 1992, s 139* (company reconstructions involving transfer of business — see 13.10 COMPANIES);
- *TCGA 1992, s 140A* (transfer of UK trade between companies in different EC member states — see 45.10 OVERSEAS MATTERS);
- *TCGA 1992, s 140E* (formation of SE by merger leaving assets within UK tax charge — see 13.18 COMPANIES); and
- *TCGA 1992, s 171(1)* (intra-group transfers — see 27.2 GROUPS OF COMPANIES).

TCGA 1992, s 127 (reorganisation of share capital — see 58.1 SHARES AND SECURITIES) and *TCGA 1992, s 116(10)* (reorganisations involving QUALIFYING CORPORATE BONDS (50.3)) do not apply to a substantial holding in a QIS. A transaction which would otherwise have fallen within either of those provisions is treated as involving a disposal and subsequent acquisition of the holding. The acquisition is treated as made at the market value of the holding immediately before the acquisition.

[*SI 2006 No 964, Regs 60–69*].

65.8 COURT INVESTMENT FUNDS

These are common investment funds established under *Administration of Justice Act 1982, s 42*. The Accountant General is deemed to hold the funds (together with other funds in court) as nominee or bare trustee as in 57.2 SETTLEMENTS. [*TCGA 1992, s 61, s 100*(*3*)].

Gains realised by court investment funds are not chargeable gains. [*TCGA 1992, s 100*(*1*)].

65.9 INVESTMENT CLUBS

An investment club is a group of people who join together to invest, primarily in the stock market. Each club will have its own rules, which will, *inter alia*, determine each member's proportionate entitlement to the club's investments, which will change frequently as capital is invested and withdrawn. Members share income, gains and losses according to their entitlement and are personally responsible for declaring the income etc. and personally liable for tax thereon. There are two ways in which members can return their shares of gains (and income) in a particular tax year:

- in accordance with a standard form of agreement (available from HMRC) whereby the secretary or other responsible officer makes a return of the gains based on less detailed computations than are statutorily required; or
- in accordance with strict statutory requirements, which, in addition to requiring gains (and income) to be returned by individual members, may also involve special returns being made by the treasurer and the person in whose name the club investments are held.

For 2001/02 and earlier years, there was a third method, the simplified scheme, which could be used by smaller clubs. Under the simplified scheme:

- an officer of the club applied on form 185–1 for the club to be included for a particular year;
- all capital gains were apportioned to the members as agreed by them;
- the share of gains to date of a member who left partway through the year had to be either accepted by him or apportioned between the other members as agreed by them;
- details of transactions, members and their shares of gains and income were included on the form 185–1; and
- upon agreement of the figures, the club gave each member a form 185–2 showing his shares of gains and income, which he then included in his personal tax return.

An investment club was eligible for the simplified scheme for a particular year if:

- it had no more than 20 members at any one time;
- the annual subscription did not exceed £1,000 per member;
- the net gains did not exceed £5,000;
- the average investment per head, based on cost price, did not exceed £5,000; and
- all members agreed the division of the capital gains.

The simplified scheme is withdrawn for 2002/03 and subsequent years.

(HMRC Capital Gains Manual CG 20600–20650).

65.10 VENTURE CAPITAL TRUSTS

Chargeable gains of venture capital trusts are not chargeable gains. See 66.10 VENTURE CAPITAL TRUSTS below.

66 Venture Capital Trusts

Simon's Direct Tax Service. See Division C3.11.

66.1 From 6 April 1995, the venture capital trust scheme described at 66.2 *et seq.* below was introduced to encourage individuals to invest in unquoted trading companies through such trusts. The provisions dealing with the approval of companies as venture capital trusts, and with the reliefs for investors, were introduced in *FA 1995, ss 70–72, Schs 14–16*. The Treasury has wide powers to make regulations governing all aspects of the reliefs applicable to venture capital trust investments, and for the requirements as regards returns, records and provision of information by the trust. [*FA 1995, s 73; FA 2002, s 109, Sch 33 paras 14–16; ITTOIA 2005, Sch 1 para 477*]. See *SI 1995 No 1979*.

See also HMRC Venture Capital Schemes Manual VCM 10000 *et seq.* and 60000 *et seq.*

From 25 September 2000, a centralised service became operational for companies newly raising money under the venture capital trust scheme. All enquiries about whether a company meets the requirements should be made to Small Company Enterprise Centre, Ty Glas, Llanishen, Cardiff, CF14 5ZG (Tel. 029 2032 7400; fax 029 2032 7398; e-mail: enterprise.centre@ir.gsi.gov.uk). This initial point of contact is supported by specialist HMRC units that also deal with the corporation tax affairs, and the monitoring, of such companies as well as companies raising money under other types of venture capital scheme or granting options under enterprise management incentives. (Revenue Press Release 25 September 2000). The approval of venture capital trusts themselves is dealt with by HMRC (CTTG) (see 66.2 below).

66.2 CONDITIONS FOR APPROVAL

A '*venture capital trust*' ('VCT') is a company approved for this purpose by HMRC. Close companies (see Tolley's Corporation Tax under Close Companies) are excluded. The time from which an approval takes effect is specified in the approval, and may not be earlier than the time the application for approval was made.

Except as detailed further below, approval may not be given unless HMRC are satisfied that the following conditions are met.

(*a*) The company's income in its most recent complete accounting period has been derived wholly or mainly from shares or securities, and no more than 15% of its income from shares and securities has been retained.

(*b*) Throughout that period at least 70% by value of the company's 'investments' has been represented by shares or securities in 'qualifying holdings' (see 66.3 below), at least 30% of which (by value) has been represented by holdings of '*eligible shares*', i.e. ordinary shares carrying no present or future preferential right to dividends or to assets on a winding up and no present or future right (before 6 April 1998, present or future preferential right) to redemption. In practice HMRC will not seek to withdraw approval where the company breaches this requirement inadvertently, so long as the position is corrected, and HMRC is informed, without delay after discovery (HMRC Venture Capital Schemes Manual VCM 60420).

(*c*) The company's ordinary shares (or each class thereof) have been listed in the Official List of the Stock Exchange throughout that period.

(*d*) No holding in any company other than a VCT (or a company which could be a VCT but for (*c*) above) has at any time in that period represented more than 15% of the value of the company's investments.

As regards (*a*) and (*d*) above, the provisions which apply to the similar restrictions on investment trusts (see 65.3 UNIT TRUSTS ETC.) apply here with appropriate modification.

'Securities' for these purposes are deemed to include liabilities in respect of certain loans not repayable within five years, and in relation to which any stocks or securities are not re-purchasable or redeemable within five years of issue. In practice HMRC will not regard a standard event of default clause in a loan agreement made on normal commercial terms as a provision which would disqualify the loan being a security. A clause in an agreement would not be regarded as standard if it entitled the lender or a third party to exercise any action which would cause the borrower to default (HMRC Statement of Practice 8/95).

For the purposes of applying (*b*) and (*d*) above on or after 6 April 2007, a company's 'investments' are taken to include any money in the company's possession and any sum owed to the company by another person where

- the company has a right (whether or not its exercise is subject to conditions) to require that person to pay out the sum or part of the sum to the company or at the company's direction, and
- the sum is owed to the company as a result either of amounts having been paid to the other person by or for the company or of that person having identified a sum in respect of which the company may exercise such a right.

The above does not require a company's investments to be taken to include anything to which the company is not beneficially entitled, but for this purpose a company is treated as beneficially entitled to any sums subscribed for shares issued by it and anything to which it is entitled that represents (directly or indirectly) any such sums.

Where (*a*)–(*d*) above are met, HMRC must also be satisfied that they will be met in the accounting period current at the time of application for approval. Where any of (*a*)–(*d*) above are not met, approval may nevertheless be given where HMRC are satisfied that:

(i) in the case of (*a*), (*c*) or (*d*), the condition will be met in the accounting period current when the application for approval is made or in the following accounting period;

(ii) in the case of (*b*), the condition will be met in an accounting period beginning no more than three years after the earlier of the time approval is given and the time it takes effect; and

(iii) in any case, that the condition will continue to be fulfilled in accounting periods following that referred to in (i) or (ii).

On a second and subsequent issues by an approved VCT, the use to which the money raised is put, and the use of any money deriving from that use, is disregarded in determining whether the requirements of condition (*b*) above are met in relation to the accounting period of the further issue or any later accounting period ending no more than three years after the making of the further issue. For shares issued after 5 April 2004, this provision applies conditionally on the money being raised by the further issue for the purposes of the VCT acquiring additional investments which fulfil the tests at (*b*) above. If any of the money raised (or any assets directly or indirectly derived from it) is used other than for such a purpose, the provision is treated as not applying to the further issue from the time immediately before that use. Where, as a result of that use, the tests at (*b*) above have to be applied, the money raised by the further issue (or assets derived from it) is treated for the purposes of the tests as forming part of the company's investments.

The above condition as to the purposes of raising money by a further issue is, in particular, treated as not fulfilled where

- any of the money (or any assets deriving from it) is used for the VCT to purchase any of its own shares and either HMRC consider that the shares being purchased are not insignificant in relation to the issued ordinary share capital of the VCT or the purchase is made as a result of a general offer to members (with or without exceptions for persons connected with the VCT); and

- the shares are issued for new consideration, any of the money raised (or any assets deriving from it) is used for the purpose of the successor company purchasing shares in any of the merging companies and the money so raised exceeds the least of: 20% of the money raised by the shares issued for new consideration (or of the aggregate of those amounts if there has been more than one such issue); 5% of the aggregate of all amounts subscribed for eligible shares in the successor company and the merging companies before the merger; and £3,000,000.

The value of any investment for the purposes of (*b*) and (*d*) above is the value when the investment was acquired, except that where it is added to by a further holding of an investment of the same description, or a payment is made in discharge of any obligation attached to it which increases its value, it is the value immediately after the most recent such addition or payment.

[*ICTA 1988, s 842AA(1)–(5)(5A)(5B)(11A)–(12)(14); FA 1995, s 70(1); FA 1996, Sch 38 para 7; FA 1997, s 75; FA 1998, s 73(1); FA 2002, ss 82, 109, Sch 25 para 57, Sch 33 paras 11–13; FA 2006, Sch 14 para 8; SI 2004 No 2199 Regs 1, 14*].

For the detailed requirements as regards granting and refusal (and withdrawal) of approval, and appeals procedures, see *SI 1995 No 1979, Pt II*.

Applications for approval should be made to HMRC (CTTG), Sapphire House, 550 Streetsbrook Road, Solihull, B91 1QU.

Company restructuring and share conversions. With effect from 16 June 1999, certain transactions in shares held by a VCT are in effect disregarded in considering the value of holdings for the purposes of the 70%, 30% and 15% tests in (*b*) and (*d*) above. The transactions concerned are as follows.

- Where, as part of a restructuring, shares or securities in a company are exchanged for corresponding shares and securities in a new holding company. Certain deemed securities (see above) which are not thus acquired by the new company may be disregarded where these provisions would otherwise be prevented from applying.
- Where a VCT exercises conversion rights in respect of certain convertible shares and securities.

In these circumstances, and subject to detailed conditions (see *ICTA 1988, Sch 28B paras 10C, 10D* introduced by *FA 1999, s 69*), the value of the new shares is taken to be the same as the value of the old shares when they were last valued for these purposes.

Where, after 20 March 2000 under a *company reorganisation, takeover or scheme of reconstruction*,

- a VCT exchanges a qualifying holding for other shares or securities (with or without other consideration), and
- the exchange is for *bona fide* commercial reasons and not part of a tax avoidance scheme or arrangements,

regulations provide a formula which values the new shares or securities, for the purposes of the 70%, 30% and 15% tests in (*b*) and (*d*) above, by reference to the proportion of the value of the old shares or securities that the market value of the new shares or securities bears to the total consideration receivable. If no other consideration is receivable, the value of the new is identical to that of the old. The provisions extend to new shares or securities received in pursuance of an earn-out right (see 58.5 SHARES AND SECURITIES) conferred in exchange for a qualifying holding, in which case an election is available (under *Reg 10*) to modify the formula by effectively disregarding the earn-out right itself.

[*ICTA 1988, s 842AA(5AA)–(5AE), Sch 28B para 11B; FA 1999, s 69(4)(5); FA 2000, s 65, Sch 18 para 8; SI 2002 No 2661*].

Withdrawal of approval. Approval may be withdrawn where there are reasonable grounds for believing that either:

(A) the conditions for approval were not satisfied at the time the approval was given; or

(B) a condition that HMRC were satisfied (as above) would be met has not been or will not be met; or

(C) where (ii) above applies, any other conditions prescribed by regulation in relation to the three-year period have not been met; or

(D) in either the most recent complete accounting period or the current one, one of conditions (*a*)–(*d*) above has failed or will fail to be met (unless the failure was allowed for under (i)–(iii) above); or

(E) where, in relation to a second or further issue by an approved VCT, (*b*) above does not have to be met in the period of issue or certain following accounting periods (see above), one of conditions (*a*)–(*d*) above will fail to be met in the first period for which (*b*) above must be met; or

(F) any other conditions prescribed by regulations have not been met in relation to, or to part of, an accounting period for which (*b*) above does not have to be met.

The withdrawal is effective from the time the company is notified of it, except that:

(1) where approval is given under (i)–(iii) above, and is withdrawn before all the conditions in (*a*)–(*d*) above have been satisfied in relation to either a complete twelve-month accounting period or successive complete accounting periods constituting a continuous period of twelve months or more, the approval is deemed never to have been given; and

(2) for the purposes of relief for capital gains accruing to a VCT under *TCGA 1992, s 100* (see 66.10 below), withdrawal may be effective from an earlier date, but not before the start of the accounting period in which the failure occurred (or is expected to occur).

An assessment consequent on the withdrawal of approval may, where otherwise out of time, be made within three years from the time notice of the withdrawal was given.

[*ICTA 1988, s 842AA(6)–(10); FA 1995, s 70(1)*].

Mergers. For mergers of two or more VCTs which take place after 16 April 2002, regulations enable the merging VCTs to retain VCT status and provide for investors in the merged VCTs who continue as investors in the 'successor company' not to lose their tax reliefs. This treatment can apply to two types of merger:

1 where shares in one of the merging companies (company A) are issued to members of the other merging company or companies in exchange for their shares in that other company or by way of consideration for a transfer to company A of the whole or part of the business of that other company;

2 where shares in a company (company B) which is not one of the merging companies are issued to members of the merging companies in exchange for their shares in those companies or as consideration for a transfer to company B of the whole or part of the businesses of those companies.

Company A or, as appropriate, company B is the '*successor company*'.

For the regulations to apply, a merging company or the successor company must apply to HMRC for approval, and approval must be granted before the merger takes place. For the procedure for obtaining approval see *SI 2004 No 2199, Reg 10*. HMRC will not approve the merger unless they are satisfied that strict conditions are met, including that the merger is for *bona fide* commercial reasons and not part of a scheme or arrangements with a tax avoidance purpose. For the detailed conditions, see *SI 2004 No 2199, Reg 9(3)*. Where approval is obtained, the following apply:

- income tax investment relief within 66.7 below cannot be obtained in respect of any shares issued to effect the merger by the successor company, and such shares are ignored in determining whether the 'permitted maximum' at 66.9 below has been exceeded;
- the conditions at (*a*), (*b*) and (*d*) above, and the provisions at 66.3 below apply to the successor company
  - (i) as if the property of the merging companies were vested in the successor company (so that transfers between a merging company and the successor company are disregarded);
  - (ii) disregarding, in the hands of the successor company, any assets consisting in rights against, or shares or securities of, another company which is a merging company; and
  - (iii) disregarding, in the hands of the successor company, the use of any money which, in the hands of another company which is a merging company, would have been disregarded under *ICTA 1988, s 842AA(5B)* (disregard for the purposes of (*b*) above of money raised by second and subsequent issue of shares — see above), for the same periods as are mentioned in that provision;
- a disposal by a merging company to the successor company after the merger of an asset held by the merging company immediately before, or in the period during which, the merger takes place is not prevented by *TCGA 1992, s 171(2)(cc)* (see 27.2(via) GROUPS OF COMPANIES) from being treated as at no gain/no loss;
- for the purposes of the income tax reliefs at 66.7–66.9 below and capital gains tax deferral relief at 66.12 below,
  - any share for share exchange or share for business transfer is not treated as a disposal of the 'old shares' (i.e. the shares for which the shares issued to effect the merger (the '*new shares*') were issued or, in the case of a share for business transfer, the shares in respect of which the new shares were issued) or as a chargeable event within 66.12 below;
  - any other act (including the giving of relief) carried out, of failure to act, in relation to the old shares is treated as carried out, or omitted, in relation to the corresponding new shares; and
  - references to the company in which the old shares were held are to be read as references to the successor company;
- for the purposes of capital gains tax relief on disposal at 66.11 below, if the successor company is not otherwise a VCT at the time the shares issued to effect the merger are acquired but is a VCT at the time of a subsequent disposal of the shares, it is treated as a VCT at and from the time of acquisition;
- where any of the qualifying holding requirements at 66.3 below (other than the qualifying subsidiaries requirement) were satisfied to any extent or for any period in relation to an investment held by a merging company immediately before the merger, they are treated as satisfied to the same extent or for the same period when held by the successor company, as if the two companies were the same company;
- for the purposes of the 15% test at (*d*) above and the qualifying subsidiaries requirement at 66.3 below, the period in which the merger takes place is disregarded and if as a result of the merger that test or requirement is no longer met, it is treated as met for a period of one year;
- for the purposes of the conditions at (*b*) and (*d*) above and the eligible shares requirement at 66.3 below, the value of investments in the hands of the successor

company immediately after the merger is taken to be their value when last valued before the merger in accordance with the rules governing those conditions and that requirement, unless there has been a transaction other than the merger as a result of which the investments would fall to be revalued; and

- where provisional approval of a merging company other than the successor company is withdrawn following the merger, the withdrawal takes effect from the time the company is notified of it (and the approval is not deemed never to have been given).

[*FA 2002, s 109, Sch 33 paras 8–10; SI 2004 No 2199, Regs 1, 9–13*].

Winding-up. Regulations enable a VCT commencing winding-up after 16 April 2002 to retain its VCT status during a 'prescribed winding-up period', thereby enabling investors' reliefs to continue for that period.

A VCT-in-liquidation can obtain this treatment if either it has been approved as a VCT continuously for at least three years ending with the commencement of the winding-up (five years where the VCT, having previously obtained approval, issues ordinary share capital between 6 April 2004 and 5 April 2006, without having done so before 6 April 2004) or, where the winding-up is by court order, it is approved as a VCT immediately before the commencement. The winding-up must be for *bona fide* commercial reasons and not part of tax avoidance arrangements and the VCT-in-liquidation must notify HMRC of the commencement. A VCT-in-liquidation which has been at any time a merger company (see above) without being a successor company does not qualify. The '*prescribed winding-up period*' for these purposes is the three years beginning with the commencement of the winding-up, but if the winding-up ends, the company ceases to be wound up or is dissolved, the period comes to an end with the earliest of those events.

Where the VCT-in-liquidation fulfils the above requirements, the following apply.

(I) For the purposes of the income tax relief on investments (see 66.7 below), the commencement of the winding-up does not affect the status of the VCT-in-liquidation as a VCT (i.e. the commencement itself is not treated as an event leading to the withdrawal of approval and the provisions for withdrawal of relief at 66.8 below are not triggered by it).

(II) Gains accruing to the VCT-in-liquidation during the prescribed winding-up period on disposal of assets acquired before the commencement of the winding-up are not chargeable gains (and losses are not allowable losses).

(III) Capital gains tax relief on disposal of VCT shares (see 66.11 below) is available (provided that the other conditions for that relief are met) for disposals in the prescribed winding-up period as if the VCT-in-liquidation were a VCT. If, at the end of that period the VCT-in-liquidation still exists and the conditions for approval as a VCT (see above) are not then fulfilled, approval is treated, for the purposes of that relief, as withdrawn at that time (with the consequences described at 66.10 below).

(IV) For the purposes of capital gains tax deferral relief on reinvestment in VCT shares (see 66.12 below), the VCT-in-liquidation is treated throughout the prescribed winding-up period as a VCT and no chargeable event can occur during that time by reason of withdrawal of approval (see 66.12(F) below). If the VCT-in-liquidation still exists at the end of the period, a chargeable event is deemed to occur immediately after that time (see 66.12(H) below).

[*FA 2002, s 109, Sch 33 paras 1–8; SI 2004 No 2199, Regs 1–7*].

66.3 QUALIFYING HOLDINGS

Shares or securities in a company are comprised in a VCT's '*qualifying holdings*' at any time if they were first issued to the VCT, and have been held by it ever since, and the following requirements are satisfied at that time. [*ICTA 1988, s 842AA(13), Sch 28B para 1(2); FA 1995, Sch 14*]. See 66.4 below for further relevant provisions.

Companies wishing to raise money under the venture capital trust scheme may make enquiries as to whether they meet the conditions and/or request informal advance clearance, by contacting HMRC's Small Company Enterprise Centre (see 66.1 above).

Unquoted status requirement. The company is an '*unquoted company*' (whether or not UK resident), i.e. none of its shares, stocks, debentures or other securities is

(i) listed on a recognised stock exchange (see 58.23 SHARES AND SECURITIES), or a designated exchange outside the UK, or

(ii) dealt in on the Unlisted Securities Market, or outside the UK by such means as may be designated for the purpose by order.

If the company ceases to be an unquoted company at a time when its shares are comprised in the qualifying holdings of the VCT, this condition is treated as continuing to be met, in relation to shares or securities acquired before that time, for the following five years.

[*ICTA 1988, Sch 28B para 2; FA 1995, Sch 14 para 2*].

Company's business requirements. Both of the following requirements must be met.

(*a*) Either

(i) the company must exist wholly for the purpose of carrying on one or more 'qualifying trades' (see 66.5 below), disregarding any purpose having no significant effect on the extent of its activities as a whole. (The case of *Lord v Tustain*; *Lord v Chapple Ch D 1993, 65 TC 761* concerned the question whether a company exists for the purposes of carrying on a trade), or

(ii) it must be the 'parent company of a trading group'; and

(*b*) When the shares or securities were issued to the VCT and ever since, a 'qualifying company' (whether or not the same company throughout) must have been carrying on a qualifying trade wholly or mainly in the UK, or preparing to carry on such a trade intended to be carried on wholly or mainly in the UK by such a company. In the latter case, there is a time limit of two years from the issue of the shares etc. for the trade to be commenced as intended. For this purpose, a '*qualifying company*' is the company issuing the shares etc. to the VCT or a 'relevant qualifying subsidiary' of that company, and any carrying on of a trade by a subsidiary before it became a relevant qualifying subsidiary is disregarded in determining when the trade commences. In relation to shares or securities issued to a VCT before 17 March 2004, this requirement has to be met throughout by one qualifying company (i.e. either the trade must be carried on throughout by the same company or the same company must prepare to carry on, and subsequently carry on, the trade).

In considering whether a trade is carried on 'wholly or mainly in the UK' for the purposes of (*b*) above, HMRC will take into account the totality of the activities of the trade; a company can satisfy the requirement if the major part of the trade, i.e. over half of the trading activity, taken as a whole, is carried on within the UK (see HMRC Statement of Practice 3/00).

Parent company of a trading group. A company is the '*parent company of a trading group*' if it has one or more subsidiaries, each of which is a 'qualifying subsidiary', and if, taking all the activities of the company and its subsidiaries as one business, neither that business nor a substantial part of it consists in either or both of:

- activities within 66.5(A)–(L) below (but with the same let-outs applying as regards (D)); and
- non-trading activities.

Activities are for these purposes disregarded to the extent that they consist in:

(1) holding shares in or securities of, or making loans to, one or more of the company's subsidiaries; or

(2) holding and managing property used by the company or any of its subsidiaries for the purposes or either

(i) research and development (as defined — see 66.5 below) from which it is intended that a qualifying trade to be carried on by the company or any of its subsidiaries will be derived, or

(ii) one or more qualifying trades so carried on.

Activities of a subsidiary are similarly disregarded to the extent that they consist in the making of loans to the company or, where the subsidiary exists wholly for the purpose of carrying on one or more qualifying trades (apart from '*insignificant purposes*', i.e. purposes capable of having no significant effect, other than in relation to incidental matters, on the extent of the subsidiary's activities), of activities carried on in pursuance of those insignificant purposes.

Qualifying subsidiary. A subsidiary is a '*qualifying subsidiary*' of a parent company if

(A) in relation to shares or securities issued to the VCT after 16 March 2004, it is a 51% subsidiary (within *ICTA 1988, s 838*) of that company;

(B) in relation to shares or securities issued to the VCT before 17 March 2004, the parent company, or another of its subsidiaries, possesses at least 75% (90% before 6 April 1998) of both the issued share capital and the voting power, and is beneficially entitled to at least 75% (90% before 6 April 1998) of the assets available for distribution to equity holders on a winding-up etc. (see *ICTA 1988, Sch 18 paras 1, 3*) and of the profits available for distribution to equity holders;

(C) no other person has control (within *ICTA 1988, s 840*) of the subsidiary; and

(D) no arrangements exist whereby (A), (B) or (C) could cease to be satisfied.

The fact that a subsidiary, or, in respect of shares etc. issued after 16 March 2004, any other company, is wound up does not mean that the subsidiary ceases to be a qualifying subsidiary provided that the winding-up is for genuine commercial reasons and is not part of a tax avoidance scheme or arrangements. In relation to shares etc. issued after 16 March 2004, the fact that a subsidiary or any other company goes into administration or receivership (both as defined) does not mean that the subsidiary ceases to be a qualifying subsidiary provided that the entry into, and everything done as a consequence of being in, administration or receivership is for genuine commercial reasons and is not part of a tax avoidance scheme or arrangements. Similarly, the fact that arrangements may exist to dispose of the entire interest held in the subsidiary does not prevent it from being a qualifying subsidiary if the disposal is to be for commercial reasons and is not part of a tax avoidance scheme or arrangements.

Relevant qualifying subsidiary. A subsidiary is a '*relevant qualifying subsidiary*' of the company issuing the shares or securities to the VCT at any time when

(*aa*) that company possesses at least 90% of both the issued share capital of, and the voting power in, the subsidiary, and is beneficially entitled to at least 90% of the assets available for distribution to equity holders on a winding-up etc. (see *ICTA 1988, Sch 18 paras 1, 3*) and of the profits available for distribution to equity holders,

(*bb*) no other person has control (within *ICTA 1988, s 840*) of the subsidiary, and

(*cc*) no arrangements exist whereby (*aa*) or (*bb*) could cease to be satisfied.

The provisions above relating to winding-up, administration and disposal of qualifying subsidiaries apply to relevant qualifying subsidiaries as they apply to qualifying subsidiaries.

[*ICTA 1988, Sch 28B paras 3, 5A, 10; FA 1995, Sch 14; FA 1997, Sch 9 paras 2, 5, 6; FA 1998, s 73*(2)(3); *FA 2001, s 64, Sch 16 para 1; FA 2004, Sch 19 paras 9, 10, 12, 16, Sch 27 para 5*(2), *Sch 42 Pt 2*(12)].

After 20 March 2000, a company does not cease to meet the requirements of (*a*) or (*b*) above by reason only of anything done as a consequence of its being in administration or receivership, provided everything so done and the making of the relevant order are for *bona fide* commercial (and not tax avoidance) reasons. [*ICTA 1988, Sch 28B para 11A; FA 2000, s 65, Sch 18 paras 4, 7; FA 2004, Sch 19 para 15*].

The Treasury have power by order to modify the above requirements (including the definition of a qualifying trade at 66.5 below) as they consider expedient. [*ICTA 1988, Sch 28B para 12*(*a*); *FA 1995, Sch 14; FA 1998, s 70*(3)].

Use of money raised requirement. The money raised by the issue of shares to the VCT must be employed *wholly* (disregarding insignificant amounts) for the purposes of the qualifying trade. At any time within 12 months after the issue (or after the date of commencement of the qualifying trade where this is later than the date of issue) this condition is treated as satisfied if at least 80% of that money has been, or is intended to be, so employed. At any time within the following 12 months, the condition is treated as satisfied if at least 80% of that money *has been* so employed. The above treatment applies for the purpose of determining whether any shares or securities are, as at any time after 6 March 2001, to be regarded as comprised in the qualifying holdings of the VCT. Previously, the condition was treated as satisfied at any time within the first 12-month period if *all* the money was intended to be so employed. No special treatment applied in the following 12 months.

In this connection, money is used 'for the purposes of' a trade if it is used for the purpose of preparing to carry on a trade or for the purpose of research and development leading to a trade. Money whose retention can reasonably be regarded as necessary or advisable for financing current business requirements is regarded as employed for trade purposes. (HMRC Venture Capital Schemes Manual VCM 12070, 12080, 62150–62153).

If this requirement would be met as to only part of the money raised by the issue, and the holding is not otherwise capable of being treated as separate holdings, it is treated as two separate holdings, one from which that part of the money was raised, the other from which the rest was raised, with the value being apportioned accordingly to each holding. This does not require an insignificant amount applied for non-trade purposes to be treated as a separate holding.

In relation to shares or securities issued to a VCT after 16 March 2004, this requirement is treated as not met if the required qualifying trade (or preparations for the trade) (see (*b*) above) is carried on at any time after the issue of the shares or securities by any person other than a qualifying company (see (*b*) above). The requirement is not, however, treated as not met by virtue of this provision:

(I) by reason only of the carrying on of the trade by a person other than a qualifying company at a time when such a company has not yet carried on the trade but is preparing to do so;

(II) by reason only of the carrying on of the trade by the partners in a partnership of which a qualifying company is a member;

(III) by reason only of the carrying on of the trade by the parties to a joint venture to which a qualifying company is a party; or

(IV) if, by reason only of anything done as a consequence of any company being in administration or receivership or of any company being wound up or dissolved without winding-up, the trade ceases to be carried on by a qualifying company and is subsequently carried on by any person who has not been connected (within *ICTA 1988, s 839*) with the issuing company at any time in the period beginning one year before the issue of the shares or securities to the VCT. The winding-up etc. or the entry into, and everything done as a consequence of being in, administration or receivership must be for genuine commercial reasons and not part of a tax avoidance scheme or arrangements.

In relation to shares or securities issued to a VCT before 17 March 2004, where the company is a parent company of a trading group (see above), the requirement is not treated as met unless the '*trader company*' (i.e. the company carrying on (or preparing to carry on) the required qualifying trade) either:

- satisfies the requirements in (*a*)(i) above; or
- is a company in relation to which those requirements would be satisfied if activities within (1) and (2) above, or consisting of a subsidiary making loans to its parent, were disregarded; or
- is a relevant qualifying subsidiary (see above) which either
  - exists wholly for the purpose of carrying on activities within (2) above (disregarding purposes capable of having no significant effect (other than in relation to incidental matters) on the extent of its activities), or
  - has no corporation tax profits and no part of its business consists in the making of investments.

[*ICTA 1988, Sch 28B paras 1(3), 6, 13(4); FA 1995, Sch 14; FA 1997, Sch 9 paras 4, 6; FA 1998, s 73(4); FA 2001, Sch 16 para 2; FA 2004, Sch 19 paras 11, 16, Sch 42 Pt 2(12)*].

In relation to buy-outs (and in particular management buy-outs), HMRC will usually accept that where a company is formed to acquire a trade, and the funds raised from the VCT are applied to that purchase, the requirement that the funds be employed for the purposes of the trade is satisfied. Where the company is formed to acquire another company and its trade, or a holding company and its trading subsidiaries, this represents an investment rather than employment for the purposes of the trade. However, HMRC will usually accept that the requirement is satisfied if the trade of the company, or all the activities of the holding company and its subsidiaries, are hived up to the acquiring company as soon as possible after the acquisition. In the case of a holding company and its subsidiaries, to the extent that the trades are not hived up, the holding cannot be a qualifying holding (Revenue Tax Bulletin August 1995 pp 243, 244).

Maximum qualifying investment requirement. The aggregate of money raised from shares issued by the company to the VCT must not have exceeded the 'maximum qualifying investment' of £1 million in the period from six months before the issue in question (or, if earlier, the beginning of the year of assessment of the issue) to the time of the issue in question. Disposals are treated as far as possible as eliminating any such excess. The £1 million limit is proportionately reduced where, at the time of the issue, the qualifying trade is carried on, or to be carried on, in partnership or as a joint venture, and one or more of the other parties is a company.

If this requirement would be met as to only part of the money raised by the issue, and the holding is not otherwise capable of being treated as separate holdings, it is treated as two separate holdings, one from which that part of the money was raised, the other from which the rest was raised, with the value being apportioned accordingly to each holding.

The Treasury have power by order to alter the above cash limit.

[*ICTA 1988, Sch 28B paras 1(3), 7, 12(b); FA 1995, Sch 14*].

Gross assets requirement. The value of the company's assets as a whole did not exceed £7 million immediately before the issue and did not exceed £8 million immediately afterwards. As regards shares and securities issued by investee companies before 6 April 2006, these limits were £15 million and £16 million respectively. The latter limits continue to apply in relation to shares or securities acquired using money raised by the issue of shares or securities in the VCT before 6 April 2006 or money derived from the investment by the VCT of any such money. As regards shares and securities issued by investee companies before 6 April 1998, the limits were £10 million and £11 million.

For this purpose, value means the value of the gross assets of the company at a time when it did not have any qualifying subsidiaries (see above), or the aggregate value of the gross assets of all the companies in the group where it does have such subsidiaries (but disregarding any rights against, or shares in or securities of, another group member). The Treasury have power by order to alter the cash limits.

[*ICTA 1988, Sch 28B paras 8, 12*(*b*); *FA 1995, Sch 14; FA 1998, s 73*(*5*); *FA 2006, Sch 14 para 2, Sch 26 Pt 3*(*16*)].

HMRC's approach is that the value of a company's gross assets at any time is the aggregate of the values of its assets (without any deduction for liabilities) as would be shown in a balance sheet drawn up as at that time. Any advance payment received for the share issue itself is ignored immediately before the issue but the right to the unpaid portion of shares issued partly paid is taken as included in gross assets immediately after the issue. See HMRC Statement of Practice 2/00.

Qualifying subsidiaries requirement. The company must not control (within *ICTA 1988, s 416*, see Tolley's Corporation Tax under Close Companies, as modified by *ICTA 1988, Sch 28B para 13*(*2*)(*3*)(*5*)(*6*), and with or without connected persons) any company other than a qualifying subsidiary (see above), nor must another company (or another company and a person connected with it) control it. Neither must arrangements be in existence by virtue of which such control could arise. [*ICTA 1988, Sch 28B para 9; FA 1995, Sch 14; FA 1996, s 161*(*1*)(*2*), *Sch 41 Pt V*(*22*)]. The control test disregards all fixed rate preference shares (unless and until they carry voting rights) and loans held by the VCT and by any other investor (Revenue Press Release 4 March 1996). See Revenue Tax Bulletin October 1997 pp 471, 472 for HMRC's views on the application of the control test where two or more co-investors (including a VCT) invest in a company alongside each other.

Property managing subsidiaries requirement. In relation to shares or securities issued after 16 March 2004, the company must not have a 'property managing subsidiary' other than one which is its relevant qualifying subsidiary (see above). For this purpose, a '*property managing subsidiary*' is a qualifying subsidiary (see above) whose business consists wholly or mainly in the holding or managing of land or any property deriving its value from land (and the terms 'land' and 'property deriving its value from land' have the same meaning as in 38.4 LAND). [*ICTA 1988, Sch 28B para 10ZA; FA 2004, Sch 19 paras 13, 16*].

No guaranteed loans requirement. The holding in question must not include any securities (as defined in 66.2 above) relating to a guaranteed loan. A security relates to a guaranteed loan if there are arrangements entitling the VCT to receive anything (directly or indirectly) from a 'third party' in the event of a failure by any person to comply with the terms of the security or the loan to which it relates. It is immaterial whether or not the arrangements apply in all such cases. '*Third party*' includes any person other than the investee company itself and, if it is a parent company of a trading group (see above), its subsidiaries. This condition applies for accounting periods (of the VCT) ending after 1 July 1997, but does not apply in the case of shares or securities acquired by the VCT by means of investing money raised by the issue by it before 2 July 1997 of shares or securities (or money derived from the investment of any such money raised). [*ICTA 1988, Sch 28B para 10A; FA 1998, s 72*(*1*)(*4*)].

Eligible shares requirement. At least 10% (by value) of the VCT's *total* holding of shares in and securities of the company must consist of 'eligible shares' (as defined in 66.2(b) above — broadly, ordinary, non-preferential, shares). For this purpose, the value of shares etc. at any time is taken to be their value immediately after the most recent of the events listed below, except that it cannot thereby be taken to be less than the amount of consideration given by the VCT for the shares etc. The said events are as follows.

- The acquisition of the shares etc. by the VCT.
- The acquisition by the VCT (other than by way of bonus issue for no consideration) of any other shares etc. in the same company which are of the same description as those already held.
- The making of any payment in discharge (or part discharge) of any obligation attached to the shares etc. in a case where such discharge increases the value of the shares etc.

This condition applies for accounting periods (of the VCT) ending after 1 July 1997, but, if necessary in order to satisfy the condition, one may disregard shares and securities acquired by the VCT by means of investing money raised by the issue by it before 2 July 1997 of shares or securities (or money derived from the investment of any such money raised).

[*ICTA 1988, Sch 28B para 10B; FA 1998, s 72*(2)(5)(6)].

66.4 **Supplementary provisions** *Company wound up.* Where the company is being wound up, none of the requirements in 66.3 above are regarded on that account as not being satisfied provided that those requirements would be met apart from the winding up, and that the winding up is for *bona fide* commercial reasons and not part of a scheme or arrangement a main purpose of which is the avoidance of tax. [*ICTA 1988, Sch 28B para 11; FA 1995, Sch 14; FA 2004, Sch 19 para 14, Sch 42 Pt 2*(12)].

Disregard of certain transactions in shares. With effect from 16 June 1999, certain transactions in shares held by a VCT are in effect disregarded in considering whether the requirements in 66.3 above (other than the unquoted status and no guaranteed loan requirements) are met. The transactions concerned are as follows.

(A) Where, as part of a restructuring, shares or securities in a company are exchanged for corresponding shares and securities in a new holding company. Certain deemed securities (see 66.2 above) which are not thus acquired by the new company may be disregarded where these provisions would otherwise be prevented from applying.

(B) Where a VCT exercises conversion rights in respect of certain convertible shares and securities.

In these circumstances, and subject to detailed conditions, to the extent that the condition was satisfied in relation to the old shares, it will generally be taken to be satisfied in relation to the new shares. [*ICTA 1988, Sch 28B paras 10C, 10D; FA 1999, s 69*(2)(5)].

Company reorganisations involving exchange of shares. Where, after 20 March 2000 under a company reorganisation, takeover or scheme of reconstruction,

- a VCT exchanges a qualifying holding for other shares or securities (with or without other consideration), and
- the exchange is for *bona fide* commercial reasons and not part of a tax avoidance scheme or arrangements,

the new shares or securities may be treated as being qualifying holdings for a specified period even if some or all of the above requirements are not otherwise satisfied. Regulations specify the circumstances in which, and conditions subject to which, they apply and which requirements are to be treated as met. Where the new shares or securities are those of a different company than before and they do not meet any one or more of the requirements in 66.3 above (disregarding the use of money raised and maximum qualifying investment requirements), those requirements are treated as met for, broadly, three years in the case of shares or five years in the case of securities, reduced in either case to, broadly, two years where the company is not, or ceases to be, an unquoted company. A formula is provided for valuing the new shares or securities for the purposes of the eligible shares requirement. The provisions extend to new shares or securities received in pursuance of an earn-out right (see 58.5 SHARES AND SECURITIES) conferred in exchange for a qualifying holding, in which case an election is available (under *Reg 10*) to modify the said valuation formula by effectively disregarding the earn-out right itself. [*ICTA 1988 s 842AA(5AD)(5AE), Sch 28B para 11B; FA 2000, s 65, Sch 18 paras 4, 8(1)(4); SI 2002 No 2661*].

Investments transferred from VCT-in-liquidation. Regulations enable certain investments comprised in the qualifying holdings of a VCT-in-liquidation (VCT1) which are transferred by it during its prescribed winding-up period (see 66.2 above under 'Winding-up') to another VCT (VCT2) to be treated as comprised in the qualifying holdings of VCT2. Where any of the qualifying holding requirements (see 66.3 above) which are listed below have been satisfied to any extent or for any period in relation to the investment when held by VCT1 (whether before or after the commencement of its winding-up), they are treated as satisfied to the same extent or for the same period in relation to the investment when held by VCT2. The requirements are:

- that the shares or securities concerned were first issued to the VCT-in-liquidation and have been held by it ever since;
- the use of money raised requirement;
- the maximum qualifying investment requirement; and
- the gross assets requirement.

This treatment applies where

- VCT1 commences winding-up after 16 April 2002;
- the winding-up is for bona fide commercial reasons and not part of tax avoidance arrangements;
- VCT1 has made all reasonable endeavours to sell the shares or securities at or as near as possible to their market value but has been unable to do so;
- the transfer to VCT2 is by way of a bargain made at arm's length or at not less than market value; and
- the value of all shares or securities transferred by VCT1 to other VCTs in its prescribed winding-up period does not exceed 7.5% of the aggregate value of its investments at the commencement of the winding-up. For this purpose, the value of VCT1's investments at the commencement of the winding-up are taken to be those used in its statement of affairs, or, where this does not provide a value for an investment, its market value at that time.

[*FA 2002, s 109, Sch 33 paras 1, 5; SI 2004 No 2199, Regs 1(2), 8*].

66.5 **Qualifying trades.** A trade is a '*qualifying trade*' for the purposes of 66.3 above if it does not, or not substantially (see below), consist of any of the activities at (A)–(L) below. 'Research and development' from which it is intended that there will be derived a qualifying trade carried on wholly or mainly in the UK is treated as the carrying on of a qualifying trade. For the purpose of determining whether shares or securities issued after 5 April 2000 are to be regarded as comprised in a VCT's qualifying holdings, '*research and development*' has the meaning given by *ICTA 1988, s 837A* (see Tolley's Income Tax). Previously, it meant any activity intended to result in a patentable invention (within *Patents Act 1977*) or in a computer program.

(A) Dealing in land, in commodities or futures or in shares, securities or other financial instruments.

(B) Dealing in goods otherwise than in the case of an 'ordinary' trade of wholesale or retail distribution.

(C) Banking, insurance, money-lending, debt-factoring, hire-purchase financing or other financial activities.

(D) Leasing (including letting ships on charter or other assets on hire) or receiving royalties or licence fees.

(E) Providing legal or accountancy services.

(F) 'Property development' (see below).

(G) Farming or market gardening.

(H) Holding, managing or occupying woodlands, any other forestry activities or timber production.

(J) Operating or managing hotels or comparable establishments (including guest houses, hostels and other establishments whose main purpose is to offer overnight accommodation with or without catering) or property used as such.

(K) Operating or managing nursing homes or residential care homes (both as defined in *ICTA 1988, Sch 28B para 5(1)*) or property used as such.

(L) Providing services or facilities for any trade, profession or vocation within (A)–(K) above and which is carried on by another person (other than a parent company), where one person has a 'controlling interest' in both trades.

Exclusions (F)–(K) (and the reference to those in exclusion (L)) apply for the purpose of determining whether any shares or securities are, as at any time **after 16 March 1998**, to be regarded as comprised in the qualifying holdings of the VCT. However, those exclusions **do not apply** in relation to shares and securities acquired by the VCT by means of the investment of

- money raised by the issue **before 17 March 1998** of shares in or securities of the VCT; or
- money derived from the investment by the VCT of money so raised.

Exclusions (J) and (K) apply only if the person carrying on the activity in question has an estate or interest (e.g. a lease) in the property concerned or occupies that property.

Adventures and concerns in the nature of trade, and trades not carried on commercially and with a view to the realisation of profits, are also excluded.

Activities accounting in aggregate for less than 20% of the trade, judged normally by reference to turnover or capital employed, are not normally regarded as a 'substantial' part of the trade (HMRC Venture Capital Schemes Manual VCM 17040). As regards (A) above, dealing in land includes cases where steps are taken, before selling the land, to make it more attractive to a purchaser; such steps might include the refurbishment of existing buildings (HMRC Venture Capital Schemes Manual VCM 17050).

As regards (B) above, a trade of wholesale or retail distribution is a trade consisting of the offer of goods for sale either to persons for resale (or processing and resale) (which resale must be to members of the general public) by them ('*wholesale*') or to the general public ('*retail*') and a trade is not an ordinary wholesale or retail trade if it consists to a substantial extent of dealing in goods collected or held as an investment (or of that and any other activity within (A)–(L) above), and a substantial proportion of such goods is held for a significantly longer period than might reasonably be expected for a vendor trying to dispose of them at market value. Whether such trades are '*ordinary*' is to be judged having regard to the following features, those under (1) supporting the categorisation as 'ordinary', those under (2) being indicative to the contrary.

(1)

(*a*) The breaking of bulk.

(*b*) The purchase and sale of goods in different markets.

(*c*) The employment of staff and incurring of trade expenses other than the cost of goods or the remuneration of persons connected (within *ICTA 1988, s 839*) with a company carrying on the trade.

(2)

(*a*) The purchase or sale of goods from or to persons connected (within *ICTA 1988, s 839*) with the trader.

(*b*) The matching of purchases with sales.

(*c*) The holding of goods for longer than might normally be expected.

(*d*) The carrying on of the trade at a place not commonly used for wholesale or retail trading.

(*e*) The absence of physical possession of the goods by the trader.

As regards (D) above as it applies for determining whether shares or securities issued before 6 April 2000 are to be regarded as comprised in a VCT's qualifying holdings, the trade of a company engaged in the production of original master films, tapes or discs is not excluded by reason only of the receipt of royalties or licence fees, provided that all royalties and licence fees received by the company are in respect of films, etc. produced by it since the issue of the shares to the VCT or in respect of by-products arising therefrom. The company may also be engaged in the distribution of films produced by it since those shares were issued. Similarly the trade of a company engaged in research and development (as defined) is not excluded by reason only of the receipt of royalties and licence fees attributable to that research and development.

As regards (D) above as it applies for determining whether shares or securities issued after 5 April 2000 are to be regarded as comprised in a VCT's qualifying holdings, a trade is not excluded from being a qualifying trade solely because it consists to a substantial extent in the receiving of royalties or licence fees substantially attributable (in terms of value) to the exploitation of 'relevant intangible assets'. An intangible asset is an asset falling to be treated as such under generally accepted UK accounting practice. A '*relevant intangible asset*' is an asset the whole or greater part of which (in terms of value) has been created by the company carrying on the trade or by a company which throughout the creation of the asset was the 'parent company' of that company or a 'qualifying subsidiary' (within *ICTA 1988, Sch 28B para 10* as modified for this purpose) of that parent company. A '*parent company*' is for these purposes a company with one or more 51% subsidiaries which is not itself a 51% subsidiary. Where the asset is 'intellectual property', it is treated as created by a company only if the right to exploit it vests in that company (alone or with others). The term '*intellectual property*' incorporates patents, trade marks, copyrights, design rights etc. and foreign equivalents.

Where the grant of a licence is merely incidental to an activity of supplying *services*, the fees are not excluded by (D) above (see Revenue Tax Bulletin August 2001 p 878).

Also as regards (D) above, a trade carried on by a company will not be excluded by reason only of its consisting of chartering ships, other than ships of a kind primarily used for sport or recreation or (in determining whether shares or securities issued on or after 6 April 2004 are to be regarded as comprised in a VCT's qualifying holding) offshore installations (within *ICTA 1988, s 837C*) or (in relation to shares and securities issued before that date) oil rigs (as defined), provided that

(I) the company beneficially owns all the ships it so lets,

(II) every ship beneficially owned by the company is UK-registered,

(III) the company is solely responsible for arranging the marketing of the services of its ships, and

(IV) in relation to every letting on charter, certain conditions as to length and terms of charter, and the arm's length character of the transaction, are met,

and if any of (I)–(IV) above is not met in relation to certain lettings, only those lettings (together with any other excluded activities) are taken into account in determining whether a substantial part of the trade consists of excluded activities.

See Revenue Tax Bulletin August 2001 p 877 for a note on the letting of other assets on hire (also within the exclusion at (D) above), with particular reference to car hire.

As regards (E) above, the provision of accounting staff by a company to a firm of accountants was held in an EIS case to be synonymous with the provision of accountancy services, with the result that the company's trade was not a qualifying trade (*Castleton Management Service Ltd v Kirkwood (Sp C 276), [2001] SSCD 95*).

'*Property development*' in (F) above means the development of land by a company, which has (or has had at any time) an 'interest in the land' (as defined by *ICTA 1988, Sch 28B para 5*(*5*)(*7*)), with the sole or main object of realising a gain from the disposal of an interest in the developed land.

As regards (L) above, a person has a '*controlling interest*' in a trade carried on by a company if he controls the company (within *ICTA 1988, s 416*, see Tolley's Corporation Tax under Close Companies, as modified by *ICTA 1988, Sch 28B para 13*(*2*)(*3*)(*5*)(*6*)); or if the company is close (see Tolley's Corporation Tax under Close Companies) and he or an 'associate' (within *ICTA 1988, s 417*, see Tolley's Corporation Tax under Close Companies, but excluding a brother or sister) is a director of the company and the beneficial owner of, or able to control, more than 30% of its ordinary share capital; or if at least half of its ordinary share capital is directly or indirectly owned by him. In any other case, it is obtained by his being entitled to at least one-half of the assets used for, or income arising from, the trade. Rights and powers of 'associates' (as above) are taken into account for these purposes.

[*ICTA 1988, Sch 28B paras 4, 5, 13*(*2*)–(*5*); *FA 1995, Sch 14; FA 1997, Sch 9 paras 3, 6; FA 1998, Sch 12 paras 3, 4; FA 2000, s 65, Sch 18 paras 4–6; FA 2002, s 103*(*4*); *FA 2004, Sch 27 para 5*(*3*)–(*6*), *Sch 42 Pt 2*(*18*)].

66.6 **INCOME TAX RELIEFS** [*ICTA 1988, s 332A, Sch 15B; FA 1995, s 71, Sch 15; ITTOIA 2005, ss 709–712, Sch 1 paras 140, 346; FA 2006, Sch 14 paras 4, 7*]

Relief from income tax is granted for 1995/96 and subsequent years in respect of both investments in VCTs and dividends from such trusts. See also 66.2 above as regards mergers and winding-up of VCTs.

66.7 **Relief in respect of investments.** Subject to the conditions described below, an individual may claim relief for a year of assessment for the amount (or aggregate amounts) subscribed by him on his own behalf for 'eligible shares' issued to him in a year of assessment by a VCT (or VCTs) for raising money. There is a limit of **£200,000** for 2004/05 and subsequent years on the relief which may be claimed for any year of assessment. For 2003/04 and earlier years the limit is £100,000.

'*Eligible shares*' means new ordinary shares in a VCT which, throughout the five years following issue (three years for shares issued after 5 April 2000 and before 6 April 2006), carry no present or future preferential right to dividends or to assets on a winding up and no present or future right (before 6 April 1998, present or future preferential right) to redemption.

Relief is given by a reduction in what would otherwise be the individual's income tax liability for the year of assessment by the lesser of

(i) in relation to shares issued on or after 6 April 2006, 30% of the amount(s) subscribed, and

(ii) an amount sufficient to reduce that liability to nil.

In relation to shares issued after 5 April 2004 and before 6 April 2006, the reduction is the lesser of 40% of the amount(s) subscribed, and the amount needed to reduce the tax liability to nil. In relation to shares issued before 6 April 2004, the reduction is the lesser of 20% of the amount(s) subscribed, and the amount needed to reduce the tax liability to nil.

The income tax reduction under this chapter is made in priority to any of the following:

- an income tax reduction due in respect of personal reliefs or qualifying maintenance payments (see Tolley's Income Tax under, respectively, Allowances and Tax Rates and Married Persons);
- an income tax reduction due in respect of interest relief (see Tolley's Income Tax under Interest Payable);
- an income tax reduction due in respect of medical insurance (see Tolley's Income Tax under Medical Insurance);
- an income tax reduction due in respect of EIS investments (see 21.2(b) ENTERPRISE INVESTMENT SCHEME);
- an income tax reduction due in respect of community investment tax relief (see Tolley's Income Tax);
- a reduction of liability to tax by way of DOUBLE TAX RELIEF (19).

In determining the individual's income tax liability from which the reduction under this chapter is to be made, no account is taken of any basic rate tax on income the tax on which the individual is entitled to charge against any other person or to deduct, retain or satisfy out of any payment. This includes any basic rate tax deemed to have been deducted at source from a charitable donation made after 5 April 2000 under the Gift Aid scheme (see 10.7 CHARITIES). Any such basic rate tax cannot, therefore, be extinguished by income tax relief on VCT investments.

An individual is **not** entitled to relief where:

(*a*) he was under 18 years of age at the time of issue of the shares;

(*b*) circumstances have arisen which, had the relief already been given, would have resulted in the withdrawal or reduction of the relief (see 66.8 below);

(*c*) the shares were issued or subscribed for other than for *bona fide* commercial purposes or as part of a scheme or arrangement a main purpose of which was the avoidance of tax;

(*d*) a loan is made to the individual (or to an 'associate' within *ICTA 1988, s 417*, see Tolley's Corporation Tax under Close Companies, but excluding a brother or sister) by any person at any time in the period beginning with the incorporation of the VCT (or, if later, two years before the date of issue of the shares) and ending five years after the date of issue of the shares (three years for shares issued after 5 April 2000 and before 6 April 2006), and the loan would not have been made, or would not have been made on the same terms, if he had not subscribed, or had not been proposing to subscribe, for the shares. For HMRC's views on 'loan-linked' investments, see HMRC Statement of Practice 6/98. The granting of credit to, or the assignment of a debt due from, the individual or associate is counted as a loan for these purposes; or

(*e*) the shares were treated as issued by virtue of *FA 2003, s 195(8)* (company disposing of treasury shares — see 58.14 SHARES AND SECURITIES). Where a venture capital trust issues eligible shares to an individual in such circumstances it must give notice to the individual stating that he is not eligible for relief, and a copy of the notice must be sent to an HMRC officer within three months after the issue of the shares.

[*ICTA 1988, Sch 15B paras 1, 2, 6; FA 1995, Sch 15 paras 1, 2, 6; FA 1998, s 73(1)(6), Sch 27 Pt III(13); FA 2000, Sch 18, para 1(2)(4), para 3; FA 2001, Sch 16 para 3; FA 2002, s 57, Sch 17 para 3; FA 2003, s 195(10), Sch 40 para 1; FA 2004, s 94(1)(3), Sch 19 paras 1, 3; FA 2006, Sch 14 paras 4(1)(3), 7(2)(4)(5), Sch 26 Pt 3(16)*].

An individual subscribing for eligible shares may obtain from the VCT a certificate giving details of the subscription and certifying that certain conditions for relief are satisfied. [*SI 1995 No 1979, Reg 9*].

Example

On 1 August 2006, A Ventura, a 44 year old married man whose salary is £60,000 p.a. from UK employment, subscribes for 50,000 eligible £1 shares issued at par to raise money by VCT plc, an approved venture capital trust. On 1 March 2007 he purchases a further 190,000 £1 shares in VCT plc for £170,000 on the open market. The trust makes no distribution in 2006/07. Mr Ventura's other income for 2006/07 consists of dividends of £16,200 (net).

Mr Ventura's tax computation for 2006/07 is as follows.

	£	£
Earnings from UK employment		60,000.00
Dividends	16,200.00	
Add Tax credits	1,800.00	18,000.00
Total income		78,000.00
Deduct personal allowance		5,035.00
Taxable income		£72,965.00
Tax payable:		£
2,150 @ 10%		215.00
31,150 @ 22%		6,853.00
21,665 @ 40%		8,666.00
18,000 @ 32.5%		5,850.00
		21,584.00
Deduct Relief in respect of investment in VCT plc:		
Lower of 30% of £50,000 subscribed and £21,584.00		15,000.00
		6,584.00
Deduct Tax credits on dividends		1,800.00
Net tax payable (subject to PAYE deductions from salary)		£4,784.00

66.8 **Withdrawal of relief on investment.** *Disposal of investment.* Where an individual disposes of eligible shares, in respect of which relief has been claimed as under 66.7 above, within five years of their issue (three years for shares issued after 5 April 2000 and before 6 April 2006) and other than to a spouse or civil partner when they are living together (see below), then:

(*a*) if the disposal is otherwise than at arm's length, relief given by reference to those shares is withdrawn;

(*b*) if the disposal is at arm's length, the relief given by reference to those shares is reduced by an amount equivalent to 30% of the consideration received for the disposal (40% for shares issued after 5 April 2004 and before 6 April 2006 and 20% for shares issued before 6 April 2004) or is withdrawn if the relief exceeds that amount.

Relief is **not** withdrawn where the disposal is by one spouse or civil partner to the other at a time when they are living together. However, on any subsequent disposal the spouse or partner to whom the shares were transferred is treated as if he or she were the person who subscribed for the shares, as if the shares had been issued to him or her at the time they were issued to the transferor spouse or partner, and as if his or her liability to income tax had been reduced by reference to those shares by the same amount, and for the same year of assessment, as applied on the subscription by the transferor spouse or partner. Any assessment for reducing or withdrawing relief is made on the transferee spouse or partner.

Identification of shares. For the above purposes, disposals of eligible shares in a VCT are identified with those acquired earlier rather than later. As between eligible shares acquired on the same day, shares by reference to which relief has been given are treated as disposed of after any other eligible shares.

Withdrawal of approval. Where approval of a company as a VCT is withdrawn (but not treated as never having been given) (see 66.2 above), relief given by reference to eligible shares in the VCT is withdrawn as if on a non-arm's length disposal immediately before the withdrawal of approval. See 66.2(I) above for the position where a VCT enters liquidation.

Assessments withdrawing or reducing relief, whether because relief is subsequently found not to have been due or under the above provisions, are made (before *ITTOIA 2005* came into effect, under Schedule D, Case VI) for the year of assessment for which the relief was given. No such assessment is, however, to be made by reason of an event occurring after the death of the person to whom the shares were issued.

Information. Particulars of all events leading to the reduction or withdrawal of relief must be notified to the inspector by the person to whom the relief was given within 60 days of his coming to know of the event. Where the inspector has reason to believe that a notice so required has not been given, he may require that person to furnish him, within a specified time not being less than 60 days, with such information relating to the event as he may reasonably require. The requirements of secrecy do not prevent the inspector disclosing to a VCT that relief has been given or claimed by reference to a particular number or proportion of its shares. Penalties under *TMA 1970, s 98* apply for failure to comply with these requirements.

[*ICTA 1988, Sch 15B paras 3–5; FA 1995, s 71(3), Sch 15 paras 3–5; FA 2000, Sch 18 para 1(3), para 3; FA 2004, s 94(2); ITTOIA 2005, Sch 1 para 346(2); SI 2005 No 3229, Reg 102; FA 2006, Sch 14 paras 4(2)(3), 7(3)(5)*].

Example

On 1 August 2008, A Ventura in the *Example* at 66.7 above, who since 2006/07 has neither acquired nor disposed of any shares in VCT plc, gives 30,000 shares to his son. On 1 March 2009 he disposes of the remaining 210,000 shares for £195,000. The relief given in 66.7 above is withdrawn as follows.

Disposal on 1 August 2008

The shares disposed of are identified with 30,000 of those subscribed for, and, since the disposal was not at arm's length, the relief given on those shares is fully withdrawn.

	£
Relief withdrawn 30,000/50,000 × £15,000 =	9,000

Disposal on 1 March 2009

The balance of £6,000 of the relief originally given was in respect of 20,000 of the shares disposed of. The disposal consideration for those 20,000 shares is

	£
$195{,}000 \times \dfrac{20{,}000}{210{,}000} =$	18,571

The relief withdrawn is the lesser of the relief originally given and 30% of the consideration received, i.e.
30% of £18,571 = £5,571.

Relief withdrawn is therefore	£5,571
The 2006/07 income tax assessment is therefore	£14,571

66.9 **Relief on dividends.** A 'VCT dividend' to which a 'qualifying investor' is beneficially entitled is not treated as income for income tax purposes, provided, for dividends made before 6 April 1999, that certain conditions are fulfilled as regards the obtaining of an 'enduring declaration' from the investor, and that the VCT claims the related tax credit, which it is required to pass on to the investor. Dividends made after 5 April 1999 remain exempt from income tax but, in line with general tax changes, tax credits are not repayable.

A '*qualifying investor*' is an individual aged 18 or over who is beneficially entitled to the dividend either as the holder of the shares or through a nominee (including the trustees of a bare trust).

A '*VCT dividend*' is a dividend (including a capital dividend) in respect of ordinary shares in a company which is a VCT which were acquired at a time when it was a VCT by the recipient of the dividend, and which were not shares acquired in excess of the 'permitted maximum' for the year of assessment. Shares acquired after 8 March 1999 must also have been acquired for *bona fide* commercial purposes and not as part of a tax avoidance scheme or arrangements. A VCT dividend does not include any dividend paid in respect of profits or gains of any accounting period ending when the company was not a VCT.

Shares are acquired in excess of the '*permitted maximum*' for a year where the aggregate of the market values of ordinary shares acquired in VCTs by the individual or his nominee(s) in that year exceeds £200,000 (£100,000 for 2003/04 and earlier years), disregarding shares acquired other than for *bona fide* commercial reasons or as part of a scheme or arrangement a main purpose of which is the avoidance of tax. Shares acquired later in the year are identified as representing the excess before those acquired earlier, and in relation to same-day acquisition of different shares, a proportionate part of each description of share is treated as representing any excess arising on that day. Shares acquired at a time when a company was not a VCT are for these purposes treated as disposed of before other shares in the VCT. Otherwise, disposals are identified with earlier acquisitions before later ones, except that as between shares acquired on the same day, shares acquired in excess of the permitted maximum are treated as disposed of before any other shares. There are provisions for effectively disregarding acquisitions arising out of share exchanges where, for capital gains purposes, the new shares are treated as the same assets as the old.

[*ITTOIA 2005, ss 709–712, Sch 1 para 346(3); ICTA 1988, Sch 15B paras 7–9; FA 1995, Sch 15 paras 7–9; FA 1999, s 70; FA 2004, Sch 19 paras 2, 3; SI 1995 No 1979, Reg 10; SI 1999 No 819, Reg 4*].

For the detailed requirements as regards obtaining relief for dividends, including the obtaining of the 'enduring declaration' and the claiming of tax credits, see *SI 1995 No 1979, Pt III Ch II*, repealed with effect from 6 April 1999 by *SI 1999 No 819, Reg 4*.

66.10 **CAPITAL GAINS TAX RELIEFS** [*TCGA 1992, ss 151A, 151B, Sch 5C; FA 1995, s 72, Sch 16; FA 2002, Sch 9 paras 5(9), 7; FA 2004, Sch 19 paras 4–7, Sch 42 Pt 2(12); ITTOIA 2005, Sch 1 para 437; SI 2005 No 3229, Reg 128*]

The capital gains of a VCT are not chargeable gains. [*TCGA 1992, s 100(1); FA 1995, s 72(2)*]. In addition, individual investors in VCTs are entitled to two reliefs:

(*a*) on disposal of VCT shares (see 66.11 below); and

(*b*) by deferral of chargeable gains on re-investment in VCT share issues before 6 April 2004 (see 66.12 below).

Various provisions of *TCGA 1992* which are superseded for these purposes by specific provisions (as below) are disapplied or applied separately to parts of holdings which do not fall within the reliefs.

See also 66.2 above for the effect on the reliefs where a VCT enters liquidation or there is a merger of VCTs..

Withdrawal of approval. Where approval of a company as a VCT is withdrawn (but not treated as never having been given) (see 66.2 above), shares which (apart from the withdrawal) would be eligible for the relief on disposal (see 66.11 below) are treated as disposed of at their market value at the time of the withdrawal. For the purposes of the relief on disposal, the disposal is treated as taking place while the company is still a VCT, but the re-acquisition is treated as taking place immediately after it ceases to be so.

66.11 **Relief on disposal.** A gain or loss accruing to an individual on a 'qualifying disposal' of ordinary shares in a company which was a VCT throughout his period of ownership is not a chargeable gain or an allowable loss. A disposal is a '*qualifying disposal*' if:

(*a*) the individual is 18 years of age or more at the time of the disposal;

(*b*) the shares were not acquired in excess of the 'permitted maximum' for any year of assessment; and

(*c*) the shares were acquired for *bona fide* commercial purposes and not as part of a scheme or arrangement a main purpose of which was the avoidance of tax.

The identification of those shares which were acquired in excess of the '*permitted maximum*' is as under 66.9 above, i.e. where the aggregate of the market values of ordinary shares acquired in VCTs by the individual or his nominee(s) in that year exceeds £200,000 (£100,000 for 2003/04 and earlier years), disregarding shares acquired other than for *bona fide* commercial reasons or as part of a scheme or arrangement a main purpose of which is the avoidance of tax. Shares acquired later in the year are identified as representing the excess before those acquired earlier, and in relation to same-day acquisition of different shares, a proportionate part of each description of share is treated as representing any excess arising on that day. Shares acquired at a time when a company was not a VCT are for these purposes treated as disposed of before other shares in the VCT. Otherwise, disposals are identified with earlier acquisitions before later ones, except that as between shares acquired on the same day, shares acquired in excess of the permitted maximum are treated as disposed of before any other shares. See the examples at HMRC Venture Capital Schemes Manual VCM 66800, 66850.

The normal rules for the pooling of shares and identification of disposals in *TCGA 1992, ss 104, 105, 106A, 107* (see 59.2, 59.3 SHARES AND SECURITIES—IDENTIFICATION RULES) are disapplied in respect of shares which are eligible for the above relief.

There are provisions (see below) for effectively disregarding acquisitions arising out of share exchanges where, for capital gains purposes, the new shares are treated as the same assets as the old.

Where an individual holds ordinary shares in a VCT which fall into more than one of the following groups:

(1) shares eligible for relief on disposal (as above) and by reference to which he has been given or is entitled to claim relief under the provisions in 66.7 above (income tax relief on investments);

(2) shares eligible for relief on disposal but by reference to which he has not been given or will be unable to claim relief under the provisions in 66.7 above;

(3) shares by reference to which he has been given or is entitled to claim relief under the provisions in 66.7 above but which are not eligible for relief on disposal;

(4) shares not within (1)–(3) above,

then, if there is a reorganisation under *TCGA 1992, s 126*, the provisions in *TCGA 1992, s 127* (equation of original shares with new holding) (see 58.1 SHARES AND SECURITIES above) will apply separately to each group of shares (if any) in order that they continue to be kept within their respective groups.

Where an individual holds ordinary shares in a company ('the existing holding') and there is, by virtue of an allotment for payment within *TCGA 1992, s 126(2)(a)* (e.g. a rights issue), a reorganisation affecting the existing holding immediately following which the shares or allotted holding are shares falling within (1)–(3) above, the provisions in *TCGA 1992, ss 127–130* will not apply in relation to that existing holding. The effect is that the rights issue will be treated as an acquisition.

Where holding consists of shares falling within (1) or (2) above and it is exchanged or is deemed to be exchanged for a second holding which does not consist of ordinary shares in a VCT, then the provisions in *TCGA 1992, ss 135, 136* will not apply (see 58.4 and 58.6 SHARES AND SECURITIES above). The effect is that there will be or deemed to be a disposal and acquisition.

[*TCGA 1992, ss 151A, 151B; FA 1995, s 72(3); FA 1998, s 124(6); FA 2002, Sch 9 paras 5(9), 7; ITTOIA 2005, Sch 1 para 437*].

See 66.10 above as regards relief on withdrawal of approval of the VCT.

Example

On the disposals in the *Example* at 66.8 above, a chargeable gain or allowable loss arises only on the disposal of the shares acquired in excess of the permitted maximum for 2006/07. The shares in VCT plc were acquired in 2006/07 for £220,000, so that there is a £20,000 excess over the permitted maximum. The 50,000 shares first acquired for £50,000 are first identified, so that shares representing the excess are two-seventeenths of the 190,000 shares subsequently acquired for £170,000 on 1 March 2007, i.e. 22,353 of those shares. The disposal identified with those shares is a corresponding proportion of the 210,000 shares disposed of for a consideration of £195,000 on 1 March 2009.

Mr Ventura's capital gains tax computation for 2008/09 is as follows.

Disposal consideration for 22,353 shares:	£
$£195{,}000 \times \dfrac{22{,}353}{210{,}000} =$	20,756
Deduct Cost:	
$£170{,}000 \times \dfrac{22{,}353}{190{,}000} =$	20,000
Chargeable gain (subject to taper relief)	£756

66.12 **Deferral relief on reinvestment.** The relief described below is **abolished** for shares issued on or after **6 April 2004**.

TCGA 1992, Sch 5C applies where:

(*a*) a chargeable gain accrues to an individual after 5 April 1995

- on the disposal by him of any asset; or
- on the occurrence of a chargeable event under these provisions or the similar provisions governing reinvestment into EIS shares (see 21.10 ENTERPRISE INVESTMENT SCHEME);

(*b*) the individual makes a 'qualifying investment' before 6 April 2004; and

(*c*) the individual is UK resident or ordinarily resident both when the chargeable gain accrues to him and when he makes the 'qualifying investment', and is not, at the latter time, regarded as resident outside the UK for the purposes of any double taxation arrangements the effect of which would be that he would not be liable to tax on a gain arising on a disposal, immediately after their acquisition, of the shares comprising the 'qualifying investment', disregarding the exemption under *TCGA 1992, s 151A*(*1*) (see 66.11 above).

A '*qualifying investment*' is a subscription for shares in a company which is a VCT, by reference to which income tax investment relief is obtained under 66.7 above, within twelve months (extendible by HMRC) before or after the time of the accrual of the chargeable gain in question, and, if before, provided that the shares are still held at that time. The shares are not deemed to be issued by reason only of a letter of allotment.

Broadly, the detailed provisions below allow a claim for the chargeable gain to be rolled over into the VCT shares, and for the gain to become chargeable on certain events in relation to those shares (including, in particular, on their disposal).

Postponement of original gain. Where a chargeable gain would otherwise accrue to an individual ('the investor') and he acquires a qualifying investment, a claim can be made by him to defer the whole or part of that gain against a corresponding amount of his qualifying investment up to the amount of the gain, or for an amount so claimed, whichever is the smaller. The gain eligible for deferral is the gain after all available reliefs (including indexation allowance and (for disposals before 6 April 2003) retirement relief where available) other than taper relief (see 61.15 TAPER RELIEF) (HMRC Venture Capital Schemes Manual VCM 68020). The amount of qualifying investment available for set-off is restricted to the amount on which income tax investment relief has been given under 66.7 above (maximum **£100,000** per tax year), less any amount already utilised against other gains. If income tax investment relief is restricted because the investor's income tax liability is insufficient to fully absorb the relief, deferral relief is still available on the full amount of the investment that would otherwise have qualified for the income tax relief. It is, however, necessary for *some* income tax investment relief to have been given; no deferral relief is available if the investor's income tax liability is nil without taking account of income tax investment relief. (HMRC Venture Capital Schemes Manual VCM 68030).

Subject to what is said at 12.2 CLAIMS re claims being included in a self-assessment tax return if possible, there is no statutory form in which a claim must be made. Deferral cannot be given until income tax relief has been given in respect of the VCT shares, which may not be until after the end of the tax year in which they are issued. (HMRC Venture Capital Schemes Manual VCM 69000). The deferral claim must be made by the fifth anniversary of 31 January following the 'relevant tax year'. The '*relevant tax year*' is the tax year in which the *later* of the following events occurred:

- the gain to be deferred arose;
- the VCT shares were issued.

(HMRC Venture Capital Schemes Manual VCM 69010).

Chargeable event. The original gain deferred through the making of the above claim will subsequently crystallise if one of the following circumstances arise:

(A) the investor disposes of the shares in his qualifying investment ('the relevant shares') otherwise than under *TCGA 1992, s 58* (a transfer between spouses or civil partners);

(B) the relevant shares are disposed of by the spouse or civil partner of the investor (otherwise than by a transfer back to him), the spouse or partner having first acquired them from the investor under *TCGA 1992, s 58*;

(C) where shares falling within 66.11(3) above are exchanged or treated as exchanged for any non-VCT holdings and under *TCGA 1992, s 135* or *TCGA 1992, s 136* (see 58.4 and 58.6 SHARES AND SECURITIES above) there is a requirement (or, but for *TCGA 1992, s 116* (see 50 QUALIFYING CORPORATE BONDS above) there would be a requirement) for those holdings to be regarded as the same assets as those shares;

(D) the investor becomes neither resident nor ordinarily resident in the UK whilst holding the relevant shares and within three years of the making of the qualifying investment (five years as regards shares issued before 6 April 2000);

(E) an individual who acquired the relevant shares through a transfer under *TCGA 1992, s 58* becomes neither resident nor ordinarily resident in the UK whilst holding those shares and within period referred to in (D) above;

(F) the company in which the relevant shares are held has its approval as a VCT withdrawn (in a case in which approval is not treated as never having been given) (see 66.2 above);

(G) the relief given under 66.7 above by reference to relevant shares is withdrawn or reduced in circumstances not falling within (A)–(F) above;

(H) the 'prescribed winding-up period' of a VCT-in-liquidation comes to an end, the VCT-in-liquidation then still being in existence (see 66.2(IV) above).

In the case of (D) or (E) above, the original gain will not crystallise where the individual concerned became neither resident nor ordinarily resident in the UK through temporarily working abroad and he again becomes UK resident or ordinarily resident in the UK within three years of that event, without having disposed of any of the relevant shares in the meantime. An assessment will be issued by HMRC when it is clear that the individual will not regain UK resident status within the three-year period.

There is no crystallisation of the original gain where an event within (A)–(H) above occurs at or after the time of death of the investor or a person to whom the relevant shares were transferred under *TCGA 1992, s 58*.

Without prejudice to the following provisions in a case falling within (F) (or (H)) above, any reference above to a disposal excludes a reference to the disposal deemed to occur on the withdrawal of approval (or the deemed withdrawal at the end of the prescribed winding-up period (see 66.2(III) above) within 66.10 above.

Crystallisation of original gain. Where a chargeable event mentioned in (A)–(H) above relating to relevant shares occurs for the first time in connection with those shares, a chargeable gain is deemed to accrue at that time equal to so much of the expenditure on those shares which was set against the original gain.

Identification of shares. In determining whether any shares to which a chargeable gain relates are shares the expenditure on which has been set against the whole or part of any gain, disposals of shares are identified with those subscribed for earlier rather than later, and as between shares in a company acquired on the same day, those the expenditure on which has been set against a gain are treated as disposed of after any other shares in that company. The normal rules at 59.2 SHARES AND SECURITIES—IDENTIFICATION RULES are disapplied (regardless of whether or not the shares are eligible for CGT relief under 66.11 above). For a practical illustration, see the *Example* below and, for a more complex example, HMRC Venture Capital Schemes Manual VCM 68320.

Assets. Where at the time of a chargeable event relevant shares are regarded as represented by assets which consist of or include assets other than relevant shares, the expenditure on those shares is apportioned between those assets on a just and reasonable basis. As between different assets regarded as representing the same relevant shares, the identification of those assets will be determined on a similar basis to the identification of shares.

Persons assessable. The chargeable gain is treated as accruing, as the case may be:

(i) to the individual who makes the disposal;

(ii) to the individual who holds the shares in question at the time of the exchange or deemed exchange;

(iii) to the individual who becomes non-UK resident etc.;

(iv) to the individual who holds the shares in question when the withdrawal of the approval takes effect;

(v) to the individual who holds the shares in question immediately following the end of the VCT-in-liquidation's prescribed winding-up period; or

(vi) to the individual who holds the shares in question when the circumstances arise in respect of which the relief is withdrawn or reduced.

A chargeable gain is computed separately for the investor without reference to any shares held at the time of the chargeable event by a recipient to the investor from a *TCGA 1992, s 58* transfer.

[*TCGA 1992, Sch 5C; FA 1995, Sch 16; FA 1998, s 124(6); FA 2000, Sch 18 paras 2, 3; FA 2004, Sch 19 paras 4, 5, 7, Sch 42 Pt 2(12); SI 2004 No 2199, Reg 7; SI 2005 No 3229, Reg 128*].

See 61.15 TAPER RELIEF for the application of that relief to the deferred gain.

The above relief is abolished for shares issued on or after 6 April 2004.

Example

On 1 August 2003, Mr Truman subscribes for 50,000 eligible £1 shares issued at par to raise money by VCT2 plc, an approved venture capital trust. On 1 March 2004 he purchases a further 90,000 £1 shares in VCT2 plc for £70,000 on the open market. Mr Truman sells a painting on 1 November 2003, realising a chargeable gain of £26,900.

In addition to the relief against income tax he receives, he also claims deferral of the gain against his subscription for shares in VCT2 plc up to an amount of £19,000, leaving £7,900 to be covered by his annual exemption.

On 1 August 2005, Mr Truman, who since 2003/04 has neither acquired nor disposed of any shares in VCT2 plc, gives 30,000 shares to his son. On 1 March 2006 he disposes of the remaining 110,000 shares for £95,000. The gain of £19,000 deferred on the disposal of the painting crystallises and forms part of his gains for 2005/06 as follows.

1 August 2005 disposal

The 30,000 shares disposed of on 1 August 2005 are initially identified on a first in/first out basis with the 50,000 shares subscribed for on 1 August 2003. Of those 50,000 shares acquired on the same day, deferral relief is attributable to 19,000 shares (acquired for £19,000, the amount of the deferred gain). The disposal is matched firstly with the shares to which no deferral relief is attributable, i.e. 31,000 shares. [*TCGA 1992, Sch 5C para 4(3); FA 1995, Sch 16*]. The disposal therefore includes none of the 19,000 shares to which deferral relief is attributable. See also HMRC Venture Capital Schemes Manual VCM 68320.

1 March 2006 disposal

This disposal of 110,000 shares is firstly identified on a first in/first out basis with the remaining 20,000 of the shares subscribed for on 1 August 2003. Of those 20,000 shares acquired on the same day, deferral relief is attributable to 19,000 shares. The disposal is matched firstly with the shares to which no deferral relief is attributable, i.e. 1,000 shares, and then with the 19,000 shares to which deferral relief is attributable. The disposal includes all of the 19,000 shares to which deferral relief is attributable. Therefore, the whole of the £19,000 deferred gain is brought into charge on 1 March 2006.

The above interpretation of the rules for identifying disposals of VCT shares to which deferral relief is attributable is HMRC's interpretation at Venture Capital Schemes Manual VCM 68320. Where, as in this example, part disposals are involved, they act to the taxpayer's advantage (although in this example both part disposals are in the same tax year in any case). Note the contrast between the application of these rules and those for EIS deferral relief illustrated in the example at 21.10 ENTERPRISE INVESTMENT SCHEME.

NB: any taper relief available is disregarded for the purposes of this example, but see 61.15 TAPER RELIEF for a further example.

67 Wasting Assets

Cross-references. See 6.6 ASSETS for plant or machinery lease under a long finance lease; 22.4 EXEMPTIONS AND RELIEFS for tangible movable assets generally and 22.11 for private passenger motor vehicles; 38.13–38.23 LAND for leases of land which are wasting assets; and 55.7 ROLLOVER RELIEF for the relief available where assets are, or will within ten years, become wasting assets.

Simon's Direct Tax Service. See Division C2.9.

67.1 Subject to the following, where an asset disposed of is a 'wasting asset'

(*a*) the original cost, etc. (see 15.4 COMPUTATION OF GAINS AND LOSSES) less predictable residual value, is treated as diminishing evenly day by day over the asset's life, and

(*b*) additional expenditure (see 15.4 COMPUTATION OF GAINS AND LOSSES) is similarly treated as diminishing evenly over the remaining life of the asset as from the date the expenditure was first reflected in the state or nature of the asset

and only so much of the original cost and additional expenditure as, on the above basis, remains at the date of disposal is then deductible. If additional expenditure under (*b*) above creates or increases a residual value, then the new residual value is taken into account in (*a*) above. [*TCGA 1992, s 46*].

A '*wasting asset*' is an asset with a predictable 'life' not exceeding 50 years and, in relation to tangible movable property, '*life*' means 'useful life', having regard to the purpose for which the tangible assets were acquired or provided by the person making the disposal. However, plant and machinery are always regarded as having a predictable life of less than 50 years and that life is to be based on normal usage. Freehold land is never a wasting asset, whatever its nature and whatever the nature of the building or works on it. The predictable life and predictable residual value, if not immediately ascertainable by the nature of the asset, are to be taken on a disposal as they were known or ascertainable at the time when the asset was acquired by the person making the disposal. [*TCGA 1992, s 44*].

Milk quota (see 6.9 ASSETS) is not regarded by HMRC as a wasting asset (HMRC Capital Gains Manual CG 77940).

No restriction of allowable expenditure as above occurs where an asset, throughout the ownership of the person making the disposal, is used solely for the purposes of a trade, profession or vocation, and capital allowances have, or could have, been claimed in respect of its cost, or in respect of any enhancement expenditure. This also applies where an asset has otherwise qualified in full for any capital allowances. Where, however, the asset disposed of has been used partly for non-business purposes, or has only partly qualified for capital allowances, the expenditure and consideration are apportioned and the restrictions imposed above applied to that portion of expenditure which has not qualified for capital allowances, or which relates to the period of non-business use. [*TCGA 1992, s 47*].

Tangible movable assets (chattels) which are wasting assets are exempt subject to certain conditions. See 22.4 EXEMPTIONS AND RELIEFS. Chattels such as antique clocks and certain motor vehicles may be 'machinery' and thus exempt subject to those conditions (which broadly correspond to those of *TCGA 1992, s 47* above). See Revenue Tax Bulletin, October 1994, pp 166, 167 for HMRC's meaning of machinery.

Example

V bought an aircraft on 31 May 2001 at a cost of £90,000 for use in his air charter business. It has been agreed that V's non-business use of the aircraft amounts to one-tenth, on a flying hours basis, and capital allowances and running costs have accordingly been restricted for income tax purposes. On 1 February 2007, V sells the aircraft for £185,000. The aircraft is agreed as having a useful life of 20 years at the date it was acquired.

	£	£
Amount qualifying for capital allowances		
Relevant portion of disposal consideration 9/10 × £185,000		166,500
Relevant portion of acquisition cost 9/10 × £90,000		81,000
Chargeable gain 2006/07 (subject to TAPER RELIEF (61))		£85,500
Amount not qualifying for capital allowances		
Relevant portion of disposal consideration 1/10 × £185,000		18,500
Relevant portion of acquisition cost		
1/10 × £90,000	9,000	
Deduct wasted $£9{,}000 \times \frac{5y\ 8m}{20y}$	2,550	6,450
Gain		£12,050

The whole of the £12,050 is exempt.

The total chargeable gain (before taper relief) is therefore £85,500

67.2 OPTIONS AND FUTURES CONTRACTS

Generally speaking, options are treated as wasting assets and are subject to the rules outlined in 67.1 above. However, there are specific statutory exceptions to this and these, together with further rules relating to options generally, are covered in 6.7 ASSETS. For employee share options, see 20 EMPLOYEE SHARE SCHEMES. See 22.56 EXEMPTIONS AND RELIEFS and 65.2 UNIT TRUSTS ETC. for options held by pension schemes and authorised unit trusts respectively.

See 6.8 ASSETS for certain commodity and financial futures which are excepted from wasting asset treatment.

67.3 LEASES OF PROPERTY OTHER THAN LAND

In accordance with the definition of a wasting asset given in 67.1 above a 'lease of property other than land' may be or become a wasting asset. Such a lease which is a wasting asset is subject to the rules in 67.1 above, and in particular those regarding allowable expenditure. This treatment should be compared with leases of land which are wasting assets where, instead of allowable expenditure being written off at a uniform rate, a special basis is used (see 38.14 LAND). Despite this, the legislation regarding leases of property other than land is mainly by direct reference to that covering leases of land with 'necessary modifications'. [*TCGA 1992, ss 44, 46, 47, 240, Sch 8 para 9*(*1*)].

A '*lease of property other than land*' means any kind of agreement or arrangement under which payments are made for the use of, or otherwise in respect of, property and '*lessor*', '*lessee*' and '*rent*' are construed accordingly. [*TCGA 1992, Sch 8 para 10*(*1*)(*b*)].

Duration of a lease. The duration of a lease is to be decided by reference to the facts known or ascertainable at the time when the lease was acquired or created. In determining the duration, the following provisions apply.

(*a*) Where the terms of the lease include provision for the determination of the lease by notice given by the lessor, the lease is not to be treated as granted for a term longer than one ending at the earliest date on which it could be determined by notice given by the lessor.

(*b*) Where any of the terms of the lease or any other circumstances rendered it unlikely that the lease will continue beyond a date earlier than the expiration of the terms of the lease, the lease is not to be treated as having been granted for a longer term than one ending on that date. This applies in particular where the lease provides for rent to go up after a given date, or for the lessee's obligation to become more onerous after a given date, but includes provision for the determination of the lease on that date, by notice given by the lessee, and those provisions render it unlikely that the lease will continue beyond that date.

(*c*) Where the terms of the lease include provision for the extension of the lease beyond a given date by notice given by the lessee, the duration of the lease applies as if the term of the lease extended for as long as it could be extended by the lessee, but subject to any right of the lessor to determine the lease by notice.

(*d*) In the case of a lease of an asset which itself is a wasting asset and also movable property, the lease is assumed to terminate not later than the end of the life of the wasting asset.

[*TCGA 1992, Sch 8 para 8, para 9(3)*].

67.4 **Premiums for leases.** Where the payment of a 'premium' is required under a lease (or otherwise under the terms subject to which the lease is granted) there is a part disposal of the asset or other interest out of which that lease is granted.

In the part disposal computation (which follows the normal rules in *TCGA 1992, s 42*, see 15.7 COMPUTATION OF GAINS AND LOSSES) the property which remains undisposed of includes a right to any rent or other payments (other than a premium) payable under the lease, and that right is valued at the time of the part disposal. [*TCGA 1992, Sch 8 para 2*].

'*Premium*' includes any like sum, whether payable to the intermediate or superior lessor and includes any sum (other than rent) paid on or in connection with the granting of a lease except in so far as the other sufficient consideration for the payment is shown to have been given. Other capital sums payable by a tenant may fall to be treated as premiums (see 38.15 LAND).

Where by reference to any capital sum within the meaning of *ICTA 1988, s 781* (assets leased to traders and others) any amount of that capital sum is charged to income tax then that amount is deducted from the consideration for capital gains tax purposes but not so as to convert a gain into a loss or increase a loss. [*TCGA 1992, Sch 8 para 9(2)*].

67.5 **Sub-leases granted out of short leases.** Where a sub-lease is granted out of a head-lease with less than 50 years to run, the normal part disposal rules do not apply. Instead, subject to below, a proportion of the cost and enhancement expenditure attributable to the lease is apportioned to the part disposed of as follows

$$\frac{P(1)}{P(2)}$$

where

P(1) = the duration of the sub-lease

P(2) = the duration of the lease at the date of acquisition (for apportionment of cost) or the duration of the lease at the date when expenditure is first reflected in the nature of the lease (for apportionment of enhancement expenditure).

If the amount of the premium is less than what would be obtainable by way of premium for the sub-lease if the rent payable under the sub-lease were the same as the rent payable under the lease, the percentage attributable to the sub-lease as calculated above must be multiplied by the premium received over the premium so obtainable before being applied to cost or enhancement expenditure. [*TCGA 1992, Sch 8 para 4(1)(2)*].

Example

P purchases a 40-year lease of a non-wasting asset (other than land) in 2001 for £15,000. In 2006 he grants a sub-lease of the asset to Q for 20 years for a premium of £8,000. Had the rent under head-lease and sub-lease been the same the premium would have been £10,000. The expenditure attributable to the part disposal of the sub-lease is given by

$$£15{,}000 \times \frac{20}{40} \times \frac{8{,}000}{10{,}000} = 0.4 \times £\,15{,}000 = £\,6{,}000$$

Where the sub-lease is a sub-lease of part only of the asset comprised in the lease, the cost and enhancement expenditure of the head-lease must be apportioned between the sub-lease and the remainder in proportion to their respective values. [*TCGA 1992, Sch 8 para 4(3)*].

67.6 **LIFE INTERESTS**

Life interests in settled property within 67.1 above are treated as wasting assets when the expectation of life of the life tenant is 50 years or less. The predictable life of life tenants and annuities is ascertained from actuarial tables which have HMRC approval. [*TCGA 1992, s 44(1)(d)*]. See 57.14 SETTLEMENTS for the disposal of interests in settled property generally.

Example

N is a beneficiary under a settlement. On 30 June 1992, when her actuarially estimated life expectancy was 40 years, she sold her life interest to an unrelated individual, R, for £50,000. N dies on 31 December 2006, and the life interest is extinguished.

R will have an allowable loss for 2006/07 as follows

	£	£
Disposal consideration on death of N		Nil
Allowable cost	50,000	
Deduct wasted $\frac{14y\ 6m}{40y} \times £\,50{,}000$	18,125	
		31,875
Allowable loss		£31,875

Note to the example

(*a*) The amount of the cost wasted is computed by reference to the predictable life, not the actual life, of the wasting asset.

68 Finance Act 2006—Summary of CGT Provisions

The following is a brief summary of the main provisions of the current Finance Act that are concerned with, or impinge upon, capital gains tax (CGT) and/or corporation tax on chargeable gains. For an exhaustive list of current Finance Act provisions covered in Tolley's Capital Gains Tax, which may also include, for example, taxes management provisions of more general application, see 71 TABLE OF STATUTES.

(Royal Assent 19 July 2006)

s 23 — **Rates of tax.** For 2006/07, the starting rate, basic rate and higher rate of income tax (and thus, effectively, CGT) are established (the starting rate limit and basic rate limit being set by statutory instrument). See 2.1 ANNUAL RATES AND EXEMPTIONS.

s 54 — **Charities: transactions with substantial donors.** Anti-avoidance provisions are introduced to restrict the transactions that can take place between a 'substantial donor' and a charity without loss of tax exemptions. The provisions apply, broadly, to transactions occurring on or after 22 March 2006. See 10.4 CHARITIES.

s 55 — **Charities: non-charitable expenditure.** For chargeable periods beginning on or after 22 March 2006, where a charity incurs non-charitable expenditure, the amount of tax relief given under certain exemptions, including in respect of chargeable gains, is reduced by an amount equal to that expenditure. See 10.4 CHARITIES.

s 64 — **Payments in respect of Nazi persecution.** An exemption is introduced for gains accruing on disposal of rights to receive payments of interest under certain compensation schemes for deposits made on or before 5 June 1945 by, or on behalf of, victims of Nazi persecution. The exemption applies with retrospective effect to disposals on or after 6 April 1996. See 22.13 EXEMPTIONS AND RELIEFS.

ss 65–68 — **London Olympic Games 2012.** A number of tax exemptions relating to the Games are introduced. See 22.52 EXEMPTIONS AND RELIEFS.

s 69 — **Restrictions on a company's allowable losses.** For corporation tax purposes only, a loss accruing on a disposal on or after 5 December 2005 directly or indirectly in consequence of, or otherwise in connection with, any arrangements the main purpose of which, or one of the main purposes of which, is to secure a tax advantage is not an allowable loss. See 13.4 COMPANIES.

s 70 — **Restrictions on companies buying losses or gains.** With effect, broadly, for accounting periods ending on or after 5 December 2005, anti-avoidance provisions are introduced to restrict the use of capital losses where there is a change of ownership of a company as a result of arrangements with a tax avoidance purpose. See 27.18 GROUPS OF COMPANIES. The provisions apply in priority to the original loss buying provisions (see 27.20 GROUPS OF COMPANIES) and replace the original gain buying provisions, which are repealed (see 27.31 GROUPS OF COMPANIES).

s 71	**Avoidance involving losses of companies.** Further anti-avoidance provisions are introduced to ensure that capital losses of companies cannot be used against income profits. The provisions target two types of avoidance scheme. The first is to turn an income receipt into capital. The second is to generate a deduction from income as part of arrangements to crystallise a capital gain. The provisions apply to disposals on or after 5 December 2005. See 13.5 COMPANIES.
s 72	**Repeal of *TCGA 1992, s 106*.** The special identification rules for shares acquired and disposed of by a company within a short period are repealed for disposals on or after 5 December 2005. See 13.14 COMPANIES.
s 73	**Policies of insurance and non-deferred annuities.** For disposals on or after 5 December 2005, the exemption for disposals of rights under a contract for a 'non-deferred annuity' is extended to annuities granted otherwise than by a company. See 22.3 EXEMPTIONS AND RELIEFS. For disposals on or after 5 December 2005, the provisions providing for exemption for disposal of rights conferred by a 'non-life insurance policy' are clarified so as explicitly to include capital redemption policies. See 22.10 EXEMPTIONS AND RELIEFS.
s 74	**Exception to bed and breakfasting rules.** For acquisitions on or after 22 March 2006, '30-day' capital gains tax share identification rule does not require shares to be identified with shares which the person making the disposal acquires at a time when he is neither resident nor ordinarily resident in the UK or when he is treaty non-resident. See 59.2 SHARES AND SECURITIES — IDENTIFICATION RULES.
s 77	**Intangible fixed assets.** Anti-avoidance provisions are introduced, broadly, to treat an asset created after the commencement of the corporation tax intangible fixed assets regime and acquired by a company from a related party as excluded from the regime by its commencement provisions where either the asset is derived from assets themselves so excluded or the acquisition is directly or indirectly in consequence of, or in connection with, the disposal of an excluded asset. The provisions apply, broadly, on or after 5 December 2005. See 14.13 COMPANIES — CORPORATE FINANCE AND INTANGIBLES.
s 88, Sch 12	**Settlements.** A number of changes are made to the capital gains provisions for settlements. The main changes are as follows. A new standard definition of 'settlor' is introduced for most capital gains purposes with effect from 6 April 2006. See 57.3 SETTLEMENTS. For the purposes of the charge on settlors with an interest in a settlement, the rules determining when a settlor has an interest are amended with effect from 6 April 2006 to include cases where property is payable to, or benefits are enjoyed by, a dependent child of the settlor. See 57.5 SETTLEMENTS. For 2006/07 onwards, trustees of a settlement can make an election under which a specified part of the settled property is treated for capital gains tax purposes as a separate settlement (a sub-fund settlement). See 57.8 SETTLEMENTS. The rules determining the residence status of trustees are amended for 2007/08 onwards. See 44.1 OFFSHORE SETTLEMENTS.

s 91, Sch 14	**Venture capital schemes.** Amendments are made to the enterprise investment scheme, the corporate venturing scheme and the venture capital trusts rules. In particular the income tax relief rate for investments in venture capital trusts is reduced to 30% and the minimum period for holding shares is increased to five years for shares issued on or after 6 April 2006. See 66.7 VENTURE CAPITAL TRUSTS. The maximum investment qualifying for income tax relief under the enterprise investment scheme is increased to £400,000 for 2006/07 onwards. See 21.2 ENTERPRISE INVESTMENT SCHEME.
s 92	**Employee share schemes.** The extended definition of shares at 21.2 EMPLOYEE SHARE SCHEMES is further amended with reference to options with retrospective effect from 2 December 2004.
ss 103–145, Schs 16, 17	**Real estate investment trusts.** For accounting periods beginning on or after 1 January 2007, companies meeting the necessary conditions can elect to become real estate investment trusts. A special tax regime applies to the property business of such a trust, the business being effectively ring-fenced with profits and gains exempt from corporation tax. See 65.4 UNIT TRUSTS, ETC.

69 Tax Case Digest

Cases referred to in this chapter are cross-referenced to the relevant paragraph of this edition. Statutory references marked with an asterisk (*) are to legislation which has replaced that involved in the case summarised.

Aberdeen Construction Group Ltd v CIR 15.1, 22.5

Loan waiver condition of sale of shares — 'debt on a security'

A company sold its shares in a subsidiary for £250,000, a condition of the sale being that it waived repayment of unsecured loans of £500,000 it had made to the subsidiary. It was assessed on its gain from the sale of the shares with no allowance for the £500,000. The HL rejected the company's contentions that the loan was a 'debt on a security' within *TCGA 1992, s 251(1)** or that *TCGA 1992, s 43** applied, but held that the waiver of the loan was part of the consideration for the £250,000. The appeal was remitted to the Commissioners to make an appropriate apportionment under *TCGA 1992, s 52(4)**. *Aberdeen Construction Group Ltd v CIR HL 1978, 52 TC 281; [1978] STC 127; [1978] 2 WLR 648; [1978] 1 All ER 962.*

Allison v Murray 15.4

Insurance premium paid as part of trust variation

A settlement in Scots form was varied by agreement on 3 March 1965 on terms whereby 60% of the trust fund, less £10,000, became absolutely vested in Mrs M who was required at her own expense to effect a single-premium policy in favour of the trustees against the event of her predeceasing Mrs W. In the event, Mrs W died on 1 March 1966, survived by Mrs M. Mrs M's husband was assessed for 1966/67 on the gain on the sale by the trustees of investments appropriated to Mrs M by reference to their market value at 6 April 1965. The assessment was upheld and a deduction refused for the insurance premium as not falling within *TCGA 1992, s 38(1)(a) or (b)**. Certain other contentions by the husband (who conducted his appeal in person) were rejected. *Allison v Murray Ch D 1975, 51 TC 57; [1975] STC 524; [1975] 1 WLR 1578; [1975] 3 All ER 561.*

Anders Utkilens Rederi AS v OY Lovisa Stevedoring Co AB 15.7

Compromise agreement for sale of defendant's property — whether a part disposal

A Norwegian company obtained judgement against another company for a liquidated sum. The defendant company appealed, but a compromise agreement was reached whereby the defendant's premises, plant and machinery were to be sold and the proceeds divided between the parties. The defendant subsequently went into voluntary liquidation, and the property was sold a year later. The Ch D held that the compromise agreement effected a part disposal of the property by the defendant to the plaintiff, and that each party subsequently disposed of its interest then held to the ultimate purchaser. *Anders Utkilens Rederi AS v OY Lovisa Stevedoring Co AB & Another Ch D 1984, [1985] STC 301; [1985] 2 All ER 669.*

Aspden v Hildesley 16.1, 42.4

Transfer of assets under Court Order on divorce

The taxpayer and his wife had jointly owned certain property, not the private residence of either. They had been separated since 1970 and were divorced by decree nisi on 12 February 1976. The Court Order (by consent) provided, inter alia, for the taxpayer's half share of the property to be transferred to his wife, while she undertook to give an irrevocable order to her personal representatives that, should she die before 10 December 1984 and before her husband, a sum equal to half the equity in the property was to be paid to him out of her estate. The taxpayer was assessed on the footing that he had disposed of his share in the property on 12 February 1976, and that by virtue of *CGTA 1979, s 19(3)(a)** and *TCGA 1992, ss 18, 286** the consideration was to be taken as the market value. The Ch D upheld the assessment, reversing the decision of the Commissioners. On the facts, the taxpayer's interest in the property was transferred at the time of the decree nisi, the consent order being an unconditional contract for the transfer. As the decree was not then absolute, the parties were still married and *CGTA 1979, s 19(3)(a)** applied by virtue of *TCGA 1992, s 18(2)*, s 286(2)*. Aspden v Hildesley Ch D 1981, 55 TC 609; [1982] STC 206; [1982] 1 WLR 264; [1982] 2 All ER 53.* (Note. *CGTA 1979, s 19(3)* was repealed by *FA 1981* and replaced by what is now *TCGA 1992, s 17.*)

Atkinson v Dancer 53.4

Retirement relief

A taxpayer farmed 89 acres and sold nine of them. He was assessed and claimed retirement relief, contending that the sale was a disposal of part of his business. The Ch D, reversing the Commissioners' decision, held that no relief was due, applying *McGregor v Adcock. Atkinson v Dancer Ch D 1988, 61 TC 598; [1988] STC 758.* (Note. Retirement relief is abolished for disposals after 5 April 2003 (see 53.1 RETIREMENT RELIEF).)

Barrett v Powell 53.4

Retirement relief — surrender of agricultural tenancy by farmer — continuation of farming under temporary licence

In March 1990 a tenant farmer received £120,000 from his landlord as compensation for surrendering his agricultural tenancy. He was allowed to continue to farm the land in question, under a temporary licence, until September 1991. The Revenue assessed the compensation to capital gains tax for 1989/90. The farmer appealed, contending that the payment of compensation qualified for retirement relief. The Ch D rejected this contention and upheld the assessment. On the evidence, the payment was made for the disposal of an asset, but was not made for the disposal of the whole or part of the farmer's business, since he had been able to continue farming the land in question for two summers under the temporary licence. *Jarmin v Rawlings* distinguished. *Barrett v Powell Ch D 1998, 70 TC 432; [1998] STC 283.* (Note. Retirement relief is abolished for disposals after 5 April 2003 (see 53.1 RETIREMENT RELIEF).)

Batey v Wakefield 49.1

Bungalow separated from main residence — whether part of dwelling-house

A taxpayer owned a house in Marlborough, built on 1.1 acres of land, but lived with his family in a London flat during the working week, returning to the house at weekends. He had elected under *TCGA 1992, s 222(5)** for the house to be treated as his main residence. Following a number of local burglaries, he had a bungalow built on the land, physically separate from the house and with separate road access. He arranged for the bungalow to be occupied by a farm labourer who acted as caretaker. In 1974 the taxpayer began living in the house on a full-time basis and, no longer needing a caretaker, sold the bungalow with 0.2 acres of land. The Revenue assessed the resulting gain to CGT and he appealed, contending that the bungalow had formed part of his dwelling-house and was exempt under *TCGA 1992, s 222**. The General Commissioners allowed his appeal, finding that the bungalow had been built for the purpose of providing services for the benefit of the main house, and holding that the occupation by the caretaker amounted to occupation by the taxpayer as part of his residence. The CA upheld the Commissioners' decision as one of fact, holding that they were entitled to conclude that the bungalow was part of the taxpayer's residence. *Batey v Wakefield CA 1981, 55 TC 550; [1981] STC 521; [1982] 1 All ER 61.* (Note. *Dicta* of Fox LJ were subsequently disapproved by the CA in *Lewis v Rook* below.)

Bayley v Rogers 38.14

Sale of new lease — whether a continuation of old lease

A taxpayer's 14-year lease of his business premises expired in December 1974 and, following proceedings under the *Landlord and Tenant Act 1954,* he was granted a new lease. He disposed of the new lease in 1976 and was assessed on the gain on the footing that the new lease was a separate asset from the old. He appealed, contending that the new lease was a continuation of the old and that the straightline basis over the period from 1960 should be used by virtue of *TCGA 1992, Sch 2 para 16**. The Ch D, reversing the Commissioners' decision, held that the two leases were separate assets, and the second lease was not derived from the first within the meaning of *TCGA 1992, s 43**. *Bayley v Rogers Ch D 1980, 53 TC 420; [1980] STC 544.*

Baylis v Gregory 3.1, 4.7, 5.1

Avoidance Schemes

The managing director of a company (PGI) controlled the company through his own and trustee shareholdings. Another company, C, entered into negotiations to acquire PGI, and the taxpayer and his associates set up a Manx company to exchange their shares in PGI with shares in the Manx company. However, C ended the negotiations. Nevertheless the share exchange was proceeded with and completed in March 1974. No further steps were taken to sell PGI until May 1975 when a third company, H, became interested in it. Eventually, the Manx company sold the PGI shares to H. The Special Commissioners allowed the taxpayer's appeals and their decision was upheld by the Ch D, the CA, and the HL. The transactions were not a 'pre-ordained series of transactions'. (The case was heard with *Craven v White*, in the CA and HL.) *Baylis v Gregory HL 1988, 62 TC 1; [1988] STC 476; [1988] 3 WLR 423; [1988] 3 All ER 495.*

Begg-McBrearty v Stilwell 57.12

Exercise of power of appointment in favour of grandchildren of settlor — whether grandchildren acquiring an interest in possession at age of 18 or 21

In 1975 the trustees of a settlement made in 1959 exercised their power of appointment in favour of the settlor's three grandchildren, and thereafter held the trust fund contingently for the grandchildren contingently on their reaching the age of 21. The eldest grandchild became 21 in 1990, and thus became absolutely entitled to a one-third share of the settled property. The Revenue issued a 1990/91 assessment on one of the trustees, charging CGT on the deemed disposal to the grandchild in accordance with *TCGA, s 71**. The trustee appealed, contending that the gain should be held over by virtue of *TCGA, s 260(2)(d)**. The Ch D upheld the assessment. The disposal could not be held over under *TCGA, s 260(2)(d)** because the grandchild had become entitled to an interest in possession in her share of the settled property in 1987, when she reached the age of 18. Before the exercise of the power of appointment, the grandchild had had only a revocable interest in the trust property. Her relevant interest arose from the power of appointment. Since this had been exercised in 1975, it fell within the provisions of Family Law Reform Act 1969 (which had reduced the age of majority to 18 with effect from 1 January 1970), even though the original settlement had been made before the date on which that act took effect. *Begg-McBrearty v Stilwell Ch D 1996, 68 TC 426; [1996] STC 413; [1996] 1 WLR 951; [1996] 4 All ER 205.*

Bentley v Pike 15.4

Rate of exchange where gain realised abroad

Under German law, the taxpayer's wife and her sister became equally entitled to real property in Germany under the intestacy of their father, resident and domiciled abroad. The father died on 31 October 1967. Following the issue of the German equivalent of Letters of Administration, the sisters were entered in the German Land Registry in July

1972 as tenants in common of the property. The property was sold in July 1973, the sisters receiving their shares of the net proceeds in Deutschmarks. The Ch D upheld the Commissioners' decision that the taxpayer had been correctly assessed on his wife's gain taken as the difference between the Deutschmark value of her share of the property at her father's death, converted into sterling at the then ruling exchange rate, and the Deutschmarks she received on the sale, converted into sterling at the rate ruling at the date of sale. The taxpayer's contentions that the date of acquisition was the date his wife was entered in the Land Registry, and that the gain was the difference between the two Deutschmark figures converted at the rate at the time of disposal, were rejected. On the evidence, under German law, his wife became absolutely entitled on her father's death. This was the date of acquisition by virtue of *TCGA 1992, s 62(1)(a)**. The unit of account for assessment was sterling and the market value of the deemed acquisition on the death must be arrived at using the exchange rate at the time. *Bentley v Pike Ch D 1981, 53 TC 590; [1981] STC 360.*

Billows v Hammond 41.4

Value of unquoted shares

In December 1986 the controlling director of a company gave most of his shares in the company to his two children. The Revenue issued an estimated CGT assessment, and the director appealed, contending that the shares had no value at the time of the transfer. The Special Commissioner rejected this contention and upheld the assessment in principle, holding on the evidence that the shares transferred had an open market value of £195 each. *Billows v Hammond (Sp C 252), [2000] SSCD 430.* (Note. The director had failed to notify the gift on his tax return and the Commissioner held that this constituted 'negligent conduct' within *TMA 1970, s 36* (see 23.4 FRAUDULENT OR NEGLIGENT CONDUCT). In separate proceedings, the CA had previously held that the company's accounts were unreliable.)

Bond v Pickford 57.12

Power of Appointment

In 1972 the trustees of a discretionary settlement, which had been established in 1961, executed two deeds to allocate part of the settled property. The allocated funds continued to be held by the trustees of the main settlement and were subject to the administrative powers of that settlement. The trustees were assessed on the basis that there had been a deemed disposal under *TCGA 1992, s 71(1)**. The Special Commissioners allowed their appeal and this decision was upheld by the Ch D and the CA. Applying dicta of Wilberforce J in *Roome v Edwards*, it would not be natural for a person with knowledge of the legal context of 'settlement', and applying that knowledge in a practical and common-sense manner to the facts, to say that separate settlements had been made by the allocations. There is a distinction between powers to alter the trusts of a settlement expressly or by necessary implication authorising the trustees to remove assets altogether from the original settlement (without rendering any person absolutely entitled to them), and powers which do not confer on the trustees such authority. The relevant powers here were of the latter type. *Bond v Pickford CA 1983, 57 TC 301; [1983] STC 517.*

Booth v Ellard 57.2

Shares transferred to trustees under pooling agreement — whether a disposal

Twelve shareholders in a company entered into an agreement under which their shares were transferred to trustees. This was done so that they and their families could retain effective control of the company if its shares were dealt with on the Stock Exchange. The agreement was for 15 years but subject to determination by shareholders who, between them, held a specified proportion of the shares transferred. The broad effect of the agreement was that the shares were pooled. The participants received the trust income proportionate to the shares they transferred and they were able to direct the trustees how to exercise the votes attaching to the shares or decide should there be a rights issue, etc. Provisions ensured that the shares would remain in the family should a participant die or wish to sell. CGT assessments were made on the footing that the agreement was a settlement of the shares. The CA allowed on appeal by one of the shareholders, reversing the decision of the Commissioners. The shareholders collectively had power to end the trust, and although their interests in their shares were subject to restraints, they did not lose their beneficial interests. They were absolutely entitled to their shares as against the trustees, within *TCGA 1992, s 60(1)**; hence the transfer to the trustees was not a chargeable disposal. *Booth v Ellard CA 1980, 53 TC 393; [1980] STC 555; [1980] 1 WLR 1443; [1980] 3 All ER 569.*

Bullivant Holdings Ltd v CIR 41.1

Acquisition of shares — whether TCGA 1992, s 17 applicable*

A company (B) acquired two 25% shareholdings in a publishing company, from different vendors, for a total of £25,000. It subsequently lodged a claim that *TCGA 1992, s 17** should be treated as applying to the acquisitions, so that its acquisition cost should be treated as market value rather than as £25,000. The Revenue rejected the claim and the Special Commissioner dismissed B's appeal. On the evidence, the shares had been acquired at arm's length and the consideration of £25,000 appeared to be 'a full and fair price'. Accordingly, *TCGA 1992, s 17** did not apply. The Ch D upheld this decision. *Bullivant Holdings Ltd v CIR Ch D 1998, 71 TC 22; [1998] STC 905.*

Burca v Parkinson 15.2

Beneficial ownership of asset

The controlling director of a publishing company sold his shareholding in 1988. In his tax return, he only accounted for tax on part of the consideration which he had received. Subsequently the Revenue issued assessments charging CGT on the balance of the gain. The director appealed, contending that he had passed 60% of the shares to his parents in 1987. The Special Commissioner reviewed the evidence, rejected this contention, and upheld the assessments, finding that although the director had borrowed money from his parents, there was 'no evidence … of the taxpayer completing (either in writing or orally) a declaration of trust in favour of his parents or of his agreeing to hold shares for them as nominee'. The director appealed to the Ch D, which upheld the Commissioner's decision. *Burca v Parkinson Ch D 2001, 74 TC 125; [2001] STC 1298.*

Burman v Hedges & Butler Ltd 27.9

Avoidance scheme — whether TCGA 1992, s 171 (transfers within a group) applicable*

A company (H) owned the share capital of B Ltd and was itself wholly owned by BC Ltd. BC Ltd agreed, subject to contract, to sell B Ltd to S Ltd, an unconnected company. To avoid the chargeable gain of about £½m which would have arisen on a direct sale, the following scheme was carried out. V Ltd was formed with capital of 76 £1 participating preference shares held by the taxpayer and 24 £1 ordinary shares held by S Ltd. Z Ltd was formed with share capital owned by V Ltd. Z Ltd bought the shares in B Ltd out of a loan to it by S Ltd. V Ltd then went into liquidation, the liquidator transferring its shares in Z Ltd to S Ltd as the ordinary shareholder of V Ltd. H was assessed on the basis that it had sold the shares in B Ltd to S Ltd. The Commissioners discharged the assessment, rejecting the Revenue's contention that V Ltd and Z Ltd had acted throughout as nominees or agents for S Ltd, and holding that the sale from H to Z Ltd was within *TCGA 1992, s 171**. Their decision was upheld by the Ch D. *Burman v Hedges & Butler Ltd Ch D 1978, 52 TC 501; [1979] STC 136; [1979] 1 WLR 160.*

Burman v Westminster Press Ltd 22.4

Wasting assets — whether TCGA 1992, s 45(2)(b) applicable where capital allowances withdrawn*

In 1973 a company (W), which published regional newspapers, agreed to purchase a printing press. The purchase price was paid by instalments beginning in 1973 and ending in 1977. The press was not delivered until 1976, by which time it was surplus to W's requirements. It was never used in W's trade and was kept in storage until 1978 when it was sold to a Dutch company at a profit of more than £650,000. W had been given first-year allowances on the instalments of the purchase price, but these were subsequently withdrawn under *FA 1971, s 41(2)*. The Revenue included the profit on the sale of the press in a CT assessment on W. W appealed, contending that the press was a wasting asset within *TCGA 1992, s 45** and had not qualified in full for a capital allowance within the meaning of *TCGA 1992, s 45(2)(b)**, so that the gain was exempt under *TCGA 1992, s 45(1)**. The Special Commissioner allowed W's appeal and the Ch D upheld this decision. The expenditure on the press had not fulfilled the necessary conditions to attract a capital allowance, so that *TCGA 1992, s 45(2)(b)** did not apply. *Burman v Westminster Press Ltd Ch D 1987, 60 TC 418; [1987] STC 669.*

Campbell Connelly & Co Ltd v Barnett 55.1, 55.3, 55.5

Rollover relief — whether new premises used for trading purposes 'on' acquisition

A music publishing company (C) sold its trading premises in 1984, and moved into the premises of its parent company. In January 1986, it purchased the freehold of another property, but was unable to obtain vacant possession because the property was occupied by lessees. In September 1986, C's parent company purchased the leasehold interest. C then moved into the property and began using it for trading purposes. C claimed rollover relief in respect of the gain on the sale of its previous premises. The Revenue refused to allow relief, considering that the premises had not been taken into trade use 'on the acquisition', as required by *TCGA 1992, s 152(1)**, and that the acquisition into which the gain could have been rolled over was the purchase of the leasehold interest, which had been carried out by the parent and not by C. The General Commissioners dismissed the company's appeal and the Ch D and CA upheld their decision. The premises had not been used for the purposes of C's trade on the acquisition of the freehold, and neither could the acquisitions of the freehold and leasehold interests by different legal persons be regarded as one transaction. Accordingly, relief was not due. *Campbell Connelly & Co Ltd v Barnett CA 1993, 66 TC 380; [1994] STC 50.* (Note. *TCGA 1992, s 152* has subsequently been amended by *FA 1995, s 48*.)

Cann v Woods 40.10

Irrecoverable loans to company ?whether TCGA 1992, s 253(12) applicable

In 1988 a wealthy investor (C) purchased a majority shareholding in a company (BG) which had four subsidiaries. The group was suffering financial difficulties. From 1989 to 1992 C made loans of more than £2,000,000 to one of BG's subsidiaries (B). However, B continued to suffer financial problems. In March 1994 BG sold its shareholding in B to another company (GD), and a week later B sold its net assets to GD. GD did not take over B's overdraft or the loans from C. C claimed relief under *TCGA 1992, s 253(3)* for his loans to B. The Revenue rejected the claim, considering that *TCGA 1992, s 253(12)* applied, on the basis that the loans had become irrecoverable as a result of an 'act ... by the lender', namely the sale of B's shares and assets. C appealed, contending that the loans had become irrecoverable as a result of the commercial situation. The Special Commissioner accepted this contention and allowed the appeal. When C had first invested in B, he believed that it had commercial potential. However, he could not be expected to fund B indefinitely. By February 1994 B had become insolvent and C's loans had become irrecoverable. Such 'acts' as took place at the end of March played no part in their becoming irrecoverable at or before the end of February. Accordingly C was entitled to relief. (The Special Commissioner also rejected, as not supported by the evidence, an alternative contention by the Revenue that the loans had not been recoverable when they had been made and thus could not have 'become irrecoverable'.) *Cann v Woods (Sp C 183), [1999] SSCD 77.*

Capcount Trading v Evans 15.4

Computation of loss on asset purchased and sold in foreign currency

Bentley v Pike (see above) was applied in this subsequent case where a company had made a loss on the disposal of shares in a Canadian company. The shares had been purchased and sold for Canadian dollars, and the Revenue computed the resulting loss by translating the dollar purchase price and the dollar sale price into sterling at the spot rates prevailing at, respectively, the date of purchase and the date of sale, and deducting the sterling equivalent of the sale price from the sterling equivalent of the purchase price. The company appealed, contending that the loss should be computed by deducting the dollar sale price from the dollar cost, and translating the resulting sum into sterling at the spot rate prevailing at the date of disposal. The Special Commissioner rejected this contention and dismissed the company's appeal. The CA upheld the Commissioner's decision. For the purpose of tax on capital gains, foreign currency was not money but was an asset. Therefore, when the company acquired the Canadian shares for Canadian dollars, it gave a consideration in money's worth which fell to be valued in sterling at that time. *Pattison v Marine Midland Ltd* distinguished. *Capcount Trading v Evans CA 1992, 65 TC 545; [1993] STC 11; [1993] All ER 125.*

Caton's Administrators v Couch 15.4

Costs of appealing against valuation of unquoted shares — whether 'incidental costs of disposal'

In a share valuation case, the administrators of a deceased's estate contended that the costs of their appeal qualified as incidental costs of disposal. The Ch D rejected this contention and the CA dismissed the administrators' appeal. Morritt LJ held that, although the costs of an initial valuation were deductible, *TCGA** did not permit a liability to tax to be diminished (or even extinguished) by contesting it. If such expenses were to be treated as deductible, there would be a positive deterrent to reaching a sensible agreement as to the quantum of the liability. Applying *Smith's Potato Estates Ltd v Bolland*, there was a distinction between the costs of producing accounts from which to compute profits and the conduct of a tax controversy with the Revenue. The costs and expenses which a taxpayer might deduct under *TCGA 1992, s 38(2)(b)** were limited to those incurred in complying with the requirements of *TMA 1970, s 12* [and presumably *TMA 1970, s 8* under self-assessment from 1996/97], and did not extend to costs incurred in contesting the tax liability arising from a disposal. *Caton's Administrators v Couch CA 1997, 70 TC 10; [1997] STC 970.*

Chaloner v Pellipar Investments Ltd 15.3

*Development agreement providing for 'money's worth' in the form of site works — whether within TCGA 1992, s 22**

Under a development agreement made in 1987, a company received 'money's worth' in the form of site works. The works were not completed until 1991. The Revenue considered that the effect of *TCGA 1992, s 28** was that the consideration was assessable in the company's accounting period ending June 1988, by reference to the date of the contract. The company appealed, contending that the consideration was a capital sum derived from an asset, within *TCGA 1992, s 22**, so that it was not assessable until the period in which it was received. The Special Commissioner allowed the company's appeal but the Ch D reversed this decision, holding that, since the benefit to the company of the development of the site represented consideration for a lease rather than a licence, it did not fall within *TCGA 1992, s 22(1)(d)*. *Chaloner v Pellipar Investments Ltd Ch D 1996, 68 TC 238; [1996] STC 234.*

Chaney v Watkis 15.4

Deductible money liability replaced by non-monetary obligation — whether money's worth and deductible

The taxpayer had owned a house, occupied by his mother-in-law Mrs W as a protected tenant. He was offered £7,200 for the house subject to the tenancy but refused it. Subsequently he agreed with Mrs W that, if she would vacate the house, he would compensate her by paying her half the difference between the tenanted value and the actual sale price. The house was sold in 1981 for £26,000, but prior to completion he agreed with Mrs W that he would provide her with rent-free accommodation for life if in return she released him from his obligation to pay her £9,400 under their previous agreement. In the event she came to live in an extension to his own residence built for some £25,000. The appeal was against an assessment on the gain from the disposal of the house with no deduction for the £9,400. The Ch D allowed the appeal (reversing the decision of the Commissioners). It was common ground that, had the £9,400 been paid, it would have been deductible under *TCGA 1992, s 38(1)(b)**. The obligation to pay this sum was replaced by an obligation capable of being valued in money terms, despite the domestic nature of the agreement, which, applying *Oram v Johnson*, gave rise to an allowable deduction. The case was remitted to the Commissioners to determine the appeal in accordance with the judgment. *Chaney v Watkis Ch D 1985, 58 TC 707; [1986] STC 89.*

Chinn v Collins 57.12

Whether shares sold held under non-resident settlement

Under a 1960 settlement, shares in L Ltd, a public quoted company, were held on discretionary trusts. A scheme was subsequently carried out to mitigate the incidence of CGT. The existing (resident) trustees were replaced by non-resident trustees and on 28 October 1969 the following transactions were effected. With the settlor's permission, 184,500 of the shares held by the trustees were appointed to each of two brothers, discretionary beneficiaries under the trust, contingently on their surviving three days; each brother assigned his contingent interest to a Jersey company for £352,705; that company contracted to sell each brother 184,500 shares in L Ltd for £355,162 (their then market value), the contract to be completed on 1 November. The brothers survived the three days. The upshot was that they had acquired the shares for their full price, the cost being financed by their disposal of their contingent interests (exempt under *TCGA 1992, s 76(1)**). The brothers were assessed on the basis that *FA 1965, s 42(2)* applied. Their appeals against the assessments were dismissed by the HL. The scheme was an arrangement within the definition of 'settlement' in *FA 1965, s 42(7)*. Although, following *CIR v Plummer*, a settlement must include an element of bounty, there was here an act of bounty in favour of the sons. The settlor's bounty was incomplete when he divested himself of the shares settled. *Chinn v Collins*; *Chinn v Hochstrasser HL 1980, 54 TC 311; [1981] STC 1; [1981] 2 WLR 14; [1981] 1 All ER 189.*

CIR v Beveridge 7.10

*Share exchange on takeover — application of TCGA 1992, Sch 2 para 19**

In a case in which the issue was the application of *TCGA 1992, Sch 2 para 19**, the relevant shares were originally ordinary shares in S Ltd, a private company, acquired before 6 April 1965, exchanged for ordinary shares in L Ltd in 1967 on a takeover, and disposed of in 1974. There had been a substantial fall in the value of the shares between 1967 and 1974. The assessment was on the basis that *TCGA 1992, Sch 2 para 19(3)** applied. The taxpayer appealed, contending that it did not apply, because the shares in S Ltd were subject to a restriction on transfer to which those in L Ltd were not subject, and consequently not of the same class. The Commissioners allowed his appeal and the CS upheld their decision. The CS also held that *TCGA 1992, Sch 2 para 19(3)** was inapplicable as 'reorganisation of a company's share capital' cannot be construed to cover an amalgamation of two companies. *CIR v Beveridge CS 1979, 53 TC 178; [1979] STC 592.* (Note. See also SP 14/79.)

CIR v Burmah Oil Co 3.1, 58.1

Avoidance Schemes

A company (H), which was a member of a group, was dormant but owned stock with a market value substantially less than its acquisition cost. Its parent company (B) carried out a series of transactions including a capital reorganisation and the loan of £160 million to H via another company in the same group. At the end of these transactions, B held the stock previously held by H, which had been put into liquidation. B claimed that it had made a loss of £160 million on the disposal of its shareholding in H. The HL rejected the claim (reversing the decision of the CS). The whole and only purpose of the scheme had been the avoidance of tax. Applying *WT Ramsay Ltd*, the transactions had 'no commercial purpose apart from the avoidance of a liability to tax', and should be disregarded. *CIR v Burmah Oil Co Ltd HL 1981, 54 TC 200; [1982] STC 30.*

CIR v Chubb's Trustee 15.4

Expenses of terminating trust

Under a marriage settlement, a fund was settled on the wife for life with remainder to the issue of the marriage. The husband had died before the relevant period and the only child was a married daughter with infant children. Arrangements were made under which the trust was terminated and the trust fund vested absolutely in the widow and the daughter. In an appeal against the resultant assessment made under *TCGA 1992, s 71(1)**, the trustee claimed to deduct the cost of legal expenses (including fees to counsel for advice), stamp duty and other expenses as necessarily incurred to bring about the chargeable occasion under *TCGA 1992, s 71(1)**. The Commissioners allowed the deduction and the CS upheld their decision. *CIR v Chubb's Trustee CS 1971, 47 TC 353.*

CIR v John Lewis Properties plc 15.7, 55.3

Assignment of rentals for five-year period—whether income within Schedule A or capital

In 1995 a property-holding company assigned to a bank its right to receive rental income for a five-year period, in return for a lump sum payment (a type of transaction generally known as rent factoring). The Revenue issued a corporation tax assessment on the basis that the payment was income chargeable under Schedule A. The company appealed, contending that the payment was a capital receipt for the part disposal of its interests in the properties (so that it was entitled to rollover relief). The Special Commissioner accepted this contention and allowed the appeal, and the CA upheld this decision. Applying *dicta* of Dixon J in the Australian case of *Hallstroms Property Ltd v Federal Commissioner of Taxation CA(A) 1946, 72 CLR 634*, the question of whether the money was received as capital or income 'depends on what the expenditure is calculated to effect from a practical and business point of view, rather than upon the juristic classification of the legal rights, if any, secured, employed or exhausted in the process'. Dyson LJ held that 'the payment made by the bank was one of capital. The sum was substantial, it was a single payment for the once and for all disposal by (J) of six years' rents, which resulted in a diminution in the value of its reversionary interests.' He observed that 'if J had granted the bank six-year leases at nominal rents, the premiums payable would have been capital payments ... the differences between such a transaction and the one which they in fact entered into are not sufficiently significant that they should lead to a different fiscal result'. *CIR v John Lewis Properties plc CA 2002, [2003] STC 117.* (*Notes.* (1) With effect for transactions after 20 March 2000, rent factoring receipts are taxable as income under Schedule A — see Tolley's Corporation Tax under Property Income. (2) The Revenue's further submission that, if not chargeable as income, the full proceeds should be taken into account for corporation tax on chargeable gains, without the deduction of any acquisition cost, was rejected by the Special Commissioner; the disposal was a part disposal within *TCGA 1992, s 42*).

CIR v Montgomery 9.1

Sale of rights to insurance recoveries

Property was extensively damaged by fire with the result that the owners (trustees of a will trust) became entitled to insurance recoveries of £75,192. The owners assigned their rights under the policies to G in consideration of £75,192 and were assessed on the resultant gain. The taxpayers' contention that there was no chargeable gain was upheld. The £75,192 was derived from the sale of the rights under the policies and no more and *TCGA 1992, s 22** was confined to cases where no asset was acquired by the person paying the capital sum. *CIR v Montgomery Ch D 1974, 49 TC 679; [1975] STC 182; [1975] 1 All ER 664*. (Note. The law was amended for disposals after 19 December 1974. See now *TCGA 1992, s 225*. *Dicta* of Walton J were disapproved by the HL in *Marren v Ingles*.)

CIR v Richards' Executors 18.8, 15.4

Expenses of obtaining confirmation (*probate*)

The executors of a deceased person were assessed on their gains from disposals of investments forming part of the estate. On appeal, the Commissioners allowed their claim for the deduction for a proportionate amount of the fees paid to solicitors for valuing the estate, paying the estate duty, obtaining confirmation, etc. and for commission paid to them for their work done in disposing of the investments. The HL upheld this decision. *CIR v Richards' Executors HL 1971, 46 TC 626; [1971] 1 WLR 571; [1971] 1 All ER 785*.

Clark (Clark's Executor) v Green & CIR 41.4

*Valuation of unquoted shares — TCGA 1992, s 273(3)**

A taxpayer held a 3.16% shareholding in a substantial unquoted company. She died in September 1987. The company's accounts for the year ending 31 August 1987 (which had not been published at the time of the taxpayer's death) showed pre-tax profits of £2,350,000. In April 1988 all the issued share capital of the company was sold. The Revenue issued a CGT assessment on the basis that the value of the shares at the time of the taxpayer's death was 30p each. (This valuation was computed by applying a gross price/earnings ratio of 12 to the earnings per share, and discounting it by 65% for unmarketability, leaving a net price/earnings ratio of 4.2.) Her executor appealed, contending that the shares should be valued at 18p each, since the Revenue's valuation took account of unpublished information concerning the company's profits which should have been ignored. The Special Commissioner dismissed the appeal and upheld the Revenue's valuation, holding that the effect of *TCGA 1992, s 273(3)** was that the unpublished information concerning the company's profits should be taken into account, and that the Revenue's valuation had been made on a reasonable basis. The Commissioner observed that *TCGA 1992, s 273** (which derived from *FA 1973, s 51*) had been enacted to overturn the decision in Lynall. Although the shareholding was a small minority holding, the hypothetical purchaser was 'considering an investment of something in the region of £100,000 – £169,000'. The Commissioner also considered that the Revenue's valuation was 'if anything, rather low', and noted that the valuation was significantly less than the valuation of shares in the same company in *Caton's Administrators v Couch (Sp C 6), [1995] SSCD 34*, but observed that 'the difference between the two valuations reflects the difference in the size of the shareholdings which, in turn, reflects the amount of information assumed to be available'. (The valuation in *Caton's Administrators v Couch* was based on the assumption that the prospective purchaser would know that the company's entire share capital was likely to be sold in the near future, which was not the case here since the shareholding here was significantly smaller.) *Clark (Clark's Executor) v Green & CIR (Sp C 5), [1995] SSCD 99*.

Clarke v Mayo 53.6

*Associated disposals — TCGA 1992, s 164(7)**

A company was incorporated in 1954 to take over a retail business which had previously been carried on by a father and son in partnership. The father acquired 50.01% of the company's shares, and the son acquired the remaining 49.99%. In June 1988, when the son was aged 60, contracts were exchanged for the sale of premises which the company occupied (and in which the son had a 25% interest) to an unrelated company. On 25 January 1989 the father died, bequeathing his shareholding to his son. On 31 January 1989 the sale of the property was completed. On 28 February 1989 the company ceased trading. On 28 February 1990 the son transferred his original 49.99% holding in the company's shares to his children. He claimed retirement relief. The inspector rejected the claim, on the grounds that the conditions of *TCGA 1992, s 164(7)(b)** were not satisfied, since the company had ceased to occupy the property four weeks before the date on which the company ceased trading. The Commissioners allowed the son's appeal, holding that the disposal of the shares was a 'material disposal' within *TCGA 1992, s 163(5)**, that the disposal of the property was an 'associated disposal' within *TCGA 1992, s 164(6)**, and that, although the company had ceased to occupy the property four weeks before it ceased trading, the property qualified as having been used by the company 'immediately before' the cessation of the business. The Ch D upheld the Commissioners' decision. Evans-Lombe J held that the words 'immediately before ... the cessation of the business' should not be construed in isolation, but in the context of *TCGA 1992, ss 163, 164** as a whole. The words 'immediately before' could be construed as meaning 'sufficiently proximate in time to the material disposal or cessation so as to justify the conclusion that the transaction in question formed part of it'. (The Revenue had conceded that the Commissioners were entitled to find that the disposal of the son's interest in the property was an 'associated disposal' within *TCGA 1992, s 164(6)** even though the transfer of his shares in the company did not take place until 56 weeks later.) *Clarke v Mayo Ch D 1994, 66 TC 728; [1994] STC 570.* (Note. Retirement relief is abolished for disposals after 5 April 2003 (see 53.1 RETIREMENT RELIEF).)

Clarke v United Real (Moorgate) Ltd 38.15

Grant of lease of freehold property after development — whether reimbursement of development expenditure a premium within TCGA 1992, Sch 8 para 2(1), para 10(2)

M, a company carrying on property investment and development, agreed in 1978 with contractors for the development of a freehold site it owned. In 1979 it signed an 'agreement for a lease' with another company, N, under which N agreed to reimburse M's expenditure on the development, on completion of which M was to grant N a long lease of the property at a rent below the market value, the formula for which was directly related to N's payments in reimbursement of M's development expenditure. The Ch D, reversing the decision of the Special Commissioner, held that the reimbursement of the expenditure was a premium within *TCGA 1992, Sch 8 para 2(1), para 10(2)**. M's contention that it had been reimbursed the expenditure in its capacity of property developer, and not in its capacity of landlord, was rejected. M developed the site for itself and not for N, which was not a party to the development contracts. *Clarke v United Real (Moorgate) Ltd Ch D 1987, 61 TC 353; [1988] STC 273.*

Cleveleys Investment Trust Co v CIR (No 1) 22.5

Advance for payment of shares — incorporeal rights

C, an investment company, advanced £25,000 to F Ltd, which undertook to reconstruct its share capital, allotting a 51% holding to C. The £25,000 was to be used to acquire the shares. F Ltd accepted a bill of exchange for £25,000 drawn on it by C. F Ltd went into voluntary liquidation before its capital had been reconstructed and the £25,000 was not recovered. The CS held that the advance of £25,000 was part of a composite single transaction conferring incorporeal rights on C — see *TCGA 1992, s 21(1)(a)** — and its loss was an allowable loss. *Cleveleys Investment Trust Co v CIR (No 1) CS 1971, 47 TC 300.*

Cleveleys Investment Trust Co v CIR (No 2) 15.4

Guarantee payment — whether chargeable asset acquired

An investment company guaranteed the bank overdraft of another company and paid £27,351 in pursuance of the guarantee. It contended that in so doing it had acquired the bank's rights as a creditor of the other company, that these rights were an asset for CGT purposes the value of which had become negligible within *TCGA 1992, s 24(2)**, and that accordingly it had an allowable loss of £27,351. The CS rejected this contention. The company's acquisition of the bank's worthless claim was an incident of its discharge of its obligation to the bank. *Cleveleys Investment Trust Co v CIR (No 2) CS 1975, 51 TC 26; [1975] STC 457.*

Coates v Arndale Properties Ltd 3.1, 27.4

Avoidance scheme — whether TCGA 1992, s 173(1) applicable*

Three companies, members of the same group, entered into transactions, not disputed to be genuine, but admittedly to secure expected favourable tax consequences. One company, SPI, had acquired and developed at a cost of £5,313,822 property the market value of which had fallen by March 1973 to £3,100,000. On 30 March 1973 it assigned the property to a property dealing company, A, for a consideration of £3,090,000. On the same day, A assigned the property for £3,100,000 to an investment company, APT. No cash passed, the matter being dealt with by book entries. A then purported to make an election under *TCGA 1992, s 161(3)**; the consequence would be that, by virtue of *TCGA 1992, s 171(1)**, the transfer from SPI to A would give rise to no loss or gain for CGT purposes, and in computing A's Case I profits it could treat the cost of the property as its market value plus the CGT loss which would have accrued under *TCGA 1992, s 161(1)** if the election had not been made. The Revenue assessed A under Case I on the footing that the election was invalid, contending that A had not acquired the property as trading stock within the meaning of *TCGA 1992, s 173(1)**. The HL upheld the assessment, holding that A never did decide to acquire, and never did acquire, the lease as trading stock. The transfer of the lease from SPI to A and from A to APT was procured with the object of obtaining group relief without in fact changing the lease from a capital asset to a trading asset. A lent its name to the transaction but it did not trade and never had any intention of trading with the lease. In these circumstances it was unnecessary to consider the principles enunciated in *CIR v Burmah Oil Co* and *Furniss v Dawson* or the dividend-stripping cases which had been considered in the courts below. *Coates v Arndale Properties Ltd HL 1984, 59 TC 516; [1984] STC 637; [1984] 1 WLR 1328; [1985] 1 All ER 15.*

Cooper v Billingham; Fisher v Edwards 44.14

Trustees making demand loans to settlor & quest; whether any 'capital payments' within TCGA 1992, s 87(4)

In 1987 a UK resident (C) established a settlement, the trustees of which were resident in Switzerland and the Cayman Islands. The trustees made a number of interest-free loans, repayable on demand, to C. The Revenue issued CGT assessments on the basis that C should be treated as having received capital payments, within *TCGA 1992, s 87(4)*, from the trustees of the settlement, the amount of such payments being the interest that would have been payable had the loans from the trustees been made on a commercial basis. C appealed, contending that, while there had been a nominal payment of capital when each initial loan was made, there was no further capital payment while that loan remained outstanding. The Ch D rejected this contention and upheld the assessments. Lloyd J held that, when the trustees had made a loan which was repayable on demand, they conferred a benefit on C 'by leaving the loan outstanding for any period, even for a single day'. The effect of *TCGA 1992, s 97* was that the benefits were to be treated as capital payments for the purposes of *TCGA 1992, s 87(4)*. The CA unanimously dismissed C's appeal against this decision. Applying *dicta* of Viscount Simon LC in *Nokes v Doncaster Amalgamated Collieries HL, [1940] AC 1014; [1940] 3 All ER 549*, 'if the choice is between two interpretations, the narrower of which would fail to achieve the manifest purpose of the legislation, we should avoid a construction which would reduce the legislation to futility and should rather accept the bolder construction based on the view that Parliament would legislate only for the purpose of bringing about an effective result'. Robert Walker LJ held that 'the whole scheme of the legislation requires the court to see what benefit a beneficiary actually receives, in cash or in kind, otherwise than as income or under an arm's length transaction. Any pre-existing beneficial interest belonging to the beneficiary is irrelevant.' *Cooper v Billingham; Fisher v Edwards CA 2001, 74 TC 139; [2001] STC 1177.*

Cottle v Coldicott 6.9

Sale of milk quota — whether part of cost of land deductible from gain

A farmer owned 56.68 acres of land and was entitled to 120,000 litres of milk quota. In September 1991, he sold 60,000 litres of milk quota to a company. On the same day, but under separate agreements, he granted the company a tenancy of 10.39 acres of his land for a ten-month period, and the company appointed him as its agent to enter into occupation of that part of the land. The land subject to the tenancy was not to be used for milk production, this short-term let being necessary to ensure a permanent and effective transfer of the milk quota, since milk quota could not be used or sold without the land to which it was attached. The Revenue issued a CGT assessment on the gain. The farmer appealed, contending that the sale of the milk quota should be treated as a part disposal of his land, so that part of the acquisition cost of the land should be allowed as a deduction and that on this basis he had made a capital loss rather than a capital gain. The Special Commissioners rejected this contention and rejected the farmer's appeal. The milk quota was a separate asset from the land. Although milk quota corresponded to a holding of land, it did not 'correspond to any particular parcel of land in that holding'. Milk quota did not derive from the occupier's land, but was 'an advantage derived from the context of the common organisation of the market in milk'. Milk quota was a valuable asset, and those holding it had the right (subject to restrictions laid down in EC law) to dispose of it for profit. *Dicta* of the European Court of Justice in *R v Ministry of Agriculture, Fisheries and Food (ex p. Bostock), CJEC [1994] 1 ECR 955* applied. The sale of the milk quota was not a part disposal of the farmer's land within *TCGA 1992, s 21(2)(b)**, and was not a capital sum derived from the land within *TCGA 1992, s 22(1)**. Since the value of the quota did not derive from the holding, *TCGA 1992, s 43** did not apply. *Cottle v Coldicott (Sp C 40), [1995] SSCD 239.*

Craven v White 3.1

Anti-avoidance

Three members of a family owned all the shares in a UK company (Q), which owned a number of shops. From 1973 they conducted negotiations with various other companies with a view to selling Q or merging it with a similar business. In July 1976, at a time when they were negotiating with two unconnected companies, they exchanged their shares for shares in an Isle of Man company (M). Nineteen days later M sold the shares in Q to one of the two companies with which negotiations had been in progress at the time of the share exchange. The sale proceeds were paid by M to the shareholders over a period of five years. The Revenue issued CGT assessments for 1976/77 on the basis that, applying the Ramsay principle, the disposal of the shares to M and their subsequent sale by M should be treated as a single composite transaction and that the transfer of the shares to M was a fiscal nullity. The Special Commissioners reduced the assessments, holding that the transfer could not be treated as a fiscal nullity but that the shareholders were assessable on the amounts they had received from M at the time of receipt. The Revenue's appeals against this decision were dismissed by the Ch D, the CA, and (by a 3–2 majority) the HL. In giving the leading judgement for the majority, Lord Oliver indicated the limitations of the principle adopted in *CIR v Ramsay*, as defined by Lord Brightman in *Furniss v Dawson*. The principle in question — that the Commissioners are not bound to consider individually each step in a composite transaction intended to be carried through as a whole — applied only where there was a 'pre-ordained series of transactions' or 'one single composite transaction' and where steps were inserted which had no commercial purpose apart from the avoidance of a liability to tax. Although the decision in *Furniss v Dawson* extended the *Ramsay* principle, by applying it to a linear transaction as opposed to a circular self-cancelling one, it did no more than apply that principle to different events. It did not lay down any proposition that a transaction entered into with the motive of minimising tax was to be ignored or struck down. In the *Ramsay* case, Lord Wilberforce had emphasised the continuing validity and application of the principle enunciated by Lord Tomlin in *CIR v Duke of Westminster*. Lord Fraser had echoed this view, as had Lord Bridge in *Furniss v Dawson*. (The speech of Lord Roskill in that case, which implied the contrary, did not appear to represent the view of the majority.) The criteria by reference to which the Ramsay principle applied were not logically capable of expansion so as to apply to any similar case except one in which, when the intermediate transaction or transactions took place, the end result which in fact occurred was so certain of fulfilment that it was intellectually and practically possible to conclude that there had indeed taken place one single and indivisible process. For the principle to apply, the intermediate steps had to serve no purpose other than that of saving tax; all stages of the composite transaction had to be pre-ordained with a degree of certainty with the taxpayer having control over the end result at the time when the intermediate steps were taken; and there should be no interruption between the intermediate transaction and the disposal to the ultimate purchaser. In this case, however, the transactions that the Crown sought to reconstruct into a single direct disposal were not contemporaneous. Nor were they pre-ordained since, at the time of the share exchange, it was not certain what the ultimate destination of the property would be. Lord Jauncey considered that 'a step in a linear transaction which has no business purpose apart from the avoidance or deferment of tax liability will be treated as forming part of a pre-ordained series of transactions or of a composite transaction if it was taken at a time when negotiations or arrangements for the carrying through as a continuous process of a subsequent transaction which actually takes place had reached a stage when there was no real likelihood that such subsequent transaction would not take place and if thereafter such negotiations or arrangements were carried through to completion without genuine interruption'. Lord Oliver concurred with this definition. *Craven v White HL 1988, 62 TC 1; [1988] STC 476; [1988] 3 WLR 423; [1988] 3 All ER 495.*

Davenport v Chilver 6.1

*Compensation for confiscation of asset — application of TCGA 1992, s 22(1)**

In 1940 the USSR nationalised private property in Latvia. Following the *Foreign Compensation (USSR) Order 1969 (SI 1969 No 735)*, a woman who was resident in the UK made a claim in respect of such property in Latvia, some of which she had held in her own right and some of which had been held by her mother. In 1972/73 she received a payment in respect of the claim. She appealed against a CGT assessment on the payment. The Ch D held that the compensation for the loss of the assets she had held was within *TCGA 1992, s 22(1)(a)**, and that the compensation for the assets her mother had held was within *TCGA 1992, s 21(a)**. The case was remitted to the Special Commissioner for figures to be determined. *Davenport v Chilver Ch D 1983, 57 TC 661; [1983] STC 426; [1983] 3 WLR 481.* (Note. See now *TCGA 1992, s 17.*)

Davis v Henderson 9.1

Statutory compensation for disturbance on surrender of agricultural lease

Davis v Powell (see below) was applied in a subsequent case in which a farmer had surrendered an agricultural tenancy to his landlord under an agreement providing for payment of £455,180 as compensation for disturbance under *Agricultural Holdings Act 1986, s 60*, and £520,000 as additional compensation. The Revenue issued an assessment charging CGT on both payments. The farmer appealed, accepting that the £520,000 was chargeable to CGT but contending that the £455,180 was not taxable. The Special Commissioners accepted this contention and allowed the appeal, holding that the payment was statutory compensation under *Agricultural Holdings Act 1986*, and was therefore not taxable. The Commissioners held that 'the notice to quit need not necessarily be the sole or proximate cause of the termination of a tenancy: it may be sufficient for the notice to quit to be one of a number of links in a chain of causal events'. The Revenue's contention that the tenancy had been terminated by agreement was rejected. *Davis v Henderson (Sp C 46), [1995] SSCD 308.*

Davis v Powell 9.1

Statutory compensation for disturbance on surrender of agricultural lease

A farmer surrendered to the Milton Keynes Development Corporation part of land he leased, receiving compensation of £5,971 from the Corporation. Included in this was £591 equal to one year's rent and representing compensation for disturbance under *Agricultural Holdings Act 1948, s 34*. The Ch D held that no gain could be made out of a sum of money given to compensate for loss or expense which was unavoidably incurred after the lease has gone and the £591 was not a capital sum 'derived from' the lease or 'received in return for ... surrender of rights' (*TCGA 1992, s 22(1)**) and not liable to capital gains tax. (There was no dispute as to the tax treatment of the balance of the £5,971.) *Davis v Powell Ch D 1976, 51 TC 492; [1977] STC 32; [1977] 1 WLR 258; [1977] 1 All ER 471.*

De Rothschild v Lawrenson 44.14

*Interaction of TCGA 1992, s 77 and 87(2)**

In 1989 the trustees of two non-resident settlements, which had been established in 1982 by a UK resident, sold the trust funds and resolved to pay the whole amount realised to the settlor. The Revenue raised an assessment on the settlor under *TCGA 1992, s 87(2)**, charging CGT on the amount on which the trustees would have been chargeable to tax if they had been resident or ordinarily resident in the UK. The settlor appealed, contending that the effect of *TCGA 1992, s 77** was that the gains of the settlements were not to be treated as accruing to the trustees and that the assessment should be reduced to nil. The Special Commissioners dismissed his appeal and the Ch D upheld their decision. *TCGA 1992, s 77** did not apply, since it dealt with cases where trustees were in fact chargeable to tax on realised gains. In a case within *TCGA 1992, s 87(2)**, gains were to be computed on the amount on which the trustees would have been chargeable to tax if they had been resident or ordinarily resident in the UK. That provision did not make the trustees themselves chargeable to tax, and the gains so computed were to be treated as chargeable gains accruing to the beneficiary. *De Rothschild v Lawrenson CA 1995, 67 TC 300; [1995] STC 623.*

Director v Inspector of Taxes 40.9

*Relief under TCGA 1992, s 24(2) (assets of negligible value)**

An individual (D) was allotted 30,000 £1 shares in a company, in consideration of future services to the company. Shortly after being allotted these shares, he was appointed a director of the company. The company's liabilities exceeded its assets, and it subsequently became insolvent. After correspondence, the Revenue accepted for Schedule E purposes that the shares had a nil market value at the time of their allotment. Three years later, D submitted a claim for relief under *TCGA 1992, s 24(2)* in respect of the shares. The Revenue rejected this claim and the Special Commissioner dismissed D's appeal. Under *TCGA 1992, s 17*, the shares were deemed to have been acquired for a consideration equal to their market value, which was clearly nil. Since the shares had a market value of nil when they were acquired, they were not capable of becoming of negligible value, within *section 24(2)*. (The Commissioner observed that D had 'sought both to have his cake and to eat it'.) *Director v Inspector of Taxes (Sp C 161), [1998] SSCD 172.*

Drummond v Austin Brown 9.1

Statutory compensation for disturbance on termination of tenancy of business premises

Davis v Powell was followed in a case in which the taxpayer had for many years carried on practice as a solicitor in premises leased to him by a bank. The bank required the premises for the purposes of its own business and gave him notice under *Part II* of the *Landlord and Tenant Act 1954* that it would oppose a renewal of his lease. He did not oppose the notice and his tenancy was terminated from 1 April 1978. He received compensation of £31,384 under *Landlord and Tenant Act 1954, s 37*. The Revenue assessed him on this sum for 1977/78 on the footing that it was a capital sum derived from an asset within *TCGA 1992, s 22**. His appeal was allowed by the Special Commissioners, and the Ch D and CA upheld their decision. The right to the compensation was a statutory one. There was no entitlement to it under the lease and it was therefore not derived from the lease. Nor was it, as the Revenue contended, for the loss of an asset. The lease had expired, but it was never 'lost'. *Drummond v Austin Brown CA 1984, 58 TC 67; [1984] STC 321; [1984] 3 WLR 381; [1984] 2 All ER 699.*

Dunlop International AG v Pardoe 27.9

*Principal group company becoming non-resident — application of TCGA 1992, s 179**

In May 1978, D, which had been the principal member of a group of companies, became non-resident. The Revenue issued an assessment on the basis that *TCGA 1992, s 179** applied, so that D was deemed to have sold and immediately re-acquired shares in a subsidiary company, which it had acquired from another group member in March 1978. The Special Commissioners upheld the assessment, observing that the change of residence 'was an appropriate point at which to bring to an end the deferral of any gain or loss'. The Ch D and the CA dismissed D's appeal against this decision. Chadwick LJ observed that the object of *section 179** was 'to prevent the transferee company from taking the asset out of the group in circumstances in which the gain will not crystallise on a subsequent disposal — because there will be no subsequent disposal'. *Dunlop International AG v Pardoe CA 1999, 72 TC 71.*

Dunstan v Young Austen Young Ltd 3.1, 58.1

Whether issue of new shares not acquired at arm's length constituted a capital reorganisation

The taxpayer company (Y) carried on business as a mechanical engineering contractor. In 1977 it acquired for £16,100 the 1,000 issued £1 shares of a company (J) in the same line of business. Shortly afterwards it joined a large group; one of the shares in J was registered in the name of a fellow-subsidiary (T), the remainder being registered in its own name. J was not trading profitably. By March 1979 it had incurred debts of £200,911 to other companies in the group, mainly to Y, and it was decided to sell it. An arm's length purchaser was found, and J issued a further 200,000 £1 shares on 12 June 1979. These were allotted to Y for £200,000 cash, which was promptly repaid to Y to clear its indebtedness. On 29 June an agreement was completed between Y, T and the purchaser for the sale of the 201,000 shares for £38,000. The appeal was against an assessment for the year to September 1979. The profits were agreed at nil and the substantive issue was whether Y had incurred a capital loss on its disposal of the shares in J and, if so, of what amount. It was common ground that Y acquired the additional 200,000 shares 'otherwise than by a bargain made at arm's length' and by virtue of *CGTA 1979, s 19(3)** the consideration for them should be taken to be their market value, which the Special Commissioner found to be nil 'or so near to it as to make no matter'. However, Y contended that the issue of the further 200,000 shares constituted a reorganisation of J's capital within *TCGA 1992,* *ss 126, 128**, with the consequence that the new shares would not be treated as a separate acquisition and that the £200,000 would be treated as having been given for the original 1,000 shares, making their cost £216,100 and the loss £178,100. This contention was upheld by the CA, reversing the decision of the Ch D and restoring that of the Special Commissioner. Properly construed, the phrase 'reorganisation of a company's share capital' in *TCGA 1992, s 126** included an increase in a company's share capital and the allotment of the new shares to its parent company for cash. *Dunstan v Young Austen Young Ltd, CA 1988, 61 TC 448; [1989] STC 69.* (Note. *CGTA 1979, s 19(3)* was repealed by *FA 1981*. See now *TCGA 1992, s 128(2)* as regards reorganisations on or after 10 March 1981.)

Durrant v CIR 53.8

Definition of 'chargeable business asset' — TCGA 1992, Sch 6 para 12(2)

An accountant retired from an accountancy partnership. He had held 11.11% of the shares in the partnership's service company, and disposed of these shares on his retirement. He claimed retirement relief, but the Revenue rejected his claim, considering that the shares were not 'chargeable business assets' within *TCGA 1992, Sch 6 para 12(2)**. The Special Commissioner dismissed the accountant's appeal against this decision. *Durrant v CIR (Sp C 24), [1995] SSCD 145.* (Note. Retirement relief is abolished for disposals after 5 April 2003 (see 53.1 RETIREMENT RELIEF).)

Eastham v Leigh London & Provincial Properties Ltd 15.3

Date of acquisition

On 22 June 1962, a company agreed with the owners of land to erect on the land a building to be leased, on completion, to the company for 125 years from 24 June 1962. The building was completed and the lease granted in May 1964. On 28 July 1965, the company disposed of the lease at a large gain which was assessed on the basis that the acquisition and disposal of the lease took place within three years and *FA 1965, s 82(2)(3)* (interim charge of tax) applied. The company contended that the lease was acquired under the 1962 agreement. The Revenue contended that the 1962 agreement comprised two contracts, a building agreement and an agreement for a lease, the latter being a conditional contract within the meaning of *FA 1962, Sch 9 para 1* (compare *TCGA 1992, s 28(2)*), or alternatively, that there was a single but conditional contract. The CA held that the 1962 agreement was a single and absolute contract. *Eastham v Leigh London & Provincial Properties Ltd CA 1971, 46 TC 687; [1971] Ch 871; [1971] 2 All ER 811.*

Eilbeck v Rawling 3.1, 57.12

Anti-avoidance — scheme of arrangement

A taxpayer made a chargeable gain of £355,094 in 1974/75 as to which there was no dispute. Later in the same year he entered into a chain of transactions with the object of creating a commensurate allowable loss, at a cost to him of only £370 apart from the fees, etc. paid for the scheme, which was an 'off the peg' avoidance device obtained from a Jersey company. The central feature of the scheme involved his acquiring reversionary interests in two trust funds, one held by Jersey trustees and the other by Gibraltar trustees. Under a special power of appointment, the Gibraltar trustees advanced £315,000 to the Jersey trustees to be held on the trusts of the Jersey settlement. The taxpayer then sold both reversionary interests, making a gain on the sale of his interest under the Jersey settlement (claimed to be exempt under *TCGA 1992, s 76(1)**) and a matching loss of £312,470 on the sale of his interest under the Gibraltar settlement (claimed as an allowable loss). The CA refused the claim on the ground, inter alia, that the exercise of the power of appointment did not take the £315,000 outside the Gibraltar settlement; hence the sale of his reversionary interest in the £315,000 was a part sale of his interest under the Gibraltar settlement. The taxpayer appealed to the HL. The appeal was considered with W T Ramsay Ltd, and dismissed for the same general reason that, on the facts, the scheme was to be looked at as a composite transaction under which there was neither gain nor loss apart from the £370. Furthermore, the HL upheld the CA decision that the sale of the reversionary interest in the £315,000 was a sale of part of the taxpayer's reversionary interest in the Gibraltar settlement. *Eilbeck v Rawling HL 1981, 54 TC 101; [1981] STC 174; [1981] 2 WLR 449; [1981] 1 All ER 865*. (Note. The device would also now be caught by the value shifting provisions of *TCGA 1992, s 30*.)

Emmerson v Computer Time International Ltd 15.6

Assignment of lease — whether arrears of rent deductible

A company discontinued its trade and went into voluntary liquidation. It owed rent in respect of its business premises, held under leases with several years to run but which could not be assigned without the landlord's consent. The landlord gave his consent subject to payment of the arrears. The liquidator accordingly sold the leases for £93,135 and paid the landlord the arrears of rent including £6,131 for the period of liquidation after trading had ceased. The company claimed to deduct the £6,131 in arriving at the gain on the disposal of the leases on the ground that it was a payment to enhance the value of the leases or a capital payment for the right to assign them. The CA rejected the claim. The £6,131 was in discharge of the company's obligations under its lease and not within *TCGA 1992, s 38(1)(b)**. Further, even if it were within that provision, deduction would be precluded by *TCGA 1992, s 39(2)**. *Emmerson v Computer Time International Ltd CA 1977, 50 TC 628; [1977] STC 170; [1977] 1 WLR 734; [1977] 2 All ER 545.*

EV Booth (Holdings) Ltd v Buckwell 15.7

Sale of shares accompanied by waiver of debt — amount of consideration

A company entered into an agreement under which it sold shares in a subsidiary for £35,000 and, in addition, accepted £20,969 in full satisfaction of a debt of £55,839 owed to it by the subsidiary. The debt was not a 'debt on a security'. The Ch D held that there were two disposals and that the consideration for the disposal of the shares was the £35,000. *Aberdeen Construction Group Ltd v CIR* distinguished. *EV Booth (Holdings) Ltd v Buckwell Ch D 1980, 53 TC 425; [1980] STC 578.*

Fallon and Another (Executors of Morgan deceased) v Fellows 58.6

TCGA 1992, s 136 — reconstruction involving issue of securities*

A company (F) had carried on business through two divisions. In 1979 its directors decided, for commercial reasons, that each division should be carried on through a separate company, owned by different groups of shareholders. To achieve this, a number of transactions were carried out on 1 April 1980. F was placed in members' voluntary liquidation, and its shareholders received shares in one of two new companies. In 1987 one of the shareholders (M) sold a substantial number of shares in one of the new companies (L). The Revenue issued a CGT assessment, computed on the basis that the transactions carried out in April 1980 fell within *TCGA 1992, s 136**, so that the acquisition cost of the shares in L was the original acquisition cost of the shares in F. M appealed, contending that the transactions did not fall within *TCGA 1992, s 136**, so that the acquisition cost of the shares in L was the market value of the shares in F at 1 April 1980. The Ch D accepted this contention and allowed the appeal. Park J held that the transactions in question constituted a partition, rather than a 'reconstruction', and were not within *TCGA 1992, s 136**. *Fallon and Another (Executors of Morgan deceased) v Fellows Ch D 2001, 74 TC 232; [2001] STC 1409.* (Note. For shares or debentures issued after 16 April 2002, a new definition of 'scheme of reconstruction' (see 58.6 SHARES AND SECURITIES) is intended to reverse the effect of the decision in this case (Treasury Explanatory Notes to Finance Bill 2002)).

Fielder v Vedlynn Ltd 41.1

Consideration for sale of companies with tax losses — whether to include sums payable under guarantees by reference to amount of losses

In December 1977 a company (V) sold shares in eight subsidiary companies to an unconnected company (M). The subsidiary companies had incurred capital losses which had not been quantified at the date of the sale. The shares were sold for their market value of £19,529, but under the agreement M provided a guarantee that each of the eight companies should pay V an amount equal to 7.5% of their allowable capital losses. In December 1979 the losses in question were agreed at £19.5 million, and the amounts in question were paid to V by the subsidiaries. The Revenue issued a CGT assessment on V for the period ending 31 December 1977, including the amount received by V from the subsidiaries as part of the consideration for the sale of the shares. V appealed, contending that the consideration should be restricted to the £19,529 which was agreed to be the market value of the companies in December 1977. The Special Commissioner allowed V's appeal and the Ch D upheld this decision. The guarantees were terms of the sale agreements, and no additional monetary value could or should be placed on them. Further, even if they were to be regarded as part of the consideration, they were incapable of valuation within the meaning of *FA 1965, s 22(4)*. *Fielder v Vedlynn Ltd Ch D 1992, 65 TC 145; [1992] STC 553*. (Note. *FA 1965, s 22(4)* became *CGTA, s 19(3)*, which was repealed by *FA 1981, s 90* with effect from 10 March 1981 and replaced by what is now *TCGA 1992, s 17*.)

Figg v Clarke 57.15

'Absolutely entitled as against the trustee' (TCGA 1992, s 60)
Date on which beneficiaries absolutely entitled

In 1963 the trustees of a settlement made an appointment whereby certain investments and income should be held 'upon trust for such of the children (of the settlor) now living or hereafter to be born … as shall attain the age of 21'. In 1964 the settlor was paralysed in an accident, leaving no realistic possibility that he could beget any more children. The settlor's youngest child became 21 in 1976 and the settlor died in 1990. The Special Commissioner held that the children became absolutely entitled as against the trustees in 1990 (rather than 1976). The Ch D upheld this decision. Blackburne J held that the court could not have regard to the impossibility of a person having children in the future. *Figg v Clarke Ch D 1996, 68 TC 645; [1997] STC 247*.

Fisher v Edwards

See *Cooper v Billingham* above.

Floor v Davis 3.5, 16.6

*Arrangements to reduce liability — interpretation of TCGA 1992, s 29(2)**

It had been arranged that, subject to contract, the share capital of a company (IDM) would be sold (at a substantial profit to the shareholders) to another company (KDI). F and his two sons-in-law, who together controlled IDM, carried out a scheme under which the following transactions took place shortly after each other. They transferred their IDM shares to FNW, a company set up for the purpose, for preferred shares in FNW; FNW sold the IDM shares to KDI for cash; a Cayman Islands company, D, acquired a relatively insignificant holding of preferred shares in FNW; following a rights issue open to all preferred shareholders but accepted only by D, D became the sole ordinary shareholder in FNW; FNW went into liquidation and because of the differing rights attached to the two classes of shares, D, as the ordinary shareholder, became entitled to six-sevenths of the assets of FNW. The upshot was that the greater part of the proceeds of sale of the IDM shares reached D. The CA held (Eveleigh LJ dissenting), that F had disposed of his IDM shares to FNW (and not, as contended by the Revenue, to KDI) with the consequence that under *TCGA 1992, s 135** his FNW shares were treated as the IDM shares he originally held. However, the CA unanimously held that value had passed out of the FNW shares within the meaning of *TCGA 1992, s 29(2)** and F was assessable accordingly, on the grounds that (i) 'person' in *TCGA 1992, s 29(2)** includes the plural by virtue of *Interpretation Act 1889, s 1(1)(b)* and the definition of 'control' (see *TCGA 1992, s 288(1)**) and (ii) F and his sons-in-law had exercised their control, notwithstanding that two of them had not voted on the resolution to wind up FNW. The HL rejected F's appeal on this point. (The Revenue's contention that F had disposed of the shares to KDI was therefore not argued in the HL. See now as to this *Furniss v Dawson*, in which the dissenting judgement of Eveleigh LJ, who upheld the Revenue's contention that the shares had been disposed of to KDI, was approved.) *Floor v Davis HL 1979, 52 TC 609; [1979] STC 379; [1979] 2 WLR 830; [1979] 2 All ER 677.* (Notes. (1) The relevant transactions took place in 1969. See now for value-shifting transactions after 13 March 1989, *TCGA 1992, ss 30–34*. (2) The *Interpretation Act 1889* has since been repealed. See now *Interpretation Act 1978, s 6(c)*.)

Foster v Williams; Horan v Williams 58.22

Cash bonuses received on takeover of building society

A building society transferred its business to a banking company. Shareholders and depositors were paid lump sums of £500 and percentage bonus payments calculated by reference to the balance on their accounts. Two shareholders appealed against CGT assessments, contending that they had made a complete disposal of their existing assets and that there was no chargeable gain. The Special Commissioner accepted this contention and allowed the appeals in principle, holding that there had been a total disposal of the relevant assets. With regard to the share accounts, the amount of the credit balance on each account was allowable expenditure within *TCGA 1992, s 38*. With regard to the deposit accounts, the effect of *TCGA 1992, s 251* was that there was no chargeable gain. Since payments were made to shareholders and depositors alike, none of the expenditure could be attributed to the shareholders' equity rights. *Foster v Williams; Horan v Williams (Sp C 113), [1997] SSCD 112.*

Fulford-Dobson, ex p., R v Inspector of Taxes 52.3

Gift by wife to husband about to become non-resident — application of ESC D2

On 18 August 1980 an individual (F) entered into a contract of employment in Germany. He was required to begin work on 15 September and he left the UK for this purpose on 29 August 1980. From that date he became resident in Germany, having previously been resident and ordinarily resident in the UK. Acting on professional advice, and admittedly to take advantage of Revenue Extra-Statutory Concession D2, his wife transferred to him on that date a farm which she had inherited in 1977 and had been considering selling in 1980. The farm was in fact sold by auction on 17 September. The Revenue assessed F to CGT for 1980/81 on the gain on the sale. He applied for judicial review to quash the assessment, contending that the Revenue should have applied Revenue Extra-Statutory Concession D2. The QB rejected this contention and dismissed the application, holding that the Revenue had been entitled to refuse to apply the concession. It was clearly stated inside the front cover of Revenue Pamphlet IR1, listing the extra-statutory concessions in operation, that a 'concession will not be given in any case where an attempt is made to use it for tax avoidance'. *R v Inspector of Taxes (ex p. Fulford-Dobson), QB 1987, 60 TC 168; [1987] STC 344; [1987] 3 WLR 277.*

Furniss v Dawson 3.1, 53.9, 59.3

Anti-avoidance

The shareholders in two family companies wished to dispose of their shares, and found an unconnected company (W) willing to acquire the shares at an agreed price. Before disposing of the shares, they exchanged them for shares in a Manx company which in turn sold them to W. The Revenue issued assessments on the basis that the shares should be treated as having been disposed of directly to W, since the interposition of the Manx company had been designed solely to take advantage of the law then in force with regard to company reconstructions and amalgamations. The HL unanimously upheld the assessments (reversing the decision of the CA). Applying *WT Ramsay Ltd*, the transactions should be regarded as a single composite transaction. Lord Bridge of Harwich observed that 'the distinction between form and substance ... can usefully be drawn in determining the tax consequences of composite transactions'. Lord Brightman held that the *Ramsay* principle applied in cases where there was a 'pre-ordained series of transactions; or ... one single composite transaction' and steps were 'inserted which have no commercial (business) purpose apart from the avoidance of a liability to tax — not "no business effect". If these two ingredients exist, the inserted steps are to be disregarded for fiscal purposes. The court must look at the end result.' *Furniss v Dawson HL 1984, 55 TC 324; [1984] STC 153; [1984] 2 WLR 226; [1984] 1 All ER 530*. (Notes. (1) See also *TCGA 1992, s 137*. (2) Although the decision was unanimous, there was implicit disagreement as to the continuing validity of the Duke of Westminster principle. Lords Bridge and Scarman indicated that the principle still applied, but Lord Roskill specifically refrained from endorsing the Westminster decision. For subsequent developments, see the judgement of Lord Templeman in *Ensign Tankers (Leasing) Ltd v Stokes*, and that of Lord Keith in *Countess Fitzwilliam v CIR*.)

Garner v Pounds Shipowners & Shipbreakers Ltd (and related appeal) 6.7, 15.4, 15.6

Grant of option to purchase land—treatment of payment for release of restrictive covenants

A company (P) granted an option to purchase freehold land which was subject to certain restrictive covenants. P undertook to use its best endeavours to obtain the release of the covenants but the exercise of the option was not dependent on their release. The purchaser paid £399,750 for the option, this amount being held by P's solicitors as stakeholders pending the release of the covenants. P subsequently paid £90,000 to obtain the release of the covenants. The option was not, in fact, exercised. The Revenue issued an assessment charging tax on the consideration of £399,750 without allowing a deduction for the £90,000. The HL unanimously dismissed P's appeal and upheld the assessment. Lord Jauncey held that 'no payment by the company to a third party can alter the value of the cash sum of £399,750 paid by (the purchaser) in terms of the agreement as a consideration for the disposal, i.e. the grant of the option'. *Randall v Plumb* distinguished. Furthermore, the £90,000 was not allowable expenditure within *TCGA 1992, s 38**. The implementation of the obligation to obtain the release of the covenants was 'not a prerequisite of the option being exercised'. Accordingly, the expenditure was not 'wholly and exclusively incurred by (P) in providing' the option. Additionally, 'the expenditure referred to in *s 38(1)** must be expenditure which is extraneous to the asset rather than part of it'. On a sale of the land itself, there would be strong grounds for claiming the £90,000 as allowable expenditure, as the value of the land would have been enhanced by removal of the restrictive covenants. *Garner v Pounds Shipowners & Shipbreakers Ltd (and related appeal) HL 2000, 72 TC 561; [2000] STC 420.*

Golding v Kaufman 6.7

Amount received for release of put option

An employee of an investment company owned 25% of the shares of that company. He entered into an agreement with the company under which he could require the company to purchase his shareholding. In 1969 the company paid him £5,000 to relinquish his rights under this agreement. The Revenue included the £5,000 in a CGT assessment on him for 1968/69. He appealed, contending that, by virtue of *FA 1965, Sch 7 para 14(3)*, there had been no disposal of any asset. The Special Commissioners allowed his appeal but the Ch D reversed their decision and restored the assessment. A sum paid to a person who had the right to call on another person to buy property from him (a put option) was a capital sum derived from an asset. *FA 1965, Sch 7 para 14(3)* provided that the exercise of a put option would not be treated as a disposal for the purpose of creating allowable losses, but it did not exempt a gain made from such a transaction. *Golding v Kaufman Ch D 1985, 58 TC 296; [1985] STC 152*. (Note. *FA 1965, Sch 7 para 14(3)* was modified by *FA 1971*. See now *TCGA 1992, s 144(3)(4)*.)

Goodbrand v Loffland Bros North Sea Inc 15.6

Deferred consideration (TCGA 1992, s 48)
Exchange rate fluctuations — whether TCGA 1992, s 48 applicable*

In 1985 a company (L) sold various assets under a lease-purchase agreement for $38,610,000. The Revenue issued an assessment on the basis that the sterling equivalent of the disposal proceeds, at the then exchange rate, was £33,313,000. As a result of subsequent fluctuations in the exchange rate, L only received £23,853,000. It claimed relief under *TCGA 1992, s 48** for the balance of £9,500,000. The Ch D upheld the Revenue's rejection of the claim, and the CA dismissed the company's appeal, holding that the 'consideration ... brought into account' was the contractual consideration, rather than its sterling equivalent. The tax computation merely involved a valuation exercise, rather than an actual conversion of dollars into sterling. L had anticipated receiving $38,610,000 and had received that amount. The exchange loss of £9,500,000 was not irrecoverable consideration within the meaning of *TCGA 1992, s 48**. *Goodbrand v Loffland Bros North Sea Inc CA 1998, 71 TC 57; [1998] STC 930*.

Goodwin v Curtis 49.2

Private residence exemption (TCGA 1992, ss 222–225)
Farmhouse inhabited by claimant for only 32 days — whether eligible for relief under TCGA 1992, s 222.*

In 1983 a company had exchanged contracts for the purchase of a farm, which included a nine-bedroomed farmhouse. It agreed that, following completion of the purchase, it would sell the farmhouse to one of its directors (G). The company did not complete the purchase of the farmhouse until 7 March 1985, and the sale to G was completed on 1 April 1985. G, who was in the process of separating from his wife, had already instructed estate agents with regard to the sale of the farmhouse, but moved into it immediately. On 3 April 1985 G completed the purchase of a small cottage, and on 11 April 1985 he advertised the farmhouse for sale. He continued to live in the farmhouse until 3 May 1985, when he completed the sale of the farmhouse and moved into the cottage. He appealed against a CGT assessment, contending that the gain on the sale of the farmhouse was eligible for relief under *TCGA 1992, s 222**. The General Commissioners rejected this contention, finding that G had not intended to occupy the farmhouse as his permanent residence, and holding that the gain did not qualify for relief. The CA upheld their decision. G had only lived in the farmhouse for 32 days, and the Commissioners had been entitled to find that he had not intended to occupy it as his permanent residence. *Dicta* of Viscount Cave in *Levene v CIR* applied. *Goodwin v Curtis CA 1998, 70 TC 478; [1998] STC 475*.

Gordon v CIR 33.10

Whether business transferred as a going concern

A farmer entered into an agreement with his wife to farm an estate in partnership. Five days later the partnership agreed to transfer its business to an unlimited company which the farmer and his wife had formed in the previous month. The Revenue issued a capital gains tax assessment charging tax on the transfer of the business to the company. The farmer appealed, contending that the business had been transferred as a going concern, so that rollover relief was available. The Special Commissioner dismissed his appeal, finding that, although the 'whole assets of the business' had been transferred, the farmer had intended that the company should sell the estate to an outside purchaser, and that the company had not taken over the business until contracts for the sale of the estate had been exchanged. Accordingly, the business had not been transferred as a going concern, since 'its end was too clearly and too closely in sight'. The CS allowed the farmer's appeal against this decision. Although contracts for the sale of the estate to an outside purchaser had been exchanged by the time when the company took over the farming of the estate, no such sale had been agreed at the time when the partnership had agreed to transfer the estate to the company. Accordingly, the company could have continued to operate the business if it had so wished. Furthermore, the company subsequently continued to farm an estate elsewhere, using machinery and cattle transferred to it from the partnership. Lord Hope held that 'a planned move of the entire assets of a business from one place to another is not inconsistent with the continuation of its trade'. On the facts found by the Commissioner, the only reasonable conclusion was that the company had received the whole assets of the business as a going concern. *Robroyston Brickworks Ltd* applied. *Gordon v CIR CS 1991, 64 TC 173; [1991] STC 174.*

Green v CIR 49.1

Whether wing of mansion part of residence — whether TCGA 1992, s 224(2) applicable*

In 1975 a taxpayer sold a mansion house and grounds which he had acquired in 1971. The building comprised a central block with 33 rooms, and two wings connected to it by corridors. Some work of reconstruction and redecoration had been carried out, during which the taxpayer and various members of his family and others had occupied parts of the central block, while a flat had been made in one of the wings for a gardener. The taxpayer claimed that the whole of the gain was within the private residence exemption. The General Commissioners held that the two wings were not part of the residence and that the gain on their sale was not within the relief. As regards the main block, they applied *TCGA 1992, s 224(2)**, adjusting the relief in respect of a 'change in what is occupied as the individual's residence', and allowed relief on one-third of the gain. The CS held that there was no factual material before the Commissioners which entitled them to adjust the relief under *TCGA 1992, s 224(2)**. Accordingly, the whole of the gain on the sale of the central block and grounds was exempt. Applying *Batey v Wakefield*, whether the wings were part of the residence was a matter of degree for the Commissioners, and their decision was not inconsistent with the evidence. Accordingly, the appeal failed as regards the gain on the sale of the wings. *Green v CIR CS 1982, 56 TC 10; [1982] STC 485.*

Griffin v Citibank Investments Ltd 6.7

Whether gain from certain transactions in financial options taxable as chargeable gain or as income

The Revenue contended that two options, purchased by the taxpayer company from the same fellow group company, intended to have effect together, and undoubtedly financial options within *TCGA 1992, s 144(8)(c)(i)* when considered separately, should be regarded as a single composite transaction that was not a financial option but a loan, the 'gain' on which should be taxed as income under Schedule D, Case III. The taxpayer company had unused capital losses and had wished to receive funds in the form of capital gains. In allowing the company's appeal, the Special Commissioners held that, even if the options were a single composite transaction (which in their judgement was not the case), to re-characterise them as a loan would be to disregard the legal form and nature of the transactions and to go behind them to some supposed underlying substance. This was not possible in the absence of artificial steps as in *Ramsay* (see 3.1 ANTI-AVOIDANCE). The Ch D upheld this decision. On the evidence, the Commissioners were entitled to conclude that the options were not to be regarded as a single composite transaction. *Citibank Investments Ltd v Griffin Ch D 2000, 73 TC 352; [2000] STC 1010.*

Griffin v Craig-Harvey 49.4

Main residence relief

A taxpayer, who owned a house in Stockwell, acquired a house in Winchester on 12 August 1985. On 9 July 1986 he sold his house in Stockwell and bought another house in Clapham. On 21 January 1988 he submitted a notice under *TCGA 1992, s 222(5)** declaring that the house in Winchester should be treated as his main residence. On 26 January 1989 he sold that house, realising a capital gain of around £225,000. The inspector issued a CGT assessment on the basis that $^{11}/_{41.5}$ of the gain was chargeable, considering that the period from August 1985 to June 1986 was not covered by the notice submitted in January 1988, since that notice was for the purpose of determining whether the Winchester house or the Clapham house should be treated as the taxpayer's main residence, and any notice determining whether the Stockwell house or the Winchester house had been the taxpayer's main residence would have had to have been lodged within two years of the taxpayer's acquisition of the Winchester house in August 1985. The taxpayer appealed, contending that the notice should be treated as effective from January 1986, so that only $^{5.5}/_{41.5}$ of the gain was chargeable. The Ch D upheld the assessment (reversing the Special Commissioner's decision). The two-year period of *TCGA 1992, s 222(5)(a)* began to run from the time when it first became necessary to determine which of two specific residences should be treated as a taxpayer's main residence. The taxpayer had made no election covering the period when he owned a house in Stockwell as well as the house in Winchester. The election which he had made in January 1988 was an election between his house in Clapham and the house in Winchester. Since he had not acquired the house in Clapham until July 1986, the notice could not cover any period before that time. (Vinelott J observed that *TCGA 1992, s 222(5)** derived from *FA 1965*, and that during the relevant Parliamentary debates the Financial Secretary had stated that the intention of the clause was so that a taxpayer could 'exercise a choice within two years from the time when he acquires the second house'.) *Griffin v Craig-Harvey Ch D 1993, 66 TC 396; [1994] STC 54.*

Gubay v Kington 42.4, 52.3

*Gift by resident husband to non-resident wife — application of TCGA 1992, s 58(1)**

The taxpayer's wife took up residence in the Isle of Man on 4 April 1972. The taxpayer remained resident and ordinarily resident in the UK until October 1972, but meanwhile he visited his wife and lived with her in the Isle of Man most weekends. In July 1972 he gave his wife some valuable shares. He appealed against a 1972/73 assessment on him in respect of the resultant gain. The HL allowed his appeal (Lord Scarman dissenting), holding that the combined effect of *ICTA 1988, s 282* and *TCGA 1992, s 58(1)** was that no CGT was payable on the gift of the shares. *Gubay v Kington HL 1984, 57 TC 601; [1984] STC 99; [1984] 1 WLR 163; [1984] 1 All ER 513.*

Hart v Briscoe and Others 57.12

*TCGA 1992, s 71(1)** — *'absolutely entitled' — whether beneficial entitlement required*

Two cases concerning *TCGA 1992, s 71(1)** were heard together. In *Hart v Briscoe*, trustees, acting under a 1955 settlement, declared that the whole of the settled property should be held on the trusts of a 1972 settlement, made for the purpose by the same settlor with the same trustees. In *Hoare Trustees,* trustees used a power of advancement in a settlement to declare trusts of assets advanced. It was held in both that the 'new' trustees had become absolutely entitled to settled property as against the old. 'Absolutely entitled' in *TCGA 1992, s 71(1)** does not imply beneficial ownership but whether an advancement is a continuance of the existing trust or a new trust is a question of fact and degree. *Hart v Briscoe and Others Ch D 1977, 52 TC 53; [1978] STC 89; [1978] 2 WLR 832; [1978] 1 All ER 791.* (See now *Roome v Edwards* and HMRC Statement of Practice SP 9/81.)

Hatt v Newman 53.3

Retirement relief — sale of let property

A married couple purchased a property in 1967, parts of which they let, furnished, to tenants and other parts of which were used by the husband as a workshop and a store for his business as a haulage contractor which ceased in 1990. The couple sold the property in 1995 and claimed retirement relief. The Revenue rejected the claim and the husband appealed. The Special Commissioner dismissed the appeal, and the Ch D upheld this decision. Applying *Griffiths v Jackson Ch D 1982, 52 TC 583; [1983] STC 184*, the letting of furnished rooms was not a trade. Furthermore, the period between the cessation of the husband's business as a contractor and the disposal of the property exceeded the one-year time limit permitted by *TCGA 1992, s 163, Sch 6* (see 53.4(*b*) RETIREMENT RELIEF). *Hatt v Newman Ch D 2000, 72 TC 462; [2000] STC 113.* (Notes. (1) The husband appeared in person. (2) The Commissioner and Ch D also upheld the Revenue's contention that, by virtue of *TCGA 1992, s 28*, the disposal took place in 1994/95 when the contract was signed and the condition to which it was subject was fulfilled, rather than in 1995/96 when the contract was completed. (3) Retirement relief is abolished for disposals after 5 April 2003 (see 53.1 RETIREMENT RELIEF).)

Hawkings-Byass v Sassen 41.4

Valuation of unquoted shares

In three appeals heard together, members of the same family disposed of shares in an unquoted Cayman Islands company which was the holding company of a trading group concerned principally with the production and sale of sherry. Under the company's Articles of Association, the company could refuse to register the transfer of shares to anyone who was not a member of the two families which had originally formed the company (and the disposals were to members of the other family in question). The valuation of the shares at 31 March 1982 was disputed. The Special Commissioners reviewed the evidence in detail, holding that in the particular circumstances, it was not appropriate to value the shares on an earnings basis or on a dividend basis, but that the company should be valued on an assets basis and on a turnover basis to arrive at a notional quoted value which should be uplifted by a 'control premium' of 30% to arrive at an entirety value of £46,000,000. The shares should then be valued on the basis that the two smaller shareholdings (comprising 11.09% and 9.09% of the total shares respectively) could have been acquired with a bid of two-thirds of their 'entirety value' (i.e. at £256 each) and that, for the largest shareholding (comprising 18.16% of the share capital), a 20% premium should be added to this (arriving at a value of £307 each). *Hawkings-Byass v Sassen (and related appeals) (Sp C 88), [1996] SSCD 319.*

Henderson v Karmel's Executors 41.7

Election for 6 April 1965 valuation — whether land subject to a tenancy

In 1975 a married woman (K) sold land which she had held for many years. From 1961 to 1972 it had been farmed by a company which she controlled, and from then until the sale she had farmed it in partnership. The company had originally paid an annual rental of £2,000, but this was waived in 1966. The Revenue issued a CGT assessment to the executors of K's husband, charging tax on the disposal. The executors appealed, contending that the land should be valued on the basis of vacant possession of the land at 6 April 1965. The Ch D rejected this contention and upheld the assessment (reversing the decision of the General Commissioners). On the evidence, at 6 April 1965 the land had clearly been subject to a tenancy. *Henderson v Karmel's Executors Ch D 1984, 58 TC 201; [1984] STC 572.*

Hepworth v Smith 53.3

Family company — whether voting rights not exercised are 'exercisable'

In a claim to retirement relief in which the facts are complex, the issue was whether S Ltd was a 'family company' in relation to the claimant. S Ltd had an issued capital of 100 shares of which the taxpayer, his wife and a business associate each held one. The remaining 97 shares were held by B Ltd which had, however, never appointed a representative to exercise its voting rights. The taxpayer contended that, for the purposes of *TCGA 1992, Sch 6 para 1(2)**, S Ltd was a family company, as he held one-third of the voting rights actually exercised. The Ch D, reversing the Commissioners' decision, held that voting rights 'exercisable' were those capable of being exercised. Accordingly, the voting rights of the shares held by B Ltd were 'exercisable' and S Ltd was not a family company. *Hepworth v Smith Ch D 1981, 54 TC 396; [1981] STC 354.* (Notes. (1) *TCGA 1992, s 163, TCGA 1992, Sch 6 para 1(2)* has subsequently been amended by *FA 1993, s 87, Sch 7.* The references in *TCGA 1992, s 163* to a 'family company' have been replaced by references to a 'personal company'. (2) Retirement relief is abolished for disposals after 5 April 2003 (see 53.1 RETIREMENT RELIEF).)

Hinchcliffe v Crabtree 7.2, 41.3

Value of quoted shares while secret takeover negotiations in progress

A taxpayer was liable on his gain from the disposal during 1965/66 of certain quoted shares in a manufacturing company of which he was a joint managing director. The question at issue was their market value at 6 April 1965. At that date, takeover negotiations were in progress but had not been made public and the Commissioners accepted evidence that, had they been public, the quoted price at that date would have been substantially higher than the actual quoted price. The HL held that the mere fact that directors of a company possessed information which if made public would affect the quoted prices of its shares was not a special circumstance. (There was no evidence of impropriety in withholding the relevant information.) *Hinchcliffe v Crabtree HL 1971, 47 TC 419; [1972] AC 725; [1971] 3 All ER 967.*

Hirsch v Crowthers Cloth Ltd 35.1

*Machinery and plant — exclusion of amounts taken into account in computing balancing charge — TCGA 1992, s 37**

In 1980 a company sold for £715,967 looms which it had purchased for £545,930. The sale gave rise to a balancing charge under *CAA 1990, s 24**. The company appealed against a CGT assessment on the overall gain of £170,037, contending that, by virtue of *TCGA 1992, s 37(1)**, the acquisition cost of the looms should be excluded from the disposal consideration, since it had been taken into account in computing the balancing charge. The Ch D, reversing the Commissioner's decision, held that the acquisition cost was not to be excluded from the disposal consideration. Although *TCGA 1992, s 37(2)**, which specifically excluded from the scope of *TCGA 1992, s 37(1)** amounts taken into account in making a balancing charge under *CAA 1968*, had subsequently been amended by *FA 1980* to refer also to amounts taken into account under *FA 1971*, this was merely making explicit what was already implicit in *TCGA 1992, s 37(1)**. Where legislation was ambiguously worded, it was necessary to have regard to the context and scheme of the Act under consideration, and to strive to find an interpretation which avoided injustice or absurdity. The words 'taken into account' in *TCGA 1992, s 37(1)** should be read as referring to sums which had to be brought directly into the computation. The purpose of the limitation of the disposal value to the cost of acquisition was to avoid double taxation of any profit on disposal. It would be paradoxical to find that the cost of acquisition was itself to be deducted from the disposal consideration, thereby ensuring that the gain escaped altogether the charge to tax. *Hirsch v Crowthers Cloth Ltd Ch D 1989, 62 TC 759; [1990] STC 174.*

Honour v Norris 49.1

Whether self-contained flat formed part of dwelling-house

The owner of four separate flats, located in separate buildings in the same square within 95 yards of each other, sold one of them, which had been used to provide occasional bedroom accommodation for his children and guests and, on rare occasions, sleeping accommodation for him and his wife. He appealed against an assessment on the gain, claiming relief under *TCGA 1992, s 222**. (The square contained 32 houses, most of which were divided into flats.) The Ch D rejected the claim and upheld the assessment (reversing the decision of the Commissioners). The flat was a separate dwelling-house, which could not be regarded as part of a common entity with the flat in which the owner and his wife lived. The fact that the owner had sometimes used it to accommodate his children or guests did not make it a part of his private residence. *Honour v Norris Ch D 1992, 64 TC 599; [1992] STC 304.*

Innocent v Whaddon Estates Ltd 27.2

*Transfers within a group — construction of TCGA 1992, s 171(2)**

In 1961 the taxpayer company received, on the liquidation of a subsidiary, a capital distribution of shares in a public quoted company which at the time had a market value of 13s 4d each. The value fell to 6s 3d by Budget Day 1965, although this still exceeded their cost to the subsidiary. The company made various sales of the shares and appealed against assessments on the gains arrived at by treating the consideration for the shares as 6s 3d each. The Ch D upheld the assessments, rejecting the company's contention that the cost should be taken as 13s 4d each. The reference in *TCGA 1992, s 171(2)** to *TCGA 1992, s 122** applied to its disposal of its shares in the subsidiary, but not to the shares it acquired on the liquidation. *Innocent v Whaddon Estates Ltd Ch D 1981, 55 TC 476; [1982] STC 115.*

Jarmin v Rawlings 53.4

Retirement relief

A farmer owned 64 acres with a milking parlour and yard, and had a dairy herd of 34 animals. In October 1988 he sold the parlour and yard, and during the next three months he sold 14 of the animals. He transferred most of the remaining animals to a farm three miles away which belonged to his wife. He ceased dairy farming and used his land for rearing and finishing store cattle, although he retained and leased the milk quota, with a view to enhancing the value of the land on an eventual sale. The Revenue issued an assessment charging CGT on the sale of the parlour and yard. He appealed, claiming retirement relief. The Revenue rejected his claim on the grounds that he had only sold assets of his business, rather than a part of his business. The Commissioners allowed his appeal, holding that the dairy farming had been 'a separate and distinguishable part of the taxpayer's business', that he had sold a part of his business and that the sale qualified for retirement relief. The Ch D upheld the Commissioners' decision. Knox J held that the Commissioners were entitled to find that the dairy farming was a separate business from the rearing and finishing of store cattle, and that 'the sale by auction and completion of that sale of the milking parlour and yard, coupled with the cessation at completion of all milking operations for the taxpayer's benefit, amounted to a disposal by him of his dairy farming business'. *Jarmin v Rawlings Ch D 1994, 67 TC 130; [1994] STC 1005.* (Note. Retirement relief is abolished for disposals after 5 April 2003 (see 53.1 RETIREMENT RELIEF).)

Jerome v Kelly 15.3

Date of disposal/identity of disponor

In April 1987 a married couple signed a contract to dispose of three plots of land. The sale of the first plot was not completed until 1990, and the sale of the final plot was not completed until 1992. Meanwhile, in 1989, the couple had assigned half of their beneficial interests in the land to the trustee of two Bermudan settlements which they had created. The Revenue issued a CGT assessment on the basis that the effect of *TCGA 1992, s 28** was that the couple had disposed of the whole of their interests in the land in 1987/88 (the year the contract was made). The husband (J) appealed, contending that the disposal in 1987/88 should be treated as being limited to the half of the beneficial interests which they still held when the sales were completed, and should not be treated as also covering the half of the beneficial interests which they had assigned in 1989. The HL accepted this contention and allowed the appeal. Lord Hoffmann observed that the draftsman responsible for (*TCGA 1992, s 28(1)**) 'did not think about what should happen in the situation which has arisen in this case'. He held that it would be wrong 'to attribute to Parliament an intention to impose a liability to tax upon a person who would not be treated as having made a disposal under the carefully constructed scheme for taxing the disposals of assets held on trust'. (*TCGA 1992, s 28(1)**) should be treated as 'concerned solely with fixing the time of disposal by a person whose identity is to be ascertained by other means. It follows that the disposal under the conveyance to the purchasers was made by the Bermudan trustees and not by (Mr and Mrs J).' Lord Walker of Gestingthorpe observed that 'the contingent way in which (*TCGA 1992, s 28(1)**) operates creates an obvious problem for a taxpayer who has entered into a contract to sell an asset, with completion postponed until a later tax year. Should he assume that the contract will be duly completed and, on that assumption, return a chargeable gain accruing on the date of the contract? The Revenue acknowledge that this is a flaw in the capital gains tax legislation. Good legislative practice requires that a taxpayer should not be left in doubt as to whether or not he has incurred a tax charge.' *Jerome v Kelly HL, [2004] STC 887; [2004] UKHL 25; [2004] All ER(D) 168(May).*

Johnson v Edwards 15.3

*Application of TCGA 1992, s 28(1)**

In a case where the facts were complex, the owner of certain shares agreed on 25 February 1965 to sell them. The date of completion was fixed as 31 January 1970, but in fact completion did not take place until 1971/72. The Revenue assessed the resulting gain in 1971/72 and the taxpayer appealed, contending that, by virtue of *TCGA 1992, s 28(1)**, the date of disposal was 25 February 1965. The Ch D dismissed his appeal, holding that the words 'where an asset is disposed of under a contract' in *TCGA 1992, s 28* apply to a disposal after 5 April 1971 under a contract entered into after that date, but not to a disposal after that date under a contract entered into before that date. *Johnson v Edwards Ch D 1981, 54 TC 488; [1981] STC 660.*

Jones v Wilcock 49.7

Loss on sale of property — whether TCGA, s 224(3) applicable

In 1988 an accountant and his wife purchased a house for more than £120,000. They subsequently incurred considerable expenditure on improvements, but, following a general fall in house prices, sold the house for £97,000 in 1993. The husband had other capital gains in the year of disposal, and claimed that the loss on the house should be set against such gains. The Revenue rejected the claim, on the basis that the house had been the couple's private residence, so that the effect of *TCGA 1992, s 16, s 223(1)* was that the loss was not allowable. The husband appealed, contending that the house had been purchased 'wholly or partly for the purpose of realising a gain', within *TCGA 1992, s 224(3)*, so that *TCGA 1992, s 223* did not apply. The Special Commissioner rejected this contention and dismissed the appeal. On the evidence, the couple's purpose in buying the house was to use it as their home. Their hope that they would be able to make a profit on its eventual sale 'was not a purpose within *TCGA 1992, s 224(3)*'. *Jones v Wilcock (Sp C 92), [1996] SSCD 389.*

Joseph Carter & Sons Ltd v Baird; Wear Ironmongers & Sons Ltd v Baird 55.1

Companies claiming rollover relief in respect of land purchased by associated company

Two associated companies (C and W) disposed of some land in Sunderland. Their controlling director purchased a farm in France, and transferred its ownership to a French company, the shares in which were owned by C and W. C and W claimed rollover relief. The Revenue rejected the claim on the grounds that neither the land in Sunderland, nor the farm in France, had been used for the purpose of the trades of C and W, and that the disposals and acquisition had not been by the same person, as required by *TCGA 1992, s 152**. The Commissioners dismissed the companies' appeals and the Ch D upheld their decision. *Joseph Carter & Sons Ltd v Baird; Wear Ironmongers & Sons Ltd v Baird Ch D 1998, 72 TC 303; [1999] STC 120.*

Kirby v Thorn EMI plc 6.1, 9.1

Whether consideration for a non-competition covenant a capital sum derived from an asset

A holding company (T) held the shares of M. In December 1977 an elaborate agreement between T, M and an American corporation (G) was completed, under which T procured the sale to G of three subsidiaries of M, engaged mainly in the repairing of electrical motors and generators, with the benefit of a covenant by T under which broadly it undertook that it and its subsidiaries would not engage in a competing business in the UK before 1983. The consideration was $1.73m of which $.575m (then equivalent to £315,934) was apportioned to the covenant. The CA accepted this contention, holding that the sum received in respect of the covenant gave rise to a chargeable gain (reversing the decisions of the Special Commissioners and the Ch D). The Revenue's contention that, by the covenant, T conferred rights on G, and the asset thus created had been disposed of by T to G, was rejected by the Commissioners, the Ch D and the CA. However, an alternative Revenue contention, not advanced in the Ch D, was that if a pre-existing asset was needed for the tax to apply to it, the goodwill of T was such an asset, of which it made a part disposal by the covenant, or from which it derived a capital sum. The CA accepted this contention, holding that the disputed amount was a capital sum derived from T's goodwill. Since the extent and valuation of this goodwill had not been canvassed before the Commissioners, Nicholls LJ considered that the case should be remitted to them, to reconsider the company's appeal in the light of his judgement. (Subsequently the Court agreed that there should be no such remitter and that both the Commissioners' determination and the judgement of the Ch D should be varied in specified terms set out in a schedule of 'terms of compromise'.) *Kirby v Thorn EMI plc CA 1987, 60 TC 519; [1987] STC 621; 1988 STI 90; [1988] 1 WLR 445; [1988] 2 All ER 947.*

Larner v Warrington 4.13

*Assets of negligible value — whether dissipated within TCGA 1992, s 24(1)**

The taxpayer made a substantial gain on the disposal of shares in M Ltd in 1973/74. Shortly after the disposal, he and his wife invested in two companies, the shares in which had become of negligible value by 5 April 1974. He was assessed on his 1973/74 gain in 1978 and appealed against the assessment, claiming relief under *TCGA 1992, s 24(2)** for 1973/74. The General Commissioners heard the appeal in July 1979 and allowed the taxpayer's claim in principle, adjourning the appeal for the value of the shares in M Ltd to be agreed. The appeal was restored for hearing in February 1984. In the interval *Williams v Bullivant* had been decided in the Ch D, and the Commissioners permitted the Revenue to raise the new argument that the notional loss provided for by *TCGA 1992, s 24(2)** took place not earlier than the making of the claim in 1978/79. The Commissioners accepted this, and determined the assessment accordingly. The taxpayer appealed to the Ch D, where he appeared in person and contended that the Commissioners should not have permitted their 1979 decision in his favour to be reopened. Further, since the shares in the companies in which he and his wife had invested had lost their value by April 1974, they had by then been dissipated within *TCGA 1992, s 24(1)**. Both contentions were rejected. There had been no final decision on any matter raised at the July 1979 hearing, as the value of the M Ltd shares was unsettled. The taxpayer had not been prejudiced, for if the final decision had been in his favour, the Revenue could, and no doubt would, have appealed to the Ch D. The relevant assets remained in existence, although they had become valueless, and loss in value as distinct from the loss, destruction, dissipation or extinction of an asset falls under *TCGA 1992, s 24(2)** and not under TCGA 1992, s 24(1)*. *Larner v Warrington Ch D 1985, 58 TC 557; [1985] STC 442.*

Lee v Jewitt 15.4

Legal costs relating to partnership dispute — whether within TCGA 1992, s 38(1)(b)

In 1981 an accountancy partnership admitted three new partners. The new partners paid a total of £150,000 to the original partners. In the relevant agreements, 20% of this was attributed to goodwill. Following disagreements, the new partners took legal proceedings, seeking a dissolution of the partnership and the repayment of the £75,000 paid to one of the original partners (L). L incurred legal costs of some £13,000 in defending the proceedings. The Ch D ordered that the partnership should be dissolved, but rejected the claim for repayment. The Revenue issued a 1981/82 CGT assessment on L in respect of the partial disposal of the partnership goodwill. L appealed, contending that the legal costs should be allowed as a deduction. The Special Commissioner accepted this contention and allowed the appeal. In his view, there was clear evidence that the taxpayer was defending his title to the goodwill, for what the new partners were alleging was that the goodwill had turned out not to have existed at the time of their admittance. *Lee v Jewitt (Sp C 257), [2000] SSCD 517.*

Leisureking Ltd v Cushing 40.10

Loss relief for payment made under guarantee

In 1985 a company (L), and ten companies in the same group, entered into a composite joint and several guarantee with a bank whereby the liabilities to the bank of each of the companies were guaranteed by all the other ten companies as co-guarantors. In 1988 the bank sought repayment of liabilities incurred by two of the associated companies, which were no longer solvent. L made a payment of £2,115,000 to the bank, and did not seek to recover any contributions from its co-guarantors. L claimed relief for the payment under *TCGA 1992, s 253(4)**. The Revenue considered that the relief should be restricted to take account of the fact that the liability was shared between L and the other companies which had acted as guarantors. The Special Commissioner found on the evidence that only three of the co-guarantors remained solvent at the time when L had made the payment in question, and held that L was entitled to relief in respect of one-third of the payment. The Ch D dismissed L's appeal against this decision. The amount of the relief had to be restricted to take account of potential contributions from the co-guarantors. (Chadwick J also observed that the Commissioner had apparently been wrong to disregard any possibility of recovery from a liquidation of the eight co-guarantors which were no longer solvent, but declined to remit the matter to the Commissioner to reconsider this point, since the Revenue had not appealed against the decision.) *Leisureking Ltd v Cushing Ch D 1992, 65 TC 400; [1993] STC 46.*

Lewis v Rook 49.1

In 1968 a taxpayer purchased a large house, ten acres of land, and two cottages. In 1979 she sold one of the cottages, which was 190 yards from her house and had been occupied by a gardener. The Revenue issued an assessment on the gain and she appealed, contending that *TCGA 1992, s 222** applied. The Commissioners allowed her appeal but the CA reversed this decision and restored the assessment. Applying the non-tax cases of *Methuen Campbell v Walters [1979] 1 QB 525* and *Dyer v Dorset County Council [1989] QB 346*, the true test was whether the cottage was within the curtilage of, and appurtenant to, the main property, so as to be part of the entity which, together with the main property, constituted the dwelling-house occupied by the taxpayer as her main residence. This was not the case here, where the cottage was some way from the main building and separated by a large garden. *Lewis v Rook CA 1992, 64 TC 567, [1992] STC 171; [1992] 1 WLR 662.*

Lewis v Walters 38.14

Whether lease a wasting asset

On the death of their mother in 1982, a brother and sister inherited the freehold interest in a house. The house was subject to a lease, for a term of 99 years from 1904, in favour of their father. He died in 1985 and the brother and sister then acquired the lease as his executors. Neither of them lived in the house, and in 1987 they sold the freehold and leasehold interests to the same purchaser. The Revenue issued a CGT assessment in which the value of the house was apportioned between the leasehold and freehold interests. In the assessment the lease was treated as a wasting asset, so that its value at the date of acquisition was written down in accordance with *TCGA 1992, Sch 8**. The executors appealed, contending that, by virtue of *Leasehold Reform Act 1967*, the lease should not be treated as a wasting asset. Their appeal was dismissed by the General Commissioners and the Ch D. The lease as granted did not contain any express term providing for its extension beyond 2003. The rights conferred by the *Leasehold Reform Act* did not constitute a provision 'for the extension of the lease beyond a given date' within the meaning of *TCGA 1992, Sch 8 para 8(5)**. Furthermore, the executors' father had not given notice of any desire to extend the lease and the executors had no power to extend the lease either in their capacity as executors or as the heirs of his estate. Accordingly, the lease was a wasting asset and the assessment had been computed on the correct basis. *Lewis v Walters Ch D 1992, 64 TC 489; [1992] STC 97.*

Liddell v CIR 8.3

Whether Revenue acting unreasonably in refusing to allow late election under TCGA 1992, s 35(5) (universal re-basing election)

An individual (L) held shares in three associated companies at 31 March 1982. In 1986 he exchanged these shares for shares in the parent company of the group. In 1991 he sold some shares in an unrelated company (R). This sale gave rise to a chargeable gain which was below the annual exemption limit. In April 1992 the parent company of the group went into receivership, so that its shares became worthless. Consequently, the time limit for making an election under *TCGA 1992, s 35(5)*, to treat the value of the shares at 31 March 1982 as their cost of acquisition, expired on 5 April 1994. L failed to make such an election within the statutory time limit, but in March 1995 he applied for an extension of the time limit under *section 35(6)(b)*. The Revenue rejected the application. L applied for judicial review, contending that the sale of his shares in R should not be regarded as a relevant disposal, and that the Revenue's refusal to allow a late election was unreasonable. The SCS rejected this contention and dismissed the application. Lord Eassie observed that the circumstances did not fall within Revenue Statement of Practice SP 4/92, or within the scope of a Ministerial Statement issued in December 1985 in relation to the extension of time limits. Furthermore, there was 'a clear distinction between disposals upon which the gain, irrespective of amount, will not be chargeable and those which will give rise to a chargeable gain, which may possibly not give rise to actual liability to tax by virtue of the exemption afforded by *TCGA 1992, s 3.* The chartered accountants acting for the petitioner effectively invited the Board to alter or erase that boundary. In its response the Board adhered to its analysis by emphasising that chargeable gains remained chargeable even in the event that their net amount is sufficiently low to come within the annual exempt amount.' The Revenue had been entitled to take the view that 'oversight by the professional advisers was not a sufficient reason for their granting an extension of the time limit.' *Liddell v CIR SCS 1997, 72 TC 62.* (*Note.* For the text of the Ministerial Statement in question, see HMRC Capital Gains Manual CG 13802.)

Longson v Baker 49.1

Private residence exemption — area required for reasonable enjoyment

An individual (L) separated from his wife in 1990 and moved out of the matrimonial home, which was a farmhouse including stables and 7.56 hectares of land. L and his family kept horses at the farm and had erected a further building for use as a riding school. In 1995 the couple divorced, and L disposed of his beneficial interest in the property to his former wife. The Revenue issued a CGT assessment on the basis that only 1.054 hectares qualified for private residence relief within *TCGA 1992, s 222(3)*. (It was accepted that L was entitled to relief by virtue of ESC D6, although he had not lived in the property since 1990.) L appealed against the assessment, contending that all 7.56 hectares had been 'required for the reasonable enjoyment of the dwelling-house'. The Special Commissioner rejected this contention and dismissed the appeal, holding that 'it cannot be correct that the dwelling-house ... *requires* an area of land amounting to 7.56 hectares in order to ensure its reasonable enjoyment as a residence, having regard to its size and character.' While it may have been 'desirable or convenient' for L to have such an area, it was not *required* for the reasonable enjoyment of the dwelling-house. *In Re Newhill Compulsory Purchase Order* applied; *Green v CIR* distinguished. The Ch D upheld this decision as one of fact. Evans-Lombe J held that *section 222(3)* imposed an objective test. It is not objectively required, i.e. necessary, to keep horses at a house to enjoy it as a residence. An individual taxpayer may subjectively wish to do so but that is not the same thing. *Longson v Baker Ch D 2000, 73 TC 415; [2001] STC 6.*

In re Lynall 41.4

Value of unquoted shares while public flotation under consideration

In an estate duty case the question at issue was the price which certain unquoted shares 'would fetch if sold in the open market at the time of the death of the deceased'. (*FA 1894, s 7(5)*. Compare *TCGA 1992, s 272(1)*.) At the time of the death, the directors were considering public flotation and favourable confidential reports had been made to them for that purpose by a firm of accountants and a firm of stockbrokers. The HL held, *inter alia*, that although no general rule could be laid down as to the information a hypothetical purchaser in an open market may be deemed to have, the board could not be deemed to disclose confidential information which, if published prematurely, might prejudice the company's interests, including reports on the possibility of a public issue. *In re Lynall HL 1971, 47 TC 375; [1972] AC 680; [1971] 3 All ER 904.* (Note. See now *FA 1973, s 51*, re-enacted as *TCGA 1992, s 273*, as to disposals after 5 July 1973. The substantive decision here is therefore now of limited application, but the judgements include a useful review of estate duty cases dealing with the valuation of unquoted shares. See also *Battle v CIR* and *CIR v Crossman*, and the 1995 cases of *Caton's Administrators v Couch* and *Clark (Clark's Executor) v CIR*.)

Lyon v Pettigrew 15.3

Consideration for disposal paid in instalments

In 1979/80 a taxi-cab proprietor contracted to sell some of his cabs together with their licences. Under the contract for each, the purchase price was £6,000, payable in instalments of £40 over 150 weeks. The contract provided that the licence would not be transferred until 'payment of all monies hereunder'. The Revenue issued an assessment on the basis that the cabs had been disposed of in 1979/80. The proprietor appealed, contending that the sales had been conditional within *TCGA 1992, s 28(2)**, so that the disposal had not taken place until the date on which the final instalment was paid. The Commissioners allowed his appeal but the Ch D reversed their decision and restored the assessment. By virtue of the *Town Police Clauses Act 1847*, it was not possible to sever the licences from the taxicabs. The contracts as a whole were not conditional, and the full amount of the consideration was chargeable in 1979/80. *Eastham v Leigh London & Provincial Properties Ltd* applied. *Lyon v Pettigrew, Ch D 1985, 58 TC 452; [1985] STC 369.*

McGregor v Adcock 53.4

Sale of part of land by farmer

A taxpayer, aged 70, had farmed 35 acres for over 10 years. He sold some 5 acres for which outline planning permission had been obtained. He was assessed on the large resulting gain and claimed retirement relief. The Ch D, reversing the decision of the Commissioners, held that no relief was due. The only reasonable conclusion on the facts was that there had been a sale of an asset of the business and not of part of the business. *McGregor v Adcock Ch D 1977, 51 TC 692; [1977] STC 206; [1977] 1 WLR 864; [1977] 3 All ER 65.* (Note. Retirement relief is abolished for disposals after 5 April 2003 (see 53.1 RETIREMENT RELIEF).)

MacPherson v Hall 59.6

Identification of shares disposed of

The rules for the identification of securities, etc. disposed of, introduced by *FA 1982, ss 88, 89*, are similar to those which had been in force for Sch D, Case VII (abolished from 6 April 1971). In a Case VII appeal, the taxpayer sold 6,000 shares of a company on the London Stock Exchange on 14 September 1964, the delivery date being 14 October. He had bought 6,000 shares of the same company some months previously and he also bought 6,000 on 11 September, the delivery date for which was 22 September. The Ch D held that under the legislation in force (the wording of *TCGA 1992, s 108(4)(b)* is identical) the shares disposed of should be identified with those acquired on 11 September, resulting in a loss of £20. (It was unsuccessfully contended for the taxpayer that the provision applied only to shares acquired on or after the date of disposal and that the shares sold should have been matched with those first purchased, producing a loss of £3,702.) *MacPherson v Hall Ch D 1972, 48 TC 210.*

Magnavox Electronics Co Ltd (in liquidation) v Hall 3.1

Anti-avoidance

In September 1978 a company (M) exchanged contracts for the sale of a factory to another company (J) for £1,400,000. Completion was arranged for February 1979, but for financial reasons J was unable to complete the purchase, and forfeited its deposit. Meanwhile, M had gone into voluntary liquidation in December 1978. The liquidator did not rescind the contract of sale, but arranged for M to acquire an 'off-the-shelf' company (S), to which it assigned its beneficial interest under the contract on 6 July 1979. Three days later certain variations in the contract were agreed, including a reduction of the purchase price to £1,150,000 and a new completion date of 9 October 1979. On the same day S exchanged contracts with a fourth company (B) for the sale of the factory on terms practically identical with those in the original contract as varied. B duly completed. The Revenue issued an assessment on the basis that the disposal had taken place after M had gone into liquidation. M appealed, contending that the disposal had taken place in September 1978 (so that trading losses of that accounting period could be set against the gain). The Special Commissioners dismissed M's appeal, and the Ch D and CA upheld their decision. The disposal to B was not under the 1978 contract, but under a new contract made in July 1979. Furthermore, the interposition of S was part of an artificial avoidance scheme which could be disregarded, applying *Furniss v Dawson. Magnavox Electronics Co Ltd (in liquidation) v Hall, CA 1986, 59 TC 610; [1986] STC 561.*

Makins v Elson 49.1

Whether caravan a dwelling-house

A taxpayer purchased land on which to build a house on which construction had commenced. Meanwhile, he lived with his family in a wheeled caravan jacked up and resting on bricks on the land, with water, electricity and telephone installed. Before completing the house, he sold the site, with the caravan, and was assessed on the resultant gain. The Ch D held that the caravan was a dwelling-house for the relevant period and that the gain was within the private residence exemption. *Makins v Elson Ch D 1976, 51 TC 437; [1977] STC 46; [1977] 1 WLR 221; [1977] 1 All ER 572.*

Mannion v Johnston 53.4

Retirement relief

A taxpayer who farmed 78 acres sold 17 of them in April 1984 and a further 18 acres in December 1984. He was assessed and claimed retirement relief, contending that the sales were a disposal of part of his business. The Ch D, reversing the Commissioners' decision, held that no relief was due, applying *McGregor v Adcock*. Each of the two dispositions had to be considered separately and the changes caused by each one were merely limited changes of scale. *Mannion v Johnston Ch D 1988, 61 TC 598; [1988] STC 758.* (Notes. (1) The case was heard in the Ch D with *Atkinson v Dancer*. (2) Retirement relief is abolished for disposals after 5 April 2003 (see 53.1 RETIREMENT RELIEF).)

Mansworth v Jelley 6.7, 20.6, 20.24

Acquisition of shares under share option scheme — application of TCGA 1992, s 17

An employee (J) was granted options to acquire shares in his employer's parent company. He was not resident in the UK at the time he was granted these options, but subsequently became UK-resident, exercised the options, and then sold the shares. The Revenue issued CGT assessments on the basis that the base value of the shares was the sum of the price paid for the shares on the exercise of the options and the market value of the options when they were originally granted (which was treated as nil). J appealed, contending that the base value of the shares was their market value when the options were exercised. The Special Commissioner accepted this contention and allowed the appeal, and the Ch D and CA upheld this decision. Chadwick LJ held that the acquisition of the shares was clearly 'an incident of the taxpayer's employment', and was therefore within *TCGA 1992, s 17(1)(b)**. Accordingly, in the CGT computation, the cost of acquisition was 'the market value of the underlying asset', i.e. the shares, at the time when the options were exercised. *Mansworth v Jelley CA 2002, 75 TC 1; [2003] STC 53.*

Markey v Sanders 49.1

Private residence exemption

In 1951, the taxpayer's mother purchased a small country estate of 4 acres with a main house and outbuildings reached by a 130 metre drive from the main entrance gates. In 1963, this was sold to the taxpayer, who had earlier (in 1956) acquired adjoining land of nearly 9 acres. In 1965, the taxpayer built a three-bedroom bungalow by the entrance gates, with a quarter-acre garden, which was occupied rent-free by a gardener and housekeeper. The bungalow was not separately rated. In September 1980, the whole estate, including the bungalow, was sold to a single purchaser. The issue in the appeal was whether the gain on the sale of the bungalow was within the private residence exemption. Walton J, reversing the Commissioners' decision and applying *Batey v Wakefield* held that it was not. Batey decided that 'residence' need not mean a single building, and a relevant fact there was that the bungalow was 'very closely adjacent' to the main residence. 'Very closely adjacent' is an imprecise test; he preferred to ask whether the relevant group of buildings, looked on as a whole, could be fairly regarded as a single dwelling-house used as the taxpayer's main residence. Here the only reasonable conclusion from the facts was that the bungalow was not part of the taxpayer's residence. *Markey v Sanders Ch D 1987, 60 TC 245; [1987] STC 256; [1987] 1 WLR 864.*

Marren v Ingles 6.1, 9.1, 22.5, 58.5

*Deferred sale consideration — application of TCGA 1992, s 22(1)**

Under an agreement of 15 September 1970, shares in a private company were sold for an immediate payment of £750 per share plus a further amount to be calculated by reference to the quoted price of shares representing them on the first dealing day following a proposed flotation of the company. In the event, the relevant dealing day was 5 December

1972 and the further consideration was agreed at £2,825 per share. It was common ground that, in arriving at the gain on the disposal of the shares, the £750 and the value at 15 September 1970 of the contingent right to further consideration were to be taken into account. A 1972/73 assessment was issued on the basis that the right to receive the further consideration, being a chose in action, was an asset from which a capital sum was derived on 5 December 1972; that there was a deemed disposal under *TCGA 1992, s 22(1)**; and that this right was not a debt within *TCGA 1992, s 251(1)**. The HL upheld the assessment. *Dicta* of Walton J in *CIR v Montgomery* on which the taxpayer relied, were disapproved. *Marren v Ingles HL 1980, 54 TC 76; [1980] STC 500; [1980] 1 WLR 983; [1980] 3 All ER 95.* See now *TCGA 1992, s 138A* at 58.5 SHARES AND SECURITIES.

Marriott v Lane 53.4

Retirement relief

TCGA, s 163(4)(c)— date of cessation of business*

A taxpayer (M) owned land and buildings which were used as an aircraft museum by a company of which he was the controlling director. The museum was closed to the public in October 1988, and in September 1989 the premises were sold to a subsidiary company which had been incorporated to undertake the residential development of the site. The Revenue issued an assessment charging CGT on the disposal, and M appealed, claiming retirement relief. The General Commissioners dismissed the appeal, finding that at the time of the sale, the company had hoped to reopen the museum at different premises, so that the trade had not then ceased and that retirement relief was not therefore due. The Ch D allowed M's appeal, holding that since the museum had never in fact reopened, the fact that the company had originally hoped to reopen it was not conclusive. Accordingly, the business should be treated as having ceased in October 1988, and M qualified for retirement relief under *TCGA 1992, s 163*. Marriott v Lane Ch D 1996, 69 TC 157; [1996] STC 704; [1996] 1 WLR 111.* (Note. Retirement relief is abolished for disposals after 5 April 2003 (see 53.1 RETIREMENT RELIEF).)

Marshall v Kerr 18.6, 44.14

Whether TCGA 1992, s 62(6) applicable to non-resident settlement established by a UK-resident beneficiary of a non-resident testator*

K's father-in-law (B) died in 1977, resident and ordinarily resident in Jersey. Half of B's personal estate was bequeathed to K's wife, who was a UK resident. By a deed of family arrangement in 1978 she settled her share of the estate on Jersey trustees, to be held on discretionary trusts for herself and her family. The administration of the estate was not completed until 1979 and the assets were at no time vested in K's wife. Between 1981 and 1985 the settlement trustees made capital payments to K's wife. The Revenue issued assessments under *TCGA 1992, ss 87–98**. K appealed, contending that, by virtue of *TCGA 1992, s 62(6)**, B should be deemed to be the settlor of the trusts, so that, since he had been neither resident or ordinarily resident in the UK, there was no CGT liability. The HL upheld the assessments (restoring the decision of the Ch D which had reversed that of the Special Commissioner). The arrangement did not settle any specific assets comprised in the estate, but settled the legatee's half-share in the residuary estate, which had not by then been constituted. The property settled by the legatee constituted a separate chose in action. Where a legatee varied her entitlement under a will by means of a family arrangement, the making of the variation was deemed not to be a disposal in itself. However, *TCGA 1992, s 62(6)** did not have the further effect of treating the assets vested in the legatee as acquired from the deceased at the date of death. Accordingly, the legatee was the settlor of the arrangement for the purposes of *TCGA 1992, s 87**. *Marshall v Kerr HL 1994, 67 TC 56; [1994] STC 638; [1994] 3 WLR 299; [1994] 2 All ER 106.*

Marson v Marriage 9.1, 15.6, 22.5

Deferred sale consideration — whether TCGA 1992, s 48 applicable*

A taxpayer agreed on 31 March 1965 to sell to a development company 47 acres of land with development possibilities. The consideration was £47,040 payable immediately with future payments of £7,500 for each acre developed and provision for compensation to the taxpayer should the land be compulsorily purchased from the company. In the event, the company developed the land in 1975 and paid £348,250 to the taxpayer in settlement of the agreement. He was assessed to CGT for 1975/76 on the basis that the £348,250 was a taxable receipt. The Ch D upheld the assessment, following *Marren v Ingles* and holding that the provision for compensation should the land be compulsorily purchased meant that the future consideration was not ascertainable at 31 March 1965. (The taxpayer had contended that, by virtue of *TCGA 1992, s 48**, the consideration could have been brought into account at that date.) *Marson v Marriage Ch D 1979, 54 TC 59; [1980] STC 177.*

Mashiter v Pearmain 7.6

Land value

A taxpayer sold land in 1976 for consideration exceeding its current use value. The land had been acquired by gift in 1960, and the Revenue issued an assessment computed on the basis that the land should be treated as having been sold on 6 April 1965 and re-acquired at its market value on that date. The taxpayer appealed, contending that the gain should be time-apportioned over the whole period from 1960 to 1976. The CA rejected this contention and upheld the assessment. *Mashiter v Pearmain, CA 1984, 58 TC 334; [1985] STC 165.*

Mayes v Woods 53.3

TCGA, s 163(1)(b) — whether claimant had 'retired on ill-health grounds'.

A greengrocer (M) sold his business and claimed retirement relief on the basis that he had retired on ill-health grounds after suffering chest pains. The Revenue rejected the claim, since a medical report had suggested that the pains were attributable to anxiety or hypertension, rather than to any heart condition. The Special Commissioner reviewed the medical evidence and dismissed M's appeal, finding that M did not satisfy the conditions of *TCGA 1992, s 163(1)(b)** and *Sch 6 para 3(1)**. *Mayes v Woods (Sp C 126), [1997] SSCD 206*. (Note. Retirement relief is abolished for disposals after 5 April 2003 (see 53.1 RETIREMENT RELIEF).)

Moore v Thompson 49.1

Whether a caravan a dwelling house

Makins v Elson was distinguished in a subsequent case where the General Commissioners held that a caravan installed in a small farm while the farmhouse was being renovated was not within the exemption of *TCGA 1992, s 222**, and the Ch D upheld their decision. The caravan was disposed of when the farmhouse was sold. The farmhouse was never occupied by the taxpayer, and the evidence was that she had never used the caravan as a permanent residence. *Moore v Thompson Ch D 1986, 61 TC 15; [1986] STC 170.*

Morgan v Gibson 7.6

Land reflecting development value

In 1948 a taxpayer acquired an interest in land which had an agreed value of £15,545. In 1984 the land was sold to the British Airports Authority for £160,000, with the condition that, should the Authority obtain planning permission within 30 years, a further sum of up to £350,000 would be payable. The Revenue issued an assessment on the basis that the consideration received on disposal included development value and that therefore *TCGA*

*1992, Sch 2 para 9** applied. The taxpayer appealed, contending that the conditions of *TCGA 1992, Sch 2 para 9(1)(b)** were not satisfied, and that the assessment should be computed on a straight-line apportionment basis. The Ch D rejected this contention and upheld the assessment (reversing the General Commissioners' decision). There was a clear finding of fact that the sale price included an element of 'hope value', which was equivalent to anticipated development value. That being so, the provisions of *TCGA 1992, Sch 2 para 9** had to be applied. *Morgan v Gibson Ch D 1989, 61 TC 654; [1989] STC 568.*

Newman v Pepper; Newman v Morgan 57.2

Date of disposal

*Assets held as nominee for other persons — TCGA 1992, s 60**

In 1982 a landowner (N) conveyed an area of farmland to his two sons as trustees. Two days later he and his sons granted a building company (W) an option to purchase most of the land. Under the option agreement, W covenanted to 'use all reasonable endeavours' to obtain the inclusion of the land 'in any relevant local plan or planning policy document for the area as land suitable for residential development'. In 1985 W assigned the benefit of the option to two other companies (M and C). Later that year the local council granted outline planning permission for residential development on 11.3 hectares of land. M and C subsequently exercised the option in respect of those 11.3 hectares, and paid more than £700,000 to N and his children in accordance with the agreement. In 1986 N and his sons released C from some of its obligations under the option agreement in return for a payment of £175,000. The Revenue issued CGT assessments on N's sons, against which they appealed. The Special Commissioners dismissed their appeals, holding that the date of disposal for CGT purposes was the date on which the option was exercised, and that, applying *Marren v Ingles* (see above), the value of the right to receive further consideration must be added to the cash actually received on the disposal. The effect of *TCGA 1992, s 60** was that N's sons were chargeable to CGT. *Newman v Pepper; Newman v Morgan (Sp C 243), [2000] SSCD 345.* (*Notes.* (1) The appellants appeared in person. (2) Appeals against assessments under *ICTA 1988, s 776* were also dismissed. (3) The Commissioners also found that N and his sons had submitted a hold-over election under *FA 1980, s 79* (see 33.9 HOLD-OVER RELIEFS), rejecting a contention by one of N's sons that their signatures had been forged.)

O'Brien v Benson's Hosiery (Holdings) Ltd 6.1

Payment from employee for release from service agreement

A company, on acquiring the shares of another, entered into a seven-year service agreement with B, the sales director of the other company. After two years in which B carried out his duties with conspicuous success, he was released from the agreement on paying £50,000 to the first company, which was assessed on the £50,000 as a chargeable gain. The HL upheld the assessment (reversing the CA decision). The rights, although not assignable, could be turned to account in the hands of the employer and were an asset within the general scheme of the legislation. The concept of market value is introduced for certain purposes; it cannot be deduced from this that all assets within CGT must have a market value. *O'Brien v Benson's Hosiery (Holdings) Ltd HL 1979, 53 TC 241; [1979] STC 735; [1979] 3 WLR 572; [1979] 3 All ER 652.*

O'Rourke v Binks 58.7, 58.10

*Capital distribution — TCGA 1992, s 122**

The taxpayer held a large number of shares in a company (C). The total allowable expenditure on any disposal of those shares was £214,000. Under a merger agreement between C and a public company, he exchanged his shares for 840,000 shares in the public company and 75,000 shares in a subsidiary company (the market value of these being

£246,000). The transfer to the taxpayer of the shares in the subsidiary company was treated as a capital distribution and thus as a partial disposal of his shares in C. The Revenue issued a CGT assessment in which the total allowable expenditure was apportioned in accordance with *TCGA 1992, s 42**. The taxpayer appealed, contending that, since the total allowable expenditure was less than the value of the shares in the subsidiary, he was entitled to elect that the amount of the distribution should be reduced by the total allowable expenditure, in accordance with *TCGA 1992, s 122(4)**. The Special Commissioner allowed the appeal but the CA reversed this decision and restored the assessment. The words of *TCGA 1992, s 122(4)** were ambiguous, and in the circumstances the court should give effect to the presumed intention of the legislature by inserting words into the subsection. The taxpayer could not make an election under *TCGA 1992, s 122(4)** unless the distribution was 'small', within *TCGA 1992, s 122(2)**. The capital distribution here (which amounted to 15.58% of the total expenditure) was not small for the purposes of *TCGA 1992, s 122(2)**. *O'Rourke v Binks CA 1992, 65 TC 165; [1992] STC 703.*

Owen v Elliott 49.8

*Private residence partly used as guest house — relief under TCGA 1992, s 223(4)**

A taxpayer and his wife had carried on a private guest house business from premises they owned and lived in. They had occupied different parts of the premises at different times of the year in such a way that every part of the premises had, at some time during their period of ownership, constituted their main residence. When the property was sold it was agreed that one-third of the gain was exempt under *TCGA 1992, s 222** and *s 223(2)**. The taxpayer appealed against an assessment on the gain, contending that further relief was due under *TCGA 1992, s 223(4)**. The CA allowed his appeal (reversing the decision of the Ch D). The phrase 'let by him as residential accommodation' in *TCGA 1992, s 223(4)** did not, directly or by association, mean premises let which were likely to be occupied as a home. It referred to living accommodation as distinct, for example, from office accommodation. The lettings undertaken by the taxpayer were within the words 'residential accommodation'. *Owen v Elliott CA 1990, 63 TC 319; [1990] STC 469; [1990] 3 WLR 133.*

Palmer v Maloney and Shipleys 53.3

Retirement relief — meaning of 'full-time working officer or employee'

A trader (P) was also the majority shareholder in a company, to which he devoted most of his working time. He wished to retire and, on the advice of his accountants, he caused the company to realise the value of his shares by paying an interim dividend. Subsequently he took legal action against the accountants, contending that they had been negligent in that they should have advised him to realise the value of his shares by a capital distribution, so that he could have claimed retirement relief. The CA accepted this contention (by a 2–1 majority, Nourse LJ dissenting) and ordered the accountants to pay P damages. Aldous LJ held that, since P worked for the company for 42½ hours each week, he qualified as a 'full-time working officer or employee' of the company, within *TCGA 1992, s 163(5)*. The fact that he also worked for a separate business for 7½ hours each week was not material. *Palmer v Maloney and Shipleys CA 1999, 71 TC 502; [1999] STC 890.* (Notes. (1) For HMRC's interpretation of the phrase 'full-time working officer or employee', see HMRC Capital Gains Manual CG 63621. For the Revenue's practice following the earlier Ch D decision in favour of the defendants and pending a final outcome to the case, see Revenue Tax Bulletin April 1999 p 653. (2) Retirement relief is abolished for disposals after 5 April 2003 (see 53.1 RETIREMENT RELIEF).)

Pepper v Daffurn 53.4

Retirement relief

A farmer had owned 113 acres of land, on which he had reared and grazed cattle, for several years. He gradually ceased to rear cattle, and sold 83 acres in 1986. In 1987 he obtained planning permission in respect of a covered cattle yard comprising 0.6 acres, which he sold in 1988. Thereafter his only activity was cattle grazing. The Revenue issued a CGT assessment on the sale of the cattle yard, and the farmer appealed, contending that he was entitled to retirement relief. The Ch D upheld the assessment (reversing the decision of the General Commissioners). On the evidence, the farmer had changed the nature of his activities from rearing cattle to grazing them in preparation for the sale of the yard. Following this change, the yard was no longer necessary to the farmer's business, so that its sale did not constitute a disposal of a part of that business. *Pepper v Daffurn Ch D 1993, 66 TC 68; [1993] STC 466.* (Note. Retirement relief is abolished for disposals after 5 April 2003 (see 53.1 RETIREMENT RELIEF).)

Plumbly & Others (Harbour's Personal Representatives) v Spencer 53.4

Sale of land leased to family company — whether vendor entitled to retirement relief

In 1988 an individual (H), who was 60 years of age, disposed of 163 acres of land which had been used by a trading company, of which he was a director and shareholder, for the purposes of its business (which was discontinued at the time of the sale). The company, which had paid rent to H for the use of the land, qualified as H's 'family company' under *TCGA 1992, s 163** as then in force. The Revenue issued a CGT assessment, and H's personal representatives appealed, contending that the sale of the land qualified for retirement relief under *TCGA 1992, s 163**. The CA accepted this contention and allowed the appeal, holding that where there was a disposal of assets in a discontinued business, it was not essential that the business must have been the business of the individual making the disposal, and relief could still be claimed where the conditions of *s 163(3)** were satisfied. The CA observed that it would be 'anomalous if (H) had been denied any business relief, after the company had been farming for 40 years, because of his (or his advisers') omission to take one or other of two otherwise fairly pointless steps (that is the transfer of the farming business to (H) personally just before its cessation, or the disposal of his shares in the dormant company)'. *Plumbly & Others (Harbour's Personal Representatives) v Spencer CA 1999, 71 TC 399; [1999] STC 677.* (Notes. (1) The references in *TCGA 1992, s 163* to a 'family company' were subsequently replaced by references to a 'personal company'. (2) Retirement relief is abolished for disposals after 5 April 2003 (see 53.1 RETIREMENT RELIEF).)

Powlson v Welbeck Securities Ltd 6.7, 15.3

Surrender of an option

In 1961 a company acquired an option to participate in a property development. In 1971 it began proceedings to enforce its option, but these were settled by consent in 1974, the company receiving £2,000,000 in return for agreeing to 'release and abandon' the option. The Revenue assessed the amount as a chargeable gain and the company appealed, contending that, by virtue of *TCGA 1992, s 144(4)**, the surrender of the option did not constitute the disposal of an asset. The CA dismissed the company's appeal, holding that *TCGA 1992, s 144(3)** constituted an exception to the operation of *TCGA 1992, s 24(1)** but did not confer any exemption from the chargeable disposal which arose under *TCGA 1992, s 22(1)** when the company received a capital sum for the surrender of the option. *Powlson v Welbeck Securities Ltd CA 1987, 60 TC 269; [1987] STC 468.*

Prest v Bettinson 10.6

Residuary legatees of estate subject to annuities include charities — whether charitable exemption applies

Under a will the residuary estate was held on the usual trusts for sale and conversion for the benefit of five institutions, equally and absolutely, subject to certain annuities. The income was more than sufficient to cover the annuities and no annuity fund was set up. Assets of the estate were sold, so permitting capital distributions to the residuary legatees, and the gains were assessed on the trustee. Four of the residuary legatees were charities, and the trustee contended that four-fifths of the gains accrued to charities and were exempted by *TCGA 1992, s 256(1)**. The Ch D rejected this contention and upheld the assessment. *Prest v Bettinson Ch D 1980, 53 TC 437; [1980] STC 607.*

Purves v Harrison 53.4

Sale of premises nine months before sale of business — whether sale of premises qualifying for retirement relief

The proprietor of a coach and a minibus service wished to retire. In March 1990 he sold his business premises. However, the purchaser granted him a licence to continue to occupy the premises, and he continued to carry on the business until December 1990, when he sold it to the same purchaser. He claimed retirement relief in respect of the sale of the business, including the premises. The Revenue accepted the claim in respect of the business sold in December 1990, but rejected the claim in respect of the earlier sale of the premises. The Ch D upheld the Revenue's ruling. Blackburne J held that the sales could not be treated as a single transaction. The sale of the premises in March could not be treated as part of the sale of the business in December. *Purves v Harrison Ch D 2000, 73 TC 390; [2001] STC 267.* (Note. Retirement relief is abolished for disposals after 5 April 2003 (see 53.1 RETIREMENT RELIEF).)

Quinn v Cooper 22.20

Indexation allowance — Business Expansion Scheme — TCGA 1992, s 150

An individual (C) had purchased a number of shares which entitled him to relief under the Business Expansion Scheme. He subsequently sold the shares at a loss. The Revenue issued CGT assessments on the basis that the effect of *TCGA 1992, s 150*(*3*)* was that indexation allowance only applied to the sale proceeds of the shares. C appealed, contending that the effect of *TCGA 1992, s 53* and *s 150* was that indexation allowance should be applied to the original purchase price of the shares. The Ch D rejected this contention and upheld the assessments (reversing the decision of the Special Commissioner). Lightman J held that, having regard to the interrelationship of the relevant statutory provisions, indexation should only be applied to the cost as reduced by *section 150*(*3*). *Quinn v Cooper Ch D 1998, 71 TC 44; [1998] STC 772.*

W T Ramsay Ltd v CIR 3.1, 22.5

Artificial avoidance scheme — whether a nullity for tax purposes

A company, having made a substantial gain on the sale of a farm, carried out a number of share and loan transactions with the object of creating a large allowable loss at little cost to itself. The loss emerged as one of about £175,000 on shares it subscribed for in a company formed for the scheme, the success of which depended on its establishing that a loan to the same company, sold at a profit of about £173,000, was not a debt on a security within *TCGA 1992, s 251(1)**. The acceptance of the offer of the loan was given orally, but evidenced by a statutory declaration (vide *Statutory Declarations Act 1835*) by a director of the borrowing company. The CA held that the loan, being evidenced by the statutory declaration, which represented a marketable security, was a debt on a security. The scheme therefore failed. The company appealed to the HL, where the appeal was considered with that in *Eilbeck v Rawling* and in both cases the Revenue advanced the new argument that the scheme should be treated as a fiscal nullity producing neither loss nor gain (other than a loss of £370 in *Eilbeck v Rawling*). The HL accepted this approach. Lord Wilberforce held that although the Duke of Westminster principle prevented a court from looking behind a genuine document or transaction to some supposed underlying substance, it did not compel the court to view a document or transaction in blinkers, isolated from its context. A finding that a document or transaction is genuine does not preclude the Commissioners from considering whether, on the facts, what is in issue is a composite transaction or a number of independent transactions. The Commissioners are not 'bound to consider individually each separate step in a composite transaction intended to be carried through as a whole'. The question of whether what is in issue is a composite transaction or a number of independent transactions is a matter of law, reviewable by the courts. Such an approach does not introduce a new principle when dealing with legal avoidance, but applies existing legislation to new and sophisticated legal devices; 'while the techniques of tax avoidance progress, the courts are not obliged to stand still'. Turning to the facts here, it was clear that the scheme was for tax avoidance with no commercial justification, and that it was the intention to proceed through all its stages to completion once set in motion. It would therefore be wrong to consider one step in isolation. The true view was that, regarding the scheme as a whole, there was neither gain nor loss. The company's appeal was dismissed. Furthermore, although this ended the appeal, the CA had been correct in holding that the relevant debt was a 'debt on a security'. *W T Ramsay Ltd v CIR HL 1981, 54 TC 101; [1981] STC 174; [1981] 2 WLR 449; [1981] 1 All ER 865.*

Randall v Plumb 6.7, 38.24

Option payment contingently repayable

The owner of some land granted a gravel company an option to purchase the land for £100,000. He received £25,000 for the option. The agreement included a proviso that he would repay the £25,000 to the company if, after ten years, the company had not obtained planning permission to extract sand and gravel from the land. The Revenue assessed the £25,000 to CGT for the year in which the option was granted. The Ch D allowed his appeal against the assessment, holding that the consideration should not be the full amount of the £25,000, but that the £25,000 should be brought in at a valuation taking the contingency into account. *Randall v Plumb Ch D 1974, 50 TC 392; [1975] STC 191; [1975] 1 All ER 734.*

Rank Xerox Ltd v Lane 4.21, 22.3

*Annual payments under covenant — TCGA 1992, s 237(c)**

R surrendered to X its licence from X to make use of the 'xerographic' process in certain areas in return for a 'royalty' of 5% of certain sales by X in those areas. The relevant agreements to pay the 'royalties' were made under seal. Subsequently, R distributed the 'royalty' rights in specie to its shareholders, who in turn surrendered them to X for a consideration. R was assessed to corporation tax on its gain from the disposal and appealed, contending that the 'royalties' were annual payments due under a covenant within *TCGA 1992, s 237(c)**. The HL rejected this contention and upheld the assessment. 'Covenant' here must be construed in its context and annual payments under a covenant are payments made gratuitously, the promise to pay them being enforceable only because of the form in which it was given, i.e. (in England) given under seal. Here the payments were for consideration and the presence of a seal on the relevant agreement added nothing to the obligation to pay them. *Rank Xerox Ltd v Lane HL 1979, 53 TC 185; [1979] STC 740; [1979] 3 WLR 594; [1979] 3 All ER 657.*

Reed v Nova Securities Ltd 3.1, 27.4

Acquisition 'as trading stock' commercial justification

The taxpayer company (N) had traded in shares and securities since 1955. In March 1973 it was acquired by the well-known Littlewoods group. On 17 August 1973 Littlewoods sold to it shares owned by Littlewoods in, and debts owing to Littlewoods by, certain foreign companies. The sale price for the assets was £30,000, their market value, but their capital gains cost to Littlewoods was nearly £4m. When offering the assets to N, Littlewoods' Board said that about £55,000 would be received in part repayment of the debts and N had received a payment of £35,447 in 1979. They were not part of Littlewoods' trading stock. N purported to make an election under *TCGA 1992, s 161(3)** in respect of the assets acquired, and the issue in the appeal was whether they were trading stock, as defined in *ICTA 1988, s 100(2)** (see *TCGA 1992, s 288**). The General Commissioners found that they were and their decision was upheld by the Ch D and the CA. The HL unanimously upheld the decision as regards the debts but reversed it as regards the shares. The Commissioners had determined the appeal on the basis of an agreed statement of facts, without recourse to oral evidence, and no reasonable body of Commissioners could have concluded that the company had acquired the shares as trading stock; its acquisition of shares that had no value was without commercial justification. *Reed v Nova Securities Ltd HL 1985, 59 TC 516; [1985] STC 124; [1985] 1 WLR 193; [1985] 1 All ER 686.*

Roome v Edwards 57.12

Exercise of power of appointment or advancement

Under a 1944 marriage settlement (as varied), the trust fund, worth some £912,000, was held on trust for the wife for life with remainder to the husband for life with remainder to two daughters (born in 1948 and 1951) absolutely in equal shares. In March 1972 the beneficiaries assigned their respective interests to two Cayman Islands companies for sums totalling £868,000. The trustees were replaced by Cayman Islands trustees and in 1972/73 one of the companies assigned its interests to the other which, as a consequence, became absolutely entitled to the trust fund as against the trustees. In 1955, pursuant to powers in the 1944 settlement, investments in the fund worth some £13,000 had been appointed in trust for the elder daughter absolutely on attaining 25. There had been no relevant transaction regarding the 1955 fund, which had been administered separately from the 1944 fund and the trustees of which were UK residents. The substantial gain which arose under *TCGA 1992, s 71(1)** as a result of the transactions relating to the 1944 fund was assessed on the trustees of the 1955 fund on the footing that under *TCGA 1992, s 69(3)** the two sets of trustees fell to be treated as a single body of which the UK members could be assessed under *TCGA 1992, s 65(1)**. The HL upheld the assessment, reversing the decisions of the Ch D and CA. Whether a particular set of facts amounts to a settlement should be approached by asking what a person, with knowledge of the legal context of the word under established doctrine and applying this knowledge in a practical and common-sense manner to the facts under examination, would conclude. Here the intention throughout was to treat the 1955 fund as being held on the trusts of the 1944 settlement as added to and varied by the 1955 appointment. Further, the words 'accruing to the trustees of a settlement' in *TCGA 1992, s 65(1)** are to be read in the light of the situation created by *TCGA 1992, s 69(1)(3)**. *TCGA 1992, s 69(3)** is not restricted to cases where property vested in two sets of trustees is held on identical trusts. *Roome and Another v Edwards HL 1981, 54 TC 359; [1981] STC 96; [1981] 2 WLR 268; [1981] 1 All ER 736.* (For HMRC practice following this decision, see HMRC Statement of Practice 7/84.)

Sansom v Peay 49.5

Occupation of residence under discretionary trust

The trustees of a discretionary trust permitted certain beneficiaries (as they were enabled to do under the trust) to occupy as their residence a house subject to the trust. The house was exchanged and it was held that the resultant gain was exempt under *TCGA 1992, s 225**. The Ch D rejected the Revenue's contention that the beneficiaries were not 'entitled' to occupy the house, because they had no absolute right under the trust. While the beneficiaries were in occupation with the trustees' permission they were entitled to occupy it. *Sansom & Another v Peay Ch D 1976, 52 TC 1; [1976] STC 494; [1976] 1 WLR 1073; [1976] 3 All ER 375.*

Shepherd v Lyntress 3.1

Applicability of Ramsay principle where subsidiary company acquired with accumulated tax losses

A major public company (N) had acquired shares in companies that had appreciated in value. It decided to acquire companies which had accumulated tax losses so that the gains on the holdings could be realised and the accrued losses could be set off against them. Accordingly, in 1979 N acquired the issued share capital of L, a company claiming to have £4m of accumulated tax losses available for set-off. In 1980 N sold part of its holding of appreciated assets to L, and a few days later L realised the gains by disposing of the assets on the Stock Exchange. The Revenue raised assessments on N on the basis that the Ramsay principle applied, and that the sale of the assets by N to L was to be ignored for fiscal purposes, so that the transactions would fall to be treated as disposals on the Stock Exchange by N, and on L on the basis that, again applying the *Ramsay* principle, the losses incurred within the company's former group were not available against gains accruing to a company outside that group. The Special Commissioners reduced the assessment on L, rejecting the Revenue's contention that the accumulated losses were not available for set-off. However, they upheld the assessment on N. Both sides appealed to the Ch D. Vinelott J allowed N's appeal and upheld the Commissioners' decision with regard to the assessment on L. On the facts, the Commissioners were clearly correct in rejecting the Revenue's contention that L's losses were not available for set-off. The real question in the case was whether the Commissioners were justified in concluding that the transfer and sale of the assets were part of a single composite transaction. Following *Craven v White*, this could not be held to be the case here, because no arrangements to sell the shares on the Stock Exchange had been made at the time when they were transferred from N to L. It was therefore impossible to conclude that the transfer of the shares to L, and their subsequent sale by L, was a single composite transaction within the *Ramsay* principle. L had an allowable loss at the time when its share capital was acquired by N. That loss remained an allowable loss after N had acquired L's share capital, and the gains which were realised when the transferred assets were sold on the Stock Exchange were gains realised by L at a time when it was a member of the same group of companies as N. *Shepherd v Lyntress Ltd; News International plc v Shepherd Ch D 1989, 62 TC 495; [1989] STC 617.* (Note. See now *TCGA 1992, Sch 7A*, introduced by *FA 1993, s 88*.)

Smallwood v HMRC 15.6

Losses on disposal of units in enterprise zone unit trust—whether TCGA 1992, s 41(2) applicable.

In 1989 an individual (S) invested £10,000 in an enterprise zone unit trust. The trustees used the funds to acquire land and buildings, and claimed capital allowances. S was credited with some of these allowances under *Income Tax (Definition of Unit Trusts Schemes) Regulations 1998 (SI 1998 No 267)*. Subsequently the property was disposed of and S received distributions, which were treated for CGT purposes as part disposals of S's units. S claimed that these disposals gave rise to allowable losses. The Revenue rejected the claim on the basis that the effect of *TCGA 1992, s 41(2)* was that S's allowable expenditure had to be restricted by the capital allowances. S appealed, contending that *section 41(2)* did not apply because it was the trustees' expenditure, rather than his expenditure, which gave rise to capital allowances. The Special Commissioner accepted this contention and allowed S's appeal, holding that 'once the step has been taken of treating the unit trust as a company and the rights of the unitholders as shares in that company, then for CGT purposes … the computation of gains on disposals of units must be treated in the same way as the computation of gains on disposals of shares'. Accordingly, the expression 'any expenditure to the extent to which any capital allowance … has been or may be made in respect of it' in *TCGA 1992, s 41(2)* had to be construed as 'referring to expenditure comprised in the consideration given wholly and exclusively for the acquisition of the relevant asset, i.e. the £10,000 given by (S) for his units. Capital allowances were not given in respect of that expenditure. Thus *section 41(2)* does not apply.' *Smallwood v HMRC, Sp C 2005 (Sp C 509), [2006] SSCD 12.*

Smith v Schofield 7.7

Indexation allowance — interaction with time-apportionment

A taxpayer had acquired two chattels in 1952. She sold them in 1987. Her chargeable gain fell to be time-apportioned in accordance with *TCGA 1992, Sch 2 para 16(2)**. The

Revenue deducted the indexation allowance from the unindexed gain before time-apportionment. She appealed, contending that the indexation allowance should be deducted only from the amount of the post-1965 gain. The HL rejected this contention and upheld the assessment (reversing the decision of the CA and restoring that of the Ch D). The issue had to be determined by construing the relevant statutory provisions against the underlying philosophy of the legislation, rather than by detailed consideration of hypothetical examples producing apparently anomalous results. The effect of the legislation was that the indexation allowance had to be applied to the gross gain before time-apportionment, and could not be set only against that part of the gain apportioned to the period after 6 April 1965. *Smith v Schofield HL 1993, 65 TC 669; [1993] STC 268; [1993] 1 WLR 398.*

Spectros International plc v Madden 15.1

Consideration for sale of company with substantial debt to bank

A company (S) owned a number of subsidiary companies, one of which operated a liquid chromatography business. Another company (B) wished to purchase this business. S wished to structure the sale in such a way as to minimise its tax liability. In July 1986 one of S's wholly-owned subsidiary companies (H) declared a cash dividend of $20,000,000. It was offered an overdraft facility of this amount by a bank, the overdraft being secured by a deposit of that amount by S (so that, on payment of the dividend, the $20,000,000 effectively travelled in a circle). In September 1986 S sold a number of its subsidiary companies, including H, to B, and agreed not to compete with B in the liquid chromatography business. The agreement provided that B should pay $23,000,000 in total, of which $20,000,000 should be paid to the bank to clear the loan to H, and that $1,000 of the $23,000,000 related to the common stock of H. S appealed against an estimated assessment, contending that the consideration which it had received for the sale of H was only $1,000. The Special Commissioners rejected this contention and dismissed the appeal, holding that the effect of the agreement was that the consideration paid for the common stock of H was $20,001,000, since S 'could and did direct how that sum should be applied'. (The Commissioners noted that neither S nor the Revenue contended that the $20,000,000 should be apportioned between the assets of the liquid chromatography business.) The Ch D upheld the Commissioners' decision. Lightman J observed that, if the parties had intended that the sale of the common stock should be for $1,000, it would have been very simple to say so. Where a holding company sold a solvent subsidiary and the purchaser agreed to discharge a debt owed by that subsidiary, the amount of the debt would not necessarily constitute consideration for the shares in the subsidiary. However, in the case under appeal, the parties had specifically agreed that the amount of the debt should be allocated to the purchase price. Accordingly, on the wording of the specific agreements, the consideration for the common stock was $20,001,000. *Spectros International plc v Madden Ch D 1996, 70 TC 349; [1997] STC 114.*

Stanton v Drayton Commercial Investment Co Ltd 15.4

*Consideration satisfied by issue of shares — definition of 'value' in TCGA 1992, s 38(1)(a)**

In September 1972 a company (D) agreed to acquire investments from an insurance company for £3,937,632, to be paid by means of 2,461,226 shares in D at their issue price of 160p per share. The agreement was conditional on permission being obtained for the shares to be dealt in on the Stock Exchange. The agreement became unconditional on 11 October, when the shares were issued. On 12 October, when they were first quoted on the Stock Exchange, their middle market price was 125p per share. Subsequently D sold some of the investments it had acquired from the insurance company. The Revenue issued an assessment on the gains, in which the cost of the investments was computed on the basis that the shares in D should be valued at 125p each. D appealed, contending that the shares should be valued at 160p each. The CA allowed D's appeal and the HL upheld this decision. There had been an honest arm's length agreement in which the shares had been valued at 160p, and there was no reason for going behind this agreed value. Market value was only relevant where no agreed value was available. *Stanton v Drayton Commercial Investment Co Ltd HL 1982, 55 TC 286; [1982] STC 585; [1982] 3 WLR 214; [1982] 2 All ER 942.*

Steibelt v Paling 55.1, 55.3, 55.4

Rollover relief — extension of three-year time limit for replacing assets; whether trades carried on successively; application of ESC D24

A publican sold his business in October 1986 for approximately £130,000 realising a chargeable gain of approximately £52,000. In February 1988 he purchased a barge for £20,000, which he intended to convert into a wine bar and restaurant. Between December 1989 and November 1994 he incurred enhancement expenditure of approximately £160,000 on the barge. He eventually began to trade from it in August 1995. He claimed rollover relief in respect of the 1986 gain. The Ch D rejected the claim (reversing the General Commissioners' decision). Sir Richard Scott V-C held that whilst the Revenue's decision not to exercise their statutory discretion to extend the three-year time limit laid down by *TCGA 1992, s 152(3)* might be challenged by judicial review, it was not reviewable by the Commissioners. In any case, the two trades, separated by a gap of nine years, could not be said to be carried on 'successively' as required by *TCGA 1992, s 152(8)*. In addition, the terms of ESC D24 (assets not brought immediately into trading use) were not satisfied. *Steibelt v Paling Ch D 1999, 71 TC 376; [1999] STC 594.*

Stephenson v Barclays Bank Trust Co Ltd 57.2

Trust fund subject to annuities — whether beneficiaries absolutely entitled

Under a will, a fund was held in trust for such of the testator's grandchildren who should attain 21 years, subject to the payment of annuities to three daughters during widowhood. There were two grandchildren, both of whom had attained 21 before the relevant year. Under a deed of family arrangement entered into in 1968/69, a fund was appropriated for the annuities and a sum advanced to the grandchildren to purchase further income for the daughters with the intent that the balance of the trust fund, comprising mainly shares, should be transferred forthwith to the grandchildren. The trustees were assessed for 1968/69 on the footing of a notional disposal under *TCGA 1992, s 71(1)**, the grandchildren having become 'absolutely entitled as against' the trustees when the deed of family arrangement was entered into. The assessment was upheld. The trustees' contentions that the annuities were 'outgoings' within *TCGA 1992, s 60(2)** (with the result that the grandchildren became absolutely entitled when the younger attained 21) were rejected. *Kidson v Macdonald* followed as regards the construction of 'jointly' in *TCGA 1992, s 60(1)**. *Stephenson v Barclays Bank Trust Co Ltd Ch D 1974, 50 TC 374; [1975] STC 151; [1975] 1 WLR 882; [1975] 1 All ER 625.*

Strand Options and Futures Ltd v Vojak 58.14

Company purchasing own shares from another company — whether chargeable gain of vendor — whether excluded by ICTA 1988, s 208 or TCGA 1992, s 37

In September 1995, a company (C) purchased 89,700 of its own shares from another company (S). The payment for the shares fell to be treated as a distribution. The Revenue applied SP 4/89 and thus took the view that the distribution should be included in the consideration for the disposal of the shares for the purposes of charging corporation tax on chargeable gains. S appealed, contending that the effect of *ICTA 1988, s 208* was that the consideration should not be treated as chargeable to corporation tax. The Special Commissioners rejected this contention and dismissed the appeal, holding that *ICTA 1988, s 208* did not provide 'a complete exemption', but simply exempted the consideration from Schedule F. The CA unanimously upheld the Commissioners' decision. Carnwath LJ held that *section 208* should be construed as preventing the imposition of 'a tax which is directly charged on the dividends as such, rather than indirectly as part of the computation of a taxable amount'. *Strand Options & Futures Ltd v Vojak, CA, [2003] EWCA Civ 1457; [2003] All ER(D) 358(Oct).*

Strange v Openshaw 6.7

Grant of option to purchase land — whether a part disposal

Four brothers owned some agricultural land and their mother owned some adjoining land. They granted a company an option, exercisable within 10 years, to purchase the land on prescribed terms. (In the event, the option was not exercised.) The company paid £125,000 for the option, and the Revenue issued assessments on the brothers charging CGT on the amount each received. They appealed, contending that, by virtue of *TCGA 1992, s 144(2)**, no assessment should be raised until the option was exercised or abandoned. The Commissioners rejected this contention, holding that there had been a part disposal. Both sides appealed. The Ch D allowed the Revenue's cross-appeal and upheld the assessments, holding that *TCGA 1992, s 144** was not intended to supersede *TCGA 1992, s 21**, but provided how the chargeable gain on the grant of an option was to be computed. Accordingly, the whole amount of the option price, less the costs of granting it, was a chargeable gain under the general provisions of *TCGA 1992, s 144(1)**. The part disposal rules were not applicable to the grant of an option. *Strange v Openshaw (and related appeals) Ch D 1983, 57 TC 544; [1983] STC 416.*

Swires v Renton 57.12

Exercise of power of appointment — whether a deemed disposal

The trustees of a settlement executed a deed of appointment by which the trust fund was divided into two parts. One part of the fund was appointed to the settlor's daughter. The second part was placed on trust, the income to be paid to the daughter for life. It was accepted that the absolute appointment to the daughter gave rise to a deemed disposal of that part of the trust fund under *TCGA 1992, s 71(1)**, and CGT was assessed and paid accordingly. The inspector took the view that there had also been a deemed disposal of the second part of the fund, and issued a further CGT assessment on the grounds that a new and separate settlement of the appointed fund had been created. The principal trustee appealed, contending that the exercise of the power of appointment had not created a new settlement of the fund and had not amounted to a deemed disposal under *TCGA 1992, s 71(1)**. The Special Commissioner allowed the trustee's appeal and the Ch D upheld this decision. On the evidence, the assets of the appointed fund remained subject to the trusts of the original settlement as varied by the deed of appointment, and had not become subject to the trusts of a new settlement. Accordingly, the trustees' exercise of the power of appointment had not amounted to a deemed disposal under *TCGA 1992, s 71(1)**. *Swires v Renton Ch D 1991, 64 TC 315; [1991] STC 490.*

Tarmac Roadstone Holdings Ltd v Williams 22.5

Dollar floating rate notes — whether debts 'on a security'

In July 1986 a US company issued its UK parent company twelve loan notes of $5,000,000 each. The notes could only be transferred with the prior consent of the issuing company, which could be refused without any reason being given, and the issuing company could redeem them at any time. They were redeemed at par in December 1987. Because of the fall in value of the dollar, the UK company made a loss of more than £6,000,000. It claimed that this loss should be allowed against its chargeable gains. The Revenue rejected the claim, considering that the effect of *TCGA 1992, s 251(1)** was that there was no chargeable gain or allowable loss. The company appealed, contending that the loans were debts 'on a security', so that the loss was allowable. The Special Commissioners rejected this contention and dismissed the appeal. The distinguishing feature of a debt on a security was that it is 'in the nature of an investment which can be dealt in as such'. The loan notes in this case were not in the nature of investments, since they could only be transferred with the prior consent of the issuing company and that company could redeem them at any time. *Aberdeen Group Construction Ltd v CIR* and *dicta* in *WT Ramsay Ltd v CIR* applied. *Tarmac Roadstone Holdings Ltd v Williams (Sp C 95), [1996] SSCD 409.*

Taylor Clark International Ltd v Lewis 22.5

Loan to overseas subsidiary secured on property — whether a 'debt on a security'

In 1984 a company gave a promissory note for $15,193,000, repayable on demand, to a US subsidiary. The loan in question was repaid in two stages, in 1986 and 1992. Because of the fall in value of the dollar, the company made a loss on the loan. The company appealed against an assessment for its accounting period ending in 1992, contending that the loan was a 'debt on a security' and that the loss could be set against its chargeable gains. The Special Commissioners dismissed the appeal, holding that the loan was not a 'debt on a security', and the CA upheld their decision. The fact that a debt was secured did not necessarily mean that it qualified as a 'debt on a security'. On the evidence, the debt here was not a marketable security in any realistic sense. *Aberdeen Group Construction Ltd v CIR*, and *dicta* in *WT Ramsay Ltd v CIR*, applied. *Taylor Clark International Ltd v Lewis CA 1998, 71 TC 226; [1998] STC 1259.*

Thompson v Salah 15.3

Sale coupled with mortgage to purchaser

A taxpayer's wife, having received an offer of £20,000 for land she owned, effected the sale by mortgaging the land to the purchaser for £20,000 and conveying the fee simple the next day in consideration of a release from her obligation to repay the £20,000. The taxpayer was assessed under Sch D, Case VII on the basis that the land had been sold for £20,000. He appealed, contending that the actual conveyance was for the equity of redemption of a nil market value. The Ch D held that the two transactions together constituted a conveyance on sale of the property free of the legal charge. *Thompson v Salah Ch D 1971, 47 TC 559; [1972] 1 All ER 530.*

Tod v Mudd 55.6

Quantum of relief where new asset used partly for business and partly owned by taxpayer as tenant in common

The taxpayer sold a business asset (part of the goodwill of his practice as accountant) for a chargeable gain of £155,688 in April 1982. On 1 June 1982 he and his wife entered into partnership to carry on business as hoteliers at a house being purchased in their joint names. The business was to be carried on in the part of the premises 'attributable to the share provided by' the taxpayer. The total cost of the property with the furniture and fittings and expenses was £209,093, and it was common ground that 75% of this cost (i.e. £156,820) was provided by the taxpayer, and that the premises were used as to 75% for business purposes. The property was transferred to the husband and wife upon trust as to 75% for the taxpayer and 25% for his wife as tenants in common. In an appeal against an assessment on the gain of £155,688 the issue was the taxpayer's entitlement to rollover relief. The Ch D held that since the taxpayer and his wife, as tenants in common, were entitled to an interest in every part of the property, the relief was 75% of the taxpayer's contribution to the cost (i.e. £117,615, being 75% of £156,820) and not £156,820 as contended by the taxpayer. *Tod v Mudd Ch D 1986, 60 TC 237; [1987] STC 141.*

Trennery v West 57.5, 57.19

Whether settlor benefiting from 'derived property' — TCGA 1992, s 77

A company director (T) held 10,000 shares in an unquoted company. He executed a scheme designed to 'avoid and reduce' the CGT liability on his disposal of these shares.

Under the scheme, on 4 April 1995 he transferred 8,000 shares to a settlement which he had executed a few days earlier, and in which he was a beneficiary. On the same day the trustees borrowed cash, using the shares as security, and advanced the cash to a second settlement, in which T had an interest. On 5 April 1995 the trustees of the first settlement executed a deed of exclusion, excluding T and his wife from being beneficiaries of the first settlement, leaving other beneficiaries (their children) with an interest in possession. On 13 April 1995 the trustees of the first settlement sold the shares. The Revenue issued a CGT assessment for 1995/96, on the basis that T had benefited from 'derived property', within *TCGA 1992, s 77*. The HL unanimously upheld the assessment. Lord Millett observed that the purpose of *section 77* was 'to prevent taxpayers from obtaining the benefit of the lower rate of tax by transferring assets pregnant with capital gains into a settlement in which they retain an interest before procuring the trustees to dispose of them'. The effect of *section 77(2)* was that T was to be regarded as having had an interest in the first settlement during 1995/96. The trust funds of the second settlement, and the income paid to T, were 'derived property' within *section 77(8)*. Lord Millett also observed that 'the fact that the settlor obtained his right to income under the trusts of the second settlement is immaterial if the income represented the income of the proceeds of property comprised in the first settlement'. *Trennery v West (and related appeals) (aka Tee v HM Inspector of Taxes), HL 2005, [2005] STC 214, [2005] UKHL 5.* (*Note*. See now *TCGA 1992, Sch 4B* at 57.19 SETTLEMENTS designed to counter the scheme used in this case.)

Unilever (UK) Holdings Ltd v Smith 7.10, 58.1

Shares held on 6 April 1965 — whether subsequent Scheme of Arrangement a 'reorganisation'

A company (U) had acquired all the ordinary shares in a subsidiary company (B) before 6 April 1965. On 29 April 1965 B's share capital was the subject of a Scheme of Arrangement which involved the cancellation of all its preference shares, leaving only the ordinary shares. Before the Scheme of Arrangement, U had held 62% of the voting rights in B; after the Scheme, it held 100% of the voting rights. The issued ordinary share capital had not, however, increased. U sold its ordinary shares in B, at a loss, in 1992. It sought to set this loss against a subsequent gain, and contended that the shares should be treated as having been acquired at market value on 29 April 1965, on the basis that they had been concerned in a 'reorganisation' on that date within *TCGA 1992, s 126** with the result that *TCGA 1992, Sch 2 para 19(2)* applied. The Revenue rejected the claim on the basis that the ordinary shares had not been concerned in a 'reorganisation', so that the loss should be computed on a straight-line time apportionment basis. The Special Commissioners dismissed the company's appeal and the Ch D and CA upheld this decision. Jonathan Parker LJ held that the cancellation of the preference shares did not amount to a 'reorganisation', since it did not 'alter the rights attaching either to the ordinary shares or to the preference shares'. *Unilever (UK) Holdings Ltd v Smith CA, 2002 STI 1806.*

Van Arkadie v Plunket 45.5

*Foreign assets — delayed remittances — effect of TCGA 1992, s 279**

A UK resident (P) owned one-third of the share capital of a Rhodesian company, which would have been a close company if it had been resident in the UK. The company made gains on the sale of assets outside the UK. Under *TCGA 1992, s 13**, part of the gains were treated as accruing to P, although the company did not make any distributions. Regulations imposed by the de facto Rhodesian government (which had made a unilateral declaration of independence from the UK) prohibited the company from paying dividends to shareholders resident in the UK. P claimed relief under *TCGA 1992, s 279**. The Ch D held that the relief was not due (reversing the General Commissioners' decision). *TCGA 1992, s 279** applied only where a gain was represented by money or money's worth in the hands of the taxpayer. P could not receive the money because the company had not made any distributions, so that *TCGA 1992, s 279** did not apply. *Van Arkadie v Plunket Ch D 1982, 56 TC 310; [1983] STC 54.*

Varty v Lynes 49.1

Part of garden retained on sale of house and subsequently sold

A taxpayer owned and occupied a house and garden (of less than one acre). He sold the house and part of the garden in June 1971. In May 1972, he sold at a substantial profit the rest of the garden for which he had meanwhile obtained planning permission. The Ch D upheld an assessment on the gain, rejecting the taxpayer's contention that it was exempted by *TCGA 1992, s 222**. *TCGA 1992, s 222(1)(b)** related only to the actual moment of disposal of the land and *TCGA 1992, s 222(2)** did not extend to a subsequent disposal. *Varty v Lynes Ch D 1976, 51 TC 419; [1976] STC 508; [1976] 1 WLR 1091; [1976] 3 All ER 447.*

Wardhaugh v Penrith Rugby Union Football Club 15.6, 55.1

Non-effect of TCGA 1992, s 50 on quantum of rollover relief

In 1995 a rugby club sold some land for £315,105, resulting in a chargeable gain of £204,165. The club used the proceeds of the land to build a new clubhouse. The clubhouse cost £600,459. The club received a grant of £409,000 from the Sports Council (which was accepted as a 'public authority' within *TCGA 1992, s 50*). The club claimed rollover relief under *TCGA 1992, s 152* in respect of the total cost of the new clubhouse. The Revenue ruled that the effect of *TCGA 1992, s 50* on rollover relief was that the consideration given for the acquisition of the new clubhouse was the net amount of £191,459 after deducting the Sports Council grant and that, consequently, not all of the proceeds of the land had been reinvested in the new asset. The General Commissioners allowed the club's appeal, holding that the only computation of a gain which *section 50* would affect would be the computation on a subsequent disposal of the clubhouse. The Ch D upheld this decision. Ferris J held that there was nothing in *section 152* which required *section 50* to be applied before giving effect to rollover relief, and 'no words in *section 50* itself which are capable of producing this result'. *Wardhaugh v Penrith Rugby Union Football Club Ch D 2002, 74 TC 499; [2002] STC 776.*

Wase v Bourke 53.4

Retirement relief — sale of milk quota following cessation of dairy farming

In March 1988 a dairy farmer sold his entire herd. In February 1989, having reached the age of 60, he sold his milk quota. He appealed against a CGT assessment on the gain, contending that he was entitled to retirement relief on the basis that the sale of the milk quota was 'a disposal of the whole or part of a business'. The Ch D held that retirement relief was not due, since the milk quota was simply an asset and that its disposal was not the disposal of part of a business. The relevant business activity had ceased in March 1988 when the herd was sold. The subsequent disposal of another asset did not amount to the disposal of part of the business. *Atkinson v Dancer* applied; *Jarmin v Rawlings* distinguished. *Wase v Bourke Ch D 1995, 68 TC 109; [1996] STC 18.* (Note. Retirement relief is abolished for disposals after 5 April 2003 (see 53.1 RETIREMENT RELIEF).)

Watton v Tippett 55.1

Rollover relief (TCGA 1992, ss 152–162) — purchase of single property followed by sale of part of property

In 1988 a trader purchased some business premises. In 1989 he sold part of the premises at a profit. The Revenue issued a CGT assessment and he appealed, contending that he was entitled to treat the proceeds of sale as having been used in acquiring the balance of the premises, so that he was entitled to rollover relief under *TCGA 1992, s 152**. The CA rejected this contention and upheld the assessment. The disposal had been a part disposal of the original asset. The consideration which the trader had paid for the premises could not be divided and treated as partly attributable to the part of the premises which he subsequently sold and as partly attributable to the part which he retained. The premises had been acquired 'as a single asset and for an unapportioned consideration', and continued to constitute a single asset until the part disposal. *Watton v Tippett CA 1997, 69 TC 491; [1997] STC 893.*

Whitaker v Cameron 7.8

*Election for 6 April 1965 valuation — construction of TCGA 1992, Sch 2 para 17(1)(2)**

A taxpayer disposed in 1973 of land he had acquired in 1957; his appeal was against an assessment on the gain made on the time apportionment basis. The market value at 6 April 1965 was slightly above the disposal figure, but there had been no timeous application for a 6 April 1965 valuation under *TCGA 1992, Sch 2 para 17(1)**, and an extension of the time limit had been refused. If there had been a timeous application there would have been a no loss/no gain situation as a result of *Sch 2 para 17(2)**, and the taxpayer contended that it was unnecessary to make a 6 April 1965 valuation election where it would produce a no loss/no gain result. The Ch D rejected the contention. The two sub-paragraphs are closely bound up and *Sch 2 para 17(2)** has effect only if there has been an election under *Sch 2 para 17(1)**. *Whitaker v Cameron Ch D 1982, 56 TC 97; [1982] STC 665.*

Whittles v Uniholdings Ltd (No 3) 15.4

Company borrowing US dollars and entering forward contract to purchase sufficient dollars to repay loan — whether transactions to be taxed separately

In May 1982 a company borrowed some US dollars to finance an investment (the rate of interest on the dollar loan being less than the company could have obtained on a sterling loan). It simultaneously entered into a forward contract to purchase sufficient dollars to repay the loan when it matured some ten months later. During the intervening ten months the pound sterling depreciated substantially against the dollar. The Revenue treated the two transactions as separate, with the result that the company had made a loss on the dollar loan which was not allowable for CGT purposes, and had made a chargeable gain on the disposal of its rights under the forward contract. The CA upheld the Revenue's contentions (reversing the decision of the Special Commissioner). Nourse LJ held that the loan and the forward contract had to be considered separately. The fact that the subject matter of the forward contract was currency did not mean that the company had acquired a 'debt' within *TCGA 1992, s 251*. The forward contract was in substance no different from any contract for the sale of real or personal property with a deferred date for completion. In the absence of any specific provision to the contrary, it would be wrong in principle to value the acquisition cost of an asset on any date other than the actual date of acquisition. The cost of acquiring the US dollars had to be valued at May 1982 and their cost to the company was the value of its promise to repay them in March 1983, together with interest during that period. *Whittles v Uniholdings Ltd (No 3) CA, [1996] STC 914.*

Williams v Evans 55.3

Relief claimed on movable machinery

A civil engineering partnership sold some earth-moving vehicles at a profit and reinvested the proceeds in two similar machines. They appealed against a CGT assessment on the gain, claiming roll over relief. The Ch D dismissed their appeals. *TCGA 1992, s 155* (*Class 1, Head B*)* confined the relief to fixed plant and fixed machinery. The relief did not extend to movable machinery. *Williams v Evans & related appeals Ch D 1982, 59 TC 509; [1982] STC 498; [1982] 1 WLR 972.*

Williams v Merrylees 49.1

Private residence exemption

A taxpayer bought in 1956 a small estate in Sussex comprising a main house with 4 acres of garden and land and a lodge at the entrance of the estate, about 200 metres from the main house. The house became his main residence and the lodge was occupied by Mr and Mrs L whom he employed as caretaker/gardener and domestic help respectively. The house and lodge were rated together. Mrs L died in 1969. In 1976 the taxpayer sold the main house and estate apart from the lodge and a garden of less than an acre, and went to live in Cornwall in a house he had previously bought as a holiday home. He retained the lodge and allowed Mr L to live in it, in case he and his wife did not like their Cornwall house and decided to return to Sussex and live in the lodge. Mr L died in 1979 and the taxpayer then sold the lodge to the purchaser of the main house. The Commissioners held that the gain on the sale of the lodge was within the private residence exemption, finding as a matter of fact that from 1956 to 1976 the lodge had been part of the taxpayer's only or main residence and within the curtilage of the property and appurtenant to the main house. Vinelott J, after reviewing *Batey v Wakefield* and *Markey v Sanders*, considered that the test was whether there is an entity which can be sensibly described as being a dwelling-house although split up into different buildings performing different functions. The propinquity of the buildings is a relevant factor but should not be considered in isolation. Here, after considerable hesitation, he felt that it would be wrong for him to interfere with the Commissioners' decision as one inconsistent with the facts. *Williams v Merrylees Ch D 1987, 60 TC 297; [1987] STC 445; [1987] 1 WLR 1511.*

Willson v Hooker 45.3

*Sale of land — whether UK resident assessable as agent for Isle of Man company — TMA 1970, s 78**

An Isle of Man company realised a gain from the purchase and sale of land in Wales. The Revenue assessed the gain on an individual (W) who was resident in the UK, considering that he was acting as an agent of the company, within *TMA 1970, s 78*. The General Commissioners upheld the assessment and W appealed, contending that he was not assessable because he was not carrying on a 'regular agency', within *TMA 1970, s 82*. The Ch D rejected this contention and dismissed W's appeal, holding on the evidence that W 'was the person through whom all the transactions of (the company) in the United Kingdom were carried out during the relevant period'. *Willson v Hooker Ch D 1995, 67 TC 585; [1995] STC 1142.*

Young v Phillips 6.2

Location of letters of allotment

Two brothers resident and ordinarily resident in the UK, but domiciled in South Africa, owned equally the ordinary shares of three associated UK companies, each with substantial sums to the credit of its profit and loss account. On professional advice, during 1978/79 they implemented a pre-arranged scheme with the aim of 'exporting' the shares outside the UK (and so taking them outside the scope of capital transfer tax) without incurring any CGT liability. In brief, each company created new preferred ordinary shares, ranking pari passu with the existing ordinary shares save for priority in a capital repayment on a winding up; capitalised the amounts credited to profit and loss; appropriated these amounts to the taxpayers and used them in paying up, in full, new preferred ordinary shares issued to them, in respect of which the company issued to them renounceable letters of allotment. Shortly afterwards two Channel Island companies, set up for the purpose, issued to the taxpayers shares at a premium of £1,364,216 and resolved to buy from them (by now directors of the Channel Island companies) their preferred ordinary shares in the UK companies for £1,364,216. The taxpayers then went to Sark with their letters of allotment and the scheme was completed by, inter alia, letters of renunciation in favour of the Channel Island companies. CGT assessments were made on the basis that there had been a disposal of assets situated in the UK. The Special Commissioners dismissed the taxpayers' appeals, and the Ch D upheld their decision. Nicholls J held that there had been a disposal of rights against the UK companies, and that these were situated in the UK irrespective of where the letters of allotment happened to be. Further, even had he held that there had been a disposal of assets outside the UK, *W T Ramsay Ltd* and *Furniss v Dawson*, would have applied, and he would have accepted an alternative Revenue contention that *TCGA 1992, s 29(2)** applied, the relieving provisions of *TCGA 1992, ss 127, 135** being curtailed by *TCGA 1992, s 137(1)** because one of the main purposes of the issuing of the shares in the UK companies was the avoidance of liability to tax. *Young and Another v Phillips Ch D 1984, 58 TC 232; [1984] STC 520.*

Zim Properties Ltd v Proctor 6.1, 9.1

Amount received as part of out-of-court settlement — whether derived from an asset

In July 1973 a company (Z) contracted to sell three properties. The date of completion was fixed for 12 July 1974. However, the sale of the properties was not completed, because the original conveyance to one of them had been lost and Z was unable to provide proof of ownership. The purchaser refused to complete and successfully sued Z for the return of its deposit. Z issued a writ against its solicitors, claiming damages of more than £100,000. Following negotiations, Z agreed to accept payment of £69,000 in two instalments, in settlement of its claim. The Revenue included the amount of the first instalment as a chargeable gain in a CT assessment. Z appealed, contending that the gain was not chargeable since it had not been derived from an asset. The Special Commissioners held that the amount was a capital sum derived from Z's right against its solicitors, and that it was acquired for the purposes of *CGTA 1979, s 19(3)* otherwise than by way of an arm's length agreement, so that its market value was deductible. The Ch D upheld this decision (against which both sides had appealed) and referred the case back to the Commissioners for figures to be agreed. *O'Brien v Benson's Hosiery (Holdings) Ltd* applied. *Zim Properties Ltd v Proctor (and cross-appeal) Ch D 1984, 58 TC 371; [1985] STC 90.* (Notes. (1) See now ESC D33. (2) *CGTA 1979, s 19(3)* was subsequently repealed; see now *TCGA 1992, s 17.*)

70 Table of Cases

Where the CIR, HMRC (or, in Scotland, the Lord Advocate) are a party, the case is listed under the name of the other party only. Judicial review cases are listed under the name of the applicant and the person who is the subject of the review but again excluding the CIR etc.

Hedges & Butler Ltd, Burman *v* 27.9; 69
Ch D 1978: 52 TC 501; [1979] STC 136; [1979] 1 WLR 160; [1978] TR 409.
Helen Slater Charitable Trust Ltd, CIR *v* 10.3
CA 1981: 55 TC 230; [1981] STC 471; [1982] Ch 49; [1981] 3 WLR 377; [1981] 3 All E R 98.
Henderson, Davis *v* 9.1; 69
(Sp C 46), [1995] SSCD 308.
Henderson *v* Karmel's Exors 41.7; 69
Ch D 1984: 58 TC 201; [1984] STC 572.
Hepworth *v* Smith 33.1; 53.3; 55.1; 69
Ch D 1981: 54 TC 396; [1981] STC 354.
Herbert Berry Associates Ltd *v* CIR 47.7
HL 1977: 52 TC 113; [1977] 1 WLR 1437; [1978] 1 All E R 161.
Heron, ex p., R *v* Wokingham Commrs 4.13
QB 1984: [1984] STI 710.
Hicks, Davies *v* 59.2
Ch D 2005: [2005] STC 850.
High Wycombe Commrs and CIR, Stoll *v* 48.18
Ch D 1992: 64 TC 587; [1992] STC 179.
Hildesley, Aspden *v* 16.1; 42.4; 69
Ch D 1981: 55 TC 609; [1982] STC 206; [1982] 1 WLR 264; [1982] 2 All E R 53.
Hill, Anson *v* 4.21
CA 1968: [1968] TR 125; 47 ATC 143.
Hillenbrand *v* CIR 23.2
CS 1966: 42 TC 617; [1966] TR 201.
Hilton, Schuldenfrei *v* 4.7
CA 1999: 72 TC 167; [1999] STC 821.
Hinchcliffe *v* Crabtree 7.2; 41.3; 69
HL 1971: 47 TC 419; [1972] AC 707; [1971] 3 WLR 821; [1971] 3 All E R 967; [1971] TR 321; 50 ATC 358.
Hirsch *v* Crowthers Cloth Ltd 35.1; 69
Ch D 1989: 62 TC 759; [1990] STC 174.
Hitch and Others *v* Stone 3.1
CA 2001: [2001] STC 214.
Hoare Trustees *v* Gardner 57.12
Ch D 1977: 52 TC 53; [1978] STC 89; [1979] Ch 10; [1978] 2 WLR 839; [1978] 1 All E R 789; [1977] TR 293.
Holden, Wood and another *v* 52.6
CA 2006: [2006] STC 443.
Hollebone's Agreement, Re 47.7
CA 1959: [1959] 1 WLR 536; [1959] 2 All E R 152; [1959] TR 147; 38 ATC 142.
Holly and another *v* Inspector of Taxes 54.8
1999 (Sp C 225), [2000] SSCD 50.
Holyhead Commrs, R *v*, ex p. Roberts 4.10
QB 1982: 56 TC 127.
Honig and Another *v* Sarsfield 5.7
CA 1986: 59 TC 337; [1986] STC 246.
Honour *v* Norris 49.1; 69
Ch D 1992: 64 TC 599; [1992] STC 304.
Honourable Company of Master Mariners *v* CIR 10.2
KB 1932: 17 TC 298; 11 ATC 277.
Hood Barrs, R *v* 4.12
CA 1943: [1943] KB 455; [1943] 1 All E R 665.
Hood Barrs *v* CIR (No 3) 4.24
CA 1960: 39 TC 209; [1960] TR 113; 39 ATC 87.

Morgan, Newman *v* 57.2; 69
(Sp C 243), [2000] SSCD 345.

Morgan Grenfell & Co Ltd, oao, R *v* Special Commr 23.8; 54.10
HL 2002: [2002] STC 786.

Morleston & Litchurch Commrs, R *v* 4.13
KB 1951: 32 TC 335.

Morris, Nicholson *v* 23.2
CA 1977: 51 TC 95; [1977] STC 162; [1977] TR 1.

Morton, Marson *v* 38.3
Ch D 1986: 59 TC 381; [1986] STC 463; [1986] 1 WLR 1343.

Moschi, ex p., R *v* Special Commr 4.12
CA 1981: [1981] STC 465.

Moschi *v* Kensington Commrs 48.23
Ch D 1979: 54 TC 403; [1980] STC 1; [1979] TR 353.

Mother *v* Inspector of Taxes 54.10
(Sp C 211), [1999] SSCD 279.

Moyse, Thomson *v* 51.2
HL 1960: 39 TC 291; [1961] AC 967; [1960] 3 All E R 684; [1960] TR 309.

Mudd, Tod *v* 55.6; 69
Ch D 1986: 60 TC 237; [1987] STC 141.

Muir *v* CIR 4.24
CA 1966: 43 TC 367; [1966] 1 WLR 1269; [1966] 3 All E R 38; [1966] TR 165; 45 ATC 185.

Murphy *v* Elders 4.6
Ch D 1973: 49 TC 135; [1974] STC 34; [1973] TR 291; 52 ATC 353.

Murray, Allison *v* 15.4; 69
Ch D 1975: 51 TC 57; [1975] STC 524; [1975] 1 WLR 1578; [1975] 3 All E R 561.

Mylam, Alabama Coal, Iron, Land & Colonization Co Ltd *v* 38.3
KB 1926: 11 TC 232; 6 ATC 24.

N Ltd *v* HM Inspector of Taxes 27.4
(Sp C 90), [1996] SSCD 346.

NAP Holdings UK Ltd *v* Whittles 27.2; 58.4
HL 1994: 67 TC 166; [1994] STC 979.

Napier *v* Farnham Commrs 48.23
CA 1978: [1978] TR 403.

Napier, ex p., R *v* Special Commr 4.22; 4.26
CA 1988: 61 TC 206; [1988] STC 573; [1988] 3 All E R 166.

National Anti-Vivisection Society, CIR *v* 10.2
HL 1947: 28 TC 311; [1948] AC 31; [1947] 2 All E R 217; 26 ATC 309.

National Federation of Self-Employed and Small Businesses Ltd, ex p., R *v* CIR 4.26; 28.3; 48.10
HL 1981: 55 TC 133; [1981] STC 260; [1982] AC 617; [1981] 2 WLR 722; [1981] 2 All E R 93.

National Westminster Bank plc and another *v* CIR 21.4; 22.20
HL 1994: 67 TC 1; [1994] STC 580; [1994] 3 WLR 159; [1994] 3 All E R 1.

Neubergh *v* CIR 52.3
Ch D 1977: 52 TC 79; [1978] STC 181.

New Angel Court Ltd *v* Adam 27.4
CA 2004: [2004] STC 779; [2004] EWCA Civ 242.

New Zealand Commissioner of Inland Revenue *v* Challenge Corporation Ltd 3.1
PC 1986: [1986] STC 548; [1987] AC 155; [1987] 2 WLR 24.

New Zealand Commissioner of Inland Revenue *v* Wattie and another 38.15
PC 1998: 72 TC 639; [1998] STC 1160.

New Zealand Shipping Co Ltd *v* Thew 52.6
HL 1922: 8 TC 208; 1 ATC 90.

R (oao Barnett) *v* CIR 55.1
QB 2003: [2004] STC 763.
R (oao Browallia Cal Ltd) *v* CIR 4.4
QB 2003: [2004] STC 296.
R (oao Carvill) *v* CIR 4.26
Ch D 2002: [2002] STC 1167.
R (oao Devine) *v* CIR 21.10
QB 2003: TL 3713.
R (oao H) *v* CIR 23.10
QB 2002: 75 TC 377; [2002] STC 1354.
R (oao Morgan Grenfell & Co Ltd) *v* Special Commr 23.8; 54.10
HL 2002: [2002] STC 786.
R (oao Spring Salmon and Seafood Ltd) v CIR 54.8
CS 2004: [2004] STC 444.
Ramsay (W T) Ltd *v* CIR 3.1; 22.5; 69
HL 1981: 54 TC 101; [1981] STC 174; [1982] AC 300; [1981] 2 WLR 449; [1981] 1 All E R 865; [1981] TR 123.
Rand *v* Alberni Land Co Ltd 38.3
KB 1920: 7 TC 629.
Randall, Pilkington *v* 38.3
CA 1966: 42 TC 662; [1966] TR 33; 45 ATC 32.
Randall, Walsh *v* 51.2
KB 1940: 23 TC 55.
Randall *v* Plumb 6.7; 38.24; 69
Ch D 1974: 50 TC 392; [1975] STC 191; [1975] 1 WLR 633; [1975] 1 All E R 734; [1974] TR 371; 53 ATC 384.
Rank Xerox Ltd *v* Lane 4.21; 22.3; 69
HL 1979: 53 TC 185; [1979] STC 740; [1981] AC 269; [1979] 3 WLR 594; [1979] 3 All E R 657.
Rawling, Eilbeck *v* 3.1; 57.12; 69
HL 1981: 54 TC 101; [1981] STC 174; [1981] 2 WLR 449; [1981] 1 All E R 865; [1981] TR 123.
Rawlings, Jarmin *v* 53.4; 69
Ch D 1994: 67 TC 130; [1994] STC 1005.
Redden, Owton Fens Properties Ltd *v* 4.2
Ch D 1984: 58 TC 218; [1984] STC 618.
Reed *v* Clark 52.3; 52.4
Ch D 1985: 58 TC 528; [1985] STC 323; [1986] Ch 1; [1985] 3 WLR 142.
Reed *v* Nova Securities Ltd 3.1; 27.4; 69
HL 1985: 59 TC 516; [1985] STC 124; [1985] 1 WLR 193; [1985] 1 All E R 686.
Reeves *v* Evans, Boyce & Northcott Syndicate 38.3
Ch D 1971: 48 TC 495; [1971] TR 483; 50 ATC 487.
Regent Oil Co Ltd, Strick *v* 35.1
HL 1965: 43 TC 1; [1966] AC 295; [1965] 3 WLR 696; [1965] 3 All E R 174; [1965] TR 277; 44 ATC 264.
Reid *v* CIR 52.4
CS 1926: 10 TC 673; [1926] SLT 365; 5 ATC 357.
Reinhold, CIR *v* 38.3
CS 1953: 34 TC 389; [1953] SLT 94; [1953] TR 11; 32 ATC 10.
Rellim Ltd *v* Vise 38.3
CA 1951: 32 TC 254; [1951] TR 109; 30 ATC 105.
Renton, Swires *v* 57.12; 69
Ch D 1991: 64 TC 315; [1991] STC 490.
Reynolds' Exors *v* Bennett 52.7
KB 1943: 25 TC 401; 22 ATC 233.

Warrington, Larner *v* 4.13; 69
Ch D 1985: 58 TC 557; [1985] STC 442.
Warrington *v* Brown 38.12; 57.2
Ch D 1989: 62 TC 226; [1989] STC 577; [1989] 1 WLR 1163.
Wase *v* Bourke 53.4; 69
Ch D 1995: 68 TC 109; [1996] STC 18.
Waterson, Talib *v* 4.12
Ch D 1980: [1980] STC 563; [1980] TR 253.
Watkis, Chaney *v* 15.4; 69
Ch D 1985: 58 TC 707; [1986] STC 89.
Watson *v* Samson Bros 4.24
Ch D 1959: 38 TC 346.
Wattie and another, New Zealand Commissioner of Inland Revenue *v* 38.15
PC 1998: 72 TC 639; [1998] STC 1160.
Watton *v* Tippett 55.1; 69
CA 1997: 69 TC 491; [1997] STC 893.
Way *v* Underdown (No 1) 4.24
CA 1974: 49 TC 215; [1974] STC 11; [1974] 2 All E R 595; 52 ATC 342.
Wear Ironmongers & Sons Ltd *v* Baird 55.1; 69
Ch D 1998: 72 TC 303; [1999] STC 120.
Webb (Lance) Estates Ltd *v* Aller 38.3
Ch D 1954: 35 TC 305.
Welbeck Securities Ltd, Powlson *v* 6.7; 15.3; 69
CA 1987: 60 TC 269; [1987] STC 468.
Wells *v* Croydon Commrs 48.23
Ch D 1968: [1968] TR 265; 47 ATC 356.
Wells Commrs, Brodt *v* 48.23
Ch D 1987: 60 TC 436; [1987] STC 207.
West, CIR *v* 4.7
CA 1991: 64 TC 196; [1991] STC 357.
West, Trennery *v* 57.5; 57.19; 69
HL 2005: [2005] STC 214; [2005] UKHL 5.
West Brixton Commrs, Sparks *v* 48.23
Ch D 1977: [1977] STC 212.
Westcott *v* Woolcombers Ltd 27.2; 58.4
CA 1987: 60 TC 575; [1987] STC 600.
Westminster Bank Ltd *v* Burton-Butler and Others, re Waring dec'd 4.24
Ch D 1948: [1948] Ch 221; [1948] 1 All E R 257.
Westminster (Duke of) *v* CIR 3.1
HL 1935: 19 TC 490; [1936] AC 1; [1935] All E R 259; 14 ATC 77.
Westminster Press Ltd, Burman *v* 22.4; 69
Ch D 1987: 60 TC 418; [1987] STC 669.
Westmoreland Investments Ltd, MacNiven *v* 3.1; 4.7
HL 2001: 73 TC 1; [2001] STC 237.
Weston *v* Garnett 50.2
CA 2005: [2005] STC 1134.
Whaddon Estates Ltd, Innocent *v* 27.2; 69
Ch D 1981: 55 TC 476; [1982] STC 115; [1981] TR 379.
Whalley, Frowd *v* 4.24
Ch D 1965: 42 TC 599; [1965] TR 47; 44 ATC 423.
Whalley, Woodrow *v* 23.2
Ch D 1964: 42 TC 249; [1964] TR 409; 43 ATC 441.
Whitaker *v* Cameron 7.8; 69
Ch D 1982: 56 TC 97; [1982] STC 665.

71 Table of Statutes

Miscellaneous legislation
(in alphabetical order)

72 Table of Statutory Instruments

Note. Statutory Instruments (SIs) referred to at 19.2, 19.3, 19.9 double tax relief are not listed below. Also not listed are those SIs which do no more than confirm indexed rises in tax rates and allowances as announced in the Budget or which alter the rates of interest on overpaid and unpaid tax, though these are referred to in the text where appropriate.

The list below is in date order.

Year	Statutory Instrument	Reference
1955	No 1954 International Finance Corporation Order 1955	22.50
1960	No 1383 International Development Association Order 1960	22.50
1967	No 149 Capital Gains Tax Regulations 1967	4.3
1971	No 1035 Mineral Royalties (Tax) Regulations 1971	43.1
1984	No 1836 Finance Act 1984 (Commencement No 2) Order 1984	4.6
1986	No 387 Capital Gains Tax (Parallel Pooling) Regulations 1986	59.7
	No 1925 Insolvency Rules 1986	13.8
1987	No 412 Pension Scheme Surpluses (Valuation) Regulations 1987	22.56
1988	No 266 Capital Gains Tax (Definition of Unit Trust Scheme) Regulations 1988	65.2
1989	No 469 Personal Equity Plan Regulations 1989	58.18
	No 1297 Taxes (Interest Rate) Regulations 1989	36.1; 36.2; 37.1; 37.5
	No 1299 IT (Stock Lending) Regulations 1989	58.21
1990	No 678 Personal Equity Plan (Amendment) Regulations 1990	58.18
1991	No 724 High Court and County Courts Jurisdiction Order 1991	47.7
	No 733 Personal Equity Plan (Amendment) Regulations 1991	58.18
	No 1877 County Court Appeals Order 1991	47.7
	No 2774 Personal Equity Plan (Amendment No 2) Regulations 1991	58.18
1992	No 623 Personal Equity Plan (Amendment) Regulations 1992	58.18
	No 572 IT (Stock Lending) (Amendment) Regulations 1992	58.21
	No 3066 Corporation Tax Acts (Provisions for Payment of Tax and Returns), (Appointed Days) Order 1992	13.10; 47.2; 54.18
1993	No 236 Finance (No 2) Act 1992, Schedule 9, (Appointed Day) Order 1993	22.47
	No 756 Personal Equity Plan (Amendment) Regulations 1993	58.18
	No 950 Capital Gains Tax (Gilt-edged Securities) Order 1993	26.2
	No 2003 IT (Stock Lending) (Amendment) Regulations 1993	58.21
	No 2212 Taxes (Interest Rate) (Amendment No 3) Regulations 1993	36.2; 37.5
1994	No 87 Finance Act 1989, Section 152, (Appointed Day) Order 1994	47.7
	No 236 Distraint by Collectors (Fees, Costs and Charges) Regulations 1994	47.7
	No 1811 Special Commissioners (Jurisdiction and Procedure) Regulations 1994	4.9; 4.17–4.19; 4.25; 48.18
	No 1812 General Commissioners (Jurisdiction and Procedure) Regulations 1994	4.9–4.15; 4.21–4.23; 48.18
	No 1813 General and Special Commissioners (Amendment of Enactments) Regulations 1994	4.13; 4.15; 4.21; 4.24; 4.25; 47.4; 48.18–48.20
	No 2656 Capital Gains Tax (Gilt-edged Securities) Order 1994	26.2
	No 3227 Exchange Gains and Losses (Alternative Method of Calculation of Gain or Loss) Regulations 1994	14.15; 60.23
1995	No 353 Lloyd's Underwriters (Special Reserve Funds) Regulations 1995	64.1
	No 1185 Lloyd's Underwriters (Special Reserve Funds) (Amendment) Regulations 1995	64.1
	No 1283 IT (Stock Lending) (Amendment) Regulations 1995	58.21
	No 1539 Personal Equity Plan (Amendment) Regulations 1995	58.18
	No 1979 Venture Capital Trust Regulations 1995	66.1; 66.2; 66.7; 66.9
	No 2151 Distraint by Collectors (Fees, Costs and Charges) (Amendment) Regulations 1995	47.7
	No 3219 IT (Stock Lending) (Amendment No 2) Regulations 1995	58.21
	No 3287 Personal Equity Plan (Amendment No 2) Regulations 1995	58.18

1996 No 846 Personal Equity Plan (Amendment) Regulations 1996 58.18
No 1031 Capital Gains Tax (Gilt-edged Securities) Order 1996 26.2
No 1355 Personal Equity Plan (Amendment No 2) Regulations 1996 58.18
No 1654 Income Tax (Payments on Account) Regulations 1996 56.4
No 2325 Housing Act 1996 (Consequential Provisions) Order 1996 22.49; 22.58
No 3187 Taxes (Interest Rate) (Amendment No 4) Regulations 1996 36.1; 37.1
1997 No 57 Electronic Lodgement of Tax Returns Order 1997 54.22
No 511 Personal Equity Plan (Amendment) Regulations 1997 58.18
No 991 Finance Act 1997, Schedule 10, (Appointed Day) Order 1997 58.21
No 1154 Open-ended Investment Companies (Tax) Regulations 1997 10.4; 65.6
No 1603 Finance Act 1997, Section 110, (Appointed Day) Order 1997 29.2
No 1715 Open-ended Investment Companies (Tax) (Amendment) Regulations 1997 65.6
No 1716 Personal Equity Plan (Amendment No 2) Regulations 1997 58.18
No 2491 Income Tax (Payments on Account) (Amendment) Regulations 1997 56.4
No 2681 Lloyd's Underwriters (Scottish Limited Partnerships) (Tax) Regulations 1997 64.3
1998 No 310 Taxes (Interest Rate) (Amendment) Regulations 1998 37.1
No 311 Finance Act 1989, Section 178(1), (Appointed Day) Order 1998 37.1; 48.14
No 1869 Personal Equity Plan (Amendment) Regulations 1998 58.18
No 1870 Individual Savings Account Regulations 1998 22.29
No 1871 Individual Savings Account (Insurance Companies) Regulations 1998 22.29
No 2244 Government of Wales Act 1998 (Commencement No 1) Order 1998 22.49; 22.58
No 3173 Finance Act 1994, Section 199, (Appointed Day) Order 1998 56.2
No 3174 Individual Savings Account (Amendment) Regulations 1998 22.29
No 3175 Corporation Tax (Instalment Payments) Regulations 1998 36.2; 37.5; 47.2
No 3176 Taxes (Interest Rate) (Amendment No 2) Regulations 1998 36.2; 37.5
No 3177 European Single Currency (Taxes) Regulations 1998 6.1; 6.7; 13.1; 22.5; 45.1; 58.7; 58.21
1999 No 527 Social Security Contributions (Transfer of Functions, etc) Act 1999 (Commencement No 1 and Transitional Provisions) Order 1999 29.4
No 564 Finance Act 1993, Section 86(2), (Fish Quota) Order 1999 55.3
No 819 Venture Capital Trust (Amendment) Regulations 1999 66.9
No 1928 Taxes (Interest Rate) (Amendment No 2) Regulations 1999 36.2
No 1929 Corporation Tax (Instalment Payments) (Amendment) Regulations 1999 47.2
No 1953 Capital Gains Tax (Definition of Permanent Interest Bearing Share) Regulations 1999 50.2
No 2975 Corporation Tax (Simplified Arrangements for Group Relief) Regulations 1999 54.18
No 3292 Special Commissioners (Jurisdiction and Procedure) (Amendment) Regulations 1999 4.19
No 3293 General Commissioners (Jurisdiction and Procedure) (Amendment) Regulations 1999 4.13; 4.14; 4.21
No 3294 Special Commissioners (Amendment of the Taxes Management Act 1970) Regulations 1999 4.25
No 3308 Lloyd's Underwriters (Special Reserve Funds) Regulations 1999 64.1
2000 No 809 Individual Savings Account (Amendment) Regulations 2000 22.29
No 892 Corporation Tax (Instalment Payments) (Amendment) Regulations 2000 47.2
No 893 Taxes (Interest Rate) (Amendment) Regulations 2000 37.5
No 945 Income Tax (Electronic Communications) Regulations 2000 54.3
No 2074 Donations to Charity by Individuals (Appropriate Declarations) Regulations 2000 10.7
No 2079 Individual Savings Account (Amendment No 2) Regulations 2000 22.29
No 2550 Capital Gains Tax (Definition of Unit Trust Scheme) (Amendment) Regulations 2000 65.2
No 2875 Orders for the Delivery of Documents (Procedure) Regulations 2000 23.9
No 3109 Personal Equity Plan (Amendment) Regulations 2000 58.18
No 3112 Individual Savings Account (Amendment No 3) Regulations 2000 22.29

2000 No 3315 Exchange Gains and Losses (Miscellaneous Modifications) Regulations 2000 14.15
No 3316 Limited Liability Partnerships Act 2000 (Commencement) Order 2000 46.19
2001 No 56 Income Tax (Electronic Communications) (Incentive Payments) Regulations 2001 28.8
No 204 Taxes (Interest Rate) (Amendment No 1) Regulations 2001 37.5
No 544 Financial Services and Markets Act 2000 (Regulated Activities) Order 2001 6.7; 6.8
No 908 Individual Savings Account (Amendment) Regulations 2001 22.29
No 916 Access to Justice Act 1999 (Commencement No 7, Transitional Provisions and Savings) Order 2001 4.15
No 923 Personal Equity Plan (Amendment) Regulations 2001 58.18
No 1081 Income Tax (Electronic Communications) (Miscellaneous Amendments) Regulations 2001 28.8
No 1122 Capital Gains Tax (Gilt-edged Securities) Order 2001 26.2
No 1304 General Commissioners of Income Tax (Costs) Regulations 2001 4.15
No 3629 Financial Services and Markets Act 2000 (Consequential Amendments) (Taxes) Order 2001 10.4; 13.10; 22.8; 22.29; 27.2; 41.3; 45.3; 50.2; 54.18; 58.18; 61.25; 64.1; 65.1; 65.6
No 3777 Personal Equity Plan (Amendment No 2) Regulations 2001 58.18
No 3778 Individual Savings Account (Amendment No 2) Regulations 2001 22.29
No 3799 Enterprise Management Incentives (Gross Asset Requirement) Order 2001 20.24
No 4024 Referrals to the Special Commissioners Regulations 2001 54.13
2002 No 453 Individual Savings Account (Amendment) Regulations 2002 22.29
No 1727 Tax Credits Act 2002 (Commencement No 1) Order 2002 29.2–29.4
No 1966 Relief for Community Amateur Sports Clubs (Designation) Order 2002 10.8
No 1967 Corporation Tax (Finance Leasing of Intangible Assets) Regulations 2002 14.14
No 1970 Exchange Gains and Losses (Bringing into Account Gains or Losses) Regulations 2002 14.3; 14.15
No 1974 Individual Savings Account (Amendment No 2) Regulations 2002 22.29
No 2661 Venture Capital Trust (Exchange of Shares and Securities) Regulations 200266.2; 66.4
No 2849 Capital Gains Tax (Gilt-edged Securities) Order 2002 26.2
No 2976 General Commissioners and Special Commissioners (Jurisdiction and Procedure) (Amendment) Regulations 2002 4.12; 4.19
No 3036 Tax Credits (Administrative Arrangements) Regulations 2002 29.2
No 3158 Individual Savings Account (Amendment No 3) Regulations 2002 22.29
2003 No 120 Proceeds of Crime Act 2002 (Commencement No 4, Transitional Provisions and Savings) Order 2003 29.2
No 282 The Income and Corporation Taxes (Electronic Communications) Regulations 200328.8
No 1116 Companies (Acquisition of Own Shares) (Treasury Shares) Regulations 2003 58.14
No 1997 Finance Act 2003, Schedule 22, Paragraph 3(1) (Appointed Day) Order 2003 20.6; 20.14–20.17
No 2093 Enterprise Act 2002 (Commencement No. 4 and Transitional Provisions and Savings) Order 2003 4.12
No 2747 Individual Savings Account (Amendment) Regulations 2003 22.29
No 2748 Personal Equity Plan (Amendment) Regulations 2003 58.18
No 3077 Finance Act 2003, Section 195 and Schedule 40 (Appointed Day) Order 2003 58.14
2004 No 438 Capital Gains Tax (Gilt-Edged Securities) Order 2004 26.2
No 674 Recovery of Duties and Taxes Etc. Due in Other Member States (Corresponding UK Claims, Procedure and Supplementary) Regulations 2004 47.8
No 1676 Personal Equity Plan (Amendment) Regulations 2004 58.18
No 1450 Child Trust Funds Regulations 2004
Regs 24–38 22.22
No 1677 Individual Savings Account (Amendment) Regulations 2004 22.29
No 1863 Tax Avoidance Schemes (Prescribed Descriptions of Arrangements) Regulations 2004 3.2
No 1864 Tax Avoidance Schemes (Information) Regulations 2004 3.2

73 Index

This index is referenced to the chapter number or to the chapter and paragraph number. The entries printed in bold capitals are chapter headings in the text.

E

G

H

U